OSW
OFFICIAL SCRABBLE® WORDS

OSW

OFFICIAL SCRABBLE® WORDS

Second edition

Chambers

First edition 1988.
Second edition © W & R Chambers Ltd 1990.

This paperback edition published 1991 by
W & R Chambers Ltd, 43–45 Annandale Street,
Edinburgh EH7 4AZ.

British Library Cataloguing in Publication Data

Francis, Darryl
    OSW: Official Scrabble Words.
    2nd ed, by *Darryl Francis, Philip Nelkon, Allan Simmons*
    1. Scrabble
    I. Title   II. Nelkon, Philip   III. Simmons, Allan
    793.7

ISBN 0 550 19023 6

The publishers wish to acknowledge the computing help
of Peter Schwarz in the compilation and revision of
Official Scrabble® Words.

The book was prepared and revised on a Sirius
microcomputer using programs run under the UCSD-p
system and the large-file editor ASE. The text was sorted
on the Edinburgh University Multi-Access System
(EMAS).

Typeset by Pillans & Wilson Specialist Litho Printers Ltd,
Edinburgh.

Printed in England by Clays Ltd, St Ives plc.

Preface to first edition

At last we have the book which Scrabble® players have been wanting for many years. *Official Scrabble® Words (OSW)* is the definitive work which will save family arguments in social games and enable challenges to be dealt with quickly and efficiently in Scrabble Clubs and tournaments.

J W Spear & Sons and Chambers have had a close relationship going back to when the UK Scrabble Club movement adopted *Chambers 20th Century Dictionary* as its reference work. *Chambers* (now published as *Chambers English Dictionary*) is loved by Scrabble players throughout most of the English-speaking world because of the rich fund of useful Scrabble words it contains.

Official Scrabble Words uses this source so it almost certainly contains your pet Scrabble words and thousands of others. *OSW* is complementary to *Chambers English Dictionary,* which remains the reference work when you want to check a definition.

The task of adjudicating on well over 150,000 words was a mammoth one. I would like to thank the main adjudicating committee, the groups of volunteer Scrabble players who acted as the initial adjudicators (all named below) and, of course, Catherine Schwarz and her colleagues at Chambers for the dedicated way they handled the many problems. I also thank the members of the Australian Scrabble Players' Association who have made their contribution in helping Chambers' editorial team.

I am sure that the work they all have done will add to the enjoyment and satisfaction that you obtain from playing Scrabble.

Francis A Spear
Chairman
J W Spear & Sons PLC

Main committee

Darryl Francis, *London Scrabble League*
Leonard Hodge, *Scrabble Club Co-ordinator and Chairman*
Angus Macdonald, *Mapperley Scrabble Club*
Philip Nelkon, *London Scrabble League*
Allan Simmons, *Postal Scrabble Club*

Initial adjudicating committee

Steve Ablitt-Jones, *Croydon SC*
Olive Behan, *Glenthorn SC*
Jackie Fallows, *Isle of Wight SC*
Raye Green, *Leicester SC*
Mary Grylls, *Grantham SC*
Ian Gucklhorn, *London Scrabble League*
Josef Kollar, *Hythe SC*
Kevin Morris, *Bristol SC*
Jane McLeman, *Frodsham SC*
Norman Smith, *Edinburgh SC*
Roy Upton, *Derby SC*
Mike Willis, *Milton Keynes SC*
Dorothy Harrison, *Plymouth SC*

Preface to second edition

Since its publication in 1988 *Official Scrabble® Words* has proved its worth as the Scrabble-players' authority from fireside to National championship finals.

In the course of using it, and its source and contemporary, *Chambers English Dictionary*, Scrabble players and dictionary users have brought to light a number of inconsistencies and infelicities. These have been scrutinised, extended, decided on and dealt with by original main committee members Darryl Francis, Philip Nelkon and Allan Simmons, in conjunction with Catherine Schwarz of Chambers. As before, we are grateful to members of the Australian Scrabble Players' Association for their constructive and courteous contribution. With *Chambers English Dictionary* complementing it for meanings and longer words, the revised *Official Scrabble Words* now takes its predecessor's place as the definitive Scrabble adjudication tool.

Francis A Spear
Chairman
J W Spear & Sons PLC

Introduction

This revised edition of *Official Scrabble® Words* is the final authority on allowed Scrabble® words. It is based on the 1988 edition of *Chambers English Dictionary*. All words listed in that dictionary are permitted in Scrabble except:

> those only spelt with an initial capital letter;
>
> abbreviations;
>
> prefixes and suffixes;
>
> those requiring apostrophes and hyphens.

Official Scrabble Words fully takes account of the 1988 revision of the rules used for the National Scrabble Championship and other official Scrabble events. The differences between the revised rules and the earlier rules can be summarised here:

> foreign words are allowed;
>
> names of letters and letter sounds are allowed;
>
> obsolete words and words from the works of Shakespeare, Spenser and Milton are allowed;
>
> adverbs are only allowed if in *Chambers*.

Let us look at these differences in slightly more detail, as well as at the approaches that have been taken towards certain groups of words.

Foreign words

Foreign words appearing in *Chambers English Dictionary* have been included in *Official Scrabble Words*. Where a specific plural form appears in *Chambers*, we have included only that form, but where no plural is shown in the dictionary, we have used our judgment, and the appropriate plural form has been included. In some instances, this will be a foreign plural; in others, it will be an English plural (usually the addition of an -S); occasionally both types of plural will be included. Do be aware that not all plural forms in *OSW* are explicitly shown in *Chambers*. For example, as no plural form is shown in the dictionary for DEUS, we have included the plural forms DEI and DI in preference to an unlisted -ES plural of DEUS.

Letters and letter sounds

Names of letters and letter sounds appearing in *Chambers English Dictionary* are included in *Official Scrabble Words*. The reasons for barring these from the National Scrabble Championship and other official events were never clear, and these words are now welcomed back into the realm of valid Scrabble words. This allows the inclusion here of a flurry of words such as MU, NU and XI, as well as AITCH, VAU and YPSILON. Their plural forms are also included.

Obsolete words

Obsolete words are included in *Official Scrabble Words*, along with many of their relevant inflected forms (such as plurals and verb inflections). We have included plurals of most obsolete nouns. We have included verb inflections of most, but not all, obsolete verbs. We have not included comparative and superlative forms of obsolete adjectives. We have not included derivatives of obsolete words, unless explicitly shown in *Chambers*. (For example, BROACH and BROACHER are both allowable words, and BROCH is in the dictionary as an obsolete spelling of BROACH – so BROACH, BROACHER and BROCH are all allowable, but we have not included the assumed BROCHER.)

Words marked in *Chambers* as being from the works of Shakespeare, Spenser and Milton have been treated in the same way as obsolete words.

Adverbs

Adverbs have only been included in *Official Scrabble Words* if they are included in *Chambers*. No attempt has been made to include adverbial forms which are not explicitly shown in the dictionary.

Users of OSW may find it helpful if we outline our thinking on certain other groups of words, as well as on the word lengths included in the book.

Plurals

With few exceptions, we have included in *Official Scrabble Words* the plurals of all nouns. Plural forms have been shown for all nouns ending in -ISM, -ITY and -NESS. While these plurals may be little used in regular English, all are available for use if needed in the English language. We have also included the plural forms of chemicals, chemical elements, minerals, man-made materials, natural materials, fibres, drugs, gases, rocks, oils, vitamins, enzymes, diseases, illnesses, and the like.

Comparatives and superlatives

We have included a wide range of comparatives and superlatives in *Official Scrabble Words*. We have considered the possible comparative and superlative forms of all adjectives in *OSW*, and we have based our final selection on a range of criteria. These have included commonness or familiarity of the adjective, number of syllables, meaning, and whether the adjective is dialect, obsolete or foreign. We also took into account the euphony of the -ER and -EST forms, current usage, and listings in other dictionaries. We cannot say that we have applied a mechanical formula in deciding which comparatives and superlatives to include. We have allowed the -IER and -IEST forms of most one- and two-syllable adjectives ending in -Y, and some of three syllables, but not all. We have excluded comparative and superlative forms of obsolete and archaic adjectives ending in -Y. We have not excluded the comparatives and superlatives of all adjectives of three syllables or more – some have been included. We have not excluded the comparatives and superlatives of all adjectives ending with certain specific groups of letters, such as -ATE, -ENT, -CTE and -ID. We have certainly included some of these comparatives and superlatives. This revised edition of *Official Scrabble Words* contains many more comparative and superlative forms than the original edition, having taken into account comments from Scrabble players around the world.

Interjections

Interjections are treated not as nouns, but as parts of speech which do not permit plurals. In *Official Scrabble Words*, an interjection has no inflected forms, unless explicitly indicated in *Chambers*. A plural is only allowed if an interjection is also shown to be a noun; and verb forms are only allowed if an interjection is shown to be a verb. Some examples:

> AH, QUOTHA and UM are interjections only, so no inflected forms are allowed;
>
> EH is an interjection and a verb, so the inflected verb forms EHS, EHED and EHING are allowed;
>
> OOH is an interjection, verb and noun, so the verb forms OOHS, OOHED and OOHING are allowed; OOHS is also the plural form of the noun.

If *Chambers* quite clearly lists a plural form of an interjection (for example, as at LO), then that is allowable.

Accents

Accented letters have been retained in *Official Scrabble Words*, even though there are no accents in English-language Scrabble sets. Accents are to be ignored. Occasionally, two forms of an allowable Scrabble word are given in *OSW*, one accented, one not. An example is PATE and PÂTÉ. Retention of accents has been considered desirable because we have anticipated that *OSW* may well be used as the authority for other word-games which do *not* allow accented words. Inclusion of the accents will enable the players of those other games to discard accented words if they wish to.

Word lengths

Official Scrabble Words users may well want to understand what criteria have been employed in considering word lengths. In compiling *OSW* we began by listing all the valid but uninflected words of length up to (and including) 9 letters. We then allowed the relevant inflections of these (namely plurals, verb forms, and comparatives and superlatives), resulting in words up to 13 letters long. (It is possible for a 9-letter verb to double a final consonant before adding -ING, giving 13 letters in all!) Here are some examples:

> the 9-letter noun CACODEMON gives rise to the 10-letter plural CACODEMONS;
>
> the 9-letter noun CACOPHONY gives rise to the 11-letter plural CACOPHONIES;
>
> the 9-letter noun CANTHARIS gives rise to the 11-letter plural CANTHARIDES;
>
> the 9-letter verb CALCULATE gives rise to these verb inflections: CALCULATED, CALCULATES and CALCULATING, having 10 or 11 letters;
>
> the 8-letter verb CARBURET gives rise to these verb inflections: CARBURETS, CARBURETTED and CARBURETTING, having 9, 11 or 12 letters.

If any inflected form of a 9-letter word is also a singular noun in its own right, then a plural form of that noun is also included. For example:

> the 9-letter verb CATERWAUL gives rise to these verb inflections: CATERWAULS, CATERWAULED and CATERWAULING; but since CATERWAULING is also shown in *Chambers* as a noun, the plural form CATERWAULINGS has been included here;
>
> the 8-letter verb CROSSCUT gives rise to these verb inflections: CROSSCUTS and CROSSCUTTING; but since CROSSCUTTING is also shown in *Chambers* as a noun, the plural form CROSSCUTTINGS has been included here.

There are a few instances of 9-letter adjectives which add an -S to become 10-letter nouns. For example, CANONICAL is an adjective only, yet CANONICALS is a noun. In such cases, we have included the -S form. After all, if CANONICAL was a noun rather than an adjective, we would have included its plural form CANONICALS. There are instances of singular nouns having more than 9 letters, but with plurals of 9 letters or less. The singulars have not been included here, but the plurals have. For example, the singular CYNOMOLGUS has 10 letters, so hasn't been included, but its plural CYNOMOLGI has 9 letters, so is included.

Order of words

All the words in *Official Scrabble Words* are listed in strict alphabetical sequence regardless of length. It is important to bear this in mind, particularly when checking the validity of plurals. For example:

> the plural of FAD is not listed immediately after FAD but is shown at its correct alphabetical place beween FADOS and FADY;
>
> to determine whether FAB has a plural or not, it is necessary to check between the entries FABRICS and FABULAR. It is not listed there, so FABS is not allowed.

Official Scrabble Words does not list the definitions of any words. If you wish to discover the meaning of a word included, then it is necessary to consult *Chambers English Dictionary*.

Apparent misspellings

There are some instances where it may appear that a word has been misspelt. This can occur when the normal spelling is greater than 9 letters and therefore excluded, but an older or obsolete spelling of the same word qualifies for inclusion. For example:

> SENSUALTY and its plural form SENSUALTIES both appear in *Official Scrabble Words* because SENSUALTY is a 9-letter noun. The regular spelling SENSUALITY and its plural form SENSUALITIES are not listed because SENSUALITY is longer than 9 letters.

Official Scrabble Words will not answer every possible enquiry regarding the validity of words. For uninflected words longer than 9 letters, you will have to turn to

Chambers itself. For example, CYNOMOLGUS, mentioned above, is perfectly valid for use in Scrabble; it's just that it isn't included here. There are plenty of other 10-15 letter words which could be played on a Scrabble board and are in *Chambers*. However, we felt that such words fell outside the scope of *OSW*.

Why a revised edition?

This revised edition of *Official Scrabble Words* contains about 1300 words *not* listed in the original edition. Some were accidentally omitted from the original edition, but many are added as the result of reconsidering derivative forms. This is especially the case with comparatives and superlatives of adjectives ending in -Y, and the verbal derivatives of obsolete words. While these 1300 new words represent less than 1% of the total stock of words in *Official Scrabble Words*, it is felt that Scrabble players will welcome their introduction here in an attempt to make this revised edition as accurate and consistent as possible.

The revised *Official Scrabble Words* omits about 500 words which appeared in the original edition. Some were too long, some were misprints, and some were inappropriate plurals and other derivative forms. Again, although these deletions represent about one-third of 1% of the stock of words in *Official Scrabble Words*, it is felt that Scrabble players everywhere will welcome this improved level of accuracy and consistency.

The 1300 additions and the 500 deletions have all been individually and carefully considered. Many other words have been considered for inclusion and exclusion, but have remained excluded or included. In several cases it has been particularly difficult to decide over a word's validity for inclusion (or otherwise) here. However, if after considering the guidelines here you believe you have found an error, either of inclusion or omission, then please write to Catherine Schwarz at W and R Chambers, Edinburgh.

Darryl Francis, Leonard Hodge,
Philip Nelkon, Allan Simmons
UK *Official Scrabble® Words Committee*

A

AA
AARDVARK
AARDVARKS
AARDWOLF
AARDWOLVES
AAS
AASVOGEL
AASVOGELS
ABA
ABAC
ABACA
ABACAS
ABACI
ABACK
ABACS
ABACTINAL
ABACTOR
ABACTORS
ABACUS
ABACUSES
ABAFT
ABALONE
ABALONES
ABAMPERE
ABAMPERES
ABAND
ABANDED
ABANDING
ABANDON
ABANDONED
ABANDONEE
ABANDONEES
ABANDONING
ABANDONS
ABANDS
ABAS
ABASE
ABASED
ABASEMENT
ABASEMENTS
ABASES
ABASING
ABASH
ABASHED
ABASHES
ABASHING
ABASHLESS
ABASHMENT
ABASHMENTS
ABASING
ABASK
ABATABLE
ABATE
ABATED
ABATEMENT
ABATEMENTS
ABATES
ABATING
ABATIS
ABATOR
ABATORS
ABATTIS
ABATTOIR
ABATTOIRS

ABATTU
ABATURE
ABATURES
ABAXIAL
ABAYA
ABAYAS
ABB
ABBA
ABBACIES
ABBACY
ABBAS
ABBATIAL
ABBÉ
ABBÉS
ABBESS
ABBESSES
ABBEY
ABBEYS
ABBOT
ABBOTS
ADDOTSHIP
ABBOTSHIPS
ABBS
ABCEE
ABCEES
ABDABS
ABDICABLE
ABDICANT
ABDICATE
ABDICATED
ABDICATES
ABDICATING
ABDOMEN
ABDOMENS
ABDOMINAL
ABDUCE
ABDUCED
ABDUCENT
ABDUCES
ABDUCING
ABDUCT
ABDUCTED
ABDUCTEE
ABDUCTEES
ABDUCTING
ABDUCTION
ABDUCTIONS
ABDUCTOR
ABDUCTORS
ABDUCTS
ABEAM
ABEAR
ABEARING
ABEARS
ABED
ABEIGH
ABELE
ABELES
ABELIA
ABELIAS
ABERRANCE
ABERRANCES
ABERRANCIES

ABERRANCY
ABERRANT
ABERRATE
ABERRATED
ABERRATES
ABERRATING
ABESSIVE
ABESSIVES
ABET
ABETMENT
ABETMENTS
ABETS
ABETTED
ABETTER
ABETTERS
ABETTING
ABETTOR
ABETTORS
ABEYANCE
ABEYANCES
ABEYANCIES
ABEYANCY
ABEYANT
ABHOR
ABHORRED
ABHORRENT
ABHORRER
ABHORRERS
ABHORRING
ABHORRINGS
ADHORS
ABID
ABIDANCE
ABIDANCES
ABIDDEN
ABIDE
ABIDED
ABIDES
ABIDING
ABIDINGLY
ABIDINGS
ABIES
ABIGAIL
ABIGAILS
ABILITIES
ABILITY
ABIOSES
ABIOSIS
ABIOTIC
ABJECT
ABJECTED
ABJECTING
ABJECTION
ABJECTIONS
ABJECTLY
ABJECTS
ABJOINT
ABJOINTED
ABJOINTING
ABJOINTS
ABJURE
ABJURED
ABJURER

ABJURERS
ABJURES
ABJURING
ABLATE
ABLATED
ABLATES
ABLATING
ABLATION
ABLATIONS
ABLATIVAL
ABLATIVE
ABLATIVES
ABLATOR
ABLATORS
ABLAUT
ABLAUTS
ABLAZE
ABLE
ABLED
ABLER
ABLES
ABLEST
ABLET
ABLETS
ABLING
ABLINS
ABLOOM
ABLOW
ABLUSH
ABLUTION
ABLUTIONS
ABLY
ABNEGATE
ABNEGATED
ABNEGATES
ABNEGATING
ABNEGATOR
ABNEGATORS
ABNORMAL
ABNORMITIES
ABNORMITY
ABNORMOUS
ABOARD
ABODE
ABODED
ABODEMENT
ABODEMENTS
ABODES
ABODING
ABOIDEAU
ABOIDEAUS
ABOIL
ABOITEAU
ABOITEAUS
ABOLISH
ABOLISHED
ABOLISHES
ABOLISHING
ABOLITION
ABOLITIONS
ABOLLA
ABOLLAE
ABOLLAS

ABOMASA
ABOMASUM
ABOMASUS
ABOMASUSES
ABOMINATE
ABOMINATED
ABOMINATES
ABOMINATING
ABONDANCE
ABONDANCES
ABORAL
ABORD
ABORDED
ABORDING
ABORDS
ABORE
ABORIGEN
ABORIGENS
ABORIGIN
ABORIGINE
ABORIGINES
ABORIGINS
ABORNE
ABORT
ABORTED
ABORTING
ABORTION
ABORTIONS
ABORTIVE
ABORTS
ABOUGHT
ABOULIA
ABOULIAS
ABOUND
ABOUNDED
ABOUNDING
ABOUNDS
ABOUT
ABOUTS
ABOVE
ABRADANT
ABRADANTS
ABRADE
ABRADED
ABRADES
ABRADING
ABRAID
ABRAIDED
ABRAIDING
ABRAIDS
ABRAM
ABRASION
ABRASIONS
ABRASIVE
ABRASIVES
ABRAXAS
ABRAXASES
ABRAY
ABRAYED
ABRAYING
ABRAYS
ABRAZO
ABRAZOS

ABREACT
ABREACTED
ABREACTING
ABREACTS
ABREAST
ABRÉGÉ
ABRÉGÉS
ABRICOCK
ABRICOCKS
ABRIDGE
ABRIDGED
ABRIDGER
ABRIDGERS
ABRIDGES
ABRIDGING
ABRIM
ABRIN
ABRINS
ABROACH
ABROAD
ABROADS
ABROGATE
ABROGATED
ABROGATES
ABROGATING
ABROGATOR
ABROGATORS
ABROOKE
ABROOKED
ABROOKES
ABROOKING
ABRUPT
ABRUPTER
ABRUPTEST
ABRUPTION
ABRUPTIONS
ABRUPTLY
ABRUPTS
ABSCESS
ABSCESSES
ABSCIND
ABSCINDED
ABSCINDING
ABSCINDS
ABSCISE
ABSCISED
ABSCISES
ABSCISIN
ABSCISING
ABSCISINS
ABSCISS
ABSCISSA
ABSCISSAE
ABSCISSAS
ABSCISSE
ABSCISSES
ABSCISSIN
ABSCISSINS
ABSCOND
ABSCONDED
ABSCONDER
ABSCONDERS
ABSCONDING
ABSCONDS
ABSEIL
ABSEILED
ABSEILING
ABSEILINGS
ABSEILS
ABSENCE

ABSENCES
ABSENT
ABSENTED
ABSENTEE
ABSENTEES
ABSENTING
ABSENTLY
ABSENTS
ABSEY
ABSEYS
ABSINTH
ABSINTHE
ABSINTHES
ABSINTHS
ABSIT
ABSITS
ABSOLUTE
ABSOLUTES
ABSOLVE
ABSOLVED
ABSOLVER
ABSOLVERS
ABSOLVES
ABSOLVING
ABSONANT
ABSORB
ABSORBATE
ABSORBATES
ABSORBED
ABSORBENT
ABSORBENTS
ABSORBER
ABSORBERS
ABSORBING
ABSORBS
ABSTAIN
ABSTAINED
ABSTAINER
ABSTAINERS
ABSTAINING
ABSTAINS
ABSTERGE
ABSTERGED
ABSTERGES
ABSTERGING
ABSTINENT
ABSTRACT
ABSTRACTED
ABSTRACTER
ABSTRACTEST
ABSTRACTING
ABSTRACTS
ABSTRICT
ABSTRICTED
ABSTRICTING
ABSTRICTS
ABSTRUSE
ABSTRUSER
ABSTRUSEST
ABSURD
ABSURDER
ABSURDEST
ABSURDITIES
ABSURDITY
ABSURDLY
ABTHANE
ABTHANES
ABULIA
ABULIAS
ABUNA

ABUNAS
ABUNDANCE
ABUNDANCES
ABUNDANCIES
ABUNDANCY
ABUNDANT
ABUNE
ABURST
ABUSAGE
ABUSAGES
ABUSE
ABUSED
ABUSER
ABUSERS
ABUSES
ABUSING
ABUSION
ABUSIONS
ABUSIVE
ABUSIVELY
ABUT
ABUTILON
ABUTILONS
ABUTMENT
ABUTMENTS
ABUTS
ABUTTAL
ABUTTALS
ABUTTED
ABUTTER
ABUTTERS
ABUTTING
ABUZZ
ABVOLT
ABVOLTS
ABY
ABYE
ABYEING
ABYES
ABYING
ABYSM
ABYSMAL
ABYSMALLY
ABYSMS
ABYSS
ABYSSAL
ABYSSES
ACACIA
ACACIAS
ACADEME
ACADEMES
ACADEMIA
ACADEMIAS
ACADEMIC
ACADEMICS
ACADEMIES
ACADEMIST
ACADEMISTS
ACADEMY
ACAJOU
ACAJOUS
ACALEPH
ACALEPHA
ACALEPHAN
ACALEPHANS
ACALEPHAS
ACALEPHE
ACALEPHES
ACALEPHS
ACANTH

ACANTHA
ACANTHAS
ACANTHIN
ACANTHINE
ACANTHINS
ACANTHOID
ACANTHOUS
ACANTHS
ACANTHUS
ACANTHUSES
ACAPNIA
ACAPNIAS
ACARI
ACARIAN
ACARIASES
ACARIASIS
ACARICIDE
ACARICIDES
ACARID
ACARIDAN
ACARIDANS
ACARIDEAN
ACARIDEANS
ACARIDIAN
ACARIDIANS
ACARIDS
ACARINE
ACAROID
ACAROLOGIES
ACAROLOGY
ACARPOUS
ACARUS
ACATER
ACATERS
ACATES
ACATOUR
ACATOURS
ACAUDAL
ACAUDATE
ACAULINE
ACAULOSE
ACCABLÉ
ACCEDE
ACCEDED
ACCEDENCE
ACCEDENCES
ACCEDER
ACCEDERS
ACCEDES
ACCEDING
ACCEND
ACCENDED
ACCENDING
ACCENDS
ACCENSION
ACCENSIONS
ACCENT
ACCENTED
ACCENTING
ACCENTOR
ACCENTORS
ACCENTS
ACCENTUAL
ACCEPT
ACCEPTANT
ACCEPTANTS
ACCEPTED
ACCEPTER
ACCEPTERS
ACCEPTING

ACCEPTIVE
ACCEPTOR
ACCEPTORS
ACCEPTS
ACCESS
ACCESSARIES
ACCESSARY
ACCESSED
ACCESSES
ACCESSING
ACCESSION
ACCESSIONED
ACCESSIONING
ACCESSIONS
ACCESSORIES
ACCESSORY
ACCIDENCE
ACCIDENCES
ACCIDENT
ACCIDENTS
ACCIDIE
ACCIDIES
ACCINGE
ACCINGED
ACCINGES
ACCINGING
ACCITE
ACCITED
ACCITES
ACCITING
ACCLAIM
ACCLAIMED
ACCLAIMING
ACCLAIMS
ACCLIMATE
ACCLIMATED
ACCLIMATES
ACCLIMATING
ACCLIVITIES
ACCLIVITY
ACCLIVOUS
ACCLOY
ACCLOYED
ACCLOYING
ACCLOYS
ACCOAST
ACCOASTED
ACCOASTING
ACCOASTS
ACCOIED
ACCOIL
ACCOILS
ACCOLADE
ACCOLADES
ACCOMPANIED
ACCOMPANIES
ACCOMPANY
ACCOMPANYING
ACCOMPT
ACCOMPTED
ACCOMPTING
ACCOMPTS
ACCORAGE
ACCORAGED
ACCORAGES
ACCORAGING
ACCORD
ACCORDANT
ACCORDED
ACCORDER

ACCORDERS
ACCORDING
ACCORDION
ACCORDIONS
ACCORDS
ACCOST
ACCOSTED
ACCOSTING
ACCOSTS
ACCOUNT
ACCOUNTED
ACCOUNTING
ACCOUNTINGS
ACCOUNTS
ACCOURAGE
ACCOURAGED
ACCOURAGES
ACCOURAGING
ACCOURT
ACCOURTED
ACCOURTING
ACCOURTS
ACCOUTRE
ACCOUTRED
ACCOUTRES
ACCOUTRING
ACCOY
ACCOYED
ACCOYING
ACCOYLD
ACCOYS
ACCREDIT
ACCREDITED
ACCREDITING
ACCREDITS
ACCRETE
ACCRETED
ACCRETES
ACCRETING
ACCRETION
ACCRETIONS
ACCRETIVE
ACCREW
ACCREWED
ACCREWING
ACCREWS
ACCRUAL
ACCRUALS
ACCRUE
ACCRUED
ACCRUES
ACCRUING
ACCUMBENT
ACCURACIES
ACCURACY
ACCURATE
ACCURSE
ACCURSED
ACCURSES
ACCURSING
ACCURST
ACCUSABLE
ACCUSAL
ACCUSALS
ACCUSE
ACCUSED
ACCUSER
ACCUSERS
ACCUSES
ACCUSING

ACCUSTOM
ACCUSTOMED
ACCUSTOMING
ACCUSTOMS
ACE
ACED
ACEDIA
ACEDIAS
ACELLULAR
ACERB
ACERBATE
ACERBATED
ACERBATES
ACERBATING
ACERBER
ACERBEST
ACERBIC
ACERBITIES
ACERBITY
ACEROSE
ACEROUS
ACERVATE
ACES
ACESCENCE
ACESCENCES
ACESCENCIES
ACESCENCY
ACESCENT
ACETABULA
ACETAL
ACETALS
ACETAMIDE
ACETAMIDES
ACETATE
ACETATES
ACETIC
ACETIFIED
ACETIFIES
ACETIFY
ACETIFYING
ACETONE
ACETONES
ACETOSE
ACETOUS
ACETYL
ACETYLENE
ACETYLENES
ACETYLS
ACHAENIUM
ACHAENIUMS
ACHAGE
ACHAGES
ACHARNE
ACHARYA
ACHARYAS
ACHATES
ACHE
ACHED
ACHENE
ACHENES
ACHENIAL
ACHENIUM
ACHENIUMS
ACHES
ACHIER
ACHIEST
ACHIEVE
ACHIEVED
ACHIEVER
ACHIEVERS

ACHIEVES
ACHIEVING
ACHIMENES
ACHING
ACHINGS
ACHKAN
ACHKANS
ACHROMAT
ACHROMATS
ACHY
ACICULAR
ACICULATE
ACID
ACIDER
ACIDEST
ACIDFREAK
ACIDFREAKS
ACIDIC
ACIDIFIED
ACIDIFIES
ACIDIFY
ACIDIFYING
ACIDITIES
ACIDITY
ACIDOSES
ACIDOSIS
ACIDS
ACIDULATE
ACIDULATED
ACIDULATES
ACIDULATING
ACIDULOUS
ACIERAGE
ACIERAGES
ACIERATE
ACIERATED
ACIERATES
ACIERATING
ACIFORM
ACING
ACINI
ACINIFORM
ACINOSE
ACINOUS
ACINUS
ACKEE
ACKEES
ACKERS
ACKNEW
ACKNOW
ACKNOWING
ACKNOWN
ACKNOWNE
ACKNOWS
ACLINIC
ACME
ACMES
ACMITE
ACMITES
ACNE
ACNES
ACOCK
ACOEMETI
ACOLD
ACOLUTHIC
ACOLYTE
ACOLYTES
ACOLYTH
ACOLYTHS
ACONITE

ACONITES
ACONITIC
ACONITINE
ACONITINES
ACONITUM
ACONITUMS
ACORN
ACORNED
ACORNS
ACOSMISM
ACOSMISMS
ACOSMIST
ACOSMISTS
ACOUCHIES
ACOUCHY
ACOUSTIC
ACOUSTICS
ACQUAINT
ACQUAINTED
ACQUAINTING
ACQUAINTS
ACQUEST
ACQUESTS
ACQUIESCE
ACQUIESCED
ACQUIESCES
ACQUIESCING
ACQUIGHT
ACQUIGHTING
ACQUIGHTS
ACQUINAL
ACQUIRALS
ACQUIRE
ACQUIRED
ACQUIRES
ACQUIRING
ACQUIST
ACQUISTS
ACQUIT
ACQUITE
ACQUITES
ACQUITING
ACQUITS
ACQUITTAL
ACQUITTALS
ACQUITTED
ACQUITTING
ACRAWL
ACRE
ACREAGE
ACREAGES
ACRED
ACRES
ACRID
ACRIDER
ACRIDEST
ACRIDIN
ACRIDINE
ACRIDINES
ACRIDINS
ACRIDITIES
ACRIDITY
ACRIMONIES
ACRIMONY
ACROBAT
ACROBATIC
ACROBATICS
ACROBATS
ACROGEN
ACROGENS

ACROLEIN
ACROLEINS
ACROLITH
ACROLITHS
ACROMIAL
ACROMION
ACROMIONS
ACRONYM
ACRONYMIC
ACRONYMS
ACROPETAL
ACROPHONIES
ACROPHONY
ACROPOLIS
ACROPOLISES
ACROSPIRE
ACROSPIRES
ACROSS
ACROSTIC
ACROSTICS
ACROTER
ACROTERIA
ACROTERS
ACROTISM
ACROTISMS
ACRYLIC
ACRYLICS
ACT
ACTA
ACTED
ACTIN
ACTINAL
ACTING
ACTINGS
ACTINIA
ACTINIAE
ACTINIAN
ACTINIANS
ACTINIAS
ACTINIC
ACTINIDE
ACTINIDES
ACTINISM
ACTINISMS
ACTINIUM
ACTINIUMS
ACTINOID
ACTINOIDS
ACTINON
ACTINONS
ACTINS
ACTION
ACTIONIST
ACTIONISTS
ACTIONS
ACTIVATE
ACTIVATED
ACTIVATES
ACTIVATING
ACTIVATOR
ACTIVATORS
ACTIVE
ACTIVELY
ACTIVISM
ACTIVISMS
ACTIVIST
ACTIVISTS
ACTIVITIES
ACTIVITY
ACTON

ACTONS
ACTOR
ACTORS
ACTRESS
ACTRESSES
ACTS
ACTUAL
ACTUALISE
ACTUALISED
ACTUALISES
ACTUALISING
ACTUALIST
ACTUALISTS
ACTUALITIES
ACTUALITY
ACTUALIZE
ACTUALIZED
ACTUALIZES
ACTUALIZING
ACTUALLY
ACTUARIAL
ACTUARIES
ACTUARY
ACTUATE
ACTUATED
ACTUATES
ACTUATING
ACTUATION
ACTUATIONS
ACTUATOR
ACTUATORS
ACTURE
ACTURES
ACUITIES
ACUITY
ACULEATE
ACULEATED
ACUMEN
ACUMENS
ACUMINATE
ACUMINATED
ACUMINATES
ACUMINATING
ACUPOINTS
ACUSHLA
ACUSHLAS
ACUTE
ACUTELY
ACUTENESS
ACUTENESSES
ACUTER
ACUTES
ACUTEST
ACYCLIC
ACYCLOVIR
ACYCLOVIRS
ACYL
ACYLS
AD
ADAGE
ADAGES
ADAGIO
ADAGIOS
ADAMANT
ADAMANTS
ADAPT
ADAPTABLE
ADAPTED
ADAPTER
ADAPTERS

ADAPTING
ADAPTION
ADAPTIONS
ADAPTIVE
ADAPTOR
ADAPTORS
ADAPTS
ADAW
ADAWED
ADAWING
ADAWS
ADAXIAL
ADAYS
ADD
ADDAX
ADDAXES
ADDED
ADDEEM
ADDEEMED
ADDEEMING
ADDEEMS
ADDEND
ADDENDA
ADDENDS
ADDENDUM
ADDER
ADDERS
ADDERWORT
ADDERWORTS
ADDICT
ADDICTED
ADDICTING
ADDICTION
ADDICTIONS
ADDICTIVE
ADDICTS
ADDING
ADDIO
ADDIOS
ADDITION
ADDITIONS
ADDITIVE
ADDITIVES
ADDLE
ADDLED
ADDLEMENT
ADDLEMENTS
ADDLES
ADDLING
ADDOOM
ADDOOMED
ADDOOMING
ADDOOMS
ADDORSED
ADDRESS
ADDRESSED
ADDRESSEE
ADDRESSEES
ADDRESSER
ADDRESSERS
ADDRESSES
ADDRESSING
ADDRESSOR
ADDRESSORS
ADDREST
ADDS
ADDUCE
ADDUCED
ADDUCENT
ADDUCER

ADDUCERS
ADDUCES
ADDUCIBLE
ADDUCING
ADDUCT
ADDUCTED
ADDUCTING
ADDUCTION
ADDUCTIONS
ADDUCTIVE
ADDUCTOR
ADDUCTORS
ADDUCTS
ADEEM
ADEEMED
ADEEMING
ADEEMS
ADEMPTION
ADEMPTIONS
ADENINE
ADENINES
ADENITIS
ADENITISES
ADENOID
ADENOIDAL
ADENOIDS
ADENOMA
ADENOMAS
ADENOMATA
ADENOSINE
ADENOSINES
ADEPT
ADEPTER
ADEPTEST
ADEPTNESS
ADEPTNESSES
ADEPTS
ADEQUACIES
ADEQUACY
ADEQUATE
ADERMIN
ADERMINS
ADESPOTA
ADESSIVE
ADESSIVES
ADHARMA
ADHARMAS
ADHERE
ADHERED
ADHERENCE
ADHERENCES
ADHERENT
ADHERENTS
ADHERER
ADHERERS
ADHERES
ADHERING
ADHESION
ADHESIONS
ADHESIVE
ADHESIVES
ADHIBIT
ADHIBITED
ADHIBITING
ADHIBITS
ADIABATIC
ADIAPHORA
ADIEU
ADIEUS
ADIEUX

ADIOS
ADIPIC
ADIPOCERE
ADIPOCERES
ADIPOSE
ADIPOSITIES
ADIPOSITY
ADIT
ADITS
ADJACENCIES
ADJACENCY
ADJACENT
ADJECTIVE
ADJECTIVES
ADJOIN
ADJOINED
ADJOINING
ADJOINS
ADJOINT
ADJOINTS
ADJOURN
ADJOURNED
ADJOURNING
ADJOURNS
ADJUDGE
ADJUDGED
ADJUDGES
ADJUDGING
ADJUNCT
ADJUNCTLY
ADJUNCTS
ADJURE
ADJURED
ADJURES
ADJURING
ADJUST
ADJUSTED
ADJUSTER
ADJUSTERS
ADJUSTING
ADJUSTOR
ADJUSTORS
ADJUSTS
ADJUTAGE
ADJUTAGES
ADJUTANCIES
ADJUTANCY
ADJUTANT
ADJUTANTS
ADJUVANCIES
ADJUVANCY
ADJUVANT
ADJUVANTS
ADMASS
ADMASSES
ADMEASURE
ADMEASURED
ADMEASURES
ADMEASURING
ADMIN
ADMINICLE
ADMINICLES
ADMINS
ADMIRABLE
ADMIRABLY
ADMIRAL
ADMIRALS
ADMIRANCE
ADMIRANCES
ADMIRE

ADMIRED
ADMIRER
ADMIRERS
ADMIRES
ADMIRING
ADMISSION
ADMISSIONS
ADMISSIVE
ADMIT
ADMITS
ADMITTED
ADMITTING
ADMIX
ADMIXED
ADMIXES
ADMIXING
ADMIXTURE
ADMIXTURES
ADMONISH
ADMONISHED
ADMONISHES
ADMONISHING
ADMONITOR
ADMONITORS
ADNASCENT
ADNATE
ADNATION
ADNATIONS
ADO
ADOBE
ADOBES
ADONISE
ADONISED
ADONISES
ADONISING
ADONIZE
ADONIZED
ADONIZES
ADONIZING
ADOORS
ADOPT
ADOPTED
ADOPTER
ADOPTERS
ADOPTING
ADOPTION
ADOPTIONS
ADOPTIOUS
ADOPTIVE
ADOPTS
ADORABLE
ADORABLY
ADORATION
ADORATIONS
ADORE
ADORED
ADORER
ADORERS
ADORES
ADORING
ADORINGLY
ADORN
ADORNED
ADORNING
ADORNMENT
ADORNMENTS
ADORNS
ADOS
ADOWN
ADPRESS

ADPRESSED	ADVECTION	ADVOWSONS	AEROBOMB	AESTIVATES
ADPRESSES	ADVECTIONS	ADWARD	AEROBOMBS	AESTIVATING
ADPRESSING	ADVENE	ADWARDED	AEROBUS	AETHER
ADRAD	ADVENED	ADWARDING	AEROBUSES	AETHERS
ADREAD	ADVENES	ADWARDS	AERODART	AETIOLOGIES
ADREADED	ADVENING	ADYNAMIA	AERODARTS	AETIOLOGY
ADREADING	ADVENT	ADYNAMIAS	AERODROME	AFALD
ADREADS	ADVENTIVE	ADYNAMIC	AERODROMES	AFAR
ADRED	ADVENTIVES	ADYTA	AERODYNE	AFARA
ADRENAL	ADVENTS	ADYTUM	AERODYNES	AFARAS
ADRENALS	ADVENTURE	ADZE	AEROFOIL	AFAWLD
ADRIFT	ADVENTURED	ADZES	AEROFOILS	AFEAR
ADROIT	ADVENTURES	AE	AEROGRAM	AFEARD
ADROITER	ADVENTURING	AECIA	AEROGRAMS	AFEARED
ADROITEST	ADVERB	AECIDIA	AEROGRAPH	AFEARING
ADROITLY	ADVERBIAL	AECIDIUM	AEROGRAPHS	AFEARS
ADRY	ADVERBS	AECIUM	AEROLITE	AFFABLE
ADS	ADVERSARIES	AEDILE	AEROLITES	AFFABLY
ADSCRIPT	ADVERSARY	AEDILES	AEROLITH	AFFAIR
ADSCRIPTS	ADVERSE	AEFALD	AEROLITHS	AFFAIRE
ADSORB	ADVERSELY	AEFAULD	AEROLITIC	AFFAIRES
ADSORBATE	ADVERSER	AEFAWLD	AEROLOGIES	AFFAIRS
ADSORBATES	ADVERSEST	AEGIRINE	AEROLOGY	AFFEAR
ADSORBED	ADVERSITIES	AEGIRINES	AEROMANCIES	AFFEARD
ADSORBENT	ADVERSITY	AEGIRITE	AEROMANCY	AFFEARE
ADSORBENTS	ADVERT	AEGIRITES	AEROMETER	AFFEARED
ADSORBING	ADVERTED	AEGIS	AEROMETERS	AFFEARES
ADSORBS	ADVERTENT	AEGISES	AEROMETRIES	AFFEARING
ADSUM	ADVERTING	AEGLOGUE	AEROMETRY	AFFEARS
ADULARIA	ADVERTISE	AEGLOGUES	AEROMOTOR	AFFECT
ADULARIAS	ADVERTISED	AEGROTAT	AEROMOTORS	AFFECTED
ADULATE	ADVERTISES	AEGROTATS	AERONAUT	AFFECTER
ADULATED	ADVERTISING	AEMULE	AERONAUTS	AFFECTERS
ADULATES	ADVERTISINGS	AEMULED	AERONOMIES	AFFECTING
ADULATING	ADVERTS	AEMULES	AERONOMY	AFFECTION
ADULATION	ADVEW	AEMULING	AEROPHONE	AFFECTIONED
ADULATIONS	ADVEWED	AEOLIAN	AEROPHONES	AFFECTIONING
ADULATOR	ADVEWING	AEOLIPILE	AEROPHYTE	AFFECTIONS
ADULATORS	ADVEWS	AEOLIPILES	AEROPHYTES	AFFECTIVE
ADULATORY	ADVICE	AEOLIPYLE	AEROPLANE	AFFECTS
ADULT	ADVICEFUL	AEOLIPYLES	AEROPLANES	AFFEER
ADULTERER	ADVICES	AEON	AEROSHELL	AFFEERED
ADULTERERS	ADVISABLE	AEONIAN	AEROSHELLS	AFFEERING
ADULTERIES	ADVISABLY	AEONS	AEROSOL	AFFEERS
ADULTERY	ADVISE	AERATE	AEROSOLS	AFFERENT
ADULTHOOD	ADVISED	AERATED	AEROSPACE	AFFIANCE
ADULTHOODS	ADVISEDLY	AERATES	AEROSPACES	AFFIANCED
ADULTS	ADVISER	AERATING	AEROSTAT	AFFIANCES
ADUMBRATE	ADVISERS	AERATION	AEROSTATS	AFFIANCING
ADUMBRATED	ADVISES	AERATIONS	AEROTAXES	AFFICHE
ADUMBRATES	ADVISING	AERATOR	AEROTAXIS	AFFICHES
ADUMBRATING	ADVISINGS	AERATORS	AEROTRAIN	AFFIDAVIT
ADUNC	ADVISOR	AERIAL	AEROTRAINS	AFFIDAVITS
ADUNCATE	ADVISORS	AERIALIST	AERY	AFFIED
ADUNCATED	ADVISORY	AERIALISTS	AESC	AFFIES
ADUNCITIES	ADVOCAAT	AERIALITIES	AESCES	AFFILIATE
ADUNCITY	ADVOCAATS	AERIALITY	AESCULIN	AFFILIATED
ADUNCOUS	ADVOCACIES	AERIALLY	AESCULINS	AFFILIATES
ADUST	ADVOCACY	AERIALS	AESIR	AFFILIATING
ADUSTED	ADVOCATE	AERIE	AESTHESES	AFFINE
ADUSTING	ADVOCATED	AERIER	AESTHESIA	AFFINED
ADUSTS	ADVOCATES	AERIES	AESTHESIAS	AFFINES
ADVANCE	ADVOCATING	AERIEST	AESTHESIS	AFFINITIES
ADVANCED	ADVOCATOR	AERIFORM	AESTHETE	AFFINITY
ADVANCES	ADVOCATORS	AEROBE	AESTHETES	AFFIRM
ADVANCING	ADVOUTRER	AEROBES	AESTHETIC	AFFIRMANT
ADVANTAGE	ADVOUTRERS	AEROBIC	AESTHETICS	AFFIRMANTS
ADVANTAGED	ADVOUTRIES	AEROBICS	AESTIVAL	AFFIRMED
ADVANTAGES	ADVOUTRY	AEROBIONT	AESTIVATE	AFFIRMER
ADVANTAGING	ADVOWSON	AEROBIONTS	AESTIVATED	AFFIRMERS

AFFIRMING
AFFIRMS
AFFIX
AFFIXED
AFFIXES
AFFIXING
AFFLATED
AFFLATION
AFFLATIONS
AFFLATUS
AFFLATUSES
AFFLICT
AFFLICTED
AFFLICTING
AFFLICTINGS
AFFLICTS
AFFLUENCE
AFFLUENCES
AFFLUENT
AFFLUENTS
AFFLUX
AFFLUXES
AFFLUXION
AFFLUXIONS
AFFOORD
AFFOORDED
AFFOORDING
AFFOORDS
AFFORCE
AFFORCED
AFFORCES
AFFORCING
AFFORD
AFFORDED
AFFORDING
AFFORDS
AFFOREST
AFFORESTED
AFFORESTING
AFFORESTS
AFFRAP
AFFRAPPED
AFFRAPPING
AFFRAPS
AFFRAY
AFFRAYED
AFFRAYING
AFFRAYS
AFFRENDED
AFFRET
AFFRETS
AFFRICATE
AFFRICATES
AFFRIGHT
AFFRIGHTED
AFFRIGHTING
AFFRIGHTS
AFFRONT
AFFRONTÉ
AFFRONTED
AFFRONTÉE
AFFRONTEE
AFFRONTING
AFFRONTINGS
AFFRONTS
AFFUSION
AFFUSIONS
AFFY
AFFYDE
AFFYING

AFGHAN
AFGHANS
AFIELD
AFIRE
AFLAJ
AFLAME
AFLATOXIN
AFLATOXINS
AFLOAT
AFOOT
AFORE
AFOREHAND
AFORESAID
AFORETIME
AFOUL
AFRAID
AFREET
AFREETS
AFRESH
AFRIT
AFRITS
AFRO
AFRONT
AFROS
AFT
AFTER
AFTERCARE
AFTERCARES
AFTEREYE
AFTEREYED
AFTEREYEING
AFTEREYES
AFTEREYING
AFTERGAME
AFTERGAMES
AFTERGLOW
AFTERGLOWS
AFTERINGS
AFTERMATH
AFTERMATHS
AFTERMOST
AFTERNOON
AFTERNOONS
AFTERS
AFTERTIME
AFTERTIMES
AFTERWARD
AFTERWARDS
AFTERWORD
AFTERWORDS
AFTMOST
AGA
AGAÇANT
AGAÇANTE
AGACERIE
AGACERIES
AGAIN
AGAINST
AGALACTIA
AGALACTIAS
AGALLOCH
AGALLOCHS
AGAMI
AGAMIC
AGAMID
AGAMIDS
AGAMIS
AGAMOID
AGAMOIDS
AGAMOUS

AGAPAE
AGAPE
AGAR
AGARIC
AGARICS
AGARS
AGAS
AGAST
AGATE
AGATES
AGAVE
AGAVES
AGAZE
AGAZED
AGE
AGED
AGEDNESS
AGEDNESSES
AGEE
AGEING
AGEINGS
AGEISM
AGEISMS
AGEIST
AGEISTS
AGELAST
AGELASTIC
AGELASTS
AGELESS
AGELONG
AGEN
AGENCIES
AGENCY
AGENDA
AGENDAS
AGENE
AGENES
AGENT
AGENTED
AGENTIAL
AGENTING
AGENTS
AGES
AGGER
AGGERS
AGGRACE
AGGRACED
AGGRACES
AGGRACING
AGGRADE
AGGRADED
AGGRADES
AGGRADING
AGGRATE
AGGRATED
AGGRATES
AGGRATING
AGGRAVATE
AGGRAVATED
AGGRAVATES
AGGRAVATING
AGGREGATE
AGGREGATED
AGGREGATES
AGGREGATING
AGGRESS
AGGRESSED
AGGRESSES
AGGRESSING
AGGRESSOR

AGGRESSORS
AGGRI
AGGRIEVE
AGGRIEVED
AGGRIEVES
AGGRIEVING
AGGRO
AGGROS
AGGRY
AGHA
AGHAS
AGHAST
AGILA
AGILAS
AGILE
AGILELY
AGILER
AGILEST
AGILITIES
AGILITY
AGIN
AGING
AGINGS
AGINNER
AGINNERS
AGIO
AGIOS
AGIOTAGE
AGIOTAGES
AGIST
AGISTED
AGISTER
AGISTERS
AGISTING
AGISTMENT
AGISTMENTS
AGISTOR
AGISTORS
AGISTS
AGITATE
AGITATED
AGITATES
AGITATING
AGITATION
AGITATIONS
AGITATIVE
AGITATO
AGITATOR
AGITATORS
AGITPROP
AGITPROPS
AGLEE
AGLET
AGLETS
AGLEY
AGLIMMER
AGLITTER
AGLOW
AGMA
AGMAS
AGNAIL
AGNAILS
AGNAME
AGNAMED
AGNAMES
AGNATE
AGNATES
AGNATIC
AGNATICAL
AGNATION

AGNATIONS
AGNISE
AGNISED
AGNISES
AGNISING
AGNIZE
AGNIZED
AGNIZES
AGNIZING
AGNOMEN
AGNOMENS
AGNOMINA
AGNOSTIC
AGNOSTICS
AGO
AGOG
AGOGE
AGOGES
AGOGIC
AGOGICS
AGOING
AGON
AGONE
AGONIC
AGONIES
AGONISE
AGONISED
AGONISES
AGONISING
AGONIST
AGONISTES
AGONISTIC
AGONISTICS
AGONISTS
AGONIZE
AGONIZED
AGONIZES
AGONIZING
AGONS
AGONY
AGOOD
AGORA
AGORAS
AGOROT
AGOUTA
AGOUTAS
AGOUTI
AGOUTIES
AGOUTIS
AGOUTY
AGRAFFE
AGRAFFES
AGRAPHA
AGRAPHIA
AGRAPHIAS
AGRAPHIC
AGRAPHON
AGRARIAN
AGRASTE
AGRAVIC
AGREE
AGREEABLE
AGREEABLY
AGREED
AGREEING
AGREEMENT
AGREEMENTS
AGREES
AGRÉGÉ
AGRÉGÉS

.GRÉMENS	AIDANCES	AIRIER	AITCH	ALARM
.GRÉMENT	AIDANT	AIRIEST	AITCHBONE	ALARMED
.GRÉMENTS	AIDE	AIRILY	AITCHBONES	ALARMEDLY
.GRESTAL	AIDED	AIRINESS	AITCHES	ALARMING
.GRESTIAL	AIDER	AIRINESSES	AITS	ALARMISM
.GRESTIC	AIDERS	AIRING	AITU	ALARMISMS
.GRIMONIES	AIDES	AIRINGS	AITUS	ALARMIST
.GRIMONY	AIDFUL	AIRLESS	AIZLE	ALARMISTS
.GRIN	AIDING	AIRLIFT	AIZLES	ALARMS
.GRIOLOGIES	AIDLESS	AIRLIFTED	AJAR	ALARUM
.GRIOLOGY	AIDOI	AIRLIFTING	AJEE	ALARUMED
.GRISE	AIDOS	AIRLIFTS	AJOWAN	ALARUMING
.GRISED	AIDS	AIRLINE	AJOWANS	ALARUMS
.GRISES	AIERIES	AIRLINER	AJUTAGE	ALARY
.GRISING	AIERY	AIRLINERS	AJUTAGES	ALAS
.GRIZE	AIGLET	AIRLINES	AJWAN	ALASTRIM
.GRIZED	AIGLETS	AIRMAIL	AJWANS	ALASTRIMS
.GRIZES	AIGRETTE	AIRMAILED	AKE	ALATE
.GRIZING	AIGRETTES	AIRMAILING	AKED	ALATED
.GROLOGIES	AIGUILLE	AIRMAILS	AKEDAH	ALAY
.GROLOGY	AIGUILLES	AIRMAN	AKEDAHS	ALAYED
.GRONOMIC	AIKIDO	AIRMEN	AKEE	ALAYING
.GRONOMICS	AIKIDOS	AIRN	AKEES	ALAYS
.GRONOMIES	AIKONA	AIRNED	AKENE	ALB
.GHONOMY	AIL	AIRNING	AKENES	ALBACORE
.GROUND	AILANTHUS	AIRNS	AKES	ALBACORES
.GRYZE	AILANTHUSES	AIRPLANE	AKIMBO	ALBARELLI
.GRYZED	AILANTO	AIRPLANES	AKIN	ALBARELLO
.GRYZES	AILANTOS	AIRPORT	AKINESIA	ALBARELLOS
.GRYZING	AILED	AIRPORTS	AKINESIAS	ALBATA
.GUACATE	AILERON	AIRS	AKINESIS	ALBATAS
.GUACATES	AILERONS	AIRSCREW	AKING	ALBATROSS
.GUE	AILETTE	AIRSCREWS	AKKAS	ALBATROSSES
.GUED	AILETTES	AIRSHAFT	AKOLUTHOS	ALBE
.GUES	AILING	AIRSHAFTS	AKOLUTHOSES	ALBEDO
.GUISE	AILMENT	AIRSHIP	AKVAVIT	ALBEDOS
.GUISED	AILMENTS	AIRSHIPS	AKVAVITS	ALBEE
.GUISES	AILS	AIRSICK	ALA	ALBEIT
.GUISH	AIM	AIRSPACE	ALAAP	ALBERGHI
.GUISHLY	AIMED	AIRSPACES	ALAAPS	ALBERGO
.GUISING	AIMING	AIRSTOP	ALABAMINE	ALBERT
.GUIZE	AIMLESS	AIRSTOPS	ALABAMINES	ALBERTITE
.GUIZED	AIMLESSLY	AIRSTREAM	ALABASTER	ALBERTITES
.GUIZES	AIMS	AIRSTREAMS	ALABASTERS	ALBERTS
.GUIZING	AIN	AIRSTRIP	ALACK	ALBESCENT
.GUTI	AÎNÉ	AIRSTRIPS	ALACRITIES	ALBESPINE
.GUTIS	AÎNÉE	AIRT	ALACRITY	ALBESPINES
.H	AIOLI	AIRTED	ALAE	ALBESPYNE
.HA	AIOLIS	AIRTIGHT	ALAIMENT	ALBESPYNES
.HEAD	AIR	AIRTIME	ALAIMENTS	ALBICORE
.HEAP	AIRBORNE	AIRTIMES	ALALAGMOI	ALBICORES
.HEIGHT	AIRBURST	AIRTING	ALALAGMOS	ALBINESS
.HEM	AIRBURSTS	AIRTS	ALALIA	ALBINESSES
.HIGH	AIRCRAFT	AIRWARD	ALALIAS	ALBINISM
.HIMSA	AIRDRAWN	AIRWARDS	ALAMEDA	ALBINISMS
.HIMSAS	AIRDROME	AIRWAVE	ALAMEDAS	ALBINO
.HIND	AIRDROMES	AIRWAVES	ALAMODE	ALBINOISM
.HINT	AIRED	AIRWAY	ALAMODES	ALBINOISMS
.HOLD	AIRER	AIRWAYS	ALAMORT	ALBINOS
.HORSE	AIRERS	AIRWOMAN	ALAND	ALBINOTIC
.HOY	AIRFIELD	AIRWOMEN	ALANG	ALBITE
.HULL	AIRFIELDS	AIRWORTHY	ALANGS	ALBITES
.HUNGERED	AIRFRAME	AIRY	ALANNAH	ALBITISE
.HUNGRY	AIRFRAMES	AIS	ALANNAHS	ALBITISED
.I	AIRGAP	AISLE	ALAP	ALBITISES
.IA	AIRGAPS	AISLED	ALAPA	ALBITISING
.IAS	AIRGRAPH	AISLES	ALAPAS	ALBITIZE
.IBLINS	AIRGRAPHS	AISLING	ALAPS	ALBITIZED
.ID	AIRHOLE	AISLINGS	ALAR	ALBITIZES
.IDANCE	AIRHOLES	AIT		ALBITIZING

ALBRICIAS
ALBS
ALBUGO
ALBUGOS
ALBUM
ALBUMEN
ALBUMENS
ALBUMIN
ALBUMINS
ALBUMS
ALBURNOUS
ALBURNUM
ALBURNUMS
ALCAHEST
ALCAHESTS
ALCAIDE
ALCAIDES
ALCALDE
ALCALDES
ALCARRAZA
ALCARRAZAS
ALCATRAS
ALCATRASES
ALCAYDE
ALCAYDES
ALCÁZAR
ALCÁZARS
ALCHEMIC
ALCHEMIES
ALCHEMIST
ALCHEMISTS
ALCHEMY
ALCHERA
ALCHERAS
ALCHYMIES
ALCHYMY
ALCOHOL
ALCOHOLIC
ALCOHOLICS
ALCOHOLS
ALCORZA
ALCORZAS
ALCOVE
ALCOVES
ALDEA
ALDEAS
ALDEHYDE
ALDEHYDES
ALDER
ALDERMAN
ALDERMEN
ALDERN
ALDERS
ALDOSE
ALDOSES
ALDRIN
ALDRINS
ALE
ALEATORIC
ALEATORIES
ALEATORY
ALEBENCH
ALEBENCHES
ALECOST
ALECOSTS
ALECTRYON
ALECTRYONS
ALEE
ALEFT
ALEGAR

ALEGARS
ALEGGE
ALEGGED
ALEGGES
ALEGGING
ALEMBIC
ALEMBICS
ALEMBROTH
ALEMBROTHS
ALENGTH
ALEPH
ALEPHS
ALEPINE
ALEPINES
ALERCE
ALERCES
ALERION
ALERIONS
ALERT
ALERTED
ALERTER
ALERTEST
ALERTING
ALERTLY
ALERTNESS
ALERTNESSES
ALERTS
ALES
ALEURON
ALEURONE
ALEURONES
ALEURONS
ALEVIN
ALEVINS
ALEW
ALEWASHED
ALEWIFE
ALEWIVES
ALEWS
ALEXIA
ALEXIAS
ALEXIC
ALEXIN
ALEXINS
ALEYE
ALEYED
ALEYES
ALEYING
ALFA
ALFALFA
ALFALFAS
ALFAQUÍ
ALFAQUÍS
ALFAS
ALFÉRECES
ALFÉREZ
ALFORJA
ALFORJAS
ALFRESCO
ALGA
ALGAE
ALGAL
ALGAROBA
ALGAROBAS
ALGARROBA
ALGARROBAS
ALGARROBO
ALGARROBOS
ALGATE
ALGATES

ALGEBRA
ALGEBRAIC
ALGEBRAS
ALGERINE
ALGERINES
ALGESES
ALGESIA
ALGESIAS
ALGESIS
ALGICIDE
ALGICIDES
ALGID
ALGIDITIES
ALGIDITY
ALGIN
ALGINATE
ALGINATES
ALGINIC
ALGINS
ALGOID
ALGOLOGIES
ALGOLOGY
ALGORISM
ALGORISMS
ALGORITHM
ALGORITHMS
ALGUACIL
ALGUACILS
ALGUAZIL
ALGUAZILS
ALGUM
ALGUMS
ALIAS
ALIASES
ALIBI
ALIBIS
ALICANT
ALICANTS
ALICYCLIC
ALIDAD
ALIDADE
ALIDADES
ALIDADS
ALIEN
ALIENABLE
ALIENAGE
ALIENAGES
ALIENATE
ALIENATED
ALIENATES
ALIENATING
ALIENATOR
ALIENATORS
ALIENED
ALIENEE
ALIENEES
ALIENING
ALIENISM
ALIENISMS
ALIENIST
ALIENISTS
ALIENOR
ALIENORS
ALIENS
ALIFORM
ALIGARTA
ALIGARTAS
ALIGHT
ALIGHTED
ALIGHTING

ALIGHTS
ALIGN
ALIGNED
ALIGNING
ALIGNMENT
ALIGNMENTS
ALIGNS
ALIKE
ALIMENT
ALIMENTAL
ALIMENTED
ALIMENTING
ALIMENTS
ALIMONIES
ALIMONY
ALINE
ALINED
ALINEMENT
ALINEMENTS
ALINES
ALINING
ALIPED
ALIPEDS
ALIPHATIC
ALIQUANT
ALIQUOT
ALISMA
ALISMAS
ALIT
ALIUNDE
ALIVE
ALIZARI
ALIZARIN
ALIZARINE
ALIZARINES
ALIZARINS
ALIZARIS
ALKAHEST
ALKAHESTS
ALKALI
ALKALIES
ALKALIFIED
ALKALIFIES
ALKALIFY
ALKALIFYING
ALKALINE
ALKALIS
ALKALISE
ALKALISED
ALKALISES
ALKALISING
ALKALIZE
ALKALIZED
ALKALIZES
ALKALIZING
ALKALOID
ALKALOIDS
ALKALOSES
ALKALOSIS
ALKANE
ALKANES
ALKANET
ALKANETS
ALKENE
ALKENES
ALKYD
ALKYDS
ALKYL
ALKYLS
ALKYNE

ALKYNES
ALL
ALLANTOIC
ALLANTOID
ALLANTOIDS
ALLANTOIS
ALLANTOISES
ALLATIVE
ALLATIVES
ALLAY
ALLAYED
ALLAYER
ALLAYERS
ALLAYING
ALLAYINGS
ALLAYMENT
ALLAYMENTS
ALLAYS
ALLEDGE
ALLEDGED
ALLEDGES
ALLEDGING
ALLÉE
ALLÉES
ALLEGE
ALLEGED
ALLEGEDLY
ALLEGER
ALLEGERS
ALLEGES
ALLEGGE
ALLEGGED
ALLEGGES
ALLEGGING
ALLEGIANT
ALLEGING
ALLEGORIC
ALLEGORIES
ALLEGORY
ALLEGRO
ALLEGROS
ALLEL
ALLELE
ALLELES
ALLELS
ALLELUIA
ALLELUIAH
ALLELUIAHS
ALLELUIAS
ALLEMANDE
ALLEMANDES
ALLENARLY
ALLERGEN
ALLERGENS
ALLERGIC
ALLERGICS
ALLERGIES
ALLERGY
ALLERION
ALLERIONS
ALLEVIATE
ALLEVIATED
ALLEVIATES
ALLEVIATING
ALLEY
ALLEYED
ALLEYS
ALLEYWAY
ALLEYWAYS
ALLHEAL

LLHEALS	ALLOTTERIES	ALMONRIES	ALPINISTS	ALUMINA
LLIANCE	ALLOTTERY	ALMONRY	ALPS	ALUMINAS
LLIANCES	ALLOTTING	ALMOST	ALREADY	ALUMINATE
LLICE	ALLOW	ALMOUS	ALRIGHT	ALUMINATES
LLICES	ALLOWABLE	ALMS	ALS	ALUMINISE
LLICHOLIES	ALLOWABLY	ALMUG	ALSIKE	ALUMINISED
LLICHOLY	ALLOWANCE	ALMUGS	ALSIKES	ALUMINISES
LLIED	ALLOWANCED	ALNAGE	ALSO	ALUMINISING
LLIES	ALLOWANCES	ALNAGER	ALSOON	ALUMINIUM
LLIGARTA	ALLOWANCING	ALNAGERS	ALSOONE	ALUMINIUMS
LLIGARTAS	ALLOWED	ALNAGES	ALT	ALUMINIZE
LLIGATE	ALLOWEDLY	ALOD	ALTAR	ALUMINIZED
LLIGATED	ALLOWING	ALODIAL	ALTARAGE	ALUMINIZES
LLIGATES	ALLOWS	ALODIUM	ALTARAGES	ALUMINIZING
LLIGATING	ALLOY	ALODIUMS	ALTARS	ALUMINOUS
LLIGATOR	ALLOYED	ALODS	ALTARWISE	ALUMINUM
LLIGATORS	ALLOYING	ALOE	ALTER	ALUMINUMS
LLIS	ALLOYS	ALOED	ALTERABLE	ALUMISH
LLISES	ALLS	ALOES	ALTERANT	ALUMIUM
LLNESS	ALLSEED	ALOETIC	ALTERANTS	ALUMIUMS
LLNESSES	ALLSEEDS	ALOETICS	ALTERCATE	ALUMNA
LLNIGHT	ALLSPICE	ALOFT	ALTERCATED	ALUMNAE
LLOCABLE	ALLSPICES	ALOGIA	ALTERCATES	ALUMNI
LLOCARPIES	ALLUDE	ALOGIAS	ALTERCATING	ALUMNUS
LLOCARPY	ALLUDED	ALOGICAL	ALTERED	ALUMS
LLOCATE	ALLUDES	ALOHA	ALTERING	ALUNITE
LLOCATED	ALLUDING	ALOHAS	ALTERITIES	ALUNITES
LLOCATES	ALLURE	ALONE	ALTERITY	ALURE
LLOCATING	ALLURED	ALONELY	ALTERN	ALURES
LLOD	ALLURER	ALONENESS	ALTERNANT	ALVEARIES
LLODIAL	ALLURERS	ALONENESSES	ALTERNANTS	ALVEARY
LLODIUM	ALLURES	ALONG	ALTERNAT	ALVEATED
LLODIUMS	ALLURING	ALONGSIDE	ALTERNATE	ALVEOLAR
LLODS	ALLUSION	ALONGST	ALTERNATED	ALVEOLATE
LLOGAMIES	ALLUSIONS	ALOOF	ALTERNATES	ALVEOLE
LLOGAMY	ALLUSIVE	ALOOFLY	ALTERNATING	ALVEOLES
LLOGRAPH	ALLUVIA	ALOOFNESS	ALTERNATS	ALVEOLI
LLOGRAPHS	ALLUVIAL	ALOOFNESSES	ALTERNE	ALVEOLUS
LLOMETRIES	ALLUVION	ALOPECIA	ALTERNES	ALVINE
LLOMETRY	ALLUVIONS	ALOPECIAS	ALTERS	ALWAY
LLOMORPH	ALLUVIUM	ALOPECOID	ALTESSE	ALWAYS
LLOMORPHS	ALLY	ALOUD	ALTESSES	ALYSSUM
LLONGE	ALLYCHOLIES	ALOW	ALTEZA	ALYSSUMS
LLONGES	ALLYCHOLY	ALOWE	ALTEZAS	AM
LLONS	ALLYING	ALP	ALTEZZA	AMABILE
LLONYM	ALLYL	ALPACA	ALTEZZAS	AMADAVAT
LLONYMS	ALLYLS	ALPACAS	ALTHAEA	AMADAVATS
LLOPATH	ALMA	ALPARGATA	ALTHAEAS	AMADOU
LLOPATHIES	ALMAH	ALPARGATAS	ALTHORN	AMADOUS
LLOPATHS	ALMAHS	ALPEEN	ALTHORNS	AMAH
LLOPATHY	ALMAIN	ALPEENS	ALTHOUGH	AMAHS
LLOPHONE	ALMAINS	ALPENHORN	ALTIMETER	AMAIN
LLOPHONES	ALMANAC	ALPENHORNS	ALTIMETERS	AMALGAM
LLOPLASM	ALMANACS	ALPHA	ALTISSIMO	AMALGAMS
LLOPLASMS	ALMANDINE	ALPHABET	ALTITUDE	AMANDINE
LLOSAUR	ALMANDINES	ALPHABETED	ALTITUDES	AMANDINES
LLOSAURS	ALMAS	ALPHABETING	ALTO	AMANITA
LLOSTERIES	ALME	ALPHABETS	ALTOS	AMANITAS
LLOSTERY	ALMEH	ALPHAS	ALTRICES	AMARACUS
LLOT	ALMEHS	ALPHASORT	ALTRICIAL	AMARACUSES
LLOTMENT	ALMERIES	ALPHASORTED	ALTRUISM	AMARANT
LLOTMENTS	ALMERY	ALPHASORTING	ALTRUISMS	AMARANTH
LLOTROPE	ALMES	ALPHASORTS	ALTRUIST	AMARANTHS
LLOTROPES	ALMIGHTY	ALPHORN	ALTRUISTS	AMARANTIN
LLOTROPIES	ALMIRAH	ALPHORNS	ALTS	AMARANTS
LLOTROPY	ALMIRAHS	ALPINE	ALUDEL	AMARYLLID
LLOTS	ALMOND	ALPINES	ALUDELS	AMARYLLIDS
LLOTTED	ALMONDS	ALPINISM	ALULA	AMARYLLIS
LLOTTEE	ALMONER	ALPINISMS	ALULAS	AMARYLLISES
LLOTTEES	ALMONERS	ALPINIST	ALUM	AMASS

AMASSABLE	AMBITION	AMENAUNCES	AMITY	AMOROSA
AMASSED	AMBITIONS	AMEND	AMLA	AMOROSAS
AMASSES	AMBITIOUS	AMENDABLE	AMLAS	AMOROSITIES
AMASSING	AMBITS	AMENDE	AMMAN	AMOROSITY
AMASSMENT	AMBITTY	AMENDED	AMMANS	AMOROSO
AMASSMENTS	AMBIVERT	AMENDER	AMMETER	AMOROSOS
AMATE	AMBIVERTS	AMENDERS	AMMETERS	AMOROUS
AMATED	AMBLE	AMENDES	AMMIRAL	AMOROUSLY
AMATES	AMBLED	AMENDING	AMMIRALS	AMORPHISM
AMATEUR	AMBLER	AMENDMENT	AMMO	AMORPHISMS
AMATEURS	AMBLERS	AMENDMENTS	AMMON	AMORPHOUS
AMATING	AMBLES	AMENDS	AMMONAL	AMORT
AMATION	AMBLING	AMENE	AMMONALS	AMORTISE
AMATIONS	AMBLINGS	AMENED	AMMONIA	AMORTISED
AMATIVE	AMBLYOPIA	AMENING	AMMONIAC	AMORTISES
AMATOL	AMBLYOPIAS	AMENITIES	AMMONIAS	AMORTISING
AMATOLS	AMBO	AMENITY	AMMONITE	AMORTIZE
AMATORIAL	AMBONES	AMENS	AMMONITES	AMORTIZED
AMATORIAN	AMBOS	AMENT	AMMONIUM	AMORTIZES
AMATORY	AMBRIES	AMENTA	AMMONIUMS	AMORTIZING
AMAUROSES	AMBROID	AMENTAL	AMMONOID	AMOSITE
AMAUROSIS	AMBROIDS	AMENTIA	AMMONOIDS	AMOSITES
AMAUROTIC	AMBROSIA	AMENTIAS	AMMONS	AMOUNT
AMAZE	AMBROSIAL	AMENTS	AMMOS	AMOUNTED
AMAZED	AMBROSIAN	AMENTUM	AMNESIA	AMOUNTING
AMAZEDLY	AMBROSIAS	AMERCE	AMNESIAC	AMOUNTS
AMAZEMENT	AMBROTYPE	AMERCED	AMNESIACS	AMOUR
AMAZEMENTS	AMBROTYPES	AMERCES	AMNESIAS	AMOURETTE
AMAZES	AMBRY	AMERCING	AMNESIC	AMOURETTES
AMAZING	AMBULACRA	AMERICIUM	AMNESICS	AMOURS
AMAZINGLY	AMBULANCE	AMERICIUMS	AMNESTIED	AMOVE
AMAZON	AMBULANCES	AMETHYST	AMNESTIES	AMOVED
AMAZONIAN	AMBULANT	AMETHYSTS	AMNESTY	AMOVES
AMAZONITE	AMBULANTS	AMI	AMNESTYING	AMOVING
AMAZONITES	AMBULATE	AMIABLE	AMNIA	AMP
AMAZONS	AMBULATED	AMIABLY	AMNION	AMPASSIES
AMBAGE	AMBULATES	AMIANTHUS	AMNIOTIC	AMPASSY
AMBAGES	AMBULATING	AMIANTHUSES	AMOEBA	AMPERAGE
AMBAGIOUS	AMBULATOR	AMIANTUS	AMOEBAE	AMPERAGES
AMBAN	AMBULATORS	AMIANTUSES	AMOEBAEAN	AMPERE
AMBANS	AMBUSCADE	AMICABLE	AMOEBAS	AMPERES
AMBASSAGE	AMBUSCADED	AMICABLY	AMOEBIC	AMPERSAND
AMBASSAGES	AMBUSCADES	AMICE	AMOEBOID	AMPERSANDS
AMBASSIES	AMBUSCADING	AMICES	AMOK	AMPERZAND
AMBASSY	AMBUSCADO	AMID	AMOMUM	AMPERZANDS
AMBATCH	AMBUSCADOES	AMIDE	AMOMUMS	AMPHIBIAN
AMBATCHES	AMBUSCADOS	AMIDES	AMONG	AMPHIBIANS
AMBER	AMBUSH	AMIDMOST	AMONGST	AMPHIBOLE
AMBERED	AMBUSHED	AMIDSHIPS	AMOOVE	AMPHIBOLES
AMBERGRIS	AMBUSHES	AMIDST	AMOOVED	AMPHIBOLIES
AMBERGRISES	AMBUSHING	AMIE	AMOOVES	AMPHIBOLY
AMBERITE	AMEARST	AMIES	AMOOVING	AMPHIGORIES
AMBERITES	AMEBA	AMIGO	AMORAL	AMPHIGORY
AMBERJACK	AMEBAE	AMIGOS	AMORALISM	AMPHIOXUS
AMBERJACKS	AMEBAS	AMILDAR	AMORALISMS	AMPHIOXUSES
AMBEROID	AMEBIC	AMILDARS	AMORALIST	AMPHIPOD
AMBEROIDS	AMEER	AMINE	AMORALISTS	AMPHIPODS
AMBEROUS	AMEERS	AMINES	AMORCE	AMPHOLYTE
AMBERS	AMELCORN	AMIR	AMORCES	AMPHOLYTES
AMBERY	AMELCORNS	AMIRS	AMORET	AMPHORA
AMBIANCE	AMELIA	AMIS	AMORETS	AMPHORAE
AMBIANCES	AMELIAS	AMISES	AMORETTI	AMPHORIC
AMBIENCE	AMEN	AMISS	AMORETTO	AMPLE
AMBIENCES	AMENABLE	AMISSES	AMORINI	AMPLENESS
AMBIENT	AMENABLY	AMISSIBLE	AMORINO	AMPLENESSES
AMBIENTS	AMENAGE	AMISSING	AMORISM	AMPLER
AMBIGUITIES	AMENAGED	AMITIES	AMORISMS	AMPLEST
AMBIGUITY	AMENAGES	AMITOSES	AMORIST	AMPLIFIED
AMBIGUOUS	AMENAGING	AMITOSIS	AMORISTS	AMPLIFIER
AMBIT	AMENAUNCE	AMITOTIC	AMORNINGS	AMPLIFIERS

AMPLIFIES	AMYLOPSINS	ANALOGIZES	ANARCHS	ANCLE
AMPLIFY	AMYLS	ANALOGIZING	ANARCHY	ANCLES
AMPLIFYING	AMYLUM	ANALOGON	ANAS	ANCOME
AMPLITUDE	AMYLUMS	ANALOGONS	ANASARCA	ANCOMES
AMPLITUDES	AN	ANALOGOUS	ANASARCAS	ANCON
AMPLOSOME	ANA	ANALOGS	ANASTASES	ANCONES
AMPLOSOMES	ANABAS	ANALOGUE	ANASTASIS	ANCORA
AMPLY	ANABASES	ANALOGUES	ANASTATIC	ANCRESS
AMPOULE	ANABASIS	ANALOGY	ANATASE	ANCRESSES
AMPOULES	ANABATIC	ANALYSAND	ANATASES	AND
AMPS	ANABIOSES	ANALYSANDS	ANATHEMA	ANDANTE
AMPUL	ANABIOSIS	ANALYSE	ANATHEMAS	ANDANTES
AMPULE	ANABIOTIC	ANALYSED	ANATOMIC	ANDANTINO
AMPULES	ANABLEPS	ANALYSER	ANATOMIES	ANDANTINOS
AMPULLA	ANABLEPSES	ANALYSERS	ANATOMISE	ANDESINE
AMPULLAE	ANABOLIC	ANALYSES	ANATOMISED	ANDESINES
AMPULS	ANABOLISM	ANALYSING	ANATOMISES	ANDESITE
AMPUTATE	ANABOLISMS	ANALYSIS	ANATOMISING	ANDESITES
AMPUTATED	ANABRANCH	ANALYST	ANATOMIST	ANDESITIC
AMPUTATES	ANABRANCHES	ANALYSTS	ANATOMISTS	ANDIRON
AMPUTATING	ANACHARIS	ANALYTIC	ANATOMIZE	ANDIRONS
AMPUTATOR	ANACHARISES	ANALYTICS	ANATOMIZED	ANDROECIA
AMPUTATORS	ANACONDA	ANALYZE	ANATOMIZES	ANDROGEN
AMPUTEE	ANACONDAS	ANALYZED	ANATOMIZING	ANDROGENS
AMPUTEES	ANACRUSES	ANALYZER	ANATOMY	ANDROGYNE
AMRIT	ANACRUSIS	ANALYZERS	ANATROPIES	ANDROGYNES
AMRITA	ANADEM	ANALYZES	ANATROPY	ANDROGYNIES
AMRITAS	ANADEMS	ANALYZING	ANATTA	ANDROGYNY
AMRITS	ANAEMIA	ANAMNESES	ANATTAS	ANDROID
AMTMAN	ANAEMIAS	ANAMNESIS	ANATTO	ANDROIDS
AMTMANS	ANAEMIC	ANAN	ANATTOS	ANDROLOGIES
AMTRACK	ANAEROBE	ANANA	ANBURIES	ANDROLOGY
AMTRACKS	ANAEROBES	ANANAS	ANBURY	ANDROMEDA
AMUCK	ANAEROBIC	ANANAOEO	ANCE	ANDROMEDAS
AMULET	ANAGLYPH	ANANDROUS	ANCESTOR	ANDS
AMULETIC	ANAGLYPHS	ANANKE	ANCESTORS	ANDVILE
AMULETS	ANAGOGE	ANANKES	ANCESTRAL	ANDVILES
AMUSABLE	ANAGOGES	ANANTHOUS	ANCESTRIES	ANE
AMUSE	ANAGOGIC	ANAPAEST	ANCESTRY	ANEAR
AMUSED	ANAGOGIES	ANAPAESTS	ANCHOR	ANEARED
AMUSEDLY	ANAGOGY	ANAPEST	ANCHORAGE	ANEARING
AMUSEMENT	ANAGRAM	ANAPESTS	ANCHORAGES	ANEARS
AMUSEMENTS	ANAGRAMMED	ANAPHASE	ANCHORED	ANEATH
AMUSER	ANAGRAMMING	ANAPHASES	ANCHORESS	ANECDOTAL
AMUSERS	ANAGRAMS	ANAPHORA	ANCHORESSES	ANECDOTE
AMUSES	ANAL	ANAPHORAS	ANCHORET	ANECDOTES
AMUSETTE	ANALCIME	ANAPHORIC	ANCHORETS	ANECHOIC
AMUSETTES	ANALCIMES	ANAPLASTIES	ANCHORING	ANELACE
AMUSING	ANALCITE	ANAPLASTY	ANCHORITE	ANELACES
AMUSINGLY	ANALCITES	ANAPTYXES	ANCHORITES	ANELE
AMUSIVE	ANALECTA	ANAPTYXIS	ANCHORS	ANELED
AMYGDAL	ANALECTIC	ANARAK	ANCHOVETA	ANELES
AMYGDALA	ANALECTS	ANARAKS	ANCHOVETAS	ANELING
AMYGDALAS	ANALEPTIC	ANARCH	ANCHOVIES	ANEMIA
AMYGDALE	ANALGESIA	ANARCHAL	ANCHOVY	ANEMIAS
AMYGDALES	ANALGESIAS	ANARCHIAL	ANCHYLOSE	ANEMIC
AMYGDALIN	ANALGESIC	ANARCHIC	ANCHYLOSED	ANEMOGRAM
AMYGDALINS	ANALGESICS	ANARCHIES	ANCHYLOSES	ANEMOGRAMS
AMYGDALS	ANALLY	ANARCHISE	ANCHYLOSING	ANEMOLOGIES
AMYGDULE	ANALOG	ANARCHISED	ANCHYLOSIS	ANEMOLOGY
AMYGDULES	ANALOGIC	ANARCHISES	ANCIENT	ANEMONE
AMYL	ANALOGIES	ANARCHISING	ANCIENTLY	ANEMONES
AMYLASE	ANALOGISE	ANARCHISM	ANCIENTRIES	ANENT
AMYLASES	ANALOGISED	ANARCHISMS	ANCIENTRY	ANERLY
AMYLENE	ANALOGISES	ANARCHIST	ANCIENTS	ANEROID
AMYLENES	ANALOGISING	ANARCHISTS	ANCILE	ANEROIDS
AMYLOID	ANALOGIST	ANARCHIZE	ANCILES	ANES
AMYLOIDAL	ANALOGISTS	ANARCHIZED	ANCILLARIES	ANESTRA
AMYLOIDS	ANALOGIZE	ANARCHIZES	ANCILLARY	ANESTRI
AMYLOPSIN	ANALOGIZED	ANARCHIZING	ANCIPITAL	ANESTROUS

ANESTRUM
ANESTRUS
ANETIC
ANEURIN
ANEURINS
ANEURISM
ANEURISMS
ANEURYSM
ANEURYSMS
ANEW
ANGARIES
ANGARY
ANGEKKOK
ANGEKKOKS
ANGEKOK
ANGEKOKS
ANGEL
ANGELHOOD
ANGELHOODS
ANGELIC
ANGELICA
ANGELICAL
ANGELICAS
ANGELS
ANGELUS
ANGELUSES
ANGER
ANGERED
ANGERING
ANGERLESS
ANGERLY
ANGERS
ANGICO
ANGICOS
ANGINA
ANGINAL
ANGINAS
ANGIOGRAM
ANGIOGRAMS
ANGIOMA
ANGIOMAS
ANGIOMATA
ANGLE
ANGLED
ANGLER
ANGLERS
ANGLES
ANGLESITE
ANGLESITES
ANGLEWISE
ANGLICE
ANGLICISE
ANGLICISED
ANGLICISES
ANGLICISING
ANGLICISM
ANGLICISMS
ANGLICIST
ANGLICISTS
ANGLICIZE
ANGLICIZED
ANGLICIZES
ANGLICIZING
ANGLIFIED
ANGLIFIES
ANGLIFY
ANGLIFYING
ANGLING
ANGLINGS
ANGLIST

ANGLISTS
ANGLOPHIL
ANGLOPHILS
ANGORA
ANGORAS
ANGRIER
ANGRIES
ANGRIEST
ANGRILY
ANGRINESS
ANGRINESSES
ANGRY
ANGST
ANGSTROM
ANGSTROMS
ANGSTS
ANGUIFORM
ANGUINE
ANGUIPED
ANGUIPEDE
ANGUISH
ANGUISHED
ANGUISHES
ANGUISHING
ANGULAR
ANGULATE
ANGULATED
ANHEDONIA
ANHEDONIAS
ANHEDRAL
ANHUNGRED
ANHYDRIDE
ANHYDRIDES
ANHYDRITE
ANHYDRITES
ANHYDROUS
ANICONIC
ANICONISM
ANICONISMS
ANICONIST
ANICONISTS
ANICUT
ANICUTS
ANIGH
ANIGHT
ANIL
ANILE
ANILINE
ANILINES
ANILITIES
ANILITY
ANILS
ANIMA
ANIMAL
ANIMALIC
ANIMALISE
ANIMALISED
ANIMALISES
ANIMALISING
ANIMALISM
ANIMALISMS
ANIMALIST
ANIMALISTS
ANIMALITIES
ANIMALITY
ANIMALIZE
ANIMALIZED
ANIMALIZES
ANIMALIZING
ANIMALLY

ANIMALS
ANIMAS
ANIMATE
ANIMATED
ANIMATES
ANIMATING
ANIMATION
ANIMATIONS
ANIMATISM
ANIMATISMS
ANIMATOR
ANIMATORS
ANIMÉ
ANIME
ANIMÉS
ANIMES
ANIMISM
ANIMISMS
ANIMIST
ANIMISTIC
ANIMISTS
ANIMOSITIES
ANIMOSITY
ANIMUS
ANIMUSES
ANION
ANIONIC
ANIONS
ANISE
ANISEED
ANISEEDS
ANISES
ANISETTE
ANISETTES
ANKER
ANKERITE
ANKERITES
ANKERS
ANKH
ANKHS
ANKLE
ANKLED
ANKLES
ANKLET
ANKLETS
ANKUS
ANKUSES
ANKYLOSE
ANKYLOSED
ANKYLOSES
ANKYLOSING
ANKYLOSIS
ANLACE
ANLACES
ANLAGE
ANLAGES
ANN
ANNA
ANNAL
ANNALISE
ANNALISED
ANNALISES
ANNALISING
ANNALIST
ANNALISTS
ANNALIZE
ANNALIZED
ANNALIZES
ANNALIZING
ANNALS

ANNAS
ANNAT
ANNATES
ANNATS
ANNATTA
ANNATTAS
ANNATTO
ANNATTOS
ANNEAL
ANNEALED
ANNEALER
ANNEALERS
ANNEALING
ANNEALINGS
ANNEALS
ANNECTENT
ANNELID
ANNELIDS
ANNEX
ANNEXE
ANNEXED
ANNEXES
ANNEXING
ANNEXION
ANNEXIONS
ANNEXMENT
ANNEXMENTS
ANNEXURE
ANNEXURES
ANNICUT
ANNICUTS
ANNO
ANNOTATE
ANNOTATED
ANNOTATES
ANNOTATING
ANNOTATOR
ANNOTATORS
ANNOUNCE
ANNOUNCED
ANNOUNCER
ANNOUNCERS
ANNOUNCES
ANNOUNCING
ANNOY
ANNOYANCE
ANNOYANCES
ANNOYED
ANNOYING
ANNOYS
ANNS
ANNUAL
ANNUALISE
ANNUALISED
ANNUALISES
ANNUALISING
ANNUALIZE
ANNUALIZED
ANNUALIZES
ANNUALIZING
ANNUALLY
ANNUALS
ANNUITANT
ANNUITANTS
ANNUITIES
ANNUITY
ANNUL
ANNULAR
ANNULARS
ANNULATE

ANNULATED
ANNULATES
ANNULET
ANNULETS
ANNULI
ANNULLED
ANNULLING
ANNULMENT
ANNULMENTS
ANNULOSE
ANNULS
ANNULUS
ANOA
ANOAS
ANODAL
ANODE
ANODES
ANODIC
ANODISE
ANODISED
ANODISES
ANODISING
ANODIZE
ANODIZED
ANODIZES
ANODIZING
ANODYNE
ANODYNES
ANOESES
ANOESIS
ANOESTRA
ANOESTRI
ANOESTRUM
ANOESTRUS
ANOETIC
ANOINT
ANOINTED
ANOINTING
ANOINTS
ANOMALIES
ANOMALOUS
ANOMALY
ANOMIC
ANOMIE
ANOMIES
ANOMY
ANON
ANONYM
ANONYMA
ANONYMAS
ANONYMITIES
ANONYMITY
ANONYMOUS
ANONYMS
ANOPHELES
ANORAK
ANORAKS
ANORECTIC
ANORECTICS
ANORETIC
ANORETICS
ANOREXIA
ANOREXIAS
ANOREXIC
ANOREXICS
ANOREXIES
ANOREXY
ANORTHIC
ANORTHITE
ANORTHITES

ANOSMIA	ANTHEM	ANTINOMIC	ANTRORSE	APAYD
ANOSMIAS	ANTHEMED	ANTINOMIES	ANTRUM	APAYING
ANOTHER	ANTHEMIA	ANTINOMY	ANTRUMS	APAYS
ANOUGH	ANTHEMING	ANTIPAPAL	ANTS	APE
ANOUROUS	ANTHEMION	ANTIPASTO	ANUCLEATE	APEAK
ANOW	ANTHEMS	ANTIPASTOS	ANURIA	APED
ANOXIA	ANTHER	ANTIPATHIES	ANURIAS	APEDOM
ANOXIAS	ANTHERS	ANTIPATHY	ANUROUS	APEDOMS
ANOXIC	ANTHESES	ANTIPHON	ANUS	APEEK
ANSATE	ANTHESIS	ANTIPHONIES	ANUSES	APEHOOD
ANSATED	ANTHOCARP	ANTIPHONS	ANVIL	APEHOODS
ANSERINE	ANTHOCARPS	ANTIPHONY	ANVILS	APEMAN
ANSWER	ANTHOCYAN	ANTIPODAL	ANXIETIES	APEMEN
ANSWERED	ANTHOCYANS	ANTIPODE	ANXIETY	APEPSIA
ANSWERER	ANTHOID	ANTIPODES	ANXIOUS	APEPSIAS
ANSWERERS	ANTHOLOGIES	ANTIPOLE	ANXIOUSLY	APEPSIES
ANSWERING	ANTHOLOGY	ANTIPOLES	ANY	APEPSY
ANSWERS	ANTHRACIC	ANTIPOPE	ANYBODIES	APERÇU
ANT	ANTHRAX	ANTIPOPES	ANYBODY	APERÇUS
ANTA	ANTHRAXES	ANTIQUARIES	ANYHOW	APERIENT
ANTACID	ANTHROPIC	ANTIQUARK	ANYONE	APERIENTS
ANTACIDS	ANTHURIUM	ANTIQUARKS	ANYONES	APERIES
ANTAE	ANTHURIUMS	ANTIQUARY	ANYROAD	APERIODIC
ANTAR	ANTI	ANTIQUATE	ANYTHING	APÉRITIF
ANTARS	ANTIAR	ANTIQUATED	ANYTHINGS	APÉRITIFS
ANTBEAR	ANTIARS	ANTIQUATES	ANYTIME	APERITIVE
ANTBEARS	ANTIBODIES	ANTIQUATING	ANYWAY	APERITIVES
ANTE	ANTIBODY	ANTIQUE	ANYWAYS	APERT
ANTECEDE	ANTIC	ANTIQUED	ANYWHEN	APERTNESS
ANTECEDED	ANTICHLOR	ANTIQUELY	ANYWHERE	APERTNESSES
ANTECEDES	ANTICHLORS	ANTIQUES	ANYWISE	APERTURE
ANTECEDING	ANTICIVIC	ANTIQUING	ANZIANI	APERTURES
ANTECHOIR	ANTICIZE	ANTIQUITIES	AORIST	APERY
ANTECHOIRS	ANTICIZED	ANTIQUITY	AORISTIC	APES
ANTED	ANTICIZES	ANTIS	AORISTS	APETALIES
ANTEDATE	ANTICIZING	ANTISCIAN	AORTA	APETALOUS
ANTEDATED	ANTICK	ANTISCIANS	AORTAL	APETALY
ANTEDATES	ANTICKE	ANTISERA	AORTAS	APEX
ANTEDATING	ANTICKED	ANTISERUM	AORTIC	APEXES
ANTEFIX	ANTICKING	ANTISERUMS	AORTITIS	APHAGIA
ANTEFIXA	ANTICLINE	ANTISHIP	AORTITISES	APHAGIAS
ANTEFIXAL	ANTICLINES	ANTISPAST	AOUDAD	APHANITE
ANTEFIXES	ANTICOUS	ANTISPASTS	AOUDADS	APHANITES
ANTEING	ANTICS	ANTISTAT	APACE	APHASIA
ANTELOPE	ANTIDOTAL	ANTISTATS	APACHE	APHASIAC
ANTELOPES	ANTIDOTE	ANTITHET	APACHES	APHASIACS
ANTELUCAN	ANTIDOTES	ANTITHETS	APAGE	APHASIAS
ANTENATAL	ANTIENT	ANTITOXIC	APAGOGE	APHASIC
ANTENATI	ANTIENTS	ANTITOXIN	APAGOGES	APHELIA
ANTENNA	ANTIGEN	ANTITOXINS	APAGOGIC	APHELIAN
ANTENNAE	ANTIGENIC	ANTITRADE	APAID	APHELIC
ANTENNAL	ANTIGENS	ANTITRADES	APANAGE	APHELION
ANTENNARY	ANTIHELICES	ANTITRAGI	APANAGED	APHELIONS
ANTENNAS	ANTIHELIX	ANTITYPAL	APANAGES	APHERESIS
ANTENNULE	ANTIKNOCK	ANTITYPE	APART	APHESES
ANTENNULES	ANTIKNOCKS	ANTITYPES	APARTHEID	APHESIS
ANTEPAST	ANTILOG	ANTITYPIC	APARTHEIDS	APHETIC
ANTEPASTS	ANTILOGIES	ANTIVENIN	APARTMENT	APHETISE
ANTERIOR	ANTILOGS	ANTIVENINS	APARTMENTS	APHETISED
ANTEROOM	ANTILOGY	ANTIVIRAL	APARTNESS	APHETISES
ANTEROOMS	ANTIMASK	ANTLER	APARTNESSES	APHETISING
ANTES	ANTIMASKS	ANTLERED	APATETIC	APHETIZE
ANTEVERT	ANTIMONIC	ANTLERS	APATHATON	APHETIZED
ANTEVERTED	ANTIMONIES	ANTLIA	APATHATONS	APHETIZES
ANTEVERTING	ANTIMONY	ANTLIAE	APATHETIC	APHETIZING
ANTEVERTS	ANTING	ANTLIATE	APATHIES	APHICIDE
ANTHELIA	ANTINGS	ANTONYM	APATHY	APHICIDES
ANTHELICES	ANTINODAL	ANTONYMS	APATITE	APHID
ANTHELION	ANTINODE	ANTRE	APATITES	APHIDES
ANTHELIX	ANTINODES	ANTRES	APAY	APHIDIAN

APHIDIANS
APHIDICAL
APHIDS
APHIS
APHONIA
APHONIAS
APHONIC
APHONIES
APHONOUS
APHONY
APHORISE
APHORISED
APHORISER
APHORISERS
APHORISES
APHORISING
APHORISM
APHORISMS
APHORIST
APHORISTS
APHORIZE
APHORIZED
APHORIZER
APHORIZERS
APHORIZES
APHORIZING
APHOTIC
APHTHA
APHTHAE
APHTHOUS
APHYLLIES
APHYLLOUS
APHYLLY
APIAN
APIARIAN
APIARIES
APIARIST
APIARISTS
APIARY
APICAL
APICALLY
APICES
APICULATE
APIECE
APING
APIOL
APIOLS
APISH
APISHLY
APISHNESS
APISHNESSES
APISM
APISMS
APIVOROUS
APLANAT
APLANATIC
APLANATS
APLASIA
APLASIAS
APLASTIC
APLENTY
APLITE
APLITES
APLOMB
APLOMBS
APLUSTRE
APLUSTRES
APNEA
APNEAS
APNOEA

APNOEAS
APOCOPATE
APOCOPATED
APOCOPATES
APOCOPATING
APOCOPE
APOCOPES
APOCRINE
APOCRYPHA
APOD
APODAL
APODE
APODES
APODICTIC
APODOSES
APODOSIS
APODOUS
APODS
APOENZYME
APOENZYMES
APOGAEIC
APOGAMIES
APOGAMOUS
APOGAMY
APOGEAL
APOGEAN
APOGEE
APOGEES
APOGRAPH
APOGRAPHS
APOLLINE
APOLLO
APOLLOS
APOLOGIA
APOLOGIAS
APOLOGIES
APOLOGISE
APOLOGISED
APOLOGISES
APOLOGISING
APOLOGIST
APOLOGISTS
APOLOGIZE
APOLOGIZED
APOLOGIZES
APOLOGIZING
APOLOGUE
APOLOGUES
APOLOGY
APOMICTIC
APOMIXES
APOMIXIS
APOOP
APOPHATIC
APOPHYGE
APOPHYGES
APOPHYSES
APOPHYSIS
APOPLEX
APOPLEXED
APOPLEXES
APOPLEXIES
APOPLEXING
APOPLEXY
APORIA
APORIAS
APORT
APOSITIA
APOSITIAS
APOSPORIES

APOSPORY
APOSTASIES
APOSTASY
APOSTATE
APOSTATES
APOSTATIC
APOSTIL
APOSTILLE
APOSTILLES
APOSTILS
APOSTLE
APOSTLES
APOSTOLIC
APOTHECIA
APOTHEGM
APOTHEGMS
APOTHEM
APOTHEMS
APOZEM
APOZEMS
APPAID
APPAIR
APPAIRED
APPAIRING
APPAIRS
APPAL
APPALLED
APPALLING
APPALS
APPALTI
APPALTO
APPANAGE
APPANAGED
APPANAGES
APPARAT
APPARATS
APPARATUS
APPARATUSES
APPAREL
APPARELLED
APPARELLING
APPARELS
APPARENCIES
APPARENCY
APPARENT
APPARENTS
APPARITOR
APPARITORS
APPAY
APPAYD
APPAYING
APPAYS
APPEACH
APPEACHED
APPEACHES
APPEACHING
APPEAL
APPEALED
APPEALING
APPEALS
APPEAR
APPEARED
APPEARER
APPEARERS
APPEARING
APPEARS
APPEASE
APPEASED
APPEASES
APPEASING

APPELLANT
APPELLANTS
APPELLATE
APPEND
APPENDAGE
APPENDAGES
APPENDANT
APPENDANTS
APPENDED
APPENDICES
APPENDING
APPENDIX
APPENDIXES
APPENDS
APPERIL
APPERILL
APPERILLS
APPERILS
APPERTAIN
APPERTAINED
APPERTAINING
APPERTAINS
APPESTAT
APPESTATS
APPETENCE
APPETENCES
APPETENCIES
APPETENCY
APPETENT
APPETIBLE
APPETISE
APPETISED
APPETISER
APPETISERS
APPETISES
APPETISING
APPETITE
APPETITES
APPETIZE
APPETIZED
APPETIZER
APPETIZERS
APPETIZES
APPETIZING
APPLAUD
APPLAUDED
APPLAUDER
APPLAUDERS
APPLAUDING
APPLAUDS
APPLAUSE
APPLAUSES
APPLE
APPLES
APPLIABLE
APPLIANCE
APPLIANCES
APPLICANT
APPLICANTS
APPLICATE
APPLIED
APPLIES
APPLIQUÉ
APPLIQUÉS
APPLY
APPLYING
APPOINT
APPOINTED
APPOINTEE
APPOINTEES

APPOINTING
APPOINTOR
APPOINTORS
APPOINTS
APPORT
APPORTION
APPORTIONED
APPORTIONING
APPORTIONS
APPORTS
APPOSE
APPOSED
APPOSER
APPOSERS
APPOSES
APPOSING
APPOSITE
APPRAISAL
APPRAISALS
APPRAISE
APPRAISED
APPRAISER
APPRAISERS
APPRAISES
APPRAISING
APPREHEND
APPREHENDED
APPREHENDING
APPREHENDS
APPRESS
APPRESSED
APPRESSES
APPRESSING
APPRISE
APPRISED
APPRISES
APPRISING
APPRIZE
APPRIZED
APPRIZER
APPRIZERS
APPRIZES
APPRIZING
APPRIZINGS
APPROACH
APPROACHED
APPROACHES
APPROACHING
APPROBATE
APPROBATED
APPROBATES
APPROBATING
APPROOF
APPROOFS
APPROVAL
APPROVALS
APPROVE
APPROVED
APPROVER
APPROVERS
APPROVES
APPROVING
APPUI
APPUIED
APPUIS
APPULSE
APPULSES
APPUY
APPUYED
APPUYING

APPUYS	AQUANAUTS	ARAK	ARCADE	ARCHIVOLT
APRAXIA	AQUAPLANE	ARAKS	ARCADED	ARCHIVOLTS
APRAXIAS	AQUAPLANED	ARALIA	ARCADES	ARCHLET
APRÈS	AQUAPLANES	ARALIAS	ARCADING	ARCHLETS
APRICATE	AQUAPLANING	ARAME	ARCADINGS	ARCHLUTE
APRICATED	AQUAPLANINGS	ARAMES	ARCANA	ARCHLUTES
APRICATES	AQUARELLE	ARANEID	ARCANE	ARCHLY
APRICATING	AQUARELLES	ARANEIDS	ARCANELY	ARCHNESS
APRICOCK	AQUARIA	ARANEOUS	ARCANIST	ARCHNESSES
APRICOCKS	AQUARIAN	ARAPAIMA	ARCANISTS	ARCHOLOGIES
APRICOT	AQUARIANS	ARAPAIMAS	ARCANUM	ARCHOLOGY
APRICOTS	AQUARIIST	ARAPONGA	ARCCOS	ARCHON
APRIORISM	AQUARIISTS	ARAPONGAS	ARCCOSES	ARCHONS
APRIORISMS	AQUARIST	ARAPUNGA	ARCED	ARCHONTIC
APRIORIST	AQUARISTS	ARAPUNGAS	ARCH	ARCHWAY
APRIORISTS	AQUARIUM	ARAR	ARCHAEI	ARCHWAYS
APRIORITIES	AQUARIUMS	ARAROBA	ARCHAEUS	ARCHWISE
APRIORITY	AQUAS	ARAROBAS	ARCHAIC	ARCING
APRON	AQUATIC	ARARS	ARCHAISE	ARCINGS
APRONED	AQUATICS	ARAUCARIA	ARCHAISED	ARCKED
APRONFUL	AQUATINT	ARAUCARIAS	ARCHAISER	ARCKING
APRONFULS	AQUATINTA	ARAYSE	ARCHAISERS	ARCKINGS
APRONING	AQUATINTAS	ARAYSED	ARCHAISES	ARCO
APRONS	AQUATINTED	ARAYSES	ARCHAISING	ARCS
APROPOS	AQUATINTING	ARAYSING	ARCHAISM	ARCSECOND
APSE	AQUATINTS	ARBA	ARCHAISMS	ARCSECONDS
APSES	AQUAVIT	ARBALEST	ARCHAIST	ARCSIN
APSIDAL	AQUAVITS	ARBALESTS	ARCHAISTS	ARCSINS
APSIDES	AQUEDUCT	ARBALIST	ARCHAIZE	ARCTAN
APSIDIOLE	AQUEDUCTS	ARBALISTS	ARCHAIZED	ARCTANS
APSIDIOLES	AQUEOUS	ARBAS	ARCHAIZER	ARCTIC
APSIS	AQUIFER	ARBITER	ARCHAIZERS	ARCTICS
APT	AQUIFERS	ARBITERS	ARCHAIZES	ARCTOID
APTED	AQUILEGIA	ARBITRAGE	ARCHAIZING	ARCTOPHIL
APTER	AQUILEGIAS	ARBITRAGED	ARCHANGEL	ARCTOPHILS
APTERAL	AQUILINE	ARBITRAGES	ARCHANGELS	ARCUATE
APTERIA	AQUIVER	ARBITRAGING	ARCHDUCAL	ARCUATED
APTERIUM	AR	ARBITRAL	ARCHDUCHIES	ARCUATION
APTEROUS	ARABA	ARBITRARY	ARCHDUCHY	ARCUATIONS
APTERYX	ARABAS	ARBITRATE	ARCHDUKE	ARCUS
APTERYXES	ARABESQUE	ARBITRATED	ARCHDUKES	ARCUSES
APTEST	ARABESQUES	ARBITRATES	ARCHED	ARDEB
APTING	ARABICA	ARBITRATING	ARCHEI	ARDEBS
APTITUDE	ARABICAS	ARBITRESS	ARCHER	ARDENCIES
APTITUDES	ARABIN	ARBITRESSES	ARCHERESS	ARDENCY
APTLY	ARABINOSE	ARBITRIUM	ARCHERESSES	ARDENT
APTNESS	ARABINOSES	ARBITRIUMS	ARCHERIES	ARDENTLY
APTNESSES	ARABINS	ARBLAST	ARCHERS	ARDOUR
APTOTE	ARABISE	ARBLASTER	ARCHERY	ARDOURS
APTOTES	ARABISED	ARBLASTERS	ARCHES	ARDRI
APTOTIC	ARABISES	ARBLASTS	ARCHEST	ARDRIGH
APTS	ARABISING	ARBOR	ARCHETYPE	ARDRIGHS
APYRETIC	ARABIZE	ARBOREAL	ARCHETYPES	ARDRIS
APYREXIA	ARABIZED	ARBOREOUS	ARCHEUS	ARDUOUS
APYREXIAS	ARABIZES	ARBORET	ARCHIL	ARDUOUSLY
AQUA	ARABIZING	ARBORETA	ARCHILOWE	ARE
AQUABATIC	ARABLE	ARBORETS	ARCHILOWES	AREA
AQUABATICS	ARACEOUS	ARBORETUM	ARCHILS	AREACH
AQUABOARD	ARACHIS	ARBORIST	ARCHIMAGE	AREACHED
AQUABOARDS	ARACHISES	ARBORISTS	ARCHIMAGES	AREACHES
AQUACADE	ARACHNID	ARBOROUS	ARCHING	AREACHING
AQUACADES	ARACHNIDS	ARBORS	ARCHITECT	AREAD
AQUADROME	ARACHNOID	ARBOUR	ARCHITECTED	AREADING
AQUADROMES	ARACHNOIDS	ARBOURED	ARCHITECTING	AREADS
AQUAE	ARAGONITE	ARBOURS	ARCHITECTS	AREAL
AQUAFER	ARAGONITES	ARBUTE	ARCHIVAL	AREAR
AQUAFERS	ARAISE	ARBUTES	ARCHIVE	AREAS
AQUALUNG	ARAISED	ARBUTUS	ARCHIVES	ARECA
AQUALUNGS	ARAISES	ARBUTUSES	ARCHIVIST	ARECAS
AQUANAUT	ARAISING	ARC	ARCHIVISTS	ARED

AREDD
AREDE
AREDES
AREDING
AREFIED
AREFIES
AREFY
AREFYING
ARENA
ARENAS
ARENATION
ARENATIONS
AREOLA
AREOLAE
AREOLAR
AREOLATE
AREOLATED
AREOLE
AREOLES
AREOMETER
AREOMETERS
AREOSTYLE
AREOSTYLES
ARERE
ARES
ARET
ARÊTE
ARÊTES
ARETS
ARETT
ARETTED
ARETTING
ARETTS
AREW
ARGAL
ARGALA
ARGALAS
ARGALI
ARGALIS
ARGAN
ARGAND
ARGANDS
ARGANS
ARGEMONE
ARGEMONES
ARGENT
ARGENTINE
ARGENTINES
ARGENTITE
ARGENTITES
ARGENTS
ARGHAN
ARGHANS
ARGIL
ARGILLITE
ARGILLITES
ARGILS
ARGININE
ARGININES
ARGOL
ARGOLS
ARGON
ARGONAUT
ARGONAUTS
ARGONS
ARGOSIES
ARGOSY
ARGOT
ARGOTS
ARGUABLE

ARGUABLY
ARGUE
ARGUED
ARGUER
ARGUERS
ARGUES
ARGUFIED
ARGUFIES
ARGUFY
ARGUFYING
ARGUING
ARGULI
ARGULUS
ARGUMENT
ARGUMENTS
ARGUS
ARGUSES
ARGUTE
ARGUTELY
ARGYLE
ARGYLES
ARGYRIA
ARGYRIAS
ARGYRITE
ARGYRITES
ARHYTHMIA
ARHYTHMIAS
ARHYTHMIC
ARIA
ARIAS
ARID
ARIDER
ARIDEST
ARIDITIES
ARIDITY
ARIDLY
ARIDNESS
ARIDNESSES
ARIEL
ARIELS
ARIETTA
ARIETTAS
ARIETTE
ARIETTES
ARIGHT
ARIL
ARILLARY
ARILLATE
ARILLATED
ARILLI
ARILLODE
ARILLODES
ARILLUS
ARILS
ARIOSI
ARIOSO
ARIOSOS
ARIOT
ARIPPLE
ARIS
ARISE
ARISEN
ARISES
ARISH
ARISHES
ARISING
ARISTA
ARISTAE
ARISTAS
ARISTATE

ARISTO
ARISTOS
ARK
ARKED
ARKING
ARKITE
ARKITES
ARKOSE
ARKOSES
ARKS
ARLES
ARLESED
ARLESES
ARLESING
ARM
ARMADA
ARMADAS
ARMADILLO
ARMADILLOS
ARMAMENT
ARMAMENTS
ARMATURE
ARMATURES
ARMBAND
ARMBANDS
ARMCHAIR
ARMCHAIRS
ARMED
ARMET
ARMETS
ARMFUL
ARMFULS
ARMGAUNT
ARMHOLE
ARMHOLES
ARMIES
ARMIGER
ARMIGERAL
ARMIGERO
ARMIGEROS
ARMIGERS
ARMIL
ARMILLA
ARMILLAE
ARMILLARY
ARMILLAS
ARMILS
ARMING
ARMISTICE
ARMISTICES
ARMLESS
ARMLET
ARMLETS
ARMLOCK
ARMLOCKS
ARMOIRE
ARMOIRES
ARMOR
ARMORIAL
ARMORIALS
ARMORIES
ARMORIST
ARMORISTS
ARMORS
ARMORY
ARMOUR
ARMOURED
ARMOURER
ARMOURERS
ARMOURIES

ARMOURS
ARMOURY
ARMOZEEN
ARMOZEENS
ARMOZINE
ARMOZINES
ARMPIT
ARMPITS
ARMS
ARMURE
ARMURES
ARMY
ARNA
ARNAS
ARNICA
ARNICAS
ARNOTTO
ARNOTTOS
ARNUT
ARNUTS
AROBA
AROBAS
AROID
AROIDS
AROINT
AROINTED
AROINTING
AROINTS
AROLLA
AROLLAS
AROMA
AROMAS
AROMATIC
AROMATICS
AROMATISE
AROMATISED
AROMATISES
AROMATISING
AROMATIZE
AROMATIZED
AROMATIZES
AROMATIZING
AROSE
AROUND
AROUSAL
AROUSALS
AROUSE
AROUSED
AROUSER
AROUSERS
AROUSES
AROUSING
AROW
AROYNT
AROYNTED
AROYNTING
AROYNTS
ARPEGGIO
ARPEGGIOS
ARPENT
ARPENTS
ARQUEBUS
ARQUEBUSE
ARQUEBUSES
ARRACACHA
ARRACACHAS
ARRACK
ARRACKS
ARRAH
ARRAIGN

ARRAIGNED
ARRAIGNER
ARRAIGNERS
ARRAIGNING
ARRAIGNINGS
ARRAIGNS
ARRANGE
ARRANGED
ARRANGER
ARRANGERS
ARRANGES
ARRANGING
ARRANT
ARRANTLY
ARRAS
ARRASED
ARRASENE
ARRASENES
ARRASES
ARRAUGHT
ARRAY
ARRAYED
ARRAYING
ARRAYMENT
ARRAYMENTS
ARRAYS
ARREAR
ARREARAGE
ARREARAGES
ARREARS
ARRECT
ARREEDE
ARREEDES
ARREEDING
ARREST
ARRESTED
ARRESTEE
ARRESTEES
ARRESTER
ARRESTERS
ARRESTING
ARRESTIVE
ARRESTOR
ARRESTORS
ARRESTS
ARRÊT
ARRÊTS
ARRIAGE
ARRIAGES
ARRIDE
ARRIDED
ARRIDES
ARRIDING
ARRIÉRÉ
ARRIERO
ARRIEROS
ARRIS
ARRISES
ARRISH
ARRISHES
ARRIVAL
ARRIVALS
ARRIVANCE
ARRIVANCES
ARRIVANCIES
ARRIVANCY
ARRIVE
ARRIVED
ARRIVES
ARRIVING

ARRIVISME
ARRIVISMES
ARRIVISTE
ARRIVISTES
ARROBA
ARROBAS
ARROGANCE
ARROGANCES
ARROGANCIES
ARROGANCY
ARROGANT
ARROGATE
ARROGATED
ARROGATES
ARROGATING
ARROW
ARROWED
ARROWING
ARROWROOT
ARROWROOTS
ARROWS
ARROWWOOD
ARROWWOODS
ARROWY
ARROYO
ARROYOS
ARS
ARSE
ARSEHOLE
ARSEHOLES
ARSENAL
ARSENALS
ARSENATE
ARSENATES
ARSENIATE
ARSENIATES
ARSENIC
ARSENICAL
ARSENICS
ARSENIDE
ARSENIDES
ARSENIOUS
ARSENITE
ARSENITES
ARSES
ARSHEEN
ARSHEENS
ARSHIN
ARSHINE
ARSHINES
ARSHINS
ARSINE
ARSINES
ARSIS
ARSON
ARSONIST
ARSONISTS
ARSONITE
ARSONITES
ARSONS
ART
ARTAL
ARTEFACT
ARTEFACTS
ARTEL
ARTELS
ARTEMISIA
ARTEMISIAS
ARTERIAL
ARTERIES

ARTERIOLE
ARTERIOLES
ARTERITIS
ARTERITISES
ARTERY
ARTESIAN
ARTFUL
ARTFULLY
ARTHRITIC
ARTHRITICS
ARTHRITIS
ARTHRITISES
ARTHROPOD
ARTHROPODS
ARTHROSES
ARTHROSIS
ARTIC
ARTICHOKE
ARTICHOKES
ARTICLE
ARTICLED
ARTICLES
ARTICLING
ARTICS
ARTICULAR
ARTIER
ARTIEST
ARTIFACT
ARTIFACTS
ARTIFICE
ARTIFICER
ARTIFICERS
ARTIFICES
ARTILLERIES
ARTILLERY
ARTISAN
ARTISANAL
ARTISANS
ARTIST
ARTISTE
ARTISTES
ARTISTIC
ARTISTRIES
ARTISTRY
ARTISTS
ARTLESS
ARTLESSLY
ARTS
ARTSIER
ARTSIEST
ARTSMAN
ARTSMEN
ARTSY
ARTWORK
ARTWORKS
ARTY
ARUM
ARUMS
ARVAL
ARVO
ARVOS
ARY
ARYBALLOS
ARYBALLOSES
ARYL
ARYLS
ARYTENOID
ARYTENOIDS
AS
ASAFETIDA

ASAFETIDAS
ASANA
ASANAS
ASAR
ASARUM
ASARUMS
ASBESTIC
ASBESTINE
ASBESTOS
ASBESTOSES
ASBESTOUS
ASCARID
ASCARIDES
ASCARIDS
ASCARIS
ASCAUNT
ASCEND
ASCENDANT
ASCENDANTS
ASCENDED
ASCENDENT
ASCENDENTS
ASCENDER
ASCENDERS
ASCENDING
ASCENDS
ASCENSION
ASCENSIONS
ASCENSIVE
ASCENT
ASCENTS
ASCERTAIN
ASCERTAINED
ASCERTAINING
ASCERTAINS
ASCESES
ASCESIS
ASCETIC
ASCETICAL
ASCETICS
ASCI
ASCIAN
ASCIANS
ASCIDIA
ASCIDIAN
ASCIDIANS
ASCIDIUM
ASCITES
ASCITIC
ASCITICAL
ASCLEPIAD
ASCLEPIADS
ASCLEPIAS
ASCLEPIASES
ASCONCE
ASCORBATE
ASCORBATES
ASCORBIC
ASCOSPORE
ASCOSPORES
ASCOT
ASCOTS
ASCRIBE
ASCRIBED
ASCRIBES
ASCRIBING
ASCUS
ASEISMIC
ASEITIES
ASEITY

ASEPALOUS
ASEPSES
ASEPSIS
ASEPTATE
ASEPTIC
ASEPTICS
ASEXUAL
ASEXUALLY
ASH
ASHAKE
ASHAME
ASHAMED
ASHAMEDLY
ASHAMES
ASHAMING
ASHEN
ASHERIES
ASHERY
ASHES
ASHET
ASHETS
ASHIER
ASHIEST
ASHINE
ASHIVER
ASHLAR
ASHLARED
ASHLARING
ASHLARINGS
ASHLARS
ASHLER
ASHLERED
ASHLERING
ASHLERINGS
ASHLERS
ASHORE
ASHRAM
ASHRAMA
ASHRAMAS
ASHRAMS
ASHY
ASIDE
ASIDES
ASINICO
ASINICOS
ASININE
ASININITIES
ASININITY
ASK
ASKANCE
ASKANCED
ASKANCES
ASKANCING
ASKANT
ASKANTED
ASKANTING
ASKANTS
ASKARI
ASKARIS
ASKED
ASKER
ASKERS
ASKESES
ASKESIS
ASKEW
ASKING
ASKLENT
ASKS
ASLAKE
ASLAKED

ASLAKES
ASLAKING
ASLANT
ASLEEP
ASLOPE
ASMEAR
ASMOULDER
ASOCIAL
ASP
ASPARAGUS
ASPARAGUSES
ASPARTAME
ASPARTAMES
ASPECT
ASPECTED
ASPECTING
ASPECTS
ASPECTUAL
ASPEN
ASPENS
ASPER
ASPERATE
ASPERATED
ASPERATES
ASPERATING
ASPERGE
ASPERGED
ASPERGER
ASPERGERS
ASPERGES
ASPERGILL
ASPERGILLS
ASPERGING
ASPERITIES
ASPERITY
ASPEROUS
ASPERS
ASPERSE
ASPERSED
ASPERSES
ASPERSING
ASPERSION
ASPERSIONS
ASPERSIVE
ASPERSOIR
ASPERSOIRS
ASPERSORIES
ASPERSORY
ASPHALT
ASPHALTED
ASPHALTIC
ASPHALTING
ASPHALTS
ASPHALTUM
ASPHALTUMS
ASPHODEL
ASPHODELS
ASPHYXIA
ASPHYXIAS
ASPHYXIES
ASPHYXY
ASPIC
ASPICK
ASPICKS
ASPICS
ASPIDIA
ASPIDIOID
ASPIDIUM
ASPINE
ASPINES

ASPIRANT
ASPIRANTS
ASPIRATE
ASPIRATED
ASPIRATES
ASPIRATING
ASPIRATOR
ASPIRATORS
ASPIRE
ASPIRED
ASPIRES
ASPIRIN
ASPIRING
ASPIRINS
ASPORT
ASPORTED
ASPORTING
ASPORTS
ASPOUT
ASPRAWL
ASPREAD
ASPROUT
ASPS
ASQUAT
ASQUINT
ASS
ASSAGAI
ASSAGAIED
ASSAGAIING
ASSAGAIS
ASSAI
ASSAIL
ASSAILANT
ASSAILANTS
ASSAILED
ASSAILING
ASSAILS
ASSAIS
ASSART
ASSARTED
ASSARTING
ASSARTS
ASSASSIN
ASSASSINS
ASSAULT
ASSAULTED
ASSAULTER
ASSAULTERS
ASSAULTING
ASSAULTS
ASSAY
ASSAYABLE
ASSAYED
ASSAYER
ASSAYERS
ASSAYING
ASSAYINGS
ASSAYS
ASSEGAAI
ASSEGAAIED
ASSEGAAIING
ASSEGAAIS
ASSEGAI
ASSEGAIED
ASSEGAIING
ASSEGAIS
ASSEMBLE
ASSEMBLÉ
ASSEMBLED
ASSEMBLER

ASSEMBLERS
ASSEMBLES
ASSEMBLÉS
ASSEMBLIES
ASSEMBLING
ASSEMBLY
ASSENT
ASSENTED
ASSENTER
ASSENTERS
ASSENTING
ASSENTIVE
ASSENTOR
ASSENTORS
ASSENTS
ASSERT
ASSERTED
ASSERTER
ASSERTERS
ASSERTING
ASSERTION
ASSERTIONS
ASSERTIVE
ASSERTOR
ASSERTORS
ASSERTORY
ASSERTS
ASSES
ASSESS
ASSESSED
ASSESSES
ASSESSING
ASSESSOR
ASSESSORS
ASSET
ASSETS
ASSEVER
ASSEVERED
ASSEVERING
ASSEVERS
ASSHOLE
ASSHOLES
ASSIDUITIES
ASSIDUITY
ASSIDUOUS
ASSIEGE
ASSIEGED
ASSIEGES
ASSIEGING
ASSIENTO
ASSIENTOS
ASSIGN
ASSIGNAT
ASSIGNATS
ASSIGNED
ASSIGNEE
ASSIGNEES
ASSIGNING
ASSIGNOR
ASSIGNORS
ASSIGNS
ASSIST
ASSISTANT
ASSISTANTS
ASSISTED
ASSISTING
ASSISTS
ASSIZE
ASSIZED
ASSIZER

ASSIZERS
ASSIZES
ASSIZING
ASSOCIATE
ASSOCIATED
ASSOCIATES
ASSOCIATING
ASSOIL
ASSOILED
ASSOILING
ASSOILS
ASSOILZIE
ASSOILZIED
ASSOILZIEING
ASSOILZIES
ASSONANCE
ASSONANCES
ASSONANT
ASSONATE
ASSONATED
ASSONATES
ASSONATING
ASSORT
ASSORTED
ASSORTER
ASSORTERS
ASSORTING
ASSORTS
ASSOT
ASSOTS
ASSOTT
ASSOTTED
ASSOTTING
ASSUAGE
ASSUAGED
ASSUAGES
ASSUAGING
ASSUAGINGS
ASSUASIVE
ASSUETUDE
ASSUETUDES
ASSUMABLE
ASSUMABLY
ASSUME
ASSUMED
ASSUMEDLY
ASSUMES
ASSUMING
ASSUMINGS
ASSUMPSIT
ASSUMPSITS
ASSURABLE
ASSURANCE
ASSURANCES
ASSURE
ASSURED
ASSUREDLY
ASSUREDS
ASSURER
ASSURERS
ASSURES
ASSURGENT
ASSURING
ASSWAGE
ASSWAGED
ASSWAGES
ASSWAGING
ASTABLE
ASTARE
ASTART

ASTARTED
ASTARTING
ASTARTS
ASTATIC
ASTATINE
ASTATINES
ASTATKI
ASTATKIS
ASTEISM
ASTEISMS
ASTELIC
ASTELIES
ASTELY
ASTER
ASTERIA
ASTERIAS
ASTERID
ASTERIDS
ASTERISK
ASTERISKED
ASTERISKING
ASTERISKS
ASTERISM
ASTERISMS
ASTERN
ASTEROID
ASTEROIDS
ASTERS
ASTERT
ASTERTED
ASTERTING
ASTERTS
ASTHENIA
ASTHENIAS
ASTHENIC
ASTHENICS
ASTHMA
ASTHMAS
ASTHMATIC
ASTHORE
ASTHORES
ASTICHOUS
ASTIGMIA
ASTIGMIAS
ASTILBE
ASTILBES
ASTIR
ASTOMOUS
ASTONE
ASTONED
ASTONES
ASTONIED
ASTONIES
ASTONING
ASTONISH
ASTONISHED
ASTONISHES
ASTONISHING
ASTONY
ASTONYING
ASTOOP
ASTOUND
ASTOUNDED
ASTOUNDING
ASTOUNDS
ASTRADDLE
ASTRAGAL
ASTRAGALS
ASTRAKHAN
ASTRAKHANS

ASTRAL
ASTRAND
ASTRAY
ASTRICT
ASTRICTED
ASTRICTING
ASTRICTS
ASTRIDE
ASTRINGE
ASTRINGED
ASTRINGER
ASTRINGERS
ASTRINGES
ASTRINGING
ASTRODOME
ASTRODOMES
ASTROFELL
ASTROFELLS
ASTROID
ASTROIDS
ASTROLABE
ASTROLABES
ASTROLOGIES
ASTROLOGY
ASTRONAUT
ASTRONAUTS
ASTRONOMIES
ASTRONOMY
ASTROPHEL
ASTROPHELS
ASTRUT
ASTUCIOUS
ASTUCITIES
ASTUCITY
ASTUN
ASTUNNED
ASTUNNING
ASTUNS
ASTUTE
ASTUTELY
ASTUTER
ASTUTEST
ASTYLAR
ASUDDEN
ASUNDER
ASWARM
ASWAY
ASWIM
ASWING
ASWIRL
ASWOON
ASYLUM
ASYLUMS
ASYMMETRIES
ASYMMETRY
ASYMPTOTE
ASYMPTOTES
ASYNDETIC
ASYNDETON
ASYNDETONS
ASYNERGIA
ASYNERGIAS
ASYSTOLE
ASYSTOLES
AT
ATABAL
ATABALS
ATABEG
ATABEGS
ATABEK

ATABEKS	ATHETISES	ATOMISTIC	ATTACKS	ATTITUDE
ATABRIN	ATHETISING	ATOMISTS	ATTAIN	ATTITUDES
ATABRINS	ATHETIZE	ATOMIZE	ATTAINDER	ATTOLLENT
ATACAMITE	ATHETIZED	ATOMIZED	ATTAINDERS	ATTOLLENTS
ATACAMITES	ATHETIZES	ATOMIZER	ATTAINED	ATTONCE
ATACTIC	ATHETIZING	ATOMIZERS	ATTAINING	ATTONE
ATAGHAN	ATHETOID	ATOMIZES	ATTAINS	ATTONES
ATAGHANS	ATHETOIDS	ATOMIZING	ATTAINT	ATTORN
ATALAYA	ATHETOSES	ATOMS	ATTAINTED	ATTORNED
ATALAYAS	ATHETOSIS	ATOMY	ATTAINTING	ATTORNEY
ATAMAN	ATHIRST	ATONAL	ATTAINTS	ATTORNEYED
ATAMANS	ATHLETA	ATONALISM	ATTAP	ATTORNEYING
ATAP	ATHLETAS	ATONALISMS	ATTAPS	ATTORNEYS
ATAPS	ATHLETE	ATONALITIES	ATTAR	ATTORNING
ATARACTIC	ATHLETES	ATONALITY	ATTARS	ATTORNS
ATARACTICS	ATHLETIC	ATONE	ATTASK	ATTRACT
ATARAXIA	ATHLETICS	ATONED	ATTASKED	ATTRACTED
ATARAXIAS	ATHRILL	ATONEMENT	ATTASKING	ATTRACTING
ATARAXIC	ATHROB	ATONEMENTS	ATTASKS	ATTRACTOR
ATARAXICS	ATHROCYTE	ATONER	ATTASKT	ATTRACTORS
ATARAXIES	ATHROCYTES	ATONERS	ATTEMPER	ATTRACTS
ATARAXY	ATHWART	ATONES	ATTEMPERED	ATTRAHENT
ATAVISM	ATILT	ATONIC	ATTEMPERING	ATTRAHENTS
ATAVISMS	ATIMIES	ATONICITIES	ATTEMPERS	ATTRAP
ATAVISTIC	ATIMY	ATONICITY	ATTEMPT	ATTRAPPED
ATAXIA	ATINGLE	ATONIES	ATTEMPTED	ATTRAPPING
ATAXIAS	ATLAS	ATONING	ATTEMPTER	ATTRAPS
ATAXIC	ATLASES	ATONINGLY	ATTEMPTERS	ATTRIBUTE
ATAXIES	ATMAN	ATONY	ATTEMPTING	ATTRIBUTED
ATAXY	ATMANS	ATOP	ATTEMPTS	ATTRIBUTES
ATOMISE	ATMOLOGIES	ATOPIC	ATTEND	ATTRIBUTING
ATCHIEVED	ATMOLOGY	ATOPIES	ATTENDANT	ATTRIST
ATCHIEVES	ATMOLYSE	ATOPY	ATTENDANTS	ATTRISTED
ATCHIEVING	ATMOLYSED	ATRAMENT	ATTENDED	ATTRISTING
ATE	ATMOLYSES	ATRAMENTS	ATTENDEE	ATTRISTS
ATEBRIN	ATMOLYSING	ATREMBLE	ATTENDEES	ATTRITE
ATEBRINS	ATMOLYSIS	ATRESIA	ATTENDER	ATTRITION
ATELIER	ATMOLYZE	ATRESIAS	ATTENDERS	ATTRITIONS
ATELIERS	ATMOLYZED	ATRIA	ATTENDING	ATTUENT
ATHANASIES	ATMOLYZES	ATRIAL	ATTENDS	ATTUITE
ATHANASY	ATMOLYZING	ATRIP	ATTENT	ATTUITED
ATHANOR	ATMOMETER	ATRIUM	ATTENTAT	ATTUITES
ATHANORS	ATMOMETERS	ATROCIOUS	ATTENTATS	ATTUITING
ATHEISE	ATOC	ATROCITIES	ATTENTION	ATTUITION
ATHEISED	ATOCIA	ATROCITY	ATTENTIONS	ATTUITIONS
ATHEISES	ATOCIAS	ATROPHIED	ATTENTIVE	ATTUITIVE
ATHEISING	ATOCS	ATROPHIES	ATTENTS	ATTUNE
ATHEISM	ATOK	ATROPHY	ATTENUANT	ATTUNED
ATHEISMS	ATOKAL	ATROPHYING	ATTENUANTS	ATTUNES
ATHEIST	ATOKE	ATROPIA	ATTENUATE	ATTUNING
ATHEISTIC	ATOKES	ATROPIAS	ATTENUATED	ATWAIN
ATHEISTS	ATOKOUS	ATROPIN	ATTENUATES	ATWEEL
ATHEIZE	ATOKS	ATROPINE	ATTENUATING	ATWEEN
ATHEIZED	ATOLL	ATROPINES	ATTERCOP	ATWIXT
ATHEIZES	ATOLLS	ATROPINS	ATTERCOPS	ATYPICAL
ATHEIZING	ATOM	ATROPISM	ATTEST	AUBADE
ATHELING	ATOMIC	ATROPISMS	ATTESTED	AUBADES
ATHELINGS	ATOMICAL	ATROPOUS	ATTESTER	AUBERGE
ATHEMATIC	ATOMICITIES	ATTABOY	ATTESTERS	AUBERGES
ATHEOLOGIES	ATOMICITY	ATTACH	ATTESTING	AUBERGINE
ATHEOLOGY	ATOMIES	ATTACHÉ	ATTESTOR	AUBERGINES
ATHEOUS	ATOMISE	ATTACHED	ATTESTORS	AUBRIETIA
ATHERINE	ATOMISED	ATTACHES	ATTESTS	AUBRIETIAS
ATHERINES	ATOMISER	ATTACHÉS	ATTIC	AUBURN
ATHEROMA	ATOMISERS	ATTACHING	ATTICS	AUCEPS
ATHEROMAS	ATOMISES	ATTACK	ATTIRE	AUCEPSES
ATHETESES	ATOMISING	ATTACKED	ATTIRED	AUCTION
ATHETESIS	ATOMISM	ATTACKER	ATTIRES	AUCTIONED
ATHETISE	ATOMISMS	ATTACKERS	ATTIRING	AUCTIONING
ATHETISED	ATOMIST	ATTACKING	ATTIRINGS	AUCTIONS

AUCTORIAL
AUCUBA
AUCUBAS
AUDACIOUS
AUDACITIES
AUDACITY
AUDIBLE
AUDIBLY
AUDIENCE
AUDIENCES
AUDIENT
AUDIENTS
AUDILE
AUDILES
AUDIO
AUDIOGRAM
AUDIOGRAMS
AUDIOLOGIES
AUDIOLOGY
AUDIOPHIL
AUDIOPHILS
AUDIOS
AUDIPHONE
AUDIPHONES
AUDIT
AUDITED
AUDITING
AUDITION
AUDITIONED
AUDITIONING
AUDITIONS
AUDITIVE
AUDITOR
AUDITORIA
AUDITORIES
AUDITORS
AUDITORY
AUDITRESS
AUDITRESSES
AUDITS
AUF
AUFGABE
AUFGABES
AUFS
AUGER
AUGERS
AUGHT
AUGHTS
AUGITE
AUGITES
AUGITIC
AUGMENT
AUGMENTED
AUGMENTER
AUGMENTERS
AUGMENTING
AUGMENTOR
AUGMENTORS
AUGMENTS
AUGUR
AUGURAL
AUGURED
AUGURER
AUGURERS
AUGURIES
AUGURING
AUGURS
AUGURSHIP
AUGURSHIPS
AUGURY

AUGUST
AUGUSTE
AUGUSTER
AUGUSTES
AUGUSTEST
AUGUSTLY
AUGUSTS
AUK
AUKLET
AUKLETS
AUKS
AULA
AULARIAN
AULARIANS
AULAS
AULD
AULDER
AULDEST
AULIC
AULNAGE
AULNAGER
AULNAGERS
AULNAGES
AULOI
AULOS
AUMAIL
AUMAILED
AUMAILING
AUMAILS
AUMBRIES
AUMBRY
AUMIL
AUMILS
AUNT
AUNTER
AUNTERS
AUNTIE
AUNTIES
AUNTS
AUNTY
AURA
AURAE
AURAL
AURALLY
AURAS
AURATE
AURATED
AURATES
AUREATE
AUREI
AUREITIES
AUREITY
AURELIA
AURELIAN
AURELIANS
AURELIAS
AUREOLA
AUREOLAS
AUREOLE
AUREOLED
AUREOLES
AUREUS
AURIC
AURICLE
AURICLED
AURICLES
AURICULA
AURICULAR
AURICULAS
AURIFIED

AURIFIES
AURIFORM
AURIFY
AURIFYING
AURISCOPE
AURISCOPES
AURIST
AURISTS
AUROCHS
AUROCHSES
AURORA
AURORAE
AURORAL
AURORALLY
AURORAS
AUROREAN
AUROUS
AUSPICATE
AUSPICATED
AUSPICATES
AUSPICATING
AUSPICE
AUSPICES
AUSTENITE
AUSTENITES
AUSTERE
AUSTERELY
AUSTERER
AUSTEREST
AUSTERITIES
AUSTERITY
AUSTRAL
AUTACOID
AUTACOIDS
AUTARCHIC
AUTARCHIES
AUTARCHY
AUTARKIC
AUTARKIES
AUTARKIST
AUTARKISTS
AUTARKY
AUTEUR
AUTEURS
AUTHENTIC
AUTHOR
AUTHORED
AUTHORESS
AUTHORESSES
AUTHORIAL
AUTHORING
AUTHORINGS
AUTHORISE
AUTHORISED
AUTHORISES
AUTHORISH
AUTHORISING
AUTHORISM
AUTHORISMS
AUTHORITIES
AUTHORITY
AUTHORIZE
AUTHORIZED
AUTHORIZES
AUTHORIZING
AUTHORS
AUTISM
AUTISMS
AUTISTIC
AUTO

AUTOBAHN
AUTOBAHNS
AUTOBUS
AUTOBUSES
AUTOCADE
AUTOCADES
AUTOCAR
AUTOCARP
AUTOCARPS
AUTOCARS
AUTOCLAVE
AUTOCLAVES
AUTOCRACIES
AUTOCRACY
AUTOCRAT
AUTOCRATS
AUTOCROSS
AUTOCROSSES
AUTOCUE
AUTOCUES
AUTOCYCLE
AUTOCYCLES
AUTODYNE
AUTOFLARE
AUTOFLARES
AUTOGAMIC
AUTOGAMIES
AUTOGAMY
AUTOGENIC
AUTOGENICS
AUTOGENIES
AUTOGENY
AUTOGIRO
AUTOGIROS
AUTOGRAFT
AUTOGRAFTED
AUTOGRAFTING
AUTOGRAFTS
AUTOGRAPH
AUTOGRAPHED
AUTOGRAPHING
AUTOGRAPHS
AUTOGYRO
AUTOGYROS
AUTOHARP
AUTOHARPS
AUTOLATRIES
AUTOLATRY
AUTOLOGIES
AUTOLOGY
AUTOLYSE
AUTOLYSED
AUTOLYSES
AUTOLYSING
AUTOLYSIS
AUTOLYTIC
AUTOLYZE
AUTOLYZED
AUTOLYZES
AUTOLYZING
AUTOMAT
AUTOMATA
AUTOMATE
AUTOMATED
AUTOMATES
AUTOMATIC
AUTOMATICS
AUTOMATING
AUTOMATON
AUTOMATONS

AUTOMATS
AUTONOMIC
AUTONOMICS
AUTONOMIES
AUTONOMY
AUTONYM
AUTONYMS
AUTOPHAGIES
AUTOPHAGY
AUTOPHOBIES
AUTOPHOBY
AUTOPHONIES
AUTOPHONY
AUTOPILOT
AUTOPILOTS
AUTOPISTA
AUTOPISTAS
AUTOPOINT
AUTOPOINTS
AUTOPSIA
AUTOPSIAS
AUTOPSIED
AUTOPSIES
AUTOPSY
AUTOPSYING
AUTOPTIC
AUTOROUTE
AUTOROUTES
AUTOS
AUTOSCOPIES
AUTOSCOPY
AUTOSOMAL
AUTOSOME
AUTOSOMES
AUTOTELIC
AUTOTIMER
AUTOTIMERS
AUTOTOMIES
AUTOTOMY
AUTOTOXIN
AUTOTOXINS
AUTOTROPH
AUTOTROPHS
AUTOTYPE
AUTOTYPED
AUTOTYPES
AUTOTYPING
AUTOVAC
AUTOVACS
AUTUMN
AUTUMNAL
AUTUMNS
AUTUMNY
AUTUNITE
AUTUNITES
AUXESES
AUXESIS
AUXETIC
AUXETICS
AUXILIAR
AUXILIARIES
AUXILIARS
AUXILIARY
AUXIN
AUXINS
AUXOMETER
AUXOMETERS
AVA
AVADAVAT
AVADAVATS

AVAIL	AVERTABLE	AVOIDING	AWARNED	AX
AVAILABLE	AVERTED	AVOIDS	AWARNING	AXE
AVAILABLY	AVERTEDLY	AVOISION	AWARNS	AXED
AVAILE	AVERTIBLE	AVOISIONS	AWASH	AXEL
AVAILED	AVERTING	AVOSET	AWATCH	AXELS
AVAILES	AVERTS	AVOSETS	AWAVE	AXES
AVAILFUL	AVES	AVOUCH	AWAY	AXIAL
AVAILING	AVGAS	AVOUCHED	AWAYES	AXIALLY
AVAILS	AVGASES	AVOUCHES	AWAYS	AXIL
AVAL	AVIAN	AVOUCHING	AWDL	AXILE
AVALANCHE	AVIARIES	AVOUE	AWDLS	AXILLA
AVALANCHED	AVIARIST	AVOUES	AWE	AXILLAE
AVALANCHES	AVIARISTS	AVOURE	AWEARIED	AXILLAR
AVALANCHING	AVIARY	AVOURES	AWEARY	AXILLARY
AVALE	AVIATE	AVOUTERER	AWED	AXILS
AVALED	AVIATED	AVOUTERERS	AWEEL	AXING
AVALES	AVIATES	AVOUTRER	AWELESS	AXINITE
AVALING	AVIATING	AVOUTRERS	AWES	AXINITES
AVANT	AVIATION	AVOUTRIES	AWESOME	AXIOLOGIES
AVANTI	AVIATIONS	AVOUTRY	AWESOMELY	AXIOLOGY
AVARICE	AVIATOR	AVOW	AWESTRIKE	AXIOM
AVARICES	AVIATORS	AVOWABLE	AWESTRIKES	AXIOMATIC
AVAS	AVIATRIX	AVOWAL	AWESTRIKING	AXIOMATICS
AVAST	AVIATRIXES	AVOWALS	AWESTRUCK	AXIOME
AVATAR	AVID	AVOWED	AWETO	AXIS
AVATARS	AVIDER	AVOWEDLY	AWETOS	AXISES
AVAUNT	AVIDEST	AVOWING	AWFUL	AXLE
AVAUNTED	AVIDITIES	AVOWRIES	AWFULLER	AXLES
AVAUNTING	AVIDITY	AVOWRY	AWFULLEST	AXOID
AVAUNTS	AVIDLY	AVOWS	AWFULLY	AXOIDS
AVE	AVIETTE	AVOYER	AWFULNESS	AXOLOTL
AVENGE	AVIETTES	AVOYERS	AWFULNESSES	AXOLOTLS
AVENGED	AVIFAUNA	AVULSE	AWHAPE	AXON
AVENGEFUL	AVIFAUNAE	AVULSED	AWHAPED	AXONS
AVENGER	AVIFAUNAS	AVULSES	AWHAPES	AXOPLASM
AVENGERS	AVIFORM	AVULSING	AWHAPING	AXOPLASMS
AVENGES	AVINE	AVULSION	AWHEEL	AY
AVENGING	AVION	AVULSIONS	AWHEELS	AYAH
AVENIR	AVIONIC	AVUNCULAR	AWHILE	AYAHS
AVENIRS	AVIONICS	AVYZE	AWING	AYAHUASCO
AVENS	AVIONS	AVYZED	AWKWARD	AYAHUASCOS
AVENSES	AVISANDUM	AVYZES	AWKWARDER	AYATOLLAH
AVENTAIL	AVISANDUMS	AVYZING	AWKWARDEST	AYATOLLAHS
AVENTAILE	AVISE	AW	AWKWARDLY	AYE
AVENTAILES	AVISED	AWA	AWL	AYELP
AVENTAILS	AVISEMENT	AWAIT	AWLBIRD	AYENBITE
AVENTRE	AVISEMENTS	AWAITED	AWLBIRDS	AYENBITES
AVENTRED	AVISES	AWAITING	AWLS	AYES
AVENTRES	AVISING	AWAITS	AWMOUS	AYGRE
AVENTRING	AVISO	AWAKE	AWMRIE	AYONT
AVENTURE	AVISOS	AWAKED	AWMRIES	AYRE
AVENTURES	AVITAL	AWAKEN	AWMRY	AYRES
AVENUE	AVIZANDUM	AWAKENED	AWN	AYRIE
AVENUES	AVIZANDUMS	AWAKENING	AWNED	AYRIES
AVER	AVIZE	AWAKENINGS	AWNER	AYU
AVERAGE	AVIZED	AWAKENS	AWNERS	AYURVEDIC
AVERAGED	AVIZEFULL	AWAKES	AWNIER	AYUS
AVERAGES	AVIZES	AWAKING	AWNIEST	AYWORD
AVERAGING	AVIZING	AWAKINGS	AWNING	AYWORDS
AVERMENT	AVOCADO	AWANTING	AWNINGS	AZALEA
AVERMENTS	AVOCADOS	AWARD	AWNLESS	AZALEAS
AVERRED	AVOCATION	AWARDED	AWNS	AZAN
AVERRING	AVOCATIONS	AWARDING	AWNY	AZANS
AVERS	AVOCET	AWARDS	AWOKE	AZEOTROPE
AVERSE	AVOCETS	AWARE	AWOKEN	AZEOTROPES
AVERSELY	AVOID	AWARENESS	AWORK	AZIDE
AVERSION	AVOIDABLE	AWARENESSES	AWRACK	AZIDES
AVERSIONS	AVOIDANCE	AWARER	AWRONG	AZIMUTH
AVERSIVE	AVOIDANCES	AWAREST	AWRY	AZIMUTHAL
AVERT	AVOIDED	AWARN	AWSOME	AZIMUTHS

AZIONE
AZIONES
AZOIC
AZOLLA
AZOLLAS
AZONAL
AZONIC
AZOTE
AZOTES

AZOTH
AZOTHS
AZOTIC
AZOTISE
AZOTISED
AZOTISES
AZOTISING
AZOTIZE
AZOTIZED

AZOTIZES
AZOTIZING
AZOTOUS
AZULEJO
AZULEJOS
AZURE
AZUREAN
AZURES
AZURINE

AZURINES
AZURITE
AZURITES
AZURN
AZURY
AZYGIES
AZYGOUS
AZYGY
AZYM

AZYME
AZYMES
AZYMITE
AZYMITES
AZYMOUS
AZYMS

B

BA
BAA
BAAED
BAAING
BAAINGS
BAAS
BAASES
BAASSKAP
BAASSKAPS
BABA
BABACOOTE
BABACOOTES
BABAS
BABASSU
BABASSUS
BABBITT
BABBITTED
BABBITTING
BABBITTS
BABBLE
BABBLED
BABBLER
BABBLERS
BABBLES
BABBLIER
BABBLIEST
BABBLING
BABBLINGS
BABBLY
BABE
BABEL
BABELDOM
BABELDOMS
BABELISH
BABELISM
BABELISMS
BABELS
BABES
BABICHE
BABICHES
BABIED
BABIER
BABIES
BABIEST
BABIRUSSA
BABIRUSSAS
BABLAH
BABLAHS
BABOO
BABOON
BABOONERIES
BABOONERY
BABOONISH
BABOONS
BABOOS
BABOOSH
BABOOSHES
BABOUCHE
BABOUCHES
BABU
BABUCHE
BABUCHES
BABUDOM

BABUDOMS
BABUISM
BABUISMS
BABUL
BABULS
BABUS
BABUSHKA
BABUSHKAS
BABY
BABYFOOD
BABYFOODS
BABYHOOD
BABYHOODS
BABYING
BABYISH
BACCA
BACCAE
BACCARA
BACCARAS
BACCARAT
BACCARATS
BACCARE
BACCAS
BACCATE
BACCHANAL
BACCHANALS
BACCHANT
BACCHANTE
BACCHANTES
BACCHANTS
BACCHIAC
BACCHII
BACCHIUS
BACCIES
BACCIFORM
BACCO
BACCOES
BACCOS
BACCY
BACH
BACHARACH
BACHARACHS
BACHED
BACHELOR
BACHELORS
BACHES
BACHING
BACILLAR
BACILLARY
BACILLI
BACILLUS
BACK
BACKACHE
BACKACHES
BACKARE
BACKBAND
BACKBANDS
BACKBIT
BACKBITE
BACKBITER
BACKBITERS
BACKBITES
BACKBITING

BACKBITINGS
BACKBITTEN
BACKBOND
BACKBONDS
BACKBONE
BACKBONED
BACKBONES
BACKCHAT
BACKCHATS
BACKCHATTED
BACKCHATTING
BACKCOURT
BACKCOURTS
BACKDOWN
BACKDOWNS
BACKDROP
BACKDROPS
BACKED
BACKER
BACKERS
BACKET
BACKETS
BACKFALL
BACKFALLS
BACKFILL
BACKFILLED
BACKFILLING
BACKFILLS
BACKFIRE
BACKFIRED
BACKFIRES
BACKFIRING
BACKFISCH
BACKFISCHES
BACKHAND
BACKHANDS
BACKHOE
BACKHOES
BACKING
BACKINGS
BACKLASH
BACKLASHES
BACKLIST
BACKLISTS
BACKLOG
BACKLOGS
BACKMOST
BACKPACK
BACKPACKED
BACKPACKING
BACKPACKINGS
BACKPACKS
BACKPAY
BACKPAYS
BACKPIECE
BACKPIECES
BACKROOM
BACKS
BACKSAW
BACKSAWS
BACKSET
BACKSETS
BACKSEY

BACKSEYS
BACKSHISH
BACKSHISHES
BACKSIDE
BACKSIDES
BACKSIGHT
BACKSIGHTS
BACKSLID
BACKSLIDE
BACKSLIDES
BACKSLIDING
BACKSLIDINGS
BACKSPACE
BACKSPACED
BACKSPACES
BACKSPACING
BACKSPEER
BACKSPEERED
BACKSPEERING
BACKSPEERS
BACKSPEIR
BACKSPEIRED
BACKSPEIRING
BACKSPEIRS
BACKSPIN
BACKSPINS
BACKSTAGE
BACKSTALL
BACKSTALLS
BACKSTAYS
BACKSTOP
BACKSTOPS
BACKSWORD
BACKSWORDS
BACKTRACK
BACKTRACKED
BACKTRACKING
BACKTRACKINGS
BACKTRACKS
BACKVELD
BACKVELDS
BACKWARD
BACKWARDS
BACKWASH
BACKWASHED
BACKWASHES
BACKWASHING
BACKWATER
BACKWATERS
BACKWOODS
BACKWORD
BACKWORDS
BACKWORK
BACKWORKS
BACKYARD
BACKYARDS
BACLAVA
BACLAVAS
BACON
BACONS
BACTERIA
BACTERIAL
BACTERIAN

BACTERIC
BACTERISE
BACTERISED
BACTERISES
BACTERISING
BACTERIUM
BACTERIZE
BACTERIZED
BACTERIZES
BACTERIZING
BACTEROID
BACTEROIDS
BACULINE
BACULITE
BACULITES
DAD
BADDIE
BADDIES
BADDISH
BADDY
BADE
BADGE
BADGER
BADGERED
BADGERING
BADGERLY
BADGERS
BADGES
BADINAGE
BADINAGES
BADIOUS
BADLANDS
BADLY
BADMAN
BADMASH
BADMASHES
BADMEN
BADMINTON
BADMINTONS
BADMOUTH
BADMOUTHED
BADMOUTHING
BADMOUTHS
BADNESS
BADNESSES
BAEL
BAELS
BAETYL
BAETYLS
BAFF
BAFFED
BAFFIES
BAFFING
BAFFLE
BAFFLED
BAFFLEGAB
BAFFLEGABS
BAFFLER
BAFFLERS
BAFFLES
BAFFLING
BAFFS
BAFFY

BAFT
BAFTS
BAG
BAGARRE
BAGARRES
BAGASSE
BAGASSES
BAGATELLE
BAGATELLES
BAGEL
BAGELS
BAGFUL
BAGFULS
BAGGAGE
BAGGAGES
BAGGED
BAGGIER
BAGGIEST
BAGGILY
BAGGING
BAGGINGS
BAGGIT
BAGGITS
BAGGY
BAGMAN
BAGMEN
BAGNIO
BAGNIOS
BAGPIPE
BAGPIPER
BAGPIPERS
BAGPIPES
BAGPIPING
BAGPIPINGS
BAGS
BAGUETTE
BAGUETTES
BAGUIO
BAGUIOS
BAGWASH
BAGWASHES
BAGWIG
BAGWIGS
BAH
BAHADA
BAHADAS
BAHT
BAHTS
BAHUVRIHI
BAHUVRIHIS
BAIGNOIRE
BAIGNOIRES
BAIL
BAILABLE
BAILBOND
BAILBONDS
BAILED
BAILEE
BAILEES
BAILER
BAILERS
BAILEY
BAILEYS
BAILIE
BAILIES
BAILIFF
BAILIFFS
BAILING
BAILIWICK
BAILIWICKS

BAILLI
BAILLIAGE
BAILLIAGES
BAILLIE
BAILLIES
BAILLIS
BAILMENT
BAILMENTS
BAILOR
BAILORS
BAILS
BAILSMAN
BAILSMEN
BAININ
BAININS
BAIRN
BAIRNLIKE
BAIRNLY
BAIRNS
BAISEMAIN
BAISEMAINS
BAIT
BAITED
BAITER
BAITERS
BAITFISH
BAITFISHES
BAITING
BAITINGS
BAITS
BAIZE
BAIZED
BAIZES
BAIZING
BAJADA
BAJADAS
BAJAN
BAJANS
BAJRA
BAJRAS
BAJREE
BAJREES
BAJRI
BAJRIS
BAKE
BAKEAPPLE
BAKEAPPLES
BAKEBOARD
BAKEBOARDS
BAKED
BAKEHOUSE
BAKEHOUSES
BAKEMEAT
BAKEMEATS
BAKEN
BAKER
BAKERIES
BAKERS
BAKERY
BAKES
BAKESTONE
BAKESTONES
BAKEWARE
BAKEWARES
BAKHSHISH
BAKHSHISHES
BAKING
BAKINGS
BAKLAVA
BAKLAVAS

BAKSHEESH
BAKSHEESHES
BALADIN
BALADINE
BALADINES
BALADINS
BALALAIKA
BALALAIKAS
BALANCE
BALANCED
BALANCER
BALANCERS
BALANCES
BALANCING
BALANITIS
BALANITISES
BALAS
BALASES
BALATA
BALATAS
BALBOA
BALBOAS
BALCONET
BALCONETS
BALCONIED
BALCONIES
BALCONY
BALD
BALDACHIN
BALDACHINS
BALDAQUIN
BALDAQUINS
BALDER
BALDEST
BALDING
BALDISH
BALDLY
BALDMONEY
BALDMONEYS
BALDNESS
BALDNESSES
BALDPATE
BALDPATED
BALDPATES
BALDRIC
BALDRICK
BALDRICKS
BALDRICS
BALE
BALECTION
BALECTIONS
BALED
BALEEN
BALEENS
BALEFUL
BALEFULLY
BALER
BALERS
BALES
BALING
BALISTA
BALISTAE
BALISTAS
BALK
BALKANISE
BALKANISED
BALKANISES
BALKANISING
BALKANIZE
BALKANIZED

BALKANIZES
BALKANIZING
BALKED
BALKER
BALKERS
BALKIER
BALKIEST
BALKINESS
BALKINESSES
BALKING
BALKINGLY
BALKINGS
BALKLINE
BALKLINES
BALKS
BALKY
BALL
BALLABILE
BALLABILES
BALLABILI
BALLAD
BALLADE
BALLADED
BALLADEER
BALLADEERED
BALLADEERING
BALLADEERS
BALLADES
BALLADIN
BALLADINE
BALLADINES
BALLADING
BALLADINS
BALLADIST
BALLADISTS
BALLADRIES
BALLADRY
BALLADS
BALLAN
BALLANS
BALLANT
BALLANTS
BALLAST
BALLASTED
BALLASTING
BALLASTS
BALLAT
BALLATS
BALLCOCK
BALLCOCKS
BALLED
BALLERINA
BALLERINAS
BALLERINE
BALLET
BALLETIC
BALLETS
BALLING
BALLINGS
BALLISTA
BALLISTAE
BALLISTAS
BALLISTIC
BALLISTICS
BALLIUM
BALLIUMS
BALLOCKS
BALLOCKSED
BALLOCKSES
BALLOCKSING

BALLON
BALLONET
BALLONETS
BALLONS
BALLOON
BALLOONED
BALLOONING
BALLOONINGS
BALLOONS
BALLOT
BALLOTED
BALLOTEE
BALLOTEES
BALLOTING
BALLOTS
BALLOW
BALLOWS
BALLPARK
BALLS
BALLY
BALLYHOO
BALLYHOOS
BALLYRAG
BALLYRAGGED
BALLYRAGGING
BALLYRAGS
BALM
BALMED
BALMIER
BALMIEST
BALMILY
BALMINESS
BALMINESSES
BALMING
BALMORAL
BALMORALS
BALMS
BALMY
BALNEAL
BALNEARIES
BALNEARY
BALONEY
BALONEYS
BALOO
BALOOS
BALSA
BALSAM
BALSAMED
BALSAMIC
BALSAMING
BALSAMS
BALSAMY
BALSAS
BALTHASAR
BALTHASARS
BALTHAZAR
BALTHAZARS
BALU
BALUS
BALUSTER
BALUSTERS
BALZARINE
BALZARINES
BAM
BAMBINI
BAMBINO
BAMBINOS
BAMBOO
BAMBOOS
BAMBOOZLE

BAMBOOZLED
BAMBOOZLES
BAMBOOZLING
BAMMED
BAMMER
BAMMERS
BAMMING
BAMPOT
BAMPOTS
BAMS
BAN
BANAL
BANALER
BANALEST
BANALITIES
BANALITY
BANALLY
BANANA
BANANAS
BANAUSIAN
BANAUSIC
BANC
BANCO
BANCOS
BANCS
BAND
BANDAGE
BANDAGED
BANDAGES
BANDAGING
BANDALORE
BANDALORES
BANDANA
BANDANAS
BANDANNA
BANDANNAS
BANDAR
BANDARS
BANDBRAKE
BANDBRAKES
BANDEAU
BANDEAUX
BANDED
BANDELET
BANDELETS
BANDELIER
BANDELIERS
BANDEROL
BANDEROLE
BANDEROLES
BANDEROLS
BANDH
BANDHED
BANDHING
BANDHS
BANDICOOT
BANDICOOTED
BANDICOOTING
BANDICOOTS
BANDIED
BANDIER
BANDIES
BANDIEST
BANDING
BANDINGS
BANDIT
BANDITRIES
BANDITRY
BANDITS
BANDITTI

BANDITTIS
BANDOBAST
BANDOBASTS
BANDOG
BANDOGS
BANDOLEER
BANDOLEERS
BANDOLERO
BANDOLEROS
BANDOLIER
BANDOLIERS
BANDOLINE
BANDOLINES
BANDOOK
BANDOOKS
BANDORA
BANDORAS
BANDORE
BANDORES
BANDROL
BANDROLS
BANDS
BANDSMAN
BANDSMEN
BANDSTAND
BANDSTANDS
BANDSTER
BANDSTERS
BANDURA
BANDURAS
BANDWAGON
BANDWAGONS
BANDWIDTH
BANDWIDTHS
BANDY
BANDYING
BANDYINGS
BANDYMAN
BANDYMEN
BANE
BANEBERRIES
BANEBERRY
BANED
BANEFUL
BANEFULLY
BANES
BANG
BANGED
BANGER
BANGERS
BANGING
BANGLE
BANGLED
BANGLES
BANGS
BANGSRING
BANGSRINGS
BANGSTER
BANGSTERS
BANI
BANIA
BANIAN
BANIANS
BANIAS
BANING
BANISH
BANISHED
BANISHES
BANISHING
BANISTER

BANISTERS
BANJAX
BANJAXED
BANJAXES
BANJAXING
BANJO
BANJOES
BANJOIST
BANJOISTS
BANJOS
BANJULELE
BANJULELES
BANK
BANKABLE
BANKED
BANKER
BANKERS
BANKET
BANKETS
BANKING
BANKINGS
BANKROLL
BANKROLLED
BANKROLLING
BANKROLLS
BANKRUPT
BANKRUPTED
BANKRUPTING
BANKRUPTS
BANKS
BANKSIA
BANKSIAS
BANKSMAN
BANKSMEN
BANLIEUE
BANLIEUES
BANNED
BANNER
BANNERALL
BANNERALLS
BANNERED
BANNERET
BANNERETS
BANNEROL
BANNEROLS
BANNERS
BANNING
BANNOCK
BANNOCKS
BANNS
BANQUET
BANQUETED
BANQUETER
BANQUETERS
BANQUETING
BANQUETINGS
BANQUETS
BANQUETTE
BANQUETTES
BANS
BANSHEE
BANSHEES
BANT
BANTAM
BANTAMS
BANTED
BANTENG
BANTENGS
BANTER
BANTERED

BANTERER
BANTERERS
BANTERING
BANTERINGS
BANTERS
BANTING
BANTINGS
BANTLING
BANTLINGS
BANTS
BANXRING
BANXRINGS
BANYAN
BANYANS
BANZAI
BAOBAB
BAOBABS
BAP
BAPS
BAPTISE
BAPTISED
BAPTISES
BAPTISING
BAPTISM
BAPTISMAL
BAPTISMS
BAPTIST
BAPTISTRIES
BAPTISTRY
BAPTISTS
BAPTIZE
BAPTIZED
BAPTIZES
BAPTIZING
BAPU
BAPUS
BAR
BARACAN
BARACANS
BARAGOUIN
BARAGOUINS
BARATHEA
BARATHEAS
BARATHRUM
BARATHRUMS
BARB
BARBARIAN
BARBARIANS
BARBARIC
BARBARISE
BARBARISED
BARBARISES
BARBARISING
BARBARISM
BARBARISMS
BARBARITIES
BARBARITY
BARBARIZE
BARBARIZED
BARBARIZES
BARBARIZING
BARBAROUS
BARBASCO
BARBASCOS
BARBASTEL
BARBASTELS
BARBATE
BARBATED
BARBE
BARBECUE

BARBECUED
BARBECUES
BARBECUING
BARBED
BARBEL
BARBELS
BARBER
BARBERED
BARBERING
BARBERRIES
BARBERRY
BARBERS
BARBES
BARBET
BARBETS
BARBETTE
BARBETTES
BARBICAN
BARBICANS
BARBICEL
BARBICELS
BARBIE
BARBIES
BARBING
BARBITAL
BARBITALS
BARBITONE
BARBITONES
BARBOLA
BARBOLAS
BARBOTINE
BARBOTINES
BARBS
BARBULE
BARBULES
BARCA
BARCAROLE
BARCAROLES
BARCAS
BARCHAN
BARCHANE
BARCHANES
BARCHANS
BARD
BARDASH
BARDASHES
BARDED
BARDIC
BARDIER
BARDIEST
BARDING
BARDLING
BARDLINGS
BARDS
BARDSHIP
BARDSHIPS
BARDY
BARE
BAREBACK
BAREBOAT
BAREBONE
BAREBONES
BARED
BAREFACED
BAREFOOT
BAREGE
BAREGES
BAREGINE
BAREGINES
BARELY

BARENESS	BARKLESS	BAROSTAT	BARRIERED	BASEMENT
BARENESSES	BARKS	BAROSTATS	BARRIERING	BASEMENTS
BARER	BARKY	BAROUCHE	BARRIERS	BASENESS
BARES	BARLEY	BAROUCHES	BARRING	BASENESSES
BARESARK	BARLEYS	BARP	BARRINGS	BASENJI
BARESARKS	BARM	BARPERSON	BARRIO	BASENJIS
BAREST	BARMAID	BARPERSONS	BARRIOS	BASEPLATE
BARF	BARMAIDS	BARPS	BARRISTER	BASEPLATES
BARFED	BARMAN	BARQUE	BARRISTERS	BASER
BARFING	BARMBRACK	BARQUES	BARROW	BASES
BARFLIES	BARMBRACKS	BARRACAN	BARROWS	BASEST
BARFLY	BARMEN	BARRACANS	BARRULET	BASH
BARFS	BARMIER	BARRACE	BARRULETS	BASHAW
BARFUL	BARMIEST	BARRACES	BARS	BASHAWISM
BARGAIN	BARMINESS	BARRACK	BARTENDER	BASHAWISMS
BARGAINED	BARMINESSES	BARRACKED	BARTENDERS	BASHAWS
BARGAINER	BARMIZVAH	BARRACKER	BARTER	BASHED
BARGAINERS	BARMIZVAHS	BARRACKERS	BARTERED	BASHER
BARGAINING	BARMKIN	BARRACKING	BARTERER	BASHERS
BARGAINS	BARMKINS	BARRACKINGS	BARTERERS	BASHES
BARGAIST	BARMS	BARRACKS	BARTERING	BASHFUL
BARGAISTS	BARMY	BARRACOON	BARTERS	BASHFULLY
BARGANDER	BARN	BARRACOONS	BARTISAN	BASHING
BARGANDERS	BARNACLE	BARRACUDA	BARTISANED	BASHINGS
BARGE	BARNACLED	BARRACUDAS	BARTISANS	BASHLESS
BARGED	BARNACLES	BARRAGE	BARTIZAN	BASHLYK
BARGEE	BARNED	BARRAGES	BARTIZANS	BASHLYKS
BARGEES	BARNEY	BARRANCA	BARTON	BASIC
BARGEESE	BARNEYS	BARRANCAS	BARTONS	BASICALLY
BARGELLO	BARNING	BARRANCO	BARWOOD	BASICITIES
BARGELLOS	BARNS	BARRANCOS	BARWOODS	BASICITY
BARGEMAN	BARNSTORM	BARRAT	BARYE	BASICS
BARGEMEN	BARNSTORMED	BARRATOR	BARYES	BASIDIA
BARGEPOLE	BARNSTORMING	BARRATORS	BARYON	BASIDIAL
BARGEPOLES	BARNSTORMS	BARRATRIES	BARYONS	BASIDIUM
BARGES	BARNYARD	BARRATRY	BARYTA	BASIFIXED
BARGEST	BARNYARDS	BARRATS	BARYTAS	BASIFUGAL
BARGESTS	BAROCCO	BARRÉ	BARYTES	BASIL
BARGHEST	BAROCCOS	BARRE	BARYTIC	BASILAR
BARGHESTS	BAROCK	BARRED	BARYTON	BASILICA
BARGING	BAROCKS	BARREFULL	BARYTONE	BASILICAL
BARGOOSE	BAROGRAM	BARREL	BARYTONES	BASILICAN
BARIC	BAROGRAMS	BARRELAGE	BARYTONS	BASILICAS
BARILLA	BAROGRAPH	BARRELAGES	BAS	BASILICON
BARILLAS	BAROGRAPHS	BARRELFUL	BASAL	BASILICONS
BARING	BAROMETER	BARRELFULS	BASALT	BASILISK
BARISH	BAROMETERS	BARRELLED	BASALTIC	BASILISKS
BARITE	BAROMETRIES	BARRELLING	BASALTS	BASILS
BARITES	BAROMETRY	BARRELS	BASAN	BASIN
BARITONE	BAROMETZ	BARREN	BASANITE	BASINET
BARITONES	BAROMETZES	BARRENER	BASANITES	BASINETS
BARIUM	BARON	BARRENEST	BASANS	BASINFUL
BARIUMS	BARONAGE	BARRES	BASBLEU	BASINFULS
BARK	BARONAGES	BARRET	BASBLEUS	BASING
BARKAN	BARONESS	BARRETS	BASCULE	BASINS
BARKANS	BARONESSES	BARRETTE	BASCULES	BASIPETAL
BARKED	BARONET	BARRETTES	BASE	BASIS
BARKEEPER	BARONETCIES	BARRICADE	BASEBALL	BASK
BARKEEPERS	BARONETCY	BARRICADED	BASEBALLS	BASKED
BARKEN	BARONETS	BARRICADES	BASEBOARD	BASKET
BARKENED	BARONIAL	BARRICADING	BASEBOARDS	BASKETFUL
BARKENING	BARONIES	BARRICADO	BASECOURT	BASKETFULS
BARKENS	BARONNE	BARRICADOED	BASECOURTS	BASKETRIES
BARKER	BARONNES	BARRICADOES	BASED	BASKETRY
BARKERS	BARONS	BARRICADOING	BASELARD	BASKETS
BARKHAN	BARONY	BARRICADOS	BASELARDS	BASKING
BARKHANS	BAROQUE	BARRICO	BASELESS	BASKS
BARKIER	BAROQUES	BARRICOES	BASELY	BASMIZVAH
BARKIEST	BAROSCOPE	BARRICOS	BASEMAN	BASMIZVAHS
BARKING	BAROSCOPES	BARRIER	BASEMEN	BASNET

BASNETS	BATABLE	BATONED	BAUCHLING	BAYARD
BASOCHE	BATATA	BATONING	BAUD	BAYARDS
BASOCHES	BATATAS	BATONS	BAUDEKIN	BAYBERRIES
BASON	BATCH	BATOON	BAUDEKINS	BAYBERRY
BASONS	BATCHED	BATOONED	BAUDRIC	BAYE
BASQUE	BATCHES	BATOONING	BAUDRICK	BAYED
BASQUED	BATCHING	BATOONS	BAUDRICKE	BAYES
BASQUES	BATE	BATRACHIA	BAUDRICKES	BAYING
BASQUINE	BATEAU	BATS	BAUDRICKS	BAYLE
BASQUINES	BATEAUX	BATSMAN	BAUDRICS	BAYLES
BASS	BATED	BATSMEN	BAUDS	BAYONET
BASSE	BATELESS	BATSWING	BAUERA	BAYONETED
BASSED	BATELEUR	BATSWINGS	BAUERAS	BAYONETING
BASSER	BATELEURS	BATT	BAUHINIA	BAYONETS
BASSES	BATEMENT	BATTA	BAUHINIAS	BAYOU
BASSEST	BATEMENTS	BATTALIA	BAUK	BAYOUS
BASSET	BATES	BATTALIAS	BAUKED	BAYS
BASSETED	BATH	BATTALION	BAUKING	BAYT
BASSETING	BATHCUBE	BATTALIONS	BAUKS	BAYTED
BASSETS	BATHCUBES	BATTAS	BAULK	BAYTING
BASSI	BATHE	BATTED	BAULKED	BAYTS
BASSIER	BATHED	BATTEL	BAULKING	BAZAAR
BASSIEST	BATHER	BATTELED	BAULKS	BAZAARS
BASSINET	BATHERS	BATTELER	BAUR	BAZAR
BASSINETS	BATHES	BATTELERS	BAURS	BAZARS
BASSING	BATHETIC	BATTELING	BAUSOND	BAZAZZ
BASSIST	BATHHOUSE	BATTELS	BAUXITE	BAZAZZES
BASSISTS	BATHHOUSES	BATTELMENT	BAUXITES	BAZOOKA
BASSO	BATHING	BATTEMENTS	BAUXITIC	BAZOOKAS
BASSOON	BATHMIC	BATTEN	BAVARDAGE	BDELLIUM
BASSOONS	BATHMISM	BATTENED	BAVARDAGES	BDELLIUMS
BASSOS	BATHMISMS	BATTENING	BAVIN	BE
BASSWOOD	BATHOLITE	BATTENINGS	BAVINS	BEACH
BASSWOODS	BATHOLITES	BATTENS	BAWBEE	BEACHED
BASSY	BATHOLITH	BATTER	BAWBEES	BEACHES
BAST	BATHOLITHS	BATTERED	BAWBLE	BEACHHEAD
BASTA	BATHORSE	BATTERIE	BAWBLES	BEACHHEADS
BASTARD	BATHORSES	BATTERIES	BAWCOCK	BEACHIER
BASTARDIES	BATHOS	BATTERING	BAWCOCKS	BEACHIEST
BASTARDLY	BATHOSES	BATTERO	BAWD	BEACHING
BASTARDS	BATHROBE	BATTEROS	BAWDIER	BEACHY
BASTARDY	BATHROBES	BATTERS	BAWDIES	BEACON
BASTE	BATHROOM	BATTERY	BAWDIEST	BEACONED
BASTED	BATHROOMS	BATTIER	BAWDILY	BEACONING
BASTER	BATHS	BATTIEST	BAWDINESS	BEACONS
BASTERS	BATHTUB	BATTILL	BAWDINESSES	BEAD
BASTES	BATHTUBS	BATTING	BAWDKIN	BEADED
BASTIDE	BATHYAL	BATTINGS	BAWDKINS	BEADIER
BASTIDES	BATHYBIUS	BATTLE	BAWDRIES	BEADIEST
BASTILLE	BATHYBIUSES	BATTLED	BAWDRY	BEADING
BASTILLES	BATHYLITE	BATTLER	BAWDS	BEADINGS
BASTINADE	BATHYLITES	BATTLERS	BAWDY	BEADLE
BASTINADED	BATHYLITH	BATTLES	BAWL	BEADLEDOM
BASTINADES	BATHYLITHS	BATTLING	BAWLED	BEADLEDOMS
BASTINADING	BATIK	BATTOLOGIES	BAWLER	BEADLES
BASTINADO	BATIKS	BATTOLOGY	BAWLERS	BEADMAN
BASTINADOED	BATING	BATTS	BAWLEY	BEADMEN
BASTINADOES	BATISTE	BATTUE	BAWLEYS	BEADS
BASTINADOING	BATISTES	BATTUES	BAWLING	BEADSMAN
BASTING	BATLER	BATTUTA	BAWLINGS	BEADSMEN
BASTINGS	BATLERS	BATTUTAS	BAWLS	BEADY
BASTION	BATLET	BATTY	BAWN	BEAGLE
BASTIONED	BATLETS	BATWOMAN	BAWNS	BEAGLED
BASTIONS	BATMAN	BATWOMEN	BAWR	BEAGLER
BASTLE	BATMEN	BAUBLE	BAWRS	BEAGLERS
BASTLES	BATMIZVAH	BAUBLES	BAXTER	BEAGLES
BASTO	BATMIZVAHS	BAUBLING	BAXTERS	BEAGLING
BASTOS	BATOLOGIES	BAUCHLE	BAY	BEAGLINGS
BASTS	BATOLOGY	BAUCHLED	BAYADÈRE	BEAK
BAT	BATON	BAUCHLES	BAYADÈRES	BEAKED

BEAKER
BEAKERS
BEAKS
BEAM
BEAMED
BEAMER
BEAMERS
BEAMIER
BEAMIEST
BEAMILY
BEAMINESS
BEAMINESSES
BEAMING
BEAMINGLY
BEAMINGS
BEAMISH
BEAMLESS
BEAMS
BEAMY
BEAN
BEANED
BEANFEAST
BEANFEASTS
BEANIE
BEANIES
BEANING
BEANO
BEANOS
BEANPOLE
BEANPOLES
BEANS
BEANSTALK
BEANSTALKS
BEAR
BEARABLE
BEARABLY
BEARBINE
BEARBINES
BEARD
BEARDED
BEARDIE
BEARDIES
BEARDING
BEARDLESS
BEARDS
BEARE
BEARED
BEARER
BEARERS
BEARES
BEARING
BEARINGS
BEARISH
BÉARNAISE
BÉARNAISES
BEARS
BEARSKIN
BEARSKINS
BEARWARD
BEARWARDS
BEAST
BEASTHOOD
BEASTHOODS
BEASTIE
BEASTIES
BEASTILY
BEASTINGS
BEASTLIER
BEASTLIEST
BEASTLIKE

BEASTLY
BEASTS
BEAT
BEATABLE
BEATEN
BEATER
BEATERS
BEATH
BEATHED
BEATHING
BEATHS
BEATIFIC
BEATIFIED
BEATIFIES
BEATIFY
BEATIFYING
BEATING
BEATINGS
BEATITUDE
BEATITUDES
BEATNIK
BEATNIKS
BEATS
BEAU
BEAUFET
BEAUFETS
BEAUFFET
BEAUFFETS
BEAUFIN
BEAUFINS
BEAUISH
BEAUT
BEAUTEOUS
BEAUTIED
BEAUTIES
BEAUTIFIED
BEAUTIFIES
BEAUTIFUL
BEAUTIFY
BEAUTIFYING
BEAUTS
BEAUTY
BEAUTYING
BEAUX
BEAUXITE
BEAUXITES
BEAVER
BEAVERED
BEAVERIES
BEAVERS
BEAVERY
BEBEERINE
BEBEERINES
BEBEERU
BEBEERUS
BEBOP
BEBOPPED
BEBOPPING
BEBOPS
BEBUNG
BEBUNGS
BECALL
BECALLED
BECALLING
BECALLS
BECALM
BECALMED
BECALMING
BECALMS
BECAME

BÉCASSE
BÉCASSES
BECAUSE
BECCACCIA
BECCACCIAS
BECCAFICO
BECCAFICOS
BÉCHAMEL
BÉCHAMELS
BECHANCE
BECHANCED
BECHANCES
BECHANCING
BECHARM
BECHARMED
BECHARMING
BECHARMS
BECK
BECKE
BECKED
BECKES
BECKET
BECKETS
BECKING
BECKON
BECKONED
BECKONING
BECKONS
BECKS
BECLOUD
BECLOUDED
BECLOUDING
BECLOUDS
BECOME
BECOMES
BECOMING
BECQUEREL
BECQUERELS
BECURL
BECURLED
BECURLING
BECURLS
BED
BEDABBLE
BEDABBLED
BEDABBLES
BEDABBLING
BEDAD
BEDAGGLE
BEDAGGLED
BEDAGGLES
BEDAGGLING
BEDARKEN
BEDARKENED
BEDARKENING
BEDARKENS
BEDASH
BEDASHED
BEDASHES
BEDASHING
BEDAUB
BEDAUBED
BEDAUBING
BEDAUBS
BEDAWIN
BEDAWINS
BEDAZE
BEDAZED
BEDAZES
BEDAZING

BEDAZZLE
BEDAZZLED
BEDAZZLES
BEDAZZLING
BEDBUG
BEDBUGS
BEDCOVER
BEDCOVERS
BEDDABLE
BEDDED
BEDDER
BEDDERS
BEDDING
BEDDINGS
BEDE
BEDEAFEN
BEDEAFENED
BEDEAFENING
BEDEAFENS
BEDECK
BEDECKED
BEDECKING
BEDECKS
BEDEGUAR
BEDEGUARS
BEDEL
BEDELL
BEDELLS
BEDELS
BEDELSHIP
BEDELSHIPS
BEDEMAN
BEDEMEN
BEDERAL
BEDERALS
BEDES
BEDESMAN
BEDESMEN
BEDEVIL
BEDEVILLED
BEDEVILLING
BEDEVILS
BEDEW
BEDEWED
BEDEWING
BEDEWS
BEDFAST
BEDFELLOW
BEDFELLOWS
BEDIDE
BEDIGHT
BEDIGHTING
BEDIGHTS
BEDIM
BEDIMMED
BEDIMMING
BEDIMMINGS
BEDIMS
BEDIZEN
BEDIZENED
BEDIZENING
BEDIZENS
BEDLAM
BEDLAMISM
BEDLAMISMS
BEDLAMITE
BEDLAMITES
BEDLAMS
BEDMAKER
BEDMAKERS

BEDOUIN
BEDOUINS
BEDPAN
BEDPANS
BEDPOST
BEDPOSTS
BEDRAGGLE
BEDRAGGLED
BEDRAGGLES
BEDRAGGLING
BEDRAL
BEDRALS
BEDRENCH
BEDRENCHED
BEDRENCHES
BEDRENCHING
BEDRID
BEDRIDDEN
BEDRIGHT
BEDRIGHTS
BEDRITE
BEDRITES
BEDROCK
BEDROCKS
BEDROOM
BEDROOMS
BEDROP
BEDROPPED
BEDROPPING
BEDROPS
BEDROPT
BEDS
BEDSIDE
BEDSIDES
BEDSOCKS
BEDSORE
BEDSORES
BEDSPREAD
BEDSPREADS
BEDSTEAD
BEDSTEADS
BEDSTRAW
BEDSTRAWS
BEDTICK
BEDTICKS
BEDTIME
BEDTIMES
BEDUCK
BEDUCKED
BEDUCKING
BEDUCKS
BEDUIN
BEDUINS
BEDUNG
BEDUNGED
BEDUNGING
BEDUNGS
BEDUST
BEDUSTED
BEDUSTING
BEDUSTS
BEDWARD
BEDWARDS
BEDWARF
BEDWARFED
BEDWARFING
BEDWARFS
BEDYDE
BEDYE
BEDYED

BEDYEING
BEDYES
BEE
BEECH
BEECHEN
BEECHES
BEEF
BEEFALO
BEEFALOES
BEEFALOS
BEEFCAKE
BEEFCAKES
BEEFEATER
BEEFEATERS
BEEFED
BEEFIER
BEEFIEST
BEEFING
BEEFS
BEEFSTEAK
BEEFSTEAKS
BEEFY
BEEGAH
BEEGAHS
BEEHIVE
BEEHIVES
BEEKEEPER
BEEKEEPERS
BEEN
BEENAH
BEENAHS
BEEP
BEEPED
BEEPER
BEEPERS
BEEPING
BEEPS
BEER
BEERHALL
BEERHALLS
BEERIER
BEERIEST
BEERINESS
BEERINESSES
BEERS
BEERY
BEES
BEESOME
BEESTINGS
BEESWAX
BEESWAXED
BEESWAXES
BEESWAXING
BEESWING
BEESWINGED
BEESWINGS
BEET
BEETED
BEETING
BEETLE
BEETLED
BEETLES
BEETLING
BEETROOT
BEETROOTS
BEETS
BEEVES
BEFALL
BEFALLEN
BEFALLING

BEFALLS
BEFANA
BEFANAS
BEFELD
BEFELL
BEFFANA
BEFFANAS
BEFIT
BEFITS
BEFITTED
BEFITTING
BEFLOWER
BEFLOWERED
BEFLOWERING
BEFLOWERS
BEFLUM
BEFLUMMED
BEFLUMMING
BEFLUMS
BEFOAM
BEFOAMED
BEFOAMING
BEFOAMS
BEFOG
BEFOGGED
BEFOGGING
BEFOGS
BEFOOL
BEFOOLED
BEFOOLING
BEFOOLS
BEFORE
BEFORTUNE
BEFORTUNED
BEFORTUNES
BEFORTUNING
BEFOUL
BEFOULED
BEFOULING
BEFOULS
BEFRIEND
BEFRIENDED
BEFRIENDING
BEFRIENDS
BEFRINGE
BEFRINGED
BEFRINGES
BEFRINGING
BEFUDDLE
BEFUDDLED
BEFUDDLES
BEFUDDLING
BEG
BEGAD
BEGAN
BEGAR
BEGARS
BEGAT
BEGEM
BEGEMMED
BEGEMMING
BEGEMS
BEGET
BEGETS
BEGETTER
BEGETTERS
BEGETTING
BEGGAR
BEGGARDOM
BEGGARDOMS

BEGGARED
BEGGARIES
BEGGARING
BEGGARLY
BEGGARS
BEGGARY
BEGGED
BEGGING
BEGGINGLY
BEGGINGS
BEGHARD
BEGHARDS
BEGIFT
BEGIFTED
BEGIFTING
BEGIFTS
BEGILD
BEGILDED
BEGILDING
BEGILDS
BEGILT
BEGIN
BEGINNE
BEGINNER
BEGINNERS
BEGINNES
BEGINNING
BEGINNINGS
BEGINS
BEGIRD
BEGIRDED
BEGIRDING
BEGIRDS
BEGIRT
BEGLAMOUR
BEGLAMOURED
BEGLAMOURING
BEGLAMOURS
BEGLERBEG
BEGLERBEGS
BEGLOOM
BEGLOOMED
BEGLOOMING
BEGLOOMS
BEGNAW
BEGNAWED
BEGNAWING
BEGNAWS
BEGO
BEGOES
BEGOING
BEGONE
BEGONIA
BEGONIAS
BEGORED
BEGORRA
BEGORRAH
BEGOT
BEGOTTEN
BEGRIME
BEGRIMED
BEGRIMES
BEGRIMING
BEGRUDGE
BEGRUDGED
BEGRUDGES
BEGRUDGING
BEGS
BEGUILE
BEGUILED

BEGUILER
BEGUILERS
BEGUILES
BEGUILING
BEGUIN
BEGUINAGE
BEGUINAGES
BEGUINE
BEGUINES
BEGUINS
BEGUM
BEGUMS
BEGUN
BEGUNK
BEGUNKED
BEGUNKING
BEGUNKS
BEHALF
BEHALVES
BEHAPPEN
BEHAPPENED
BEHAPPENING
BEHAPPENS
BEHAVE
BEHAVED
BEHAVES
BEHAVING
BEHAVIOR
BEHAVIORS
BEHAVIOUR
BEHAVIOURS
BEHEAD
BEHEADAL
BEHEADALS
BEHEADED
BEHEADING
BEHEADINGS
BEHEADS
BEHELD
BEHEMOTH
BEHEMOTHS
BEHEST
BEHESTS
BEHIGHT
BEHIGHTING
BEHIGHTS
BEHIND
BEHINDS
BEHOLD
BEHOLDEN
BEHOLDER
BEHOLDERS
BEHOLDING
BEHOLDINGS
BEHOLDS
BEHOOF
BEHOOFS
BEHOOVE
BEHOOVED
BEHOOVES
BEHOOVING
BEHOTE
BEHOTES
BEHOTING
BEHOVE
BEHOVED
BEHOVEFUL
BEHOVELY
BEHOVES

BEHOVING
BEHOWL
BEHOWLED
BEHOWLING
BEHOWLS
BEIGE
BEIGEL
BEIGELS
BEIGES
BEIGNET
BEIGNETS
BEIN
BEING
BEINGLESS
BEINGNESS
BEINGNESSES
BEINGS
BEINKED
BEINNESS
BEINNESSES
BEJABERS
BEJADE
BEJADED
BEJADES
BEJADING
BEJANT
BEJANTS
BEJESUIT
BEJESUITED
BEJESUITING
BEJESUITS
BEJEWEL
BEJEWELLED
BEJEWELLING
BEJEWELS
BEKAH
BEKAHS
BEKISS
BEKISSED
BEKISSES
BEKISSING
BEKNAVE
BEKNAVED
BEKNAVES
BEKNAVING
BEKNOWN
BEL
BELABOUR
BELABOURED
BELABOURING
BELABOURS
BELACE
BELACED
BELACES
BELACING
BELAH
BELAHS
BELAID
BELAMIES
BELAMOURE
BELAMOURES
BELAMY
BELATE
BELATED
BELATES
BELATING
BELAUD
BELAUDED
BELAUDING
BELAUDS

BELAY
BELAYING
BELAYS
BELCH
BELCHED
BELCHER
BELCHERS
BELCHES
BELCHING
BELDAM
BELDAME
BELDAMES
BELDAMS
BELEAGUER
BELEAGUERED
BELEAGUERING
BELEAGUERS
BELEE
BELEED
BELEEING
BELEES
BELEMNITE
BELEMNITES
BELFRIED
BELFRIES
BELFRY
BELGA
BELGARD
BELGARDS
BELGAS
BELIE
BELIED
BELIEF
BELIEFS
BELIER
BELIERS
BELIES
BELIEVE
BELIEVED
BELIEVER
BELIEVERS
BELIEVES
BELIEVING
BELIKE
BELITTLE
BELITTLED
BELITTLES
BELITTLING
BELIVE
BELL
BELLBIND
BELLBINDS
BELLCOTE
BELLCOTES
BELLE
BELLED
BELLES
BELLETER
BELLETERS
BELLHOP
BELLHOPS
BELLIBONE
BELLIBONES
BELLICOSE
BELLIED
BELLIES
BELLING
BELLMAN
BELLMEN
BELLOW

BELLOWED
BELLOWER
BELLOWERS
BELLOWING
BELLOWS
BELLPUSH
BELLPUSHES
BELLS
BELLWORT
BELLWORTS
BELLY
BELLYFUL
BELLYFULS
BELLYING
BELLYINGS
BELOMANCIES
BELOMANCY
BELONG
BELONGED
BELONGER
BELONGERS
BELONGING
BELONGINGS
BELONGS
BELOVE
BELOVED
BELOVEDS
BELOVES
BELOVING
BELOW
BELS
BELT
BELTED
BELTER
BELTERS
BELTING
BELTINGS
BELTS
BELTWAY
BELTWAYS
BELUGA
BELUGAS
BELVEDERE
BELVEDERES
BELYING
BEMA
BEMAD
BEMADDED
BEMADDING
BEMADS
BEMAS
BEMATA
BEMAUL
BEMAULED
BEMAULING
BEMAULS
BEMAZED
BEMEAN
BEMEANED
BEMEANING
BEMEANS
BEMEANT
BEMEDAL
BEMEDALLED
BEMEDALLING
BEMEDALS
BEMETE
BEMETED
BEMETES
BEMETING

BEMIRE
BEMIRED
BEMIRES
BEMIRING
BEMOAN
BEMOANED
BEMOANER
BEMOANERS
BEMOANING
BEMOANINGS
BEMOANS
BEMOCK
BEMOCKED
BEMOCKING
BEMOCKS
BEMOIL
BEMOILED
BEMOILING
BEMOILS
BEMONSTER
BEMONSTERED
BEMONSTERING
BEMONSTERS
BEMOUTH
BEMOUTHED
BEMOUTHING
BEMOUTHS
BEMUD
BEMUDDED
BEMUDDING
BEMUDDLE
BEMUDDLED
BEMUDDLES
BEMUDDLING
BEMUDS
BEMUFFLE
BEMUFFLED
BEMUFFLES
BEMUFFLING
BEMUSE
BEMUSED
BEMUSES
BEMUSING
BEN
BENAME
BENAMED
BENAMES
BENAMING
BENCH
BENCHED
BENCHER
BENCHERS
BENCHES
BENCHING
BEND
BENDED
BENDER
BENDERS
BENDIER
BENDIEST
BENDING
BENDINGLY
BENDINGS
BENDLET
BENDLETS
BENDS
BENDWISE
BENDY
BENE
BENEATH

BENEDICT
BENEDIGHT
BENEFACT
BENEFACTED
BENEFACTING
BENEFACTS
BENEFIC
BENEFICE
BENEFICED
BENEFICES
BENEFIT
BENEFITED
BENEFITING
BENEFITS
BENEMPT
BENES
BENET
BENETS
BENETTED
BENETTING
BENGALINE
BENGALINES
BENI
BENIGHT
BENIGHTED
BENIGHTEN
BENIGHTENED
BENIGHTENING
BENIGHTENINGS
BENIGHTENS
BENIGHTER
BENIGHTERS
BENIGHTING
BENIGHTINGS
BENIGHTS
BENIGN
BENIGNANT
BENIGNER
BENIGNEST
BENIGNITIES
BENIGNITY
BENIGNLY
BENIS
BENISEED
BENISEEDS
BENISON
BENISONS
BÉNITIER
BÉNITIERS
BENJ
BENJAMIN
BENJAMINS
BENJES
BENNE
BENNES
BENNET
BENNETS
BENNI
BENNIES
BENNIS
BENNY
BENS
BENT
BENTHIC
BENTHOAL
BENTHONIC
BENTHOS
BENTHOSES
BENTIER
BENTIEST

BENTONITE
BENTONITES
BENTS
BENTWOOD
BENTWOODS
BENTY
BENUMB
BENUMBED
BENUMBING
BENUMBS
BENZAL
BENZALS
BENZENE
BENZENES
BENZIDINE
BENZIDINES
BENZIL
BENZILS
BENZINE
BENZINES
BENZOATE
BENZOATES
BENZOIC
BENZOIN
BENZOINS
BENZOL
BENZOLE
BENZOLES
BENZOLINE
BENZOLINES
BENZOLS
BENZOYL
BENZOYLS
BENZYL
BENZYLS
BEPAINT
BEPAINTED
BEPAINTING
BEPAINTS
BEPAT
BEPATCHED
BEPATS
BEPATTED
BEPATTING
BEPEARL
BEPEARLED
BEPEARLING
BEPEARLS
BEPELT
BEPELTED
BEPELTING
BEPELTS
BEPEPPER
BEPEPPERED
BEPEPPERING
BEPEPPERS
BEPESTER
BEPESTERED
BEPESTERING
BEPESTERS
BEPITIED
BEPITIES
BEPITY
BEPITYING
BEPLASTER
BEPLASTERED
BEPLASTERING
BEPLASTERS
BEPLUMED
BEPOMMEL

BEPOMMELLED	BERGHAANS	BESCREENED	BESLAVED	BESPICED
BEPOMMELLING	BERGMEHL	BESCREENING	BESLAVER	BESPICES
BEPOMMELS	BERGMEHLS	BESCREENS	BESLAVERED	BESPICING
BEPOWDER	BERGOMASK	BESCRIBBLE	BESLAVERING	BESPIT
BEPOWDERED	BERGOMASKS	BESCRIBBLED	BESLAVERS	BESPITS
BEPOWDERING	BERGS	BESCRIBBLES	BESLAVES	BESPITTING
BEPOWDERS	BERGYLT	BESCRIBBLING	BESLAVING	BESPOKE
BEPRAISE	BERGYLTS	BESEE	BESLOBBER	BESPOKEN
BEPRAISED	BERIBERI	BESEECH	BESLOBBERED	BESPORT
BEPRAISES	BERIBERIS	BESEECHED	BESLOBBERING	BESPORTED
BEPRAISING	BERK	BESEECHER	BESLOBBERS	BESPORTING
BEPROSE	BERKELIUM	BESEECHERS	BESLUBBER	BESPORTS
BEPROSED	BERKELIUMS	BESEECHES	BESLUBBERED	BESPOT
BEPROSES	BERKS	BESEECHING	BESLUBBERING	BESPOTS
BEPROSING	BERLEY	BESEECHINGS	BESLUBBERS	BESPOTTED
BEPUFF	BERLEYS	BESEEING	BESMEAR	BESPOTTING
BEPUFFED	BERLIN	BESEEKE	BESMEARED	BESPOUT
BEPUFFING	BERLINE	BESEEKES	BESMEARING	BESPOUTED
BEPUFFS	BERLINES	BESEEKING	BESMEARS	BESPOUTING
BEQUEATH	BERLINS	BESEEM	BESMIRCH	BESPOUTS
BEQUEATHED	BERM	BESEEMED	BESMIRCHED	BESPREAD
BEQUEATHING	BERMS	BESEEMING	BESMIRCHES	BESPREADING
BEQUEATHS	BEROB	BESEEMINGS	BESMIRCHING	BESPREADS
BEQUEST	BEROBBED	BESEEMLY	BESMUT	BESPRENT
BEQUESTS	BEROBBING	BESEEMS	BESMUTCH	BEST
BERATE	BEROBS	BESEEN	BESMUTCHED	BESTAD
BERATED	BERRET	BESEES	BESMUTCHES	BESTADDE
BERATES	BERRETS	BESET	BESMUTCHING	BESTAIN
BERATING	BERRIED	BESETMENT	BESMUTS	BESTAINED
BERAY	BERRIES	BESETMENTS	BESMUTTED	BESTAINING
BERAYED	BERRY	BESETS	BESMUTTING	BESTAINS
BERAYING	BERRYING	BESETTER	BESOGNIO	BESTAR
BERAYS	BERRYINGS	BESETTERS	BESOGNIOS	BESTARRED
BERBERINE	BERSERK	BESETTING	BESOIN	BESTARRING
BERBERINES	BERSERKER	BESHADOW	BESOINS	BESTARS
BERBERIS	BERSERKERS	BESHADOWED	BESOM	BESTEAD
BERBERISES	BERSERKLY	BESHADOWING	BESOMS	BESTEADED
BERCEAU	BERSERKS	BESHADOWS	BESORT	BESTEADING
BERCEAUX	BERTH	BESHAME	BESORTED	BESTEADS
BERCEUSE	BERTHA	BESHAMED	BESORTING	BESTED
BERCEUSES	BERTHAGE	BESHAMES	BESORTS	BESTIAL
BERDACHE	BERTHAGES	BESHAMING	BESOT	BESTIALS
BERDACHES	BERTHAS	BESHINE	BESOTS	BESTIARIES
BERDASH	BERTHE	BESHINES	BESOTTED	BESTIARY
BERDASHES	BERTHED	BESHINING	BESOTTING	BESTICK
BERE	BERTHES	BESHONE	BESOUGHT	BESTICKING
BEREAVE	BERTHING	BESHREW	BESOULED	BESTICKS
BEREAVED	BERTHS	BESHREWED	BESPAKE	BESTILL
BEREAVEN	BERYL	BESHREWING	BESPANGLE	BESTILLED
BEREAVES	BERYLLIA	BESHREWS	BESPANGLED	BESTILLING
BEREAVING	BERYLLIAS	BESIDE	BESPANGLES	BESTILLS
BEREFT	BERYLLIUM	BESIDES	BESPANGLING	BESTING
BERES	BERYLLIUMS	BESIEGE	BESPAT	BESTIR
BERET	BERYLS	BESIEGED	BESPATE	BESTIRRED
BERETS	BESAINT	BESIEGER	BESPATTER	BESTIRRING
BERG	BESAINTED	BESIEGERS	BESPATTERED	BESTIRS
BERGAMA	BESAINTING	BESIEGES	BESPATTERING	BESTORM
BERGAMAS	BESAINTS	BESIEGING	BESPATTERS	BESTORMED
BERGAMASK	BESANG	BESIEGINGS	BESPEAK	BESTORMING
BERGAMASKS	BESAT	BESIGH	BESPEAKING	BESTORMS
BERGAMOT	BESAW	BESIGHED	BESPEAKS	BESTOW
BERGAMOTS	BESCATTER	BESIGHING	BESPECKLE	BESTOWAL
BERGANDER	BESCATTERED	BESIGHS	BESPECKLED	BESTOWALS
BERGANDERS	BESCATTERING	BESING	BESPECKLES	BESTOWED
BERGENIA	BESCATTERS	BESINGING	BESPECKLING	BESTOWER
BERGENIAS	BESCRAWL	BESINGS	BESPED	BESTOWERS
BERGÈRE	BESCRAWLED	BESIT	BESPEED	BESTOWING
BERGFALL	BESCRAWLING	BESITS	BESPEEDING	BESTOWS
BERGFALLS	BESCRAWLS	BESITTING	BESPEEDS	BESTREAK
BERGHAAN	BESCREEN	BESLAVE	BESPICE	BESTREAKED

BESTREAKING
BESTREAKS
BESTREW
BESTREWED
BESTREWING
BESTREWN
BESTREWS
BESTRID
BESTRIDDEN
BESTRIDE
BESTRIDES
BESTRIDING
BESTRODE
BESTROWN
BESTS
BESTSELL
BESTSELLING
BESTSELLS
BESTSOLD
BESTUCK
BESTUD
BESTUDDED
BESTUDDING
BESTUDS
BESUNG
BET
BETA
BETACISM
BETACISMS
BETAINE
BETAINES
BETAKE
BETAKEN
BETAKES
BETAKING
BETAS
BETATRON
BETATRONS
BÊTE
BETE
BETED
BETEEM
BETEEME
BETEEMED
BETEEMES
BETEEMING
BETEEMS
BETEL
BETELS
BÊTES
BETES
BETH
BETHANKIT
BETHANKITS
BETHEL
BETHELS
BETHESDA
BETHESDAS
BETHINK
BETHINKING
BETHINKS
BETHOUGHT
BETHRALL
BETHRALLED
BETHRALLING
BETHRALLS
BETHS
BETHUMB
BETHUMBED
BETHUMBING

BETHUMBS
BETHUMP
BETHUMPED
BETHUMPING
BETHUMPS
BETHWACK
BETHWACKED
BETHWACKING
BETHWACKS
BETID
BETIDE
BETIDED
BETIDES
BETIDING
BETIGHT
BETIME
BETIMED
BETIMES
BETIMING
BETING
BÊTISE
BÊTISES
BETITLE
BETITLED
BETITLES
BETITLING
BETOIL
BETOILED
BETOILING
BETOILS
BETOKEN
BETOKENED
BETOKENING
BETOKENS
BÉTON
BETONIES
BÉTONS
BETONY
BETOOK
BETOSS
BETOSSED
BETOSSES
BETOSSING
BETRAY
BETRAYAL
BETRAYALS
BETRAYED
BETRAYER
BETRAYERS
BETRAYING
BETRAYS
BETREAD
BETREADING
BETREADS
BETRIM
BETRIMMED
BETRIMMING
BETRIMS
BETROD
BETRODDEN
BETROTH
BETROTHAL
BETROTHALS
BETROTHED
BETROTHEDS
BETROTHING
BETROTHS
BETS
BETTED
BETTER

BETTERED
BETTERING
BETTERINGS
BETTERS
BETTIES
BETTING
BETTINGS
BETTOR
BETTORS
BETTY
BETUMBLED
BETWEEN
BETWEENS
BETWIXT
BEURRÉ
BEURRE
BEURRÉS
BEURRES
BEVATRON
BEVATRONS
BEVEL
BEVELLED
BEVELLER
BEVELLERS
BEVELLING
BEVELLINGS
BEVELMENT
BEVELMENTS
BEVELS
BEVER
BEVERAGE
BEVERAGES
BEVERS
BEVIES
BEVUE
BEVUES
BEVVIED
BEVVIES
BEVVY
BEVY
BEWAIL
BEWAILED
BEWAILING
BEWAILINGS
BEWAILS
BEWARE
BEWARED
BEWARES
BEWARING
BEWEEP
BEWEEPING
BEWEEPS
BEWENT
BEWEPT
BEWET
BEWETS
BEWETTED
BEWETTING
BEWHORE
BEWHORED
BEWHORES
BEWHORING
BEWIG
BEWIGGED
BEWIGGING
BEWIGS
BEWILDER
BEWILDERED
BEWILDERING
BEWILDERS

BEWITCH
BEWITCHED
BEWITCHES
BEWITCHING
BEWRAY
BEWRAYED
BEWRAYING
BEWRAYS
BEY
BEYOND
BEYONDS
BEYS
BEZ
BEZANT
BEZANTS
BEZAZZ
BEZAZZES
BEZEL
BEZELS
BEZES
BEZIQUE
BEZIQUES
BEZOAR
BEZOARDIC
BEZOARS
BEZONIAN
BEZONIANS
BEZZLE
BEZZLED
BEZZLES
BEZZLING
BHAJAN
BHAJANS
BHAKTI
BHAKTIS
BHANG
BHANGS
BHARAL
BHARALS
BHEESTIE
BHEESTIES
BHEESTY
BHEL
BHELS
BHINDI
BHINDIS
BHISTEE
BHISTEES
BHISTI
BHISTIS
BIANNUAL
BIAS
BIASED
BIASES
BIASING
BIASINGS
BIASSED
BIASSES
BIASSING
BIATHLON
BIATHLONS
BIAXAL
BIAXIAL
BIB
BIBACIOUS
BIBATION
BIBATIONS
BIBBED
BIBBER
BIBBERS

BIBBING
BIBCOCK
BIBCOCKS
BIBELOT
BIBELOTS
BIBLE
BIBLES
BIBLICAL
BIBLICISM
BIBLICISMS
BIBLICIST
BIBLICISTS
BIBLIST
BIBLISTS
BIBS
BIBULOUS
BICAMERAL
BICARB
BICARBS
BICE
BICEPS
BICEPSES
BICES
BICHORD
BICIPITAL
BICKER
BICKERED
BICKERING
BICKERS
BICONCAVE
BICONVEX
BICUSPID
BICUSPIDS
BICYCLE
BICYCLED
BICYCLES
BICYCLING
BICYCLIST
BICYCLISTS
BID
BIDDABLE
BIDDEN
BIDDER
BIDDERS
BIDDIES
BIDDING
BIDDINGS
BIDDY
BIDE
BIDED
BIDENT
BIDENTAL
BIDENTALS
BIDENTATE
BIDENTS
BIDES
BIDET
BIDETS
BIDING
BIDINGS
BIDON
BIDONS
BIDS
BIELD
BIELDIER
BIELDIEST
BIELDS
BIELDY
BIEN
BIENNIAL

BIENNIALS
BIER
BIERS
BIESTINGS
BIFACIAL
BIFARIOUS
BIFF
BIFFED
BIFFIN
BIFFING
BIFFINS
BIFFS
BIFID
BIFILAR
BIFOCAL
BIFOCALS
BIFOLD
BIFOLIATE
BIFORM
BIFURCATE
BIFURCATED
BIFURCATES
BIFURCATING
BIG
BIGA
BIGAE
BIGAMIES
BIGAMIST
BIGAMISTS
BIGAMOUS
BIGAMY
BIGENER
BIGENERIC
BIGENERS
BIGG
BIGGED
BIGGER
BIGGEST
BIGGIE
BIGGIES
BIGGIN
BIGGING
BIGGINS
BIGGISH
BIGGS
BIGGY
BIGHA
BIGHAS
BIGHEADED
BIGHORN
BIGHORNS
BIGHT
BIGHTS
BIGNESS
BIGNESSES
BIGOT
BIGOTED
BIGOTRIES
BIGOTRY
BIGOTS
BIGS
BIGWIG
BIGWIGS
BIJECTION
BIJECTIONS
BIJOU
BIJOUX
BIJWONER
BIJWONERS
BIKE

BIKED
BIKER
BIKERS
BIKES
BIKIE
BIKIES
BIKING
BIKINGS
BIKINI
BIKINIS
BILABIAL
BILABIALS
BILABIATE
BILANDER
BILANDERS
BILATERAL
BILBERRIES
BILBERRY
BILBO
BILBOES
BILBOS
BILE
BILES
BILGE
BILGED
BILGES
BILGIER
BILGIEST
BILGING
BILGY
BILHARZIA
BILHARZIAS
BILIAN
BILIANS
BILIARIES
BILIARY
BILIMBI
BILIMBING
BILIMBINGS
BILIMBIS
BILINGUAL
BILIOUS
BILIOUSLY
BILIRUBIN
BILIRUBINS
BILITERAL
BILK
BILKED
BILKER
BILKERS
BILKING
BILKS
BILL
BILLABONG
BILLABONGS
BILLBOARD
BILLBOARDS
BILLBOOK
BILLBOOKS
BILLED
BILLET
BILLETED
BILLETING
BILLETS
BILLFOLD
BILLFOLDS
BILLHEAD
BILLHEADS
BILLHOOK
BILLHOOKS

BILLIARD
BILLIARDS
BILLIE
BILLIES
BILLING
BILLINGS
BILLION
BILLIONS
BILLIONTH
BILLIONTHS
BILLMAN
BILLMEN
BILLON
BILLONS
BILLOW
BILLOWED
BILLOWIER
BILLOWIEST
BILLOWING
BILLOWS
BILLOWY
BILLS
BILLY
BILLYBOY
BILLYBOYS
BILLYCOCK
BILLYCOCKS
BILOBAR
BILOBATE
BILOBED
BILOBULAR
BILOCULAR
BILTONG
BILTONGS
BIMANAL
BIMANOUS
BIMBASHI
BIMBASHIS
BIMBO
BIMBOS
BIMONTHLY
BIN
BINARIES
BINARY
BINATE
BINAURAL
BIND
BINDER
BINDERIES
BINDERS
BINDERY
BINDING
BINDINGS
BINDS
BINDWEED
BINDWEEDS
BINE
BINERVATE
BINES
BING
BINGE
BINGED
BINGEING
BINGER
BINGERS
BINGES
BINGING
BINGLE
BINGLED
BINGLES

BINGLING
BINGO
BINGOS
BINGS
BINK
BINKS
BINNACLE
BINNACLES
BINNED
BINNING
BINOCLE
BINOCLES
BINOCULAR
BINOCULARS
BINOMIAL
BINOMIALS
BINOMINAL
BINS
BINT
BINTS
BINTURONG
BINTURONGS
BIO
BIOASSAY
BIOASSAYS
BIOBLAST
BIOBLASTS
BIOCIDAL
BIOCIDE
BIOCIDES
BIODATA
BIOETHICS
BIOG
BIOGAS
BIOGASES
BIOGEN
BIOGENIC
BIOGENIES
BIOGENOUS
BIOGENS
BIOGENY
BIOGRAPH
BIOGRAPHIES
BIOGRAPHS
BIOGRAPHY
BIOGS
BIOHAZARD
BIOHAZARDS
BIOLOGIES
BIOLOGIST
BIOLOGISTS
BIOLOGY
BIOMASS
BIOMASSES
BIOME
BIOMES
BIOMETRIC
BIOMETRICS
BIOMETRIES
BIOMETRY
BIOMORPH
BIOMORPHS
BIONIC
BIONICS
BIONOMIC
BIONOMICS
BIONT
BIONTIC
BIONTS
BIOPARENT

BIOPARENTS
BIOPHOR
BIOPHORE
BIOPHORES
BIOPHORS
BIOPIC
BIOPICS
BIOPLASM
BIOPLASMS
BIOPLAST
BIOPLASTS
BIOPSIES
BIOPSY
BIOS
BIOSCOPE
BIOSCOPES
BIOSPHERE
BIOSPHERES
BIOSTABLE
BIOTA
BIOTAS
BIOTIC
BIOTIN
BIOTINS
BIOTITE
BIOTITES
BIOTYPE
BIOTYPES
BIPAROUS
BIPARTITE
BIPED
BIPEDAL
BIPEDS
BIPHENYL
BIPHENYLS
BIPINNATE
BIPLANE
BIPLANES
BIPOD
BIPODS
BIPOLAR
BIPYRAMID
BIPYRAMIDS
BIRCH
BIRCHED
BIRCHEN
BIRCHES
BIRCHING
BIRD
BIRDBATH
BIRDBATHS
BIRDCAGE
BIRDCAGES
BIRDCALL
BIRDCALLS
BIRDED
BIRDER
BIRDERS
BIRDIE
BIRDIED
BIRDIEING
BIRDIES
BIRDING
BIRDINGS
BIRDMAN
BIRDMEN
BIRDS
BIRDSEED
BIRDSEEDS
BIRDSHOT

BIRDSHOTS	BISHES	BITTERLY	BLACKBIRD	BLAEST
BIRDWING	BISHOP	BITTERN	BLACKBIRDS	BLAG
BIRDWINGS	BISHOPDOM	BITTERNS	BLACKBOY	BLAGGED
BIREME	BISHOPDOMS	BITTERS	BLACKBOYS	BLAGGING
BIREMES	BISHOPED	BITTIE	BLACKBUCK	BLAGS
BIRETTA	BISHOPESS	BITTIER	BLACKBUCKS	BLAGUE
BIRETTAS	BISHOPESSES	BITTIES	BLACKCAP	BLAGUES
BIRIYANI	BISHOPING	BITTIEST	BLACKCAPS	BLAGUEUR
BIRIYANIS	BISHOPRIC	BITTING	BLACKCOCK	BLAGUEURS
BIRK	BISHOPRICS	BITTOCK	BLACKCOCKS	BLAH
BIRKEN	BISHOPS	BITTOCKS	BLACKED	BLAHED
BIRKIE	BISK	BITTOR	BLACKEN	BLAHING
BIRKIES	BISKS	BITTORS	BLACKENED	BLAHS
BIRKS	BISMAR	BITTOUR	BLACKENING	BLAIN
BIRL	BISMARS	BITTOURS	BLACKENS	BLAINS
BIRLE	BISMILLAH	BITTS	BLACKER	BLAISE
BIRLED	BISMUTH	BITTUR	BLACKEST	BLAIZE
BIRLER	BISMUTHS	BITTURS	BLACKFISH	BLAMABLE
BIRLERS	BISON	BITTY	BLACKFISHES	BLAMABLY
BIRLES	BISONS	BITUMED	BLACKGAME	BLAME
BIRLIEMAN	BISQUE	BITUMEN	BLACKGAMES	BLAMEABLE
BIRLIEMEN	BISQUES	BITUMENS	BLACKHEAD	BLAMEABLY
BIRLING	BISSON	BIVALENCE	BLACKHEADS	BLAMED
BIRLINGS	BISTABLE	BIVALENCES	BLACKING	BLAMEFUL
BIRLINN	BISTER	BIVALENCIES	BLACKINGS	BLAMELESS
BIRLINNS	BISTERS	BIVALENCY	BLACKISH	BLAMES
BIRLS	BISTORT	BIVALENT	BLACKJACK	BLAMING
BIRR	BISTORTS	BIVALENTS	BLACKJACKS	BLANCH
BIRRS	BISTOURIES	BIVALVE	BLACKLEAD	BLANCHED
BIRSE	BISTOURY	BIVALVES	BLACKLEADS	BLANCHES
BIRSES	BISTRE	BIVARIANT	BLACKLEG	BLANCHING
BIRSIER	BISTRED	BIVARIANTS	BLACKLEGGED	BLANCO
BIRSIEST	BISTRES	BIVARIATE	BLACKLEGGING	BLANCOED
BIRSLE	BISTRO	BIVARIATES	BLACKLEGS	BLANCOING
BIRSLED	BISTROS	BIVIOUS	BLACKLIST	BLANCOS
BIRSLES	BISULCATE	BIVIUM	BLACKLISTED	BLAND
BIRSLING	BIT	BIVIUMS	BLACKLISTING	BLANDER
BIRSY	BITCH	BIVOUAC	BLACKLISTINGS	BLANDEST
BIRTH	BITCHED	BIVOUACKED	BLACKLISTS	BLANDISH
BIRTHDAY	BITCHERIES	BIVOUACKING	BLACKMAIL	BLANDISHED
BIRTHDAYS	BITCHERY	BIVOUACS	BLACKMAILED	BLANDISHES
BIRTHDOM	BITCHES	BIVVIED	BLACKMAILING	BLANDISHING
BIRTHDOMS	BITCHIER	BIVVIES	BLACKMAILS	BLANDLY
BIRTHMARK	BITCHIEST	BIVVY	BLACKNESS	BLANDNESS
BIRTHMARKS	BITCHILY	BIVVYING	BLACKNESSES	BLANDNESSES
BIRTHS	BITCHING	BIZ	BLACKOUT	BLANDS
BIRTHWORT	BITCHY	BIZARRE	BLACKOUTS	BLANK
BIRTHWORTS	BITE	BIZAZZ	BLACKS	BLANKED
BIRYANI	BITER	BIZAZZES	BLACKTOP	BLANKER
BIRYANIS	BITERS	BIZCACHA	BLACKTOPS	BLANKEST
BIS	BITES	BIZCACHAS	BLACKWASH	BLANKET
BISCACHA	BITING	BIZONAL	BLACKWASHES	BLANKETED
BISCACHAS	BITINGS	BIZONE	BLACKWOOD	BLANKETIES
BISCUIT	BITO	BIZONES	BLACKWOODS	BLANKETING
BISCUITS	BITONAL	BIZZES	BLAD	BLANKETINGS
BISCUITY	BITOS	BLAB	BLADDED	BLANKETS
BISE	BITS	BLABBED	BLADDER	BLANKETY
BISECT	BITSIER	BLABBER	BLADDERED	BLANKIES
BISECTED	BITSIEST	BLABBERS	BLADDERS	BLANKING
BISECTING	BITSY	BLABBING	BLADDERY	BLANKINGS
BISECTION	BITT	BLABBINGS	BLADDING	BLANKLY
BISECTIONS	BITTACLE	BLABS	BLADE	BLANKNESS
BISECTOR	BITTACLES	BLACK	BLADED	BLANKNESSES
BISECTORS	BITTE	BLACKBALL	BLADES	BLANKS
BISECTS	BITTED	BLACKBALLED	BLADS	BLANKY
BISERIAL	BITTEN	BLACKBALLING	BLAE	BLANQUET
BISERRATE	BITTER	BLACKBALLINGS	BLAEBERRIES	BLANQUETS
BISES	BITTERER	BLACKBALLS	BLAEBERRY	BLARE
BISEXUAL	BITTEREST	BLACKBAND	BLAER	BLARED
BISH	BITTERISH	BLACKBANDS	BLAES	BLARES

BLARING
BLARNEY
BLARNEYED
BLARNEYING
BLARNEYS
BLASÉ
BLASH
BLASHES
BLASHIER
BLASHIEST
BLASHY
BLASPHEME
BLASPHEMED
BLASPHEMES
BLASPHEMIES
BLASPHEMING
BLASPHEMY
BLAST
BLASTED
BLASTEMA
BLASTEMAS
BLASTER
BLASTERS
BLASTING
BLASTINGS
BLASTMENT
BLASTMENTS
BLASTOID
BLASTOIDS
BLASTS
BLASTULA
BLASTULAE
BLASTULAR
BLASTULAS
BLAT
BLATANT
BLATANTLY
BLATE
BLATER
BLATEST
BLATHER
BLATHERED
BLATHERING
BLATHERS
BLATS
BLATT
BLATTANT
BLATTED
BLATTER
BLATTERED
BLATTERING
BLATTERS
BLATTING
BLATTS
BLAUBOK
BLAUBOKS
BLAUD
BLAUDED
BLAUDING
BLAUDS
BLAWORT
BLAWORTS
BLAY
BLAYS
BLAZE
BLAZED
BLAZER
BLAZERS
BLAZES
BLAZING

BLAZON
BLAZONED
BLAZONER
BLAZONERS
BLAZONING
BLAZONRIES
BLAZONRY
BLAZONS
BLEACH
BLEACHED
BLEACHER
BLEACHERIES
BLEACHERS
BLEACHERY
BLEACHES
BLEACHING
BLEACHINGS
BLEAK
BLEAKER
BLEAKEST
BLEAKIER
BLEAKIEST
BLEAKLY
BLEAKNESS
BLEAKNESSES
BLEAKS
BLEAKY
BLEAR
BLEARED
BLEARER
BLEAREST
BLEAREYED
BLEARIER
BLEARIEST
BLEARING
BLEARS
BLEARY
BLEAT
BLEATED
BLEATER
BLEATERS
BLEATING
BLEATINGS
BLEATS
BLEB
BLEBS
BLED
BLEE
BLEED
BLEEDER
BLEEDERS
BLEEDING
BLEEDINGS
BLEEDS
BLEEP
BLEEPED
BLEEPER
BLEEPERS
BLEEPING
BLEEPS
BLEES
BLEMISH
BLEMISHED
BLEMISHES
BLEMISHING
BLENCH
BLENCHED
BLENCHES
BLENCHING
BLEND

BLENDE
BLENDED
BLENDER
BLENDERS
BLENDES
BLENDING
BLENDINGS
BLENDS
BLENNIES
BLENNY
BLENT
BLESBOK
BLESBOKS
BLESS
BLESSED
BLESSEDER
BLESSEDEST
BLESSEDLY
BLESSES
BLESSING
BLESSINGS
BLEST
BLET
BLETHER
BLETHERED
BLETHERING
BLETHERINGS
BLETHERS
BLETS
BLETTED
BLETTING
BLEUÂTRE
BLEW
BLEWART
BLEWARTS
BLEWITS
BLEWITSES
BLEY
BLEYS
BLIGHT
BLIGHTED
BLIGHTER
BLIGHTERS
BLIGHTIES
BLIGHTING
BLIGHTINGS
BLIGHTS
BLIGHTY
BLIMBING
BLIMBINGS
BLIMEY
BLIMP
BLIMPISH
BLIMPS
BLIMY
BLIN
BLIND
BLINDAGE
BLINDAGES
BLINDED
BLINDER
BLINDERS
BLINDEST
BLINDFISH
BLINDFISHES
BLINDFOLD
BLINDFOLDED
BLINDFOLDING
BLINDFOLDS
BLINDING

BLINDINGS
BLINDLESS
BLINDLY
BLINDNESS
BLINDNESSES
BLINDS
BLINDWORM
BLINDWORMS
BLINI
BLINIS
BLINK
BLINKARD
BLINKARDS
BLINKED
BLINKER
BLINKERED
BLINKERING
BLINKERS
BLINKING
BLINKS
BLINNED
BLINNING
BLINS
BLINTZ
BLINTZE
BLINTZES
BLIP
BLIPPED
BLIPPING
BLIPS
BLISS
BLISSES
BLISSFUL
BLISSLESS
BLIST
BLISTER
BLISTERED
BLISTERING
BLISTERS
BLISTERY
BLITE
BLITES
BLITHE
BLITHELY
BLITHER
BLITHERED
BLITHERING
BLITHEST
BLITZ
BLITZED
BLITZES
BLITZING
BLIVE
BLIZZARD
BLIZZARDS
BLOAT
BLOATED
BLOATER
BLOATERS
BLOATING
BLOATINGS
BLOATS
BLOB
BLOBBED
BLOBBING
BLOBS
BLOC
BLOCK
BLOCKADE

BLOCKADED
BLOCKADES
BLOCKADING
BLOCKAGE
BLOCKAGES
BLOCKED
BLOCKER
BLOCKERS
BLOCKHEAD
BLOCKHEADS
BLOCKHOLE
BLOCKHOLES
BLOCKIER
BLOCKIEST
BLOCKING
BLOCKINGS
BLOCKISH
BLOCKS
BLOCKWORK
BLOCKWORKS
BLOCKY
BLOCS
BLOKE
BLOKES
BLONCKET
BLOND
BLONDE
BLONDER
BLONDES
BLONDEST
BLONDS
BLOOD
BLOODED
BLOODHEAT
BLOODHEATS
BLOODIED
BLOODIER
BLOODIES
BLOODIEST
BLOODILY
BLOODING
BLOODLESS
BLOODLUST
BLOODLUSTS
BLOODROOT
BLOODROOTS
BLOODS
BLOODSHED
BLOODSHEDS
BLOODSHOT
BLOODWOOD
BLOODWOODS
BLOODY
BLOODYING
BLOOM
BLOOMED
BLOOMER
BLOOMERIES
BLOOMERS
BLOOMERY
BLOOMIER
BLOOMIEST
BLOOMING
BLOOMLESS
BLOOMS
BLOOMY
BLOOP
BLOOPED
BLOOPER
BLOOPERS

BLOOPING
BLOOPS
BLOOSME
BLOOSMED
BLOOSMES
BLOOSMING
BLORE
BLORES
BLOSSOM
BLOSSOMED
BLOSSOMING
BLOSSOMINGS
BLOSSOMS
BLOSSOMY
BLOT
BLOTCH
BLOTCHED
BLOTCHES
BLOTCHIER
BLOTCHIEST
BLOTCHING
BLOTCHINGS
BLOTCHY
BLOTS
BLOTTED
BLOTTER
BLOTTERS
BLOTTIER
BLOTTIEST
BLOTTING
BLOTTINGS
BLOTTO
BLOTTY
BLOUBOK
BLOUBOKS
BLOUSE
BLOUSED
BLOUSES
BLOUSING
BLOUSON
BLOUSONS
BLOW
BLOWBALL
BLOWBALLS
BLOWDOWN
BLOWDOWNS
BLOWED
BLOWER
BLOWERS
BLOWFLIES
BLOWFLY
BLOWGUN
BLOWGUNS
BLOWHARD
BLOWHARDS
BLOWHOLE
BLOWHOLES
BLOWIE
BLOWIER
BLOWIES
BLOWIEST
BLOWING
BLOWLAMP
BLOWLAMPS
BLOWN
BLOWPIPE
BLOWPIPES
BLOWS
BLOWSE
BLOWSED

BLOWSES
BLOWSIER
BLOWSIEST
BLOWSY
BLOWTORCH
BLOWTORCHES
BLOWY
BLOWZE
BLOWZED
BLOWZES
BLOWZIER
BLOWZIEST
BLOWZY
BLUB
BLUBBED
BLUBBER
BLUBBERED
BLUBBERING
BLUBBERS
BLUBBING
BLUBS
BLUCHER
BLUCHERS
BLUDE
BLUDES
BLUDGE
BLUDGED
BLUDGEON
BLUDGEONED
BLUDGEONING
BLUDGEONS
BLUDGER
BLUDGERS
BLUDGES
BLUDGING
BLUDIE
BLUDIER
BLUDIEST
BLUDY
BLUE
BLUEBACK
BLUEBACKS
BLUEBEARD
BLUEBEARDS
BLUEBELL
BLUEBELLS
BLUEBERRIES
BLUEBERRY
BLUEBIRD
BLUEBIRDS
BLUEBUCK
BLUEBUCKS
BLUECAP
BLUECAPS
BLUECOAT
BLUECOATS
BLUED
BLUEFISH
BLUEFISHES
BLUEGOWN
BLUEGOWNS
BLUEGRASS
BLUEGRASSES
BLUEING
BLUEINGS
BLUENESS
BLUENESSES
BLUENOSE
BLUENOSES
BLUEPRINT

BLUEPRINTED
BLUEPRINTING
BLUEPRINTS
BLUER
BLUES
BLUESIER
BLUESIEST
BLUEST
BLUESTONE
BLUESTONES
BLUESY
BLUETTE
BLUETTES
BLUEWEED
BLUEWEEDS
BLUEWING
BLUEWINGS
BLUEY
BLUEYS
BLUFF
BLUFFED
BLUFFER
BLUFFERS
BLUFFEST
BLUFFING
BLUFFLY
BLUFFNESS
BLUFFNESSES
BLUFFS
BLUGGY
BLUID
BLUIDIER
BLUIDIEST
BLUIDS
BLUIDY
BLUIER
BLUIEST
BLUING
BLUINGS
BLUISH
BLUNDER
BLUNDERED
BLUNDERER
BLUNDERERS
BLUNDERING
BLUNDERINGS
BLUNDERS
BLUNGE
BLUNGED
BLUNGER
BLUNGERS
BLUNGES
BLUNGING
BLUNK
BLUNKED
BLUNKER
BLUNKERS
BLUNKING
BLUNKS
BLUNT
BLUNTED
BLUNTER
BLUNTEST
BLUNTING
BLUNTISH
BLUNTLY
BLUNTNESS
BLUNTNESSES
BLUNTS
BLUR

BLURB
BLURBS
BLURRED
BLURRING
BLURS
BLURT
BLURTED
BLURTING
BLURTINGS
BLURTS
BLUSH
BLUSHED
BLUSHER
BLUSHERS
BLUSHES
BLUSHET
BLUSHETS
BLUSHFUL
BLUSHING
BLUSHINGS
BLUSHLESS
BLUSTER
BLUSTERED
BLUSTERER
BLUSTERERS
BLUSTERIER
BLUSTERIEST
BLUSTERING
BLUSTERINGS
BLUSTERS
BLUSTERY
BLUSTROUS
BLUTWURST
BLUTWURSTS
BO
BOA
BOAK
BOAKED
BOAKING
BOAKS
BOAR
BOARD
BOARDED
BOARDER
BOARDERS
BOARDING
BOARDINGS
BOARDROOM
BOARDROOMS
BOARDS
BOARDWALK
BOARDWALKS
BOARFISH
BOARFISHES
BOARISH
BOARS
BOART
BOARTS
BOAS
BOAST
BOASTED
BOASTER
BOASTERS
BOASTFUL
BOASTING
BOASTINGS
BOASTLESS
BOASTS
BOAT
BOATBILL

BOATBILLS
BOATED
BOATEL
BOATELS
BOATER
BOATERS
BOATHOUSE
BOATHOUSES
BOATING
BOATINGS
BOATMAN
BOATMEN
BOATRACE
BOATRACES
BOATS
BOATSWAIN
BOATSWAINS
BOATTAIL
BOATTAILS
BOB
BOBA
BOBAC
BOBACS
BOBAK
BOBAKS
BOBAS
BOBBED
BOBBERIES
BOBBERY
BOBBIES
BOBBIN
BOBBINET
BOBBINETS
BOBBING
BOBBINS
BOBBISH
BOBBLE
BOBBLED
BOBBLES
BOBBLING
BOBBY
BOBBYSOCK
BOBBYSOCKS
BOBCAT
BOBCATS
BOBOLINK
BOBOLINKS
BOBS
BOBSLED
BOBSLEDS
BOBSLEIGH
BOBSLEIGHS
BOBSTAYS
BOBTAIL
BOBTAILED
BOBTAILING
BOBTAILS
BOBWHEEL
BOBWHEELS
BOBWIG
BOBWIGS
BOCAGE
BOCAGES
BOCCA
BOCCAS
BOCHE
BOCHES
BOCK
BOCKED
BOCKING

BOCKS
BOD
BODACH
BODACHS
BODDLE
BODDLES
BODE
BODED
BODEFUL
BODEGA
BODEGAS
BODEGUERO
BODEGUEROS
BODEMENT
BODEMENTS
BODES
BODGE
BODGED
BODGER
BODGERS
BODGES
BODGIE
BODGIES
BODGING
BODICE
BODICES
BODIED
BODIES
BODIKIN
BODIKINS
BODILESS
BODILY
BODING
BODINGS
BODKIN
BODKINS
BODLE
BODLES
BODRAG
BODRAGS
BODS
BODY
BODYGUARD
BODYGUARDS
BODYING
BODYLINE
BODYLINES
BODYSHELL
BODYSHELLS
BODYWORK
BODYWORKS
BOEREWORS
BOEREWORSES
BOFF
BOFFED
BOFFIN
BOFFING
BOFFINS
BOFFS
BOG
BOGAN
BOGANS
BOGBEAN
BOGBEANS
BOGEY
BOGEYISM
BOGEYISMS
BOGEYS
BOGGARD
BOGGARDS

BOGGART
BOGGARTS
BOGGED
BOGGIER
BOGGIEST
BOGGINESS
BOGGINESSES
BOGGING
BOGGLE
BOGGLED
BOGGLER
BOGGLERS
BOGGLES
BOGGLING
BOGGY
BOGIE
BOGIES
BOGLAND
BOGLANDS
BOGLE
BOGLES
BOGOAK
BOGOAKS
BOGONG
BOGONGS
BOGS
BOGUS
BOGY
BOGYISM
BOGYISMS
BOH
BOHEA
BOHEAS
BOHUNK
BOHUNKS
BOIL
BOILED
BOILER
BOILERIES
BOILERS
BOILERY
BOILING
BOILINGS
BOILS
BOING
BOINGED
BOINGING
BOINGS
BOINK
BOINKED
BOINKING
BOINKS
BOK
BOKE
BOKED
BOKES
BOKING
BOKO
BOKOS
BOKS
BOLAS
BOLASES
BOLD
BOLDEN
BOLDENED
BOLDENING
BOLDENS
BOLDER
BOLDEST
BOLDLY

BOLDNESS
BOLDNESSES
BOLE
BOLECTION
BOLECTIONS
BOLERO
BOLEROS
BOLES
BOLETI
BOLETUS
BOLETUSES
BOLIDE
BOLIDES
BOLIVAR
BOLIVARS
BOLIVIANO
BOLIVIANOS
BOLIX
BOLIXES
BOLL
BOLLARD
BOLLARDS
BOLLED
BOLLEN
BOLLETRIE
BOLLETRIES
BOLLING
BOLLIX
BOLLIXES
BOLLOCK
BOLLOCKED
BOLLOCKING
BOLLOCKINGS
BOLLOCKS
BOLLOCKSED
BOLLOCKSES
BOLLOCKSING
BOLLS
BOLO
BOLOMETER
BOLOMETERS
BOLOMETRIES
BOLOMETRY
BOLONEY
BOLONEYS
BOLOS
BOLSHEVIK
BOLSHEVIKS
BOLSHIE
BOLSHIER
BOLSHIES
BOLSHIEST
BOLSHY
BOLSTER
BOLSTERED
BOLSTERING
BOLSTERINGS
BOLSTERS
BOLT
BOLTED
BOLTER
BOLTERS
BOLTHEAD
BOLTHEADS
BOLTHOLE
BOLTHOLES
BOLTING
BOLTINGS
BOLTS

BOLUS
BOLUSES
BOMA
BOMAS
BOMB
BOMBARD
BOMBARDED
BOMBARDING
BOMBARDON
BOMBARDONS
BOMBARDS
BOMBASINE
BOMBASINES
BOMBAST
BOMBASTED
BOMBASTIC
BOMBASTING
BOMBASTS
BOMBAX
BOMBAXES
BOMBAZINE
BOMBAZINES
BOMBE
BOMBED
BOMBER
BOMBERS
BOMBES
BOMBILATE
BOMBILATED
BOMBILATES
BOMBILATING
BOMBINATE
BOMBINATED
BOMBINATES
BOMBINATING
BOMBING
BOMBO
BOMBORA
BOMBORAS
BOMBOS
BOMBS
BOMBSHELL
BOMBSHELLS
BOMBSITE
BOMBSITES
BOMBYCID
BOMBYCIDS
BON
BONA
BONAMANI
BONAMANO
BONANZA
BONANZAS
BONASSUS
BONASSUSES
BONASUS
BONASUSES
BONBON
BONBONS
BONCE
BONCES
BOND
BONDAGE
BONDAGER
BONDAGERS
BONDAGES
BONDED
BONDER
BONDERS

BONDING
BONDINGS
BONDMAID
BONDMAIDS
BONDMAN
BONDMEN
BONDS
BONDSMAN
BONDSMEN
BONDSTONE
BONDSTONES
BONDUC
BONDUCS
BONE
BONED
BONEHEAD
BONEHEADS
BONELESS
BONER
BONERS
BONES
BONESET
BONESETS
BONEYARD
BONEYARDS
BONFIRE
BONFIRES
BONG
BONGED
BONGING
BONGO
BONGOS
BONGRACE
BONGRACES
BONGS
BONHOMIE
BONHOMIES
BONHOMMIE
BONHOMMIES
BONHOMOUS
BONIBELL
BONIBELLS
BONIE
BONIER
BONIEST
BONIFACE
BONIFACES
BONILASSE
BONILASSES
BONINESS
BONINESSES
BONING
BONINGS
BONISM
BONISMS
BONIST
BONISTS
BONITO
BONITOS
BONJOUR
BONK
BONKED
BONKERS
BONKING
BONKS
BONNE
BONNES
BONNET
BONNETED
BONNETING

BONNETS
BONNIBELL
BONNIBELLS
BONNIE
BONNIER
BONNIES
BONNIEST
BONNILY
BONNINESS
BONNINESSES
BONNY
BONSAI
BONSAIS
BONSOIR
BONSPIEL
BONSPIELS
BONTEBOK
BONTEBOKS
BONUS
BONUSES
BONXIE
BONXIES
BONY
BONZE
BONZER
BONZES
BOO
BOOB
BOOBED
BOOBIES
BOOBING
BOOBOO
BOOBOOK
BOOBOOKS
BOOBOOS
BOOBS
BOOBY
BOOBYISH
BOOBYISM
BOOBYISMS
BOODIE
BOODIED
BOODIES
BOODLE
BOODLES
BOODY
BOODYING
BOOED
BOOGIE
BOOGIED
BOOGIEING
BOOGIES
BOOH
BOOHED
BOOHING
BOOHS
BOOING
BOOK
BOOKABLE
BOOKCASE
BOOKCASES
BOOKED
BOOKFUL
BOOKIE
BOOKIER
BOOKIES
BOOKIEST
BOOKING
BOOKINGS
BOOKISH

BOOKLAND
BOOKLANDS
BOOKLESS
BOOKLET
BOOKLETS
BOOKLICE
BOOKLORE
BOOKLORES
BOOKLOUSE
BOOKMAKER
BOOKMAKERS
BOOKMAN
BOOKMARK
BOOKMARKS
BOOKMEN
BOOKPLATE
BOOKPLATES
BOOKREST
BOOKRESTS
BOOKS
BOOKSHELF
BOOKSHELVES
BOOKSHOP
BOOKSHOPS
BOOKSIE
BOOKSIER
BOOKSIEST
BOOKSTALL
BOOKSTALLS
BOOKSTAND
BOOKSTANDS
BOOKSTORE
BOOKSTORES
BOOKSY
BOOKWORK
BOOKWORKS
BOOKWORM
BOOKWORMS
BOOKY
BOOM
BOOMED
BOOMER
BOOMERANG
BOOMERANGED
BOOMERANGING
BOOMERANGS
BOOMERS
BOOMING
BOOMINGS
BOOMS
BOOMSLANG
BOOMSLANGS
BOON
BOONDOCKS
BOONG
BOONGS
BOONIES
BOONS
BOOR
BOORD
BOORDE
BOORDES
BOORDS
BOORISH
BOORISHLY
BOORS
BOORTREE
BOORTREES
BOOS
BOOSE

BOOSED
BOOSES
BOOSING
BOOST
BOOSTED
BOOSTER
BOOSTERS
BOOSTING
BOOSTS
BOOT
BOOTBLACK
BOOTBLACKS
BOOTED
BOOTEE
BOOTEES
BOOTH
BOOTHOSE
BOOTHS
BOOTIES
BOOTIKIN
BOOTIKINS
BOOTING
BOOTLACE
BOOTLACES
BOOTLAST
BOOTLASTS
BOOTLEG
BOOTLEGGED
BOOTLEGGING
BOOTLEGGINGS
BOOTLEGS
BOOTLESS
BOOTLICK
BOOTLICKED
BOOTLICKING
BOOTLICKINGS
BOOTLICKS
BOOTMAKER
BOOTMAKERS
BOOTS
BOOTTREE
BOOTTREES
BOOTY
BOOZE
BOOZED
BOOZER
BOOZERS
BOOZES
BOOZEY
BOOZIER
BOOZIEST
BOOZILY
BOOZING
BOOZY
BOP
BOPPED
BOPPER
BOPPERS
BOPPING
BOPS
BOR
BORA
BORACHIO
BORACHIOS
BORACIC
BORACITE
BORACITES
BORAGE
BORAGES
BORANE

BORANES
BORAS
BORATE
BORATES
BORAX
BORAXES
BORAZON
BORAZONS
BORD
BORDAR
BORDARS
BORDE
BORDEL
BORDELLO
BORDELLOS
BORDELS
BORDER
BORDEREAU
BORDEREAUX
BORDERED
BORDERER
BORDERERS
BORDERING
BORDERS
BORDES
BORDS
BORDURE
BORDURES
BORE
BOREAL
BORECOLE
BORECOLES
BORED
BOREDOM
BOREDOMS
BOREE
BOREEN
BOREENS
BOREES
BOREHOLE
BOREHOLES
BOREL
BORER
BORERS
BORES
BORGHETTO
BORGHETTOS
BORGO
BORGOS
BORIC
BORIDE
BORIDES
BORING
BORINGS
BORN
BORNE
BORNÉ
BORNITE
BORNITES
BORON
BORONIA
BORONIAS
BORONS
BOROUGH
BOROUGHS
BORREL
BORRELL
BORROW
BORROWED
BORROWER

BORROWERS
BORROWING
BORROWINGS
BORROWS
BORS
BORSCH
BORSCHES
BORSCHT
BORSCHTS
BORSTAL
BORSTALL
BORSTALLS
BORSTALS
BORT
BORTS
BORTSCH
BORTSCHES
BORTSCHT
BORTSCHTS
BORZOI
BORZOIS
BOS
BOSBOK
BOSBOKS
BOSCAGE
BOSCAGES
BOSCHBOK
BOSCHBOKS
BOSCHE
BOSCHES
BOSCHVELD
BOSCHVELDS
BOSH
BOSHES
BOSHTA
BOSHTER
BOSK
BOSKER
BOSKET
BOSKETS
BOSKIER
BOSKIEST
BOSKINESS
BOSKINESSES
BOSKS
BOSKY
BOSOM
BOSOMED
BOSOMING
BOSOMS
BOSOMY
BOSON
BOSONS
BOSS
BOSSED
BOSSER
BOSSES
BOSSEST
BOSSIER
BOSSIEST
BOSSILY
BOSSINESS
BOSSINESSES
BOSSING
BOSSY
BOSTANGI
BOSTANGIS
BOSTON
BOSTONS
BOSTRYX

BOSTRYXES
BOSUN
BOSUNS
BOT
BOTANIC
BOTANICAL
BOTANICALS
BOTANIES
BOTANISE
BOTANISED
BOTANISES
BOTANISING
BOTANIST
BOTANISTS
BOTANIZE
BOTANIZED
BOTANIZES
BOTANIZING
BOTANY
BOTARGO
BOTARGOES
BOTARGOS
BOTCH
BOTCHED
BOTCHER
BOTCHERIES
BOTCHERS
BOTCHERY
BOTCHES
BOTCHIER
BOTCHIEST
BOTCHING
BOTCHINGS
BOTCHY
BOTEL
BOTELS
BOTFLIES
BOTFLY
BOTH
BOTHAN
BOTHANS
BOTHER
BOTHERED
BOTHERING
BOTHERS
BOTHIE
BOTHIES
BOTHOLE
BOTHOLES
BOTHY
BOTHYMAN
BOTHYMEN
BOTONE
BOTRYOID
BOTRYOSE
BOTS
BOTT
BOTTE
BOTTED
BOTTEGA
BOTTEGAS
BOTTES
BOTTIES
BOTTINE
BOTTINES
BOTTING
BOTTLE
BOTTLED
BOTTLEFUL
BOTTLEFULS

BOTTLER
BOTTLERS
BOTTLES
BOTTLING
BOTTOM
BOTTOMED
BOTTOMING
BOTTOMS
BOTTONY
BOTTS
BOTTY
BOTULISM
BOTULISMS
BOUCHE
BOUCHÉ
BOUCHÉE
BOUCHÉES
BOUCHES
BOUCHÉS
BOUCLÉ
BOUCLÉS
BOUDERIE
BOUDERIES
BOUDOIR
BOUDOIRS
BOUFFANT
BOUGE
BOUGED
BOUGES
BOUGET
BOUGETS
BOUGH
BOUGHPOT
BOUGHPOTS
BOUGHS
BOUGHT
BOUGHTEN
BOUGHTS
BOUGIE
BOUGIES
BOUGING
BOUILLI
BOUILLIS
BOUILLON
BOUILLONS
BOUK
BOUKS
BOULDER
BOULDERS
BOULE
BOULES
BOULEVARD
BOULEVARDS
BOULLE
BOULLES
BOULT
BOULTED
BOULTER
BOULTERS
BOULTING
BOULTINGS
BOULTS
BOUN
BOUNCE
BOUNCED
BOUNCER
BOUNCERS
BOUNCES
BOUNCIER
BOUNCIEST

BOUNCILY
BOUNCING
BOUNCY
BOUND
BOUNDARIES
BOUNDARY
BOUNDED
BOUNDEN
BOUNDER
BOUNDERS
BOUNDING
BOUNDLESS
BOUNDS
BOUNED
BOUNING
BOUNS
BOUNTEOUS
BOUNTIES
BOUNTIFUL
BOUNTREE
BOUNTREES
BOUNTY
BOUNTYHED
BOUNTYHEDS
BOUQUET
BOUQUETS
BOURASQUE
BOURASQUES
BOURBON
BOURDONS
BOURD
BOURDER
BOURDERS
BOURDON
BOURDONS
BOURDS
BOURG
BOURGEOIS
BOURGEOISES
BOURGEON
BOURGEONED
BOURGEONING
BOURGEONS
BOURGS
BOURKHA
BOURKHAS
BOURLAW
BOURLAWS
BOURN
BOURNE
BOURNES
BOURNS
BOURREE
BOURREES
BOURSE
BOURSES
BOURSIER
BOURSIERS
BOURTREE
BOURTREES
BOUSE
BOUSED
BOUSES
BOUSIER
BOUSIEST
BOUSING
BOUSY
BOUT
BOUTADE
BOUTADES

BOUTIQUE
BOUTIQUES
BOUTON
BOUTONNÉ
BOUTONNÉE
BOUTONS
BOUTS
BOUZOUKI
BOUZOUKIS
BOVATE
BOVATES
BOVINE
BOVVER
BOVVERS
BOW
BOWAT
BOWATS
BOWBENT
BOWED
BOWEL
BOWELLED
BOWELLING
BOWELS
BOWER
BOWERED
BOWERIES
BOWERING
BOWERS
BOWERY
BOWES
BOWET
BOWETS
BOWFIN
BOWFINS
BOWGET
BOWGETS
BOWHEAD
BOWHEADS
BOWING
BOWL
BOWLDER
BOWLDERS
BOWLED
BOWLER
BOWLERED
BOWLERING
BOWLERS
BOWLINE
BOWLINES
BOWLING
BOWLINGS
BOWLS
BOWMAN
BOWMEN
BOWNE
BOWNED
BOWNES
BOWNING
BOWPOT
BOWPOTS
BOWR
BOWRS
BOWS
BOWSE
BOWSED
BOWSER
BOWSERS
BOWSES
BOWSHOT
BOWSHOTS

BOWSING
BOWSPRIT
BOWSPRITS
BOWSTRING
BOWSTRINGED
BOWSTRINGING
BOWSTRINGS
BOWSTRUNG
BOWWOW
BOWWOWS
BOWYER
BOWYERS
BOX
BOXCAR
BOXCARS
BOXED
BOXEN
BOXER
BOXERS
BOXES
BOXFUL
BOXFULS
BOXIER
BOXIEST
BOXINESS
BOXINESSES
BOXING
BOXINGS
BOXKEEPER
BOXKEEPERS
BOXROOM
BOXROOMS
BOXWALLAH
BOXWALLAHS
BOXWOOD
BOXWOODS
BOXY
BOY
BOYAR
BOYARS
BOYAU
BOYAUX
BOYCOTT
BOYCOTTED
BOYCOTTING
BOYCOTTS
BOYED
BOYFRIEND
BOYFRIENDS
BOYG
BOYGS
BOYHOOD
BOYHOODS
BOYING
BOYISH
BOYISHLY
BOYO
BOYOS
BOYS
BOZZETTI
BOZZETTO
BRA
BRABBLE
BRABBLED
BRABBLES
BRADDLING
BRACCATE
BRACCIA
BRACCIO
BRACE

BRACED
BRACELET
BRACELETS
BRACER
BRACERS
BRACES
BRACH
BRACHES
BRACHET
BRACHETS
BRACHIAL
BRACING
BRACK
BRACKEN
BRACKENS
BRACKET
BRACKETED
BRACKETING
BRACKETS
BRACKISH
BRACKS
BRACT
BRACTEAL
BRACTEATE
BRACTEATES
BRACTEOLE
BRACTEOLES
BRACTLESS
BRACTLET
BRACTLETS
BRACTS
BRAD
BRADAWL
BRADAWLS
BRADS
BRAE
BRAES
BRAG
BRAGGART
BRAGGARTS
BRAGGED
BRAGGING
BRAGLY
BRAGS
BRAID
BRAIDE
BRAIDED
BRAIDER
BRAIDEST
BRAIDING
BRAIDINGS
BRAIDS
BRAIL
BRAILED
BRAILING
BRAILS
BRAIN
BRAINCASE
BRAINCASES
BRAINED
BRAINIER
BRAINIEST
BRAINING
BRAINISH
BRAINLESS
BRAINPAN
BRAINPANS
BRAINS
BRAINSICK
BRAINWASH

BRAINWASHED
BRAINWASHES
BRAINWASHING
BRAINWASHINGS
BRAINY
BRAIRD
BRAIRDED
BRAIRDING
BRAIRDS
BRAISE
BRAISED
BRAISES
BRAISING
BRAIZE
BRAIZES
BRAKE
BRAKED
BRAKELESS
BRAKEMAN
BRAKEMEN
BRAKES
BRAKIER
BRAKIEST
BRAKING
BRAKY
BRALESS
BRAMBLE
BRAMBLES
BRAMBLIER
BRAMBLIEST
BRAMBLING
BRAMBLINGS
BRAMBLY
BRAME
BRAMES
BRAN
BRANCARD
BRANCARDS
BRANCH
BRANCHED
BRANCHER
BRANCHERIES
BRANCHERS
BRANCHERY
BRANCHES
BRANCHIA
BRANCHIAE
BRANCHIAL
BRANCHIER
BRANCHIEST
BRANCHING
BRANCHINGS
BRANCHLET
BRANCHLETS
BRANCHY
BRAND
BRANDADE
BRANDADES
BRANDED
BRANDER
BRANDERED
BRANDERING
BRANDERS
BRANDIED
BRANDIES
BRANDING
BRANDISE
BRANDISES
BRANDISH
BRANDISHED

BRANDISHES
BRANDISHING
BRANDLING
BRANDLINGS
BRANDRETH
BRANDRETHS
BRANDS
BRANDY
BRANGLE
BRANGLED
BRANGLES
BRANGLING
BRANGLINGS
BRANK
BRANKED
BRANKIER
BRANKIEST
BRANKING
BRANKS
BRANKY
BRANLE
BRANLES
BRANNIER
BRANNIEST
BRANNY
BRANS
BRANSLE
BRANSLES
BRANTLE
BRANTLES
BRAS
BRASERO
BRASEROS
BRASES
BRASH
BRASHED
BRASHER
BRASHES
BRASHEST
BRASHIER
BRASHIEST
BRASHING
BRASHY
BRASIER
BRASIERS
BRASS
BRASSARD
BRASSARDS
BRASSART
BRASSARTS
BRASSERIE
BRASSERIES
BRASSES
BRASSET
BRASSETS
BRASSICA
BRASSICAS
BRASSIE
BRASSIER
BRASSIÈRE
BRASSIÈRES
BRASSIES
BRASSIEST
BRASSILY
BRASSY
BRAST
BRASTING
BRASTS
BRAT
BRATCHET

BRATCHETS
BRATLING
BRATLINGS
BRATS
BRATTICE
BRATTICED
BRATTICES
BRATTICING
BRATTICINGS
BRATTIER
BRATTIEST
BRATTISH
BRATTISHED
BRATTISHES
BRATTISHING
BRATTISHINGS
BRATTLE
BRATTLED
BRATTLES
BRATTLING
BRATTLINGS
BRATTY
BRATWURST
BRATWURSTS
BRAUNCH
BRAUNCHED
BRAUNCHES
BRAUNCHING
BRAVA
BRAVADO
BRAVADOED
BRAVADOES
BRAVADOING
BRAVADOS
BRAVE
BRAVED
BRAVELY
BRAVER
BRAVERIES
BRAVERY
BRAVES
BRAVEST
BRAVI
BRAVING
BRAVO
BRAVOES
BRAVOS
BRAVURA
BRAVURAS
BRAW
BRAWER
BRAWEST
BRAWL
BRAWLED
BRAWLER
BRAWLERS
BRAWLIER
BRAWLIEST
BRAWLING
BRAWLINGS
BRAWLS
BRAWLY
BRAWN
BRAWNED
BRAWNIER
BRAWNIEST
BRAWNS
BRAWNY
BRAWS
BRAXIES

BRAXY
BRAY
BRAYED
BRAYER
BRAYERS
BRAYING
BRAYS
BRAZE
BRAZED
BRAZELESS
BRAZEN
BRAZENED
BRAZENING
BRAZENLY
BRAZENRIES
BRAZENRY
BRAZENS
BRAZES
BRAZIER
BRAZIERS
BRAZIL
BRAZILS
BRAZING
BREACH
BREACHED
BREACHES
BREACHING
BREAD
BREADED
BREADHEAD
BREADHEADS
BREADING
BREADLINE
BREADLINES
BREADNUT
BREADNUTS
BREADROOM
BREADROOMS
BREADROOT
BREADROOTS
BREADS
BREADTH
BREADTHS
BREAK
BREAKABLE
BREAKABLES
BREAKAGE
BREAKAGES
BREAKAWAY
BREAKAWAYS
BREAKBACK
BREAKDOWN
BREAKDOWNS
BREAKER
BREAKERS
BREAKFAST
BREAKFASTED
BREAKFASTING
BREAKFASTS
BREAKING
BREAKINGS
BREAKNECK
BREAKS
BREAM
BREAMED
BREAMING
BREAMS
BREARE
BREARES
BREASKIT

BREASKITS	BRENNING	BRICKED	BRIGADES	BRIOCHE
BREAST	BRENS	BRICKEN	BRIGADIER	BRIOCHES
BREASTED	BRENT	BRICKIE	BRIGADIERS	BRIONIES
BREASTING	BRENTER	BRICKIER	BRIGADING	BRIONY
BREASTPIN	BRENTEST	BRICKIES	BRIGAND	BRIOS
BREASTPINS	BRER	BRICKIEST	BRIGANDRIES	BRIQUET
BREASTS	BRERE	BRICKING	BRIGANDRY	BRIQUETS
BREATH	BRERES	BRICKINGS	BRIGANDS	BRIQUETTE
BREATHE	BRERS	BRICKLE	BRIGHT	BRIQUETTES
BREATHED	BRETASCHE	BRICKS	BRIGHTEN	BRISÉ
BREATHER	BRETASCHES	BRICKWALL	BRIGHTENED	BRISÉS
BREATHERS	BRETESSE	BRICKWALLS	BRIGHTENING	BRISK
BREATHES	BRETESSES	BRICKWORK	BRIGHTENS	BRISKED
BREATHFUL	BRETHREN	BRICKWORKS	BRIGHTER	BRISKEN
BREATHIER	BRETON	BRICKY	BRIGHTEST	BRISKENED
BREATHIEST	BRETONS	BRICKYARD	BRIGHTLY	BRISKENING
BREATHILY	BRETTICE	BRICKYARDS	BRIGS	BRISKENS
BREATHING	BRETTICED	BRICOLE	BRIGUE	BRISKER
BREATHINGS	BRETTICES	BRICOLES	BRIGUED	BRISKEST
BREATHS	BRETTICING	BRIDAL	BRIGUES	BRISKET
BREATHY	BREVE	BRIDALS	BRIGUING	BRISKETS
BRECCIA	BREVES	BRIDE	BRIGUINGS	BRISKING
BRECCIAS	BREVET	BRIDECAKE	BRILL	BRISKISH
BRECHAM	BREVETE	BRIDECAKES	BRILLIANT	BRISKLY
BRECHAMS	BREVETED	BRIDED	BRILLIANTED	BRISKNESS
BRED	BREVETING	BRIDEMAID	BRILLIANTING	BRISKNESSES
BREDE	BREVETS	BRIDEMAIDS	BRILLIANTS	BRISKS
BREDED	BREVETTED	BRIDEMAN	BRILLS	BRISKY
BREDES	BREVETTING	BRIDEMEN	BRIM	BRISLING
BREDING	BREVIARIES	BRIDES	BRIMFUL	BRISLINGS
BREE	BREVIARY	BRIDESMAN	BRIMING	BRISTLE
BREECH	BREVIATE	BRIDESMEN	BRIMINGS	BRISTLED
BREECHED	BREVIATES	BRIDEWELL	BRIMLESS	BRISTLES
BREECHES	BREVIER	BRIDEWELLS	BRIMMED	BRISTLIER
BREECHING	BREVIERS	BRIDGE	BRIMMER	BRISTLIEST
BREECHINGS	BREVITIES	BRIDGED	BRIMMERS	BRISTLING
BREED	BREVITY	BRIDGES	BRIMMING	BRISTLY
BREEDER	BREW	BRIDGING	BRIMS	BRISTOLS
BREEDERS	BREWAGE	BRIDGINGS	BRIMSTONE	BRISURE
BREEDING	BREWAGES	BRIDIE	BRIMSTONES	BRISURES
BREEDINGS	BREWED	BRIDIES	BRIMSTONY	BRIT
BREEDS	BREWER	BRIDING	BRINDED	BRITCHES
BREEKS	BREWERIES	BRIDLE	BRINDISI	BRITS
BREEM	BREWERS	BRIDLED	BRINDISIS	BRITSCHKA
BREER	BREWERY	BRIDLER	BRINDLE	BRITSCHKAS
BREERED	BREWING	BRIDLERS	BRINDLED	BRITSKA
BREERING	BREWINGS	BRIDLES	BRINDLES	BRITSKAS
BREERS	BREWIS	BRIDLING	BRINE	BRITTLE
BREES	BREWISES	BRIDOON	BRINED	BRITTLER
BREESE	BREWS	BRIDOONS	BRINES	BRITTLES
BREESES	BREWSTER	BRIEF	BRING	BRITTLEST
BREEZE	BREWSTERS	BRIEFED	BRINGER	BRITZKA
BREEZED	BRIAR	BRIEFER	BRINGERS	BRITZKAS
BREEZES	BRIARED	BRIEFEST	BRINGING	BRITZSKA
BREEZIER	BRIARS	BRIEFING	BRINGINGS	BRITZSKAS
BREEZIEST	BRIBE	BRIEFINGS	BRINGS	BRIZE
BREEZILY	BRIBED	BRIEFLESS	BRINIER	BRIZES
BREEZING	BRIBER	BRIEFLY	BRINIEST	BRO
BREEZY	BRIBERIES	BRIEFNESS	BRINING	BROACH
BREGMA	BRIBERS	BRIEFNESSES	BRINISH	BROACHED
BREGMATA	BRIBERY	BRIEFS	BRINJAL	BROACHER
BREGMATIC	BRIBES	BRIER	BRINJALS	BROACHERS
BREHON	BRIBING	BRIERED	BRINJARRIES	BROACHES
BREHONS	BRICABRAC	BRIERIER	BRINJARRY	BROACHING
BRELOQUE	BRICABRACS	BRIERIEST	BRINK	BROAD
BRELOQUES	BRICK	BRIERS	BRINKMAN	BROADBAND
BREME	BRICKBAT	BRIERY	BRINKMEN	BROADCAST
BREN	BRICKBATS	BRIG	BRINKS	BROADCASTED
BRENNE	BRICKCLAY	BRIGADE	BRINY	BROADCASTING
BRENNES	BRICKCLAYS	BRIGADED	BRIO	BROADCASTINGS

BROADCASTS
BROADEN
BROADENED
BROADENING
BROADENS
BROADER
BROADEST
BROADISH
BROADLOOM
BROADLY
BROADNESS
BROADNESSES
BROADS
BROADSIDE
BROADSIDES
BROADTAIL
BROADTAILS
BROADWAY
BROADWAYS
BROADWISE
BROCADE
BROCADED
BROCADES
BROCAGE
BROCAGES
BROCARD
BROCARDS
BROCATEL
BROCATELS
BROCCOLI
BROCCOLIS
BROCH
BROCHAN
BROCHANS
BROCHÉ
BROCHÉS
BROCHS
BROCHURE
BROCHURES
BROCK
BROCKAGE
BROCKAGES
BROCKED
BROCKET
BROCKETS
BROCKIT
BROCKRAM
BROCKRAMS
BROCKS
BROD
BRODDED
BRODDING
BRODEKIN
BRODEKINS
BRODKIN
BRODKINS
BRODS
BROG
BROGAN
BROGANS
BROGGED
BROGGING
BROGH
BROGHS
BROGS
BROGUE
BROGUES
BROIDER
BROIDERED
BROIDERER

BROIDERERS
BROIDERIES
BROIDERING
BROIDERINGS
BROIDERS
BROIDERY
BROIL
BROILED
BROILER
BROILERS
BROILING
BROILS
BROKAGE
BROKAGES
BROKE
BROKED
BROKEN
BROKENLY
BROKER
BROKERAGE
BROKERAGES
BROKERIES
BROKERS
BROKERY
BROKES
BROKING
BROKINGS
BROLGA
BROLGAS
BROLLIES
BROLLY
BROMATE
BROMATES
BROMELIA
BROMELIAD
BROMELIADS
BROMELIAS
BROMIC
BROMIDE
BROMIDES
BROMIDIC
BROMINE
BROMINES
BROMMER
BROMMERS
BROMOFORM
BROMOFORMS
BRONCHI
BRONCHIA
BRONCHIAL
BRONCHO
BRONCHOS
BRONCHUS
BRONCO
BRONCOS
BROND
BRONDS
BRONDYRON
BRONDYRONS
BRONZE
BRONZED
BRONZEN
BRONZES
BRONZIER
BRONZIEST
BRONZIFIED
BRONZIFIES
BRONZIFY
BRONZIFYING
BRONZING

BRONZINGS
BRONZITE
BRONZITES
BRONZY
BROO
BROOCH
BROOCHED
BROOCHES
BROOCHING
BROOD
BROODED
BROODER
BROODERS
BROODIER
BROODIEST
BROODING
BROODMARE
BROODMARES
BROODS
BROODY
BROOK
BROOKED
BROOKING
BROOKITE
BROOKITES
BROOKLET
BROOKLETS
BROOKLIME
BROOKLIMES
BROOKS
BROOKWEED
BROOKWEEDS
BROOL
BROOLS
BROOM
BROOMBALL
BROOMBALLS
BROOMED
BROOMIER
BROOMIEST
BROOMING
BROOMRAPE
BROOMRAPES
BROOMS
BROOMY
BROOS
BROOSE
BROOSES
BROS
BROSE
BROSES
BROTH
BROTHEL
BROTHELS
BROTHER
BROTHERLY
BROTHERS
BROTHS
BROUGH
BROUGHAM
BROUGHAMS
BROUGHS
BROUGHT
BROUHAHA
BROUHAHAS
BROUZE
BROUZES
BROW
BROWBEAT
BROWBEATEN

BROWBEATING
BROWBEATS
BROWLESS
BROWN
BROWNED
BROWNER
BROWNEST
BROWNIE
BROWNIER
BROWNIES
BROWNIEST
BROWNING
BROWNINGS
BROWNISH
BROWNNESS
BROWNNESSES
BROWNOUT
BROWNOUTS
BROWNS
BROWNY
BROWS
BROWSE
BROWSED
BROWSES
BROWSING
BROWSINGS
BROWST
BROWSTS
BRUCHID
BRUCHIDS
BRUCINE
BRUCINES
BRUCITE
BRUCITES
BRUCKLE
BRUHAHA
BRUHAHAS
BRUILZIE
BRUILZIES
BRUISE
BRUISED
BRUISER
BRUISERS
BRUISES
BRUISING
BRUISINGS
BRUIT
BRUITED
BRUITING
BRUITS
BRÛLÉ
BRULYIE
BRULYIES
BRULZIE
BRULZIES
BRUMAL
BRUMBIES
BRUMBY
BRUME
BRUMES
BRUMMER
BRUMMERS
BRUMOUS
BRUNCH
BRUNCHES
BRUNET
BRUNETS
BRUNETTE
BRUNETTES
BRUNT

BRUNTED
BRUNTING
BRUNTS
BRUSH
BRUSHED
BRUSHER
BRUSHERS
BRUSHES
BRUSHIER
BRUSHIEST
BRUSHING
BRUSHINGS
BRUSHWOOD
BRUSHWOODS
BRUSHWORK
BRUSHWORKS
BRUSHY
BRUSQUE
BRUSQUELY
BRUSQUER
BRUSQUEST
BRUST
BRUSTING
BRUSTS
BRUT
BRUTAL
BRUTALISE
BRUTALISED
BRUTALISES
BRUTALISING
BRUTALISM
BRUTALISMS
BRUTALIST
BRUTALISTS
BRUTALITIES
BRUTALITY
BRUTALIZE
BRUTALIZED
BRUTALIZES
BRUTALIZING
BRUTALLY
BRUTE
BRUTED
BRUTENESS
BRUTENESSES
BRUTES
BRUTIFIED
BRUTIFIES
BRUTIFY
BRUTIFYING
BRUTING
BRUTISH
BRUTISHLY
BRUXISM
BRUXISMS
BRYOLOGIES
BRYOLOGY
BRYONIES
BRYONY
BRYOPHYTE
BRYOPHYTES
BUAT
BUATS
BUAZE
BUAZES
BUB
BUBA
BUBAL
BUBALINE
BUBALIS

BUBALISES
BUBALS
BUBAS
BUBBIES
BUBBLE
BUBBLED
BUBBLES
BUBBLIER
BUBBLIES
BUBBLIEST
BUBBLING
BUBBLY
BUBBY
BUBINGA
BUBINGAS
BUBO
BUBOES
BUBONIC
BUBS
BUBUKLE
BUBUKLES
BUCCAL
BUCCANEER
BUCCANEERED
BUCCANEERING
BUCCANEERINGS
BUCCANEERS
BUCCANIER
BUCCANIERED
BUCCANIERING
BUCCANIERS
BUCCINA
BUCCINAS
BUCELLAS
BUCELLASES
BUCHU
BUCHUS
BUCK
BUCKAROO
BUCKAROOS
BUCKAYRO
BUCKAYROS
BUCKBEAN
BUCKBEANS
BUCKBOARD
BUCKBOARDS
BUCKCART
BUCKCARTS
BUCKED
BUCKEEN
BUCKEENS
BUCKER
BUCKEROO
BUCKEROOS
BUCKERS
BUCKET
BUCKETED
BUCKETFUL
BUCKETFULS
BUCKETING
BUCKETINGS
BUCKETS
BUCKHORN
BUCKHORNS
BUCKHOUND
BUCKHOUNDS
BUCKIE
BUCKIES
BUCKING
BUCKINGS

BUCKISH
BUCKLE
BUCKLED
BUCKLER
BUCKLERS
BUCKLES
BUCKLING
BUCKLINGS
BUCKO
BUCKOES
BUCKRA
BUCKRAM
BUCKRAMED
BUCKRAMING
BUCKRAMS
BUCKRAS
BUCKS
BUCKSAW
BUCKSAWS
BUCKSHEE
BUCKSHEES
BUCKSHISH
BUCKSHISHES
BUCKSHOT
BUCKSHOTS
BUCKSKIN
BUCKSKINS
BUCKSOM
BUCKTEETH
BUCKTHORN
BUCKTHORNS
BUCKTOOTH
BUCKU
BUCKUS
BUCKWHEAT
BUCKWHEATS
BUCOLIC
BUCOLICAL
BUCOLICS
BUD
BUDDED
BUDDIER
BUDDIES
BUDDIEST
BUDDING
BUDDINGS
BUDDLE
BUDDLED
BUDDLEIA
BUDDLEIAS
BUDDLES
BUDDLING
BUDDY
BUDGE
BUDGED
BUDGER
BUDGEREE
BUDGERO
BUDGEROS
BUDGEROW
BUDGEROWS
BUDGERS
BUDGES
BUDGET
BUDGETARY
BUDGETED
BUDGETING
BUDGETS
BUDGIE
BUDGIES

BUDGING
BUDLESS
BUDMASH
BUDMASHES
BUDO
BUDOS
BUDS
BUFF
BUFFA
BUFFALO
BUFFALOED
BUFFALOES
BUFFALOING
BUFFE
BUFFED
BUFFER
BUFFERED
BUFFERING
BUFFERS
BUFFET
BUFFETED
BUFFETING
BUFFETINGS
BUFFETS
BUFFI
BUFFING
BUFFO
BUFFOON
BUFFOONS
BUFFS
BUFO
BUFOS
BUG
BUGABOO
BUGABOOS
BUGBANE
BUGBANES
BUGBEAR
BUGBEARS
BUGGAN
BUGGANE
BUGGANES
BUGGANS
BUGGED
BUGGER
BUGGERED
BUGGERIES
BUGGERING
BUGGERS
BUGGERY
BUGGIES
BUGGIN
BUGGING
BUGGINGS
BUGGINS
BUGGY
BUGHOUSE
BUGHOUSES
BUGLE
BUGLED
BUGLER
BUGLERS
BUGLES
BUGLET
BUGLETS
BUGLING
BUGLOSS
BUGLOSSES
BUGONG
BUGONGS

BUGS
BUGWORT
BUGWORTS
BUHL
BUHLS
BUHRSTONE
BUHRSTONES
BUIK
BUIKS
BUILD
BUILDED
BUILDER
BUILDERS
BUILDING
BUILDINGS
BUILDS
BUILT
BUIRDLIER
BUIRDLIEST
BUIRDLY
BUIST
BUISTED
BUISTING
BUISTS
BUKE
BUKES
BUKSHEE
BUKSHEES
BUKSHI
BUKSHIS
BULB
BULBAR
BULBED
BULBIL
BULBILS
BULBING
BULBOUS
BULBS
BULBUL
BULBULS
BULGE
BULGED
BULGER
BULGERS
BULGES
BULGIER
BULGIEST
BULGINE
BULGINES
BULGINESS
BULGINESSES
BULGING
BULGY
BULIMIA
BULIMIAS
BULIMIC
BULIMICS
BULIMIES
BULIMUS
BULIMUSES
BULIMY
BULK
BULKED
BULKER
BULKERS
BULKHEAD
BULKHEADS
BULKIER
BULKIEST
BULKILY

BULKINESS
BULKINESSES
BULKING
BULKS
BULKY
BULL
BULLA
BULLACE
BULLACES
BULLAE
BULLARIES
BULLARY
BULLAS
BULLATE
BULLBAT
BULLBATS
BULLDOG
BULLDOGGED
BULLDOGGING
BULLDOGS
BULLDOZE
BULLDOZED
BULLDOZER
BULLDOZERS
BULLDOZES
BULLDOZING
BULLDUST
BULLDUSTS
BULLED
BULLER
BULLERED
BULLERING
BULLERS
BULLET
BULLETIN
BULLETINS
BULLETRIE
BULLETRIES
BULLETS
BULLFIGHT
BULLFIGHTS
BULLFINCH
BULLFINCHES
BULLFROG
BULLFROGS
BULLGINE
BULLGINES
BULLHEAD
BULLHEADS
BULLIED
BULLIER
BULLIES
BULLIEST
BULLING
BULLION
BULLIONS
BULLISH
BULLISHLY
BULLOCK
BULLOCKS
BULLS
BULLSHIT
BULLSHITS
BULLSHITTED
BULLSHITTING
BULLWHACK
BULLWHACKED
BULLWHACKING
BULLWHACKS
BULLY

BULLYING
BULLYISM
BULLYISMS
BULLYRAG
BULLYRAGGED
BULLYRAGGING
BULLYRAGS
BULRUSH
BULRUSHES
BULRUSHY
BULSE
BULSES
BULWARK
BULWARKED
BULWARKING
BULWARKS
BUM
BUMALO
BUMBAZE
BUMBAZED
BUMBAZES
BUMBAZING
BUMBLE
BUMBLED
BUMBLES
BUMBLING
BUMBO
BUMBOS
BUMF
BUMFS
BUMKIN
BUMKINS
BUMMALO
BUMMALOTI
BUMMALOTIS
BUMMAREE
BUMMAREES
BUMMED
BUMMEL
BUMMELS
BUMMER
BUMMERS
BUMMING
BUMMLE
BUMMLED
BUMMLES
BUMMLING
BUMMOCK
BUMMOCKS
BUMP
BUMPED
BUMPER
BUMPERED
BUMPERING
BUMPERS
BUMPH
BUMPHS
BUMPIER
BUMPIEST
BUMPINESS
BUMPINESSES
BUMPING
BUMPKIN
BUMPKINS
BUMPOLOGIES
BUMPOLOGY
BUMPS
BUMPTIOUS
BUMPY
BUMS

BUMSUCKER
BUMSUCKERS
BUN
BUNA
BUNAS
BUNCE
BUNCED
BUNCES
BUNCH
BUNCHED
BUNCHES
BUNCHIER
BUNCHIEST
BUNCHING
BUNCHINGS
BUNCHY
BUNCING
BUNCO
BUNCOED
BUNCOING
BUNCOMBE
BUNCOMBES
BUNCOS
BUND
BUNDED
BUNDING
BUNDLE
BUNDLED
BUNDLES
BUNDLING
BUNDLINGS
BUNDOBUST
BUNDOBUSTS
BUNDOOK
BUNDOOKS
BUNDS
BUNDU
BUNDUS
BUNG
BUNGALOID
BUNGALOIDS
BUNGALOW
BUNGALOWS
BUNGED
BUNGEE
BUNGEES
BUNGEY
BUNGEYS
BUNGIE
BUNGIES
BUNGING
BUNGLE
BUNGLED
BUNGLER
BUNGLERS
BUNGLES
BUNGLING
BUNGLINGS
BUNGS
BUNGY
BUNIA
BUNIAS
BUNION
BUNIONS
BUNJE
BUNJEE
BUNJEES
BUNJES
BUNJIE
BUNJIES

BUNJY
BUNK
BUNKED
BUNKER
BUNKERED
BUNKERING
BUNKERS
BUNKHOUSE
BUNKHOUSES
BUNKING
BUNKO
BUNKOED
BUNKOING
BUNKOS
BUNKS
BUNKUM
BUNKUMS
BUNNIA
BUNNIAS
BUNNIES
BUNNY
BUNODONT
BUNRAKU
BUNRAKUS
BUNS
BUNT
BUNTED
BUNTER
BUNTERS
BUNTIER
BUNTIEST
BUNTING
BUNTINGS
BUNTLINE
BUNTLINES
BUNTS
BUNTY
BUNYA
BUNYAS
BUNYIP
BUNYIPS
BUONAMANI
BUONAMANO
BUOY
BUOYAGE
BUOYAGES
BUOYANCE
BUOYANCES
BUOYANCIES
BUOYANCY
BUOYANT
BUOYED
BUOYING
BUOYS
BUPLEVER
BUPLEVERS
BUR
BURAN
BURANS
BURBLE
BURBLED
BURBLES
BURBLING
BURBLINGS
BURBOT
BURBOTS
BURD
BURDASH
BURDASHES
BURDEN

BURDENED
BURDENING
BURDENOUS
BURDENS
BURDIE
BURDIES
BURDOCK
BURDOCKS
BURDS
BUREAU
BUREAUS
BUREAUX
BURETTE
BURETTES
BURG
BURGAGE
BURGAGES
BURGANET
BURGANETS
BURGEE
BURGEES
BURGEON
BURGEONED
BURGEONING
BURGEONS
BURGER
BURGERS
BURGESS
BURGESSES
BURGH
BURGHAL
BURGHER
BURGHERS
BURGHS
BURGLAR
BURGLARED
BURGLARIES
BURGLARING
BURGLARS
BURGLARY
BURGLE
BURGLED
BURGLES
BURGLING
BURGONET
BURGONETS
BURGOO
BURGOOS
BURGRAVE
BURGRAVES
BURGS
BURGUNDIES
BURGUNDY
BURHEL
BURHELS
BURIAL
BURIALS
BURIED
BURIES
BURIN
BURINIST
BURINISTS
BURINS
BURITI
BURITIS
BURK
BURKA
BURKAS
BURKE
BURKED

BURKES
BURKHA
BURKHAS
BURKING
BURKS
BURL
BURLAP
BURLAPS
BURLED
BURLER
BURLERS
BURLESQUE
BURLESQUED
BURLESQUES
BURLESQUING
BURLETTA
BURLETTAS
BURLEY
BURLEYS
BURLIER
BURLIEST
BURLINESS
BURLINESSES
BURLING
BURLS
BURLY
BURN
BURNED
BURNER
BURNERS
BURNET
BURNETS
BURNING
BURNINGS
BURNISH
BURNISHED
BURNISHER
BURNISHERS
BURNISHES
BURNISHING
BURNISHINGS
BURNOUS
BURNOUSE
BURNOUSES
BURNS
BURNSIDE
BURNSIDES
BURNT
BUROO
BUROOS
BURP
BURPED
BURPING
BURPS
BURQA
BURQAS
BURR
BURRED
BURREL
BURRELL
BURRELLS
BURRELS
BURRHEL
BURRHELS
BURRIER
BURRIEST
BURRING
BURRO
BURROS
BURROW

BURROWED	BUSHINESS	BUSTLES	BUTTES	BYCOKETS
BURROWING	BUSHINESSES	BUSTLING	BUTTIES	BYE
BURROWS	BUSHING	BUSTS	BUTTING	BYES
BURRS	BUSHMAN	BUSTY	BUTTLE	BYGOING
BURRSTONE	BUSHMEN	BUSY	BUTTLED	BYGOINGS
BURRSTONES	BUSHVELD	BUSYBODIES	BUTTLES	BYGONE
BURRY	BUSHVELDS	BUSYBODY	BUTTLING	BYGONES
BURS	BUSHWALK	BUSYING	BUTTOCK	BYKE
BURSA	BUSHWALKED	BUSYNESS	BUTTOCKED	BYKED
BURSAE	BUSHWALKING	BUSYNESSES	BUTTOCKING	BYKES
BURSAL	BUSHWALKINGS	BUT	BUTTOCKS	BYKING
BURSAR	BUSHWALKS	BUTADIENE	BUTTON	BYLANDER
BURSARIAL	BUSHWHACK	BUTADIENES	BUTTONED	BYLANDERS
BURSARIES	BUSHWHACKED	BUTANE	BUTTONING	BYLAW
BURSARS	BUSHWHACKING	BUTANES	BUTTONS	BYLAWS
BURSARY	BUSHWHACKINGS	BUTANOL	BUTTONY	BYLINE
BURSE	BUSHWHACKS	BUTANOLS	BUTTRESS	BYLINES
BURSES	BUSHY	BUTCH	BUTTRESSED	BYLIVE
BURSIFORM	BUSIED	BUTCHER	BUTTRESSES	BYNEMPT
BURSITIS	BUSIER	BUTCHERED	BUTTRESSING	BYPASS
BURSITISES	BUSIES	BUTCHERIES	BUTTS	BYPASSED
BURST	BUSIEST	BUTCHERING	BUTTY	BYPASSES
BURSTED	BUSILY	BUTCHERINGS	BUTTYMAN	BYPASSING
BURSTEN	BUSINESS	BUTCHERLY	BUTTYMEN	BYPATH
BURSTER	BUSINESSES	BUTCHERS	BUTYL	BYPATHS
BURSTERS	BUSING	BUTCHERY	BUTYLENE	BYPLACE
BURSTING	BUSINGS	BUTCHES	BUTYLENES	BYPLACES
BURSTS	BUSK	BUTCHEST	BUTYLS	BYRE
BURTHEN	BUSKED	BUTCHING	BUTYRATE	BYREMAN
BURTHENED	BUSKER	BUTCHINGS	BUTYRATES	BYREMEN
BURTHENING	BUSKERS	BUTE	BUTYRIC	BYRES
BURTHENS	BUSKET	BUTENE	BUVETTE	BYREWOMAN
BURTON	BUSKETS	BUTENES	BUVETTES	BYREWOMEN
BURTONS	BUSKIN	BUTES	BUXOM	BYRLADY
BURWEED	BUSKINED	BUTLER	BUXOMER	BYRLAKIN
BURWEEDS	BUSKING	BUTLERAGE	BUXOMEST	BYRLAW
BURY	BUSKINGS	BUTLERAGES	BUXOMNESS	BYRLAWS
BURYING	BUSKINS	BUTLERED	BUXOMNESSES	BYRNIE
BUS	BUSKS	BUTLERIES	BUY	BYRNIES
BUSBIES	BUSKY	BUTLERING	BUYABLE	BYROAD
BUSBOY	BUSMAN	BUTLERS	BUYABLES	BYROADS
BUSBOYS	BUSMEN	BUTLERY	BUYER	BYROOM
BUSBY	BUSS	BUTMENT	BUYERS	BYROOMS
BUSED	BUSSED	BUTMENTS	BUYING	BYS
BUSES	BUSSES	BUTS	BUYS	BYSSAL
BUSGIRL	BUSSING	BUTT	BUZZ	BYSSINE
BUSGIRLS	BUSSINGS	BUTTE	BUZZARD	BYSSOID
BUSH	BUSSU	BUTTED	BUZZARDS	BYSSUS
BUSHCRAFT	BUSSUS	BUTTER	BUZZED	BYSSUSES
BUSHCRAFTS	BUST	BUTTERBUR	BUZZER	BYSTANDER
BUSHED	BUSTARD	BUTTERBURS	BUZZERS	BYSTANDERS
BUSHEL	BUSTARDS	BUTTERCUP	BUZZES	BYTE
BUSHELLED	BUSTED	BUTTERCUPS	BUZZIER	BYTES
BUSHELLER	BUSTEE	BUTTERED	BUZZIEST	BYTOWNITE
BUSHELLERS	BUSTEES	BUTTERFLIES	BUZZING	BYTOWNITES
BUSHELLING	BUSTER	BUTTERFLY	BUZZINGLY	BYWAY
BUSHELLINGS	BUSTERS	BUTTERIER	BUZZINGS	BYWAYS
BUSHELS	BUSTIER	BUTTERIES	BUZZY	BYWONER
BUSHES	BUSTIERS	BUTTERIEST	BWANA	BYWONERS
BUSHFIRE	BUSTIEST	BUTTERINE	BWANAS	BYWORD
BUSHFIRES	BUSTING	BUTTERINES	BWAZI	BYWORDS
BUSHIDO	BUSTINGS	BUTTERING	BWAZIS	BYWORK
BUSHIDOS	BUSTLE	BUTTERNUT	BY	BYWORKS
BUSHIER	BUSTLED	BUTTERNUTS	BYCATCH	BYZANT
BUSHIES	BUSTLER	BUTTERS	BYCATCHES	BYZANTS
BUSHIEST	BUSTLERS	BUTTERY	BYCOKET	

C

CAATINGA
CAATINGAS
CAB
CABA
CABAL
CABALA
CABALAS
CABALETTA
CABALETTAS
CABALETTE
CABALISM
CABALISMS
CABALIST
CABALISTS
CABALLED
CABALLER
CABALLERO
CABALLEROS
CABALLERS
CABALLINE
CABALLING
CABALS
CABANA
CABANAS
CABARET
CABARETS
CABAS
CABBAGE
CABBAGED
CABBAGES
CABBAGING
CABBAGY
CABBALA
CABBALAS
CABBALISM
CABBALISMS
CABBALIST
CABBALISTS
CABBIE
CABBIES
CABBY
CABER
CABERS
CABIN
CABINED
CABINET
CABINETS
CABINING
CABINS
CABLE
CABLED
CABLEGRAM
CABLEGRAMS
CABLES
CABLEWAY
CABLEWAYS
CABLING
CABLINGS
CABMAN
CABMEN
CABOB
CABOBS
CABOC

CABOCEER
CABOCEERS
CABOCHED
CABOCHON
CABOCHONS
CABOCS
CABOODLE
CABOODLES
CABOOSE
CABOOSES
CABOSHED
CABOTAGE
CABOTAGES
CABRÉ
CABRIE
CABRIES
CABRIOLE
CABRIOLES
CABRIOLET
CABRIOLETS
CABRIT
CABRITS
CABS
CACAFOGO
CACAFOGOS
CACAFUEGO
CACAFUEGOS
CACAO
CACAOS
CACHAEMIA
CACHAEMIAS
CACHAEMIC
CACHALOT
CACHALOTS
CACHE
CACHECTIC
CACHED
CACHES
CACHET
CACHETS
CACHEXIA
CACHEXIAS
CACHEXIES
CACHEXY
CACHING
CACHOLONG
CACHOLONGS
CACHOLOT
CACHOLOTS
CACHOU
CACHOUS
CACHUCHA
CACHUCHAS
CACIQUE
CACIQUES
CACIQUISM
CACIQUISMS
CACKLE
CACKLED
CACKLER
CACKLERS
CACKLES
CACKLING

CACODEMON
CACODEMONS
CACODOXIES
CACODOXY
CACODYL
CACODYLIC
CACODYLS
CACOEPIES
CACOEPY
CACOETHES
CACOLET
CACOLETS
CACOLOGIES
CACOLOGY
CACOMIXL
CACOMIXLS
CACOON
CACOONS
CACOPHONIES
CACOPHONY
CACOTOPIA
CACOTOPIAS
CACTI
CACTIFORM
CACTUS
CACTUSES
CACUMEN
CACUMENS
CACUMINAL
CAD
CADASTRAL
CADASTRE
CADASTRES
CADAVER
CADAVERIC
CADAVERS
CADDICE
CADDICES
CADDIE
CADDIED
CADDIES
CADDIS
CADDISES
CADDISH
CADDY
CADDYING
CADDYSS
CADDYSSES
CADE
CADEAU
CADEAUX
CADENCE
CADENCED
CADENCES
CADENCIES
CADENCY
CADENT
CADENTIAL
CADENZA
CADENZAS
CADES
CADET
CADETS

CADETSHIP
CADETSHIPS
CADGE
CADGED
CADGER
CADGERS
CADGES
CADGIER
CADGIEST
CADGING
CADGY
CADI
CADIE
CADIES
CADIS
CADMIUM
CADMIUMS
CADRANS
CADRANSES
CADRE
CADRES
CADS
CADUAC
CADUACS
CADUCEAN
CADUCEI
CADUCEUS
CADUCITIES
CADUCITY
CADUCOUS
CAECA
CAECAL
CAECILIAN
CAECILIANS
CAECUM
CAERULE
CAERULEAN
CAESAR
CAESARS
CAESE
CAESIOUS
CAESIUM
CAESIUMS
CAESTUS
CAESTUSES
CAESURA
CAESURAL
CAESURAS
CAFARD
CAFARDS
CAFÉ
CAFÉS
CAFETERIA
CAFETERIAS
CAFF
CAFFEINE
CAFFEINES
CAFFEISM
CAFFEISMS
CAFFILA
CAFFILAS
CAFFS
CAFILA

CAFILAS
CAFTAN
CAFTANS
CAGE
CAGEBIRD
CAGEBIRDS
CAGED
CAGELING
CAGELINGS
CAGES
CAGEWORK
CAGEWORKS
CAGEY
CAGEYNESS
CAGEYNESSES
CAGIER
CAGIEST
CAGILY
CAGINESS
CAGINESSES
CAGING
CAGOT
CAGOTS
CAGOUL
CAGOULE
CAGOULES
CAGOULS
CAGY
CAGYNESS
CAGYNESSES
CAHIER
CAHIERS
CAHOOT
CAHOOTS
CAILLACH
CAILLACHS
CAILLEACH
CAILLEACHS
CAILLIACH
CAILLIACHS
CAIMAC
CAIMACAM
CAIMACAMS
CAIMACS
CAIMAN
CAIMANS
CAIN
CAINS
CAÏQUE
CAIQUE
CAÏQUES
CAIQUES
CAIRD
CAIRDS
CAIRN
CAIRNED
CAIRNGORM
CAIRNGORMS
CAIRNS
CAISSON
CAISSONS
CAITIFF
CAITIFFS

CAITIVE
CAITIVES
CAJEPUT
CAJEPUTS
CAJOLE
CAJOLED
CAJOLER
CAJOLERIES
CAJOLERS
CAJOLERY
CAJOLES
CAJOLING
CAJUN
CAJUPUT
CAJUPUTS
CAKE
CAKED
CAKES
CAKEWALK
CAKEWALKED
CAKEWALKING
CAKEWALKS
CAKIER
CAKIEST
CAKING
CAKINGS
CAKY
CALABASH
CALADASHES
CALABOOSE
CALABOOSES
CALABRESE
CALABRESES
CALAMANCO
CALAMANCOS
CALAMARIES
CALAMARY
CALAMI
CALAMINE
CALAMINES
CALAMINT
CALAMINTS
CALAMITE
CALAMITES
CALAMITIES
CALAMITY
CALAMUS
CALANDO
CALANDRIA
CALANDRIAS
CALANTHE
CALANTHES
CALASH
CALASHES
CALAVANCE
CALAVANCES
CALCANEAL
CALCANEAN
CALCANEUM
CALCANEUMS
CALCAR
CALCARATE
CALCARINE
CALCARS
CALCEATE
CALCEATED
CALCEATES
CALCEATING
CALCED
CALCEDONIES

CALCEDONY
CALCES
CALCIC
CALCICOLE
CALCIFIC
CALCIFIED
CALCIFIES
CALCIFUGE
CALCIFY
CALCIFYING
CALCINE
CALCINED
CALCINES
CALCINING
CALCITE
CALCITES
CALCIUM
CALCIUMS
CALCSPAR
CALCSPARS
CALCULAR
CALCULARY
CALCULATE
CALCULATED
CALCULATES
CALCULATING
CALCULI
CALCULOUL
CALCULOUS
CALCULUS
CALCULUSES
CALDARIA
CALDARIUM
CALDARIUMS
CALDERA
CALDERAS
CALDRON
CALDRONS
CALEFIED
CALEFIES
CALEFY
CALEFYING
CALEMBOUR
CALEMBOURS
CALENDAR
CALENDARED
CALENDARING
CALENDARS
CALENDER
CALENDERED
CALENDERING
CALENDERINGS
CALENDERS
CALENDRER
CALENDRERS
CALENDRIES
CALENDRY
CALENDS
CALENDULA
CALENDULAS
CALENTURE
CALENTURES
CALF
CALFDOZER
CALFDOZERS
CALFLESS
CALFS
CALFSKIN
CALFSKINS
CALIATOUR

CALIATOURS
CALIBER
CALIBERED
CALIBERS
CALIBRATE
CALIBRATED
CALIBRATES
CALIBRATING
CALIBRE
CALIBRED
CALIBRES
CALICES
CALICHE
CALICHES
CALICO
CALICOES
CALICOS
CALID
CALIDITIES
CALIDITY
CALIF
CALIFS
CALIGO
CALIGOES
CALIGOS
CALIOLOGIES
CALIOLOGY
CALIPASH
CALIPASHES
CALIPEE
CALIPEES
CALIPER
CALIPERS
CALIPH
CALIPHAL
CALIPHATE
CALIPHATES
CALIPHS
CALISAYA
CALISAYAS
CALIVER
CALIVERS
CALIX
CALIXES
CALK
CALKED
CALKER
CALKERS
CALKIN
CALKING
CALKINS
CALKS
CALL
CALLA
CALLANT
CALLANTS
CALLAS
CALLED
CALLER
CALLERS
CALLET
CALLETS
CALLID
CALLIDITIES
CALLIDITY
CALLIGRAM
CALLIGRAMS
CALLING
CALLINGS
CALLIOPE

CALLIOPES
CALLIPER
CALLIPERED
CALLIPERING
CALLIPERS
CALLOSITIES
CALLOSITY
CALLOUS
CALLOUSLY
CALLOW
CALLOWER
CALLOWEST
CALLOWS
CALLS
CALLUS
CALLUSES
CALM
CALMANT
CALMANTS
CALMATIVE
CALMATIVES
CALMED
CALMER
CALMEST
CALMIER
CALMIEST
CALMING
CALMLY
CALMNESS
CALMNESSES
CALMS
CALMSTANE
CALMSTANES
CALMSTONE
CALMSTONES
CALMY
CALOMEL
CALOMELS
CALORIC
CALORICS
CALORIE
CALORIES
CALORIFIC
CALORIST
CALORISTS
CALOTTE
CALOTTES
CALOTYPE
CALOTYPES
CALOYER
CALOYERS
CALP
CALPA
CALPAC
CALPACK
CALPACKS
CALPACS
CALPAS
CALPS
CALQUE
CALQUED
CALQUES
CALQUING
CALTHA
CALTHAS
CALTHROP
CALTHROPS
CALTRAP
CALTRAPS
CALTROP

CALTROPS
CALUMBA
CALUMBAS
CALUMET
CALUMETS
CALUMNIES
CALUMNY
CALVE
CALVED
CALVER
CALVERED
CALVERING
CALVERS
CALVES
CALVING
CALVITIES
CALX
CALXES
CALYCES
CALYCINAL
CALYCINE
CALYCLE
CALYCLED
CALYCLES
CALYCOID
CALYCULE
CALYCULES
CALYPSO
CALYPSOS
CALYPTRA
CALYPTRAS
CALYX
CALYXES
CALZONE
CALZONES
CALZONI
CAM
CAMAIEU
CAMAIEUX
CAMAN
CAMANACHD
CAMANACHDS
CAMANS
CAMARILLA
CAMARILLAS
CAMARON
CAMARONS
CAMAS
CAMASES
CAMASH
CAMASHES
CAMASS
CAMASSES
CAMBER
CAMBERED
CAMBERING
CAMBERS
CAMBIAL
CAMBIFORM
CAMBISM
CAMBISMS
CAMBIST
CAMBISTRIES
CAMBISTRY
CAMBISTS
CAMBIUM
CAMBIUMS
CAMBOGE
CAMBOGES
CAMBREL

CAMBRELS
CAMBRIC
CAMBRICS
CAMCORDER
CAMCORDERS
CAME
CAMEL
CAMELBACK
CAMELBACKS
CAMELEER
CAMELEERS
CAMELEON
CAMELEONS
CAMELID
CAMELIDS
CAMELINE
CAMELINES
CAMELISH
CAMELLIA
CAMELLIAS
CAMELOID
CAMELOIDS
CAMELOT
CAMELOTS
CAMELRIES
CAMELRY
CAMELS
CAMEO
CAMEOS
CAMERA
CAMERAL
CAMERAMAN
CAMERAMEN
CAMERAS
CAMERATED
CAMES
CAMESE
CAMESES
CAMION
CAMIONS
CAMIS
CAMISADE
CAMISADES
CAMISADO
CAMISADOS
CAMISARD
CAMISARDS
CAMISE
CAMISES
CAMISOLE
CAMISOLES
CAMLET
CAMLETS
CAMMED
CAMMING
CAMOMILE
CAMOMILES
CAMOUFLET
CAMOUFLETS
CAMP
CAMPAGNA
CAMPAGNAS
CAMPAIGN
CAMPAIGNED
CAMPAIGNING
CAMPAIGNS
CAMPANA
CAMPANAS
CAMPANERO
CAMPANEROS

CAMPANILE
CAMPANILES
CAMPANILI
CAMPANIST
CAMPANISTS
CAMPEADOR
CAMPEADORS
CAMPED
CAMPER
CAMPERS
CAMPESINO
CAMPESINOS
CAMPEST
CAMPHANE
CAMPHANES
CAMPHENE
CAMPHENES
CAMPHINE
CAMPHINES
CAMPHIRE
CAMPHIRES
CAMPHOR
CAMPHORIC
CAMPHORS
CAMPIER
CAMPIEST
CAMPING
CAMPION
CAMPIONS
CAMPLE
CAMPLED
CAMPLES
CAMPLING
CAMPS
CAMPSITE
CAMPSITES
CAMPUS
CAMPUSES
CAMPY
CAMS
CAMSHAFT
CAMSHAFTS
CAMSHEUGH
CAMSHO
CAMSHOCH
CAMSTAIRY
CAMSTANE
CAMSTANES
CAMSTEARY
CAMSTONE
CAMSTONES
CAMUS
CAMUSES
CAN
CAÑADA
CAÑADAS
CANAIGRE
CANAIGRES
CANAILLE
CANAILLES
CANAKIN
CANAKINS
CANAL
CANALISE
CANALISED
CANALISES
CANALISING
CANALIZE
CANALIZED
CANALIZES

CANALIZING
CANALS
CANAPÉ
CANAPÉS
CANARD
CANARDS
CANARIED
CANARIES
CANARY
CANARYING
CANASTA
CANASTAS
CANASTER
CANASTERS
CANCAN
CANCANS
CANCEL
CANCELEER
CANCELEERED
CANCELEERING
CANCELEERS
CANCELIER
CANCELIERED
CANCELIERING
CANCELIERS
CANCELLED
CANCELLI
CANCELLING
CANCELS
CANCER
CANCERATE
CANCERATED
CANCERATES
CANCERATING
CANCEROUS
CANCERS
CANCRINE
CANCROID
CANCROIDS
CANDELA
CANDELAS
CANDENT
CANDID
CANDIDA
CANDIDACIES
CANDIDACY
CANDIDAS
CANDIDATE
CANDIDATES
CANDIDER
CANDIDEST
CANDIDLY
CANDIE
CANDIED
CANDIES
CANDLE
CANDLED
CANDLES
CANDLING
CANDOCK
CANDOCKS
CANDOR
CANDORS
CANDOUR
CANDOURS
CANDY
CANDYING
CANDYTUFT
CANDYTUFTS
CANE

CANED
CANEFRUIT
CANEFRUITS
CANEH
CANEHS
CANELLA
CANELLAS
CANEPHOR
CANEPHORA
CANEPHORAS
CANEPHORE
CANEPHORES
CANEPHORS
CANES
CANESCENT
CANFUL
CANFULS
CANG
CANGLE
CANGLED
CANGLES
CANGLING
CANGS
CANGUE
CANGUES
CANICULAR
CANID
CANIDS
CANIER
CANIEST
CANIKIN
CANIKINS
CANINE
CANINES
CANING
CANINGS
CANINITIES
CANINITY
CANISTER
CANISTERED
CANISTERING
CANISTERS
CANITIES
CANKER
CANKERED
CANKERING
CANKEROUS
CANKERS
CANKERY
CANN
CANNA
CANNABIC
CANNABIN
CANNABINS
CANNABIS
CANNABISES
CANNACH
CANNACHS
CANNAE
CANNAS
CANNED
CANNEL
CANNELS
CANNELURE
CANNELURES
CANNER
CANNERIES
CANNERS
CANNERY
CANNIBAL

CANNIBALS
CANNIER
CANNIEST
CANNIKIN
CANNIKINS
CANNILY
CANNINESS
CANNINESSES
CANNING
CANNON
CANNONADE
CANNONADED
CANNONADES
CANNONADING
CANNONED
CANNONEER
CANNONEERS
CANNONIER
CANNONIERS
CANNONING
CANNONRIES
CANNONRY
CANNONS
CANNOT
CANNS
CANNULA
CANNULAE
CANNULAS
CANNULATE
CANNY
CANOE
CANOED
CANOEING
CANOEINGS
CANOEIST
CANOEISTS
CANOES
CANON
CAÑON
CANONESS
CANONESSES
CANONIC
CANONICAL
CANONICALS
CANONISE
CANONISED
CANONISES
CANONISING
CANONIST
CANONISTS
CANONIZE
CANONIZED
CANONIZES
CANONIZING
CANONRIES
CANONRY
CANONS
CAÑONS
CANOODLE
CANOODLED
CANOODLES
CANOODLING
CANOPIED
CANOPIES
CANOPY
CANOPYING
CANOROUS
CANS
CANST
CANSTICK

CANSTICKS
CANT
CANTABANK
CANTABANKS
CANTABILE
CANTABILES
CANTALOUP
CANTALOUPS
CANTAR
CANTARS
CANTATA
CANTATAS
CANTATE
CANTATES
CANTDOG
CANTDOGS
CANTED
CANTEEN
CANTEENS
CANTER
CANTERED
CANTERING
CANTERS
CANTEST
CANTHARI
CANTHARID
CANTHARIDES
CANTHARIDS
CANTHARIS
CANTHARUS
CANTHI
CANTHOOK
CANTHOOKS
CANTHUS
CANTICLE
CANTICLES
CANTICO
CANTICOED
CANTICOING
CANTICOS
CANTICOY
CANTICOYED
CANTICOYING
CANTICOYS
CANTICUM
CANTICUMS
CANTIER
CANTIEST
CANTILENA
CANTILENAS
CANTINA
CANTINAS
CANTINESS
CANTINESSES
CANTING
CANTINGS
CANTION
CANTIONS
CANTLE
CANTLED
CANTLES
CANTLET
CANTLETS
CANTLING
CANTO
CANTON
CANTONAL
CANTONED
CANTONING
CANTONS

CANTOR
CANTORIAL
CANTORIS
CANTORS
CANTOS
CANTRED
CANTREDS
CANTREF
CANTREFS
CANTRIP
CANTRIPS
CANTS
CANTUS
CANTY
CANVAS
CANVASED
CANVASES
CANVASING
CANVASS
CANVASSED
CANVASSER
CANVASSERS
CANVASSES
CANVASSING
CANY
CANYON
CANYONS
CANZONA
CANZONAS
CANZONE
CANZONET
CANZONETS
CANZONI
CAP
CAPA
CAPABLE
CAPABLER
CAPABLEST
CAPACIOUS
CAPACITIES
CAPACITOR
CAPACITORS
CAPACITY
CAPARISON
CAPARISONED
CAPARISONING
CAPARISONS
CAPAS
CAPE
CAPED
CAPELET
CAPELETS
CAPELIN
CAPELINE
CAPELINES
CAPELINS
CAPELLET
CAPELLETS
CAPELLINE
CAPELLINES
CAPER
CAPERED
CAPERER
CAPERERS
CAPERING
CAPERS
CAPES
CAPIAS
CAPIASES
CAPILLARIES

CAPILLARY
CAPING
CAPITA
CAPITAL
CAPITALLY
CAPITALS
CAPITAN
CAPITANI
CAPITANO
CAPITANOS
CAPITANS
CAPITATE
CAPITAYN
CAPITAYNS
CAPITELLA
CAPITULA
CAPITULAR
CAPITULARS
CAPITULUM
CAPLE
CAPLES
CAPLIN
CAPLINS
CAPO
CAPOCCHIA
CAPOCCHIAS
CAPON
CAPONIER
CAPONIERE
CAPONIERES
CAPONIERS
CAPONISE
CAPONISED
CAPONISES
CAPONISING
CAPONIZE
CAPONIZED
CAPONIZES
CAPONIZING
CAPONS
CAPORAL
CAPORALS
CAPOS
CAPOT
CAPOTASTO
CAPOTASTOS
CAPOTE
CAPOTES
CAPOTS
CAPOTTED
CAPOTTING
CAPPED
CAPPER
CAPPERS
CAPPING
CAPPINGS
CAPRATE
CAPRATES
CAPRIC
CAPRICCI
CAPRICCIO
CAPRICCIOS
CAPRICE
CAPRICES
CAPRID
CAPRIDS
CAPRIFIED
CAPRIFIES
CAPRIFIG
CAPRIFIGS

CAPRIFOIL
CAPRIFOILS
CAPRIFOLE
CAPRIFOLES
CAPRIFORM
CAPRIFY
CAPRIFYING
CAPRINE
CAPRIOLE
CAPRIOLED
CAPRIOLES
CAPRIOLING
CAPROATE
CAPROATES
CAPROIC
CAPRYLATE
CAPRYLATES
CAPRYLIC
CAPS
CAPSAICIN
CAPSAICINS
CAPSICUM
CAPSICUMS
CAPSID
CAPSIDS
CAPSIZAL
CAPSIZALS
CAPSIZE
CAPSIZED
CAPSIZES
CAPSIZING
CAPSTAN
CAPSTANS
CAPSTONES
CAPSULAR
CAPSULARY
CAPSULATE
CAPSULE
CAPSULES
CAPSULISE
CAPSULISED
CAPSULISES
CAPSULISING
CAPSULIZE
CAPSULIZED
CAPSULIZES
CAPSULIZING
CAPTAIN
CAPTAINCIES
CAPTAINCY
CAPTAINED
CAPTAINING
CAPTAINRIES
CAPTAINRY
CAPTAINS
CAPTAN
CAPTANS
CAPTION
CAPTIONED
CAPTIONING
CAPTIONS
CAPTIOUS
CAPTIVATE
CAPTIVATED
CAPTIVATES
CAPTIVATING
CAPTIVE
CAPTIVED
CAPTIVES

CAPTIVING
CAPTIVITIES
CAPTIVITY
CAPTOR
CAPTORS
CAPTURE
CAPTURED
CAPTURES
CAPTURING
CAPUCCIO
CAPUCCIOS
CAPUCHE
CAPUCHES
CAPUCHIN
CAPUCHINS
CAPUL
CAPULS
CAPUT
CAPYBARA
CAPYBARAS
CAR
CARABIN
CARABINE
CARABINES
CARABINS
CARACAL
CARACALS
CARACARA
CARACARAS
CARACK
CARACKS
CARACOL
CARACOLE
CARACOLED
CARACOLES
CARACOLING
CARACOLLED
CARACOLLING
CARACOLS
CARACT
CARACTS
CARACUL
CARACULS
CARAFE
CARAFES
CARAMBA
CARAMBOLA
CARAMBOLAS
CARAMBOLE
CARAMBOLED
CARAMBOLES
CARAMBOLING
CARAMEL
CARAMELLED
CARAMELLING
CARAMELS
CARANGID
CARANGIDS
CARANGOID
CARANGOIDS
CARANNA
CARANNAS
CARANX
CARAP
CARAPACE
CARAPACES
CARAPS
CARAT
CARATS
CARAUNA

CARAUNAS
CARAVAN
CARAVANCE
CARAVANCES
CARAVANED
CARAVANER
CARAVANERS
CARAVANING
CARAVANNED
CARAVANNING
CARAVANS
CARAVEL
CARAVELS
CARAWAY
CARAWAYS
CARB
CARBAMATE
CARBAMATES
CARBAMIDE
CARBAMIDES
CARBARYL
CARBARYLS
CARBIDE
CARBIDES
CARBINE
CARBINEER
CARBINEERS
CARBINES
CARBINIER
CARBINIERS
CARBOLIC
CARBOLICS
CARBON
CARBONADE
CARBONADES
CARBONADO
CARBONADOED
CARBONADOES
CARBONADOING
CARBONADOS
CARBONATE
CARBONATED
CARBONATES
CARBONATING
CARBONIC
CARBONISE
CARBONISED
CARBONISES
CARBONISING
CARBONIZE
CARBONIZED
CARBONIZES
CARBONIZING
CARBONS
CARBONYL
CARBONYLS
CARBOXYL
CARBOXYLS
CARBOY
CARBOYS
CARBS
CARBUNCLE
CARBUNCLES
CARBURATE
CARBURATED
CARBURATES
CARBURATING
CARBURET
CARBURETS
CARBURETTED

CARBURETTING
CARBURISE
CARBURISED
CARBURISES
CARBURISING
CARBURIZE
CARBURIZED
CARBURIZES
CARBURIZING
CARCAJOU
CARCAJOUS
CARCAKE
CARCAKES
CARCANET
CARCANETS
CARCASE
CARCASED
CARCASES
CARCASING
CARCASS
CARCASSED
CARCASSES
CARCASSING
CARCINOMA
CARCINOMAS
CARCINOMATA
CARD
CARDAMINE
CARDAMINES
CARDAMOM
CARDAMOMS
CARDAMON
CARDAMONS
CARDAMUM
CARDAMUMS
CARDBOARD
CARDBOARDS
CARDECU
CARDECUE
CARDECUES
CARDECUS
CARDED
CARDER
CARDERS
CARDI
CARDIAC
CARDIACAL
CARDIACS
CARDIALGIES
CARDIALGY
CARDIES
CARDIGAN
CARDIGANS
CARDINAL
CARDINALS
CARDING
CARDIOID
CARDIOIDS
CARDIS
CARDITIS
CARDITISES
CARDOON
CARDOONS
CARDPUNCH
CARDPUNCHES
CARDS
CARDUUS
CARDUUSES
CARDY
CARE

CARED
CAREEN
CAREENAGE
CAREENAGES
CAREENED
CAREENING
CAREENS
CAREER
CAREERED
CAREERING
CAREERISM
CAREERISMS
CAREERIST
CAREERISTS
CAREERS
CAREFREE
CAREFUL
CAREFULLY
CARELESS
CARÈME
CARÈMES
CARER
CARERS
CARES
CARESS
CARESSED
CARESSES
CARESSING
CARESSINGS
CARET
CARETAKE
CARETAKEN
CARETAKER
CARETAKERS
CARETAKES
CARETAKING
CARETOOK
CARETS
CAREWORN
CAREX
CARFAX
CARFAXES
CARFOX
CARFOXES
CARFUFFLE
CARFUFFLED
CARFUFFLES
CARFUFFLING
CARGEESE
CARGO
CARGOED
CARGOES
CARGOING
CARGOOSE
CARIACOU
CARIACOUS
CARIAMA
CARIAMAS
CARIBE
CARIBES
CARIBOU
CARIBOUS
CARICES
CARIERE
CARIERES
CARIES
CARILLON
CARILLONED
CARILLONING
CARILLONS

CARINA
CARINAS
CARINATE
CARING
CARIOCA
CARIOCAS
CARIOLE
CARIOLES
CARIOUS
CARITAS
CARITATES
CARJACOU
CARJACOUS
CARK
CARKED
CARKING
CARKS
CARL
CARLINE
CARLINES
CARLISH
CARLOAD
CARLOADS
CARLOCK
CARLOCKS
CARLOT
CARLOTS
CARLS
CARMAN
CARMELITE
CARMELITES
CARMEN
CARMINE
CARMINES
CARNAGE
CARNAGES
CARNAHUBA
CARNAHUBAS
CARNAL
CARNALISE
CARNALISED
CARNALISES
CARNALISING
CARNALISM
CARNALISMS
CARNALIST
CARNALISTS
CARNALITIES
CARNALITY
CARNALIZE
CARNALIZED
CARNALIZES
CARNALIZING
CARNALLED
CARNALLING
CARNALLY
CARNALS
CARNATION
CARNATIONS
CARNAUBA
CARNAUBAS
CARNELIAN
CARNELIANS
CARNEOUS
CARNET
CARNETS
CARNEY
CARNEYED
CARNEYING
CARNEYS

CARNIED
CARNIER
CARNIES
CARNIEST
CARNIFEX
CARNIFEXES
CARNIVAL
CARNIVALS
CARNIVORE
CARNIVORES
CARNOSE
CARNOSITIES
CARNOSITY
CARNOTITE
CARNOTITES
CARNY
CARNYING
CAROB
CAROBS
CAROCHE
CAROCHES
CAROL
CAROLLED
CAROLLER
CAROLLERS
CAROLLING
CAROLS
CAROM
CAROMED
CAROMEL
CAROMELLED
CAROMELLING
CAROMELS
CAROMING
CAROMS
CAROTENE
CAROTENES
CAROTID
CAROTIN
CAROTINS
CAROUSAL
CAROUSALS
CAROUSE
CAROUSED
CAROUSEL
CAROUSELS
CAROUSER
CAROUSERS
CAROUSES
CAROUSING
CARP
CARPAL
CARPALS
CARPARK
CARPARKS
CARPED
CARPEL
CARPELS·
CARPENTER
CARPENTERED
CARPENTERING
CARPENTERS
CARPENTRIES
CARPENTRY
CARPER
CARPERS
CARPET
CARPETED
CARPETING
CARPETINGS

CARPETS
CARPING
CARPINGLY
CARPINGS
CARPORT
CARPORTS
CARPS
CARPUS
CARPUSES
CARR
CARRACK
CARRACKS
CARRACT
CARRACTS
CARRAGEEN
CARRAGEENS
CARRAT
CARRATS
CARRAWAY
CARRAWAYS
CARRECT
CARRECTS
CARREL
CARRELL
CARRELLS
CARRELS
CARRIAGE
CARRIAGES
CARRIED
CARRIER
CARRIERS
CARRIES
CARRIOLE
CARRIOLES
CARRION
CARRIONS
CARRITCH
CARRITCHES
CARRONADE
CARRONADES
CARROT
CARROTS
CARROTY
CARROUSEL
CARROUSELS
CARRS
CARRY
CARRYCOT
CARRYCOTS
CARRYING
CARRYTALE
CARRYTALES
CARS
CARSE
CARSES
CART
CARTA
CARTAGE
CARTAGES
CARTAS
CARTE
CARTED
CARTEL
CARTELISE
CARTELISED
CARTELISES
CARTELISING
CARTELIZE
CARTELIZED
CARTELIZES

CARTELIZING
CARTELS
CARTER
CARTERS
CARTES
CARTILAGE
CARTILAGES
CARTING
CARTLOAD
CARTLOADS
CARTOGRAM
CARTOGRAMS
CARTOLOGIES
CARTOLOGY
CARTON
CARTONAGE
CARTONAGES
CARTONED
CARTONING
CARTONS
CARTOON
CARTOONED
CARTOONING
CARTOONS
CARTOUCH
CARTOUCHE
CARTOUCHES
CARTRIDGE
CARTRIDGES
CARTROAD
CARTROADS
CARTS
CARTULARIES
CARTULARY
CARTWAY
CARTWAYS
CARTWHEEL
CARTWHEELED
CARTWHEELING
CARTWHEELS
CARUCAGE
CARUCAGES
CARUCATE
CARUCATES
CARUNCLE
CARUNCLES
CARVACROL
CARVACROLS
CARVE
CARVED
CARVEL
CARVELS
CARVEN
CARVER
CARVERS
CARVES
CARVIES
CARVING
CARVINGS
CARVY
CARYATIC
CARYATID
CARYATIDES
CARYATIDS
CARYOPSES
CARYOPSIDES
CARYOPSIS
CASA
CASAS
CASBAH

CASBAHS
CASCABEL
CASCABELS
CASCADE
CASCADED
CASCADES
CASCADING
CASCARA
CASCARAS
CASCHROM
CASCHROMS
CASCO
CASCOS
CASE
CASEATION
CASEATIONS
CASEBOOK
CASEBOOKS
CASED
CASEIN
CASEINS
CASEMAKER
CASEMAKERS
CASEMAN
CASEMATE
CASEMATED
CASEMATES
CASEMEN
CASEMENT
CASEMENTS
CASEOUS
CASERN
CASERNE
CASERNES
CASERNS
CASES
CASH
CASHAW
CASHAWS
CASHED
CASHES
CASHEW
CASHEWS
CASHIER
CASHIERED
CASHIERER
CASHIERERS
CASHIERING
CASHIERINGS
CASHIERS
CASHING
CASHLESS
CASHMERE
CASHMERES
CASING
CASINGS
CASINO
CASINOS
CASK
CASKED
CASKET
CASKETS
CASKING
CASKS
CASQUE
CASQUES
CASSAREEP
CASSAREEPS
CASSARIPE
CASSARIPES

CASSATA
CASSATAS
CASSATION
CASSATIONS
CASSAVA
CASSAVAS
CASSEROLE
CASSEROLED
CASSEROLES
CASSEROLING
CASSETTE
CASSETTES
CASSIA
CASSIAS
CASSIMERE
CASSIMERES
CASSINO
CASSINOS
CASSIS
CASSISES
CASSOCK
CASSOCKED
CASSOCKS
CASSONADE
CASSONADES
CASSONE
CASSONES
CASSOULET
CASSOULETS
CASSOWARIES
CASSOWARY
CAST
CASTANETS
CASTAWAY
CASTAWAYS
CASTE
CASTED
CASTELESS
CASTELLA
CASTELLAN
CASTELLANS
CASTELLUM
CASTELLUMS
CASTER
CASTERS
CASTES
CASTIGATE
CASTIGATED
CASTIGATES
CASTIGATING
CASTING
CASTINGS
CASTLE
CASTLED
CASTLES
CASTLING
CASTOCK
CASTOCKS
CASTOR
CASTOREUM
CASTOREUMS
CASTORIES
CASTORS
CASTORY
CASTRAL
CASTRATE
CASTRATED
CASTRATES
CASTRATI
CASTRATING

CASTRATO
CASTS
CASUAL
CASUALISE
CASUALISED
CASUALISES
CASUALISING
CASUALISM
CASUALISMS
CASUALIZE
CASUALIZED
CASUALIZES
CASUALIZING
CASUALLY
CASUALS
CASUALTIES
CASUALTY
CASUARINA
CASUARINAS
CASUIST
CASUISTIC
CASUISTRIES
CASUISTRY
CASUISTS
CAT
CATACLASM
CATACLASMS
CATACLYSM
CATACLYSMS
CATACOMB
CATACOMBS
CATAFALCO
CATAFALCOES
CATALASE
CATALASES
CATALEPSIES
CATALEPSY
CATALEXES
CATALEXIS
CATALO
CATALOES
CATALOG
CATALOGED
CATALOGER
CATALOGERS
CATALOGING
CATALOGS
CATALOGUE
CATALOGUED
CATALOGUES
CATALOGUING
CATALOS
CATALPA
CATALPAS
CATALYSE
CATALYSED
CATALYSER
CATALYSERS
CATALYSES
CATALYSING
CATALYSIS
CATALYST
CATALYSTS
CATALYTIC
CATALYZE
CATALYZED
CATALYZER
CATALYZERS
CATALYZES
CATALYZING

CATAMARAN	CATE	CATHEDRALS	CAUDAL	CAUSERIE
CATAMARANS	CATECHISE	CATHEDRAS	CAUDATE	CAUSERIES
CATAMENIA	CATECHISED	CATHETER	CAUDATED	CAUSERS
CATAMITE	CATECHISES	CATHETERS	CAUDEX	CAUSES
CATAMITES	CATECHISING	CATHETUS	CAUDEXES	CAUSEWAY
CATAMOUNT	CATECHISINGS	CATHETUSES	CAUDICES	CAUSEWAYED
CATAMOUNTS	CATECHISM	CATHEXES	CAUDICLE	CAUSEWAYING
CATAPAN	CATECHISMS	CATHEXIS	CAUDICLES	CAUSEWAYS
CATAPANS	CATECHIST	CATHISMA	CAUDILLO	CAUSEY
CATAPHYLL	CATECHISTS	CATHISMAS	CAUDILLOS	CAUSEYED
CATAPHYLLS	CATECHIZE	CATHODAL	CAUDLE	CAUSEYING
CATAPLASM	CATECHIZED	CATHODE	CAUDLED	CAUSEYS
CATAPLASMS	CATECHIZES	CATHODES	CAUDLES	CAUSING
CATAPLEXIES	CATECHIZING	CATHODIC	CAUDLING	CAUSTIC
CATAPLEXY	CATECHIZINGS	CATHOLIC	CAUDRON	CAUSTICS
CATAPULT	CATECHOL	CATHOOD	CAUDRONS	CAUTEL
CATAPULTED	CATECHOLS	CATHOODS	CAUF	CAUTELOUS
CATAPULTING	CATECHU	CATHOUSE	CAUGHT	CAUTELS
CATAPULTS	CATECHUS	CATHOUSES	CAUK	CAUTER
CATARACT	CATEGORIES	CATION	CAUKER	CAUTERANT
CATARACTS	CATEGORY	CATIONS	CAUKERS	CAUTERANTS
CATARHINE	CATELOG	CATKIN	CAUKS	CAUTERIES
CATARRH	CATELOGS	CATKINS	CAUL	CAUTERISE
CATARRHAL	CATENA	CATLING	CAULD	CAUTERISED
CATARRHS	CATENAE	CATLINGS	CAULDER	CAUTERISES
CATASTA	CATENARIES	CATMINT	CAULDEST	CAUTERISING
CATASTAS	CATENARY	CATMINTS	CAULDRIFE	CAUTERISM
CATATONIA	CATENAS	CATNAP	CAULDRON	CAUTERISMS
CATATONIAS	CATENATE	CATNAPS	CAULDRONS	CAUTERIZE
CATATONIC	CATENATED	CATNEP	CAULDS	CAUTERIZED
CATATONICS	CATENATES	CATNEPS	CAULES	CAUTERIZES
CATATONIES	CATENATING	CATNIP	CAULICLE	CAUTERIZING
CATATONY	CATER	CATNIPS	CAULICLES	CAUTERS
CATAWBA	CATERAN	CATOPTRIC	CAULIFORM	CAUTERY
CATAWBAS	CATERANS	CATOPTRICS	CAULINARY	CAUTION
CATBIRD	CATERED	CATS	CAULINE	CAUTIONED
CATBIRDS	CATERER	CATSKIN	CAULIS	CAUTIONER
CATBOAT	CATERERS	CATSKINS	CAULK	CAUTIONERS
CATBOATS	CATERESS	CATSUIT	CAULKED	CAUTIONING
CATCALL	CATERESSES	CATSUITS	CAULKER	CAUTIONRIES
CATCALLED	CATERING	CATSUP	CAULKERS	CAUTIONRY
CATCALLING	CATERINGS	CATSUPS	CAULKING	CAUTIONS
CATCALLS	CATERS	CATTABU	CAULKINGS	CAUTIOUS
CATCH	CATERWAUL	CATTABUS	CAULKS	CAUVES
CATCHABLE	CATERWAULED	CATTALO	CAULOME	CAVALCADE
CATCHED	CATERWAULING	CATTALOES	CAULOMES	CAVALCADED
CATCHEN	CATERWAULINGS	CATTALOS	CAULS	CAVALCADES
CATCHER	CATERWAULS	CATTED	CAUM	CAVALCADING
CATCHERS	CATES	CATTERIES	CAUMED	CAVALIER
CATCHES	CATFISH	CATTERY	CAUMING	CAVALIERED
CATCHFLIES	CATFISHES	CATTIER	CAUMS	CAVALIERING
CATCHFLY	CATGUT	CATTIES	CAUMSTANE	CAVALIERO
CATCHIER	CATGUTS	CATTIEST	CAUMSTANES	CAVALIEROS
CATCHIEST	CATHARISE	CATTILY	CAUMSTONE	CAVALIERS
CATCHING	CATHARISED	CATTINESS	CAUMSTONES	CAVALLA
CATCHINGS	CATHARISES	CATTINESSES	CAUP	CAVALLAS
CATCHMENT	CATHARISING	CATTING	CAUPS	CAVALLIES
CATCHMENTS	CATHARIZE	CATTISH	CAUSAL	CAVALLY
CATCHPOLE	CATHARIZED	CATTISHLY	CAUSALITIES	CAVALRIES
CATCHPOLES	CATHARIZES	CATTLE	CAUSALITY	CAVALRY
CATCHPOLL	CATHARIZING	CATTLEMAN	CAUSALLY	CAVASS
CATCHPOLLS	CATHARSES	CATTLEMEN	CAUSATION	CAVASSES
CATCHT	CATHARSIS	CATTY	CAUSATIONS	CAVATINA
CATCHUP	CATHARTIC	CAUCHEMAR	CAUSATIVE	CAVATINAS
CATCHUPS	CATHARTICS	CAUCHEMARS	CAUSATIVES	CAVE
CATCHWEED	CATHEAD	CAUCUS	CAUSE	CAVEAT
CATCHWEEDS	CATHEADS	CAUCUSED	CAUSED	CAVEATS
CATCHWORD	CATHECTIC	CAUCUSES	CAUSELESS	CAVED
CATCHWORDS	CATHEDRA	CAUCUSING	CAUSEN	CAVEL
CATCHY	CATHEDRAL	CAUDAD	CAUSER	CAVELS

CAVEMAN	CAZIQUES	CELERY	CEMENTUM	CENTNERS
CAVEMEN	CEAS	CELESTA	CEMETERIES	CENTO
CAVENDISH	CEASE	CELESTAS	CEMETERY	CENTOIST
CAVENDISHES	CEASED	CELESTE	CEMITARE	CENTOISTS
CAVER	CEASELESS	CELESTES	CEMITARES	CENTONATE
CAVERN	CEASES	CELESTIAL	CENACLE	CENTONEL
CAVERNED	CEASING	CELESTIALS	CENACLES	CENTONELL
CAVERNING	CEASINGS	CELESTINE	CENDRÉ	CENTONELLS
CAVERNOUS	CEAZE	CELESTINES	CENOBITE	CENTONELS
CAVERNS	CEAZED	CELIAC	CENOBITES	CENTONIST
CAVERS	CEAZES	CELIACS	CENOTAPH	CENTONISTS
CAVES	CEAZING	CELIBACIES	CENOTAPHS	CENTOS
CAVESSON	CEBADILLA	CELIBACY	CENOTE	CENTRAL
CAVESSONS	CEBADILLAS	CELIBATE	CENOTES	CENTRALLY
CAVETTI	CECA	CELIBATES	CENSE	CENTRE
CAVETTO	CECILS	CELL	CENSED	CENTRED
CAVIAR	CECITIES	CELLA	CENSER	CENTREING
CAVIARE	CECITY	CELLAE	CENSERS	CENTREINGS
CAVIARES	CECUM	CELLAR	CENSES	CENTRES
CAVIARIE	CEDAR	CELLARAGE	CENSING	CENTRIC
CAVIARIES	CEDARED	CELLARAGES	CENSOR	CENTRICAL
CAVIARS	CEDARN	CELLARED	CENSORED	CENTRIES
CAVICORN	CEDARS	CELLARER	CENSORIAL	CENTRING
CAVICORNS	CEDARWOOD	CELLARERS	CENSORIAN	CENTRINGS
CAVIE	CEDARWOODS	CELLARET	CENSORING	CENTRISM
CAVIER	CEDE	CELLARETS	CENSORS	CENTRISMS
CAVIERS	CEDED	CELLARING	CENSUAL	CENTRIST
CAVIES	CEDES	CELLARIST	CENSURE	CENTRISTS
CAVIL	CEDI	CELLARISTS	CENSURED	CENTRODE
CAVILLED	CEDILLA	CELLARMAN	CENSURES	CENTRODES
CAVILLER	CEDILLAS	CELLARMEN	CENSURING	CENTROID
CAVILLERS	CEDING	CELLAROUS	CENSUS	CENTROIDS
CAVILLING	CEDIS	CELLARS	CENSUSED	CENTRUM
CAVILLINGS	CEDRATE	CELLED	CENSUSES	CENTRUMS
CAVILS	CEDRATES	CELLIST	CENSUSING	CENTRY
CAVING	CEDRINE	CELLISTS	CENT	CENTS
CAVINGS	CEDULA	CELLO	CENTAGE	CENTUM
CAVITATE	CEDULAS	CELLOS	CENTAGES	CENTUMS
CAVITATED	CEE	CELLPHONE	CENTAL	CENTUMVIR
CAVITATES	CEES	CELLPHONES	CENTALS	CENTUMVIRI
CAVITATING	CEIL	CELLS	CENTAUR	CENTUPLE
CAVITIED	CEILED	CELLULAR	CENTAURIES	CENTUPLED
CAVITIES	CEILI	CELLULE	CENTAURS	CENTUPLES
CAVITY	CEILIDH	CELLULES	CENTAURY	CENTUPLING
CAVORT	CEILIDHS	CELLULITE	CENTAVO	CENTURIAL
CAVORTED	CEILING	CELLULITES	CENTAVOS	CENTURIES
CAVORTING	CEILINGED	CELLULOID	CENTENARIES	CENTURION
CAVORTS	CEILINGS	CELLULOIDS	CENTENARY	CENTURIONS
CAVY	CEILIS	CELLULOSE	CENTENIER	CENTURY
CAW	CEILS	CELLULOSES	CENTENIERS	CEORL
CAWED	CEINTURE	CELOM	CENTER	CEORLS
CAWING	CEINTURES	CELOMS	CENTERED	CEP
CAWINGS	CEL	CELS	CENTERING	CEPHALAD
CAWK	CELADON	CELSITUDE	CENTERINGS	CEPHALATE
CAWKER	CELADONS	CELSITUDES	CENTERS	CEPHALIC
CAWKERS	CELANDINE	CELT	CENTESES	CEPHALICS
CAWKS	CELANDINES	CELTS	CENTESIS	CEPHALOUS
CAWS	CELEBRANT	CEMBALIST	CENTIARE	CEPHEID
CAXON	CELEBRANTS	CEMBALISTS	CENTIARES	CEPHEIDS
CAXONS	CELEBRATE	CEMBALO	CENTIGRAM	CEPS
CAY	CELEBRATED	CEMBALOS	CENTIGRAMS	CERACEOUS
CAYENNE	CELEBRATES	CEMBRA	CENTIME	CERAMET
CAYENNED	CELEBRATING	CEMBRAS	CENTIMES	CERAMETS
CAYENNES	CELEBRITIES	CEMENT	CENTINEL	CERAMIC
CAYMAN	CELEBRITY	CEMENTA	CENTINELL	CERAMICS
CAYMANS	CELERIAC	CEMENTED	CENTINELLS	CERAMIST
CAYS	CELERIACS	CEMENTING	CENTINELS	CERAMISTS
CAYUSE	CELERIES	CEMENTITE	CENTIPEDE	CERASIN
CAYUSES	CELERITIES	CEMENTITES	CENTIPEDES	CERASINS
CAZIQUE	CELERITY	CEMENTS	CENTNER	CERASTES

CERATE
CERATED
CERATES
CERATITIS
CERATITISES
CERATODUS
CERATODUSES
CERATOID
CERBERIAN
CERCAL
CERCARIA
CERCARIAE
CERCARIAN
CERCARIAS
CERCI
CERCUS
CERCUSES
CERE
CEREAL
CEREALIST
CEREALISTS
CEREALS
CEREBELLA
CEREBRAL
CEREBRATE
CEREBRATED
CEREBRATES
CEREBRATING
CEREBRIC
CEREBRUM
CEREBRUMS
CERED
CEREMENT
CEREMENTS
CEREMONIES
CEREMONY
CEREOUS
CERES
CERESIN
CERESINE
CERESINES
CERESINS
CERGE
CERGES
CERIA
CERIAS
CERING
CERIPH
CERIPHS
CERISE
CERISES
CERITE
CERITES
CERIUM
CERIUMS
CERMET
CERMETS
CERNE
CERNED
CERNES
CERNING
CERNUOUS
CEROGRAPH
CEROGRAPHS
CEROMANCIES
CEROMANCY
CEROON
CEROONS
CERRIAL
CERRIS

CERRISES
CERT
CERTAIN
CERTAINLY
CERTAINTIES
CERTAINTY
CERTES
CERTIFIED
CERTIFIER
CERTIFIERS
CERTIFIES
CERTIFY
CERTIFYING
CERTITUDE
CERTITUDES
CERTS
CERULEAN
CERULEIN
CERULEINS
CERULEOUS
CERUMEN
CERUMENS
CERUSE
CERUSES
CERUSITE
CERUSITES
CERUSSITE
CERUSSITES
CERVELAT
CERVELATS
CERVICAL
CERVINE
CERVIX
CERVIXES
CESAREVNA
CESAREVNAS
CESIUM
CESIUMS
CESPITOSE
CESS
CESSATION
CESSATIONS
CESSE
CESSED
CESSER
CESSERS
CESSES
CESSING
CESSION
CESSIONS
CESSPIT
CESSPITS
CESSPOOL
CESSPOOLS
CESTODE
CESTODES
CESTOID
CESTOIDS
CESTUI
CESTUIS
CESTUS
CESTUSES
CESURA
CESURAS
CESURE
CESURES
CETACEAN
CETACEANS
CETACEOUS
CETANE

CETANES
CETE
CETERACH
CETERACHS
CETES
CETOLOGIES
CETOLOGY
CETYL
CETYLS
CETYWALL
CETYWALLS
CEVADILLA
CEVADILLAS
CEYLANITE
CEYLANITES
CEYLONITE
CEYLONITES
CH
CHA
CHABAZITE
CHABAZITES
CHABOUK
CHABOUKS
CHACE
CHACED
CHACES
CHACING
CHACK
CHACKED
CHACKING
CHACKS
CHACMA
CHACMAS
CHACO
CHACOES
CHACONNE
CHACONNES
CHACOS
CHAD
CHADAR
CHADARS
CHADDAR
CHADDARS
CHADOR
CHADORS
CHADS
CHAETA
CHAETAE
CHAETODON
CHAETODONS
CHAETOPOD
CHAETOPODS
CHAFE
CHAFED
CHAFER
CHAFERS
CHAFES
CHAFF
CHAFFED
CHAFFER
CHAFFERED
CHAFFERER
CHAFFERERS
CHAFFERIES
CHAFFERING
CHAFFERS
CHAFFERY
CHAFFIER
CHAFFIEST
CHAFFINCH

CHAFFINCHES
CHAFFING
CHAFFINGS
CHAFFLESS
CHAFFRON
CHAFFRONS
CHAFFS
CHAFFY
CHAFING
CHAFT
CHAFTS
CHAGAN
CHAGANS
CHAGRIN
CHAGRINED
CHAGRINING
CHAGRINS
CHAI
CHAIN
CHAINED
CHAINING
CHAINLESS
CHAINLET
CHAINLETS
CHAINS
CHAINSAW
CHAINSAWS
CHAINWORK
CHAINWORKS
CHAIR
CHAIRDAYS
CHAIRED
CHAIRING
CHAIRLIFT
CHAIRLIFTS
CHAIRMAN
CHAIRMEN
CHAIRS
CHAIS
CHAISE
CHAISES
CHAKRA
CHAKRAS
CHAL
CHALAN
CHALANED
CHALANING
CHALANS
CHALAZA
CHALAZAE
CHALAZAS
CHALDAISM
CHALDAISMS
CHALDER
CHALDERS
CHALDRON
CHALDRONS
CHALET
CHALETS
CHALICE
CHALICED
CHALICES
CHALK
CHALKED
CHALKFACE
CHALKFACES
CHALKIER
CHALKIEST
CHALKING
CHALKPIT

CHALKPITS
CHALKS
CHALKY
CHALLAN
CHALLANED
CHALLANING
CHALLANS
CHALLENGE
CHALLENGED
CHALLENGES
CHALLENGING
CHALLIS
CHALLISES
CHALONE
CHALONES
CHALONIC
CHALS
CHALUMEAU
CHALUMEAUX
CHALYBITE
CHALYBITES
CHAM
CHAMADE
CHAMADES
CHAMBER
CHAMBERED
CHAMBERER
CHAMBERERS
CHAMBERING
CHAMBERINGS
CHAMBERS
CHAMBRÉ
CHAMELEON
CHAMELEONS
CHAMELOT
CHAMELOTS
CHAMFER
CHAMFERED
CHAMFERING
CHAMFERS
CHAMFRAIN
CHAMFRAINS
CHAMFRON
CHAMFRONS
CHAMISAL
CHAMISALS
CHAMISE
CHAMISES
CHAMISO
CHAMISOS
CHAMLET
CHAMLETS
CHAMOIS
CHAMOMILE
CHAMOMILES
CHAMP
CHAMPAC
CHAMPACS
CHAMPAGNE
CHAMPAGNES
CHAMPAIGN
CHAMPAIGNS
CHAMPAK
CHAMPAKS
CHAMPART
CHAMPARTS
CHAMPED
CHAMPERS
CHAMPERTIES
CHAMPERTY

CHAMPING	CHAOTIC	CHARADES	CHAROSETS	CHASTISING
CHAMPION	CHAP	CHARAS	CHARPIE	CHASTITIES
CHAMPIONED	CHAPARRAL	CHARASES	CHARPIES	CHASTITY
CHAMPIONING	CHAPARRALS	CHARCOAL	CHARPOY	CHASUBLE
CHAMPIONS	CHAPATI	CHARCOALS	CHARPOYS	CHASUBLES
CHAMPLEVÉ	CHAPATIS	CHARD	CHARQUI	CHAT
CHAMPLEVÉS	CHAPATTI	CHARDS	CHARQUIS	CHÂTEAU
CHAMPS	CHAPATTIS	CHARE	CHARR	CHÂTEAUX
CHAMS	CHAPBOOK	CHARED	CHARRED	CHÂTELAIN
CHANCE	CHAPBOOKS	CHARES	CHARRING	CHÂTELAINS
CHANCED	CHAPE	CHARET	CHARRS	CHATON
CHANCEFUL	CHAPEAU	CHARETS	CHARRY	CHATONS
CHANCEL	CHAPEAUS	CHARGE	CHARS	CHATOYANT
CHANCELS	CHAPEL	CHARGED	CHART	CHATS
CHANCER	CHAPELESS	CHARGEFUL	CHARTA	CHATTA
CHANCERS	CHAPELRIES	CHARGER	CHARTAS	CHATTAS
CHANCES	CHAPELRY	CHARGERS	CHARTED	CHATTED
CHANCIER	CHAPELS	CHARGES	CHARTER	CHATTEL
CHANCIEST	CHAPERON	CHARGING	CHARTERED	CHATTELS
CHANCING	CHAPERONE	CHARIER	CHARTERER	CHATTER
CHANCRE	CHAPERONED	CHARIEST	CHARTERERS	CHATTERED
CHANCRES	CHAPERONES	CHARILY	CHARTERING	CHATTERER
CHANCROID	CHAPERONING	CHARINESS	CHARTERS	CHATTERERS
CHANCROIDS	CHAPERONS	CHARINESSES	CHARTING	CHATTERING
CHANCROUS	CHAPES	CHARING	CHARTISM	CHATTERINGS
CHANCY	CHAPESS	CHARIOT	CHARTISMS	CHATTERS
CHANDLER	CHAPESSES	CHARIOTED	CHARTIST	CHATTIER
CHANDLERIES	CHAPITER	CHARIOTING	CHARTISTS	CHATTIES
CHANDLERS	CHAPITERS	CHARIOTS	CHARTLESS	CHATTIEST
CHANDLERY	CHAPKA	CHARISM	CHARTS	CHATTING
CHANGE	CHAPKAS	CHARISMA	CHARWOMAN	CHATTY
CHANGED	CHAPLAIN	CHARISMAS	CHARWOMEN	CHAUFE
CHANGEFUL	CHAPLAINS	CHARISMS	CHARY	CHAUFED
CHANGER	CHAPLESS	CHARITIES	CHAS	CHAUFES
CHANGERS	CHAPLET	CHARITY	CHASE	CHAUFF
CHANGES	CHAPLETED	CHARIVARI	CHASED	CHAUFFED
CHANGING	CHAPLETS	CHARIVARIS	CHASER	CHAUFFER
CHANK	CHAPMAN	CHARK	CHASERS	CHAUFFERS
CHANKS	CHAPMEN	CHARKED	CHASES	CHAUFFEUR
CHANNEL	CHAPPED	CHARKING	CHASING	CHAUFFEURED
CHANNELLED	CHAPPESS	CHARKS	CHASINGS	CHAUFFEURING
CHANNELLING	CHAPPESSES	CHARLADIES	CHASM	CHAUFFEURS
CHANNELS	CHAPPIE	CHARLADY	CHASMED	CHAUFFING
CHANOYU	CHAPPIER	CHARLATAN	CHASMIC	CHAUFFS
CHANOYUS	CHAPPIES	CHARLATANS	CHASMIER	CHAUFING
CHANSON	CHAPPIEST	CHARLEY	CHASMIEST	CHAUMER
CHANSONS	CHAPPING	CHARLEYS	CHASMS	CHAUMERS
CHANT	CHAPPY	CHARLIE	CHASMY	CHAUNCE
CHANTAGE	CHAPRASSI	CHARLIES	CHASSÉ	CHAUNCED
CHANTAGES	CHAPRASSIS	CHARLOCK	CHASSE	CHAUNCES
CHANTED	CHAPS	CHARLOCKS	CHASSÉED	CHAUNCING
CHANTER	CHAPTER	CHARLOTTE	CHASSÉING	CHAUNGE
CHANTERS	CHAPTERED	CHARLOTTES	CHASSÉS	CHAUNGED
CHANTEUSE	CHAPTERING	CHARM	CHASSES	CHAUNGES
CHANTEUSES	CHAPTERS	CHARMED	CHASSEUR	CHAUNGING
CHANTEY	CHAPTREL	CHARMER	CHASSEURS	CHAUNT
CHANTEYS	CHAPTRELS	CHARMERS	CHASSIS	CHAUNTED
CHANTIE	CHAR	CHARMEUSE	CHASTE	CHAUNTER
CHANTIES	CHARA	CHARMEUSES	CHASTELY	CHAUNTERS
CHANTING	CHARABANC	CHARMFUL	CHASTEN	CHAUNTING
CHANTOR	CHARABANCS	CHARMING	CHASTENED	CHAUNTRIES
CHANTORS	CHARACIN	CHARMLESS	CHASTENER	CHAUNTRY
CHANTRESS	CHARACINS	CHARMS	CHASTENERS	CHAUNTS
CHANTRESSES	CHARACT	CHARNECO	CHASTENING	CHAUSSES
CHANTRIES	CHARACTER	CHARNECOS	CHASTENS	CHAUSSURE
CHANTRY	CHARACTERED	CHARNEL	CHASTER	CHAUSSURES
CHANTS	CHARACTERING	CHARNELS	CHASTEST	CHAUVIN
CHANTY	CHARACTERS	CHAROSET	CHASTISE	CHAUVINS
CHAOS	CHARACTS	CHAROSETH	CHASTISED	CHAVE
CHAOSES	CHARADE	CHAROSETHS	CHASTISES	CHAVENDER

CHAVENDERS
CHAW
CHAWDRON
CHAWDRONS
CHAWED
CHAWING
CHAWS
CHAY
CHAYA
CHAYAS
CHAYOTE
CHAYOTES
CHAYS
CHE
CHEAP
CHEAPEN
CHEAPENED
CHEAPENER
CHEAPENERS
CHEAPENING
CHEAPENS
CHEAPER
CHEAPEST
CHEAPIE
CHEAPIES
CHEAPLY
CHEAPNESS
CHEAPNESSES
CHEAPO
CHEAPS
CHEAPY
CHEAT
CHEATED
CHEATER
CHEATERS
CHEATERIES
CHEATERS
CHEATERY
CHEATING
CHEATS
CHECHAKO
CHECHAKOES
CHECHAKOS
CHECHAQUA
CHECHAQUAS
CHECHAQUO
CHECHAQUOS
CHÉCHIA
CHÉCHIAS
CHECK
CHECKED
CHECKER
CHECKERED
CHECKERS
CHECKIER
CHECKIEST
CHECKING
CHECKLIST
CHECKLISTS
CHECKMATE
CHECKMATED
CHECKMATES
CHECKMATING
CHECKROOM
CHECKROOMS
CHECKS
CHECKY
CHEECHAKO
CHEECHAKOES
CHEECHAKOS
CHEEK

CHEEKED
CHEEKIER
CHEEKIEST
CHEEKILY
CHEEKING
CHEEKS
CHEEKY
CHEEP
CHEEPED
CHEEPER
CHEEPERS
CHEEPING
CHEEPS
CHEER
CHEERED
CHEERER
CHEERERS
CHEERFUL
CHEERFULLER
CHEERFULLEST
CHEERIER
CHEERIEST
CHEERILY
CHEERING
CHEERIO
CHEERIOS
CHEERLESS
CHEERLY
CHEERO
CHEEROS
CHEERS
CHEERY
CHEESE
CHEESED
CHEESES
CHEESIER
CHEESIEST
CHEESING
CHEESY
CHEETAH
CHEETAHS
CHEEWINK
CHEEWINKS
CHEF
CHEFS
CHEKA
CHEKAS
CHEKIST
CHEKISTS
CHELA
CHELAE
CHELAS
CHELASHIP
CHELASHIPS
CHELATE
CHELATED
CHELATES
CHELATING
CHELATION
CHELATIONS
CHELATOR
CHELATORS
CHELICERA
CHELICERAE
CHELIPED
CHELIPEDS
CHELOID
CHELOIDAL
CHELOIDS
CHELONIAN

CHELONIANS
CHEMIC
CHEMICAL
CHEMICALS
CHEMICKED
CHEMICKING
CHEMICS
CHEMISE
CHEMISES
CHEMISM
CHEMISMS
CHEMIST
CHEMISTRIES
CHEMISTRY
CHEMISTS
CHEMITYPE
CHEMITYPES
CHEMITYPIES
CHEMITYPY
CHEMMIES
CHEMMY
CHEMOSTAT
CHEMOSTATS
CHEMURGIC
CHEMURGIES
CHEMURGY
CHENAR
CHENARS
CHENET
CHENETS
CHENILLE
CHENILLES
CHENIX
CHENIXES
CHEQUE
CHEQUER
CHEQUERED
CHEQUERING
CHEQUERS
CHEQUES
CHEQUIER
CHEQUIEST
CHEQUY
CHER
CHERALITE
CHERALITES
CHÈRE
CHERIMOYA
CHERIMOYAS
CHERISH
CHERISHED
CHERISHES
CHERISHING
CHERNOZEM
CHERNOZEMS
CHEROOT
CHEROOTS
CHERRIED
CHERRIER
CHERRIES
CHERRIEST
CHERRY
CHERRYING
CHERT
CHERTIER
CHERTIEST
CHERTS
CHERTY
CHERUB
CHERUBIC

CHERUBIM
CHERUBIMS
CHERUBIN
CHERUBINS
CHERUBS
CHERUP
CHERUPED
CHERUPING
CHERUPS
CHERVIL
CHERVILS
CHESIL
CHESILS
CHESNUT
CHESNUTS
CHESS
CHESSEL
CHESSELS
CHESSES
CHESSMAN
CHESSMEN
CHEST
CHESTED
CHESTFUL
CHESTFULS
CHESTIER
CHESTIEST
CHESTNUT
CHESTNUTS
CHESTS
CHESTY
CHEVALET
CHEVALETS
CHEVALIER
CHEVALIERS
CHEVELURE
CHEVELURES
CHEVEN
CHEVENS
CHEVEREL
CHEVERELS
CHEVERIL
CHEVERILS
CHEVERON
CHEVERONS
CHEVERYE
CHEVERYES
CHEVIED
CHEVIES
CHEVILLE
CHEVILLES
CHEVIN
CHEVINS
CHEVRETTE
CHEVRETTES
CHEVRON
CHEVRONED
CHEVRONS
CHEVRONY
CHEVY
CHEVYING
CHEW
CHEWED
CHEWET
CHEWETS
CHEWIER
CHEWIEST
CHEWING
CHEWINK
CHEWINKS

CHEWS
CHEWY
CHEZ
CHI
CHIACK
CHIACKED
CHIACKING
CHIACKINGS
CHIACKS
CHIAO
CHIASM
CHIASMA
CHIASMAS
CHIASMS
CHIASMUS
CHIASMUSES
CHIASTIC
CHIAUS
CHIAUSED
CHIAUSES
CHIAUSING
CHIBOL
CHIBOLS
CHIBOUK
CHIBOUKS
CHIBOUQUE
CHIBOUQUES
CHIC
CHICA
CHICANE
CHICANED
CHICANER
CHICANERIES
CHICANERS
CHICANERY
CHICANES
CHICANING
CHICANINGS
CHICANO
CHICANOS
CHICAS
CHICCORIES
CHICCORY
CHICER
CHICEST
CHICH
CHICHA
CHICHAS
CHICHES
CHICHI
CHICHIS
CHICK
CHICKADEE
CHICKADEES
CHICKAREE
CHICKAREES
CHICKEN
CHICKENED
CHICKENING
CHICKENS
CHICKLING
CHICKLINGS
CHICKS
CHICKWEED
CHICKWEEDS
CHICLE
CHICLES
CHICLY
CHICON
CHICONS

CHICORIES
CHICORY
CHICS
CHID
CHIDDEN
CHIDE
CHIDED
CHIDER
CHIDERS
CHIDES
CHIDING
CHIDINGS
CHIDLINGS
CHIEF
CHIEFDOM
CHIEFDOMS
CHIEFER
CHIEFERIES
CHIEFERY
CHIEFESS
CHIEFESSES
CHIEFEST
CHIEFLESS
CHIEFLING
CHIEFLINGS
CHIEFLY
CHIEFRIES
CHIEFRY
CHIEFS
CHIEFSHIP
CHIEFSHIPS
CHIEFTAIN
CHIEFTAINS
CHIFI
CHIELD
CHIELDS
CHIELS
CHIFFON
CHIFFONS
CHIGGER
CHIGGERS
CHIGNON
CHIGNONS
CHIGOE
CHIGOES
CHIGRE
CHIGRES
CHIHUAHUA
CHIHUAHUAS
CHIK
CHIKARA
CHIKARAS
CHIKHOR
CHIKHORS
CHIKOR
CHIKORS
CHIKS
CHILBLAIN
CHILBLAINS
CHILD
CHILDBED
CHILDBEDS
CHILDE
CHILDED
CHILDER
CHILDHOOD
CHILDHOODS
CHILDING
CHILDISH
CHILDLESS

CHILDLIKE
CHILDLY
CHILDNESS
CHILDNESSES
CHILDREN
CHILDS
CHILE
CHILES
CHILI
CHILIAD
CHILIADS
CHILIAGON
CHILIAGONS
CHILIARCH
CHILIARCHS
CHILIASM
CHILIASMS
CHILIAST
CHILIASTS
CHILIS
CHILL
CHILLED
CHILLER
CHILLERS
CHILLEST
CHILLI
CHILLIER
CHILLIES
CHILLIEST
CHILLILY
CHILLING
CHILLINGS
CHILLIS
CHILLNESS
CHILLNESSES
CHILLS
CHILLUM
CHILLUMS
CHILLY
CHIMAERA
CHIMAERAS
CHIMAERID
CHIMAERIDS
CHIMB
CHIMBS
CHIME
CHIMED
CHIMER
CHIMERA
CHIMERE
CHIMERES
CHIMERIC
CHIMERS
CHIMES
CHIMING
CHIMLEY
CHIMLEYED
CHIMLEYS
CHIMNEY
CHIMNEYED
CHIMNEYING
CHIMNEYS
CHIMP
CHIMPS
CHIN
CHINA
CHINAMPA
CHINAMPAS

CHINAR
CHINAROOT
CHINAROOTS
CHINARS
CHINAS
CHINCAPIN
CHINCAPINS
CHINCH
CHINCHES
CHINCOUGH
CHINCOUGHS
CHINDIT
CHINDITS
CHINÉ
CHINE
CHINED
CHINES
CHINESE
CHINING
CHINK
CHINKAPIN
CHINKAPINS
CHINKARA
CHINKARAS
CHINKED
CHINKIE
CHINKIER
CHINKIES
CHINKIEST
CHINKING
CHINKS
CHINKY
CHINLESS
CHINO
CHINOOK
CHINOOKS
CHINOS
CHINOVNIK
CHINOVNIKS
CHINS
CHINSTRAP
CHINSTRAPS
CHINTZ
CHINTZES
CHINTZIER
CHINTZIEST
CHINTZY
CHINWAG
CHINWAGGED
CHINWAGGING
CHINWAGS
CHIP
CHIPBOARD
CHIPBOARDS
CHIPMUCK
CHIPMUCKS
CHIPMUNK
CHIPMUNKS
CHIPOCHIA
CHIPOCHIAS
CHIPOLATA
CHIPOLATAS
CHIPPED
CHIPPER
CHIPPIE
CHIPPIER
CHIPPIES
CHIPPIEST
CHIPPING
CHIPPINGS

CHIPPY
CHIPS
CHIRAGRA
CHIRAGRAS
CHIRAGRIC
CHIRAL
CHIRALITIES
CHIRALITY
CHIRIMOYA
CHIRIMOYAS
CHIRK
CHIRKED
CHIRKING
CHIRKS
CHIRL
CHIRLED
CHIRLING
CHIRLS
CHIRM
CHIRMED
CHIRMING
CHIRMS
CHIROLOGIES
CHIROLOGY
CHIRONOMIES
CHIRONOMY
CHIROPODIES
CHIROPODY
CHIRP
CHIRPED
CHIRPER
CHIRPERS
CHIRPIER
CHIRPIEST
CHIRPILY
CHIRPING
CHIRPS
CHIRPY
CHIRR
CHIRRED
CHIRRING
CHIRRS
CHIRRUP
CHIRRUPED
CHIRRUPING
CHIRRUPS
CHIRRUPY
CHIRT
CHIRTED
CHIRTING
CHIRTS
CHIS
CHISEL
CHISELLED
CHISELLING
CHISELLINGS
CHISELS
CHIT
CHITAL
CHITALS
CHITCHAT
CHITCHATS
CHITCHATTED
CHITCHATTING
CHITIN
CHITINOUS
CHITINS
CHITLINGS
CHITON
CHITONS

CHITS
CHITTED
CHITTER
CHITTERED
CHITTERING
CHITTERINGS
CHITTERS
CHITTIER
CHITTIES
CHITTIEST
CHITTING
CHITTY
CHIV
CHIVALRIC
CHIVALRIES
CHIVALRY
CHIVE
CHIVED
CHIVES
CHIVIED
CHIVIES
CHIVING
CHIVS
CHIVVED
CHIVVIED
CHIVVIES
CHIVVING
CHIVVY
CHIVVYING
CHIVY
CHIVYING
CHLAMYDES
CHLAMYDIA
CHLAMYDIAS
CHLAMYS
CHLOASMA
CHLOASMAS
CHLORACNE
CHLORACNES
CHLORAL
CHLORALS
CHLORATE
CHLORATES
CHLORDAN
CHLORDANE
CHLORDANES
CHLORDANS
CHLORIC
CHLORIDE
CHLORIDES
CHLORINE
CHLORINES
CHLORITE
CHLORITES
CHLORITIC
CHLOROSES
CHLOROSIS
CHLOROTIC
CHLOROUS
CHOBDAR
CHOBDARS
CHOC
CHOCHO
CHOCHOS
CHOCK
CHOCKED
CHOCKER
CHOCKING
CHOCKS
CHOCOLATE

CHOCOLATES	CHONDRIFIES	CHORINE	CHRISTOM	CHUFFS
CHOCS	CHONDRIFY	CHORINES	CHRISTOMS	CHUFFY
CHOCTAW	CHONDRIFYING	CHORIOID	CHRISTY	CHUG
CHOCTAWS	CHONDRIN	CHORIOIDS	CHROMA	CHUGGED
CHODE	CHONDRINS	CHORION	CHROMAKEY	CHUGGING
CHOENIX	CHONDRITE	CHORIONIC	CHROMAKEYS	CHUGS
CHOENIXES	CHONDRITES	CHORISES	CHROMAS	CHUKAR
CHOICE	CHONDROID	CHORISIS	CHROMATE	CHUKARS
CHOICEFUL	CHONDRULE	CHORIST	CHROMATES	CHUKKA
CHOICELY	CHONDRULES	CHORISTER	CHROMATIC	CHUKKAS
CHOICER	CHONDRUS	CHORISTERS	CHROMATICS	CHUKKER
CHOICES	CHOOK	CHORISTS	CHROMATIN	CHUKKERS
CHOICEST	CHOOKIE	CHORIZO	CHROMATINS	CHUKOR
CHOIR	CHOOKIES	CHORIZONT	CHROME	CHUKORS
CHOIRBOY	CHOOKS	CHORIZONTS	CHROMED	CHUM
CHOIRBOYS	CHOOM	CHORIZOS	CHROMES	CHUMLEY
CHOIRED	CHOOMS	CHOROID	CHROMIC	CHUMLEYED
CHOIRING	CHOOSE	CHOROIDS	CHROMIDIA	CHUMLEYING
CHOIRMAN	CHOOSER	CHOROLOGIES	CHROMING	CHUMLEYS
CHOIRMEN	CHOOSERS	CHOROLOGY	CHROMITE	CHUMMAGE
CHOIRS	CHOOSES	CHORTLE	CHROMITES	CHUMMAGES
CHOKE	CHOOSEY	CHORTLED	CHROMIUM	CHUMMED
CHOKEBORE	CHOOSIER	CHORTLES	CHROMIUMS	CHUMMIER
CHOKEBORES	CHOOSIEST	CHORTLING	CHROMO	CHUMMIES
CHOKED	CHOOSING	CHORUS	CHROMOS	CHUMMIEST
CHOKEDAMP	CHOOSY	CHORUSED	CHRONIC	CHUMMING
CHOKEDAMPS	CHOP	CHORUSES	CHRONICAL	CHUMMY
CHOKER	CHOPIN	CHORUSING	CHRONICLE	CHUMP
CHOKERS	CHOPINE	CHOSE	CHRONICLED	CHUMPS
CHOKES	CHOPINES	CHOSEN	CHRONICLES	CHUMS
CHOKEY	CHOPINS	CHOSES	CHRONICLING	CHUNDER
CHOKEYS	CHOPPED	CHOU	CHRONICS	CHUNDERED
CHOKIDAR	CHOPPER	CHOUGH	CHRONON	CHUNDERING
CHOKIDARS	CHOPPERS	CHOUGHS	CHRONONS	CHUNDERS
CHOKIER	CHOPPIER	CHOULTRIES	CHRYSALID	CHUNK
CHOKIES	CHOPPIEST	CHOULTRY	CHRYSALIDES	CHUNKIER
CHOKIEST	CHOPPING	CHOUNTER	CHRYSALIDS	CHUNKIEST
CHOKING	CHOPPINGS	CHOUNTERED	CHRYSALIS	CHUNKS
CHOKY	CHOPPY	CHOUNTERING	CHRYSALISES	CHUNKY
CHOLAEMIA	CHOPS	CHOUNTERS	CHRYSANTH	CHUNNEL
CHOLAEMIAS	CHORAGI	CHOUSE	CHRYSANTHS	CHUNNELS
CHOLAEMIC	CHORAGIC	CHOUSED	CHTHONIAN	CHUNNER
CHOLECYST	CHORAGUS	CHOUSES	CHTHONIC	CHUNNERED
CHOLECYSTS	CHORAGUSES	CHOUSING	CHUB	CHUNNERING
CHOLELITH	CHORAL	CHOUT	CHUBBED	CHUNNERS
CHOLELITHS	CHORALE	CHOUTS	CHUBBIER	CHUNTER
CHOLER	CHORALES	CHOUX	CHUBBIEST	CHUNTERED
CHOLERA	CHORALLY	CHOW	CHUBBY	CHUNTERING
CHOLERAIC	CHORALS	CHOWDER	CHUBS	CHUNTERS
CHOLERAS	CHORD	CHOWDERS	CHUCK	CHUPATI
CHOLERIC	CHORDAL	CHOWKIDAR	CHUCKED	CHUPATIS
CHOLERS	CHORDATE	CHOWKIDARS	CHUCKIE	CHUPATTI
CHOLI	CHORDATES	CHOWRI	CHUCKIES	CHUPATTIS
CHOLIAMB	CHORDS	CHOWRIES	CHUCKING	CHUPRASSIES
CHOLIAMBS	CHORE	CHOWRIS	CHUCKLE	CHUPRASSY
CHOLIC	CHOREA	CHOWRY	CHUCKLED	CHURCH
CHOLINE	CHOREAS	CHOWS	CHUCKLES	CHURCHED
CHOLINES	CHOREE	CHRISM	CHUCKLING	CHURCHES
CHOLIS	CHOREES	CHRISMAL	CHUCKLINGS	CHURCHIER
CHOLTRIES	CHOREGI	CHRISMALS	CHUCKS	CHURCHIEST
CHOLTRY	CHOREGIC	CHRISMS	CHUDDAH	CHURCHING
CHOMP	CHOREGUS	CHRISOM	CHUDDAHS	CHURCHINGS
CHOMPED	CHOREGUSES	CHRISOMS	CHUDDAR	CHURCHISM
CHOMPING	CHORES	CHRISTEN	CHUDDARS	CHURCHISMS
CHOMPS	CHOREUS	CHRISTENED	CHUFA	CHURCHLY
CHONDRAL	CHOREUSES	CHRISTENING	CHUFAS	CHURCHMAN
CHONDRE	CHORIA	CHRISTENINGS	CHUFF	CHURCHMEN
CHONDRES	CHORIAMB	CHRISTENS	CHUFFED	CHURCHWAY
CHONDRI	CHORIAMBS	CHRISTIE	CHUFFIER	CHURCHWAYS
CHONDRIFIED	CHORIC	CHRISTIES	CHUFFIEST	CHURCHY

CHURINGA
CHURINGAS
CHURL
CHURLISH
CHURLS
CHURN
CHURNED
CHURNING
CHURNINGS
CHURNS
CHURR
CHURRED
CHURRING
CHURRS
CHURRUS
CHURRUSES
CHUSE
CHUSES
CHUSING
CHUT
CHUTE
CHUTES
CHUTIST
CHUTISTS
CHUTNEY
CHUTNEYS
CHUTZPAH
CHUTZPAHS
CHYACK
CHYACKED
CHYACKING
CHYACKS
CHYLDE
CHYLE
CHYLES
CHYLURIA
CHYLURIAS
CHYME
CHYMES
CHYMIFIED
CHYMIFIES
CHYMIFY
CHYMIFYING
CHYMISTRIES
CHYMISTRY
CHYMOUS
CHYND
CHYPRE
CHYPRES
CIAO
CIAOS
CIBATION
CIBATIONS
CIBOL
CIBOLS
CIBORIA
CIBORIUM
CICADA
CICADAS
CICALA
CICALAS
CICATRICE
CICATRICES
CICATRISE
CICATRISED
CICATRISES
CICATRISING
CICATRIX
CICATRIXES
CICATRIZE

CICATRIZED
CICATRIZES
CICATRIZING
CICELIES
CICELY
CICERO
CICERONE
CICERONED
CICERONEING
CICERONES
CICERONI
CICEROS
CICHLID
CICHLIDS
CICHLOID
CICINNUS
CICINNUSES
CICISBEI
CICISBEO
CICLATON
CICLATONS
CICLATOUN
CICLATOUNS
CICUTA
CICUTAS
CIDARIS
CIDARISES
CIDE
CIDED
CIDER
CIDERKIN
CIDERKINS
CIDERS
CIDERY
CIDES
CIDING
CIEL
CIELED
CIELING
CIELINGS
CIELS
CIERGE
CIERGES
CIG
CIGAR
CIGARETTE
CIGARETTES
CIGARILLO
CIGARILLOS
CIGARS
CIGGIE
CIGGIES
CIGGY
CIGS
CILIA
CILIARY
CILIATE
CILIATED
CILICE
CILICES
CILICIOUS
CILIOLATE
CILIUM
CILL
CILLS
CIMAR
CIMARS
CIMELIA
CIMEX
CIMICES

CIMIER
CIMIERS
CIMINITE
CIMINITES
CIMOLITE
CIMOLITES
CINCH
CINCHED
CINCHES
CINCHING
CINCHONA
CINCHONAS
CINCHONIC
CINCINNUS
CINCINNUSES
CINCT
CINCTURE
CINCTURED
CINCTURES
CINCTURING
CINDER
CINDERS
CINDERY
CINEAST
CINEASTE
CINEASTE
CINEASTES
CINÉASTES
CINEASTS
CINEMA
CINEMAS
CINEMATIC
CINEOL
CINEOLE
CINEOLES
CINEOLS
CINERAMIC
CINERARIA
CINERARIAS
CINERARY
CINERATOR
CINERATORS
CINEREA
CINEREAL
CINEREAS
CINEREOUS
CINGULUM
CINGULUMS
CINNABAR
CINNABARS
CINNAMIC
CINNAMON
CINNAMONS
CINQUAIN
CINQUAINS
CINQUE
CINQUES
CION
CIONS
CIPHER
CIPHERED
CIPHERING
CIPHERINGS
CIPHERS
CIPOLIN
CIPOLINS
CIPOLLINO
CIPOLLINOS
CIPPI
CIPPUS

CIRCA
CIRCADIAN
CIRCAR
CIRCARS
CIRCINATE
CIRCITER
CIRCLE
CIRCLED
CIRCLER
CIRCLERS
CIRCLES
CIRCLET
CIRCLETS
CIRCLING
CIRCLINGS
CIRCS
CIRCUIT
CIRCUITED
CIRCUITIES
CIRCUITING
CIRCUITRIES
CIRCUITRY
CIRCUITS
CIRCUITY
CIRCULAR
CIRCULARS
CIRCULATE
CIRCULATED
CIRCULATES
CIRCULATING
CIRCULATINGS
CIRCUS
CIRCUSES
CIRCUSSY
CIRCUSY
CIRÉ
CIRÉS
CIRL
CIRLS
CIRQUE
CIRQUES
CIRRATE
CIRRHOPOD
CIRRHOPODS
CIRRHOSES
CIRRHOSIS
CIRRHOTIC
CIRRI
CIRRIFORM
CIRRIPED
CIRRIPEDE
CIRRIPEDES
CIRRIPEDS
CIRROSE
CIRROUS
CIRRUS
CISCO
CISCOES
CISCOS
CISELEUR
CISELEURS
CISELURE
CISELURES
CISLUNAR
CISSIER
CISSIES
CISSIEST
CISSOID
CISSOIDS
CISSY

CIST
CISTED
CISTERN
CISTERNS
CISTIC
CISTRON
CISTRONS
CISTS
CISTUS
CISTUSES
CISTVAEN
CISTVAENS
CIT
CITABLE
CITADEL
CITADELS
CITAL
CITALS
CITATION
CITATIONS
CITATORY
CITE
CITED
CITER
CITERS
CITES
CITESS
CITESSES
CITHARA
CITHARAS
CITHARIST
CITHARISTS
CITHER
CITHERN
CITHERNS
CITHERS
CITIES
CITIFIED
CITIFIES
CITIFY
CITIFYING
CITIGRADE
CITING
CITIZEN
CITIZENRIES
CITIZENRY
CITIZENS
CITO
CITOLE
CITOLES
CITRANGE
CITRANGES
CITRATE
CITRATES
CITREOUS
CITRIC
CITRIN
CITRINE
CITRINES
CITRINS
CITRON
CITRONS
CITROUS
CITRUS
CITRUSES
CITS
CITTERN
CITTERNS
CITY
CITYSCAPE

CITYSCAPES	CLAGGIEST	CLANGS	CLARTIEST	CLAUSTRAL
CIVE	CLAGGING	CLANK	CLARTING	CLAUSTRUM
CIVES	CLAGGY	CLANKED	CLARTS	CLAUSULA
CIVET	CLAGS	CLANKING	CLARTY	CLAUSULAE
CIVETS	CLAIM	CLANKINGS	CLARY	CLAUSULAR
CIVIC	CLAIMABLE	CLANKLESS	CLASH	CLAUT
CIVICALLY	CLAIMANT	CLANKS	CLASHED	CLAUTED
CIVICS	CLAIMANTS	CLANNISH	CLASHES	CLAUTING
CIVIL	CLAIMED	CLANS	CLASHING	CLAUTS
CIVILIAN	CLAIMER	CLANSHIP	CLASHINGS	CLAVATE
CIVILIANS	CLAIMERS	CLANSHIPS	CLASP	CLAVATED
CIVILISE	CLAIMING	CLANSMAN	CLASPED	CLAVATION
CIVILISED	CLAIMS	CLANSMEN	CLASPER	CLAVATIONS
CIVILISER	CLAM	CLAP	CLASPERS	CLAVE
CIVILISERS	CLAMANCIES	CLAPBOARD	CLASPING	CLAVECIN
CIVILISES	CLAMANCY	CLAPBOARDS	CLASPINGS	CLAVECINS
CIVILISING	CLAMANT	CLAPBREAD	CLASPS	CLAVER
CIVILIST	CLAMANTLY	CLAPBREADS	CLASS	CLAVERED
CIVILISTS	CLAMBAKE	CLAPDISH	CLASSABLE	CLAVERING
CIVILITIES	CLAMBAKES	CLAPDISHES	CLASSED	CLAVERS
CIVILITY	CLAMBE	CLAPNET	CLASSES	CLAVES
CIVILIZE	CLAMBER	CLAPNETS	CLASSIBLE	CLAVICLE
CIVILIZED	CLAMBERED	CLAPPED	CLASSIC	CLAVICLES
CIVILIZER	CLAMBERING	CLAPPER	CLASSICAL	CLAVICORN
CIVILIZERS	CLAMBERS	CLAPPERED	CLASSICS	CLAVICORNS
CIVILIZES	CLAME	CLAPPERING	CLASSIER	CLAVICULA
CIVILIZING	CLAMES	CLAPPERINGS	CLASSIEST	CLAVICULAS
CIVILLY	CLAMMED	CLAPPERS	CLASSIFIC	CLAVIE
CIVISM	CLAMMIER	CLAPPING	CLASSIFIED	CLAVIER
CIVISMS	CLAMMIEST	CLAPPINGS	CLASSIFIES	CLAVIERS
CIVVIES	CLAMMILY	CLAPS	CLASSIFY	CLAVIES
CIVVY	CLAMMING	CLAPTRAP	CLASSIFYING	CLAVIFORM
CIZERS	CLAMMY	CLAPTRAPS	CLASSING	CLAVIGER
CLABBER	CLAMOR	CLAQUE	CLASSIS	CLAVIGERS
CLABBERS	CLAMORED	CLAQUES	CLASSLESS	CLAVIS
CLACHAN	CLAMORING	CLAQUEUR	CLASSMAN	CLAVULATE
CLACHANS	CLAMOROUS	CLAQUEURS	CLASSMATE	CLAW
CLACK	CLAMORS	CLARENCE	CLASSMATES	CLAWBACK
CLACKBOX	CLAMOUR	CLARENCES	CLASSMEN	CLAWBACKS
CLACKBOXES	CLAMOURED	CLARENDON	CLASSROOM	CLAWED
CLACKDISH	CLAMOURER	CLARENDONS	CLASSROOMS	CLAWING
CLACKDISHES	CLAMOURERS	CLARET	CLASSY	CLAWLESS
CLACKED	CLAMOURING	CLARETED	CLASTIC	CLAWS
CLACKER	CLAMOURS	CLARETING	CLAT	CLAY
CLACKERS	CLAMP	CLARETS	CLATCH	CLAYED
CLACKING	CLAMPDOWN	CLARIES	CLATCHED	CLAYEY
CLACKS	CLAMPDOWNS	CLARIFIED	CLATCHES	CLAYIER
CLAD	CLAMPED	CLARIFIER	CLATCHING	CLAYIEST
CLADDED	CLAMPER	CLARIFIERS	CLATHRATE	CLAYING
CLADDER	CLAMPERED	CLARIFIES	CLATS	CLAYISH
CLADDERS	CLAMPERING	CLARIFY	CLATTED	CLAYMORE
CLADDING	CLAMPERS	CLARIFYING	CLATTER	CLAYMORES
CLADDINGS	CLAMPING	CLARINET	CLATTERED	CLAYPAN
CLADE	CLAMPS	CLARINETS	CLATTERER	CLAYPANS
CLADES	CLAMS	CLARINI	CLATTERERS	CLAYS
CLADISM	CLAN	CLARINO	CLATTERING	CLEAN
CLADISMS	CLANG	CLARINOS	CLATTERS	CLEANED
CLADIST	CLANGED	CLARION	CLATTING	CLEANER
CLADISTIC	CLANGER	CLARIONET	CLAUCHT	CLEANERS
CLADISTICS	CLANGERS	CLARIONETS	CLAUCHTED	CLEANEST
CLADISTS	CLANGING	CLARIONS	CLAUCHTING	CLEANING
CLADODE	CLANGINGS	CLARITIES	CLAUCHTS	CLEANINGS
CLADODES	CLANGOR	CLARITY	CLAUGHT	CLEANLIER
CLADOGRAM	CLANGORED	CLARKIA	CLAUGHTED	CLEANLIEST
CLADOGRAMS	CLANGORING	CLARKIAS	CLAUGHTING	CLEANLY
CLADS	CLANGORS	CLARSACH	CLAUGHTS	CLEANNESS
CLAES	CLANGOUR	CLARSACHS	CLAUSAL	CLEANNESSES
CLAG	CLANGOURED	CLART	CLAUSE	CLEANS
CLAGGED	CLANGOURING	CLARTED	CLAUSES	CLEANSE
CLAGGIER	CLANGOURS	CLARTIER	CLAUSTRA	CLEANSED

CLEANSER
CLEANSERS
CLEANSES
CLEANSING
CLEANSINGS
CLEANSKIN
CLEANSKINS
CLEAR
CLEARAGE
CLEARAGES
CLEARANCE
CLEARANCES
CLEARCOLE
CLEARCOLES
CLEARED
CLEARER
CLEARERS
CLEAREST
CLEARING
CLEARINGS
CLEARLY
CLEARNESS
CLEARNESSES
CLEARS
CLEARSKIN
CLEARSKINS
CLEARWAY
CLEARWAYS
CLEARWING
CLEARWINGS
CLEAT
CLEATED
CLEATING
CLEATS
CLEAVABLE
CLEAVAGE
CLEAVAGES
CLEAVE
CLEAVED
CLEAVER
CLEAVERS
CLEAVES
CLEAVING
CLEAVINGS
CLECHÉ
CLECK
CLECKED
CLECKING
CLECKINGS
CLECKS
CLEEK
CLEEKED
CLEEKING
CLEEKIT
CLEEKS
CLEEP
CLEEPED
CLEEPING
CLEEPS
CLEEVE
CLEEVES
CLEF
CLEFS
CLEFT
CLEFTS
CLEG
CLEGS
CLEITHRAL
CLEM
CLEMATIS

CLEMATISES
CLEMENCE
CLEMENCES
CLEMENCIES
CLEMENCY
CLEMENT
CLEMENTLY
CLEMMED
CLEMMING
CLEMS
CLENCH
CLENCHED
CLENCHES
CLENCHING
CLEPE
CLEPED
CLEPES
CLEPING
CLEPSYDRA
CLEPSYDRAS
CLERECOLE
CLERECOLES
CLERGIES
CLERGY
CLERGYMAN
CLERGYMEN
CLERIC
CLERICAL
CLERICALS
CLERICATE
CLERICATES
CLERICITIES
CLERICITY
CLERICS
CLERIHEW
CLERIHEWS
CLERISIES
CLERISY
CLERK
CLERKDOM
CLERKDOMS
CLERKED
CLERKESS
CLERKESSES
CLERKING
CLERKISH
CLERKLESS
CLERKLIER
CLERKLIEST
CLERKLING
CLERKLINGS
CLERKLY
CLERKS
CLERKSHIP
CLERKSHIPS
CLERUCH
CLERUCHIA
CLERUCHIAS
CLERUCHIES
CLERUCHS
CLERUCHY
CLEUCH
CLEUCHS
CLEUGH
CLEUGHS
CLEVE
CLEVEITE
CLEVEITES
CLEVER
CLEVERER

CLEVEREST
CLEVERISH
CLEVERLY
CLEVES
CLEVIS
CLEVISES
CLEW
CLEWED
CLEWING
CLEWS
CLIANTHUS
CLIANTHUSES
CLICHÉ
CLICHÉD
CLICHÉS
CLICK
CLICKED
CLICKER
CLICKERS
CLICKET
CLICKETED
CLICKETING
CLICKETS
CLICKING
CLICKINGS
CLICKS
CLIED
CLIENT
CLIENTAGE
CLIENTAGES
CLIENTAL
CLIENTÈLE
CLIENTÈLES
CLIENTS
CLIES
CLIFF
CLIFFED
CLIFFHANG
CLIFFHANGING
CLIFFHANGINGS
CLIFFHANGS
CLIFFHUNG
CLIFFIER
CLIFFIEST
CLIFFS
CLIFFY
CLIFT
CLIFTED
CLIFTIER
CLIFTIEST
CLIFTS
CLIFTY
CLIMACTIC
CLIMATAL
CLIMATE
CLIMATED
CLIMATES
CLIMATIC
CLIMATING
CLIMATISE
CLIMATISED
CLIMATISES
CLIMATISING
CLIMATIZE
CLIMATIZED
CLIMATIZES
CLIMATIZING
CLIMATURE
CLIMATURES
CLIMAX

CLIMAXED
CLIMAXES
CLIMAXING
CLIMB
CLIMBABLE
CLIMBED
CLIMBER
CLIMBERS
CLIMBING
CLIMBINGS
CLIMBS
CLIME
CLIMES
CLINAMEN
CLINAMENS
CLINCH
CLINCHED
CLINCHER
CLINCHERS
CLINCHES
CLINCHING
CLINE
CLINES
CLING
CLINGER
CLINGERS
CLINGIER
CLINGIEST
CLINGING
CLINGS
CLINGY
CLINIC
CLINICAL
CLINICIAN
CLINICIANS
CLINICS
CLINIQUE
CLINIQUES
CLINK
CLINKED
CLINKER
CLINKERS
CLINKING
CLINKS
CLINOAXES
CLINOAXIS
CLINQUANT
CLINQUANTS
CLINT
CLINTS
CLIP
CLIPBOARD
CLIPBOARDS
CLIPE
CLIPED
CLIPES
CLIPING
CLIPPED
CLIPPER
CLIPPERS
CLIPPIE
CLIPPIES
CLIPPING
CLIPPINGS
CLIPS
CLIPT
CLIQUE
CLIQUES
CLIQUEY
CLIQUIER

CLIQUIEST
CLIQUISH
CLIQUISM
CLIQUISMS
CLIQUY
CLITELLA
CLITELLAR
CLITELLUM
CLITHRAL
CLITIC
CLITICS
CLITORAL
CLITORIS
CLITORISES
CLITTER
CLITTERED
CLITTERING
CLITTERS
CLIVERS
CLOACA
CLOACAE
CLOACAL
CLOACALIN
CLOACINAL
CLOAK
CLOAKED
CLOAKING
CLOAKROOM
CLOAKROOMS
CLOAKS
CLOAM
CLOAMS
CLOBBER
CLOBBERED
CLOBBERING
CLOBBERS
CLOCHARD
CLOCHARDS
CLOCHE
CLOCHES
CLOCK
CLOCKED
CLOCKER
CLOCKERS
CLOCKING
CLOCKS
CLOCKWISE
CLOCKWORK
CLOCKWORKS
CLOD
CLODDED
CLODDIER
CLODDIEST
CLODDING
CLODDISH
CLODDY
CLODPATE
CLODPATED
CLODPATES
CLODPOLE
CLODPOLES
CLODPOLL
CLODPOLLS
CLODS
CLOFF
CLOFFS
CLOG
CLOGDANCE
CLOGDANCES

CLOGGED
CLOGGER
CLOGGERS
CLOGGIER
CLOGGIEST
CLOGGING
CLOGGY
CLOGS
CLOISON
CLOISONNÉ
CLOISONNÉS
CLOISONS
CLOISTER
CLOISTERED
CLOISTERING
CLOISTERS
CLOISTRAL
CLOKE
CLOKED
CLOKES
CLOKING
CLOMB
CLONAL
CLONE
CLONED
CLONES
CLONIC
CLONING
CLONK
CLONKED
CLONKING
CLONKS
CLONUS
CLONUSES
CLOOP
CLOOPS
CLOOT
CLOOTS
CLOP
CLOPPED
CLOPPING
CLOPS
CLOQUÉ
CLOQUÉS
CLOSE
CLOSED
CLOSELY
CLOSENESS
CLOSENESSES
CLOSER
CLOSERS
CLOSES
CLOSEST
CLOSET
CLOSETED
CLOSETING
CLOSETS
CLOSING
CLOSINGS
CLOSURE
CLOSURED
CLOSURES
CLOSURING
CLOT
CLOTBUR
CLOTBURS
CLOTE
CLOTEBUR
CLOTEBURS
CLOTES

CLOTH
CLOTHE
CLOTHED
CLOTHES
CLOTHIER
CLOTHIERS
CLOTHING
CLOTHINGS
CLOTHS
CLOTPOLL
CLOTPOLLS
CLOTS
CLOTTED
CLOTTER
CLOTTERED
CLOTTERING
CLOTTERS
CLOTTIER
CLOTTIEST
CLOTTING
CLOTTINGS
CLOTTY
CLOTURE
CLOTURED
CLOTURES
CLOTURING
CLOU
CLOUD
CLOUDAGE
CLOUDAGES
CLOUDED
CLOUDIER
CLOUDIEST
CLOUDILY
CLOUDING
CLOUDINGS
CLOUDLAND
CLOUDLANDS
CLOUDLESS
CLOUDLET
CLOUDLETS
CLOUDS
CLOUDY
CLOUGH
CLOUGHS
CLOUR
CLOURED
CLOURING
CLOURS
CLOUS
CLOUT
CLOUTED
CLOUTER
CLOUTERLY
CLOUTERS
CLOUTING
CLOUTS
CLOVE
CLOVEN
CLOVER
CLOVERED
CLOVERS
CLOVERY
CLOVES
CLOW
CLOWDER
CLOWDERS
CLOWN
CLOWNED
CLOWNERIES

CLOWNERY
CLOWNING
CLOWNINGS
CLOWNISH
CLOWNS
CLOWNSHIP
CLOWNSHIPS
CLOWS
CLOY
CLOYE
CLOYED
CLOYES
CLOYING
CLOYLESS
CLOYMENT
CLOYMENTS
CLOYS
CLOYSOME
CLOZE
CLUB
CLUBABLE
CLUBBABLE
CLUBBED
CLUBBING
CLUBBINGS
CLUBBISH
CLUBBISM
CLUBBISMS
CLUBBIST
CLUBBISTS
CLUBHOUSE
CLUBHOUSES
CLUBLAND
CLUBLANDS
CLUBMAN
CLUBMEN
CLUBROOM
CLUBROOMS
CLUBROOT
CLUBROOTS
CLUBS
CLUBWOMAN
CLUBWOMEN
CLUCK
CLUCKED
CLUCKIER
CLUCKIEST
CLUCKS
CLUCKY
CLUDGIE
CLUDGIES
CLUE
CLUED
CLUEING
CLUELESS
CLUES
CLUING
CLUMBER
CLUMBERS
CLUMP
CLUMPED
CLUMPIER
CLUMPIEST
CLUMPING
CLUMPS
CLUMPY
CLUMSIER
CLUMSIEST
CLUMSILY

CLUMSY
CLUNCH
CLUNCHES
CLUNG
CLUNK
CLUNKED
CLUNKING
CLUNKS
CLUPEID
CLUPEIDS
CLUPEOID
CLUPEOIDS
CLUSIA
CLUSIAS
CLUSTER
CLUSTERED
CLUSTERING
CLUSTERS
CLUSTERY
CLUTCH
CLUTCHED
CLUTCHES
CLUTCHING
CLUTTER
CLUTTERED
CLUTTERING
CLUTTERS
CLY
CLYING
CLYPE
CLYPEAL
CLYPEATE
CLYPED
CLYPEI
CLYPES
CLYPEUS
CLYPING
CLYSTER
CLYSTERS
CNIDA
CNIDAE
CNIDARIA
COACH
COACHDOG
COACHDOGS
COACHED
COACHEE
COACHEES
COACHER
COACHERS
COACHES
COACHIES
COACHING
COACHINGS
COACHMAN
COACHMEN
COACHWHIP
COACHWHIPS
COACHWORK
COACHWORKS
COACHY
COACT
COACTED
COACTING
COACTION
COACTIONS
COACTIVE
COACTS
COADJUTOR
COADJUTORS

COADUNATE
COADUNATED
COADUNATES
COADUNATING
COAGULANT
COAGULANTS
COAGULATE
COAGULATED
COAGULATES
COAGULATING
COAGULUM
COAGULUMS
COAITA
COAITAS
COAL
COALBALL
COALBALLS
COALED
COALER
COALERS
COALESCE
COALESCED
COALESCES
COALESCING
COALFIELD
COALFIELDS
COALFISH
COALFISHES
COALIER
COALIEST
COALING
COALISE
COALISED
COALISES
COALISING
COALITION
COALITIONS
COALIZE
COALIZED
COALIZES
COALIZING
COALMAN
COALMEN
COALS
COALY
COAMING
COAMINGS
COAPT
COAPTED
COAPTING
COAPTS
COARB
COARBS
COARCTATE
COARSE
COARSELY
COARSEN
COARSENED
COARSENING
COARSENS
COARSER
COARSEST
COARSISH
COAST
COASTAL
COASTED
COASTER
COASTERS
COASTING
COASTINGS

OASTLINE	COBURG	COCKERED	COCOA	COELOMATE
OASTLINES	COBURGS	COCKEREL	COCOANUT	COELOMATES
OASTS	COBWEB	COCKERELS	COCOANUTS	COELOME
OASTWARD	COBWEBBED	COCKERING	COCOAS	COELOMES
OASTWARDS	COBWEBBIER	COCKERS	COCONUT	COELOMIC
OASTWISE	COBWEBBIEST	COCKET	COCONUTS	COELOMS
OAT	COBWEBBING	COCKETS	COCOON	COELOSTAT
OATE	COBWEBBY	COCKEYE	COCOONED	COELOSTATS
OATED	COBWEBS	COCKEYED	COCOONERIES	COEMPTION
OATEE	COCA	COCKEYES	COCOONERY	COEMPTIONS
OATEES	COCAINE	COCKFIGHT	COCOONING	COENOBIA
OATER	COCAINES	COCKFIGHTS	COCOONS	COENOBITE
OATERS	COCAINISE	COCKHORSE	COCOPLUM	COENOBITES
OATES	COCAINISED	COCKHORSES	COCOPLUMS	COENOBIUM
OATI	COCAINISES	COCKIER	COCOS	COENOSARC
OATING	COCAINISING	COCKIES	COCOTTE	COENOSARCS
OATINGS	COCAINISM	COCKIEST	COCOTTES	COENZYME
OATIS	COCAINISMS	COCKILY	COCTILE	COENZYMES
OATLESS	COCAINIST	COCKINESS	COCTION	COEQUAL
OATRACK	COCAINISTS	COCKINESSES	COCTIONS	COEQUALLY
OATRACKS	COCAINIZE	COCKING	COD	COEQUALS
OATS	COCAINIZED	COCKLAIRD	CODA	COERCE
OATSTAND	COCAINIZES	COCKLAIRDS	CODAS	COERCED
OATSTANDS	COCAINIZING	COCKLE	CODDED	COERCES
OAX	COCAS	COCKLED	CODDING	COERCIBLE
OAXED	COCCAL	COCKLES	CODDLE	COERCIBLY
OAXER	COCCI	COCKLING	CODDLED	COERCING
OAXERS	COCCID	COCKLOFT	CODDLES	COERCION
OAXES	COCCIDIA	COCKLOFTS	CODDLING	COERCIONS
OAXIAL	COCCIDIUM	COCKMATCH	CODE	COERCIVE
OAXIALLY	COCCIDS	COCKMATCHES	CODED	COEVAL
OAXING	COCCO	COCKNEY	CODEINE	COEVALS
OAXINGLY	COCCOID	COCKNEYFIED	CODEINES	COFF
OB	COCCOLITE	COCKNEYFIES	CODES	COFFEE
OBALT	COCCOLITES	COCKNEYFY	CODEX	COFFEES
OBALTIC	COCCOLITH	COCKNEYFYING	CODFISH	COFFER
OBALTITE	COCCOLITHS	COCKNEYS	CODFISHES	COFFERED
OBALTITES	COCCOS	COCKPIT	CODGER	COFFERING
OBALTS	COCCUS	COCKPITS	CODGERS	COFFERS
OBB	COCCYGEAL	COCKROACH	CODICES	COFFIN
OBBED	COCCYGES	COCKROACHES	CODICIL	COFFINED
OBBER	COCCYGIAN	COCKS	CODICILS	COFFING
OBBERS	COCCYX	COCKSCOMB	CODIFIED	COFFINING
OBBIER	COCH	COCKSCOMBS	CODIFIER	COFFINITE
OBBIEST	COCHES	COCKSFOOT	CODIFIERS	COFFINITES
OBBING	COCHINEAL	COCKSFOOTS	CODIFIES	COFFINS
OBBLE	COCHINEALS	COCKSHIES	CODIFY	COFFLE
OBBLED	COCHLEA	COCKSHOOT	CODIFYING	COFFLES
OBBLER	COCHLEAE	COCKSHOOTS	CODILLA	COFFRET
OBBLERIES	COCHLEAR	COCKSHOT	CODILLAS	COFFRETS
OBBLERS	COCHLEARE	COCKSHOTS	CODILLE	COFFS
OBBLERY	COCHLEARES	COCKSHUT	CODILLES	COFT
OBBLES	COCHLEARS	COCKSHUTS	CODING	COG
OBBLING	COCHLEAS	COCKSHY	CODINGS	COGENCE
OBBLINGS	COCHLEATE	COCKSIER	CODIST	COGENCES
OBBS	COCK	COCKSIEST	CODISTS	COGENCIES
OBBY	COCKADE	COCKSPUR	CODLIN	COGENCY
OBIA	COCKADES	COCKSPURS	CODLING	COGENER
OBIAS	COCKATEEL	COCKSURE	CODLINGS	COGENERS
OBLE	COCKATEELS	COCKSWAIN	CODLINS	COGENT
OBLES	COCKATIEL	COCKSWAINED	CODON	COGENTLY
OBLOAF	COCKATIELS	COCKSWAINING	CODONS	COGGED
OBLOAVES	COCKATOO	COCKSWAINS	CODS	COGGER
OBNUT	COCKATOOS	COCKSY	COED	COGGERS
OBNUTS	COCKBIRD	COCKTAIL	COEDS	COGGIE
OBRA	COCKBIRDS	COCKTAILS	COEHORN	COGGIES
OBRAS	COCKBOAT	COCKY	COEHORNS	COGGING
OBRIC	COCKBOATS	COCKYOLLIES	COELIAC	COGGLE
OBRIFORM	COCKED	COCKYOLLY	COELIACS	COGGLED
OBS	COCKER	COCO	COELOM	COGGLES

COGGLIER
COGGLIEST
COGGLING
COGGLY
COGIE
COGIES
COGITABLE
COGITATE
COGITATED
COGITATES
COGITATING
COGNATE
COGNATES
COGNATION
COGNATIONS
COGNISANT
COGNISE
COGNISED
COGNISES
COGNISING
COGNITION
COGNITIONS
COGNITIVE
COGNIZANT
COGNIZE
COGNIZED
COGNIZES
COGNIZING
COGNOMEN
COGNOMENS
COGNOMINA
COGNOSCE
COGNOSCED
COGNOSCES
COGNOSCING
COGNOVIT
COGNOVITS
COGS
COGUE
COGUES
COHABIT
COHABITED
COHABITEE
COHABITEES
COHABITING
COHABITS
COHERE
COHERED
COHERENCE
COHERENCES
COHERENCIES
COHERENCY
COHERENT
COHERER
COHERERS
COHERES
COHERING
COHERITOR
COHERITORS
COHESIBLE
COHESION
COHESIONS
COHESIVE
COHIBIT
COHIBITED
COHIBITING
COHIBITS
COHO
COHOE
COHOES

COHOG
COHOGS
COHORN
COHORNS
COHORT
COHORTS
COHOS
COHUNE
COHUNES
COIF
COIFED
COIFFEUR
COIFFEURS
COIFFEUSE
COIFFEUSES
COIFFURE
COIFFURED
COIFFURES
COIFFURING
COIFING
COIFS
COIGN
COIGNE
COIGNED
COIGNES
COIGNING
COIGNS
COIL
COILED
COILING
COILS
COIN
COINAGE
COINAGES
COINCIDE
COINCIDED
COINCIDES
COINCIDING
COINED
COINER
COINERS
COINING
COININGS
COINS
COIR
COIRS
COISTREL
COISTRELS
COISTRIL
COISTRILS
COITAL
COITION
COITIONS
COITUS
COITUSES
COJOIN
COJOINED
COJOINING
COJOINS
COKE
COKED
COKERNUT
COKERNUTS
COKES
COKESES
COKIER
COKIEST
COKING
COKY
COL

COLA
COLANDER
COLANDERS
COLAS
COLATION
COLATIONS
COLATURE
COLATURES
COLCANNON
COLCANNONS
COLCHICA
COLCHICUM
COLCHICUMS
COLCOTHAR
COLCOTHARS
COLD
COLDBLOOD
COLDBLOODS
COLDER
COLDEST
COLDHOUSE
COLDHOUSES
COLDISH
COLDLY
COLDNESS
COLDNESSES
COLDS
COLE
COLES
COLEUS
COLEUSES
COLEY
COLEYS
COLIBRI
COLIBRIS
COLIC
COLICKY
COLICS
COLIFORM
COLIFORMS
COLIN
COLINS
COLISEUM
COLISEUMS
COLITIS
COLITISES
COLL
COLLAGE
COLLAGEN
COLLAGENS
COLLAGES
COLLAGIST
COLLAGISTS
COLLAPSE
COLLAPSED
COLLAPSES
COLLAPSING
COLLAR
COLLARD
COLLARDS
COLLARED
COLLARING
COLLARS
COLLATE
COLLATED
COLLATES
COLLATING
COLLATION
COLLATIONS
COLLATIVE

COLLATOR
COLLATORS
COLLEAGUE
COLLEAGUED
COLLEAGUES
COLLEAGUING
COLLECT
COLLECTED
COLLECTING
COLLECTINGS
COLLECTOR
COLLECTORS
COLLECTS
COLLED
COLLEEN
COLLEENS
COLLEGE
COLLEGER
COLLEGERS
COLLEGES
COLLEGIA
COLLEGIAL
COLLEGIAN
COLLEGIANS
COLLEGIUM
COLLEGIUMS
COLLET
COLLETS
COLLIDE
COLLIDED
COLLIDES
COLLIDING
COLLIE
COLLIED
COLLIER
COLLIERIES
COLLIERS
COLLIERY
COLLIES
COLLIGATE
COLLIGATED
COLLIGATES
COLLIGATING
COLLIMATE
COLLIMATED
COLLIMATES
COLLIMATING
COLLINEAR
COLLING
COLLINGS
COLLISION
COLLISIONS
COLLOCATE
COLLOCATED
COLLOCATES
COLLOCATING
COLLODION
COLLODIONS
COLLOGUE
COLLOGUED
COLLOGUES
COLLOGUING
COLLOID
COLLOIDAL
COLLOIDS
COLLOP
COLLOPS
COLLOQUE
COLLOQUED
COLLOQUES

COLLOQUIA
COLLOQUIED
COLLOQUIES
COLLOQUING
COLLOQUY
COLLOQUYING
COLLOTYPE
COLLOTYPES
COLLS
COLLUDE
COLLUDED
COLLUDER
COLLUDERS
COLLUDES
COLLUDING
COLLUSION
COLLUSIONS
COLLUSIVE
COLLUVIES
COLLY
COLLYING
COLLYRIA
COLLYRIUM
COLLYRIUMS
COLOBI
COLOBUS
COLOBUSES
COLOCYNTH
COLOCYNTHS
COLON
COLONEL
COLONELCIES
COLONELCY
COLONELS
COLONES
COLONIAL
COLONIALS
COLONIC
COLONICS
COLONIES
COLONISE
COLONISED
COLONISES
COLONISING
COLONIST
COLONISTS
COLONIZE
COLONIZED
COLONIZES
COLONIZING
COLONNADE
COLONNADES
COLONS
COLONY
COLOPHON
COLOPHONIES
COLOPHONS
COLOPHONY
COLOR
COLORANT
COLORANTS
COLORED
COLORIFIC
COLORING
COLORS
COLOSSAL
COLOSSEUM
COLOSSEUMS
COLOSSI
COLOSSUS

COLOSSUSES
COLOSTOMIES
COLOSTOMY
COLOSTRIC
COLOSTRUM
COLOSTRUMS
COLOTOMIES
COLOTOMY
COLOUR
COLOURANT
COLOURANTS
COLOURED
COLOUREDS
COLOURER
COLOURERS
COLOURFUL
COLOURING
COLOURINGS
COLOURIST
COLOURISTS
COLOURMAN
COLOURMEN
COLOURS
COLOURY
COLS
COLT
COLTED
COLTER
COLTERS
COLTING
COLTISH
COLTS
COLTSFOOT
COLTSFOOTS
COLTWOOD
COLTWOODS
COLUBER
COLUBERS
COLUBRIAD
COLUBRIADS
COLUBRINE
COLUGO
COLUGOS
COLUMBARIES
COLUMBARY
COLUMBATE
COLUMBATES
COLUMBIC
COLUMBINE
COLUMBINES
COLUMDITE
COLUMBITES
COLUMBIUM
COLUMBIUMS
COLUMEL
COLUMELLA
COLUMELLAE
COLUMELS
COLUMN
COLUMNAL
COLUMNAR
COLUMNED
COLUMNIST
COLUMNISTS
COLUMNS
COLURE
COLURES
COLZA
COLZAS
COMA

COMAE
COMAL
COMARB
COMARBS
COMART
COMARTS
COMAS
COMATE
COMATES
COMATOSE
COMB
COMBAT
COMBATANT
COMBATANTS
COMBATED
COMBATING
COMBATIVE
COMBATS
COMBE
COMBED
COMBER
COMBERS
COMBES
COMBIER
COMBIEST
COMBINATE
COMBINE
COMBINED
COMBINES
COMBING
COMBINGS
COMBINING
COMBLE
COMBLES
COMBLOOM
COMBO
COMBOS
COMBRETUM
COMBRETUMS
COMBS
COMBUST
COMBUSTED
COMBUSTING
COMBUSTS
COMBWISE
COMBY
COME
COMEDIAN
COMEDIANS
COMEDIC
COMEDIES
COMEDO
COMEDOS
COMEDOWN
COMEDOWNS
COMEDY
COMELIER
COMELIEST
COMELY
COMER
COMERS
COMES
COMET
COMETARY
COMETHER
COMETHERS
COMETIC
COMETS
COMFIER
COMFIEST

COMFIT
COMFITS
COMFITURE
COMFITURES
COMFORT
COMFORTED
COMFORTER
COMFORTERS
COMFORTING
COMFORTS
COMFREY
COMFREYS
COMFY
COMIC
COMICAL
COMICALLY
COMICS
COMING
COMINGS
COMIQUE
COMIQUES
COMITADJI
COMITADJIS
COMITAL
COMITATUS
COMITATUSES
COMITIA
COMITIES
COMITY
COMMA
COMMAND
COMMANDED
COMMANDER
COMMANDERS
COMMANDING
COMMANDO
COMMANDOS
COMMANDS
COMMAS
COMMENCE
COMMENCED
COMMENCES
COMMENCING
COMMEND
COMMENDAM
COMMENDAMS
COMMENDED
COMMENDING
COMMENDS
COMMENSAL
COMMENSALS
COMMENT
COMMENTED
COMMENTER
COMMENTERS
COMMENTING
COMMENTOR
COMMENTORS
COMMENTS
COMMER
COMMERCE
COMMERCED
COMMERCES
COMMERCING
COMMÈRE
COMMÈRES
COMMERGE
COMMERGED
COMMERGES
COMMERGING

COMMERS
COMMIE
COMMIES
COMMINATE
COMMINATED
COMMINATES
COMMINATING
COMMINGLE
COMMINGLED
COMMINGLES
COMMINGLING
COMMINUTE
COMMINUTED
COMMINUTES
COMMINUTING
COMMIS
COMMISSAR
COMMISSARS
COMMIT
COMMITS
COMMITTAL
COMMITTALS
COMMITTED
COMMITTEE
COMMITTEES
COMMITTING
COMMIX
COMMIXED
COMMIXES
COMMIXING
COMMO
COMMODE
COMMODES
COMMODITIES
COMMODITY
COMMODORE
COMMODORES
COMMON
COMMONAGE
COMMONAGES
COMMONED
COMMONER
COMMONERS
COMMONEST
COMMONEY
COMMONEYS
COMMONING
COMMONLY
COMMONS
COMMORANT
COMMORANTS
COMMOS
COMMOT
COMMOTE
COMMOTES
COMMOTION
COMMOTIONS
COMMOTS
COMMOVE
COMMOVED
COMMOVES
COMMOVING
COMMUNAL
COMMUNARD
COMMUNARDS
COMMUNE
COMMUNED
COMMUNES
COMMUNING
COMMUNINGS

COMMUNION
COMMUNIONS
COMMUNISE
COMMUNISED
COMMUNISES
COMMUNISING
COMMUNISM
COMMUNISMS
COMMUNIST
COMMUNISTS
COMMUNITIES
COMMUNITY
COMMUNIZE
COMMUNIZED
COMMUNIZES
COMMUNIZING
COMMUTATE
COMMUTATED
COMMUTATES
COMMUTATING
COMMUTE
COMMUTED
COMMUTER
COMMUTERS
COMMUTES
COMMUTING
COMMUTUAL
COMOSE
COMOUS
COMP
COMPACT
COMPACTED
COMPACTER
COMPACTEST
COMPACTING
COMPACTLY
COMPACTOR
COMPACTORS
COMPACTS
COMPAGE
COMPAGES
COMPANDER
COMPANDERS
COMPANDOR
COMPANDORS
COMPANIED
COMPANIES
COMPANING
COMPANION
COMPANIONED
COMPANIONING
COMPANIONS
COMPANY
COMPANYING
COMPARE
COMPARED
COMPARES
COMPARING
COMPART
COMPARTED
COMPARTING
COMPARTS
COMPASS
COMPASSED
COMPASSES
COMPASSING
COMPASSINGS
COMPAST
COMPEAR
COMPEARED

COMPEARING
COMPEARS
COMPEER
COMPEERED
COMPEERING
COMPEERS
COMPEL
COMPELLED
COMPELLING
COMPELS
COMPEND
COMPENDIA
COMPENDS
COMPERE
COMPERED
COMPERES
COMPERING
COMPESCE
COMPESCED
COMPESCES
COMPESCING
COMPETE
COMPETED
COMPETENT
COMPETES
COMPETING
COMPILE
COMPILED
COMPILER
COMPILERS
COMPILES
COMPILING
COMPITAL
COMPLAIN
COMPLAINED
COMPLAINING
COMPLAININGS
COMPLAINS
COMPLAINT
COMPLAINTS
COMPLEAT
COMPLECT
COMPLECTED
COMPLECTING
COMPLECTS
COMPLETE
COMPLETED
COMPLETER
COMPLETES
COMPLETEST
COMPLETING
COMPLEX
COMPLEXED
COMPLEXER
COMPLEXES
COMPLEXEST
COMPLEXING
COMPLEXLY
COMPLEXUS
COMPLEXUSES
COMPLIANT
COMPLICE
COMPLICES
COMPLIED
COMPLIER
COMPLIERS
COMPLIES
COMPLIN
COMPLINE
COMPLINES

COMPLINS
COMPLISH
COMPLISHED
COMPLISHES
COMPLISHING
COMPLOT
COMPLOTS
COMPLOTTED
COMPLOTTING
COMPLUVIA
COMPLY
COMPLYING
COMPO
COMPONÉ
COMPONENT
COMPONENTS
COMPONY
COMPORT
COMPORTED
COMPORTING
COMPORTS
COMPOS
COMPOSE
COMPOSED
COMPOSER
COMPOSERS
COMPOSES
COMPOSING
COMPOSITE
COMPOSITED
COMPOSITES
COMPOSITING
COMPOST
COMPOSTED
COMPOSTER
COMPOSTERS
COMPOSTING
COMPOSTS
COMPOSURE
COMPOSURES
COMPOT
COMPOTE
COMPOTES
COMPOTIER
COMPOTIERS
COMPOTS
COMPOUND
COMPOUNDED
COMPOUNDING
COMPOUNDS
COMPRADOR
COMPRADORS
COMPRESS
COMPRESSED
COMPRESSES
COMPRESSING
COMPRINT
COMPRINTED
COMPRINTING
COMPRINTS
COMPRISAL
COMPRISALS
COMPRISE
COMPRISED
COMPRISES
COMPRISING
COMPS
COMPT
COMPTABLE
COMPTED

COMPTER
COMPTERS
COMPTIBLE
COMPTING
COMPTROLL
COMPTROLLED
COMPTROLLING
COMPTROLLS
COMPTS
COMPULSE
COMPULSED
COMPULSES
COMPULSING
COMPUTANT
COMPUTANTS
COMPUTE
COMPUTED
COMPUTER
COMPUTERS
COMPUTES
COMPUTING
COMPUTIST
COMPUTISTS
COMRADE
COMRADELY
COMRADES
COMS
COMUS
COMUSES
CON
CONACRE
CONACRED
CONACRES
CONACRING
CONARIA
CONARIAL
CONARIUM
CONATION
CONATIONS
CONATIVE
CONATUS
CONCAUSE
CONCAUSES
CONCAVE
CONCAVED
CONCAVELY
CONCAVES
CONCAVING
CONCAVITIES
CONCAVITY
CONCEAL
CONCEALED
CONCEALING
CONCEALS
CONCEDE
CONCEDED
CONCEDER
CONCEDERS
CONCEDES
CONCEDING
CONCEIT
CONCEITED
CONCEITING
CONCEITS
CONCEITY
CONCEIVE
CONCEIVED
CONCEIVES
CONCEIVING
CONCENT

CONCENTED
CONCENTER
CONCENTERED
CONCENTERING
CONCENTERS
CONCENTING
CONCENTRE
CONCENTRED
CONCENTRES
CONCENTRING
CONCENTS
CONCEPT
CONCEPTI
CONCEPTS
CONCEPTUS
CONCEPTUSES
CONCERN
CONCERNED
CONCERNING
CONCERNS
CONCERT
CONCERTED
CONCERTING
CONCERTO
CONCERTOS
CONCERTS
CONCETTI
CONCETTO
CONCH
CONCHA
CONCHAE
CONCHATE
CONCHE
CONCHED
CONCHES
CONCHIE
CONCHIES
CONCHING
CONCHITIS
CONCHITISES
CONCHOID
CONCHOIDS
CONCHS
CONCHY
CONCIERGE
CONCIERGES
CONCILIAR
CONCISE
CONCISED
CONCISELY
CONCISER
CONCISES
CONCISEST
CONCISING
CONCISION
CONCISIONS
CONCLAVE
CONCLAVES
CONCLUDE
CONCLUDED
CONCLUDES
CONCLUDING
CONCOCT
CONCOCTED
CONCOCTER
CONCOCTERS
CONCOCTING
CONCOCTOR
CONCOCTORS
CONCOCTS

CONCOLOR
CONCORD
CONCORDAT
CONCORDATS
CONCORDED
CONCORDING
CONCORDS
CONCOURS
CONCOURSE
CONCOURSES
CONCREATE
CONCREATED
CONCREATES
CONCREATING
CONCRETE
CONCRETED
CONCRETES
CONCRETING
CONCREW
CONCREWED
CONCREWING
CONCREWS
CONCUBINE
CONCUBINES
CONCUPIES
CONCUPY
CONCUR
CONCURRED
CONCURRING
CONCURS
CONCUSS
CONCUSSED
CONCUSSES
CONCUSSING
CONCYCLIC
COND
CONDEMN
CONDEMNED
CONDEMNING
CONDEMNS
CONDENSE
CONDENSED
CONDENSER
CONDENSERS
CONDENSES
CONDENSING
CONDER
CONDERS
CONDIDDLE
CONDIDDLED
CONDIDDLES
CONDIDDLING
CONDIGN
CONDIGNLY
CONDIMENT
CONDIMENTED
CONDIMENTING
CONDIMENTS
CONDITION
CONDITIONED
CONDITIONING
CONDITIONINGS
CONDITIONS
CONDOLE
CONDOLED
CONDOLENT
CONDOLES
CONDOLING
CONDOM
CONDOMS

CONDONE
CONDONED
CONDONES
CONDONING
CONDOR
CONDORS
CONDUCE
CONDUCED
CONDUCES
CONDUCING
CONDUCIVE
CONDUCT
CONDUCTED
CONDUCTI
CONDUCTING
CONDUCTOR
CONDUCTORS
CONDUCTS
CONDUCTUS
CONDUIT
CONDUITS
CONDYLAR
CONDYLE
CONDYLES
CONDYLOID
CONDYLOMA
CONDYLOMATA
CONE
CONED
CONES
CONEY
CONEYS
CONFAB
CONFABBED
CONFABBING
CONFABS
CONFECT
CONFECTED
CONFECTING
CONFECTS
CONFER
CONFEREE
CONFEREES
CONFERRED
CONFERRER
CONFERRERS
CONFERRING
CONFERS
CONFERVA
CONFERVAE
CONFESS
CONFESSED
CONFESSES
CONFESSING
CONFESSOR
CONFESSORS
CONFEST
CONFESTLY
CONFETTI
CONFIDANT
CONFIDANTS
CONFIDE
CONFIDED
CONFIDENT
CONFIDENTS
CONFIDER
CONFIDERS
CONFIDES
CONFIDING
CONFIGURE

CONFIGURED
CONFIGURES
CONFIGURING
CONFINE
CONFINED
CONFINER
CONFINERS
CONFINES
CONFINING
CONFIRM
CONFIRMED
CONFIRMEE
CONFIRMEES
CONFIRMER
CONFIRMERS
CONFIRMING
CONFIRMINGS
CONFIRMOR
CONFIRMORS
CONFIRMS
CONFISEUR
CONFISEURS
CONFIT
CONFITEOR
CONFITEORS
CONFITS
CONFITURE
CONFITURES
CONFIX
CONFIXED
CONFIXES
CONFIXING
CONFLATE
CONFLATED
CONFLATES
CONFLATING
CONFLICT
CONFLICTED
CONFLICTING
CONFLICTS
CONFLUENT
CONFLUENTS
CONFLUX
CONFLUXES
CONFORM
CONFORMAL
CONFORMED
CONFORMER
CONFORMERS
CONFORMING
CONFORMS
CONFOUND
CONFOUNDED
CONFOUNDING
CONFOUNDS
CONFRÈRE
CONFRÈRES
CONFRÉRIE
CONFRÉRIES
CONFRONT
CONFRONTÉ
CONFRONTED
CONFRONTING
CONFRONTS
CONFUSE
CONFUSED
CONFUSES
CONFUSING
CONFUSION
CONFUSIONS

CONFUTE
CONFUTED
CONFUTES
CONFUTING
CONGA
CONGAED
CONGAING
CONGAS
CONGÉ
CONGEAL
CONGEALED
CONGEALING
CONGEALS
CONGÉD
CONGEE
CONGEED
CONGEEING
CONGEES
CONGÉING
CONGENER
CONGENERS
CONGENIAL
CONGER
CONGERIES
CONGERS
CONGERY
CONGÉS
CONGEST
CONGESTED
CONGESTING
CONGESTS
CONGIARIES
CONGIARY
CONGLOBE
CONGLOBED
CONGLOBES
CONGLOBING
CONGO
CONGOS
CONGOU
CONGOUS
CONGREE
CONGREED
CONGREEING
CONGREES
CONGREET
CONGREETED
CONGREETING
CONGREETS
CONGRESS
CONGRESSED
CONGRESSES
CONGRESSING
CONGRUE
CONGRUED
CONGRUENT
CONGRUES
CONGRUING
CONGRUITIES
CONGRUITY
CONGRUOUS
CONIA
CONIAS
CONIC
CONICAL
CONICALLY
CONICS
CONIDIA
CONIDIAL
CONIDIUM

CONIES
CONIFER
CONIFERS
CONIFORM
CONIINE
CONIINES
CONIMA
CONIMAS
CONINE
CONINES
CONING
CONJECT
CONJECTED
CONJECTING
CONJECTS
CONJEE
CONJEED
CONJEEING
CONJEES
CONJOIN
CONJOINED
CONJOINING
CONJOINS
CONJOINT
CONJUGAL
CONJUGANT
CONJUGANTS
CONJUGATE
CONJUGATED
CONJUGATES
CONJUGATING
CONJUGATINGS
CONJUNCT
CONJURE
CONJURED
CONJURER
CONJURERS
CONJURES
CONJURIES
CONJURING
CONJURINGS
CONJUROR
CONJURORS
CONJURY
CONK
CONKED
CONKER
CONKERS
CONKIES
CONKING
CONKS
CONKY
CONN
CONNATE
CONNATION
CONNATIONS
CONNATURE
CONNATURES
CONNE
CONNECT
CONNECTED
CONNECTER
CONNECTERS
CONNECTING
CONNECTOR
CONNECTORS
CONNECTS
CONNED
CONNER
CONNERS

CONNES
CONNEXION
CONNEXIONS
CONNEXIVE
CONNING
CONNINGS
CONNIVE
CONNIVED
CONNIVENT
CONNIVER
CONNIVERS
CONNIVES
CONNIVING
CONNOTATE
CONNOTATED
CONNOTATES
CONNOTATING
CONNOTE
CONNOTED
CONNOTES
CONNOTING
CONNOTIVE
CONNS
CONNUBIAL
CONODONT
CONODONTS
CONOID
CONOIDAL
CONOIDIC
CONOIDS
CONQUER
CONQUERED
CONQUERING
CONQUEROR
CONQUERORS
CONQUERS
CONQUEST
CONQUESTS
CONS
CONSCIENT
CONSCIOUS
CONSCIOUSES
CONSCRIBE
CONSCRIBED
CONSCRIBES
CONSCRIBING
CONSCRIPT
CONSCRIPTED
CONSCRIPTING
CONSCRIPTS
CONSEIL
CONSEILS
CONSENSUS
CONSENSUSES
CONSENT
CONSENTED
CONSENTING
CONSENTS
CONSERVE
CONSERVED
CONSERVER
CONSERVERS
CONSERVES
CONSERVING
CONSIDER
CONSIDERED
CONSIDERING
CONSIDERINGS
CONSIDERS
CONSIGN

CONSIGNED
CONSIGNEE
CONSIGNEES
CONSIGNER
CONSIGNERS
CONSIGNING
CONSIGNOR
CONSIGNORS
CONSIGNS
CONSIST
CONSISTED
CONSISTING
CONSISTS
CONSOLATE
CONSOLATED
CONSOLATES
CONSOLATING
CONSOLE
CONSOLED
CONSOLER
CONSOLERS
CONSOLES
CONSOLING
CONSOLS
CONSOMMÉ
CONSOMMÉS
CONSONANT
CONSONANTS
CONSONOUS
CONSORT
CONSORTED
CONSORTER
CONSORTERS
CONSORTIA
CONSORTING
CONSORTS
CONSPIRE
CONSPIRED
CONSPIRER
CONSPIRERS
CONSPIRES
CONSPIRING
CONSTABLE
CONSTABLES
CONSTANCIES
CONSTANCY
CONSTANT
CONSTANTS
CONSTATE
CONSTATED
CONSTATES
CONSTATING
CONSTER
CONSTERED
CONSTERING
CONSTERS
CONSTRAIN
CONSTRAINED
CONSTRAINING
CONSTRAINS
CONSTRICT
CONSTRICTED
CONSTRICTING
CONSTRICTS
CONSTRUCT
CONSTRUCTED
CONSTRUCTING
CONSTRUCTS
CONSTRUE
CONSTRUED

CONSTRUER
CONSTRUERS
CONSTRUES
CONSTRUING
CONSUL
CONSULAGE
CONSULAGES
CONSULAR
CONSULARS
CONSULATE
CONSULATES
CONSULS
CONSULT
CONSULTA
CONSULTAS
CONSULTED
CONSULTEE
CONSULTEES
CONSULTER
CONSULTERS
CONSULTING
CONSULTOR
CONSULTORS
CONSULTS
CONSUME
CONSUMED
CONSUMER
CONSUMERS
CONSUMES
CONSUMING
CONSUMINGS
CONSUMPT
CONSUMPTS
CONTACT
CONTACTED
CONTACTING
CONTACTOR
CONTACTORS
CONTACTS
CONTADINA
CONTADINAS
CONTADINE
CONTADINI
CONTADINO
CONTAGION
CONTAGIONS
CONTAGIUM
CONTAGIUMS
CONTAIN
CONTAINED
CONTAINER
CONTAINERS
CONTAINING
CONTAINS
CONTANGO
CONTANGOED
CONTANGOING
CONTANGOS
CONTE
CONTECK
CONTECKS
CONTEMN
CONTEMNED
CONTEMNER
CONTEMNERS
CONTEMNING
CONTEMNOR
CONTEMNORS
CONTEMNS
CONTEMPER

CONTEMPERED
CONTEMPERING
CONTEMPERS
CONTEMPT
CONTEMPTS
CONTEND
CONTENDED
CONTENDER
CONTENDERS
CONTENDING
CONTENDINGS
CONTENDS
CONTENT
CONTENTED
CONTENTING
CONTENTS
CONTES
CONTEST
CONTESTED
CONTESTER
CONTESTERS
CONTESTING
CONTESTS
CONTEXT
CONTEXTS
CONTICENT
CONTINENT
CONTINENTS
CONTINUA
CONTINUAL
CONTINUE
CONTINUED
CONTINUER
CONTINUERS
CONTINUES
CONTINUING
CONTINUO
CONTINUOS
CONTINUUM
CONTLINE
CONTLINES
CONTO
CONTORNO
CONTORNOS
CONTORT
CONTORTED
CONTORTING
CONTORTS
CONTOS
CONTOUR
CONTOURED
CONTOURING
CONTOURS
CONTRA
CONTRACT
CONTRACTED
CONTRACTING
CONTRACTS
CONTRAIL
CONTRAILS
CONTRAIR
CONTRALTI
CONTRALTO
CONTRALTOS
CONTRARIED
CONTRARIES
CONTRARY
CONTRARYING
CONTRAS
CONTRAST

CONTRASTED
CONTRASTING
CONTRASTS
CONTRASTY
CONTRATE
CONTRIST
CONTRISTED
CONTRISTING
CONTRISTS
CONTRITE
CONTRIVE
CONTRIVED
CONTRIVER
CONTRIVERS
CONTRIVES
CONTRIVING
CONTROL
CONTROLLED
CONTROLLING
CONTROLS
CONTROUL
CONTROULED
CONTROULING
CONTROULS
CONTUMACIES
CONTUMACY
CONTUMELIES
CONTUMELY
CONTUND
CONTUNDED
CONTUNDING
CONTUNDS
CONTUSE
CONTUSED
CONTUSES
CONTUSING
CONTUSION
CONTUSIONS
CONTUSIVE
CONUNDRUM
CONUNDRUMS
CONURBAN
CONURBIA
CONURBIAS
CONVECTOR
CONVECTORS
CONVENE
CONVENED
CONVENER
CONVENERS
CONVENES
CONVENING
CONVENOR
CONVENORS
CONVENT
CONVENTED
CONVENTING
CONVENTS
CONVERGE
CONVERGED
CONVERGES
CONVERGING
CONVERSE
CONVERSED
CONVERSES
CONVERSING
CONVERT
CONVERTED
CONVERTER
CONVERTERS

CONVERTING
CONVERTOR
CONVERTORS
CONVERTS
CONVEX
CONVEXED
CONVEXES
CONVEXITIES
CONVEXITY
CONVEXLY
CONVEY
CONVEYAL
CONVEYALS
CONVEYED
CONVEYER
CONVEYERS
CONVEYING
CONVEYOR
CONVEYORS
CONVEYS
CONVICT
CONVICTED
CONVICTING
CONVICTS
CONVINCE
CONVINCED
CONVINCES
CONVINCING
CONVIVE
CONVIVED
CONVIVES
CONVIVIAL
CONVIVING
CONVOCATE
CONVOCATED
CONVOCATES
CONVOCATING
CONVOKE
CONVOKED
CONVOKES
CONVOKING
CONVOLUTE
CONVOLVE
CONVOLVED
CONVOLVES
CONVOLVING
CONVOY
CONVOYED
CONVOYING
CONVOYS
CONVULSE
CONVULSED
CONVULSES
CONVULSING
CONY
COO
COOED
COOEE
COOEED
COOEEING
COOEES
COOEY
COOEYED
COOEYING
COOEYS
COOF
COOFS
COOING
COOINGLY
COOINGS

COOK
COOKABLE
COOKED
COOKER
COOKERIES
COOKERS
COOKERY
COOKHOUSE
COOKHOUSES
COOKIE
COOKIES
COOKING
COOKMAID
COOKMAIDS
COOKOUT
COOKOUTS
COOKROOM
COOKROOMS
COOKS
COOKSHOP
COOKSHOPS
COOKWARE
COOKWARES
COOKY
COOL
COOLABAH
COOLABAHS
COOLABAR
COOLABARS
COOLAMON
COOLAMONS
COOLANT
COOLANTS
COOLED
COOLER
COOLERS
COOLEST
COOLIBAH
COOLIBAHS
COOLIBAR
COOLIBARS
COOLIE
COOLIES
COOLING
COOLISH
COOLLY
COOLNESS
COOLNESSES
COOLS
COOLTH
COOLTHS
COOLY
COOM
COOMB
COOMBS
COOMED
COOMIER
COOMIEST
COOMING
COOMS
COOMY
COON
COONS
COONTIE
COONTIES
COONTY
COOP
COOPED
COOPER
COOPERAGE

COOPERAGES
COOPERANT
COOPERATE
COOPERATED
COOPERATES
COOPERATING
COOPERED
COOPERIES
COOPERING
COOPERINGS
COOPERS
COOPERY
COOPING
COOPS
COOS
COOSEN
COOSENED
COOSENING
COOSENS
COOSER
COOSERS
COOSIN
COOSINED
COOSINING
COOSINS
COOST
COOT
COOTIKIN
COOTIKINS
COOTS
COP
COPACETIC
COPAIBA
COPAIBAS
COPAIVA
COPAIVAS
COPAL
COPALS
COPARTNER
COPARTNERS
COPATAINE
COPATRIOT
COPATRIOTS
COPE
COPECK
COPECKS
COPED
COPEPOD
COPEPODS
COPER
COPERED
COPERING
COPERS
COPES
COPIED
COPIER
COPIERS
COPIES
COPILOT
COPILOTS
COPING
COPINGS
COPIOUS
COPIOUSLY
COPITA
COPITAS
COPPED
COPPER
COPPERAS
COPPERASES

COPPERED
COPPERING
COPPERINGS
COPPERISH
COPPERS
COPPERY
COPPICE
COPPICED
COPPICES
COPPICING
COPPICINGS
COPPIES
COPPIN
COPPING
COPPINS
COPPLE
COPPLES
COPPY
COPRA
COPRAS
COPRESENT
COPROLITE
COPROLITES
COPROLOGIES
COPROLOGY
COPS
COPSE
COPSED
COPSES
COPSEWOOD
COPSEWOODS
COPSIER
COPSIEST
COPSING
COPSY
COPULA
COPULAR
COPULAS
COPULATE
COPULATED
COPULATES
COPULATING
COPY
COPYBOOK
COPYBOOKS
COPYHOLD
COPYHOLDS
COPYING
COPYISM
COPYISMS
COPYIST
COPYISTS
COPYRIGHT
COPYRIGHTED
COPYRIGHTING
COPYRIGHTS
COQUET
COQUETRIES
COQUETRY
COQUETS
COQUETTE
COQUETTED
COQUETTES
COQUETTING
COQUILLA
COQUILLAS
COQUILLE
COQUILLES
COQUITO
COQUITOS

COR
CORACLE
CORACLES
CORACOID
CORACOIDS
CORAGGIO
CORAGGIOS
CORAL
CORALLA
CORALLINE
CORALLINES
CORALLITE
CORALLITES
CORALLOID
CORALLUM
CORALS
CORAMINE
CORAMINES
CORANACH
CORANACHS
CORANTO
CORANTOES
CORANTOS
CORBAN
CORBANS
CORBE
CORBEAU
CORBEAUS
CORBEIL
CORBEILLE
CORBEILLES
CORBEILS
CORBEL
CORBELLED
CORBELS
CORBES
CORBICULA
CORBICULAE
CORBIE
CORBIES
CORCASS
CORCASSES
CORD
CORDAGE
CORDAGES
CORDATE
CORDED
CORDIAL
CORDIALLY
CORDIALS
CORDIFORM
CORDINER
CORDINERS
CORDING
CORDINGS
CORDITE
CORDITES
CORDLESS
CÓRDOBA
CÓRDOBAS
CORDON
CORDONED
CORDONING
CORDONS
CORDOTOMIES
CORDOTOMY
CORDOVAN
CORDOVANS
CORDS
CORDUROY

CORDUROYS
CORDWAIN
CORDWAINS
CORDYLINE
CORDYLINES
CORE
CORED
CORELESS
CORELLA
CORELLAS
COREOPSIS
COREOPSISES
CORER
CORERS
CORES
CORF
CORGI
CORGIS
CORIA
CORIANDER
CORIANDERS
CORING
CORIOUS
CORIUM
CORIUMS
CORK
CORKAGE
CORKAGES
CORKED
CORKER
CORKERS
CORKIER
CORKIEST
CORKINESS
CORKINESSES
CORKING
CORKIR
CORKIRS
CORKS
CORKWING
CORKWINGS
CORKWOOD
CORKWOODS
CORKY
CORM
CORMORANT
CORMORANTS
CORMOUS
CORMS
CORMUS
CORMUSES
CORN
CORNACRE
CORNACRES
CORNAGE
CORNAGES
CORNBRASH
CORNBRASHES
CORNCRAKE
CORNCRAKES
CORNEA
CORNEAL
CORNEAS
CORNED
CORNEL
CORNELIAN
CORNELIANS
CORNELS
CORNEMUSE
CORNEMUSES

CORNEOUS
CORNER
CORNERED
CORNERING
CORNERS
CORNET
CORNETCIES
CORNETCY
CORNETIST
CORNETISTS
CORNETS
CORNETT
CORNETTI
CORNETTO
CORNETTS
CORNFIELD
CORNFIELDS
CORNFLIES
CORNFLOUR
CORNFLOURS
CORNFLY
CORNHUSK
CORNHUSKS
CORNI
CORNICE
CORNICED
CORNICES
CORNICHE
CORNICHES
CORNICING
CORNICLE
CORNICLES
CORNIER
CORNIEST
CORNIFIC
CORNIFORM
CORNING
CORNIST
CORNISTS
CORNLAND
CORNLANDS
CORNLOFT
CORNLOFTS
CORNO
CORNOPEAN
CORNOPEANS
CORNPIPE
CORNPIPES
CORNS
CORNSTALK
CORNSTALKS
CORNSTONE
CORNSTONES
CORNU
CORNUA
CORNUAL
CORNUTE
CORNUTED
CORNUTES
CORNUTING
CORNUTO
CORNUTOS
CORNWORM
CORNWORMS
CORNY
COROCORE
COROCORES
COROCORO
COROCOROS
CORODIES

CORODY
COROLLA
COROLLARIES
COROLLARY
COROLLAS
COROLLINE
CORONA
CORONACH
CORONACHS
CORONAE
CORONAL
CORONALS
CORONARIES
CORONARY
CORONAS
CORONATE
CORONATED
CORONER
CORONERS
CORONET
CORONETED
CORONETS
CORONIS
CORONISES
CORONIUM
CORONIUMS
CORONOID
COROZO
COROZOS
CORPORA
CORPORAL
CORPORALS
CORPORAS
CORPORASES
CORPORATE
CORPOREAL
CORPORIFIED
CORPORIFIES
CORPORIFY
CORPORIFYING
CORPOSANT
CORPOSANTS
CORPS
CORPSE
CORPSED
CORPSES
CORPSING
CORPULENT
CORPUS
CORPUSCLE
CORPUSCLES
CORRADE
CORRADED
CORRADES
CORRADING
CORRAL
CORRALLED
CORRALLING
CORRALS
CORRASION
CORRASIONS
CORRECT
CORRECTED
CORRECTER
CORRECTEST
CORRECTING
CORRECTLY
CORRECTOR
CORRECTORS
CORRECTS

CORRELATE
CORRELATED
CORRELATES
CORRELATING
CORRIDA
CORRIDAS
CORRIDOR
CORRIDORS
CORRIE
CORRIES
CORRIGENT
CORRIGENTS
CORRIVAL
CORRIVALLED
CORRIVALLING
CORRIVALS
CORRODE
CORRODED
CORRODENT
CORRODENTS
CORRODES
CORRODIES
CORRODING
CORRODY
CORROSION
CORROSIONS
CORROSIVE
CORROSIVES
CORRUGATE
CORRUGATED
CORRUGATES
CORRUGATING
CORRUPT
CORRUPTED
CORRUPTER
CORRUPTERS
CORRUPTEST
CORRUPTING
CORRUPTLY
CORRUPTS
CORS
CORSAGE
CORSAGES
CORSAIR
CORSAIRS
CORSE
CORSELET
CORSELETS
CORSES
CORSET
CORSETED
CORSETIER
CORSETIERS
CORSETING
CORSETRIES
CORSETRY
CORSETS
CORSIVE
CORSIVES
CORSLET
CORSLETED
CORSLETS
CORSNED
CORSNEDS
CORSO
CORSOS
CORTÈGE
CORTÈGES
CORTEX
CORTEXES

CORTICAL
CORTICATE
CORTICES
CORTICOID
CORTICOIDS
CORTILE
CORTILES
CORTISOL
CORTISOLS
CORTISONE
CORTISONES
CORUNDUM
CORUNDUMS
CORUSCANT
CORUSCATE
CORUSCATED
CORUSCATES
CORUSCATING
CORVÉE
CORVÉES
CORVES
CORVET
CORVETED
CORVETING
CORVETS
CORVETTE
CORVETTED
CORVETTES
CORVETTING
CORVID
CORVIDS
CORVINE
CORVUS
CORVUSES
CORYBANT
CORYBANTES
CORYBANTS
CORYMB
CORYMBOSE
CORYMBS
CORYPHAEI
CORYPHE
CORYPHEE
CORYPHEES
CORYPHENE
CORYPHENES
CORYPHES
CORYZA
CORYZAS
COS
COSE
COSECANT
COSECANTS
COSECH
COSECHS
COSED
COSEISMAL
COSEISMIC
COSES
COSH
COSHED
COSHER
COSHERED
COSHERER
COSHERERS
COSHERIES
COSHERING
COSHERINGS
COSHERS
COSHERY

COSHES
COSHING
COSIER
COSIERS
COSIES
COSIEST
COSILY
COSINE
COSINES
COSINESS
COSINESSES
COSING
COSMEA
COSMEAS
COSMESES
COSMESIS
COSMETIC
COSMETICS
COSMIC
COSMICAL
COSMISM
COSMISMS
COSMIST
COSMISTS
COSMOCRAT
COSMOCRATS
COSMOGENIES
COSMOGENY
COSMOGONIES
COSMOGONY
COSMOLOGIES
COSMOLOGY
COSMONAUT
COSMONAUTS
COSMORAMA
COSMORAMAS
COSMOS
COSMOSES
COSMOTRON
COSMOTRONS
COSPONSOR
COSPONSORED
COSPONSORING
COSPONSORS
COSS
COSSES
COSSET
COSSETED
COSSETING
COSSETS
COSSIE
COSSIES
COST
COSTA
COSTAE
COSTAL
COSTALS
COSTARD
COSTARDS
COSTATE
COSTATED
COSTE
COSTEAN
COSTEANED
COSTEANING
COSTEANINGS
COSTEANS
COSTED
COSTER
COSTERS

COSTES
COSTING
COSTIVE
COSTIVELY
COSTLIER
COSTLIEST
COSTLY
COSTMARIES
COSTMARY
COSTREL
COSTRELS
COSTS
COSTUME
COSTUMED
COSTUMER
COSTUMERS
COSTUMES
COSTUMIER
COSTUMIERS
COSTUMING
COSTUS
COSTUSES
COSY
COT
COTANGENT
COTANGENTO
COTE
COTEAU
COTEAUX
COTED
CÔTELETTE
CÔTELETTES
COTELINE
COTELINES
COTERIE
CÔTERIES
COTES
COTH
COTHS
COTHURN
COTHURNI
COTHURNS
COTHURNUS
COTICULAR
COTILLION
COTILLIONS
COTILLON
COTILLONS
COTING
COTINGA
COTINGAS
COTISE
COTISED
COTISES
COTISING
COTLAND
COTLANDS
COTQUEAN
COTQUEANS
COTS
COTT
COTTA
COTTABUS
COTTABUSES
COTTAGE
COTTAGED
COTTAGER
COTTAGERS
COTTAGES
COTTAGEY

COTTAR
COTTARS
COTTAS
COTTED
COTTER
COTTERS
COTTIER
COTTIERS
COTTISE
COTTISED
COTTISES
COTTISING
COTTOID
COTTOIDS
COTTON
COTTONADE
COTTONADES
COTTONED
COTTONING
COTTONS
COTTONY
COTTOWN
COTTOWNS
COTTS
COTWAL
COTWAL
OOTWALO
COTYLAE
COTYLE
COTYLEDON
COTYLEDONS
COTYLES
COTYLOID
COUCAL
COUCALS
COUCH
COUCHANT
COUCHÉ
COUCHED
COUCHEE
COUCHÉE
COUCHEES
COUCHÉES
COUCHÉS
COUCHES
COUCHETTE
COUCHETTES
COUCHING
COUCHINGS
COUDÉ
COUGAR
COUGARS
COUGH
COUGHED
COUGHER
COUGHERS
COUGHING
COUGHINGS
COUGHS
COUGUAR
COUGUARS
COULD
COULÉE
COULÉES
COULIS
COULISSE
COULISSES
COULOIR
COULOIRS
COULOMB
COULOMBS

COULTER
COULTERS
COUMARIC
COUMARIN
COUMARINS
COUNCIL
COUNCILOR
COUNCILORS
COUNCILS
COUNSEL
COUNSELLED
COUNSELLING
COUNSELLINGS
COUNSELS
COUNT
COUNTABLE
COUNTED
COUNTER
COUNTERED
COUNTERING
COUNTERS
COUNTESS
COUNTESSES
COUNTIES
COUNTING
COUNTLESS
COUNTRIES
COUNTROL
COUNTROLLED
COUNTROLLING
COUNTROLS
COUNTRY
COUNTS
COUNTSHIP
COUNTSHIPS
COUNTY
COUP
COUPE
COUPÉ
COUPED
COUPEE
COUPEES
COUPER
COUPERS
COUPES
COUPÉS
COUPING
COUPLE
COUPLED
COUPLER
COUPLERS
COUPLES
COUPLET
COUPLETS
COUPLING
COUPLINGS
COUPON
COUPONS
COUPS
COUPURE
COUPURES
COUR
COURAGE
COURAGES
COURANT
COURANTE
COURANTES
COURANTS
COURB
COURBARIL

COURBARILS
COURBED
COURBETTE
COURBETTES
COURBING
COURBS
COURD
COURE
COURED
COURES
COURGETTE
COURGETTES
COURIER
COURIERS
COURING
COURLAN
COURLANS
COURS
COURSE
COURSED
COURSER
COURSERS
COURSES
COURSING
COURSINGS
COURT
COURTED
COURTEOUS
COURTESAN
COURTESANS
COURTESIED
COURTESIES
COURTESY
COURTESYING
COURTEZAN
COURTEZANS
COURTIER
COURTIERS
COURTING
COURTINGS
COURTLET
COURTLETS
COURTLIER
COURTLIEST
COURTLIKE
COURTLING
COURTLINGS
COURTLY
COURTROOM
COURTROOMS
COURTS
COURTSHIP
COURTSHIPS
COURTYARD
COURTYARDS
COUSCOUS
COUSCOUSES
COUSIN
COUSINAGE
COUSINAGES
COUSINLY
COUSINRIES
COUSINRY
COUSINS
COUTER
COUTERS
COUTH
COUTHER
COUTHEST
COUTHIE

COUTHIER
COUTHIEST
COUTHY
COUTIL
COUTILLE
COUTILLES
COUTILS
COUTURE
COUTURES
COUTURIER
COUTURIERS
COUVADE
COUVADES
COUVERT
COUVERTS
COVALENCIES
COVALENCY
COVALENT
COVARIANT
COVARIANTS
COVARIED
COVARIES
COVARY
COVARYING
COVE
COVED
COVELET
COVELETS
COVELLITE
COVELLITES
COVEN
COVENANT
COVENANTED
COVENANTING
COVENANTO
COVENS
COVENT
COVENTS
COVER
COVERAGE
COVERAGES
COVERALL
COVERALLS
COVERED
COVERING
COVERINGS
COVERLET
COVERLETS
COVERLID
COVERLIDS
COVERS
COVERSLIP
COVERSLIPS
COVERT
COVERTLY
COVERTS
COVERTURE
COVERTURES
COVES
COVET
COVETABLE
COVETED
COVETING
COVETISE
COVETISES
COVETOUS
COVETS
COVEY
COVEYS
COVIN

COVING
COVINGS
COVINOUS
COVINS
COVYNE
COVYNES
COW
COWAGE
COWAGES
COWAN
COWANS
COWARD
COWARDED
COWARDICE
COWARDICES
COWARDING
COWARDLY
COWARDREE
COWARDREES
COWARDRIES
COWARDRY
COWARDS
COWBANE
COWBANES
COWBELL
COWBELLS
COWBERRIES
COWBERRY
COWBIRD
COWBIRDS
COWBOY
COWBOYS
COWED
COWER
COWERED
COWERING
COWERS
COWFEEDER
COWFEEDERS
COWFISH
COWFISHES
COWGIRL
COWGIRLS
COWGRASS
COWGRASSES
COWHAGE
COWHAGES
COWHAND
COWHANDS
COWHEARD
COWHEARDS
COWHEEL
COWHEELS
COWHERD
COWHERDS
COWHIDE
COWHIDED
COWHIDES
COWHIDING
COWHOUSE
COWHOUSES
COWING
COWISH
COWITCH
COWITCHES
COWL
COWLED
COWLICK
COWLICKS
COWLING

COWLINGS
COWLS
COWMAN
COWMEN
COWP
COWPAT
COWPATS
COWPED
COWPING
COWPOKE
COWPOKES
COWPOX
COWPOXES
COWPS
COWRIE
COWRIES
COWRY
COWS
COWSHED
COWSHEDS
COWSLIP
COWSLIPS
COX
COXA
COXAE
COXAL
COXALGIA
COXALGIAS
COXCOMB
COXCOMBIC
COXCOMBRIES
COXCOMBRY
COXCOMBS
COXED
COXES
COXIER
COXIEST
COXINESS
COXINESSES
COXING
COXSWAIN
COXSWAINED
COXSWAINING
COXSWAINS
COXY
COY
COYED
COYER
COYEST
COYING
COYISH
COYISHLY
COYLY
COYNESS
COYNESSES
COYOTE
COYOTES
COYPU
COYPUS
COYS
COYSTREL
COYSTRELS
COYSTRIL
COYSTRILS
COZ
COZE
COZED
COZEN
COZENAGE
COZENAGES

COZENED
COZENER
COZENERS
COZENING
COZENS
COZES
COZIER
COZIERS
COZIES
COZIEST
COZING
COZY
COZZES
CRAB
CRABBED
CRABBEDLY
CRABBIER
CRABBIEST
CRABBILY
CRABBING
CRABBY
CRABLIKE
CRABS
CRABSTICK
CRABSTICKS
CRABWISE
CRACK
CRACKDOWN
CRACKDOWNS
CRACKED
CRACKER
CRACKERS
CRACKING
CRACKJAW
CRACKLE
CRACKLED
CRACKLES
CRACKLIER
CRACKLIEST
CRACKLING
CRACKLINGS
CRACKLY
CRACKNEL
CRACKNELS
CRACKPOT
CRACKPOTS
CRACKS
CRACKSMAN
CRACKSMEN
CRACOWE
CRACOWES
CRADLE
CRADLED
CRADLES
CRADLING
CRADLINGS
CRAFT
CRAFTED
CRAFTIER
CRAFTIEST
CRAFTILY
CRAFTING
CRAFTLESS
CRAFTS
CRAFTSMAN
CRAFTSMEN
CRAFTWORK
CRAFTWORKS
CRAFTY
CRAG

CRAGFAST
CRAGGED
CRAGGIER
CRAGGIEST
CRAGGY
CRAGS
CRAGSMAN
CRAGSMEN
CRAIG
CRAIGS
CRAKE
CRAKED
CRAKES
CRAKING
CRAM
CRAMBO
CRAMBOES
CRAME
CRAMES
CRAMESIES
CRAMESY
CRAMMABLE
CRAMMED
CRAMMER
CRAMMERS
CRAMMING
CRAMOISIES
CRAMOISY
CRAMP
CRAMPED
CRAMPET
CRAMPETS
CRAMPIER
CRAMPIEST
CRAMPING
CRAMPIT
CRAMPITS
CRAMPON
CRAMPONS
CRAMPS
CRAMPY
CRAMS
CRAN
CRANAGE
CRANAGES
CRANBERRIES
CRANBERRY
CRANCH
CRANCHED
CRANCHES
CRANCHING
CRANE
CRANED
CRANES
CRANIA
CRANIAL
CRANING
CRANIUM
CRANIUMS
CRANK
CRANKCASE
CRANKCASES
CRANKED
CRANKER
CRANKEST
CRANKIER
CRANKIEST
CRANKILY
CRANKING
CRANKLE

CRANKLED
CRANKLES
CRANKLING
CRANKNESS
CRANKNESSES
CRANKS
CRANKY
CRANNIED
CRANNIES
CRANNOG
CRANNOGS
CRANNY
CRANNYING
CRANREUCH
CRANREUCHS
CRANS
CRANTS
CRANTSES
CRAP
CRAPE
CRAPED
CRAPES
CRAPIER
CRAPIEST
CRAPING
CRAPLE
CRAPLES
CRAPPED
CRAPPING
CRAPS
CRAPULENT
CRAPULOUS
CRAPY
CRARE
CRARES
CRASES
CRASH
CRASHED
CRASHES
CRASHING
CRASHPAD
CRASHPADS
CRASIS
CRASS
CRASSER
CRASSEST
CRASSLY
CRASSNESS
CRASSNESSES
CRATCH
CRATCHES
CRATE
CRATED
CRATER
CRATEROUS
CRATERS
CRATES
CRATING
CRATON
CRATONS
CRATUR
CRATURS
CRAUNCH
CRAUNCHED
CRAUNCHES
CRAUNCHING
CRAVAT
CRAVATS
CRAVATTED
CRAVATTING

CRAVE
CRAVED
CRAVEN
CRAVENED
CRAVENING
CRAVENLY
CRAVENS
CRAVER
CRAVERS
CRAVES
CRAVING
CRAVINGS
CRAW
CRAWFISH
CRAWFISHES
CRAWL
CRAWLED
CRAWLER
CRAWLERS
CRAWLIER
CRAWLIEST
CRAWLING
CRAWLINGS
CRAWLS
CRAWLY
CRAWS
CRAYER
CRAYERS
CRAYFISH
CRAYFISHES
CRAYON
CRAYONED
CRAYONING
CRAYONS
CRAZE
CRAZED
CRAZES
CRAZIER
CRAZIES
CRAZIEST
CRAZILY
CRAZINESS
CRAZINESSES
CRAZING
CRAZY
CREACH
CREACHS
CREAGH
CREAGHS
CREAK
CREAKED
CREAKIER
CREAKIEST
CREAKILY
CREAKING
CREAKS
CREAKY
CREAM
CREAMED
CREAMER
CREAMERIES
CREAMERS
CREAMERY
CREAMIER
CREAMIEST
CREAMING
CREAMS
CREAMY
CREANCE
CREANCES

CREANT
CREASE
CREASED
CREASES
CREASIER
CREASIEST
CREASING
CREASOTE
CREASOTED
CREASOTES
CREASOTING
CREASY
CREATABLE
CREATE
CREATED
CREATES
CREATIC
CREATINE
CREATINES
CREATING
CREATION
CREATIONS
CREATIVE
CREATOR
CREATORS
CREATRESS
CREATRESSES
CREATRIX
CREATRIXES
CREATURAL
CREATURE
CREATURES
CRÈCHE
CRÈCHES
CREDAL
CREDENCE
CREDENCES
CREDENDA
CREDENDUM
CREDENT
CREDENZA
CREDENZAS
CREDIBLE
CREDIBLY
CREDIT
CREDITED
CREDITING
CREDITOR
CREDITORS
CREDITS
CREDO
CREDOS
CREDULITIES
CREDULITY
CREDULOUS
CREE
CREED
CREEDAL
CREEDS
CREEING
CREEK
CREEKIER
CREEKIEST
CREEKS
CREEKY
CREEL
CREELS
CREEP
CREEPER
CREEPERED

CREEPERS
CREEPIE
CREEPIER
CREEPIES
CREEPIEST
CREEPING
CREEPS
CREEPY
CREES
CREESE
CREESED
CREESES
CREESH
CREESHED
CREESHES
CREESHING
CREESHY
CREESING
CREMASTER
CREMASTERS
CREMATE
CREMATED
CREMATES
CREMATING
CREMATION
CREMATIONS
CREMATOR
CREMATORIES
CREMATORS
CREMATORY
CREME
CRÈME
CRÈMES
CRÈMES
CREMOCARP
CREMOCARPS
CREMONA
CREMONAS
CREMOR
CREMORNE
CREMORNES
CREMORS
CREMOSIN
CREMSIN
CRENA
CRENAS
CRENATE
CRENATED
CRENATION
CRENATIONS
CRENATURE
CRENATURES
CRENEL
CRENELATE
CRENELATED
CRENELATES
CRENELATING
CRENELLED
CRENELLING
CRENELS
CRENULATE
CREODONT
CREODONTS
CREOLE
CREOLES
CREOLIAN
CREOLIANS
CREOLIST
CREOLISTS
CREOSOTE

CREOSOTED
CREOSOTES
CREOSOTING
CREPANCE
CREPANCES
CRÊPE
CRÊPED
CRÊPES
CRÊPIER
CRÊPIEST
CRÊPING
CREPITANT
CREPITATE
CREPITATED
CREPITATES
CREPITATING
CREPITUS
CREPITUSES
CREPOLINE
CREPOLINES
CREPON
CREPONS
CREPT
CREPUSCLE
CREPUSCLES
CREPY
CRESCENDO
CRESCENDOED
CRESCENDOING
CRESCENDOS
CRESCENT
CRESCENTO
CRESCIVE
CRESOL
CRESOLS
CRESS
CRESSES
CRESSET
CRESSETS
CRESSIER
CRESSIEST
CRESSY
CREST
CRESTED
CRESTING
CRESTLESS
CRESTS
CRETIC
CRETICS
CRETIN
CRETINISM
CRETINISMS
CRETINOID
CRETINOUS
CRETINS
CRETISM
CRETISMS
CRETONNE
CRETONNES
CREUTZER
CREUTZERS
CREVASSE
CREVASSED
CREVASSES
CREVASSING
CREVICE
CREVICES
CREW
CREWE
CREWED

CREWEL
CREWELIST
CREWELISTS
CREWELLED
CREWELLING
CREWELS
CREWES
CREWING
CREWS
CRIANT
CRIB
CRIBBAGE
CRIBBAGES
CRIBBED
CRIBBING
CRIBBLE
CRIBBLED
CRIBBLES
CRIBBLING
CRIBELLA
CRIBELLAR
CRIBELLUM
CRIBLÉ
CRIBRATE
CRIBROSE
CRIBS
CRIBWORK
CRIBWORKS
CRICK
CRICKED
CRICKET
CRICKETED
CRICKETER
CRICKETERS
CRICKETING
CRICKETINGS
CRICKETS
CRICKEY
CRICKING
CRICKS
CRICKY
CRICOID
CRICOIDS
CRIED
CRIER
CRIERS
CRIES
CRIKEY
CRIME
CRIMED
CRIMEFUL
CRIMELESS
CRIMES
CRIMINAL
CRIMINALS
CRIMINATE
CRIMINATED
CRIMINATES
CRIMINATING
CRIMINE
CRIMING
CRIMINI
CRIMINOUS
CRIMMER
CRIMMERS
CRIMP
CRIMPED
CRIMPER
CRIMPERS
CRIMPIER

CRIMPIEST
CRIMPING
CRIMPLE
CRIMPLED
CRIMPLES
CRIMPLING
CRIMPS
CRIMPY
CRIMSON
CRIMSONED
CRIMSONING
CRIMSONS
CRINAL
CRINATE
CRINATED
CRINE
CRINED
CRINES
CRINGE
CRINGED
CRINGER
CRINGERS
CRINGES
CRINGING
CRINGINGS
CRINGLE
CRINGLES
CRINING
CRINITE
CRINITES
CRINKLE
CRINKLED
CRINKLES
CRINKLIER
CRINKLIES
CRINKLIEST
CRINKLING
CRINKLY
CRINOID
CRINOIDAL
CRINOIDS
CRINOLINE
CRINOLINES
CRINOSE
CRINUM
CRINUMS
CRIOLLO
CRIOLLOS
CRIPES
CRIPPLE
CRIPPLED
CRIPPLES
CRIPPLING
CRIPPLINGS
CRISE
CRISES
CRISIS
CRISP
CRISPATE
CRISPATED
CRISPED
CRISPER
CRISPERS
CRISPEST
CRISPIER
CRISPIEST
CRISPIN
CRISPING
CRISPINS
CRISPLY

CRISPNESS
CRISPNESSES
CRISPS
CRISPY
CRISSA
CRISSUM
CRISTA
CRISTAE
CRISTATE
CRIT
CRITERIA
CRITERION
CRITH
CRITHS
CRITIC
CRITICAL
CRITICISE
CRITICISED
CRITICISES
CRITICISING
CRITICISM
CRITICISMS
CRITICIZE
CRITICIZED
CRITICIZES
CRITICIZING
CRITICS
CRITIQUE
CRITIQUES
CRITS
CRITTER
CRITTERS
CRITTUR
CRITTURS
CRIVENS
CRIVVENS
CROAK
CROAKED
CROAKER
CROAKERS
CROAKIER
CROAKIEST
CROAKILY
CROAKING
CROAKINGS
CROAKS
CROAKY
CROC
CROCEATE
CROCEOUS
CROCHE
CROCHES
CROCHET
CROCHETED
CROCHETING
CROCHETINGS
CROCHETS
CROCK
CROCKED
CROCKERIES
CROCKERY
CROCKET
CROCKETS
CROCKING
CROCKS
CROCODILE
CROCODILES
CROCOITE
CROCOITES
CROCS

CROCUS
CROCUSES
CROFT
CROFTER
CROFTERS
CROFTING
CROFTINGS
CROFTS
CROISSANT
CROISSANTS
CROMACK
CROMACKS
CROMB
CROMBED
CROMBIE
CROMBIES
CROMBING
CROMBS
CROME
CROMED
CROMES
CROMING
CROMLECH
CROMLECHS
CROMORNA
CROMORNAS
CROMORNE
CROMORNES
CRONE
CRONES
CRONET
CRONETS
CRONIES
CRONK
CRONKER
CRONKEST
CRONY
CRONYISM
CRONYISMS
CROODLE
CROODLED
CROODLES
CROODLING
CROOK
CROOKBACK
CROOKBACKS
CROOKED
CROOKEDER
CROOKEDEST
CROOKEDLY
CROOKER
CROOKEST
CROOKING
CROOKS
CROON
CROONED
CROONER
CROONERS
CROONING
CROONINGS
CROONS
CROP
CROPBOUND
CROPFUL
CROPFULL
CROPFULS
CROPLAND
CROPLANDS
CROPPED
CROPPER

CROPPERS
CROPPIES
CROPPING
CROPPINGS
CROPPY
CROPS
CROPSICK
CROQUET
CROQUETED
CROQUETING
CROQUETS
CROQUETTE
CROQUETTES
CROQUIS
CRORE
CRORES
CROSIER
CROSIERED
CROSIERS
CROSS
CROSSBAND
CROSSBANDS
CROSSBAR
CROSSBARS
CROSSBEAM
CROSSBEAMS
CROSSBILL
CROSSBILLS
CROSSBIT
CROSSBITE
CROSSBITES
CROSSBITING
CROSSBITTEN
CROSSBOW
CROSSBOWS
CROSSBRED
CROSSCUT
CROSSCUTS
CROSSCUTTING
CROSSCUTTINGS
CROSSE
CROSSED
CROSSER
CROSSES
CROSSEST
CROSSETTE
CROSSETTES
CROSSFALL
CROSSFALLS
CROSSFIRE
CROSSFIRES
CROSSFISH
CROSSFISHES
CROSSING
CROSSINGS
CROSSISH
CROSSJACK
CROSSJACKS
CROSSLET
CROSSLETS
CROSSLY
CROSSNESS
CROSSNESSES
CROSSOVER
CROSSOVERS
CROSSROAD
CROSSROADS
CROSSTREE
CROSSTREES
CROSSWALK

CROSSWALKS
CROSSWAY
CROSSWAYS
CROSSWIND
CROSSWINDS
CROSSWISE
CROSSWORD
CROSSWORDS
CROSSWORT
CROSSWORTS
CROST
CROTAL
CROTALA
CROTALINE
CROTALISM
CROTALISMS
CROTALS
CROTALUM
CROTCH
CROTCHED
CROTCHES
CROTCHET
CROTCHETS
CROTCHETY
CROTON
CROTONS
CROTTLE
CROTTLES
CROUCH
CROUCHED
CROUCHES
CROUCHING
CROUP
CROUPADE
CROUPADES
CROUPE
CROUPED
CROUPER
CROUPERS
CROUPES
CROUPIER
CROUPIERS
CROUPIEST
CROUPING
CROUPON
CROUPONS
CROUPOUS
CROUPS
CROUPY
CROUSE
CROUSELY
CROUSTADE
CROUSTADES
CROUT
CROÛTE
CROÛTES
CROÛTON
CROÛTONS
CROUTS
CROW
CROWD
CROWDED
CROWDER
CROWDERS
CROWDIE
CROWDIES
CROWDING
CROWDS
CROWED
CROWFEET

CROWFOOT
CROWFOOTS
CROWING
CROWN
CROWNED
CROWNER
CROWNERS
CROWNET
CROWNETS
CROWNING
CROWNINGS
CROWNLESS
CROWNLET
CROWNLETS
CROWNS
CROWNWORK
CROWNWORKS
CROWS
CROZE
CROZES
CROZIER
CROZIERS
CRU
CRUBEEN
CRUBEENS
CRUCES
CRUCIAL
CRUCIAN
CRUCIANS
CRUCIATE
CRUCIATED
CRUCIATES
CRUCIATING
CRUCIBLE
CRUCIBLES
CRUCIFER
CRUCIFERS
CRUCIFIED
CRUCIFIER
CRUCIFIERS
CRUCIFIES
CRUCIFIX
CRUCIFIXES
CRUCIFORM
CRUCIFY
CRUCIFYING
CRUCK
CRUCKS
CRUD
CRUDDIER
CRUDDIEST
CRUDDLE
CRUDDLED
CRUDDLES
CRUDDLING
CRUDDY
CRUDE
CRUDELY
CRUDENESS
CRUDENESSES
CRUDER
CRUDES
CRUDEST
CRUDITÉS
CRUDITIES
CRUDITY
CRUDS
CRUDY
CRUE
CRUEL

CRUELLER
CRUELLEST
CRUELLS
CRUELLY
CRUELNESS
CRUELNESSES
CRUELS
CRUELTIES
CRUELTY
CRUES
CRUET
CRUETS
CRUISE
CRUISED
CRUISER
CRUISERS
CRUISES
CRUISEWAY
CRUISEWAYS
CRUISIE
CRUISIES
CRUISING
CRUIVE
CRUIVES
CRULLER
CRULLERS
CRUMB
CRUMBED
CRUMBIER
CRUMBIEST
CRUMBING
CRUMBLE
CRUMBLED
CRUMBLES
CRUMBLIER
CRUMBLIES
CRUMBLIEST
CRUMBLING
CRUMBLY
CRUMBS
CRUMBY
CRUMEN
CRUMENAL
CRUMENALS
CRUMENS
CRUMHORN
CRUMHORNS
CRUMMACK
CRUMMACKS
CRUMMIER
CRUMMIES
CRUMMIEST
CRUMMOCK
CRUMMOCKS
CRUMMY
CRUMP
CRUMPED
CRUMPER
CRUMPEST
CRUMPET
CRUMPETS
CRUMPIER
CRUMPIEST
CRUMPING
CRUMPLE
CRUMPLED
CRUMPLES
CRUMPLING
CRUMPLINGS
CRUMPS

CRUMPY
CRUNCH
CRUNCHED
CRUNCHES
CRUNCHIER
CRUNCHIEST
CRUNCHING
CRUNCHY
CRUNKLE
CRUNKLED
CRUNKLES
CRUNKLING
CRUOR
CRUORS
CRUPPER
CRUPPERS
CRURAL
CRUS
CRUSADE
CRUSADED
CRUSADER
CRUSADERS
CRUSADES
CRUSADING
CRUSADO
CRUSADOS
CRUSE
CRUSES
CRUSET
CRUSETS
CRUSH
CRUSHABLE
CRUSHED
CRUSHER
CRUSHERS
CRUSHES
CRUSHING
CRUSIAN
CRUSIANS
CRUSIE
CRUSIES
CRUST
CRUSTA
CRUSTAE
CRUSTAL
CRUSTATE
CRUSTATED
CRUSTED
CRUSTIER
CRUSTIEST
CRUSTILY
CRUSTING
CRUSTLESS
CRUSTS
CRUSTY
CRUTCH
CRUTCHED
CRUTCHES
CRUTCHING
CRUVE
CRUVES
CRUX
CRUXES
CRUZEIRO
CRUZEIROS
CRWTH
CRWTHS
CRY
CRYING

CRYINGS
CRYOGEN
CRYOGENIC
CRYOGENICS
CRYOGENIES
CRYOGENS
CRYOGENY
CRYOLITE
CRYOLITES
CRYOMETER
CRYOMETERS
CRYONIC
CRYONICS
CRYOPROBE
CRYOPROBES
CRYOSCOPE
CRYOSCOPES
CRYOSCOPY
CRYOSTAT
CRYOSTATS
CRYOTRON
CRYOTRONS
CRYPT
CRYPTADIA
CRYPTAL
CRYPTIC
CRYPTICAL
CRYPTO
CRYPTOGAM
CRYPTOGAMS
CRYPTON
CRYPTONS
CRYPTONYM
CRYPTONYMS
CRYPTOS
CRYPTS
CRYSTAL
CRYSTALS
CSARDAS
CSÁRDÁSES
CTENE
CTENES
CTENIFORM
CTENOID
CUB
CUBAGE
CUBAGES
CUBATURE
CUBATURES
CUBBED
CUBBIES
CUBBING
CUBBINGS
CUBBISH
CUBBY
CUBE
CUBEB
CUBEBS
CUBED
CUBES
CUBHOOD
CUBHOODS
CUBIC
CUBICA
CUBICAL
CUBICALLY
CUBICAS
CUBICLE
CUBICLES

CUBIFORM
CUBING
CUBISM
CUBISMS
CUBIST
CUBISTS
CUBIT
CUBITAL
CUBITS
CUBITUS
CUBITUSES
CUBLESS
CUBOID
CUBOIDAL
CUBOIDS
CUBS
CUCKOLD
CUCKOLDED
CUCKOLDING
CUCKOLDLY
CUCKOLDOM
CUCKOLDOMS
CUCKOLDRIES
CUCKOLDRY
CUCKOLDS
CUCKOLDY
CUCKOO
CUCKOOS
CUCULLATE
CUCUMBER
CUCUMBERS
CUCURBIT
CUCURBITS
CUD
CUDBEAR
CUDBEARS
CUDDEEHIH
CUDDEEHIHS
CUDDEN
CUDDENS
CUDDIE
CUDDIES
CUDDIN
CUDDINS
CUDDLE
CUDDLED
CUDDLES
CUDDLIER
CUDDLIEST
CUDDLING
CUDDLY
CUDDY
CUDGEL
CUDGELLED
CUDGELLER
CUDGELLERS
CUDGELLING
CUDGELLINGS
CUDGELS
CUDWEED
CUDWEEDS
CUE
CUED
CUEING
CUEIST
CUEISTS
CUES
CUESTA
CUESTAS

CUFF
CUFFED
CUFFIN
CUFFING
CUFFINS
CUFFLE
CUFFLED
CUFFLES
CUFFLING
CUFFO
CUFFS
CUIF
CUIFS
CUING
CUIRASS
CUIRASSED
CUIRASSES
CUIRASSING
CUISH
CUISHES
CUISINE
CUISINES
CUISINIER
CUISINIERS
CUISSE
CUISSER
CUISSERS
CUISSES
CUIT
CUITER
CUITERED
CUITERING
CUITERS
CUITIKIN
CUITIKINS
CUITS
CUITTLE
CUITTLED
CUITTLES
CUITTLING
CULCH
CULCHES
CULET
CULETS
CULEX
CULICES
CULICID
CULICIDS
CULICINE
CULINARY
CULL
CULLED
CULLENDER
CULLENDERS
CULLER
CULLERS
CULLET
CULLETS
CULLIED
CULLIES
CULLING
CULLINGS
CULLION
CULLIONLY
CULLIONS
CULLIS
CULLISES
CULLS
CULLY
CULLYING

CULLYISM
CULLYISMS
CULM
CULMED
CULMEN
CULMENS
CULMINANT
CULMINATE
CULMINATED
CULMINATES
CULMINATING
CULMING
CULMS
CULOTTE
CULOTTES
CULPABLE
CULPABLY
CULPATORY
CULPRIT
CULPRITS
CULT
CULTCH
CULTCHES
CULTER
CULTERS
CULTIC
CULTIGEN
CULTIGENS
CULTISH
CULTISM
CULTISMS
CULTIST
CULTISTS
CULTIVAR
CULTIVARS
CULTIVATE
CULTIVATED
CULTIVATES
CULTIVATING
CULTORIST
CULTORISTS
CULTRATE
CULTRATED
CULTS
CULTURAL
CULTURE
CULTURED
CULTURES
CULTURING
CULTURIST
CULTURISTS
CULTUS
CULTUSES
CULVER
CULVERIN
CULVERINS
CULVERS
CULVERT
CULVERTS
CUM
CUMARIN
CUMARINS
CUMBENT
CUMBER
CUMBERED
CUMBERER
CUMBERERS
CUMBERING
CUMBERS
CUMBRANCE

CUMBRANCES
CUMBROUS
CUMEC
CUMECS
CUMIN
CUMINS
CUMMER
CUMMERS
CUMMIN
CUMMINS
CUMQUAT
CUMQUATS
CUMSHAW
CUMSHAWS
CUMULATE
CUMULATED
CUMULATES
CUMULATING
CUMULI
CUMULOSE
CUMULUS
CUNABULA
CUNCTATOR
CUNCTATORS
CUNEAL
CUNEATE
CUNEATIC
CUNEIFORM
CUNEIFORMS
CUNETTE
CUNETTES
CUNJEVOI
CUNJEVOIS
CUNNER
CUNNERS
CUNNING
CUNNINGLY
CUNNINGS
CUNT
CUNTS
CUP
CUPBEARER
CUPBEARERS
CUPBOARD
CUPBOARDED
CUPBOARDING
CUPBOARDS
CUPEL
CUPELLED
CUPELLING
CUPELS
CUPFUL
CUPFULS
CUPGALL
CUPGALLS
CUPHEAD
CUPHEADS
CUPID
CUPIDITIES
CUPIDITY
CUPIDS
CUPMAN
CUPMEN
CUPOLA
CUPOLAED
CUPOLAING
CUPOLAR
CUPOLAS
CUPOLATED
CUPPA

CUPPAS
CUPPED
CUPPER
CUPPERS
CUPPING
CUPPINGS
CUPREOUS
CUPRIC
CUPRITE
CUPRITES
CUPROUS
CUPS
CUPULAR
CUPULATE
CUPULE
CUPULES
CUR
CURABLE
CURAÇAO
CURAÇAOS
CURACIES
CURAÇOA
CURAÇOAS
CURACY
CURARA
CURARAS
CURARE
CURARES
CURARI
CURARINE
CURARINES
CURARIS
CURARISE
CURARISED
CURARISES
CURARISING
CURARIZE
CURARIZED
CURARIZES
CURARIZING
CURASSOW
CURASSOWS
CURAT
CURATE
CURATES
CURATIVE
CURATOR
CURATORS
CURATORY
CURATRIX
CURATRIXES
CURATS
CURB
CURBABLE
CURBED
CURBING
CURBLESS
CURBS
CURCH
CURCHES
CURCULIO
CURCULIOS
CURCUMA
CURCUMAS
CURCUMINE
CURCUMINES
CURD
CURDED
CURDIER
CURDIEST

CURDINESS
CURDINESSES
CURDING
CURDLE
CURDLED
CURDLES
CURDLING
CURDS
CURDY
CURE
CURÉ
CURED
CURELESS
CURER
CURERS
CURES
CURÉS
CURETTAGE
CURETTAGES
CURETTE
CURETTED
CURETTES
CURETTING
CURFEW
CURFEWS
CURFUFFLE
CURFUFFLED
CURFUFFLES
CURFUFFLING
CURIA
CURIAE
CURIALISM
CURIALISMS
CURIALIST
CURIALISTS
CURIAS
CURIE
CURIES
CURIET
CURIETS
CURING
CURIO
CURIOS
CURIOSA
CURIOSITIES
CURIOSITY
CURIOUS
CURIOUSER
CURIOUSLY
CURIUM
CURIUMS
CURL
CURLED
CURLER
CURLERS
CURLEW
CURLEWS
CURLICUE
CURLICUES
CURLIER
CURLIEST
CURLINESS
CURLINESSES
CURLING
CURLINGS
CURLS
CURLY
CURN
CURNEY
CURNIER

CURNIEST
CURNS
CURNY
CURPEL
CURPELS
CURR
CURRACH
CURRACHS
CURRAGH
CURRAGHS
CURRAJONG
CURRAJONGS
CURRANT
CURRANTS
CURRANTY
CURRAWONG
CURRAWONGS
CURRED
CURRENCIES
CURRENCY
CURRENT
CURRENTLY
CURRENTS
CURRICLE
CURRICLES
CURRICULA
CURRIE
CURRIED
CURRIER
CURRIERS
CURRIES
CURRING
CURRISH
CURRISHLY
CURRS
CURRY
CURRYING
CURRYINGS
CURS
CURSAL
CURSE
CURSED
CURSEDLY
CURSENARY
CURSER
CURSERS
CURSES
CURSING
CURSINGS
CURSITOR
CURSITORS
CURSITORY
CURSIVE
CURSIVELY
CURSOR
CURSORARY
CURSORES
CURSORIAL
CURSORILY
CURSORS
CURSORY
CURST
CURSTNESS
CURSTNESSES
CURSUS
CURSUSES
CURT
CURTAIL
CURTAILED
CURTAILING

CURTAILS
CURTAIN
CURTAINED
CURTAINING
CURTAINS
CURTAL
CURTALS
CURTANA
CURTANAS
CURTATE
CURTATION
CURTATIONS
CURTAXE
CURTAXES
CURTER
CURTEST
CURTILAGE
CURTILAGES
CURTLY
CURTNESS
CURTNESSES
CURTSEY
CURTSEYED
CURTSEYING
CURTSEYS
CURTSIED
CURTSIES
CURTSY
CURTSYING
CURULE
CURVATE
CURVATED
CURVATION
CURVATIONS
CURVATIVE
CURVATURE
CURVATURES
CURVE
CURVED
CURVES
CURVESOME
CURVET
CURVETED
CURVETING
CURVETS
CURVETTED
CURVETTING
CURVIER
CURVIEST
CURVIFORM
CURVING
CURVITAL
CURVITIES
CURVITY
CURVY
CUSCUS
CUSCUSES
CUSEC
CUSECS
CUSH
CUSHAT
CUSHATS
CUSHAW
CUSHAWS
CUSHES
CUSHIER
CUSHIEST
CUSHION
CUSHIONED
CUSHIONET

CUSHIONETS
CUSHIONING
CUSHIONS
CUSHIONY
CUSHY
CUSK
CUSKS
CUSP
CUSPATE
CUSPED
CUSPID
CUSPIDAL
CUSPIDATE
CUSPIDOR
CUSPIDORE
CUSPIDORES
CUSPIDORS
CUSPS
CUSS
CUSSED
CUSSER
CUSSERS
CUSSES
CUSSING
CUSTARD
CUSTARDS
CUSTOCK
CUSTOCKS
CUSTODE
CUSTODES
CUSTODIAL
CUSTODIAN
CUSTODIANS
CUSTODIER
CUSTODIERS
CUSTODIES
CUSTODY
CUSTOM
CUSTOMARIES
CUSTOMARY
CUSTOMED
CUSTOMER
CUSTOMERS
CUSTOMISE
CUSTOMISED
CUSTOMISES
CUSTOMISING
CUSTOMIZE
CUSTOMIZED
CUSTOMIZES
CUSTOMIZING
CUSTOMS
CUSTOS
CUSTREL
CUSTRELS
CUSTUMARIES
CUSTUMARY
CUT
CUTANEOUS
CUTAWAY
CUTAWAYS
CUTBACK
CUTBACKS
CUTCH
CUTCHA
CUTCHERIES
CUTCHERRIES
CUTCHERRY
CUTCHERY
CUTCHES

CUTE
CUTER
CUTES
CUTESIER
CUTESIEST
CUTEST
CUTESY
CUTEY
CUTEYS
CUTICLE
CUTICLES
CUTICULAR
CUTIE
CUTIES
CUTIKIN
CUTIKINS
CUTIN
CUTINISE
CUTINISED
CUTINISES
CUTINISING
CUTINIZE
CUTINIZED
CUTINIZES
CUTINIZING
CUTINS
CUTIS
CUTISES
CUTLASS
CUTLASSES
CUTLER
CUTLERIES
CUTLERS
CUTLERY
CUTLET
CUTLETS
CUTLINE
CUTLINES
CUTPURSE
CUTPURSES
CUTS
CUTTER
CUTTERS
CUTTIER
CUTTIES
CUTTIEST
CUTTING
CUTTINGS
CUTTLE
CUTTLES
CUTTO
CUTTOE
CUTTOES
CUTTY
CUTWORM
CUTWORMS
CUVÉE
CUVÉES
CUVETTE
CUVETTES
CUZ
CUZZES
CWM
CWMS
CYAN
CYANAMIDE
CYANAMIDES
CYANATE
CYANATES
CYANIC

CYANIDE
CYANIDED
CYANIDES
CYANIDING
CYANIDINGS
CYANIN
CYANINE
CYANINES
CYANINS
CYANISE
CYANISED
CYANISES
CYANISING
CYANITE
CYANITES
CYANIZE
CYANIZED
CYANIZES
CYANIZING
CYANOGEN
CYANOGENS
CYANOSED
CYANOSES
CYANOSIS
CYANOTIC
CYANOTYPE
CYANOTYPES
CYANS
CYANURET
CYANURETS
CYATHI
CYATHIA
CYATHIUM
CYATHUS
CYATHUSES
CYCAD
CYCADS
CYCLAMATE
CYCLAMATES
CYCLAMEN
CYCLAMENS
CYCLE
CYCLED
CYCLER
CYCLERS
CYCLES
CYCLEWAY
CYCLEWAYS
CYCLIC
CYCLICAL
CYCLICISM
CYCLICISMS
CYCLICITIES
CYCLICITY
CYCLING
CYCLINGS
CYCLIST
CYCLISTS
CYCLO
CYCLOID
CYCLOIDAL
CYCLOIDS
CYCLOLITH
CYCLOLITHS
CYCLONE
CYCLONES
CYCLONIC
CYCLOPEAN
CYCLOPES
CYCLOPIAN

CYCLOPIC
CYCLOPS
CYCLORAMA
CYCLORAMAS
CYCLOS
CYCLOSES
CYCLOSIS
CYCLOTRON
CYCLOTRONS
CYCLUS
CYCLUSES
CYDER
CYDERS
CYESES
CYESIS
CYGNET
CYGNETS
CYLICES
CYLINDER
CYLINDERS
CYLINDRIC
CYLIX
CYMA
CYMAGRAPH
CYMAGRAPHS
CYMAR
CYMARS
CYMAS
CYMATIUM

CYMATIUMS
CYMBAL
CYMBALIST
CYMBALISTS
CYMBALO
CYMBALOES
CYMBALOS
CYMBALS
CYMBIDIA
CYMBIDIUM
CYMBIDIUMS
CYMBIFORM
CYME
CYMES
CYMOGRAPH
CYMOGRAPHS
CYMOID
CYMOPHANE
CYMOPHANES
CYMOSE
CYMOUS
CYNANCHE
CYNANCHES
CYNEGETIC
CYNIC
CYNICAL
CYNICALLY
CYNICISM
CYNICISMS

CYNICS
CYNOMOLGI
CYNOSURE
CYNOSURES
CYPHER
CYPHERED
CYPHERING
CYPHERS
CYPRESS
CYPRESSES
CYPRIAN
CYPRIANS
CYPRID
CYPRIDES
CYPRIDS
CYPRINE
CYPRINOID
CYPRIS
CYPRUS
CYPRUSES
CYST
CYSTIC
CYSTID
CYSTIDEAN
CYSTIDEANS
CYSTIDS
CYSTIFORM
CYSTITIS
CYSTITISES

CYSTOCARP
CYSTOCARPS
CYSTOCELE
CYSTOCELES
CYSTOID
CYSTOIDS
CYSTOLITH
CYSTOLITHS
CYSTOTOMIES
CYSTOTOMY
CYSTS
CYTASE
CYTASES
CYTE
CYTES
CYTISI
CYTISINE
CYTISINES
CYTISUS
CYTODE
CYTODES
CYTOID
CYTOKININ
CYTOKININS
CYTOLOGIES
CYTOLOGY
CYTOLYSES
CYTOLYSIS
CYTON

CYTONS
CYTOPLASM
CYTOPLASMS
CYTOSINE
CYTOSINES
CYTOTOXIC
CYTOTOXIN
CYTOTOXINS
CZAPKA
CZAPKAS
CZAR
CZARDAS
CZARDASES
CZARDOM
CZARDOMS
CZAREVICH
CZAREVICHES
CZAREVNA
CZAREVNAS
CZARINA
CZARINAS
CZARISM
CZARISMS
CZARIST
CZARISTS
CZARITZA
CZARITZAS
CZARS

D

DA
DAB
DABBED
DABBER
DABBERS
DABBING
DABBITIES
DABBITY
DABBLE
DABBLED
DABBLER
DABBLERS
DABBLES
DABBLING
DABBLINGS
DABCHICK
DABCHICKS
DABS
DABSTER
DABSTERS
DACE
DACES
DACHA
DACHAS
DACHSHUND
DACHSHUNDS
DACITE
DACITES
DACKER
DACKERED
DACKERING
DACKERS
DACOIT
DACOITAGE
DACOITAGES
DACOITIES
DACOITS
DACOITY
DACTYL
DACTYLAR
DACTYLIC
DACTYLIST
DACTYLISTS
DACTYLS
DAD
DADDED
DADDIES
DADDING
DADDLE
DADDLED
DADDLES
DADDLING
DADDOCK
DADDOCKS
DADDY
DADO
DADOED
DADOES
DADOING
DADOS
DADS
DAEDAL
DAEDALE

DAEDALIC
DAEMON
DAEMONIC
DAEMONS
DAFF
DAFFED
DAFFIER
DAFFIES
DAFFIEST
DAFFING
DAFFINGS
DAFFODIL
DAFFODILS
DAFFS
DAFFY
DAFT
DAFTAR
DAFTARS
DAFTER
DAFTEST
DAFTIE
DAFTIES
DAFTLY
DAFTNESS
DAFTNESSES
DAG
DAGABA
DAGABAS
DAGGA
DAGGAS
DAGGED
DAGGER
DAGGERS
DAGGING
DAGGLE
DAGGLED
DAGGLES
DAGGLING
DAGLOCK
DAGLOCKS
DAGO
DAGOBA
DAGOBAS
DAGOES
DAGS
DAGWOOD
DAGWOODS
DAH
DAHABEEAH
DAHABEEAHS
DAHABIEH
DAHABIEHS
DAHABIYAH
DAHABIYAHS
DAHABIYEH
DAHABIYEHS
DAHL
DAHLIA
DAHLIAS
DAHLS
DAHS
DAIDLE
DAIDLED

DAIDLES
DAIDLING
DAIKER
DAIKERED
DAIKERING
DAIKERS
DAIKON
DAIKONS
DAILIES
DAILY
DAIMEN
DAIMIO
DAIMIOS
DAIMON
DAIMONIC
DAIMONS
DAINE
DAINED
DAINES
DAINING
DAINT
DAINTIER
DAINTIES
DAINTIEST
DAINTILY
DAINTY
DAIQUIRI
DAIQUIRIS
DAIRIES
DAIRY
DAIRYING
DAIRYINGS
DAIRYMAID
DAIRYMAIDS
DAIRYMAN
DAIRYMEN
DAIS
DAISES
DAISIED
DAISIES
DAISY
DAK
DAKER
DAKERED
DAKERING
DAKERS
DAKOIT
DAKOITI
DAKOITIS
DAKOITS
DAKS
DAL
DALE
DALES
DALESMAN
DALESMEN
DALI
DALIS
DALLE
DALLES
DALLIANCE
DALLIANCES
DALLIED

DALLIER
DALLIERS
DALLIES
DALLOP
DALLOPS
DALLY
DALLYING
DALMAHOY
DALMAHOYS
DALMATIC
DALMATICS
DALS
DALT
DALTON
DALTONS
DALTS
DAM
DAMAGE
DAMAGED
DAMAGES
DAMAGING
DAMAN
DAMANS
DAMAR
DAMARS
DAMASCENE
DAMASCENED
DAMASCENES
DAMASCENING
DAMASCENINGS
DAMASK
DAMASKED
DAMASKEEN
DAMASKEENED
DAMASKEENING
DAMASKEENS
DAMASKIN
DAMASKINED
DAMASKING
DAMASKINING
DAMASKINS
DAMASKS
DAMASQUIN
DAMASQUINED
DAMASQUINING
DAMASQUINS
DAMASSIN
DAMASSINS
DAMBOARD
DAMBOARDS
DAMBROD
DAMBRODS
DAME
DAMES
DAMFOOL
DAMMAR
DAMMARS
DAMME
DAMMED
DAMMER
DAMMERS
DAMMING
DAMMIT

DAMN
DAMNABLE
DAMNABLY
DAMNATION
DAMNATIONS
DAMNATORY
DAMNED
DAMNEDER
DAMNEDEST
DAMNIFIED
DAMNIFIES
DAMNIFY
DAMNIFYING
DAMNING
DAMNS
DAMOISEL
DAMOISELS
DAMOSEL
DAMOSELS
DAMOZEL
DAMOZELS
DAMP
DAMPED
DAMPEN
DAMPENED
DAMPENING
DAMPENS
DAMPER
DAMPERS
DAMPEST
DAMPIER
DAMPIEST
DAMPING
DAMPINGS
DAMPISH
DAMPLY
DAMPNESS
DAMPNESSES
DAMPS
DAMPY
DAMS
DAMSEL
DAMSELFLIES
DAMSELFLY
DAMSELS
DAMSON
DAMSONS
DAN
DANCE
DANCEABLE
DANCED
DANCER
DANCERS
DANCES
DANCETTE
DANCETTÉ
DANCETTEE
DANCETTES
DANCETTY
DANCING
DANCINGS
DANDELION
DANDELIONS

DANDER
DANDERED
DANDERING
DANDERS
DANDIACAL
DANDIER
DANDIES
DANDIEST
DANDIFIED
DANDIFIES
DANDIFY
DANDIFYING
DANDILY
DANDIPRAT
DANDIPRATS
DANDLE
DANDLED
DANDLER
DANDLERS
DANDLES
DANDLING
DANDRIFF
DANDRIFFS
DANDRUFF
DANDRUFFS
DANDY
DANDYFUNK
DANDYFUNKS
DANDYISH
DANDYISM
DANDYISMS
DANDYPRAT
DANDYPRATS
DANEGELD
DANEGELDS
DANEGELT
DANEGELTS
DANELAGH
DANELAGHS
DANELAW
DANELAWS
DANG
DANGED
DANGER
DANGERED
DANGERING
DANGEROUS
DANGERS
DANGING
DANGLE
DANGLED
DANGLER
DANGLERS
DANGLES
DANGLING
DANGLINGS
DANGS
DANIO
DANIOS
DANK
DANKER
DANKEST
DANKISH
DANKNESS
DANKNESSES
DANKS
DANNEBROG
DANNEBROGS
DANS
DANSEUR

DANSEURS
DANSEUSE
DANSEUSES
DANT
DANTED
DANTING
DANTON
DANTONED
DANTONING
DANTONS
DANTS
DAP
DAPHNE
DAPHNES
DAPHNID
DAPHNIDS
DAPPED
DAPPER
DAPPERER
DAPPEREST
DAPPERLY
DAPPERS
DAPPING
DAPPLE
DAPPLED
DAPPLES
DAPPLING
DAPS
DAPSONE
DAPSONES
DARAF
DARAFS
DARBIES
DARE
DARED
DAREFUL
DARES
DARG
DARGA
DARGAS
DARGLE
DARGLES
DARGS
DARI
DARIC
DARICS
DARING
DARINGLY
DARINGS
DARIOLE
DARIOLES
DARIS
DARK
DARKEN
DARKENED
DARKENING
DARKENS
DARKER
DARKEST
DARKEY
DARKEYS
DARKIE
DARKIES
DARKISH
DARKLE
DARKLED
DARKLES
DARKLING
DARKLINGS
DARKLY

DARKMANS
DARKNESS
DARKNESSES
DARKROOM
DARKROOMS
DARKS
DARKSOME
DARKY
DARLING
DARLINGS
DARN
DARNED
DARNEDER
DARNEDEST
DARNEL
DARNELS
DARNER
DARNERS
DARNING
DARNINGS
DARNS
DARRAIGN
DARRAIGNE
DARRAIGNED
DARRAIGNES
DARRAIGNING
DARRAIGNS
DARRAIN
DARRAINE
DARRAINED
DARRAINES
DARRAINING
DARRAINS
DARRAYN
DARRAYNED
DARRAYNING
DARRAYNS
DARRE
DARRED
DARRES
DARRING
DARSHAN
DARSHANS
DART
DARTED
DARTER
DARTERS
DARTING
DARTINGLY
DARTLE
DARTLED
DARTLES
DARTLING
DARTRE
DARTRES
DARTROUS
DARTS
DARZI
DARZIS
DAS
DASH
DASHBOARD
DASHBOARDS
DASHED
DASHEEN
DASHEENS
DASHEKI
DASHEKIS
DASHER
DASHERS

DASHES
DASHIKI
DASHIKIS
DASHING
DASHINGLY
DASSIE
DASSIES
DASTARD
DASTARDIES
DASTARDLY
DASTARDS
DASTARDY
DASYPOD
DASYPODS
DASYURE
DASYURES
DATA
DATABANK
DATABANKS
DATABASE
DATABASES
DATABLE
DATABUS
DATABUSES
DATAL
DATALLER
DATALLERS
DATALS
DATARIA
DATARIAS
DATARIES
DATARY
DATE
DATEABLE
DATED
DATELESS
DATER
DATERS
DATES
DATING
DATINGS
DATIVAL
DATIVE
DATIVES
DATOLITE
DATOLITES
DATUM
DATURA
DATURAS
DATURINE
DATURINES
DAUB
DAUBE
DAUBED
DAUBER
DAUBERS
DAUBERIES
DAUBERY
DAUBES
DAUBIER
DAUBIEST
DAUBING
DAUBINGS
DAUBS
DAUBY
DAUD
DAUDED
DAUDING
DAUDS
DAUGHTER

DAUGHTERS
DAULT
DAULTS
DAUNDER
DAUNDERED
DAUNDERING
DAUNDERS
DAUNER
DAUNERED
DAUNERING
DAUNERS
DAUNT
DAUNTED
DAUNTER
DAUNTERS
DAUNTING
DAUNTLESS
DAUNTON
DAUNTONED
DAUNTONING
DAUNTONS
DAUNTS
DAUPHIN
DAUPHINE
DAUPHINES
DAUPHINS
DAUR
DAURED
DAURING
DAURS
DAUT
DAUTED
DAUTIE
DAUTIES
DAUTING
DAUTS
DAVENPORT
DAVENPORTS
DAVIT
DAVITS
DAW
DAWBRIES
DAWBRY
DAWCOCK
DAWCOCKS
DAWD
DAWDED
DAWDING
DAWDLE
DAWDLED
DAWDLER
DAWDLERS
DAWDLES
DAWDLING
DAWDS
DAWED
DAWING
DAWISH
DAWK
DAWKS
DAWN
DAWNED
DAWNER
DAWNERED
DAWNERING
DAWNERS
DAWNING
DAWNINGS
DAWNS
DAWS

DAWT
DAWTED
DAWTIE
DAWTIES
DAWTING
DAWTS
DAY
DAYBREAK
DAYBREAKS
DAYDREAM
DAYDREAMED
DAYDREAMING
DAYDREAMS
DAYDREAMT
DAYGLO
DAYLIGHT
DAYLIGHTS
DAYLONG
DAYMARK
DAYMARKS
DAYNT
DAYS
DAYSMAN
DAYSMEN
DAYSPRING
DAYSPRINGS
DAYSTAR
DAYSTARS
DAYTALE
DAYTALER
DAYTALERS
DAYTALES
DAYTIME
DAYTIMES
DAZE
DAZED
DAZEDLY
DAZES
DAZING
DAZZLE
DAZZLED
DAZZLER
DAZZLERS
DAZZLES
DAZZLING
DAZZLINGS
DEACON
DEACONESS
DEACONESSES
DEACONRIES
DEACONRY
DEACONS
DEAD
DEADED
DEADEN
DEADENED
DEADENER
DEADENERS
DEADENING
DEADENINGS
DEADENS
DEADER
DEADERS
DEADEST
DEADHOUSE
DEADHOUSES
DEADING
DEADLIER
DEADLIEST
DEADLINE

DEADLINES
DEADLOCK
DEADLOCKED
DEADLOCKING
DEADLOCKS
DEADLY
DEADNESS
DEADNESSES
DEADPAN
DEADPANS
DEADS
DEAF
DEAFEN
DEAFENED
DEAFENING
DEAFENINGS
DEAFENS
DEAFER
DEAFEST
DEAFLY
DEAFNESS
DEAFNESSES
DEAL
DEALBATE
DEALER
DEALERS
DEALFISH
DEALFISHES
DEALING
DEALINGS
DEALS
DEALT
DEAN
DEANER
DEANERIES
DEANERS
DEANERY
DEANS
DEANSHIP
DEANSHIPS
DEAR
DEARE
DEARED
DEARER
DEARES
DEAREST
DEARIE
DEARIES
DEARING
DEARLING
DEARLINGS
DEARLY
DEARN
DEARNESS
DEARNESSES
DEARNFUL
DEARNLY
DEARNS
DEARS
DEARTH
DEARTHS
DEARY
DEASIL
DEASILS
DEASIUL
DEASIULS
DEASOIL
DEASOILS
DEATH
DEATHFUL

DEATHIER
DEATHIEST
DEATHLESS
DEATHLIER
DEATHLIEST
DEATHLIKE
DEATHLY
DEATHS
DEATHSMAN
DEATHSMEN
DEATHWARD
DEATHWARDS
DEATHY
DEAVE
DEAVED
DEAVES
DEAVING
DEAW
DEAWIE
DEAWS
DEAWY
DEB
DEBACLE
DÉBÂCLE
DEBACLES
DÉBÂCLES
DEBAG
DEBAGGED
DEBAGGING
DEBAGGINGS
DEBAGS
DEBAR
DEBARK
DEBARKED
DEBARKING
DEBARKS
DEBARMENT
DEBARMENTS
DEBARRASS
DEBARRASSED
DEBARRASSES
DEBARRASSING
DEBARRED
DEBARRING
DEBARS
DEBASE
DEBASED
DEBASER
DEBASERS
DEBASES
DEBASING
DEBATABLE
DEBATE
DEBATED
DEBATEFUL
DEBATER
DEBATERS
DEBATES
DEBATING
DEBAUCH
DEBAUCHED
DEBAUCHEE
DEBAUCHEES
DEBAUCHER
DEBAUCHERS
DEBAUCHES
DEBAUCHING
DEBBIER
DEBBIES
DEBBIEST

DEBBY
DEBEL
DEBELLED
DEBELLING
DEBELS
DEBENTURE
DEBENTURES
DEBILE
DEBILITIES
DEBILITY
DEBIT
DEBITED
DEBITING
DEBITOR
DEBITORS
DEBITS
DEBONAIR
DEBOSH
DEBOSHED
DEBOSHES
DEBOSHING
DEBOUCH
DÉBOUCHÉ
DEBOUCHED
DÉBOUCHÉS
DEBOUCHES
DEBOUCHING
DEBRIDE
DEBRIDED
DEBRIDES
DEBRIDING
DEBRIEF
DEBRIEFED
DEBRIEFING
DEBRIEFINGS
DEBRIEFS
DEBRIS
DEBRUISED
DEBS
DEBT
DEBTED
DEBTEE
DEBTEES
DEBTOR
DEBTORS
DEBTS
DEBUG
DEBUGGED
DEBUGGING
DEBUGS
DEBUNK
DEBUNKED
DEBUNKING
DEBUNKS
DEBUS
DEBUSSED
DEBUSSES
DEBUSSING
DÉBUT
DÉBUTANT
DEBUTANTE
DEBUTANTES
DÉBUTANTS
DÉBUTS
DECACHORD
DECACHORDS
DECAD
DECADAL
DECADE
DECADENCE

DECADENCES
DECADENCIES
DECADENCY
DECADENT
DECADENTS
DECADES
DECADS
DECAGON
DECAGONAL
DECAGONS
DECAGRAM
DECAGRAMS
DECAL
DECALCIFIED
DECALCIFIES
DECALCIFY
DECALCIFYING
DECALITRE
DECALITRES
DECALOGUE
DECALOGUES
DECALS
DECAMETRE
DECAMETRES
DECAMP
DECAMPED
DECAMPING
DECAMPS
DECANAL
DECANE
DECANES
DECANI
DECANT
DECANTATE
DECANTATED
DECANTATES
DECANTATING
DECANTED
DECANTER
DECANTERS
DECANTING
DECANTS
DECAPOD
DECAPODAL
DECAPODAN
DECAPODS
DECARB
DECARBED
DECARBING
DECARBS
DECARE
DECARES
DECASTERE
DECASTERES
DECASTICH
DECASTICHS
DECASTYLE
DECASTYLES
DECATHLON
DECATHLONS
DECAUDATE
DECAUDATED
DECAUDATES
DECAUDATING
DECAY
DECAYED
DECAYING
DECAYS
DECCIE
DECCIES

DECEASE
DECEASED
DECEASES
DECEASING
DECEDENT
DECEDENTS
DECEIT
DECEITFUL
DECEITS
DECEIVE
DECEIVED
DECEIVER
DECEIVERS
DECEIVES
DECEIVING
DECEMVIR
DECEMVIRI
DECEMVIRS
DECENCIES
DECENCY
DECENNARIES
DECENNARY
DECENNIA
DECENNIAL
DECENNIUM
DECENNIUMS
DECENT
DECENTER
DECENTEST
DECENTLY
DECEPTION
DECEPTIONS
DECEPTIVE
DECEPTORY
DECERN
DECERNED
DECERNING
DECERNS
DECESSION
DECESSIONS
DÉCHÉANCE
DÉCHÉANCES
DECIARE
DECIARES
DECIBEL
DECIBELS
DECIDABLE
DECIDE
DECIDED
DECIDEDLY
DECIDER
DECIDERS
DECIDES
DECIDING
DECIDUA
DECIDUAL
DECIDUAS
DECIDUATE
DECIDUOUS
DECIGRAM
DECIGRAMS
DECILITRE
DECILITRES
DECILLION
DECILLIONS
DECIMAL
DECIMALLY
DECIMALS
DECIMATE
DECIMATED

DECIMATES
DECIMATING
DECIMATOR
DECIMATORS
DÉCIME
DÉCIMES
DECIMETRE
DECIMETRES
DECIPHER
DECIPHERED
DECIPHERING
DECIPHERS
DECISION
DECISIONS
DECISIVE
DECISORY
DECISTERE
DECISTERES
DECK
DECKCHAIR
DECKCHAIRS
DECKED
DECKER
DECKERS
DECKING
DECKINGS
DECKLE
DECKLED
DECKLES
DECKO
DECKOED
DECKOING
DECKOS
DECKS
DECLAIM
DECLAIMED
DECLAIMER
DECLAIMERS
DECLAIMING
DECLAIMINGS
DECLAIMS
DECLARANT
DECLARANTS
DECLARE
DECLARED
DECLARER
DECLARERS
DECLARES
DECLARING
DECLASS
DÉCLASSÉ
DECLASSED
DÉCLASSÉE
DECLASSES
DECLASSING
DECLINAL
DECLINANT
DECLINATE
DECLINE
DECLINED
DECLINES
DECLINING
DECLIVITIES
DECLIVITY
DECLIVOUS
DECLUTCH
DECLUTCHED
DECLUTCHES
DECLUTCHING
DECO

DECOCT
DECOCTED
DECOCTING
DECOCTION
DECOCTIONS
DECOCTIVE
DECOCTS
DECOCTURE
DECOCTURES
DECODE
DECODED
DECODER
DECODERS
DECODES
DECODING
DECOHERER
DECOHERERS
DECOKE
DECOKED
DECOKES
DECOKING
DECOLLATE
DECOLLATED
DECOLLATES
DECOLLATING
DÉCOLLETÉ
DECOLOR
DECOLORED
DECOLORING
DECOLORS
DECOLOUR
DECOLOURED
DECOLOURING
DECOLOURS
DECOMPLEX
DECOMPOSE
DECOMPOSED
DECOMPOSES
DECOMPOSING
DECONGEST
DECONGESTED
DECONGESTING
DECONGESTS
DECONTROL
DECONTROLLED
DECONTROLLING
DECONTROLS
DÉCOR
DECORATE
DECORATED
DECORATES
DECORATING
DECORATOR
DECORATORS
DECOROUS
DÉCORS
DECORUM
DECORUMS
DECOUPAGE
DECOUPAGES
DECOUPLE
DECOUPLED
DECOUPLES
DECOUPLING
DECOUPLINGS
DECOY
DECOYED
DECOYING
DECOYS
DECREASE

DECREASED
DECREASES
DECREASING
DECREE
DECREED
DECREEING
DECREES
DECREET
DECREETS
DECREMENT
DECREMENTED
DECREMENTING
DECREMENTS
DECREPIT
DECRETAL
DECRETALS
DECRETIST
DECRETISTS
DECRETIVE
DECRETORY
DECREW
DECREWED
DECREWING
DECREWS
DECRIAL
DECRIALS
DECRIED
DECRIER
DECRIERS
DECRIES
DECROWN
DECROWNED
DECROWNING
DECROWNS
DECRY
DECRYING
DECRYPT
DECRYPTED
DECRYPTING
DECRYPTS
DECTET
DECTETS
DECUBITI
DECUBITUS
DECUMAN
DECUMANS
DECUMBENT
DECUPLE
DECUPLED
DECUPLES
DECUPLING
DECURIA
DECURIAS
DECURIES
DECURION
DECURIONS
DECURRENT
DECURSION
DECURSIONS
DECURSIVE
DECURVE
DECURVED
DECURVES
DECURVING
DECURY
DECUSSATE
DECUSSATED
DECUSSATES
DECUSSATING
DEDAL

DEDALIAN
DEDANS
DEDICANT
DEDICANTS
DEDICATE
DEDICATED
DEDICATEE
DEDICATEES
DEDICATES
DEDICATING
DEDICATOR
DEDICATORS
DEDIMUS
DEDIMUSES
DEDUCE
DEDUCED
DEDUCES
DEDUCIBLE
DEDUCING
DEDUCT
DEDUCTED
DEDUCTING
DEDUCTION
DEDUCTIONS
DEDUCTIVE
DEDUCTS
DEE
DEED
DEEDED
DEEDER
DEEDEST
DEEDFUL
DEEDIER
DEEDIEST
DEEDILY
DEEDING
DEEDLESS
DEEDS
DEEDY
DEEING
DEEJAY
DEEJAYED
DEEJAYING
DEEJAYS
DEEM
DEEMED
DEEMING
DEEMS
DEEMSTER
DEEMSTERS
DEEN
DEENS
DEEP
DEEPEN
DEEPENED
DEEPENING
DEEPENS
DEEPER
DEEPEST
DEEPFELT
DEEPIE
DEEPIES
DEEPLY
DEEPMOST
DEEPNESS
DEEPNESSES
DEEPS
DEER
DEERBERRIES
DEERBERRY

DEERE
DEERHORN
DEERHORNS
DEERLET
DEERLETS
DEERSKIN
DEERSKINS
DEES
DEEV
DEEVE
DEEVED
DEEVES
DEEVING
DEEVS
DEFACE
DEFACED
DEFACER
DEFACERS
DEFACES
DEFACING
DEFAECATE
DEFAECATED
DEFAECATES
DEFAECATING
DEFALCATE
DEFALCATED
DEFALCATES
DEFALCATING
DEFAME
DEFAMED
DEFAMES
DEFAMING
DEFAMINGS
DEFAST
DEFASTE
DEFAT
DEFATS
DEFATTED
DEFATTING
DEFAULT
DEFAULTED
DEFAULTER
DEFAULTERS
DEFAULTING
DEFAULTS
DEFEAT
DEFEATED
DEFEATING
DEFEATISM
DEFEATISMS
DEFEATIST
DEFEATISTS
DEFEATS
DEFEATURE
DEFEATURED
DEFEATURES
DEFEATURING
DEFECATE
DEFECATED
DEFECATES
DEFECATING
DEFECATOR
DEFECATORS
DEFECT
DEFECTED
DEFECTING
DEFECTION
DEFECTIONS
DEFECTIVE
DEFECTIVES

DEFECTOR
DEFECTORS
DEFECTS
DEFENCE
DEFENCED
DEFENCES
DEFEND
DEFENDANT
DEFENDANTS
DEFENDED
DEFENDER
DEFENDERS
DEFENDING
DEFENDS
DEFENSE
DEFENSES
DEFENSIVE
DEFENSIVES
DEFER
DEFERABLE
DEFERENCE
DEFERENCES
DEFERENT
DEFERENTS
DEFERMENT
DEFERMENTS
DEFERRAL
DEFERRALS
DEFERRED
DEFERRER
DEFERRERS
DEFERRING
DEFERS
DEFFLY
DEFIANCE
DEFIANCES
DEFIANT
DEFIANTLY
DEFICIENT
DEFICIENTS
DEFICIT
DEFICITS
DEFIED
DEFIER
DEFIERS
DEFIES
DEFILADE
DEFILADED
DEFILADES
DEFILADING
DEFILE
DEFILED
DEFILER
DEFILERS
DEFILES
DEFILING
DEFINABLE
DEFINABLY
DEFINE
DEFINED
DEFINER
DEFINERS
DEFINES
DEFINING
DEFINITE
DEFLATE
DEFLATED
DEFLATER
DEFLATERS
DEFLATES

DEFLATING
DEFLATION
DEFLATIONS
DEFLATOR
DEFLATORS
DEFLECT
DEFLECTED
DEFLECTING
DEFLECTOR
DEFLECTORS
DEFLECTS
DEFLEX
DEFLEXED
DEFLEXES
DEFLEXING
DEFLEXION
DEFLEXIONS
DEFLEXURE
DEFLEXURES
DEFLORATE
DEFLORATED
DEFLORATES
DEFLORATING
DEFLOWER
DEFLOWERED
DEFLOWERING
DEFLOWERS
DEFLUENT
DEFLUXION
DEFLUXIONS
DEFOLIANT
DEFOLIANTS
DEFOLIATE
DEFOLIATED
DEFOLIATES
DEFOLIATING
DEFORCE
DEFORCED
DEFORCES
DEFORCING
DEFOREST
DEFORESTED
DEFORESTING
DEFORESTS
DEFORM
DEFORMED
DEFORMER
DEFORMERS
DEFORMING
DEFORMITIES
DEFORMITY
DEFORMS
DEFOUL
DEFOULED
DEFOULING
DEFOULS
DEFRAUD
DEFRAUDED
DEFRAUDER
DEFRAUDERS
DEFRAUDING
DEFRAUDS
DEFRAY
DEFRAYAL
DEFRAYALS
DEFRAYED
DEFRAYER
DEFRAYERS
DEFRAYING
DEFRAYS

DEFREEZE
DEFREEZES
DEFREEZING
DEFROCK
DEFROCKED
DEFROCKING
DEFROCKS
DEFROST
DEFROSTED
DEFROSTER
DEFROSTERS
DEFROSTING
DEFROSTS
DEFROZE
DEFROZEN
DEFT
DEFTER
DEFTEST
DEFTLY
DEFTNESS
DEFTNESSES
DEFUNCT
DEFUNCTS
DEFUSE
DEFUSED
DEFUSES
DEFUSING
DEFUZE
DEFUZED
DEFUZES
DEFUZING
DEFY
DEFYING
DÉGAGÉ
DEGARNISH
DEGARNISHED
DEGARNISHES
DEGARNISHING
DEGAS
DEGASSED
DEGASSES
DEGASSING
DEGAUSS
DEGAUSSED
DEGAUSSES
DEGAUSSING
DEGENDER
DEGENDERED
DEGENDERING
DEGENDERS
DÉGOÛT
DÉGOÛTS
DEGRADE
DEGRADED
DEGRADES
DEGRADING
DEGRAS
DEGREASE
DEGREASED
DEGREASES
DEGREASING
DEGREE
DEGREES
DEGUM
DEGUMMED
DEGUMMING
DEGUMS
DEGUST
DEGUSTATE
DEGUSTATED

DEGUSTATES
DEGUSTATING
DEGUSTED
DEGUSTING
DEGUSTS
DEHISCE
DEHISCED
DEHISCENT
DEHISCES
DEHISCING
DEHORN
DEHORNED
DEHORNER
DEHORNERS
DEHORNING
DEHORNS
DEHORT
DEHORTED
DEHORTER
DEHORTERS
DEHORTING
DEHORTS
DEHYDRATE
DEHYDRATED
DEHYDRATES
DEHYDRATING
DEI
DEICIDAL
DEICIDE
DEICIDES
DEICTIC
DEICTICS
DEID
DEIDER
DEIDEST
DEIDS
DEIFIC
DEIFICAL
DEIFIED
DEIFIER
DEIFIERS
DEIFIES
DEIFORM
DEIFY
DEIFYING
DEIGN
DEIGNED
DEIGNING
DEIGNS
DEIL
DEILS
DEINOSAUR
DEINOSAURS
DEIPAROUS
DEISEAL
DEISEALS
DEISHEAL
DEISHEALS
DEISM
DEISMS
DEIST
DEISTIC
DEISTICAL
DEISTS
DEITIES
DEITY
DEIXES
DEIXIS
DEJECT
DEJECTA

DEJECTED
DEJECTING
DEJECTION
DEJECTIONS
DEJECTORY
DEJECTS
DEJEUNE
DÉJEUNER
DÉJEUNERS
DEJEUNES
DEKALOGIES
DEKALOGY
DEKKO
DEKKOED
DEKKOING
DEKKOS
DEL
DELAINE
DELAINES
DELAPSE
DELAPSED
DELAPSES
DELAPSING
DELAPSION
DELAPSIONS
DELATE
DELATED
DELATES
DELATING
DELATION
DELATIONS
DELATOR
DELATORS
DELAY
DELAYED
DELAYER
DELAYERS
DELAYING
DELAYS
DELE
DELEBLE
DELED
DELEGABLE
DELEGACIES
DELEGACY
DELEGATE
DELEGATED
DELEGATES
DELEGATING
DELEING
DELENDA
DELES
DELETE
DELETED
DELETES
DELETING
DELETION
DELETIONS
DELETIVE
DELETORY
DELF
DELFS
DELFT
DELFTS
DELI
DELIBATE
DELIBATED
DELIBATES
DELIBATING
DELIBLE

DELICACIES
DELICACY
DELICATE
DELICATES
DELICE
DELICES
DELICIOUS
DELICT
DELICTS
DELIGHT
DELIGHTED
DELIGHTING
DELIGHTS
DELIMIT
DELIMITED
DELIMITING
DELIMITS
DELINEATE
DELINEATED
DELINEATES
DELINEATING
DELIQUIUM
DELIQUIUMS
DELIRIA
DELIRIANT
DELIRIANTS
DELIRIOUS
DELIRIUM
DELIRIUMS
DELIS
DELIVER
DELIVERED
DELIVERER
DELIVERERS
DELIVERIES
DELIVERING
DELIVERLY
DELIVERS
DELIVERY
DELL
DELLS
DELOUSE
DELOUSED
DELOUSES
DELOUSING
DELPH
DELPHIC
DELPHIN
DELPHINIA
DELPHS
DELS
DELTA
DELTAIC
DELTAS
DELTOID
DELUBRUM
DELUBRUMS
DELUDABLE
DELUDE
DELUDED
DELUDER
DELUDERS
DELUDES
DELUDING
DELUGE
DELUGED
DELUGES
DELUGING
DELUNDUNG
DELUNDUNGS

DELUSION
DELUSIONS
DELUSIVE
DELUSORY
DELVE
DELVED
DELVER
DELVERS
DELVES
DELVING
DEMAGOGIC
DEMAGOGIES
DEMAGOGUE
DEMAGOGUES
DEMAGOGY
DEMAIN
DEMAINE
DEMAINES
DEMAINS
DEMAN
DEMAND
DEMANDANT
DEMANDANTS
DEMANDED
DEMANDER
DEMANDERS
DEMANDING
DEMANDS
DEMANNED
DEMANNING
DEMANNINGS
DEMANS
DEMARCATE
DEMARCATED
DEMARCATES
DEMARCATING
DÉMARCHE
DÉMARCHES
DEMARK
DEMARKED
DEMARKING
DEMARKS
DEMAYNE
DEMAYNES
DEME
DEMEAN
DEMEANE
DEMEANED
DEMEANES
DEMEANING
DEMEANOR
DEMEANORS
DEMEANOUR
DEMEANOURS
DEMEANS
DEMENT
DEMENTATE
DEMENTATED
DEMENTATES
DEMENTATING
DEMENTED
DÉMENTI
DEMENTIA
DEMENTIAS
DEMENTING
DÉMENTIS
DEMENTS
DEMERARA
DEMERARAS
DEMERGE

DEMERGED
DEMERGER
DEMERGERS
DEMERGES
DEMERGING
DEMERIT
DEMERITS
DEMERSAL
DEMERSE
DEMERSED
DEMERSES
DEMERSING
DEMERSION
DEMERSIONS
DEMES
DEMESNE
DEMESNES
DEMIC
DEMIES
DEMIGOD
DEMIGODS
DEMIJOHN
DEMIJOHNS
DEMIPIQUE
DEMIPIQUES
DEMIREP
DEMIREPS
DEMISABLE
DEMISE
DEMISED
DEMISES
DEMISING
DEMISS
DEMISSION
DEMISSIONS
DEMISSIVE
DEMISSLY
DEMIST
DEMISTED
DEMISTER
DEMISTERS
DEMISTING
DEMISTS
DEMIT
DEMITASSE
DEMITASSES
DEMITS
DEMITTED
DEMITTING
DEMIURGE
DEMIURGES
DEMIURGIC
DEMIURGUS
DEMIURGUSES
DEMO
DEMOB
DEMOBBED
DEMOBBING
DEMOBS
DEMOCRACIES
DEMOCRACY
DEMOCRAT
DEMOCRATIES
DEMOCRATS
DEMOCRATY
DÉMODÉ
DEMODED
DEMOLISH
DEMOLISHED
DEMOLISHES

DEMOLISHING
DEMOLOGIES
DEMOLOGY
DEMON
DEMONESS
DEMONESSES
DEMONIAC
DEMONIACS
DEMONIAN
DEMONIC
DEMONISE
DEMONISED
DEMONISES
DEMONISING
DEMONISM
DEMONISMS
DEMONIST
DEMONISTS
DEMONIZE
DEMONIZED
DEMONIZES
DEMONIZING
DEMONRIES
DEMONRY
DEMONS
DEMOS
DEMOSES
DEMOTE
DEMOTED
DEMOTES
DEMOTIC
DEMOTING
DEMOTION
DEMOTIONS
DEMOTIST
DEMOTISTS
DEMOUNT
DEMOUNTED
DEMOUNTING
DEMOUNTS
DEMPSTER
DEMPSTERS
DEMPT
DEMULCENT
DEMULCENTS
DEMULSIFIED
DEMULSIFIES
DEMULSIFY
DEMULSIFYING
DEMUR
DEMURE
DEMURED
DEMURELY
DEMURER
DEMURES
DEMUREST
DEMURING
DEMURRAGE
DEMURRAGES
DEMURRAL
DEMURRALS
DEMURRED
DEMURRER
DEMURRERS
DEMURRING
DEMURS
DEMY
DEMYSHIP
DEMYSHIPS
DEMYSTIFIED

DEMYSTIFIES
DEMYSTIFY
DEMYSTIFYING
DEN
DENARIES
DENARII
DENARIUS
DENARY
DENATURE
DENATURED
DENATURES
DENATURING
DENAY
DENAYED
DENAYING
DENAYS
DENAZIFIED
DENAZIFIES
DENAZIFY
DENAZIFYING
DENDRITE
DENDRITES
DENDRITIC
DENDROID
DENDRON
DENDRONS
DENE
DENES
DENGUE
DENGUES
DENIABLE
DENIABLY
DENIAL
DENIALS
DENIED
DENIER
DENIERS
DENIES
DENIGRATE
DENIGRATED
DENIGRATES
DENIGRATING
DENIM
DENIMS
DENITRATE
DENITRATED
DENITRATES
DENITRATING
DENITRIFIED
DENITRIFIES
DENITRIFY
DENITRIFYING
DENIZEN
DENIZENED
DENIZENING
DENIZENS
DENNED
DENNET
DENNETS
DENNING
DENOTABLE
DENOTATE
DENOTATED
DENOTATES
DENOTATING
DENOTE
DENOTED
DENOTES
DENOTING
DENOUNCE

DENOUNCED
DENOUNCER
DENOUNCERS
DENOUNCES
DENOUNCING
DENS
DENSE
DENSELY
DENSENESS
DENSENESSES
DENSER
DENSEST
DENSIFIED
DENSIFIER
DENSIFIERS
DENSIFIES
DENSIFY
DENSIFYING
DENSITIES
DENSITY
DENT
DENTAL
DENTALIA
DENTALIUM
DENTALIUMS
DENTALS
DENTARIA
DENTARIAS
DENTARIES
DENTARY
DENTATE
DENTATED
DENTATION
DENTATIONS
DENTED
DENTEL
DENTELLE
DENTELLES
DENTELS
DENTEX
DENTEXES
DENTICLE
DENTICLES
DENTIFORM
DENTIL
DENTILS
DENTIN
DENTINE
DENTINES
DENTING
DENTINS
DENTIST
DENTISTRIES
DENTISTRY
DENTISTS
DENTITION
DENTITIONS
DENTOID
DENTS
DENTURE
DENTURES
DENUDATE
DENUDATED
DENUDATES
DENUDATING
DENUDE
DENUDED
DENUDES
DENUDING
DENY

DENYING
DENYINGLY
DEODAND
DEODANDS
DEODAR
DEODARS
DEODATE
DEODATES
DEODORANT
DEODORANTS
DEODORISE
DEODORISED
DEODORISES
DEODORISING
DEODORIZE
DEODORIZED
DEODORIZES
DEODORIZING
DEONTIC
DEONTICS
DEOXIDATE
DEOXIDATED
DEOXIDATES
DEOXIDATING
DEOXIDISE
DEOXIDISED
DEOXIDISES
DEOXIDISING
DEOXIDIZE
DEOXIDIZED
DEOXIDIZES
DEOXIDIZING
DEPAINT
DEPAINTED
DEPAINTING
DEPAINTS
DEPART
DEPARTED
DEPARTER
DEPARTERS
DEPARTING
DEPARTINGS
DEPARTS
DEPARTURE
DEPARTURES
DEPASTURE
DEPASTURED
DEPASTURES
DEPASTURING
DÉPÊCHE
DÉPÊCHES
DEPEINCT
DEPEINCTED
DEPEINCTING
DEPEINCTS
DEPEND
DEPENDANT
DEPENDANTS
DEPENDED
DEPENDENT
DEPENDENTS
DEPENDING
DEPENDS
DEPICT
DEPICTED
DEPICTER
DEPICTERS
DEPICTING
DEPICTION
DEPICTIONS

DEPICTIVE
DEPICTOR
DEPICTORS
DEPICTS
DEPICTURE
DEPICTURED
DEPICTURES
DEPICTURING
DEPILATE
DEPILATED
DEPILATES
DEPILATING
DEPILATOR
DEPILATORS
DEPLANE
DEPLANED
DEPLANES
DEPLANING
DEPLETE
DEPLETED
DEPLETES
DEPLETING
DEPLETION
DEPLETIONS
DEPLETIVE
DEPLETORY
DEPLORE
DEPLORED
DEPLORES
DEPLORING
DEPLOY
DEPLOYED
DEPLOYING
DEPLOYS
DEPLUME
DEPLUMED
DEPLUMES
DEPLUMING
DEPONE
DEPONED
DEPONENT
DEPONENTS
DEPONES
DEPONING
DEPORT
DEPORTED
DEPORTEE
DEPORTEES
DEPORTING
DEPORTS
DEPOSABLE
DEPOSAL
DEPOSALS
DEPOSE
DEPOSED
DEPOSER
DEPOSERS
DEPOSES
DEPOSING
DEPOSIT
DEPOSITED
DEPOSITING
DEPOSITOR
DEPOSITORS
DEPOSITS
DEPOT
DEPOTS
DEPRAVE
DEPRAVED
DEPRAVES

DEPRAVING
DEPRAVITIES
DEPRAVITY
DEPRECATE
DEPRECATED
DEPRECATES
DEPRECATING
DEPREDATE
DEPREDATED
DEPREDATES
DEPREDATING
DEPREHEND
DEPREHENDED
DEPREHENDING
DEPREHENDS
DEPRESS
DEPRESSED
DEPRESSES
DEPRESSING
DEPRESSOR
DEPRESSORS
DEPRIVAL
DEPRIVALS
DEPRIVE
DEPRIVED
DEPRIVES
DEPRIVING
DEPROGRAM
DEPROGRAMMED
DEPROGRAMMING
DEPROGRAMS
DEPSIDE
DEPSIDES
DEPTH
DEPTHLESS
DEPTHS
DEPURANT
DEPURANTS
DEPURATE
DEPURATED
DEPURATES
DEPURATING
DEPURATOR
DEPURATORS
DEPUTE
DEPUTED
DEPUTES
DEPUTIES
DEPUTING
DEPUTISE
DEPUTISED
DEPUTISES
DEPUTISING
DEPUTIZE
DEPUTIZED
DEPUTIZES
DEPUTIZING
DEPUTY
DÉRACINÉ
DERAIGN
DERAIGNED
DERAIGNING
DERAIGNS
DERAIL
DERAILED
DERAILER
DERAILERS
DERAILING
DERAILS
DERANGE

DERANGED
DERANGES
DERANGING
DERATE
DERATED
DERATES
DERATING
DERATINGS
DERATION
DERATIONED
DERATIONING
DERATIONS
DERAY
DERAYED
DERAYING
DERAYS
DERBIES
DERBY
DERE
DERED
DERELICT
DERELICTS
DERES
DERHAM
DERHAMS
DERIDE
DERIDED
DERIDER
DERIDERS
DERIDES
DERIDING
DERING
DERISIBLE
DERISION
DERISIONS
DERISIVE
DERISORY
DERIVABLE
DERIVABLY
DERIVATE
DERIVATES
DERIVE
DERIVED
DERIVES
DERIVING
DERM
DERMA
DERMAL
DERMAS
DERMATIC
DERMATOID
DERMATOME
DERMATOMES
DERMIC
DERMIS
DERMISES
DERMOID
DERMOIDS
DERMS
DERN
DERNFUL
DERNIER
DERNLY
DERNS
DEROGATE
DEROGATED
DEROGATES
DEROGATING
DERRICK
DERRICKED

DERRICKING
DERRICKS
DERRIÈRE
DERRIÈRES
DERRIES
DERRINGER
DERRINGERS
DERRIS
DERRISES
DERRY
DERTH
DERTHS
DERV
DERVISH
DERVISHES
DERVS
DESALT
DESALTED
DESALTING
DESALTINGS
DESALTS
DESCALE
DESCALED
DESCALES
DESCALING
DESCANT
DESCANTED
DESCANTING
DESCANTS
DESCEND
DESCENDED
DESCENDER
DESCENDERS
DESCENDING
DESCENDINGS
DESCENDS
DESCENT
DESCENTS
DESCHOOL
DESCHOOLED
DESCHOOLING
DESCHOOLINGS
DESCHOOLS
DESCRIBE
DESCRIBED
DESCRIBER
DESCRIBERS
DESCRIBES
DESCRIBING
DESCRIED
DESCRIES
DESCRIVE
DESCRIVED
DESCRIVES
DESCRIVING
DESCRY
DESCRYING
DESECRATE
DESECRATED
DESECRATES
DESECRATING
DESELECT
DESELECTED
DESELECTING
DESELECTS
DESERT
DESERTED
DESERTER
DESERTERS
DESERTING

DESERTION
DESERTIONS
DESERTS
DESERVE
DESERVED
DESERVER
DESERVERS
DESERVES
DESERVING
DESEX
DESEXED
DESEXES
DESEXING
DESICCANT
DESICCANTS
DESICCATE
DESICCATED
DESICCATES
DESICCATING
DESIGN
DESIGNATE
DESIGNATED
DESIGNATES
DESIGNATING
DESIGNED
DESIGNER
DESIGNERS
DESIGNFUL
DESIGNING
DESIGNINGS
DESIGNS
DESILVER
DESILVERED
DESILVERING
DESILVERS
DESINE
DESINED
DESINENCE
DESINENCES
DESINENT
DESINES
DESINING
DESIPIENT
DESIRABLE
DESIRABLES
DESIRABLY
DESIRE
DESIRED
DESIRER
DESIRERS
DESIRES
DESIRING
DESIROUS
DESIST
DESISTED
DESISTING
DESISTS
DESK
DESKBOUND
DESKILL
DESKILLED
DESKILLING
DESKILLS
DESKS
DESKTOP
DESMAN
DESMANS
DESMID
DESMIDS
DESMINE

DESMINES
DESMODIUM
DESMODIUMS
DESMOID
DESMOSOME
DESMOSOMES
DÉSOEUVRÉ
DESOLATE
DESOLATED
DESOLATER
DESOLATERS
DESOLATES
DESOLATING
DESOLATOR
DESOLATORS
DESORB
DESORBED
DESORBING
DESORBS
DESPAIR
DESPAIRED
DESPAIRING
DESPAIRS
DESPATCH
DESPATCHED
DESPATCHES
DESPATCHING
DESPERADO
DESPERADOES
DESPERADOS
DESPERATE
DESPIGHT
DESPIGHTS
DESPISAL
DESPISALS
DESPISE
DESPISED
DESPISER
DESPISERS
DESPISES
DESPISING
DESPITE
DESPITES
DESPOIL
DESPOILED
DESPOILER
DESPOILERS
DESPOILING
DESPOILS
DESPOND
DESPONDED
DESPONDING
DESPONDINGS
DESPONDS
DESPOT
DESPOTAT
DESPOTATE
DESPOTATES
DESPOTATS
DESPOTIC
DESPOTISM
DESPOTISMS
DESPOTS
DESPUMATE
DESPUMATED
DESPUMATES
DESPUMATING
DESSE
DESSERT
DESSERTS

DESSES
DESTEMPER
DESTEMPERED
DESTEMPERING
DESTEMPERS
DESTINATE
DESTINATED
DESTINATES
DESTINATING
DESTINE
DESTINED
DESTINES
DESTINIES
DESTINING
DESTINY
DESTITUTE
DESTITUTED
DESTITUTES
DESTITUTING
DESTRIER
DESTRIERS
DESTROY
DESTROYED
DESTROYER
DESTROYERS
DESTROYING
DESTROYS
DESTRUCT
DESTRUCTED
DESTRUCTING
DESTRUCTS
DESUETUDE
DESUETUDES
DESULPHUR
DESULPHURED
DESULPHURING
DESULPHURS
DESULTORY
DESYATIN
DESYATINS
DESYNE
DESYNED
DESYNES
DESYNING
DETACH
DETACHED
DETACHES
DETACHING
DETAIL
DETAILED
DETAILING
DETAILS
DETAIN
DETAINED
DETAINEE
DETAINEES
DETAINER
DETAINERS
DETAINING
DETAINS
DETECT
DETECTED
DETECTING
DETECTION
DETECTIONS
DETECTIVE
DETECTIVES
DETECTOR
DETECTORS
DETECTS

DETENT	DETRACTINGS	DEVELOPING	DEVLINGS	DEXTER
DÉTENTE	DETRACTOR	DEVELOPS	DEVOICE	DEXTERITIES
DÉTENTES	DETRACTORS	DEVELS	DEVOICED	DEXTERITY
DETENTION	DETRACTS	DEVEST	DEVOICES	DEXTEROUS
DETENTIONS	DETRAIN	DEVESTED	DEVOICING	DEXTERS
DETENTS	DETRAINED	DEVESTING	DEVOID	DEXTRAL
DÉTENU	DETRAINING	DEVESTS	DEVOIR	DEXTRALLY
DÉTENUE	DETRAINS	DEVIANCE	DEVOIRS	DEXTRAN
DÉTENUES	DÉTRAQUÉ	DEVIANCES	DEVOLVE	DEXTRANS
DÉTENUS	DÉTRAQUÉE	DEVIANCIES	DEVOLVED	DEXTRIN
DETER	DÉTRAQUÉES	DEVIANCY	DEVOLVES	DEXTRINE
DETERGE	DÉTRAQUÉS	DEVIANT	DEVOLVING	DEXTRINES
DETERGED	DETRIMENT	DEVIANTS	DEVONPORT	DEXTRINS
DETERGENT	DETRIMENTS	DEVIATE	DEVONPORTS	DEXTRORSE
DETERGENTS	DETRITAL	DEVIATED	DÉVOT	DEXTROSE
DETERGES	DETRITION	DEVIATES	DEVOTE	DEXTROSES
DETERGING	DETRITIONS	DEVIATING	DEVOTED	DEXTROUS
DETERMENT	DETRITUS	DEVIATION	DEVOTEDLY	DEY
DETERMENTS	DETRUDE	DEVIATIONS	DEVOTEE	DEYS
DETERMINE	DETRUDED	DEVIATOR	DEVOTEES	DHAK
DETERMINED	DETRUDES	DEVIATORS	DEVOTES	DHAKS
DETERMINES	DETRUDING	DEVIATORY	DEVOTING	DHAL
DETERMINING	DETRUSION	DEVICE	DEVOTION	DHALS
DETERRED	DETRUSIONS	DEVICEFUL	DEVOTIONS	DHARMA
DETERRENT	DEUCE	DEVICES	DÉVOTS	DHARMAS
DETERRENTS	DEUCED	DEVIL	DEVOUR	DHARMSALA
DETERRING	DEUCEDLY	DEVILDOM	DEVOURED	DHARMSALAS
DETERS	DEUCES	DEVILDOMS	DEVOURER	DHARNA
DETERSION	DEUDDARN	DEVILESS	DEVOURERS	DHARNAS
DETERSIONS	DEUDDARNS	DEVILESSES	DEVOURING	DHOBI
DETERSIVE	DEUS	DEVILET	DEVOURS	DHOBIS
DETERSIVES	DEUTERATE	DEVILETS	DEVOUT	DHOLE
DETEST	DEUTERATED	DEVILING	DEVOUTER	DHOLES
DETESTED	DEUTERATES	DEVILINGS	DEVOUTEST	DHOLL
DETESTING	DEUTERATING	DEVILISH	DEVOUTLY	DHOLLS
DETESTS	DEUTERIDE	DEVILISM	DEVVEL	DHOOLIES
DETHRONE	DEUTERIDES	DEVILISMS	DEVVELLED	DHOOLY
DETHRONED	DEUTERIUM	DEVILKIN	DEVVELLING	DHOOTI
DETHRONER	DEUTERIUMS	DEVILKINS	DEVVELS	DHOOTIS
DETHRONERS	DEUTERON	DEVILLED	DEW	DHOTI
DETHRONES	DEUTERONS	DEVILLING	DEWAN	DHOTIS
DETHRONING	DEUTON	DEVILMENT	DEWANI	DHOW
DETHRONINGS	DEUTONS	DEVILMENTS	DEWANIS	DHOWS
DETINUE	DEVA	DEVILRIES	DEWANNIES	DHURRA
DETINUES	DEVALL	DEVILRY	DEWANNY	DHURRAS
DETONATE	DEVALLED	DEVILS	DEWANS	DHURRIE
DETONATED	DEVALLING	DEVILSHIP	DEWATER	DHURRIES
DETONATES	DEVALLS	DEVILSHIPS	DEWATERED	DI
DETONATING	DEVALUATE	DEVILTRIES	DEWATERING	DIABASE
DETONATOR	DEVALUATED	DEVILTRY	DEWATERS	DIABASES
DETONATORS	DEVALUATES	DEVIOUS	DEWED	DIABASIC
DETORSION	DEVALUATING	DEVIOUSLY	DEWFULL	DIABETES
DETORSIONS	DEVALUE	DEVISABLE	DEWIER	DIABETIC
DETORT	DEVALUED	DEVISAL	DEWIEST	DIABETICS
DETORTED	DEVALUES	DEVISALS	DEWILY	DIABLERIE
DETORTING	DEVALUING	DEVISE	DEWINESS	DIABLERIES
DETORTION	DEVAS	DEVISED	DEWINESSES	DIABLERY
DETORTIONS	DEVASTATE	DEVISEE	DEWING	DIABOLIC
DETORTS	DEVASTATED	DEVISEES	DEWITT	DIABOLISE
DETOUR	DEVASTATES	DEVISER	DEWITTED	DIABOLISED
DETOURED	DEVASTATING	DEVISERS	DEWITTING	DIABOLISES
DETOURING	DEVEL	DEVISES	DEWITTS	DIABOLISING
DETOURS	DEVELLED	DEVISING	DEWLAP	DIABOLISM
DETOXIFIED	DEVELLING	DEVISOR	DEWLAPPED	DIABOLISMS
DETOXIFIES	DEVELOP	DEVISORS	DEWLAPS	DIABOLIZE
DETOXIFY	DEVELOPE	DEVITRIFIED	DEWLAPT	DIABOLIZED
DETOXIFYING	DEVELOPED	DEVITRIFIES	DEWPOINT	DIABOLIZES
DETRACT	DEVELOPER	DEVITRIFY	DEWPOINTS	DIABOLIZING
DETRACTED	DEVELOPERS	DEVITRIFYING	DEWS	DIABOLO
DETRACTING	DEVELOPES	DEVLING	DEWY	DIABOLOGIES

DIABOLOGY	DIALOGIZED	DIAPYETICS	DIAZO	DICKIES
DIABOLOS	DIALOGIZES	DIARCH	DIAZOES	DICKIEST
DIACHYLON	DIALOGIZING	DIARCHAL	DIAZOS	DICKS
DIACHYLONS	DIALOGS	DIARCHIC	DIB	DICKTIER
DIACHYLUM	DIALOGUE	DIARCHIES	DIBASIC	DICKTIEST
DIACHYLUMS	DIALOGUED	DIARCHY	DIBBED	DICKTY
DIACID	DIALOGUES	DIARIAL	DIBBER	DICKY
DIACODION	DIALOGUING	DIARIAN	DIBBERS	DICLINISM
DIACODIONS	DIALS	DIARIES	DIBBING	DICLINISMS
DIACODIUM	DIALYSE	DIARISE	DIBBLE	DICLINOUS
DIACODIUMS	DIALYSED	DIARISED	DIBBLED	DICOT
DIACONAL	DIALYSER	DIARISES	DIBBLER	DICOTS
DIACONATE	DIALYSERS	DIARISING	DIBBLERS	DICROTIC
DIACONATES	DIALYSES	DIARIST	DIBBLES	DICROTISM
DIACRITIC	DIALYSING	DIARISTS	DIBBLING	DICROTISMS
DIACRITICS	DIALYSIS	DIARIZE	DIBBS	DICROTOUS
DIACT	DIALYTIC	DIARIZED	DIBS	DICT
DIACTINAL	DIALYZE	DIARIZES	DIBUTYL	DICTA
DIACTINE	DIALYZED	DIARIZING	DICACIOUS	DICTATE
DIACTINIC	DIALYZER	DIARRHEA	DICACITIES	DICTATED
DIADEM	DIALYZERS	DIARRHEAL	DICACITY	DICTATES
DIADEMED	DIALYZES	DIARRHEAS	DICAST	DICTATING
DIADEMS	DIALYZING	DIARRHEIC	DICASTERIES	DICTATION
DIADOCHI	DIAMAGNET	DIARRHOEA	DICASTERY	DICTATIONS
DIADROM	DIAMAGNETS	DIARRHOEAS	DICASTIC	DICTATOR
DIADROMS	DIAMANTÉ	DIARY	DICASTS	DICTATORS
DIAERESES	DIAMANTÉS	DIASCOPE	DICE	DICTATORY
DIAERESIS	DIAMETER	DIASCOPES	DICED	DICTATRIX
DIAGLYPH	DIAMETERS	DIASPORA	DICENTRA	DICTATRIXES
DIAGLYPHS	DIAMETRAL	DIASPORAS	DICENTRAS	DICTATURE
DIAGNOSE	DIAMETRIC	DIASPORE	DICER	DICTATURES
DIAGNOSED	DIAMOND	DIASPORES	DICERS	DICTED
DIAGNOSES	DIAMONDED	DIASTASE	DICES	DICTIER
DIAGNOSING	DIAMONDS	DIASTASES	DICEY	DICTIEST
DIAGNOSIS	DIAMYL	DIASTASIC	DICH	DICTING
DIAGONAL	DIANDRIES	DIASTASIS	DICHASIA	DICTION
DIAGONALS	DIANDROUS	DIASTATIC	DICHASIAL	DICTIONS
DIAGRAM	DIANDRY	DIASTEMA	DICHASIUM	DICTS
DIAGRAMS	DIANETICS®	DIASTEMATA	DICHOGAMIES	DICTUM
DIAGRAPH	DIANODAL	DIASTER	DICHOGAMY	DICTY
DIAGRAPHS	DIANOETIC	DIASTERS	DICHORD	DICTYOGEN
DIAGRID	DIANTHUS	DIASTOLE	DICHORDS	DICTYOGENS
DIAGRIDS	DIANTHUSES	DIASTOLES	DICHOTOMIES	DICYCLIC
DIAL	DIAPASE	DIASTOLIC	DICHOTOMY	DID
DIALECT	DIAPASES	DIASTYLE	DICHROIC	DIDACTIC
DIALECTAL	DIAPASON	DIASTYLES	DICHROISM	DIDACTICS
DIALECTIC	DIAPASONS	DIATHERMIES	DICHROISMS	DIDACTYL
DIALECTICS	DIAPAUSE	DIATHERMY	DICHROITE	DIDACTYLS
DIALECTS	DIAPAUSES	DIATHESES	DICHROITES	DIDAKAI
DIALIST	DIAPENTE	DIATHESIS	DICHROMAT	DIDAKAIS
DIALISTS	DIAPENTES	DIATHETIC	DICHROMATS	DIDAKEI
DIALLAGE	DIAPER	DIATOM	DICHROMIC	DIDAKEIS
DIALLAGES	DIAPERED	DIATOMIC	DICHT	DIDAPPER
DIALLAGIC	DIAPERING	DIATOMIST	DICHTED	DIDAPPERS
DIALLED	DIAPERINGS	DIATOMISTS	DICHTING	DIDDER
DIALLER	DIAPERS	DIATOMITE	DICHTS	DIDDERED
DIALLERS	DIAPHONE	DIATOMITES	DICIER	DIDDERING
DIALLING	DIAPHONES	DIATOMS	DICIEST	DIDDERS
DIALLINGS	DIAPHRAGM	DIATONIC	DICING	DIDDICOI
DIALOG	DIAPHRAGMS	DIATRETUM	DICINGS	DIDDICOIS
DIALOGIC	DIAPHYSES	DIATRETUMS	DICK	DIDDICOY
DIALOGISE	DIAPHYSIS	DIATRIBE	DICKENS	DIDDICOYS
DIALOGISED	DIAPIR	DIATRIBES	DICKER	DIDDLE
DIALOGISES	DIAPIRIC	DIATROPIC	DICKERED	DIDDLED
DIALOGISING	DIAPIRISM	DIAXON	DICKERING	DIDDLER
DIALOGIST	DIAPIRISMS	DIAXONS	DICKERS	DIDDLERS
DIALOGISTS	DIAPIRS	DIAZEPAM	DICKEY	DIDDLES
DIALOGITE	DIAPYESES	DIAZEPAMS	DICKEYS	DIDDLING
DIALOGITES	DIAPYESIS	DIAZEUXES	DICKIE	DIDELPHIC
DIALOGIZE	DIAPYETIC	DIAZEUXIS	DICKIER	DIDELPHID

DIDELPHIDS
DIDICOI
DIDICOIS
DIDICOY
DIDICOYS
DIDO
DIDOES
DIDOS
DIDRACHM
DIDRACHMA
DIDRACHMAS
DIDRACHMS
DIDST
DIDYMIUM
DIDYMIUMS
DIDYMOUS
DIE
DIEB
DIEBACK
DIEBACKS
DIEBS
DIED
DIEDRAL
DIEDRALS
DIEDRE
DIEDRES
DIEGESES
DIEGESIS
DIELDRIN
DIELDRINS
DIELYTRA
DIELYTRAS
DIENE
DIENES
DIERESES
DIERESIS
DIES
DIESEL
DIESELISE
DIESELISED
DIESELISES
DIESELISING
DIESELIZE
DIESELIZED
DIESELIZES
DIESELIZING
DIESELS
DIESES
DIESIS
DIESTRUS
DIESTRUSES
DIET
DIETARIAN
DIETARIANS
DIETARIES
DIETARY
DIETED
DIETER
DIETERS
DIETETIC
DIETETICS
DIETHYL
DIETICIAN
DIETICIANS
DIETINE
DIETINES
DIETING
DIETIST
DIETISTS
DIETITIAN

DIETITIANS
DIETS
DIFFER
DIFFERED
DIFFERENT
DIFFERING
DIFFERS
DIFFICILE
DIFFICULT
DIFFIDENT
DIFFLUENT
DIFFORM
DIFFRACT
DIFFRACTED
DIFFRACTING
DIFFRACTS
DIFFUSE
DIFFUSED
DIFFUSELY
DIFFUSER
DIFFUSERS
DIFFUSES
DIFFUSING
DIFFUSION
DIFFUSIONS
DIFFUSIVE
DIG
DIGAMIES
DIGAMIST
DIGAMISTS
DIGAMMA
DIGAMMAS
DIGAMOUS
DIGAMY
DIGASTRIC
DIGEST
DIGESTED
DIGESTER
DIGESTERS
DIGESTING
DIGESTION
DIGESTIONS
DIGESTIVE
DIGESTIVES
DIGESTS
DIGGABLE
DIGGED
DIGGER
DIGGERS
DIGGING
DIGGINGS
DIGHT
DIGHTED
DIGHTING
DIGHTS
DIGIT
DIGITAL
DIGITALIN
DIGITALINS
DIGITALIS
DIGITALISES
DIGITALS
DIGITATE
DIGITATED
DIGITISE
DIGITISED
DIGITISER
DIGITISERS
DIGITISES
DIGITISING

DIGITIZE
DIGITIZED
DIGITIZER
DIGITIZERS
DIGITIZES
DIGITIZING
DIGITS
DIGLOT
DIGLOTS
DIGLYPH
DIGLYPHS
DIGNIFIED
DIGNIFIES
DIGNIFY
DIGNIFYING
DIGNITARIES
DIGNITARY
DIGNITIES
DIGNITY
DIGONAL
DIGRAPH
DIGRAPHS
DIGRESS
DIGRESSED
DIGRESSES
DIGRESSING
DIGS
DIGYNIAN
DIGYNOUS
DIHEDRAL
DIHEDRALS
DIHEDRON
DIHEDRONS
DIHYBRID
DIHYBRIDS
DIHYDRIC
DIKA
DIKAS
DIKAST
DIKASTS
DIKE
DIKED
DIKER
DIKERS
DIKES
DIKEY
DIKIER
DIKIEST
DIKING
DIKTAT
DIKTATS
DILATABLE
DILATANCIES
DILATANCY
DILATANT
DILATATOR
DILATATORS
DILATE
DILATED
DILATER
DILATERS
DILATES
DILATING
DILATION
DILATIONS
DILATIVE
DILATOR
DILATORS
DILATORY
DILDO

DILDOE
DILDOES
DILDOS
DILEMMA
DILEMMAS
DILIGENCE
DILIGENCES
DILIGENT
DILL
DILLI
DILLIER
DILLIES
DILLIEST
DILLING
DILLINGS
DILLIS
DILLS
DILLY
DILUENT
DILUENTS
DILUTABLE
DILUTABLES
DILUTE
DILUTED
DILUTEES
DILUTER
DILUTERS
DILUTES
DILUTING
DILUTION
DILUTIONS
DILUTOR
DILUTORS
DILUVIA
DILUVIAL
DILUVIAN
DILUVION
DILUVIONS
DILUVIUM
DILUVIUMS
DIM
DIMBLE
DIMBLES
DIME
DIMENSION
DIMENSIONED
DIMENSIONING
DIMENSIONS
DIMER
DIMERIC
DIMERISE
DIMERISED
DIMERISES
DIMERISING
DIMERISM
DIMERISMS
DIMERIZE
DIMERIZED
DIMERIZES
DIMERIZING
DIMEROUS
DIMERS
DIMES
DIMETER
DIMETERS
DIMETHYL
DIMETHYLS
DIMETRIC
DIMIDIATE

DIMIDIATED
DIMIDIATES
DIMIDIATING
DIMINISH
DIMINISHED
DIMINISHES
DIMINISHING
DIMINISHINGS
DIMISSORY
DIMITIES
DIMITY
DIMLY
DIMMED
DIMMER
DIMMERS
DIMMEST
DIMMING
DIMMISH
DIMNESS
DIMNESSES
DIMORPH
DIMORPHIC
DIMORPHS
DIMPLE
DIMPLED
DIMPLES
DIMPLIER
DIMPLIEST
DIMPLING
DIMPLY
DIMS
DIMWIT
DIMWITS
DIMYARIAN
DIN
DINAR
DINARCHIES
DINARCHY
DINARS
DINDLE
DINDLED
DINDLES
DINDLING
DINE
DINED
DINER
DINERS
DINES
DINETTE
DINETTES
DINFUL
DING
DINGBAT
DINGBATS
DINGE
DINGED
DINGER
DINGERS
DINGES
DINGESES
DINGEY
DINGEYS
DINGHIES
DINGHY
DINGIER
DINGIES
DINGIEST
DINGINESS
DINGINESSES
DINGING

DINGLE
DINGLES
DINGO
DINGOES
DINGS
DINGUS
DINGUSES
DINGY
DINIC
DINICS
DINING
DINK
DINKED
DINKER
DINKEST
DINKIER
DINKIES
DINKIEST
DINKING
DINKS
DINKUM
DINKY
DINMONT
DINMONTS
DINNED
DINNER
DINNERED
DINNERING
DINNERS
DINNING
DINNLE
DINNLED
DINNLES
DINNLING
DINOSAUR
DINOSAURS
DINS
DINT
DINTED
DINTING
DINTS
DIOCESAN
DIOCESANS
DIOCESE
DIOCESES
DIODE
DIODES
DIOECIOUS
DIOECISM
DIOECISMS
DIOESTRUS
DIOESTRUSES
DIOPSIDE
DIOPSIDES
DIOPTASE
DIOPTASES
DIOPTER
DIOPTERS
DIOPTRATE
DIOPTRE
DIOPTRES
DIOPTRIC
DIOPTRICS
DIORAMA
DIORAMAS
DIORAMIC
DIORISM
DIORISMS
DIORISTIC
DIORITE

DIORITES
DIORITIC
DIOSGENIN
DIOSGENINS
DIOTA
DIOTAS
DIOXAN
DIOXANE
DIOXANES
DIOXANS
DIOXIDE
DIOXIDES
DIOXIN
DIOXINS
DIP
DIPCHICK
DIPCHICKS
DIPEPTIDE
DIPEPTIDES
DIPHENYL
DIPHENYLS
DIPHONE
DIPHONES
DIPHTHONG
DIPHTHONGS
DIPHYSITE
DIPHYSITES
DIPLEX
DIPLOE
DIPLOES
DIPLOGEN
DIPLOGENS
DIPLOID
DIPLOIDIES
DIPLOIDY
DIPLOMA
DIPLOMACIES
DIPLOMACY
DIPLOMAED
DIPLOMAING
DIPLOMAS
DIPLOMAT
DIPLOMATE
DIPLOMATED
DIPLOMATES
DIPLOMATING
DIPLOMATS
DIPLON
DIPLONS
DIPLONT
DIPLONTS
DIPLOPIA
DIPLOPIAS
DIPNOAN
DIPNOANS
DIPNOOUS
DIPODIES
DIPODY
DIPOLAR
DIPOLE
DIPOLES
DIPPED
DIPPER
DIPPERS
DIPPIER
DIPPIEST
DIPPING
DIPPINGS
DIPPY
DIPS

DIPSADES
DIPSAS
DIPSO
DIPSOS
DIPTERAL
DIPTERAN
DIPTERANS
DIPTERIST
DIPTERISTS
DIPTEROI
DIPTEROS
DIPTEROSES
DIPTEROUS
DIPTYCH
DIPTYCHS
DIRDAM
DIRDAMS
DIRDUM
DIRDUMS
DIRE
DIRECT
DIRECTED
DIRECTER
DIRECTEST
DIRECTING
DIRECTION
DIRECTIONS
DIRECTIVE
DIRECTIVES
DIRECTLY
DIRECTOR
DIRECTORIES
DIRECTORS
DIRECTORY
DIRECTRICES
DIRECTRIX
DIRECTRIXES
DIRECTS
DIREFUL
DIREFULLY
DIREMPT
DIREMPTED
DIREMPTING
DIREMPTS
DIRER
DIREST
DIRGE
DIRGES
DIRHAM
DIRHAMS
DIRHEM
DIRHEMS
DIRIGE
DIRIGENT
DIRIGES
DIRIGIBLE
DIRIGIBLES
DIRIGISM
DIRIGISME
DIRIGISMES
DIRIGISMS
DIRIGISTE
DIRIMENT
DIRK
DIRKE
DIRKED
DIRKES
DIRKING
DIRKS
DIRL

DIRLED
DIRLING
DIRLS
DIRNDL
DIRNDLS
DIRT
DIRTED
DIRTIED
DIRTIER
DIRTIES
DIRTIEST
DIRTILY
DIRTINESS
DIRTINESSES
DIRTING
DIRTS
DIRTY
DIRTYING
DISA
DISABLE
DISABLED
DISABLES
DISABLING
DISABUSE
DISABUSED
DISABUSES
DISABUSING
DISACCORD
DISACCORDED
DISACCORDING
DISACCORDS
DISADORN
DISADORNED
DISADORNING
DISADORNS
DISAFFECT
DISAFFECTED
DISAFFECTING
DISAFFECTS
DISAFFIRM
DISAFFIRMED
DISAFFIRMING
DISAFFIRMS
DISAGREE
DISAGREED
DISAGREEING
DISAGREES
DISALLIED
DISALLIES
DISALLOW
DISALLOWED
DISALLOWING
DISALLOWS
DISALLY
DISALLYING
DISANCHOR
DISANCHORED
DISANCHORING
DISANCHORS
DISANNEX
DISANNEXED
DISANNEXES
DISANNEXING
DISANNUL
DISANNULLED
DISANNULLING
DISANNULLINGS
DISANNULS
DISANOINT
DISANOINTED

DISANOINTING
DISANOINTS
DISAPPEAR
DISAPPEARED
DISAPPEARING
DISAPPEARS
DISAPPLIED
DISAPPLIES
DISAPPLY
DISAPPLYING
DISARM
DISARMED
DISARMER
DISARMERS
DISARMING
DISARMS
DISARRAY
DISARRAYED
DISARRAYING
DISARRAYS
DISAS
DISASTER
DISASTERS
DISATTIRE
DISATTIRED
DISATTIRES
DISATTIRING
DISATTUNE
DISATTUNED
DISATTUNES
DISATTUNING
DISAVOUCH
DISAVOUCHED
DISAVOUCHES
DISAVOUCHING
DISAVOW
DISAVOWAL
DISAVOWALS
DISAVOWED
DISAVOWING
DISAVOWS
DISBAND
DISBANDED
DISBANDING
DISBANDS
DISBAR
DISBARK
DISBARKED
DISBARKING
DISBARKS
DISBARRED
DISBARRING
DISBARS
DISBELIEF
DISBELIEFS
DISBENCH
DISBENCHED
DISBENCHES
DISBENCHING
DISBODIED
DISBOSOM
DISBOSOMED
DISBOSOMING
DISBOSOMS
DISBOWEL
DISBOWELLED
DISBOWELLING
DISBOWELS
DISBRANCH
DISBRANCHED

DISBRANCHES
DISBRANCHING
DISBUD
DISBUDDED
DISBUDDING
DISBUDS
DISBURDEN
DISBURDENED
DISBURDENING
DISBURDENS
DISBURSAL
DISBURSALS
DISBURSE
DISBURSED
DISBURSES
DISBURSING
DISC
DISCAGE
DISCAGED
DISCAGES
DISCAGING
DISCAL
DISCALCED
DISCANDIE
DISCANDIED
DISCANDIES
DISCANDY
DISCANDYING
DISCANDYINGS
DISCANT
DISCANTED
DISCANTING
DISCANTS
DISCARD
DISCARDED
DISCARDING
DISCARDS
DISCASE
DISCASED
DISCASES
DISCASING
DISCED
DISCEPT
DISCEPTED
DISCEPTING
DISCEPTS
DISCERN
DISCERNED
DISCERNER
DISCERNERS
DISCERNING
DISCERNS
DISCERP
DISCERPED
DISCERPING
DISCERPS
DISCHARGE
DISCHARGED
DISCHARGES
DISCHARGING
DISCHURCH
DISCHURCHED
DISCHURCHES
DISCHURCHING
DISCIDE
DISCIDED
DISCIDES
DISCIDING
DISCINCT
DISCING

DISCIPLE
DISCIPLED
DISCIPLES
DISCIPLING
DISCLAIM
DISCLAIMED
DISCLAIMING
DISCLAIMS
DISCLOSE
DISCLOSED
DISCLOSES
DISCLOSING
DISCLOST
DISCO
DISCOBOLI
DISCOER
DISCOERS
DISCOID
DISCOIDAL
DISCOLOUR
DISCOLOURED
DISCOLOURING
DISCOLOURS
DISCOMFIT
DISCOMFITED
DISCOMFITING
DISCOMFITS
DISCOMMON
DISCOMMONED
DISCOMMONING
DISCOMMONS
DISCORD
DISCORDED
DISCORDING
DISCORDS
DISCOS
DISCOUNT
DISCOUNTED
DISCOUNTING
DISCOUNTS
DISCOURE
DISCOURED
DISCOURES
DISCOURING
DISCOURSE
DISCOURSED
DISCOURSES
DISCOURSING
DISCOVER
DISCOVERED
DISCOVERIES
DISCOVERING
DISCOVERS
DISCOVERT
DISCOVERY
DISCREDIT
DISCREDITED
DISCREDITING
DISCREDITS
DISCREET
DISCREETER
DISCREETEST
DISCRETE
DISCRETER
DISCRETEST
DISCROWN
DISCROWNED
DISCROWNING
DISCROWNS
DISCS

DISCUMBER
DISCUMBERED
DISCUMBERING
DISCUMBERS
DISCURE
DISCURED
DISCURES
DISCURING
DISCURSUS
DISCURSUSES
DISCUS
DISCUSES
DISCUSS
DISCUSSED
DISCUSSES
DISCUSSING
DISDAIN
DISDAINED
DISDAINING
DISDAINS
DISEASE
DISEASED
DISEASES
DISEASING
DISEDGE
DISEDGED
DISEDGES
DISEDGING
DISEMBARK
DISEMBARKED
DISEMBARKING
DISEMBARKS
DISEMBODIED
DISEMBODIES
DISEMBODY
DISEMBODYING
DISEMPLOY
DISEMPLOYED
DISEMPLOYING
DISEMPLOYS
DISENABLE
DISENABLED
DISENABLES
DISENABLING
DISENDOW
DISENDOWED
DISENDOWING
DISENDOWS
DISENGAGED
DISENGAGES
DISENGAGING
DISENROL
DISENROLLED
DISENROLLING
DISENROLS
DISENTAIL
DISENTAILED
DISENTAILING
DISENTAILS
DISENTOMB
DISENTOMBED
DISENTOMBING
DISENTOMBS
DISESTEEM
DISESTEEMED
DISESTEEMING
DISESTEEMS
DISEUR
DISEURS

DISEUSE
DISEUSES
DISFAME
DISFAMES
DISFAVOR
DISFAVORED
DISFAVORING
DISFAVORS
DISFAVOUR
DISFAVOURED
DISFAVOURING
DISFAVOURS
DISFIGURE
DISFIGURED
DISFIGURES
DISFIGURING
DISFLESH
DISFLESHED
DISFLESHES
DISFLESHING
DISFLUENT
DISFOREST
DISFORESTED
DISFORESTING
DISFORESTS
DISFORM
DISFORMED
DISFORMING
DISFORMS
DISFROCK
DISFROCKED
DISFROCKING
DISFROCKS
DISGAVEL
DISGAVELLED
DISGAVELLING
DISGAVELS
DISGEST
DISGESTED
DISGESTING
DISGESTS
DISGODDED
DISGORGE
DISGORGED
DISGORGES
DISGORGING
DISGOWN
DISGOWNED
DISGOWNING
DISGOWNS
DISGRACE
DISGRACED
DISGRACER
DISGRACERS
DISGRACES
DISGRACING
DISGRADE
DISGRADED
DISGRADES
DISGRADING
DISGUISE
DISGUISED
DISGUISER
DISGUISERS
DISGUISES
DISGUISING
DISGUISINGS
DISGUST
DISGUSTED
DISGUSTING

DISGUSTS
DISH
DISHABIT
DISHABITED
DISHABITING
DISHABITS
DISHABLE
DISHABLED
DISHABLES
DISHABLING
DISHALLOW
DISHALLOWED
DISHALLOWING
DISHALLOWS
DISHED
DISHELM
DISHELMED
DISHELMING
DISHELMS
DISHERIT
DISHERITED
DISHERITING
DISHERITS
DISHES
DISHEVEL
DISHEVELLED
DISHEVELLING
DISHEVELS
DISHFUL
DISHFULS
DISHIER
DISHIEST
DISHING
DISHINGS
DISHOME
DISHOMED
DISHOMES
DISHOMING
DISHONEST
DISHONOR
DISHONORED
DISHONORING
DISHONORS
DISHONOUR
DISHONOURED
DISHONOURING
DISHONOURS
DISHORN
DISHORNED
DISHORNING
DISHORNS
DISHORSE
DISHORSED
DISHORSES
DISHORSING
DISHOUSE
DISHOUSED
DISHOUSES
DISHOUSING
DISHUMOUR
DISHUMOURED
DISHUMOURING
DISHUMOURS
DISHY
DISILLUDE
DISILLUDED
DISILLUDES
DISILLUDING
DISIMMURE
DISIMMURED

DISIMMURES
DISIMMURING
DISINFECT
DISINFECTED
DISINFECTING
DISINFECTS
DISINFEST
DISINFESTED
DISINFESTING
DISINFESTS
DISINHUME
DISINHUMED
DISINHUMES
DISINHUMING
DISINTER
DISINTERRED
DISINTERRING
DISINTERS
DISINURE
DISINURED
DISINURES
DISINURING
DISINVEST
DISINVESTED
DISINVESTING
DISINVESTS
DISJASKIT
DISJECT
DISJECTED
DISJECTING
DISJECTS
DISJOIN
DISJOINED
DISJOINING
DISJOINS
DISJOINT
DISJOINTED
DISJOINTING
DISJOINTS
DISJUNCT
DISJUNCTS
DISJUNE
DISJUNES
DISK
DISKED
DISKETTE
DISKETTES
DISKING
DISKS
DISLEAF
DISLEAFED
DISLEAFING
DISLEAFS
DISLEAL
DISLEAVE
DISLEAVED
DISLEAVES
DISLEAVING
DISLIKE
DISLIKED
DISLIKEN
DISLIKENED
DISLIKENING
DISLIKENS
DISLIKES
DISLIKING
DISLIMB
DISLIMBED
DISLIMBING
DISLIMBS

DISLIMN
DISLIMNED
DISLIMNING
DISLIMNS
DISLINK
DISLINKED
DISLINKING
DISLINKS
DISLOAD
DISLOADED
DISLOADING
DISLOADS
DISLOCATE
DISLOCATED
DISLOCATES
DISLOCATING
DISLODGE
DISLODGED
DISLODGES
DISLODGING
DISLOIGN
DISLOIGNED
DISLOIGNING
DISLOIGNS
DISLOYAL
DISLUSTRE
DISLUSTRED
DISLUSTRES
DISLUSTRING
DISMAL
DISMALITIES
DISMALITY
DISMALLER
DISMALLEST
DISMALLY
DISMALS
DISMAN
DISMANNED
DISMANNING
DISMANS
DISMANTLE
DISMANTLED
DISMANTLES
DISMANTLING
DISMASK
DISMASKED
DISMASKING
DISMASKS
DISMAST
DISMASTED
DISMASTING
DISMASTS
DISMAY
DISMAYD
DISMAYED
DISMAYFUL
DISMAYING
DISMAYL
DISMAYLED
DISMAYLING
DISMAYLS
DISMAYS
DISME
DISMEMBER
DISMEMBERED
DISMEMBERING
DISMEMBERS
DISMES
DISMISS
DISMISSAL

DISMISSALS
DISMISSED
DISMISSES
DISMISSING
DISMODED
DISMOUNT
DISMOUNTED
DISMOUNTING
DISMOUNTS
DISNEST
DISNESTED
DISNESTING
DISNESTS
DISOBEY
DISOBEYED
DISOBEYING
DISOBEYS
DISOBLIGE
DISOBLIGED
DISOBLIGES
DISOBLIGING
DISORBED
DISORDER
DISORDERED
DISORDERING
DISORDERS
DISORIENT
DISORIENTED
DISORIENTING
DISORIENTS
DISOWN
DISOWNED
DISOWNING
DISOWNS
DISPACE
DISPACED
DISPACES
DISPACING
DISPARAGE
DISPARAGED
DISPARAGES
DISPARAGING
DISPARATE
DISPARATES
DISPARITIES
DISPARITY
DISPARK
DISPARKED
DISPARKING
DISPARKS
DISPART
DISPARTED
DISPARTING
DISPARTS
DISPATCH
DISPATCHED
DISPATCHES
DISPATCHING
DISPATHIES
DISPATHY
DISPAUPER
DISPAUPERED
DISPAUPERING
DISPAUPERS
DISPEACE
DISPEACES
DISPEL
DISPELLED
DISPELLING
DISPELS

DISPENCE
DISPENCED
DISPENCES
DISPENCING
DISPEND
DISPENDED
DISPENDING
DISPENDS
DISPENSE
DISPENSED
DISPENSER
DISPENSERS
DISPENSES
DISPENSING
DISPEOPLE
DISPEOPLED
DISPEOPLES
DISPEOPLING
DISPERSAL
DISPERSALS
DISPERSE
DISPERSED
DISPERSER
DISPERSERS
DISPERSES
DISPERSING
DISPIRIT
DISPIRITED
DISPIRITING
DISPIRITS
DISPLACE
DISPLACED
DISPLACES
DISPLACING
DISPLANT
DISPLANTED
DISPLANTING
DISPLANTS
DISPLAY
DISPLAYED
DISPLAYER
DISPLAYERS
DISPLAYING
DISPLAYS
DISPLE
DISPLEASE
DISPLEASED
DISPLEASES
DISPLEASING
DISPLED
DISPLES
DISPLING
DISPLODE
DISPLODED
DISPLODES
DISPLODING
DISPLUME
DISPLUMED
DISPLUMES
DISPLUMING
DISPONDEE
DISPONDEES
DISPONE
DISPONED
DISPONEE
DISPONEES
DISPONER
DISPONERS
DISPONES
DISPONGE

DISPONGED
DISPONGES
DISPONGING
DISPONING
DISPORT
DISPORTED
DISPORTING
DISPORTS
DISPOSAL
DISPOSALS
DISPOSE
DISPOSED
DISPOSER
DISPOSERS
DISPOSES
DISPOSING
DISPOSINGS
DISPOST
DISPOSTED
DISPOSTING
DISPOSTS
DISPOSURE
DISPOSURES
DISPRAD
DISPRAISE
DISPRAISED
DISPRAISES
DISPRAISING
DISPREAD
DISPREADING
DISPREADS
DISPRED
DISPREDDEN
DISPREDDING
DISPREDS
DISPRISON
DISPRISONED
DISPRISONING
DISPRISONS
DISPRIZE
DISPRIZED
DISPRIZES
DISPRIZING
DISPROFIT
DISPROFITS
DISPROOF
DISPROOFS
DISPROOVE
DISPROOVED
DISPROOVES
DISPROOVING
DISPROVAL
DISPROVALS
DISPROVE
DISPROVED
DISPROVEN
DISPROVES
DISPROVING
DISPUNGE
DISPUNGED
DISPUNGES
DISPUNGING
DISPURSE
DISPURSED
DISPURSES
DISPURSING
DISPURVEY
DISPURVEYED
DISPURVEYING
DISPURVEYS

DISPUTANT
DISPUTANTS
DISPUTE
DISPUTED
DISPUTER
DISPUTERS
DISPUTES
DISPUTING
DISQUIET
DISQUIETED
DISQUIETING
DISQUIETS
DISRANK
DISRANKED
DISRANKING
DISRANKS
DISRATE
DISRATED
DISRATES
DISRATING
DISREGARD
DISREGARDED
DISREGARDING
DISRELIANDS
DISRELISH
DISRELISHED
DISRELISHES
DISRELISHING
DISREPAIR
DISREPUTE
DISREPUTES
DISROBE
DISROBED
DISROBES
DISROBING
DISROOT
DISROOTED
DISROOTING
DISROOTS
DISRUPT
DISRUPTED
DISRUPTER
DISRUPTERS
DISRUPTING
DISRUPTOR
DISRUPTORS
DISRUPTS
DISS
DISSEAT
DISSEATED
DISSEATING
DISSEATS
DISSECT
DISSECTED
DISSECTING
DISSECTINGS
DISSECTOR
DISSECTORS
DISSECTS
DISSEISE
DISSEISED
DISSEISES
DISSEISIN
DISSEISING
DISSEISINS
DISSEISOR
DISSEISORS
DISSEIZE
DISSEIZED

DISSEIZES
DISSEIZIN
DISSEIZING
DISSEIZINS
DISSEIZOR
DISSEIZORS
DISSEMBLE
DISSEMBLED
DISSEMBLES
DISSEMBLIES
DISSEMBLING
DISSEMBLINGS
DISSEMBLY
DISSENT
DISSENTED
DISSENTER
DISSENTERS
DISSENTING
DISSENTS
DISSERT
DISSERTED
DISSERTING
DISSERTS
DISSERVE
DISSERVED
DISSERVES
DISSERVING
DISSES
DISSEVEN
DISSEVERED
DISSEVERING
DISSEVENO
DISSHIVER
DISSHIVERED
DISSHIVERING
DISSHIVERS
DISSIDENT
DISSIDENTS
DISSIGHT
DISSIGHTS
DISSIMILE
DISSIMILES
DISSIPATE
DISSIPATED
DISSIPATES
DISSIPATING
DISSOCIAL
DISSOLUTE
DISSOLUTES
DISSOLVE
DISSOLVED
DISSOLVES
DISSOLVING
DISSOLVINGS
DISSONANT
DISSUADE
DISSUADED
DISSUADER
DISSUADERS
DISSUADES
DISSUADING
DISSUNDER
DISSUNDERED
DISSUNDERING
DISSUNDERS
DISTAFF
DISTAFFS
DISTAIN
DISTAINED
DISTAINING

DISTAINS
DISTAL
DISTALLY
DISTANCE
DISTANCED
DISTANCES
DISTANCING
DISTANT
DISTANTLY
DISTASTE
DISTASTED
DISTASTES
DISTASTING
DISTEMPER
DISTEMPERED
DISTEMPERING
DISTEMPERS
DISTEND
DISTENDED
DISTENDING
DISTENDS
DISTENT
DISTHENE
DISTHENES
DISTHRONE
DISTHRONED
DISTHRONES
DISTHRONING
DIETICH
DISTICHAL
DISTICHS
DISTIL
DISTILL
DISTILLED
DISTILLER
DISTILLERS
DISTILLING
DISTILLINGS
DISTILS
DISTILS
DISTINCT
DISTINCTER
DISTINCTEST
DISTINGUÉ
DISTORT
DISTORTED
DISTORTING
DISTORTS
DISTRACT
DISTRACTED
DISTRACTING
DISTRACTS
DISTRAIN
DISTRAINED
DISTRAINING
DISTRAINS
DISTRAINT
DISTRAINTS
DISTRAIT
DISTRAITE
DISTRESS
DISTRESSED
DISTRESSES
DISTRESSING
DISTRICT
DISTRICTED
DISTRICTING
DISTRICTS
DISTRUST
DISTRUSTED

DISTRUSTING
DISTRUSTS
DISTUNE
DISTUNED
DISTUNES
DISTUNING
DISTURB
DISTURBED
DISTURBER
DISTURBERS
DISTURBING
DISTURBS
DISTYLE
DISTYLES
DISUNION
DISUNIONS
DISUNITE
DISUNITED
DISUNITES
DISUNITIES
DISUNITING
DISUNITY
DISUSAGE
DISUSE
DISUSED
DISUSES
DISUSING
DISVALUE
DISVALUED
DISVALUES
DISVALUING
DISVOUCH
DISVOUCHED
DISVOUCHES
DISVOUCHING
DISYOKE
DISYOKED
DISYOKES
DISYOKING
DIT
DITA
DITAL
DITALS
DITAS
DITCH
DITCHED
DITCHER
DITCHERS
DITCHES
DITCHING
DITE
DITED
DITES
DITHECAL
DITHECOUS
DITHEISM
DITHEISMS
DITHEIST
DITHEISTS
DITHELETE
DITHELETES
DITHELISM
DITHELISMS
DITHER
DITHERED
DITHERER
DITHERERS
DITHERIER
DITHERIEST

DITHERING
DITHERS
DITHERY
DITHYRAMB
DITHYRAMBS
DITING
DITOKOUS
DITONE
DITONES
DITROCHEE
DITROCHEES
DITS
DITT
DITTANDER
DITTANDERS
DITTANIES
DITTANY
DITTAY
DITTAYS
DITTED
DITTIED
DITTIES
DITTING
DITTIT
DITTO
DITTOED
DITTOING
DITTOLOGIES
DITTOLOGY
DITTOS
DITTS
DITTY
DITTYING
DIURESES
DIURESIS
DIURETIC
DIURETICS
DIURNAL
DIURNALLY
DIURNALS
DIUTURNAL
DIV
DIVA
DIVAGATE
DIVAGATED
DIVAGATES
DIVAGATING
DIVALENT
DIVALENTS
DIVAN
DIVANS
DIVAS
DIVE
DIVED
DIVELLENT
DIVER
DIVERGE
DIVERGED
DIVERGENT
DIVERGES
DIVERGING
DIVERS
DIVERSE
DIVERSED
DIVERSELY
DIVERSES
DIVERSIFIED
DIVERSIFIES
DIVERSIFY
DIVERSIFYING

DIVERSING
DIVERSION
DIVERSIONS
DIVERSITIES
DIVERSITY
DIVERSLY
DIVERT
DIVERTED
DIVERTING
DIVERTIVE
DIVERTS
DIVES
DIVEST
DIVESTED
DIVESTING
DIVESTS
DIVI
DIVIDABLE
DIVIDANT
DIVIDE
DIVIDED
DIVIDEDLY
DIVIDEND
DIVIDENDS
DIVIDER
DIVIDERS
DIVIDES
DIVIDING
DIVIDINGS
DIVIDIVI
DIVIDIVIS
DIVIDUAL
DIVIDUOUS
DIVIED
DIVIING
DIVINATOR
DIVINATORS
DIVINE
DIVINED
DIVINELY
DIVINER
DIVINERS
DIVINES
DIVINEST
DIVING
DIVINGS
DIVINIFIED
DIVINIFIES
DIVINIFY
DIVINIFYING
DIVINING
DIVINISE
DIVINISED
DIVINISES
DIVINISING
DIVINITIES
DIVINITY
DIVINIZE
DIVINIZED
DIVINIZES
DIVINIZING
DIVIS
DIVISIBLE
DIVISIBLY
DIVISIM
DIVISION
DIVISIONS
DIVISIVE
DIVISOR
DIVISORS

DIVORCE
DIVORCED
DIVORCEE
DIVORCEES
DIVORCER
DIVORCERS
DIVORCES
DIVORCING
DIVORCIVE
DIVOT
DIVOTS
DIVS
DIVULGATE
DIVULGATED
DIVULGATES
DIVULGATING
DIVULGE
DIVULGED
DIVULGES
DIVULGING
DIVULSION
DIVULSIONS
DIVULSIVE
DIVVIED
DIVVIES
DIVVY
DIVVYING
DIWAN
DIWANS
DIXI
DIXIE
DIXIES
DIXY
DIZAIN
DIZAINS
DIZEN
DIZENED
DIZENING
DIZENS
DIZYGOTIC
DIZZARD
DIZZARDS
DIZZIED
DIZZIER
DIZZIES
DIZZIEST
DIZZILY
DIZZINESS
DIZZINESSES
DIZZY
DIZZYING
DJEBEL
DJEBELS
DJELLABA
DJELLABAH
DJELLABAHS
DJELLABAS
DJIBBAH
DJIBBAHS
DJINN
DJINNI
DO
DOAB
DOABLE
DOABS
DOAT
DOATED
DOATER
DOATERS
DOATING

DOATINGS
DOATS
DOB
DOBBED
DOBBER
DOBBERS
DOBBIE
DOBBIES
DOBBIN
DOBBING
DOBBINS
DOBBY
DOBCHICK
DOBCHICKS
DOBHASH
DOBHASHES
DOBS
DOC
DOCENT
DOCENTS
DOCHMIAC
DOCHMII
DOCHMIUS
DOCHMIUSES
DOCHT
DOCIBLE
DOCILE
DOCILER
DOCILEST
DOCILITIES
DOCILITY
DOCIMASIES
DOCIMASY
DOCK
DOCKAGE
DOCKAGES
DOCKED
DOCKEN
DOCKENS
DOCKER
DOCKERS
DOCKET
DOCKETED
DOCKETING
DOCKETS
DOCKING
DOCKINGS
DOCKISE
DOCKISED
DOCKISES
DOCKISING
DOCKIZE
DOCKIZED
DOCKIZES
DOCKIZING
DOCKLAND
DOCKLANDS
DOCKS
DOCKYARD
DOCKYARDS
DOCQUET
DOCQUETED
DOCQUETING
DOCQUETS
DOCS
DOCTOR
DOCTORAL
DOCTORAND
DOCTORANDS
DOCTORATE

DOCTORATED
DOCTORATES
DOCTORATING
DOCTORED
DOCTORESS
DOCTORESSES
DOCTORIAL
DOCTORING
DOCTORLY
DOCTORS
DOCTRESS
DOCTRESSES
DOCTRINAL
DOCTRINE
DOCTRINES
DOCUDRAMA
DOCUDRAMAS
DOCUMENT
DOCUMENTED
DOCUMENTING
DOCUMENTS
DOD
DODDARD
DODDED
DODDER
DODDERED
DODDERER
DODDERERS
DODDERIER
DODDERIEST
DODDERING
DODDERS
DODDERY
DODDIER
DODDIES
DODDIEST
DODDING
DODDIPOLL
DODDIPOLLS
DODDLE
DODDLES
DODDY
DODDYPOLL
DODDYPOLLS
DODECAGON
DODECAGONS
DODGE
DODGED
DODGEM
DODGEMS
DODGER
DODGERIES
DODGERS
DODGERY
DODGES
DODGIER
DODGIEST
DODGING
DODGY
DODKIN
DODKINS
DODMAN
DODMANS
DODO
DODOES
DODOS
DODS
DOE
DOEN
DOER

DOERS
DOES
DOEST
DOETH
DOFF
DOFFED
DOFFER
DOFFERS
DOFFING
DOFFS
DOG
DOGARESSA
DOGARESSAS
DOGATE
DOGATES
DOGBANE
DOGBANES
DOGBERRIES
DOGBERRY
DOGBOLT
DOGBOLTS
DOGCART
DOGCARTS
DOGDAYS
DOGE
DOGEATE
DOGEATES
DOGES
DOGESHIP
DOGESHIPS
DOGFIGHT
DOGFIGHTS
DOGFISH
DOGFISHES
DOGFOX
DOGFOXES
DOGGED
DOGGEDER
DOGGEDEST
DOGGEDLY
DOGGER
DOGGEREL
DOGGERELS
DOGGERIES
DOGGERMAN
DOGGERMEN
DOGGERS
DOGGERY
DOGGESS
DOGGESSES
DOGGIE
DOGGIER
DOGGIES
DOGGIEST
DOGGINESS
DOGGINESSES
DOGGING
DOGGINGS
DOGGISH
DOGGISHLY
DOGGO
DOGGONE
DOGGONED
DOGGREL
DOGGRELS
DOGGY
DOGHOLE
DOGHOLES
DOGIE
DOGIES

DOGMA
DOGMAS
DOGMATIC
DOGMATICS
DOGMATISE
DOGMATISED
DOGMATISES
DOGMATISING
DOGMATISM
DOGMATISMS
DOGMATIST
DOGMATISTS
DOGMATIZE
DOGMATIZED
DOGMATIZES
DOGMATIZING
DOGMATORY
DOGS
DOGSBODIES
DOGSBODY
DOGSHIP
DOGSHIPS
DOGSHORES
DOGSKIN
DOGSKINS
DOGSLEEP
DOGSLEEPS
DOGTEETH
DOGTOOTH
DOGTOWN
DOGTOWNS
DOGTROT
DOGTROTS
DOGVANE
DOGVANES
DOGWOOD
DOGWOODS
DOGY
DOH
DOHS
DOILED
DOILIES
DOILT
DOILTER
DOILTEST
DOILY
DOING
DOINGS
DOIT
DOITED
DOITIT
DOITKIN
DOITKINS
DOITS
DOJO
DOJOS
DOLCE
DOLCES
DOLDRUMS
DOLE
DOLED
DOLEFUL
DOLEFULLY
DOLENT
DOLERITE
DOLERITES
DOLERITIC
DOLES
DOLESOME
DOLIA

DOLICHOS
DOLICHOSES
DOLING
DOLIUM
DOLL
DOLLAR
DOLLARED
DOLLARS
DOLLDOM
DOLLDOMS
DOLLED
DOLLHOOD
DOLLHOODS
DOLLIED
DOLLIER
DOLLIERS
DOLLIES
DOLLINESS
DOLLINESSES
DOLLING
DOLLISH
DOLLOP
DOLLOPS
DOLLS
DOLLY
DOLLYING
DOLMA
DOLMADES
DOLMAN
DOLMANS
DOLMAS
DOLMEN
DOLMENS
DOLOMITE
DOLOMITES
DOLOMITIC
DOLORIFIC
DOLOROSO
DOLOROUS
DOLOUR
DOLOURS
DOLPHIN
DOLPHINET
DOLPHINETS
DOLPHINS
DOLT
DOLTISH
DOLTISHLY
DOLTS
DOMAIN
DOMAINAL
DOMAINS
DOMAL
DOMANIAL
DOMATIA
DOMATIUM
DOME
DOMED
DOMES
DOMESTIC
DOMESTICS
DOMETT
DOMETTS
DOMICAL
DOMICIL
DOMICILE
DOMICILED
DOMICILES
DOMICILING
DOMICILS

DOMIER
DOMIEST
DOMINANCE
DOMINANCES
DOMINANCIES
DOMINANCY
DOMINANT
DOMINANTS
DOMINATE
DOMINATED
DOMINATES
DOMINATING
DOMINATOR
DOMINATORS
DOMINEER
DOMINEERED
DOMINEERING
DOMINEERS
DOMING
DOMINICAL
DOMINIE
DOMINIES
DOMINION
DOMINIONS
DOMINO
DOMINOES
DOMINOS
DOMY
DON
DONA
DONAH
DONARIES
DONARY
DONAS
DONATARIES
DONATARY
DONATE
DONATED
DONATES
DONATING
DONATION
DONATIONS
DONATISM
DONATISMS
DONATIVE
DONATIVES
DONATOR
DONATORIES
DONATORS
DONATORY
DONEE
DONEES
DONENESS
DONENESSES
DONG
DONGA
DONGAS
DONGED
DONGING
DONGLE
DONGLES
DONGS
DONING
DONINGS
DONJON
DONJONS
DONKEY
DONKEYS

DONNARD
DONNART
DONNAT
DONNATS
DONNÉ
DONNE
DONNED
DONNÉE
DONNÉES
DONNERD
DONNERED
DONNERT
DONNÉS
DONNING
DONNISH
DONNISM
DONNISMS
DONNOT
DONNOTS
DONOR
DONORS
DONS
DONSHIP
DONSHIPS
DONSIE
DONSIER
DONSIEST
DONUT
DONUTS
DONZEL
DONZELS
DOO
DOOB
DOOBS
DOOCOT
DOOCOTS
DOODAD
DOODADS
DOODAH
DOODAHS
DOODLE
DOODLEBUG
DOODLEBUGS
DOODLED
DOODLER
DOODLERS
DOODLES
DOODLING
DOOK
DOOKED
DOOKET
DOOKETS
DOOKING
DOOKS
DOOL
DOOLE
DOOLES
DOOLIE
DOOLIES
DOOLS
DOOM
DOOMED
DOOMFUL
DOOMIER
DOOMIEST
DOOMING
DOOMS
DOOMSDAY
DOOMSDAYS
DOOMSMAN

DOOMSMEN
DOOMSTER
DOOMSTERS
DOOMWATCH
DOOMWATCHED
DOOMWATCHES
DOOMWATCHING
DOOMWATCHINGS
DOOMY
DOOR
DOORBELL
DOORBELLS
DOORKNOB
DOORKNOBS
DOORKNOCK
DOORKNOCKED
DOORKNOCKING
DOORKNOCKS
DOORMAT
DOORMATS
DOORN
DOORNAIL
DOORNAILS
DOORNS
DOORPOST
DOORPOSTS
DOORS
DOORSTEP
DOORSTEPPED
DOORSTEPPING
DOORSTEPPINGS
DOORSTEP
DOORSTONE
DOORSTONES
DOORSTOP
DOORSTOPS
DOORWAY
DOORWAYS
DOOS
DOP
DOPA
DOPAMINE
DOPAMINES
DOPANT
DOPANTS
DOPAS
DOPE
DOPED
DOPER
DOPERS
DOPES
DOPEY
DOPIER
DOPIEST
DOPING
DOPINGS
DOPPED
DOPPER
DOPPERS
DOPPIE
DOPPIES
DOPPING
DOPPINGS
DOPS
DOPY
DOR
DORAD
DORADO
DORADOS
DORADS

DOREE	DOSAGE	DOTTY	DOUPS	DOWELLED
DOREES	DOSAGES	DOTY	DOUR	DOWELLING
DORHAWK	DOSE	DOUANE	DOURA	DOWELLINGS
DORHAWKS	DOSED	DOUANES	DOURAS	DOWELS
DORIDOID	DOSEH	DOUANIER	DOURER	DOWER
DORIDOIDS	DOSEHS	DOUANIERS	DOUREST	DOWERED
DORIES	DOSES	DOUAR	DOURINE	DOWERING
DORISE	DOSIMETER	DOUARS	DOURINES	DOWERLESS
DORISED	DOSIMETERS	DOUBLE	DOURNESS	DOWERS
DORISES	DOSIMETRIES	DOUBLED	DOURNESSES	DOWF
DORISING	DOSIMETRY	DOUBLER	DOUSE	DOWFNESS
DORIZE	DOSING	DOUBLERS	DOUSED	DOWFNESSES
DORIZED	DOSIOLOGIES	DOUBLES	DOUSER	DOWIE
DORIZES	DOSIOLOGY	DOUBLET	DOUSERS	DOWIER
DORIZING	DOSOLOGIES	DOUBLETON	DOUSES	DOWIEST
DORLACH	DOSOLOGY	DOUBLETONS	DOUSING	DOWING
DORLACHS	DOSS	DOUBLETS	DOUT	DOWL
DORM	DOSSAL	DOUBLING	DOUTED	DOWLAS
DORMANCIES	DOSSALS	DOUBLINGS	DOUTER	DOWLASES
DORMANCY	DOSSED	DOUBLOON	DOUTERS	DOWLE
DORMANT	DOSSEL	DOUBLOONS	DOUTING	DOWLES
DORMANTS	DOSSELS	DOUBLY	DOUTS	DOWLNE
DORMER	DOSSER	DOUBT	DOUZEPER	DOWLNES
DORMERS	DOSSERS	DOUBTABLE	DOUZEPERS	DOWLNEY
DORMICE	DOSSES	DOUBTED	DOVE	DOWLS
DORMIE	DOSSIER	DOUBTER	DOVECOT	DOWN
DORMIENT	DOSSIERS	DOUBTERS	DOVECOTE	DOWNA
DORMITION	DOSSIL	DOUBTFUL	DOVECOTES	DOWNBEAT
DORMITIONS	DOSSILS	DOUBTFULS	DOVECOTS	DOWNBEATS
DORMITIVE	DOSSING	DOUBTING	DOVED	DOWNBOW
DORMITIVES	DOST	DOUBTINGS	DOVEISH	DOWNBOWS
DORMITORIES	DOT	DOUBTLESS	DOVEKIE	DOWNCAST
DORMITORY	DOTAGE	DOUBTS	DOVEKIES	DOWNCASTS
DORMOUSE	DOTAGES	DOUC	DOVELET	DOWNED
DORMS	DOTAL	DOUCE	DOVELETS	DOWNER
DORMY	DOTANT	DOUCELY	DOVER	DOWNERS
DORNICK	DOTANTS	DOUCENESS	DOVERED	DOWNFALL
DORNICKS	DOTARD	DOUCENESSES	DOVERING	DOWNFALLS
DORP	DOTARDS	DOUCEPERE	DOVERS	DOWNFLOW
DORPS	DOTATION	DOUCEPERES	DOVES	DOWNFLOWS
DORR	DOTATIONS	DOUCER	DOVETAIL	DOWNFORCE
DORRED	DOTE	DOUCEST	DOVETAILED	DOWNFORCES
DORRING	DOTED	DOUCET	DOVETAILING	DOWNGRADE
DORRS	DOTER	DOUCETS	DOVETAILINGS	DOWNGRADED
DORS	DOTERS	DOUCEUR	DOVETAILS	DOWNGRADES
DORSA	DOTES	DOUCEURS	DOVIE	DOWNGRADING
DORSAL	DOTH	DOUCHE	DOVIER	DOWNHILL
DORSALLY	DOTIER	DOUCHED	DOVIEST	DOWNHILLS
DORSALS	DOTIEST	DOUCHES	DOVING	DOWNIER
DORSE	DOTING	DOUCHING	DOVISH	DOWNIEST
DORSEL	DOTINGS	DOUCINE	DOW	DOWNINESS
DORSELS	DOTISH	DOUCINES	DOWABLE	DOWNINESSES
DORSER	DOTS	DOUCS	DOWAGER	DOWNING
DORSERS	DOTTED	DOUGH	DOWAGERS	DOWNLAND
DORSES	DOTTEREL	DOUGHIER	DOWAR	DOWNLANDS
DORSIFLEX	DOTTERELS	DOUGHIEST	DOWARS	DOWNMOST
DORSUM	DOTTIER	DOUGHNUT	DOWD	DOWNPIPE
DORT	DOTTIEST	DOUGHNUTS	DOWDIER	DOWNPIPES
DORTED	DOTTINESS	DOUGHS	DOWDIES	DOWNPOUR
DORTER	DOTTINESSES	DOUGHT	DOWDIEST	DOWNPOURS
DORTERS	DOTTING	DOUGHTIER	DOWDILY	DOWNRIGHT
DORTIER	DOTTIPOLL	DOUGHTIEST	DOWDINESS	DOWNRUSH
DORTIEST	DOTTIPOLLS	DOUGHTILY	DOWDINESSES	DOWNRUSHES
DORTING	DOTTLE	DOUGHTY	DOWDS	DOWNS
DORTOUR	DOTTLED	DOUGHY	DOWDY	DOWNSTAGE
DORTOURS	DOTTLER	DOULEIA	DOWDYISH	DOWNSTAIR
DORTS	DOTTLES	DOULEIAS	DOWDYISM	DOWNSTAIRS
DORTY	DOTTLEST	DOUMA	DOWDYISMS	DOWNSWING
DORY	DOTTREL	DOUMAS	DOWED	DOWNSWINGS
DOS	DOTTRELS	DOUP	DOWEL	DOWNTIME

DOWNTIMES	DRABBLING	DRAGONISING	DRAPERIED	DREADLY
DOWNTREND	DRABBLINGS	DRAGONISM	DRAPERIES	DREADS
DOWNTRENDS	DRABBY	DRAGONISMS	DRAPERS	DREAM
DOWNTURN	DRABETTE	DRAGONIZE	DRAPERY	DREAMBOAT
DOWNTURNS	DRABETTES	DRAGONIZED	DRAPERYING	DREAMBOATS
DOWNWARD	DRABLER	DRAGONIZES	DRAPES	DREAMED
DOWNWARDS	DRABLERS	DRAGONIZING	DRAPET	DREAMER
DOWNWIND	DRABLY	DRAGONNÉ	DRAPETS	DREAMERIES
DOWNY	DRABNESS	DRAGONS	DRAPIER	DREAMERS
DOWP	DRABNESSES	DRAGOON	DRAPIERS	DREAMERY
DOWPS	DRABS	DRAGOONED	DRAPING	DREAMFUL
DOWRIES	DRACHM	DRAGOONING	DRAPPED	DREAMHOLE
DOWRY	DRACHMA	DRAGOONS	DRAPPIE	DREAMHOLES
DOWS	DRACHMAE	DRAGS	DRAPPIES	DREAMIER
DOWSE	DRACHMAI	DRAGSMAN	DRAPPING	DREAMIEST
DOWSED	DRACHMAS	DRAGSMEN	DRAPPY	DREAMILY
DOWSER	DRACHMS	DRAGSTER	DRAPS	DREAMING
DOWSERS	DRACONE	DRAGSTERS	DRASTIC	DREAMINGS
DOWSES	DRACONES	DRAIL	DRASTICS	DREAMLESS
DOWSET	DRACONIAN	DRAILED	DRAT	DREAMS
DOWSETS	DRACONIC	DRAILING	DRATCHELL	DREAMT
DOWSING	DRACONISM	DRAILS	DRATCHELLS	DREAMTIME
DOWT	DRACONISMS	DRAIN	DRATTED	DREAMTIMES
DOWTS	DRACONTIC	DRAINABLE	DRAUGHT	DREAMY
DOXIES	DRAD	DRAINAGE	DRAUGHTED	DREAR
DOXOLOGIES	DRAFF	DRAINAGES	DRAUGHTER	DREARE
DOXOLOGY	DRAFFIER	DRAINED	DRAUGHTERS	DREARER
DOXY	DRAFFIEST	DRAINER	DRAUGHTIER	DREARES
DOYEN	DRAFFISH	DRAINERS	DRAUGHTIEST	DREAREST
DOYENNE	DRAFFS	DRAINING	DRAUGHTING	DREARIER
DOYENNES	DRAFFY	DRAINS	DRAUGHTS	DREARIEST
DOYENS	DRAFT	DRAISENE	DRAUGHTY	DREARILY
DOYLEY	DRAFTED	DRAISENES	DRAUNT	DREARING
DOYLEYS	DRAFTEE	DRAISINE	DRAUNTED	DREARINGS
DOYLIES	DRAFTEES	DRAISINES	DRAUNTING	DREARS
DOYLY	DRAFTER	DRAKE	DRAUNTS	DREARY
DOZE	DRAFTERS	DRAKES	DRAVE	DRECK
DOZED	DRAFTING	DRAM	DRAW	DRECKS
DOZEN	DRAFTS	DRAMA	DRAWABLE	DREDGE
DOZENED	DRAFTSMAN	DRAMAS	DRAWBACK	DREDGED
DOZENING	DRAFTSMEN	DRAMATIC	DRAWBACKS	DREDGER
DOZENS	DRAG	DRAMATICS	DRAWEE	DREDGERS
DOZENTH	DRAGÉE	DRAMATISE	DRAWEES	DREDGES
DOZENTHS	DRAGÉES	DRAMATISED	DRAWER	DREDGING
DOZER	DRAGGED	DRAMATISES	DRAWERS	DREE
DOZERS	DRAGGIER	DRAMATISING	DRAWING	DREED
DOZES	DRAGGIEST	DRAMATIST	DRAWINGS	DREEING
DOZIER	DRAGGING	DRAMATISTS	DRAWL	DREES
DOZIEST	DRAGGLE	DRAMATIZE	DRAWLED	DREGGIER
DOZINESS	DRAGGLED	DRAMATIZED	DRAWLER	DREGGIEST
DOZINESSES	DRAGGLES	DRAMATIZES	DRAWLERS	DREGGY
DOZING	DRAGGLING	DRAMATIZING	DRAWLING	DREGS
DOZINGS	DRAGGY	DRAMATURG	DRAWLS	DREICH
DOZY	DRAGHOUND	DRAMATURGS	DRAWN	DREICHER
DRAB	DRAGHOUNDS	DRAMMACH	DRAWS	DREICHEST
DRABBED	DRAGLINE	DRAMMACHS	DRAY	DRENCH
DRABBER	DRAGLINES	DRAMMED	DRAYAGE	DRENCHED
DRABBERS	DRAGOMAN	DRAMMING	DRAYAGES	DRENCHER
DRABBEST	DRAGOMANS	DRAMMOCK	DRAYMAN	DRENCHERS
DRABBET	DRAGON	DRAMMOCKS	DRAYMEN	DRENCHES
DRABBETS	DRAGONESS	DRAMS	DRAYS	DRENCHING
DRABBIER	DRAGONESSES	DRANK	DRAZEL	DRENT
DRABBIEST	DRAGONET	DRANT	DRAZELS	DREPANIUM
DRABBING	DRAGONETS	DRANTED	DREAD	DREPANIUMS
DRABBISH	DRAGONFLIES	DRANTING	DREADED	DRERE
DRABBLE	DRAGONFLY	DRANTS	DREADER	DRERES
DRABBLED	DRAGONISE	DRAP	DREADERS	DRERYHEAD
DRABBLER	DRAGONISED	DRAPE	DREADFUL	DRERYHEADS
DRABBLERS	DRAGONISES	DRAPED	DREADING	DRESS
DRABBLES	DRAGONISH	DRAPER	DREADLESS	DRESSAGE

DRESSAGES	DRINKERS	DROLLNESSES	DROSERA	DRUG
DRESSED	DRINKING	DROLLS	DROSERAS	DRUGGED
DRESSER	DRINKINGS	DROLLY	DROSHKIES	DRUGGER
DRESSERS	DRINKS	DROME	DROSHKY	DRUGGERS
DRESSES	DRIP	DROMEDARE	DROSKIES	DRUGGET
DRESSIER	DRIPPED	DROMEDARES	DROSKY	DRUGGETS
DRESSIEST	DRIPPIER	DROMEDARIES	DROSS	DRUGGING
DRESSING	DRIPPIEST	DROMEDARY	DROSSES	DRUGGIST
DRESSINGS	DRIPPING	DROMES	DROSSIER	DRUGGISTS
DRESSY	DRIPPINGS	DROMIC	DROSSIEST	DRUGS
DREST	DRIPPY	DROMICAL	DROSSY	DRUID
DREVILL	DRIPS	DROMOI	DROSTDIES	DRUIDESS
DREVILLS	DRISHEEN	DROMON	DROSTDY	DRUIDESSES
DREW	DRISHEENS	DROMOND	DROSTDYS	DRUIDIC
DREY	DRIVABLE	DROMONDS	DROUGHT	DRUIDICAL
DREYS	DRIVE	DROMONS	DROUGHTIER	DRUIDISM
DRIB	DRIVEABLE	DROMOS	DROUGHTIEST	DRUIDISMS
DRIBBED	DRIVEL	DRONE	DROUGHTS	DRUIDS
DRIBBER	DRIVELLED	DRONED	DROUGHTY	DRUM
DRIBBERS	DRIVELLER	DRONES	DROUK	DRUMBEAT
DRIBBING	DRIVELLERS	DRONGO	DROUKED	DRUMBEATS
DRIBBLE	DRIVELLING	DRONGOES	DROUKING	DRUMBLE
DRIBBLED	DRIVELS	DRONGOS	DROUKINGS	DRUMBLED
DRIBBLER	DRIVEN	DRONIER	DROUKIT	DRUMBLES
DRIBBLERS	DRIVER	DRONIEST	DROUKS	DRUMBLING
DRIBBLES	DRIVERS	DRONING	DROUTH	DRUMFIRE
DRIBBLET	DRIVES	DRONINGLY	DROUTHIER	DRUMFIRES
DRIBBLETS	DRIVEWAY	DRONISH	DROUTHIEST	DRUMFISH
DRIBBLIER	DRIVEWAYS	DRONISHLY	DROUTHS	DRUMFISHES
DRIBBLIEST	DRIVING	DRONY	DROUTHY	DRUMHEAD
DRIBBLING	DRIZZLE	DROOK	DROVE	DRUMHEADS
DRIBBLY	DRIZZLED	DROOKED	DROVER	DRUMLIER
DRIBLET	DRIZZLES	DROOKING	DROVERS	DRUMLIEST
DRIBLETS	DRIZZLIER	DROOKINGS	DROVES	DRUMLIN
DRIBS	DRIZZLIEST	DROOKIT	DROW	DRUMLINS
DRICKSIE	DRIZZLING	DROOKS	DROWN	DRUMLY
DRICKSIER	DRIZZLY	DROOL	DROWNDED	DRUMMED
DRICKSIEST	DROGER	DROOLED	DROWNED	DRUMMER
DRIED	DROGERS	DROOLING	DROWNER	DRUMMERS
DRIER	DROGHER	DROOLS	DROWNERS	DRUMMING
DRIERS	DROGHERS	DROOME	DROWNING	DRUMMOCK
DRIES	DROGUE	DROOMES	DROWNINGS	DRUMMOCKS
DRIEST	DROGUES	DROOP	DROWNS	DRUMS
DRIFT	DROGUET	DROOPED	DROWS	DRUMSTICK
DRIFTAGE	DROGUETS	DROOPIER	DROWSE	DRUMSTICKS
DRIFTAGES	DROICH	DROOPIEST	DROWSED	DRUNK
DRIFTED	DROICHIER	DROOPILY	DROWSES	DRUNKARD
DRIFTER	DROICHIEST	DROOPING	DROWSIER	DRUNKARDS
DRIFTERS	DROICHS	DROOPS	DROWSIEST	DRUNKEN
DRIFTIER	DROICHY	DROOPY	DROWSIHED	DRUNKENLY
DRIFTIEST	DROIL	DROP	DROWSIHEDS	DRUNKER
DRIFTING	DROILED	DROPFLIES	DROWSILY	DRUNKEST
DRIFTLESS	DROILING	DROPFLY	DROWSING	DRUNKS
DRIFTPIN	DROILS	DROPLET	DROWSY	DRUPE
DRIFTPINS	DROIT	DROPLETS	DRUB	DRUPEL
DRIFTS	DROITS	DROPPED	DRUBBED	DRUPELET
DRIFTY	DRÔLE	DROPPER	DRUBBING	DRUPELETS
DRILL	DRÔLER	DROPPERS	DRUBBINGS	DRUPELS
DRILLED	DRÔLES	DROPPING	DRUBS	DRUPES
DRILLER	DRÔLEST	DROPPINGS	DRUCKEN	DRUSE
DRILLERS	DROLL	DROPPLE	DRUDGE	DRUSES
DRILLING	DROLLED	DROPPLES	DRUDGED	DRUSIER
DRILLINGS	DROLLER	DROPS	DRUDGER	DRUSIEST
DRILLS	DROLLERIES	DROPSICAL	DRUDGERIES	DRUSY
DRILLSHIP	DROLLERY	DROPSIED	DRUDGERS	DRUXIER
DRILLSHIPS	DROLLEST	DROPSIES	DRUDGERY	DRUXIEST
DRILY	DROLLING	DROPSTONE	DRUDGES	DRUXY
DRINK	DROLLINGS	DROPSTONES	DRUDGING	DRY
DRINKABLE	DROLLISH	DROPSY	DRUDGISM	DRYAD
DRINKER	DROLLNESS	DROPWISE	DRUDGISMS	DRYADES

DRYADS
DRYBEAT
DRYBEATEN
DRYBEATING
DRYBEATS
DRYER
DRYERS
DRYING
DRYINGS
DRYISH
DRYLY
DRYMOUTH
DRYMOUTHS
DRYNESS
DRYNESSES
DRYSALTER
DRYSALTERS
DSO
DSOBO
DSOBOS
DSOMO
DSOMOS
DSOS
DUAD
DUADS
DUAL
DUALIN
DUALINS
DUALISM
DUALISMS
DUALIST
DUALISTIC
DUALISTS
DUALITIES
DUALITY
DUALLY
DUALS
DUAN
DUANS
DUAR
DUARCHIES
DUARCHY
DUARS
DUB
DUBBED
DUBBIN
DUBBING
DUBBINGS
DUBBINS
DUBIETIES
DUBIETY
DUBIOSITIES
DUBIOSITY
DUBIOUS
DUBIOUSLY
DUBITABLE
DUBITABLY
DUBITANCIES
DUBITANCY
DUBITATE
DUBITATED
DUBITATES
DUBITATING
DUBS
DUCAL
DUCALLY
DUCAT
DUCATOON
DUCATOONS
DUCATS

DUCDAME
DUCE
DUCES
DUCHESS
DUCHESSE
DUCHESSES
DUCHIES
DUCHY
DUCK
DUCKBILL
DUCKBILLS
DUCKED
DUCKER
DUCKERS
DUCKIER
DUCKIES
DUCKIEST
DUCKING
DUCKINGS
DUCKLING
DUCKLINGS
DUCKMOLE
DUCKMOLES
DUCKS
DUCKSHOVE
DUCKSHOVED
DUCKSHOVES
DUCKSHOVING
DUCKWEED
DUCKWEEDS
DUCKY
DUCT
DUCTED
DUCTILE
DUCTILITIES
DUCTILITY
DUCTING
DUCTLESS
DUCTS
DUD
DUDDER
DUDDERIES
DUDDERS
DUDDERY
DUDDIE
DUDDIER
DUDDIEST
DUDE
DUDEEN
DUDEENS
DUDES
DUDGEON
DUDGEONS
DUDHEEN
DUDHEENS
DUDISH
DUDISM
DUDISMS
DUDS
DUE
DUED
DUEFUL
DUEL
DUELLED
DUELLER
DUELLERS
DUELLING
DUELLINGS
DUELLIST
DUELLISTS

DUELLO
DUELLOS
DUELS
DUELSOME
DUENNA
DUENNAS
DUES
DUET
DUETS
DUETT
DUETTED
DUETTI
DUETTING
DUETTINO
DUETTINOS
DUETTIST
DUETTISTS
DUETTO
DUETTOS
DUETTS
DUFF
DUFFED
DUFFEL
DUFFELS
DUFFER
DUFFERDOM
DUFFERDOMS
DUFFERISM
DUFFERISMS
DUFFERS
DUFFEST
DUFFING
DUFFINGS
DUFFLE
DUFFLES
DUFFS
DUG
DUGONG
DUGONGS
DUGOUT
DUGOUTS
DUGS
DUIKER
DUIKERS
DUING
DUKE
DUKED
DUKEDOM
DUKEDOMS
DUKELING
DUKELINGS
DUKERIES
DUKERY
DUKES
DUKESHIP
DUKESHIPS
DUKING
DULCAMARA
DULCAMARAS
DULCET
DULCIAN
DULCIANA
DULCIANAS
DULCIANS
DULCIFIED
DULCIFIES
DULCIFY
DULCIFYING
DULCIMER
DULCIMERS

DULCITE
DULCITES
DULCITOL
DULCITOLS
DULCITUDE
DULCITUDES
DULCOSE
DULCOSES
DULE
DULES
DULIA
DULIAS
DULL
DULLARD
DULLARDS
DULLED
DULLER
DULLEST
DULLIER
DULLIEST
DULLING
DULLISH
DULLNESS
DULLNESSES
DULLS
DULLY
DULNESS
DULNESSES
DULOCRACIES
DULOCRACY
DULOSES
DULOSIS
DULOTIC
DULSE
DULSES
DULY
DUMA
DUMAIST
DUMAISTS
DUMAS
DUMB
DUMBED
DUMBER
DUMBEST
DUMBFOUND
DUMBFOUNDED
DUMBFOUNDING
DUMBFOUNDS
DUMBING
DUMBLY
DUMBNESS
DUMBNESSES
DUMBS
DUMDUM
DUMDUMS
DUMFOUND
DUMFOUNDED
DUMFOUNDING
DUMFOUNDS
DUMKA
DUMKY
DUMMERER
DUMMERERS
DUMMIED
DUMMIER
DUMMIES
DUMMIEST
DUMMINESS
DUMMINESSES
DUMMY

DUMMYING
DUMOSE
DUMOSITIES
DUMOSITY
DUMOUS
DUMP
DUMPBIN
DUMPBINS
DUMPED
DUMPER
DUMPERS
DUMPIER
DUMPIES
DUMPIEST
DUMPINESS
DUMPINESSES
DUMPING
DUMPISH
DUMPISHLY
DUMPLE
DUMPLED
DUMPLES
DUMPLING
DUMPLINGS
DUMPS
DUMPY
DUN
DUNCE
DUNCEDOM
DUNCEDOMS
DUNCERIES
DUNCERY
DUNCES
DUNCH
DUNCHED
DUNCHES
DUNCHING
DUNDER
DUNDERS
DUNE
DUNES
DUNG
DUNGAREE
DUNGAREES
DUNGED
DUNGEON
DUNGEONED
DUNGEONER
DUNGEONERS
DUNGEONING
DUNGEONS
DUNGIER
DUNGIEST
DUNGING
DUNGMERE
DUNGMERES
DUNGS
DUNGY
DUNITE
DUNITES
DUNK
DUNKED
DUNKING
DUNKS
DUNLIN
DUNLINS
DUNNAGE
DUNNAGES
DUNNAKIN
DUNNAKINS

DUNNED
DUNNER
DUNNEST
DUNNIER
DUNNIES
DUNNIEST
DUNNING
DUNNINGS
DUNNISH
DUNNITE
DUNNITES
DUNNO
DUNNOCK
DUNNOCKS
DUNNY
DUNS
DUNSH
DUNSHED
DUNSHES
DUNSHING
DUNT
DUNTED
DUNTING
DUNTS
DUO
DUODECIMO
DUODECIMOS
DUODENA
DUODENAL
DUODENARY
DUODENUM
DUOLOGUE
DUOLOGUES
DUOMI
DUOMO
DUOMOS
DUOPOLIES
DUOPOLY
DUOS
DUOTONE
DUOTONES
DUP
DUPABLE
DUPE
DUPED
DUPER
DUPERIES
DUPERS
DUPERY
DUPES
DUPING
DUPION
DUPIONS
DUPLE
DUPLET
DUPLETS
DUPLEX
DUPLEXES
DUPLICAND
DUPLICANDS
DUPLICATE
DUPLICATED
DUPLICATES
DUPLICATING
DUPLICITIES
DUPLICITY
DUPLIED
DUPLIES
DUPLY
DUPLYING

DUPONDII
DUPONDIUS
DUPPED
DUPPIES
DUPPING
DUPPY
DUPS
DURA
DURABLE
DURABLES
DURABLY
DURAL
DURALS
DURALUMIN
DURALUMINS
DURAMEN
DURAMENS
DURANCE
DURANCES
DURANT
DURANTS
DURAS
DURATION
DURATIONS
DURBAR
DURBARS
DURDUM
DURDUMS
DURE
DURED
DUREFUL
DURES
DURESS
DURESSE
DURESSES
DURGAN
DURGANS
DURGIER
DURGIEST
DURGY
DURIAN
DURIANS
DURING
DURION
DURIONS
DURMAST
DURMASTS
DURN
DURNS
DURO
DUROS
DUROY
DUROYS
DURRA
DURRAS
DURRIE
DURRIES
DURST
DURUKULI
DURUKULIS
DURUM
DURUMS
DUSH
DUSHED
DUSHES
DUSHING
DUSK
DUSKED
DUSKEN
DUSKENED

DUSKENING
DUSKENS
DUSKER
DUSKEST
DUSKIER
DUSKIEST
DUSKILY
DUSKINESS
DUSKINESSES
DUSKING
DUSKISH
DUSKISHLY
DUSKLY
DUSKNESS
DUSKNESSES
DUSKS
DUSKY
DUST
DUSTBIN
DUSTBINS
DUSTED
DUSTER
DUSTERS
DUSTIER
DUSTIEST
DUSTILY
DUSTINESS
DUSTINESSES
DUSTING
DUSTLESS
DUSTMAN
DUSTMEN
DUSTPROOF
DUSTS
DUSTY
DUTCH
DUTCHES
DUTEOUS
DUTEOUSLY
DUTIABLE
DUTIED
DUTIES
DUTIFUL
DUTIFULLY
DUTY
DUUMVIR
DUUMVIRAL
DUUMVIRI
DUUMVIRS
DUVET
DUVETINE
DUVETINES
DUVETS
DUVETYN
DUVETYNE
DUVETYNES
DUVETYNS
DUX
DUXELLES
DUXES
DUYKER
DUYKERS
DVANDVA
DVANDVAS
DVORNIK
DVORNIKS
DWALE
DWALES
DWALM
DWALMED

DWALMING
DWALMS
DWAM
DWAMMED
DWAMMING
DWAMS
DWARF
DWARFED
DWARFING
DWARFISH
DWARFISM
DWARFISMS
DWARFS
DWARVES
DWAUM
DWAUMED
DWAUMING
DWAUMS
DWELL
DWELLED
DWELLER
DWELLERS
DWELLING
DWELLINGS
DWELLS
DWELT
DWINDLE
DWINDLED
DWINDLES
DWINDLING
DWINE
DWINED
DWINES
DWINING
DYABLE
DYAD
DYADIC
DYADS
DYARCHIES
DYARCHY
DYBBUK
DYBBUKS
DYE
DYEABLE
DYED
DYEING
DYEINGS
DYELINE
DYELINES
DYER
DYERS
DYES
DYESTER
DYESTERS
DYESTUFF
DYESTUFFS
DYING
DYINGLY
DYINGNESS
DYINGNESSES
DYINGS
DYKE
DYKED
DYKES
DYKEY
DYKIER
DYKIEST
DYKING
DYNAMIC
DYNAMICAL

DYNAMICS
DYNAMISE
DYNAMISED
DYNAMISES
DYNAMISING
DYNAMISM
DYNAMISMS
DYNAMIST
DYNAMISTS
DYNAMITE
DYNAMITED
DYNAMITER
DYNAMITERS
DYNAMITES
DYNAMITING
DYNAMIZE
DYNAMIZED
DYNAMIZES
DYNAMIZING
DYNAMO
DYNAMOS
DYNAMOTOR
DYNAMOTORS
DYNAST
DYNASTIC
DYNASTIES
DYNASTS
DYNASTY
DYNATRON
DYNATRONS
DYNE
DYNES
DYNODE
DYNODES
DYSCHROA
DYSCHROAS
DYSCHROIA
DYSCHROIAS
DYSCRASIA
DYSCRASIAS
DYSENTERIES
DYSENTERY
DYSGENIC
DYSGENICS
DYSLECTIC
DYSLECTICS
DYSLEXIA
DYSLEXIAS
DYSLEXIC
DYSLEXICS
DYSLOGIES
DYSLOGY
DYSMELIA
DYSMELIAS
DYSMELIC
DYSODIL
DYSODILE
DYSODILES
DYSODILS
DYSODYLE
DYSODYLES
DYSPATHIES
DYSPATHY
DYSPEPSIA
DYSPEPSIAS
DYSPEPSIES
DYSPEPSY
DYSPEPTIC
DYSPEPTICS
DYSPHAGIA

DYSPHAGIAS
DYSPHAGIC
DYSPHAGIES
DYSPHAGY
DYSPHASIA
DYSPHASIAS
DYSPHONIA
DYSPHONIAS
DYSPHONIC
DYSPHORIA
DYSPHORIAS

DYSPHORIC
DYSPLASIA
DYSPLASIAS
DYSPNEA
DYSPNEAL
DYSPNEAS
DYSPNEIC
DYSPNOEA
DYSPNOEAL
DYSPNOEAS
DYSPNOEIC

DYSPRAXIA
DYSPRAXIAS
DYSTECTIC
DYSTHESIA
DYSTHESIAS
DYSTHETIC
DYSTHYMIA
DYSTHYMIAS
DYSTHYMIC
DYSTOPIA
DYSTOPIAN

DYSTOPIAS
DYSTROPHIES
DYSTROPHY
DYSURIA
DYSURIAS
DYSURIC
DYSURIES
DYSURY
DYTISCID
DYTISCIDS
DYVOUR

DYVOURIES
DYVOURS
DYVOURY
DZEREN
DZERENS
DZIGGETAI
DZIGGETAIS
DZO
DZOS

E

EA
EACH
EACHWHERE
EADISH
EADISHES
EAGER
EAGERLY
EAGERNESS
EAGERNESSES
EAGERS
EAGLE
EAGLES
EAGLET
EAGLETS
EAGLEWOOD
EAGLEWOODS
EAGRE
EAGRES
EALDORMAN
EALDORMEN
EALE
EALES
EAN
EANED
EANING
EANLING
EANLINGS
EANS
EAR
EARACHE
EARACHES
EARBASH
EARBASHED
EARBASHES
EARBASHING
EARBOB
EARBOBS
EARD
EARDED
EARDING
EARDROP
EARDROPS
EARDRUM
EARDRUMS
EARDS
EARED
EARFLAP
EARFLAPS
EARFUL
EARFULS
EARING
EARINGS
EARL
EARLAP
EARLAPS
EARLDOM
EARLDOMS
EARLESS
EARLIER
EARLIEST
EARLINESS
EARLINESSES
EARLOCK

EARLOCKS
EARLS
EARLY
EARMARK
EARMARKED
EARMARKING
EARMARKS
EARMUFFS
EARN
EARNED
EARNER
EARNERS
EARNEST
EARNESTLY
EARNESTS
EARNING
EARNINGS
EARNS
EARPHONE
EARPHONES
EARPICK
EARPICKS
EARPIECE
EARPIECES
EARPLUG
EARPLUGS
EARRING
EARRINGS
EARS
EARST
EARTH
EARTHBORN
EARTHED
EARTHEN
EARTHFALL
EARTHFALLS
EARTHFAST
EARTHFLAX
EARTHFLAXES
EARTHIER
EARTHIEST
EARTHING
EARTHLIER
EARTHLIES
EARTHLIEST
EARTHLING
EARTHLINGS
EARTHLY
EARTHMAN
EARTHMEN
EARTHS
EARTHWARD
EARTHWAX
EARTHWAXES
EARTHWOLF
EARTHWOLVES
EARTHWORK
EARTHWORKS
EARTHWORM
EARTHWORMS
EARTHY
EARWAX
EARWAXES

EARWIG
EARWIGGED
EARWIGGING
EARWIGGY
EARWIGS
EAS
EASE
EASED
EASEFUL
EASEL
EASELS
EASEMENT
EASEMENTS
EASES
EASIER
EASIEST
EASILY
EASINESS
EASINESSES
EASING
EASLE
EASLES
EASSEL
EASSIL
EAST
EASTED
EASTER
EASTERLIES
EASTERLY
EASTERN
EASTERNER
EASTERNERS
EASTING
EASTINGS
EASTLAND
EASTLANDS
EASTLIN
EASTLING
EASTLINGS
EASTLINS
EASTMOST
EASTS
EASTWARD
EASTWARDS
EASY
EAT
EATABLE
EATABLES
EATAGE
EATAGES
EATCHE
EATCHES
EATEN
EATER
EATERIES
EATERS
EATERY
EATH
EATHE
EATHLY
EATING
EATINGS
EATS

EAU
EAUS
EAUX
EAVES
EAVESDRIP
EAVESDRIPS
EAVESDROP
EAVESDROPPED
EAVESDROPPING
EAVESDROPPINGS
EAVESDROPS
ÉBAUCHE
ÉBAUCHES
EBB
EBBED
EBBING
EBBLESS
EBBS
EBBTIDE
EBBTIDES
EBENEZER
EBENEZERS
ÉBÉNISTE
ÉBÉNISTES
EBIONISE
EBIONISED
EBIONISES
EBIONISING
EBIONISM
EBIONISMS
EBIONITIC
EBIONIZE
EBIONIZED
EBIONIZES
EBIONIZING
EBON
EBONIES
EBONISE
EBONISED
EBONISES
EBONISING
EBONIST
EBONISTS
EBONITE
EBONITES
EBONIZE
EBONIZED
EBONIZES
EBONIZING
EBONS
EBONY
EBRIATE
EBRIATED
EBRIETIES
EBRIETY
EBRILLADE
EBRILLADES
EBRIOSE
EBRIOSITIES
EBRIOSITY
EBULLIENT
EBURNEAN
EBURNEOUS

ECAD
ECADS
ÉCARTÉ
ÉCARTÉS
ECAUDATE
ECBOLE
ECBOLES
ECBOLIC
ECBOLICS
ECCE
ECCENTRIC
ECCENTRICS
ECCLESIA
ECCLESIAL
ECCLESIAS
ECCO
ECCRINE
ECCRISES
ECCRISIS
ECCRITIC
ECCRITICS
ECDYSES
ECDYSIAST
ECDYSIASTS
ECDYSIS
ECH
ÉCHAPPÉ
ÉCHAPPÉS
ECHE
ECHED
ECHELON
ECHELONS
ECHES
ECHEVERIA
ECHEVERIAS
ECHIDNA
ECHIDNAS
ECHIDNINE
ECHIDNINES
ECHINATE
ECHINATED
ECHING
ECHINI
ECHINOID
ECHINOIDS
ECHINUS
ECHINUSES
ECHO
ECHOED
ECHOER
ECHOERS
ECHOES
ECHOGRAM
ECHOGRAMS
ECHOIC
ECHOING
ECHOISE
ECHOISED
ECHOISES
ECHOISING
ECHOISM
ECHOISMS
ECHOIST

CHOISTS
CHOIZE
CHOIZED
CHOIZES
CHOIZING
CHOLALIA
CHOLALIAS
CHOLESS
CHT
CLAIR
CLAIRS
CLAMPSIA
CLAMPSIAS
CLAMPSIES
CLAMPSY
CLAMPTIC
CLAT
CLATS
CLECTIC
CLECTICS
CLIPSE
CLIPSED
CLIPSES
CLIPSING
CLIPTIC
CLIPTICS
CLOGITE
CLOGITES
CLOGUE
CLOGUES
CLOSE
CLOSED
CLOSES
CLOSING
CLOSION
CLOSIONS
COCIDE
COCIDES
COFREAK
COFREAKS
COLOGIC
COLOGIES
COLOGIST
COLOGISTS
COLOGY
CONOMIC
CONOMICS
CONOMIES
CONOMISE
CONOMISED
CONOMISES
CONOMISING
CONOMISM
CONOMISMS
CONOMIST
CONOMISTS
CONOMIZE
CONOMIZED
CONOMIZES
CONOMIZING
CONUT
CONUTS
COPHOBIA
COPHOBIAS
CORCHÉ
CORCHÉS
COSPHERE
COSPHERES
COSSAISE

ÉCOSSAISES
ECOSTATE
ECOSYSTEM
ECOSYSTEMS
ECOTYPE
ECOTYPES
ÉCRASEUR
ÉCRASEURS
ÉCRITOIRE
ÉCRITOIRES
ECRU
ECRUS
ECSTASES
ECSTASIED
ECSTASIES
ECSTASIS
ECSTASISE
ECSTASISED
ECSTASISES
ECSTASISING
ECSTASIZE
ECSTASIZED
ECSTASIZES
ECSTASIZING
ECSTASY
ECSTASYING
ECSTATIC
ECSTATICS
ECTASES
ECTASIS
ECTHYMA
ECTHYMAS
ECTOBLAST
ECTOBLASTS
ECTOCRINE
ECTOCRINES
ECTODERM
ECTODERMS
ECTOGENIC
ECTOGENIES
ECTOGENY
ECTOMORPH
ECTOMORPHS
ECTOPHYTE
ECTOPHYTES
ECTOPIA
ECTOPIAS
ECTOPIC
ECTOPIES
ECTOPLASM
ECTOPLASMS
ECTOPY
ECTOSARC
ECTOSARCS
ECTOTHERM
ECTOTHERMS
ECTOZOA
ECTOZOAN
ECTOZOANS
ECTOZOIC
ECTOZOON
ECTROPIC
ECTROPION
ECTROPIONS
ECTROPIUM
ECTROPIUMS
ECTYPAL
ECTYPE
ECTYPES
ECU

ÉCUELLE
ÉCUELLES
ECUMENIC
ECUMENICS
ECUMENISM
ECUMENISMS
ÉCURIE
ÉCURIES
ECUS
ECZEMA
ECZEMAS
EDACIOUS
EDACITIES
EDACITY
EDAPHIC
EDDIED
EDDIES
EDDISH
EDDISHES
EDDO
EDDOES
EDDY
EDDYING
EDELWEISS
EDELWEISSES
EDEMA
EDEMAS
EDEMATOSE
EDEMATOUS
EDENTAL
EDENTATE
EDENTATES
EDGE
EDGEBONE
EDGEBONES
EDGED
EDGELESS
EDGER
EDGERS
EDGES
EDGEWAYS
EDGEWISE
EDGIER
EDGIEST
EDGINESS
EDGINESSES
EDGING
EDGINGS
EDGY
EDH
EDHS
EDIBILITIES
EDIBILITY
EDIBLE
EDIBLES
EDICT
EDICTAL
EDICTALLY
EDICTS
EDIFICE
EDIFICES
EDIFICIAL
EDIFIED
EDIFIER
EDIFIERS
EDIFIES
EDIFY
EDIFYING
EDILE
EDILES

EDIT
EDITED
EDITING
EDITION
EDITIONS
EDITOR
EDITORIAL
EDITORIALS
EDITORS
EDITRESS
EDITRESSES
EDITS
EDUCABLE
EDUCATE
EDUCATED
EDUCATES
EDUCATING
EDUCATION
EDUCATIONS
EDUCATIVE
EDUCATOR
EDUCATORS
EDUCATORY
EDUCE
EDUCED
EDUCEMENT
EDUCEMENTS
EDUCES
EDUCIBLE
EDUCING
EDUCT
EDUCTION
EDUCTIONS
EDUCTOR
EDUCTORS
EDUCTS
EDUSKUNTA
EDUSKUNTAS
EE
EECH
EECHED
EECHES
EECHING
EEK
EEL
EELFARE
EELFARES
EELGRASS
EELGRASSES
EELIER
EELIEST
EELPOUT
EELPOUTS
EELS
EELWORM
EELWORMS
EELWRACK
EELWRACKS
EELY
EEN
EERIE
EERIER
EERIEST
EERILY
EERINESS
EERINESSES
EERY
EEVEN
EEVENS
EEVN

EEVNING
EEVNINGS
EEVNS
EF
EFF
EFFABLE
EFFACE
EFFACED
EFFACES
EFFACING
EFFECT
EFFECTED
EFFECTER
EFFECTERS
EFFECTING
EFFECTIVE
EFFECTIVES
EFFECTOR
EFFECTORS
EFFECTS
EFFECTUAL
EFFED
EFFEIR
EFFEIRED
EFFEIRING
EFFEIRS
EFFENDI
EFFENDIS
EFFERE
EFFERED
EFFERENCE
EFFERENCES
EFFERENT
EFFERES
EFFERING
EFFETE
EFFETELY
EFFICACIES
EFFICACY
EFFICIENT
EFFICIENTS
EFFIERCE
EFFIERCED
EFFIERCES
EFFIERCING
EFFIGIES
EFFIGY
EFFING
EFFLUENCE
EFFLUENCES
EFFLUENT
EFFLUENTS
EFFLUVIA
EFFLUVIAL
EFFLUVIUM
EFFLUX
EFFLUXES
EFFLUXION
EFFLUXIONS
EFFORCE
EFFORCED
EFFORCES
EFFORCING
EFFORT
EFFORTFUL
EFFORTS
EFFRAIDE
EFFRAY
EFFRAYS
EFFS

EFFULGE
EFFULGED
EFFULGENT
EFFULGES
EFFULGING
EFFUSE
EFFUSED
EFFUSES
EFFUSING
EFFUSION
EFFUSIONS
EFFUSIVE
EFS
EFT
EFTEST
EFTS
EFTSOONS
EGAD
EGAL
EGALITIES
EGALITY
EGALLY
EGAREMENT
EGAREMENTS
EGENCE
EGENCES
EGENCIES
EGENCY
EGER
EGERS
EGEST
EGESTA
EGESTED
EGESTING
EGESTION
EGESTIONS
EGESTIVE
EGESTS
EGG
EGGAR
EGGARS
EGGCUP
EGGCUPS
EGGED
EGGER
EGGERIES
EGGERS
EGGERY
EGGHEAD
EGGHEADS
EGGIER
EGGIEST
EGGING
EGGLER
EGGLERS
EGGMASS
EGGMASSES
EGGNOG
EGGNOGS
EGGS
EGGSHELL
EGGSHELLS
EGGY
EGIS
EGISES
EGLANTINE
EGLANTINES
EGLATERE
EGLATERES
EGMA

EGMAS
EGO
EGOISM
EGOISMS
EGOIST
EGOISTIC
EGOISTS
EGOITIES
EGOITY
EGOMANIA
EGOMANIAC
EGOMANIACS
EGOMANIAS
EGOS
EGOTHEISM
EGOTHEISMS
EGOTISE
EGOTISED
EGOTISES
EGOTISING
EGOTISM
EGOTISMS
EGOTIST
EGOTISTIC
EGOTISTS
EGOTIZE
EGOTIZED
EGOTIZES
EGOTIZING
EGREGIOUS
EGRESS
EGRESSES
EGRESSION
EGRESSIONS
EGRET
EGRETS
EH
EHED
EHING
EHS
EIDENT
EIDER
EIDERDOWN
EIDERDOWNS
EIDERS
EIDETIC
EIDETICS
EIDOGRAPH
EIDOGRAPHS
EIDOLA
EIDOLON
EIGENTONE
EIGENTONES
EIGHT
EIGHTEEN
EIGHTEENS
EIGHTFOIL
EIGHTFOILS
EIGHTFOLD
EIGHTFOOT
EIGHTH
EIGHTHLY
EIGHTHS
EIGHTIES
EIGHTIETH
EIGHTIETHS
EIGHTS
EIGHTSMAN
EIGHTSMEN
EIGHTSOME

EIGHTSOMES
EIGHTVO
EIGHTVOS
EIGHTY
EIGNE
EIK
EIKED
EIKING
EIKON
EIKONS
EIKS
EILD
EILDING
EILDINGS
EILDS
EINE
EIRACK
EIRACKS
EIRENIC
EIRENICON
EIRENICONS
EISEL
EISELL
EISELLS
EISELS
EITHER
EJACULATE
EJACULATED
EJACULATES
EJACULATING
EJECT
EJECTA
EJECTED
EJECTING
EJECTION
EJECTIONS
EJECTIVE
EJECTMENT
EJECTMENTS
EJECTOR
EJECTORS
EJECTS
EKE
EKED
EKES
EKING
EKISTIC
EKISTICS
EKKA
EKKAS
EKLOGITE
EKLOGITES
EKPWELE
EKPWELES
EKUELE
EL
ELABORATE
ELABORATED
ELABORATES
ELABORATING
ELAEOLITE
ELAEOLITES
ÉLAN
ELANCE
ELANCED
ELANCES
ELANCING
ELAND
ELANDS
ELANET

ELANETS
ÉLANS
ELAPHINE
ELAPSE
ELAPSED
ELAPSES
ELAPSING
ELASTANCE
ELASTANCES
ELASTASE
ELASTASES
ELASTIC
ELASTICS
ELASTIN
ELASTINS
ELASTOMER
ELASTOMERS
ELATE
ELATED
ELATEDLY
ELATER
ELATERIN
ELATERINS
ELATERITE
ELATERITES
ELATERIUM
ELATERIUMS
ELATERS
ELATES
ELATING
ELATION
ELATIONS
ELATIVE
ELATIVES
ELBOW
ELBOWED
ELBOWING
ELBOWS
ELCHEE
ELCHEES
ELCHI
ELCHIS
ELD
ELDER
ELDERLIES
ELDERLY
ELDERS
ELDERSHIP
ELDERSHIPS
ELDEST
ELDIN
ELDING
ELDINGS
ELDINS
ELDRITCH
ELDS
ELECT
ELECTABLE
ELECTED
ELECTING
ELECTION
ELECTIONS
ELECTIVE
ELECTIVES
ELECTOR
ELECTORAL
ELECTORS
ELECTRESS
ELECTRESSES
ELECTRET

ELECTRETS
ELECTRIC
ELECTRICS
ELECTRIFIED
ELECTRIFIES
ELECTRIFY
ELECTRIFYING
ELECTRISE
ELECTRISED
ELECTRISES
ELECTRISING
ELECTRIZE
ELECTRIZED
ELECTRIZES
ELECTRIZING
ELECTRO
ELECTRODE
ELECTRODES
ELECTRON
ELECTRONS
ELECTROS
ELECTRUM
ELECTRUMS
ELECTS
ELECTUARIES
ELECTUARY
ELEGANCE
ELEGANCES
ELEGANCIES
ELEGANCY
ELEGANT
ELEGANTLY
ELEGIAC
ELEGIACAL
ELEGIACS
ELEGIAST
ELEGIASTS
ELEGIES
ELEGISE
ELEGISED
ELEGISES
ELEGISING
ELEGIST
ELEGISTS
ELEGIT
ELEGITS
ELEGIZE
ELEGIZED
ELEGIZES
ELEGIZING
ELEGY
ELEMENT
ELEMENTAL
ELEMENTALS
ELEMENTS
ELEMI
ELEMIS
ELENCH
ELENCHI
ELENCHS
ELENCHUS
ELENCTIC
ELEPHANT
ELEPHANTS
ELEUTHERI
ELEVATE
ELEVATED
ELEVATEDS
ELEVATES
ELEVATING

ELEVATION
ELEVATIONS
ELEVATOR
ELEVATORS
ELEVATORY
ELEVEN
ELEVENS
ELEVENSES
ELEVENTH
ELEVENTHS
ELEVON
ELEVONS
ELF
ELFED
ELFHOOD
ELFHOODS
ELFIN
ELFING
ELFINS
ELFISH
ELFLAND
ELFLANDS
ELFLOCKS
ELFS
ELIAD
ELIADS
ELICIT
ELICITED
ELICITING
ELICITOR
ELICITORS
ELICITO
ELIDE
ELIDED
ELIDES
ELIDING
ELIGIBLE
ELIGIBLES
ELIGIBLY
ELIMINANT
ELIMINANTS
ELIMINATE
ELIMINATED
ELIMINATES
ELIMINATING
ELISION
ELISIONS
ELITE
ÉLITES
ELITISM
ELITISMS
ELITIST
ELITISTS
ELIXIR
ELIXIRS
ELK
ELKHOUND
ELKHOUNDS
ELKS
ELL
ELLAGIC
ELLIPSE
ELLIPSES
ELLIPSIS
ELLIPSOID
ELLIPSOIDS
ELLIPTIC
ELLOPS
ELLOPSES
ELLS

ELLWAND
ELLWANDS
ELM
ELMEN
ELMIER
ELMIEST
ELMS
ELMWOOD
ELMWOODS
ELMY
ELOCUTE
ELOCUTED
ELOCUTES
ELOCUTING
ELOCUTION
ELOCUTIONS
ELOCUTORY
ÉLOGE
ÉLOGES
ELOGIES
ELOGIST
ELOGISTS
ELOGIUM
ELOGIUMS
ELOGY
ELOIGN
ELOIGNED
ELOIGNER
ELOIGNERS
ELOIGNING
ELOIGNS
ELOIN
ELOINED
ELOINER
ELOINERS
ELOINING
ELOINMENT
ELOINMENTS
ELOINS
ELONGATE
ELONGATED
ELONGATES
ELONGATING
ELOPE
ELOPED
ELOPEMENT
ELOPEMENTS
ELOPER
ELOPERS
ELOPES
ELOPING
ELOPS
ELOPSES
ELOQUENCE
ELOQUENCES
ELOQUENT
ELPEE
ELPEES
ELS
ELSE
ELSEWHERE
ELSEWISE
ELSHIN
ELSHINS
ELSIN
ELSINS
ELT
ELTCHI
ELTCHIS
ELTS

ELUANT
ELUANTS
ELUATE
ELUATES
ELUCIDATE
ELUCIDATED
ELUCIDATES
ELUCIDATING
ELUDE
ELUDED
ELUDER
ELUDERS
ELUDES
ELUDIBLE
ELUDING
ELUENT
ELUENTS
ELUSION
ELUSIONS
ELUSIVE
ELUSIVELY
ELUSORY
ELUTE
ELUTED
ELUTES
ELUTING
ELUTION
ELUTIONS
ELUTOR
ELUTORS
ELUTRIATE
ELUTRIATED
ELUTRIATES
ELUTRIATING
ELUVIA
ELUVIAL
ELUVIUM
ELUVIUMS
ELVAN
ELVANITE
ELVANITES
ELVANS
ELVER
ELVERS
ELVES
ELVISH
ELYTRA
ELYTRAL
ELYTRON
ELYTRUM
EM
EMACIATE
EMACIATED
EMACIATES
EMACIATING
EMALANGENI
EMANANT
EMANATE
EMANATED
EMANATES
EMANATING
EMANATION
EMANATIONS
EMANATIST
EMANATISTS
EMANATIVE
EMANATORY
EMBACE
EMBACES
EMBACING

EMBAIL
EMBAILED
EMBAILING
EMBAILS
EMBALE
EMBALED
EMBALES
EMBALING
EMBALL
EMBALLED
EMBALLING
EMBALLINGS
EMBALLS
EMBALM
EMBALMED
EMBALMER
EMBALMERS
EMBALMING
EMBALMINGS
EMBALMS
EMBANK
EMBANKED
EMBANKER
EMBANKERS
EMBANKING
EMBANKS
EMBAR
EMBARGO
EMBARGOED
EMBARGOES
EMBARGOING
EMBARK
EMBARKED
EMBARKING
EMBARKS
EMBARRASS
EMBARRASSED
EMBARRASSES
EMBARRASSING
EMBARRED
EMBARRING
EMBARRINGS
EMBARS
EMBASE
EMBASED
EMBASES
EMBASING
EMBASSADE
EMBASSADES
EMBASSAGE
EMBASSAGES
EMBASSIES
EMBASSY
EMBASTE
EMBATHE
EMBATHED
EMBATHES
EMBATHING
EMBATTLE
EMBATTLED
EMBATTLES
EMBATTLING
EMBAY
EMBAYED
EMBAYING
EMBAYLD
EMBAYMENT
EMBAYMENTS
EMBAYS
EMBED

EMBEDDED
EMBEDDING
EMBEDMENT
EMBEDMENTS
EMBEDS
EMBELLISH
EMBELLISHED
EMBELLISHES
EMBELLISHING
EMBER
EMBERS
EMBEZZLE
EMBEZZLED
EMBEZZLER
EMBEZZLERS
EMBEZZLES
EMBEZZLING
EMBITTER
EMBITTERED
EMBITTERING
EMBITTERINGS
EMBITTERS
EMBLAZE
EMBLAZED
EMBLAZES
EMBLAZING
EMBLAZON
EMBLAZONED
EMBLAZONING
EMBLAZONS
EMBLEM
EMBLEMA
EMBLEMATA
EMBLEMED
EMBLEMING
EMBLEMISE
EMBLEMISED
EMBLEMISES
EMBLEMISING
EMBLEMIZE
EMBLEMIZED
EMBLEMIZES
EMBLEMIZING
EMBLEMS
EMBLIC
EMBLICS
EMBLOOM
EMBLOOMED
EMBLOOMING
EMBLOOMS
EMBLOSSOM
EMBLOSSOMED
EMBLOSSOMING
EMBLOSSOMS
EMBODIED
EMBODIES
EMBODY
EMBODYING
EMBOG
EMBOGGED
EMBOGGING
EMBOGS
EMBOGUE
EMBOGUED
EMBOGUES
EMBOGUING
EMBOIL
EMBOILED
EMBOILING
EMBOILS

EMBOLDEN	EMBRASURE	EMCEES	ÉMIGRÉS	EMPACKETED
EMBOLDENED	EMBRASURES	EME	EMINENCE	EMPACKETING
EMBOLDENING	EMBRAVE	EMEER	EMINENCES	EMPACKETS
EMBOLDENS	EMBRAVED	EMEERS	EMINENCIES	EMPAESTIC
EMBOLI	EMBRAVES	EMEND	EMINENCY	EMPAIRE
EMBOLIC	EMBRAVING	EMENDABLE	EMINENT	EMPAIRED
EMBOLIES	EMBRAZURE	EMENDALS	EMINENTLY	EMPAIRES
EMBOLISM	EMBRAZURES	EMENDATE	EMIR	EMPAIRING
EMBOLISMS	EMBREAD	EMENDATED	EMIRATE	EMPALE
EMBOLUS	EMBREADED	EMENDATES	EMIRATES	EMPALED
EMBOLUSES	EMBREADING	EMENDATING	EMIRS	EMPALES
EMBOLY	EMBREADS	EMENDATOR	EMISSARIES	EMPALING
EMBORDER	EMBREATHE	EMENDATORS	EMISSARY	EMPANEL
EMBORDERED	EMBREATHED	EMENDED	EMISSILE	EMPANELLED
EMBORDERING	EMBREATHES	EMENDING	EMISSION	EMPANELLING
EMBORDERS	EMBREATHING	EMENDS	EMISSIONS	EMPANELS
EMBOSCATA	EMBREWE	EMERALD	EMISSIVE	EMPANOPLIED
EMBOSCATAS	EMBREWED	EMERALDS	EMIT	EMPANOPLIES
EMBOSOM	EMBREWES	EMERAUDE	EMITS	EMPANOPLY
EMBOSOMED	EMBREWING	EMERAUDES	EMITTED	EMPANOPLYING
EMBOSOMING	EMBRITTLE	EMERGE	EMITTING	EMPARE
EMBOSOMS	EMBRITTLED	EMERGED	EMMA	EMPARED
EMBOSS	EMBRITTLES	EMERGENCE	EMMARBLE	EMPARES
EMBOSSED	EMBRITTLING	EMERGENCES	EMMARBLED	EMPARING
EMBOSSER	EMBROCATE	EMERGENCIES	EMMARBLES	EMPART
EMBOSSERS	EMBROCATED	EMERGENCY	EMMARBLING	EMPARTED
EMBOSSES	EMBROCATES	EMERGENT	EMMAS	EMPARTING
EMBOSSING	EMBROCATING	EMERGES	EMMER	EMPARTS
EMBOST	EMBROGLIO	EMERGING	EMMERS	EMPATHIC
EMBOUND	EMBROGLIOS	EMERIED	EMMESH	EMPATHIES
EMBOUNDED	EMBROIDER	EMERIES	EMMESHED	EMPATHISE
EMBOUNDING	EMBROIDERED	EMERITI	EMMESHES	EMPATHISED
EMBOUNDS	EMBROIDERING	EMERITUS	EMMESHING	EMPATHISES
EMBOW	EMBROIDERS	EMERODS	EMMET	EMPATHISING
EMBOWED	EMBROIL	EMERSED	EMMETROPE	EMPATHIZE
EMBOWEL	EMBROILED	EMERSION	EMMETROPES	EMPATHIZED
EMBOWELLED	EMBROILING	EMERSIONS	EMMETS	EMPATHIZES
EMBOWELLING	EMBROILS	EMERY	EMMEW	EMPATHIZING
EMBOWELS	EMBROWN	EMERYING	EMMEWED	EMPATHY
EMBOWER	EMBROWNED	EMES	EMMEWING	EMPATRON
EMBOWERED	EMBROWNING	EMESES	EMMEWS	EMPATRONED
EMBOWERING	EMBROWNS	EMESIS	EMMOVE	EMPATRONING
EMBOWERS	EMBRUE	EMETIC	EMMOVED	EMPATRONS
EMBOWING	EMBRUED	EMETICAL	EMMOVES	EMPAYRE
EMBOWS	EMBRUES	EMETICS	EMMOVING	EMPAYRED
EMBOX	EMBRUING	EMETIN	EMOLLIATE	EMPAYRES
EMBOXED	EMBRUTE	EMETINE	EMOLLIATED	EMPAYRING
EMBOXES	EMBRUTED	EMETINES	EMOLLIATES	EMPEACH
EMBOXING	EMBRUTES	EMETINS	EMOLLIATING	EMPEACHED
EMBRACE	EMBRUTING	EMEU	EMOLLIENT	EMPEACHES
EMBRACED	EMBRYO	EMEUS	EMOLLIENTS	EMPEACHING
EMBRACEOR	EMBRYON	ÉMEUTE	EMOLUMENT	EMPENNAGE
EMBRACEORS	EMBRYONAL	ÉMEUTES	EMOLUMENTS	EMPENNAGES
EMBRACER	EMBRYONIC	EMICANT	EMONG	EMPEOPLE
EMBRACERIES	EMBRYONS	EMICATE	EMONGES	EMPEOPLED
EMBRACERS	EMBRYOS	EMICATED	EMONGST	EMPEOPLES
EMBRACERY	EMBRYOTIC	EMICATES	EMONGST	EMPEOPLING
EMBRACES	EMBUS	EMICATING	EMOTE	EMPERCE
EMBRACING	EMBUSIED	EMICATION	EMOTED	EMPERCED
EMBRACIVE	EMBUSIES	EMICATIONS	EMOTES	EMPERCES
EMBRAID	EMBUSQUÉ	EMICTION	EMOTING	EMPERCING
EMBRAIDED	EMBUSQUÉS	EMICTIONS	EMOTION	EMPERIES
EMBRAIDING	EMBUSSED	EMICTORY	EMOTIONAL	EMPERISE
EMBRAIDS	EMBUSSES	EMIGRANT	EMOTIONS	EMPERISED
EMBRANGLE	EMBUSSING	EMIGRANTS	EMOTIVE	EMPERISES
EMBRANGLED	EMBUSY	EMIGRATE	EMOVE	EMPERISH
EMBRANGLES	EMBUSYING	EMIGRATED	EMOVED	EMPERISHED
EMBRANGLING	EMCEE	EMIGRATES	EMOVES	EMPERISHES
EMBRASOR	EMCEED	EMIGRATING	EMOVING	EMPERISHING
EMBRASORS	EMCEEING	ÉMIGRÉ	EMPACKET	EMPERISING

EMPERIZE	EMPOLDER	EMULING	ENARCHES	ENCHEASON
EMPERIZED	EMPOLDERED	EMULOUS	ENARCHING	ENCHEASONS
EMPERIZES	EMPOLDERING	EMULOUSLY	ENARM	ENCHEER
EMPERIZING	EMPOLDERS	EMULSIFIED	ENARMED	ENCHEERED
EMPEROR	EMPORIA	EMULSIFIES	ENARMING	ENCHEERING
EMPERORS	EMPORIUM	EMULSIFY	ENARMS	ENCHEERS
EMPERY	EMPORIUMS	EMULSIFYING	ENATE	ENCHILADA
EMPHASES	EMPOWER	EMULSIN	ENATION	ENCHILADAS
EMPHASIS	EMPOWERED	EMULSINS	ENATIONS	ENCHORIAL
EMPHASISE	EMPOWERING	EMULSION	ENAUNTER	ENCHORIC
EMPHASISED	EMPOWERS	EMULSIONS	ENCAENIA	ENCIPHER
EMPHASISES	EMPRESS	EMULSIVE	ENCAENIAS	ENCIPHERED
EMPHASISING	EMPRESSE	EMULSOID	ENCAGE	ENCIPHERING
EMPHASIZE	EMPRESSES	EMULSOIDS	ENCAGED	ENCIPHERS
EMPHASIZED	EMPRISE	EMULSOR	ENCAGES	ENCIRCLE
EMPHASIZES	EMPRISES	EMULSORS	ENCAGING	ENCIRCLED
EMPHASIZING	EMPTIED	EMUNCTORIES	ENCALM	ENCIRCLES
EMPHATIC	EMPTIER	EMUNCTORY	ENCALMED	ENCIRCLING
EMPHLYSES	EMPTIERS	EMUNGE	ENCALMING	ENCIRCLINGS
EMPHLYSIS	EMPTIES	EMUNGED	ENCALMS	ENCLASP
EMPHYSEMA	EMPTIEST	EMUNGES	ENCAMP	ENCLASPED
EMPHYSEMAS	EMPTILY	EMUNGING	ENCAMPED	ENCLASPING
EMPIERCE	EMPTINESS	EMURE	ENCAMPING	ENCLASPS
EMPIERCED	EMPTINESSES	EMURED	ENCAMPS	ENCLAVE
EMPIERCES	EMPTION	EMURES	ENCANTHIS	ENCLAVED
EMPIERCING	EMPTIONAL	EMURING	ENCANTHISES	ENCLAVES
EMPIGHT	EMPTIONS	EMUS	ENCARPUS	ENCLAVING
EMPIRE	EMPTY	EMYDES	ENCARPUSES	ENCLISES
EMPIRES	EMPTYING	EMYS	ENCASE	ENCLISIS
EMPIRIC	EMPTYINGS	EN	ENCASED	ENCLITIC
EMPIRICAL	EMPTYSES	ENABLE	ENCASES	ENCLITICS
EMPIRICS	EMPTYSIS	ENABLED	ENCASH	ENCLOSE
EMPLACE	EMPURPLE	ENABLER	ENCASHED	ENCLOSED
EMPLACED	EMPURPLED	ENABLERS	ENCASHES	ENCLOSER
EMPLACES	EMPURPLES	ENABLES	ENCASHING	ENCLOSERS
EMPLACING	EMPURPLING	ENABLING	ENCASING	ENCLOSES
EMPLANE	EMPUSA	ENACT	ENCAUSTIC	ENCLOSING
EMPLANED	EMPUSAS	ENACTED	ENCAUSTICS	ENCLOSURE
EMPLANES	EMPUSE	ENACTING	ENCAVE	ENCLOSURES
EMPLANING	EMPUSES	ENACTION	ENCAVED	ENCLOTHE
EMPLASTER	EMPYEMA	ENACTIONS	ENCAVES	ENCLOTHED
EMPLASTERED	EMPYEMAS	ENACTIVE	ENCAVING	ENCLOTHES
EMPLASTERING	EMPYESES	ENACTMENT	ENCEINTE	ENCLOTHING
EMPLASTERS	EMPYESIS	ENACTMENTS	ENCEINTES	ENCLOUD
EMPLASTIC	EMPYREAL	ENACTOR	ENCHAFE	ENCLOUDED
EMPLASTICS	EMPYREAN	ENACTORS	ENCHAFED	ENCLOUDING
EMPLECTON	EMPYREANS	ENACTS	ENCHAFES	ENCLOUDS
EMPLECTONS	EMPYREUMA	ENACTURE	ENCHAFING	ENCODE
EMPLECTUM	EMPYREUMATA	ENACTURES	ENCHAIN	ENCODED
EMPLECTUMS	EMS	ENALLAGE	ENCHAINED	ENCODES
EMPLONGE	EMU	ENALLAGES	ENCHAINING	ENCODING
EMPLONGED	EMULATE	ENAMEL	ENCHAINS	ENCOLOUR
EMPLONGES	EMULATED	ENAMELLED	ENCHANT	ENCOLOURED
EMPLONGING	EMULATES	ENAMELLER	ENCHANTED	ENCOLOURING
EMPLOY	EMULATING	ENAMELLERS	ENCHANTER	ENCOLOURS
EMPLOYED	EMULATION	ENAMELLING	ENCHANTERS	ENCOLPION
EMPLOYEE	EMULATIONS	ENAMELLINGS	ENCHANTING	ENCOLPIONS
EMPLOYEES	EMULATIVE	ENAMELS	ENCHANTS	ENCOLPIUM
EMPLOYER	EMULATOR	ENAMOR	ENCHARGE	ENCOLPIUMS
EMPLOYERS	EMULATORS	ENAMORADO	ENCHARGED	ENCOLURE
EMPLOYING	EMULE	ENAMORADOS	ENCHARGES	ENCOLURES
EMPLOYS	EMULED	ENAMORED	ENCHARGING	ENCOMIA
EMPLUME	EMULES	ENAMORING	ENCHARM	ENCOMIAST
EMPLUMED	EMULGE	ENAMORS	ENCHARMED	ENCOMIASTS
EMPLUMES	EMULGED	ENAMOUR	ENCHARMING	ENCOMION
EMPLUMING	EMULGENCE	ENAMOURED	ENCHARMS	ENCOMIUM
EMPOISON	EMULGENCES	ENAMOURING	ENCHASE	ENCOMIUMS
EMPOISONED	EMULGENT	ENAMOURS	ENCHASED	ENCOMPASS
EMPOISONING	EMULGES	ENARCH	ENCHASES	ENCOMPASSED
EMPOISONS	EMULGING	ENARCHED	ENCHASING	ENCOMPASSES

ENCOMPASSING
ENCORE
ENCORED
ENCORES
ENCORING
ENCOUNTER
ENCOUNTERED
ENCOUNTERING
ENCOUNTERS
ENCOURAGE
ENCOURAGED
ENCOURAGES
ENCOURAGING
ENCOURAGINGS
ENCRADLE
ENCRADLED
ENCRADLES
ENCRADLING
ENCRATIES
ENCRATY
ENCREASE
ENCREASED
ENCREASES
ENCREASING
ENCRIMSON
ENCRIMSONED
ENCRIMSONING
ENCRIMSONS
ENCRINAL
ENCRINIC
ENCRINITE
ENCRINITES
ENCROACH
ENCROACHED
ENCROACHES
ENCROACHING
ENCRUST
ENCRUSTED
ENCRUSTING
ENCRUSTS
ENCRYPT
ENCRYPTED
ENCRYPTING
ENCRYPTS
ENCUMBER
ENCUMBERED
ENCUMBERING
ENCUMBERS
ENCURTAIN
ENCURTAINED
ENCURTAINING
ENCURTAINS
ENCYCLIC
ENCYCLICS
ENCYST
ENCYSTED
ENCYSTING
ENCYSTS
END
ENDAMAGE
ENDAMAGED
ENDAMAGES
ENDAMAGING
ENDAMOEBA
ENDAMOEBAE
ENDAMOEBAS
ENDANGER
ENDANGERED
ENDANGERING
ENDANGERS

ENDARCH
ENDART
ENDARTED
ENDARTING
ENDARTS
ENDEAR
ENDEARED
ENDEARING
ENDEARS
ENDEAVOUR
ENDEAVOURED
ENDEAVOURING
ENDEAVOURS
ENDECAGON
ENDECAGONS
ENDED
ENDEICTIC
ENDEIXES
ENDEIXIS
ENDEIXISES
ENDEMIAL
ENDEMIC
ENDEMICAL
ENDEMICS
ENDEMISM
ENDEMISMS
ENDENIZEN
ENDENIZENED
ENDENIZENING
ENDENIZENS
ENDERMIC
ENDERON
ENDERONS
ENDEW
ENDEWED
ENDEWING
ENDEWS
ENDGAME
ENDGAMES
ENDING
ENDINGS
ENDIRON
ENDIRONS
ENDITE
ENDITED
ENDITES
ENDITING
ENDIVE
ENDIVES
ENDLANG
ENDLESS
ENDLESSLY
ENDLONG
ENDMOST
ENDOBLAST
ENDOBLASTS
ENDOCARP
ENDOCARPS
ENDOCRINE
ENDOCRINES
ENDODERM
ENDODERMS
ENDODYNE
ENDOGAMIC
ENDOGAMIES
ENDOGAMY
ENDOGEN
ENDOGENIC
ENDOGENIES
ENDOGENS

ENDOGENY
ENDOLYMPH
ENDOLYMPHS
ENDOMIXES
ENDOMIXIS
ENDOMIXISES
ENDOMORPH
ENDOMORPHS
ENDOPHAGIES
ENDOPHAGY
ENDOPHYTE
ENDOPHYTES
ENDOPLASM
ENDOPLASMS
ENDORPHIN
ENDORPHINS
ENDORSE
ENDORSED
ENDORSEE
ENDORSEES
ENDORSER
ENDORSERS
ENDORSES
ENDORSING
ENDOSARC
ENDOSARCS
ENDOSCOPE
ENDOSCOPES
ENDOSCOPIES
ENDOSCOPY
ENDOSMOSE
ENDOSMOSES
ENDOSPERM
ENDOSPERMS
ENDOSPORE
ENDOSPORES
ENDOSS
ENDOSSED
ENDOSSES
ENDOSSING
ENDOSTEAL
ENDOSTEUM
ENDOSTEUMS
ENDOW
ENDOWED
ENDOWER
ENDOWERS
ENDOWING
ENDOWMENT
ENDOWMENTS
ENDOWS
ENDOZOA
ENDOZOIC
ENDOZOON
ENDS
ENDSHIP
ENDSHIPS
ENDUE
ENDUED
ENDUES
ENDUING
ENDUNGEON
ENDUNGEONED
ENDUNGEONING
ENDUNGEONS
ENDURABLE
ENDURABLY
ENDURANCE
ENDURANCES
ENDURE

ENDURED
ENDURER
ENDURERS
ENDURES
ENDURING
ENDWAYS
ENDWISE
ENE
ENEMA
ENEMAS
ENEMATA
ENEMIES
ENEMY
ENERGETIC
ENERGETICS
ENERGIC
ENERGID
ENERGIDS
ENERGIES
ENERGISE
ENERGISED
ENERGISES
ENERGISING
ENERGIZE
ENERGIZED
ENERGIZES
ENERGIZING
ENERGUMEN
ENERGUMENS
ENERGY
ENERVATE
ENERVATED
ENERVATES
ENERVATING
ENERVE
ENERVED
ENERVES
ENERVING
ENES
ENEW
ENEWED
ENEWING
ENEWS
ENFACE
ENFACED
ENFACES
ENFACING
ENFANT
ENFANTS
ENFEEBLE
ENFEEBLED
ENFEEBLES
ENFEEBLING
ENFELON
ENFELONED
ENFELONING
ENFELONS
ENFEOFF
ENFEOFFED
ENFEOFFING
ENFEOFFS
ENFESTED
ENFETTER
ENFETTERED
ENFETTERING
ENFETTERS
ENFIERCE
ENFIERCED
ENFIERCES
ENFIERCING

ENFILADE
ENFILADED
ENFILADES
ENFILADING
ENFILED
ENFIRE
ENFIRED
ENFIRES
ENFIRING
ENFIX
ENFIXED
ENFIXES
ENFIXING
ENFLESH
ENFLESHED
ENFLESHES
ENFLESHING
ENFLOWER
ENFLOWERED
ENFLOWERING
ENFLOWERS
ENFOLD
ENFOLDED
ENFOLDING
ENFOLDS
ENFORCE
ENFORCED
ENFORCES
ENFORCING
ENFOREST
ENFORESTED
ENFORESTING
ENFORESTS
ENFORM
ENFORMED
ENFORMING
ENFORMS
ENFRAME
ENFRAMED
ENFRAMES
ENFRAMING
ENFREE
ENFREED
ENFREEDOM
ENFREEDOMED
ENFREEDOMING
ENFREEDOMS
ENFREEING
ENFREES
ENFREEZE
ENFREEZES
ENFREEZING
ENFROSEN
ENFROZE
ENFROZEN
ENG
ENGAGÉ
ENGAGE
ENGAGED
ENGAGER
ENGAGERS
ENGAGES
ENGAGING
ENGAOL
ENGAOLED
ENGAOLING
ENGAOLS
ENGARLAND
ENGARLANDED
ENGARLANDING

ENGARLANDS
ENGENDER
ENGENDERED
ENGENDERING
ENGENDERS
ENGENDURE
ENGENDURES
ENGILD
ENGILDED
ENGILDING
ENGILDS
ENGILT
ENGINE
ENGINED
ENGINEER
ENGINEERED
ENGINEERING
ENGINEERINGS
ENGINEERS
ENGINER
ENGINERIES
ENGINERY
ENGINES
ENGINING
ENGIRD
ENGIRDING
ENGIRDLE
ENGIRDLED
ENGIRDLES
ENGIRDLING
ENGIRDS
ENGIRT
ENGISCOPE
ENGISCOPES
ENGLOBE
ENGLOBED
ENGLOBES
ENGLOBING
ENGLOOM
ENGLOOMED
ENGLOOMING
ENGLOOMS
ENGLUT
ENGLUTS
ENGLUTTED
ENGLUTTING
ENGOBE
ENGOBES
ENGORE
ENGORED
ENGORES
ENGORGE
ENGORGED
ENGORGES
ENGORGING
ENGOULED
ENGOÛMENT
ENGOÛMENTS
ENGRACE
ENGRACED
ENGRACES
ENGRACING
ENGRAFF
ENGRAFFED
ENGRAFFING
ENGRAFFS
ENGRAFT
ENGRAFTED

ENGRAFTING
ENGRAFTS
ENGRAIL
ENGRAILED
ENGRAILING
ENGRAILS
ENGRAIN
ENGRAINED
ENGRAINER
ENGRAINERS
ENGRAINING
ENGRAINS
ENGRAM
ENGRAMMA
ENGRAMMAS
ENGRAMS
ENGRASP
ENGRASPED
ENGRASPING
ENGRASPS
ENGRAVE
ENGRAVED
ENGRAVEN
ENGRAVER
ENGRAVERIES
ENGRAVERS
ENGRAVERY
ENGRAVES
ENGRAVING
ENGRAVINGS
ENGRENAGE
ENGRENAGES
ENGRIEVE
ENGRIEVED
ENGRIEVES
ENGRIEVING
ENGROOVE
ENGROOVED
ENGROOVES
ENGROOVING
ENGROSS
ENGROSSED
ENGROSSER
ENGROSSERS
ENGROSSES
ENGROSSING
ENGS
ENGUARD
ENGUARDED
ENGUARDING
ENGUARDS
ENGULF
ENGULFED
ENGULFING
ENGULFS
ENGULPH
ENGULPHED
ENGULPHING
ENGULPHS
ENGYSCOPE
ENGYSCOPES
ENHALO
ENHALOED
ENHALOES
ENHALOING
ENHALOS
ENHANCE
ENHANCED
ENHANCES
ENHANCING

ENHANCIVE
ENHEARSE
ENHEARSED
ENHEARSES
ENHEARSING
ENHEARTEN
ENHEARTENED
ENHEARTENING
ENHEARTENS
ENHUNGER
ENHUNGERED
ENHUNGERING
ENHUNGERS
ENHYDRITE
ENHYDRITES
ENHYDROS
ENHYDROSES
ENHYDROUS
ENIAC
ENIACS
ENIGMA
ENIGMAS
ENIGMATIC
ENISLE
ENISLED
ENISLES
ENISLING
ENJAMB
ENJAMBED
ENJAMBING
ENJAMBS
ENJOIN
ENJOINED
ENJOINER
ENJOINERS
ENJOINING
ENJOINS
ENJOY
ENJOYABLE
ENJOYABLY
ENJOYED
ENJOYER
ENJOYERS
ENJOYING
ENJOYMENT
ENJOYMENTS
ENJOYS
ENKERNEL
ENKERNELLED
ENKERNELLING
ENKERNELS
ENKINDLE
ENKINDLED
ENKINDLES
ENKINDLING
ENLACE
ENLACED
ENLACES
ENLACING
ENLARD
ENLARDED
ENLARDING
ENLARDS
ENLARGE
ENLARGED
ENLARGEN
ENLARGENED
ENLARGENING
ENLARGENS
ENLARGER

ENLARGERS
ENLARGES
ENLARGING
ENLEVÉ
ENLIGHT
ENLIGHTED
ENLIGHTEN
ENLIGHTENED
ENLIGHTENING
ENLIGHTENS
ENLIGHTING
ENLIGHTS
ENLINK
ENLINKED
ENLINKING
ENLINKS
ENLIST
ENLISTED
ENLISTING
ENLISTS
ENLIT
ENLIVEN
ENLIVENED
ENLIVENER
ENLIVENERS
ENLIVENING
ENLIVENS
ENLOCK
ENLOCKED
ENLOCKING
ENLOCKS
ENLUMINE
ENLUMINED
ENLUMINES
ENLUMINING
ENMESH
ENMESHED
ENMESHES
ENMESHING
ENMEW
ENMEWED
ENMEWING
ENMEWS
ENMITIES
ENMITY
ENMOSSED
ENMOVE
ENMOVED
ENMOVES
ENMOVING
ENNEAD
ENNEADIC
ENNEADS
ENNEAGON
ENNEAGONS
ENNOBLE
ENNOBLED
ENNOBLES
ENNOBLING
ENNUI
ENNUIED
ENNUIS
ENNUYÉ
ENNUYED
ENNUYING
ENODAL
ENOMOTIES
ENOMOTY
ENORM
ENORMITIES

ENORMITY
ENORMOUS
ENOSES
ENOSIS
ENOUGH
ENOUGHS
ENOUNCE
ENOUNCED
ENOUNCES
ENOUNCING
ENOW
ENPRINT
ENPRINTS
ENQUIRE
ENQUIRED
ENQUIRER
ENQUIRERS
ENQUIRES
ENQUIRIES
ENQUIRING
ENQUIRY
ENRACE
ENRACED
ENRACES
ENRACING
ENRAGE
ENRAGE
ENRAGED
ENRAGES
ENRAGING
ENRANCKLE
ENRANCKLED
ENRANCKLES
ENRANCKLING
ENRANGE
ENRANGED
ENRANGES
ENRANGING
ENRANK
ENRANKED
ENRANKING
ENRANKS
ENRAPT
ENRAPTURE
ENRAPTURED
ENRAPTURES
ENRAPTURING
ENRAUNGE
ENRAUNGED
ENRAUNGES
ENRAUNGING
ENRAVISH
ENRAVISHED
ENRAVISHES
ENRAVISHING
ENRHEUM
ENRHEUMED
ENRHEUMING
ENRHEUMS
ENRICH
ENRICHED
ENRICHES
ENRICHING
ENRIDGED
ENRING
ENRINGED
ENRINGING
ENRINGS
ENRIVEN
ENROBE

ENROBED	ENSHIELDS	ENSUES	ENTERTAKE	ENTRAIL
ENROBES	ENSHRINE	ENSUING	ENTERTAKEN	ENTRAILED
ENROBING	ENSHRINED	ENSURE	ENTERTAKES	ENTRAILING
ENROL	ENSHRINES	ENSURED	ENTERTAKING	ENTRAILS
ENROLL	ENSHRINING	ENSURER	ENTERTOOK	ENTRAIN
ENROLLED	ENSHROUD	ENSURERS	ENTÊTÉ	ENTRAINED
ENROLLER	ENSHROUDED	ENSURES	ENTÊTÉE	ENTRAINING
ENROLLERS	ENSHROUDING	ENSURING	ENTHALPIES	ENTRAINS
ENROLLING	ENSHROUDS	ENSWATHE	ENTHALPY	ENTRALL
ENROLLS	ENSIFORM	ENSWATHED	ENTHETIC	ENTRALLES
ENROLMENT	ENSIGN	ENSWATHES	ENTHRAL	ENTRAMMEL
ENROLMENTS	ENSIGNCIES	ENSWATHING	ENTHRALL	ENTRAMMELLED
ENROLS	ENSIGNCY	ENSWEEP	ENTHRALLED	ENTRAMMELLING
ENROOT	ENSIGNED	ENSWEEPING	ENTHRALLING	ENTRAMMELS
ENROOTED	ENSIGNING	ENSWEEPS	ENTHRALLS	ENTRANCE
ENROOTING	ENSIGNS	ENSWEPT	ENTHRALS	ENTRANCED
ENROOTS	ENSILAGE	ENTAIL	ENTHRONE	ENTRANCES
ENROUGH	ENSILAGED	ENTAILED	ENTHRONED	ENTRANCING
ENROUGHED	ENSILAGES	ENTAILER	ENTHRONES	ENTRANT
ENROUGHING	ENSILAGING	ENTAILERS	ENTHRONING	ENTRANTS
ENROUGHS	ENSILE	ENTAILING	ENTHUSE	ENTRAP
ENROUND	ENSILED	ENTAILS	ENTHUSED	ENTRAPPED
ENROUNDED	ENSILES	ENTAME	ENTHUSES	ENTRAPPER
ENROUNDING	ENSILING	ENTAMED	ENTHUSING	ENTRAPPERS
ENROUNDS	ENSKIED	ENTAMES	ENTHYMEME	ENTRAPPING
ENS	ENSKIES	ENTAMING	ENTHYMEMES	ENTRAPS
ENSAMPLE	ENSKY	ENTAMOEBA	ENTIA	ENTREAT
ENSAMPLED	ENSKYING	ENTAMOEBAE	ENTICE	ENTREATED
ENSAMPLES	ENSLAVE	ENTAMOEBAS	ENTICED	ENTREATIES
ENSAMPLING	ENSLAVED	ENTANGLE	ENTICER	ENTREATING
ENSATE	ENSLAVER	ENTANGLED	ENTICERS	ENTREATS
ENSCONCE	ENSLAVERS	ENTANGLES	ENTICES	ENTREATY
ENSCONCED	ENSLAVES	ENTANGLING	ENTICING	ENTRECHAT
ENSCONCES	ENSLAVING	ENTASES	ENTICINGS	ENTRECHATS
ENSCONCING	ENSNARE	ENTASIS	ENTIRE	ENTRECÔTE
ENSEAL	ENSNARED	ENTAYLE	ENTIRELY	ENTRECÔTES
ENSEALED	ENSNARES	ENTAYLED	ENTIRES	ENTRÉE
ENSEALING	ENSNARING	ENTAYLES	ENTIRETIES	ENTRÉES
ENSEALS	ENSNARL	ENTAYLING	ENTIRETY	ENTREMES
ENSEAM	ENSNARLED	ENTELECHIES	ENTITIES	ENTREMETS
ENSEAMED	ENSNARLING	ENTELECHY	ENTITLE	ENTRENCH
ENSEAMING	ENSNARLS	ENTELLUS	ENTITLED	ENTRENCHED
ENSEAMS	ENSORCELL	ENTELLUSES	ENTITLES	ENTRENCHES
ENSEAR	ENSORCELLED	ENTENDER	ENTITLING	ENTRENCHING
ENSEARED	ENSORCELLING	ENTENDERED	ENTITY	ENTREPOT
ENSEARING	ENSORCELLS	ENTENDERING	ENTOBLAST	ENTREPOTS
ENSEARS	ENSOUL	ENTENDERS	ENTOBLASTS	ENTRESOL
ENSEMBLE	ENSOULED	ENTENTE	ENTODERM	ENTRESOLS
ENSEMBLES	ENSOULING	ENTENTES	ENTODERMS	ENTREZ
ENSEW	ENSOULS	ENTER	ENTOIL	ENTRIES
ENSEWED	ENSPHERE	ENTERA	ENTOILED	ENTRISM
ENSEWING	ENSPHERED	ENTERABLE	ENTOILING	ENTRISMS
ENSEWS	ENSPHERES	ENTERAL	ENTOILS	ENTRIST
ENSHEATH	ENSPHERING	ENTERATE	ENTOMB	ENTRISTS
ENSHEATHE	ENSTAMP	ENTERED	ENTOMBED	ENTROLD
ENSHEATHED	ENSTAMPED	ENTERER	ENTOMBING	ENTROPIES
ENSHEATHES	ENSTAMPING	ENTERERS	ENTOMBS	ENTROPION
ENSHEATHING	ENSTAMPS	ENTERIC	ENTOMIC	ENTROPIONS
ENSHEATHS	ENSTATITE	ENTERICS	ENTOPHYTE	ENTROPIUM
ENSHELL	ENSTATITES	ENTERING	ENTOPHYTES	ENTROPIUMS
ENSHELLED	ENSTEEP	ENTERINGS	ENTOPIC	ENTROPY
ENSHELLING	ENSTEEPED	ENTERITIS	ENTOPTIC	ENTRUST
ENSHELLS	ENSTEEPING	ENTERITISES	ENTOPTICS	ENTRUSTED
ENSHELTER	ENSTEEPS	ENTERON	ENTOTIC	ENTRUSTING
ENSHELTERED	ENSTYLE	ENTERS	ENTOURAGE	ENTRUSTS
ENSHELTERING	ENSTYLED	ENTERTAIN	ENTOURAGES	ENTRY
ENSHELTERS	ENSTYLES	ENTERTAINED	ENTOZOA	ENTRYISM
ENSHIELD	ENSTYLING	ENTERTAINING	ENTOZOAL	ENTRYISMS
ENSHIELDED	ENSUE	ENTERTAININGS	ENTOZOIC	ENTRYIST
ENSHIELDING	ENSUED	ENTERTAINS	ENTOZOON	ENTRYISTS

ENTWINE
ENTWINED
ENTWINES
ENTWINING
ENTWIST
ENTWISTED
ENTWISTING
ENTWISTS
ENUCLEATE
ENUCLEATED
ENUCLEATES
ENUCLEATING
ENUMERATE
ENUMERATED
ENUMERATES
ENUMERATING
ENUNCIATE
ENUNCIATED
ENUNCIATES
ENUNCIATING
ENURE
ENURED
ENURES
ENURESES
ENURESIS
ENURETIC
ENURETICS
ENURING
ENVASSAL
ENVASSALLED
ENVASSALLING
ENVASSALS
ENVAULT
ENVAULTED
ENVAULTING
ENVAULTS
ENVEIGLE
ENVEIGLED
ENVEIGLES
ENVEIGLING
ENVELOP
ENVELOPE
ENVELOPED
ENVELOPES
ENVELOPING
ENVELOPS
ENVENOM
ENVENOMED
ENVENOMING
ENVENOMS
ENVERMEIL
ENVERMEILED
ENVERMEILING
ENVERMEILS
ENVIABLE
ENVIABLY
ENVIED
ENVIER
ENVIERS
ENVIES
ENVIOUS
ENVIOUSLY
ENVIRON
ENVIRONED
ENVIRONING
ENVIRONS
ENVISAGE
ENVISAGED
ENVISAGES
ENVISAGING

ENVISION
ENVISIONED
ENVISIONING
ENVISIONS
ENVOI
ENVOIS
ENVOY
ENVOYS
ENVOYSHIP
ENVOYSHIPS
ENVY
ENVYING
ENVYINGS
ENWALL
ENWALLED
ENWALLING
ENWALLOW
ENWALLOWED
ENWALLOWING
ENWALLOWS
ENWALLS
ENWHEEL
ENWHEELED
ENWHEELING
ENWHEELS
ENWIND
ENWINDING
ENWINDS
ENWOMB
ENWOMBED
ENWOMBING
ENWOMBS
ENWOUND
ENWRAP
ENWRAPPED
ENWRAPPING
ENWRAPPINGS
ENWRAPS
ENWREATHE
ENWREATHED
ENWREATHES
ENWREATHING
ENZIAN
ENZIANS
ENZONE
ENZONES
ENZONING
ENZOOTIC
ENZOOTICS
ENZYMATIC
ENZYME
ENZYMES
ENZYMIC
EOAN
ÉOLIENNE
ÉOLIENNES
EOLIPILE
EOLIPILES
EOLITH
EOLITHIC
EOLITHS
EON
EONISM
EONISMS
EONS
EORL
EORLS
EOSIN
EOSINS

EOTHEN
EPACRID
EPACRIDS
EPACRIS
EPACRISES
EPACT
EPACTS
EPAENETIC
EPAGOGE
EPAGOGES
EPAGOGIC
EPAINETIC
EPANODOS
EPANODOSES
EPARCH
EPARCHATE
EPARCHATES
EPARCHIES
EPARCHS
EPARCHY
ÉPATANT
EPAULE
EPAULES
EPAULET
EPAULETS
EPAULETTE
EPAULETTES
EPAXIAL
EPEDAPHIC
ÉPÉE
ÉPÉES
EPEIRA
EPEIRAS
EPEIRID
EPEIRIDS
EPEOLATRIES
EPEOLATRY
ÉPERDU
ÉPERDUE
EPERGNE
EPERGNES
EPHA
EPHAH
EPHAHS
EPHAS
EPHEBE
EPHEBI
EPHEBIC
EPHEBOS
EPHEBUS
EPHEDRA
EPHEDRAS
EPHEDRINE
EPHEDRINES
EPHELIDES
EPHELIS
EPHEMERA
EPHEMERAE
EPHEMERAL
EPHEMERALS
EPHEMERAS
EPHEMERID
EPHEMERIDES
EPHEMERIDS
EPHEMERIS
EPHEMERON
EPHIALTES
EPHOD
EPHODS
EPHOR

EPHORALTIES
EPHORALTY
EPHORS
EPIBLAST
EPIBLASTS
EPIC
EPICAL
EPICALLY
EPICALYCES
EPICALYX
EPICALYXES
EPICANTHI
EPICARP
EPICARPS
EPICEDE
EPICEDES
EPICEDIA
EPICEDIAL
EPICEDIAN
EPICEDIUM
EPICENE
EPICENES
EPICENTRE
EPICENTRES
EPICIER
EPICIERS
EPICISM
EPICISMS
EPICIST
EPICISTS
EPICLESES
EPICLESIS
EPICOTYL
EPICOTYLS
EPICRITIC
EPICS
EPICURE
EPICUREAN
EPICUREANS
EPICURES
EPICURISE
EPICURISED
EPICURISES
EPICURISING
EPICURISM
EPICURISMS
EPICURIZE
EPICURIZED
EPICURIZES
EPICURIZING
EPICYCLE
EPICYCLES
EPICYCLIC
EPIDEMIC
EPIDEMICS
EPIDERMAL
EPIDERMIC
EPIDERMIS
EPIDERMISES
EPIDOSITE
EPIDOSITES
EPIDOTE
EPIDOTES
EPIDOTIC
EPIDURAL
EPIDURALS
EPIFOCAL
EPIGAEAL
EPIGAEAN
EPIGAEOUS

EPIGAMIC
EPIGEAL
EPIGEAN
EPIGENE
EPIGEOUS
EPIGON
EPIGONE
EPIGONES
EPIGONI
EPIGONS
EPIGRAM
EPIGRAMS
EPIGRAPH
EPIGRAPHED
EPIGRAPHIES
EPIGRAPHING
EPIGRAPHS
EPIGRAPHY
EPIGYNIES
EPIGYNOUS
EPIGYNY
EPILATE
EPILATED
EPILATES
EPILATING
EPILATION
EPILATIONS
EPILATOR
EPILATORS
EPILEPSIES
EPILEPSY
EPILEPTIC
EPILEPTICS
EPILOBIUM
EPILOBIUMS
EPILOGIC
EPILOGISE
EPILOGISED
EPILOGISES
EPILOGISING
EPILOGIZE
EPILOGIZED
EPILOGIZES
EPILOGIZING
EPILOGUE
EPILOGUES
EPIMER
EPIMERIC
EPIMERS
EPINASTIC
EPINASTIES
EPINASTY
EPINICIAN
EPINICION
EPINICIONS
EPINIKIAN
EPINIKION
EPINIKIONS
EPINOSIC
EPIPHANIC
EPIPHRAGM
EPIPHRAGMS
EPIPHYSES
EPIPHYSIS
EPIPHYTAL
EPIPHYTE
EPIPHYTES
EPIPHYTIC
EPIPLOIC
EPIPLOON

EPIPLOONS
EPIPOLIC
EPIPOLISM
EPIPOLISMS
EPIRRHEMA
EPIRRHEMAS
EPISCOPAL
EPISCOPE
EPISCOPES
EPISCOPIES
EPISCOPY
EPISEMON
EPISEMONS
EPISODAL
EPISODE
EPISODES
EPISODIAL
EPISODIC
EPISOME
EPISOMES
EPISPERM
EPISPERMS
EPISPORE
EPISPORES
EPISTASES
EPISTASIS
EPISTATIC
EPISTAXES
EPISTAXIS
EPISTAXISES
EPISTEMIC
EPISTEMICS
EPISTLE
EPISTLED
EPISTLER
EPISTLERS
EPISTLES
EPISTLING
EPISTOLER
EPISTOLERS
EPISTOLET
EPISTOLETS
EPISTOLIC
EPISTYLE
EPISTYLES
EPITAPH
EPITAPHED
EPITAPHER
EPITAPHERS
EPITAPHIC
EPITAPHING
EPITAPHS
EPITASES
EPITASIS
EPITAXIAL
EPITAXIES
EPITAXY
EPITHEM
EPITHEMA
EPITHEMATA
EPITHEMS
EPITHESES
EPITHESIS
EPITHET
EPITHETED
EPITHETIC
EPITHETING
EPITHETON
EPITHETONS
EPITHETS

EPITOME
EPITOMES
EPITOMIC
EPITOMISE
EPITOMISED
EPITOMISES
EPITOMISING
EPITOMIST
EPITOMISTS
EPITOMIZE
EPITOMIZED
EPITOMIZES
EPITOMIZING
EPITONIC
EPITRITE
EPITRITES
EPIZEUXES
EPIZEUXIS
EPIZEUXISES
EPIZOA
EPIZOAN
EPIZOANS
EPIZOIC
EPIZOON
EPIZOOTIC
EPIZOOTICS
EPOCH
EPOCHA
EPOCHAL
EPOCHAS
EPOCHS
EPODE
EPODES
EPODIC
EPONYM
EPONYMOUS
EPONYMS
EPOPEE
EPOPEES
EPOPOEIA
EPOPOEIAS
EPOPT
EPOPTS
EPOS
EPOSES
EPOXIDE
EPOXIDES
EPOXIES
EPOXY
ÉPRIS
ÉPRISE
EPSILON
EPSILONS
EPSOMITE
EPSOMITES
ÉPUISÉ
ÉPUISÉE
EPULARY
EPULATION
EPULATIONS
EPULIDES
EPULIS
EPULISES
EPULOTIC
EPULOTICS
EPURATE
EPURATED
EPURATES
EPURATING
EPURATION

EPURATIONS
EPYLLION
EPYLLIONS
EQUABLE
EQUABLY
EQUAL
EQUALISE
EQUALISED
EQUALISER
EQUALISERS
EQUALISES
EQUALISING
EQUALITIES
EQUALITY
EQUALIZE
EQUALIZED
EQUALIZER
EQUALIZERS
EQUALIZES
EQUALIZING
EQUALLED
EQUALLING
EQUALLY
EQUALNESS
EQUALNESSES
EQUALS
EQUANT
EQUANTS
EQUATE
EQUATED
EQUATES
EQUATING
EQUATION
EQUATIONS
EQUATOR
EQUATORS
EQUERRIES
EQUERRY
EQUINAL
EQUINE
EQUINIA
EQUINIAS
EQUINITIES
EQUINITY
EQUINOX
EQUINOXES
EQUIP
EQUIPAGE
EQUIPAGED
EQUIPAGES
EQUIPAGING
ÉQUIPE
ÉQUIPES
EQUIPMENT
EQUIPMENTS
EQUIPOISE
EQUIPOISED
EQUIPOISES
EQUIPOISING
EQUIPPED
EQUIPPING
EQUIPS
EQUISETA
EQUISETIC
EQUISETUM
EQUISETUMS
EQUITABLE
EQUITABLY
EQUITANT
EQUITIES

EQUITY
EQUIVALVE
EQUIVOCAL
EQUIVOKE
EQUIVOKES
EQUIVOQUE
EQUIVOQUES
ER
ERA
ERADIATE
ERADIATED
ERADIATES
ERADIATING
ERADICATE
ERADICATED
ERADICATES
ERADICATING
ERAS
ERASABLE
ERASE
ERASED
ERASEMENT
ERASEMENTS
ERASER
ERASERS
ERASES
ERASING
ERASION
ERASIONS
ERASURE
ERASURES
ERATHEM
ERATHEMS
ERBIA
ERBIAS
ERBIUM
ERBIUMS
ERE
ERECT
ERECTED
ERECTER
ERECTERS
ERECTILE
ERECTING
ERECTION
ERECTIONS
ERECTIVE
ERECTLY
ERECTNESS
ERECTNESSES
ERECTOR
ERECTORS
ERECTS
ERED
ERELONG
EREMIC
EREMITAL
EREMITE
EREMITES
EREMITIC
EREMITISM
EREMITISMS
ERENOW
EREPSIN
EREPSINS
ERES
ERETHISM
ERETHISMS
ERETHITIC
EREWHILE

ERF
ERG
ERGATANER
ERGATANERS
ERGATE
ERGATES
ERGATOID
ERGO
ERGODIC
ERGOGRAM
ERGOGRAMS
ERGOGRAPH
ERGOGRAPHS
ERGOMETER
ERGOMETERS
ERGON
ERGONOMIC
ERGONOMICS
ERGONS
ERGOT
ERGOTISE
ERGOTISED
ERGOTISES
ERGOTISING
ERGOTISM
ERGOTISMS
ERGOTIZE
ERGOTIZED
ERGOTIZES
ERGOTIZING
ERGOTS
ERGS
ERIACH
ERIACHS
ERIC
ERICA
ERICAS
ERICK
ERICKS
ERICOID
ERICS
ERIGERON
ERIGERONS
ERING
ERINGO
ERINGOES
ERINGOS
ERINITE
ERINITES
ERIOMETER
ERIOMETERS
ERIONITE
ERIONITES
ERISTIC
ERISTICAL
ERK
ERKS
ERMELIN
ERMELINS
ERMINE
ERMINED
ERMINES
ERN
ERNE
ERNED
ERNES
ERNING
ERNS
ERODE
ERODED

ERODENT
ERODENTS
ERODES
ERODING
ERODIUM
ERODIUMS
EROGENIC
EROGENOUS
EROSE
EROSION
EROSIONS
EROSIVE
EROSTRATE
EROTEMA
EROTEMAS
EROTEME
EROTEMES
EROTESES
EROTESIS
EROTETIC
EROTIC
EROTICA
EROTICAL
EROTICISM
EROTICISMS
EROTICIST
EROTICISTS
EROTICS
EROTISM
EROTISMS
ERR
ERRABLE
ERRAND
ERRANDS
ERRANT
ERRANTLY
ERRANTRIES
ERRANTRY
ERRANTS
ERRATA
ERRATIC
ERRATICAL
ERRATICS
ERRATUM
ERRED
ERRHINE
ERRHINES
ERRING
ERRINGLY
ERRINGS
ERRONEOUS
ERROR
ERRORIST
ERRORISTS
ERRORS
ERRS
ERS
ERSATZ
ERSATZES
ERSES
ERST
ERSTWHILE
ERUCIFORM
ERUCT
ERUCTATE
ERUCTATED
ERUCTATES
ERUCTATING
ERUCTED
ERUCTING

ERUCTS
ERUDITE
ERUDITELY
ERUDITES
ERUDITION
ERUDITIONS
ERUPT
ERUPTED
ERUPTING
ERUPTION
ERUPTIONS
ERUPTIVE
ERUPTS
ERVALENTA
ERVALENTAS
ERVEN
ERYNGIUM
ERYNGIUMS
ERYNGO
ERYNGOES
ERYNGOS
ERYTHEMA
ERYTHEMAL
ERYTHEMAS
ERYTHRINA
ERYTHRINAS
ERYTHRISM
ERYTHRISMS
ERYTHRITE
ERYTHRITES
ES
ESCALADE
ESCALADED
ESCALADES
ESCALADING
ESCALADO
ESCALADOES
ESCALATE
ESCALATED
ESCALATES
ESCALATING
ESCALATOR
ESCALATORS
ESCALIER
ESCALIERS
ESCALLOP
ESCALLOPS
ESCALOP
ESCALOPE
ESCALOPES
ESCALOPS
ESCAPABLE
ESCAPADE
ESCAPADES
ESCAPADO
ESCAPADOES
ESCAPE
ESCAPED
ESCAPEE
ESCAPEES
ESCAPER
ESCAPERS
ESCAPES
ESCAPING
ESCAPISM
ESCAPISMS
ESCAPIST
ESCAPISTS
ESCARGOT
ESCARGOTS

ESCAROLE
ESCAROLES
ESCARP
ESCARPED
ESCARPING
ESCARPS
ESCHALOT
ESCHALOTS
ESCHAR
ESCHARS
ESCHEAT
ESCHEATED
ESCHEATING
ESCHEATOR
ESCHEATORS
ESCHEATS
ESCHEW
ESCHEWED
ESCHEWING
ESCHEWS
ESCLANDRE
ESCLANDRES
ESCOLAR
ESCOLARS
ESCOPETTE
ESCOPETTES
ESCORT
ESCORTAGE
ESCORTAGES
ESCORTED
ESCORTING
ESCORTS
ESCOT
ESCOTS
ESCOTTED
ESCOTTING
ESCRIBANO
ESCRIBANOS
ESCRIBE
ESCRIBED
ESCRIBES
ESCRIBING
ESCROC
ESCROCS
ESCROL
ESCROLL
ESCROLLS
ESCROLS
ESCROW
ESCROWS
ESCUAGE
ESCUAGES
ESCUDO
ESCUDOS
ESCULENT
ESCULENTS
ESEMPLASIES
ESEMPLASY
ESILE
ESILES
ESKAR
ESKARS
ESKER
ESKERS
ESKIES
ESKY®
ESLOIN
ESLOINED
ESLOINING
ESLOINS

ESLOYNE
ESLOYNED
ESLOYNES
ESLOYNING
ESNE
ESNECIES
ESNECY
ESNES
ESOPHAGI
ESOPHAGUS
ESOTERIC
ESOTERICA
ESOTERIES
ESOTERISM
ESOTERISMS
ESOTERY
ESPADA
ESPADAS
ESPAGNOLE
ESPAGNOLES
ESPALIER
ESPALIERED
ESPALIERING
ESPALIERS
ESPARTO
ESPARTOS
ESPECIAL
ESPERANCE
ESPERANCES
ESPIAL
ESPIALS
ESPIED
ESPIÈGLE
ESPIES
ESPIONAGE
ESPIONAGES
ESPLANADE
ESPLANADES
ESPOUSAL
ESPOUSALS
ESPOUSE
ESPOUSED
ESPOUSER
ESPOUSERS
ESPOUSES
ESPOUSING
ESPRESSO
ESPRESSOS
ESPRIT
ESPRITS
ESPUMOSO
ESPUMOSOS
ESPY
ESPYING
ESQUIRE
ESQUIRES
ESQUISSE
ESQUISSES
ESS
ESSAY
ESSAYED
ESSAYER
ESSAYERS
ESSAYETTE
ESSAYETTES
ESSAYING
ESSAYISH
ESSAYIST
ESSAYISTS
ESSAYS

ESSE
ESSENCE
ESSENCES
ESSENTIAL
ESSENTIALS
ESSES
ESSIVE
ESSIVES
ESSOIN
ESSOINER
ESSOINERS
ESSOINS
ESSONITE
ESSONITES
ESSOYNE
ESSOYNES
ESTABLISH
ESTABLISHED
ESTABLISHES
ESTABLISHING
ESTACADE
ESTACADES
ESTAFETTE
ESTAFETTES
ESTAMINET
ESTAMINETO
ESTANCIA
ESTANCIAS
ESTATE
ESTATED
ESTATES
ESTATING
ESTEEM
ESTEEMED
ESTEEMING
ESTEEMS
ESTER
ESTERIFIED
ESTERIFIES
ESTERIFY
ESTERIFYING
ESTERS
ESTHESES
ESTHESIA
ESTHESIAS
ESTHESIS
ESTHETE
ESTHETES
ESTHETIC
ESTHETICS
ESTIMABLE
ESTIMABLY
ESTIMATE
ESTIMATED
ESTIMATES
ESTIMATING
ESTIMATOR
ESTIMATORS
ESTIVAL
ESTIVATE
ESTIVATED
ESTIVATES
ESTIVATING
ESTOC
ESTOCS
ESTOILE
ESTOILES
ESTOP
ESTOPPAGE
ESTOPPAGES

ESTOPPED
ESTOPPEL
ESTOPPELS
ESTOPPING
ESTOPS
ESTOVER
ESTOVERS
ESTRADE
ESTRADES
ESTRADIOL
ESTRADIOLS
ESTRAL
ESTRANGE
ESTRANGED
ESTRANGER
ESTRANGERS
ESTRANGES
ESTRANGING
ESTRAPADE
ESTRAPADES
ESTRAY
ESTRAYED
ESTRAYING
ESTRAYS
ESTREAT
ESTREATED
ESTREATING
ESTREATS
ESTREPE
ESTREPED
ESTREPES
ESTREPING
ESTRICH
ESTRICHES
ESTRIDGE
ESTRIDGES
ESTRILDID
ESTRILDIDS
ESTRO
ESTROGEN
ESTROGENS
ESTROS
ESTROUS
ESTRUM
ESTRUMS
ESTRUS
ESTRUSES
ESTUARIAL
ESTUARIAN
ESTUARIES
ESTUARINE
ESTUARY
ESURIENCE
ESURIENCES
ESURIENCIES
ESURIENCY
ESURIENT
ETA
ETACISM
ETACISMS
ETAERIO
ETAERIOS
ÉTAGE
ÉTAGÈRE
ÉTAGÈRES
ÉTAGES
ÉTALAGE
ÉTALAGES
ETALON
ETALONS

ÉTAPE
ÉTAPES
ETAS
ÉTAT
ÉTATISME
ÉTATISMES
ÉTATISTE
ÉTATISTES
ÉTATS
ETCH
ETCHANT
ETCHANTS
ETCHED
ETCHER
ETCHERS
ETCHES
ETCHING
ETCHINGS
ETEN
ETENS
ETERNAL
ETERNALLY
ETERNE
ETERNISE
ETERNISED
ETERNISES
ETERNISING
ETERNITIES
ETERNITY
ETERNIZE
ETERNIZED
ETERNIZES
ETERNIZING
ETESIAN
ETH
ETHAL
ETHALS
ETHANE
ETHANES
ETHANOL
ETHANOLS
ETHE
ETHENE
ETHENES
ETHER
ETHERCAP
ETHERCAPS
ETHEREAL
ETHEREOUS
ETHERIAL
ETHERIC
ETHERICAL
ETHERION
ETHERIONS
ETHERISE
ETHERISED
ETHERISES
ETHERISING
ETHERISM
ETHERISMS
ETHERIST
ETHERISTS
ETHERIZE
ETHERIZED
ETHERIZES
ETHERIZING
ETHERS
ETHIC
ETHICAL
ETHICALLY

ETHICALS
ETHICISE
ETHICISED
ETHICISES
ETHICISING
ETHICISM
ETHICISMS
ETHICIST
ETHICISTS
ETHICIZE
ETHICIZED
ETHICIZES
ETHICIZING
ETHICS
ETHIOPS
ETHIOPSES
ETHMOID
ETHMOIDAL
ETHNARCH
ETHNARCHIES
ETHNARCHS
ETHNARCHY
ETHNIC
ETHNICAL
ETHNICISM
ETHNICISMS
ETHNICITIES
ETHNICITY
ETHNICS
ETHNOCIDE
ETHNOCIDES
ETHNOLOGIES
ETHNOLOGY
ETHOLOGIC
ETHOLOGIES
ETHOLOGY
ETHOS
ETHOSES
ETHS
ETHYL
ETHYLATE
ETHYLATED
ETHYLATES
ETHYLATING
ETHYLENE
ETHYLENES
ETHYLS
ETHYNE
ETHYNES
ETIOLATE
ETIOLATED
ETIOLATES
ETIOLATING
ETIOLIN
ETIOLINS
ETIOLOGIES
ETIOLOGY
ETIQUETTE
ETIQUETTES
ETNA
ETNAS
ÉTOILE
ÉTOILES
ÉTOURDI
ÉTOURDIE
ÉTRANGER
ÉTRANGÈRE
ÉTRANGÈRES
ÉTRANGERS
ÉTRENNE

ÉTRENNES
ÉTRIER
ÉTRIERS
ETTERCAP
ETTERCAPS
ETTIN
ETTINS
ETTLE
ETTLED
ETTLES
ETTLING
ÉTUDE
ÉTUDES
ETUI
ETUIS
ETWEE
ETWEES
ETYMA
ETYMIC
ETYMOLOGIES
ETYMOLOGY
ETYMON
ETYMONS
ETYPIC
ETYPICAL
EUCAIN
EUCAINE
EUCAINES
EUCAINS
EUCALYPT
EUCALYPTI
EUCALYPTS
EUCARYON
EUCARYONS
EUCARYOT
EUCARYOTE
EUCARYOTES
EUCARYOTS
EUCHARIS
EUCHARISES
EUCHLORIC
EUCHOLOGIES
EUCHOLOGY
EUCHRE
EUCHRED
EUCHRES
EUCHRING
EUCLASE
EUCLASES
EUCRITE
EUCRITES
EUCRITIC
EUCYCLIC
EUDAEMONIES
EUDAEMONY
EUDEMONIA
EUDEMONIAS
EUDEMONIC
EUDEMONICS
EUDEMONIES
EUDEMONY
EUDIALYTE
EUDIALYTES
EUGE
EUGENIC
EUGENICS
EUGENISM
EUGENISMS
EUGENIST
EUGENISTS

EUGENOL
EUGENOLS
EUGH
EUGHEN
EUGHS
EUK
EUKARYON
EUKARYONS
EUKARYOT
EUKARYOTE
EUKARYOTES
EUKARYOTS
EUKED
EUKING
EUKS
EULACHON
EULACHONS
EULOGIA
EULOGIES
EULOGISE
EULOGISED
EULOGISES
EULOGISING
EULOGIST
EULOGISTS
EULOGIUM
EULOGIUMS
EULOGIZE
EULOGIZED
EULOGIZES
EULOGIZING
EULOGY
EUMELANIN
EUMELANINS
EUMERISM
EUMERISMS
EUNUCH
EUNUCHISE
EUNUCHISED
EUNUCHISES
EUNUCHISING
EUNUCHISM
EUNUCHISMS
EUNUCHIZE
EUNUCHIZED
EUNUCHIZES
EUNUCHIZING
EUNUCHOID
EUNUCHOIDS
EUNUCHS
EUOI
EUONYMIN
EUONYMINS
EUONYMUS
EUONYMUSES
EUOUAE
EUOUAES
EUPAD
EUPADS
EUPATRID
EUPATRIDAE
EUPATRIDS
EUPEPSIA
EUPEPSIAS
EUPEPSIES
EUPEPSY
EUPEPTIC
EUPHAUSID
EUPHAUSIDS
EUPHEMISE

EUPHEMISED	EUSTACY	EVANISHED	EVERYWHEN	EVOLUTION
EUPHEMISES	EUSTASIES	EVANISHES	EVES	EVOLUTIONS
EUPHEMISING	EUSTASY	EVANISHING	EVET	EVOLUTIVE
EUPHEMISM	EUSTATIC	EVANITION	EVETS	EVOLVABLE
EUPHEMISMS	EUSTYLE	EVANITIONS	EVHOE	EVOLVE
EUPHEMIZE	EUSTYLES	EVAPORATE	EVICT	EVOLVED
EUPHEMIZED	EUTAXIES	EVAPORATED	EVICTED	EVOLVENT
EUPHEMIZES	EUTAXITE	EVAPORATES	EVICTING	EVOLVES
EUPHEMIZING	EUTAXITES	EVAPORATING	EVICTION	EVOLVING
EUPHENICS	EUTAXITIC	EVAPORITE	EVICTIONS	EVOVAE
EUPHOBIA	EUTAXY	EVAPORITES	EVICTOR	EVOVAES
EUPHOBIAS	EUTECTIC	EVASIBLE	EVICTORS	EVULGATE
EUPHON	EUTECTICS	EVASION	EVICTS	EVULGATED
EUPHONIA	EUTECTOID	EVASIONS	EVIDENCE	EVULGATES
EUPHONIAS	EUTECTOIDS	EVASIVE	EVIDENCED	EVULGATING
EUPHONIC	EUTEXIA	EVASIVELY	EVIDENCES	EVULSE
EUPHONIES	EUTEXIAS	EVE	EVIDENCING	EVULSED
EUPHONISE	EUTHANASIES	EVECTION	EVIDENT	EVULSES
EUPHONISED	EUTHANASY	EVECTIONS	EVIDENTLY	EVULSING
EUPHONISES	EUTHENICS	EVEJAR	EVIDENTS	EVULSION
EUPHONISING	EUTHENIST	EVEJARS	EVIL	EVULSIONS
EUPHONIUM	EUTHENISTS	EVEN	EVILLER	EVZONE
EUPHONIUMS	EUTHERIAN	EVENED	EVILLEST	EVZONES
EUPHONIZE	EUTHERIANS	ÉVÉNEMENT	EVILLY	EWE
EUPHONIZED	EUTRAPELIES	ÉVÉNEMENTS	EVILNESS	EWER
EUPHONIZES	EUTRAPELY	EVENER	EVILNESSES	EWERS
EUPHONIZING	EUTROPHIC	EVENEST	EVILS	EWES
EUPHONS	EUTROPHIES	EVENFALL	EVINCE	EWEST
EUPHONY	EUTROPHY	EVENFALLS	EVINCED	EWFTES
EUPHORBIA	EUTROPIC	EVENING	EVINCES	EWGHEN
EUPHORBIAS	EUTROPIES	EVENINGS	EVINCIBLE	EWHOW
EUPHORIA	EUTROPOUS	EVENLY	EVINCIBLY	EWK
EUPHORIAS	EUTROPY	EVENNESS	EVINCING	EWKED
EUPHORIC	EUXENITE	EVENNESSES	EVINCIVE	EWKING
EUPHORIES	EUXENITES	EVENS	EVINCIVE	EWKS
EUPHORY	EVACUANT	EVENS	EVIRATE	EWT
EUPHRASIES	EVACUANTS	EVENSONG	EVIRATED	EWTS
EUPHRASY	EVACUATE	EVENSONGS	EVIRATES	EX
EUPHROE	EVACUATED	EVENT	EVIRATING	EXACT
EUPHROES	EVACUATES	EVENTER	EVITABLE	EXACTED
EUPHUISE	EVACUATING	EVENTERS	EVITATE	EXACTER
EUPHUISED	EVACUATOR	EVENTFUL	EVITATED	EXACTERS
EUPHUISES	EVACUATORS	EVENTIDE	EVITATES	EXACTEST
EUPHUISING	EVACUEE	EVENTIDES	EVITATING	EXACTING
EUPHUISM	EVACUEES	EVENTING	EVITATION	EXACTION
EUPHUISMS	EVADABLE	EVENTINGS	EVITATIONS	EXACTIONS
EUPHUIST	EVADE	EVENTS	EVITE	EXACTLY
EUPHUISTS	EVADED	EVENTUAL	EVITED	EXACTMENT
EUPHUIZE	EVADES	EVENTUATE	EVITERNAL	EXACTMENTS
EUPHUIZED	EVADING	EVENTUATED	EVITES	EXACTNESS
EUPHUIZES	EVAGATION	EVENTUATES	EVITING	EXACTNESSES
EUPHUIZING	EVAGATIONS	EVENTUATING	EVOCATE	EXACTOR
EUREKA	EVAGINATE	EVER	EVOCATED	EXACTORS
EUREKAS	EVAGINATED	EVERGLADE	EVOCATES	EXACTRESS
EURHYTHMIES	EVAGINATES	EVERGLADES	EVOCATING	EXACTRESSES
EURHYTHMY	EVAGINATING	EVERGREEN	EVOCATION	EXACTS
EURIPI	EVALUATE	EVERGREENS	EVOCATIONS	EXALT
EURIPUS	EVALUATED	EVERMORE	EVOCATIVE	EXALTED
EURIPUSES	EVALUATES	EVERSIBLE	EVOCATORY	EXALTING
EURO	EVALUATING	EVERSION	EVOE	EXALTS
EUROPIUM	EVANESCE	EVERSIONS	EVOHE	EXAM
EUROPIUMS	EVANESCED	EVERT	EVOKE	EXAMEN
EUROS	EVANESCES	EVERTED	EVOKED	EXAMENS
EURYTHERM	EVANESCING	EVERTING	EVOKES	EXAMINANT
EURYTHERMS	EVANGEL	EVERTS	EVOKING	EXAMINANTS
EURYTHMIES	EVANGELIC	EVERY	ÉVOLUÉ	EXAMINATE
EURYTHMY	EVANGELIES	EVERYBODY	ÉVOLUÉS	EXAMINATES
EUSOL	EVANGELS	EVERYDAY	EVOLUTE	EXAMINE
EUSOLS	EVANGELY	EVERYDAYS	EVOLUTED	EXAMINED
EUSTACIES	EVANISH	EVERYONE	EVOLUTES	EXAMINEE
		EVERYWAY	EVOLUTING	

EXAMINEES
EXAMINER
EXAMINERS
EXAMINES
EXAMINING
EXAMPLAR
EXAMPLARS
EXAMPLE
EXAMPLED
EXAMPLES
EXAMPLING
EXAMS
EXANIMATE
EXANTHEM
EXANTHEMA
EXANTHEMATA
EXANTHEMS
EXARATE
EXARATION
EXARATIONS
EXARCH
EXARCHATE
EXARCHATES
EXARCHIES
EXARCHIST
EXARCHISTS
EXARCHS
EXARCHY
EXCAMB
EXCAMBED
EXCAMBING
EXCAMBION
EXCAMBIONS
EXCAMBIUM
EXCAMBIUMS
EXCAMBS
EXCARNATE
EXCARNATED
EXCARNATES
EXCARNATING
EXCAUDATE
EXCAVATE
EXCAVATED
EXCAVATES
EXCAVATING
EXCAVATOR
EXCAVATORS
EXCEED
EXCEEDED
EXCEEDING
EXCEEDS
EXCEL
EXCELLED
EXCELLENT
EXCELLING
EXCELS
EXCELSIOR
EXCELSIORS
EXCENTRIC
EXCENTRICS
EXCEPT
EXCEPTANT
EXCEPTANTS
EXCEPTED
EXCEPTING
EXCEPTION
EXCEPTIONS
EXCEPTIVE
EXCEPTOR
EXCEPTORS

EXCEPTS
EXCERPT
EXCERPTA
EXCERPTED
EXCERPTING
EXCERPTINGS
EXCERPTOR
EXCERPTORS
EXCERPTS
EXCERPTUM
EXCESS
EXCESSES
EXCESSIVE
EXCHANGE
EXCHANGED
EXCHANGER
EXCHANGERS
EXCHANGES
EXCHANGING
EXCHEAT
EXCHEATS
EXCHEQUER
EXCHEQUERED
EXCHEQUERING
EXCHEQUERS
EXCIDE
EXCIDED
EXCIDES
EXCIDING
EXCIPIENT
EXCIPIENTS
EXCISABLE
EXCISE
EXCISED
EXCISEMAN
EXCISEMEN
EXCISES
EXCISING
EXCISION
EXCISIONS
EXCITABLE
EXCITANCIES
EXCITANCY
EXCITANT
EXCITANTS
EXCITE
EXCITED
EXCITER
EXCITERS
EXCITES
EXCITING
EXCITON
EXCITONS
EXCITOR
EXCITORS
EXCLAIM
EXCLAIMED
EXCLAIMING
EXCLAIMS
EXCLAVE
EXCLAVES
EXCLOSURE
EXCLOSURES
EXCLUDE
EXCLUDED
EXCLUDEE
EXCLUDEES
EXCLUDES
EXCLUDING
EXCLUSION

EXCLUSIONS
EXCLUSIVE
EXCLUSIVES
EXCLUSORY
EXCORIATE
EXCORIATED
EXCORIATES
EXCORIATING
EXCREMENT
EXCREMENTS
EXCRETA
EXCRETE
EXCRETED
EXCRETES
EXCRETING
EXCRETION
EXCRETIONS
EXCRETIVE
EXCRETORIES
EXCRETORY
EXCUBANT
EXCUDIT
EXCULPATE
EXCULPATED
EXCULPATES
EXCULPATING
EXCURRENT
EXCURSE
EXCURSED
EXCURSES
EXCURSING
EXCURSION
EXCURSIONED
EXCURSIONING
EXCURSIONS
EXCURSIVE
EXCURSUS
EXCURSUSES
EXCUSABLE
EXCUSABLY
EXCUSAL
EXCUSALS
EXCUSE
EXCUSED
EXCUSER
EXCUSERS
EXCUSES
EXCUSING
EXCUSIVE
EXEAT
EXEATS
EXECRABLE
EXECRABLY
EXECRATE
EXECRATED
EXECRATES
EXECRATING
EXECUTANT
EXECUTANTS
EXECUTE
EXECUTED
EXECUTER
EXECUTERS
EXECUTES
EXECUTING
EXECUTION
EXECUTIONS
EXECUTIVE
EXECUTIVES
EXECUTOR

EXECUTORS
EXECUTORY
EXECUTRICES
EXECUTRIES
EXECUTRIX
EXECUTRIXES
EXECUTRY
EXEDRA
EXEDRAE
EXEEM
EXEEMED
EXEEMING
EXEEMS
EXEGESES
EXEGESIS
EXEGETE
EXEGETES
EXEGETIC
EXEGETICS
EXEGETIST
EXEGETISTS
EXEME
EXEMED
EXEMES
EXEMING
EXEMPLA
EXEMPLAR
EXEMPLARS
EXEMPLARY
EXEMPLE
EXEMPLES
EXEMPLIFIED
EXEMPLIFIES
EXEMPLIFY
EXEMPLIFYING
EXEMPLUM
EXEMPT
EXEMPTED
EXEMPTING
EXEMPTION
EXEMPTIONS
EXEMPTS
EXEQUATUR
EXEQUATURS
EXEQUIAL
EXEQUIES
EXEQUY
EXERCISE
EXERCISED
EXERCISER
EXERCISERS
EXERCISES
EXERCISING
EXERGUAL
EXERGUE
EXERGUES
EXERT
EXERTED
EXERTING
EXERTION
EXERTIONS
EXERTIVE
EXERTS
EXES
EXEUNT
EXFOLIATE
EXFOLIATED
EXFOLIATES
EXFOLIATING
EXHALABLE

EXHALANT
EXHALANTS
EXHALE
EXHALED
EXHALES
EXHALING
EXHAUST
EXHAUSTED
EXHAUSTER
EXHAUSTERS
EXHAUSTING
EXHAUSTS
EXHEDRA
EXHEDRAE
EXHIBIT
EXHIBITED
EXHIBITER
EXHIBITERS
EXHIBITING
EXHIBITOR
EXHIBITORS
EXHIBITS
EXHORT
EXHORTED
EXHORTER
EXHORTERS
EXHORTING
EXHORTS
EXHUMATE
EXHUMATED
EXHUMATES
EXHUMATING
EXHUME
EXHUMED
EXHUMER
EXHUMERS
EXHUMES
EXHUMING
EXIES
EXIGEANT
EXIGEANTE
EXIGENCE
EXIGENCES
EXIGENCIES
EXIGENCY
EXIGENT
EXIGENTS
EXIGIBLE
EXIGUITIES
EXIGUITY
EXIGUOUS
EXILE
EXILED
EXILEMENT
EXILEMENTS
EXILES
EXILIAN
EXILIC
EXILING
EXILITIES
EXILITY
EXIMIOUS
EXINE
EXINES
EXIST
EXISTED
EXISTENCE
EXISTENCES
EXISTENT
EXISTING

EXISTS
EXIT
EXITANCE
EXITANCES
EXITED
EXITING
EXITS
EXOCARP
EXOCARPS
EXOCRINE
EXOCRINES
EXODE
EXODERM
EXODERMAL
EXODERMIS
EXODERMISES
EXODERMS
EXODES
EXODIC
EXODIST
EXODISTS
EXODUS
EXODUSES
EXOENZYME
EXOENZYMES
EXOERGIC
EXOGAMIC
EXOGAMIES
EXOGAMOUS
EXOGAMY
EXOGEN
EXOGENOUS
EXOGENS
EXOMION
EXOMIONS
EXOMIS
EXOMISES
EXON
EXONERATE
EXONERATED
EXONERATES
EXONERATING
EXONS
EXONYM
EXONYMS
EXOPHAGIES
EXOPHAGY
EXOPLASM
EXOPLASMS
EXOPOD
EXOPODITE
EXOPODITES
EXOPODS
EXORABLE
EXORATION
EXORATIONS
EXORCISE
EXORCISED
EXORCISER
EXORCISERS
EXORCISES
EXORCISING
EXORCISM
EXORCISMS
EXORCIST
EXORCISTS
EXORCIZE
EXORCIZED
EXORCIZER
EXORCIZERS

EXORCIZES
EXORCIZING
EXORDIA
EXORDIAL
EXORDIUM
EXORDIUMS
EXOSMOSE
EXOSMOSES
EXOSMOSIS
EXOSMOTIC
EXOSPHERE
EXOSPHERES
EXOSPORAL
EXOSPORE
EXOSPORES
EXOSTOSES
EXOSTOSIS
EXOTERIC
EXOTIC
EXOTICA
EXOTICISM
EXOTICISMS
EXOTICS
EXOTOXIC
EXOTOXIN
EXOTOXINS
EXPAND
EXPANDED
EXPANDER
EXPANDERS
EXPANDING
EXPANDOR
EXPANDORS
EXPANDS
EXPANSE
EXPANSES
EXPANSILE
EXPANSION
EXPANSIONS
EXPANSIVE
EXPAT
EXPATIATE
EXPATIATED
EXPATIATES
EXPATIATING
EXPATS
EXPECT
EXPECTANT
EXPECTANTS
EXPECTED
EXPECTER
EXPECTERS
EXPECTING
EXPECTINGS
EXPECTS
EXPEDIENT
EXPEDIENTS
EXPEDITE
EXPEDITED
EXPEDITES
EXPEDITING
EXPEL
EXPELLANT
EXPELLANTS
EXPELLED
EXPELLEE
EXPELLEES
EXPELLENT
EXPELLENTS
EXPELLING

EXPELS
EXPEND
EXPENDED
EXPENDER
EXPENDERS
EXPENDING
EXPENDS
EXPENSE
EXPENSES
EXPENSIVE
EXPERT
EXPERTED
EXPERTING
EXPERTISE
EXPERTISED
EXPERTISES
EXPERTISING
EXPERTIZE
EXPERTIZED
EXPERTIZES
EXPERTIZING
EXPERTLY
EXPERTS
EXPIABLE
EXPIATE
EXPIATED
EXPIATES
EXPIATING
EXPIATION
EXPIATIONS
EXPIATOR
EXPIATORS
EXPIATORY
EXPIRABLE
EXPIRANT
EXPIRANTS
EXPIRE
EXPIRED
EXPIRES
EXPIRIES
EXPIRING
EXPIRY
EXPISCATE
EXPISCATED
EXPISCATES
EXPISCATING
EXPLAIN
EXPLAINED
EXPLAINER
EXPLAINERS
EXPLAINING
EXPLAINS
EXPLANT
EXPLANTED
EXPLANTING
EXPLANTS
EXPLETIVE
EXPLETIVES
EXPLETORY
EXPLICATE
EXPLICATED
EXPLICATES
EXPLICATING
EXPLICIT
EXPLICITS
EXPLODE
EXPLODED
EXPLODER
EXPLODERS
EXPLODES

EXPLODING
EXPLOIT
EXPLOITED
EXPLOITER
EXPLOITERS
EXPLOITING
EXPLOITS
EXPLORE
EXPLORED
EXPLORER
EXPLORERS
EXPLORES
EXPLORING
EXPLOSION
EXPLOSIONS
EXPLOSIVE
EXPLOSIVES
EXPO
EXPONENT
EXPONENTS
EXPONIBLE
EXPORT
EXPORTED
EXPORTER
EXPORTERS
EXPORTING
EXPORTS
EXPOS
EXPOSAL
EXPOSALS
EXPOSE
EXPOSÉ
EXPOSED
EXPOSER
EXPOSERS
EXPOSÉS
EXPOSES
EXPOSING
EXPOSITOR
EXPOSITORS
EXPOSTURE
EXPOSTURES
EXPOSURE
EXPOSURES
EXPOUND
EXPOUNDED
EXPOUNDER
EXPOUNDERS
EXPOUNDING
EXPOUNDS
EXPRESS
EXPRESSED
EXPRESSES
EXPRESSING
EXPRESSLY
EXPRESSO
EXPRESSOS
EXPUGN
EXPUGNED
EXPUGNING
EXPUGNS
EXPULSE
EXPULSED
EXPULSES
EXPULSING
EXPULSION
EXPULSIONS
EXPULSIVE
EXPUNCT
EXPUNCTED

EXPUNCTING
EXPUNCTS
EXPUNGE
EXPUNGED
EXPUNGER
EXPUNGERS
EXPUNGES
EXPUNGING
EXPURGATE
EXPURGATED
EXPURGATES
EXPURGATING
EXPURGE
EXPURGED
EXPURGES
EXPURGING
EXQUISITE
EXQUISITES
EXSCIND
EXSCINDED
EXSCINDING
EXSCINDS
EXSECT
EXSECTED
EXSECTING
EXSECTION
EXSECTIONS
EXSECTS
EXSERT
EXSERTED
EXSERTILE
EXSERTING
EXSERTION
EXSERTIONS
EXSERTS
EXSICCANT
EXSICCATE
EXSICCATED
EXSICCATES
EXSICCATING
EXSUCCOUS
EXTANT
EXTASIES
EXTASY
EXTATIC
EXTEMPORE
EXTEMPORES
EXTEND
EXTENDANT
EXTENDED
EXTENDER
EXTENDERS
EXTENDING
EXTENDS
EXTENSE
EXTENSILE
EXTENSION
EXTENSIONS
EXTENSITIES
EXTENSITY
EXTENSIVE
EXTENSOR
EXTENSORS
EXTENT
EXTENTS
EXTENUATE
EXTENUATED
EXTENUATES
EXTENUATING
EXTENUATINGS

EXTERIOR
EXTERIORS
EXTERMINE
EXTERMINED
EXTERMINES
EXTERMINING
EXTERN
EXTERNAL
EXTERNALS
EXTERNAT
EXTERNATS
EXTERNE
EXTERNES
EXTERNS
EXTINCT
EXTINCTED
EXTINE
EXTINES
EXTIRP
EXTIRPATE
EXTIRPATED
EXTIRPATES
EXTIRPATING
EXTIRPED
EXTIRPING
EXTIRPS
EXTOL
EXTOLD
EXTOLLED
EXTOLLER
EXTOLLERS
EXTOLLING
EXTOLMENT
EXTOLMENTS
EXTOLS
EXTORSIVE
EXTORT
EXTORTED
EXTORTING

EXTORTION
EXTORTIONS
EXTORTIVE
EXTORTS
EXTRA
EXTRACT
EXTRACTED
EXTRACTING
EXTRACTOR
EXTRACTORS
EXTRACTS
EXTRADITE
EXTRADITED
EXTRADITES
EXTRADITING
EXTRADOS
EXTRADOSES
EXTRAIT
EXTRAITS
EXTRAS
EXTRAUGHT
EXTRAVERT
EXTRAVERTED
EXTRAVERTING
EXTRAVERTS
EXTREAT
EXTREATS
EXTREME
EXTREMELY
EXTREMER
EXTREMES
EXTREMEST
EXTREMISM
EXTREMISMS
EXTREMIST
EXTREMISTS
EXTREMITIES
EXTREMITY
EXTRICATE

EXTRICATED
EXTRICATES
EXTRICATING
EXTRINSIC
EXTRORSE
EXTROVERT
EXTROVERTED
EXTROVERTING
EXTROVERTS
EXTRUDE
EXTRUDED
EXTRUDER
EXTRUDERS
EXTRUDES
EXTRUDING
EXTRUSION
EXTRUSIONS
EXTRUSIVE
EXTRUSORY
EXUBERANT
EXUBERATE
EXUBERATED
EXUBERATES
EXUBERATING
EXUDATE
EXUDATES
EXUDATION
EXUDATIONS
EXUDATIVE
EXUDE
EXUDED
EXUDES
EXUDING
EXUL
EXULS
EXULT
EXULTANCE
EXULTANCES
EXULTANCIES

EXULTANCY
EXULTANT
EXULTED
EXULTING
EXULTS
EXURB
EXURBAN
EXURBIA
EXURBIAS
EXURBS
EXUVIAE
EXUVIAL
EXUVIATE
EXUVIATED
EXUVIATES
EXUVIATING
EYALET
EYALETS
EYAS
EYASES
EYE
EYEBALL
EYEBALLED
EYEBALLING
EYEBALLS
EYEBOLT
EYEBOLTS
EYEBRIGHT
EYEBRIGHTS
EYEBROW
EYEBROWED
EYEBROWING
EYEBROWS
EYED
EYEFUL
EYEFULS
EYEGLASS
EYEGLASSES
EYEHOOK

EYEHOOKS
EYEING
EYELASH
EYELASHES
EYELESS
EYELET
EYELETED
EYELETING
EYELETS
EYELIAD
EYELIADS
EYELID
EYELIDS
EYELINER
EYELINERS
EYES
EYESHADE
EYESHADES
EYESIGHT
EYESIGHTS
EYESORE
EYESORES
EYESTALK
EYESTALKS
EYESTRAIN
EYESTRAINS
EYING
EYLIAD
EYLIADS
EYNE
EYOT
EYOTS
EYRA
EYRAS
EYRE
EYRES
EYRIE
EYRIES
EYRY

F

FA	FACILITIES	FADDISMS	FAHLERZ	FAIRING
FAB	FACILITY	FADDIST	FAHLERZES	FAIRINGS
FABACEOUS	FACING	FADDISTS	FAHLORE	FAIRISH
FABBER	FACINGS	FADDLE	FAHLORES	FAIRLY
FABBEST	FAÇONNÉ	FADDLED	FAHS	FAIRNESS
FABLE	FAÇONNÉS	FADDLES	FAIBLE	FAIRNESSES
FABLED	FACSIMILE	FADDLING	FAIBLES	FAIRS
FABLER	FACSIMILED	FADDY	FAÏENCE	FAIRWAY
FABLERS	FACSIMILEING	FADE	FAIENCE	FAIRWAYS
FABLES	FACSIMILES	FADED	FAÏENCES	FAIRY
FABLIAU	FACT	FADEDLY	FAIENCES	FAIRYDOM
FABLIAUX	FACTION	FADEDNESS	FAIK	FAIRYDOMS
FABLING	FACTIONAL	FADEDNESSES	FAIKED	FAIRYHOOD
FABLINGS	FACTIONS	FADELESS	FAIKES	FAIRYHOODS
FABRIC	FACTIOUS	FADES	FAIKING	FAIRYISM
FABRICANT	FACTITIVE	FADEUR	FAIKS	FAIRYISMS
FABRICANTS	FACTIVE	FADEURS	FAIL	FAIRYLAND
FABRICATE	FACTOID	FADGE	FAILED	FAIRYLANDS
FABRICATED	FACTOIDS	FADGED	FAILING	FAIRYLIKE
FABRICATES	FACTOR	FADGES	FAILINGS	FAITH
FABRICATING	FACTORAGE	FADGING	FAILLE	FAITHED
FABRICKED	FACTORAGES	FADIER	FAILLES	FAITHFUL
FABRICKING	FACTORED	FADIEST	FAILS	FAITHING
FABRICS	FACTORIAL	FADING	FAILURE	FAITHLESS
FABULAR	FACTORIALS	FADINGS	FAILURES	FAITHS
FABULISE	FACTORIES	FADO	FAIN	FAITOR
FABULISED	FACTORING	FADOS	FAINE	FAITORS
FABULISES	FACTORINGS	FADS	FAINÉANCE	FAITOUR
FABULISING	FACTORISE	FADY	FAINÉANCES	FAITOURS
FABULIST	FACTORISED	FAECAL	FAINÉANCIES	FAIX
FABULISTS	FACTORISES	FAECES	FAINÉANCY	FAKE
FABULIZE	FACTORISING	FAERIE	FAINÉANT	FAKED
FABULIZED	FACTORIZE	FAERIES	FAINÉANTS	FAKEMENT
FABULIZES	FACTORIZED	FAERY	FAINED	FAKEMENTS
FABULIZING	FACTORIZES	FAFF	FAINER	FAKER
FABULOUS	FACTORIZING	FAFFED	FAINES	FAKERIES
FABURDEN	FACTORS	FAFFING	FAINEST	FAKERS
FABURDENS	FACTORY	FAFFS	FAINING	FAKERY
FAÇADE	FACTOTUM	FAG	FAINITES	FAKES
FAÇADES	FACTOTUMS	FAGACEOUS	FAINLY	FAKING
FACE	FACTS	FAGGED	FAINNESS	FAKIR
FACED	FACTUAL	FAGGERIES	FAINNESSES	FAKIRISM
FACELESS	FACTUM	FAGGERY	FAINS	FAKIRISMS
FACEMAN	FACTUMS	FAGGING	FAINT	FAKIRS
FACEMEN	FACTURE	FAGGINGS	FAINTED	FALAFEL
FACER	FACTURES	FAGGOT	FAINTER	FALAFELS
FACERS	FACULA	FAGGOTED	FAINTEST	FALAJ
FACES	FACULAE	FAGGOTING	FAINTIER	FALANGISM
FACET	FACULAR	FAGGOTINGS	FAINTIEST	FALANGISMS
FACETE	FACULTIES	FAGGOTS	FAINTING	FALANGIST
FACETED	FACULTY	FAGOT	FAINTINGS	FALANGISTS
FACETIAE	FACUNDITIES	FAGOTED	FAINTISH	FALBALA
FACETING	FACUNDITY	FAGOTING	FAINTLY	FALBALAS
FACETIOUS	FAD	FAGOTINGS	FAINTNESS	FALCADE
FACETS	FADABLE	FAGOTS	FAINTNESSES	FALCADES
FACIA	FADAISE	FAGOTTI	FAINTS	FALCATE
FACIAL	FADAISES	FAGOTTIST	FAINTY	FALCATED
FACIALLY	FADDIER	FAGOTTISTS	FAIR	FALCATION
FACIALS	FADDIEST	FAGOTTO	FAIRED	FALCATIONS
FACIAS	FADDINESS	FAGS	FAIRER	FALCES
FACIES	FADDINESSES	FAH	FAIREST	FALCHION
FACILE	FADDISH	FAHLBAND	FAIRIES	FALCHIONS
FACILELY	FADDISM	FAHLBANDS	FAIRILY	FALCIFORM

FALCON	FALTER	FANFOLD	FANTIGUES	FARFET
FALCONER	FALTERED	FANG	FANTOD	FARINA
FALCONERS	FALTERING	FANGED	FANTODS	FARINAS
FALCONET	FALTERINGS	FANGING	FANTOM	FARING
FALCONETS	FALTERS	FANGLE	FANTOMS	FARINOSE
FALCONINE	FALX	FANGLED	FANTOOSH	FARL
FALCONRIES	FAME	FANGLES	FANZINE	FARLE
FALCONRY	FAMED	FANGLESS	FANZINES	FARLES
FALCONS	FAMELESS	FANGLING	FAP	FARLS
FALCULA	FAMES	FANGO	FAQUIR	FARM
FALCULAS	FAMILIAL	FANGOS	FAQUIRS	FARMED
FALCULATE	FAMILIAR	FANGS	FAR	FARMER
FALDAGE	FAMILIARS	FANION	FARAD	FARMERESS
FALDAGES	FAMILIES	FANIONS	FARADAY	FARMERESSES
FALDERAL	FAMILISM	FANK	FARADAYS	FARMERIES
FALDERALS	FAMILISMS	FANKLE	FARADIC	FARMERS
FALDETTA	FAMILY	FANKLED	FARADISE	FARMERY
FALDETTAS	FAMINE	FANKLES	FARADISED	FARMHOUSE
FALDSTOOL	FAMINES	FANKLING	FARADISES	FARMHOUSES
FALDSTOOLS	FAMING	FANKS	FARADISING	FARMING
FALL	FAMISH	FANLIGHT	FARADISM	FARMINGS
FALLACIES	FAMISHED	FANLIGHTS	FARADISMS	FARMOST
FALLACY	FAMISHES	FANNED	FARADIZE	FARMS
FALLAL	FAMISHING	FANNEL	FARADIZED	FARMSTEAD
FALLALERIES	FAMOUS	FANNELL	FARADIZES	FARMSTEADS
FALLALERY	FAMOUSED	FANNELLS	FARADIZING	FARMYARD
FALLALS	FAMOUSES	FANNELS	FARADS	FARMYARDS
FALLEN	FAMOUSING	FANNER	FARAND	FARNESOL
FALLIBLE	FAMOUSLY	FANNERS	FARANDINE	FARNESOLS
FALLIBLY	FAMULUS	FANNIES	FARANDINES	FARNESS
FALLING	FAMULUSES	FANNING	FARANDOLE	FARNESSES
FALLINGS	FAN	FANNINGS	FARANDOLES	FARO
FALLOW	FANAL	FANNY	FARAWAY	FAROS
FALLOWED	FANALS	FANON	FARAWAYS	FAROUCHE
FALLOWER	FANATIC	FANONS	FARCE	FARRAGO
FALLOWEST	FANATICAL	FANS	FARCED	FARRAGOES
FALLOWING	FANATICS	FANTAD	FARCES	FARRAND
FALLOWS	FANCIED	FANTADS	FARCEUR	FARRANT
FALLS	FANCIER	FANTAIL	FARCEURS	FARRED
FALSE	FANCIERS	FANTAILED	FARCEUSE	FARREN
FALSED	FANCIES	FANTAILS	FARCEUSES	FARRENS
FALSEHOOD	FANCIEST	FANTASIA	FARCI	FARRIER
FALSEHOODS	FANCIFUL	FANTASIAS	FARCICAL	FARRIERIES
FALSELY	FANCILESS	FANTASIED	FARCIED	FARRIERS
FALSENESS	FANCY	FANTASIES	FARCIES	FARRIERY
FALSENESSES	FANCYING	FANTASISE	FARCIFIED	FARRING
FALSER	FANCYWORK	FANTASISED	FARCIFIES	FARROW
FALSERS	FANCYWORKS	FANTASISES	FARCIFY	FARROWED
FALSES	FAND	FANTASISING	FARCIFYING	FARROWING
FALSEST	FANDANGLE	FANTASIST	FARCIN	FARROWS
FALSETTO	FANDANGLES	FANTASISTS	FARCING	FARRUCA
FALSETTOS	FANDANGO	FANTASIZE	FARCINGS	FARRUCAS
FALSEWORK	FANDANGOS	FANTASIZED	FARCINS	FARS
FALSEWORKS	FANDED	FANTASIZES	FARCY	FARSE
FALSIE	FANDING	FANTASIZING	FARD	FARSED
FALSIES	FANDOM	FANTASM	FARDAGE	FARSES
FALSIFIED	FANDOMS	FANTASMS	FARDAGES	FARSING
FALSIFIER	FANDS	FANTASQUE	FARDED	FART
FALSIFIERS	FANE	FANTASQUES	FARDEL	FARTED
FALSIFIES	FANES	FANTAST	FARDELS	FARTHEL
FALSIFY	FANFARADE	FANTASTIC	FARDEN	FARTHELS
FALSIFYING	FANFARADES	FANTASTICS	FARDENS	FARTHER
FALSING	FANFARE	FANTASTRIES	FARDING	FARTHEST
FALSISH	FANFARED	FANTASTRY	FARDINGS	FARTHING
FALSISM	FANFARES	FANTASTS	FARDS	FARTHINGS
FALSISMS	FANFARING	FANTASY	FARE	FARTING
FALSITIES	FANFARON	FANTASYING	FARED	FARTS
FALSITY	FANFARONA	FANTEEG	FARES	FAS
FALTBOAT	FANFARONAS	FANTEEGS	FAREWELL	FASCES
FALTBOATS	FANFARONS	FANTIGUE	FAREWELLS	FASCI

FASCIA
FASCIAL
FASCIAS
FASCIATE
FASCIATED
FASCICLE
FASCICLED
FASCICLES
FASCICULE
FASCICULES
FASCICULI
FASCINATE
FASCINATED
FASCINATES
FASCINATING
FASCINE
FASCINES
FASCIO
FASCIOLA
FASCIOLAS
FASCIOLE
FASCIOLES
FASCISM
FASCISMI
FASCISMO
FASCISMS
FASCIST
FASCISTA
FASCISTI
FASCISTIC
FASCISTS
FASH
FASHED
FASHERIES
FASHERY
FASHES
FASHING
FASHION
FASHIONED
FASHIONER
FASHIONERS
FASHIONING
FASHIONS
FASHIOUS
FAST
FASTBACK
FASTBACKS
FASTED
FASTEN
FASTENED
FASTENER
FASTENERS
FASTENING
FASTENINGS
FASTENS
FASTER
FASTERS
FASTEST
FASTI
FASTIGIUM
FASTIGIUMS
FASTING
FASTINGS
FASTISH
FASTLY
FASTNESS
FASTNESSES
FASTS
FASTUOUS
FAT

FATAL
FATALISM
FATALISMS
FATALIST
FATALISTS
FATALITIES
FATALITY
FATALLY
FATE
FATED
FATEFUL
FATEFULLY
FATES
FATHER
FATHERED
FATHERING
FATHERLY
FATHERS
FATHOM
FATHOMED
FATHOMING
FATHOMS
FATIDICAL
FATIGABLE
FATIGATE
FATIGATED
FATIGATES
FATIGATING
FATIGUE
FATIGUED
FATIGUES
FATIGUING
FATISCENT
FATLING
FATLINGS
FATLY
FATNESS
FATNESSES
FATS
FATSO
FATSOES
FATSOS
FATSTOCK
FATSTOCKS
FATTED
FATTEN
FATTENED
FATTENER
FATTENERS
FATTENING
FATTENINGS
FATTENS
FATTER
FATTEST
FATTIER
FATTIES
FATTIEST
FATTINESS
FATTINESSES
FATTING
FATTISH
FATTRELS
FATTY
FATUITIES
FATUITOUS
FATUITY
FATUOUS
FAUBOURG
FAUBOURGS
FAUCAL

FAUCES
FAUCET
FAUCETS
FAUCHION
FAUCHIONS
FAUCHON
FAUCHONS
FAUCIAL
FAUGH
FAULCHIN
FAULCHINS
FAULCHION
FAULCHIONS
FAULT
FAULTED
FAULTFUL
FAULTIER
FAULTIEST
FAULTILY
FAULTING
FAULTLESS
FAULTS
FAULTY
FAUN
FAUNA
FAUNAE
FAUNAL
FAUNAS
FAUNIST
FAUNISTIC
FAUNISTS
FAUNS
FAURD
FAUSTIAN
FAUTEUIL
FAUTEUILS
FAUTOR
FAUTORS
FAUVETTE
FAUVETTES
FAUX
FAVEL
FAVELA
FAVELAS
FAVELL
FAVEOLATE
FAVISM
FAVISMS
FAVOR
FAVORED
FAVORING
FAVORS
FAVOSE
FAVOUR
FAVOURED
FAVOURER
FAVOURERS
FAVOURING
FAVOURITE
FAVOURITES
FAVOURS
FAVOUS
FAVRILE
FAVRILES
FAVUS
FAVUSES
FAW
FAWN
FAWNED
FAWNER

FAWNERS
FAWNING
FAWNINGLY
FAWNINGS
FAWNS
FAWS
FAX
FAXED
FAXES
FAXING
FAY
FAYALITE
FAYALITES
FAYED
FAYENCE
FAYENCES
FAYER
FAYEST
FAYING
FAYNE
FAYNED
FAYNES
FAYNING
FAYS
FAZE
FAZED
FAZES
FAZING
FEAGUE
FEAGUED
FEAGUES
FEAGUING
FEAL
FEALED
FEALING
FEALS
FEALTIES
FEALTY
FEAR
FEARE
FEARED
FEARES
FEARFUL
FEARFULLY
FEARING
FEARLESS
FEARS
FEARSOME
FEASIBLE
FEASIBLY
FEAST
FEASTED
FEASTER
FEASTERS
FEASTFUL
FEASTING
FEASTINGS
FEASTS
FEAT
FEATED
FEATEOUS
FEATHER
FEATHERED
FEATHERIER
FEATHERIEST
FEATHERING
FEATHERINGS
FEATHERS
FEATHERY
FEATING

FEATLY
FEATOUS
FEATS
FEATUOUS
FEATURE
FEATURED
FEATURELY
FEATURES
FEATURING
FEBLESSE
FEBLESSES
FEBRICITIES
FEBRICITY
FEBRICULA
FEBRICULAS
FEBRICULE
FEBRICULES
FEBRIFIC
FEBRIFUGE
FEBRIFUGES
FEBRILE
FEBRILITIES
FEBRILITY
FECAL
FECES
FECHT
FECHTER
FECHTERS
FECHTING
FECHTS
FECIAL
FECIT
FECK
FECKLESS
FECKLY
FECKS
FECULA
FECULAS
FECULENCE
FECULENCES
FECULENCIES
FECULENCY
FECULENT
FECUND
FECUNDATE
FECUNDATED
FECUNDATES
FECUNDATING
FECUNDITIES
FECUNDITY
FED
FEDARIE
FEDARIES
FEDAYEE
FEDAYEEN
FEDELINI
FEDELINIS
FEDERACIES
FEDERACY
FEDERAL
FEDERALS
FEDERARIE
FEDERARIES
FEDERARY
FEDERATE
FEDERATED
FEDERATES
FEDERATING
FEDORA
FEDORAS

FEDS
FEE
FÉE
FEEBLE
FEEBLED
FEEBLER
FEEBLES
FEEBLEST
FEEBLING
FEEBLISH
FEEBLY
FEED
FEEDBACK
FEEDBACKS
FEEDER
FEEDERS
FEEDING
FEEDINGS
FEEDLOT
FEEDLOTS
FEEDS
FEEDSTOCK
FEEDSTOCKS
FEEDSTUFF
FEEDSTUFFS
FEEING
FEEL
FEELER
FEELERS
FEELING
FEELINGLY
FEELINGS
FEELS
FEER
FEERED
FÉERIE
FÉERIES
FEERIN
FEERING
FEERINGS
FEERINS
FEERS
FEES
FEESE
FEESED
FEESES
FEESING
FEET
FEETLESS
FEEZE
FEEZED
FEEZES
FEEZING
FEGARIES
FEGARY
FEGS
FEHM
FEHME
FEHMIC
FEIGN
FEIGNED
FEIGNEDLY
FEIGNING
FEIGNINGS
FEIGNS
FEINT
FEINTED
FEINTER
FEINTEST
FEINTING

FEINTS
FEIS
FEISEANNA
FEISTIER
FEISTIEST
FEISTY
FELAFEL
FELAFELS
FELDGRAU
FELDGRAUS
FELDSHER
FELDSHERS
FELDSPAR
FELDSPARS
FELDSPATH
FELDSPATHS
FELICIFIC
FELICITER
FELICITIES
FELICITY
FELINE
FELINES
FELINITIES
FELINITY
FELL
FELLA
FELLABLE
FELLAH
FELLAHÎN
FELLAHS
FELLAS
FELLATE
FELLATED
FELLATES·
FELLATING
FELLATIO
FELLATION
FELLATIONS
FELLATIOS
FELLED
FELLER
FELLERS
FELLEST
FELLIES
FELLING
FELLNESS
FELLNESSES
FELLOE
FELLOES
FELLOW
FELLOWLY
FELLOWS
FELLS
FELLY
FELON
FELONIES
FELONIOUS
FELONOUS
FELONRIES
FELONRY
FELONS
FELONY
FELSITE
FELSITES
FELSITIC
FELSPAR
FELSPARS
FELSTONE
FELSTONES
FELT

FELTED
FELTER
FELTERED
FELTERING
FELTERS
FELTING
FELTINGS
FELTS
FELUCCA
FELUCCAS
FELWORT
FELWORTS
FEMAL
FEMALE
FEMALES
FEMALITIES
FEMALITY
FEMALS
FEME
FEMERALL
FEMERALLS
FEMES
FEMETARIES
FEMETARY
FEMINAL
FEMINEITIES
FEMINEITY
FEMININE
FEMININES
FEMINISE
FEMINISED
FEMINISES
FEMINISING
FEMINISM
FEMINISMS
FEMINIST
FEMINISTS
FEMINITIES
FEMINITY
FEMINIZE
FEMINIZED
FEMINIZES
FEMINIZING
FEMITER
FEMITERS
FEMME
FEMMES
FEMORA
FEMORAL
FEMUR
FEMURS
FEN
FENCE
FENCED
FENCELESS
FENCER
FENCERS
FENCES
FENCIBLE
FENCIBLES
FENCING
FENCINGS
FEND
FENDED
FENDER
FENDERS
FENDIER
FENDIEST
FENDING
FENDS

FENDY
FENESTRA
FENESTRAL
FENESTRALS
FENESTRAS
FENITAR
FENITARS
FENKS
FENLAND
FENLANDS
FENMAN
FENMEN
FENNEC
FENNECS
FENNEL
FENNELS
FENNIER
FENNIEST
FENNISH
FENNY
FENS
FENT
FENTS
FENUGREEK
FENUGREEKS
FEOD
FEODAL
FEODARIES
FEODARY
FEODS
FEOFF
FEOFFED
FEOFFEE
FEOFFEES
FEOFFER
FEOFFERS
FEOFFING
FEOFFMENT
FEOFFMENTS
FEOFFOR
FEOFFORS
FEOFFS
FERACIOUS
FERACITIES
FERACITY
FERAL
FERALISED
FERALIZED
FERE
FERER
FERES
FEREST
FERETORIES
FERETORY
FERIAL
FERINE
FERITIES
FERITY
FERLIED
FERLIER
FERLIES
FERLIEST
FERLY
FERLYING
FERM
FERMATA
FERMATAS
FERMENT
FERMENTED
FERMENTING

FERMENTS
FERMI
FERMION
FERMIONS
FERMIS
FERMIUM
FERMIUMS
FERMS
FERN
FERNBIRD
FERNBIRDS
FERNERIES
FERNERY
FERNIER
FERNIEST
FERNING
FERNINGS
FERNS
FERNSHAW
FERNSHAWS
FERNTICLE
FERNTICLES
FERNY
FEROCIOUS
FEROCITIES
FEROCITY
FERRATE
FERRATES
FERREL
FERRELS
FERREOUS
FERRET
FERRETED
FERRETER
FERRETERS
FERRETING
FERRETS
FERRETY
FERRIAGE
FERRIAGES
FERRIC
FERRIED
FERRIES
FERRITE
FERRITES
FERRITIC
FERROTYPE
FERROTYPES
FERROUS
FERRUGO
FERRUGOS
FERRULE
FERRULES
FERRY
FERRYING
FERRYMAN
FERRYMEN
FERTILE
FERTILELY
FERTILER
FERTILEST
FERTILISE
FERTILISED
FERTILISES
FERTILISING
FERTILITIES
FERTILITY
FERTILIZE
FERTILIZED
FERTILIZES

FERTILIZING
FERULA
FERULAS
FERULE
FERULES
FERVENCIES
FERVENCY
FERVENT
FERVENTER
FERVENTEST
FERVENTLY
FERVID
FERVIDER
FERVIDEST
FERVIDITIES
FERVIDITY
FERVIDLY
FERVOROUS
FERVOUR
FERVOURS
FESCUE
FESCUES
FESS
FESSE
FESSES
FEST
FESTA
FESTAL
FESTALLY
FESTALS
FESTAS
FESTER
FESTERED
FESTERING
FESTERS
FESTILOGIES
FESTILOGY
FESTINATE
FESTINATED
FESTINATES
FESTINATING
FESTIVAL
FESTIVALS
FESTIVE
FESTIVELY
FESTIVITIES
FESTIVITY
FESTIVOUS
FESTOLOGIES
FESTOLOGY
FESTOON
FESTOONED
FESTOONING
FESTOONS
FESTS
FET
FETA
FETAL
FETAS
FETCH
FETCHED
FETCHES
FETCHING
FÊTE
FÊTED
FÊTES
FETIAL
FETICH
FETICHE
FETICHES

FETICHISE
FETICHISED
FETICHISES
FETICHISING
FETICHISM
FETICHISMS
FETICHIST
FETICHISTS
FETICHIZE
FETICHIZED
FETICHIZES
FETICHIZING
FETICIDAL
FETICIDE
FETICIDES
FETID
FETIDER
FETIDEST
FETIDNESS
FETIDNESSES
FÊTING
FETISH
FETISHES
FETISHISE
FETISHISED
FETISHISES
FETISHISING
FETISHISM
FETISHISMS
FETISHIST
FETISHISTS
FETISHIZE
FETISHIZED
FETISHIZES
FETISHIZING
FETLOCK
FETLOCKED
FETLOCKS
FETOR
FETORS
FETOSCOPIES
FETOSCOPY
FETS
FETT
FETTA
FETTAS
FETTED
FETTER
FETTERED
FETTERING
FETTERS
FETTING
FETTLE
FETTLED
FETTLER
FETTLERS
FETTLES
FETTLING
FETTLINGS
FETTS
FETTUCINE
FETTUCINES
FETTUCINI
FETTUCINIS
FETUS
FETUSES
FETWA
FETWAS
FEU
FEUAR

FEUARS
FEUD
FEUDAL
FEUDALISE
FEUDALISED
FEUDALISES
FEUDALISING
FEUDALISM
FEUDALISMS
FEUDALIST
FEUDALISTS
FEUDALITIES
FEUDALITY
FEUDALIZE
FEUDALIZED
FEUDALIZES
FEUDALIZING
FEUDALLY
FEUDARIES
FEUDARY
FEUDATORIES
FEUDATORY
FEUDED
FEUDING
FEUDINGS
FEUDIST
FEUDISTS
FEUDS
FEUED
FEUILLETÉ
FEUILLETÉS
FEUING
FEUS
FEUTRE
FEUTRED
FEUTRES
FEUTRING
FEVER
FEVERED
FEVERFEW
FEVERFEWS
FEVERING
FEVERISH
FEVEROUS
FEVERS
FEW
FEWER
FEWEST
FEWMET
FEWMETS
FEWNESS
FEWNESSES
FEWTER
FEWTERED
FEWTERING
FEWTERS
FEWTRILS
FEY
FEYED
FEYER
FEYEST
FEYING
FEYS
FEZ
FEZES
FEZZED
FEZZES
FIACRE
FIACRES
FIANCÉ

FIANCÉE
FIANCÉES
FIANCÉS
FIAR
FIARS
FIASCO
FIASCOES
FIASCOS
FIAT
FIATED
FIATING
FIATS
FIAUNT
FIAUNTS
FIB
FIBBED
FIBBER
FIBBERIES
FIBBERS
FIBBERY
FIBBING
FIBER
FIBERS
FIBRE
FIBRED
FIBRELESS
FIBRES
FIBRIFORM
FIBRIL
FIBRILLA
FIBRILLAE
FIBRILLAR
FIBRILS
FIBRIN
FIBRINOUS
FIBRINS
FIBRO
FIBROCYTE
FIBROCYTES
FIBROID
FIBROIDS
FIBROIN
FIBROINS
FIBROLINE
FIBROLINES
FIBROLITE
FIBROLITES
FIBROMA
FIBROMAS
FIBROMATA
FIBROS
FIBROSE
FIBROSED
FIBROSES
FIBROSING
FIBROSIS
FIBROTIC
FIBROUS
FIBS
FIBSTER
FIBSTERS
FIBULA
FIBULAR
FIBULAS
FICHE
FICHES
FICHU
FICHUS
FICKLE
FICKLED

FICKLER
FICKLES
FICKLEST
FICKLING
FICO
FICOS
FICTILE
FICTION
FICTIONAL
FICTIONS
FICTIVE
FICTOR
FICTORS
FID
FIDDIOUS
FIDDIOUSED
FIDDIOUSES
FIDDIOUSING
FIDDLE
FIDDLED
FIDDLER
FIDDLERS
FIDDLES
FIDDLEY
FIDDLEYS
FIDDLIER
FIDDLIEST
FIDDLING
FIDDLY
FIDEISM
FIDEISMS
FIDEISTIC
FIDELITIES
FIDELITY
FIDGE
FIDGED
FIDGES
FIDGET
FIDGETED
FIDGETING
FIDGETS
FIDGETY
FIDGING
FIDIBUS
FIDIBUSES
FIDS
FIDUCIAL
FIDUCIARIES
FIDUCIARY
FIE
FIEF
FIEFS
FIELD
FIELDED
FIELDER
FIELDERS
FIELDFARE
FIELDFARES
FIELDING
FIELDINGS
FIELDMICE
FIELDS
FIELDSMAN
FIELDSMEN
FIELDWARD
FIELDWARDS
FIELDWORK
FIELDWORKS
FIEND
FIENDISH

FIENDS
FIENT
FIENTS
FIERCE
FIERCELY
FIERCER
FIERCEST
FIERE
FIERES
FIERIER
FIERIEST
FIERILY
FIERINESS
FIERINESSES
FIERY
FIESTA
FIESTAS
FIFE
FIFED
FIFER
FIFERS
FIFES
FIFING
FIFTEEN
FIFTEENER
FIFTEENERS
FIFTEENS
FIFTEENTH
FIFTEENTHS
FIFTH
FIFTHLY
FIFTHS
FIFTIES
FIFTIETH
FIFTIETHS
FIFTY
FIFTYISH
FIG
FIGGED
FIGGERIES
FIGGERY
FIGGING
FIGHT
FIGHTABLE
FIGHTBACK
FIGHTBACKS
FIGHTER
FIGHTERS
FIGHTING
FIGHTINGS
FIGHTS
FIGMENT
FIGMENTS
FIGO
FIGOS
FIGS
FIGULINE
FIGULINES
FIGURABLE
FIGURAL
FIGURANT
FIGURANTE
FIGURANTES
FIGURANTS
FIGURATE
FIGURE
FIGURED
FIGURES
FIGURINE
FIGURINES

FIGURING
FIGURIST
FIGURISTS
FIGWORT
FIGWORTS
FIKE
FIKED
FIKERIES
FIKERY
FIKES
FIKIER
FIKIEST
FIKING
FIKISH
FIKY
FIL
FILABEG
FILABEGS
FILACEOUS
FILACER
FILACERS
FILAGREE
FILAGREES
FILAMENT
FILAMENTS
FILANDER
FILANDERS
FILAR
FILARIA
FILARIAL
FILARIAS
FILASSE
FILASSES
FILATORIES
FILATORY
FILATURE
FILATURES
FILAZER
FILAZERS
FILBERD
FILBERDS
FILBERT
FILBERTS
FILCH
FILCHED
FILCHER
FILCHERS
FILCHES
FILCHING
FILCHINGS
FILE
FILED
FILEMOT
FILEMOTS
FILER
FILERS
FILES
FILET
FILETS
FILFOT
FILFOTS
FILIAL
FILIALLY
FILIATE
FILIATED
FILIATES
FILIATING
FILIATION
FILIATIONS
FILIBEG

FILIBEGS
FILICIDE
FILICIDES
FILIFORM
FILIGRAIN
FILIGRAINS
FILIGRANE
FILIGRANES
FILIGREE
FILIGREES
FILING
FILINGS
FILIOQUE
FILIOQUES
FILL
FILLE
FILLED
FILLER
FILLERS
FILLES
FILLET
FILLETED
FILLETING
FILLETS
FILLIBEG
FILLIBEGS
FILLIES
FILLING
FILLINGS
FILLIP
FILLIPED
FILLIPEEN
FILLIPEENS
FILLIPING
FILLIPS
FILLISTER
FILLISTERS
FILLS
FILLY
FILM
FILMABLE
FILMDOM
FILMDOMS
FILMED
FILMGOER
FILMGOERS
FILMIC
FILMIER
FILMIEST
FILMINESS
FILMINESSES
FILMING
FILMISH
FILMLAND
FILMLANDS
FILMS
FILMSET
FILMSETS
FILMSETTING
FILMSETTINGS
FILMY
FILOPLUME
FILOPLUMES
FILOPODIA
FILOSE
FILOSELLE
FILOSELLES
FILS
FILTER

FILTERED
FILTERING
FILTERS
FILTH
FILTHIER
FILTHIEST
FILTHILY
FILTHS
FILTHY
FILTRABLE
FILTRATE
FILTRATED
FILTRATES
FILTRATING
FIMBLE
FIMBLES
FIMBRIA
FIMBRIAS
FIMBRIATE
FIMBRIATED
FIMBRIATES
FIMBRIATING
FIN
FINABLE
FINAGLE
FINAGLED
FINAGLES
FINAGLING
FINAL
FINALE
FINALES
FINALISE
FINALISED
FINALISES
FINALISING
FINALISM
FINALISMS
FINALIST
FINALISTS
FINALITIES
FINALITY
FINALIZE
FINALIZED
FINALIZES
FINALIZING
FINALLY
FINALS
FINANCE
FINANCED
FINANCES
FINANCIAL
FINANCIER
FINANCIERED
FINANCIERING
FINANCIERS
FINANCING
FINBACK
FINBACKS
FINCH
FINCHED
FINCHES
FIND
FINDER
FINDERS
FINDING
FINDINGS
FINDRAM
FINDRAMS
FINDS
FINE

FINED
FINEER
FINEERED
FINEERING
FINEERS
FINEISH
FINELESS
FINELY
FINENESS
FINENESSES
FINER
FINERIES
FINERS
FINERY
FINES
FINESSE
FINESSED
FINESSER
FINESSERS
FINESSES
FINESSING
FINESSINGS
FINEST
FINGAN
FINGANS
FINGER
FINGERED
FINGERING
FINGERINGS
FINGERS
FINGERTIP
FINGERTIPS
FINIAL
FINIALS
FINICAL
FINICALLY
FINICKIER
FINICKIEST
FINICKING
FINICKINGS
FINICKY
FINIKIN
FINING
FININGS
FINIS
FINISH
FINISHED
FINISHER
FINISHERS
FINISHES
FINISHING
FINISHINGS
FINITE
FINITELY
FINITUDE
FINITUDES
FINJAN
FINJANS
FINK
FINKED
FINKING
FINKS
FINLESS
FINNAC
FINNACK
FINNACKS
FINNACS
FINNAN
FINNANS
FINNED

FINNER
FINNERS
FINNESKO
FINNIER
FINNIEST
FINNOCHIO
FINNOCHIOS
FINNOCK
FINNOCKS
FINNSKO
FINNY
FINO
FINOCCHIO
FINOCCHIOS
FINOCHIO
FINOCHIOS
FINOS
FINS
FINSKO
FIORD
FIORDS
FIORIN
FIORINS
FIORITURA
FIORITURE
FIPPENCE
FIPPENCES
FIPPLE
FIPPLES
FIR
FIRE
FIREARM
FIREARMS
FIREBALL
FIREBALLS
FIREBRAND
FIREBRANDS
FIREBRAT
FIREBRATS
FIREBRICK
FIREBRICKS
FIREBUG
FIREBUGS
FIRECREST
FIRECRESTS
FIRED
FIREDAMP
FIREDAMPS
FIREDOG
FIREDOGS
FIREFLIES
FIREFLOAT
FIREFLOATS
FIREFLY
FIREGUARD
FIREGUARDS
FIREHOUSE
FIREHOUSES
FIRELESS
FIRELIGHT
FIRELIGHTS
FIRELOCK
FIRELOCKS
FIREMAN
FIREMARK
FIREMARKS
FIREMEN
FIREPAN
FIREPANS
FIREPLACE

FIREPLACES
FIREPOT
FIREPOTS
FIREPROOF
FIREPROOFED
FIREPROOFING
FIREPROOFINGS
FIREPROOFS
FIRER
FIRERS
FIRES
FIRESHIP
FIRESHIPS
FIRESIDE
FIRESIDES
FIRESTONE
FIRESTONES
FIRETHORN
FIRETHORNS
FIREWEED
FIREWEEDS
FIREWOMAN
FIREWOMEN
FIREWOOD
FIREWOODS
FIREWORK
FIREWORKS
FIREWORM
FIREWORMS
FIRING
FIRINGS
FIRK
FIRKED
FIRKIN
FIRKING
FIRKINS
FIRKS
FIRLOT
FIRLOTS
FIRM
FIRMAMENT
FIRMAMENTS
FIRMAN
FIRMANS
FIRMED
FIRMER
FIRMERS
FIRMEST
FIRMING
FIRMLESS
FIRMLY
FIRMNESS
FIRMNESSES
FIRMS
FIRMWARE
FIRMWARES
FIRN
FIRNS
FIRRIER
FIRRIEST
FIRRING
FIRRINGS
FIRRY
FIRS
FIRST
FIRSTLING
FIRSTLINGS
FIRSTLY
FIRSTS
FIRTH

FIRTHS
FISC
FISCAL
FISCALS
FISCS
FISGIG
FISGIGS
FISH
FISHABLE
FISHBALL
FISHBALLS
FISHCAKE
FISHCAKES
FISHED
FISHER
FISHERIES
FISHERMAN
FISHERMEN
FISHERS
FISHERY
FISHES
FISHEYE
FISHEYES
FISHFUL
FISHGIG
FISHGIGS
FISHIER
FISHIEST
FISHIFIED
FISHIFIES
FISHIFY
FISHIFYING
FISHINESS
FISHINESSES
FISHING
FISHINGS
FISHSKIN
FISHSKINS
FISHWIFE
FISHWIVES
FISHY
FISHYBACK
FISHYBACKS
FISK
FISKED
FISKING
FISKS
FISNOMIE
FISNOMIES
FISSILE
FISSILITIES
FISSILITY
FISSION
FISSIONS
FISSIPED
FISSIPEDE
FISSIPEDES
FISSIPEDS
FISSIVE
FISSLE
FISSLED
FISSLES
FISSLING
FISSURE
FISSURED
FISSURES
FISSURING
FIST
FISTED
FISTFUL

FISTFULS
FISTIANA
FISTIANAS
FISTIC
FISTICAL
FISTICUFF
FISTICUFFS
FISTIER
FISTIEST
FISTING
FISTMELE
FISTMELES
FISTS
FISTULA
FISTULAE
FISTULAR
FISTULAS
FISTULOSE
FISTULOUS
FISTY
FIT
FITCH
FITCHÉ
FITCHEE
FITCHES
FITCHET
FITCHETS
FITCHEW
FITCHEWS
FITCHY
FITFUL
FITFULLY
FITLIER
FITLIEST
FITLY
FITMENT
FITMENTS
FITNESS
FITNESSES
FITS
FITT
FITTE
FITTED
FITTER
FITTERS
FITTES
FITTEST
FITTING
FITTINGLY
FITTINGS
FITTS
FIVE
FIVEFOLD
FIVEPENCE
FIVEPENCES
FIVEPENNY
FIVEPIN
FIVEPINS
FIVER
FIVERS
FIVES
FIX
FIXABLE
FIXATE
FIXATED
FIXATES
FIXATING
FIXATION
FIXATIONS
FIXATIVE

FIXATIVES
FIXATURE
FIXATURES
FIXED
FIXEDLY
FIXEDNESS
FIXEDNESSES
FIXER
FIXERS
FIXES
FIXING
FIXINGS
FIXITIES
FIXITY
FIXIVE
FIXTURE
FIXTURES
FIXURE
FIXURES
FIZ
FIZGIG
FIZGIGS
FIZZ
FIZZED
FIZZEN
FIZZENS
FIZZER
FIZZERS
FIZZES
FIZZGIG
FIZZGIGS
FIZZIER
FIZZIEST
FIZZING
FIZZINGS
FIZZLE
FIZZLED
FIZZLES
FIZZLING
FIZZY
FJORD
FJORDS
FLAB
FLABBIER
FLABBIEST
FLABBY
FLABELLA
FLABELLUM
FLABELLUMS
FLABS
FLACCID
FLACCIDER
FLACCIDEST
FLACCIDLY
FLACK
FLACKER
FLACKERED
FLACKERING
FLACKERS
FLACKET
FLACKETS
FLACKS
FLACON
FLACONS
FLAFF
FLAFFED
FLAFFER
FLAFFERED
FLAFFERING
FLAFFERS

FLAFFING
FLAFFS
FLAG
FLAGELLA
FLAGELLUM
FLAGEOLET
FLAGEOLETS
FLAGGED
FLAGGIER
FLAGGIEST
FLAGGING
FLAGGINGS
FLAGGY
FLAGITATE
FLAGITATED
FLAGITATES
FLAGITATING
FLAGON
FLAGONS
FLAGPOLE
FLAGPOLES
FLAGRANCE
FLAGRANCES
FLAGRANCIES
FLAGRANCY
FLAGRANT
FLAGS
FLAGSHIP
FLAGSHIPS
FLAGSTAFF
FLAGSTAFFS
FLAGSTICK
FLAGSTICKS
FLAGSTONE
FLAGSTONES
FLAIL
FLAILED
FLAILING
FLAILS
FLAIR
FLAIRS
FLAK
FLAKE
FLAKED
FLAKES
FLAKIER
FLAKIEST
FLAKINESS
FLAKINESSES
FLAKING
FLAKS
FLAKY
FLAM
FLAMBÉ
FLAMBEAU
FLAMBEAUS
FLAMBEAUX
FLAMBÉED
FLAME
FLAMED
FLAMELESS
FLAMELET
FLAMELETS
FLAMEN
FLAMENCO
FLAMENCOS
FLAMENS
FLAMES
FLAMFEW
FLAMFEWS

FLAMIER
FLAMIEST
FLAMINES
FLAMING
FLAMINGLY
FLAMINGO
FLAMINGOES
FLAMINGOS
FLAMM
FLAMMABLE
FLAMMED
FLAMMING
FLAMMS
FLAMMULE
FLAMMULES
FLAMS
FLAMY
FLAN
FLANCH
FLANCHED
FLANCHES
FLANCHING
FLANCHINGS
FLÂNERIE
FLÂNERIES
FLÂNEUR
FLÂNEURS
FLANGE
FLANGED
FLANGES
FLANGING
FLANK
FLANKED
FLANKER
FLANKERED
FLANKERING
FLANKERS
FLANKING
FLANKS
FLANNEL
FLANNELLED
FLANNELLING
FLANNELLY
FLANNELS
FLANNEN
FLANNENS
FLANS
FLAP
FLAPJACK
FLAPJACKS
FLAPPABLE
FLAPPED
FLAPPER
FLAPPERS
FLAPPING
FLAPPINGS
FLAPS
FLAPTRACK
FLAPTRACKS
FLARE
FLARED
FLARES
FLARIER
FLARIEST
FLARING
FLARINGLY
FLARY
FLASER
FLASERS
FLASH

FLASHCUBE
FLASHCUBES
FLASHED
FLASHER
FLASHERS
FLASHES
FLASHEST
FLASHIER
FLASHIEST
FLASHILY
FLASHING
FLASHINGS
FLASHY
FLASK
FLASKET
FLASKETS
FLASKS
FLAT
FLATBACK
FLATBACKS
FLATBOAT
FLATBOATS
FLATFISH
FLATFISHES
FLATHEAD
FLATHEADS
FLATIRON
FLATIRONS
FLATLET
FLATLETS
FLATLING
FLATLINGS
FLATLONG
FLATLY
FLATMATE
FLATMATES
FLATNESS
FLATNESSES
FLATS
FLATTED
FLATTEN
FLATTENED
FLATTENING
FLATTENS
FLATTER
FLATTERED
FLATTERER
FLATTERERS
FLATTERIES
FLATTERING
FLATTERS
FLATTERY
FLATTEST
FLATTING
FLATTINGS
FLATTISH
FLATULENT
FLATUOUS
FLATUS
FLATUSES
FLATWARE
FLATWARES
FLATWAYS
FLATWISE
FLATWORM
FLATWORMS
FLAUGHT
FLAUGHTED
FLAUGHTER
FLAUGHTERED

FLAUGHTERING
FLAUGHTERS
FLAUGHTING
FLAUGHTS
FLAUNCH
FLAUNCHED
FLAUNCHES
FLAUNCHING
FLAUNCHINGS
FLAUNE
FLAUNES
FLAUNT
FLAUNTED
FLAUNTER
FLAUNTERS
FLAUNTIER
FLAUNTIEST
FLAUNTING
FLAUNTS
FLAUNTY
FLAUTIST
FLAUTISTS
FLAVIN
FLAVINE
FLAVINES
FLAVINS
FLAVONE
FLAVONES
FLAVOROUS
FLAVOUR
FLAVOURED
FLAVOURING
FLAVOURINGS
FLAVOURS
FLAW
FLAWED
FLAWIER
FLAWIEST
FLAWING
FLAWLESS
FLAWN
FLAWNS
FLAWY
FLAX
FLAXEN
FLAXES
FLAXIER
FLAXIEST
FLAXY
FLAY
FLAYED
FLAYER
FLAYERS
FLAYING
FLAYS
FLEA
FLEAM
FLEAMS
FLEAS
FLEASOME
FLÈCHE
FLÈCHES
FLECHETTE
FLÉCHETTE
FLECHETTES
FLÉCHETTES
FLECK
FLECKED
FLECKER

FLECKERED
FLECKERING
FLECKERS
FLECKING
FLECKLESS
FLECKS
FLECTION
FLECTIONS
FLED
FLEDGE
FLEDGED
FLEDGES
FLEDGIER
FLEDGIEST
FLEDGING
FLEDGLING
FLEDGLINGS
FLEDGY
FLEE
FLEECE
FLEECED
FLEECER
FLEECERS
FLEECES
FLEECH
FLEECHED
FLEECHES
FLEECHING
FLEECHINGS
FLEECIER
FLEECIEST
FLEECING
FLEECY
FLEEING
FLEER
FLEERED
FLEERER
FLEERERS
FLEERING
FLEERINGS
FLEERS
FLEES
FLEET
FLEETED
FLEETER
FLEETEST
FLEETING
FLEETLY
FLEETNESS
FLEETNESSES
FLEETS
FLEG
FLEGGED
FLEGGING
FLEGS
FLEME
FLEMES
FLEMING
FLEMISH
FLEMISHED
FLEMISHES
FLEMISHING
FLEMIT
FLENCH
FLENCHED
FLENCHES
FLENCHING
FLENSE
FLENSED
FLENSES

FLENSING
FLESH
FLESHED
FLESHER
FLESHERS
FLESHES
FLESHHOOD
FLESHHOODS
FLESHIER
FLESHIEST
FLESHING
FLESHINGS
FLESHLESS
FLESHLIER
FLESHLIEST
FLESHLING
FLESHLINGS
FLESHLY
FLESHMENT
FLESHMENTS
FLESHWORM
FLESHWORMS
FLESHY
FLETCH
FLETCHED
FLETCHER
FLETCHERS
FLETCHES
FLETCHING
FLETTON
FLETTONS
FLEURET
FLEURETS
FLEURETTE
FLEURETTES
FLEURON
FLEURONS
FLEURY
FLEW
FLEWED
FLEWS
FLEX
FLEXED
FLEXES
FLEXIBLE
FLEXIBLY
FLEXILE
FLEXING
FLEXION
FLEXIONS
FLEXITIME
FLEXITIMES
FLEXOR
FLEXORS
FLEXUOSE
FLEXUOUS
FLEXURAL
FLEXURE
FLEXURES
FLEY
FLEYED
FLEYING
FLEYS
FLIC
FLICHTER
FLICHTERED
FLICHTERING
FLICHTERS
FLICK
FLICKED

FLICKER
FLICKERED
FLICKERING
FLICKERS
FLICKING
FLICKS
FLICS
FLIER
FLIERS
FLIES
FLIEST
FLIGHT
FLIGHTED
FLIGHTIER
FLIGHTIEST
FLIGHTILY
FLIGHTING
FLIGHTS
FLIGHTY
FLIMP
FLIMPED
FLIMPING
FLIMPS
FLIMSIER
FLIMSIES
FLIMSIEST
FLIMSILY
FLIMSY
FLINCH
FLINCHED
FLINCHER
FLINCHERS
FLINCHES
FLINCHING
FLINCHINGS
FLINDER
FLINDERS
FLING
FLINGER
FLINGERS
FLINGING
FLINGS
FLINT
FLINTIER
FLINTIEST
FLINTIFIED
FLINTIFIES
FLINTIFY
FLINTIFYING
FLINTILY
FLINTLOCK
FLINTLOCKS
FLINTS
FLINTY
FLIP
FLIPFLOP
FLIPFLOPS
FLIPPANCIES
FLIPPANCY
FLIPPANT
FLIPPED
FLIPPER
FLIPPERS
FLIPPEST
FLIPPING
FLIPS
FLIRT
FLIRTED
FLIRTIER
FLIRTIEST

FLIRTING
FLIRTINGS
FLIRTISH
FLIRTS
FLIRTY
FLISK
FLISKED
FLISKIER
FLISKIEST
FLISKING
FLISKS
FLISKY
FLIT
FLITCH
FLITCHES
FLITE
FLITED
FLITES
FLITING
FLITS
FLITT
FLITTED
FLITTER
FLITTERED
FLITTERING
FLITTERN
FLITTERNS
FLITTERS
FLITTING
FLIVVER
FLIVVERS
FLIX
FLIXED
FLIXES
FLIXING
FLOAT
FLOATABLE
FLOATAGE
FLOATAGES
FLOATANT
FLOATANTS
FLOATED
FLOATEL
FLOATELS
FLOATER
FLOATERS
FLOATIER
FLOATIEST
FLOATING
FLOATINGS
FLOATS
FLOATY
FLOCCI
FLOCCOSE
FLOCCULAR
FLOCCULE
FLOCCULES
FLOCCULI
FLOCCULUS
FLOCCUS
FLOCK
FLOCKED
FLOCKING
FLOCKS
FLOE
FLOES
FLOG
FLOGGED
FLOGGING

FLOGGINGS
FLOGS
FLONG
FLONGS
FLOOD
FLOODED
FLOODGATE
FLOODGATES
FLOODING
FLOODINGS
FLOODLIT
FLOODMARK
FLOODMARKS
FLOODS
FLOODTIDE
FLOODTIDES
FLOODWALL
FLOODWALLS
FLOODWAY
FLOODWAYS
FLOOR
FLOORED
FLOORER
FLOORERS
FLOORHEAD
FLOORHEADS
FLOORING
FLOORINGS
FLOORS
FLOOZIE
FLOOSIES
FLOOSY
FLOOZIE
FLOOZIES
FLOOZY
FLOP
FLOPHOUSE
FLOPHOUSES
FLOPPED
FLOPPIER
FLOPPIEST
FLOPPILY
FLOPPING
FLOPPY
FLOPS
FLOR
FLORA
FLORAE
FLORAL
FLORALLY
FLORAS
FLOREAT
FLOREATED
FLORENCE
FLORENCES
FLORET
FLORETS
FLORIATED
FLORID
FLORIDEAN
FLORIDEANS
FLORIDER
FLORIDEST
FLORIDITIES
FLORIDITY
FLORIDLY
FLORIER
FLORIEST
FLORIFORM
FLORIGEN

FLORIGENS
FLORIN
FLORINS
FLORIST
FLORISTIC
FLORISTICS
FLORISTRIES
FLORISTRY
FLORISTS
FLORS
FLORUIT
FLORUITS
FLORY
FLOSCULAR
FLOSCULE
FLOSCULES
FLOSH
FLOSHES
FLOSS
FLOSSES
FLOSSIER
FLOSSIEST
FLOSSY
FLOTA
FLOTAGE
FLOTAGES
FLOTANT
FLOTAS
FLOTATION
FLOTATIONS
FLOTE
FLOTEL
FLOTELS
FLOTES
FLOTILLA
FLOTILLAS
FLOTSAM
FLOTSAMS
FLOUNCE
FLOUNCED
FLOUNCES
FLOUNCING
FLOUNCINGS
FLOUNDER
FLOUNDERED
FLOUNDERING
FLOUNDERS
FLOUR
FLOURED
FLOURIER
FLOURIEST
FLOURING
FLOURISH
FLOURISHED
FLOURISHES
FLOURISHING
FLOURISHY
FLOURS
FLOURY
FLOUSE
FLOUSED
FLOUSES
FLOUSH
FLOUSHED
FLOUSHES
FLOUSHING
FLOUSING
FLOUT
FLOUTED
FLOUTING

FLOUTS
FLOW
FLOWAGE
FLOWAGES
FLOWED
FLOWER
FLOWERAGE
FLOWERAGES
FLOWERED
FLOWERER
FLOWERERS
FLOWERET
FLOWERETS
FLOWERIER
FLOWERIEST
FLOWERING
FLOWERINGS
FLOWERPOT
FLOWERPOTS
FLOWERS
FLOWERY
FLOWING
FLOWINGLY
FLOWMETER
FLOWMETERS
FLOWN
FLOWS
FLU
FLUATE
FLUATES
FLUB
FLUBBED
FLUBBING
FLUBS
FLUCTUANT
FLUCTUATE
FLUCTUATED
FLUCTUATES
FLUCTUATING
FLUE
FLUELLIN
FLUELLINS
FLUENCE
FLUENCES
FLUENCIES
FLUENCY
FLUENT
FLUENTLY
FLUENTS
FLUES
FLUEWORK
FLUEWORKS
FLUEY
FLUFF
FLUFFED
FLUFFIER
FLUFFIEST
FLUFFING
FLUFFS
FLUFFY
FLUGEL
FLUGELMAN
FLUGELMEN
FLUGELS
FLUID
FLUIDAL
FLUIDIC
FLUIDICS
FLUIDIFIED
FLUIDIFIES

FLUIDIFY
FLUIDIFYING
FLUIDISE
FLUIDISED
FLUIDISES
FLUIDISING
FLUIDITIES
FLUIDITY
FLUIDIZE
FLUIDIZED
FLUIDIZES
FLUIDIZING
FLUIDNESS
FLUIDNESSES
FLUIDS
FLUIER
FLUIEST
FLUKE
FLUKED
FLUKES
FLUKEY
FLUKIER
FLUKIEST
FLUKING
FLUKY
FLUME
FLUMES
FLUMMERIES
FLUMMERY
FLUMMOX
FLUMMOXED
FLUMMOXES
FLUMMOXING
FLUMP
FLUMPED
FLUMPING
FLUMPS
FLUNG
FLUNK
FLUNKED
FLUNKEY
FLUNKEYS
FLUNKIES
FLUNKING
FLUNKS
FLUNKY
FLUOR
FLUORESCE
FLUORESCED
FLUORESCES
FLUORESCING
FLUORIC
FLUORIDE
FLUORIDES
FLUORINE
FLUORINES
FLUORITE
FLUORITES
FLUOROSES
FLUOROSIS
FLUORS
FLUORSPAR
FLUORSPARS
FLURR
FLURRED
FLURRIED
FLURRIES
FLURRING
FLURRS
FLURRY

FLURRYING
FLUS
FLUSH
FLUSHED
FLUSHER
FLUSHERS
FLUSHES
FLUSHEST
FLUSHIER
FLUSHIEST
FLUSHING
FLUSHINGS
FLUSHNESS
FLUSHNESSES
FLUSHY
FLUSTER
FLUSTERED
FLUSTERING
FLUSTERS
FLUSTERY
FLUSTRATE
FLUSTRATED
FLUSTRATES
FLUSTRATING
FLUTE
FLUTED
FLUTER
FLUTERS
FLUTES
FLUTIER
FLUTIEST
FLUTINA
FLUTINAS
FLUTING
FLUTINGS
FLUTIST
FLUTISTS
FLUTTER
FLUTTERED
FLUTTERING
FLUTTERS
FLUTY
FLUVIAL
FLUVIATIC
FLUX
FLUXED
FLUXES
FLUXING
FLUXION
FLUXIONAL
FLUXIONS
FLUXIVE
FLY
FLYABLE
FLYAWAY
FLYBANE
FLYBANES
FLYBELT
FLYBELTS
FLYBLOW
FLYBLOWS
FLYBOAT
FLYBOATS
FLYBOOK
FLYBOOKS
FLYER
FLYERS
FLYEST
FLYING
FLYINGS

FLYLEAF
FLYLEAVES
FLYMAKER
FLYMAKERS
FLYOVER
FLYOVERS
FLYPAPER
FLYPAPERS
FLYPE
FLYPED
FLYPES
FLYPING
FLYSCH
FLYSCHES
FLYTE
FLYTED
FLYTES
FLYTING
FLYTINGS
FLYTRAP
FLYTRAPS
FLYWAY
FLYWAYS
FLYWEIGHT
FLYWEIGHTS
FLYWHEEL
FLYWHEELS
FOAL
FOALED
FOALFOOT
FOALFOOTS
FOALING
FOALS
FOAM
FOAMED
FOAMIER
FOAMIEST
FOAMILY
FOAMINESS
FOAMINESSES
FOAMING
FOAMINGLY
FOAMINGS
FOAMLESS
FOAMS
FOAMY
FOB
FOBBED
FOBBING
FOBS
FOCAL
FOCALISE
FOCALISED
FOCALISES
FOCALISING
FOCALIZE
FOCALIZED
FOCALIZES
FOCALIZING
FOCALLY
FOCI
FOCIMETER
FOCIMETERS
FOCUS
FOCUSED
FOCUSES
FOCUSING
FOCUSSED
FOCUSSES
FOCUSSING

FODDER
FODDERED
FODDERER
FODDERERS
FODDERING
FODDERINGS
FODDERS
FOE
FOEDARIE
FOEDARIES
FOEDERATI
FOEHN
FOEHNS
FOEMAN
FOEMEN
FOEN
FOES
FOETAL
FOETICIDE
FOETICIDES
FOETID
FOETIDER
FOETIDEST
FOETOR
FOETORS
FOETUS
FOETUSES
FOG
FOGASH
FOGASHES
FOGBOUND
FOGEY
FOGEYS
FOGGAGE
FOGGAGED
FOGGAGES
FOGGAGING
FOGGED
FOGGER
FOGGERS
FOGGIER
FOGGIEST
FOGGILY
FOGGINESS
FOGGINESSES
FOGGING
FOGGY
FOGHORN
FOGHORNS
FOGIES
FOGLE
FOGLES
FOGLESS
FOGMAN
FOGMEN
FOGRAM
FOGRAMITE
FOGRAMITES
FOGRAMITIES
FOGRAMITY
FOGRAMS
FOGS
FOGY
FOGYDOM
FOGYDOMS
FOGYISH
FOGYISM
FOGYISMS
FOH
FÖHN

FÖHNS	FOLKROCK	FOODIES	FOOTPACES	FORAY
FOIBLE	FOLKROCKS	FOODLESS	FOOTPAD	FORAYED
FOIBLES	FOLKS	FOODS	FOOTPADS	FORAYER
FOIL	FOLKSIER	FOODSTUFF	FOOTPAGE	FORAYERS
FOILED	FOLKSIEST	FOODSTUFFS	FOOTPAGES	FORAYING
FOILING	FOLKSY	FOOL	FOOTPATH	FORAYS
FOILINGS	FOLKWAY	FOOLED	FOOTPATHS	FORBAD
FOILS	FOLKWAYS	FOOLERIES	FOOTPLATE	FORBADE
FOIN	FOLLICLE	FOOLERY	FOOTPLATES	FORBEAR
FOINED	FOLLICLES	FOOLHARDY	FOOTPOST	FORBEARING
FOINING	FOLLIED	FOOLING	FOOTPOSTS	FORBEARS
FOININGLY	FOLLIES	FOOLINGS	FOOTPRINT	FORBID
FOINS	FOLLOW	FOOLISH	FOOTPRINTS	FORBIDDAL
FOISON	FOLLOWED	FOOLISHER	FOOTRA	FORBIDDALS
FOISONS	FOLLOWER	FOOLISHEST	FOOTRAS	FORBIDDEN
FOIST	FOLLOWERS	FOOLISHLY	FOOTREST	FORBIDDER
FOISTED	FOLLOWING	FOOLPROOF	FOOTRESTS	FORBIDDERS
FOISTER	FOLLOWINGS	FOOLS	FOOTROT	FORBIDDING
FOISTERS	FOLLOWS	FOOLSCAP	FOOTROTS	FORBIDDINGS
FOISTING	FOLLY	FOOLSCAPS	FOOTRULE	FORBIDS
FOISTS	FOLLYING	FOOT	FOOTRULES	FORBODE
FOLACIN	FOMENT	FOOTAGE	FOOTS	FORBODES
FOLACINS	FOMENTED	FOOTAGES	FOOTSLOG	FORBORE
FOLATE	FOMENTER	FOOTBALL	FOOTSLOGGED	FORBORNE
FOLD	FOMENTERS	FOOTBALLS	FOOTSLOGGING	FORBY
FOLDABLE	FOMENTING	FOOTBAR	FOOTSLOGGINGS	FORBYE
FOLDAWAY	FOMENTS	FOOTBARS	FOOTSLOGS	FORÇAT
FOLDBOAT	FOMES	FOOTBOARD	FOOTSORE	FORÇATS
FOLDBOATS	FOMITES	FOOTBOARDS	FOOTSTALK	FORCE
FOLDED	FON	FOOTBOY	FOOTSTALKS	FORCED
FOLDER	FOND	FOOTBOYS	FOOTSTEP	FORCEDLY
FOLDEROL	FONDA	FOOTCLOTH	FOOTSTEPS	FORCEFUL
FOLDEROLS	FONDANT	FOOTCLOTHS	FOOTSTOOL	FORCELESS
FOLDERS	FONDANTS	FOOTED	FOOTSTOOLS	FORCEMEAT
FOLDING	FONDAS	FOOTER	FOOTWAY	FORCEMEATS
FOLDINGS	FONDED	FOOTERS	FOOTWAYS	FORCEPS
FOLDS	FONDER	FOOTFALL	FOOTWEAR	FORCEPSES
FOLIA	FONDEST	FOOTFALLS	FOOTWEARS	FORCER
FOLIAGE	FONDING	FOOTFAULT	FOOTWORK	FORCERS
FOLIAGED	FONDLE	FOOTFAULTED	FOOTWORKS	FORCES
FOLIAGES	FONDLED	FOOTFAULTING	FOOTWORN	FORCIBLE
FOLIAR	FONDLER	FOOTFAULTS	FOOTY	FORCIBLY
FOLIATE	FONDLERS	FOOTGEAR	FOOZLE	FORCING
FOLIATED	FONDLES	FOOTGEARS	FOOZLED	FORCIPATE
FOLIATES	FONDLING	FOOTHILL	FOOZLER	FORCIPES
FOLIATING	FONDLINGS	FOOTHILLS	FOOZLERS	FORD
FOLIATION	FONDLY	FOOTHOLD	FOOZLES	FORDABLE
FOLIATIONS	FONDNESS	FOOTHOLDS	FOOZLING	FORDED
FOLIATURE	FONDNESSES	FOOTIER	FOOZLINGS	FORDID
FOLIATURES	FONDS	FOOTIEST	FOP	FORDING
FOLIE	FONDUE	FOOTING	FOPLING	FORDO
FOLIES	FONDUES	FOOTINGS	FOPLINGS	FORDOES
FOLIO	FONE	FOOTLE	FOPPERIES	FORDOING
FOLIOED	FONLY	FOOTLED	FOPPERY	FORDONE
FOLIOING	FONNED	FOOTLES	FOPPISH	FORDS
FOLIOLATE	FONNING	FOOTLESS	FOPPISHLY	FORE
FOLIOLE	FONS	FOOTLIGHT	FOPS	FOREANENT
FOLIOLES	FONT	FOOTLIGHTS	FOR	FOREARM
FOLIOLOSE	FONTAL	FOOTLING	FORA	FOREARMED
FOLIOS	FONTANEL	FOOTLINGS	FORAGE	FOREARMING
FOLIOSE	FONTANELS	FOOTLOOSE	FORAGED	FOREARMS
FOLIUM	FONTANGE	FOOTMAN	FORAGER	FOREBEAR
FOLK	FONTANGES	FOOTMARK	FORAGERS	FOREBEARS
FOLKLAND	FONTICULI	FOOTMARKS	FORAGES	FOREBITT
FOLKLANDS	FONTLET	FOOTMEN	FORAGING	FOREBITTS
FOLKLORE	FONTLETS	FOOTMUFF	FORAMEN	FOREBODE
FOLKLORES	FONTS	FOOTMUFFS	FORAMINA	FOREBODED
FOLKLORIC	FOOD	FOOTNOTE	FORAMINAL	FOREBODER
FOLKMOOT	FOODFUL	FOOTNOTES ·	FORANE	FOREBODERS
FOLKMOOTS	FOODIE	FOOTPACE	FORASMUCH	FOREBODES

FOREBODING	FORELAID	FORERUNNING	FORESTER	FORFEND
FOREBODINGS	FORELAIN	FORERUNS	FORESTERS	FORFENDED
FOREBY	FORELAND	FORES	FORESTINE	FORFENDING
FORECABIN	FORELANDS	FORESAID	FORESTING	FORFENDS
FORECABINS	FORELAY	FORESAIL	FORESTRIES	FORFEX
FORECAR	FORELAYING	FORESAILS	FORESTRY	FORFEXES
FORECARS	FORELAYS	FORESAW	FORESTS	FORFICATE
FORECAST	FORELEG	FORESAY	FORETASTE	FORGAT
FORECASTED	FORELEGS	FORESAYING	FORETASTED	FORGATHER
FORECASTING	FORELEND	FORESAYS	FORETASTES	FORGATHERED
FORECASTS	FORELENDING	FORESEE	FORETASTING	FORGATHERING
FORECLOSE	FORELENDS	FORESEEING	FORETAUGHT	FORGATHERS
FORECLOSED	FORELENT	FORESEEN	FORETEACH	FORGAVE
FORECLOSES	FORELIE	FORESEES	FORETEACHES	FORGE
FORECLOSING	FORELIES	FORESHEW	FORETEACHING	FORGEABLE
FORECLOTH	FORELIFT	FORESHEWED	FORETEETH	FORGED
FORECLOTHS	FORELIFTED	FORESHEWING	FORETELL	FORGEMAN
FORECOURT	FORELIFTING	FORESHEWN	FORETELLING	FORGEMEN
FORECOURTS	FORELIFTS	FORESHEWS	FORETELLS	FORGER
FOREDATE	FORELIMB	FORESHIP	FORETHINK	FORGERIES
FOREDATED	FORELIMBS	FORESHIPS	FORETHINKING	FORGERS
FOREDATES	FORELOCK	FORESHOCK	FORETHINKS	FORGERY
FOREDATING	FORELOCKS	FORESHOCKS	FORETHOUGHT	FORGES
FOREDECK	FORELS	FORESHORE	FORETHOUGHTS	FORGET
FOREDECKS	FORELYING	FORESHORES	FORETIME	FORGETFUL
FOREDOOM	FOREMAN	FORESHOW	FORETIMES	FORGETIVE
FOREDOOMED	FOREMAST	FORESHOWED	FORETOKEN	FORGETS
FOREDOOMING	FOREMASTS	FORESHOWING	FORETOKENED	FORGETTER
FOREDOOMS	FOREMEAN	FORESHOWN	FORETOKENING	FORGETTERS
FOREFEEL	FOREMEANING	FORESHOWS	FORETOKENINGS	FORGETTING
FOREFEELING	FOREMEANS	FORESIDE	FORETOKENS	FORGETTINGS
FOREFEELS	FOREMEANT	FORESIDES	FORETOLD	FORGING
FOREFEET	FOREMEN	FORESIGHT	FORETOOTH	FORGINGS
FOREFELT	FOREMOST	FORESIGHTS	FORETOP	FORGIVE
FOREFOOT	FORENAME	FORESKIN	FORETOPS	FORGIVEN
FOREFRONT	FORENAMED	FORESKINS	FOREVER	FORGIVES
FOREFRONTS	FORENAMES	FORESKIRT	FOREVERS	FORGIVING
FOREGLEAM	FORENIGHT	FORESKIRTS	FOREWARD	FORGO
FOREGLEAMS	FORENIGHTS	FORESLACK	FOREWARDS	FORGOES
FOREGO	FORENOON	FORESLACKED	FOREWARN	FORGOING
FOREGOER	FORENOONS	FORESLACKING	FOREWARNED	FORGONE
FOREGOERS	FORENSIC	FORESLACKS	FOREWARNING	FORGOT
FOREGOES	FORENSICS	FORESLOW	FOREWARNINGS	FORGOTTEN
FOREGOING	FOREPART	FORESLOWED	FOREWARNS	FORHAILE
FOREGOINGS	FOREPARTS	FORESLOWING	FOREWEIGH	FORHAILED
FOREGONE	FOREPAST	FORESLOWS	FOREWEIGHED	FORHAILES
FOREGUT	FOREPAW	FORESPEAK	FOREWEIGHING	FORHAILING
FOREGUTS	FOREPAWS	FORESPEAKING	FOREWEIGHS	FORHENT
FOREHAND	FOREPEAK	FORESPEAKS	FOREWENT	FORHENTING
FOREHANDS	FOREPEAKS	FORESPEND	FOREWIND	FORHENTS
FOREHEAD	FOREPLAN	FORESPENDING	FOREWINDS	FORHOO
FOREHEADS	FOREPLANNED	FORESPENDS	FOREWING	FORHOOED
FOREHENT	FOREPLANNING	FORESPENT	FOREWINGS	FORHOOIE
FOREHENTING	FOREPLANS	FORESPOKE	FOREWOMAN	FORHOOIED
FOREHENTS	FOREPLAY	FORESPOKEN	FOREWOMEN	FORHOOIEING
FOREIGN	FOREPLAYS	FOREST	FOREWORD	FORHOOIES
FOREIGNER	FOREPOINT	FORESTAGE	FOREWORDS	FORHOOING
FOREIGNERS	FOREPOINTED	FORESTAGES	FORFAIR	FORHOOS
FOREJUDGE	FOREPOINTING	FORESTAIR	FORFAIRED	FORHOW
FOREJUDGED	FOREPOINTS	FORESTAIRS	FORFAIRING	FORHOWED
FOREJUDGES	FORERAN	FORESTAL	FORFAIRN	FORHOWING
FOREJUDGING	FOREREACH	FORESTALL	FORFAIRS	FORHOWS
FOREKING	FOREREACHED	FORESTALLED	FORFAULT	FORINSEC
FOREKINGS	FOREREACHES	FORESTALLING	FORFAULTS	FORINT
FOREKNEW	FOREREACHING	FORESTALLINGS	FORFEIT	FORINTS
FOREKNOW	FOREREAD	FORESTALLS	FORFEITED	FORJASKIT
FOREKNOWING	FOREREADING	FORESTAY	FORFEITER	FORJESKIT
FOREKNOWN	FOREREADINGS	FORESTAYS	FORFEITERS	FORJUDGE
FOREKNOWS	FOREREADS	FORESTEAL	FORFEITING	FORJUDGED
FOREL	FORERUN	FORESTED	FORFEITS	FORJUDGES

FORJUDGING
FORK
FORKED
FORKEDLY
FORKER
FORKERS
FORKHEAD
FORKHEADS
FORKIER
FORKIEST
FORKINESS
FORKINESSES
FORKING
FORKS
FORKTAIL
FORKTAILS
FORKY
FORLANA
FORLANAS
FORLEND
FORLENDING
FORLENDS
FORLENT
FORLESE
FORLESES
FORLESING
FORLORE
FORLORN
FORLORNER
FORLORNLY
FORLORNS
FORM
FORMABLE
FORMAL
FORMALIN
FORMALINS
FORMALISE
FORMALISED
FORMALISES
FORMALISING
FORMALISM
FORMALISMS
FORMALIST
FORMALISTS
FORMALITIES
FORMALITY
FORMALIZE
FORMALIZED
FORMALIZES
FORMALIZING
FORMALLY
FORMANT
FORMANTS
FORMAT
FORMATE
FORMATED
FORMATES
FORMATING
FORMATION
FORMATIONS
FORMATIVE
FORMATIVES
FORMATS
FORMATTED
FORMATTER
FORMATTERS
FORMATTING
FORME
FORMED

FORMER
FORMERLY
FORMERS
FORMES
FORMIATE
FORMIATES
FORMIC
FORMICANT
FORMICARIES
FORMICARY
FORMICATE
FORMING
FORMINGS
FORMLESS
FORMOL
FORMOLS
FORMS
FORMULA
FORMULAE
FORMULAIC
FORMULAR
FORMULARIES
FORMULARY
FORMULAS
FORMULATE
FORMULATED
FORMULATES
FORMULATING
FORMULISE
FORMULISED
FORMULISES
FORMULISING
FORMULISM
FORMULISMS
FORMULIST
FORMULISTS
FORMULIZE
FORMULIZED
FORMULIZES
FORMULIZING
FORMWORK
FORMWORKS
FORNENST
FORNENT
FORNICAL
FORNICATE
FORNICATED
FORNICATES
FORNICATING
FORNIX
FORNIXES
FORPET
FORPETS
FORPINE
FORPINED
FORPINES
FORPINING
FORPIT
FORPITS
FORRAD
FORRADER
FORRAY
FORRAYED
FORRAYING
FORRAYS
FORREN
FORRIT
FORSAID
FORSAKE
FORSAKEN

FORSAKES
FORSAKING
FORSAKINGS
FORSAY
FORSAYING
FORSAYS
FORSLACK
FORSLACKED
FORSLACKING
FORSLACKS
FORSLOE
FORSLOED
FORSLOEING
FORSLOES
FORSLOW
FORSLOWED
FORSLOWING
FORSLOWS
FORSOOK
FORSOOTH
FORSPEAK
FORSPEAKING
FORSPEAKS
FORSPEND
FORSPENDING
FORSPENDS
FORSPENT
FORSPOKE
FORSPOKEN
FORSWATT
FORSWEAR
FORSWEARING
FORSWEARS
FORSWINK
FORSWINKED
FORSWINKING
FORSWINKS
FORSWONCK
FORSWORE
FORSWORN
FORSWUNK
FORSYTHIA
FORSYTHIAS
FORT
FORTALICE
FORTALICES
FORTE
FORTED
FORTES
FORTH
FORTHCAME
FORTHCOME
FORTHCOMES
FORTHCOMING
FORTHINK
FORTHINKING
FORTHINKS
FORTHOUGHT
FORTHWITH
FORTHY
FORTIES
FORTIETH
FORTIETHS
FORTIFIED
FORTIFIER
FORTIFIERS
FORTIFIES
FORTIFY
FORTIFYING
FORTILAGE

FORTILAGES
FORTING
FORTIS
FORTITUDE
FORTITUDES
FORTLET
FORTLETS
FORTNIGHT
FORTNIGHTS
FORTRESS
FORTRESSED
FORTRESSES
FORTRESSING
FORTS
FORTUITIES
FORTUITY
FORTUNATE
FORTUNE
FORTUNED
FORTUNES
FORTUNING
FORTUNIZE
FORTUNIZED
FORTUNIZES
FORTUNIZING
FORTY
FORTYISH
FORUM
FORUMS
FORWANDER
FORWANDERED
FORWANDERING
FORWANDERS
FORWARD
FORWARDED
FORWARDER
FORWARDERS
FORWARDEST
FORWARDING
FORWARDINGS
FORWARDLY
FORWARDS
FORWARN
FORWARNED
FORWARNING
FORWARNS
FORWASTE
FORWASTED
FORWASTES
FORWASTING
FORWEARIED
FORWEARIES
FORWEARY
FORWEARYING
FORWENT
FORWHY
FORWORN
FORZANDI
FORZANDO
FORZANDOS
FORZATI
FORZATO
FORZATOS
FOSS
FOSSA
FOSSAE
FOSSAS
FOSSE
FOSSED
FOSSES

FOSSETTE
FOSSETTES
FOSSICK
FOSSICKED
FOSSICKER
FOSSICKERS
FOSSICKING
FOSSICKINGS
FOSSICKS
FOSSIL
FOSSILISE
FOSSILISED
FOSSILISES
FOSSILISING
FOSSILIZE
FOSSILIZED
FOSSILIZES
FOSSILIZING
FOSSILS
FOSSOR
FOSSORIAL
FOSSORS
FOSSULA
FOSSULAS
FOSSULATE
FOSTER
FOSTERAGE
FOSTERAGES
FOSTERED
FOSTERER
FOSTERERS
FOSTERING
FOSTERINGS
FOSTERS
FOSTRESS
FOSTRESSES
FOTHER
FOTHERED
FOTHERING
FOTHERS
FOU
FOUAT
FOUATS
FOUD
FOUDRIE
FOUDRIES
FOUDS
FOUER
FOUEST
FOUET
FOUETTE
FOUETTES
FOUGADE
FOUGADES
FOUGASSE
FOUGASSES
FOUGHT
FOUGHTEN
FOUGHTIER
FOUGHTIEST
FOUGHTY
FOUL
FOULARD
FOULARDS
FOULDER
FOULDERED
FOULDERING
FOULDERS
FOULÉ

FOULED	FOVEOLE	FRACTURE	FRANGIBLE	FRAZILS
FOULER	FOVEOLES	FRACTURED	FRANION	FRAZZLE
FOULÉS	FOWL	FRACTURES	FRANIONS	FRAZZLED
FOULEST	FOWLED	FRACTURING	FRANK	FRAZZLES
FOULING	FOWLER	FRAE	FRANKED	FRAZZLING
FOULLY	FOWLERS	FRAENA	FRANKER	FREAK
FOULMART	FOWLING	FRAENUM	FRANKEST	FREAKED
FOULMARTS	FOWLINGS	FRAGILE	FRANKING	FREAKFUL
FOULNESS	FOWLS	FRAGILELY	FRANKLIN	FREAKIER
FOULNESSES	FOWTH	FRAGILER	FRANKLINS	FREAKIEST
FOULS	FOWTHS	FRAGILEST	FRANKLY	FREAKING
FOUMART	FOX	FRAGILITIES	FRANKNESS	FREAKISH
FOUMARTS	FOXBERRIES	FRAGILITY	FRANKNESSES	FREAKS
FOUND	FOXBERRY	FRAGMENT	FRANKS	FREAKY
FOUNDED	FOXED	FRAGMENTED	FRANTIC	FRECKLE
FOUNDER	FOXES	FRAGMENTING	FRANTICLY	FRECKLED
FOUNDERED	FOXGLOVE	FRAGMENTS	FRANZIER	FRECKLES
FOUNDERING	FOXGLOVES	FRAGOR	FRANZIEST	FRECKLIER
FOUNDERS	FOXHOLE	FRAGORS	FRANZY	FRECKLIEST
FOUNDING	FOXHOLES	FRAGRANCE	FRAP	FRECKLING
FOUNDINGS	FOXHOUND	FRAGRANCED	FRAPPANT	FRECKLINGS
FOUNDLING	FOXHOUNDS	FRAGRANCES	FRAPPÉ	FRECKLY
FOUNDLINGS	FOXIER	FRAGRANCIES	FRAPPED	FREDAINE
FOUNDRESS	FOXIEST	FRAGRANCING	FRAPPÉE	FREDAINES
FOUNDRESSES	FOXINESS	FRAGRANCY	FRAPPING	FREE
FOUNDRIES	FOXINESSES	FRAGRANT	FRAPS	FREEBEE
FOUNDRY	FOXING	FRAÎCHEUR	FRAS	FREEBEES
FOUNDS	FOXINGS	FRAÎCHEURS	FRASS	FREEBIE
FOUNT	FOXSHARK	FRAIL	FRASSES	FREEBIES
FOUNTAIN	FOXSHARKS	FRAILER	FRATCH	FREEBOOTIES
FOUNTAINED	FOXSHIP	FRAILEST	FRATCHES	FREEBOOTY
FOUNTAINING	FOXSHIPS	FRAILISH	FRATCHETY	FREEBORN
FOUNTAINS	FOXTROT	FRAILLY	FRATCHIER	FREED
FOUNTFUL	FOXTROTS	FRAILNESS	FRATCHIEST	FREEDMAN
FOUNTS	FOXTROTTED	FRAILNESSES	FRATCHING	FREEDMEN
FOUR	FOXTROTTING	FRAILS	FRATCHY	FREEDOM
FOURFOLD	FOXY	FRAILTEE	FRATE	FREEDOMS
FOURGON	FOY	FRAILTEES	FRATER	FREEHOLD
FOURGONS	FOYER	FRAILTIES	FRATERIES	FREEHOLDS
FOURPENCE	FOYERS	FRAILTY	FRATERNAL	FREEING
FOURPENCES	FOYLE	FRAIM	FRATERS	FREELOAD
FOURPENNIES	FOYLED	FRAIMS	FRATERY	FREELOADED
FOURPENNY	FOYLES	FRAISE	FRATI	FREELOADING
FOURS	FOYLING	FRAISED	FRATRIES	FREELOADINGS
FOURSCORE	FOYNE	FRAISES	FRATRY	FREELOADS
FOURSES	FOYNED	FRAISING	FRAU	FREELY
FOURSOME	FOYNES	FRAME	FRAUD	FREEMAN
FOURSOMES	FOYNING	FRAMED	FRAUDFUL	FREEMASON
FOURTEEN	FOYS	FRAMER	FRAUDS	FREEMASONS
FOURTEENS	FOZIER	FRAMERS	FRAUDSMAN	FREEMEN
FOURTH	FOZIEST	FRAMES	FRAUDSMEN	FREENESS
FOURTHLY	FOZINESS	FRAMEWORK	FRAUDSTER	FREENESSES
FOURTHS	FOZINESSES	FRAMEWORKS	FRAUDSTERS	FREER
FOUS	FOZY	FRAMING	FRAUGHT	FREERS
FOUSSA	FRA	FRAMINGS	FRAUGHTED	FREES
FOUSSAS	FRAB	FRAMPAL	FRAUGHTER	FREESHEET
FOUTER	FRABBED	FRAMPLER	FRAUGHTEST	FREESHEETS
FOUTERS	FRABBING	FRAMPLERS	FRAUGHTING	FREESIA
FOUTH	FRABBIT	FRAMPOLD	FRAUGHTS	FREESIAS
FOUTHS	FRABJOUS	FRANC	FRÄULEIN	FREEST
FOUTRA	FRABS	FRANCHISE	FRÄULEINS	FREESTONE
FOUTRAS	FRACAS	FRANCHISED	FRAUS	FREESTONES
FOUTRE	FRACK	FRANCHISES	FRAUTAGE	FREESTYLE
FOUTRES	FRACT	FRANCHISING	FRAUTAGES	FREESTYLES
FOVEA	FRACTED	FRANCIUM	FRAY	FREET
FOVEAE	FRACTING	FRANCIUMS	FRAYED	FREETIER
FOVEAL	FRACTION	FRANCO	FRAYING	FREETIEST
FOVEATE	FRACTIONS	FRANCOLIN	FRAYINGS	FREETS
FOVEOLA	FRACTIOUS	FRANCOLINS	FRAYS	FREETY
FOVEOLAS	FRACTS	FRANCS	FRAZIL	FREEWAY

FREEWAYS
FREEWOMAN
FREEWOMEN
FREEZABLE
FREEZE
FREEZER
FREEZERS
FREEZES
FREEZING
FREEZINGS
FREIGHT
FREIGHTED
FREIGHTER
FREIGHTERS
FREIGHTING
FREIGHTS
FREIT
FREITIER
FREITIEST
FREITS
FREITY
FREMD
FREMDS
FREMIT
FREMITS
FREMITUS
FREMITUSES
FRENA
FRENCH
FRENETIC
FRENETICS
FRENNE
FRENNES
FRENUM
FRENZICAL
FRENZIED
FRENZIES
FRENZY
FRENZYING
FREON
FREONS
FREQUENCE
FREQUENCES
FREQUENCIES
FREQUENCY
FREQUENT
FREQUENTED
FREQUENTER
FREQUENTERS
FREQUENTEST
FREQUENTING
FREQUENTS
FRÈRE
FRÈRES
FRESCADE
FRESCADES
FRESCO
FRESCOED
FRESCOER
FRESCOERS
FRESCOES
FRESCOING
FRESCOINGS
FRESCOIST
FRESCOISTS
FRESCOS
FRESH
FRESHED

FRESHEN
FRESHENED
FRESHENER
FRESHENERS
FRESHENING
FRESHENS
FRESHER
FRESHERS
FRESHES
FRESHEST
FRESHET
FRESHETS
FRESHING
FRESHISH
FRESHLY
FRESHMAN
FRESHMEN
FRESHNESS
FRESHNESSES
FRET
FRETFUL
FRETFULLY
FRETS
FRETSAW
FRETSAWS
FRETTED
FRETTIER
FRETTIEST
FRETTING
FRETTINGS
FRETTY
FRETWORK
FRETWORKS
FRIABLE
FRIAND
FRIANDE
FRIANDES
FRIANDS
FRIAR
FRIARBIRD
FRIARBIRDS
FRIARIES
FRIARLY
FRIARS
FRIARY
FRIBBLE
FRIBBLED
FRIBBLER
FRIBBLERS
FRIBBLES
FRIDDLING
FRIBBLISH
FRICADEL
FRICADELS
FRICASSEE
FRICASSEED
FRICASSEEING
FRICASSEES
FRICATIVE
FRICATIVES
FRICHT
FRICHTED
FRICHTING
FRICHTS
FRICTION
FRICTIONS
FRIDGE
FRIDGED

FRIDGES
FRIDGING
FRIED
FRIEDCAKE
FRIEDCAKES
FRIEND
FRIENDED
FRIENDING
FRIENDINGS
FRIENDLIER
FRIENDLIES
FRIENDLIEST
FRIENDLY
FRIENDS
FRIER
FRIERS
FRIES
FRIEZE
FRIEZED
FRIEZES
FRIEZING
FRIG
FRIGATE
FRIGATES
FRIGATOON
FRIGATOONS
FRIGES
FRIGGED
FRIGGER
FRIGGERS
FRIGGING
FRIGGINGS
FRIGHT
FRIGHTED
FRIGHTEN
FRIGHTENED
FRIGHTENING
FRIGHTENS
FRIGHTFUL
FRIGHTING
FRIGHTS
FRIGID
FRIGIDER
FRIGIDEST
FRIGIDITIES
FRIGIDITY
FRIGIDLY
FRIGOT
FRIGOTS
FRIGS
FRIJOL
FRIJOLE
FRIJOLES
FRIKKADEL
FRIKKADELS
FRILL
FRILLED
FRILLIER
FRILLIES
FRILLIEST
FRILLING
FRILLINGS
FRILLS
FRILLY
FRINGE
FRINGED
FRINGES
FRINGIER

FRINGIEST
FRINGING
FRINGY
FRIPON
FRIPONS
FRIPPER
FRIPPERER
FRIPPERERS
FRIPPERIES
FRIPPERS
FRIPPERY
FRIS
FRISES
FRISETTE
FRISETTES
FRISEUR
FRISEURS
FRISK
FRISKA
FRISKAS
FRISKED
FRISKER
FRISKERS
FRISKET
FRISKETS
FRISKFUL
FRISKIER
FRISKIEST
FRISKILY
FRISKING
FRISKINGS
FRISKS
FRISKY
FRISSON
FRISSONS
FRIST
FRISTED
FRISTING
FRISTS
FRISURE
FRISURES
FRIT
FRITFLIES
FRITFLY
FRITH
FRITHBORH
FRITHBORHS
FRITHGILD
FRITHGILDS
FRITHS
FRITS
FRITTED
FRITTER
FRITTERED
FRITTERER
FRITTERERS
FRITTERING
FRITTERS
FRITTING
FRITURE
FRITURES
FRIVOL
FRIVOLITIES
FRIVOLITY
FRIVOLLED
FRIVOLLING
FRIVOLOUS
FRIVOLS

FRIZ
FRIZE
FRIZES
FRIZING
FRIZZ
FRIZZANTE
FRIZZED
FRIZZES
FRIZZIER
FRIZZIEST
FRIZZING
FRIZZLE
FRIZZLED
FRIZZLES
FRIZZLIER
FRIZZLIEST
FRIZZLING
FRIZZLY
FRIZZY
FRO
FROCK
FROCKED
FROCKING
FROCKINGS
FROCKLESS
FROCKS
FROG
FROGBIT
FROGBITS
FROGGED
FROGGERIES
FROGGERY
FROGGIER
FROGGIEST
FROGGING
FROGGINGS
FROGGY
FROGLET
FROGLETS
FROGLING
FROGLINGS
FROGMAN
FROGMOUTH
FROGMOUTHS
FROGS
FROISE
FROISES
FROLIC
FROLICKED
FROLICKING
FROLICS
FROM
FROMENTIES
FROMENTY
FROND
FRONDAGE
FRONDAGES
FRONDED
FRONDENT
FRONDEUR
FRONDEURS
FRONDOSE
FRONDS
FRONT
FRONTAGE
FRONTAGER
FRONTAGERS

FRONTAGES
FRONTAL
FRONTALS
FRONTED
FRONTIER
FRONTIERED
FRONTIERING
FRONTIERS
FRONTING
FRONTLESS
FRONTLET
FRONTLETS
FRONTMAN
FRONTMEN
FRONTON
FRONTONS
FRONTOON
FRONTOONS
FRONTS
FRONTWARD
FRONTWARDS
FRONTWAYS
FRONTWISE
FRORE
FROREN
FRORN
FRORNE
FRORY
FROST
FROSTBIT
FROSTBITE
FROSTBITES
FROSTBITING
FROSTBITTEN
FROSTED
FROSTIER
FROSTIEST
FROSTILY
FROSTING
FROSTINGS
FROSTLESS
FROSTS
FROSTWORK
FROSTWORKS
FROSTY
FROTH
FROTHED
FROTHERIES
FROTHERY
FROTHIER
FROTHIEST
FROTHILY
FROTHING
FROTHLESS
FROTHS
FROTHY
FROTTAGE
FROTTAGES
FROTTEUR
FROTTEURS
FROUGHIER
FROUGHIEST
FROUGHY
FROUNCE
FROUNCED
FROUNCES
FROUNCING
FROW

FROWARD
FROWARDLY
FROWARDS
FROWIE
FROWIER
FROWIEST
FROWN
FROWNED
FROWNING
FROWNS
FROWS
FROWSIER
FROWSIEST
FROWST
FROWSTED
FROWSTER
FROWSTERS
FROWSTIER
FROWSTIEST
FROWSTING
FROWSTS
FROWSTY
FROWSY
FROWY
FROWZIER
FROWZIEST
FROWZY
FROZE
FROZEN
FRUCTED
FRUCTIFIED
FRUCTIFIES
FRUCTIFY
FRUCTIFYING
FRUCTOSE
FRUCTOSES
FRUCTUARIES
FRUCTUARY
FRUCTUATE
FRUCTUATED
FRUCTUATES
FRUCTUATING
FRUCTUOUS
FRUGAL
FRUGALIST
FRUGALISTS
FRUGALITIES
FRUGALITY
FRUGALLY
FRUICT
FRUICTS
FRUIT
FRUITAGE
FRUITAGES
FRUITED
FRUITER
FRUITERER
FRUITERERS
FRUITERIES
FRUITERS
FRUITERY
FRUITFUL
FRUITIER
FRUITIEST
FRUITING
FRUITINGS
FRUITION
FRUITIONS

FRUITIVE
FRUITLESS
FRUITLET
FRUITLETS
FRUITS
FRUITWOOD
FRUITWOODS
FRUITY
FRUMENTIES
FRUMENTY
FRUMP
FRUMPED
FRUMPIER
FRUMPIEST
FRUMPING
FRUMPISH
FRUMPLE
FRUMPLED
FRUMPLES
FRUMPLING
FRUMPS
FRUMPY
FRUSH
FRUSHED
FRUSHES
FRUSHING
FRUST
FRUSTA
FRUSTRATE
FRUSTRATED
FRUSTRATES
FRUSTRATING
FRUSTS
FRUSTULE
FRUSTULES
FRUSTUM
FRUSTUMS
FRUTEX
FRUTICES
FRUTICOSE
FRUTIFIED
FRUTIFIES
FRUTIFY
FRUTIFYING
FRY
FRYER
FRYERS
FRYING
FRYINGS
FUB
FUBBED
FUBBERIES
FUBBERY
FUBBIER
FUBBIEST
FUBBING
FUBBY
FUBS
FUBSIER
FUBSIEST
FUBSY
FUCHSIA
FUCHSIAS
FUCHSINE
FUCHSINES
FUCHSITE
FUCHSITES
FUCI

FUCK
FUCKED
FUCKER
FUCKERS
FUCKING
FUCKINGS
FUCKS
FUCOID
FUCOIDAL
FUCOIDS
FUCUS
FUCUSED
FUCUSES
FUD
FUDDLE
FUDDLED
FUDDLER
FUDDLERS
FUDDLES
FUDDLING
FUDDLINGS
FUDGE
FUDGED
FUDGES
FUDGING
FUDS
FUEL
FUELLED
FUELLER
FUELLERS
FUELLING
FUELS
FUERO
FUEROS
FUFF
FUFFED
FUFFIER
FUFFIEST
FUFFING
FUFFS
FUFFY
FUG
FUGACIOUS
FUGACITIES
FUGACITY
FUGAL
FUGALLY
FUGATO
FUGATOS
FUGGED
FUGGIER
FUGGIEST
FUGGING
FUGGY
FUGHETTA
FUGHETTAS
FUGIE
FUGIES
FUGITIVE
FUGITIVES
FUGLE
FUGLED
FUGLEMAN
FUGLEMEN
FUGLES
FUGLING
FUGS
FUGUE

FUGUES
FUGUIST
FUGUISTS
FULCRATE
FULCRUM
FULCRUMS
FULFIL
FULFILLED
FULFILLER
FULFILLERS
FULFILLING
FULFILLINGS
FULFILS
FULGENCIES
FULGENCY
FULGENT
FULGENTLY
FULGID
FULGOR
FULGOROUS
FULGORS
FULGOUR
FULGOURS
FULGURAL
FULGURANT
FULGURATE
FULGURATED
FULGURATES
FULGURATING
FULGURITE
FULGURITES
FULGUROUS
FULHAM
FULHAMS
FULL
FULLAGE
FULLAGES
FULLAM
FULLAMS
FULLAN
FULLANS
FULLED
FULLER
FULLERS
FULLEST
FULLING
FULLISH
FULLNESS
FULLNESSES
FULLS
FULLY
FULMAR
FULMARS
FULMINANT
FULMINANTS
FULMINATE
FULMINATED
FULMINATES
FULMINATING
FULMINE
FULMINED
FULMINES
FULMINING
FULMINOUS
FULNESS
FULNESSES
FULSOME

FULSOMELY
FULSOMER
FULSOMEST
FULVID
FULVOUS
FUM
FUMADO
FUMADOES
FUMADOS
FUMAGE
FUMAGES
FUMAROLE
FUMAROLES
FUMATORIA
FUMATORIES
FUMATORY
FUMBLE
FUMBLED
FUMBLER
FUMBLERS
FUMBLES
FUMBLING
FUME
FUMED
FUMEROLE
FUMEROLES
FUMES
FUMET
FUMETS
FUMETTE
FUMETTES
FUMETTI
FUMETTO
FUMIER
FUMIEST
FUMIGANT
FUMIGANTS
FUMIGATE
FUMIGATED
FUMIGATES
FUMIGATING
FUMIGATOR
FUMIGATORS
FUMING
FUMITORIES
FUMITORY
FUMOSITIES
FUMOSITY
FUMOUS
FUMS
FUMY
FUN
FUNCTION
FUNCTIONED
FUNCTIONING
FUNCTIONS
FUND
FUNDABLE
FUNDAMENT
FUNDAMENTS
FUNDED
FUNDER
FUNDERS
FUNDI
FUNDING
FUNDINGS
FUNDIS
FUNDLESS

FUNDS
FUNDUS
FUNEBRAL
FUNÈBRE
FUNEBRIAL
FUNERAL
FUNERALS
FUNERARY
FUNEREAL
FUNEST
FUNFAIR
FUNFAIRS
FUNG
FUNGAL
FUNGI
FUNGIBLES
FUNGICIDE
FUNGICIDES
FUNGIFORM
FUNGOID
FUNGOIDAL
FUNGOSITIES
FUNGOSITY
FUNGOUS
FUNGS
FUNGUS
FUNGUSES
FUNICLE
FUNICLES
FUNICULAR
FUNICULI
FUNICULUS
FUNK
FUNKED
FUNKHOLE
FUNKHOLES
FUNKIA
FUNKIAS
FUNKIER
FUNKIEST
FUNKINESS
FUNKINESSES
FUNKING
FUNKS
FUNKY
FUNNED
FUNNEL
FUNNELLED
FUNNELLING
FUNNELS
FUNNIER
FUNNIES
FUNNIEST
FUNNILY
FUNNINESS
FUNNINESSES
FUNNING
FUNNY
FUNS
FUR
FURACIOUS
FURACITIES
FURACITY
FURAL
FURALS
FURAN
FURANE
FURANES

FURANS
FURBELOW
FURBELOWED
FURBELOWING
FURBELOWS
FURBISH
FURBISHED
FURBISHER
FURBISHERS
FURBISHES
FURBISHING
FURCAL
FURCATE
FURCATED
FURCATION
FURCATIONS
FURCULA
FURCULAR
FURCULAS
FURDER
FUREUR
FUREURS
FURFAIR
FURFAIRS
FURFUR
FURFURALS
FURFURAN
FURFURANS
FURFUROL
FURFUROLE
FURFUROLES
FURFUROLS
FURFUROUS
FURFURS
FURIBUND
FURIES
FURIOSITIES
FURIOSITY
FURIOSO
FURIOSOS
FURIOUS
FURIOUSLY
FURL
FURLANA
FURLANAS
FURLED
FURLING
FURLONG
FURLONGS
FURLOUGH
FURLOUGHED
FURLOUGHING
FURLOUGHS
FURLS
FURMENTIES
FURMENTY
FURMETIES
FURMETY
FURMITIES
FURMITY
FURNACE
FURNACED
FURNACES
FURNACING
FURNIMENT
FURNIMENTS
FURNISH

FURNISHED
FURNISHER
FURNISHERS
FURNISHES
FURNISHING
FURNISHINGS
FURNITURE
FURNITURES
FUROL
FUROLE
FUROLES
FUROLS
FUROR
FURORE
FURORES
FURORS
FURPHIES
FURPHY
FURR
FURRED
FURRIER
FURRIERIES
FURRIERS
FURRIERY
FURRIEST
FURRING
FURRINGS
FURROW
FURROWED
FURROWING
FURROWS
FURROWY
FURRS
FURRY
FURS
FURTH
FURTHER
FURTHERED
FURTHERER
FURTHERERS
FURTHERING
FURTHERS
FURTHEST
FURTIVE
FURTIVELY
FURTIVER
FURTIVEST
FURUNCLE
FURUNCLES
FURY
FURZE
FURZES
FURZIER
FURZIEST
FURZY
FUSAIN
FUSAINS
FUSAROL
FUSAROLE
FUSAROLES
FUSAROLS
FUSC
FUSCOUS
FUSE
FUSED
FUSEE
FUSEES
FUSELAGE

FUSELAGES
FUSES
FUSHION
FUSHIONS
FUSIBLE
FUSIFORM
FUSIL
FUSILE
FUSILEER
FUSILEERS
FUSILIER
FUSILIERS
FUSILLADE
FUSILLADES
FUSILS
FUSING
FUSION
FUSIONISM
FUSIONISMS
FUSIONIST
FUSIONISTS
FUSIONS
FUSS
FUSSED
FUSSER
FUSSERS
FUSSES
FUSSIER
FUSSIEST
FUSSILY
FUSSINESS
FUSSINESSES
FUSSING
FUSSY
FUST
FUSTED
FUSTET
FUSTETS
FUSTIAN
FUSTIANS
FUSTIC
FUSTICS
FUSTIER
FUSTIEST
FUSTIGATE
FUSTIGATED
FUSTIGATES
FUSTIGATING
FUSTILUGS
FUSTILY
FUSTINESS
FUSTINESSES
FUSTING
FUSTOC
FUSTOCS
FUSTS
FUSTY
FUTCHEL
FUTCHELS
FUTHARK
FUTHARKS
FUTHORC
FUTHORCS
FUTHORK
FUTHORKS
FUTILE
FUTILELY
FUTILER

FUTILEST
FUTILITIES
FUTILITY
FUTON
FUTONS
FUTTOCK
FUTTOCKS
FUTURE
FUTURES
FUTURISM

FUTURISMS
FUTURIST
FUTURISTS
FUTURITIES
FUTURITY
FUZE
FUZEE
FUZEES
FUZES
FUZZ

FUZZED
FUZZES
FUZZIER
FUZZIEST
FUZZILY
FUZZINESS
FUZZINESSES
FUZZING
FUZZLE
FUZZLED

FUZZLES
FUZZLING
FUZZY
FY
FYKE
FYKED
FYKES
FYKING
FYLE
FYLES

FYLFOT
FYLFOTS
FYNBOS
FYNBOSES
FYRD
FYRDS
FYTTE
FYTTES

G

GAB
GABARDINE
GABARDINES
GABBARD
GABBARDS
GABBART
GABBARTS
GABBED
GABBER
GABBERS
GABBIER
GABBIEST
GABBING
GABBLE
GABBLED
GABBLER
GABBLERS
GABBLES
GABBLING
GABBLINGS
GABBRO
GABBROIC
GABBROID
GABBROS
GABBY
GABELLE
GABELLER
GABELLERS
GABELLES
GABERDINE
GABERDINES
GABFEST
GABFESTS
GABIES
GABION
GABIONADE
GABIONADES
GABIONAGE
GABIONAGES
GABIONED
GABIONS
GABLE
GABLED
GABLES
GABLET
GABLETS
GADNASH
GABNASHES
GABS
GABY
GAD
GADABOUT
GADABOUTS
GADDED
GADDER
GADDERS
GADDING
GADE
GADES
GADFLIES
GADFLY
GADGE
GADGES

GADGET
GADGETEER
GADGETEERS
GADGETRIES
GADGETRY
GADGETS
GADGIE
GADGIES
GADI
GADIS
GADJE
GADJES
GADLING
GADLINGS
GADOID
GADOIDS
GADROON
GADROONED
GADROONS
GADS
GADSMAN
GADSMEN
GADSO
GADSOS
GADWALL
GADWALLS
GADZOOKS
GAE
GAED
GAELICISE
GAELICISED
GAELICISES
GAELICISING
GAELICISM
GAELICISMS
GAELICIZE
GAELICIZED
GAELICIZES
GAELICIZING
GAES
GAFF
GAFFE
GAFFED
GAFFER
GAFFERS
GAFFES
GAFFING
GAFFINGS
GAFFS
GAG
GAGA
GAGAKU
GAGAKUS
GAGE
GAGED
GAGES
GAGGED
GAGGER
GAGGERS
GAGGING
GAGGLE
GAGGLED
GAGGLES

GAGGLING
GAGGLINGS
GAGING
GAGMAN
GAGMEN
GAGS
GAGSTER
GAGSTERS
GAHNITE
GAHNITES
GAID
GAIDS
GAIETIES
GAIETY
GAILLARD
GAILLARDE
GAILY
GAIN
GAINABLE
GAINED
GAINER
GAINERS
GAINEST
GAINFUL
GAINFULLY
GAINING
GAININGS
GAINLESS
GAINLIER
GAINLIEST
GAINLY
GAINS
GAINSAID
GAINSAY
GAINSAYER
GAINSAYERS
GAINSAYING
GAINSAYINGS
GAINSAYS
GAIR
GAIRFOWL
GAIRFOWLS
GAIRS
GAIT
GAITED
GAITER
GAITERS
GAITS
GAITT
GAITTS
GAJO
GAJOS
GAL
GALA
GALABEA
GALABEAH
GALABEAHS
GALABEAS
GALABIA
GALABIAH
GALABIAHS
GALABIAS
GALABIEH

GALABIEHS
GALABIYA
GALABIYAH
GALABIYAHS
GALABIYAS
GALABIYEH
GALABIYEHS
GALACTIC
GALACTOSE
GALACTOSES
GALAGE
GALAGES
GALAH
GALAHS
GALANGA
GALANGAL
GALANGALS
GALANGAS
GALANT
GALANTINE
GALANTINES
GALAPAGO
GALAPAGOS
GALAS
GALATEA
GALATEAS
GALAXIES
GALAXY
GALBANUM
GALBANUMS
GALDRAGON
GALDRAGONS
GALE
GALEA
GALEAS
GALEATE
GALEATED
GALENA
GALENAS
GALENGALE
GALENGALES
GALENITE
GALENITES
GALENOID
GALERE
GALERES
GALES
GALILEE
GALILEES
GALINGALE
GALINGALES
GALIONGEE
GALIONGEES
GALIOT
GALIOTS
GALIPOT
GALIPOTS
GALL
GALLABEA
GALLABEAH
GALLABEAHS
GALLABEAS
GALLABIA

GALLABIAH
GALLABIAHS
GALLABIAS
GALLABIEH
GALLABIEHS
GALLABIYA
GALLABIYAS
GALLANT
GALLANTER
GALLANTEST
GALLANTLY
GALLANTRIES
GALLANTRY
GALLANTS
GALLATE
GALLATES
GALLEASS
GALLEASSES
GALLED
GALLEON
GALLEONS
GALLERIED
GALLERIES
GALLERY
GALLERYING
GALLET
GALLETED
GALLETING
GALLETS
GALLEY
GALLEYS
GALLIARD
GALLIARDS
GALLIASS
GALLIASSES
GALLICISE
GALLICISED
GALLICISES
GALLICISING
GALLICISM
GALLICISMS
GALLICIZE
GALLICIZED
GALLICIZES
GALLICIZING
GALLIED
GALLIES
GALLINAZO
GALLINAZOS
GALLING
GALLINGLY
GALLINULE
GALLINULES
GALLIOT
GALLIOTS
GALLIPOT
GALLIPOTS
GALLISE
GALLISED
GALLISES
GALLISING
GALLISISE
GALLISISED

GALLISISES
GALLISISING
GALLISIZE
GALLISIZED
GALLISIZES
GALLISIZING
GALLIUM
GALLIUMS
GALLIVANT
GALLIVANTED
GALLIVANTING
GALLIVANTS
GALLIVAT
GALLIVATS
GALLIWASP
GALLIWASPS
GALLIZE
GALLIZED
GALLIZES
GALLIZING
GALLON
GALLONAGE
GALLONAGES
GALLONS
GALLOON
GALLOONED
GALLOONS
GALLOP
GALLOPADE
GALLOPADED
GALLOPADES
GALLOPADING
GALLOPED
GALLOPER
GALLOPERS
GALLOPHIL
GALLOPHILS
GALLOPING
GALLOPS
GALLOW
GALLOWED
GALLOWING
GALLOWS
GALLOWSES
GALLS
GALLUMPH
GALLUMPHED
GALLUMPHING
GALLUMPHS
GALLUS
GALLUSES
GALLY
GALLYING
GALOCHE
GALOCHED
GALOCHES
GALOCHING
GALOOT
GALOOTS
GALOP
GALOPED
GALOPIN
GALOPING
GALOPINS
GALOPPED
GALOPPING
GALOPS
GALORE
GALOSH
GALOSHED

GALOSHES
GALOSHING
GALOWSES
GALRAVAGE
GALRAVAGED
GALRAVAGES
GALRAVAGING
GALS
GALTONIA
GALTONIAS
GALUMPH
GALUMPHED
GALUMPHER
GALUMPHERS
GALUMPHING
GALUMPHS
GALUT
GALUTH
GALUTHS
GALUTS
GALVANIC
GALVANISE
GALVANISED
GALVANISES
GALVANISING
GALVANISM
GALVANISMS
GALVANIST
GALVANISTS
GALVANIZE
GALVANIZED
GALVANIZES
GALVANIZING
GAM
GAMASH
GAMASHES
GAMB
GAMBA
GAMBADO
GAMBADOES
GAMBADOS
GAMBAS
GAMBESON
GAMBESONS
GAMBET
GAMBETS
GAMBIER
GAMBIERS
GAMBIR
GAMBIRS
GAMBIST
GAMBISTS
GAMBIT
GAMBITED
GAMBITING
GAMBITS
GAMBLE
GAMBLED
GAMBLER
GAMBLERS
GAMBLES
GAMBLING
GAMBLINGS
GAMBOGE
GAMBOGES
GAMBOGIAN
GAMBOGIC
GAMBOL
GAMBOLLED
GAMBOLLING

GAMBOLS
GAMBREL
GAMBRELS
GAMBROON
GAMBROONS
GAMBS
GAME
GAMED
GAMELAN
GAMELANS
GAMELY
GAMENESS
GAMENESSES
GAMER
GAMES
GAMESIER
GAMESIEST
GAMESOME
GAMEST
GAMESTER
GAMESTERS
GAMESY
GAMETAL
GAMETE
GAMETES
GAMETIC
GAMIC
GAMIER
GAMIEST
GAMIN
GAMINE
GAMINERIE
GAMINERIES
GAMINES
GAMING
GAMINGS
GAMINS
GAMMA
GAMMADION
GAMMADIONS
GAMMAS
GAMMATION
GAMMATIONS
GAMME
GAMMED
GAMMER
GAMMERS
GAMMES
GAMMIER
GAMMIEST
GAMMING
GAMMOCK
GAMMOCKED
GAMMOCKING
GAMMOCKS
GAMMON
GAMMONED
GAMMONER
GAMMONERS
GAMMONING
GAMMONINGS
GAMMONS
GAMMY
GAMP
GAMPISH
GAMPS
GAMS
GAMUT
GAMUTS
GAMY

GAN
GANCH
GANCHED
GANCHES
GANCHING
GANDER
GANDERISM
GANDERISMS
GANDERS
GANE
GANG
GANGBOARD
GANGBOARDS
GANGED
GANGER
GANGERS
GANGING
GANGINGS
GANGLAND
GANGLANDS
GANGLIA
GANGLIAR
GANGLIATE
GANGLIER
GANGLIEST
GANGLING
GANGLION
GANGLIONS
GANGLY
GANGPLANK
GANGPLANKS
GANGREL
GANGRELS
GANGRENE
GANGRENED
GANGRENES
GANGRENING
GANGS
GANGSMAN
GANGSMEN
GANGSTER
GANGSTERS
GANGUE
GANGUES
GANGWAY
GANGWAYS
GANISTER
GANISTERS
GANJA
GANJAS
GANNET
GANNETRIES
GANNETRY
GANNETS
GANNISTER
GANNISTERS
GANOID
GANOIDS
GANOIN
GANOINS
GANT
GANTED
GANTING
GANTLET
GANTLETS
GANTLINE
GANTLINES
GANTLOPE
GANTLOPES
GANTRIES

GANTRY
GANTS
GAOL
GAOLED
GAOLER
GAOLERESS
GAOLERESSES
GAOLERS
GAOLING
GAOLS
GAP
GAPE
GAPED
GAPER
GAPERS
GAPES
GAPESEED
GAPESEEDS
GAPEWORM
GAPEWORMS
GAPING
GAPINGLY
GAPINGS
GAPÓ
GAPÓS
GAPPED
GAPPIER
GAPPIEST
GAPPING
GAPPY
GAPS
GAR
GARAGE
GARAGED
GARAGES
GARAGING
GARAGINGS
GARB
GARBAGE
GARBAGES
GARBANZO
GARBANZOS
GARBE
GARBED
GARBES
GARBING
GARBLE
GARBLED
GARBLER
GARBLERS
GARBLES
GARBLING
GARBLINGS
GARBO
GARBOARD
GARBOARDS
GARBOIL
GARBOILS
GARBOS
GARBS
GARÇON
GARÇONS
GARDA
GARDAI
GARDANT
GARDANTS
GARDEN
GARDENED
GARDENER
GARDENERS

GARDENIA
GARDENIAS
GARDENING
GARDENINGS
GARDENS
GARDEROBE
GARDEROBES
GARDYLOO
GARDYLOOS
GARE
GAREFOWL
GAREFOWLS
GARFISH
GARFISHES
GARGANEY
GARGANEYS
GARGARISE
GARGARISED
GARGARISES
GARGARISING
GARGARISM
GARGARISMS
GARGARIZE
GARGARIZED
GARGARIZES
GARGARIZING
GARGET
GARGETS
GARGLE
GARGLED
GARGLES
GARGLING
GARGOYLE
GARGOYLES
GARIAL
GARIALS
GARIBALDI
GARIBALDIS
GARIGUE
GARIGUES
GARISH
GARISHED
GARISHES
GARISHING
GARISHLY
GARJAN
GARJANS
GARLAND
GARLANDED
GARLANDING
GARLANDRIES
GARLANDRY
GARLANDS
GARLIC
GARLICKY
GARLICS
GARMENT
GARMENTED
GARMENTING
GARMENTS
GARNER
GARNERED
GARNERING
GARNERS
GARNET
GARNETS
GARNI
GARNISH
GARNISHED
GARNISHEE

GARNISHEED
GARNISHEEING
GARNISHEES
GARNISHER
GARNISHERS
GARNISHES
GARNISHING
GARNISHINGS
GARNISHRIES
GARNISHRY
GARNITURE
GARNITURES
GAROTTE
GAROTTED
GAROTTER
GAROTTERS
GAROTTES
GAROTTING
GAROTTINGS
GARPIKE
GARPIKES
GARRAN
GARRANS
GARRE
GARRED
GARRES
GARRET
GARRETED
GARRETEER
GARRETEERS
GARRETS
GARRIGUE
GARRIGUES
GARRING
GARRISON
GARRISONED
GARRISONING
GARRISONS
GARRON
GARRONS
GARROT
GARROTE
GARROTED
GARROTES
GARROTING
GARROTS
GARROTTE
GARROTTED
GARROTTER
GARROTTERS
GARROTTES
GARROTTING
GARROTTINGS
GARRULITIES
GARRULITY
GARRULOUS
GARRYA
GARRYAS
GARRYOWEN
GARRYOWENS
GARS
GART
GARTER
GARTERED
GARTERING
GARTERS
GARTH
GARTHS
GARUDA
GARUDAS

GARUM
GARUMS
GARVIE
GARVIES
GARVOCK
GARVOCKS
GAS
GASAHOL
GASAHOLS
GASALIER
GASALIERS
GASCON
GASCONADE
GASCONADED
GASCONADES
GASCONADING
GASCONISM
GASCONISMS
GASCONS
GASEITIES
GASEITY
GASELIER
GASELIERS
GASEOUS
GASES
GASFIELD
GASFIELDS
GASH
GASHED
GASHES
GASHFUL
GASHING
GASHLY
GASIFIED
GASIFIER
GASIFIERS
GASIFIES
GASIFORM
GASIFY
GASIFYING
GASKET
GASKETS
GASKIN
GASKINS
GASLIGHT
GASLIGHTS
GASLIT
GASMAN
GASMEN
GASOGENE
GASOGENES
GASOHOL
GASOHOLS
GASOLENE
GASOLENES
GASOLIER
GASOLIERS
GASOLINE
GASOLINES
GASOMETER
GASOMETERS
GASOMETRIES
GASOMETRY
GASP
GASPED
GASPER
GASPEREAU
GASPEREAUS
GASPERS
GASPIER

GASPIEST
GASPINESS
GASPINESSES
GASPING
GASPINGLY
GASPINGS
GASPS
GASPY
GASSED
GASSES
GASSIER
GASSIEST
GASSINESS
GASSINESSES
GASSING
GASSINGS
GASSY
GAST
GASTED
GASTFULL
GASTING
GASTNESS
GASTNESSE
GASTNESSES
GASTRAEA
GASTRAEAS
GASTRAEUM
GASTRAEUMS
GASTRIC
GASTRIN
GASTRINS
GASTRITIS
GASTRITISES
GASTROPOD
GASTROPODS
GASTRULA
GASTRULAE
GASTRULAS
GASTS
GAT
GATE
GÂTEAU
GÂTEAUS
GÂTEAUX
GATECRASH
GATECRASHED
GATECRASHES
GATECRASHING
GATED
GATEFOLD
GATEFOLDS
GATELEG
GATELESS
GATES
GATEWAY
GATEWAYS
GATH
GATHER
GATHERED
GATHERER
GATHERERS
GATHERING
GATHERINGS
GATHERS
GATHS
GATING
GATINGS
GATS
GAU
GAUCHE

GAUCHER
GAUCHERIE
GAUCHERIES
GAUCHESCO
GAUCHEST
GAUCHO
GAUCHOS
GAUCIE
GAUCIER
GAUCIEST
GAUCY
GAUD
GAUDEAMUS
GAUDEAMUSES
GAUDED
GAUDERIES
GAUDERY
GAUDGIE
GAUDGIES
GAUDIER
GAUDIES
GAUDIEST
GAUDILY
GAUDINESS
GAUDINESSES
GAUDINO
GAUDS
GAUDY
GAUFER
GAUFERS
GAUFRE
GAUFRES
GAUGE
GAUGEABLE
GAUGED
GAUGER
GAUGERS
GAUGES
GAUGING
GAUGINGS
GAUJE
GAUJES
GAULEITER
GAULEITERS
GAULT
GAULTER
GAULTERS
GAULTS
GAUM
GAUMED
GAUMIER
GAUMIEST
GAUMING
GAUMLESS
GAUMS
GAUMY
GAUN
GAUNCH
GAUNCHED
GAUNCHES
GAUNCHING
GAUNT
GAUNTED
GAUNTER
GAUNTEST
GAUNTING
GAUNTLET
GAUNTLETS
GAUNTLY
GAUNTNESS

GAUNTNESSES
GAUNTREE
GAUNTREES
GAUNTRIES
GAUNTRY
GAUNTS
GAUP
GAUPED
GAUPER
GAUPERS
GAUPING
GAUPS
GAUPUS
GAUPUSES
GAUR
GAURS
GAUS
GAUSS
GAUSSES
GAUSSIAN
GAUZE
GAUZES
GAUZIER
GAUZIEST
GAUZINESS
GAUZINESSES
GAUZY
GAVAGE
GAVAGES
GAVE
GAVEL
GAVELKIND
GAVELKINDS
GAVELMAN
GAVELMEN
GAVELOCK
GAVELOCKS
GAVELS
GAVIAL
GAVIALS
GAVOTTE
GAVOTTES
GAWCIER
GAWCIEST
GAWCY
GAWD
GAWDS
GAWK
GAWKED
GAWKER
GAWKERS
GAWKIER
GAWKIES
GAWKIEST
GAWKIHOOD
GAWKIHOODS
GAWKINESS
GAWKINESSES
GAWKING
GAWKS
GAWKY
GAWP
GAWPED
GAWPER
GAWPERS
GAWPING
GAWPS
GAWPUS
GAWPUSES
GAWSIER

GAWSIEST
GAWSY
GAY
GAYAL
GAYALS
GAYER
GAYEST
GAYNESS
GAYNESSES
GAYS
GAYSOME
GAZAL
GAZALS
GAZE
GAZEBO
GAZEBOES
GAZEBOS
GAZED
GAZEFUL
GAZEL
GAZELLE
GAZELLES
GAZELS
GAZEMENT
GAZEMENTS
GAZER
GAZERS
GAZES
GAZETTE
GAZETTED
GAZETTEER
GAZETTEERED
GAZETTEERING
GAZETTEERS
GAZETTES
GAZETTING
GAZIER
GAZIEST
GAZING
GAZOGENE
GAZOGENES
GAZON
GAZONS
GAZOO
GAZOOKA
GAZOOKAS
GAZOON
GAZOONS
GAZOOS
GAZPACHO
GAZPACHOS
GAZUMP
GAZUMPED
GAZUMPING
GAZUMPS
GAZY
GEAL
GEALED
GEALING
GEALOUS
GEALOUSIES
GEALOUSY
GEALS
GEAN
GEANS
GEAR
GEARBOX
GEARBOXES
GEARE
GEARED

GEARES
GEARING
GEARINGS
GEARLESS
GEARS
GEASON
GEAT
GEATS
GEBUR
GEBURS
GECK
GECKED
GECKING
GECKO
GECKOES
GECKOS
GECKS
GED
GEDS
GEE
GEEBUNG
GEEBUNGS
GEED
GEEING
GEES
GEESE
GEEZER
GEEZERS
GEFUFFLE
GEFUFFLED
GEFUFFLES
GEFUFFLING
GEISHA
GEISHAS
GEIST
GEISTS
GEIT
GEITS
GEL
GELADA
GELADAS
GELASTIC
GELATI
GELATIN
GELATINE
GELATINES
GELATINS
GELATION
GELATIONS
GELATO
GELD
GELDED
GELDER
GELDERS
GELDING
GELDINGS
GELDS
GELID
GELIDER
GELIDEST
GELIDITIES
GELIDITY
GELIDLY
GELIDNESS
GELIDNESSES
GELIGNITE
GELIGNITES
GELLED
GELLING
GELLY

GELOSIES
GELOSY
GELS
GELSEMINE
GELSEMINES
GELSEMIUM
GELSEMIUMS
GELT
GELTS
GEM
GEMATRIA
GEMATRIAS
GEMEL
GEMELS
GEMINATE
GEMINATED
GEMINATES
GEMINATING
GEMINI
GEMINIES
GEMINOUS
GEMINY
GEMMA
GEMMAE
GEMMAN
GEMMATE
GEMMATED
GEMMATES
GEMMATING
GEMMATION
GEMMATIONS
GEMMATIVE
GEMMED
GEMMEN
GEMMEOUS
GEMMERIES
GEMMERY
GEMMIER
GEMMIEST
GEMMING
GEMMOLOGIES
GEMMOLOGY
GEMMULE
GEMMULES
GEMMY
GEMOLOGIES
GEMOLOGY
GEMONY
GEMOT
GEMOTS
GEMS
GEMSBOK
GEMSBOKS
GEMSTONE
GEMSTONES
GEMÜTLICH
GEN
GENA
GENAL
GENAPPE
GENAPPES
GENAS
GENDARME
GENDARMES
GENDER
GENDERED
GENDERING
GENDERS
GENE
GENEALOGIES

GENEALOGY
GENERA
GENERABLE
GENERAL
GENERALE
GENERALIA
GENERALLED
GENERALLING
GENERALLY
GENERALS
GENERANT
GENERANTS
GENERATE
GENERATED
GENERATES
GENERATING
GENERATOR
GENERATORS
GENERIC
GENERICAL
GENERICS
GENEROUS
GENES
GENESES
GENESIS
GENET
GENETIC
GENETICAL
GENETICS
GENETRICES
GENETRIX
GENETRIXES
GENETS
GENETTE
GENETTES
GENEVA
GENEVAS
GENIAL
GENIALISE
GENIALISED
GENIALISES
GENIALISING
GENIALITIES
GENIALITY
GENIALIZE
GENIALIZED
GENIALIZES
GENIALIZING
GENIALLY
GENIC
GENIE
GENIES
GENII
GENIP
GENIPAP
GENIPAPS
GENIPS
GENISTA
GENISTAS
GENITAL
GENITALIA
GENITALIC
GENITALS
GENITIVAL
GENITIVE
GENITIVES
GENITOR
GENITORS
GENITRICES
GENITRIX

GENITRIXES
GENITURE
GENITURES
GENIUS
GENIUSES
GENIZAH
GENIZAHS
GENNET
GENNETS
GENOA
GENOAS
GENOCIDAL
GENOCIDE
GENOCIDES
GENOM
GENOME
GENOMES
GENOMS
GENOTYPE
GENOTYPES
GENOTYPIC
GENRE
GENRES
GENS
GENSDARMES
GENT
GENTEEL
GENTEELER
GENTEELEST
GENTEELLY
GENTES
GENTIAN
GENTIANS
GENTIER
GENTIEST
GENTILE
GENTILES
GENTILIC
GENTILISE
GENTILISED
GENTILISES
GENTILISH
GENTILISING
GENTILISM
GENTILISMS
GENTILITIES
GENTILITY
GENTILIZE
GENTILIZED
GENTILIZES
GENTILIZING
GENTLE
GENTLED
GENTLEMAN
GENTLEMEN
GENTLER
GENTLES
GENTLEST
GENTLING
GENTLY
GENTOO
GENTOOS
GENTRICE
GENTRICES
GENTRIES
GENTRIFIED
GENTRIFIES
GENTRIFY
GENTRIFYING
GENTRY

GENTS
GENTY
GENU
GENUFLECT
GENUFLECTED
GENUFLECTING
GENUFLECTS
GENUINE
GENUINELY
GENUS
GENUSES
GEO
GEOCARPIC
GEOCARPIES
GEOCARPY
GEODE
GEODES
GEODESIC
GEODESIES
GEODESIST
GEODESISTS
GEODESY
GEODETIC
GEODETICS
GEODIC
GEOGENIES
GEOGENY
GEOGNOSES
GEOGNOSIS
GEOGNOST
GEOGNOSTS
GEOGNOSY
GEOGONIC
GEOGONIES
GEOGONY
GEOGRAPHIES
GEOGRAPHY
GEOID
GEOIDAL
GEOIDS
GEOLATRIES
GEOLATRY
GEOLOGER
GEOLOGERS
GEOLOGIAN
GEOLOGIANS
GEOLOGIC
GEOLOGIES
GEOLOGISE
GEOLOGISED
GEOLOGISES
GEOLOGISING
GEOLOGIST
GEOLOGISTS
GEOLOGIZE
GEOLOGIZED
GEOLOGIZES
GEOLOGIZING
GEOLOGY
GEOMANCER
GEOMANCERS
GEOMANCIES
GEOMANCY
GEOMANTIC
GEOMETER
GEOMETERS
GEOMETRIC
GEOMETRID
GEOMETRIDS

GEOMETRIES
GEOMETRY
GEOMYOID
GEOPHAGIES
GEOPHAGY
GEOPHILIC
GEOPHONE
GEOPHONES
GEOPHYTE
GEOPHYTES
GEOPHYTIC
GEOPONIC
GEOPONICS
GEORDIE
GEORDIES
GEORGETTE
GEORGETTES
GEORGIC
GEORGICS
GEOS
GEOSPHERE
GEOSPHERES
GEOSTATIC
GEOSTATICS
GEOTACTIC
GEOTAXES
GEOTAXIS
GEOTROPIC
GERAH
GERAHS
GERANIOL
GERANIOLS
GERANIUM
GERANIUMS
GERBE
GERBERA
GERBERAS
GERBES
GERBIL
GERBILLE
GERBILLES
GERBILS
GERE
GERENT
GERENTS
GERENUK
GERENUKS
GERES
GERFALCON
GERFALCONS
GERIATRIC
GERIATRICS
GERIATRIES
GERIATRY
GERLE
GERLES
GERM
GERMAIN
GERMAINE
GERMAINES
GERMAINS
GERMAN
GERMANDER
GERMANDERS
GERMANE
GERMANELY
GERMANIUM
GERMANIUMS
GERMANS
GERMED

GERMEN
GERMENS
GERMICIDE
GERMICIDES
GERMIN
GERMINAL
GERMINANT
GERMINATE
GERMINATED
GERMINATES
GERMINATING
GERMING
GERMINS
GERMS
GERNE
GERNED
GERNES
GERNING
GERONTIC
GEROPIGA
GEROPIGAS
GERUND
GERUNDIAL
GERUNDIVE
GERUNDIVES
GERUNDS
GESNERIA
GESNERIAS
GESSAMINE
GESSAMINES
GESSE
GESSED
GESSES
GESSING
GESSO
GESSOES
GEST
GESTALT
GESTALTS
GESTANT
GESTATE
GESTATED
GESTATES
GESTATING
GESTATION
GESTATIONS
GESTATIVE
GESTATORY
GESTE
GESTES
GESTIC
GESTS
GESTURAL
GESTURE
GESTURED
GESTURES
GESTURING
GET
GETA
GETAS
GETAWAY
GETAWAYS
GETS
GETTABLE
GETTER
GETTERED
GETTERING
GETTERINGS
GETTERS
GETTING

GETTINGS
GEUM
GEUMS
GEWGAW
GEWGAWS
GEY
GEYAN
GEYER
GEYEST
GEYSER
GEYSERITE
GEYSERITES
GEYSERS
GHARIAL
GHARIALS
GHARRI
GHARRIES
GHARRIS
GHARRY
GHAST
GHASTED
GHASTFUL
GHASTFULL
GHASTING
GHASTLIER
GHASTLIEST
GHASTLY
GHASTNESS
GHASTNESSES
GHASTS
GHAT
GHATS
GHAUT
GHAUTS
GHAZAL
GHAZALS
GHAZEL
GHAZELS
GHAZI
GHAZIS
GHEE
GHEES
GHERAO
GHERAOED
GHERAOING
GHERAOS
GHERKIN
GHERKINS
GHESSE
GHESSED
GHESSES
GHESSING
GHEST
GHETTOES
GHETTOISE
GHETTOISED
GHETTOISES
GHETTOISING
GHETTOIZE
GHETTOIZED
GHETTOIZES
GHETTOIZING
GHETTOS
GHI
GHILGAI
GHILGAIS
GHILLIE
GHILLIED
GHILLIES

GHILLYING
GHIS
GHOST
GHOSTED
GHOSTIER
GHOSTIEST
GHOSTING
GHOSTLIER
GHOSTLIEST
GHOSTLY
GHOSTS
GHOSTY
GHOUL
GHOULISH
GHOULS
GHYLL
GHYLLS
GI
GIAMBEUX
GIANT
GIANTESS
GIANTESSES
GIANTHOOD
GIANTHOODS
GIANTISM
GIANTISMS
GIANTLIER
GIANTLIEST
GIANTLY
GIANTRIES
GIANTRY
GIANTS
GIANTSHIP
GIANTSHIPS
GIAOUR
GIAOURS
GIB
GIBBED
GIBBER
GIBBERED
GIBBERING
GIBBERISH
GIBBERISHES
GIBBERS
GIBBET
GIBBETED
GIBBETING
GIBBETS
GIBBING
GIBBON
GIBBONS
GIBBOSE
GIBBOSITIES
GIBBOSITY
GIBBOUS
GIBBOUSLY
GIBBSITE
GIBBSITES
GIBE
GIBED
GIBEL
GIBELS
GIBER
GIBERS
GIBES
GIBING
GIBINGLY
GIBLET
GIBLETS
GIBS

GIBUS
GIBUSES
GID
GIDDIED
GIDDIER
GIDDIES
GIDDIEST
GIDDILY
GIDDINESS
GIDDINESSES
GIDDY
GIDDYING
GIDGEE
GIDGEES
GIDJEE
GIDJEES
GIDS
GIE
GIED
GIEING
GIEN
GIES
GIF
GIFT
GIFTED
GIFTEDLY
GIFTING
GIFTS
GIG
GIGA
GIGAHERTZ
GIGAHERTZES
GIGANTEAN
GIGANTIC
GIGANTISM
GIGANTISMS
GIGAS
GIGAWATT
GIGAWATTS
GIGGED
GIGGING
GIGGIT
GIGGITED
GIGGITING
GIGGITS
GIGGLE
GIGGLED
GIGGLER
GIGGLERS
GIGGLES
GIGGLIER
GIGGLIEST
GIGGLING
GIGGLINGS
GIGGLY
GIGLET
GIGLETS
GIGLOT
GIGLOTS
GIGMAN
GIGMANITIES
GIGMANITY
GIGMEN
GIGOLO
GIGOLOS
GIGOT
GIGOTS
GIGS
GIGUE
GIGUES

GILA
GILAS
GILBERT
GILBERTS
GILCUP
GILCUPS
GILD
GILDED
GILDEN
GILDER
GILDERS
GILDING
GILDINGS
GILDS
GILET
GILETS
GILGAI
GILGAIS
GILGIE
GILGIES
GILL
GILLAROO
GILLAROOS
GILLED
GILLET
GILLETS
GILLFLIRT
GILLFLIRTS
GILLIE
GILLIED
GILLIES
GILLING
GILLION
GILLIONS
GILLS
GILLY
GILLYING
GILLYVOR
GILLYVORS
GILPEY
GILPEYS
GILPIES
GILPY
GILRAVAGE
GILRAVAGED
GILRAVAGES
GILRAVAGING
GILT
GILTCUP
GILTCUPS
GILTS
GILTWOOD
GIMBAL
GIMBALS
GIMCRACK
GIMCRACKS
GIMLET
GIMLETED
GIMLETING
GIMLETS
GIMMAL
GIMMALLED
GIMMALS
GIMME
GIMMER
GIMMERS
GIMMES
GIMMICK
GIMMICKIER
GIMMICKIEST

GIMMICKRIES
GIMMICKRY
GIMMICKS
GIMMICKY
GIMMOR
GIMMORS
GIMP
GIMPED
GIMPING
GIMPS
GIN
GING
GINGAL
GINGALL
GINGALLS
GINGALS
GINGELLIES
GINGELLY
GINGER
GINGERADE
GINGERADES
GINGERED
GINGERING
GINGERLY
GINGEROUS
GINGERS
GINGERY
GINGHAM
GINGHAMS
GINGILI
GINGILIS
GINGIVAL
GINGKO
GINGKOES
GINGLE
GINGLED
GINGLES
GINGLING
GINGLYMI
GINGLYMUS
GINGS
GINHOUSE
GINHOUSES
GINK
GINKGO
GINKGOES
GINKS
GINN
GINNED
GINNEL
GINNELS
GINNER
GINNERIES
GINNERS
GINNERY
GINNING
GINS
GINSENG
GINSENGS
GINSHOP
GINSHOPS
GIO
GIOCOSO
GIOS
GIP
GIPPIES
GIPPO
GIPPOS
GIPPY
GIPS

GIPSEN
GIPSENS
GIPSIED
GIPSIES
GIPSY
GIPSYING
GIRAFFE
GIRAFFES
GIRAFFID
GIRAFFINE
GIRAFFOID
GIRANDOLA
GIRANDOLAS
GIRANDOLE
GIRANDOLES
GIRASOL
GIRASOLE
GIRASOLES
GIRASOLS
GIRD
GIRDED
GIRDER
GIRDERS
GIRDING
GIRDINGS
GIRDLE
GIRDLED
GIRDLER
GIRDLERS
GIRDLES
GIRDLING
GIRDS
GIRKIN
GIRKINS
GIRL
GIRLHOOD
GIRLHOODS
GIRLIE
GIRLIES
GIRLISH
GIRLISHLY
GIRLOND
GIRLONDS
GIRLS
GIRLY
GIRN
GIRNED
GIRNEL
GIRNELS
GIRNIE
GIRNIER
GIRNIEST
GIRNING
GIRNS
GIRO
GIRON
GIRONS
GIROS
GIROSOL
GIROSOLS
GIRR
GIRRS
GIRT
GIRTED
GIRTH
GIRTHED
GIRTHING
GIRTHLINE
GIRTHLINES
GIRTHS

GIRTING
GIRTLINE
GIRTLINES
GIRTS
GIS
GISARME
GISARMES
GISM
GISMO
GISMOS
GISMS
GIST
GISTS
GIT
GITANA
GITANAS
GITANO
GITANOS
GITE
GITES
GITS
GITTERN
GITTERNED
GITTERNING
GITTERNS
GIUST
GIUSTED
GIUSTING
GIUSTO
GIUSTS
GIVE
GIVEAWAY
GIVEAWAYS
GIVED
GIVEN
GIVENNESS
GIVENNESSES
GIVER
GIVERS
GIVES
GIVING
GIVINGS
GIZMO
GIZMOS
GIZZ
GIZZARD
GIZZARDS
GIZZEN
GIZZENED
GIZZENING
GIZZENS
GIZZES
GJU
GJUS
GLABELLA
GLABELLAE
GLABELLAR
GLABRATE
GLABROUS
GLACÉ
GLACÉED
GLACÉING
GLACÉS
GLACIAL
GLACIALS
GLACIATE
GLACIATED
GLACIATES
GLACIATING
GLACIER

GLACIERS
GLACIS
GLACISES
GLAD
GLADDED
GLADDEN
GLADDENED
GLADDENING
GLADDENS
GLADDER
GLADDEST
GLADDIE
GLADDIES
GLADDING
GLADDON
GLADDONS
GLADE
GLADES
GLADFUL
GLADIATE
GLADIATOR
GLADIATORS
GLADIER
GLADIEST
GLADIOLE
GLADIOLES
GLADIOLI
GLADIOLUS
GLADIOLUSES
GLADIUS
GLADIUSES
GLADLY
GLADNESS
GLADNESSES
GLADS
GLADSOME
GLADY
GLAIK
GLAIKET
GLAIKIT
GLAIKS
GLAIR
GLAIRED
GLAIREOUS
GLAIRIER
GLAIRIEST
GLAIRIN
GLAIRING
GLAIRINS
GLAIRS
GLAIRY
GLAIVE
GLAIVED
GLAIVES
GLAM
GLAMOR
GLAMORED
GLAMORING
GLAMORISE
GLAMORISED
GLAMORISES
GLAMORISING
GLAMORIZE
GLAMORIZED
GLAMORIZES
GLAMORIZING
GLAMOROUS
GLAMORS
GLAMOUR
GLAMOURED

GLAMOURING
GLAMOURS
GLANCE
GLANCED
GLANCES
GLANCING
GLANCINGS
GLAND
GLANDERED
GLANDERS
GLANDES
GLANDS
GLANDULAR
GLANDULE
GLANDULES
GLANS
GLARE
GLAREAL
GLARED
GLAREOUS
GLARES
GLARIER
GLARIEST
GLARING
GLARINGLY
GLARY
GLASNOST
GLASNOSTS
GLASS
GLASSED
GLASSEN
GLASSES
GLASSFUL
GLASSFULS
GLASSIER
GLASSIEST
GLASSIFIED
GLASSIFIES
GLASSIFY
GLASSIFYING
GLASSILY
GLASSINE
GLASSINES
GLASSING
GLASSLIKE
GLASSMAN
GLASSMEN
GLASSWARE
GLASSWARES
GLASSWORK
GLASSWORKS
GLASSWORT
GLASSWORTS
GLASSY
GLAUCOMA
GLAUCOMAS
GLAUCOUS
GLAUM
GLAUMED
GLAUMING
GLAUMS
GLAUR
GLAURIER
GLAURIEST
GLAURS
GLAURY
GLAZE
GLAZED
GLAZEN
GLAZER

GLAZERS
GLAZES
GLAZIER
GLAZIERS
GLAZIEST
GLAZING
GLAZINGS
GLAZY
GLEAM
GLEAMED
GLEAMIER
GLEAMIEST
GLEAMING
GLEAMINGS
GLEAMS
GLEAMY
GLEAN
GLEANED
GLEANER
GLEANERS
GLEANING
GLEANINGS
GLEANS
GLEAVE
GLEAVES
GLEBE
GLEBES
GLEBOUS
GLEBY
GLED
GLEDE
GLEDES
GLEDGE
GLEDGED
GLEDGES
GLEDGING
GLEDS
GLEE
GLEED
GLEEDS
GLEEFUL
GLEEING
GLEEK
GLEEKED
GLEEKING
GLEEKS
GLEEMAN
GLEEMEN
GLEES
GLEESOME
GLEET
GLEETED
GLEETIER
GLEETIEST
GLEETING
GLEETS
GLEETY
GLEG
GLEGGER
GLEGGEST
GLEI
GLEIS
GLEN
GLENGARRIES
GLENGARRY
GLENOID
GLENOIDAL
GLENOIDS
GLENS
GLENT

GLENTED
GLENTING
GLENTS
GLEY
GLEYED
GLEYING
GLEYS
GLIA
GLIADIN
GLIADINE
GLIADINES
GLIADINS
GLIAL
GLIAS
GLIB
GLIBBED
GLIBBER
GLIBBERY
GLIBBEST
GLIBBING
GLIBLY
GLIBNESS
GLIBNESSES
GLIBS
GLID
GLIDDEN
GLIDDERY
GLIDDEST
GLIDE
GLIDED
GLIDER
GLIDERS
GLIDES
GLIDING
GLIDINGLY
GLIDINGS
GLIFF
GLIFFING
GLIFFINGS
GLIFFS
GLIFT
GLIFTS
GLIKE
GLIKES
GLIM
GLIMMER
GLIMMERED
GLIMMERING
GLIMMERINGS
GLIMMERS
GLIMMERY
GLIMPSE
GLIMPSED
GLIMPSES
GLIMPSING
GLIMS
GLINT
GLINTED
GLINTING
GLINTS
GLIOMA
GLIOMAS
GLIOMATA
GLIOSES
GLIOSIS
GLISK
GLISKS
GLISSADE
GLISSADED
GLISSADES

GLISSADING
GLISSANDO
GLISSANDOS
GLISTEN
GLISTENED
GLISTENING
GLISTENS
GLISTER
GLISTERED
GLISTERING
GLISTERS
GLIT
GLITCH
GLITCHES
GLITS
GLITTER
GLITTERED
GLITTERING
GLITTERINGS
GLITTERS
GLITTERY
GLITZ
GLITZES
GLITZIER
GLITZIEST
GLITZY
GLOAMING
GLOAMINGS
GLOAT
GLOATED
GLOATING
GLOATS
GLOB
GLOBAL
GLOBALISE
GLOBALISED
GLOBALISES
GLOBALISING
GLOBALIZE
GLOBALIZED
GLOBALIZES
GLOBALIZING
GLOBALLY
GLOBATE
GLOBATED
GLOBE
GLOBED
GLOBES
GLOBIN
GLOBING
GLOBINS
GLOBOID
GLOBOIDS
GLOBOSE
GLOBOSES
GLOBOSITIES
GLOBOSITY
GLOBOUS
GLOBS
GLOBULAR
GLOBULE
GLOBULES
GLOBULET
GLOBULETS
GLOBULIN
GLOBULINS
GLOBULITE
GLOBULITES
GLOBULOUS
GLOBY

GLODE
GLOGG
GLOGGS
GLOIRE
GLOIRES
GLOM
GLOMERATE
GLOMERATED
GLOMERATES
GLOMERATING
GLOMERULE
GLOMERULES
GLOMERULI
GLOMMED
GLOMMING
GLOMS
GLONOIN
GLONOINS
GLOOM
GLOOMED
GLOOMFUL
GLOOMIER
GLOOMIEST
GLOOMILY
GLOOMING
GLOOMINGS
GLOOMS
GLOOMY
GLORIA
GLORIAS
GLORIED
GLORIES
GLORIFIED
GLORIFIES
GLORIFY
GLORIFYING
GLORIOLE
GLORIOLES
GLORIOSA
GLORIOSAS
GLORIOUS
GLORY
GLORYBOX
GLORYBOXES
GLORYING
GLOSS
GLOSSA
GLOSSAE
GLOSSAL
GLOSSARIES
GLOSSARY
GLOSSAS
GLOSSATOR
GLOSSATORS
GLOSSED
GLOSSEME
GLOSSEMES
GLOSSER
GLOSSERS
GLOSSES
GLOSSIER
GLOSSIES
GLOSSIEST
GLOSSILY
GLOSSINA
GLOSSINAS
GLOSSING
GLOSSITIS
GLOSSITISES
GLOSSY

GLOTTAL
GLOTTIC
GLOTTIDES
GLOTTIS
GLOTTISES
GLOUT
GLOUTED
GLOUTING
GLOUTS
GLOVE
GLOVED
GLOVER
GLOVERS
GLOVES
GLOVING
GLOW
GLOWED
GLOWER
GLOWERED
GLOWERING
GLOWERS
GLOWING
GLOWINGLY
GLOWLAMP
GLOWLAMPS
GLOWS
GLOXINIA
GLOXINIAS
GLOZE
GLOZED
GLOZES
GLOZING
GLOZINGS
GLUCAGON
GLUCAGONS
GLUCINA
GLUCINAS
GLUCINIUM
GLUCINIUMS
GLUCINUM
GLUCINUMS
GLUCOSE
GLUCOSES
GLUCOSIC
GLUCOSIDE
GLUCOSIDES
GLUE
GLUED
GLUER
GLUERS
GLUES
GLUEY
GLUEYNESS
GLUEYNESSES
GLUG
GLUGGED
GLUGGING
GLUGS
GLÜHWEIN
GLÜHWEINS
GLUIER
GLUIEST
GLUING
GLUISH
GLUM
GLUME
GLUMELLA
GLUMELLAS
GLUMES
GLUMLY

GLUMMER
GLUMMEST
GLUMNESS
GLUMNESSES
GLUMPIER
GLUMPIEST
GLUMPISH
GLUMPS
GLUMPY
GLUON
GLUONS
GLUT
GLUTAEAL
GLUTAEI
GLUTAEUS
GLUTAMATE
GLUTAMATES
GLUTAMINE
GLUTAMINES
GLUTEAL
GLUTEI
GLUTELIN
GLUTELINS
GLUTEN
GLUTENOUS
GLUTENS
GLUTEUS
GLUTINOUS
GLUTS
GLUTTED
GLUTTING
GLUTTON
GLUTTONIES
GLUTTONS
GLUTTONY
GLYCERIC
GLYCERIDE
GLYCERIDES
GLYCERIN
GLYCERINE
GLYCERINES
GLYCERINS
GLYCEROL
GLYCEROLS
GLYCERYL
GLYCERYLS
GLYCIN
GLYCINE
GLYCINES
GLYCINS
GLYCOCOLL
GLYCOCOLLS
GLYCOGEN
GLYCOGENS
GLYCOL
GLYCOLIC
GLYCOLLIC
GLYCOLS
GLYCONIC
GLYCONICS
GLYCOSE
GLYCOSES
GLYCOSIDE
GLYCOSIDES
GLYCOSYL
GLYCOSYLS
GLYPH
GLYPHIC
GLYPHS
GLYPTIC

GLYPTICS
GMELINITE
GMELINITES
GNAR
GNARL
GNARLED
GNARLIER
GNARLIEST
GNARLING
GNARLS
GNARLY
GNARR
GNARRED
GNARRING
GNARRS
GNARS
GNASH
GNASHED
GNASHER
GNASHERS
GNASHES
GNASHING
GNAT
GNATHAL
GNATHIC
GNATHITE
GNATHITES
GNATHONIC
GNATLING
GNATLINGS
GNATS
GNAW
GNAWED
GNAWER
GNAWERS
GNAWING
GNAWN
GNAWS
GNEISS
GNEISSES
GNEISSIC
GNEISSOID
GNEISSOSE
GNOCCHI
GNOCCHIS
GNOMAE
GNOME
GNOMES
GNOMIC
GNOMISH
GNOMIST
GNOMISTS
GNOMON
GNOMONIC
GNOMONICS
GNOMONS
GNOSES
GNOSIS
GNOSTIC
GNOSTICAL
GNU
GNUS
GO
GOA
GOAD
GOADED
GOADING
GOADS
GOADSMAN
GOADSMEN

GOADSTER
GOADSTERS
GOAF
GOAFS
GOAL
GOALED
GOALIE
GOALIES
GOALING
GOALLESS
GOALMOUTH
GOALMOUTHS
GOALPOST
GOALPOSTS
GOALS
GOANNA
GOANNAS
GOARY
GOAS
GOAT
GOATEE
GOATEED
GOATEES
GOATFISH
GOATFISHES
GOATHERD
GOATHERDS
GOATIER
GOATIEST
GOATISH
GOATLING
GOATLINGS
GOATS
GOATSKIN
GOATSKINS
GOATWEED
GOATWEEDS
GOATY
GOB
GOBANG
GOBANGS
GOBBELINE
GOBBELINES
GOBBET
GOBBETS
GOBBI
GOBBLE
GOBBLED
GOBBLER
GOBBLERS
GOBBLES
GOBBLING
GOBBO
GOBIES
GOBIOID
GOBLET
GOBLETS
GOBLIN
GOBLINS
GOBO
GOBOES
GOBONY
GOBOS
GOBS
GOBURRA
GOBURRAS
GOBY
GOD
GODCHILD
GODCHILDREN

GODDAM
GODDAMN
GODDAMNED
GODDED
GODDESS
GODDESSES
GODDING
GODET
GODETIA
GODETIAS
GODETS
GODFATHER
GODFATHERS
GODHEAD
GODHEADS
GODHOOD
GODHOODS
GODLESS
GODLESSLY
GODLIER
GODLIEST
GODLIKE
GODLILY
GODLINESS
GODLINESSES
GODLING
GODLINGS
GODLY
GODMOTHER
GODMOTHERS
GODOWN
GODOWNS
GODPARENT
GODPARENTS
GODROON
GODROONS
GODS
GODSEND
GODSENDS
GODSHIP
GODSHIPS
GODSO
GODSON
GODSONS
GODSOS
GODSPEED
GODSPEEDS
GODWARD
GODWARDS
GODWIT
GODWITS
GOE
GOEL
GOELS
GOER
GOERS
GOES
GOETHITE
GOETHITES
GOETIC
GOETIES
GOETY
GOEY
GOFER
GOFERS
GOFF
GOFFED
GOFFER
GOFFERED
GOFFERING

GOFFERINGS
GOFFERS
GOFFING
GOFFS
GOG
GOGGLE
GOGGLED
GOGGLER
GOGGLERS
GOGGLES
GOGGLIER
GOGGLIEST
GOGGLING
GOGGLINGS
GOGGLY
GOGLET
GOGLETS
GOGO
GOGS
GOIER
GOIEST
GOING
GOINGS
GOITER
GOITERS
GOITRE
GOITRED
GOITRES
GOITROUS
GOLD
GOLDARN
GOLDCREST
GOLDCRESTS
GOLDEN
GOLDENED
GOLDENER
GOLDENEST
GOLDENING
GOLDENROD
GOLDENRODS
GOLDENS
GOLDER
GOLDEST
GOLDEYE
GOLDEYES
GOLDFIELD
GOLDFIELDS
GOLDFINCH
GOLDFINCHES
GOLDFINNIES
GOLDFINNY
GOLDFISH
GOLDFISHES
GOLDIER
GOLDIEST
GOLDISH
GOLDLESS
GOLDS
GOLDSINNIES
GOLDSINNY
GOLDSIZE
GOLDSIZES
GOLDSMITH
GOLDSMITHS
GOLDSPINK
GOLDSPINKS
GOLDSTICK
GOLDSTICKS
GOLDSTONE

GOLDSTONES
GOLDY
GOLE
GOLEM
GOLEMS
GOLES
GOLF
GOLFED
GOLFER
GOLFERS
GOLFIANA
GOLFIANAS
GOLFING
GOLFINGS
GOLFS
GOLIARD
GOLIARDIC
GOLIARDIES
GOLIARDS
GOLIARDY
GOLIAS
GOLIASED
GOLIASES
GOLIASING
GOLLAN
GOLLAND
GOLLANDS
GOLLANS
GOLLAR
GOLLARED
GOLLARING
GOLLARS
GOLLIES
GOLLIWOG
GOLLIWOGS
GOLLOP
GOLLOPED
GOLLOPING
GOLLOPS
GOLLY
GOLLYWOG
GOLLYWOGS
GOLOMYNKA
GOLOMYNKAS
GOLOSH
GOLOSHED
GOLOSHES
GOLOSHING
GOLP
GOLPE
GOLPES
GOLPS
GOMBEEN
GOMBEENS
GOMBO
GOMBOS
GOMBRO
GOMBROS
GOMERAL
GOMERALS
GOMERIL
GOMERILS
GOMOKU
GOMOKUS
GOMPA
GOMPAS
GOMPHOSES
GOMPHOSIS
GOMUTI
GOMUTIS

GOMUTO
GOMUTOS
GON
GONAD
GONADIAL
GONADIC
GONADS
GONDELAY
GONDELAYS
GONDOLA
GONDOLAS
GONDOLIER
GONDOLIERS
GONE
GONENESS
GONENESSES
GONER
GONERS
GONFALON
GONFALONS
GONFANON
GONFANONS
GONG
GONGED
GONGING
GONGS
GONGSTER
GONGSTERS
GONIA
GONIATITE
GONIATITES
GONIDIA
GONIDIAL
GONIDIC
GONIDIUM
GONION
GONK
GONKS
GONNA
GONOCOCCI
GONOCYTE
GONOCYTES
GONOPHORE
GONOPHORES
GONORRHEA
GONORRHEAS
GONS
GOO
GOOBER
GOOBERS
GOOD
GOODFACED
GOODIER
GOODIES
GOODIEST
GOODINESS
GOODINESSES
GOODISH
GOODLIER
GOODLIEST
GOODLY
GOODMAN
GOODMEN
GOODNESS
GOODNESSES
GOODNIGHT
GOODNIGHTS
GOODS
GOODSIRE
GOODSIRES

GOODTIME
GOODWIFE
GOODWILL
GOODWILLS
GOODWIVES
GOODY
GOODYEAR
GOODYEARS
GOOEY
GOOF
GOOFBALL
GOOFBALLS
GOOFED
GOOFIER
GOOFIEST
GOOFILY
GOOFINESS
GOOFINESSES
GOOFING
GOOFS
GOOFY
GOOGLE
GOOGLED
GOOGLES
GOOGLIES
GOOGLING
GOOGLY
GOOGOL
GOOGOLS
GOOIER
GOOIEST
GOOK
GOOKS
GOOL
GOOLD
GOOLDS
GOOLEY
GOOLEYS
GOOLIE
GOOLIES
GOOLS
GOOLY
GOON
GOONEY
GOONEYS
GOONS
GOOP
GOOPIER
GOOPIEST
GOOPS
GOOPY
GOOR
GOOROO
GOOROOS
GOORS
GOOS
GOOSANDER
GOOSANDERS
GOOSE
GOOSED
GOOSEFOOT
GOOSEFOOTS
GOOSEGOB
GOOSEGOBS
GOOSEGOG
GOOSEGOGS
GOOSEHERD
GOOSEHERDS
GOOSERIES
GOOSERY

GOOSES
GOOSEY
GOOSEYS
GOOSIER
GOOSIES
GOOSIEST
GOOSING
GOOSY
GOPAK
GOPAKS
GOPHER
GOPHERED
GOPHERING
GOPHERS
GOPURA
GOPURAM
GOPURAMS
GOPURAS
GORAL
GORALS
GORAMIES
GORAMY
GORBLIMEY
GORBLIMY
GORCOCK
GORCOCKS
GORCROW
GORCROWS
GORE
GORED
GORES
GORGE
GORGED
GORGEOUS
GORGERIN
GORGERINS
GORGES
GORGET
GORGETS
GORGIA
GORGIAS
GORGING
GORGIO
GORGIOS
GORGON
GORGONEIA
GORGONIAN
GORGONIANS
GORGONISE
GORGONISED
GORGONISES
GORGONISING
GORGONIZE
GORGONIZED
GORGONIZES
GORGONIZING
GORGONS
GORIER
GORIEST
GORILLA
GORILLAS
GORILLIAN
GORILLINE
GORILY
GORING
GORINGS
GORM
GORMAND
GORMANDS
GORMED

GORMIER
GORMIEST
GORMING
GORMLESS
GORMS
GORMY
GORSE
GORSEDD
GORSEDDS
GORSES
GORSIER
GORSIEST
GORSOON
GORSOONS
GORSY
GORY
GOS
GOSH
GOSHAWK
GOSHAWKS
GOSLARITE
GOSLARITES
GOSLET
GOSLETS
GOSLING
GOSLINGS
GOSPEL
GOSPELISE
GOSPELISED
GOSPELISES
GOSPELISING
GOSPELIZE
GOSPELIZED
GOSPELIZES
GOSPELIZING
GOSPELLED
GOSPELLER
GOSPELLERS
GOSPELLING
GOSPELS
GOSPODAR
GOSPODARS
GOSSAMER
GOSSAMERS
GOSSAMERY
GOSSAN
GOSSANS
GOSSE
GOSSES
GOSSIB
GOSSIBS
GOSSIP
GOSSIPED
GOSSIPING
GOSSIPINGS
GOSSIPRIES
GOSSIPRY
GOSSIPS
GOSSIPY
GOSSOON
GOSSOONS
GOSSYPINE
GOSSYPOL
GOSSYPOLS
GOT
GOTHICISE
GOTHICISED
GOTHICISES
GOTHICISING
GOTHICIZE

GOTHICIZED
GOTHICIZES
GOTHICIZING
GÖTHITE
GÖTHITES
GOTTA
GOTTEN
GOUACHE
GOUACHES
GOUGE
GOUGED
GOUGÈRE
GOUGÈRES
GOUGES
GOUGING
GOUJEERS
GOUJONS
GOUK
GOUKS
GOULASH
GOULASHES
GOURAMI
GOURAMIS
GOURD
GOURDE
GOURDES
GOURDIER
GOURDIEST
GOURDS
GOURDY
GOURMAND
GOURMANDS
GOURMET
GOURMETS
GOUSTIER
GOUSTIEST
GOUSTROUS
GOUSTY
GOUT
GOUTFLIES
GOUTFLY
GOUTIER
GOUTIEST
GOUTINESS
GOUTINESSES
GOUTS
GOUTTE
GOUTTES
GOUTWEED
GOUTWEEDS
GOUTWORT
GOUTWORTS
GOUTY
GOV
GOVERN
GOVERNALL
GOVERNALLS
GOVERNED
GOVERNESS
GOVERNESSED
GOVERNESSES
GOVERNESSING
GOVERNING
GOVERNOR
GOVERNORS
GOVERNS
GOVS
GOWAN
GOWANED
GOWANS

GOWANY
GOWD
GOWDER
GOWDEST
GOWDS
GOWDSPINK
GOWDSPINKS
GOWF
GOWFED
GOWFERS
GOWFING
GOWFS
GOWK
GOWKS
GOWL
GOWLAND
GOWLANDS
GOWLED
GOWLING
GOWLS
GOWN
GOWNBOY
GOWNBOYS
GOWNED
GOWNING
GOWNMAN
GOWNMEN
GOWNS
GOWNSMAN
GOWNSMEN
GOWPEN
GOWPENFUL
GOWPENFULS
GOWPENS
GOY
GOYIM
GOYISCH
GOYISH
GOZZAN
GOZZANS
GRAAL
GRAALS
GRAB
GRABBED
GRABBER
GRABBERS
GRABBING
GRABBLE
GRABBLED
GRABBLER
GRABBLERS
GRABBLES
GRABBLING
GRABEN
GRABENS
GRABS
GRACE
GRACED
GRACEFUL
GRACELESS
GRACES
GRACILE
GRACILITIES
GRACILITY
GRACING
GRACIOSO
GRACIOSOS
GRACIOUS
GRACIOUSES

GRACKLE	GRAINIER	GRANDPAPA	GRAPESHOT	GRATICULE
GRACKLES	GRAINIEST	GRANDPAPAS	GRAPESHOTS	GRATICULES
GRADABLE	GRAINING	GRANDPAS	GRAPETREE	GRATIFIED
GRADABLES	GRAININGS	GRANDS	GRAPETREES	GRATIFIER
GRADATE	GRAINS	GRANDSIRE	GRAPEVINE	GRATIFIERS
GRADATED	GRAINY	GRANDSIRES	GRAPEVINES	GRATIFIES
GRADATES	GRAIP	GRANDSON	GRAPEY	GRATIFY
GRADATIM	GRAIPS	GRANDSONS	GRAPH	GRATIFYING
GRADATING	GRAITH	GRANFER	GRAPHED	GRATING
GRADATION	GRAITHED	GRANFERS	GRAPHEME	GRATINGLY
GRADATIONS	GRAITHING	GRANGE	GRAPHEMES	GRATINGS
GRADATORY	GRAITHLY	GRANGER	GRAPHEMIC	GRATIS
GRADDAN	GRAITHS	GRANGERS	GRAPHEMICS	GRATITUDE
GRADDANED	GRAKLE	GRANGES	GRAPHIC	GRATITUDES
GRADDANING	GRAKLES	GRANITE	GRAPHICAL	GRATTOIR
GRADDANS	GRALLOCH	GRANITES	GRAPHICLY	GRATTOIRS
GRADE	GRALLOCHED	GRANITIC	GRAPHICS	GRATUITIES
GRADED	GRALLOCHING	GRANITISE	GRAPHING	GRATUITY
GRADELY	GRALLOCHS	GRANITISED	GRAPHITE	GRATULANT
GRADER	GRAM	GRANITISES	GRAPHITES	GRATULATE
GRADERS	GRAMA	GRANITISING	GRAPHITIC	GRATULATED
GRADES	GRAMARIES	GRANITITE	GRAPHIUM	GRATULATES
GRADIENT	GRAMARY	GRANITITES	GRAPHIUMS	GRATULATING
GRADIENTS	GRAMARYE	GRANITIZE	GRAPHS	GRAUPEL
GRADIN	GRAMARYES	GRANITIZED	GRAPIER	GRAUPELS
GRADINE	GRAMAS	GRANITIZES	GRAPICOT	GRAVAMEN
GRADINES	GRAMASH	GRANITIZING	GRAPING	GRAVAMINA
GRADING	GRAMASHES	GRANITOID	GRAPLE	GRAVE
GRADINI	GRAME	GRANIVORE	GRAPLES	GRAVED
GRADINO	GRAMERCIES	GRANIVORES	GRAPNEL	GRAVEL
GRADINS	GRAMERCY	GRANNAM	GRAPNELS	GRAVELESS
GRADUAL	GRAMES	GRANNAMS	GRAPPA	GRAVELLED
GRADUALLY	GRAMMAR	GRANNIE	GRAPPAS	GRAVELLING
GRADUALS	GRAMMARS	GRANNIES	GRAPPLE	GRAVELLY
GRADUAND	GRAMMATIC	GRANNY	GRAPPLED	GRAVELS
GRADUANDS	GRAMME	GRANS	GRAPPLES	GRAVELY
GRADUATE	GRAMMES	GRANT	GRAPPLING	GRAVEN
GRADUATED	GRAMOCHE	GRANTABLE	GRAPY	GRAVENESS
GRADUATES	GRAMOCHES	GRANTED	GRASP	GRAVENESSES
GRADUATING	GRAMPUS	GRANTEE	GRASPABLE	GRAVER
GRADUATOR	GRAMPUSES	GRANTEES	GRASPED	GRAVERS
GRADUATORS	GRAMS	GRANTER	GRASPER	GRAVES
GRADUS	GRAN	GRANTERS	GRASPERS	GRAVEST
GRADUSES	GRANARIES	GRANTING	GRASPING	GRAVEYARD
GRAFF	GRANARY	GRANTOR	GRASPLESS	GRAVEYARDS
GRAFFED	GRAND	GRANTORS	GRASPS	GRAVID
GRAFFING	GRANDAD	GRANTS	GRASS	GRAVIDITIES
GRAFFITI	GRANDADDIES	GRANULAR	GRASSED	GRAVIDITY
GRAFFITIS	GRANDADDY	GRANULARY	GRASSER	GRAVIES
GRAFFITO	GRANDADS	GRANULATE	GRASSERS	GRAVING
GRAFFS	GRANDAM	GRANULATED	GRASSES	GRAVINGS
GRAFT	GRANDAMS	GRANULATES	GRASSHOOK	GRAVITAS
GRAFTED	GRANDDAD	GRANULATING	GRASSHOOKS	GRAVITASES
GRAFTER	GRANDDADS	GRANULE	GRASSIER	GRAVITATE
GRAFTERS	GRANDE	GRANULES	GRASSIEST	GRAVITATED
GRAFTING	GRANDEE	GRANULITE	GRASSING	GRAVITATES
GRAFTINGS	GRANDEES	GRANULITES	GRASSINGS	GRAVITATING
GRAFTS	GRANDER	GRANULOMA	GRASSLAND	GRAVITIES
GRAIL	GRANDEST	GRANULOMAS	GRASSLANDS	GRAVITON
GRAILE	GRANDEUR	GRANULOMATA	GRASSUM	GRAVITONS
GRAILES	GRANDEURS	GRANULOSE	GRASSUMS	GRAVITY
GRAILS	GRANDIOSE	GRANULOUS	GRASSY	GRAVURE
GRAIN	GRANDLY	GRAPE	GRASTE	GRAVURES
GRAINAGE	GRANDMA	GRAPED	GRAT	GRAVY
GRAINAGES	GRANDMAMA	GRAPELESS	GRATE	GRAY
GRAINE	GRANDMAMAS	GRAPERIES	GRATED	GRAYED
GRAINED	GRANDMAS	GRAPERY	GRATEFUL	GRAYER
GRAINER	GRANDNESS	GRAPES	GRATER	GRAYEST
GRAINERS	GRANDNESSES	GRAPESEED	GRATERS	GRAYFLIES
GRAINES	GRANDPA	GRAPESEEDS	GRATES	GRAYFLY

GRAYING
GRAYLE
GRAYLES
GRAYLING
GRAYLINGS
GRAYS
GRAYWACKE
GRAYWACKES
GRAZE
GRAZED
GRAZER
GRAZERS
GRAZES
GRAZIER
GRAZIERS
GRAZING
GRAZINGS
GRAZIOSO
GREASE
GREASED
GREASER
GREASERS
GREASES
GREASIER
GREASIEST
GREASILY
GREASING
GREASY
GREAT
GREATCOAT
GREATCOATS
GREATEN
GREATENED
GREATENING
GREATENS
GREATER
GREATEST
GREATLY
GREATNESS
GREATNESSES
GREATS
GREAVE
GREAVED
GREAVES
GREAVING
GREBE
GREBES
GRECE
GRECES
GRECIAN
GRECIANS
GRECQUE
GRECQUES
GREE
GREECE
GREECES
GREED
GREEDIER
GREEDIEST
GREEDILY
GREEDS
GREEDY
GREEGREE
GREEGREES
GREEING
GREEN
GREENBACK
GREENBACKS
GREENED
GREENER

GREENERIES
GREENERY
GREENEST
GREENFLIES
GREENFLY
GREENGAGE
GREENGAGES
GREENHAND
GREENHANDS
GREENHORN
GREENHORNS
GREENIER
GREENIEST
GREENING
GREENINGS
GREENISH
GREENLET
GREENLETS
GREENLY
GREENMAIL
GREENMAILS
GREENNESS
GREENNESSES
GREENROOM
GREENROOMS
GREENS
GREENSAND
GREENSANDS
GREENTH
GREENTHS
GREENWEED
GREENWEEDS
GREENWOOD
GREENWOODS
GREENY
GREES
GREESE
GREESES
GREESING
GREESINGS
GREET
GREETE
GREETED
GREETES
GREETING
GREETINGS
GREETS
GREFFIER
GREFFIERS
GREGALE
GREGALES
GREGARIAN
GREGARINE
GREGARINES
GREGATIM
GREGE
GREGO
GREGORIES
GREGORY
GREGOS
GREIGE
GREIN
GREINED
GREINING
GREINS
GREISEN
GREISENS
GREISLY
GREMIAL
GREMIALS

GREMLIN
GREMLINS
GREN
GRENADE
GRENADES
GRENADIER
GRENADIERS
GRENADINE
GRENADINES
GRENNED
GRENNING
GRENS
GRESE
GRESES
GRESSING
GRESSINGS
GREVE
GREVES
GREW
GREWED
GREWHOUND
GREWHOUNDS
GREWING
GREWS
GREY
GREYBEARD
GREYBEARDS
GREYED
GREYER
GREYEST
GREYHEN
GREYHENS
GREYHOUND
GREYHOUNDS
GREYING
GREYISH
GREYLY
GREYNESS
GREYNESSES
GREYS
GREYWACKE
GREYWACKES
GRIBBLE
GRIBBLES
GRICE
GRICER
GRICERS
GRICES
GRICING
GRICINGS
GRID
GRIDDLE
GRIDDLES
GRIDE
GRIDED
GRIDELIN
GRIDELINS
GRIDES
GRIDING
GRIDIRON
GRIDIRONED
GRIDIRONING
GRIDIRONS
GRIDLOCK
GRIDLOCKS
GRIDS
GRIECE
GRIECED
GRIECES
GRIEF

GRIEFFUL
GRIEFLESS
GRIEFS
GRIESIE
GRIESLY
GRIESY
GRIEVANCE
GRIEVANCES
GRIEVE
GRIEVED
GRIEVER
GRIEVERS
GRIEVES
GRIEVING
GRIEVOUS
GRIFF
GRIFFE
GRIFFES
GRIFFIN
GRIFFINS
GRIFFON
GRIFFONS
GRIFFS
GRIFT
GRIFTED
GRIFTER
GRIFTERS
GRIFTING
GRIFTS
GRIG
GRIGGED
GRIGGING
GRIGRI
GRIGRIS
GRIGS
GRIKE
GRIKES
GRILL
GRILLADE
GRILLADES
GRILLAGE
GRILLAGES
GRILLE
GRILLED
GRILLES
GRILLING
GRILLINGS
GRILLS
GRILSE
GRILSES
GRIM
GRIMACE
GRIMACED
GRIMACES
GRIMACING
GRIMALKIN
GRIMALKINS
GRIME
GRIMED
GRIMES
GRIMIER
GRIMIEST
GRIMILY
GRIMINESS
GRIMINESSES
GRIMING
GRIMLY
GRIMMER
GRIMMEST
GRIMNESS

GRIMNESSES
GRIMOIRE
GRIMOIRES
GRIMY
GRIN
GRIND
GRINDED
GRINDER
GRINDERIES
GRINDERS
GRINDERY
GRINDING
GRINDINGS
GRINDS
GRINGO
GRINGOS
GRINNED
GRINNER
GRINNERS
GRINNING
GRINS
GRIOT
GRIOTS
GRIP
GRIPE
GRIPED
GRIPER
GRIPERS
GRIPES
GRIPING
GRIPINGLY
GRIPLE
GRIPPE
GRIPPED
GRIPPER
GRIPPERS
GRIPPES
GRIPPIER
GRIPPIEST
GRIPPING
GRIPPLE
GRIPPLES
GRIPPY
GRIPS
GRIPSACK
GRIPSACKS
GRIS
GRISAILLE
GRISAILLES
GRISE
GRISED
GRISELY
GRISEOUS
GRISES
GRISETTE
GRISETTES
GRISGRIS
GRISING
GRISKIN
GRISKINS
GRISLED
GRISLIER
GRISLIEST
GRISLY
GRISON
GRISONS
GRIST
GRISTLE
GRISTLES
GRISTLIER

GRISTLIEST	GROMWELL	GROUCHIER	GROWLIER	GRUMMET
GRISTLY	GROMWELLS	GROUCHIEST	GROWLIEST	GRUMMETS
GRISTS	GRONE	GROUCHILY	GROWLING	GRUMNESS
GRISY	GRONED	GROUCHING	GROWLINGS	GRUMNESSES
GRIT	GRONEFULL	GROUCHY	GROWLS	GRUMOSE
GRITH	GRONES	GROUF	GROWLY	GRUMOUS
GRITHS	GRONING	GROUFS	GROWN	GRUMPH
GRITS	GROOF	GROUND	GROWS	GRUMPHED
GRITSTONE	GROOFS	GROUNDAGE	GROWTH	GRUMPHIE
GRITSTONES	GROOLY	GROUNDAGES	GROWTHIST	GRUMPHIES
GRITTED	GROOM	GROUNDED	GROWTHISTS	GRUMPHING
GRITTER	GROOMED	GROUNDEN	GROWTHS	GRUMPHS
GRITTERS	GROOMING	GROUNDER	GROYNE	GRUMPIER
GRITTEST	GROOMS	GROUNDERS	GROYNES	GRUMPIEST
GRITTIER	GROOMSMAN	GROUNDING	GRUB	GRUMPILY
GRITTIEST	GROOMSMEN	GROUNDINGS	GRUBBED	GRUMPY
GRITTING	GROOVE	GROUNDMAN	GRUBBER	GRUNGIER
GRITTY	GROOVED	GROUNDMEN	GRUBBERS	GRUNGIEST
GRIVET	GROOVES	GROUNDS	GRUBBIER	GRUNGY
GRIVETS	GROOVIER	GROUNDSEL	GRUBBIEST	GRUNION
GRIZE	GROOVIEST	GROUNDSELS	GRUBBING	GRUNIONS
GRIZES	GROOVING	GROUP	GRUBBLE	GRUNT
GRIZZLE	GROOVY	GROUPAGE	GRUBBLED	GRUNTED
GRIZZLED	GROPE	GROUPAGES	GRUBBLES	GRUNTER
GRIZZLER	GROPED	GROUPED	GRUBBLING	GRUNTERS
GRIZZLERS	GROPER	GROUPER	GRUBBY	GRUNTING
GRIZZLES	GROPERS	GROUPERS	GRUBS	GRUNTINGS
GRIZZLIER	GROPES	GROUPIE	GRUDGE	GRUNTLE
GRIZZLIES	GROPING	GROUPIES	GRUDGED	GRUNTLED
GRIZZLIEST	GROPINGLY	GROUPING	GRUDGEFUL	GRUNTLES
GRIZZLING	GROSBEAK	GROUPINGS	GRUDGES	GRUNTLING
GRIZZLY	GROSBEAKS	GROUPIST	GRUDGING	GRUNTS
GROAN	GROSCHEN	GROUPISTS	GRUDGINGS	GRUPPETTI
GROANED	GROSCHENS	GROUPLET	GRUE	GRUPPETTO
GROANER	GROSER	GROUPLETS	GRUED	GRUTCH
GROANERS	GROSERS	GROUPS	GRUEING	GRUTCHED
GROANFUL	GROSERT	GROUPY	GRUEL	GRUTCHES
GROANING	GROSERTS	GROUSE	GRUELLED	GRUTCHING
GROANINGS	GROSET	GROUSED	GRUELLING	GRUTTEN
GROANS	GROSETS	GROUSER	GRUELLINGS	GRYCE
GROAT	GROSGRAIN	GROUSERS	GRUELS	GRYCES
GROATS	GROSGRAINS	GROUSES	GRUES	GRYDE
GROCER	GROSS	GROUSING	GRUESOME	GRYDED
GROCERIES	GROSSART	GROUT	GRUESOMER	GRYDES
GROCERS	GROSSARTS	GROUTED	GRUESOMEST	GRYDING
GROCERY	GROSSED	GROUTIER	GRUFF	GRYESLY
GROCKLE	GROSSER	GROUTIEST	GRUFFER	GRYESY
GROCKLES	GROSSES	GROUTING	GRUFFEST	GRYFON
GROG	GROSSEST	GROUTINGS	GRUFFISH	GRYFONS
GROGGED	GROSSING	GROUTS	GRUFFLY	GRYKE
GROGGERIES	GROSSNESS	GROUTY	GRUFFNESS	GRYKES
GROGGERY	GROSSNESSES	GROVE	GRUFFNESSES	GRYPE
GROGGIER	GROSSULAR	GROVEL	GRUFTED	GRYPES
GROGGIEST	GROSSULARS	GROVELLED	GRUING	GRYPHON
GROGGING	GROT	GROVELLER	GRUM	GRYPHONS
GROGGY	GROTESQUE	GROVELLERS	GRUMBLE	GRYPT
GROGRAM	GROTESQUER	GROVELLING	GRUMBLED	GRYSBOK
GROGRAMS	GROTESQUES	GROVELS	GRUMBLER	GRYSBOKS
GROGS	GROTESQUEST	GROVES	GRUMBLERS	GRYSELY
GROIN	GROTS	GROW	GRUMBLES	GRYSIE
GROINED	GROTTIER	GROWER	GRUMBLIER	GRYSELY
GROINING	GROTTIEST	GROWERS	GRUMBLIEST	GU
GROININGS	GROTTO	GROWING	GRUMBLING	GUACAMOLE
GROINS	GROTTOES	GROWINGS	GRUMBLINGS	GUACAMOLES
GROMA	GROTTOS	GROWL	GRUMBLY	GUACHARO
GROMAS	GROTTY	GROWLED	GRUME	GUACHAROS
GROMET	GROUCH	GROWLER	GRUMES	GUACO
GROMETS	GROUCHED	GROWLERIES	GRUMLY	GUACOS
GROMMET	GROUCHES	GROWLERS	GRUMMER	GUAIACUM
GROMMETS		GROWLERY	GRUMMEST	GUAIACUMS
				GUAN

GUANA
GUANACO
GUANACOS
GUANAS
GUANAZOLO
GUANAZOLOS
GUANIN
GUANINE
GUANINES
GUANINS
GUANO
GUANOS
GUANS
GUAR
GUARANÁ
GUARANÁS
GUARANI
GUARANIES
GUARANTEE
GUARANTEED
GUARANTEEING
GUARANTEES
GUARANTIED
GUARANTIES
GUARANTOR
GUARANTORS
GUARANTY
GUARANTYING
GUARD
GUARDABLE
GUARDAGE
GUARDAGES
GUARDANT
GUARDANTS
GUARDED
GUARDEDLY
GUARDEE
GUARDEES
GUARDIAN
GUARDIANS
GUARDING
GUARDLESS
GUARDS
GUARDSMAN
GUARDSMEN
GUARISH
GUARISHED
GUARISHES
GUARISHING
GUARS
GUAVA
GUAVAS
GUAYULE
GUAYULES
GUB
GUBBAH
GUBBAHS
GUBBINS
GUBS
GUCK
GUCKIER
GUCKIEST
GUCKS
GUCKY
GUDDLE
GUDDLED
GUDDLES
GUDDLING
GUDE
GUDEMAN

GUDEMEN
GUDESIRE
GUDESIRES
GUDEWIFE
GUDEWIVES
GUDGEON
GUDGEONED
GUDGEONING
GUDGEONS
GUE
GUENON
GUENONS
GUERDON
GUERDONED
GUERDONING
GUERDONS
GUEREZA
GUEREZAS
GUÉRIDON
GUÉRIDONS
GUERILLA
GUERILLAS
GUERNSEY
GUERNSEYS
GUERRILLA
GUERRILLAS
GUES
GUESS
GUESSABLE
GUESSED
GUESSER
GUESSERS
GUESSES
GUESSING
GUESSINGS
GUEST
GUESTED
GUESTEN
GUESTENED
GUESTENING
GUESTENS
GUESTING
GUESTS
GUESTWISE
GUFF
GUFFAW
GUFFAWED
GUFFAWING
GUFFAWS
GUFFS
GUGGLE
GUGGLED
GUGGLES
GUGGLING
GUICHET
GUICHETS
GUID
GUIDABLE
GUIDAGE
GUIDAGES
GUIDANCE
GUIDANCES
GUIDE
GUIDED
GUIDELESS
GUIDELINE
GUIDELINES
GUIDER
GUIDERS
GUIDES

GUIDESHIP
GUIDESHIPS
GUIDING
GUIDINGS
GUIDON
GUIDONS
GUILD
GUILDER
GUILDERS
GUILDHALL
GUILDHALLS
GUILDRIES
GUILDRY
GUILDS
GUILE
GUILED
GUILEFUL
GUILELESS
GUILER
GUILERS
GUILES
GUILING
GUILLEMOT
GUILLEMOTS
GUILLOCHE
GUILLOCHED
GUILLOCHES
GUILLOCHING
GUILT
GUILTIER
GUILTIEST
GUILTILY
GUILTLESS
GUILTS
GUILTY
GUIMBARD
GUIMBARDS
GUIMP
GUIMPE
GUIMPED
GUIMPES
GUIMPING
GUIMPS
GUINEA
GUINEAS
GUIPURE
GUIPURES
GUIRO
GUIROS
GUISARD
GUISARDS
GUISE
GUISED
GUISER
GUISERS
GUISES
GUISING
GUITAR
GUITARIST
GUITARISTS
GUITARS
GUIZER
GUIZERS
GULA
GULAG
GULAGS
GULAR
GULAS
GULCH
GULCHED

GULCHES
GULCHING
GULDEN
GULDENS
GULE
GULES
GULF
GULFED
GULFIER
GULFIEST
GULFING
GULFS
GULFY
GULL
GULLABLE
GULLED
GULLER
GULLERIES
GULLERS
GULLERY
GULLET
GULLETS
GULLEY
GULLEYED
GULLEYING
GULLEYS
GULLIBLE
GULLIED
GULLIES
GULLING
GULLISH
GULLS
GULLY
GULLYING
GULOSITIES
GULOSITY
GULP
GULPED
GULPER
GULPERS
GULPH
GULPHED
GULPHING
GULPHS
GULPING
GULPS
GULY
GUM
GUMBO
GUMBOIL
GUMBOILS
GUMBOOT
GUMBOOTS
GUMBOS
GUMDROP
GUMDROPS
GUMMA
GUMMATA
GUMMATOUS
GUMMED
GUMMIER
GUMMIEST
GUMMINESS
GUMMINESSES
GUMMING
GUMMINGS
GUMMITE
GUMMITES
GUMMOSES
GUMMOSIS

GUMMOSITIES
GUMMOSITY
GUMMOUS
GUMMY
GUMNUT
GUMNUTS
GUMP
GUMPED
GUMPHION
GUMPHIONS
GUMPING
GUMPS
GUMPTION
GUMPTIONS
GUMPTIOUS
GUMS
GUMSHIELD
GUMSHIELDS
GUMSHOE
GUMSHOED
GUMSHOEING
GUMSHOES
GUN
GUNBOAT
GUNBOATS
GUNCOTTON
GUNCOTTONS
GUNDIES
GUNDY
GUNFIGHT
GUNFIGHTING
GUNFIGHTS
GUNFIRE
GUNFIRES
GUNFLINT
GUNFLINTS
GUNFOUGHT
GUNGE
GUNGES
GUNGIER
GUNGIEST
GUNGY
GUNITE
GUNITES
GUNK
GUNKS
GUNLAYER
GUNLAYERS
GUNMAKER
GUNMAKERS
GUNMAN
GUNMEN
GUNMETAL
GUNMETALS
GUNNAGE
GUNNAGES
GUNNED
GUNNEL
GUNNELS
GUNNER
GUNNERA
GUNNERAS
GUNNERIES
GUNNERS
GUNNERY
GUNNIES
GUNNING
GUNNINGS
GUNNY
GUNPLAY

GUNPLAYS	GURNET	GUTBUCKETS	GYBE	GYPSEOUS
GUNPORT	GURNETS	GUTCHER	GYBED	GYPSIED
GUNPORTS	GURNEY	GUTCHERS	GYBES	GYPSIES
GUNPOWDER	GURNEYS	GUTLESS	GYBING	GYPSUM
GUNPOWDERS	GURNING	GUTS	GYELD	GYPSUMS
GUNROOM	GURNS	GUTSIER	GYELDS	GYPSY
GUNROOMS	GURRAH	GUTSIEST	GYLDEN	GYPSYDOM
GUNRUNNER	GURRAHS	GUTSINESS	GYM	GYPSYDOMS
GUNRUNNERS	GURRIES	GUTSINESSES	GYMBAL	GYPSYING
GUNS	GURRY	GUTSY	GYMBALS	GYPSYISM
GUNSEL	GURS	GUTTA	GYMKHANA	GYPSYISMS
GUNSELS	GURU	GUTTAE	GYMKHANAS	GYPSYWORT
GUNSHIP	GURUDOM	GUTTAS	GYMMAL	GYPSYWORTS
GUNSHIPS	GURUDOMS	GUTTATE	GYMMALS	GYRAL
GUNSHOT	GURUISM	GUTTATED	GYMNASIA	GYRALLY
GUNSHOTS	GURUISMS	GUTTATES	GYMNASIAL	GYRANT
GUNSMITH	GURUS	GUTTATING	GYMNASIC	GYRATE
GUNSMITHS	GURUSHIP	GUTTATION	GYMNASIEN	GYRATED
GUNSTICK	GURUSHIPS	GUTTATIONS	GYMNASIUM	GYRATES
GUNSTICKS	GUS	GUTTED	GYMNASIUMS	GYRATING
GUNSTOCK	GUSH	GUTTER	GYMNAST	GYRATION
GUNSTOCKS	GUSHED	GUTTERED	GYMNASTIC	GYRATIONS
GUNSTONE	GUSHER	GUTTERING	GYMNASTICS	GYRATORY
GUNSTONES	GUSHERS	GUTTERINGS	GYMNASTS	GYRE
GUNTER	GUSHES	GUTTERS	GYMNIC	GYRED
GUNTERS	GUSHIER	GUTTIES	GYMNOSOPH	GYRENE
GUNWALE	GUSHIEST	GUTTING	GYMNOSOPHS	GYRFALCON
GUNWALES	GUSHING	GUTTLE	GYMP	GYRFALCONS
GUNYAH	GUSHINGLY	GUTTLED	GYMPED	GYRI
GUNYAHS	GUSHY	GUTTLES	GYMPING	GYRING
GUP	GUSLA	GUTTLING	GYMPS	GYRO
GUPPIES	GUSLAR	GUTTURAL	GYMS	GYROCAR
GUPPY	GUSLARS	GUTTURALS	GYNAE	GYROCARS
GUPS	GUSLAS	GUTTY	GYNAECEUM	GYRODYNE
GUR	GUSLE	GUTZER	GYNAECEUMS	GYRODYNES
GURAMI	GUSLES	GUTZERS	GYNAECOID	GYROIDAL
GURAMIS	GUSLI	GUY	GYNAES	GYROMANCIES
GURDWARA	GUSLIS	GUYED	GYNANDRIES	GYROMANCY
GURDWARAS	GUSSET	GUYING	GYNANDRY	GYRON
GURGE	GUSSETED	GUYLE	GYNECIUM	GYRONNY
GURGES	GUSSETING	GUYLED	GYNECIUMS	GYRONS
GURGLE	GUSSETS	GUYLER	GYNIES	GYROPLANE
GURGLED	GUST	GUYLERS	GYNNEY	GYROPLANES
GURGLES	GUSTABLE	GUYLES	GYNNEYS	GYROS
GURGLING	GUSTABLES	GUYLING	GYNNIES	GYROSCOPE
GURGOYLE	GUSTATION	GUYOT	GYNNY	GYROSCOPES
GURGOYLES	GUSTATIONS	GUYOTS	GYNOCRACIES	GYROSE
GURJUN	GUSTATIVE	GUYS	GYNOCRACY	GYROSTAT
GURJUNS	GUSTATORY	GUYSE	GYNOECIUM	GYROSTATS
GURL	GUSTED	GUYSES	GYNOECIUMS	GYROUS
GURLED	GUSTFUL	GUZZLE	GYNOPHORE	GYROVAGUE
GURLET	GUSTIER	GUZZLED	GYNOPHORES	GYROVAGUES
GURLETS	GUSTIEST	GUZZLER	GYNY	GYRUS
GURLIER	GUSTINESS	GUZZLERS	GYP	GYRUSES
GURLIEST	GUSTINESSES	GUZZLES	GYPPED	GYTE
GURLING	GUSTING	GUZZLING	GYPPIE	GYTES
GURLS	GUSTO	GWINIAD	GYPPIES	GYTRASH
GURLY	GUSTOS	GWINIADS	GYPPING	GYTRASHES
GURN	GUSTS	GWYNIAD	GYPPO	GYVE
GURNARD	GUSTY	GWYNIADS	GYPPOS	GYVED
GURNARDS	GUT	GYAL	GYPPY	GYVES
GURNED	GUTBUCKET	GYALS	GYPS	GYVING

H

HA
HAAF
HAAFS
HAANEPOOT
HAANEPOOTS
HAAR
HAARS
HABANERA
HABANERAS
HABDABS
HABERDINE
HABERDINES
HABERGEON
HABERGEONS
HABILABLE
HABILE
HABIT
HABITABLE
HABITABLY
HABITANS
HABITANT
HABITANTS
HABITAT
HABITATS
HABITED
HABITING
HABITS
HABITUAL
HABITUALS
HABITUATE
HABITUATED
HABITUATES
HABITUATING
HABITUDE
HABITUDES
HABITUÉ
HABITUÉS
HABITUS
HABLE
HABOOB
HABOOBS
HACEK
HACEKS
HACHIS
HACHURE
HACHURED
HACHURES
HACHURING
HACIENDA
HACIENDAS
HACK
HACKAMORE
HACKAMORES
HACKBERRIES
HACKBERRY
HACKBOLT
HACKBOLTS
HACKBUT
HACKBUTS
HACKED
HACKEE
HACKEES
HACKER

HACKERIES
HACKERS
HACKERY
HACKETTE
HACKETTES
HACKING
HACKINGS
HACKLE
HACKLED
HACKLER
HACKLERS
HACKLES
HACKLET
HACKLETS
HACKLIER
HACKLIEST
HACKLING
HACKLY
HACKNEY
HACKNEYED
HACKNEYING
HACKNEYS
HACKS
HACQUETON
HACQUETONS
HAD
HADAL
HADDEN
HADDIE
HADDIES
HADDING
HADDOCK
HADDOCKS
HADE
HADED
HADES
HADING
HADITH
HADITHS
HADJ
HADJES
HADJI
HADJIS
HADROME
HADROMES
HADRON
HADRONIC
HADRONS
HADROSAUR
HADROSAURS
HADS
HADST
HAE
HAECCEITIES
HAECCEITY
HAEING
HAEM
HAEMAL
HAEMATIC
HAEMATIN
HAEMATINS
HAEMATITE
HAEMATITES

HAEMATOID
HAEMATOMA
HAEMATOMAS
HAEMIC
HAEMIN
HAEMINS
HAEMOCYTE
HAEMOCYTES
HAEMONIES
HAEMONY
HAEMOSTAT
HAEMOSTATS
HAEMS
HAET
HAETS
HAFF
HAFFET
HAFFETS
HAFFIT
HAFFITS
HAFFLIN
HAFFLINS
HAFFS
HAFNIUM
HAFNIUMS
HAFT
HAFTED
HAFTING
HAFTS
HAG
HAGBERRIES
HAGBERRY
HAGBOLT
HAGBOLTS
HAGBUT
HAGBUTS
HAGDEN
HAGDENS
HAGDON
HAGDONS
HAGDOWN
HAGDOWNS
HAGFISH
HAGFISHES
HAGG
HAGGARD
HAGGARDLY
HAGGARDS
HAGGED
HAGGING
HAGGIS
HAGGISES
HAGGISH
HAGGISHLY
HAGGLE
HAGGLED
HAGGLER
HAGGLERS
HAGGLES
HAGGLING
HAGGS
HAGIARCHIES
HAGIARCHY

HAGIOLOGIES
HAGIOLOGY
HAGLET
HAGLETS
HAGS
HAH
HAHNIUM
HAHNIUMS
HAICK
HAICKS
HAIDUK
HAIDUKS
HAIK
HAIKAI
HAIKS
HAIKU
HAIL
HAILED
HAILER
HAILERS
HAILIER
HAILIEST
HAILING
HAILS
HAILSHOT
HAILSHOTS
HAILSTONE
HAILSTONES
HAILY
HAIN
HAINCH
HAINCHED
HAINCHES
HAINCHING
HAINED
HAINING
HAININGS
HAINS
HAIQUE
HAIQUES
HAIR
HAIRBELL
HAIRBELLS
HAIRCLOTH
HAIRCLOTHS
HAIRCUT
HAIRCUTS
HAIRED
HAIRIER
HAIRIEST
HAIRINESS
HAIRINESSES
HAIRING
HAIRLESS
HAIRLIKE
HAIRLINE
HAIRLINES
HAIRPIN
HAIRPINS
HAIRS
HAIRST
HAIRSTED
HAIRSTING

HAIRSTS
HAIRSTYLE
HAIRSTYLES
HAIRY
HAITH
HAJ
HAJES
HAJI
HAJIS
HAJJ
HAJJES
HAJJI
HAJJIS
HAKA
HAKAM
HAKAMS
HAKAS
HAKE
HAKES
HAKIM
HAKIMS
HALAL
HALALLED
HALALLING
HALALS
HALATION
HALATIONS
HALAVAH
HALAVAHS
HALBERD
HALBERDS
HALBERT
HALBERTS
HALCYON
HALCYONS
HALE
HALED
HALENESS
HALENESSES
HALER
HALERS
HALES
HALEST
HALF
HALFA
HALFAS
HALFEN
HALFLIN
HALFLING
HALFLINGS
HALFLINS
HALFPACE
HALFPACES
HALFPENCE
HALFPENNIES
HALFPENNY
HALFWAY
HALIBUT
HALIBUTS
HALICORE
HALICORES
HALIDE
HALIDES

HALIDOM	HALO	HAMFATTERING	HANDBILL	HANDSEL
HALIDOMS	HALOBIONT	HAMFATTERS	HANDBILLS	HANDSELLED
HALIEUTIC	HALOBIONTS	HAMING	HANDBOOK	HANDSELLING
HALIEUTICS	HALOED	HAMLET	HANDBOOKS	HANDSELS
HALIMOT	HALOES	HAMLETS	HANDCAR	HANDSET
HALIMOTE	HALOGEN	HAMMAL	HANDCARS	HANDSETS
HALIMOTES	HALOGENS	HAMMALS	HANDCLAP	HANDSHAKE
HALIMOTS	HALOID	HAMMAM	HANDCLAPS	HANDSHAKES
HALING	HALOIDS	HAMMAMS	HANDCLASP	HANDSOME
HALIOTIS	HALOING	HAMMED	HANDCLASPS	HANDSOMER
HALITE	HALOPHILE	HAMMER	HANDCRAFT	HANDSOMEST
HALITES	HALOPHILIES	HAMMERED	HANDCRAFTS	HANDSPIKE
HALITOSES	HALOPHILY	HAMMERER	HANDCUFF	HANDSPIKES
HALITOSIS	HALOPHOBE	HAMMERERS	HANDCUFFED	HANDSTAFF
HALITOUS	HALOPHOBES	HAMMERING	HANDCUFFING	HANDSTAFFS
HALITUS	HALOPHYTE	HAMMERINGS	HANDCUFFS	HANDSTAND
HALITUSES	HALOPHYTES	HAMMERKOP	HANDED	HANDSTANDS
HALL	HALOS	HAMMERKOPS	HANDER	HANDSTAVES
HALLAL	HALOTHANE	HAMMERMAN	HANDERS	HANDSTURN
HALLALI	HALOTHANES	HAMMERMEN	HANDFAST	HANDSTURNS
HALLALIS	HALSE	HAMMERS	HANDFASTED	HANDTOWEL
HALLALLED	HALSED	HAMMIER	HANDFASTING	HANDTOWELS
HALLALLING	HALSER	HAMMIEST	HANDFASTINGS	HANDWORK
HALLALOO	HALSERS	HAMMILY	HANDFASTS	HANDWORKS
HALLALOOS	HALSES	HAMMING	HANDFUL	HANDY
HALLALS	HALSING	HAMMOCK	HANDFULS	HANDYMAN
HALLAN	HALT	HAMMOCKS	HANDGRIP	HANDYMEN
HALLANS	HALTED	HAMMY	HANDGRIPS	HANDYWORK
HALLIAN	HALTER	HAMOSE	HANDHOLD	HANDYWORKS
HALLIANS	HALTERED	HAMOUS	HANDHOLDS	HANEPOOT
HALLIARD	HALTERES	HAMPER	HANDICAP	HANEPOOTS
HALLIARDS	HALTERING	HAMPERED	HANDICAPPED	HANG
HALLING	HALTERS	HAMPERING	HANDICAPPING	HANGABLE
HALLINGS	HALTING	HAMPERS	HANDICAPS	HANGAR
HALLION	HALTINGLY	HAMPSTER	HANDIER	HANGARS
HALLIONS	HALTINGS	HAMPSTERS	HANDIEST	HANGBIRD
HALLMARK	HALTS	HAMS	HANDILY	HANGBIRDS
HALLMARKED	HALVA	HAMSTER	HANDINESS	HANGDOG
HALLMARKING	HALVAH	HAMSTERS	HANDINESSES	HANGDOGS
HALLMARKS	HALVAHS	HAMSTRING	HANDING	HANGED
HALLO	HALVAS	HAMSTRINGED	HANDIWORK	HANGER
HALLOA	HALVE	HAMSTRINGING	HANDIWORKS	HANGERS
HALLOAED	HALVED	HAMSTRINGS	HANDJAR	HANGFIRE
HALLOAING	HALVER	HAMSTRUNG	HANDJARS	HANGFIRES
HALLOAS	HALVERS	HAMULAR	HANDLE	HANGING
HALLOED	HALVES	HAMULATE	HANDLEBAR	HANGINGS
HALLOES	HALVING	HAMULI	HANDLEBARS	HANGMAN
HALLOING	HALYARD	HAMULUS	HANDLED	HANGMEN
HALLOO	HALYARDS	HAMZA	HANDLER	HANGNAIL
HALLOOED	HAM	HAMZAH	HANDLERS	HANGNAILS
HALLOOING	HAMADRYAD	HAMZAHS	HANDLES	HANGNEST
HALLOOS	HAMADRYADES	HAMZAS	HANDLESS	HANGNESTS
HALLOS	HAMADRYADS	HAN	HANDLING	HANGOUT
HALLOW	HAMAL	HANAP	HANDLINGS	HANGOUTS
HALLOWED	HAMALS	HANAPER	HANDLIST	HANGOVER
HALLOWING	HAMARTIA	HANAPERS	HANDLISTS	HANGOVERS
HALLOWS	HAMARTIAS	HANAPS	HANDMADE	HANGS
HALLS	HAMATE	HANCE	HANDMAID	HANJAR
HALLSTAND	HAMBLE	HANCES	HANDMAIDS	HANJARS
HALLSTANDS	HAMBLED	HANCH	HANDOUT	HANK
HALLUCES	HAMBLES	HANCHED	HANDOUTS	HANKED
HALLUX	HAMBLING	HANCHES	HANDOVER	HANKER
HALLWAY	HAMBURGER	HANCHING	HANDOVERS	HANKERED
HALLWAYS	HAMBURGERS	HAND	HANDPLAY	HANKERING
HALLYON	HAME	HANDBAG	HANDPLAYS	HANKERINGS
HALLYONS	HAMED	HANDBAGS	HANDRAIL	HANKERS
HALM	HAMES	HANDBALL	HANDRAILS	HANKIE
HALMA	HAMEWITH	HANDBALLS	HANDS	HANKIES
HALMAS	HAMFATTER	HANDBELL	HANDSAW	HANKING
HALMS	HAMFATTERED	HANDBELLS	HANDSAWS	HANKS

HANKY
HANSEL
HANSELLED
HANSELLING
HANSELS
HANSOM
HANSOMS
HANTLE
HANTLES
HANUMAN
HANUMANS
HAOMA
HAOMAS
HAP
HAPHAZARD
HAPHAZARDS
HAPLESS
HAPLESSLY
HAPLOID
HAPLOIDIES
HAPLOIDY
HAPLOLOGIES
HAPLOLOGY
HAPLY
HAPPED
HAPPEN
HAPPENED
HAPPENING
HAPPENINGS
HAPPENS
HAPPIED
HAPPIER
HAPPIES
HAPPIEST
HAPPILY
HAPPINESS
HAPPINESSES
HAPPING
HAPPY
HAPPYING
HAPS
HAPTERON
HAPTERONS
HAPTIC
HAPTICS
HAQUETON
HAQUETONS
HARAM
HARAMS
HARANGUE
HARANGUED
HARANGUER
HARANGUERS
HARANGUES
HARANGUING
HARASS
HARASSED
HARASSER
HARASSERS
HARASSES
HARASSING
HARASSINGS
HARBINGER
HARBINGERED
HARBINGERING
HARBINGERS
HARBOR
HARBORED
HARBORING
HARBORS

HARBOUR
HARBOURED
HARBOURER
HARBOURERS
HARBOURING
HARBOURS
HARD
HARDBACK
HARDBACKS
HARDBAKE
HARDBAKES
HARDBEAM
HARDBEAMS
HARDBOARD
HARDBOARDS
HARDCORE
HARDCORES
HARDEN
HARDENED
HARDENER
HARDENERS
HARDENING
HARDENINGS
HARDENS
HARDER
HARDEST
HARDFACE
HARDFACES
HARDGRASS
HARDGRASSES
HARDHACK
HARDHACKS
HARDHEAD
HARDHEADS
HARDIER
HARDIEST
HARDIHEAD
HARDIHEADS
HARDIHOOD
HARDIHOODS
HARDILY
HARDIMENT
HARDIMENTS
HARDINESS
HARDINESSES
HARDISH
HARDLINE
HARDLINER
HARDLINERS
HARDLY
HARDNESS
HARDNESSES
HARDNOSED
HARDOKE
HARDOKES
HARDPARTS
HARDS
HARDSHELL
HARDSHIP
HARDSHIPS
HARDTACK
HARDTACKS
HARDTOP
HARDTOPS
HARDWARE
HARDWARES
HARDWOOD
HARDWOODS
HARDY
HARE

HAREBELL
HAREBELLS
HARED
HAREEM
HAREEMS
HARELD
HARELDS
HAREM
HAREMS
HARES
HAREWOOD
HAREWOODS
HARICOT
HARICOTS
HARIGALDS
HARIGALS
HARIM
HARIMS
HARING
HARIOLATE
HARIOLATED
HARIOLATES
HARIOLATING
HARISH
HARK
HARKED
HARKEN
HARKENED
HARKENING
HARKENS
HARKING
HARKS
HARL
HARLED
HARLEQUIN
HARLEQUINED
HARLEQUINING
HARLEQUINS
HARLING
HARLINGS
HARLOT
HARLOTRIES
HARLOTRY
HARLOTS
HARLS
HARM
HARMALA
HARMALAS
HARMALIN
HARMALINE
HARMALINES
HARMALINS
HARMAN
HARMANS
HARMATTAN
HARMATTANS
HARMDOING
HARMDOINGS
HARMED
HARMEL
HARMELS
HARMFUL
HARMFULLY
HARMIN
HARMINE
HARMINES
HARMING
HARMINS
HARMLESS
HARMONIC

HARMONICA
HARMONICAS
HARMONICS
HARMONIES
HARMONISE
HARMONISED
HARMONISES
HARMONISING
HARMONIST
HARMONISTS
HARMONIUM
HARMONIUMS
HARMONIZE
HARMONIZED
HARMONIZES
HARMONIZING
HARMONY
HARMOST
HARMOSTIES
HARMOSTS
HARMOSTY
HARMOTOME
HARMOTOMES
HARMS
HARN
HARNESS
HARNESSED
HARNESSES
HARNESSING
HARNS
HARO
HAROS
HAROSET
HAROSETH
HAROSETHS
HAROSETS
HARP
HARPED
HARPER
HARPERS
HARPIES
HARPING
HARPINGS
HARPIST
HARPISTS
HARPOON
HARPOONED
HARPOONER
HARPOONERS
HARPOONING
HARPOONS
HARPS
HARPY
HARQUEBUS
HARQUEBUSES
HARRIDAN
HARRIDANS
HARRIED
HARRIER
HARRIERS
HARRIES
HARROW
HARROWED
HARROWING
HARROWS
HARRUMPH
HARRUMPHED
HARRUMPHING
HARRUMPHS
HARRY

HARRYING
HARSH
HARSHEN
HARSHENED
HARSHENING
HARSHENS
HARSHER
HARSHEST
HARSHLY
HARSHNESS
HARSHNESSES
HARSLET
HARSLETS
HART
HARTAL
HARTALS
HARTBEES
HARTBEESES
HARTELY
HARTEN
HARTENED
HARTENING
HARTENS
HARTLESSE
HARTS
HARTSHORN
HARTSHORNS
HARUSPEX
HARUSPICES
HARUSPICIES
HARUSPICY
HARVEST
HARVESTED
HARVESTER
HARVESTERS
HARVESTING
HARVESTS
HAS
HASH
HASHED
HASHEESH
HASHEESHES
HASHES
HASHIER
HASHIEST
HASHING
HASHISH
HASHISHES
HASHY
HASK
HASKS
HASLET
HASLETS
HASP
HASPED
HASPING
HASPS
HASSAR
HASSARS
HASSLE
HASSLED
HASSLES
HASSLING
HASSOCK
HASSOCKS
HASSOCKY
HAST
HASTA
HASTATE
HASTATED

HASTE
HASTED
HASTEN
HASTENED
HASTENER
HASTENERS
HASTENING
HASTENS
HASTES
HASTIER
HASTIEST
HASTILY
HASTINESS
HASTINESSES
HASTING
HASTINGS
HASTY
HAT
HATABLE
HATBAND
HATBANDS
HATBOX
HATBOXES
HATBRUSH
HATBRUSHES
HATCH
HATCHBACK
HATCHBACKS
HATCHED
HATCHEL
HATCHELLED
HATCHELLING
HATCHELS
HATCHER
HATCHERIES
HATCHERS
HATCHERY
HATCHES
HATCHET
HATCHETS
HATCHETY
HATCHING
HATCHINGS
HATCHLING
HATCHLINGS
HATCHMENT
HATCHMENTS
HATCHWAY
HATCHWAYS
HATE
HATEABLE
HATED
HATEFUL
HATEFULLY
HATELESS
HATER
HATERENT
HATERENTS
HATERS
HATES
HATFUL
HATFULS
HATGUARD
HATGUARDS
HATH
HATING
HATLESS
HATPEG
HATPEGS
HATPIN

HATPINS
HATRACK
HATRACKS
HATRED
HATREDS
HATS
HATSTAND
HATSTANDS
HATTED
HATTER
HATTERED
HATTERING
HATTERS
HATTING
HATTINGS
HATTOCK
HATTOCKS
HAUBERK
HAUBERKS
HAUD
HAUDING
HAUDS
HAUGH
HAUGHS
HAUGHT
HAUGHTIER
HAUGHTIEST
HAUGHTILY
HAUGHTY
HAUL
HAULAGE
HAULAGES
HAULD
HAULDS
HAULED
HAULER
HAULERS
HAULIER
HAULIERS
HAULING
HAULM
HAULMS
HAULS
HAULST
HAULT
HAUNCH
HAUNCHED
HAUNCHES
HAUNCHING
HAUNT
HAUNTED
HAUNTER
HAUNTERS
HAUNTING
HAUNTINGS
HAUNTS
HAURIANT
HAURIENT
HAUSE
HAUSED
HAUSES
HAUSFRAU
HAUSFRAUS
HAUSING
HAUSTELLA
HAUSTORIA
HAUT
HAUTBOIS
HAUTBOY
HAUTBOYS

HAUTE
HAUTEUR
HAUTEURS
HAÜYNE
HAÜYNES
HAVE
HAVELOCK
HAVELOCKS
HAVEN
HAVENED
HAVENING
HAVENS
HAVEOUR
HAVEOURS
HAVER
HAVERED
HAVEREL
HAVERELS
HAVERING
HAVERINGS
HAVERS
HAVERSACK
HAVERSACKS
HAVERSINE
HAVERSINES
HAVES
HAVILDAR
HAVILDARS
HAVING
HAVINGS
HAVIOUR
HAVIOURS
HAVOC
HAVOCKED
HAVOCKING
HAVOCS
HAW
HAWBUCK
HAWBUCKS
HAWED
HAWFINCH
HAWFINCHES
HAWING
HAWK
HAWKBELL
HAWKBELLS
HAWKBIT
HAWKBITS
HAWKED
HAWKER
HAWKERS
HAWKEY
HAWKEYS
HAWKIE
HAWKIES
HAWKING
HAWKINGS
HAWKISH
HAWKISHLY
HAWKIT
HAWKS
HAWKSBILL
HAWKSBILLS
HAWKWEED
HAWKWEEDS
HAWM
HAWMED
HAWMING
HAWMS
HAWS

HAWSE
HAWSED
HAWSEHOLE
HAWSEHOLES
HAWSEPIPE
HAWSEPIPES
HAWSER
HAWSERS
HAWSES
HAWSING
HAWTHORN
HAWTHORNS
HAY
HAYBAND
HAYBANDS
HAYBOX
HAYBOXES
HAYCOCK
HAYCOCKS
HAYED
HAYFIELD
HAYFIELDS
HAYFORK
HAYFORKS
HAYING
HAYINGS
HAYLE
HAYLES
HAYLOFT
HAYLOFTS
HAYMAKER
HAYMAKERS
HAYMAKING
HAYMAKINGS
HAYMOW
HAYMOWS
HAYRICK
HAYRICKS
HAYS
HAYSEED
HAYSEEDS
HAYSEL
HAYSELS
HAYSTACK
HAYSTACKS
HAYWARD
HAYWARDS
HAYWIRE
HAYWIRES
HAZARD
HAZARDED
HAZARDING
HAZARDIZE
HAZARDIZES
HAZARDOUS
HAZARDRIES
HAZARDRY
HAZARDS
HAZE
HAZED
HAZEL
HAZELLY
HAZELNUT
HAZELNUTS
HAZELS
HAZER
HAZERS
HAZES
HAZIER
HAZIEST

HAZILY
HAZINESS
HAZINESSES
HAZING
HAZINGS
HAZY
HE
HEAD
HEADACHE
HEADACHES
HEADACHIER
HEADACHIEST
HEADACHY
HEADBAND
HEADBANDS
HEADBOARD
HEADBOARDS
HEADCASE
HEADCASES
HEADCHAIR
HEADCHAIRS
HEADCLOTH
HEADCLOTHS
HEADED
HEADER
HEADERS
HEADFAST
HEADFASTS
HEADFRAME
HEADFRAMES
HEADGEAR
HEADGEARS
HEADHUNT
HEADHUNTED
HEADHUNTING
HEADHUNTINGS
HEADHUNTS
HEADIER
HEADIEST
HEADILY
HEADINESS
HEADINESSES
HEADING
HEADINGS
HEADLAMP
HEADLAMPS
HEADLAND
HEADLANDS
HEADLESS
HEADLIGHT
HEADLIGHTS
HEADLINE
HEADLINED
HEADLINER
HEADLINERS
HEADLINES
HEADLINING
HEADLOCK
HEADLOCKS
HEADLONG
HEADMAN
HEADMARK
HEADMARKS
HEADMEN
HEADMOST
HEADNOTE
HEADNOTES
HEADPEACE
HEADPEACES
HEADPHONE

HEADPHONES
HEADPIECE
HEADPIECES
HEADRACE
HEADRACES
HEADRAIL
HEADRAILS
HEADREACH
HEADREACHED
HEADREACHES
HEADREACHING
HEADREST
HEADRESTS
HEADRIG
HEADRIGS
HEADRING
HEADRINGS
HEADROOM
HEADROOMS
HEADROPE
HEADROPES
HEADS
HEADSCARF
HEADSCARVES
HEADSET
HEADSETS
HEADSHAKE
HEADSHAKES
HEADSHIP
HEADSHIPS
HEADSMAN
HEADSMEN
HEADSTALL
HEADSTALLS
HEADSTICK
HEADSTICKS
HEADSTOCK
HEADSTOCKS
HEADSTONE
HEADSTONES
HEADWAY
HEADWAYS
HEADWORD
HEADWORDS
HEADWORK
HEADWORKS
HEADY
HEAL
HEALABLE
HEALD
HEALDED
HEALDING
HEALDS
HEALED
HEALER
HEALERS
HEALING
HEALINGLY
HEALINGS
HEALS
HEALSOME
HEALTH
HEALTHFUL
HEALTHIER
HEALTHIEST
HEALTHILY
HEALTHS
HEALTHY
HEAME
HEAP

HEAPED
HEAPIER
HEAPIEST
HEAPING
HEAPS
HEAPSTEAD
HEAPSTEADS
HEAPY
HEAR
HEARD
HEARDS
HEARE
HEARER
HEARERS
HEARES
HEARIE
HEARING
HEARINGS
HEARKEN
HEARKENED
HEARKENER
HEARKENERS
HEARKENING
HEARKENS
HEARS
HEARSAY
HEARSAYS
HEARSE
HEARSED
HEARSES
HEARSIER
HEARSIEST
HEARSING
HEARSY
HEART
HEARTACHE
HEARTACHES
HEARTBURN
HEARTBURNS
HEARTED
HEARTEN
HEARTENED
HEARTENING
HEARTENS
HEARTFELT
HEARTH
HEARTHS
HEARTIER
HEARTIES
HEARTIEST
HEARTIKIN
HEARTIKINS
HEARTILY
HEARTING
HEARTLAND
HEARTLANDS
HEARTLESS
HEARTLET
HEARTLETS
HEARTLING
HEARTLINGS
HEARTLY
HEARTPEA
HEARTPEAS
HEARTS
HEARTSEED
HEARTSEEDS
HEARTSOME
HEARTWOOD
HEARTWOODS

HEARTY
HEAST
HEASTE
HEASTES
HEASTS
HEAT
HEATED
HEATER
HEATERS
HEATH
HEATHBIRD
HEATHBIRDS
HEATHCOCK
HEATHCOCKS
HEATHEN
HEATHENRIES
HEATHENRY
HEATHENS
HEATHER
HEATHERS
HEATHERY
HEATHIER
HEATHIEST
HEATHS
HEATHY
HEATING
HEATINGS
HEATS
HEATSPOT
HEATSPOTS
HEAUME
HEAUMES
HEAVE
HEAVED
HEAVEN
HEAVENLIER
HEAVENLIEST
HEAVENLY
HEAVENS
HEAVER
HEAVERS
HEAVES
HEAVIER
HEAVIES
HEAVIEST
HEAVILY
HEAVINESS
HEAVINESSES
HEAVING
HEAVINGS
HEAVY
HEBDOMAD
HEBDOMADS
HEBE
HEBEN
HEBENON
HEBENONS
HEBENS
HEBES
HEBETANT
HEBETATE
HEBETATED
HEBETATES
HEBETATING
HEBETUDE
HEBETUDES
HEBONA
HEBONAS
HECATOMB
HECATOMBS

HECH
HECHT
HECHTING
HECHTS
HECK
HECKLE
HECKLED
HECKLER
HECKLERS
HECKLES
HECKLING
HECKLINGS
HECKS
HECOGENIN
HECOGENINS
HECTARE
HECTARES
HECTIC
HECTICAL
HECTICS
HECTOGRAM
HECTOGRAMS
HECTOR
HECTORED
HECTORER
HECTORERS
HECTORING
HECTORINGS
HECTORISM
HECTORISMS
HECTORLY
HECTORS
HEDDLE
HEDDLED
HEDDLES
HEDDLING
HEDERAL
HEDERATED
HEDGE
HEDGEBILL
HEDGEBILLS
HEDGED
HEDGEHOG
HEDGEHOGS
HEDGEPIG
HEDGEPIGS
HEDGER
HEDGEROW
HEDGEROWS
HEDGERS
HEDGES
HEDGIER
HEDGIEST
HEDGING
HEDGINGS
HEDGY
HEDONIC
HEDONICS
HEDONISM
HEDONISMS
HEDONIST
HEDONISTS
HEDYPHANE
HEDYPHANES
HEED
HEEDED
HEEDFUL
HEEDFULLY
HEEDINESS
HEEDINESSES

HEEDING
HEEDLESS
HEEDS
HEEDY
HEEHAW
HEEHAWED
HEEHAWING
HEEHAWS
HEEL
HEELED
HEELER
HEELERS
HEELING
HEELINGS
HEELS
HEEZE
HEEZED
HEEZES
HEEZIE
HEEZIES
HEEZING
HEFT
HEFTE
HEFTED
HEFTIER
HEFTIEST
HEFTING
HEFTS
HEFTY
HEGEMONIC
HEGEMONIES
HEGEMONY
HEGIRA
HEGIRAS
HEID
HEIDS
HEIFER
HEIFERS
HEIGH
HEIGHT
HEIGHTEN
HEIGHTENED
HEIGHTENING
HEIGHTENS
HEIGHTS
HEIL
HEINOUS
HEINOUSLY
HEIR
HEIRDOM
HEIRDOMS
HEIRED
HEIRESS
HEIRESSES
HEIRING
HEIRLESS
HEIRLOOM
HEIRLOOMS
HEIRS
HEIRSHIP
HEIRSHIPS
HEIST
HEISTED
HEISTER
HEISTERS
HEISTING
HEISTS
HEJAB
HEJABS
HEJIRA

HEJIRAS	HELLIER	HEMIHEDRY	HENOTIC	HERBAR
HEJRA	HELLIERS	HEMINA	HENPECK	HERBARIA
HEJRAS	HELLING	HEMINAS	HENPECKED	HERBARIAN
HELCOID	HELLION	HEMIOLA	HENPECKING	HERBARIANS
HELD	HELLIONS	HEMIOLAS	HENPECKS	HERBARIES
HELE	HELLISH	HEMIOLIA	HENRIES	HERBARIUM
HELED	HELLISHLY	HEMIOLIAS	HENRY	HERBARIUMS
HELES	HELLO	HEMIOLIC	HENRYS	HERBARS
HELIAC	HELLOED	HEMIONE	HENS	HERBARY
HELIACAL	HELLOES	HEMIONES	HENT	HERBELET
HELIBUS	HELLOING	HEMIONUS	HENTING	HERBELETS
HELIBUSES	HELLOS	HEMIONUSES	HENTS	HERBICIDE
HELICAL	HELLOVA	HEMIOPIA	HEP	HERBICIDES
HELICALLY	HELLS	HEMIOPIAS	HEPAR	HERBIER
HELICES	HELLUVA	HEMIOPIC	HEPARIN	HERBIEST
HELICOID	HELLWARD	HEMIOPSIA	HEPARINS	HERBIST
HELICTITE	HELLWARDS	HEMIOPSIAS	HEPARS	HERBISTS
HELICTITES	HELM	HEMISPACE	HEPATIC	HERBIVORA
HELIDROME	HELMED	HEMISPACES	HEPATICAL	HERBIVORE
HELIDROMES	HELMET	HEMISTICH	HEPATICS	HERBIVORES
HELIMAN	HELMETED	HEMISTICHS	HEPATISE	HERBIVORIES
HELIMEN	HELMETS	HEMITROPE	HEPATISED	HERBIVORY
HELING	HELMING	HEMITROPES	HEPATISES	HERBLESS
HELIODOR	HELMINTH	HEMLOCK	HEPATISING	HERBLET
HELIODORS	HELMINTHS	HEMLOCKS	HEPATITE	HERBLETS
HELIOLOGIES	HELMLEOO	HEMMED	HEPATITES	HERBORISE
HELIOLOGY	HELMS	HEMMING	HEPATITIS	HERBORISED
HELIOSES	HELMSMAN	HEMP	HEPATITISES	HERBORISES
HELIOSIS	HELMSMEN	HEMPEN	HEPATIZE	HERBORISING
HELIOSTAT	HELOT	HEMPIER	HEPATIZED	HERBORIST
HELIOSTATS	HELOTAGE	HEMPIES	HEPATIZES	HERBORISTS
HELIOTYPE	HELOTAGES	HEMPIEST	HEPATIZING	HERBORIZE
HELIOTYPES	HELOTISM	HEMPS	HEPPER	HERBORIZED
HELIOTYPIES	HELOTISMS	HEMPY	HEPPEST	HERBORIZES
HELIOTYPY	HELOTRIES	HEMS	HEPS	HERBORIZING
HELIOZOAN	HELOTRY	HEN	HEPSTER	HERBOSE
HELIOZOANS	HELOTS	HENBANE	HEPSTERS	HERBOUS
HELIOZOIC	HELP	HENBANES	HEPT	HERBS
HELIPAD	HELPABLE	HENCE	HEPTAD	HERBY
HELIPADS	HELPED	HENCHMAN	HEPTADS	HERCOGAMIES
HELIPILOT	HELPER	HENCHMEN	HEPTAGLOT	HERCOGAMY
HELIPILOTS	HELPERS	HEND	HEPTAGLOTS	HERCULEAN
HELIPORT	HELPFUL	HENDED	HEPTAGON	HERCYNITE
HELIPORTS	HELPING	HENDIADYS	HEPTAGONS	HERCYNITES
HELISCOOP	HELPINGS	HENDIADYSES	HEPTANE	HERD
HELISCOOPS	HELPLESS	HENDING	HEPTANES	HERDBOY
HELISTOP	HELPLINE	HENDS	HEPTAPODIES	HERDBOYS
HELISTOPS	HELPLINES	HENEQUEN	HEPTAPODY	HERDED
HELIUM	HELPMATE	HENEQUENS	HEPTARCH	HERDEN
HELIUMS	HELPMATES	HENEQUIN	HEPTARCHIES	HERDENS
HELIX	HELPMEET	HENEQUINS	HEPTARCHS	HERDESS
HELIXES	HELPMEETS	HENGE	HEPTARCHY	HERDESSES
HELL	HELPS	HENGES	HER	HERDIC
HELLEBORE	HELVE	HENIQUIN	HERALD	HERDICS
HELLEBORES	HELVED	HENIQUINS	HERALDED	HERDING
HELLED	HELVES	HENNA	HERALDIC	HERDMAN
HELLENISE	HELVETIUM	HENNAED	HERALDING	HERDMEN
HELLENISED	HELVETIUMS	HENNAS	HERALDRIES	HERDS
HELLENISES	HELVING	HENNED	HERALDRY	HERDSMAN
HELLENISING	HEM	HENNER	HERALDS	HERDSMEN
HELLENIZE	HEMAL	HENNERIES	HERB	HERDWICK
HELLENIZED	HEMATITE	HENNERS	HERBAGE	HERDWICKS
HELLENIZES	HEMATITES	HENNERY	HERBAGED	HERE
HELLENIZING	HEME	HENNIER	HERBAGES	HEREABOUT
HELLER	HEMES	HENNIES	HERBAL	HEREABOUTS
HELLERS	HEMIALGIA	HENNIEST	HERBALISM	HEREAFTER
HELLHOUND	HEMIALGIAS	HENNIN	HERBALISMS	HEREAFTERS
HELLHOUNDS	HEMICYCLE	HENNING	HERBALIST	HEREAT
HELLICAT	HEMICYCLES	HENNINS	HERBALISTS	HEREAWAY
HELLICATS	HEMIHEDRIES	HENNY	HERBALS	HEREBY

HEREDITIES
HEREDITY
HEREFROM
HEREIN
HERENESS
HERENESSES
HEREOF
HEREON
HERESIES
HERESY
HERETIC
HERETICAL
HERETICS
HERETO
HEREUNDER
HEREUNTO
HEREUPON
HEREWITH
HERIED
HERIES
HERIOT
HERIOTS
HÉRISSÉ
HERISSON
HERISSONS
HERITABLE
HERITABLY
HERITAGE
HERITAGES
HERITOR
HERITORS
HERITRESS
HERITRESSES
HERITRICES
HERITRIX
HERITRIXES
HERKOGAMIES
HERKOGAMY
HERL
HERLING
HERLINGS
HERLS
HERM
HERMA
HERMAE
HERMANDAD
HERMANDADS
HERMETIC
HERMETICS
HERMIT
HERMITAGE
HERMITAGES
HERMITESS
HERMITESSES
HERMITS
HERMS
HERN
HERNIA
HERNIAL
HERNIAS
HERNIATED
HERNS
HERNSHAW
HERNSHAWS
HERO
HEROE
HEROES
HEROIC
HEROICAL
HEROICLY

HEROICS
HEROIN
HEROINE
HEROINES
HEROINS
HEROISE
HEROISED
HEROISES
HEROISING
HEROISM
HEROISMS
HEROIZE
HEROIZED
HEROIZES
HEROIZING
HERON
HERONRIES
HERONRY
HERONS
HERONSEW
HERONSEWS
HERONSHAW
HERONSHAWS
HEROON
HEROONS
HEROSHIP
HEROSHIPS
HERPES
HERPETIC
HERPETOID
HERRIED
HERRIES
HERRIMENT
HERRIMENTS
HERRING
HERRINGER
HERRINGERS
HERRINGS
HERRY
HERRYING
HERRYMENT
HERRYMENTS
HERS
HERSALL
HERSALLS
HERSE
HERSED
HERSEEMED
HERSEEMS
HERSELF
HERSES
HERSHIP
HERSHIPS
HERTZ
HERTZES
HERY
HERYE
HERYED
HERYES
HERYING
HES
HESITANCE
HESITANCES
HESITANCIES
HESITANCY
HESITANT
HESITATE
HESITATED
HESITATES
HESITATING

HESITATOR
HESITATORS
HESP
HESPED
HESPERID
HESPERIDS
HESPING
HESPS
HESSIAN
HESSIANS
HESSONITE
HESSONITES
HEST
HESTERNAL
HESTS
HET
HETAERA
HETAERAE
HETAERAS
HETAERIA
HETAERIAS
HETAERISM
HETAERISMS
HETAERIST
HETAERISTS
HETAIRA
HETAIRAI
HETAIRIA
HETAIRIAS
HETAIRISM
HETAIRISMS
HETAIRIST
HETAIRISTS
HETE
HETERODOX
HETERONYM
HETERONYMS
HETEROPOD
HETEROPODS
HETEROSES
HETEROSIS
HETEROTIC
HETES
HETHER
HETING
HETMAN
HETMANATE
HETMANATES
HETMANS
HETS
HEUCH
HEUCHS
HEUGH
HEUGHS
HEUREKA
HEUREKAS
HEURETIC
HEURETICS
HEURISM
HEURISMS
HEURISTIC
HEURISTICS
HEVEA
HEVEAS
HEW
HEWED
HEWER
HEWERS
HEWGH
HEWING

HEWINGS
HEWN
HEWS
HEX
HEXACHORD
HEXACHORDS
HEXACT
HEXACTS
HEXAD
HEXADIC
HEXADS
HEXAFOIL
HEXAFOILS
HEXAGLOT
HEXAGON
HEXAGONAL
HEXAGONS
HEXAGRAM
HEXAGRAMS
HEXAHEDRA
HEXAMETER
HEXAMETERS
HEXANE
HEXANES
HEXAPLA
HEXAPLAR
HEXAPLAS
HEXAPLOID
HEXAPLOIDS
HEXAPOD
HEXAPODIES
HEXAPODS
HEXAPODY
HEXARCH
HEXASTICH
HEXASTICHS
HEXASTYLE
HEXASTYLES
HEXED
HEXENE
HEXENES
HEXES
HEXING
HEXINGS
HEXOSE
HEXOSES
HEXYLENE
HEXYLENES
HEY
HEYDAY
HEYDAYS
HEYDUCK
HEYDUCKS
HEYED
HEYING
HEYS
HI
HIANT
HIATUS
HIATUSES
HIBACHI
HIBACHIS
HIBAKUSHA
HIBERNAL
HIBERNATE
HIBERNATED
HIBERNATES
HIBERNATING
HIBERNISE
HIBERNISED

HIBERNISES
HIBERNISING
HIBERNIZE
HIBERNIZED
HIBERNIZES
HIBERNIZING
HIBISCUS
HIBISCUSES
HIC
HICATEE
HICATEES
HICCATEE
HICCATEES
HICCOUGH
HICCOUGHED
HICCOUGHING
HICCOUGHS
HICCUP
HICCUPED
HICCUPING
HICCUPS
HICCUPY
HICK
HICKEY
HICKEYS
HICKORIES
HICKORY
HICKS
HICKWALL
HICKWALLS
HID
HIDAGE
HIDAGES
HIDALGA
HIDALGAS
HIDALGO
HIDALGOS
HIDDEN
HIDDENITE
HIDDENITES
HIDDENLY
HIDDER
HIDDERS
HIDE
HIDED
HIDEOSITIES
HIDEOSITY
HIDEOUS
HIDEOUSLY
HIDEOUT
HIDEOUTS
HIDES
HIDING
HIDINGS
HIDLING
HIDLINGS
HIDLINS
HIDROSES
HIDROSIS
HIDROTIC
HIDROTICS
HIE
HIED
HIEING
HIELAMAN
HIELAMANS
HIEMAL
HIEMS
HIERACIUM
HIERACIUMS

HIERARCH
HIERARCHIES
HIERARCHS
HIERARCHY
HIERATIC
HIERATICA
HIERATICAS
HIEROCRAT
HIEROCRATS
HIERODULE
HIERODULES
HIEROGRAM
HIEROGRAMS
HIEROLOGIES
HIEROLOGY
HIERURGIES
HIERURGY
HIES
HIGGLE
HIGGLED
HIGGLER
HIGGLERS
HIGGLES
HIGGLING
HIGGLINGS
HIGH
HIGHBALL
HIGHBALLED
HIGHBALLING
HIGHBALLS
HIGHBOY
HIGHBOYS
HIGHBROW
HIGHBROWS
HIGHED
HIGHER
HIGHERED
HIGHERING
HIGHERS
HIGHEST
HIGHING
HIGHISH
HIGHJACK
HIGHJACKED
HIGHJACKING
HIGHJACKS
HIGHLAND
HIGHLANDS
HIGHLIGHT
HIGHLIGHTED
HIGHLIGHTING
HIGHLIGHTS
HIGHLY
HIGHMAN
HIGHMEN
HIGHMOST
HIGHNESS
HIGHNESSES
HIGHROAD
HIGHROADS
HIGHS
HIGHT
HIGHTAIL
HIGHTAILED
HIGHTAILING
HIGHTAILS
HIGHTH
HIGHTHS
HIGHTING
HIGHTS

HIGHWAY
HIGHWAYS
HIJACK
HIJACKED
HIJACKER
HIJACKERS
HIJACKING
HIJACKS
HIJINKS
HIJRA
HIJRAH
HIJRAHS
HIJRAS
HIKE
HIKED
HIKER
HIKERS
HIKES
HIKING
HILA
HILAR
HILARIOUS
HILARITIES
HILARITY
HILCH
HILCHED
HILCHES
HILCHING
HILD
HILDING
HILDINGS
HILI
HILL
HILLED
HILLFOLK
HILLIER
HILLIEST
HILLINESS
HILLINESSES
HILLING
HILLMEN
HILLO
HILLOCK
HILLOCKS
HILLOCKY
HILLOED
HILLOES
HILLOING
HILLOS
HILLS
HILLSIDE
HILLSIDES
HILLTOP
HILLTOPS
HILLY
HILT
HILTED
HILTING
HILTS
HILUM
HILUS
HIM
HIMATIA
HIMATION
HIMATIONS
HIMSEEMED
HIMSEEMS
HIMSELF
HIN
HIND

HINDBERRIES
HINDBERRY
HINDER
HINDERED
HINDERER
HINDERERS
HINDERING
HINDERS
HINDFEET
HINDFOOT
HINDHEAD
HINDHEADS
HINDLEG
HINDLEGS
HINDMOST
HINDRANCE
HINDRANCES
HINDS
HINDSIGHT
HINDSIGHTS
HINDWARD
HING
HINGE
HINGED
HINGES
HINGING
HINGS
HINNIED
HINNIES
HINNY
HINNYING
HINS
HINT
HINTED
HINTING
HINTINGLY
HINTS
HIP
HIPPARCH
HIPPARCHS
HIPPED
HIPPER
HIPPEST
HIPPIATRIES
HIPPIATRY
HIPPIC
HIPPIE
HIPPIEDOM
HIPPIEDOMS
HIPPIER
HIPPIES
HIPPIEST
HIPPING
HIPPINGS
HIPPISH
HIPPO
HIPPOCRAS
HIPPOCRASES
HIPPODAME
HIPPODAMES
HIPPOLOGIES
HIPPOLOGY
HIPPOS
HIPPURIC
HIPPURITE
HIPPURITES
HIPPUS
HIPPUSES
HIPPY
HIPPYDOM

HIPPYDOMS
HIPS
HIPSTER
HIPSTERS
HIPT
HIRABLE
HIRCINE
HIRCOSITIES
HIRCOSITY
HIRE
HIREABLE
HIRED
HIRELING
HIRELINGS
HIRER
HIRERS
HIRES
HIRING
HIRINGS
HIRLING
HIRLINGS
HIRPLE
HIRPLED
HIRPLES
HIRPLING
HIRRIENT
HIRRIENTS
HIRSEL
HIRSELLED
HIRSELLING
HIRSELS
HIRSLE
HIRSLED
HIRSLES
HIRSLING
HIRSTIE
HIRSUTE
HIRUDIN
HIRUDINS
HIRUNDINE
HIS
HISH
HISHED
HISHES
HISHING
HISN
HISPID
HISPIDITIES
HISPIDITY
HISS
HISSED
HISSES
HISSING
HISSINGLY
HISSINGS
HIST
HISTAMINE
HISTAMINES
HISTED
HISTIDINE
HISTIDINES
HISTIE
HISTING
HISTIOID
HISTOGEN
HISTOGENIES
HISTOGENS
HISTOGENY
HISTOGRAM
HISTOGRAMS

HISTOID
HISTOLOGIES
HISTOLOGY
HISTONE
HISTONES
HISTORIAN
HISTORIANS
HISTORIC
HISTORIED
HISTORIES
HISTORIFIED
HISTORIFIES
HISTORIFY
HISTORIFYING
HISTORISM
HISTORISMS
HISTORY
HISTORYING
HISTRIO
HISTRION
HISTRIONS
HISTRIOS
HISTS
HIT
HITCH
HITCHED
HITCHER
HITCHERS
HITCHES
HITCHIER
HITCHIEST
HITCHILY
HITCHING
HITCHY
HITHE
HITHER
HITHERED
HITHERING
HITHERS
HITHERTO
HITHES
HITS
HITTER
HITTERS
HITTING
HIVE
HIVED
HIVELESS
HIVELIKE
HIVER
HIVERS
HIVES
HIVEWARD
HIVEWARDS
HIVING
HIYA
HIZEN
HIZENS
HIZZ
HIZZED
HIZZES
HIZZING
HO
HOA
HOACTZIN
HOACTZINS
HOAED
HOAING
HOAR
HOARD

HOARDED
HOARDER
HOARDERS
HOARDING
HOARDINGS
HOARDS
HOARED
HOARHEAD
HOARHEADS
HOARHOUND
HOARHOUNDS
HOARIER
HOARIEST
HOARILY
HOARINESS
HOARINESSES
HOARING
HOARS
HOARSE
HOARSELY
HOARSEN
HOARSENED
HOARSENING
HOARSENS
HOARSER
HOARSEST
HOARY
HOAS
HOAST
HOASTED
HOASTING
HOASTMAN
HOASTMEN
HOASTS
HOATZIN
HOATZINS
HOAX
HOAXED
HOAXER
HOAXERS
HOAXES
HOAXING
HOB
HOBBIES
HOBBISH
HOBBIT
HOBBITRIES
HOBBITRY
HOBBITS
HOBBLE
HOBBLED
HOBBLER
HOBBLERS
HOBBLES
HOBBLING
HOBBLINGS
HOBBY
HOBBYISM
HOBBYISMS
HOBBYIST
HOBBYISTS
HOBBYLESS
HOBDAY
HOBDAYED
HOBDAYING
HOBDAYS
HOBGOBLIN
HOBGOBLINS
HOBJOB
HOBJOBBED

HOBJOBBER
HOBJOBBERS
HOBJOBBING
HOBJOBBINGS
HOBJOBS
HOBNAIL
HOBNAILED
HOBNAILING
HOBNAILS
HOBNOB
HOBNOBBED
HOBNOBBING
HOBNOBBY
HOBNOBS
HOBO
HOBODOM
HOBODOMS
HOBOED
HOBOES
HOBOING
HOBOISM
HOBOISMS
HOBS
HOC
HOCK
HOCKED
HOCKER
HOCKERS
HOCKEY
HOCKEYS
HOCKING
HOCKS
HOCUS
HOCUSED
HOCUSES
HOCUSING
HOCUSSED
HOCUSSES
HOCUSSING
HOD
HODDED
HODDEN
HODDENS
HODDING
HODDLE
HODDLED
HODDLES
HODDLING
HODIERNAL
HODJA
HODJAS
HODMAN
HODMANDOD
HODMANDODS
HODMEN
HODOGRAPH
HODOGRAPHS
HODOMETER
HODOMETERS
HODOMETRIES
HODOMETRY
HODOSCOPE
HODOSCOPES
HODS
HOE
HOED
HOEDOWN
HOEDOWNS
HOEING
HOER

HOERS
HOES
HOG
HOGAN
HOGANS
HOGBACK
HOGBACKS
HOGEN
HOGENS
HOGG
HOGGED
HOGGER
HOGGEREL
HOGGERELS
HOGGERIES
HOGGERS
HOGGERY
HOGGET
HOGGETS
HOGGIN
HOGGING
HOGGINGS
HOGGINS
HOGGISH
HOGGISHLY
HOGGS
HOGH
HOGHOOD
HOGHOODS
HOGHS
HOGS
HOGSHEAD
HOGSHEADS
HOGTIE
HOGTIED
HOGTIES
HOGTYING
HOGWARD
HOGWARDS
HOGWASH
HOGWASHES
HOGWEED
HOGWEEDS
HOH
HOHED
HOHING
HOHS
HOI
HOICK
HOICKED
HOICKING
HOICKS
HOICKSED
HOICKSES
HOICKSING
HOIDEN
HOIDENS
HOIK
HOIKED
HOIKING
HOIKS
HOING
HOISE
HOISED
HOISES
HOISING
HOIST
HOISTED
HOISTER
HOISTERS

HOISTING
HOISTINGS
HOISTMAN
HOISTMEN
HOISTS
HOISTWAY
HOISTWAYS
HOKE
HOKED
HOKES
HOKEY
HOKIER
HOKIEST
HOKING
HOKKU
HOKUM
HOKUMS
HOLD
HOLDBACK
HOLDBACKS
HOLDEN
HOLDER
HOLDERBAT
HOLDERBATS
HOLDERS
HOLDFAST
HOLDFASTS
HOLDING
HOLDINGS
HOLDOVER
HOLDOVERS
HOLDS
HOLE
HOLED
HOLES
HOLESOM
HOLESOME
HOLEY
HOLIBUT
HOLIBUTS
HOLIDAY
HOLIDAYED
HOLIDAYING
HOLIDAYS
HOLIER
HOLIES
HOLIEST
HOLILY
HOLINESS
HOLINESSES
HOLING
HOLINGS
HOLISM
HOLISMS
HOLIST
HOLISTIC
HOLISTS
HOLLA
HOLLAND
HOLLANDS
HOLLAS
HOLLER
HOLLERED
HOLLERING
HOLLERS
HOLLIDAM
HOLLIDAMS
HOLLIES
HOLLO
HOLLOA

HOLLOAED
HOLLOAING
HOLLOAS
HOLLOED
HOLLOES
HOLLOING
HOLLOS
HOLLOW
HOLLOWARE
HOLLOWARES
HOLLOWED
HOLLOWER
HOLLOWEST
HOLLOWING
HOLLOWLY
HOLLOWS
HOLLY
HOLLYHOCK
HOLLYHOCKS
HOLM
HOLMIA
HOLMIAS
HOLMIC
HOLMIUM
HOLMIUMS
HOLMS
HOLOCAUST
HOLOCAUSTS
HOLOCRINE
HOLOGRAM
HOLOGRAMS
HOLOGRAPH
HOLOGRAPHED
HOLOGRAPHING
HOLOGRAPHS
HOLOPHOTE
HOLOPHOTES
HOLOPHYTE
HOLOPHYTES
HOLOPTIC
HOLOTYPE
HOLOTYPES
HOLOTYPIC
HOLOZOIC
HOLP
HOLPEN
HOLS
HOLSTER
HOLSTERED
HOLSTERS
HOLT
HOLTS
HOLY
HOLYDAM
HOLYDAME
HOLYDAMES
HOLYDAMS
HOLYSTONE
HOLYSTONED
HOLYSTONES
HOLYSTONING
HOMAGE
HOMAGED
HOMAGER
HOMAGERS
HOMAGES
HOMAGING
HOMALOID
HOMALOIDS
HOMBRE

HOMBRES
HOME
HOMEBOUND
HOMECRAFT
HOMECRAFTS
HOMED
HOMEFELT
HOMELAND
HOMELANDS
HOMELESS
HOMELIER
HOMELIEST
HOMELIKE
HOMELILY
HOMELY
HOMELYN
HOMELYNS
HOMEMAKER
HOMEMAKERS
HOMEOMERIES
HOMEOMERY
HOMEOPATH
HOMEOPATHS
HOMEOSES
HOMEOSIS
HOMIER
HOMERS
HOMES
HOMESICK
HOMESPUN
HOMESPUNS
HOMESTALL
HOMESTALLS
HOMESTEAD
HOMESTEADS
HOMEWARD
HOMEWARDS
HOMEWORK
HOMEWORKS
HOMEY
HOMICIDAL
HOMICIDE
HOMICIDES
HOMIER
HOMIEST
HOMILETIC
HOMILETICS
HOMILIES
HOMILIST
HOMILISTS
HOMILY
HOMING
HOMINGS
HOMINID
HOMINIDS
HOMINIES
HOMINOID
HOMINOIDS
HOMINY
HOMME
HOMMES
HOMMOCK
HOMMOCKS
HOMO
HOMODONT
HOMODYNE
HOMOEOSES
HOMOEOSIS
HOMOGAMIC
HOMOGAMIES

HOMOGAMY
HOMOGENIES
HOMOGENY
HOMOGRAFT
HOMOGRAFTS
HOMOGRAPH
HOMOGRAPHS
HOMOLOG
HOMOLOGIES
HOMOLOGS
HOMOLOGUE
HOMOLOGUES
HOMOLOGY
HOMOMORPH
HOMOMORPHS
HOMONYM
HOMONYMIC
HOMONYMIES
HOMONYMS
HOMONYMY
HOMOPHILE
HOMOPHILES
HOMOPHOBE
HOMOPHOBES
HOMOPHONE
HOMOPHONED
HOMOPHONIES
HOMOPHONY
HOMOPHYLIES
HOMOPHYLY
HOMOPLASIES
HOMOPLASY
HOMOPOLAR
HOMOS
HOMOTAXES
HOMOTAXIC
HOMOTAXIS
HOMOTONIC
HOMOTONIES
HOMOTONY
HOMOTYPAL
HOMOTYPE
HOMOTYPES
HOMOTYPIC
HOMOTYPIES
HOMOTYPY
HOMOUSIAN
HOMOUSIANS
HOMUNCLE
HOMUNCLES
HOMUNCULE
HOMUNCULES
HOMUNCULI
HOMY
HON
HOND
HONDS
HONE
HONED
HONES
HONEST
HONESTER
HONESTEST
HONESTIES
HONESTLY
HONESTY
HONEY
HONEYBUN
HONEYBUNS
HONEYCOMB

HONEYCOMBED
HONEYCOMBING
HONEYCOMBS
HONEYED
HONEYING
HONEYLESS
HONEYMOON
HONEYMOONED
HONEYMOONING
HONEYMOONS
HONEYPOT
HONEYPOTS
HONEYS
HONG
HONGING
HONGS
HONIED
HONING
HONK
HONKED
HONKER
HONKERS
HONKIE
HONKIES
HONKING
HONKS
HONKY
HONOR
HONORAND
HONORANDS
HONORARIA
HONORARIES
HONORARY
HONORED
HONORIFIC
HONORIFICS
HONORING
HONORS
HONOUR
HONOURED
HONOURER
HONOURERS
HONOURING
HONOURS
HONS
HOO
HOOCH
HOOCHES
HOOD
HOODED
HOODING
HOODLESS
HOODLUM
HOODLUMS
HOODMAN
HOODMEN
HOODOO
HOODOOED
HOODOOING
HOODOOS
HOODS
HOODWINK
HOODWINKED
HOODWINKING
HOODWINKS
HOOEY
HOOEYS
HOOF
HOOFBEAT
HOOFBEATS

HOOFED
HOOFER
HOOFERS
HOOFING
HOOFLESS
HOOFPRINT
HOOFPRINTS
HOOFROT
HOOFROTS
HOOFS
HOOK
HOOKA
HOOKAH
HOOKAHS
HOOKAS
HOOKED
HOOKER
HOOKERS
HOOKEY
HOOKEYS
HOOKIER
HOOKIES
HOOKIEST
HOOKING
HOOKS
HOOKY
HOOLACHAN
HOOLACHANS
HOOLEY
HOOLEYS
HOOLICAN
HOOLICANS
HOOLIER
HOOLIEST
HOOLIGAN
HOOLIGANS
HOOLOCK
HOOLOCKS
HOOLY
HOOP
HOOPED
HOOPER
HOOPERS
HOOPING
HOOPOE
HOOPOES
HOOPS
HOORAH
HOORAHED
HOORAHING
HOORAHS
HOORAY
HOORAYED
HOORAYING
HOORAYS
HOORD
HOORDS
HOOROO
HOOSEGOW
HOOSEGOWS
HOOSGOW
HOOSGOWS
HOOSH
HOOSHED
HOOSHES
HOOSHING
HOOT
HOOTCH
HOOTCHES
HOOTED

HOOTER
HOOTERS
HOOTING
HOOTNANNIES
HOOTNANNY
HOOTS
HOOVE
HOOVED
HOOVEN
HOOVER
HOOVERED
HOOVERING
HOOVERS
HOOVES
HOOVING
HOP
HOPBIND
HOPBINDS
HOPBINE
HOPBINES
HOPDOG
HOPDOGS
HOPE
HOPED
HOPEFUL
HOPEFULLY
HOPEFULS
HOPELESS
HOPER
HOPERS
HOPES
HOPING
HOPINGLY
HOPLITE
HOPLITES
HOPLOLOGIES
HOPLOLOGY
HOPPED
HOPPER
HOPPERS
HOPPIER
HOPPIEST
HOPPING
HOPPINGS
HOPPLE
HOPPLED
HOPPLES
HOPPLING
HOPPY
HOPS
HOPSACK
HOPSACKS
HORAL
HORARY
HORDE
HORDED
HORDEIN
HORDEINS
HORDEOLUM
HORDEOLUMS
HORDES
HORDING
HORDOCK
HORDOCKS
HORE
HOREHOUND
HOREHOUNDS
HORIZON
HORIZONS
HORKEY

HORKEYS	HOROSCOPE	HOSANNAS	HOTELIERS	HOUSELS
HORME	HOROSCOPES	HOSE	HOTELS	HOUSEMAID
HORMES	HOROSCOPIES	HOSED	HOTEN	HOUSEMAIDS
HORMONAL	HOROSCOPY	HOSEMAN	HOTFOOT	HOUSEMAN
HORMONE	HORRENT	HOSEMEN	HOTHEAD	HOUSEMEN
HORMONES	HORRIBLE	HOSEN	HOTHEADED	HOUSES
HORMONIC	HORRIBLY	HOSEPIPE	HOTHEADS	HOUSETOP
HORN	HORRID	HOSEPIPES	HOTHOUSE	HOUSETOPS
HORNBEAK	HORRIDER	HOSES	HOTHOUSES	HOUSEWIFE
HORNBEAKS	HORRIDEST	HOSIER	HOTLY	HOUSEWIVES
HORNBEAM	HORRIDLY	HOSIERIES	HOTNESS	HOUSEWORK
HORNBEAMS	HORRIFIC	HOSIERS	HOTNESSES	HOUSEWORKS
HORNBILL	HORRIFIED	HOSIERY	HOTPOT	HOUSING
HORNBILLS	HORRIFIES	HOSING	HOTPOTS	HOUSINGS
HORNBOOK	HORRIFY	HOSPICE	HOTS	HOUSLING
HORNBOOKS	HORRIFYING	HOSPICES	HOTSHOT	HOUT
HORNBUG	HORROR	HOSPITAGE	HOTSHOTS	HOUTS
HORNBUGS	HORRORS	HOSPITAGES	HOTTED	HOVE
HORNED	HORS	HOSPITAL	HOTTENTOT	HOVED
HORNER	HORSE	HOSPITALE	HOTTENTOTS	HOVEL
HORNERS	HORSEBACK	HOSPITALES	HOTTER	HOVELED
HORNET	HORSEBACKS	HOSPITALS	HOTTERED	HOVELING
HORNETS	HORSECAR	HOSPITIA	HOTTERING	HOVELLED
HORNFELS	HORSECARS	HOSPITIUM	HOTTERS	HOVELLER
HORNFELSES	HORSED	HOSPODAR	HOTTEST	HOVELLERS
HORNFUL	HORSEFLIES	HOSPODARS	HOTTIE	HOVELLING
HORNFULS	HORSEFLY	HOSS	HOTTIES	HOVELS
HORNGELD	HORSEHAIR	HOSSES	HOTTING	HOVEN
HORNGELDS	HORSEHAIRS	HOST	HOTTISH	HOVER
HORNIER	HORSEHIDE	HOSTA	HOUDAH	HOVERED
HORNIEST	HORSEHIDES	HOSTAGE	HOUDAHS	HOVERING
HORNINESS	HORSELESS	HOSTAGES	HOUDAN	HOVERPORT
HORNINESSES	HORSEMAN	HOSTAS	HOUDANS	HOVERPORTS
HORNING	HORSEMEAT	HOSTED	HOUF	HOVERS
HORNINGS	HORSEMEATS	HOSTEL	HOUFED	HOVES
HORNISH	HORSEMEN	HOSTELER	HOUFF	HOVING
HORNIST	HORSEMINT	HOSTELERS	HOUFFED	HOW
HORNISTS	HORSEMINTS	HOSTELLER	HOUFFING	HOWBE
HORNITO	HORSEPLAY	HOSTELLERS	HOUFFS	HOWBEIT
HORNITOS	HORSEPLAYS	HOSTELRIES	HOUFING	HOWDAH
HORNLESS	HORSEPOND	HOSTELRY	HOUFS	HOWDAHS
HORNLET	HORSEPONDS	HOSTELS	HOUGH	HOWDIE
HORNLETS	HORSES	HOSTESS	HOUGHED	HOWDIES
HORNPIPE	HORSESHOE	HOSTESSED	HOUGHING	HOWDY
HORNPIPES	HORSESHOES	HOSTESSES	HOUGHS	HOWE
HORNS	HORSETAIL	HOSTESSING	HOUND	HOWES
HORNSTONE	HORSETAILS	HOSTILE	HOUNDED	HOWEVER
HORNSTONES	HORSEWAY	HOSTILELY	HOUNDING	HOWF
HORNTAIL	HORSEWAYS	HOSTILITIES	HOUNDS	HOWFED
HORNTAILS	HORSEWHIP	HOSTILITY	HOUR	HOWFF
HORNWORK	HORSEWHIPPED	HOSTING	HOURI	HOWFFED
HORNWORKS	HORSEWHIPPING	HOSTINGS	HOURIS	HOWFFING
HORNWORM	HORSEWHIPS	HOSTLER	HOURLONG	HOWFFS
HORNWORMS	HORSIER	HOSTLERS	HOURLY	HOWFING
HORNWORT	HORSIEST	HOSTLESSE	HOURPLATE	HOWFS
HORNWORTS	HORSINESS	HOSTRIES	HOURPLATES	HOWITZER
HORNWRACK	HORSINESSES	HOSTRY	HOURS	HOWITZERS
HORNWRACKS	HORSING	HOSTS	HOUSE	HOWK
HORNY	HORSINGS	HOT	HOUSEBOY	HOWKED
HORNYHEAD	HORSON	HOTBED	HOUSEBOYS	HOWKER
HORNYHEADS	HORSONS	HOTBEDS	HOUSED	HOWKERS
HOROLOGE	HORST	HOTCH	HOUSEFUL	HOWKING
HOROLOGER	HORSTS	HOTCHED	HOUSEFULS	HOWKS
HOROLOGERS	HORSY	HOTCHES	HOUSEHOLD	HOWL
HOROLOGES	HORTATION	HOTCHING	HOUSEHOLDS	HOWLED
HOROLOGIC	HORTATIONS	HOTCHPOT	HOUSEL	HOWLER
HOROLOGIES	HORTATIVE	HOTCHPOTS	HOUSELESS	HOWLERS
HOROLOGY	HORTATORY	HOTE	HOUSELLED	HOWLET
HOROMETRIES	HOS	HOTEL	HOUSELLING	HOWLETS
HOROMETRY	HOSANNA	HOTELIER	HOUSELLINGS	HOWLING

OWLINGS
OWLS
OWRE
OWRES
OWS
OWSO
OWSOEVER
OWTOWDIE
OWTOWDIES
OX
OXED
OXES
OXING
OY
OYA
OYAS
OYDEN
OYDENISH
OYDENISMS
OYDENS
OYED
OYING
OYS
IUANAOO
IUANACOS
UB
UBBIES
IUDDUD
UBBUBOO
UBBUBOOS
UBBUBS
UBBY
UBRIS
UBRISES
UBRISTIC
UBS
UCK
UCKABACK
UCKABACKS
UCKLE
UCKLES
UCKS
UCKSTER
UCKSTERED
UCKSTERIES
UCKSTERING
UCKSTERS
UCKSTERY
UDDEN
UDDLE
UDDLED
IUDDLES
UDDLING
UDDUP
UE
UED
UELESS
UER
UERS
UES
UFF
UFFED
UFFIER
UFFIEST
UFFILY
UFFINESS
UFFINESSES
UFFING

HUFFISH
HUFFISHLY
HUFFKIN
HUFFKINS
HUFFS
HUFFY
HUG
HUGE
HUGELY
HUGENESS
HUGENESSES
HUGEOUS
HUGEOUSLY
HUGER
HUGEST
HUGGABLE
HUGGED
HUGGING
HUGS
HUGY
HUH
HUIA
HUIAS
HUISSIER
HUISSIERS
HUITAIN
HUITAINS
HULA
HULAS
HULE
HULES
HULK
HULKIER
HULKIEST
HULKING
HULKS
HULKY
HULL
HULLED
HULLIER
HULLIEST
HULLING
HULLO
HULLOED
HULLOES
HULLOING
HULLOS
HULLS
HULLY
HUM
HUMA
HUMAN
HUMANE
HUMANELY
HUMANER
HUMANEST
HUMANISE
HUMANISED
HUMANISES
HUMANISING
HUMANISM
HUMANISMS
HUMANIST
HUMANISTS
HUMANITIES
HUMANITY
HUMANIZE
HUMANIZED
HUMANIZES
HUMANIZING

HUMANKIND
HUMANLIKE
HUMANLY
HUMANNESS
HUMANNESSES
HUMANOID
HUMANOIDS
HUMANS
HUMAS
HUMBLE
HUMBLED
HUMBLER
HUMBLES
HUMBLESSE
HUMBLESSES
HUMBLEST
HUMBLING
HUMBLINGS
HUMBLY
HUMBUG
HUMBUGGED
HUMBUGGER
HUMBUGGERS
HUMBUGGING
HUMBUGS
HUMBUZZ
HUMBUZZES
HUMDINGER
HUMDINGERS
HUMDRUM
HUMDRUMS
HUMECT
HUMECTANT
HUMECTANTS
HUMECTATE
HUMECTATED
HUMECTATES
HUMECTATING
HUMECTED
HUMECTING
HUMECTIVE
HUMECTIVES
HUMECTS
HUMEFIED
HUMEFIES
HUMEFY
HUMEFYING
HUMERAL
HUMERALS
HUMERI
HUMERUS
HUMF
HUMFED
HUMFING
HUMFS
HUMHUM
HUMHUMS
HUMIC
HUMID
HUMIDER
HUMIDEST
HUMIDIFIED
HUMIDIFIES
HUMIDIFY
HUMIDIFYING
HUMIDITIES
HUMIDITY
HUMIDLY
HUMIDNESS
HUMIDNESSES

HUMIDOR
HUMIDORS
HUMIFIED
HUMIFIES
HUMIFY
HUMIFYING
HUMILIANT
HUMILIATE
HUMILIATED
HUMILIATES
HUMILIATING
HUMILITIES
HUMILITY
HUMITE
HUMITES
HUMLIE
HUMLIES
HUMMABLE
HUMMAUM
HUMMAUMS
HUMMED
HUMMEL
HUMMELLED
HUMMELLER
HUMMELLERS
HUMMELLING
HUMMELS
HUMMER
HUMMERS
HUMMING
HUMMINGS
HUMMOCK
HUMMOCKED
HUMMOCKS
HUMMOCKY
HUMMUM
HUMMUMS
HUMMUS
HUMMUSES
HUMOGEN
HUMOGENS
HUMOR
HUMORAL
HUMORALLY
HUMORED
HUMORESK
HUMORESKS
HUMORING
HUMORIST
HUMORISTS
HUMOROUS
HUMORS
HUMOUR
HUMOURED
HUMOURING
HUMOURS
HUMOUS
HUMP
HUMPBACK
HUMPBACKS
HUMPED
HUMPEN
HUMPENS
HUMPH
HUMPHED
HUMPHING
HUMPHS
HUMPIER
HUMPIES
HUMPIEST

HUMPING
HUMPS
HUMPTIES
HUMPTY
HUMPY
HUMS
HUMSTRUM
HUMSTRUMS
HUMUS
HUMUSES
HUMUSY
HUNCH
HUNCHBACK
HUNCHBACKS
HUNCHED
HUNCHES
HUNCHING
HUNDRED
HUNDREDER
HUNDREDERS
HUNDREDOR
HUNDREDORS
HUNDREDS
HUNDREDTH
HUNDREDTHS
HUNG
HUNGER
HUNGERED
HUNGERFUL
HUNGERING
HUNGERLY
HUNGERS
HUNGRIER
HUNGRIEST
HUNGRILY
HUNGRY
HUNK
HUNKER
HUNKERED
HUNKERING
HUNKERS
HUNKIER
HUNKIES
HUNKIEST
HUNKS
HUNKSES
HUNKY
HUNT
HUNTED
HUNTER
HUNTERS
HUNTING
HUNTINGS
HUNTRESS
HUNTRESSES
HUNTS
HUNTSMAN
HUNTSMEN
HUP
HUPPED
HUPPING
HUPS
HURCHEON
HURCHEONS
HURDEN
HURDENS
HURDIES
HURDLE
HURDLED
HURDLER

HURDLERS
HURDLES
HURDLING
HURDLINGS
HURDS
HURL
HURLED
HURLER
HURLERS
HURLEY
HURLEYS
HURLIES
HURLING
HURLINGS
HURLS
HURLY
HURRA
HURRAED
HURRAH
HURRAHED
HURRAHING
HURRAHS
HURRAING
HURRAS
HURRAY
HURRAYED
HURRAYING
HURRAYS
HURRICANE
HURRICANES
HURRICANO
HURRICANOES
HURRIED
HURRIEDLY
HURRIES
HURRY
HURRYING
HURRYINGS
HURST
HURSTS
HURT
HURTER
HURTERS
HURTFUL
HURTFULLY
HURTING
HURTLE
HURTLED
HURTLES
HURTLESS
HURTLING
HURTS
HUSBAND
HUSBANDED
HUSBANDING
HUSBANDLY
HUSBANDRIES
HUSBANDRY
HUSBANDS
HUSH
HUSHABIED
HUSHABIES
HUSHABY
HUSHABYING
HUSHED
HUSHER
HUSHERED
HUSHERING
HUSHERS
HUSHES

HUSHIER
HUSHIEST
HUSHING
HUSHY
HUSK
HUSKED
HUSKER
HUSKERS
HUSKIER
HUSKIES
HUSKIEST
HUSKILY
HUSKINESS
HUSKINESSES
HUSKING
HUSKINGS
HUSKS
HUSKY
HUSO
HUSOS
HUSS
HUSSAR
HUSSARS
HUSSES
HUSSIES
HUSSIF
HUSSIFS
HUSSY
HUSTINGS
HUSTLE
HUSTLED
HUSTLER
HUSTLERS
HUSTLES
HUSTLING
HUSTLINGS
HUSWIFE
HUSWIVES
HUT
HUTCH
HUTCHED
HUTCHES
HUTCHING
HUTIA
HUTIAS
HUTMENT
HUTMENTS
HUTS
HUTTED
HUTTING
HUTTINGS
HUZOOR
HUZOORS
HUZZA
HUZZAED
HUZZAING
HUZZAS
HUZZIES
HUZZY
HWYL
HWYLS
HYACINE
HYACINES
HYACINTH
HYACINTHS
HYAENA
HYAENAS
HYALINE
HYALINES
HYALINISE

HYALINISED
HYALINISES
HYALINISING
HYALINIZE
HYALINIZED
HYALINIZES
HYALINIZING
HYALITE
HYALITES
HYALOID
HYALONEMA
HYALONEMAS
HYBRID
HYBRIDISE
HYBRIDISED
HYBRIDISES
HYBRIDISING
HYBRIDISM
HYBRIDISMS
HYBRIDITIES
HYBRIDITY
HYBRIDIZE
HYBRIDIZED
HYBRIDIZES
HYBRIDIZING
HYBRIDOMA
HYBRIDOMAS
HYBRIDOUS
HYBRIDS
HYBRIS
HYBRISES
HYDATHODE
HYDATHODES
HYDATID
HYDATIDS
HYDATOID
HYDRA
HYDRAEMIA
HYDRAEMIAS
HYDRANGEA
HYDRANGEAS
HYDRANT
HYDRANTH
HYDRANTHS
HYDRANTS
HYDRAS
HYDRATE
HYDRATED
HYDRATES
HYDRATING
HYDRATION
HYDRATIONS
HYDRAULIC
HYDRAULICKED
HYDRAULICKING
HYDRAULICS
HYDRAZINE
HYDRAZINES
HYDREMIA
HYDREMIAS
HYDRIA
HYDRIAE
HYDRIAS
HYDRIC
HYDRIDE
HYDRIDES
HYDRIODIC
HYDRO
HYDROCELE
HYDROCELES

HYDROFOIL
HYDROFOILS
HYDROGEN
HYDROGENS
HYDROID
HYDROIDS
HYDROLOGIES
HYDROLOGY
HYDROLYSE
HYDROLYSED
HYDROLYSES
HYDROLYSING
HYDROLYTE
HYDROLYTES
HYDROLYZE
HYDROLYZED
HYDROLYZES
HYDROLYZING
HYDROMEL
HYDROMELS
HYDRONAUT
HYDRONAUTS
HYDROPIC
HYDROPSIES
HYDROPSY
HYDROPTIC
HYDROPULT
HYDROPULTS
HYDROS
HYDROSKI
HYDROSKIS
HYDROSOMA
HYDROSOMATA
HYDROSOME
HYDROSOMES
HYDROSTAT
HYDROSTATS
HYDROUS
HYDROVANE
HYDROVANES
HYDROXIDE
HYDROXIDES
HYDROXY
HYDROXYL
HYDROXYLS
HYDROZOA
HYDROZOAN
HYDROZOANS
HYDROZOON
HYDYNE
HYDYNES
HYE
HYED
HYEING
HYEN
HYENA
HYENAS
HYENS
HYES
HYETAL
HYETOLOGIES
HYETOLOGY
HYGIENE
HYGIENES
HYGIENIC
HYGIENICS
HYGIENIST
HYGIENISTS
HYGRISTOR
HYGRISTORS

HYGRODEIK
HYGRODEIKS
HYGROLOGIES
HYGROLOGY
HYGROPHIL
HYGROSTAT
HYGROSTATS
HYING
HYKE
HYKES
HYLDING
HYLDINGS
HYLE
HYLEG
HYLEGS
HYLES
HYLIC
HYLICISM
HYLICISMS
HYLICIST
HYLICISTS
HYLISM
HYLISMS
HYLIST
HYLISTS
HYLOBATE
HYLOBATES
HYLOIST
HYLOISTS
HYLOPHYTE
HYLOPHYTES
HYLOZOISM
HYLOZOISMS
HYLOZOIST
HYLOZOISTS
HYMEN
HYMENAEAL
HYMENAEAN
HYMENAL
HYMENEAL
HYMENEALS
HYMENEAN
HYMENIA
HYMENIAL
HYMENIUM
HYMENIUMS
HYMENS
HYMN
HYMNAL
HYMNALS
HYMNARIES
HYMNARY
HYMNED
HYMNIC
HYMNING
HYMNIST
HYMNISTS
HYMNODIES
HYMNODIST
HYMNODISTS
HYMNODY
HYMNOLOGIES
HYMNOLOGY
HYMNS
HYNDE
HYNDES
HYOID
HYOSCINE
HYOSCINES
HYP

YPALGIA
YPALGIAS
YPALLAGE
YPALLAGES
YPATE
YPATES
YPE
YPED
YPER
YPERBOLA
YPERBOLAS
YPERBOLE
YPERBOLES
YPERCUBE
YPERCUBES
YPEREMIA
YPEREMIAS
YPERGAMIES
YPERGAMY
YPERMART
YPERMARTS
YPERON
YPERONS
YPEROPIA
YPEROPIAS
YPERS
YPES
YPHA
YPHAE
YPHAL
YPHEN
YPHENATE

HYPHENATED
HYPHENATES
HYPHENATING
HYPHENED
HYPHENIC
HYPHENING
HYPHENISE
HYPHENISED
HYPHENISES
HYPHENISING
HYPHENISM
HYPHENISMS
HYPHENIZE
HYPHENIZED
HYPHENIZES
HYPHENIZING
HYPHENS
HYPING
HYPINOSES
HYPINOSIS
HYPNA
HYPNIC
HYPNICS
HYPNOGENIES
HYPNOGENY
HYPNOID
HYPNOIDAL
HYPNOLOGIES
HYPNOLOGY
HYPNONE
HYPNONES
HYPNOSES

HYPNOSIS
HYPNOTEE
HYPNOTEES
HYPNOTIC
HYPNOTICS
HYPNOTISE
HYPNOTISED
HYPNOTISES
HYPNOTISING
HYPNOTISM
HYPNOTISMS
HYPNOTIST
HYPNOTISTS
HYPNOTIZE
HYPNOTIZED
HYPNOTIZES
HYPNOTIZING
HYPNOTOID
HYPNUM
HYPNUMS
HYPO
HYPOBLAST
HYPOBLASTS
HYPOBOLE
HYPOBOLES
HYPOCAUST
HYPOCAUSTS
HYPOCIST
HYPOCISTS
HYPOCOTYL
HYPOCOTYLS
HYPOCRISIES

HYPOCRISY
HYPOCRITE
HYPOCRITES
HYPODERM
HYPODERMA
HYPODERMAS
HYPODERMS
HYPOGAEA
HYPOGAEAL
HYPOGAEAN
HYPOGAEUM
HYPOGEA
HYPOGEAL
HYPOGEAN
HYPOGENE
HYPOGEOUS
HYPOGEUM
HYPOGYNIES
HYPOGYNY
HYPOID
HYPOMANIA
HYPOMANIAS
HYPOMANIC
HYPONASTIES
HYPONASTY
HYPONYM
HYPONYMS
HYPOS
HYPOSTYLE
HYPOSTYLES
HYPOTAXES
HYPOTAXIS

HYPOTHEC
HYPOTHECS
HYPOTONIA
HYPOTONIAS
HYPOTONIC
HYPOXEMIA
HYPOXEMIAS
HYPOXEMIC
HYPOXIA
HYPOXIAS
HYPOXIC
HYPPED
HYPPING
HYPS
HYPURAL
HYRACES
HYRACOID
HYRAX
HYRAXES
HYSON
HYSONS
HYSSOP
HYSSOPS
HYSTERIA
HYSTERIAS
HYSTERIC
HYSTERICS
HYSTEROID
HYTHE
HYTHES

I

IAIDO
IAIDOS
IAMB
IAMBI
IAMBIC
IAMBICS
IAMBIST
IAMBISTS
IAMBS
IAMBUS
IAMBUSES
IANTHINE
IATRIC
IATRICAL
IATROGENIES
IATROGENY
IBEX
IBEXES
IBICES
IBIDEM
IBIS
IBISES
IBUPROFEN
IBUPROFENS
ICE
ICEBERG
ICEBERGS
ICEBLINK
ICEBLINKS
ICEBOX
ICEBOXES
ICED
ICEMAN
ICEMEN
ICEPACK
ICEPACKS
ICEPLANT
ICEPLANTS
ICER
ICERS
ICES
ICH
ICHABOD
ICHED
ICHES
ICHING
ICHNEUMON
ICHNEUMONS
ICHNITE
ICHNITES
ICHNOLITE
ICHNOLITES
ICHNOLOGIES
ICHNOLOGY
ICHOR
ICHOROUS
ICHORS
ICHTHIC
ICHTHYOID
ICHTHYOIDS
ICHTHYS
ICHTHYSES
ICICLE

ICICLES
ICIER
ICIEST
ICILY
ICINESS
ICINESSES
ICING
ICINGS
ICKER
ICKERS
ICKIER
ICKIEST
ICKY
ICON
ICONIC
ICONISE
ICONISED
ICONISES
ICONISING
ICONIZE
ICONIZED
ICONIZES
ICONIZING
ICONOLOGIES
ICONOLOGY
ICONOSTAS
ICONOSTASES
ICONS
ICTAL
ICTERIC
ICTERICAL
ICTERICALS
ICTERICS
ICTERINE
ICTERUS
ICTERUSES
ICTIC
ICTUS
ICTUSES
ICY
ID
IDANT
IDANTS
IDE
IDEA
IDEAED
IDEAL
IDEALESS
IDEALISE
IDEALISED
IDEALISER
IDEALISERS
IDEALISES
IDEALISING
IDEALISM
IDEALISMS
IDEALIST
IDEALISTS
IDEALITIES
IDEALITY
IDEALIZE
IDEALIZED
IDEALIZER

IDEALIZERS
IDEALIZES
IDEALIZING
IDEALLESS
IDEALLY
IDEALOGUE
IDEALOGUES
IDEALS
IDEAS
IDEATE
IDEATED
IDEATES
IDEATING
IDEATION
IDEATIONS
IDEATIVE
IDÉE
IDÉES
IDEM
IDENTIC
IDENTICAL
IDENTIFIED
IDENTIFIES
IDENTIFY
IDENTIFYING
IDENTIKIT
IDENTIKITS
IDENTITIES
IDENTITY
IDEOGRAM
IDEOGRAMS
IDEOGRAPH
IDEOGRAPHS
IDEOLOGIC
IDEOLOGIES
IDEOLOGUE
IDEOLOGUES
IDEOLOGY
IDEOPHONE
IDEOPHONES
IDES
IDIOBLAST
IDIOBLASTS
IDIOCIES
IDIOCY
IDIOGRAPH
IDIOGRAPHS
IDIOLECT
IDIOLECTS
IDIOM
IDIOMATIC
IDIOMS
IDIOPATHIES
IDIOPATHY
IDIOPHONE
IDIOPHONES
IDIOPLASM
IDIOPLASMS
IDIOT
IDIOTCIES
IDIOTCY
IDIOTIC
IDIOTICAL

IDIOTICON
IDIOTICONS
IDIOTISH
IDIOTISM
IDIOTISMS
IDIOTS
IDLE
IDLED
IDLEHOOD
IDLEHOODS
IDLENESS
IDLENESSES
IDLER
IDLERS
IDLES
IDLESSE
IDLESSES
IDLEST
IDLING
IDLY
IDOCRASE
IDOCRASES
IDOL
IDOLATER
IDOLATERS
IDOLATRIES
IDOLATRY
IDOLISE
IDOLISED
IDOLISER
IDOLISERS
IDOLISES
IDOLISING
IDOLISM
IDOLISMS
IDOLIST
IDOLISTS
IDOLIZE
IDOLIZED
IDOLIZER
IDOLIZERS
IDOLIZES
IDOLIZING
IDOLS
IDS
IDYL
IDYLL
IDYLLIAN
IDYLLIC
IDYLLIST
IDYLLISTS
IDYLLS
IDYLS
IF
IFF
IFFIER
IFFIEST
IFFINESS
IFFINESSES
IFFY
IFS
IGAD
IGAPO

IGAPOS
IGARAPÉ
IGARAPÉS
IGLOO
IGLOOS
IGNARO
IGNAROES
IGNAROS
IGNEOUS
IGNESCENT
IGNESCENTS
IGNITABLE
IGNITE
IGNITED
IGNITER
IGNITERS
IGNITES
IGNITIBLE
IGNITING
IGNITION
IGNITIONS
IGNITRON
IGNITRONS
IGNOBLE
IGNOBLED
IGNOBLER
IGNOBLES
IGNOBLEST
IGNOBLING
IGNOBLY
IGNOMIES
IGNOMINIES
IGNOMINY
IGNOMY
IGNORABLE
IGNORAMUS
IGNORAMUSES
IGNORANCE
IGNORANCES
IGNORANT
IGNORANTS
IGNORE
IGNORED
IGNORER
IGNORERS
IGNORES
IGNORING
IGUANA
IGUANAS
IGUANID
IGUANIDS
IHRAM
IHRAMS
IKAT
IKATS
IKEBANA
IKEBANAS
IKON
IKONS
ILEA
ILEAC
ILEITIS
ILEITISES

EUM	ILLY	IMBITTER	IMITATE	IMMINGLE
EUS	ILMENITE	IMBITTERED	IMITATED	IMMINGLED
EUSES	ILMENITES	IMBITTERING	IMITATES	IMMINGLES
EX	IMAGE	IMBITTERS	IMITATING	IMMINGLING
EXES	IMAGEABLE	IMBODIED	IMITATION	IMMISSION
IA	IMAGED	IMBODIES	IMITATIONS	IMMISSIONS
IAC	IMAGELESS	IMBODY	IMITATIVE	IMMIT
ICES	IMAGERIES	IMBODYING	IMITATOR	IMMITS
IUM	IMAGERY	IMBORDER	IMITATORS	IMMITTED
K	IMAGES	IMBORDERED	IMMANACLE	IMMITTING
KA	IMAGINAL	IMBORDERING	IMMANACLED	IMMIX
KADAY	IMAGINARY	IMBORDERS	IMMANACLES	IMMIXED
KADAYS	IMAGINE	IMBOSK	IMMANACLING	IMMIXES
KS	IMAGINED	IMBOSKED	IMMANE	IMMIXING
	IMAGINER	IMBOSKING	IMMANELY	IMMOBILE
LAPSE	IMAGINERS	IMBOSKS	IMMANENCE	IMMODEST
LAPSED	IMAGINES	IMBOSOM	IMMANENCES	IMMODESTIES
LAPSES	IMAGING	IMBOSOMED	IMMANENCIES	IMMODESTY
LAPSING	IMAGINGS	IMBOSOMING	IMMANENCY	IMMOLATE
LATION	IMAGINING	IMBOSOMS	IMMANENT	IMMOLATED
LATIONS	IMAGININGS	IMBOSS	IMMANITIES	IMMOLATES
LATIVE	IMAGINIST	IMBOSSED	IMMANITY	IMMOLATING
LATIVES	IMAGINISTS	IMBOSSES	IMMANTLE	IMMOLATOR
LEGAL	IMAGISM	IMBOSSING	IMMANTLED	IMMOLATORS
LEGALLY	IMAGISMS	IMBOWER	IMMANTLES	IMMOMENT
LEGIBLE	IMAGIST	IMBOWERED	IMMANTLING	IMMORAL
LEGIBLY	IMAGISTIC	IMBOWERING	IMMASK	IMMORALLY
LIAD	IMAGISTS	IMBOWERS	IMMASKED	IMMORTAL
LIADS	IMAGO	IMBRANGLE	IMMASKING	IMMORTALS
LICENAI	IMAGOES	IMBRANGLED	IMMASKS	IMMOVABLE
LICIT	IMAGOS	IMBRANGLES	IMMATURE	IMMOVABLY
LICITLY	IMAM	IMBRANGLING	IMMATURED	IMMUNE
LIMITED	IMAMATE	IMBRAST	IMMEDIACIES	IMMUNES
LINIUM	IMAMATES	IMBREX	IMMEDIACY	IMMUNISE
LINIUMS	IMAMS	IMBRICATE	IMMEDIATE	IMMUNISED
LIPE	IMARI	IMBRICATED	IMMENSE	IMMUNISES
LIPES	IMARIS	IMBRICATES	IMMENSELY	IMMUNISING
LIQUID	IMAUM	IMBRICATING	IMMENSER	IMMUNITIES
LISION	IMAUMS	IMBRICES	IMMENSEST	IMMUNITY
LISIONS	IMBALANCE	IMBROGLIO	IMMENSITIES	IMMUNIZE
LITE	IMBALANCES	IMBROGLIOS	IMMENSITY	IMMUNIZED
LITES	IMBAR	IMBROWN	IMMERGE	IMMUNIZES
LNESS	IMBARK	IMBROWNED	IMMERGED	IMMUNIZING
LNESSES	IMBARKED	IMBROWNING	IMMERGES	IMMUNOGEN
LOGIC	IMBARKING	IMBROWNS	IMMERGING	IMMUNOGENS
LOGICAL	IMBARKS	IMBRUE	IMMERSE	IMMURE
LOGICS	IMBARRED	IMBRUED	IMMERSED	IMMURED
LS	IMBARRING	IMBRUES	IMMERSES	IMMURES
LTH	IMBARS	IMBRUING	IMMERSING	IMMURING
LTHS	IMBASE	IMBRUTE	IMMERSION	IMMUTABLE
LUDE	IMBASED	IMBRUTED	IMMERSIONS	IMMUTABLY
LUDED	IMBASES	IMBRUTES	IMMESH	IMP
LUDES	IMBASING	IMBRUTING	IMMESHED	IMPACABLE
LUDING	IMBATHE	IMBUE	IMMESHES	IMPACT
LUME	IMBATHED	IMBUED	IMMESHING	IMPACTED
LUMED	IMBATHES	IMBUES	IMMEW	IMPACTING
LUMINE	IMBATHING	IMBUING	IMMEWED	IMPACTION
LUMINED	IMBECILE	IMBURSE	IMMEWING	IMPACTIONS
LUMINER	IMBECILES	IMBURSED	IMMEWS	IMPACTITE
LUMINERS	IMBECILIC	IMBURSES	IMMIGRANT	IMPACTITES
LUMINES	IMBED	IMBURSING	IMMIGRANTS	IMPACTS
LUMING	IMBEDDED	IMIDE	IMMIGRATE	IMPAINT
LUMINING	IMBEDDING	IMIDES	IMMIGRATED	IMPAINTED
LUPI	IMBEDS	IMINE	IMMIGRATES	IMPAINTING
LUPIS	IMBIBE	IMINES	IMMIGRATING	IMPAINTS
LUSION	IMBIBED	IMITABLE	IMMINENCE	IMPAIR
LUSIONS	IMBIBER	IMITANCIES	IMMINENCES	IMPAIRED
LUSIVE	IMBIBERS	IMITANCY	IMMINENCIES	IMPAIRING
LUSORY	IMBIBES	IMITANT	IMMINENCY	IMPAIRS
	IMBIBING	IMITANTS	IMMINENT	IMPALA

IMPALAS
IMPALE
IMPALED
IMPALES
IMPALING
IMPANATE
IMPANEL
IMPANELLED
IMPANELLING
IMPANELS
IMPANNEL
IMPANNELLED
IMPANNELLING
IMPANNELS
IMPARITIES
IMPARITY
IMPARK
IMPARKED
IMPARKING
IMPARKS
IMPARL
IMPARLED
IMPARLING
IMPARLS
IMPART
IMPARTED
IMPARTER
IMPARTERS
IMPARTIAL
IMPARTING
IMPARTS
IMPASSE
IMPASSES
IMPASSION
IMPASSIONED
IMPASSIONING
IMPASSIONS
IMPASSIVE
IMPASTE
IMPASTED
IMPASTES
IMPASTING
IMPASTO
IMPASTOED
IMPASTOS
IMPATIENS
IMPATIENT
IMPAVE
IMPAVED
IMPAVES
IMPAVID
IMPAVIDLY
IMPAVING
IMPAWN
IMPAWNED
IMPAWNING
IMPAWNS
IMPEACH
IMPEACHED
IMPEACHER
IMPEACHERS
IMPEACHES
IMPEACHING
IMPEARL
IMPEARLED
IMPEARLING
IMPEARLS
IMPECCANT
IMPED
IMPEDANCE

IMPEDANCES
IMPEDE
IMPEDED
IMPEDES
IMPEDING
IMPEL
IMPELLED
IMPELLENT
IMPELLENTS
IMPELLER
IMPELLERS
IMPELLING
IMPELS
IMPEND
IMPENDED
IMPENDENT
IMPENDING
IMPENDS
IMPERATOR
IMPERATORS
IMPERFECT
IMPERFECTS
IMPERIAL
IMPERIALS
IMPERIL
IMPERILLED
IMPERILLING
IMPERILS
IMPERIOUS
IMPERIUM
IMPERIUMS
IMPETICOS
IMPETICOSSED
IMPETICOSSES
IMPETICOSSING
IMPETIGINES
IMPETIGO
IMPETIGOS
IMPETRATE
IMPETRATED
IMPETRATES
IMPETRATING
IMPETUOUS
IMPETUS
IMPETUSES
IMPI
IMPIETIES
IMPIETY
IMPING
IMPINGE
IMPINGED
IMPINGENT
IMPINGES
IMPINGING
IMPIOUS
IMPIOUSLY
IMPIS
IMPISH
IMPISHLY
IMPLANT
IMPLANTED
IMPLANTING
IMPLANTS
IMPLATE
IMPLATED
IMPLATES
IMPLATING
IMPLEACH
IMPLEACHED
IMPLEACHES

IMPLEACHING
IMPLEAD
IMPLEADED
IMPLEADER
IMPLEADERS
IMPLEADING
IMPLEADS
IMPLEDGE
IMPLEDGED
IMPLEDGES
IMPLEDGING
IMPLEMENT
IMPLEMENTED
IMPLEMENTING
IMPLEMENTS
IMPLETE
IMPLETED
IMPLETES
IMPLETING
IMPLETION
IMPLETIONS
IMPLEX
IMPLEXES
IMPLEXION
IMPLEXIONS
IMPLICATE
IMPLICATED
IMPLICATES
IMPLICATING
IMPLICIT
IMPLIED
IMPLIEDLY
IMPLIES
IMPLODE
IMPLODED
IMPLODENT
IMPLODENTS
IMPLODES
IMPLODING
IMPLORE
IMPLORED
IMPLORER
IMPLORERS
IMPLORES
IMPLORING
IMPLOSION
IMPLOSIONS
IMPLOSIVE
IMPLOSIVES
IMPLUNGE
IMPLUNGED
IMPLUNGES
IMPLUNGING
IMPLUVIA
IMPLUVIUM
IMPLY
IMPLYING
IMPOCKET
IMPOCKETED
IMPOCKETING
IMPOCKETS
IMPOLDER
IMPOLDERED
IMPOLDERING
IMPOLDERS
IMPOLICIES
IMPOLICY
IMPOLITE
IMPOLITER
IMPOLITEST

IMPOLITIC
IMPONE
IMPONED
IMPONENT
IMPONENTS
IMPONES
IMPONING
IMPORT
IMPORTANT
IMPORTED
IMPORTER
IMPORTERS
IMPORTING
IMPORTS
IMPORTUNE
IMPORTUNED
IMPORTUNES
IMPORTUNING
IMPORTUNINGS
IMPOSABLE
IMPOSE
IMPOSED
IMPOSER
IMPOSERS
IMPOSES
IMPOSING
IMPOST
IMPOSTER
IMPOSTERS
IMPOSTOR
IMPOSTORS
IMPOSTS
IMPOSTUME
IMPOSTUMES
IMPOSTURE
IMPOSTURES
IMPOT
IMPOTENCE
IMPOTENCES
IMPOTENCIES
IMPOTENCY
IMPOTENT
IMPOTS
IMPOUND
IMPOUNDED
IMPOUNDER
IMPOUNDERS
IMPOUNDING
IMPOUNDS
IMPRECATE
IMPRECATED
IMPRECATES
IMPRECATING
IMPRECISE
IMPREGN
IMPREGNED
IMPREGNING
IMPREGNS
IMPRESA
IMPRESARI
IMPRESAS
IMPRESE
IMPRESES
IMPRESS
IMPRESSE
IMPRESSED
IMPRESSES
IMPRESSING
IMPREST
IMPRESTED

IMPRESTING
IMPRESTS
IMPRIMIS
IMPRINT
IMPRINTED
IMPRINTING
IMPRINTINGS
IMPRINTS
IMPRISON
IMPRISONED
IMPRISONING
IMPRISONS
IMPROBITIES
IMPROBITY
IMPROMPTU
IMPROMPTUS
IMPROPER
IMPROVE
IMPROVED
IMPROVER
IMPROVERS
IMPROVES
IMPROVING
IMPROVISE
IMPROVISED
IMPROVISES
IMPROVISING
IMPRUDENT
IMPS
IMPUDENCE
IMPUDENCES
IMPUDENT
IMPUGN
IMPUGNED
IMPUGNER
IMPUGNERS
IMPUGNING
IMPUGNS
IMPULSE
IMPULSES
IMPULSION
IMPULSIONS
IMPULSIVE
IMPULSORY
IMPUNITIES
IMPUNITY
IMPURE
IMPURELY
IMPURER
IMPUREST
IMPURITIES
IMPURITY
IMPURPLE
IMPURPLED
IMPURPLES
IMPURPLING
IMPUTABLE
IMPUTABLY
IMPUTE
IMPUTED
IMPUTER
IMPUTERS
IMPUTES
IMPUTING
IMSHI
IMSHY
IN
INABILITIES
INABILITY
INACTION

ACTIONS
ACTIVE
AIDABLE
AMORATA
AMORATAS
AMORATO
AMORATOS
ANE
ANELY
ANENESS
ANENESSES
ANER
ANES
ANEST
ANIMATE
ANITIES
ANITION
ANITIONS
ANITY
APT
APTLY
APTNESS
APTNESSES
ARABLE
ARCH
ANOILED
ARCHES
ARCHING
ARM
ARMED
ARMING
ARMS
AUDIBLE
AUDIBLY
AUGURAL
AUGURALS
AURATE
BEING
BEINGS
BENT
BOARD
BORN
BREAK
BREAKS
BREATHE
BREATHED
BREATHES
BREATHING
BRED
BREED
BREEDING
BREEDINGS
BREEDS
BRING
BRINGING
BRINGINGS
BRINGS
BROUGHT
BURNING
BURST
BURSTS
BY
BYE
CAGE
CAGED
CAGES
CAGING
CAPABLE
CAPABLES
CAPABLY

INCARNATE
INCARNATED
INCARNATES
INCARNATING
INCASE
INCASED
INCASES
INCASING
INCAUTION
INCAUTIONS
INCAVE
INCAVED
INCAVES
INCAVI
INCAVING
INCAVO
INCEDE
INCEDED
INCEDES
INCEDING
INCENSE
INCENSED
INCENSER
INCENSERS
INCENSES
INCENSOR
INCENSORIES
INCENSORS
INCENSORY
INCENTIVE
INCENTIVES
INCENTRE
INCENTRES
INCEPT
INCEPTED
INCEPTING
INCEPTION
INCEPTIONS
INCEPTIVE
INCEPTIVES
INCEPTOR
INCEPTORS
INCEPTS
INCERTAIN
INCESSANT
INCEST
INCESTS
INCH
INCHASE
INCHASED
INCHASES
INCHASING
INCHED
INCHES
INCHING
INCHMEAL
INCHOATE
INCHOATED
INCHOATES
INCHOATING
INCHPIN
INCHPINS
INCIDENCE
INCIDENCES
INCIDENT
INCIDENTS
INCIPIENT
INCIPIT
INCISE

INCISED
INCISES
INCISING
INCISION
INCISIONS
INCISIVE
INCISOR
INCISORS
INCISORY
INCISURE
INCISURES
INCITANT
INCITANTS
INCITE
INCITED
INCITER
INCITERS
INCITING
INCIVIL
INCIVISM
INCIVISMS
INCLASP
INCLASPED
INCLASPING
INCLASPS
INCLE
INCLEMENT
INCLES
INCLINE
INCLINED
INCLINES
INCLINING
INCLININGS
INCLIP
INCLIPPED
INCLIPPING
INCLIPS
INCLOSE
INCLOSED
INCLOSER
INCLOSERS
INCLOSES
INCLOSING
INCLOSURE
INCLOSURES
INCLUDE
INCLUDED
INCLUDES
INCLUDING
INCLUSION
INCLUSIONS
INCLUSIVE
INCOGNITA
INCOGNITAS
INCOGNITO
INCOGNITOS
INCOME
INCOMER
INCOMERS
INCOMES
INCOMING
INCOMINGS
INCOMMODE
INCOMMODED
INCOMMODES
INCOMMODING
INCONDITE
INCONIE
INCONNU

INCONNUE
INCONNUES
INCONNUS
INCONY
INCORPSE
INCORPSED
INCORPSES
INCORPSING
INCORRECT
INCORRUPT
INCREASE
INCREASED
INCREASER
INCREASERS
INCREASES
INCREASING
INCREASINGS
INCREATE
INCREMATE
INCREMATED
INCREMATES
INCREMATING
INCREMENT
INCREMENTS
INCROSS
INCROSSED
INCROSSES
INCROSSING
INCRUST
INCRUSTED
INCRUSTING
INCRUSTS
INCUBATE
INCUBATED
INCUBATES
INCUBATING
INCUBATOR
INCUBATORS
INCUBI
INCUBOUS
INCUBUS
INCUBUSES
INCUDES
INCULCATE
INCULCATED
INCULCATES
INCULCATING
INCULPATE
INCULPATED
INCULPATES
INCULPATING
INCULT
INCUMBENT
INCUMBENTS
INCUNABLE
INCUNABLES
INCUR
INCURABLE
INCURABLES
INCURABLY
INCURIOUS
INCURRED
INCURRENT
INCURRING
INCURS
INCURSION
INCURSIONS
INCURSIVE
INCURVATE
INCURVATED

INCURVATES
INCURVATING
INCURVE
INCURVED
INCURVES
INCURVING
INCURVITIES
INCURVITY
INCUS
INCUSE
INCUSED
INCUSES
INCUSING
INCUT
INDABA
INDABAS
INDAGATE
INDAGATED
INDAGATES
INDAGATING
INDAGATOR
INDAGATORS
INDART
INDARTED
INDARTING
INDARTS
INDEBTED
INDECENCIES
INDECENCY
INDECENT
INDECORUM
INDECORUMS
INDEED
INDELIBLE
INDELIBLY
INDEMNIFIED
INDEMNIFIES
INDEMNIFY
INDEMNIFYING
INDEMNITIES
INDEMNITY
INDENE
INDENES
INDENT
INDENTED
INDENTER
INDENTERS
INDENTING
INDENTION
INDENTIONS
INDENTS
INDENTURE
INDENTURED
INDENTURES
INDENTURING
INDEW
INDEWED
INDEWING
INDEWS
INDEX
INDEXED
INDEXER
INDEXERS
INDEXES
INDEXICAL
INDEXING
INDEXINGS
INDEXLESS
INDICAN
INDICANS

INDICANT	INDORSED	INDWELT	INFANTA	INFINITE
INDICANTS	INDORSES	INEARTH	INFANTAS	INFINITES
INDICATE	INDORSING	INEARTHED	INFANTE	INFINITIES
INDICATED	INDRAFT	INEARTHING	INFANTED	INFINITY
INDICATES	INDRAFTS	INEARTHS	INFANTES	INFIRM
INDICATING	INDRAUGHT	INEBRIANT	INFANTILE	INFIRMARIES
INDICATOR	INDRAUGHTS	INEBRIANTS	INFANTINE	INFIRMARY
INDICATORS	INDRAWN	INEBRIATE	INFANTING	INFIRMER
INDICES	INDRENCH	INEBRIATED	INFANTRIES	INFIRMEST
INDICIA	INDRENCHED	INEBRIATES	INFANTRY	INFIRMITIES
INDICIUM	INDRENCHES	INEBRIATING	INFANTS	INFIRMITY
INDICT	INDRENCHING	INEBRIETIES	INFARCT	INFIRMLY
INDICTED	INDRI	INEBRIETY	INFARCTS	INFIX
INDICTEE	INDRIS	INEBRIOUS	INFARE	INFIXED
INDICTEES	INDRISES	INEDIBLE	INFARES	INFIXES
INDICTING	INDUBIOUS	INEDITED	INFATUATE	INFIXING
INDICTION	INDUCE	INEFFABLE	INFATUATED	INFLAME
INDICTIONS	INDUCED	INEFFABLY	INFATUATES	INFLAMED
INDICTS	INDUCER	INELASTIC	INFATUATING	INFLAMER
INDIGENCE	INDUCERS	INELEGANT	INFAUST	INFLAMERS
INDIGENCES	INDUCES	INEPT	INFECT	INFLAMES
INDIGENCIES	INDUCIAE	INEPTER	INFECTED	INFLAMING
INDIGENCY	INDUCIBLE	INEPTEST	INFECTING	INFLATE
INDIGENE	INDUCING	INEPTLY	INFECTION	INFLATED
INDIGENES	INDUCT	INEPTNESS	INFECTIONS	INFLATES
INDIGENT	INDUCTED	INEPTNESSES	INFECTIVE	INFLATING
INDIGEST	INDUCTILE	INEQUABLE	INFECTOR	INFLATION
INDIGESTS	INDUCTING	INEQUITIES	INFECTORS	INFLATIONS
INDIGN	INDUCTION	INEQUITY	INFECTS	INFLATIVE
INDIGNANT	INDUCTIONS	INERM	INFECUND	INFLATOR
INDIGNIFIED	INDUCTIVE	INERRABLE	INFEFT	INFLATORS
INDIGNIFIES	INDUCTOR	INERRABLY	INFEFTED	INFLATUS
INDIGNIFY	INDUCTORS	INERRANCIES	INFEFTING	INFLATUSES
INDIGNIFYING	INDUCTS	INERRANCY	INFEFTS	INFLECT
INDIGNITIES	INDUE	INERRANT	INFELT	INFLECTED
INDIGNITY	INDUED	INERT	INFER	INFLECTING
INDIGO	INDUES	INERTER	INFERABLE	INFLECTS
INDIGOES	INDUING	INERTEST	INFERE	INFLEXED
INDIGOS	INDULGE	INERTIA	INFERENCE	INFLEXION
INDIGOTIN	INDULGED	INERTIAL	INFERENCES	INFLEXIONS
INDIGOTINS	INDULGENT	INERTIAS	INFERIAE	INFLEXURE
INDIRECT	INDULGER	INERTLY	INFERIOR	INFLEXURES
INDIRUBIN	INDULGERS	INERTNESS	INFERIORS	INFLICT
INDIRUBINS	INDULGES	INERTNESSES	INFERNAL	INFLICTED
INDISPOSE	INDULGING	INERUDITE	INFERNO	INFLICTING
INDISPOSED	INDULINE	INESSIVE	INFERNOS	INFLICTS
INDISPOSES	INDULINES	INESSIVES	INFERRED	INFLOW
INDISPOSING	INDULT	INEXACT	INFERRING	INFLOWING
INDITE	INDULTS	INEXACTLY	INFERS	INFLOWS
INDITED	INDUNA	INEXPERT	INFERTILE	INFLUENCE
INDITER	INDUNAS	INFALL	INFEST	INFLUENCED
INDITERS	INDURATE	INFALLS	INFESTED	INFLUENCES
INDITES	INDURATED	INFAME	INFESTING	INFLUENCING
INDITING	INDURATES	INFAMED	INFESTS	INFLUENT
INDIUM	INDURATING	INFAMES	INFICETE	INFLUENTS
INDIUMS	INDUSIA	INFAMIES	INFIDEL	INFLUENZA
INDOCIBLE	INDUSIAL	INFAMING	INFIDELS	INFLUENZAS
INDOCILE	INDUSIATE	INFAMISE	INFIELD	INFLUX
INDOL	INDUSIUM	INFAMISED	INFIELDER	INFLUXES
INDOLE	INDUSTRIES	INFAMISES	INFIELDERS	INFLUXION
INDOLENCE	INDUSTRY	INFAMISING	INFIELDS	INFLUXIONS
INDOLENCES	INDUVIAE	INFAMIZE	INFILL	INFO
INDOLENCIES	INDUVIAL	INFAMIZED	INFILLED	INFOLD
INDOLENCY	INDUVIATE	INFAMIZES	INFILLING	INFOLDED
INDOLENT	INDWELL	INFAMIZING	INFILLINGS	INFOLDING
INDOLES	INDWELLER	INFAMOUS	INFILLS	INFOLDS
INDOLS	INDWELLERS	INFAMY	INFILTER	INFORCE
INDOOR	INDWELLING	INFANCIES	INFILTERED	INFORCED
INDOORS	INDWELLINGS	INFANCY	INFILTERING	INFORCES
INDORSE	INDWELLS	INFANT	INFILTERS	INFORCING

INFORM
INFORMAL
INFORMANT
INFORMANTS
INFORMED
INFORMER
INFORMERS
INFORMING
INFORMS
INFORTUNE
INFORTUNES
INFOS
INFRA
INFRACT
INFRACTED
INFRACTING
INFRACTOR
INFRACTORS
INFRACTS
INFRINGE
INFRINGED
INFRINGES
INFRINGING
INFULA
INFULAE
INFURIATE
INFURIATED
INFURIATES
INFURIATING
INFUSCATE
INFUSE
INFUSED
INFUSER
INFUSERS
INFUSES
INFUSIBLE
INFUSING
INFUSION
INFUSIONS
INFUSIVE
INFUSORIA
INFUSORY
INGAN
INGANS
INGATE
INGATES
INGENER
INGENERS
INGENIOUS
INGENIUM
INGENIUMS
INGÉNU
INGÉNUE
INGÉNUES
INGENUITIES
INGENUITY
INGENUOUS
INGÉNUS
INGEST
INGESTA
INGESTED
INGESTING
INGESTION
INGESTIONS
INGESTIVE
INGESTS
INGINE
INGINES
INGLE
INGLES

INGLOBE
INGLOBED
INGLOBES
INGLOBING
INGLUVIAL
INGLUVIES
INGO
INGOES
INGOING
INGOINGS
INGOT
INGOTS
INGOWES
INGRAFT
INGRAFTED
INGRAFTING
INGRAFTS
INGRAIN
INGRAINED
INGRAINING
INGRAINS
INGRAM
INGRATE
INGRATES
INGRESS
INGRESSES
INGROOVE
INGROOVED
INGROOVES
INGROOVING
INGROSS
INGROSSED
INGROSSES
INGROSSING
INGROUP
INGROUPS
INGROWING
INGROWN
INGROWTH
INGROWTHS
INGRUM
INGUINAL
INGULF
INGULFED
INGULFING
INGULFS
INGULPH
INGULPHED
INGULPHING
INGULPHS
INHABIT
INHABITED
INHABITING
INHABITION
INHABITORS
INHABITS
INHALANT
INHALANTS
INHALATOR
INHALATORS
INHALE
INHALED
INHALER
INHALERS
INHALES
INHALING
INHARMONIES
INHARMONY
INHAUST
INHAUSTED

INHAUSTING
INHAUSTS
INHEARSE
INHEARSED
INHEARSES
INHEARSING
INHERCE
INHERCED
INHERCES
INHERCING
INHERE
INHERED
INHERENCE
INHERENCES
INHERENCIES
INHERENCY
INHERENT
INHERES
INHERING
INHERIT
INHERITED
INHERITING
INHERITOR
INHERITORS
INHERITS
INHESION
INHESIONS
INHIBIT
INHIBITED
INHIBITING
INHIBITOR
INHIBITORS
INHIBITS
INHOLDER
INHOLDERS
INHOOP
INHOOPED
INHOOPING
INHOOPS
INHUMAN
INHUMANE
INHUMANLY
INHUMATE
INHUMATED
INHUMATES
INHUMATING
INHUME
INHUMED
INHUMES
INHUMING
INIA
INIMICAL
INION
INIQUITIES
INIQUITY
INISLE
INISLED
INISLES
INISLING
INITIAL
INITIALLED
INITIALLING
INITIALLY
INITIALS
INITIATE
INITIATED
INITIATES
INITIATING
INITIATOR
INITIATORS

INJECT
INJECTED
INJECTING
INJECTION
INJECTIONS
INJECTOR
INJECTORS
INJECTS
INJELLIED
INJELLIES
INJELLY
INJELLYING
INJOINT
INJOINTED
INJOINTING
INJOINTS
INJUNCT
INJUNCTED
INJUNCTING
INJUNCTS
INJURANT
INJURANTS
INJURE
INJURED
INJURER
INJURERS
INJURES
INJURIES
INJURING
INJURIOUS
INJURY
INJUSTICE
INJUSTICES
INK
INKBERRIES
INKBERRY
INKED
INKER
INKERS
INKHOLDER
INKHOLDERS
INKHORN
INKHORNS
INKIER
INKIEST
INKINESS
INKINESSES
INKING
INKLE
INKLED
INKLES
INKLING
INKLINGS
INKPOT
INKPOTS
INKS
INKSPOT
INKSPOTS
INKSTAND
INKSTANDS
INKSTONE
INKSTONES
INKWELL
INKWELLS
INKY
INLACE
INLACED
INLACES
INLACING
INLAID

INLAND
INLANDER
INLANDERS
INLANDS
INLAY
INLAYER
INLAYERS
INLAYING
INLAYINGS
INLAYS
INLET
INLETS
INLIER
INLIERS
INLIEST
INLOCK
INLOCKED
INLOCKING
INLOCKS
INLY
INLYING
INMATE
INMATES
INMESH
INMESHED
INMESHES
INMESHING
INMOST
INN
INNARDS
INNATE
INNATELY
INNATIVE
INNED
INNER
INNERMOST
INNERS
INNERVATE
INNERVATED
INNERVATES
INNERVATING
INNERVE
INNERVED
INNERVES
INNERVING
INNHOLDER
INNHOLDERS
INNING
INNINGS
INNKEEPER
INNKEEPERS
INNOCENCE
INNOCENCES
INNOCENCIES
INNOCENCY
INNOCENT
INNOCENTS
INNOCUITIES
INNOCUITY
INNOCUOUS
INNOVATE
INNOVATED
INNOVATES
INNOVATING
INNOVATOR
INNOVATORS
INNOXIOUS
INNS
INNUENDO
INNUENDOED

INNUENDOES
INNUENDOING
INNUENDOS
INNYARD
INNYARDS
INOCULATE
INOCULATED
INOCULATES
INOCULATING
INOCULUM
INOCULUMS
INODOROUS
INOPINATE
INORB
INORBED
INORBING
INORBS
INORGANIC
INORNATE
INOSITOL
INOSITOLS
INOTROPIC
INPAYMENT
INPAYMENTS
INPHASE
INPOURING
INPOURINGS
INPUT
INPUTS
INPUTTER
INPUTTERS
INPUTTING
INQILAB
INQILABS
INQUERE
INQUERED
INQUERES
INQUERING
INQUEST
INQUESTS
INQUIET
INQUIETED
INQUIETING
INQUIETLY
INQUIETS
INQUILINE
INQUILINES
INQUINATE
INQUINATED
INQUINATES
INQUINATING
INQUIRE
INQUIRED
INQUIRER
INQUIRERS
INQUIRES
INQUIRIES
INQUIRING
INQUIRY
INQUORATE
INRO
INROAD
INROADS
INRUSH
INRUSHES
INRUSHING
INRUSHINGS
INS
INSANE
INSANELY

INSANER
INSANEST
INSANIE
INSANIES
INSANITIES
INSANITY
INSATIATE
INSATIETIES
INSATIETY
INSCAPE
INSCAPES
INSCIENCE
INSCIENCES
INSCIENT
INSCONCE
INSCONCED
INSCONCES
INSCONCING
INSCRIBE
INSCRIBED
INSCRIBER
INSCRIBERS
INSCRIBES
INSCRIBING
INSCROLL
INSCROLLED
INSCROLLING
INSCROLLS
INSCULP
INSCULPED
INSCULPING
INSCULPS
INSCULPT
INSEAM
INSEAMED
INSEAMING
INSEAMS
INSECT
INSECTARIES
INSECTARY
INSECTILE
INSECTION
INSECTIONS
INSECTS
INSECTY
INSECURE
INSEEM
INSEEMED
INSEEMING
INSEEMS
INSELBERG
INSELBERGE
INSENSATE
INSERT
INSERTED
INSERTER
INSERTERS
INSERTING
INSERTION
INSERTIONS
INSERTS
INSET
INSETS
INSETTING
INSHALLAH
INSHEATHE
INSHEATHED
INSHEATHES
INSHEATHING
INSHELL

INSHELLED
INSHELLING
INSHELLS
INSHELTER
INSHELTERED
INSHELTERING
INSHELTERS
INSHIP
INSHIPPED
INSHIPPING
INSHIPS
INSHORE
INSHRINE
INSHRINED
INSHRINES
INSHRINING
INSIDE
INSIDER
INSIDERS
INSIDES
INSIDIOUS
INSIGHT
INSIGHTS
INSIGNE
INSIGNES
INSIGNIA
INSIGNIAS
INSINCERE
INSINEW
INSINEWED
INSINEWING
INSINEWS
INSINUATE
INSINUATED
INSINUATES
INSINUATING
INSIPID
INSIPIDLY
INSIPIENT
INSIST
INSISTED
INSISTENT
INSISTING
INSISTS
INSISTURE
INSISTURES
INSNARE
INSNARED
INSNARES
INSNARING
INSOLATE
INSOLATED
INSOLATES
INSOLATING
INSOLE
INSOLENCE
INSOLENCES
INSOLENT
INSOLES
INSOLUBLE
INSOLUBLY
INSOLVENT
INSOLVENTS
INSOMNIA
INSOMNIAC
INSOMNIACS
INSOMNIAS
INSOMUCH
INSOOTH
INSOUL

INSOULED
INSOULING
INSOULS
INSPAN
INSPANNED
INSPANNING
INSPANS
INSPECT
INSPECTED
INSPECTING
INSPECTOR
INSPECTORS
INSPECTS
INSPHERE
INSPHERED
INSPHERES
INSPHERING
INSPIRE
INSPIRED
INSPIRER
INSPIRERS
INSPIRES
INSPIRING
INSPIRIT
INSPIRITED
INSPIRITING
INSPIRITS
INSPYRE
INSPYRED
INSPYRES
INSPYRING
INSTABLE
INSTAL
INSTALL
INSTALLED
INSTALLING
INSTALLS
INSTALS
INSTANCE
INSTANCED
INSTANCES
INSTANCIES
INSTANCING
INSTANCY
INSTANT
INSTANTER
INSTANTLY
INSTANTS
INSTAR
INSTARRED
INSTARRING
INSTARS
INSTATE
INSTATED
INSTATES
INSTATING
INSTEAD
INSTEP
INSTEPS
INSTIGATE
INSTIGATED
INSTIGATES
INSTIGATING
INSTIL
INSTILL
INSTILLED
INSTILLING
INSTILLS
INSTILS
INSTINCT

INSTINCTS
INSTITUTE
INSTITUTED
INSTITUTES
INSTITUTING
INSTRESS
INSTRESSED
INSTRESSES
INSTRESSING
INSTRUCT
INSTRUCTED
INSTRUCTING
INSTRUCTS
INSUCKEN
INSULA
INSULAE
INSULANCE
INSULANCES
INSULANT
INSULANTS
INSULAR
INSULARLY
INSULAS
INSULATE
INSULATED
INSULATES
INSULATING
INSULATOR
INSULATORS
INSULIN
INSULINS
INSULSE
INSULSITIES
INSULSITY
INSULT
INSULTANT
INSULTED
INSULTER
INSULTERS
INSULTING
INSULTS
INSURABLE
INSURANCE
INSURANCES
INSURANT
INSURANTS
INSURE
INSURED
INSURER
INSURERS
INSURES
INSURGENT
INSURGENTS
INSURING
INSWATHE
INSWATHED
INSWATHES
INSWATHING
INSWING
INSWINGER
INSWINGERS
INSWINGS
INTACT
INTAGLIO
INTAGLIOED
INTAGLIOING
INTAGLIOS
INTAKE
INTAKES
INTARSI

INTARSIA
INTARSIAS
INTARSIO
INTARSIOS
INTEGER
INTEGERS
INTEGRAL
INTEGRALS
INTEGRAND
INTEGRANDS
INTEGRANT
INTEGRATE
INTEGRATED
INTEGRATES
INTEGRATING
INTEGRITIES
INTEGRITY
INTELLECT
INTELLECTS
INTENABLE
INTEND
INTENDANT
INTENDANTS
INTENDED
INTENDEDS
INTENDER
INTENDERED
INTENDERING
INTENDERS
INTENDING
INTENDS
INTENIBLE
INTENSATE
INTENSATED
INTENSATES
INTENSATING
INTENSE
INTENSELY
INTENSER
INTENSEST
INTENSIFIED
INTENSIFIES
INTENSIFY
INTENSIFYING
INTENSION
INTENSIONS
INTENSITIES
INTENSITY
INTENSIVE
INTENSIVES
INTENT
INTENTION
INTENTIONS
INTENTIVE
INTENTLY
INTENTS
INTER
INTERACT
INTERACTED
INTERACTING
INTERACTS
INTERBANK
INTERBRED
INTERCEDE
INTERCEDED
INTERCEDES
INTERCEDING
INTERCEPT
INTERCEPTED
INTERCEPTING

INTERCEPTS
INTERCITY
INTERCOM
INTERCOMS
INTERCROP
INTERCROPPED
INTERCROPPING
INTERCROPS
INTERCUT
INTERCUTS
INTERCUTTING
INTERDASH
INTERDASHED
INTERDASHES
INTERDASHING
INTERDEAL
INTERDEALING
INTERDEALS
INTERDEALT
INTERDICT
INTERDICTED
INTERDICTING
INTERDICTS
INTERDINE
INTERDINED
INTERDINES
INTERDINING
INTERESS
INTERESSE
INTERESSED
INTERESSES
INTERESSING
INTEREST
INTERESTED
INTERESTING
INTERESTS
INTERFACE
INTERFACED
INTERFACES
INTERFACING
INTERFACINGS
INTERFERE
INTERFERED
INTERFERES
INTERFERING
INTERFLOW
INTERFLOWED
INTERFLOWING
INTERFLOWS
INTERFOLD
INTERFOLDED
INTERFOLDING
INTERFOLDS
INTERFUSE
INTERFUSED
INTERFUSES
INTERFUSING
INTERGREW
INTERGROW
INTERGROWING
INTERGROWN
INTERGROWS
INTERIM
INTERIMS
INTERIOR
INTERIORS
INTERJECT
INTERJECTED
INTERJECTING
INTERJECTS

INTERJOIN
INTERJOINED
INTERJOINING
INTERJOINS
INTERKNIT
INTERKNITS
INTERKNITTED
INTERKNITTING
INTERLACE
INTERLACED
INTERLACES
INTERLACING
INTERLAID
INTERLARD
INTERLARDED
INTERLARDING
INTERLARDS
INTERLAY
INTERLAYING
INTERLAYS
INTERLEAF
INTERLEAVES
INTERLINE
INTERLINED
INTERLINES
INTERLINING
INTERLININGS
INTERLINK
INTERLINKED
INTERLINKING
INTERLINKS
INTERLOCK
INTERLOCKED
INTERLOCKING
INTERLOCKS
INTERLOPE
INTERLOPED
INTERLOPES
INTERLOPING
INTERLUDE
INTERLUDED
INTERLUDES
INTERLUDING
INTERMENT
INTERMENTS
INTERMIT
INTERMITS
INTERMITTED
INTERMITTING
INTERMIX
INTERMIXED
INTERMIXES
INTERMIXING
INTERMURE
INTERMURED
INTERMURES
INTERMURING
INTERN
INTERNAL
INTERNALS
INTERNE
INTERNED
INTERNEE
INTERNEES
INTERNES
INTERNING
INTERNIST
INTERNISTS
INTERNODE
INTERNODES

INTERNS
INTERPAGE
INTERPAGED
INTERPAGES
INTERPAGING
INTERPLAY
INTERPLAYS
INTERPONE
INTERPONED
INTERPONES
INTERPONING
INTERPOSE
INTERPOSED
INTERPOSES
INTERPOSING
INTERPRET
INTERPRETED
INTERPRETING
INTERPRETS
INTERRED
INTERREGES
INTERREX
INTERRING
INTERRUPT
INTERRUPTED
INTERRUPTING
INTERRUPTS
INTERS
INTERSECT
INTERSECTED
INTERSECTING
INTERSECTS
INTERSERT
INTERSERTED
INTERSERTING
INTERSERTS
INTERSEX
INTERSEXES
INTERTIE
INTERTIES
INTERVAL
INTERVALE
INTERVALES
INTERVALS
INTERVEIN
INTERVEINED
INTERVEINING
INTERVEINS
INTERVENE
INTERVENED
INTERVENES
INTERVENING
INTERVIEW
INTERVIEWED
INTERVIEWING
INTERVIEWS
INTERWAR
INTERWIND
INTERWINDING
INTERWINDS
INTERWORK
INTERWORKED
INTERWORKING
INTERWORKS
INTERWOUND
INTERWOVE
INTERZONE
INTERZONES
INTESTACIES
INTESTACY

INTESTATE
INTESTATES
INTESTINE
INTESTINES
INTHRAL
INTHRALL
INTHRALLED
INTHRALLING
INTHRALLS
INTHRALS
INTIL
INTIMA
INTIMACIES
INTIMACY
INTIMAE
INTIMATE
INTIMATED
INTIMATES
INTIMATING
INTIME
INTIMISM
INTIMISMS
INTIMIST
INTIMISTE
INTIMISTES
INTIMISTS
INTIMITIES
INTIMITY
INTINE
INTINES
INTIRE
INTITULE
INTITULED
INTITULES
INTITULING
INTO
INTOED
INTOMB
INTOMBED
INTOMBING
INTOMBS
INTONATE
INTONATED
INTONATES
INTONATING
INTONATOR
INTONATORS
INTONE
INTONED
INTONER
INTONERS
INTONES
INTONING
INTONINGS
INTORSION
INTORSIONS
INTORTED
INTORTION
INTORTIONS
INTOWN
INTRA
INTRADOS
INTRADOSES
INTRANT
INTRANTS
INTREAT
INTREATED
INTREATING
INTREATS
INTRENCH

INTRENCHED	INTUMESCES	INVECTIVES	INVOCATES	IODINES
INTRENCHES	INTUMESCING	INVEIGH	INVOCATING	IODISE
INTRENCHING	INTUSE	INVEIGHED	INVOICE	IODISED
INTREPID	INTUSES	INVEIGHING	INVOICED	IODISES
INTRICACIES	INTWINE	INVEIGHS	INVOICES	IODISING
INTRICACY	INTWINED	INVEIGLE	INVOICING	IODISM
INTRICATE	INTWINES	INVEIGLED	INVOKE	IODISMS
INTRIGANT	INTWINING	INVEIGLER	INVOKED	IODIZE
INTRIGANTS	INTWIST	INVEIGLERS	INVOKES	IODIZED
INTRIGUE	INTWISTED	INVEIGLES	INVOKING	IODIZES
INTRIGUED	INTWISTING	INVEIGLING	INVOLUCEL	IODIZING
INTRIGUER	INTWISTS	INVENIT	INVOLUCELS	IODOFORM
INTRIGUERS	INULA	INVENT	INVOLUCRA	IODOFORMS
INTRIGUES	INULAS	INVENTED	INVOLUCRE	IODOPHILE
INTRIGUING	INULASE	INVENTING	INVOLUCRES	IODOUS
INTRINCE	INULASES	INVENTION	INVOLUTE	IODURET
INTRINSIC	INULIN	INVENTIONS	INVOLUTED	IODURETS
INTRO	INULINS	INVENTIVE	INVOLUTES	IODYRITE
INTRODUCE	INUMBRATE	INVENTOR	INVOLUTING	IODYRITES
INTRODUCED	INUMBRATED	INVENTORIED	INVOLVE	IOLITE
INTRODUCES	INUMBRATES	INVENTORIES	INVOLVED	IOLITES
INTRODUCING	INUMBRATING	INVENTORS	INVOLVES	ION
INTROIT	INUNCTION	INVENTORY	INVOLVING	IONIC
INTROITS	INUNCTIONS	INVENTORYING	INWALL	IONISE
INTROITUS	INUNDANT	INVENTS	INWALLED	IONISED
INTROITUSES	INUNDATE	INVERSE	INWALLING	IONISER
INTROJECT	INUNDATED	INVERSED	INWALLS	IONISERS
INTROJECTED	INUNDATES	INVERSELY	INWARD	IONISES
INTROJECTING	INUNDATING	INVERSES	INWARDLY	IONISING
INTROJECTS	INURBANE	INVERSING	INWARDS	IONIUM
INTROLD	INURE	INVERSION	INWEAVE	IONIUMS
INTROMIT	INURED	INVERSIONS	INWEAVES	IONIZE
INTROMITS	INUREMENT	INVERSIVE	INWEAVING	IONIZED
INTROMITTED	INUREMENTS	INVERT	INWICK	IONIZER
INTROMITTING	INURES	INVERTASE	INWICKED	IONIZERS
INTRON	INURING	INVERTASES	INWICKING	IONIZES
INTRONS	INURN	INVERTED	INWICKS	IONIZING
INTRORSE	INURNED	INVERTER	INWIND	IONOMER
INTROS	INURNING	INVERTERS	INWINDING	IONOMERS
INTROVERT	INURNS	INVERTIN	INWINDS	IONONE
INTROVERTED	INUSITATE	INVERTING	INWIT	IONONES
INTROVERTING	INUST	INVERTINS	INWITH	IONOPAUSE
INTROVERTS	INUSTION	INVERTOR	INWITS	IONOPAUSES
INTRUDE	INUSTIONS	INVERTORS	INWORK	IONOPHORE
INTRUDED	INUTILITIES	INVERTS	INWORKED	IONOPHORES
INTRUDER	INUTILITY	INVEST	INWORKING	IONS
INTRUDERS	INVADE	INVESTED	INWORKINGS	IOS
INTRUDES	INVADED	INVESTING	INWORKS	IOTA
INTRUDING	INVADER	INVESTOR	INWORN	IOTACISM
INTRUSION	INVADERS	INVESTORS	INWOUND	IOTACISMS
INTRUSIONS	INVADES	INVESTS	INWOVE	IOTAS
INTRUSIVE	INVADING	INVEXED	INWOVEN	IPECAC
INTRUSIVES	INVALID	INVIABLE	INWRAP	IPECACS
INTRUST	INVALIDED	INVIDIOUS	INWRAPPED	IPOMOEA
INTRUSTED	INVALIDING	INVIOLATE	INWRAPPING	IPOMOEAS
INTRUSTING	INVALIDINGS	INVIOUS	INWRAPS	IRACUND
INTRUSTS	INVALIDLY	INVISIBLE	INWREATHE	IRADE
INTUBATE	INVALIDS	INVISIBLES	INWREATHED	IRADES
INTUBATED	INVARIANT	INVISIBLY	INWREATHES	IRASCIBLE
INTUBATES	INVARIANTS	INVITE	INWREATHING	IRASCIBLY
INTUBATING	INVASION	INVITED	INWROUGHT	IRATE
INTUIT	INVASIONS	INVITEE	INYALA	IRATELY
INTUITED	INVASIVE	INVITEES	INYALAS	IRATER
INTUITING	INVEAGLE	INVITER	IO	IRATEST
INTUITION	INVEAGLED	INVITERS	IODATE	IRE
INTUITIONS	INVEAGLES	INVITES	IODATES	IREFUL
INTUITIVE	INVEAGLING	INVITING	IODIC	IREFULLY
INTUITS	INVECKED	INVITINGS	IODIDE	IRENIC
INTUMESCE	INVECTED	INVOCATE	IODIDES	IRENICAL
INTUMESCED	INVECTIVE	INVOCATED	IODINE	IRENICISM

IRENICISMS	IRONIZED	ISCHAEMIA	ISOCLINE	ISOMERIC
IRENICON	IRONIZES	ISCHAEMIAS	ISOCLINES	ISOMERISE
IRENICONS	IRONIZING	ISCHAEMIC	ISOCLINIC	ISOMERISED
IRENICS	IRONS	ISCHEMIA	ISOCLINICS	ISOMERISES
IRENOLOGIES	IRONSMITH	ISCHEMIAS	ISOCRACIES	ISOMERISING
IRENOLOGY	IRONSMITHS	ISCHEMIC	ISOCRACY	ISOMERISM
IRES	IRONSTONE	ISCHIA	ISOCRATIC	ISOMERISMS
IRID	IRONSTONES	ISCHIADIC	ISOCRYMAL	ISOMERIZE
IRIDAL	IRONWARE	ISCHIAL	ISOCRYMALS	ISOMERIZED
IRIDEAL	IRONWARES	ISCHIATIC	ISOCRYME	ISOMERIZES
IRIDES	IRONWOOD	ISCHIUM	ISOCRYMES	ISOMERIZING
IRIDIAL	IRONWOODS	ISCHURIA	ISOCYCLIC	ISOMEROUS
IRIDIAN	IRONWORK	ISCHURIAS	ISODICON	ISOMERS
IRIDIC	IRONWORKS	ISENERGIC	ISODICONS	ISOMETRIC
IRIDISE	IRONY	ISH	ISODOMA	ISOMETRICS
IRIDISED	IRRADIANT	ISHES	ISODOMON	ISOMETRIES
IRIDISES	IRRADIATE	ISINGLASS	ISODOMONS	ISOMETRY
IRIDISING	IRRADIATED	ISINGLASSES	ISODOMOUS	ISOMORPH
IRIDIUM	IRRADIATES	ISLAND	ISODOMUM	ISOMORPHS
IRIDIUMS	IRRADIATING	ISLANDED	ISODONT	ISONIAZID
IRIDIZE	IRREALITIES	ISLANDER	ISODONTAL	ISONIAZIDS
IRIDIZED	IRREALITY	ISLANDERS	ISODONTS	ISONOMIC
IRIDIZES	IRREGULAR	ISLANDING	ISOETES	ISONOMIES
IRIDIZING	IRREGULARS	ISLANDS	ISOGAMETE	ISONOMOUS
IRIDOLOGIES	IRRELATED	ISLE	ISOGAMETES	ISONOMY
IRIDOLOGY	IRRIGABLE	ISLED	ISOGAMIC	ISOPLETH
IRIDOTOMIES	IRRIGATE	ISLEMAN	ISOGAMIES	ISOPLETHS
IRIDOTOMY	IRRIGATED	ISLEMEN	ISOGAMOUS	ISOPOD
IRIDS	IRRIGATES	ISLES	ISOGAMY	ISOPODAN
IRIS	IRRIGATING	ISLESMAN	ISOGENIES	ISOPODOUS
IRISATE	IRRIGATOR	ISLESMEN	ISOGENOUS	ISOPODS
IRISATED	IRRIGATORS	ISLET	ISOGENY	ISOPOLITIES
IRISATES	IRRIGUOUS	ISLETS	ISOGLOSS	ISOPOLITY
IRISATING	IRRISION	ISLING	ISOGLOSSES	ISOPRENE
IRISATION	IRRISIONS	ISM	ISOGON	ISOPRENES
IRISATIONS	IRRISORY	ISMATIC	ISOGONAL	ISOPROPYL
IRISCOPE	IRRITABLE	ISMATICAL	ISOGONALS	ISOPROPYLS
IRISCOPES	IRRITABLY	ISMIER	ISOGONIC	ISOSCELES
IRISED	IRRITANCIES	ISMIEST	ISOGONICS	ISOSPIN
IRISES	IRRITANCY	ISMS	ISOGONS	ISOSPINS
IRISING	IRRITANT	ISMY	ISOGRAM	ISOSPORIES
IRITIC	IRRITANTS	ISOBAR	ISOGRAMS	ISOSPORY
IRITIS	IRRITATE	ISOBARE	ISOHEL	ISOSTASIES
IRITISES	IRRITATED	ISOBARES	ISOHELS	ISOSTASY
IRK	IRRITATES	ISOBARIC	ISOHYET	ISOSTATIC
IRKED	IRRITATING	ISOBARS	ISOHYETAL	ISOSTERIC
IRKING	IRRITATOR	ISOBASE	ISOHYETALS	ISOTACTIC
IRKS	IRRITATORS	ISOBASES	ISOHYETS	ISOTHERAL
IRKSOME	IRRUPT	ISOBATH	ISOKONT	ISOTHERALS
IRKSOMELY	IRRUPTED	ISOBATHIC	ISOKONTAN	ISOTHERE
IROKO	IRRUPTING	ISOBATHS	ISOKONTANS	ISOTHERES
IROKOS	IRRUPTION	ISOBRONT	ISOKONTS	ISOTHERM
IRON	IRRUPTIONS	ISOBRONTS	ISOLABLE	ISOTHERMS
IRONBARK	IRRUPTIVE	ISOCHASM	ISOLATE	ISOTONE
IRONBARKS	IRRUPTS	ISOCHASMS	ISOLATED	ISOTONES
IRONED	IS	ISOCHEIM	ISOLATES	ISOTONIC
IRONER	ISABEL	ISOCHEIMS	ISOLATING	ISOTOPE
IRONERS	ISABELLA	ISOCHIMAL	ISOLATION	ISOTOPES
IRONIC	ISABELLAS	ISOCHIMALS	ISOLATIONS	ISOTOPIC
IRONICAL	ISABELS	ISOCHIME	ISOLATIVE	ISOTOPIES
IRONIES	ISAGOGE	ISOCHIMES	ISOLATOR	ISOTOPY
IRONING	ISAGOGES	ISOCHOR	ISOLATORS	ISOTRON
IRONINGS	ISAGOGIC	ISOCHORE	ISOLINE	ISOTRONS
IRONISE	ISAGOGICS	ISOCHORES	ISOLINES	ISOTROPIC
IRONISED	ISALLOBAR	ISOCHORIC	ISOLOGOUS	ISOTROPIES
IRONISES	ISALLOBARS	ISOCHORS	ISOLOGUE	ISOTROPY
IRONISING	ISATIN	ISOCHRONE	ISOLOGUES	ISOTYPE
IRONIST	ISATINE	ISOCHRONES	ISOMER	ISOTYPES
IRONISTS	ISATINES	ISOCLINAL	ISOMERE	ISSEI
IRONIZE	ISATINS	ISOCLINALS	ISOMERES	ISSEIS

ISSUABLE	ITACISMS	ITCHWEED	ITERATES	IVORIED
ISSUABLY	ITALIC	ITCHWEEDS	ITERATING	IVORIES
ISSUANCE	ITALICISE	ITCHY	ITERATION	IVORIST
ISSUANCES	ITALICISED	ITEM	ITERATIONS	IVORISTS
ISSUANT	ITALICISES	ITEMED	ITERATIVE	IVORY
ISSUE	ITALICISING	ITEMING	ITERUM	IVRESSE
ISSUED	ITALICIZE	ITEMISE	ITINERACIES	IVRESSES
ISSUELESS	ITALICIZED	ITEMISED	ITINERACY	IVY
ISSUER	ITALICIZES	ITEMISES	ITINERANT	IWIS
ISSUERS	ITALICIZING	ITEMISING	ITINERANTS	IXIA
ISSUES	ITALICS	ITEMIZE	ITINERARIES	IXIAS
ISSUING	ITAS	ITEMIZED	ITINERARY	IXTLE
ISTHMIAN	ITCH	ITEMIZES	ITINERATE	IXTLES
ISTHMUS	ITCHED	ITEMIZING	ITINERATED	IZARD
ISTHMUSES	ITCHES	ITEMS	ITINERATES	IZARDS
ISTLE	ITCHIER	ITERANCE	ITINERATING	IZZARD
ISTLES	ITCHIEST	ITERANCES	ITS	IZZARDS
IT	ITCHINESS	ITERANT	ITSELF	IZZET
ITA	ITCHINESSES	ITERATE	IVIED	IZZETS
ITACISM	ITCHING	ITERATED	IVIES	

J

JAB
JABBED
JABBER
JABBERED
JABBERER
JABBERERS
JABBERING
JABBERINGS
JABBERS
JABBING
JABBLE
JABBLED
JABBLES
JABBLING
JABERS
JABIRU
JABIRUS
JABORANDI
JABORANDIS
JABOT
JABOTS
JABS
JACAMAR
JACAMARS
JACANA
JAÇANA
JAÇANAS
JAÇANAS
JACARANDA
JACARANDAS
JACCHUS
JACCHUSES
JACENT
JACINTH
JACINTHS
JACK
JACKAL
JACKALLED
JACKALLING
JACKALS
JACKAROO
JACKAROOED
JACKAROOING
JACKAROOS
JACKASS
JACKASSES
JACKBOOT
JACKBOOTED
JACKBOOTING
JACKBOOTS
JACKDAW
JACKDAWS
JACKED
JACKEROO
JACKEROOED
JACKEROOING
JACKEROOS
JACKET
JACKETED
JACKETING
JACKETS
JACKING
JACKMAN

JACKMEN
JACKPOT
JACKPOTS
JACKS
JACKSIE
JACKSIES
JACKSMITH
JACKSMITHS
JACKSY
JACOBUS
JACOBUSES
JACONET
JACONETS
JACQUARD
JACQUARDS
JACTATION
JACTATIONS
JACULATE
JACULATED
JACULATES
JACULATING
JACULATOR
JACULATORS
JACUZZI
JACUZZIS
JADE
JADED
JADEDLY
JADEITE
JADEITES
JADERIES
JADERY
JADES
JADING
JADISH
JAEGER
JAEGERS
JAG
JÄGER
JÄGERS
JAGGED
JAGGEDLY
JAGGER
JAGGERIES
JAGGERS
JAGGERY
JAGGIER
JAGGIEST
JAGGING
JAGGY
JAGHIR
JAGHIRDAR
JAGHIRDARS
JAGHIRE
JAGHIRES
JAGHIRS
JAGIR
JAGIRS
JAGS
JAGUAR
JAGUARS
JAIL
JAILED

JAILER
JAILERESS
JAILERESSES
JAILERS
JAILHOUSE
JAILHOUSES
JAILING
JAILOR
JAILORESS
JAILORESSES
JAILORS
JAILS
JAK
JAKE
JAKES
JAKESES
JAKS
JALAP
JALAPIC
JALAPIN
JALAPINS
JALAPS
JALOPIES
JALOPPIES
JALOPPY
JALOPY
JALOUSE
JALOUSED
JALOUSES
JALOUSIE
JALOUSIED
JALOUSIES
JALOUSING
JAM
JAMADAR
JAMADARS
JAMB
JAMBE
JAMBEAU
JAMBEAUX
JAMBEE
JAMBEES
JAMBER
JAMBERS
JAMBES
JAMBEUX
JAMBIER
JAMBIERS
JAMBIYA
JAMBIYAH
JAMBIYAHS
JAMBIYAS
JAMBO
JAMBOK
JAMBOKKED
JAMBOKKING
JAMBOKS
JAMBOLAN
JAMBOLANA
JAMBOLANAS
JAMBOLANS
JAMBONE
JAMBONES

JAMBOOL
JAMBOOLS
JAMBOREE
JAMBOREES
JAMBOS
JAMBS
JAMBU
JAMBUL
JAMBULS
JAMBUS
JAMDANI
JAMDANIS
JAMES
JAMESES
JAMJAR
JAMJARS
JAMMED
JAMMER
JAMMERS
JAMMIER
JAMMIEST
JAMMING
JAMMY
JAMPAN
JAMPANEE
JAMPANEES
JAMPANI
JAMPANIS
JAMPANS
JAMPOT
JAMPOTS
JAMS
JANE
JANES
JANGLE
JANGLED
JANGLER
JANGLERS
JANGLES
JANGLIER
JANGLIEST
JANGLING
JANGLINGS
JANGLY
JANISSARIES
JANISSARY
JANITOR
JANITORS
JANITRESS
JANITRESSES
JANITRIX
JANITRIXES
JANIZAR
JANIZARIES
JANIZARS
JANIZARY
JANKER
JANKERS
JANN
JANNOCK
JANNOCKS
JANNS
JANSKIES

JANSKY
JANTEE
JANTIER
JANTIES
JANTIEST
JANTY
JAP
JAPAN
JAPANNED
JAPANNER
JAPANNERS
JAPANNING
JAPANS
JAPE
JAPED
JAPES
JAPING
JAPONICA
JAPONICAS
JAPPED
JAPPING
JAPS
JAR
JARARACA
JARARACAS
JARARAKA
JARARAKAS
JARFUL
JARFULS
JARGON
JARGONED
JARGONEER
JARGONEERS
JARGONING
JARGONISE
JARGONISED
JARGONISES
JARGONISING
JARGONIST
JARGONISTS
JARGONIZE
JARGONIZED
JARGONIZES
JARGONIZING
JARGONS
JARGOON
JARGOONS
JARK
JARKMAN
JARKMEN
JARKS
JARL
JARLS
JAROOL
JAROOLS
JAROSITE
JAROSITES
JARRAH
JARRAHS
JARRED
JARRING
JARRINGLY
JARRINGS

JARS	JAWAN	JEELIES	JENNETINGS	JESSERANTS
JARTA	JAWANS	JEELING	JENNETS	JESSES
JARTAS	JAWARI	JEELS	JENNIES	JESSIE
JARUL	JAWARIS	JEELY	JENNY	JESSIES
JARULS	JAWBATION	JEELYING	JEOFAIL	JEST
JARVEY	JAWBATIONS	JEEP	JEOFAILS	JESTBOOK
JARVEYS	JAWBONE	JEEPERS	JEOPARD	JESTBOOKS
JARVIE	JAWBONED	JEEPNEY	JEOPARDED	JESTED
JARVIES	JAWBONES	JEEPNEYS	JEOPARDER	JESTEE
JASEY	JAWBONING	JEEPS	JEOPARDERS	JESTEES
JASEYS	JAWBONINGS	JEER	JEOPARDIED	JESTER
JASIES	JAWBOX	JEERED	JEOPARDIES	JESTERS
JASMINE	JAWBOXES	JEERER	JEOPARDING	JESTFUL
JASMINES	JAWED	JEERERS	JEOPARDS	JESTING
JASP	JAWFALL	JEERING	JEOPARDY	JESTINGLY
JASPÉ	JAWFALLS	JEERINGLY	JEOPARDYING	JESTINGS
JASPER	JAWHOLE	JEERINGS	JEQUIRITIES	JESTS
JASPERISE	JAWHOLES	JEERS	JEQUIRITY	JÉSUS
JASPERISED	JAWING	JEES	JERBIL	JET
JASPERISES	JAWINGS	JEFF	JERBILS	JETÉ
JASPERISING	JAWS	JEFFED	JERBOA	JETÉS
JASPERIZE	JAY	JEFFING	JERBOAS	JETFOIL
JASPERIZED	JAYS	JEFFS	JEREED	JETFOILS
JASPERIZES	JAYWALK	JEHAD	JEREEDS	JETLINER
JASPERIZING	JAYWALKED	JEHADS	JEREMIAD	JETLINERS
JASPEROUS	JAYWALKER	JEJUNA	JEREMIADS	JETON
JASPERS	JAYWALKERS	JEJUNE	JERFALCON	JETONS
JASPERY	JAYWALKING	JEJUNELY	JERFALCONS	JETPLANE
JASPES	JAYWALKINGS	JEJUNITIES	JERID	JETPLANES
JASPIDEAN	JAYWALKS	JEJUNITY	JERIDS	JETS
JASPIS	JAZERANT	JEJUNUM	JERK	JETSAM
JASPISES	JAZERANTS	JELAB	JERKED	JETSAMS
JASPS	JAZIES	JELABS	JERKER	JETSOM
JASY	JAZY	JELL	JERKERS	JETSOMS
JATAKA	JAZZ	JELLABA	JERKIER	JETSON
JATAKAS	JAZZED	JELLABAS	JERKIES	JETSONS
JATO	JAZZES	JELLED	JERKIEST	JETSTREAM
JATOS	JAZZIER	JELLIED	JERKIN	JETSTREAMS
JAUNCE	JAZZIEST	JELLIES	JERKINESS	JETTATURA
JAUNCED	JAZZILY	JELLIFIED	JERKINESSES	JETTATURAS
JAUNCES	JAZZINESS	JELLIFIES	JERKING	JETTED
JAUNCING	JAZZINESSES	JELLIFORM	JERKINGS	JETTIER
JAUNDICE	JAZZING	JELLIFY	JERKINS	JETTIES
JAUNDICED	JAZZMAN	JELLIFYING	JERKS	JETTIEST
JAUNDICES	JAZZMEN	JELLING	JERKY	JETTINESS
JAUNDICING	JAZZY	JELLO	JEROBOAM	JETTINESSES
JAUNSE	JEALOUS	JELLOS	JEROBOAMS	JETTING
JAUNSED	JEALOUSE	JELLS	JERQUE	JETTISON
JAUNSES	JEALOUSED	JELLY	JERQUED	JETTISONED
JAUNSING	JEALOUSES	JELLYBEAN	JERQUER	JETTISONING
JAUNT	JEALOUSIES	JELLYBEANS	JERQUERS	JETTISONS
JAUNTED	JEALOUSING	JELLYFISH	JERQUES	JETTON
JAUNTEE	JEALOUSLY	JELLYFISHES	JERQUING	JETTONS
JAUNTIE	JEALOUSY	JELLYING	JERQUINGS	JETTY
JAUNTIER	JEAN	JELUTONG	JERRICAN	JEU
JAUNTIES	JEANETTE	JELUTONGS	JERRICANS	JEUNE
JAUNTIEST	JEANETTES	JEMADAR	JERRIES	JEUX
JAUNTILY	JEANS	JEMADARS	JERRY	JEWEL
JAUNTING	JEAT	JEMIDAR	JERRYCAN	JEWELFISH
JAUNTS	JEATS	JEMIDARS	JERRYCANS	JEWELFISHES
JAUNTY	JEBEL	JEMIMA	JERSEY	JEWELLED
JAUP	JEBELS	JEMIMAS	JERSEYS	JEWELLER
JAUPED	JEE	JEMMIER	JESS	JEWELLERIES
JAUPING	JEED	JEMMIES	JESSAMIES	JEWELLERS
JAUPS	JEEING	JEMMIEST	JESSAMINE	JEWELLERY
JAVEL	JEEL	JEMMINESS	JESSAMINES	JEWELLING
JAVELIN	JEELED	JEMMINESSES	JESSAMY	JEWELRIES
JAVELINS	JEELIE	JEMMY	JESSANT	JEWELRY
JAVELS	JEELIED	JENNET	JESSED	JEWELS
JAW	JEELIEING	JENNETING	JESSERANT	JEWFISH

JEWFISHES	JILLFLIRT	JIRGA	JOCKTELEGS	JOINTURING
JEZAIL	JILLFLIRTS	JIRGAS	JOCO	JOIST
JEZAILS	JILLS	JIRKINET	JOCOROUS	JOISTED
JHALA	JILT	JIRKINETS	JOCOSE	JOISTING
JHALAS	JILTED	JISM	JOCOSELY	JOISTS
JIAO	JILTING	JISMS	JOCOSITIES	JOJOBA
JIAOS	JILTS	JISSOM	JOCOSITY	JOJOBAS
JIB	JIMCRACK	JISSOMS	JOCULAR	JOKE
JIBBAH	JIMCRACKS	JITNEY	JOCULARLY	JOKED
JIBBAHS	JIMINY	JITNEYS	JOCULATOR	JOKER
JIBBED	JIMJAM	JITTER	JOCULATORS	JOKERS
JIBBER	JIMJAMS	JITTERBUG	JOCUND	JOKES
JIBBERED	JIMMIED	JITTERBUGGED	JOCUNDITIES	JOKESMITH
JIBBERING	JIMMIES	JITTERBUGGING	JOCUNDITY	JOKESMITHS
JIBBERS	JIMMY	JITTERBUGS	JOCUNDLY	JOKESOME
JIBBING	JIMMYING	JITTERED	JODEL	JOKEY
JIBBINGS	JIMP	JITTERING	JODELLED	JOKIER
JIBE	JIMPER	JITTERS	JODELLING	JOKIEST
JIBED	JIMPEST	JITTERY	JODELS	JOKING
JIBER	JIMPIER	JIVE	JODHPURS	JOKINGLY
JIBERS	JIMPIEST	JIVED	JOE	JOKOL
JIBES	JIMPLY	JIVER	JOES	JOKY
JIBING	JIMPNESS	JIVERS	JOEY	JOLE
JIBS	JIMPNESSES	JIVES	JOEYS	JOLED
JICKAJOG	JIMPY	JIVING	JOG	JOLES
JICKAJOGS	JINGAL	JIZ	JOGGED	JOLING
JIFF	JINGALS	JIZZ	JOGGER	JOLL
JIFFIES	JINGBANG	JIZZES	JOGGERS	JOLLED
JIFFS	JINGBANGS	JO	JOGGING	JOLLIED
JIFFY	JINGLE	JOANNA	JOGGINGS	JOLLIER
JIG	JINGLED	JOANNAS	JOGGLE	JOLLIES
JIGAJIG	JINGLER	JOANNES	JOGGLED	JOLLIEST
JIGAJIGS	JINGLERS	JOANNESES	JOGGLES	JOLLIFIED
JIGAJOG	JINGLES	JOB	JOGGLING	JOLLIFIES
JIGAJOGS	JINGLET	JOBATION	JOGS	JOLLIFY
JIGAMAREE	JINGLETS	JOBATIONS	JOGTROT	JOLLIFYING
JIGAMAREES	JINGLIER	JOBBED	JOGTROTS	JOLLILY
JIGGED	JINGLIEST	JOBBER	JOHANNES	JOLLIMENT
JIGGER	JINGLING	JOBBERIES	JOHANNESES	JOLLIMENTS
JIGGERED	JINGLINGS	JOBBERS	JOHN	JOLLINESS
JIGGERING	JINGLY	JOBBERY	JOHNNIE	JOLLINESSES
JIGGERS	JINGO	JOBBING	JOHNNIES	JOLLING
JIGGING	JINGOES	JOBBINGS	JOHNNY	JOLLITIES
JIGGINGS	JINGOISH	JOBCENTRE	JOHNS	JOLLITY
JIGGISH	JINGOISM	JOBCENTRES	JOIN	JOLLS
JIGGLE	JINGOISMS	JOBE	JOINDER	JOLLY
JIGGLED	JINGOIST	JOBED	JOINDERS	JOLLYBOAT
JIGGLES	JINGOISTS	JOBERNOWL	JOINED	JOLLYBOATS
JIGGLING	JINJILI	JOBERNOWLS	JOINER	JOLLYHEAD
JIGGUMBOB	JINJILIS	JOBES	JOINERIES	JOLLYHEADS
JIGGUMBOBS	JINK	JOBING	JOINERS	JOLLYING
JIGJIG	JINKED	JOBLESS	JOINERY	JOLT
JIGJIGS	JINKER	JOBS	JOINING	JOLTED
JIGOT	JINKERS	JOBSWORTH	JOININGS	JOLTER
JIGOTS	JINKING	JOBSWORTHS	JOINS	JOLTERS
JIGS	JINKS	JOCK	JOINT	JOLTHEAD
JIGSAW	JINN	JOCKETTE	JOINTED	JOLTHEADS
JIGSAWED	JINNEE	JOCKETTES	JOINTER	JOLTIER
JIGSAWING	JINNI	JOCKEY	JOINTERS	JOLTIEST
JIGSAWN	JINNS	JOCKEYED	JOINTING	JOLTING
JIGSAWS	JINX	JOCKEYING	JOINTLESS	JOLTINGLY
JIHAD	JINXED	JOCKEYISM	JOINTLY	JOLTS
JIHADS	JINXES	JOCKEYISMS	JOINTNESS	JOLTY
JILGIE	JINXING	JOCKEYS	JOINTNESSES	JOMO
JILGIES	JIRBLE	JOCKO	JOINTRESS	JOMOS
JILL	JIRBLED	JOCKOS	JOINTRESSES	JONCANOE
JILLAROO	JIRBLES	JOCKS	JOINTS	JONCANOES
JILLAROOS	JIRBLING	JOCKSTRAP	JOINTURE	JONGLEUR
JILLET	JIRD	JOCKSTRAPS	JOINTURED	JONGLEURS
JILLETS	JIRDS	JOCKTELEG	JOINTURES	JONQUIL

JONQUILS
JONTIES
JONTY
JOOK
JOOKED
JOOKERIES
JOOKERY
JOOKING
JOOKS
JOR
JORAM
JORAMS
JORDAN
JORDANS
JORDELOO
JORDELOOS
JORS
JORUM
JORUMS
JOSEPH
JOSEPHS
JOSH
JOSHED
JOSHER
JOSHERS
JOSHES
JOSHING
JOSKIN
JOSKINS
JOSS
JOSSER
JOSSERS
JOSSES
JOSTLE
JOSTLED
JOSTLES
JOSTLING
JOSTLINGS
JOT
JOTA
JOTAS
JOTS
JOTTED
JOTTER
JOTTERS
JOTTING
JOTTINGS
JOTUN
JOTUNN
JOTUNNS
JOTUNS
JOUGS
JOUISANCE
JOUISANCES
JOUK
JOUKED
JOUKERIES
JOUKERY
JOUKING
JOUKS
JOULE
JOULED
JOULES
JOULING
JOUNCE
JOUNCED
JOUNCES
JOUNCING
JOUR
JOURNAL

JOURNALLED
JOURNALLING
JOURNALS
JOURNEY
JOURNEYED
JOURNEYER
JOURNEYERS
JOURNEYING
JOURNEYS
JOURNO
JOURNOS
JOURS
JOUST
JOUSTED
JOUSTER
JOUSTERS
JOUSTING
JOUSTS
JOVIAL
JOVIALITIES
JOVIALITY
JOVIALLY
JOW
JOWAR
JOWARI
JOWARIS
JOWARS
JOWED
JOWING
JOWL
JOWLED
JOWLER
JOWLERS
JOWLING
JOWLS
JOWS
JOY
JOYANCE
JOYANCES
JOYED
JOYFUL
JOYFULLER
JOYFULLEST
JOYFULLY
JOYING
JOYLESS
JOYLESSLY
JOYOUS
JOYOUSLY
JOYS
JUBA
JUBAS
JUBATE
JUBBAH
JUBBAHS
JUBE
JUBES
JUBILANCE
JUBILANCES
JUBILANCIES
JUBILANCY
JUBILANT
JUBILATE
JUBILATED
JUBILATES
JUBILATING
JUBILEE
JUBILEES
JUD
JUDAS

JUDASES
JUDDER
JUDDERED
JUDDERING
JUDDERS
JUDGE
JUDGED
JUDGEMENT
JUDGEMENTS
JUDGES
JUDGESHIP
JUDGESHIPS
JUDGING
JUDGMENT
JUDGMENTS
JUDICABLE
JUDICATOR
JUDICATORS
JUDICIAL
JUDICIARIES
JUDICIARY
JUDICIOUS
JUDIES
JUDO
JUDOGI
JUDOGIS
JUDOIST
JUDOISTS
JUDOKA
JUDOKAS
JUDOS
JUDS
JUDY
JUG
JUGA
JUGAL
JUGALS
JUGATE
JUGFUL
JUGFULS
JUGGED
JUGGING
JUGGINS
JUGGINSES
JUGGLE
JUGGLED
JUGGLER
JUGGLERIES
JUGGLERS
JUGGLERY
JUGGLES
JUGGLING
JUGGLINGS
JUGS
JUGULAR
JUGULARS
JUGULATE
JUGULATED
JUGULATES
JUGULATING
JUGUM
JUICE
JUICED
JUICELESS
JUICER
JUICERS
JUICES
JUICIER
JUICIEST
JUICINESS

JUICINESSES
JUICING
JUICY
JUJU
JUJUBE
JUJUBES
JUJUS
JUKE
JUKED
JUKES
JUKING
JULEP
JULEPS
JULIENNE
JULIENNES
JUMAR
JUMARRED
JUMARRING
JUMARS
JUMART
JUMARTS
JUMBAL
JUMBALS
JUMBIE
JUMBIES
JUMBLE
JUMBLED
JUMBLER
JUMBLERS
JUMBLES
JUMBLIER
JUMBLIEST
JUMBLING
JUMBLY
JUMBO
JUMBOISE
JUMBOISED
JUMBOISES
JUMBOISING
JUMBOIZE
JUMBOIZED
JUMBOIZES
JUMBOIZING
JUMBOS
JUMBUCK
JUMBUCKS
JUMBY
JUMELLE
JUMELLES
JUMP
JUMPED
JUMPER
JUMPERS
JUMPIER
JUMPIEST
JUMPILY
JUMPINESS
JUMPINESSES
JUMPING
JUMPS
JUMPY
JUNCATE
JUNCATES
JUNCO
JUNCOES
JUNCOS
JUNCTION
JUNCTIONS
JUNCTURE
JUNCTURES

JUNCUS
JUNCUSES
JUNEATING
JUNEATINGS
JUNGLE
JUNGLES
JUNGLI
JUNGLIER
JUNGLIEST
JUNGLIS
JUNGLY
JUNIOR
JUNIORITIES
JUNIORITY
JUNIORS
JUNIPER
JUNIPERS
JUNK
JUNKANOO
JUNKANOOS
JUNKED
JUNKER
JUNKERDOM
JUNKERDOMS
JUNKERISM
JUNKERISMS
JUNKERS
JUNKET
JUNKETED
JUNKETING
JUNKETINGS
JUNKETS
JUNKIE
JUNKIER
JUNKIES
JUNKIEST
JUNKING
JUNKMAN
JUNKMEN
JUNKS
JUNKY
JUNTA
JUNTAS
JUNTO
JUNTOS
JUPATI
JUPATIS
JUPON
JUPONS
JURA
JURAL
JURALLY
JURANT
JURANTS
JURAT
JURATORY
JURATS
JURE
JURIDIC
JURIDICAL
JURIES
JURIST
JURISTIC
JURISTS
JUROR
JURORS
JURY
JURYMAN
JURYMAST
JURYMASTS

JURYMEN
JURYWOMAN
JURYWOMEN
JUS
JUSSIVE
JUSSIVES
JUST
JUSTED
JUSTER
JUSTEST
JUSTICE

JUSTICER
JUSTICERS
JUSTICES
JUSTICIAR
JUSTICIARS
JUSTIFIED
JUSTIFIER
JUSTIFIERS
JUSTIFIES
JUSTIFY
JUSTIFYING

JUSTING
JUSTLE
JUSTLED
JUSTLES
JUSTLING
JUSTLY
JUSTNESS
JUSTNESSES
JUSTS
JUT
JUTE

JUTES
JUTS
JUTTED
JUTTIED
JUTTIES
JUTTING
JUTTINGLY
JUTTY
JUTTYING
JUVENAL
JUVENALS

JUVENILE
JUVENILES
JUVENILIA
JUXTAPOSE
JUXTAPOSED
JUXTAPOSES
JUXTAPOSING
JYMOLD
JYNX
JYNXES

K

KA
KAAMA
KAAMAS
KABAB
KABABS
KABALA
KABALAS
KABAYA
KABAYAS
KABBALA
KABBALAH
KABBALAHS
KABBALAS
KABELE
KABELES
KABELJOU
KABELJOUS
KABELJOUW
KABELJOUWS
KABOB
KABOBS
KABUKI
KABUKIS
KACCHA
KACCHAS
KACHA
KACHAHRI
KACHAHRIS
KACHCHA
KACHERI
KACHERIS
KACHINA
KACHINAS
KADE
KADES
KADI
KADIS
KAE
KAED
KAEING
KAES
KAFFIYEH
KAFFIYEHS
KAFILA
KAFILAS
KAFTAN
KAFTANS
KAGO
KAGOOL
KAGOOLS
KAGOS
KAGOUL
KAGOULE
KAGOULES
KAGOULS
KAHAL
KAHALS
KAI
KAIAK
KAIAKS
KAID
KAIDS
KAIE

KAIES
KAIF
KAIFS
KAIKAI
KAIKAIED
KAIKAIING
KAIKAIS
KAIL
KAILS
KAILYAIRD
KAILYAIRDS
KAILYARD
KAILYARDS
KAIM
KAIMAKAM
KAIMAKAMS
KAIMS
KAIN
KAING
KAINITE
KAINITES
KAINS
KAIS
KAISER
KAISERDOM
KAISERDOMS
KAISERIN
KAISERINS
KAISERISM
KAISERISMS
KAISERS
KAJAWAH
KAJAWAHS
KAKA
KAKAPO
KAKAPOS
KAKAS
KAKEMONO
KAKEMONOS
KAKI
KAKIEMON
KAKIEMONS
KAKIS
KAKODYL
KAKODYLS
KALAMDAN
KALAMDANS
KALAMKARI
KALAMKARIS
KALE
KALENDAR
KALENDARED
KALENDARING
KALENDARS
KALENDS
KALES
KALI
KALIAN
KALIANS
KALIF
KALIFS
KALINITE
KALINITES

KALIS
KALIUM
KALIUMS
KALLITYPE
KALLITYPES
KALMIA
KALMIAS
KALONG
KALONGS
KALOTYPE
KALOTYPES
KALPA
KALPAK
KALPAKS
KALPAS
KALPIS
KALPISES
KALUMPIT
KALUMPITS
KALYPTRA
KALYPTRAS
KAM
KAMACITE
KAMACITES
KAMALA
KAMALAS
KAME
KAMEES
KAMEESES
KAMEEZ
KAMEEZES
KAMELA
KAMELAS
KAMERAD
KAMERADED
KAMERADING
KAMERADS
KAMES
KAMI
KAMICHI
KAMICHIS
KAMIK
KAMIKAZE
KAMIKAZES
KAMIKS
KAMILA
KAMILAS
KAMIS
KAMISES
KAMME
KAMPONG
KAMPONGS
KAMSEEN
KAMSEENS
KAMSIN
KAMSINS
KANA
KANAKA
KANAKAS
KANAS
KANDIES
KANDY
KANEH

KANEHS
KANG
KANGA
KANGAROO
KANGAROOED
KANGAROOING
KANGAROOS
KANGAS
KANGHA
KANGHAS
KANGS
KANS
KANSES
KANT
KANTAR
KANTARS
KANTED
KANTELA
KANTELAS
KANTELE
KANTELES
KANTEN
KANTENS
KANTHA
KANTHAS
KANTIKOY
KANTIKOYED
KANTIKOYING
KANTIKOYS
KANTING
KANTS
KANZU
KANZUS
KAOLIANG
KAOLIANGS
KAOLIN
KAOLINE
KAOLINES
KAOLINISE
KAOLINISED
KAOLINISES
KAOLINISING
KAOLINITE
KAOLINITES
KAOLINIZE
KAOLINIZED
KAOLINIZES
KAOLINIZING
KAOLINS
KAON
KAONS
KAPOK
KAPOKS
KAPPA
KAPPAS
KAPUT
KAPUTT
KARA
KARABINER
KARABINERS
KARAISM
KARAISMS
KARAIT

KARAITS
KARAKA
KARAKAS
KARAKUL
KARAKULS
KARAS
KARAT
KARATE
KARATEIST
KARATEISTS
KARATEKA
KARATEKAS
KARATES
KARATS
KARITE
KARITES
KARMA
KARMAS
KARMIC
KAROSS
KAROSSES
KARRI
KARRIS
KARSEY
KARSEYS
KARSIES
KARST
KARSTS
KARSY
KART
KARTING
KARTINGS
KARTS
KARYOLOGIES
KARYOLOGY
KARYOSOME
KARYOSOMES
KARZIES
KARZY
KAS
KASBA
KASBAH
KASBAHS
KASBAS
KASHMIR
KASHMIRS
KAT
KATABASES
KATABASIS
KATABATIC
KATABOLIC
KATAKANA
KATAKANAS
KATANA
KATANAS
KATHAK
KATHAKALI
KATHAKALIS
KATHAKS
KATHARSES
KATHARSIS
KATHODE
KATHODES

KATI
KATION
KATIONS
KATIS
KATORGA
KATORGAS
KATS
KATTI
KATTIS
KATYDID
KATYDIDS
KAUGH
KAUGHS
KAURI
KAURIS
KAVA
KAVAS
KAVASS
KAVASSES
KAW
KAWED
KAWING
KAWS
KAY
KAYAK
KAYAKS
KAYLE
KAYLES
KAYO
KAYOED
KAYOEING
KAYOES
KAYOING
KAYOS
KAYS
KAZATZKA
KAZATZKAS
KAZI
KAZIS
KAZOO
KAZOOS
KEA
KEAS
KEASAR
KEASARS
KEB
KEBAB
KEBABS
KEBBED
KEBBIE
KEBBIES
KEBBING
KEBBOCK
KEBBOCKS
KEBBUCK
KEBBUCKS
KEBELE
KEBELES
KEBLAH
KEBLAHS
KEBOB
KEBOBS
KEBS
KECK
KECKED
KECKING
KECKLE
KECKLED
KECKLES

KECKLING
KECKLINGS
KECKS
KECKSES
KECKSIES
KECKSY
KED
KEDDAH
KEDDAHS
KEDGE
KEDGED
KEDGER
KEDGEREE
KEDGEREES
KEDGERS
KEDGES
KEDGIER
KEDGIEST
KEDGING
KEDGY
KEDS
KEECH
KEECHES
KEEK
KEEKED
KEEKER
KEEKERS
KEEKING
KEEKS
KEEL
KEELAGE
KEELAGES
KEELBOAT
KEELBOATS
KEELED
KEELER
KEELERS
KEELHAUL
KEELHAULED
KEELHAULING
KEELHAULINGS
KEELHAULS
KEELIE
KEELIES
KEELING
KEELINGS
KEELIVINE
KEELIVINES
KEELMAN
KEELMEN
KEELS
KEELSON
KEELSONS
KEELYVINE
KEELYVINES
KEEN
KEENED
KEENER
KEENERS
KEENEST
KEENING
KEENINGS
KEENLY
KEENNESS
KEENNESSES
KEENS
KEEP
KEEPER
KEEPERS
KEEPING

KEEPINGS
KEEPNET
KEEPNETS
KEEPS
KEEPSAKE
KEEPSAKES
KEEPSAKY
KEESHOND
KEESHONDS
KEEVE
KEEVES
KEF
KEFFEL
KEFFELS
KEFFIYEH
KEFFIYEHS
KEFIR
KEFIRS
KEFS
KEFUFFLE
KEFUFFLED
KEFUFFLES
KEFUFFLING
KEG
KEGS
KEIGHT
KEIR
KEIRS
KEITLOA
KEITLOAS
KEKSYE
KEKOVED
KELIM
KELIMS
KELL
KELLAUT
KELLAUTS
KELLIES
KELLS
KELLY
KELOID
KELOIDAL
KELOIDS
KELP
KELPER
KELPERS
KELPIE
KELPIES
KELPS
KELPY
KELSON
KELSONS
KELT
KELTER
KELTERS
KELTIE
KELTIES
KELTS
KELTY
KELVIN
KELVINS
KEMB
KEMBED
KEMBING
KEMBO
KEMBOED
KEMBOING
KEMBOS
KEMBS
KEMP

KEMPED
KEMPER
KEMPERS
KEMPING
KEMPINGS
KEMPLE
KEMPLES
KEMPS
KEMPT
KEN
KENAF
KENAFS
KENDO
KENDOS
KENNED
KENNEL
KENNELLED
KENNELLING
KENNELS
KENNER
KENNERS
KENNET
KENNETS
KENNING
KENNINGS
KENOSES
KENOSIS
KENOTIC
KENS
KENSPECK
KENT
KENTED
KENTING
KENTLEDGE
KENTLEDGES
KENTS
KEP
KEPHALIC
KEPHALICS
KEPHIR
KEPHIRS
KEPI
KEPIS
KEPPING
KEPPIT
KEPS
KEPT
KERAMIC
KERAMICS
KERATIN
KERATING
KERATITIS
KERATITISES
KERATOID
KERATOSE
KERATOSES
KERATOSIS
KERB
KERBS
KERBSIDE
KERBSIDES
KERBSTONE
KERBSTONES
KERCHIEF
KERCHIEFED
KERCHIEFING
KERCHIEFS
KERF
KERFS
KERFUFFLE

KERFUFFLED
KERFUFFLES
KERFUFFLING
KERMES
KERMESITE
KERMESITES
KERMESS
KERMESSE
KERMESSES
KERMIS
KERMISES
KERN
KERNE
KERNED
KERNEL
KERNELLED
KERNELLING
KERNELLY
KERNELS
KERNES
KERNING
KERNISH
KERNITE
KERNITES
KERNS
KEROGEN
KEROGENS
KEROSENE
KEROSENES
KEROSINE
KEROSINES
KERRIA
KERRIAS
KERSEY
KERSEYS
KERVE
KERVED
KERVES
KERVING
KERYGMA
KERYGMAS
KESAR
KESARS
KESH
KESHES
KEST
KESTING
KESTREL
KESTRELS
KESTS
KET
KETA
KETAS
KETCH
KETCHES
KETCHING
KETCHUP
KETCHUPS
KETONE
KETONES
KETOSE
KETOSES
KETOSIS
KETS
KETTLE
KETTLEFUL
KETTLEFULS
KETTLES
KEVEL
KEVELS

KEX	KHEDIVAL	KICKSHAWSES	KILLDEE	KINAKINAS
KEXES	KHEDIVAS	KID	KILLDEER	KINAS
KEY	KHEDIVATE	KIDDED	KILLDEERS	KINASE
KEYBOARD	KHEDIVATES	KIDDER	KILLDEES	KINASES
KEYBOARDED	KHEDIVE	KIDDERS	KILLED	KINCHIN
KEYBOARDING	KHEDIVES	KIDDIED	KILLER	KINCHINS
KEYBOARDS	KHEDIVIAL	KIDDIER	KILLERS	KINCOB
KEYBUGLE	KHILAFAT	KIDDIERS	KILLICK	KINCOBS
KEYBUGLES	KHILAFATS	KIDDIES	KILLICKS	KIND
KEYED	KHILAT	KIDDING	KILLING	KINDA
KEYHOLE	KHILATS	KIDDLE	KILLINGS	KINDED
KEYHOLES	KHILIM	KIDDLES	KILLJOY	KINDER
KEYING	KHILIMS	KIDDUSH	KILLJOYS	KINDEST
KEYLESS	KHODJA	KIDDUSHES	KILLOCK	KINDING
KEYNOTE	KHODJAS	KIDDY	KILLOCKS	KINDLE
KEYNOTED	KHOJA	KIDDYING	KILLOGIE	KINDLED
KEYNOTES	KHOJAS	KIDDYWINK	KILLOGIES	KINDLER
KEYNOTING	KHOR	KIDDYWINKS	KILLS	KINDLERS
KEYS	KHORS	KIDEL	KILLUT	KINDLES
KEYSTONE	KHOTBAH	KIDELS	KILLUTS	KINDLESS
KEYSTONED	KHOTBAHS	KIDGE	KILN	KINDLIER
KEYSTONES	KHOTBEH	KIDLING	KILNED	KINDLIEST
KEYSTONING	KHOTBEHS	KIDLINGS	KILNING	KINDLILY
KEYSTROKE	KHUD	KIDNAP	KILNS	KINDLING
KEYSTROKES	KHUDS	KIDNAPPED	KILO	KINDLINGS
KGOTLA	KHURTA	KIDNAPPER	KILOBAR	KINDLY
KGOTLAS	KHURTAS	KIDNAPPERS	KILOBARS	KINDNESS
KHADDAR	KHUSKHUS	KIDNAPPING	KILOBIT	KINDNESSES
KHADDARS	KHUSKHUSES	KIDNAPS	KILOBITS	KINDRED
KHADI	KHUTBAH	KIDNEY	KILOBYTE	KINDREDS
KHADIS	KHUTBAHS	KIDNEYS	KILOBYTES	KINDS
KHAKI	KIANG	KIDOLOGIES	KILOGRAM	KINE
KHAKIS	KIANGS	KIDOLOGY	KILOGRAMS	KINEMA
KHALAT	KIAUGH	KIDS	KILOHERTZ	KINEMAS
KHALATS	KIAUGHS	KIER	KILOHERTZES	KINEMATIC
KHALIF	KIBBLE	KIERIE	KILOJOULE	KINEMATICS
KHALIFA	KIBBLED	KIERIES	KILOJOULES	KINESES
KHALIFAH	KIBBLES	KIERS	KILOMETRE	KINESICS
KHALIFAHS	KIBBLING	KIESERITE	KILOMETRES	KINESIS
KHALIFAS	KIBBUTZ	KIESERITES	KILOS	KINETIC
KHALIFAT	KIBBUTZIM	KIEVE	KILOTON	KINETICAL
KHALIFATE	KIBE	KIEVES	KILOTONNE	KINETICS
KHALIFATES	KIBES	KIF	KILOTONNES	KINFOLK
KHALIFATS	KIBITKA	KIFS	KILOTONS	KINFOLKS
KHALIFS	KIBITKAS	KIGHT	KILOVOLT	KING
KHAMSIN	KIBITZ	KIGHTS	KILOVOLTS	KINGCRAFT
KHAMSINS	KIBITZED	KIKE	KILOWATT	KINGCRAFTS
KHAN	KIBITZER	KIKES	KILOWATTS	KINGCUP
KHANATE	KIBITZERS	KIKUMON	KILP	KINGCUPS
KHANATES	KIBITZES	KIKUMONS	KILPS	KINGDOM
KHANGA	KIBITZING	KIKUYU	KILT	KINGDOMED
KHANGAS	KIBLAH	KIKUYUS	KILTED	KINGDOMS
KHANJAR	KIBLAHS	KILD	KILTER	KINGED
KHANJARS	KIBOSH	KILDERKIN	KILTERS	KINGFISH
KHANS	KIBOSHED	KILDERKINS	KILTIE	KINGFISHES
KHANSAMA	KIBOSHES	KILERG	KILTIES	KINGHOOD
KHANSAMAH	KIBOSHING	KILERGS	KILTING	KINGHOODS
KHANSAMAHS	KICK	KILEY	KILTS	KINGING
KHANSAMAS	KICKABLE	KILEYS	KILTY	KINGLE
KHANUM	KICKBACK	KILIM	KIMBO	KINGLES
KHANUMS	KICKBACKS	KILIMS	KIMBOED	KINGLESS
KHARIF	KICKDOWN	KILL	KIMBOING	KINGLET
KHARIFS	KICKDOWNS	KILLADAR	KIMBOS	KINGLETS
KHAT	KICKED	KILLADARS	KIMMER	KINGLIER
KHATS	KICKER	KILLAS	KIMMERS	KINGLIEST
KHAYA	KICKERS	KILLASES	KIMONO	KINGLING
KHAYAS	KICKING	KILLCOW	KIMONOS	KINGLINGS
KHEDA	KICKS	KILLCOWS	KIN	KINGLY
KHEDAS	KICKSHAW	KILLCROP	KINA	KINGMAKER
KHEDIVA	KICKSHAWS	KILLCROPS	KINAKINA	KINGMAKERS

KINGPOST	KIRKTON	KITTENED	KNACKY	KNICKER
KINGPOSTS	KIRKTONS	KITTENING	KNAG	KNICKERED
KINGS	KIRKTOWN	KITTENISH	KNAGGIER	KNICKERS
KINGSHIP	KIRKTOWNS	KITTENS	KNAGGIEST	KNICKS
KINGSHIPS	KIRKWARD	KITTENY	KNAGGY	KNIFE
KINGWOOD	KIRKYAIRD	KITTIES	KNAGS	KNIFED
KINGWOODS	KIRKYAIRDS	KITTING	KNAP	KNIFELESS
KININ	KIRKYARD	KITTIWAKE	KNAPPED	KNIFES
KININS	KIRKYARDS	KITTIWAKES	KNAPPER	KNIFING
KINK	KIRMESS	KITTLE	KNAPPERS	KNIFINGS
KINKAJOU	KIRMESSES	KITTLED	KNAPPING	KNIGHT
KINKAJOUS	KIRN	KITTLER	KNAPPLE	KNIGHTAGE
KINKED	KIRNS	KITTLES	KNAPPLED	KNIGHTAGES
KINKIER	KIRPAN	KITTLEST	KNAPPLES	KNIGHTED
KINKIEST	KIRPANS	KITTLIER	KNAPPLING	KNIGHTING
KINKING	KIRS	KITTLIEST	KNAPS	KNIGHTLIER
KINKLE	KIRSCH	KITTLING	KNAPSACK	KNIGHTLIEST
KINKLES	KIRSCHES	KITTLY	KNAPSACKS	KNIGHTLY
KINKS	KIRTLE	KITTUL	KNAPSCAL	KNIGHTS
KINKY	KIRTLED	KITTULS	KNAPSCALS	KNISH
KINLESS	KIRTLES	KITTY	KNAPSCULL	KNISHES
KINO	KISAN	KIWI	KNAPSCULLS	KNIT
KINONE	KISANS	KIWIS	KNAPSKULL	KNITCH
KINONES	KISH	KLANG	KNAPSKULLS	KNITCHES
KINOS	KISHES	KLANGS	KNAPWEED	KNITS
KINRED	KISMET	KLAVIER	KNAPWEEDS	KNITTED
KINREDS	KISMETS	KLAVIERS	KNAR	KNITTER
KINS	KISS	KLAXON	KNARL	KNITTERS
KINSFOLK	KISSABLE	KLAXONS	KNARLS	KNITTING
KINSFOLKS	KISSED	KLENDUSIC	KNARRED	KNITTINGS
KINSHIP	KISSER	KLEPHT	KNARRING	KNITTLE
KINSHIPS	KISSERS	KLEPHTIC	KNARS	KNITTLES
KINSMAN	KISSES	KLEPHTISM	KNAVE	KNITWEAR
KINSMEN	KISSING	KLEPHTISMS	KNAVERIES	KNITWEARS
KINSWOMAN	KIST	KLEPHTS	KNAVERY	KNIVE
KINSWOMEN	KISTED	KLINKER	KNAVES	KNIVED
KINTLEDGE	KISTING	KLINKERS	KNAVESHIP	KNIVES
KINTLEDGES	KISTS	KLINOSTAT	KNAVESHIPS	KNIVING
KIOSK	KISTVAEN	KLINOSTATS	KNAVISH	KNOB
KIOSKS	KISTVAENS	KLIPDAS	KNAVISHLY	KNOBBED
KIP	KIT	KLIPDASES	KNAWEL	KNOBBER
KIPE	KITCHEN	KLONDIKE	KNAWELS	KNOBBERS
KIPES	KITCHENED	KLONDIKED	KNEAD	KNOBBIER
KIPP	KITCHENER	KLONDIKES	KNEADED	KNOBBIEST
KIPPAGE	KITCHENERS	KLONDIKING	KNEADER	KNOBBLE
KIPPAGES	KITCHENING	KLONDYKE	KNEADERS	KNOBBLED
KIPPED	KITCHENS	KLONDYKED	KNEADING	KNOBBLES
KIPPER	KITE	KLONDYKER	KNEADS	KNOBBLIER
KIPPERED	KITED	KLONDYKERS	KNEE	KNOBBLIEST
KIPPERER	KITES	KLONDYKES	KNEED	KNOBBLING
KIPPERERS	KITH	KLONDYKING	KNEEHOLE	KNOBBLY
KIPPERING	KITHARA	KLOOF	KNEEHOLES	KNOBBY
KIPPERS	KITHARAS	KLOOFS	KNEEING	KNOBS
KIPPING	KITHE	KLUDGE	KNEEL	KNOCK
KIPPS	KITHED	KLUDGES	KNEELED	KNOCKED
KIPS	KITHES	KLUTZ	KNEELER	KNOCKER
KIR	KITHING	KLUTZES	KNEELERS	KNOCKERS
KIRBEH	KITHS	KLYSTRON	KNEELING	KNOCKING
KIRBEHS	KITING	KLYSTRONS	KNEELS	KNOCKINGS
KIRBIGRIP	KITLING	KNACK	KNEES	KNOCKOUT
KIRBIGRIPS	KITLINGS	KNACKER	KNELL	KNOCKOUTS
KIRI	KITS	KNACKERED	KNELLED	KNOCKS
KIRIMON	KITSCH	KNACKERIES	KNELLING	KNOLL
KIRIMONS	KITSCHES	KNACKERING	KNELLS	KNOLLED
KIRIS	KITSCHIER	KNACKERS	KNELT	KNOLLING
KIRK	KITSCHIEST	KNACKERY	KNEVELL	KNOLLS
KIRKED	KITSCHILY	KNACKIER	KNEVELLED	KNOP
KIRKING	KITSCHY	KNACKIEST	KNEVELLING	KNOPS
KIRKINGS	KITTED	KNACKISH	KNEVELLS	KNOSP
KIRKS	KITTEN	KNACKS	KNEW	KNOSPS

KNOT
KNOTGRASS
KNOTGRASSES
KNOTLESS
KNOTS
KNOTTED
KNOTTER
KNOTTERS
KNOTTIER
KNOTTIEST
KNOTTING
KNOTTINGS
KNOTTY
KNOTWEED
KNOTWEEDS
KNOTWORK
KNOTWORKS
KNOUT
KNOUTED
KNOUTING
KNOUTS
KNOW
KNOWABLE
KNOWE
KNOWER
KNOWERS
KNOWES
KNOWING
KNOWINGLY
KNOWLEDGE
KNOWLEDGED
KNOWLEDGES
KNOWLEDGING
KNOWN
KNOWS
KNUB
KNUBBIER
KNUBBIEST
KNUBBLE
KNUBBLED
KNUBBLES
KNUBBLIER
KNUBBLIEST
KNUBBLING
KNUBBLY
KNUBBY
KNUBS
KNUCKLE
KNUCKLED
KNUCKLES
KNUCKLING
KNUR
KNURL
KNURLED
KNURLIER
KNURLIEST
KNURLING
KNURLINGS
KNURLS
KNURLY
KNURR
KNURRS
KNURS
KNUT
KNUTS
KO
KOA
KOALA
KOALAS
KOAN

KOANS
KOAS
KOB
KOBAN
KOBANG
KOBANGS
KOBANS
KOBOLD
KOBOLDS
KOBS
KOFF
KOFFS
KOFTA
KOFTAS
KOFTGAR
KOFTGARI
KOFTGARIS
KOFTGARS
KOFTWORK
KOFTWORKS
KOHL
KOHLRABI
KOHLRABIS
KOHLS
KOINE
KOINES
KOKRA
KOKRAS
KOKUM
KOKUMS
KOLA
KOLAS
KOLINSKIES
KOLINSKY
KOLKHOZ
KOLKHOZES
KOLO
KOLOS
KOMISSAR
KOMISSARS
KOMITAJI
KOMITAJIS
KON
KOND
KONFYT
KONFYTS
KONIMETER
KONIMETERS
KONIOLOGIES
KONIOLOGY
KONISCOPE
KONISCOPES
KONK
KONKED
KONKING
KONKS
KONNING
KONS
KOODOO
KOODOOS
KOOK
KOOKED
KOOKIE
KOOKIER
KOOKIEST
KOOKING
KOOKS
KOOKY
KOOLAH
KOOLAHS

KOP
KOPECK
KOPECKS
KOPJE
KOPJES
KOPPA
KOPPAS
KOPPIE
KOPPIES
KOPS
KORA
KORAS
KORFBALL
KORFBALLS
KORKIR
KORKIRS
KORMA
KORMAS
KORORA
KORORAS
KORUNA
KORUNAS
KOS
KOSES
KOSHER
KOSHERS
KOSMOS
KOSMOSES
KOSS
KOSSES
KOTO
KOTOS
KOTOW
KOTOWED
KOTOWING
KOTOWS
KOTTABOS
KOTTABOSES
KOTWAL
KOTWALS
KOULAN
KOULANS
KOUMISS
KOUMISSES
KOURBASH
KOURBASHED
KOURBASHES
KOURBASHING
KOUSKOUS
KOUSKOUSES
KOW
KOWHAI
KOWHAIS
KOWS
KOWTOW
KOWTOWED
KOWTOWING
KOWTOWS
KRAAL
KRAALED
KRAALING
KRAALS
KRAFT
KRAFTS
KRAIT
KRAITS
KRAKEN
KRAKENS
KRAKOWIAK
KRAKOWIAKS

KRAMERIA
KRAMERIAS
KRANG
KRANGS
KRANS
KRANSES
KRANTZ
KRANTZES
KRANZ
KRANZES
KRAUT
KRAUTS
KREASOTE
KREASOTED
KREASOTES
KREASOTING
KREATINE
KREATINES
KREESE
KREESED
KREESES
KREESING
KREMLIN
KREMLINS
KRENG
KRENGS
KREOSOTE
KREOSOTED
KREOSOTES
KREOSOTING
KREPLACH
KREUTZER
KREUTZERS
KRILL
KRILLS
KRIMMER
KRIMMERS
KRIS
KRISED
KRISES
KRISING
KROMESKIES
KROMESKY
KRONA
KRONE
KRONEN
KRONER
KRONOR
KRONUR
KRUMHORN
KRUMHORNS
KRUMMHORN
KRUMMHORNS
KRYOMETER
KRYOMETERS
KRYPSES
KRYPSIS
KRYPTON
KRYPTONS
KSAR
KSARS
KUCHCHA
KUDOS
KUDOSES
KUDU
KUDUS
KUDZU
KUDZUS
KUFFIAH
KUFFIAHS

KUFFIEH
KUFFIEHS
KUFFIYEH
KUFFIYEHS
KUFIAH
KUFIAHS
KUFIYA
KUFIYAH
KUFIYAHS
KUFIYAS
KUKRI
KUKRIS
KUKU
KUKUS
KULAK
KULAKS
KULAN
KULANS
KUMARA
KUMARAS
KUMARI
KUMARIS
KUMISS
KUMISSES
KÜMMEL
KÜMMELS
KUMQUAT
KUMQUATS
KUNKAR
KUNKARS
KUNKUR
KUNKURS
KURBASH
KURBASHED
KURBASHES
KURBASHING
KURGAN
KURGANS
KURRAJONG
KURRAJONGS
KURRE
KURRES
KURSAAL
KURSAALS
KURTA
KURTAS
KURTOSES
KURTOSIS
KURVEY
KURVEYED
KURVEYING
KURVEYOR
KURVEYORS
KURVEYS
KUTCH
KUTCHA
KUTCHES
KVASS
KVASSES
KVETCH
KVETCHED
KVETCHER
KVETCHERS
KVETCHES
KVETCHING
KWACHA
KWACHAS
KWELA
KWELAS
KY

KYANG
KYANGS
KYANISE
KYANISED
KYANISES
KYANISING
KYANITE
KYANITES
KYANIZE
KYANIZED
KYANIZES
KYANIZING

KYAT
KYATS
KYBOSH
KYBOSHED
KYBOSHES
KYBOSHING
KYDST
KYE
KYLE
KYLES
KYLEY
KYLEYS

KYLICES
KYLIE
KYLIES
KYLIN
KYLINS
KYLIX
KYLLOSES
KYLLOSIS
KYLOE
KYLOES
KYMOGRAM
KYMOGRAMS

KYMOGRAPH
KYMOGRAPHS
KYND
KYNDE
KYNDED
KYNDES
KYNDING
KYNDS
KYNE
KYPHOSES
KYPHOSIS
KYPHOTIC

KYRIELLE
KYRIELLES
KYTE
KYTES
KYTHE
KYTHED
KYTHES
KYTHING

L

LA
LAAGER
LAAGERED
LAAGERING
LAAGERS
LAB
LABARA
LABARUM
LABARUMS
LABDA
LABDACISM
LABDACISMS
LABDANUM
LABDANUMS
LABDAS
LABEL
LABELLA
LABELLED
LABELLING
LABELLOID
LABELLUM
LABELS
LABIA
LABIAL
LABIALISE
LABIALISED
LABIALISES
LABIALISING
LABIALISM
LABIALISMS
LABIALIZE
LABIALIZED
LABIALIZES
LABIALIZING
LABIALLY
LABIALS
LABIATE
LABIATES
LABILE
LABILITIES
LABILITY
LABIS
LABISES
LABIUM
LABLAB
LABLABS
LABOR
LABORED
LABORING
LABORIOUS
LABORS
LABOUR
LABOURED
LABOURER
LABOURERS
LABOURING
LABOURISM
LABOURISMS
LABOURIST
LABOURISTS
LABOURS
LABRA
LABRET

LABRETS
LABRID
LABRIDS
LABROID
LABROIDS
LABROSE
LABRUM
LABRYS
LABRYSES
LABS
LABURNUM
LABURNUMS
LABYRINTH
LABYRINTHS
LAC
LACCOLITE
LACCOLITES
LACCOLITH
LACCOLITHS
LACE
LACEBARK
LACEBARKS
LACED
LACERABLE
LACERANT
LACERATE
LACERATED
LACERATES
LACERATING
LACERTIAN
LACERTINE
LACES
LACET
LACETS
LACEY
LACHES
LACHESES
LACHRYMAL
LACHRYMALS
LACIER
LACIEST
LACING
LACINGS
LACINIA
LACINIAE
LACINIATE
LACK
LACKADAY
LACKED
LACKER
LACKERED
LACKERING
LACKERS
LACKEY
LACKEYED
LACKEYING
LACKEYS
LACKING
LACKLAND
LACKLANDS
LACKS
LACMUS
LACMUSES

LACONIC
LACONICAL
LACONISM
LACONISMS
LACQUER
LACQUERED
LACQUERER
LACQUERERS
LACQUERING
LACQUERINGS
LACQUERS
LACQUEY
LACQUEYED
LACQUEYING
LACQUEYS
LACRIMAL
LACRIMALS
LACROSSE
LACROSSES
LACRYMAL
LACRYMALS
LACS
LACTASE
LACTASES
LACTATE
LACTATED
LACTATES
LACTATING
LACTATION
LACTATIONS
LACTEAL
LACTEALS
LACTEOUS
LACTIC
LACTIFIC
LACTONE
LACTONES
LACTOSE
LACTOSES
LACUNA
LACUNAE
LACUNAL
LACUNAR
LACUNARIA
LACUNARS
LACUNARY
LACUNATE
LACUNOSE
LACY
LAD
LADANUM
LADANUMS
LADDER
LADDERED
LADDERING
LADDERS
LADDERY
LADDIE
LADDIES
LADE
LADED
LADEN
LADES

LADIES
LADIFIED
LADIFIES
LADIFY
LADIFYING
LADING
LADINGS
LADLE
LADLED
LADLEFUL
LADLEFULS
LADLES
LADLING
LADRONE
LADRONES
LADS
LADY
LADYBIRD
LADYBIRDS
LADYBUG
LADYBUGS
LADYCOW
LADYCOWS
LADYFIED
LADYFIES
LADYFLIES
LADYFLY
LADYFY
LADYFYING
LADYHOOD
LADYHOODS
LADYISH
LADYISM
LADYISMS
LADYKIN
LADYKINS
LADYLIKE
LADYSHIP
LADYSHIPS
LAER
LAERS
LAESIE
LAETARE
LAETARES
LAEVIGATE
LAEVIGATED
LAEVIGATES
LAEVIGATING
LAEVULOSE
LAEVULOSES
LAG
LAGAN
LAGANS
LAGENA
LAGENAS
LAGER
LAGERS
LAGGARD
LAGGARDS
LAGGED
LAGGEN
LAGGENS
LAGGER

LAGGERS
LAGGIN
LAGGING
LAGGINGLY
LAGGINGS
LAGGINS
LAGNIAPPE
LAGNIAPPES
LAGOMORPH
LAGOMORPHS
LAGOON
LAGOONAL
LAGOONS
LAGRIMOSO
LAGS
LAGUNE
LAGUNES
LAH
LAHAR
LAHARS
LAHS
LAIC
LAICAL
LAICISE
LAICISED
LAICISES
LAICISING
LAICITIES
LAICITY
LAICIZE
LAICIZED
LAICIZES
LAICIZING
LAICS
LAID
LAIDED
LAIDING
LAIDLY
LAIDS
LAIGH
LAIGHER
LAIGHEST
LAIGHS
LAIK
LAIKA
LAIKAS
LAIKED
LAIKING
LAIKS
LAIN
LAIR
LAIRAGE
LAIRAGES
LAIRD
LAIRDS
LAIRDSHIP
LAIRDSHIPS
LAIRED
LAIRIER
LAIRIEST
LAIRING
LAIRISE
LAIRISED

LAIRISES	LAMBENTLY	LAMMING	LANDAMMANS	LANEWAY
LAIRISING	LAMBER	LAMMINGS	LANDAU	LANEWAYS
LAIRIZE	LAMBERS	LAMMY	LANDAULET	LANG
LAIRIZED	LAMBERT	LAMP	LANDAULETS	LANGAHA
LAIRIZES	LAMBERTS	LAMPAD	LANDAUS	LANGAHAS
LAIRIZING	LAMBIE	LAMPADARIES	LANDDAMNE	LANGER
LAIRS	LAMBIES	LAMPADARY	LANDDAMNED	LANGEST
LAIRY	LAMBING	LAMPADIST	LANDDAMNES	LANGLAUF
LAISSE	LAMBITIVE	LAMPADISTS	LANDDAMNING	LANGLAUFS
LAISSES	LAMBITIVES	LAMPADS	LANDDROS	LANGOUSTE
LAITANCE	LAMBKIN	LAMPAS	LANDDROSES	LANGOUSTES
LAITANCES	LAMBKINS	LAMPASES	LANDDROST	LANGRAGE
LAITH	LAMBLING	LAMPASSE	LANDDROSTS	LANGRAGES
LAITIES	LAMBLINGS	LAMPASSES	LANDE	LANGREL
LAITY	LAMBOYS	LAMPED	LANDED	LANGRELS
LAKE	LAMBS	LAMPERN	LANDER	LANGRIDGE
LAKED	LAMBSKIN	LAMPERNS	LANDERS	LANGRIDGES
LAKELET	LAMBSKINS	LAMPHOLE	LANDES	LANGSPEL
LAKELETS	LAME	LAMPHOLES	LANDFALL	LANGSPELS
LAKER	LAMED	LAMPING	LANDFALLS	LANGSPIEL
LAKERS	LAMELLA	LAMPION	LANDFILL	LANGSPIELS
LAKES	LAMELLAE	LAMPIONS	LANDFILLS	LANGUAGE
LAKH	LAMELLAR	LAMPLIGHT	LANDFORCE	LANGUAGED
LAKHS	LAMELLATE	LAMPLIGHTS	LANDFORCES	LANGUAGES
LAKIER	LAMELLOID	LAMPOON	LANDFORM	LANGUAGING
LAKIEST	LAMELLOSE	LAMPOONED	LANDFORMS	LANGUE
LAKIN	LAMELY	LAMPOONER	LANDGRAVE	LANGUED
LAKING	LAMENESS	LAMPOONERS	LANDGRAVES	LANGUES
LAKINS	LAMENESSES	LAMPOONING	LANDING	LANGUET
LAKISH	LAMENT	LAMPOONS	LANDINGS	LANGUETS
LAKY	LAMENTED	LAMPPOST	LANDLADIES	LANGUETTE
LALANG	LAMENTING	LAMPPOSTS	LANDLADY	LANGUETTES
LALANGS	LAMENTINGS	LAMPREY	LANDLER	LANGUID
LALDIE	LAMENTS	LAMPREYS	LANDLERS	LANGUIDLY
LALDIES	LAMER	LAMPS	LANDLESS	LANGUISH
LALDY	LAMES	LAMPSHADE	LANDLOPER	LANGUISHED
LALLAN	LAMEST	LAMPSHADES	LANDLOPERS	LANGUISHES
LALLANS	LAMETER	LAMPUKA	LANDLORD	LANGUISHING
LALLATION	LAMETERS	LAMPUKAS	LANDLORDS	LANGUISHINGS
LALLATIONS	LAMIA	LAMPUKI	LANDMAN	LANGUOR
LALLING	LAMIAE	LAMPUKIS	LANDMARK	LANGUORS
LALLINGS	LAMIAS	LAMS	LANDMARKS	LANGUR
LALLYGAG	LAMIGER	LANA	LANDMASS	LANGURS
LALLYGAGGED	LAMIGERS	LANAS	LANDMASSES	LANIARD
LALLYGAGGING	LAMINA	LANATE	LANDMEN	LANIARDS
LALLYGAGS	LAMINABLE	LANCE	LANDOWNER	LANIARY
LAM	LAMINAE	LANCED	LANDOWNERS	LANK
LAMA	LAMINAR	LANCEGAY	LANDRACE	LANKED
LAMAISTIC	LAMINARY	LANCEGAYS	LANDRACES	LANKER
LAMANTIN	LAMINATE	LANCELET	LANDRAIL	LANKEST
LAMANTINS	LAMINATED	LANCELETS	LANDRAILS	LANKIER
LAMAS	LAMINATES	LANCEOLAR	LANDS	LANKIEST
LAMASERAI	LAMINATING	LANCER	LANDSCAPE	LANKINESS
LAMASERAIS	LAMINATOR	LANCERS	LANDSCAPED	LANKINESSES
LAMASERIES	LAMINATORS	LANCES	LANDSCAPES	LANKING
LAMASERY	LAMING	LANCET	LANDSCAPING	LANKLY
LAMB	LAMINGTON	LANCETED	LANDSKIP	LANKNESS
LAMBAST	LAMINGTONS	LANCETS	LANDSKIPS	LANKNESSES
LAMBASTE	LAMINITIS	LANCH	LANDSLIDE	LANKS
LAMBASTED	LAMINITISES	LANCHED	LANDSLIDES	LANKY
LAMBASTES	LAMISH	LANCHES	LANDSLIP	LANNER
LAMBASTING	LAMITER	LANCHING	LANDSLIPS	LANNERET
LAMBASTS	LAMITERS	LANCIFORM	LANDSMAN	LANNERETS
LAMBDA	LAMMED	LANCINATE	LANDSMEN	LANNERS
LAMBDAS	LAMMER	LANCINATED	LANDWARD	LANOLIN
LAMBDOID	LAMMERS	LANCINATES	LANDWARDS	LANOLINE
LAMBED	LAMMIE	LANCINATING	LANDWIND	LANOLINES
LAMBENCIES	LAMMIES	LANCING	LANDWINDS	LANOLINS
LAMBENCY	LAMMIGER	LAND	LANE	LANOSE
LAMBENT	LAMMIGERS	LANDAMMAN	LANES	LANT

LANTANA
LANTANAS
LANTERLOO
LANTERLOOS
LANTERN
LANTERNED
LANTERNING
LANTERNS
LANTHANUM
LANTHANUMS
LANTHORN
LANTHORNS
LANTS
LANTSKIP
LANTSKIPS
LANUGO
LANUGOS
LANX
LANYARD
LANYARDS
LAP
LAPDOG
LAPDOGS
LAPEL
LAPELLED
LAPELS
LAPFUL
LAPFULS
LAPIDARIES
LAPIDARY
LAPIDATE
LAPIDATED
LAPIDATES
LAPIDATING
LAPIDEOUS
LAPIDIFIC
LAPIDIFIED
LAPIDIFIES
LAPIDIFY
LAPIDIFYING
LAPILLI
LAPIS
LAPISES
LAPJE
LAPJES
LAPPED
LAPPEL
LAPPELS
LAPPER
LAPPERED
LAPPERING
LAPPERS
LAPPET
LAPPETED
LAPPETS
LAPPIE
LAPPIES
LAPPING
LAPPINGS
LAPS
LAPSABLE
LAPSANG
LAPSANGS
LAPSE
LAPSED
LAPSES
LAPSING
LAPSTONE
LAPSTONES
LAPSTREAK

LAPSTREAKS
LAPSUS
LAPSUSES
LAPTOP
LAPTOPS
LAPWING
LAPWINGS
LAPWORK
LAPWORKS
LAQUEARIA
LAR
LARBOARD
LARBOARDS
LARCENER
LARCENERS
LARCENIES
LARCENIST
LARCENISTS
LARCENOUS
LARCENY
LARCH
LARCHEN
LARCHES
LARD
LARDALITE
LARDALITES
LARDED
LARDER
LARDERER
LARDERERS
LARDERS
LARDIER
LARDIEST
LARDING
LARDON
LARDONS
LARDOON
LARDOONS
LARDS
LARDY
LARE
LARES
LARGE
LARGELY
LARGEN
LARGENED
LARGENESS
LARGENESSES
LARGENING
LARGENS
LARGER
LARGES
LARGESS
LARGESSE
LARGESSES
LARGEST
LARGHETTO
LARGHETTOS
LARGISH
LARGITION
LARGITIONS
LARGO
LARGOS
LARIAT
LARIATS
LARINE
LARK
LARKED
LARKER
LARKERS

LARKIER
LARKIEST
LARKINESS
LARKINESSES
LARKING
LARKISH
LARKS
LARKSPUR
LARKSPURS
LARKY
LARMIER
LARMIERS
LARN
LARNAKES
LARNAX
LARNED
LARNING
LARNS
LAROID
LARRIGAN
LARRIGANS
LARRIKIN
LARRIKINS
LARRUP
LARRUPED
LARRUPING
LARRUPS
LARUM
LARUMS
LARVA
LARVAE
LARVAL
LARVATE
LARVATED
LARVICIDE
LARVICIDES
LARVIFORM
LARVIKITE
LARVIKITES
LARYNGAL
LARYNGEAL
LARYNGES
LARYNX
LARYNXES
LAS
LASAGNA
LASAGNAS
LASAGNE
LASAGNES
LASCAR
LASCARS
LASE
LASED
LASER
LASERS
LASERWORT
LASERWORTS
LASES
LASH
LASHED
LASHER
LASHERS
LASHES
LASHING
LASHINGS
LASHKAR
LASHKARS
LASING
LASINGS
LASKET

LASKETS
LASQUE
LASQUES
LASS
LASSES
LASSIE
LASSIES
LASSITUDE
LASSITUDES
LASSLORN
LASSO
LASSOCK
LASSOCKS
LASSOED
LASSOES
LASSOING
LASSOS
LASSU
LASSUS
LAST
LASTAGE
LASTAGES
LASTED
LASTER
LASTERS
LASTING
LASTINGLY
LASTINGS
LASTLY
LASTS
LAT
LATCH
LATCHED
LATCHES
LATCHET
LATCHETS
LATCHING
LATCHKEY
LATCHKEYS
LATE
LATED
LATEEN
LATELY
LATEN
LATENCE
LATENCES
LATENCIES
LATENCY
LATENED
LATENESS
LATENESSES
LATENING
LATENS
LATENT
LATENTLY
LATER
LATERAL
LATERALLY
LATERALS
LATERITE
LATERITES
LATESCENT
LATEST
LATESTS
LATEWAKE
LATEWAKES
LATEX
LATEXES
LATH
LATHE

LATHED
LATHEE
LATHEES
LATHEN
LATHER
LATHERED
LATHERING
LATHERS
LATHERY
LATHES
LATHI
LATHIER
LATHIEST
LATHING
LATHINGS
LATHIS
LATHS
LATHY
LATHYRISM
LATHYRISMS
LATHYRUS
LATHYRUSES
LATICES
LATICLAVE
LATICLAVES
LATIFONDI
LATISH
LATITANCIES
LATITANCY
LATITANT
LATITAT
LATITATS
LATITUDE
LATITUDES
LATKE
LATKES
LATRANT
LATRATION
LATRATIONS
LATRIA
LATRIAS
LATRINE
LATRINES
LATROCINIES
LATROCINY
LATRON
LATRONS
LATS
LATTEN
LATTENS
LATTER
LATTERLY
LATTICE
LATTICED
LATTICES
LATTICING
LATTICINI
LATTICINO
LAUCH
LAUCHING
LAUCHS
LAUD
LAUDABLE
LAUDABLY
LAUDANUM
LAUDANUMS
LAUDATION
LAUDATIONS
LAUDATIVE
LAUDATIVES

LAUDATORIES
LAUDATORY
LAUDED
LAUDER
LAUDERS
LAUDING
LAUDS
LAUF
LAUFS
LAUGH
LAUGHABLE
LAUGHABLY
LAUGHED
LAUGHER
LAUGHERS
LAUGHFUL
LAUGHIER
LAUGHIEST
LAUGHING
LAUGHINGS
LAUGHS
LAUGHSOME
LAUGHTER
LAUGHTERS
LAUGHY
LAUNCE
LAUNCED
LAUNCES
LAUNCH
LAUNCHED
LAUNCHER
LAUNCHERS
LAUNCHES
LAUNCHING
LAUNCING
LAUND
LAUNDER
LAUNDERED
LAUNDERER
LAUNDERERS
LAUNDERING
LAUNDERS
LAUNDRESS
LAUNDRESSES
LAUNDRIES
LAUNDRY
LAUNDS
LAURA
LAURAS
LAUREATE
LAUREATED
LAUREATES
LAUREATING
LAUREL
LAURELLED
LAURELS
LAUWINE
LAUWINES
LAV
LAVA
LAVABO
LAVABOES
LAVABOS
LAVAFORM
LAVAGE
LAVAGES
LAVALIERE
LAVALIERES
LAVAS
LAVATERA

LAVATERAS
LAVATION
LAVATIONS
LAVATORIES
LAVATORY
LAVE
LAVED
LAVEER
LAVEERED
LAVEERING
LAVEERS
LAVEMENT
LAVEMENTS
LAVENDER
LAVENDERED
LAVENDERING
LAVENDERS
LAVER
LAVEROCK
LAVEROCKED
LAVEROCKING
LAVEROCKS
LAVERS
LAVES
LAVING
LAVISH
LAVISHED
LAVISHER
LAVISHES
LAVISHEST
LAVISHING
LAVISHLY
LAVOLT
LAVOLTA
LAVOLTAS
LAVOLTED
LAVOLTING
LAVOLTS
LAVRA
LAVRAS
LAVS
LAW
LAWED
LAWER
LAWEST
LAWFUL
LAWFULLY
LAWING
LAWINGS
LAWK
LAWKS
LAWLAND
LAWLANDS
LAWLESS
LAWLESSLY
LAWMAN
LAWMEN
LAWMONGER
LAWMONGERS
LAWN
LAWNIER
LAWNIEST
LAWNS
LAWNY
LAWS
LAWSUIT
LAWSUITS
LAWYER
LAWYERLY
LAWYERS

LAX
LAXATIVE
LAXATIVES
LAXATOR
LAXATORS
LAXER
LAXES
LAXEST
LAXISM
LAXISMS
LAXIST
LAXISTS
LAXITIES
LAXITY
LAXLY
LAXNESS
LAXNESSES
LAY
LAYABOUT
LAYABOUTS
LAYAWAY
LAYAWAYS
LAYBACK
LAYBACKED
LAYBACKING
LAYBACKS
LAYER
LAYERED
LAYERING
LAYERINGS
LAYERS
LAYETTE
LAYETTES
LAYING
LAYINGS
LAYLOCK
LAYLOCKS
LAYMAN
LAYMEN
LAYPERSON
LAYPERSONS
LAYS
LAYSTALL
LAYSTALLS
LAYTIME
LAYTIMES
LAZAR
LAZARET
LAZARETS
LAZARETTO
LAZARETTOS
LAZARS
LAZE
LAZED
LAZES
LAZIER
LAZIEST
LAZILY
LAZINESS
LAZINESSES
LAZING
LAZULITE
LAZULITES
LAZURITE
LAZURITES
LAZY
LAZZARONE
LAZZARONI
LAZZI
LAZZO

LEA
LEACH
LEACHATE
LEACHATES
LEACHED
LEACHES
LEACHIER
LEACHIEST
LEACHING
LEACHINGS
LEACHOUR
LEACHOURS
LEACHY
LEAD
LEADED
LEADEN
LEADENED
LEADENING
LEADENLY
LEADENS
LEADER
LEADERS
LEADIER
LEADIEST
LEADING
LEADINGS
LEADLESS
LEADS
LEADSMAN
LEADSMEN
LEADY
LEAF
LEAFAGE
LEAFAGES
LEAFBUD
LEAFBUDS
LEAFED
LEAFERIES
LEAFERY
LEAFIER
LEAFIEST
LEAFINESS
LEAFINESSES
LEAFING
LEAFLESS
LEAFLET
LEAFLETED
LEAFLETING
LEAFLETS
LEAFLETTED
LEAFLETTING
LEAFS
LEAFY
LEAGUE
LEAGUED
LEAGUER
LEAGUERED
LEAGUERING
LEAGUERS
LEAGUES
LEAGUING
LEAK
LEAKAGE
LEAKAGES
LEAKED
LEAKER
LEAKERS
LEAKIER
LEAKIEST
LEAKINESS

LEAKINESSES
LEAKING
LEAKS
LEAKY
LEAL
LEALTIES
LEALTY
LEAM
LEAMED
LEAMING
LEAMS
LEAN
LEANED
LEANER
LEANEST
LEANING
LEANINGS
LEANLY
LEANNESS
LEANNESSES
LEANS
LEANT
LEANY
LEAP
LEAPED
LEAPER
LEAPEROUS
LEAPERS
LEAPING
LEAPOROUS
LEAPROUS
LEAPS
LEAPT
LEAR
LEARE
LEARED
LEARES
LEARIER
LEARIEST
LEARING
LEARN
LEARNABLE
LEARNED
LEARNEDLY
LEARNER
LEARNERS
LEARNING
LEARNINGS
LEARNS
LEARNT
LEARS
LEARY
LEAS
LEASABLE
LEASE
LEASEBACK
LEASEBACKS
LEASED
LEASEHOLD
LEASEHOLDS
LEASER
LEASERS
LEASES
LEASH
LEASHED
LEASHES
LEASHING
LEASING
LEASINGS
LEASOW

LEASOWE
LEASOWED
LEASOWES
LEASOWING
LEASOWS
LEAST
LEASTS
LEASTWAYS
LEASTWISE
LEASURE
LEASURES
LEAT
LEATHER
LEATHERED
LEATHERING
LEATHERINGS
LEATHERN
LEATHERS
LEATHERY
LEATS
LEAVE
LEAVED
LEAVEN
LEAVENED
LEAVENING
LEAVENINGS
LEAVENOUS
LEAVENS
LEAVES
LEAVIER
LEAVIEST
LEAVING
LEAVINGS
LEAVY
LEAZE
LEAZES
LEBBEK
LEBBEKS
LECANORA
LECANORAS
LECH
LECHED
LECHER
LECHERED
LECHERIES
LECHERING
LECHEROUS
LECHERS
LECHERY
LECHES
LECHING
LECHWE
LECHWES
LECITHIN
LECITHINS
LECTERN
LECTERNS
LECTIN
LECTINS
LECTION
LECTIONS
LECTOR
LECTORATE
LECTORATES
LECTORS
LECTRESS
LECTRESSES
LECTURE
LECTURED
LECTURER

LECTURERS
LECTURES
LECTURING
LECTURN
LECTURNS
LECYTHI
LECYTHUS
LED
LEDDEN
LEDDENS
LEDGE
LEDGER
LEDGERED
LEDGERING
LEDGERS
LEDGES
LEDGIER
LEDGIEST
LEDGY
LEDUM
LEDUMS
LEE
LEEAR
LEEARS
LEECH
LEECHDOM
LEECHDOMS
LEECHED
LEECHEE
LEECHEES
LEECHES
LEECHING
LEED
LEEING
LEEK
LEEKS
LEEP
LEEPED
LEEPING
LEEPS
LEER
LEERED
LEERIER
LEERIEST
LEERING
LEERINGLY
LEERINGS
LEERS
LEERY
LEES
LEESE
LEESES
LEESING
LEET
LEETLE
LEETS
LEEWARD
LEEWARDS
LEEWAY
LEEWAYS
LEFT
LEFTE
LEFTIE
LEFTIES
LEFTISM
LEFTISMS
LEFTIST
LEFTISTS
LEFTS
LEFTWARD

LEFTWARDS
LEFTY
LEG
LEGACIES
LEGACY
LEGAL
LEGALESE
LEGALESES
LEGALISE
LEGALISED
LEGALISES
LEGALISING
LEGALISM
LEGALISMS
LEGALIST
LEGALISTS
LEGALITIES
LEGALITY
LEGALIZE
LEGALIZED
LEGALIZES
LEGALIZING
LEGALLY
LEGATARIES
LEGATARY
LEGATE
LEGATEE
LEGATEES
LEGATES
LEGATINE
LEGATION
LEGATIONS
LEGATO
LEGATOR
LEGATORS
LEGATOS
LEGEND
LEGENDARIES
LEGENDARY
LEGENDIST
LEGENDISTS
LEGENDRIES
LEGENDRY
LEGENDS
LEGER
LEGERING
LEGERINGS
LEGERITIES
LEGERITY
LEGERS
LEGES
LEGGE
LEGGED
LEGGER
LEGGERS
LEGGES
LEGGIER
LEGGIEST
LEGGINESS
LEGGINESSES
LEGGING
LEGGINGS
LEGGISM
LEGGISMS
LEGGY
LEGHORN
LEGHORNS
LEGIBLE
LEGIBLY
LEGION

LEGIONARIES
LEGIONARY
LEGIONED
LEGIONS
LEGISLATE
LEGISLATED
LEGISLATES
LEGISLATING
LEGIST
LEGISTS
LEGIT
LEGITIM
LEGITIMS
LEGLAN
LEGLANS
LEGLEN
LEGLENS
LEGLESS
LEGLET
LEGLETS
LEGLIN
LEGLINS
LEGROOM
LEGROOMS
LEGS
LEGUME
LEGUMES
LEGUMIN
LEGUMINS
LEGWORK
LEGWORKS
LEHR
LEHRJAHRE
LEHRS
LEI
LEIDGER
LEIDGERS
LEIGER
LEIGERS
LEIPOA
LEIPOAS
LEIR
LEIRED
LEIRING
LEIRS
LEIS
LEISH
LEISHER
LEISHEST
LEISLER
LEISLERS
LEISTER
LEISTERED
LEISTERING
LEISTERS
LEISURE
LEISURED
LEISURELY
LEISURES
LEISURING
LEITMOTIF
LEITMOTIFS
LEITMOTIV
LEITMOTIVS
LEK
LEKE
LEKKED
LEKKING
LEKKINGS
LEKS

LEKYTHOI
LEKYTHOS
LEMAN
LEMANS
LEME
LEMED
LEMEL
LEMELS
LEMES
LEMING
LEMMA
LEMMAS
LEMMATA
LEMMING
LEMMINGS
LEMON
LEMONADE
LEMONADES
LEMONED
LEMONING
LEMONS
LEMONY
LEMPIRA
LEMPIRAS
LEMUR
LEMURES
LEMURIAN
LEMURIANS
LEMURINE
LEMURINES
LEMUROID
LEMUROIDS
LEMURS
LEND
LENDER
LENDERS
LENDING
LENDINGS
LENDS
LENES
LENG
LENGED
LENGER
LENGEST
LENGING
LENGS
LENGTH
LENGTHEN
LENGTHENED
LENGTHENING
LENGTHENS
LENGTHFUL
LENGTHIER
LENGTHIEST
LENGTHILY
LENGTHS
LENGTHY
LENIENCE
LENIENCES
LENIENCIES
LENIENCY
LENIENT
LENIENTLY
LENIENTS
LENIFIED
LENIFIES
LENIFY
LENIFYING
LENIS
LENITIES

LENITION
LENITIONS
LENITIVE
LENITIVES
LENITY
LENO
LENOS
LENS
LENSES
LENT
LENTANDO
LENTEN
LENTI
LENTIC
LENTICEL
LENTICELS
LENTICLE
LENTICLES
LENTIFORM
LENTIGINES
LENTIGO
LENTIL
LENTILS
LENTISK
LENTISKS
LENTO
LENTOID
LENTOR
LENTORS
LENTOS
LENTOUS
LENVOY
LENVOYS
LEONE
LEONES
LEONINE
LEOPARD
LEOPARDS
LEOTARD
LEOTARDS
LEP
LEPER
LEPERS
LEPID
LEPIDOTE
LEPORINE
LEPPED
LEPPING
LEPRA
LEPRAS
LEPROSE
LEPROSERIES
LEPROSERY
LEPROSIES
LEPROSITIES
LEPROSITY
LEPROSY
LEPROUS
LEPS
LEPTA
LEPTOME
LEPTOMES
LEPTON
LEPTONIC
LEPTONS
LEPTOSOME
LEPTOSOMES
LEPTOTENE
LEPTOTENES
LERE

LERED
LERES
LERING
LERNAEAN
LERNEAN
LES
LESBIAN
LESBIANS
LESBIC
LESES
LESION
LESIONS
LESS
LESSEE
LESSEES
LESSEN
LESSENED
LESSENING
LESSENS
LESSER
LESSES
LESSON
LESSONED
LESSONING
LESSONINGS
LESSONS
LESSOR
LESSORS
LEST
LESTED
LESTING
LESTS
LET
LETCH
LETCHED
LETCHES
LETCHING
LETHAL
LETHALITIES
LETHALITY
LETHALLY
LETHARGIC
LETHARGIES
LETHARGY
LETHEAN
LETHEE
LETHEES
LETHIED
LETS
LETTABLE
LETTED
LETTER
LETTERED
LETTERER
LETTERERS
LETTERING
LETTERINGS
LETTERN
LETTERNS
LETTERS
LETTING
LETTINGS
LETTRE
LETTRES
LETTUCE
LETTUCES
LEU
LEUCAEMIA
LEUCAEMIAS
LEUCAEMIC

LEUCH
LEUCHEN
LEUCIN
LEUCINE
LEUCINES
LEUCINS
LEUCITE
LEUCITES
LEUCITIC
LEUCOCYTE
LEUCOCYTES
LEUCOMA
LEUCOMAS
LEUCOTOME
LEUCOTOMES
LEUCOTOMIES
LEUCOTOMY
LEUGH
LEUGHEN
LEUKAEMIA
LEUKAEMIAS
LEV
LEVA
LEVANT
LEVANTED
LEVANTER
LEVANTERS
LEVANTINE
LEVANTINES
LEVANTING
LEVANTS
LEVATOR
LEVATORS
LEVE
LEVEE
LEVEED
LEVEEING
LEVEES
LEVEL
LEVELLED
LEVELLER
LEVELLERS
LEVELLEST
LEVELLING
LEVELLINGS
LEVELS
LEVER
LEVERAGE
LEVERAGES
LEVERED
LEVERET
LEVERETS
LEVERING
LEVERS
LEVIABLE
LEVIATHAN
LEVIATHANS
LEVIED
LEVIES
LEVIGABLE
LEVIGATE
LEVIGATED
LEVIGATES
LEVIGATING
LEVIN
LEVINS
LEVIRATE
LEVIRATES
LEVIS
LEVITATE

LEVITATED
LEVITATES
LEVITATING
LEVITE
LEVITES
LEVITIC
LEVITICAL
LEVITIES
LEVITY
LEVULOSE
LEVULOSES
LEVY
LEVYING
LEW
LEWD
LEWDER
LEWDEST
LEWDLY
LEWDNESS
LEWDNESSES
LEWDSBIES
LEWDSBY
LEWDSTER
LEWDSTERS
LEWIS
LEWISES
LEWISITE
LEWISITES
LEWISSON
LEWISSONS
LEX
LEXEME
LEXEMES
LEXES
LEXICAL
LEXICALLY
LEXICON
LEXICONS
LEXIGRAM
LEXIGRAMS
LEXIS
LEXISES
LEY
LEYS
LEZ
LEZES
LEZZ
LEZZES
LEZZIES
LEZZY
LI
LIABILITIES
LIABILITY
LIABLE
LIAISE
LIAISED
LIAISES
LIAISING
LIAISON
LIAISONS
LIANA
LIANAS
LIANE
LIANES
LIANG
LIANGS
LIANOID
LIAR
LIARD
LIARDS

LIARS
LIART
LIB
LIBANT
LIBATE
LIBATED
LIBATES
LIBATING
LIBATION
LIBATIONS
LIBATORY
LIBBARD
LIBBARDS
LIBBED
LIBBER
LIBBERS
LIBBING
LIBECCHIO
LIBECCHIOS
LIBECCIO
LIBECCIOS
LIBEL
LIBELLANT
LIBELLANTS
LIBELLED
LIBELLEE
LIBELLEES
LIBELLER
LIBELLERS
LIBELLING
LIBELLINGS
LIBELLOUS
LIBELS
LIBER
LIBERAL
LIBERALLY
LIBERALS
LIBERATE
LIBERATED
LIBERATES
LIBERATING
LIBERATOR
LIBERATORS
LIBERS
LIBERTIES
LIBERTINE
LIBERTINES
LIBERTY
LIBIDINAL
LIBIDO
LIBIDOS
LIBKEN
LIDKENS
LIBRA
LIBRAE
LIBRAIRE
LIBRAIRES
LIBRAIRIE
LIBRAIRIES
LIBRARIAN
LIBRARIANS
LIBRARIES
LIBRARY
LIBRAS
LIBRATE
LIBRATED
LIBRATES
LIBRATING
LIBRATION
LIBRATIONS

LIBRATORY	LICORICE	LIFTING	LIGNINS	LIMAS
LIBRETTI	LICORICES	LIFTS	LIGNITE	LIMATION
LIBRETTO	LICTOR	LIFULL	LIGNITES	LIMATIONS
LIBRETTOS	LICTORS	LIG	LIGNITIC	LIMAX
LIBS	LID	LIGAMENT	LIGNUM	LIMB
LICE	LIDDED	LIGAMENTS	LIGNUMS	LIMBATE
LICENCE	LIDGER	LIGAN	LIGROIN	LIMBEC
LICENCED	LIDGERS	LIGAND	LIGROINS	LIMBECK
LICENCES	LIDLESS	LIGANDS	LIGS	LIMBECKS
LICENCING	LIDO	LIGANS	LIGULA	LIMBECS
LICENSE	LIDOCAINE	LIGATE	LIGULAE	LIMBED
LICENSED	LIDOCAINES	LIGATED	LIGULAR	LIMBER
LICENSEE	LIDOS	LIGATES	LIGULAS	LIMBERED
LICENSEES	LIDS	LIGATING	LIGULATE	LIMBERING
LICENSER	LIE	LIGATION	LIGULE	LIMBERS
LICENSERS	LIED	LIGATIONS	LIGULES	LIMBIC
LICENSES	LIEDER	LIGATURE	LIGULOID	LIMBING
LICENSING	LIEF	LIGATURED	LIGURE	LIMBLESS
LICENSOR	LIEFER	LIGATURES	LIGURES	LIMBMEAL
LICENSORS	LIEFEST	LIGATURING	LIKABLE	LIMBO
LICENSURE	LIEFS	LIGER	LIKE	LIMBOS
LICENSURES	LIEGE	LIGERS	LIKEABLE	LIMBOUS
LICH	LIEGEDOM	LIGGE	LIKED	LIMBS
LICHANOS	LIEGEDOMS	LIGGED	LIKELIER	LIME
LICHANOSES	LIEGELESS	LIGGEN	LIKELIEST	LIMED
LICHEE	LIEGEMAN	LIGGER	LIKELY	LIMEKILN
LICHEES	LIEGEMEN	LIGGERS	LIKEN	LIMEKILNS
LICHEN	LIEGER	LIGGES	LIKENED	LIMELIGHT
LICHENED	LIEGERS	LIGGING	LIKENESS	LIMELIGHTED
LICHENIN	LIEGES	LIGGINGS	LIKENESSES	LIMELIGHTING
LICHENINS	LIEN	LIGHT	LIKENING	LIMELIGHTS
LICHENISM	LIENAL	LIGHTED	LIKENS	LIMELIT
LICHENISMS	LIENS	LIGHTEN	LIKER	LIMEN
LICHENIST	LIENTERIC	LIGHTENED	LIKERS	LIMENS
LICHENISTS	LIENTERIES	LIGHTENING	LIKES	LIMEPIT
LICHENOID	LIENTERY	LIGHTENINGS	LIKEWAKE	LIMEPITS
LICHENOSE	LIER	LIGHTENS	LIKEWAKES	LIMERICK
LICHENOUS	LIERNE	LIGHTER	LIKEWALK	LIMERICKS
LICHENS	LIERNES	LIGHTERS	LIKEWALKS	LIMES
LICHES	LIERS	LIGHTEST	LIKEWISE	LIMESTONE
LICHGATE	LIES	LIGHTFAST	LIKIN	LIMESTONES
LICHGATES	LIEU	LIGHTFUL	LIKING	LIMEWASH
LICHI	LIEUS	LIGHTING	LIKINGS	LIMEWASHES
LICHIS	LIEVE	LIGHTINGS	LIKINS	LIMEWATER
LICHT	LIEVER	LIGHTISH	LILAC	LIMEWATERS
LICHTED	LIEVEST	LIGHTLESS	LILACS	LIMEY
LICHTER	LIFE	LIGHTLIED	LILANGENI	LIMEYS
LICHTEST	LIFEBELT	LIGHTLIES	LILIED	LIMIER
LICHTING	LIFEBELTS	LIGHTLY	LILIES	LIMIEST
LICHTLIED	LIFEBOAT	LIGHTLYING	LILL	LIMINAL
LICHTLIES	LIFEBOATS	LIGHTNESS	LILLED	LIMINESS
LICHTLY	LIFEFUL	LIGHTNESSES	LILLING	LIMINESSES
LICHTLYING	LIFEGUARD	LIGHTNING	LILLS	LIMING
LICHTS	LIFEGUARDS	LIGHTNINGS	LILO	LIMINGS
LICHWAKE	LIFEHOLD	LIGHTS	LILOS	LIMIT
LICHWAKES	LIFELESS	LIGHTSHIP	LILT	LIMITABLE
LICHWAY	LIFELIKE	LIGHTSHIPS	LILTED	LIMITARY
LICHWAYS	LIFELONG	LIGHTSOME	LILTING	LIMITED
LICIT	LIFER	LIGNAGE	LILTS	LIMITEDLY
LICITLY	LIFERS	LIGNAGES	LILY	LIMITEDS
LICK	LIFESOME	LIGNALOES	LIMA	LIMITER
LICKED	LIFESPAN	LIGNE	LIMACEL	LIMITERS
LICKER	LIFESPANS	LIGNEOUS	LIMACELS	LIMITES
LICKERISH	LIFETIME	LIGNES	LIMACEOUS	LIMITING
LICKERS	LIFETIMES	LIGNIFIED	LIMACES	LIMITINGS
LICKING	LIFT	LIGNIFIES	LIMACINE	LIMITLESS
LICKINGS	LIFTABLE	LIGNIFORM	LIMAÇON	LIMITS
LICKPENNIES	LIFTED	LIGNIFY	LIMAÇONS	LIMMA
LICKPENNY	LIFTER	LIGNIFYING	LIMAIL	LIMMAS
LICKS	LIFTERS	LIGNIN	LIMAILS	LIMMER

LIMMERS
LIMN
LIMNAEID
LIMNAEIDS
LIMNED
LIMNER
LIMNERS
LIMNETIC
LIMNING
LIMNOLOGIES
LIMNOLOGY
LIMNS
LIMONITE
LIMONITES
LIMONITIC
LIMOSES
LIMOSIS
LIMOUS
LIMOUSINE
LIMOUSINES
LIMP
LIMPED
LIMPER
LIMPEST
LIMPET
LIMPETS
LIMPID
LIMPIDITIES
LIMPIDITY
LIMPIDLY
LIMPING
LIMPINGLY
LIMPINGS
LIMPKIN
LIMPKINS
LIMPS
LIMULI
LIMULUS
LIMULUSES
LIMY
LIN
LINAGE
LINAGES
LINALOOL
LINALOOLS
LINCH
LINCHES
LINCHET
LINCHETS
LINCHPIN
LINCHPINS
LINCRUSTA
LINCRUSTAS
LINCTURE
LINCTURES
LINCTUS
LINCTUSES
LIND
LINDANE
LINDANES
LINDEN
LINDENS
LINDS
LINDWORM
LINDWORMS
LINE
LINEAGE
LINEAGES
LINEAL
LINEALITIES

LINEALITY
LINEALLY
LINEAMENT
LINEAMENTS
LINEAR
LINEARITIES
LINEARITY
LINEARLY
LINEATE
LINEATED
LINEATION
LINEATIONS
LINED
LINEMAN
LINEMEN
LINEN
LINENS
LINEOLATE
LINER
LINERS
LINES
LINESMAN
LINESMEN
LINEY
LING
LINGA
LINGAM
LINGAMS
LINGAS
LINGEL
LINGELS
LINGER
LINGERED
LINGERER
LINGERERS
LINGERIE
LINGERIES
LINGERING
LINGERINGS
LINGERS
LINGIER
LINGIEST
LINGLE
LINGLES
LINGO
LINGOES
LINGOT
LINGOTS
LINGS
LINGSTER
LINGSTERS
LINGUA
LINGUAE
LINGUAL
LINGUALLY
LINGUAS
LINGUINE
LINGUINI
LINGUIST
LINGUISTS
LINGULA
LINGULAE
LINGULAR
LINGULAS
LINGULATE
LINGY
LINHAY
LINHAYS
LINIER
LINIEST

LINIMENT
LINIMENTS
LININ
LINING
LININGS
LININS
LINK
LINKAGE
LINKAGES
LINKBOY
LINKBOYS
LINKED
LINKING
LINKMAN
LINKMEN
LINKS
LINKSTER
LINKSTERS
LINKWORK
LINKWORKS
LINN
LINNED
LINNET
LINNETS
LINNEY
LINNEYS
LINNIES
LINNING
LINNS
LINNY
LINO
LINOCUT
LINOCUTS
LINOLEUM
LINOLEUMS
LINOS
LINS
LINSANG
LINSANGS
LINSEED
LINSEEDS
LINSEY
LINSEYS
LINSTOCK
LINSTOCKS
LINT
LINTEL
LINTELLED
LINTELS
LINTER
LINTERO
LINTIE
LINTIER
LINTIES
LINTIEST
LINTS
LINTSEED
LINTSEEDS
LINTSTOCK
LINTSTOCKS
LINTWHITE
LINTWHITES
LINTY
LINY
LION
LIONCEL
LIONCELLE
LIONCELLES
LIONCELS
LIONEL

LIONELS
LIONESS
LIONESSES
LIONET
LIONETS
LIONISE
LIONISED
LIONISES
LIONISING
LIONISM
LIONISMS
LIONIZE
LIONIZED
LIONIZES
LIONIZING
LIONLY
LIONS
LIP
LIPARITE
LIPARITES
LIPASE
LIPASES
LIPECTOMIES
LIPECTOMY
LIPGLOSS
LIPGLOSSES
LIPID
LIPIDE
LIPIDES
LIPIDS
LIPLESS
LIPOGRAM
LIPOGRAMS
LIPOID
LIPOIDS
LIPOMA
LIPOMATA
LIPOSOMAL
LIPOSOME
LIPOSOMES
LIPPED
LIPPEN
LIPPENED
LIPPENING
LIPPENS
LIPPIE
LIPPIER
LIPPIES
LIPPIEST
LIPPING
LIPPITUDE
LIPPITUDES
LIPPY
LIPS
LIPSALVE
LIPSALVES
LIPSTICK
LIPSTICKED
LIPSTICKING
LIPSTICKS
LIQUABLE
LIQUATE
LIQUATED
LIQUATES
LIQUATING
LIQUATION
LIQUATIONS
LIQUEFIED
LIQUEFIER
LIQUEFIERS

LIQUEFIES
LIQUEFY
LIQUEFYING
LIQUESCE
LIQUESCED
LIQUESCES
LIQUESCING
LIQUEUR
LIQUEURED
LIQUEURING
LIQUEURS
LIQUID
LIQUIDATE
LIQUIDATED
LIQUIDATES
LIQUIDATING
LIQUIDISE
LIQUIDISED
LIQUIDISES
LIQUIDISING
LIQUIDITIES
LIQUIDITY
LIQUIDIZE
LIQUIDIZED
LIQUIDIZES
LIQUIDIZING
LIQUIDLY
LIQUIDS
LIQUIDUS
LIQUIDUSES
LIQUOR
LIQUORED
LIQUORICE
LIQUORICES
LIQUORING
LIQUORISH
LIQUORS
LIRA
LIRAS
LIRE
LIRIPIPE
LIRIPIPES
LIRIPOOP
LIRIPOOPS
LIRK
LIRKED
LIRKING
LIRKS
LIS
LISK
LISKS
LISLE
LISLES
LISP
LISPED
LISPER
LISPERS
LISPING
LISPINGLY
LISPINGS
LISPOUND
LISPOUNDS
LISPS
LISPUND
LISPUNDS
LISSES
LISSOM
LISSOME
LIST
LISTED

LISTEL
LISTELS
LISTEN
LISTENED
LISTENER
LISTENERS
LISTENING
LISTENS
LISTER
LISTERS
LISTETH
LISTFUL
LISTING
LISTINGS
LISTLESS
LISTS
LIT
LITANIES
LITANY
LITCHI
LITCHIS
LITE
LITED
LITER
LITERACIES
LITERACY
LITERAL
LITERALLY
LITERALS
LITERARY
LITERATE
LITERATES
LITERATI
LITERATIM
LITERATO
LITERATOR
LITERATORS
LITERATUS
LITEROSE
LITERS
LITES
LITH
LITHARGE
LITHARGES
LITHATE
LITHATES
LITHE
LITHED
LITHELY
LITHENESS
LITHENESSES
LITHER
LITHERLY
LITHES
LITHESOME
LITHEST
LITHIA
LITHIAS
LITHIASES
LITHIASIS
LITHIC
LITHING
LITHISTID
LITHISTIDS
LITHITE
LITHITES
LITHIUM
LITHIUMS
LITHO
LITHOCYST

LITHOCYSTS
LITHOID
LITHOIDAL
LITHOLOGIES
LITHOLOGY
LITHOPONE
LITHOPONES
LITHOS
LITHOTOME
LITHOTOMES
LITHOTOMIES
LITHOTOMY
LITHS
LITIGABLE
LITIGANT
LITIGANTS
LITIGATE
LITIGATED
LITIGATES
LITIGATING
LITIGIOUS
LITING
LITMUS
LITMUSES
LITOTES
LITRE
LITRES
LITTEN
LITTER
LITTERED
LITTERING
LITTERS
LITTERY
LITTLE
LITTLEANE
LITTLEANES
LITTLER
LITTLES
LITTLEST
LITTLIN
LITTLING
LITTLINGS
LITTLINS
LITTORAL
LITTORALS
LITURGIC
LITURGICS
LITURGIES
LITURGIST
LITURGISTS
LITURGY
LITUUS
LITUUSES
LIVABLE
LIVE
LIVEABLE
LIVED
LIVELIER
LIVELIEST
LIVELILY
LIVELOD
LIVELODS
LIVELONG
LIVELONGS
LIVELOOD
LIVELOODS
LIVELY
LIVEN
LIVENED
LIVENING

LIVENS
LIVER
LIVERIED
LIVERIES
LIVERISH
LIVERS
LIVERWORT
LIVERWORTS
LIVERY
LIVERYMAN
LIVERYMEN
LIVES
LIVESTOCK
LIVESTOCKS
LIVEWARE
LIVEWARES
LIVID
LIVIDER
LIVIDEST
LIVIDITIES
LIVIDITY
LIVIDNESS
LIVIDNESSES
LIVING
LIVINGS
LIVOR
LIVORS
LIVRAISON
LIVRAISONS
LIVRE
LIVRES
LIXIVIAL
LIXIVIATE
LIXIVIATED
LIXIVIATES
LIXIVIATING
LIXIVIOUS
LIXIVIUM
LIXIVIUMS
LIZARD
LIZARDS
LLAMA
LLAMAS
LLANERO
LLANEROS
LLANO
LLANOS
LO
LOACH
LOACHES
LOAD
LOADED
LOADEN
LOADENED
LOADENING
LOADENS
LOADER
LOADERS
LOADING
LOADINGS
LOADS
LOADSTAR
LOADSTARS
LOADSTONE
LOADSTONES
LOAF
LOAFED
LOAFER
LOAFERISH
LOAFERS

LOAFING
LOAFINGS
LOAFS
LOAM
LOAMED
LOAMIER
LOAMIEST
LOAMINESS
LOAMINESSES
LOAMING
LOAMS
LOAMY
LOAN
LOANABLE
LOANED
LOANING
LOANINGS
LOANS
LOAST
LOATH
LOATHE
LOATHED
LOATHER
LOATHERS
LOATHES
LOATHEST
LOATHFUL
LOATHIER
LOATHIEST
LOATHING
LOATHINGS
LOATHLY
LOATHSOME
LOATHY
LOAVE
LOAVED
LOAVES
LOAVING
LOB
LOBAR
LOBATE
LOBATION
LOBATIONS
LOBBED
LOBBIED
LOBBIES
LOBBING
LOBBY
LOBBYER
LOBBYERS
LOBBYING
LOBBYINGS
LOBBYIST
LOBBYISTS
LOBE
LOBECTOMIES
LOBECTOMY
LOBED
LOBELET
LOBELETS
LOBELIA
LOBELIAS
LOBELINE
LOBELINES
LOBES
LOBI
LOBING
LOBINGS
LOBIPED
LOBLOLLIES

LOBLOLLY
LOBO
LOBOS
LOBOSE
LOBOTOMIES
LOBOTOMY
LOBS
LOBSCOUSE
LOBSCOUSES
LOBSTER
LOBSTERS
LOBULAR
LOBULATE
LOBULATED
LOBULE
LOBULES
LOBULI
LOBULUS
LOBUS
LOBWORM
LOBWORMS
LOCAL
LOCALE
LOCALES
LOCALISE
LOCALISED
LOCALISER
LOCALISERS
LOCALISES
LOCALISING
LOCALISM
LOCALISMS
LOCALIST
LOCALISTS
LOCALITIES
LOCALITY
LOCALIZE
LOCALIZED
LOCALIZER
LOCALIZERS
LOCALIZES
LOCALIZING
LOCALLY
LOCALS
LOCATE
LOCATED
LOCATES
LOCATING
LOCATION
LOCATIONS
LOCATIVE
LOCATIVES
LOCELLATE
LOCH
LOCHAN
LOCHANS
LOCHIA
LOCHIAL
LOCHS
LOCI
LOCK
LOCKAGE
LOCKAGES
LOCKAWAY
LOCKAWAYS
LOCKED
LOCKER
LOCKERS
LOCKET
LOCKETS

LOCKFAST	LODGEPOLES	LOGLOG	LOMPISH	LOOF
LOCKFUL	LODGER	LOGLOGS	LONE	LOOFA
LOCKFULS	LODGERS	LOGO	LONELIER	LOOFAH
LOCKHOUSE	LODGES	LOGOGRAM	LONELIEST	LOOFAHS
LOCKHOUSES	LODGING	LOGOGRAMS	LONELY	LOOFAS
LOCKING	LODGINGS	LOGOGRAPH	LONENESS	LOOFED
LOCKMAN	LODGMENT	LOGOGRAPHS	LONENESSES	LOOFFUL
LOCKMEN	LODGMENTS	LOGOGRIPH	LONER	LOOFFULS
LOCKOUT	LODICULA	LOGOGRIPHS	LONERS	LOOFING
LOCKOUTS	LODICULAE	LOGOMACHIES	LONESOME	LOOFS
LOCKPICK	LODICULE	LOGOMACHY	LONESOMES	LOOING
LOCKPICKS	LODICULES	LOGORRHEA	LONG	LOOK
LOCKRAM	LOESS	LOGORRHEAS	LONGA	LOOKED
LOCKRAMS	LOESSES	LOGOS	LONGAEVAL	LOOKER
LOCKS	LOFT	LOGOTHETE	LONGAN	LOOKERS
LOCKSMAN	LOFTED	LOGOTHETES	LONGANS	LOOKING
LOCKSMEN	LOFTER	LOGOTYPE	LONGAS	LOOKINGS
LOCKSMITH	LOFTERS	LOGOTYPES	LONGBOAT	LOOKOUT
LOCKSMITHS	LOFTIER	LOGS	LONGBOATS	LOOKOUTS
LOCKSTEP	LOFTIEST	LOGWOOD	LONGBOW	LOOKS
LOCKSTEPS	LOFTILY	LOGWOODS	LONGBOWS	LOOM
LOCO	LOFTINESS	LOID	LONGCLOTH	LOOMED
LOCOED	LOFTINESSES	LOIDED	LONGCLOTHS	LOOMING
LOCOES	LOFTING	LOIDING	LONGE	LOOMS
LOCOFOCO	LOFTS	LOIDS	LONGED	LOON
LOCOFOCOS	LOFTY	LOIN	LONGEING	LOONIE
LOCOMAN	LOG	LOINS	LONGER	LOONIER
LOCOMEN	LOGAN	LOIPE	LONGERON	LOONIES
LOCOMOTE	LOGANS	LOIPES	LONGERONS	LOONIEST
LOCOMOTED	LOGAOEDIC	LOIR	LONGES	LOONING
LOCOMOTES	LOGARITHM	LOIRS	LONGEST	LOONINGS
LOCOMOTING	LOGARITHMS	LOITER	LONGEVAL	LOONS
LOCOMOTOR	LOGBOARD	LOITERED	LONGEVITIES	LOONY
LOCOMOTORS	LOGBOARDS	LOITERER	LONGEVITY	LOOP
LOCOS	LOGE	LOITERERS	LONGEVOUS	LOOPED
LOCULAR	LOGES	LOITERING	LONGHAND	LOOPER
LOCULATE	LOGGAT	LOITERINGS	LONGHANDS	LOOPERS
LOCULE	LOGGATS	LOITERS	LONGHORN	LOOPHOLE
LOCULES	LOGGED	LOKE	LONGHORNS	LOOPHOLED
LOCULI	LOGGER	LOKES	LONGICORN	LOOPHOLES
LOCULUS	LOGGERS	LOKSHEN	LONGICORNS	LOOPHOLING
LOCUM	LOGGIA	LOLL	LONGING	LOOPIER
LOCUMS	LOGGIAS	LOLLED	LONGINGLY	LOOPIEST
LOCUPLETE	LOGGIE	LOLLER	LONGINGS	LOOPING
LOCUS	LOGGING	LOLLERS	LONGISH	LOOPINGS
LOCUST	LOGGINGS	LOLLIES	LONGITUDE	LOOPS
LOCUSTA	LOGIA	LOLLING	LONGITUDES	LOOPY
LOCUSTAE	LOGIC	LOLLINGLY	LONGLY	LOOR
LOCUSTED	LOGICAL	LOLLIPOP	LONGNESS	LOORD
LOCUSTING	LOGICALLY	LOLLIPOPS	LONGNESSES	LOORDS
LOCUSTS	LOGICIAN	LOLLOP	LONGS	LOOS
LOCUTION	LOGICIANS	LOLLOPED	LONGSHIP	LOOSE
LOCUTIONS	LOGICISE	LOLLOPING	LONGSHIPS	LOOSED
LOCUTORIES	LOGICISED	LOLLOPS	LONGSHORE	LOOSELY
LOCUTORY	LOGICISES	LOLLS	LONGSOME	LOOSEN
LODE	LOGICISING	LOLLY	LONGUEUR	LOOSENED
LODEN	LOGICIZE	LOLLYGAG	LONGUEURS	LOOSENER
LODENS	LOGICIZED	LOLLYGAGGED	LONGWALL	LOOSENERS
LODES	LOGICIZES	LOLLYGAGGING	LONGWALLS	LOOSENESS
LODESMAN	LOGICIZING	LOLLYGAGS	LONGWAYS	LOOSENESSES
LODESMEN	LOGICS	LOLOG	LONGWISE	LOOSENING
LODESTAR	LOGIE	LOLOGS	LONICERA	LOOSENS
LODESTARS	LOGIES	LOMA	LONICERAS	LOOSER
LODESTONE	LOGION	LOMAS	LOO	LOOSES
LODESTONES	LOGISTIC	LOME	LOOBIER	LOOSEST
LODGE	LOGISTICS	LOMENT	LOOBIES	LOOSING
LODGED	LOGJUICE	LOMENTA	LOOBIEST	LOOT
LODGEMENT	LOGJUICES	LOMENTS	LOOBILY	LOOTED
LODGEMENTS	LOGLINE	LOMENTUM	LOOBY	LOOTEN
LODGEPOLE	LOGLINES	LOMES	LOOED	LOOTER

LOOTERS	LORICS	LOUDEN	LOUVER	LOWLILY
LOOTING	LORIES	LOUDENED	LOUVERED	LOWLINESS
LOOTS	LORIKEET	LOUDENING	LOUVERS	LOWLINESSES
LOOVES	LORIKEETS	LOUDENS	LOUVRE	LOWLY
LOP	LORIMER	LOUDER	LOUVRED	LOWN
LOPE	LORIMERS	LOUDEST	LOUVRES	LOWND
LOPED	LORINER	LOUDISH	LOVABLE	LOWNDED
LOPER	LORINERS	LOUDLY	LOVAGE	LOWNDING
LOPERS	LORING	LOUDMOUTH	LOVAGES	LOWNDS
LOPES	LORINGS	LOUDMOUTHS	LOVAT	LOWNE
LOPGRASS	LORIOT	LOUDNESS	LOVATS	LOWNED
LOPGRASSES	LORIOTS	LOUDNESSES	LOVE	LOWNES
LOPHODONT	LORIS	LOUGH	LOVEABLE	LOWNESS
LOPING	LORISES	LOUGHS	LOVEBIRD	LOWNESSES
LOPPED	LORN	LOUIS	LOVEBIRDS	LOWNING
LOPPER	LORRELL	LOUN	LOVEBITE	LOWNS
LOPPERED	LORRELLS	LOUND	LOVEBITES	LOWS
LOPPERING	LORRIES	LOUNDED	LOVED	LOWSE
LOPPERS	LORRY	LOUNDER	LOVELESS	LOWSER
LOPPING	LORY	LOUNDERED	LOVELIER	LOWSES
LOPPINGS	LOS	LOUNDERING	LOVELIES	LOWSEST
LOPS	LOSABLE	LOUNDERINGS	LOVELIEST	LOWSING
LOQUACITIES	LOSE	LOUNDERS	LOVELIGHT	LOWSIT
LOQUACITY	LOSED	LOUNDING	LOVELIGHTS	LOWT
LOQUAT	LOSEL	LOUNDS	LOVELILY	LOWTED
LOQUATS	LOSELS	LOUNED	LOVELOCK	LOWTING
LOQUITUR	LOSEN	LOUNGE	LOVELOCKS	LOWTS
LOR	LOSER	LOUNGED	LOVELORN	LOWVELD
LORAL	LOSERS	LOUNGER	LOVELY	LOWVELDS
LORAN	LOSES	LOUNGERS	LOVER	LOX
LORANS	LOSH	LOUNGES	LOVERED	LOXES
LORATE	LOSING	LOUNGING	LOVERLESS	LOXODROME
LORCHA	LOSINGLY	LOUNGINGS	LOVERLY	LOXODROMES
LORCHAS	LOSINGS	LOUNING	LOVERS	LOXODROMIES
LORD	LOSS	LOUNS	LOVES	LOXODROMY
LORDED	LOSSES	LOUP	LOVESICK	LOXYGEN
LORDING	LOSSIER	LOUPE	LOVESOME	LOXYGENS
LORDINGS	LOSSIEST	LOUPED	LOVEY	LOY
LORDKIN	LOSSY	LOUPEN	LOVEYS	LOYAL
LORDKINS	LOST	LOUPES	LOVING	LOYALIST
LORDLESS	LOT	LOUPING	LOVINGLY	LOYALISTS
LORDLIER	LOTA	LOUPIT	LOVINGS	LOYALLER
LORDLIEST	LOTAH	LOUPS	LOW	LOYALLEST
LORDLING	LOTAHS	LOUR	LOWAN	LOYALLY
LORDLINGS	LOTAS	LOURE	LOWANS	LOYALTIES
LORDLY	LOTE	LOURED	LOWBOY	LOYALTY
LORDOSES	LOTES	LOURES	LOWBOYS	LOYS
LORDOSIS	LOTH	LOURIER	LOWE	LOZELL
LORDOTIC	LOTHEFULL	LOURIEST	LOWED	LOZELLS
LORDS	LOTHER	LOURING	LOWER	LOZEN
LORDSHIP	LOTHEST	LOURINGLY	LOWERED	LOZENGE
LORDSHIPS	LOTHFULL	LOURINGS	LOWERIER	LOZENGED
LORDY	LOTIC	LOURS	LOWERIEST	LOZENGES
LORE	LOTION	LOURY	LOWERING	LOZENGY
LOREL	LOTIONS	LOUSE	LOWERINGS	LOZENS
LORELS	LOTO	LOUSED	LOWERMOST	LUAU
LORES	LOTOS	LOUSES	LOWERS	LUAUS
LORETTE	LOTOSES	LOUSIER	LOWERY	LUBBARD
LORETTES	LOTS	LOUSIEST	LOWES	LUBBARDS
LORGNETTE	LOTTED	LOUSILY	LOWEST	LUBBER
LORGNETTES	LOTTERIES	LOUSINESS	LOWING	LUBBERLY
LORGNON	LOTTERY	LOUSINESSES	LOWINGS	LUBBERS
LORGNONS	LOTTING	LOUSING	LOWLAND	LUBFISH
LORIC	LOTTO	LOUSY	LOWLANDER	LUBFISHES
LORICA	LOTTOS	LOUT	LOWLANDERS	LUBRA
LORICAE	LOTUS	LOUTED	LOWLANDS	LUBRAS
LORICATE	LOTUSES	LOUTING	LOWLIER	LUBRIC
LORICATED	LOUCHE	LOUTISH	LOWLIEST	LUBRICAL
LORICATES	LOUCHELY	LOUTISHLY	LOWLIHEAD	LUBRICANT
LORICATING	LOUD	LOUTS	LOWLIHEADS	LUBRICANTS

LUBRICATE	LUFFA	LUMINANT	LUNCHES	LURGY
LUBRICATED	LUFFAS	LUMINANTS	LUNCHING	LURID
LUBRICATES	LUFFED	LUMINARIES	LUNE	LURIDER
LUBRICATING	LUFFING	LUMINARY	LUNES	LURIDEST
LUBRICITIES	LUFFS	LUMINE	LUNETTE	LURIDLY
LUBRICITY	LUG	LUMINED	LUNETTES	LURIDNESS
LUBRICOUS	LUGE	LUMINES	LUNG	LURIDNESSES
LUCARNE	LUGED	LUMINESCE	LUNGE	LURING
LUCARNES	LUGEING	LUMINESCED	LUNGED	LURK
LUCE	LUGEINGS	LUMINESCES	LUNGEING	LURKED
LUCENCIES	LUGES	LUMINESCING	LUNGES	LURKER
LUCENCY	LUGGAGE	LUMINING	LUNGFUL	LURKERS
LUCENT	LUGGAGES	LUMINIST	LUNGFULS	LURKING
LUCERN	LUGGED	LUMINISTS	LUNGI	LURKINGS
LUCERNE	LUGGER	LUMINOUS	LUNGIE	LURKS
LUCERNES	LUGGERS	LUMME	LUNGIES	LURRIES
LUCERNS	LUGGIE	LUMMIER	LUNGING	LURRY
LUCES	LUGGIES	LUMMIEST	LUNGIS	LURS
LUCID	LUGGING	LUMMOX	LUNGS	LUSCIOUS
LUCIDER	LUGING	LUMMOXES	LUNGWORT	LUSH
LUCIDEST	LUGINGS	LUMMY	LUNGWORTS	LUSHED
LUCIDITIES	LUGS	LUMP	LUNISOLAR	LUSHER
LUCIDITY	LUGSAIL	LUMPED	LUNITIDAL	LUSHERS
LUCIDLY	LUGSAILS	LUMPEN	LUNKER	LUSHES
LUCIDNESS	LUGWORM	LUMPENLY	LUNKERS	LUSHEST
LUCIDNESSES	LUGWORMS	LUMPER	LUNKHEAD	LUSHIER
LUCIFER	LUIT	LUMPERS	LUNKHEADS	LUSHIEST
LUCIFERIN	LUITEN	LUMPFISH	LUNT	LUSHING
LUCIFERINS	LUKE	LUMPFISHES	LUNTED	LUSHLY
LUCIFERS	LUKEWARM	LUMPIER	LUNTING	LUSHNESS
LUCIGEN	LULL	LUMPIEST	LUNTS	LUSHNESSES
LUCIGENS	LULLABIED	LUMPILY	LUNULA	LUSHY
LUCK	LULLABIES	LUMPINESS	LUNULAR	LUSK
LUCKEN	LULLABY	LUMPINESSES	LUNULAS	LUSKED
LUCKIE	LULLADYING	LUMPING	LUNULATE	LUSKING
LUCKIER	LULLED	LUMPISH	LUNULATED	LUSKISH
LUCKIES	LULLING	LUMPISHLY	LUNULE	LUSKS
LUCKIEST	LULLS	LUMPKIN	LUNULES	LUST
LUCKILY	LULU	LUMPKINS	LUNYIE	LUSTED
LUCKINESS	LULUS	LUMPS	LUNYIES	LUSTER
LUCKINESSES	LUM	LUMPY	LUPIN	LUSTERED
LUCKLESS	LUMBAGO	LUNACIES	LUPINE	LUSTERING
LUCKS	LUMBAGOS	LUNACY	LUPINES	LUSTERS
LUCKY	LUMBANG	LUNANAUT	LUPINS	LUSTFUL
LUCRATIVE	LUMBANGS	LUNANAUTS	LUPPEN	LUSTFULLY
LUCRE	LUMBAR	LUNAR	LUPULIN	LUSTICK
LUCRES	LUMBER	LUNARIAN	LUPULINE	LUSTIER
LUCTATION	LUMBERED	LUNARIANS	LUPULINIC	LUSTIEST
LUCTATIONS	LUMBERER	LUNARIES	LUPULINS	LUSTIHEAD
LUCUBRATE	LUMBERERS	LUNARIST	LUPUS	LUSTIHEADS
LUCUBRATED	LUMBERING	LUNARISTS	LUPUSES	LUSTIHOOD
LUCUBRATES	LUMBERINGS	LUNARNAUT	LUR	LUSTIHOODS
LUCUBRATING	LUMBERLY	LUNARNAUTS	LURCH	LUSTILY
LUCULENT	LUMBERMAN	LUNARS	LURCHED	LUSTINESS
LUCUMA	LUMBERMEN	LUNARY	LURCHER	LUSTINESSES
LUCUMAS	LUMBERS	LUNATE	LURCHERS	LUSTING
LUCUMO	LUMBRICAL	LUNATED	LURCHES	LUSTIQUE
LUCUMONES	LUMBRICALS	LUNATIC	LURCHING	LUSTLESS
LUCUMOS	LUMBRICI	LUNATICS	LURDAN	LUSTRA
LUD	LUMBRICUS	LUNATION	LURDANE	LUSTRAL
LUDIC	LUMBRICUSES	LUNATIONS	LURDANES	LUSTRATE
LUDICROUS	LUMEN	LUNCH	LURDANS	LUSTRATED
LUDO	LUMENAL	LUNCHED	LURDEN	LUSTRATES
LUDOS	LUMENS	LUNCHEON	LURDENS	LUSTRATING
LUDS	LUMINA	LUNCHEONED	LURE	LUSTRE
LUDSHIP	LUMINAIRE	LUNCHEONING	LURED	LUSTRED
LUDSHIPS	LUMINAIRES	LUNCHEONS	LURES	LUSTRES
LUES	LUMINAL	LUNCHER	LURGI	LUSTRINE
LUETIC	LUMINANCE	LUNCHERS	LURGIES	LUSTRINES
LUFF	LUMINANCES		LURGIS	LUSTRING

LUSTRINGS
LUSTROUS
LUSTRUM
LUSTRUMS
LUSTS
LUSTY
LUTANIST
LUTANISTS
LUTE
LUTEAL
LUTECIUM
LUTECIUMS
LUTED
LUTEIN
LUTEINISE
LUTEINISED
LUTEINISES
LUTEINISING
LUTEINIZE
LUTEINIZED
LUTEINIZES
LUTEINIZING
LUTEINS
LUTENIST
LUTENISTS
LUTEOLIN
LUTEOLINS
LUTEOLOUS
LUTEOUS
LUTER
LUTERS
LUTES
LUTESCENT
LUTETIUM
LUTETIUMS
LUTHERN
LUTHERNS

LUTHIER
LUTHIERS
LUTING
LUTINGS
LUTIST
LUTISTS
LUTTEN
LUTZ
LUTZES
LUX
LUXATE
LUXATED
LUXATES
LUXATING
LUXATION
LUXATIONS
LUXE
LUXES
LUXMETER
LUXMETERS
LUXURIANT
LUXURIATE
LUXURIATED
LUXURIATES
LUXURIATING
LUXURIES
LUXURIOUS
LUXURIST
LUXURISTS
LUXURY
LUZ
LUZERN
LUZERNS
LUZZES
LYAM
LYAMS
LYART

LYCÉE
LYCÉES
LYCEUM
LYCEUMS
LYCHEE
LYCHEES
LYCHGATE
LYCHGATES
LYCHNIS
LYCHNISES
LYCOPOD
LYCOPODS
LYDDITE
LYDDITES
LYE
LYES
LYFULL
LYING
LYINGLY
LYINGS
LYKEWAKE
LYKEWAKES
LYKEWALK
LYKEWALKS
LYM
LYME
LYMES
LYMITER
LYMITERS
LYMPH
LYMPHAD
LYMPHADS
LYMPHATIC
LYMPHATICS
LYMPHOID
LYMPHOMA
LYMPHOMAS

LYMPHS
LYMS
LYNAGE
LYNAGES
LYNCEAN
LYNCH
LYNCHED
LYNCHES
LYNCHET
LYNCHETS
LYNCHING
LYNCHPIN
LYNCHPINS
LYNE
LYNES
LYNX
LYNXES
LYOMEROUS
LYOPHIL
LYOPHILE
LYOPHILIC
LYOPHOBE
LYOPHOBIC
LYRATE
LYRATED
LYRE
LYRES
LYRIC
LYRICAL
LYRICALLY
LYRICISM
LYRICISMS
LYRICIST
LYRICISTS
LYRICS
LYRIFORM
LYRISM

LYRISMS
LYRIST
LYRISTS
LYSE
LYSED
LYSERGIDE
LYSERGIDES
LYSES
LYSIGENIC
LYSIMETER
LYSIMETERS
LYSIN
LYSINE
LYSINES
LYSING
LYSINS
LYSIS
LYSOL
LYSOLS
LYSOSOME
LYSOSOMES
LYSOZYME
LYSOZYMES
LYSSA
LYSSAS
LYTE
LYTED
LYTES
LYTHE
LYTHES
LYTING
LYTTA
LYTTAS

M

MA
MAAR
MAARS
MAC
MACABRE
MACACO
MACACOS
MACADAM
MACADAMIA
MACADAMIAS
MACADAMS
MACAHUBA
MACAHUBAS
MACAQUE
MACAQUES
MACARISE
MACARISED
MACARISES
MACARISING
MACARISM
MACARISMS
MACARIZE
MACARIZED
MACARIZES
MACARIZING
MACARONI
MACARONIC
MACARONICS
MACARONIES
MACARONIS
MACAROON
MACAROONS
MACAW
MACAWS
MACCHIE
MACE
MACED
MACÉDOINE
MACÉDOINES
MACER
MACERATE
MACERATED
MACERATES
MACERATING
MACERATOR
MACERATORS
MACERS
MACES
MACHAIR
MACHAIRS
MACHAN
MACHANS
MACHETE
MACHETES
MACHINATE
MACHINATED
MACHINATES
MACHINATING
MACHINE
MACHINED
MACHINERIES
MACHINERY
MACHINES

MACHINING
MACHINIST
MACHINISTS
MACHISMO
MACHISMOS
MACHMETER
MACHMETERS
MACHO
MACHOS
MACHREE
MACHREES
MACHZOR
MACHZORIM
MACING
MACINTOSH
MACINTOSHES
MACK
MACKEREL
MACKERELS
MACKINAW
MACKINAWS
MACKLE
MACKLED
MACKLES
MACKLING
MACKS
MACLE
MACLED
MACLES
MACOYA
MACOYAS
MACRAMÉ
MACRAMÉS
MACRAMI
MACRAMIS
MACRO
MACROBIAN
MACROCODE
MACROCODES
MACROCOPIES
MACROCOPY
MACROCOSM
MACROCOSMS
MACROCYTE
MACROCYTES
MACRODOME
MACRODOMES
MACROLOGIES
MACROLOGY
MACRON
MACRONS
MACROPOD
MACROPODS
MACROS
MACRURAL
MACRUROUS
MACS
MACTATION
MACTATIONS
MACULA
MACULAE
MACULAR
MACULATE

MACULATED
MACULATES
MACULATING
MACULE
MACULES
MACULOSE
MAD
MADAM
MADAME
MADAMED
MADAMING
MADAMS
MADAROSES
MADAROSIS
MADBRAIN
MADCAP
MADCAPS
MADDED
MADDEN
MADDENED
MADDENING
MADDENS
MADDER
MADDERS
MADDEST
MADDING
MADDINGLY
MADE
MADEFIED
MADEFIES
MADEFY
MADEFYING
MADELEINE
MADELEINES
MADERISE
MADERISED
MADERISES
MADERISING
MADERIZE
MADERIZED
MADERIZES
MADERIZING
MADGE
MADQEO
MADHOUSE
MADHOUSES
MADID
MADLING
MADLINGS
MADLY
MADMAN
MADMEN
MADNESS
MADNESSES
MADOQUA
MADOQUAS
MADRAS
MADRASA
MADRASAH
MADRASAHS
MADRASAS
MADRASES
MADRASSA

MADRASSAH
MADRASSAHS
MADRASSAS
MADREPORE
MADREPORES
MADRIGAL
MADRIGALS
MADROÑA
MADROÑAS
MADROÑO
MADROÑOS
MADS
MADWOMAN
MADWOMEN
MADWORT
MADWORTS
MADZOON
MADZOONS
MAE
MAELSTROM
MAELSTROMS
MAENAD
MAENADIC
MAENADS
MAESTOSO
MAESTRI
MAESTRO
MAESTROS
MAFFIA
MAFFIAS
MAFFICK
MAFFICKED
MAFFICKER
MAFFICKERS
MAFFICKING
MAFFICKINGS
MAFFICKS
MAFFLED
MAFFLIN
MAFFLING
MAFFLINGS
MAFFLINS
MAFIA
MAFIAS
MAFIOSI
MAFIOSO
MAG
MAGAZINE
MAGAZINES
MAGDALEN
MAGDALENE
MAGDALENES
MAGDALENS
MAGE
MAGENTA
MAGENTAS
MAGES
MAGESHIP
MAGESHIPS
MAGG
MAGGED
MAGGING
MAGGOT

MAGGOTS
MAGGOTY
MAGGS
MAGI
MAGIAN
MAGIANISM
MAGIANISMS
MAGIANS
MAGIC
MAGICAL
MAGICALLY
MAGICIAN
MAGICIANS
MAGICKED
MAGICKING
MAGICS
MAGILP
MAGILPS
MAGISM
MAGISMS
MAGISTER
MAGISTERIES
MAGISTERS
MAGISTERY
MAGISTRAL
MAGISTRALS
MAGLEV
MAGMA
MAGMAS
MAGMATA
MAGMATIC
MAGNALIUM
MAGNALIUMS
MAGNATE
MAGNATES
MAGNES
MAGNESES
MAGNESIA
MAGNESIAN
MAGNESIAS
MAGNESITE
MAGNESITES
MAGNESIUM
MAGNESIUMS
MAGNET
MAGNETIC
MAGNETICS
MAGNETISE
MAGNETISED
MAGNETISES
MAGNETISING
MAGNETISM
MAGNETISMS
MAGNETIST
MAGNETISTS
MAGNETITE
MAGNETITES
MAGNETIZE
MAGNETIZED
MAGNETIZES
MAGNETIZING
MAGNETO
MAGNETON

MAGNETONS	MAIDED	MAINORS	MAKIMONO	MALIC
MAGNETOS	MAIDEN	MAINOUR	MAKIMONOS	MALICE
MAGNETRON	MAIDENISH	MAINOURS	MAKING	MALICED
MAGNETRONS	MAIDENLY	MAINPRISE	MAKINGS	MALICES
MAGNETS	MAIDENS	MAINPRISES	MAKO	MALICHO
MAGNIFIC	MAIDHOOD	MAINS	MAKOS	MALICHOS
MAGNIFICO	MAIDHOODS	MAINSAIL	MAKS	MALICING
MAGNIFICOES	MAIDING	MAINSAILS	MAL	MALICIOUS
MAGNIFIED	MAIDISH	MAINSHEET	MALACHITE	MALIGN
MAGNIFIER	MAIDISM	MAINSHEETS	MALACHITES	MALIGNANT
MAGNIFIERS	MAIDISMS	MAINSTAY	MALACIA	MALIGNANTS
MAGNIFIES	MAIDLESS	MAINSTAYS	MALACIAS	MALIGNED
MAGNIFY	MAIDS	MAINTAIN	MALADIES	MALIGNER
MAGNIFYING	MAIEUTIC	MAINTAINED	MALADROIT	MALIGNERS
MAGNITUDE	MAIEUTICS	MAINTAINING	MALADY	MALIGNING
MAGNITUDES	MAIGRE	MAINTAINS	MALAGUEÑA	MALIGNITIES
MAGNOLIA	MAIGRES	MAINTOP	MALAGUEÑAS	MALIGNITY
MAGNOLIAS	MAIK	MAINTOPS	MALAISE	MALIGNLY
MAGNOX	MAIKO	MAINYARD	MALAISES	MALIGNS
MAGNOXES	MAIKOS	MAINYARDS	MALAMUTE	MALINGER
MAGNUM	MAIKS	MAIOLICA	MALAMUTES	MALINGERED
MAGNUMS	MAIL	MAIOLICAS	MALANDER	MALINGERIES
MAGOT	MAILABLE	MAIRE	MALANDERS	MALINGERING
MAGOTS	MAILE	MAIRES	MALAPERT	MALINGERS
MAGPIE	MAILED	MAISE	MALAR	MALINGERY
MAGPIES	MAILER	MAISES	MALARIA	MALIS
MAGS	MAILERS	MAIST	MALARIAL	MALISON
MAGSMAN	MAILES	MAISTER	MALARIAN	MALISONS
MAGSMEN	MAILING	MAISTERED	MALARIAS	MALIST
MAGUEY	MAILINGS	MAISTERING	MALARIOUS	MALKIN
MAGUEYS	MAILLOT	MAISTERS	MALARKEY	MALKINS
MAGUS	MAILLOTS	MAISTRIES	MALARKEYS	MALL
MAGYAR	MAILMAN	MAISTRING	MALARKIES	MALLAM
MAHARAJA	MAILMEN	MAISTRINGS	MALARKY	MALLAMS
MAHARAJAH	MAILMERGE	MAISTRY	MALARS	MALLANDER
MAHARAJAHS	MAILMERGED	MAIZE	MALATE	MALLANDERS
MAHARAJAS	MAILMERGES	MAIZES	MALATES	MALLARD
MAHARANEE	MAILMERGING	MAJESTIC	MALAX	MALLARDS
MAHARANEES	MAILS	MAJESTIES	MALAXAGE	MALLEABLE
MAHARANI	MAIM	MAJESTY	MALAXAGES	MALLEATE
MAHARANIS	MAIMED	MAJOLICA	MALAXATE	MALLEATED
MAHARISHI	MAIMING	MAJOLICAS	MALAXATED	MALLEATES
MAHARISHIS	MAIMINGS	MAJOR	MALAXATES	MALLEATING
MAHATMA	MAIMS	MAJORAT	MALAXATING	MALLECHO
MAHATMAS	MAIN	MAJORATS	MALAXATOR	MALLECHOS
MAHLSTICK	MAINBOOM	MAJORED	MALAXATORS	MALLED
MAHLSTICKS	MAINBOOMS	MAJORETTE	MALAXED	MALLEE
MAHMAL	MAINBRACE	MAJORETTES	MALAXES	MALLEES
MAHMALS	MAINBRACES	MAJORING	MALAXING	MALLEI
MAHOE	MAINDOOR	MAJORITIES	MALE	MALLEMUCK
MAHOES	MAINDOORS	MAJORITY	MALEATE	MALLEMUCKS
MAHOGANIES	MAINED	MAJORS	MALEATES	MALLENDER
MAHOGANY	MAINER	MAJORSHIP	MALEDICT	MALLENDERS
MAHONIA	MAINEST	MAJORSHIPS	MALEDICTED	MALLEOLAR
MAHONIAS	MAINFRAME	MAJUSCULE	MALEDICTING	MALLEOLI
MAHOUT	MAINFRAMES	MAJUSCULES	MALEDICTS	MALLEOLUS
MAHOUTS	MAINING	MAK	MALEFIC	MALLEOLUSES
MAHSEER	MAINLAND	MAKABLE	MALEFICE	MALLET
MAHSEERS	MAINLANDS	MAKAR	MALEFICES	MALLETS
MAHSIR	MAINLINE	MAKARS	MALEIC	MALLEUS
MAHSIRS	MAINLINED	MAKE	MALEMUTE	MALLEUSES
MAHUA	MAINLINER	MAKEABLE	MALEMUTES	MALLING
MAHUAS	MAINLINERS	MAKEBATE	MALENGINE	MALLOW
MAHWA	MAINLINES	MAKEBATES	MALENGINES	MALLOWS
MAHWAS	MAINLINING	MAKELESS	MALES	MALLS
MAHZOR	MAINLININGS	MAKER	MALFORMED	MALM
MAHZORIM	MAINLY	MAKERS	MALGRADO	MALMAG
MAID	MAINMAST	MAKES	MALGRE	MALMAGS
MAIDAN	MAINMASTS	MAKESHIFT	MALGRES	MALMS
MAIDANS	MAINOR	MAKESHIFTS	MALI	MALMSEY

MALMSEYS
MALODOUR
MALODOURS
MALONATE
MALONATES
MALS
MALSTICK
MALSTICKS
MALT
MALTALENT
MALTALENTS
MALTASE
MALTASES
MALTED
MALTHA
MALTHAS
MALTIER
MALTIEST
MALTING
MALTINGS
MALTMAN
MALTMEN
MALTOSE
MALTOSES
MALTREAT
MALTREATED
MALTREATING
MALTREATS
MALTS
MALTSTER
MALTSTERS
MALTWORM
MALTWORMS
MALTY
MALVA
MALVAS
MALVASIA
MALVASIAS
MALVESIE
MALVESIES
MALVOISIE
MALVOISIES
MAM
MAMA
MAMAS
MAMBA
MAMBAS
MAMBO
MAMBOED
MAMBOING
MAMBOS
MAMELON
MAMELONS
MAMELUCO
MAMELUCOS
MAMILLA
MAMILLAE
MAMILLAR
MAMILLARY
MAMILLATE
MAMMA
MAMMAE
MAMMAL
MAMMALIAN
MAMMALOGIES
MAMMALOGY
MAMMALS
MAMMARY
MAMMAS
MAMMATE

MAMMEE
MAMMEES
MAMMER
MAMMERED
MAMMERING
MAMMERS
MAMMET
MAMMETRIES
MAMMETRY
MAMMETS
MAMMIES
MAMMIFER
MAMMIFERS
MAMMIFORM
MAMMILLA
MAMMILLAE
MAMMOCK
MAMMOCKED
MAMMOCKING
MAMMOCKS
MAMMOGRAM
MAMMOGRAMS
MAMMON
MAMMONISH
MAMMONISM
MAMMONISMS
MAMMONIST
MAMMONISTS
MAMMONITE
MAMMONITES
MAMMONS
MAMMOTH
MAMMOTHS
MAMMY
MAMS
MAMSELLE
MAMSELLES
MAN
MANA
MANACLE
MANACLED
MANACLES
MANACLING
MANAGE
MANAGED
MANAGER
MANAGERS
MANAGES
MANAGING
MANAKIN
MANAKINS
MAÑANA
MAÑANAS
MANAS
MANATEE
MANATEES
MANATI
MANATIS
MANCANDO
MANCHE
MANCHES
MANCHET
MANCHETS
MANCIPATE
MANCIPATED
MANCIPATES
MANCIPATING
MANCIPLE
MANCIPLES
MANCUS

MANCUSES
MAND
MANDALA
MANDALAS
MANDAMUS
MANDAMUSES
MANDARIN
MANDARINE
MANDARINES
MANDARINS
MANDATARIES
MANDATARY
MANDATE
MANDATED
MANDATES
MANDATING
MANDATOR
MANDATORIES
MANDATORS
MANDATORY
MANDIBLE
MANDIBLES
MANDILION
MANDILIONS
MANDIOC
MANDIOCA
MANDIOCAS
MANDIOCCA
MANDIOCCAS
MANDIOCS
MANDIR
MANDIRA
MANDIRAS
MANDIRS
MANDOLA
MANDOLAS
MANDOLIN
MANDOLINE
MANDOLINES
MANDOLINS
MANDOM
MANDOMS
MANDORA
MANDORAS
MANDORLA
MANDORLAS
MANDRAKE
MANDRAKES
MANDREL
MANDRELS
MANDRIL
MANDRILL
MANDRILLS
MANDRILS
MANDUCATE
MANDUCATED
MANDUCATES
MANDUCATING
MANDYLION
MANDYLIONS
MANE
MANED
MANÈGE
MANÈGED
MANÈGES
MANÈGING
MANEH
MANEHS
MANELESS
MANENT

MANES
MANET
MANEUVER
MANEUVERED
MANEUVERING
MANEUVERS
MANFUL
MANFULLY
MANGABEY
MANGABEYS
MANGAL
MANGALS
MANGANATE
MANGANATES
MANGANESE
MANGANESES
MANGANIC
MANGANITE
MANGANITES
MANGANOUS
MANGE
MANGEL
MANGELS
MANGER
MANGERS
MANGES
MANGETOUT
MANGETOUTS
MANGEY
MANGIER
MANGIEST
MANGINESS
MANGINESSES
MANGLE
MANGLED
MANGLER
MANGLERS
MANGLES
MANGLING
MANGO
MANGOES
MANGOLD
MANGOLDS
MANGONEL
MANGONELS
MANGOSTAN
MANGOSTANS
MANGOUSTE
MANGOUSTES
MANGROVE
MANGROVES
MANGY
MANHANDLE
MANHANDLED
MANHANDLES
MANHANDLING
MANHOLE
MANHOLES
MANHOOD
MANHOODS
MANHUNT
MANHUNTS
MANIA
MANIAC
MANIACAL
MANIACS
MANIAS
MANIC
MANICALLY
MANICURE

MANICURED
MANICURES
MANICURING
MANIES
MANIFEST
MANIFESTED
MANIFESTING
MANIFESTO
MANIFESTOED
MANIFESTOES
MANIFESTOING
MANIFESTOS
MANIFESTS
MANIFOLD
MANIFOLDED
MANIFOLDING
MANIFOLDS
MANIFORM
MANIHOC
MANIHOCS
MANIKIN
MANIKINS
MANILA
MANILAS
MANILLA
MANILLAS
MANILLE
MANILLES
MANIOC
MANIOCS
MANIPLE
MANIPLES
MANIPLIES
MANIPULAR
MANIPULARS
MANITO
MANITOS
MANITOU
MANITOUS
MANJACK
MANJACKS
MANKIER
MANKIEST
MANKIND
MANKINDS
MANKY
MANLIER
MANLIEST
MANLINESS
MANLINESSES
MANLY
MANNA
MANNAS
MANNED
MANNEQUIN
MANNEQUINS
MANNER
MANNERED
MANNERISM
MANNERISMS
MANNERIST
MANNERISTS
MANNERLY
MANNERS
MANNIKIN
MANNIKINS
MANNING
MANNISH
MANNITE
MANNITES

MANNITOL
MANNITOLS
MANNOSE
MANNOSES
MANOAO
MANOAOS
MANOEUVRE
MANOEUVRED
MANOEUVRES
MANOEUVRING
MANOMETER
MANOMETERS
MANOMETRIES
MANOMETRY
MANOR
MANORIAL
MANORS
MANPACK
MANPACKS
MANPOWER
MANPOWERS
MANQUÉ
MANRED
MANREDS
MANRENT
MANRENTS
MANRIDER
MANRIDERS
MANS
MANSARD
MANSARDS
MANSE
MANSES
MANSHIFT
MANSHIFTS
MANSION
MANSIONS
MANSONRIES
MANSONRY
MANSUETE
MANSWORN
MANTA
MANTAS
MANTEAU
MANTEAUS
MANTEAUX
MANTEEL
MANTEELS
MANTEL
MANTELET
MANTELETS
MANTELS
MANTIC
MANTICORA
MANTICORAS
MANTICORE
MANTICORES
MANTID
MANTIDS
MANTIES
MANTILLA
MANTILLAS
MANTIS
MANTISES
MANTISSA
MANTISSAS
MANTLE
MANTLED
MANTLES
MANTLET

MANTLETS
MANTLING
MANTLINGS
MANTO
MANTOES
MANTOS
MANTRA
MANTRAM
MANTRAMS
MANTRAP
MANTRAPS
MANTRAS
MANTUA
MANTUAS
MANTY
MANUAL
MANUALLY
MANUALS
MANUBRIA
MANUBRIAL
MANUBRIUM
MANUKA
MANUKAS
MANUL
MANULS
MANUMIT
MANUMITS
MANUMITTED
MANUMITTING
MANURANCE
MANURANCES
MANURE
MANURED
MANURER
MANURERS
MANURES
MANURIAL
MANURING
MANURINGS
MANUS
MANY
MANYFOLD
MANYPLIES
MANZANITA
MANZANITAS
MANZELLO
MANZELLOS
MAORMOR
MAORMORS
MAP
MAPLE
MAPLES
MAPPED
MAPPEMOND
MAPPEMONDS
MAPPER
MAPPERIES
MAPPERS
MAPPERY
MAPPING
MAPPIST
MAPPISTS
MAPS
MAPSTICK
MAPSTICKS
MAPWISE
MAQUETTE
MAQUETTES
MAQUI
MAQUIS

MAQUISARD
MAQUISARDS
MAR
MARA
MARABOU
MARABOUS
MARABOUT
MARABOUTS
MARACA
MARACAS
MARAGING
MARAGINGS
MARAH
MARAHS
MARAS
MARASMIC
MARASMUS
MARASMUSES
MARATHON
MARATHONS
MARAUD
MARAUDED
MARAUDER
MARAUDERS
MARAUDING
MARAUDS
MARAVEDI
MARAVEDIS
MARBLE
MARBLED
MARBLER
MARBLERS
MARBLES
MARBLIER
MARBLIEST
MARBLING
MARBLINGS
MARBLY
MARC
MARCASITE
MARCASITES
MARCATO
MARCEL
MARCELLA
MARCELLAS
MARCELLED
MARCELLING
MARCELS
MARCH
MARCHED
MARCHER
MARCHERS
MARCHES
MARCHESA
MARCHESAS
MARCHESE
MARCHESES
MARCHESI
MARCHING
MARCHMAN
MARCHMEN
MARCHPANE
MARCHPANES
MARCONI
MARCONIED
MARCONIING
MARCONIS
MARCS
MARD
MARDIED

MARDIER
MARDIES
MARDIEST
MARDY
MARDYING
MARE
MAREMMA
MAREMMAS
MARES
MARESCHAL
MARESCHALLED
MARESCHALLING
MARESCHALS
MARG
MARGARIC
MARGARIN
MARGARINE
MARGARINES
MARGARINS
MARGARITA
MARGARITAS
MARGARITE
MARGARITES
MARGAY
MARGAYS
MARGE
MARGENT
MARGENTED
MARGENTING
MARGENTS
MARGES
MARGIN
MARGINAL
MARGINALS
MARGINATE
MARGINED
MARGINING
MARGINS
MARGOSA
MARGOSAS
MARGRAVE
MARGRAVES
MARGS
MARIA
MARIACHI
MARIACHIS
MARIALITE
MARIALITES
MARID
MARIDS
MARIGOLD
MARIGOLDS
MARIGRAM
MARIGRAMS
MARIGRAPH
MARIGRAPHS
MARIHUANA
MARIHUANAS
MARIJUANA
MARIJUANAS
MARIMBA
MARIMBAS
MARINA
MARINADE
MARINADED
MARINADES
MARINADING
MARINAS
MARINATE
MARINATED

MARINATES
MARINATING
MARINE
MARINER
MARINERS
MARINES
MARINIÈRE
MARIPOSA
MARIPOSAS
MARISCHAL
MARISCHALLED
MARISCHALLING
MARISCHALS
MARISH
MARISHES
MARITAGE
MARITAGES
MARITAL
MARITALLY
MARITIME
MARJORAM
MARJORAMS
MARK
MARKED
MARKEDLY
MARKER
MARKERS
MARKET
MARKETED
MARKETEER
MARKETEERS
MARKETER
MARKETERS
MARKETING
MARKETINGS
MARKETS
MARKHOR
MARKHORS
MARKING
MARKINGS
MARKKA
MARKKAA
MARKKAS
MARKMAN
MARKMEN
MARKS
MARKSMAN
MARKSMEN
MARL
MARLE
MARLED
MARLES
MARLIER
MARLIEST
MARLIN
MARLINE
MARLINES
MARLING
MARLINGS
MARLINS
MARLS
MARLSTONE
MARLSTONES
MARLY
MARM
MARMALADE
MARMALADES
MARMARISE
MARMARISED
MARMARISES

MARMARISING
MARMARIZE
MARMARIZED
MARMARIZES
MARMARIZING
MARMITE
MARMITES
MARMOREAL
MARMOSE
MARMOSES
MARMOSET
MARMOSETS
MARMOT
MARMOTS
MARMS
MAROCAIN
MAROCAINS
MAROON
MAROONED
MAROONER
MAROONERS
MAROONING
MAROONINGS
MAROONS
MAROQUIN
MAROQUINS
MAROR
MARORS
MARPLOT
MARPLOTS
MARQUE
MARQUEE
MARQUEES
MARQUES
MARQUESS
MARQUESSES
MARQUETRIES
MARQUETRY
MARQUIS
MARQUISE
MARQUISES
MARRAM
MARRAMS
MARRED
MARRELS
MARRIAGE
MARRIAGES
MARRIED
MARRIER
MARRIERS
MARRIES
MARRING
MARROW
MARROWED
MARROWFAT
MARROWFATS
MARROWING
MARROWISH
MARROWS
MARROWSKIED
MARROWSKIES
MARROWSKY
MARROWSKYING
MARROWY
MARRUM
MARRUMS
MARRY
MARRYING
MARRYINGS
MARS

MARSH
MARSHAL
MARSHALCIES
MARSHALCY
MARSHALLED
MARSHALLING
MARSHALLINGS
MARSHALS
MARSHES
MARSHIER
MARSHIEST
MARSHLAND
MARSHLANDS
MARSHWORT
MARSHWORTS
MARSHY
MARSUPIA
MARSUPIAL
MARSUPIALS
MARSUPIUM
MARSUPIUMS
MART
MARTAGON
MARTAGONS
MARTED
MARTEL
MARTELLED
MARTELLING
MARTELLO
MARTELLOS
MARTELS
MARTEN
MARTENOT
MARTENOTS
MARTENS
MARTIAL
MARTIALLY
MARTIN
MARTINET
MARTINETS
MARTING
MARTINI
MARTINIS
MARTINS
MARTLET
MARTLETS
MARTS
MARTYR
MARTYRDOM
MARTYRDOMS
MARTYRED
MARTYRIES
MARTYRING
MARTYRISE
MARTYRISED
MARTYRISES
MARTYRISING
MARTYRIZE
MARTYRIZED
MARTYRIZES
MARTYRIZING
MARTYRS
MARTYRY
MARVEL
MARVELLED
MARVELLING
MARVELS
MARYBUD
MARYBUDS
MARZIPAN

MARZIPANS
MAS
MASCARA
MASCARAS
MASCARON
MASCARONS
MASCLE
MASCLED
MASCLES
MASCON
MASCONS
MASCOT
MASCOTS
MASCULINE
MASCULINES
MASCULY
MASE
MASED
MASER
MASERS
MASES
MASH
MASHALLAH
MASHED
MASHER
MASHERS
MASHES
MASHIE
MASHIER
MASHIES
MASHIEST
MASHING
MASHINGS
MASHLAM
MASHLAMS
MASHLIM
MASHLIMS
MASHLIN
MASHLINS
MASHLOCH
MASHLOCHS
MASHLUM
MASHLUMS
MASHMAN
MASHMEN
MASHY
MASING
MASJID
MASJIDS
MASK
MASKED
MASKER
MASKERS
MASKING
MASKS
MASLIN
MASLINS
MASOCHISM
MASOCHISMS
MASOCHIST
MASOCHISTS
MASON
MASONED
MASONIC
MASONING
MASONRIED
MASONRIES
MASONRY
MASONS
MASOOLAH

MASOOLAHS
MASQUE
MASQUER
MASQUERS
MASQUES
MASS
MASSA
MASSACRE
MASSACRED
MASSACRES
MASSACRING
MASSAGE
MASSAGED
MASSAGES
MASSAGING
MASSAGIST
MASSAGISTS
MASSAS
MASSÉ
MASSED
MASSES
MASSÉS
MASSETER
MASSETERS
MASSEUR
MASSEURS
MASSEUSE
MASSEUSES
MASSICOT
MASSICOTS
MASSIER
MASSIEST
MASSIF
MASSIFS
MASSINESS
MASSINESSES
MASSING
MASSIVE
MASSIVELY
MASSOOLA
MASSOOLAS
MASSY
MASSYMORE
MASSYMORES
MAST
MASTABA
MASTABAS
MASTED
MASTER
MASTERATE
MASTERATES
MASTERDOM
MASTERDOMS
MASTERED
MASTERFUL
MASTERIES
MASTERING
MASTERINGS
MASTERLY
MASTERS
MASTERY
MASTFUL
MASTHEAD
MASTHEADED
MASTHEADING
MASTHEADS
MASTHOUSE
MASTHOUSES
MASTIC
MASTICATE

MASTICATED
MASTICATES
MASTICATING
MASTICH
MASTICHS
MASTICOT
MASTICOTS
MASTICS
MASTIER
MASTIEST
MASTIFF
MASTIFFS
MASTING
MASTITIS
MASTITISES
MASTLESS
MASTODON
MASTODONS
MASTOID
MASTOIDAL
MASTOIDS
MASTS
MASTY
MASU
MASULA
MASULAS
MASURIUM
MASURIUMS
MASUS
MAT
MATACHIN
MATACHINS
MATADOR
MATADORE
MATADORES
MATADORS
MATAMATA
MATAMATAS
MATCH
MATCHABLE
MATCHBOX
MATCHBOXES
MATCHED
MATCHER
MATCHERS
MATCHES
MATCHING
MATCHLESS
MATCHLOCK
MATCHLOCKS
MATCHWOOD
MATCHWOODS
MATE
MATÉ
MATED
MATELASSÉ
MATELASSÉS
MATELESS
MATELOT
MATELOTE
MATELOTES
MATELOTS
MATER
MATERIAL
MATERIALS
MATÉRIEL
MATÉRIELS
MATERNAL
MATERNITIES
MATERNITY

MATERS
MATES
MATÉS
MATESHIP
MATESHIPS
MATEY
MATFELON
MATFELONS
MATGRASS
MATGRASSES
MATH
MATHESES
MATHESIS
MATHS
MATICO
MATICOS
MATIER
MATIEST
MATIN
MATINAL
MATINEE
MATINÉE
MATINEES
MATINÉES
MATING
MATINS
MATLO
MATLOS
MATLOW
MATLOWS
MATRASS
MATRASSES
MATRIARCH
MATRIARCHS
MATRIC
MATRICE
MATRICES
MATRICIDE
MATRICIDES
MATRICS
MATRICULA
MATRICULAS
MATRILINIES
MATRILINY
MATRIMONIES
MATRIMONY
MATRIX
MATRIXES
MATRON
MATRONAGE
MATRONAGES
MATRONAL
MATRONISE
MATRONISED
MATRONISES
MATRONISING
MATRONIZE
MATRONIZED
MATRONIZES
MATRONIZING
MATRONLY
MATRONS
MATROSS
MATROSSES
MATS
MATT
MATTAMORE
MATTAMORES
MATTE
MATTED

MATTER
MATTERED
MATTERFUL
MATTERING
MATTERS
MATTERY
MATTES
MATTIE
MATTIES
MATTING
MATTINGS
MATTINS
MATTOCK
MATTOCKS
MATTOID
MATTOIDS
MATTRESS
MATTRESSES
MATURABLE
MATURATE
MATURATED
MATURATES
MATURATING
MATURE
MATURED
MATURELY
MATURER
MATURES
MATUREST
MATURING
MATURITIES
MATURITY
MATUTINAL
MATUTINE
MATWEED
MATWEEDS
MATY
MATZA
MATZAH
MATZAHS
MATZAS
MATZO
MATZOH
MATZOON
MATZOONS
MATZOS
MATZOT
MATZOTH
MAUD
MAUDLIN
MAUDS
MAUGRE
MAUGRES
MAUL
MAULED
MAULERS
MAULGRE
MAULGRES
MAULING
MAULS
MAULSTICK
MAULSTICKS
MAULVI
MAULVIS
MAUMET
MAUMETRIES
MAUMETRY
MAUMETS
MAUN
MAUND

MAUNDED
MAUNDER
MAUNDERED
MAUNDERER
MAUNDERERS
MAUNDERING
MAUNDERINGS
MAUNDERS
MAUNDIES
MAUNDING
MAUNDS
MAUNDY
MAUNNA
MAUSOLEAN
MAUSOLEUM
MAUSOLEUMS
MAUTHER
MAUTHERS
MAUVAIS
MAUVAISE
MAUVE
MAUVEIN
MAUVEINE
MAUVEINES
MAUVEINS
MAUVER
MAUVES
MAUVEST
MAUVIN
MAUVINE
MAUVINES
MAUVINS
MAVERICK
MAVERICKED
MAVERICKING
MAVERICKS
MAVIN
MAVINS
MAVIS
MAVISES
MAW
MAWBOUND
MAWK
MAWKIER
MAWKIEST
MAWKIN
MAWKINS
MAWKISH
MAWKISHLY
MAWKS
MAWKY
MAWMET
MAWMETRIES
MAWMETRY
MAWMETS
MAWPUS
MAWPUSES
MAWR
MAWRS
MAWS
MAWSEED
MAWSEEDS
MAWTHER
MAWTHERS
MAX
MAXES
MAXI
MAXILLA
MAXILLAE
MAXILLARIES

MAXILLARY
MAXILLULA
MAXILLULAE
MAXIM
MAXIMA
MAXIMAL
MAXIMALLY
MAXIMIN
MAXIMINS
MAXIMISE
MAXIMISED
MAXIMISES
MAXIMISING
MAXIMIST
MAXIMISTS
MAXIMIZE
MAXIMIZED
MAXIMIZES
MAXIMIZING
MAXIMS
MAXIMUM
MAXIS
MAXIXE
MAXIXES
MAXWELL
MAXWELLS
MAY
MAYA
MAYAS
MAYBE
MAYBES
MAYDAY
MAYDAYS
MAYED
MAYEST
MAYFLIES
MAYFLOWER
MAYFLOWERS
MAYFLY
MAYHAP
MAYHEM
MAYHEMS
MAYING
MAYINGS
MAYOR
MAYORAL
MAYORALTIES
MAYORALTY
MAYORESS
MAYORESSES
MAYORS
MAYORSHIP
MAYORSHIPS
MAYPOLE
MAYPOLES
MAYS
MAYST
MAYSTER
MAYSTERS
MAYWEED
MAYWEEDS
MAZARD
MAZARDS
MAZARINE
MAZARINES
MAZE
MAZED
MAZEFUL
MAZEMENT
MAZEMENTS

MAZER
MAZERS
MAZES
MAZHBI
MAZHBIS
MAZIER
MAZIEST
MAZILY
MAZINESS
MAZINESSES
MAZING
MAZOUT
MAZOUTS
MAZUMA
MAZUMAS
MAZURKA
MAZURKAS
MAZUT
MAZUTS
MAZY
MAZZARD
MAZZARDS
ME
MEACOCK
MEACOCKS
MEAD
MEADOW
MEADOWS
MEADOWY
MEADS
MEAGRE
MEAGRELY
MEAGRER
MEAGRES
MEAGREST
MEAL
MEALED
MEALER
MEALERS
MEALIE
MEALIER
MEALIES
MEALIEST
MEALINESS
MEALINESSES
MEALING
MEALS
MEALY
MEAN
MEANDER
MEANDERED
MEANDERING
MEANDERS
MEANDRIAN
MEANDROUS
MEANE
MEANED
MEANER
MEANES
MEANEST
MEANIE
MEANIES
MEANING
MEANINGLY
MEANINGS
MEANLY
MEANNESS
MEANNESSES
MEANS
MEANT

MEANTIME
MEANTIMES
MEANWHILE
MEANWHILES
MEANY
MEARE
MEARES
MEASE
MEASED
MEASES
MEASING
MEASLE
MEASLED
MEASLES
MEASLIER
MEASLIEST
MEASLING
MEASLY
MEASURE
MEASURED
MEASURER
MEASURERS
MEASURES
MEASURING
MEASURINGS
MEAT
MEATAL
MEATH
MEATHE
MEATHEAD
MEATHEADS
MEATHES
MEATHS
MEATIER
MEATIEST
MEATINESS
MEATINESSES
MEATLESS
MEATS
MEATUS
MEATUSES
MEATY
MEAWES
MEAZEL
MEAZELS
MEBOS
MEBOSES
MECHANIC
MECHANICS
MECHANISE
MECHANISED
MECHANISES
MECHANISING
MECHANISM
MECHANISMS
MECHANIST
MECHANISTS
MECHANIZE
MECHANIZED
MECHANIZES
MECHANIZING
MECONATE
MECONATES
MECONIC
MECONIN
MECONINS
MECONIUM
MECONIUMS
MEDAEWART
MEDAEWARTS

MEDAL
MEDALET
MEDALETS
MEDALLED
MEDALLIC
MEDALLING
MEDALLION
MEDALLIONED
MEDALLIONING
MEDALLIONS
MEDALLIST
MEDALLISTS
MEDALS
MEDDLE
MEDDLED
MEDDLER
MEDDLERS
MEDDLES
MEDDLING
MEDDLINGS
MEDFLIES
MEDFLY
MEDIA
MEDIACIES
MEDIACY
MEDIAE
MEDIAEVAL
MEDIAL
MEDIALLY
MEDIALS
MEDIAN
MEDIANS
MEDIANT
MEDIANTS
MEDIATE
MEDIATED
MEDIATELY
MEDIATES
MEDIATING
MEDIATION
MEDIATIONS
MEDIATISE
MEDIATISED
MEDIATISES
MEDIATISING
MEDIATIVE
MEDIATIZE
MEDIATIZED
MEDIATIZES
MEDIATIZING
MEDIATOR
MEDIATORS
MEDIATORY
MEDIATRICES
MEDIATRIX
MEDIC
MEDICABLE
MEDICAID
MEDICAIDS
MEDICAL
MEDICALLY
MEDICALS
MEDICARE
MEDICARES
MEDICATE
MEDICATED
MEDICATES
MEDICATING
MEDICINAL
MEDICINE

MEDICINED
MEDICINER
MEDICINERS
MEDICINES
MEDICINING
MEDICK
MEDICKS
MEDICO
MEDICOS
MEDICS
MEDIEVAL
MEDII
MEDINA
MEDINAS
MEDIOCRE
MEDITATE
MEDITATED
MEDITATES
MEDITATING
MEDIUM
MEDIUMS
MEDIUS
MEDIUSES
MEDLAR
MEDLARS
MEDLE
MEDLED
MEDLES
MEDLEY
MEDLEYS
MEDLING
MEDRESSEH
MEDRESSEHS
MEDULLA
MEDULLAE
MEDULLAR
MEDULLARY
MEDULLAS
MEDULLATE
MEDUSA
MEDUSAE
MEDUSAN
MEDUSANS
MEDUSAS
MEDUSOID
MEDUSOIDS
MEED
MEEDS
MEEK
MEEKEN
MEEKENED
MEEKENING
MEEKENS
MEEKER
MEEKEST
MEEKLY
MEEKNESS
MEEKNESSES
MEER
MEERCAT
MEERCATS
MEERED
MEERING
MEERKAT
MEERKATS
MEERS
MEET
MEETER
MEETEST
MEETING

MEETINGS
MEETLY
MEETNESS
MEETNESSES
MEETS
MEGABAR
MEGABARS
MEGABIT
MEGABITS
MEGABYTE
MEGABYTES
MEGACURIE
MEGACURIES
MEGACYCLE
MEGACYCLES
MEGADEATH
MEGADEATHS
MEGADYNE
MEGADYNES
MEGAFARAD
MEGAFARADS
MEGAFAUNA
MEGAFAUNAE
MEGAFAUNAS
MEGAFLORA
MEGAFLORAL
MEGAFLORAS
MEGAFOG
MEGAFOGS
MEGAGAUSS
MEGAGAUSSES
MEGAHERTZ
MEGAHERTZES
MEGAJOULE
MEGAJOULES
MEGALITH
MEGALITHS
MEGAPHONE
MEGAPHONED
MEGAPHONES
MEGAPHONING
MEGAPODE
MEGAPODES
MEGARA
MEGARAD
MEGARADS
MEGARON
MEGARONS
MEGASCOPE
MEGASCOPES
MEGASPORE
MEGASPORES
MEGASS
MEGASSE
MEGASSES
MEGASTORE
MEGASTORES
MEGATON
MEGATONNE
MEGATONNES
MEGATONS
MEGAVOLT
MEGAVOLTS
MEGAWATT
MEGAWATTS
MEGILP
MEGILPS
MEGOHM
MEGOHMS
MEGRIM

MEGRIMS
MEIN
MEINED
MEINEY
MEINEYS
MEINIE
MEINIES
MEINING
MEINS
MEINT
MEINY
MEIOFAUNA
MEIONITE
MEIONITES
MEIOSES
MEIOSIS
MEIOTIC
MEITH
MEITHS
MEKOMETER
MEKOMETERS
MEL
MELAMINE
MELAMINES
MELAMPODE
MELAMPODES
MÉLANGE
MÉLANGES
MELANIC
MELANIN
MELANINS
MELANISM
MELANISMS
MELANITE
MELANITES
MELANO
MELANOMA
MELANOMAS
MELANOMATA
MELANOS
MELANOSES
MELANOSIS
MELANOTIC
MELANOUS
MELANURIA
MELANURIAS
MELANURIC
MELAPHYRE
MELAPHYRES
MELATONIN
MELATONINS
MELD
MELDED
MELDER
MELDERS
MELDING
MELDS
MÉLÉE
MÉLÉES
MELIC
MELICS
MELILITE
MELILITES
MELILOT
MELILOTS
MELINITE
MELINITES
MELIORATE
MELIORATED
MELIORATES

MELIORATING
MELIORISM
MELIORISMS
MELIORIST
MELIORISTS
MELIORITIES
MELIORITY
MELISMA
MELISMAS
MELISMATA
MELL
MELLAY
MELLAYS
MELLED
MELLING
MELLITE
MELLITES
MELLITIC
MELLOW
MELLOWED
MELLOWER
MELLOWEST
MELLOWING
MELLOWLY
MELLOWS
MELLOWY
MELLS
MELOCOTON
MELOCOTONS
MELODEON
MELODEONS
MELODIC
MELODICS
MELODIES
MELODION
MELODIONS
MELODIOUS
MELODISE
MELODISED
MELODISES
MELODISING
MELODIST
MELODISTS
MELODIZE
MELODIZED
MELODIZES
MELODIZING
MELODRAMA
MELODRAMAS
MELODRAME
MELODRAMES
MELODY
MELOMANIA
MELOMANIAS
MELOMANIC
MELON
MELONS
MELS
MELT
MELTDOWN
MELTDOWNS
MELTED
MELTING
MELTINGLY
MELTINGS
MELTITH
MELTITHS
MELTON
MELTONS
MELTS

MEMBER
MEMBERED
MEMBERS
MEMBRAL
MEMBRANE
MEMBRANES
MEMENTO
MEMENTOES
MEMENTOS
MEMO
MEMOIR
MEMOIRISM
MEMOIRISMS
MEMOIRIST
MEMOIRISTS
MEMOIRS
MEMORABLE
MEMORABLY
MEMORANDA
MEMORIAL
MEMORIALS
MEMORIES
MEMORISE
MEMORISED
MEMORISES
MEMORISING
MEMORITER
MEMORIZE
MEMORIZED
MEMORIZES
MEMORIZING
MEMORY
MEMOS
MEN
MENACE
MENACED
MENACER
MENACERS
MENACES
MENACING
MENADIONE
MENADIONES
MÉNAGE
MENAGERIE
MENAGERIES
MÉNAGES
MENARCHE
MENARCHES
MEND
MENDACITIES
MENDACITY
MENDED
MENDER
MENDERS
MENDICANT
MENDICANTS
MENDICITIES
MENDICITY
MENDING
MENDINGS
MENDS
MENE
MENED
MENEER
MENEERS
MENES
MENFOLK
MENFOLKS
MENG
MENGE

MENGED
MENGES
MENGING
MENGS
MENHADEN
MENHADENS
MENHIR
MENHIRS
MENIAL
MENIALS
MENING
MENINGEAL
MENINGES
MENINX
MENISCI
MENISCOID
MENISCUS
MENISCUSES
MENOLOGIES
MENOLOGY
MENOMINEE
MENOMINEES
MENOPAUSE
MENOPAUSES
MENOPOME
MENOPOMES
MENORAH
MENORAHS
MENORRHEA
MENORRHEAS
MENSAL
MENSCH
MENSCHES
MENSE
MENSED
MENSEFUL
MENSELESS
MENSES
MENSH
MENSHED
MENSHES
MENSHING
MENSING
MENSTRUA
MENSTRUAL
MENSTRUUM
MENSTRUUMS
MENSUAL
MENSURAL
MENSWEAR
MENSWEARS
MENT
MENTAL
MENTALISM
MENTALISMS
MENTALIST
MENTALISTS
MENTALITIES
MENTALITY
MENTALLY
MENTATION
MENTATIONS
MENTHOL
MENTHOLS
MENTICIDE
MENTICIDES
MENTION
MENTIONED
MENTIONING
MENTIONS

MENTOR
MENTORIAL
MENTORING
MENTORINGS
MENTORS
MENTUM
MENTUMS
MENU
MENUISIER
MENUISIERS
MENUS
MEOW
MEOWED
MEOWING
MEOWS
MEPACRINE
MEPACRINES
MEPHITIC
MEPHITIS
MEPHITISES
MEPHITISM
MEPHITISMS
MERC
MERCAPTAN
MERCAPTANS
MERCAT
MERCATS
MERCENARIES
MERCENARY
MERCER
MERCERIES
MERCERISE
MERCERISED
MERCERISES
MERCERISING
MERCERIZE
MERCERIZED
MERCERIZES
MERCERIZING
MERCERS
MERCERY
MERCHANT
MERCHANTED
MERCHANTING
MERCHANTINGS
MERCHANTS
MERCHET
MERCHETS
MERCHILD
MERCHILDREN
MERCIABLE
MERCIES
MERCIFIDE
MERCIFIED
MERCIFIES
MERCIFUL
MERCIFY
MERCIFYING
MERCILESS
MERCS
MERCURATE
MERCURATED
MERCURATES
MERCURATING
MERCURIAL
MERCURIALS
MERCURIC
MERCURIES
MERCUROUS
MERCURY

MERCY
MERE
MERED
MEREL
MERELL
MERELLS
MERELS
MERELY
MERER
MERES
MERESMAN
MERESMEN
MEREST
MERESTONE
MERESTONES
MERFOLK
MERFOLKS
MERGANSER
MERGANSERS
MERGE
MERGED
MERGENCE
MERGENCES
MERGER
MERGERS
MERGES
MERGING
MERI
MERICARP
MERICARPS
MERIDIAN
MERIDIANS
MERIL
MERILS
MERIMAKE
MERIMAKES
MERING
MERINGUE
MERINGUES
MERINO
MERINOS
MERIS
MERISM
MERISMS
MERISTEM
MERISTEMS
MERISTIC
MERIT
MERITED
MERITING
MERITS
MERK
MERKIN
MERKINS
MERKS
MERL
MERLE
MERLES
MERLIN
MERLING
MERLINGS
MERLINS
MERLON
MERLONS
MERLS
MERMAID
MERMAIDEN
MERMAIDENS
MERMAIDS
MERMAN

MERMEN
MEROGONIES
MEROGONY
MEROISTIC
MEROME
MEROMES
MEROPIDAN
MEROPIDANS
MEROSOME
MEROSOMES
MEROZOITE
MEROZOITES
MERPEOPLE
MERPEOPLES
MERRIER
MERRIES
MERRIEST
MERRILY
MERRIMENT
MERRIMENTS
MERRINESS
MERRINESSES
MERRY
MERRYMAN
MERRYMEN
MERSALYL
MERSALYLS
MERSE
MERSES
MERSION
MERSIONS
MERYCISM
MERYCISMS
MES
MESA
MESAIL
MESAILS
MESAL
MESALLY
MESARAIC
MESARCH
MESAS
MESCAL
MESCALIN
MESCALINS
MESCALISM
MESCALISMS
MESCALS
MESDAMES
MESE
MESEEMED
MESEEMS
MESEL
MESELED
MESELS
MESENTERA
MESENTERIES
MESENTERY
MESES
MESH
MESHED
MESHES
MESHIER
MESHIEST
MESHING
MESHINGS
MESHUGA
MESHUGGA
MESHUGGE
MESHY

MESIAL
MESIALLY
MESIAN
MESIC
MESMERIC
MESMERISE
MESMERISED
MESMERISING
MESMERISM
MESMERISMS
MESMERIST
MESMERISTS
MESMERIZE
MESMERIZED
MESMERIZES
MESMERIZING
MESNE
MESOBLAST
MESOBLASTS
MESOCARP
MESOCARPS
MESODERM
MESODERMS
MESOGLOEA
MESOGLOEAS
MESOLITE
MESOLITES
MESOMORPH
MESOMORPHS
MESON
MESONIC
MESONS
MESOPHYLL
MESOPHYLLS
MESOPHYTE
MESOPHYTES
MESOTRON
MESOTRONS
MESPRISE
MESPRISES
MESPRIZE
MESPRIZES
MESQUIN
MESQUINE
MESQUIT
MESQUITE
MESQUITES
MESQUITS
MESS
MESSAGE
MESSAGED
MESSAGES
MESSAGING
MESSAN
MESSANS
MESSED
MESSENGER
MESSENGERS
MESSES
MESSIER
MESSIEST
MESSIEURS
MESSILY
MESSINESS
MESSINESSES
MESSING
MESSMATE
MESSMATES
MESSUAGE

MESSUAGES
MESSY
MESTEE
MESTEES
MESTIZA
MESTIZAS
MESTIZO
MESTIZOS
MESTO
MET
METABASES
METABASIS
METABATIC
METABOLIC
METAGE
METAGES
METAIRIE
METAIRIES
METAL
METALLED
METALLIC
METALLINE
METALLING
METALLINGS
METALLISE
METALLISED
METALLISES
METALLISING
METALLIST
METALLISTS
METALLIZE
METALLIZED
METALLIZES
METALLIZING
METALLOID
METALLOIDS
METALLY
METALS
METAMER
METAMERE
METAMERES
METAMERIC
METAMERS
METANOIA
METANOIAS
METAPHASE
METAPHASES
METAPHOR
METAPHORS
METAPLASM
METAPLASMS
METATARSI
METAYAGE
METAYAGES
METAYER
METAYERS
METAZOA
METAZOAN
METAZOANS
METAZOIC
METAZOON
METCAST
METCASTS
METE
METED
METEOR
METEORIC
METEORISM
METEORISMS
METEORIST

METEORISTS
METEORITE
METEORITES
METEOROID
METEOROIDS
METEOROUS
METEORS
METER
METERED
METERING
METERS
METES
METESTICK
METESTICKS
METEWAND
METEWANDS
METEYARD
METEYARDS
METHADON
METHADONE
METHADONES
METHADONS
METHANE
METHANES
METHANOL
METHANOLS
METHEGLIN
METHEGLINS
METHINK
METHINKS
METHOD
METHODIC
METHODISE
METHODISED
METHODISES
METHODISING
METHODIST
METHODISTS
METHODIZE
METHODIZED
METHODIZES
METHODIZING
METHODS
METHOUGHT
METHS
METHYL
METHYLATE
METHYLATED
METHYLATES
METHYLATING
METHYLENE
METHYLENES
METHYLIC
METHYLS
METHYSES
METHYSIS
METHYSTIC
METIC
METICAL
METICALS
METICS
METIER
METIERS
METIF
METIFS
METING
METIS
METISSE
METISSES
METOL

METOLS
METONYM
METONYMIC
METONYMIES
METONYMS
METONYMY
METOPE
METOPES
METOPIC
METOPISM
METOPISMS
METOPON
METOPONS
METOPRYL
METOPRYLS
METRE
METRED
METRES
METRIC
METRICAL
METRICATE
METRICATED
METRICATES
METRICATING
METRICIAN
METRICIANS
METRICISE
METRICISED
METRICISES
METRICISING
METRICIST
METRICISTS
METRICIZE
METRICIZED
METRICIZES
METRICIZING
METRICS
METRIFIER
METRIFIERS
METRING
METRIST
METRISTS
METRITIS
METRITISES
METRO
METRO
METROLOGIES
METROLOGY
METRONOME
METRONOMES
METROS
METROS
METTLE
METTLED
METTLES
MEU
MEUNIERE
MEUS
MEUSE
MEUSED
MEUSES
MEUSING
MEVE
MEVED
MEVES
MEVING
MEW
MEWED
MEWING
MEWL

MEWLED	MICHING	MICRURGY	MIENS	MILDS
MEWLING	MICHINGS	MICTION	MIEVE	MILE
MEWLS	MICK	MICTIONS	MIEVED	MILEAGE
MEWS	MICKEY	MICTURATE	MIEVES	MILEAGES
MEWSED	MICKEYED	MICTURATED	MIEVING	MILER
MEWSES	MICKEYING	MICTURATES	MIFF	MILERS
MEWSING	MICKEYS	MICTURATING	MIFFED	MILES
MEYNT	MICKIES	MID	MIFFIER	MILESTONE
MEZAIL	MICKLE	MIDBRAIN	MIFFIEST	MILESTONES
MEZAILS	MICKLES	MIDBRAINS	MIFFINESS	MILFOIL
MÉZÉ	MICKS	MIDDAY	MIFFINESSES	MILFOILS
MEZE	MICKY	MIDDAYS	MIFFING	MILIARIA
MEZEREON	MICO	MIDDEN	MIFFS	MILIARIAS
MEZEREONS	MICOS	MIDDENS	MIFFY	MILIARY
MEZEREUM	MICRO	MIDDEST	MIFTY	MILIEU
MEZEREUMS	MICROBAR	MIDDIES	MIGHT	MILIEUS
MÉZÉS	MICROBARS	MIDDLE	MIGHTEST	MILIEUX
MEZES	MICROBE	MIDDLED	MIGHTFUL	MILITANCIES
MEZUZA	MICROBES	MIDDLEMAN	MIGHTIER	MILITANCY
MEZUZAH	MICROBIAL	MIDDLEMEN	MIGHTIEST	MILITANT
MEZUZAHS	MICROBIAN	MIDDLES	MIGHTILY	MILITANTS
MEZUZOTH	MICROBIC	MIDDLING	MIGHTS	MILITAR
MEZZANINE	MICROCARD	MIDDLINGS	MIGHTST	MILITARIA
MEZZANINES	MICROCARDS	MIDDY	MIGHTY	MILITARIES
MEZZO	MICROCHIP	MIDFIELD	MIGNON	MILITARY
MEZZOS	MICROCHIPS	MIDFIELDS	MIGNONNE	MILITATE
MEZZOTINT	MICROCODE	MIDGE	MIGRAINE	MILITATED
MEZZOTINTS	MICROCODES	MIDGES	MIGRAINES	MILITATES
MGANGA	MICROCOPIES	MIDGET	MIGRANT	MILITATING
MGANGAS	MICROCOPY	MIDGETS	MIGRANTS	MILITIA
MHO	MICROCOSM	MIDI	MIGRATE	MILITIAS
MHORR	MICROCOSMS	MIDINETTE	MIGRATED	MILK
MHORRS	MICROCYTE	MIDINETTES	MIGRATES	MILKED
MHOS	MICROCYTES	MIDIRON	MIGRATING	MILKEN
MI	MICRODOT	MIDIRONS	MIGRATION	MILKER
MIAOW	MICRODOTS	MIDIS	MIGRATIONS	MILKERS
MIAOWED	MICROFILM	MIDLAND	MIGRATOR	MILKFISH
MIAOWING	MICROFILMED	MIDLANDS	MIGRATORS	MILKFISHES
MIAOWS	MICROFILMING	MIDMOST	MIGRATORY	MILKIER
MIASM	MICROFILMS	MIDMOSTS	MIHRAB	MILKIEST
MIASMA	MICROFORM	MIDNIGHT	MIHRABS	MILKILY
MIASMAL	MICROFORMS	MIDNIGHTS	MIKADO	MILKINESS
MIASMAS	MICROGRAM	MIDNOON	MIKADOS	MILKINESSES
MIASMATA	MICROGRAMS	MIDNOONS	MIKE	MILKING
MIASMATIC	MICROLITE	MIDRIB	MIKES	MILKINGS
MIASMIC	MICROLITES	MIDRIBS	MIKRON	MILKLESS
MIASMOUS	MICROLITH	MIDRIFF	MIKRONS	MILKLIKE
MIASMS	MICROLITHS	MIDRIFFS	MIL	MILKMAID
MIAUL	MICROLOGIES	MIDS	MILADI	MILKMAIDS
MIAULED	MICROLOGY	MIDSHIP	MILADIES	MILKMAN
MIAULING	MICRON	MIDSHIPS	MILADIS	MILKMEN
MIAULS	MICRONS	MIDST	MILADY	MILKS
MICA	MICROPSIA	MIDSTREAM	MILAGE	MILKWOOD
MICACEOUS	MICROPSIAS	MIDSTREAMS	MILAGES	MILKWOODS
MICAS	MICROPYLE	MIDSTS	MILCH	MILKWORT
MICATE	MICROPYLES	MIDSUMMER	MILD	MILKWORTS
MICATED	MICROS	MIDSUMMERS	MILDEN	MILKY
MICATES	MICROSOME	MIDWAY	MILDENED	MILL
MICATING	MICROSOMES	MIDWAYS	MILDENING	MILLDAM
MICE	MICROTOME	MIDWIFE	MILDENS	MILLDAMS
MICELLA	MICROTOMES	MIDWIFED	MILDER	MILLE
MICELLAR	MICROTOMIES	MIDWIFERIES	MILDEST	MILLED
MICELLAS	MICROTOMY	MIDWIFERY	MILDEW	MILLENARIES
MICELLE	MICROTONE	MIDWIFES	MILDEWED	MILLENARY
MICELLES	MICROTONES	MIDWIFING	MILDEWING	MILLENNIA
MICHE	MICROWAVE	MIDWIVE	MILDEWS	MILLEPED
MICHED	MICROWAVES	MIDWIVED	MILDEWY	MILLEPEDE
MICHER	MICROWIRE	MIDWIVES	MILDLY	MILLEPEDES
MICHERS	MICROWIRES	MIDWIVING	MILDNESS	MILLEPEDS
MICHES	MICRURGIES	MIEN	MILDNESSES	MILLEPORE

MILLEPORES
MILLER
MILLERITE
MILLERITES
MILLERS
MILLES
MILLET
MILLETS
MILLIARD
MILLIARDS
MILLIARE
MILLIARES
MILLIARIES
MILLIARY
MILLIBAR
MILLIBARS
MILLIÈME
MILLIÈMES
MILLIME
MILLIMES
MILLINER
MILLINERIES
MILLINERS
MILLINERY
MILLING
MILLINGS
MILLION
MILLIONS
MILLIONTH
MILLIONTHS
MILLIPED
MILLIPEDE
MILLIPEDES
MILLIPEDS
MILLOCRAT
MILLOCRATS
MILLPOND
MILLPONDS
MILLRACE
MILLRACES
MILLRIND
MILLRINDS
MILLS
MILLSTONE
MILLSTONES
MILLTAIL
MILLTAILS
MILO
MILOMETER
MILOMETERS
MILOR
MILORD
MILORDS
MILORS
MILOS
MILREIS
MILS
MILSEY
MILSEYS
MILT
MILTED
MILTER
MILTERS
MILTING
MILTONIA
MILTONIAS
MILTS
MILTZ
MILTZES
MILVINE

MIM
MIMBAR
MIMBARS
MIME
MIMED
MIMER
MIMERS
MIMES
MIMESES
MIMESIS
MIMESTER
MIMESTERS
MIMETIC
MIMETICAL
MIMETITE
MIMETITES
MIMIC
MIMICAL
MIMICS
MIMING
MIMMER
MIMMEST
MIMMICK
MIMMICKED
MIMMICKING
MIMMICKS
MIMOSA
MIMOSAS
MIMULUS
MIMULUSES
MINA
MINACIOUS
MINACITIES
MINACITY
MINAE
MINAR
MINARET
MINARETS
MINARS
MINAS
MINATORY
MINBAR
MINBARS
MINCE
MINCED
MINCEMEAT
MINCEMEATS
MINCER
MINCERS
MINCES
MINCING
MINCINGLY
MINCINGS
MIND
MINDED
MINDER
MINDERS
MINDFUL
MINDFULLY
MINDING
MINDINGS
MINDLESS
MINDS
MINDSET

MINDSETS
MINE
MINED
MINEOLA
MINEOLAS
MINER
MINERAL
MINERALS
MINERS
MINES
MINETTE
MINETTES
MINEVER
MINEVERS
MING
MINGED
MINGIER
MINGIEST
MINGINESS
MINGINESSES
MINGING
MINGLE
MINGLED
MINGLER
MINGLERS
MINGLES
MINGLING
MINGLINGS
MINGS
MINGY
MINI
MINIATE
MINIATED
MINIATES
MINIATING
MINIATION
MINIATIONS
MINIATURE
MINIATURED
MINIATURES
MINIATURING
MINIBUS
MINIBUSES
MINICAB
MINICABS
MINICAR
MINICARS
MINIDRESS
MINIDRESSES
MINIER
MINIEST
MINIFIED
MINIFIES
MINIFY
MINIFYING
MINIKIN
MINIKINS
MINIM
MINIMA
MINIMAL
MINIMENT
MINIMENTS
MINIMISE
MINIMISED
MINIMISES
MINIMISING
MINIMISM
MINIMISMS
MINIMIST
MINIMISTS

MINIMIZE
MINIMIZED
MINIMIZES
MINIMIZING
MINIMS
MINIMUM
MINIMUS
MINIMUSES
MINING
MININGS
MINION
MINIONS
MINIPILL
MINIPILLS
MINIS
MINISCULE
MINISCULES
MINISH
MINISHED
MINISHES
MINISHING
MINISKIRT
MINISKIRTS
MINISKIS
MINISTER
MINISTERED
MINISTERING
MINISTERS
MINISTRIES
MINISTRY
MINISUB
MINISUBS
MINIUM
MINIUMS
MINIVER
MINIVERS
MINIVET
MINIVETS
MINK
MINKE
MINKES
MINKS
MINNEOLA
MINNEOLAS
MINNICK
MINNICKED
MINNICKING
MINNICKS
MINNIE
MINNIES
MINNOCK
MINNOCKED
MINNOCKING
MINNOCKS
MINNOW
MINNOWS
MINO
MINOR
MINORESS
MINORESSES
MINORITE
MINORITES
MINORITIES
MINORITY
MINORS
MINORSHIP
MINORSHIPS
MINOS
MINSTER
MINSTERS

MINSTREL
MINSTRELS
MINT
MINTAGE
MINTAGES
MINTED
MINTER
MINTERS
MINTIER
MINTIEST
MINTING
MINTS
MINTY
MINUEND
MINUENDS
MINUET
MINUETS
MINUS
MINUSCULE
MINUSCULES
MINUSES
MINUTE
MINUTED
MINUTELY
MINUTEMAN
MINUTEMEN
MINUTER
MINUTES
MINUTEST
MINUTIA
MINUTIAE
MINUTING
MINUTIOSE
MINX
MINXES
MINY
MINYAN
MINYANIM
MINYANS
MIOSES
MIOSIS
MIR
MIRABELLE
MIRABELLES
MIRABILIA
MIRABILIS
MIRABILISES
MIRABLE
MIRACLE
MIRACLES
MIRADOR
MIRADORS
MIRAGE
MIRAGES
MIRBANE
MIRBANES
MIRE
MIRED
MIREPOIX
MIRES
MIRIER
MIRIEST
MIRIFIC
MIRIFICAL
MIRINESS
MIRINESSES
MIRING
MIRITI
MIRITIS
MIRK

MIRKER	MISBESEEMS	MISDEALING	MISESTEEMING	MISGUIDES
MIRKEST	MISBESTOW	MISDEALS	MISESTEEMS	MISGUIDING
MIRKIER	MISBESTOWED	MISDEALT	MISFAITH	MISHANDLE
MIRKIEST	MISBESTOWING	MISDEED	MISFAITHS	MISHANDLED
MIRKS	MISBESTOWS	MISDEEDS	MISFALL	MISHANDLES
MIRKSOME	MISBIRTH	MISDEEM	MISFALLEN	MISHANDLING
MIRKY	MISBIRTHS	MISDEEMED	MISFALLING	MISHANTER
MIRLIER	MISBORN	MISDEEMING	MISFALLS	MISHANTERS
MIRLIEST	MISCALL	MISDEEMINGS	MISFALNE	MISHAP
MIRLIGOES	MISCALLED	MISDEEMS	MISFARE	MISHAPPED
MIRLITON	MISCALLING	MISDEMEAN	MISFARED	MISHAPPEN
MIRLITONS	MISCALLS	MISDEMEANED	MISFARES	MISHAPPENED
MIRLY	MISCARRIED	MISDEMEANING	MISFARING	MISHAPPENING
MIRROR	MISCARRIES	MISDEMEANS	MISFARINGS	MISHAPPENS
MIRRORED	MISCARRY	MISDEMPT	MISFEASOR	MISHAPPING
MIRRORING	MISCARRYING	MISDESERT	MISFEASORS	MISHAPS
MIRRORS	MISCAST	MISDESERTS	MISFEIGN	MISHAPT
MIRS	MISCASTING	MISDID	MISFEIGNED	MISHEAR
MIRTH	MISCASTS	MISDIET	MISFEIGNING	MISHEARD
MIRTHFUL	MISCEGEN	MISDIETS	MISFEIGNS	MISHEARING
MIRTHLESS	MISCEGENE	MISDIGHT	MISFELL	MISHEARS
MIRTHS	MISCEGENES	MISDIRECT	MISFILE	MISHIT
MIRY	MISCEGENS	MISDIRECTED	MISFILED	MISHITS
MIS	MISCEGINE	MISDIRECTING	MISFILES	MISHITTING
MISADVISE	MISCEGINES	MISDIRECTS	MISFILING	MISHMASH
MISADVISED	MISCHANCE	MISDO	MISFIRE	MISHMASHES
MISADVISES	MISCHANCED	MISDOER	MISFIRED	MISHMEE
MISADVISING	MISCHANCES	MISDOERS	MISFIRES	MISHMEES
MISAIM	MISCHANCING	MISDOES	MISFIRING	MISHMI
MISAIMED	MISCHANCY	MISDOING	MISFIT	MISHMIS
MISAIMING	MISCHARGE	MISDOINGS	MISFITS	MISINFORM
MISAIMS	MISCHARGED	MISDONE	MISFITTED	MISINFORMED
MISALLEGE	MISCHARGES	MISDONNE	MISFITTING	MISINFORMING
MISALLEGED	MISCHARGING	MISDOUBT	MISFORM	MISINFORMS
MISALLEGES	MISCHIEF	MISDOUBTED	MISFORMED	MISINTEND
MISALLEGING	MISCHIEFED	MISDOUBTING	MISFORMING	MISINTENDED
MISALLIED	MISCHIEFING	MISDOUBTS	MISFORMS	MISINTENDING
MISALLOT	MISCHIEFS	MISDRAW	MISGAVE	MISINTENDS
MISALLOTS	MISCIBLE	MISDRAWING	MISGIVE	MISJOIN
MISALLOTTED	MISCOLOUR	MISDRAWINGS	MISGIVEN	MISJOINED
MISALLOTTING	MISCOLOURED	MISDRAWN	MISGIVES	MISJOINING
MISANDRIES	MISCOLOURING	MISDRAWS	MISGIVING	MISJOINS
MISANDRY	MISCOLOURS	MISDREAD	MISGIVINGS	MISJUDGE
MISAPPLIED	MISCOPIED	MISDREADS	MISGO	MISJUDGED
MISAPPLIES	MISCOPIES	MISDREW	MISGOES	MISJUDGES
MISAPPLY	MISCOPY	MISE	MISGOING	MISJUDGING
MISAPPLYING	MISCOPYING	MISEASE	MISGONE	MISKEN
MISARRAY	MISCOUNT	MISEASES	MISGOTTEN	MISKENNED
MISARRAYS	MISCOUNTED	MISEMPLOY	MISGOVERN	MISKENNING
MISASSIGN	MISCOUNTING	MISEMPLOYED	MISGOVERNED	MISKENS
MISASSIGNED	MISCOUNTS	MISEMPLOYING	MISGOVERNING	MISKENT
MISASSIGNING	MISCREANT	MISEMPLOYS	MISGOVERNS	MISKNEW
MISASSIGNS	MISCREANTS	MISENTRIES	MISGRAFF	MISKNOW
MISAUNTER	MISCREATE	MISENTRY	MISGRAFFED	MISKNOWING
MISAUNTERS	MISCREDIT	MISER	MISGRAFFING	MISKNOWN
MISAVISED	MISCREDITED	MISERABLE	MISGRAFFS	MISKNOWS
MISBECAME	MISCREDITING	MISERABLES	MISGRAFT	MISLAID
MISBECOME	MISCREDITS	MISERABLY	MISGRAFTED	MISLAY
MISBECOMES	MISCREED	MISERE	MISGRAFTING	MISLAYING
MISBECOMING	MISCREEDS	MISÈRE	MISGRAFTS	MISLAYS
MISBEGOT	MISCUE	MISERERE	MISGROWTH	MISLEAD
MISBEHAVE	MISCUED	MISEREES	MISGROWTHS	MISLEADER
MISBEHAVED	MISCUEING	MISÈRES	MISGUGGLE	MISLEADERS
MISBEHAVES	MISCUES	MISERIES	MISGUGGLED	MISLEADING
MISBEHAVING	MISCUING	MISERLY	MISGUGGLES	MISLEADS
MISBELIEF	MISDATE	MISERS	MISGUGGLING	MISLEARED
MISBELIEFS	MISDATED	MISERY	MISGUIDE	MISLED
MISBESEEM	MISDATES	MISES	MISGUIDED	MISLEEKE
MISBESEEMED	MISDATING	MISESTEEM	MISGUIDER	MISLEEKED
MISBESEEMING	MISDEAL	MISESTEEMED	MISGUIDERS	MISLEEKES

MISLEEKING	MISONEISTS	MISREPORTED	MISSPEAKS	MISTIMED
MISLETOE	MISORDER	MISREPORTING	MISSPELL	MISTIMES
MISLETOES	MISORDERED	MISREPORTS	MISSPELLED	MISTIMING
MISLIGHT	MISORDERING	MISRULE	MISSPELLING	MISTINESS
MISLIGHTED	MISORDERS	MISRULED	MISSPELLINGS	MISTINESSES
MISLIGHTING	MISOS	MISRULES	MISSPELLS	MISTING
MISLIGHTS	MISPICKEL	MISRULING	MISSPELT	MISTINGS
MISLIKE	MISPICKELS	MISS	MISSPEND	MISTITLE
MISLIKED	MISPLACE	MISSA	MISSPENDING	MISTITLED
MISLIKER	MISPLACED	MISSABLE	MISSPENDS	MISTITLES
MISLIKERS	MISPLACES	MISSAID	MISSPENT	MISTITLING
MISLIKES	MISPLACING	MISSAL	MISSPOKE	MISTLE
MISLIKING	MISPLAY	MISSALS	MISSPOKEN	MISTLED
MISLIKINGS	MISPLAYED	MISSAS	MISSTATE	MISTLES
MISLIPPEN	MISPLAYING	MISSAW	MISSTATED	MISTLETOE
MISLIPPENED	MISPLAYS	MISSAY	MISSTATES	MISTLETOES
MISLIPPENING	MISPLEAD	MISSAYING	MISSTATING	MISTLING
MISLIPPENS	MISPLEADED	MISSAYINGS	MISSTEP	MISTOLD
MISLIT	MISPLEADING	MISSAYS	MISSTEPPED	MISTOOK
MISLIVE	MISPLEADINGS	MISSED	MISSTEPPING	MISTRAL
MISLIVED	MISPLEADS	MISSEE	MISSTEPS	MISTRALS
MISLIVES	MISPLEASE	MISSEEING	MISSUIT	MISTREAT
MISLIVING	MISPLEASED	MISSEEM	MISSUITED	MISTREATED
MISLUCK	MISPLEASES	MISSEEMED	MISSUITING	MISTREATING
MISLUCKED	MISPLEASING	MISSEEMING	MISSUITS	MISTREATS
MISLUCKING	MISPOINT	MISSEEMINGS	MISSUSES	MISTRESS
MISLUCKS	MISPOINTED	MISSEEMS	MISSY	MISTRESSED
MISMADE	MISPOINTING	MISSEEN	MIST	MISTRESSES
MISMAKE	MISPOINTS	MISSEES	MISTAKE	MISTRESSING
MISMAKES	MISPRAISE	MISSEL	MISTAKEN	MISTRIAL
MISMAKING	MISPRAISED	MISSELS	MISTAKES	MISTRIALS
MISMANAGE	MISPRAISES	MISSEND	MISTAKING	MISTRUST
MISMANAGED	MISPRAISING	MISSENDING	MISTAKINGS	MISTRUSTED
MISMANAGES	MISPRINT	MISSENDS	MISTAUGHT	MISTRUSTING
MISMANAGING	MISPRINTED	MISSENT	MISTEACH	MISTRUSTS
MISMARRIED	MISPRINTING	MISSES	MISTEACHES	MISTRYST
MISMARRIES	MISPRINTS	MISSET	MISTEACHING	MISTRYSTED
MISMARRY	MISPRISE	MISSETS	MISTED	MISTRYSTING
MISMARRYING	MISPRISED	MISSETTING	MISTELL	MISTRYSTS
MISMATCH	MISPRISES	MISSHAPE	MISTELLING	MISTS
MISMATCHED	MISPRISING	MISSHAPED	MISTELLS	MISTUNE
MISMATCHES	MISPRIZE	MISSHAPEN	MISTEMPER	MISTUNED
MISMATCHING	MISPRIZED	MISSHAPES	MISTEMPERED	MISTUNES
MISMATE	MISPRIZES	MISSHAPING	MISTEMPERING	MISTUNING
MISMATED	MISPRIZING	MISSHOOD	MISTEMPERS	MISTY
MISMATES	MISPROUD	MISSHOODS	MISTER	MISUSAGE
MISMATING	MISQUOTE	MISSIER	MISTERED	MISUSAGES
MISMETRE	MISQUOTED	MISSIES	MISTERIES	MISUSE
MISMETRED	MISQUOTES	MISSIEST	MISTERING	MISUSED
MISMETRES	MISQUOTING	MISSILE	MISTERM	MISUSER
MISMETRING	MISRATE	MISSILERIES	MISTERMED	MISUSERS
MISNAME	MISRATED	MISSILERY	MISTERMING	MISUSES
MISNAMED	MISRATES	MISSILES	MISTERMS	MISUSING
MISNAMES	MISRATING	MISSILRIES	MISTERS	MISUST
MISNAMING	MISREAD	MISSILRY	MISTERY	MISWEEN
MISNOMER	MISREADING	MISSING	MISTFUL	MISWEENED
MISNOMERED	MISREADINGS	MISSINGLY	MISTHINK	MISWEENING
MISNOMERING	MISREADS	MISSION	MISTHINKING	MISWEENS
MISNOMERS	MISRECKON	MISSIONED	MISTHINKS	MISWEND
MISO	MISRECKONED	MISSIONER	MISTHOUGHT	MISWENDING
MISOCLERE	MISRECKONING	MISSIONERS	MISTHOUGHTS	MISWENDS
MISOGAMIES	MISRECKONINGS	MISSIONING	MISTICO	MISWENT
MISOGAMY	MISRECKONS	MISSIONS	MISTICOS	MISWORD
MISOGYNIES	MISREGARD	MISSIS	MISTIER	MISWORDED
MISOGYNY	MISREGARDS	MISSISES	MISTIEST	MISWORDING
MISOLOGIES	MISRELATE	MISSISH	MISTIGRIS	MISWORDINGS
MISOLOGY	MISRELATED	MISSIVE	MISTIGRISES	MISWORDS
MISONEISM	MISRELATES	MISSIVES	MISTILY	MISWRITE
MISONEISMS	MISRELATING	MISSPEAK	MISTIME	MISWRITES
MISONEIST	MISREPORT	MISSPEAKING		MISWRITING

MISWRITTEN
MISWROTE
MISYOKE
MISYOKED
MISYOKES
MISYOKING
MITCH
MITCHED
MITCHES
MITCHING
MITE
MITER
MITERED
MITERING
MITERS
MITES
MITHER
MITHERED
MITHERING
MITHERS
MITICIDAL
MITICIDE
MITICIDES
MITIER
MITIEST
MITIGABLE
MITIGANT
MITIGATE
MITIGATED
MITIGATES
MITIGATING
MITIGATOR
MITIGATORS
MITOGEN
MITOGENIC
MITOGENS
MITOSES
MITOSIS
MITOTIC
MITRAILLE
MITRAILLES
MITRAL
MITRE
MITRED
MITRES
MITRIFORM
MITRING
MITT
MITTEN
MITTENED
MITTENS
MITTIMUS
MITTIMUSES
MITTS
MITY
MITZVAH
MITZVAHS
MITZVOTH
MIURUS
MIURUSES
MIX
MIXABLE
MIXED
MIXEDLY
MIXEDNESS
MIXEDNESSES
MIXEN
MIXENS
MIXER
MIXERS

MIXES
MIXIER
MIXIEST
MIXING
MIXT
MIXTION
MIXTIONS
MIXTURE
MIXTURES
MIXY
MIZ
MIZEN
MIZENS
MIZES
MIZMAZE
MIZMAZES
MIZZ
MIZZEN
MIZZENS
MIZZES
MIZZLE
MIZZLED
MIZZLES
MIZZLIER
MIZZLIEST
MIZZLING
MIZZLINGS
MIZZLY
MIZZONITE
MIZZONITES
MNA
MNAS
MNEME
MNEMES
MNEMIC
MNEMON
MNEMONIC
MNEMONICS
MNEMONIST
MNEMONISTS
MNEMONS
MO
MOA
MOAN
MOANED
MOANER
MOANERS
MOANFUL
MOANFULLY
MOANING
MOANS
MOAS
MOAT
MOATED
MOATING
MOATS
MOB
MOBBED
MOBBIE
MOBBIES
MOBBING
MOBBISH
MOBBLE
MOBBLED
MOBBLES
MOBBLING
MOBBY
MOBILE
MOBILES
MOBILISE

MOBILISED
MOBILISES
MOBILISING
MOBILITIES
MOBILITY
MOBILIZE
MOBILIZED
MOBILIZES
MOBILIZING
MOBLE
MOBLED
MOBLES
MOBLING
MOBOCRACIES
MOBOCRACY
MOBOCRAT
MOBOCRATS
MOBS
MOBSMAN
MOBSMEN
MOBSTER
MOBSTERS
MOCASSIN
MOCASSINS
MOCCASIN
MOCCASINS
MOCHA
MOCHAS
MOCHELL
MOCHELLS
MOCK
MOCKABLE
MOCKADO
MOCKADOES
MOCKAGE
MOCKAGES
MOCKED
MOCKER
MOCKERIES
MOCKERS
MOCKERY
MOCKING
MOCKINGLY
MOCKINGS
MOCKS
MOCOCK
MOCOCKS
MOCUCK
MOCUCKS
MOCUDDUM
MOCUDDUMS
MOD
MODAL
MODALISM
MODALISMS
MODALIST
MODALISTS
MODALITIES
MODALITY
MODALLY
MODE
MODEL
MODELLED
MODELLER
MODELLERS
MODELLING
MODELLINGS
MODELS
MODEM
MODEMS

MODENA
MODENAS
MODERATE
MODERATED
MODERATES
MODERATING
MODERATO
MODERATOR
MODERATORS
MODERATOS
MODERN
MODERNER
MODERNEST
MODERNISE
MODERNISED
MODERNISES
MODERNISING
MODERNISM
MODERNISMS
MODERNIST
MODERNISTS
MODERNITIES
MODERNITY
MODERNIZE
MODERNIZED
MODERNIZES
MODERNIZING
MODERNLY
MODERNS
MODES
MODEST
MODESTER
MODESTEST
MODESTIES
MODESTLY
MODESTY
MODI
MODICUM
MODICUMS
MODIFIED
MODIFIER
MODIFIERS
MODIFIES
MODIFY
MODIFYING
MODII
MODILLION
MODILLIONS
MODIOLAR
MODIOLI
MODIOLUS
MODIOLUSES
MODISH
MODISHLY
MODIST
MODISTE
MODISTES
MODISTS
MODIUS
MODIWORT
MODIWORTS
MODS
MODULAR
MODULATE
MODULATED
MODULATES
MODULATING
MODULATOR
MODULATORS
MODULE

MODULES
MODULI
MODULO
MODULUS
MODUS
MOE
MOELLON
MOELLONS
MOES
MOFETTE
MOFETTES
MOFUSSIL
MOFUSSILS
MOG
MOGGAN
MOGGANS
MOGGIE
MOGGIES
MOGGY
MOGS
MOGUL
MOGULS
MOHAIR
MOHAIRS
MOHAWK
MOHAWKS
MOHEL
MOHELS
MOHR
MOHRS
MOHUR
MOHURS
MOIDER
MOIDERED
MOIDERING
MOIDERS
MOIDORE
MOIDORES
MOIETIES
MOIETY
MOIL
MOILED
MOILER
MOILERS
MOILING
MOILS
MOINEAU
MOINEAUS
MOIRE
MOIRÉ
MOIRES
MOIRÉS
MOIST
MOISTED
MOISTEN
MOISTENED
MOISTENING
MOISTENS
MOISTER
MOISTEST
MOISTIFIED
MOISTIFIES
MOISTIFY
MOISTIFYING
MOISTING
MOISTLY
MOISTNESS
MOISTNESSES
MOISTS
MOISTURE

MOISTURES
MOIT
MOITHER
MOITHERED
MOITHERING
MOITHERS
MOITS
MOKADDAM
MOKADDAMS
MOKE
MOKES
MOKI
MOKIS
MOKO
MOKOS
MOLAL
MOLALITIES
MOLALITY
MOLAR
MOLARITIES
MOLARITY
MOLARS
MOLASSES
MOLD
MOLDED
MOLDING
MOLDS
MOLDWARP
MOLDWARPS
MOLE
MOLECAST
MOLECASTS
MOLECULAR
MOLECULE
MOLECULES
MOLEHILL
MOLEHILLS
MOLERAT
MOLERATS
MOLES
MOLESKIN
MOLESKINS
MOLEST
MOLESTED
MOLESTER
MOLESTERS
MOLESTFUL
MOLESTING
MOLESTS
MOLIES
MOLIMEN
MOLIMENS
MOLINE
MOLINES
MOLL
MOLLA
MOLLAH
MOLLAHS
MOLLAS
MOLLIE
MOLLIES
MOLLIFIED
MOLLIFIER
MOLLIFIERS
MOLLIFIES
MOLLIFY
MOLLIFYING
MOLLITIES
MOLLS
MOLLUSC

MOLLUSCAN
MOLLUSCS
MOLLUSK
MOLLUSKS
MOLLY
MOLLYMAWK
MOLLYMAWKS
MOLOCH
MOLOCHISE
MOLOCHISED
MOLOCHISES
MOLOCHISING
MOLOCHIZE
MOLOCHIZED
MOLOCHIZES
MOLOCHIZING
MOLOCHS
MOLOSSI
MOLOSSUS
MOLT
MOLTED
MOLTEN
MOLTENLY
MOLTING
MOLTO
MOLTS
MOLY
MOLYBDATE
MOLYBDATES
MOLYBDIC
MOLYBDOUS
MOM
MOME
MOMENT
MOMENTA
MOMENTANY
MOMENTARY
MOMENTLY
MOMENTOUS
MOMENTS
MOMENTUM
MOMES
MOMMA
MOMMAS
MOMMET
MOMMETS
MOMMIES
MOMMY
MOMS
MONA
MONACHAL
MONACHISM
MONACHISMS
MONACHIST
MONACID
MONACT
MONACTINE
MONAD
MONADES
MONADIC
MONADICAL
MONADISM
MONADISMS
MONADS
MONAL
MONALS
MONANDRIES
MONANDRY
MONARCH
MONARCHAL

MONARCHIC
MONARCHIES
MONARCHS
MONARCHY
MONARDA
MONARDAS
MONAS
MONASES
MONASTERIES
MONASTERY
MONASTIC
MONASTICS
MONATOMIC
MONAUL
MONAULS
MONAURAL
MONAXIAL
MONAXON
MONAXONIC
MONAXONS
MONAZITE
MONAZITES
MONDAIN
MONDAINE
MONDAINES
MONDAINS
MONDIAL
MONECIOUS
MONER
MONERA
MONERGISM
MONERGISMS
MONERON
MONERS
MONETARY
MONETH
MONETHS
MONETISE
MONETISED
MONETISES
MONETISING
MONETIZE
MONETIZED
MONETIZES
MONETIZING
MONEY
MONEYED
MONEYER
MONEYERS
MONEYLESS
MONEYS
MONEYWORT
MONEYWORTS
MONG
MONGCORN
MONGCORNS
MONGER
MONGERIES
MONGERING
MONGERINGS
MONGERS
MONGERY
MONGOL
MONGOLISM
MONGOLISMS
MONGOLOID
MONGOLOIDS
MONGOLS
MONGOOSE
MONGOOSES

MONGREL
MONGRELLY
MONGRELS
MONGS
MONIAL
MONIALS
MONICKER
MONICKERS
MONIED
MONIES
MONIKER
MONIKERS
MONILIA
MONILIAS
MONIMENT
MONIMENTS
MONIPLIES
MONISM
MONISMS
MONIST
MONISTIC
MONISTS
MONITION
MONITIONS
MONITIVE
MONITOR
MONITORED
MONITORING
MONITORS
MONITORY
MONITRESS
MONITRESSES
MONK
MONKERIES
MONKERY
MONKEY
MONKEYED
MONKEYING
MONKEYISH
MONKEYISM
MONKEYISMS
MONKEYS
MONKFISH
MONKFISHES
MONKHOOD
MONKHOODS
MONKISH
MONKS
MONKSHOOD
MONKSHOODS
MONO
MONOACID
MONOAMINE
MONOAMINES
MONOBASIC
MONOCARP
MONOCARPS
MONOCEROS
MONOCEROSES
MONOCHORD
MONOCHORDS
MONOCLE
MONOCLED
MONOCLES
MONOCLINE
MONOCLINES
MONOCOQUE
MONOCOQUES
MONOCOT
MONOCOTS

MONOCRACIES
MONOCRACY
MONOCRAT
MONOCRATS
MONOCULAR
MONOCYTE
MONOCYTES
MONODIC
MONODICAL
MONODIES
MONODIST
MONODISTS
MONODONT
MONODRAMA
MONODRAMAS
MONODY
MONOECISM
MONOECISMS
MONOFIL
MONOFILS
MONOGAMIC
MONOGAMIES
MONOGAMY
MONOGENIES
MONOGENY
MONOGLOT
MONOGLOTS
MONOGONIES
MONOGONY
MONOGRAM
MONOGRAMS
MONOGRAPH
MONOGRAPHED
MONOGRAPHING
MONOGRAPHS
MONOGYNIES
MONOGYNY
MONOHULL
MONOHULLS
MONOLATER
MONOLATERS
MONOLATRIES
MONOLATRY
MONOLITH
MONOLITHS
MONOLOGIC
MONOLOGIES
MONOLOGUE
MONOLOGUES
MONOLOGY
MONOMACHIES
MONOMACHY
MONOMANIA
MONOMANIAS
MONOMARK
MONOMARKS
MONOMER
MONOMERIC
MONOMERS
MONOMETER
MONOMETERS
MONOMIAL
MONOMIALS
MONOMODE
MONOPHAGIES
MONOPHAGY
MONOPHASE
MONOPHONIES
MONOPHONY
MONOPITCH

MONOPLANE
MONOPLANES
MONOPODE
MONOPODES
MONOPODIA
MONOPOLE
MONOPOLES
MONOPOLIES.
MONOPOLY
MONOPSONIES
MONOPSONY
MONOPTERA
MONOPTOTE
MONOPTOTES
MONORAIL
MONORAILS
MONORCHID
MONORHINE
MONORHYME
MONORHYMES
MONOS
MONOSES
MONOSIES
MONOSIS
MONOSTICH
MONOSTICHS
MONOSTYLE
MONOSY
MONOTINT
MONOTINTS
MONOTONE
MONOTONED
MONOTONES
MONOTONIC
MONOTONIES
MONOTONING
MONOTONY
MONOTREME
MONOTREMES
MONOTROCH
MONOTROCHS
MONOTYPE
MONOTYPES
MONOTYPIC
MONOXIDE
MONOXIDES
MONOXYLON
MONOXYLONS
MONSIEUR
MONSOON
MONSOONAL
MONSOONS
MONSTER
MONSTERA
MONSTERAS
MONSTERS
MONSTROUS
MONTAGE
MONTAGES
MONTANE
MONTANT
MONTANTO
MONTANTOS
MONTANTS
MONTARIA
MONTARIAS
MONTE
MONTEITH
MONTEITHS
MONTEM

MONTEMS
MONTERO
MONTEROS
MONTES
MONTH
MONTHLIES
MONTHLING
MONTHLINGS
MONTHLY
MONTHS
MONTICLE
MONTICLES
MONTICULE
MONTICULES
MONTRE
MONTRES
MONTURE
MONTURES
MONUMENT
MONUMENTED
MONUMENTING
MONUMENTS
MONY
MONYPLIES
MONZONITE
MONZONITES
MOO
MOOCH
MOOCHED
MOOCHER
MOOCHERS
MOOCHES
MOOCHING
MOOD
MOODIED
MOODIER
MOODIES
MOODIEST
MOODILY
MOODINESS
MOODINESSES
MOODS
MOODY
MOODYING
MOOED
MOOI
MOOING
MOOKTAR
MOOKTARS
MOOL
MOOLA
MOOLAH
MOOLAHS
MOOLAS
MOOLED
MOOLI
MOOLIES
MOOLING
MOOLIS
MOOLS
MOOLY
MOON
MOONBEAM
MOONBEAMS
MOONBLIND
MOONCALF
MOONCALVES
MOONED
MOONER
MOONERS

MOONEYE
MOONEYES
MOONFACE
MOONFACES
MOONIER
MOONIES
MOONIEST
MOONING
MOONISH
MOONLESS
MOONLET
MOONLETS
MOONLIGHT
MOONLIGHTS
MOONLIT
MOONQUAKE
MOONQUAKES
MOONRAKER
MOONRAKERS
MOONRISE
MOONRISES
MOONS
MOONSAIL
MOONSAILS
MOONSCAPE
MOONSCAPES
MOONSEED
MOONSEEDS
MOONSET
MOONSETS
MOONSHEE
MOONSHEES
MOONSHINE
MOONSHINES
MOONSHINY
MOONSHOT
MOONSHOTS
MOONSTONE
MOONSTONES
MOONWORT
MOONWORTS
MOONY
MOOP
MOOPED
MOOPING
MOOPS
MOOR
MOORAGE
MOORAGES
MOORCOCK
MOORCOCKS
MOORED
MOORFOWL
MOORFOWLS
MOORHEN
MOORHENS
MOORIER
MOORIEST
MOORILL
MOORILLS
MOORING
MOORINGS
MOORISH
MOORLAND
MOORLANDS
MOORLOG
MOORLOGS
MOORMAN
MOORMEN
MOORS

MOORVA
MOORVAS
MOORY
MOOS
MOOSE
MOOSEYARD
MOOSEYARDS
MOOT
MOOTABLE
MOOTED
MOOTER
MOOTERS
MOOTEST
MOOTING
MOOTINGS
MOOTMAN
MOOTMEN
MOOTS
MOOVE
MOOVED
MOOVES
MOOVING
MOP
MOPANE
MOPANES
MOPBOARD
MOPBOARDS
MOPE
MOPED
MOPEDS
MOPEHAWK
MOPEHAWKS
MOPER
MOPERS
MOPES
MOPIER
MOPIEST
MOPING
MOPINGLY
MOPISH
MOPISHLY
MOPOKE
MOPOKES
MOPPED
MOPPER
MOPPERS
MOPPET
MOPPETS
MOPPIER
MOPPIEST
MOPPING
MOPPY
MOPS
MOPSIES
MOPSTICK
MOPSTICKS
MOPSY
MOPUS
MOPUSES
MOPY
MOQUETTE
MOQUETTES
MOR
MORA
MORACEOUS
MORAINAL
MORAINE
MORAINES
MORAINIC
MORAL

MORALE
MORALES
MORALISE
MORALISED
MORALISER
MORALISERS
MORALISES
MORALISING
MORALISM
MORALISMS
MORALIST
MORALISTS
MORALITIES
MORALITY
MORALIZE
MORALIZED
MORALIZER
MORALIZERS
MORALIZES
MORALIZING
MORALL
MORALLED
MORALLER
MORALLERS
MORALLING
MORALLS
MORALLY
MORALS
MORAS
MORASS
MORASSES
MORASSY
MORAT
MORATORIA
MORATORY
MORATS
MORAY
MORAYS
MORBID
MORBIDITIES
MORBIDITY
MORBIDLY
MORBIFIC
MORBILLI
MORBUS
MORBUSES
MORCEAU
MORCEAUX
MORDACITIES
MORDACITY
MORDANCIES
MORDANCY
MORDANT
MORDANTED
MORDANTING
MORDANTLY
MORDANTS
MORDENT
MORDENTS
MORE
MOREEN
MOREENS
MOREISH
MOREL
MORELLO
MORELLOS
MORELS
MORENDO
MOREOVER
MORES

MORGANITE
MORGANITES
MORGAY
MORGAYS
MORGEN
MORGENS
MORGUE
MORGUES
MORIA
MORIAS
MORIBUND
MORICHE
MORICHES
MORION
MORIONS
MORISCO
MORISCOES
MORISCOS
MORISH
MORKIN
MORKINS
MORLING
MORLINGS
MORMAOR
MORMAORS
MORN
MORNAY
MORNAYS
MORNE
MORNE
MORNED
MORNES
MORNING
MORNINGS
MORNS
MOROCCO
MOROCCOS
MORON
MORONIC
MORONS
MOROSE
MOROSELY
MOROSER
MOROSEST
MOROSITIES
MOROSITY
MORPH
MORPHEAN
MORPHEME
MORPHEMES
MORPHEMIC
MORPHEMICS
MORPHETIC
MORPHEW
MORPHEWS
MORPHIA
MORPHIAS
MORPHIC
MORPHINE
MORPHINES
MORPHO
MORPHOS
MORPHOSES
MORPHOSIS
MORPHOTIC
MORPHS
MORRA
MORRAS
MORRHUA
MORRHUAS

MORRICE
MORRICES
MORRION
MORRIONS
MORRIS
MORRISED
MORRISES
MORRISING
MORRO
MORROS
MORROW
MORROWS
MORS
MORSAL
MORSE
MORSEL
MORSELLED
MORSELLING
MORSELS
MORSES
MORSURE
MORSURES
MORT
MORTAL
MORTALISE
MORTALISED
MORTALISES
MORTALISING
MORTALITIES
MORTALITY
MORTALIZE
MORTALIZED
MORTALIZES
MORTALIZING
MORTALLY
MORTALS
MORTAR
MORTARED
MORTARING
MORTARS
MORTBELL
MORTBELLS
MORTCLOTH
MORTCLOTHS
MORTGAGE
MORTGAGED
MORTGAGEE
MORTGAGEES
MORTGAGER
MORTGAGERS
MORTGAGES
MORTGAGING
MORTGAGOR
MORTGAGORS
MORTICE
MORTICED
MORTICER
MORTICERS
MORTICES
MORTICIAN
MORTICIANS
MORTICING
MORTIFIC
MORTIFIED
MORTIFIER
MORTIFIERS
MORTIFIES
MORTIFY
MORTIFYING
MORTIFYINGS

MORTISE
MORTISED
MORTISER
MORTISERS
MORTISES
MORTISING
MORTLING
MORTLINGS
MORTMAIN
MORTMAINS
MORTS
MORTUARIES
MORTUARY
MORULA
MORULAR
MORULAS
MORWONG
MORWONGS
MOSAIC
MOSAICISM
MOSAICISMS
MOSAICIST
MOSAICISTS
MOSAICS
MOSCHATEL
MOSCHATELS
MOSE
MOSED
MOSES
MOSEY
MOSEYED
MOSEYING
MOSEYS
MOSHAV
MOSHAVIM
MOSING
MOSKONFYT
MOSKONFYTS
MOSLINGS
MOSQUE
MOSQUES
MOSQUITO
MOSQUITOES
MOSQUITOS
MOSS
MOSSED
MOSSES
MOSSIE
MOSSIER
MOSSIES
MOSSIEST
MOSSINESS
MOSSINESSES
MOSSING
MOSSLAND
MOSSLANDS
MOSSPLANT
MOSSPLANTS
MOSSY
MOST
MOSTLY
MOSTS
MOSTWHAT
MOT
MOTE
MOTED
MOTEL
MOTELIER
MOTELIERS
MOTELS

MOTEN
MOTES
MOTET
MOTETS
MOTETT
MOTETTIST
MOTETTISTS
MOTETTS
MOTEY
MOTH
MOTHBALL
MOTHBALLED
MOTHBALLING
MOTHBALLS
MOTHED
MOTHER
MOTHERED
MOTHERING
MOTHERINGS
MOTHERLY
MOTHERS
MOTHERY
MOTHIER
MOTHIEST
MOTHS
MOTIV
MOTIER
MOTIEST
MOTIF
MOTIFO
MOTILE
MOTILES
MOTILITIES
MOTILITY
MOTION
MOTIONAL
MOTIONED
MOTIONING
MOTIONIST
MOTIONISTS
MOTIONS
MOTIVATE
MOTIVATED
MOTIVATES
MOTIVATING
MOTIVE
MOTIVED
MOTIVES
MOTIVIC
MOTIVING
MOTIVITIES
MOTIVITY
MOTLEY
MOTLEYER
MOTLEYEST
MOTLEYS
MOTLIER
MOTLIEST
MOTMOT
MOTMOTS
MOTOCROSS
MOTOCROSSES
MOTOR
MOTORABLE
MOTORAIL
MOTORAILS
MOTORCADE
MOTORCADES
MOTORED
MOTORIAL

MOTORING
MOTORISE
MOTORISED
MOTORISES
MOTORISING
MOTORIST
MOTORISTS
MOTORIUM
MOTORIUMS
MOTORIZE
MOTORIZED
MOTORIZES
MOTORIZING
MOTORMAN
MOTORMEN
MOTORS
MOTORWAY
MOTORWAYS
MOTORY
MOTOSCAFI
MOTOSCAFO
MOTS
MOTSER
MOTSERS
MOTT
MOTTE
MOTTES
MOTTIER
MOTTIEST
MOTTLE
MOTTLED
MOTTLES
MOTTLING
MOTTLINGS
MOTTO
MOTTOED
MOTTOES
MOTTS
MOTTY
MOTUCA
MOTUCAS
MOTZA
MOTZAS
MOU
MOUCH
MOUCHARD
MOUCHARDS
MOUCHED
MOUCHER
MOUCHERS
MOUCHES
MOUCHING
MOUCHOIR
MOUCHOIRS
MOUDIWART
MOUDIWARTS
MOUDIWORT
MOUDIWORTS
MOUE
MOUES
MOUFFLON
MOUFFLONS
MOUFLON
MOUFLONS
MOUGHT
MOUILLÉ
MOUJIK
MOUJIKS
MOULAGE
MOULAGES

MOULD	MOUSERY	MOVINGLY	MUCHEL	MUDÉJAR
MOULDABLE	MOUSES	MOVY	MUCHELL	MUDÉJARES
MOULDED	MOUSEY	MOW	MUCHELLS	MUDIR
MOULDER	MOUSIE	MOWA	MUCHELS	MUDIRIA
MOULDERED	MOUSIER	MOWAS	MUCHES	MUDIRIAS
MOULDERING	MOUSIES	MOWBURN	MUCHLY	MUDIRIEH
MOULDERS	MOUSIEST	MOWBURNED	MUCHNESS	MUDIRIEHS
MOULDIER	MOUSING	MOWBURNING	MUCHNESSES	MUDIRS
MOULDIEST	MOUSINGS	MOWBURNS	MUCIC	MUDLARK
MOULDING	MOUSLE	MOWBURNT	MUCID	MUDLARKED
MOULDINGS	MOUSLED	MOWDIWART	MUCIGEN	MUDLARKING
MOULDS	MOUSLES	MOWDIWARTS	MUCIGENS	MUDLARKS
MOULDWARP	MOUSLING	MOWDIWORT	MUCILAGE	MUDPACK
MOULDWARPS	MOUSMÉ	MOWDIWORTS	MUCILAGES	MUDPACKS
MOULDY	MOUSMEE	MOWED	MUCIN	MUDRA
MOULIN	MOUSMEES	MOWER	MUCINS	MUDRAS
MOULINET	MOUSMÉS	MOWERS	MUCK	MUDS
MOULINETS	MOUSSAKA	MOWING	MUCKED	MUDSCOW
MOULINS	MOUSSAKAS	MOWINGS	MUCKENDER	MUDSCOWS
MOULS	MOUSSE	MOWN	MUCKENDERS	MUDSTONE
MOULT	MOUSSES	MOWRA	MUCKER	MUDSTONES
MOULTED	MOUST	MOWRAS	MUCKERED	MUDWORT
MOULTEN	MOUSTACHE	MOWS	MUCKERING	MUDWORTS
MOULTING	MOUSTACHES	MOXA	MUCKERS	MUEDDIN
MOULTINGS	MOUSTED	MOXAS	MUCKIER	MUEDDINS
MOULTS	MOUSTING	MOXIE	MUCKIEST	MUESLI
MOUND	MOUSTS	MOXIES	MUCKINESS	MUESLIS
MOUNDED	MOUSY	MOY	MUCKINESSES	MUEZZIN
MOUNDING	MOUTAN	MOYA	MUCKING	MUEZZINS
MOUNDS	MOUTANS	MOYAS	MUCKLE	MUFF
MOUNSEER	MOUTER	MOYGASHEL	MUCKLES	MUFFED
MOUNSEERS	MOUTERED	MOYGASHELS	MUCKLUCK	MUFFETTEE
MOUNT	MOUTERER	MOYITIES	MUCKLUCKS	MUFFETTEES
MOUNTAIN	MOUTERERS	MOYITY	MUCKS	MUFFIN
MOUNTAINS	MOUTERING	MOYL	MUCKY	MUFFINEER
MOUNTANT	MOUTERS	MOYLE	MUCLUC	MUFFINEERS
MOUNTANTS	MOUTH	MOYLED	MUCLUCS	MUFFING
MOUNTED	MOUTHABLE	MOYLES	MUCOID	MUFFINS
MOUNTER	MOUTHED	MOYLING	MUCOR	MUFFLE
MOUNTERS	MOUTHER	MOYLS	MUCORS	MUFFLED
MOUNTIE	MOUTHERS	MOYS	MUCOSA	MUFFLER
MOUNTIES	MOUTHFUL	MOZ	MUCOSAE	MUFFLERS
MOUNTING	MOUTHFULS	MOZE	MUCOSITIES	MUFFLES
MOUNTINGS	MOUTHIER	MOZED	MUCOSITY	MUFFLING
MOUNTS	MOUTHIEST	MOZES	MUCOUS	MUFFS
MOUNTY	MOUTHING	MOZETTA	MUCRO	MUFLON
MOUP	MOUTHLESS	MOZETTAS	MUCRONATE	MUFLONS
MOUPED	MOUTHS	MOZING	MUCRONES	MUFTI
MOUPING	MOUTHWASH	MOZZ	MUCROS	MUFTIS
MOUPS	MOUTHWASHES	MOZZES	MUCULENT	MUG
MOURN	MOUTHY	MOZZETTA	MUCUS	MUGEARITE
MOURNED	MOUTON	MOZZETTAS	MUCUSES	MUGEARITES
MOURNER	MOUTONS	MOZZIE	MUD	MUGFUL
MOURNERS	MOVABLE	MOZZIES	MUDDED	MUGFULS
MOURNFUL	MOVABLES	MOZZLE	MUDDIED	MUGGED
MOURNING	MOVABLY	MOZZLES	MUDDIER	MUGGER
MOURNINGS	MOVE	MPRET	MUDDIES	MUGGERS
MOURNIVAL	MOVEABLE	MPRETS	MUDDIEST	MUGGIER
MOURNIVALS	MOVEABLES	MRIDAMGAM	MUDDILY	MUGGIEST
MOURNS	MOVEABLY	MRIDAMGAMS	MUDDINESS	MUGGINESS
MOUS	MOVED	MRIDANG	MUDDINESSES	MUGGINESSES
MOUSAKA	MOVELESS	MRIDANGA	MUDDING	MUGGING
MOUSAKAS	MOVEMENT	MRIDANGAM	MUDDLE	MUGGINGS
MOUSE	MOVEMENTS	MRIDANGAMS	MUDDLED	MUGGINS
MOUSED	MOVER	MRIDANGAS	MUDDLER	MUGGINSES
MOUSEKIN	MOVERS	MRIDANGS	MUDDLERS	MUGGISH
MOUSEKINS	MOVES	MU	MUDDLES	MUGGY
MOUSER	MOVIE	MUCATE	MUDDLING	MUGS
MOUSERIES	MOVIES	MUCATES	MUDDY	MUGSHOT
MOUSERS	MOVING	MUCH	MUDDYING	MUGSHOTS

MUGWORT	MULMULL	MUMMIFIES	MUNSHIS	MURLAIN
MUGWORTS	MULMULLS	MUMMIFORM	MUNSTER	MURLAINS
MUGWUMP	MULMULS	MUMMIFY	MUNSTERS	MURLAN
MUGWUMPS	MULSE	MUMMIFYING	MUNTIN	MURLANS
MUID	MULSES	MUMMING	MUNTING	MURLED
MUIDS	MULSH	MUMMINGS	MUNTINGS	MURLIER
MUIL	MULSHED	MUMMOCK	MUNTINS	MURLIEST
MUILS	MULSHES	MUMMOCKS	MUNTJAC	MURLIN
MUIR	MULSHING	MUMMS	MUNTJACS	MURLING
MUIRS	MULTEITIES	MUMMY	MUNTJAK	MURLINS
MUIST	MULTEITY	MUMMYING	MUNTJAKS	MURLS
MUISTED	MULTIFID	MUMP	MUON	MURLY
MUISTING	MULTIFIL	MUMPED	MUONIC	MURMUR
MUISTS	MULTIFILS	MUMPER	MUONIUM	MURMURED
MUJAHEDIN	MULTIFOIL	MUMPERS	MUONIUMS	MURMURER
MUJAHIDIN	MULTIFOILS	MUMPING	MUONS	MURMURERS
MUJIK	MULTIFORM	MUMPISH	MUQADDAM	MURMURING
MUJIKS	MULTIFORMS	MUMPISHLY	MUQADDAMS	MURMURINGS
MUKHTAR	MULTIHULL	MUMPS	MURAENA	MURMUROUS
MUKHTARS	MULTIHULLS	MUMPSIMUS	MURAENAS	MURMURS
MUKLUK	MULTIPARA	MUMPSIMUSES	MURAGE	MURPHIES
MUKLUKS	MULTIPARAE	MUMS	MURAGES	MURPHY
MULATTA	MULTIPARAS	MUMSIER	MURAL	MURRA
MULATTAS	MULTIPED	MUMSIEST	MURALIST	MURRAIN
MULATTO	MULTIPEDE	MUMSY	MURALISTS	MURRAINED
MULATTOS	MULTIPEDES	MUN	MUNALO	MURRAINS
MULBERRIES	MULTIPEDS	MUNCH	MURDER	MURRAM
MULBERRY	MULTIPLE	MUNCHED	MURDERED	MURRAMS
MULCH	MULTIPLES	MUNCHER	MURDERER	MURRAS
MULCHED	MULTIPLET	MUNCHERS	MURDERERS	MURRAY
MULCHES	MULTIPLETS	MUNCHES	MURDERESS	MURRAYS
MULCHING	MULTIPLEX	MUNCHING	MURDERESSES	MURRE
MULCT	MULTIPLEXED	MUNDANE	MURDERING	MURRELET
MULCTED	MULTIPLEXES	MUNDANELY	MURDEROUS	MURRELETS
MULCTING	MULTIPLEXING	MUNDANER	MURDERS	MURREN
MULCTS	MULTIPLIED	MUNDANEST	MURE	MURRENS
MULE	MULTIPLIES	MUNDANITIES	MURED	MURRES
MULES	MULTIPLY	MUNDANITY	MURENA	MURREY
MULETEER	MULTIPLYING	MUNDIC	MURENAS	MURREYS
MULETEERS	MULTITUDE	MUNDICS	MURES	MURRHA
MULEY	MULTITUDES	MUNDIFIED	MUREX	MURRHAS
MULEYS	MULTUM	MUNDIFIES	MUREXES	MURRHINE
MULGA	MULTUMS	MUNDIFY	MURGEON	MURRIES
MULGAS	MULTURE	MUNDIFYING	MURGEONED	MURRIN
MULISH	MULTURED	MUNDUNGUS	MURGEONING	MURRINE
MULISHLY	MULTURER	MUNDUNGUSES	MURGEONS	MURRINS
MULL	MULTURERS	MUNGCORN	MURIATE	MURRION
MULLAH	MULTURES	MUNGCORNS	MURIATED	MURRIONS
MULLAHS	MULTURING	MUNGO	MURIATES	MURRY
MULLED	MUM	MUNGOOSE	MURIATIC	MURTHER
MULLEIN	MUMBLE	MUNGOOSES	MURICATE	MURTHERED
MULLEINS	MUMBLED	MUNGOS	MURICATED	MURTHERER
MULLER	MUMBLER	MUNICIPAL	MURICES	MURTHERERS
MULLERS	MUMBLERS	MUNIFIED	MURIFORM	MURTHERING
MULLET	MUMBLES	MUNIFIES	MURINE	MURTHERS
MULLETS	MUMBLING	MUNIFY	MURINES	MURVA
MULLEY	MUMBLINGS	MUNIFYING	MURING	MURVAS
MULLEYS	MUMCHANCE	MUNIMENT	MURK	MUS
MULLIGAN	MUMCHANCES	MUNIMENTS	MURKER	MUSACEOUS
MULLIGANS	MUMM	MUNITE	MURKEST	MUSANG
MULLING	MUMMED	MUNITED	MURKIER	MUSANGS
MULLION	MUMMER	MUNITES	MURKIEST	MUSCADEL
MULLIONED	MUMMERIES	MUNITING	MURKILY	MUSCADELS
MULLIONS	MUMMERS	MUNITION	MURKINESS	MUSCADIN
MULLOCK	MUMMERY	MUNITIONED	MURKINESSES	MUSCADINE
MULLOCKS	MUMMIA	MUNITIONING	MURKISH	MUSCADINES
MULLOWAY	MUMMIAS	MUNITIONS	MURKS	MUSCADINS
MULLOWAYS	MUMMIED	MUNNION	MURKSOME	MUSCARINE
MULLS	MUMMIES	MUNNIONS	MURKY	MUSCARINES
MULMUL	MUMMIFIED	MUNSHI	MURL	MUSCAT

MUSCATEL
MUSCATELS
MUSCATS
MUSCID
MUSCIDS
MUSCLE
MUSCLED
MUSCLES
MUSCLING
MUSCLINGS
MUSCOID
MUSCOLOGIES
MUSCOLOGY
MUSCONE
MUSCONES
MUSCOSE
MUSCOVADO
MUSCOVADOS
MUSCOVITE
MUSCOVITES
MUSCULAR
MUSCULOUS
MUSE
MUSED
MUSEFUL
MUSEFULLY
MUSEOLOGIES
MUSEOLOGY
MUSER
MUSERS
MUSES
MUSET
MUSETS
MUSETTE
MUSETTES
MUSEUM
MUSEUMS
MUSH
MUSHA
MUSHED
MUSHER
MUSHERS
MUSHES
MUSHIER
MUSHIEST
MUSHILY
MUSHINESS
MUSHINESSES
MUSHING
MUSHROOM
MUSHROOMED
MUSHROOMING
MUSHROOMS
MUSHY
MUSIC
MUSICAL
MUSICALE
MUSICALES
MUSICALLY
MUSICALS
MUSICIAN
MUSICIANS
MUSICKED
MUSICKER
MUSICKERS
MUSICKING
MUSICS
MUSIMON
MUSIMONS
MUSING

MUSINGLY
MUSINGS
MUSIT
MUSITS
MUSIVE
MUSK
MUSKED
MUSKEG
MUSKEGS
MUSKET
MUSKETEER
MUSKETEERS
MUSKETOON
MUSKETOONS
MUSKETRIES
MUSKETRY
MUSKETS
MUSKIER
MUSKIEST
MUSKILY
MUSKINESS
MUSKINESSES
MUSKING
MUSKLE
MUSKLES
MUSKONE
MUSKONES
MUSKS
MUSKY
MUSLIN
MUSLINED
MUSLINET
MUSLINETS
MUSLINS
MUSMON
MUSMONS
MUSQUASH
MUSQUASHES
MUSROL
MUSROLS
MUSS
MUSSE
MUSSED
MUSSEL
MUSSELLED
MUSSELS
MUSSES
MUSSIER
MUSSIEST
MUSSINESS
MUSSINESSES
MUSSING
MUSSITATE
MUSSITATED
MUSSITATES
MUSSITATING
MUSSY
MUST
MUSTACHE
MUSTACHES
MUSTACHIO
MUSTACHIOS
MUSTANG
MUSTANGS
MUSTARD
MUSTARDS
MUSTED
MUSTEE
MUSTEES
MUSTELINE

MUSTELINES
MUSTER
MUSTERED
MUSTERER
MUSTERERS
MUSTERING
MUSTERS
MUSTH
MUSTHS
MUSTIER
MUSTIEST
MUSTING
MUSTS
MUSTY
MUTABLE
MUTABLY
MUTAGEN
MUTAGENIC
MUTAGENS
MUTANDA
MUTANDUM
MUTANT
MUTANTS
MUTATE
MUTATED
MUTATES
MUTATING
MUTATION
MUTATIONS
MUTATIVE
MUTATORY
MUTCH
MUTCHES
MUTCHKIN
MUTCHKINS
MUTE
MUTED
MUTELY
MUTENESS
MUTENESSES
MUTER
MUTES
MUTEST
MUTICOUS
MUTILATE
MUTILATED
MUTILATES
MUTILATING
MUTILATOR
MUTILATORS
MUTINE
MUTINED
MUTINEER
MUTINEERED
MUTINEERING
MUTINEERS
MUTINES
MUTING
MUTINIED
MUTINIES
MUTINING
MUTINOUS
MUTINY
MUTINYING
MUTISM
MUTISMS
MUTON
MUTONS
MUTOSCOPE
MUTOSCOPES

MUTT
MUTTER
MUTTERED
MUTTERER
MUTTERERS
MUTTERING
MUTTERINGS
MUTTERS
MUTTON
MUTTONS
MUTTONY
MUTTS
MUTUAL
MUTUALISE
MUTUALISED
MUTUALISES
MUTUALISING
MUTUALISM
MUTUALISMS
MUTUALITIES
MUTUALITY
MUTUALIZE
MUTUALIZED
MUTUALIZES
MUTUALIZING
MUTUALLY
MUTUCA
MUTUCAS
MUTULE
MUTULES
MUTUUM
MUTUUMS
MUX
MUXED
MUXES
MUXING
MUZHIK
MUZHIKS
MUZZIER
MUZZIEST
MUZZILY
MUZZINESS
MUZZINESSES
MUZZLE
MUZZLED
MUZZLER
MUZZLERS
MUZZLES
MUZZLING
MUZZY
MVULE
MVULES
MY
MYAL
MYALGIA
MYALGIAS
MYALGIC
MYALISM
MYALISMS
MYALL
MYALLS
MYCELIA
MYCELIAL
MYCELIUM
MYCETES
MYCETOMA
MYCETOMAS
MYCOLOGIC
MYCOLOGIES
MYCOLOGY

MYCOPHAGIES
MYCOPHAGY
MYCORHIZA
MYCORHIZAS
MYCOSES
MYCOSIS
MYCOTIC
MYCOTOXIN
MYCOTOXINS
MYDRIASES
MYDRIASIS
MYDRIATIC
MYDRIATICS
MYELIN
MYELINS
MYELITIS
MYELITISES
MYELOID
MYELOMA
MYELOMAS
MYELON
MYELONS
MYGALE
MYGALES
MYIASES
MYIASIS
MYLODON
MYLODONS
MYLODONT
MYLODONTS
MYLOHYOID
MYLOHYOIDS
MYLONITE
MYLONITES
MYLONITIC
MYNA
MYNAH
MYNAHS
MYNAS
MYNHEER
MYNHEERS
MYOBLAST
MYOBLASTS
MYOFIBRIL
MYOFIBRILS
MYOGEN
MYOGENIC
MYOGENS
MYOGLOBIN
MYOGLOBINS
MYOGRAM
MYOGRAMS
MYOGRAPH
MYOGRAPHIES
MYOGRAPHS
MYOGRAPHY
MYOID
MYOLOGIES
MYOLOGIST
MYOLOGISTS
MYOLOGY
MYOMA
MYOMANCIES
MYOMANCY
MYOMANTIC
MYOMAS
MYOPE
MYOPES
MYOPIA
MYOPIAS

MYOPIC
MYOPICS
MYOPS
MYOPSES
MYOSES
MYOSIN
MYOSINS
MYOSIS
MYOSITIC
MYOSITIS
MYOSITISES
MYOSOTE
MYOSOTES
MYOSOTIS
MYOSOTISES
MYOTIC
MYOTICS
MYOTUBE
MYOTUBES
MYRBANE
MYRBANES
MYRIAD
MYRIADS

MYRIADTH
MYRIADTHS
MYRIAPOD
MYRIAPODS
MYRINGA
MYRINGAS
MYRIOPOD
MYRIOPODS
MYRIORAMA
MYRIORAMAS
MYRISTIC
MYRMECOID
MYRMIDON
MYRMIDONS
MYROBALAN
MYROBALANS
MYRRH
MYRRHIC
MYRRHINE
MYRRHOL
MYRRHOLS
MYRRHS
MYRTLE

MYRTLES
MYSELF
MYSTAGOGIES
MYSTAGOGY
MYSTERIES
MYSTERY
MYSTIC
MYSTICAL
MYSTICISM
MYSTICISMS
MYSTICS
MYSTIFIED
MYSTIFIER
MYSTIFIERS
MYSTIFIES
MYSTIFY
MYSTIFYING
MYSTIQUE
MYSTIQUES
MYTH
MYTHIC
MYTHICAL
MYTHICISE

MYTHICISED
MYTHICISES
MYTHICISING
MYTHICISM
MYTHICISMS
MYTHICIST
MYTHICISTS
MYTHICIZE
MYTHICIZED
MYTHICIZES
MYTHICIZING
MYTHISE
MYTHISED
MYTHISES
MYTHISING
MYTHISM
MYTHISMS
MYTHIST
MYTHISTS
MYTHIZE
MYTHIZED
MYTHIZES
MYTHIZING

MYTHOLOGIES
MYTHOLOGY
MYTHOMANE
MYTHOMANES
MYTHOPOET
MYTHOPOETS
MYTHOS
MYTHOSES
MYTHS
MYTHUS
MYTHUSES
MYTILOID
MYXEDEMA
MYXEDEMAS
MYXOEDEMA
MYXOEDEMAS
MYXOMA
MYXOMATA
MYXOVIRUS
MYXOVIRUSES
MZUNGU
MZUNGUS

N

NA
NAAM
NAAMS
NAAN
NAANS
NAARTJE
NAARTJES
NAB
NABBED
NABBER
NABBERS
NABBING
NABK
NABKS
NABLA
NABLAS
NABOB
NABOBS
NABS
NACARAT
NACARATS
NACELLE
NACELLES
NACH
NACHE
NACHES
NACHTMAAL
NACHTMAALS
NACKET
NACKETS
NACRE
NACREOUS
NACRES
NACRITE
NACRITES
NACROUS
NADA
NADAS
NADIR
NADIRS
NAE
NAEBODIES
NAEBODY
NAETHING
NAETHINGS
NAEVE
NAEVES
NAEVI
NAEVOID
NAEVUS
NAFF
NAFFING
NAFFS
NAG
NAGA
NAGANA
NAGANAS
NAGAPIE
NAGAPIES
NAGARI
NAGARIS
NAGAS
NAGGED

NAGGER
NAGGERS
NAGGIER
NAGGIEST
NAGGING
NAGGY
NAGMAAL
NAGMAALS
NAGOR
NAGORS
NAGS
NAHAL
NAHALS
NAIAD
NAIADES
NAIADS
NAIANT
NAÏF
NAÏFER
NAÏFEST
NAIK
NAIKS
NAIL
NAILED
NAILER
NAILERIES
NAILERS
NAILERY
NAILING
NAILINGS
NAILS
NAIN
NAINSELL
NAINSELLS
NAINSOOK
NAINSOOKS
NAIRA
NAIRAS
NAISSANT
NAÏVE
NAÏVELY
NAÏVER
NAÏVEST
NAÏVETÉ
NAÏVETÉS
NAÏVETIES
NAÏVETY
NAKED
NAKEDER
NAKEDEST
NAKEDLY
NAKEDNESS
NAKEDNESSES
NAKER
NAKERS
NALA
NALAS
NALLA
NALLAH
NALLAHS
NALLAS
NALOXONE
NALOXONES

NAM
NAMABLE
NAMASKAR
NAMASKARS
NAMASTE
NAMASTES
NAME
NAMEABLE
NAMED
NAMELESS
NAMELY
NAMER
NAMERS
NAMES
NAMESAKE
NAMESAKES
NAMING
NAMINGS
NAMS
NAN
NANA
NANAS
NANCE
NANCES
NANCIES
NANCY
NANDINE
NANDINES
NANDOO
NANDOOS
NANDU
NANDUS
NANISM
NANISMS
NANKEEN
NANKEENS
NANKIN
NANKINS
NANNA
NANNAS
NANNIED
NANNIES
NANNY
NANNYING
NANNYISH
NANOGRAM
NANOGRAMS
NANOMETRE
NANOMETRES
NANS
NAOI
NAOS
NAOSES
NAP
NAPA
NAPALM
NAPALMS
NAPAS
NAPE
NAPERIES
NAPERY
NAPES
NAPHTHA

NAPHTHAS
NAPHTHOL
NAPHTHOLS
NAPIFORM
NAPKIN
NAPKINS
NAPLESS
NAPOLEON
NAPOLEONS
NAPOO
NAPOOED
NAPOOING
NAPOOS
NAPPA
NAPPAS
NAPPE
NAPPED
NAPPER
NAPPERS
NAPPES
NAPPIER
NAPPIES
NAPPIEST
NAPPINESS
NAPPINESSES
NAPPING
NAPPY
NAPRON
NAPRONS
NAPS
NARAS
NARASES
NARCISSI
NARCISSUS
NARCISSUSES
NARCOSES
NARCOSIS
NARCOTIC
NARCOTICS
NARCOTINE
NARCOTINES
NARCOTISE
NARCOTISED
NARCOTISES
NARCOTISING
NARCOTISM
NARCOTISMS
NARCOTIST
NARCOTISTS
NARCOTIZE
NARCOTIZED
NARCOTIZES
NARCOTIZING
NARD
NARDED
NARDING
NARDOO
NARDOOS
NARDS
NARE
NARES
NARGHILE
NARGHILES

NARGHILIES
NARGHILLIES
NARGHILLY
NARGHILY
NARGILE
NARGILEH
NARGILEHS
NARGILES
NARGILIES
NARGILLIES
NARGILLY
NARGILY
NARIAL
NARICORN
NARICORNS
NARINE
NARK
NARKED
NARKIER
NARKIEST
NARKING
NARKS
NARKY
NARQUOIS
NARRAS
NARRASES
NARRATE
NARRATED
NARRATES
NARRATING
NARRATION
NARRATIONS
NARRATIVE
NARRATIVES
NARRATOR
NARRATORS
NARRATORY
NARRE
NARROW
NARROWED
NARROWER
NARROWEST
NARROWING
NARROWINGS
NARROWLY
NARROWS
NARTHEX
NARTHEXES
NARTJIE
NARTJIES
NARWHAL
NARWHALS
NARY
NAS
NASAL
NASALISE
NASALISED
NASALISES
NASALISING
NASALITIES
NASALITY
NASALIZE
NASALIZED

NASALIZES
NASALIZING
NASALLY
NASALS
NASARD
NASARDS
NASCENCE
NASCENCES
NASCENCIES
NASCENCY
NASCENT
NASEBERRIES
NASEBERRY
NASHGAB
NASHGABS
NASION
NASIONS
NASTALIK
NASTALIKS
NASTIC
NASTIER
NASTIES
NASTIEST
NASTILY
NASTINESS
NASTINESSES
NASTY
NASUTE
NASUTES
NAT
NATAL
NATALITIES
NATALITY
NATANT
NATATION
NATATIONS
NATATORY
NATCH
NATCHES
NATES
NATHELESS
NATHEMO
NATHEMORE
NATHLESS
NATIFORM
NATION
NATIONAL
NATIONALS
NATIONS
NATIVE
NATIVELY
NATIVES
NATIVISM
NATIVISMS
NATIVIST
NATIVISTS
NATIVITIES
NATIVITY
NATRIUM
NATRIUMS
NATROLITE
NATROLITES
NATRON
NATRONS
NATS
NATTER
NATTERED
NATTERING
NATTERS
NATTERY

NATTIER
NATTIEST
NATTILY
NATTINESS
NATTINESSES
NATTY
NATURA
NATURAE
NATURAL
NATURALLY
NATURALS
NATURE
NATURED
NATURES
NATURING
NATURISM
NATURISMS
NATURIST
NATURISTS
NAUGHT
NAUGHTIER
NAUGHTIES
NAUGHTIEST
NAUGHTILY
NAUGHTS
NAUGHTY
NAUMACHIA
NAUMACHIAE
NAUMACHIAS
NAUMACHIES
NAUMACHY
NAUNT
NAUNTS
NAUPLII
NAUPLIOID
NAUPLIUS
NAUSEA
NAUSEANT
NAUSEANTS
NAUSEAS
NAUSEATE
NAUSEATED
NAUSEATES
NAUSEATING
NAUSEOUS
NAUTCH
NAUTCHES
NAUTIC
NAUTICAL
NAUTICS
NAUTILI
NAUTILUS
NAUTILUSES
NAVAID
NAVAIDS
NAVAL
NAVALISM
NAVALISMS
NAVARCH
NAVARCHIES
NAVARCHS
NAVARCHY
NAVARHO
NAVARHOS
NAVARIN
NAVARINS
NAVE
NAVEL
NAVELS
NAVELWORT

NAVELWORTS
NAVES
NAVETTE
NAVETTES
NAVEW
NAVEWS
NAVICERT
NAVICERTS
NAVICULA
NAVICULAR
NAVICULARS
NAVICULAS
NAVIES
NAVIGABLE
NAVIGATE
NAVIGATED
NAVIGATES
NAVIGATING
NAVIGATOR
NAVIGATORS
NAVVIED
NAVVIES
NAVVY
NAVVYING
NAVY
NAWAB
NAWABS
NAY
NAYS
NAYTHLES
NAYWARD
NAYWARDS
NAYWORD
NAYWORDS
NAZE
NAZES
NAZIR
NAZIRS
NE
NEAFE
NEAFES
NEAFFE
NEAFFES
NEAL
NEALED
NEALING
NEALS
NEANIC
NEAP
NEAPED
NEAPING
NEAPS
NEAPTIDE
NEAPTIDES
NEAR
NEARED
NEARER
NEAREST
NEARING
NEARLY
NEARNESS
NEARNESSES
NEARS
NEARSIDE
NEARSIDES
NEAT
NEATEN
NEATENED
NEATENING
NEATENS

NEATER
NEATEST
NEATH
NEATLY
NEATNESS
NEATNESSES
NEB
NEBBED
NEBBICH
NEBBICHS
NEBBING
NEBBISH
NEBBISHE
NEBBISHER
NEBBISHERS
NEBBISHES
NEBBUK
NEBBUKS
NEBECK
NEBECKS
NEBEK
NEBEKS
NEBEL
NEBELS
NEBISH
NEBISHES
NEBRIS
NEBRISES
NEBS
NEBULA
NEBULAE
NEBULAR
NEBULE
NEBULÉ
NEBULES
NEBULISE
NEBULISED
NEBULISER
NEBULISERS
NEBULISES
NEBULISING
NEBULIUM
NEBULIUMS
NEBULIZE
NEBULIZED
NEBULIZER
NEBULIZERS
NEBULIZES
NEBULIZING
NEBULOUS
NEBULY
NECESSARIES
NECESSARY
NECESSITIES
NECESSITY
NECK
NECKATEE
NECKATEES
NECKBEEF
NECKBEEFS
NECKED
NECKGEAR
NECKGEARS
NECKING
NECKINGS
NECKLACE
NECKLACES
NECKLET
NECKLETS
NECKLINE

NECKLINES
NECKS
NECKTIE
NECKTIES
NECKVERSE
NECKVERSES
NECKWEAR
NECKWEARS
NECKWEED
NECKWEEDS
NECROLOGIES
NECROLOGY
NECROPSIES
NECROPSY
NECROSE
NECROSED
NECROSES
NECROSING
NECROSIS
NECROTIC
NECROTISE
NECROTISED
NECROTISES
NECROTISING
NECROTIZE
NECROTIZED
NECROTIZES
NECROTIZING
NECROTOMIES
NECROTOMY
NECTAR
NECTAREAL
NECTAREAN
NECTARED
NECTARIAL
NECTARIES
NECTARINE
NECTARINES
NECTAROUS
NECTARS
NECTARY
NED
NEDDIES
NEDDY
NEDS
NÉE
NEED
NEEDED
NEEDER
NEEDERS
NEEDFUL
NEEDFULLY
NEEDIER
NEEDIEST
NEEDILY
NEEDINESS
NEEDINESSES
NEEDING
NEEDLE
NEEDLED
NEEDLEFUL
NEEDLEFULS
NEEDLER
NEEDLERS
NEEDLES
NEEDLESS
NEEDLIER
NEEDLIEST
NEEDLING
NEEDLY

NEEDMENT
NEEDMENTS
NEEDS
NEEDY
NEELD
NEELDS
NEELE
NEELES
NEEM
NEEMS
NEEP
NEEPS
NEESBERRIES
NEESBERRY
NEESE
NEESED
NEESES
NEESING
NEEZE
NEEZED
NEEZES
NEEZING
NEF
NEFANDOUS
NEFARIOUS
NEFAST
NEFS
NEGATE
NEGATED
NEGATES
NEGATING
NEGATION
NEGATIONS
NEGATIVE
NEGATIVED
NEGATIVES
NEGATIVING
NEGATORY
NEGATRON
NEGATRONS
NEGLECT
NEGLECTED
NEGLECTER
NEGLECTERS
NEGLECTING
NEGLECTS
NÉGLIGÉ
NEGLIGEE
NEGLIGEES
NEGLIGENT
NÉGLIGÉS
NÉGOCIANT
NÉGOCIANTS
NEGOTIATE
NEGOTIATED
NEGOTIATES
NEGOTIATING
NEGRESS
NEGRESSES
NEGRITUDE
NEGRITUDES
NEGRO
NEGROES
NEGROHEAD
NEGROHEADS
NEGROID
NEGROIDAL
NEGROIDS
NEGROISM
NEGROISMS

NEGROPHIL
NEGROPHILS
NEGUS
NEGUSES
NEIF
NEIFS
NEIGH
NEIGHBOR
NEIGHBORED
NEIGHBORING
NEIGHBORS
NEIGHBOUR
NEIGHBOURED
NEIGHBOURING
NEIGHBOURS
NEIGHED
NEIGHING
NEIGHS
NEIST
NEITHER
NEIVE
NEIVES
NEK
NEKS
NEKTON
NEKTONS
NELIES
NELIS
NELLIES
NELLY
NELSON
NELSONS
NELUMBIUM
NELUMBIUMS
NELUMBO
NELUMBOS
NEMATIC
NEMATODE
NEMATODES
NEMATOID
NEMERTEAN
NEMERTEANS
NEMERTIAN
NEMERTIANS
NEMERTINE
NEMERTINES
NEMESES
NEMESIA
NEMESIAS
NEMESIS
NEMN
NEMNED
NEMNING
NEMNS
NEMOPHILA
NEMOPHILAS
NEMORAL
NEMOROUS
NEMPT
NENE
NENES
NENUPHAR
NENUPHARS
NEOBLAST
NEOBLASTS
NEODYMIUM
NEODYMIUMS
NEOLITH
NEOLITHS
NEOLOGIAN

NEOLOGIANS
NEOLOGIC
NEOLOGIES
NEOLOGISE
NEOLOGISED
NEOLOGISES
NEOLOGISING
NEOLOGISM
NEOLOGISMS
NEOLOGIST
NEOLOGISTS
NEOLOGIZE
NEOLOGIZED
NEOLOGIZES
NEOLOGIZING
NEOLOGY
NEOMYCIN
NEOMYCINS
NEON
NEONATAL
NEONATE
NEONATES
NEONOMIAN
NEONOMIANS
NEONS
NEOPAGAN
NEOPAGANS
NEOPHILE
NEOPHILES
NEOPHILIA
NEOPHILIAS
NEOPHOBIA
NEOPHOBIAS
NEOPHYTE
NEOPHYTES
NEOPHYTIC
NEOPLASM
NEOPLASMS
NEOPRENE
NEOPRENES
NEOTEINIA
NEOTEINIAS
NEOTEINIC
NEOTENIC
NEOTENIES
NEOTENOUS
NEOTENY
NEOTERIC
NEOTERISE
NEOTERISED
NEOTERISES
NEOTERISING
NEOTERISM
NEOTERISMS
NEOTERIST
NEOTERISTS
NEOTERIZE
NEOTERIZED
NEOTERIZES
NEOTERIZING
NEP
NEPENTHE
NEPENTHES
NEPER
NEPERS
NEPHALISM
NEPHALISMS
NEPHALIST
NEPHALISTS
NEPHELINE

NEPHELINES
NEPHELITE
NEPHELITES
NEPHEW
NEPHEWS
NEPHOGRAM
NEPHOGRAMS
NEPHOLOGIES
NEPHOLOGY
NEPHRALGIES
NEPHRALGY
NEPHRIC
NEPHRIDIA
NEPHRITE
NEPHRITES
NEPHRITIC
NEPHRITICS
NEPHRITIS
NEPHRITISES
NEPHROID
NEPHRON
NEPHRONS
NEPHROSES
NEPHROSIS
NEPHROTIC
NEPIONIC
NEPIT
NEPITS
NEPOTIC
NEPOTISM
NEPOTISMS
NEPOTIST
NEPOTISTS
NEPS
NEPTUNIUM
NEPTUNIUMS
NERD
NERDS
NEREID
NEREIDS
NERINE
NERINES
NERITE
NERITES
NERITIC
NERKA
NERKAS
NEROLI
NEROLIS
NERVAL
NERVATE
NERVATION
NERVATIONS
NERVATURE
NERVATURES
NERVE
NERVED
NERVELESS
NERVELET
NERVELETS
NERVER
NERVERS
NERVES
NERVIER
NERVIEST
NERVINE
NERVINES
NERVINESS
NERVINESSES
NERVING

NERVOUS
NERVOUSLY
NERVULAR
NERVULE
NERVULES
NERVURE
NERVURES
NERVY
NESCIENCE
NESCIENCES
NESCIENT
NESH
NESHNESS
NESHNESSES
NESS
NESSES
NEST
NESTED
NESTER
NESTERS
NESTING
NESTLE
NESTLED
NESTLES
NESTLING
NESTLINGS
NESTS
NET
NETBALL
NETBALLS
NETE
NETES
NETFUL
NETFULS
NETHELESS
NETHER
NETS
NETSUKE
NETSUKES
NETT
NETTED
NETTIER
NETTIEST
NETTING
NETTINGS
NETTLE
NETTLED
NETTLES
NETTLING
NETTS
NETTY
NETWORK
NETWORKED
NETWORKING
NETWORKS
NEUK
NEUKS
NEUM
NEUME
NEUMES
NEUMS
NEURAL
NEURALGIA
NEURALGIAS
NEURALGIC
NEURATION
NEURATIONS
NEURILITIFS
NEURILITY
NEURINE

NEURINES	NEWMARKET	NIBBLINGS	NICTATES	NIFTIER
NEURISM	NEWMARKETS	NIBLICK	NICTATING	NIFTIEST
NEURISMS	NEWNESS	NIBLICKS	NICTATION	NIFTINESS
NEURITE	NEWNESSES	NIBS	NICTATIONS	NIFTINESSES
NEURITES	NEWS	NICCOLITE	NICTITATE	NIFTY
NEURITIC	NEWSAGENT	NICCOLITES	NICTITATED	NIGELLA
NEURITICS	NEWSAGENTS	NICE	NICTITATES	NIGELLAS
NEURITIS	NEWSBOY	NICEISH	NICTITATING	NIGER
NEURITISES	NEWSBOYS	NICELY	NID	NIGERS
NEUROGLIA	NEWSCAST	NICENESS	NIDAL	NIGGARD
NEUROGLIAS	NEWSCASTS	NICENESSES	NIDATION	NIGGARDED
NEUROGRAM	NEWSED	NICER	NIDATIONS	NIGGARDING
NEUROGRAMS	NEWSES	NICEST	NIDDERING	NIGGARDLY
NEUROLOGIES	NEWSFLASH	NICETIES	NIDDERINGS	NIGGARDS
NEUROLOGY	NEWSFLASHES	NICETY	NIDE	NIGGER
NEUROMA	NEWSGIRL	NICHE	NIDERING	NIGGERDOM
NEUROMAS	NEWSGIRLS	NICHED	NIDERINGS	NIGGERDOMS
NEURON	NEWSHAWK	NICHER	NIDERLING	NIGGERED
NEURONAL	NEWSHAWKS	NICHERED	NIDERLINGS	NIGGERING
NEURONE	NEWSHOUND	NICHERING	NIDES	NIGGERISH
NEURONES	NEWSHOUNDS	NICHERS	NIDGET	NIGGERISM
NEURONS	NEWSIER	NICHES	NIDGETS	NIGGERISMS
NEUROPATH	NEWSIES	NICHING	NIDI	NIGGERS
NEUROPATHS	NEWSIEST	NICK	NIDIFIED	NIGGERY
NEUROSES	NEWSINESS	NICKAR	NIDIFIES	NIGGLE
NEUROSIS	NEWSINESSES	NICKARS	NIDIFY	NIGGLED
NEUROTIC	NEWSING	NICKED	NIDIFYING	NIGGLER
NEUROTICS	NEWSMAN	NICKEL	NIDING	NIGGLERS
NEUROTOMIES	NEWSMEN	NICKELIC	NIDINGS	NIGGLES
NEUROTOMY	NEWSPAPER	NICKELINE	NIDOR	NIGGLIER
NEUSTON	NEWSPAPERS	NICKELINES	NIDOROUS	NIGGLIEST
NEUSTONS	NEWSPEAK	NICKELISE	NIDORS	NIGGLING
NEUTER	NEWSPEAKS	NICKELISED	NIDS	NIGGLINGS
NEUTERED	NEWSPRINT	NICKELISES	NIDUS	NIGGLY
NEUTERING	NEWSPRINTS	NICKELISING	NIE	NIGH
NEUTERS	NEWSREEL	NICKELIZE	NIECE	NIGHED
NEUTRAL	NEWSREELS	NICKELIZED	NIECES	NIGHEST
NEUTRALLY	NEWSROOM	NICKELIZES	NIED	NIGHING
NEUTRALS	NEWSROOMS	NICKELIZING	NIEF	NIGHLY
NEUTRETTO	NEWSTRADE	NICKELLED	NIEFS	NIGHNESS
NEUTRETTOS	NEWSTRADES	NICKELLING	NIELLATED	NIGHNESSES
NEUTRINO	NEWSWOMAN	NICKELOUS	NIELLI	NIGHS
NEUTRINOS	NEWSWOMEN	NICKELS	NIELLIST	NIGHT
NEUTRON	NEWSY	NICKER	NIELLISTS	NIGHTCAP
NEUTRONS	NEWT	NICKERED	NIELLO	NIGHTCAPS
NÉVÉ	NEWTON	NICKERING	NIELLOED	NIGHTED
NEVEL	NEWTONS	NICKERS	NIELLOING	NIGHTFALL
NEVELLED	NEWTS	NICKING	NIELLOS	NIGHTFALLS
NEVELLING	NEXT	NICKNAME	NIES	NIGHTFIRE
NEVELS	NEXTLY	NICKNAMED	NIEVE	NIGHTFIRES
NEVER	NEXTNESS	NICKNAMES	NIEVEFUL	NIGHTGEAR
NEVERMORE	NEXTNESSES	NICKNAMING	NIEVEFULS	NIGHTGEARS
NEVES	NEXUS	NICKS	NIEVES	NIGHTGOWN
NEW	NEXUSES	NICKSTICK	NIFE	NIGHTGOWNS
NEWBORN	NGAIO	NICKSTICKS	NIFES	NIGHTHAWK
NEWCOME	NGAIOS	NICKUM	NIFF	NIGHTHAWKS
NEWCOMER	NGWEE	NICKUMS	NIFFED	NIGHTIE
NEWCOMERS	NIACIN	NICOL	NIFFER	NIGHTIES
NEWED	NIACINS	NICOLS	NIFFERED	NIGHTJAR
NEWEL	NIAISERIE	NICOMPOOP	NIFFERING	NIGHTJARS
NEWELL	NIAISERIES	NICOMPOOPS	NIFFERS	NIGHTLESS
NEWELLED	NIB	NICOTIAN	NIFFIER	NIGHTLONG
NEWELLS	NIBBED	NICOTIANA	NIFFIEST	NIGHTLY
NEWELS	NIBBING	NICOTIANAS	NIFFING	NIGHTMARE
NEWER	NIBBLE	NICOTIANS	NIFFNAFF	NIGHTMARES
NEWEST	NIBBLED	NICOTINE	NIFFNAFFED	NIGHTMARY
NEWFANGLE	NIBBLER	NICOTINES	NIFFNAFFING	NIGHTS
NEWING	NIBBLERS	NICOTINIC	NIFFNAFFS	NIGHTSPOT
NEWISH	NIBBLES	NICTATE	NIFFS	NIGHTSPOTS
NEWLY	NIBBLING	NICTATED	NIFFY	NIGHTWARD

NIGHTWEAR
NIGHTWEARS
NIGHTY
NIGRICANT
NIGRIFIED
NIGRIFIES
NIGRIFY
NIGRIFYING
NIGRITUDE
NIGRITUDES
NIGROSINE
NIGROSINES
NIHIL
NIHILISM
NIHILISMS
NIHILIST
NIHILISTS
NIHILITIES
NIHILITY
NIHILS
NIL
NILGAI
NILGAIS
NILGAU
NILGAUS
NILL
NILLED
NILLING
NILLS
NILS
NIM
NIMBED
NIMBI
NIMBLE
NIMBLER
NIMBLESSE
NIMBLESSES
NIMBLEST
NIMBLY
NIMBUS
NIMBUSED
NIMBUSES
NIMIETIES
NIMIETY
NIMIOUS
NIMMED
NIMMER
NIMMERS
NIMMING
NIMONIC
NIMS
NINCOM
NINCOMS
NINCUM
NINCUMS
NINE
NINEFOLD
NINEHOLES
NINEPENCE
NINEPENCES
NINEPENNIES
NINEPENNY
NINEPINS
NINES
NINESCORE
NINESCORES
NINETEEN
NINETEENS
NINETIES
NINETIETH

NINETIETHS
NINETY
NINJA
NINJAS
NINNIES
NINNY
NINON
NINONS
NINTH
NINTHLY
NINTHS
NIOBATE
NIOBATES
NIOBIC
NIOBITE
NIOBITES
NIOBIUM
NIOBIUMS
NIOBOUS
NIP
NIPPED
NIPPER
NIPPERED
NIPPERING
NIPPERKIN
NIPPERKINS
NIPPERS
NIPPIER
NIPPIEST
NIPPING
NIPPINGLY
NIPPLE
NIPPLED
NIPPLES
NIPPLING
NIPPY
NIPS
NIPTER
NIPTERS
NIRL
NIRLED
NIRLIE
NIRLIER
NIRLIEST
NIRLING
NIRLIT
NIRLS
NIRLY
NIRVANA
NIRVANAS
NIS
NISBERRIES
NISBERRY
NISEI
NISEIS
NISI
NISSE
NISSES
NISUS
NISUSES
NIT
NITERIE
NITERIES
NITERY
NITHING
NITHINGS
NITID
NITON
NITONS
NITRATE

NITRATED
NITRATES
NITRATINE
NITRATINES
NITRATING
NITRATION
NITRATIONS
NITRE
NITRES
NITRIC
NITRIDE
NITRIDED
NITRIDES
NITRIDING
NITRIDINGS
NITRIFIED
NITRIFIES
NITRIFY
NITRIFYING
NITRILE
NITRILES
NITRITE
NITRITES
NITROGEN
NITROGENS
NITROUS
NITROXYL
NITROXYLS
NITRY
NITRYL
NITRYLS
NITS
NITTIER
NITTIEST
NITTY
NITWIT
NITWITS
NITWITTED
NIVAL
NIVEOUS
NIX
NIXES
NIXIE
NIXIES
NIXY
NIZAM
NIZAMS
NO
NOB
NOBBIER
NOBBIEST
NOBBILY
NOBBINESS
NOBBINESSES
NOBBLE
NOBBLED
NOBBLER
NOBBLERS
NOBBLES
NOBBLING
NOBBUT
NOBBY
NOBELIUM
NOBELIUMS
NOBILESSE
NOBILESSES
NOBILIARY
NOBILITIES
NOBILITY
NOBLE

NOBLEMAN
NOBLEMEN
NOBLENESS
NOBLENESSES
NOBLER
NOBLES
NOBLESSE
NOBLESSES
NOBLEST
NOBLY
NOBODIES
NOBODY
NOBS
NOCAKE
NOCAKES
NOCENT
NOCENTLY
NOCENTS
NOCHEL
NOCHELLED
NOCHELLING
NOCHELS
NOCK
NOCKED
NOCKET
NOCKETS
NOCKING
NOCKS
NOCTILUCA
NOCTILUCAS
NOCTUA
NOCTUARIES
NOCTUARY
NOCTUAS
NOCTUID
NOCTUIDS
NOCTULE
NOCTULES
NOCTURN
NOCTURNAL
NOCTURNALS
NOCTURNE
NOCTURNES
NOCTURNS
NOCUOUS
NOCUOUSLY
NOD
NODAL
NODALISE
NODALISED
NODALISES
NODALISING
NODALITIES
NODALITY
NODALIZE
NODALIZED
NODALIZES
NODALIZING
NODATED
NODATION
NODATIONS
NODDED
NODDER
NODDERS
NODDIES
NODDING
NODDINGS
NODDLE
NODDLED
NODDLES

NODDLING
NODDY
NODE
NODES
NODI
NODICAL
NODOSE
NODOSITIES
NODOSITY
NODOUS
NODS
NODULAR
NODULATED
NODULE
NODULED
NODULES
NODULOSE
NODULOUS
NODUS
NOËL
NOËLS
NOES
NOESES
NOESIS
NOETIC
NOG
NOGAKU
NOGGIN
NOGGING
NOGGINGS
NOGGINS
NOGS
NOH
NOHOW
NOHOWISH
NOIL
NOILS
NOINT
NOINTED
NOINTING
NOINTS
NOISE
NOISED
NOISEFUL
NOISELESS
NOISES
NOISETTE
NOISETTES
NOISIER
NOISIEST
NOISILY
NOISINESS
NOISINESSES
NOISING
NOISOME
NOISOMELY
NOISY
NOLE
NOLES
NOLITION
NOLITIONS
NOLL
NOLLS
NOM
NOMA
NOMAD
NOMADE
NOMADES
NOMADIC
NOMADIES

NOMADISE
NOMADISED
NOMADISES
NOMADISING
NOMADISM
NOMADISMS
NOMADIZE
NOMADIZED
NOMADIZES
NOMADIZING
NOMADS
NOMADY
NOMARCH
NOMARCHIES
NOMARCHS
NOMARCHY
NOMAS
NOMBRIL
NOMBRILS
NOME
NOMEN
NOMES
NOMIC
NOMINA
NOMINABLE
NUMINAL
NOMINALLY
NOMINALS
NOMINATE
NOMINATED
NOMINATES
NOMINATING
NOMINATOR
NOMINATORS
NOMINEE
NOMINEES
NOMISM
NOMISMS
NOMISTIC
NOMOCRACIES
NOMOCRACY
NOMOGENIES
NOMOGENY
NOMOGRAM
NOMOGRAMS
NOMOGRAPH
NOMOGRAPHS
NOMOI
NOMOLOGIES
NOMOLOGY
NOMOS
NOMOTHETE
NOMOTHETES
NOMU
NON
NONAGE
NONAGED
NONAGES
NONAGON
NONAGONS
NONANE
NONANES
NONARY
NONCE
NONCES
NONE
NONENTITIES
NONENTITY
NONES
NONESUCH

NONESUCHES
NONET
NONETS
NONETTE
NONETTES
NONETTI
NONETTO
NONETTOS
NONG
NONGS
NONILLION
NONILLIONS
NONJURING
NONJUROR
NONJURORS
NONNIES
NONNY
NONPAREIL
NONPAREILS
NONPAROUS
NONPLUS
NONPLUSES
NONPLUSSED
NONPLUSSES
NONPLUSSING
NONPOLAR
NONSENSE
NONSENSES
NONSUCH
NONSUCHES
NONSUIT
NONSUITED
NONSUITING
NONSUITS
NONUPLE
NONUPLET
NONUPLETS
NOODLE
NOODLED
NOODLEDOM
NOODLEDOMS
NOODLES
NOODLING
NOOK
NOOKIE
NOOKIER
NOOKIES
NOOKIEST
NOOKS
NOOKY
NOOLOGIES
NOOLOGY
NOOMETRIES
NOOMETRY
NOON
NOONDAY
NOONDAYS
NOONED
NOONING
NOONINGS
NOONS
NOONTIDE
NOONTIDES
NOOP
NOOPS
NOOSE
NOOSED
NOOSES
NOOSING
NOOSPHERE

NOOSPHERES
NOPAL
NOPALS
NOPE
NOR
NORI
NORIA
NORIAS
NORIMON
NORIMONS
NORIS
NORITE
NORITES
NORK
NORKS
NORLAND
NORLANDS
NORM
NORMA
NORMAL
NORMALCIES
NORMALCY
NORMALISE
NORMALISED
NORMALISES
NORMALISING
NORMALITIES
NORMALITY
NORMALIZE
NORMALIZED
NORMALIZES
NORMALIZING
NORMALLY
NORMALS
NORMAN
NORMANS
NORMAS
NORMATIVE
NORMS
NORSEL
NORSELLED
NORSELLER
NORSELLERS
NORSELLING
NORSELS
NORTH
NORTHED
NORTHER
NORTHERED
NORTHERING
NORTHERLIES
NORTHERLY
NORTHERN
NORTHERNS
NORTHERS
NORTHING
NORTHINGS
NORTHLAND
NORTHLANDS
NORTHMOST
NORTHS
NORTHWARD
NORTHWARDS
NORWARD
NORWARDS
NOSE
NOSEAN
NOSEANS
NOSEBAG
NOSEBAGS

NOSED
NOSEGAY
NOSEGAYS
NOSELESS
NOSELITE
NOSELITES
NOSER
NOSERS
NOSES
NOSEY
NOSEYS
NOSH
NOSHED
NOSHES
NOSHING
NOSIER
NOSIES
NOSIEST
NOSILY
NOSINESS
NOSINESSES
NOSING
NOSINGS
NOSOLOGIES
NOSOLOGY
NOSTALGIA
NOSTALGIAS
NOSTALGIC
NOSTOC
NOSTOCS
NOSTOI
NOSTOLOGIES
NOSTOLOGY
NOSTOS
NOSTRIL
NOSTRILS
NOSTRUM
NOSTRUMS
NOSY
NOT
NOTABILIA
NOTABLE
NOTABLES
NOTABLY
NOTAEUM
NOTAEUMS
NOTAL
NOTANDA
NOTANDUM
NOTAPHILIES
NOTAPHILY
NOTARIAL
NOTARIES
NOTARISE
NOTARISED
NOTARISES
NOTARISING
NOTARIZE
NOTARIZED
NOTARIZES
NOTARIZING
NOTARY
NOTATE
NOTATED
NOTATES
NOTATING
NOTATION
NOTATIONS
NOTCH
NOTCHBACK

NOTCHBACKS
NOTCHED
NOTCHEL
NOTCHELLED
NOTCHELLING
NOTCHELS
NOTCHES
NOTCHIER
NOTCHIEST
NOTCHING
NOTCHINGS
NOTCHY
NOTE
NOTEBOOK
NOTEBOOKS
NOTED
NOTEDLY
NOTEDNESS
NOTEDNESSES
NOTELESS
NOTELET
NOTELETS
NOTEPAPER
NOTEPAPERS
NOTER
NOTERO
NOTES
NOTHING
NOTHINGS
NOTICE
NOTICED
NOTICES
NOTICING
NOTIFIED
NOTIFIER
NOTIFIERS
NOTIFIES
NOTIFY
NOTIFYING
NOTING
NOTION
NOTIONAL
NOTIONIST
NOTIONISTS
NOTIONS
NOTITIA
NOTITIAS
NOTOCHORD
NOTOCHORDS
NOTORIETIES
NOTORIETY
NOTORIOUS
NOTORNIS
NOTORNISES
NOTOUR
NOTT
NOTUM
NOTUMS
NOUGAT
NOUGATS
NOUGHT
NOUGHTS
NOUL
NOULD
NOULDE
NOULE
NOULES
NOULS
NOUMENA
NOUMENAL

NOUMENON	NOVELLE	NUBBIER	NUDIE	NUMERAIRE
NOUN	NOVELS	NUBBIEST	NUDIES	NUMERAIRES
NOUNAL	NOVELTIES	NUBBIN	NUDISM	NUMERAL
NOUNIER	NOVELTY	NUBBING	NUDISMS	NUMERALLY
NOUNIEST	NOVENA	NUBBINS	NUDIST	NUMERALS
NOUNS	NOVENARIES	NUBBLE	NUDISTS	NUMERARY
NOUNY	NOVENARY	NUBBLED	NUDITIES	NUMERATE
NOUP	NOVENAS	NUBBLES	NUDITY	NUMERATED
NOUPS	NOVENNIAL	NUBBLIER	NUGAE	NUMERATES
NOURICE	NOVERCAL	NUBBLIEST	NUGATORY	NUMERATING
NOURICES	NOVERINT	NUBBLING	NUGGAR	NUMERATOR
NOURISH	NOVERINTS	NUBBLY	NUGGARS	NUMERATORS
NOURISHED	NOVICE	NUBBY	NUGGET	NUMERIC
NOURISHER	NOVICES	NUBECULA	NUGGETS	NUMERICAL
NOURISHERS	NOVICIATE	NUBECULAE	NUGGETY	NUMEROUS
NOURISHES	NOVICIATES	NUBIA	NUISANCE	NUMINA
NOURISHING	NOVITIATE	NUBIAS	NUISANCER	NUMINOUS
NOURITURE	NOVITIATES	NUBIFORM	NUISANCERS	NUMMARY
NOURITURES	NOVITIES	NUBILE	NUISANCES	NUMMULAR
NOURSLE	NOVITY	NUBILITIES	NUKE	NUMMULARY
NOURSLED	NOVODAMUS	NUBILITY	NUKED	NUMMULINE
NOURSLES	NOVODAMUSES	NUBILOUS	NUKES	NUMMULITE
NOURSLING	NOVUM	NUBS	NUKING	NUMMULITES
NOUS	NOVUMS	NUCELLAR	NULL	NUMNAH
NOUSELL	NOW	NUCELLI	NULLA	NUMNAHS
NOUSELLED	NOWADAYS	NUCELLUS	NULLAH	NUMSKULL
NOUSELLING	NOWAY	NUCELLUSES	NULLAHS	NUMSKULLS
NOUSELLS	NOWAYS	NUCHA	NULLAS	NUN
NOUSES	NOWED	NUCHAL	NULLED	NUNATAK
NOUSLE	NOWHENCE	NUCHAS	NULLIFIED	NUNATAKER
NOUSLED	NOWHERE	NUCLEAL	NULLIFIER	NUNATAKS
NOUSLES	NOWHERES	NUCLEAR	NULLIFIERS	NUNCHEON
NOUSLING	NOWHITHER	NUCLEARY	NULLIFIES	NUNCHEONS
NOUT	NOWISE	NUCLEASE	NULLIFY	NUNCIO
NOUVEAU	NOWL	NUCLEASES	NULLIFYING	NUNCIOS
NOUVELLE	NOWLS	NUCLEATE	NULLING	NUNCLE
NOUVELLES	NOWN	NUCLEATED	NULLINGS	NUNCLES
NOVA	NOWNESS	NUCLEATES	NULLIPARA	NUNCUPATE
NOVAE	NOWNESSES	NUCLEATING	NULLIPARAE	NUNCUPATED
NOVALIA	NOWS	NUCLEI	NULLIPARAS	NUNCUPATES
NOVAS	NOWT	NUCLEIDE	NULLIPORE	NUNCUPATING
NOVATION	NOWTS	NUCLEIDES	NULLIPORES	NUNDINAL
NOVATIONS	NOWY	NUCLEIN	NULLITIES	NUNDINE
NOVEL	NOXAL	NUCLEINS	NULLITY	NUNDINES
NOVELDOM	NOXIOUS	NUCLEOLAR	NULLNESS	NUNHOOD
NOVELDOMS	NOXIOUSLY	NUCLEOLE	NULLNESSES	NUNHOODS
NOVELESE	NOY	NUCLEOLES	NULLS	NUNNATION
NOVELESES	NOYADE	NUCLEOLI	NUMB	NUNNATIONS
NOVELETTE	NOYADES	NUCLEOLUS	NUMBAT	NUNNERIES
NOVELETTES	NOYANCE	NUCLEON	NUMBATS	NUNNERY
NOVELISE	NOYANCES	NUCLEONS	NUMBED	NUNNISH
NOVELISED	NOYAU	NUCLEUS	NUMBER	NUNS
NOVELISER	NOYAUS	NUCLIDE	NUMBERED	NUNSHIP
NOVELISERS	NOYED	NUCLIDES	NUMBERER	NUNSHIPS
NOVELISES	NOYES	NUCULE	NUMBERERS	NUPTIAL
NOVELISH	NOYESES	NUCULES	NUMBERING	NUPTIALS
NOVELISING	NOYING	NUDATION	NUMBERS	NUR
NOVELISM	NOYOUS	NUDATIONS	NUMBEST	NURAGHE
NOVELISMS	NOYS	NUDE	NUMBING	NURAGHI
NOVELIST	NOYSOME	NUDELY	NUMBLES	NURAGHIC
NOVELISTS	NOZZLE	NUDENESS	NUMBS	NURD
NOVELIZE	NOZZLES	NUDENESSES	NUMBSKULL	NURDS
NOVELIZED	NTH	NUDER	NUMBSKULLS	NURHAG
NOVELIZER	NU	NUDES	NUMDAH	NURHAGS
NOVELIZERS	NUANCE	NUDEST	NUMDAHS	NURL
NOVELIZES	NUANCED	NUDGE	NUMEN	NURLED
NOVELIZING	NUANCES	NUDGED	NUMERABLE	NURLING
NOVELLA	NUANCING	NUDGES	NUMERABLY	NURLS
NOVELLAE	NUB	NUDGING	NUMERACIES	NURR
NOVELLAS	NUBBED	NUDICAUL	NUMERACY	NURRS

NURS
NURSE
NURSED
NURSELIKE
NURSELING
NURSELINGS
NURSEMAID
NURSEMAIDS
NURSER
NURSERIES
NURSERS
NURSERY
NURSES
NURSING
NURSLE
NURSLED
NURSLES
NURSLING
NURSLINGS
NURTURAL
NURTURANT
NURTURE
NURTURED
NURTURER
NURTURERS
NURTURES

NURTURING
NUS
NUT
NUTANT
NUTARIAN
NUTARIANS
NUTATE
NUTATED
NUTATES
NUTATING
NUTATION
NUTATIONS
NUTCASE
NUTCASES
NUTHATCH
NUTHATCHES
NUTHOUSE
NUTHOUSES
NUTJOBBER
NUTJOBBERS
NUTLET
NUTLETS
NUTMEAL
NUTMEALS
NUTMEG
NUTMEGGED

NUTMEGGY
NUTMEGS
NUTPECKER
NUTPECKERS
NUTRIA
NUTRIAS
NUTRIENT
NUTRIENTS
NUTRIMENT
NUTRIMENTS
NUTRITION
NUTRITIONS
NUTRITIVE
NUTS
NUTSHELL
NUTSHELLS
NUTTED
NUTTER
NUTTERIES
NUTTERS
NUTTERY
NUTTIER
NUTTIEST
NUTTINESS
NUTTINESSES
NUTTING

NUTTINGS
NUTTY
NUZZER
NUZZERS
NUZZLE
NUZZLED
NUZZLES
NUZZLING
NY
NYAFF
NYAFFED
NYAFFING
NYAFFS
NYALA
NYALAS
NYANZA
NYANZAS
NYAS
NYASES
NYCTALOPES
NYCTALOPS
NYE
NYED
NYES
NYING
NYLGHAU

NYLGHAUS
NYLON
NYLONS
NYMPH
NYMPHAE
NYMPHAEA
NYMPHAEUM
NYMPHAEUMS
NYMPHAL
NYMPHALID
NYMPHALIDS
NYMPHEAN
NYMPHET
NYMPHETS
NYMPHIC
NYMPHICAL
NYMPHISH
NYMPHLY
NYMPHO
NYMPHOS
NYMPHS
NYS
NYSTAGMIC
NYSTAGMUS
NYSTAGMUSES

O

OAF	OBDURE	OBITER	OBLONG	OBSIDIANS
OAFISH	OBDURED	OBITS	OBLONGS	OBSIGN
OAFS	OBDURES	OBITUAL	OBLOQUIES	OBSIGNATE
OAK	OBDURING	OBITUARIES	OBLOQUY	OBSIGNATED
OAKEN	OBEAH	OBITUARY	OBNOXIOUS	OBSIGNATES
OAKENSHAW	OBEAHED	OBJECT	OBOE	OBSIGNATING
OAKENSHAWS	OBEAHING	OBJECTED	OBOES	OBSIGNED
OAKER	OBEAHISM	OBJECTIFIED	OBOIST	OBSIGNING
OAKERS	OBEAHISMS	OBJECTIFIES	OBOISTS	OBSIGNS
OAKIER	OBEAHS	OBJECTIFY	OBOL	OBSOLESCE
OAKIEST	OBECHE	OBJECTIFYING	OBOLARY	OBSOLESCED
OAKLING	OBECHES	OBJECTING	OBOLI	OBSOLESCES
OAKLINGS	OBEDIENCE	OBJECTION	OBOLS	OBSOLESCING
OAKS	OBEDIENCES	OBJECTIONS	OBOLUS	OBSOLETE
OAKUM	OBEDIENT	OBJECTIVE	OBOVATE	OBSTACLE
OAKUMS	OBEISANCE	OBJECTIVES	OBOVATELY	OBSTACLES
OAKY	OBEISANCES	OBJECTOR	OBOVOID	OBSTETRIC
OAR	OBEISANT	OBJECTORS	OBREPTION	OBSTETRICS
OARAGE	OBEISM	OBJECTS	OBREPTIONS	OBSTINACIES
OARAGES	OBEISMS	OBJET	OBS	OBSTINACY
OARED	OBELI	OBJETS	OBSCENE	OBSTINATE
OARIER	OBELION	OBJURE	OBSCENELY	OBSTRUCT
OARIEST	OBELIONS	OBJURED	OBSCENER	OBSTRUCTED
OARING	OBELISCAL	OBJURES	OBSCENEST	OBSTRUCTING
OARLESS	OBELISE	OBJURGATE	OBSCENITIES	OBSTRUCTS
OARS	OBELISED	OBJURGATED	OBSCENITY	OBSTRUENT
OARSMAN	OBELISES	OBJURGATES	OBSCURANT	OBSTRUENTS
OARSMEN	OBELISING	OBJURGATING	OBSCURANTS	OBTAIN
OARSWOMAN	OBELISK	OBJURING	OBSCURE	OBTAINED
OARSWOMEN	OBELISKS	OBLAST	OBSCURED	OBTAINER
OARWEED	OBELIZE	OBLASTS	OBSCURELY	OBTAINERS
OARWEEDS	OBELIZED	OBLATE	OBSCURER	OBTAINING
OARY	OBELIZES	OBLATES	OBSCURERS	OBTAINS
OASES	OBELIZING	OBLATION	OBSCURES	OBTECT
OASIS	OBELUS	OBLATIONS	OBSCUREST	OBTECTED
OAST	OBESE	OBLATORY	OBSCURING	OBTEMPER
OASTS	OBESENESS	OBLIGANT	OBSCURITIES	OBTEMPERED
OAT	OBESENESSES	OBLIGANTS	OBSCURITY	OBTEMPERING
OATCAKE	OBESER	OBLIGATE	OBSECRATE	OBTEMPERS
OATCAKES	OBESEST	OBLIGATED	OBSECRATED	OBTEND
OATEN	OBESITIES	OBLIGATES	OBSECRATES	OBTENDED
OATH	OBESITY	OBLIGATING	OBSECRATING	OBTENDING
OATHABLE	OBEY	OBLIGE	OBSEQUENT	OBTENDS
OATHS	OBEYED	OBLIGED	OBSEQUIAL	OBTENTION
OATMEAL	OBEYER	OBLIGEE	OBSEQUIE	OBTENTIONS
OATMEALS	OBEYERS	OBLIGEES	OBSEQUIES	OBTEST
OATS	OBEYING	OBLIGES	OBSEQUY	OBTESTED
OAVES	OBEYS	OBLIGING	OBSERVANT	OBTESTING
OB	OBFUSCATE	OBLIGOR	OBSERVANTS	OBTESTS
OBANG	OBFUSCATED	OBLIGORS	OBSERVE	OBTRUDE
OBANGS	OBFUSCATES	OBLIQUE	OBSERVED	OBTRUDED
OBBLIGATI	OBFUSCATING	OBLIQUED	OBSERVER	OBTRUDER
OBBLIGATO	OBI	OBLIQUELY	OBSERVERS	OBTRUDERS
OBBLIGATOS	OBIA	OBLIQUER	OBSERVES	OBTRUDES
OBCONIC	OBIAS	OBLIQUES	OBSERVING	OBTRUDING
OBCONICAL	OBIED	OBLIQUEST	OBSESS	OBTRUDINGS
OBCORDATE	OBIING	OBLIQUID	OBSESSED	OBTRUSION
OBDURACIES	OBIISM	OBLIQUING	OBSESSES	OBTRUSIONS
OBDURACY	OBIISMS	OBLIQUITIES	OBSESSING	OBTRUSIVE
OBDURATE	OBIIT	OBLIQUITY	OBSESSION	OBTUND
OBDURATED	OBIS	OBLIVION	OBSESSIONS	OBTUNDED
OBDURATES	OBIT	OBLIVIONS	OBSESSIVE	OBTUNDENT
OBDURATING	OBITAL	OBLIVIOUS	OBSIDIAN	OBTUNDENTS

OBTUNDING
OBTUNDS
OBTURATE
OBTURATED
OBTURATES
OBTURATING
OBTURATOR
OBTURATORS
OBTUSE
OBTUSELY
OBTUSER
OBTUSEST
OBTUSITIES
OBTUSITY
OBUMBRATE
OBUMBRATED
OBUMBRATES
OBUMBRATING
OBVENTION
OBVENTIONS
OBVERSE
OBVERSELY
OBVERSES
OBVERSION
OBVERSIONS
OBVERT
OBVERTED
OBVERTING
OBVERTS
OBVIATE
OBVIATED
OBVIATES
OBVIATING
OBVIATION
OBVIATIONS
OBVIOUS
OBVIOUSLY
OBVOLUTE
OBVOLUTED
OBVOLVENT
OCA
OCARINA
OCARINAS
OCAS
OCCAMIES
OCCAMY
OCCASION
OCCASIONED
OCCASIONING
OCCASIONS
OCCIDENT
OCCIDENTS
OCCIPITAL
OCCIPITALS
OCCIPUT
OCCIPUTS
OCCLUDE
OCCLUDED
OCCLUDENT
OCCLUDENTS
OCCLUDES
OCCLUDING
OCCLUSAL
OCCLUSION
OCCLUSIONS
OCCLUSIVE
OCCLUSIVES
OCCLUSOR
OCCLUSORS
OCCULT

OCCULTED
OCCULTING
OCCULTISM
OCCULTISMS
OCCULTIST
OCCULTISTS
OCCULTLY
OCCULTS
OCCUPANCE
OCCUPANCES
OCCUPANCIES
OCCUPANCY
OCCUPANT
OCCUPANTS
OCCUPATE
OCCUPATED
OCCUPATES
OCCUPATING
OCCUPIED
OCCUPIER
OCCUPIERS
OCCUPIES
OCCUPY
OCCUPYING
OCCUR
OCCURRED
OCCURRENT
OCCURRENTS
OCCURRING
OCCURS
OCEAN
OCEANAUT
OCEANAUTS
OCEANIC
OCEANID
OCEANIDES
OCEANIDS
OCEANS
OCELLAR
OCELLATE
OCELLATED
OCELLI
OCELLUS
OCELOID
OCELOT
OCELOTS
OCH
OCHE
OCHER
OCHERED
OCHERING
OCHEROUS
OCHERS
OCHERY
OCHES
OCHIDORE
OCHIDORES
OCHLOCRAT
OCHLOCRATS
OCHONE
OCHRE
OCHREA
OCHREAE
OCHREATE
OCHRED
OCHREOUS
OCHRES
OCHREY
OCHRING
OCHROID

OCHROUS
OCHRY
OCKER
OCKERISM
OCKERISMS
OCKERS
OCOTILLO
OCOTILLOS
OCREA
OCREAE
OCREATE
OCTACHORD
OCTACHORDS
OCTAD
OCTADIC
OCTADS
OCTAGON
OCTAGONAL
OCTAGONS
OCTAHEDRA
OCTAL
OCTAMETER
OCTAMETERS
OCTANE
OCTANES
OCTANTAL
OCTANTS
OCTAPLA
OCTAPLAS
OCTAPLOID
OCTAPLOIDS
OCTAPODIC
OCTAPODIES
OCTAPODY
OCTAROON
OCTAROONS
OCTASTICH
OCTASTICHS
OCTASTYLE
OCTASTYLES
OCTAVAL
OCTAVE
OCTAVES
OCTAVO
OCTAVOS
OCTENNIAL
OCTET
OCTETS
OCTETT
OCTETTE
OCTETTES
OCTETTS
OCTILLION
OCTILLIONS
OCTOFID
OCTOHEDRA
OCTONARIES
OCTONARII
OCTONARY
OCTOPI
OCTOPLOID
OCTOPLOIDS
OCTOPOD
OCTOPODES
OCTOPODS
OCTOPUS
OCTOPUSES
OCTOROON
OCTOROONS

OCTOSTYLE
OCTOSTYLES
OCTROI
OCTROIS
OCTUOR
OCTUORS
OCTUPLE
OCTUPLED
OCTUPLES
OCTUPLET
OCTUPLETS
OCTUPLING
OCULAR
OCULARIST
OCULARISTS
OCULARLY
OCULARS
OCULATE
OCULATED
OCULI
OCULIST
OCULISTS
OCULUS
OD
ODA
ODAL
ODALIQUE
ODALIQUES
ODALISK
ODALISKS
ODALISQUE
ODALISQUES
ODALLER
ODALLERS
ODALS
ODAS
ODD
ODDBALL
ODDBALLS
ODDER
ODDEST
ODDISH
ODDITIES
ODDITY
ODDLY
ODDMENT
ODDMENTS
ODDNESS
ODDNESSES
ODDS
ODDSMAN
ODDSMEN
ODE
ODEA
ODEON
ODEONS
ODES
ODEUM
ODEUMS
ODIC
ODIOUS
ODIOUSLY
ODISM
ODISMS
ODIST
ODISTS
ODIUM
ODIUMS
ODOGRAPH
ODOGRAPHS

ODOMETER
ODOMETERS
ODOMETRIES
ODOMETRY
ODONATIST
ODONATISTS
ODONTALGIES
ODONTALGY
ODONTIC
ODONTIST
ODONTISTS
ODONTOID
ODONTOMA
ODONTOMAS
ODONTOMATA
ODOR
ODORANT
ODORATE
ODOROUS
ODOROUSLY
ODORS
ODOUR
ODOURED
ODOURLESS
ODOURS
ODS
ODSO
ODSOS
ODYL
ODYLE
ODYLES
ODYLISM
ODYLISMS
ODYLS
ODYSSEY
ODYSSEYS
ODZOOKS
OE
OECIST
OECISTS
OECOLOGIES
OECOLOGY
OECUMENIC
OEDEMA
OEDEMAS
OEILLADE
OEILLADES
OENANTHIC
OENOLOGIES
OENOLOGY
OENOMANCIES
OENOMANCY
OENOMANIA
OENOMANIAS
OENOMEL
OENOMELS
OENOMETER
OENOMETERS
OENOPHIL
OENOPHILE
OENOPHILES
OENOPHILIES
OENOPHILS
OENOPHILY
OERLIKON
OERLIKONS
OERSTED
OERSTEDS
OES
OESOPHAGI

OESTRAL
OESTROGEN
OESTROGENS
OESTROUS
OESTRUM
OESTRUMS
OESTRUS
OESTRUSES
OEUVRE
OEUVRES
OF
OFAY
OFAYS
OFF
OFFAL
OFFALS
OFFBEAT
OFFCUT
OFFCUTS
OFFED
OFFENCE
OFFENCES
OFFEND
OFFENDED
OFFENDER
OFFENDERS
OFFENDING
OFFENDS
OFFENSE
OFFENSES
OFFENSIVE
OFFENSIVES
OFFER
OFFERABLE
OFFERED
OFFEREE
OFFEREES
OFFERER
OFFERERS
OFFERING
OFFERINGS
OFFEROR
OFFERORS
OFFERS
OFFERTORIES
OFFERTORY
OFFHAND
OFFHANDED
OFFICE
OFFICER
OFFICERED
OFFICERING
OFFICERS
OFFICES
OFFICIAL
OFFICIALS
OFFICIANT
OFFICIANTS
OFFICIATE
OFFICIATED
OFFICIATES
OFFICIATING
OFFICINAL
OFFICIOUS
OFFING
OFFINGS
OFFISH
OFFLOAD
OFFLOADED
OFFLOADING

OFFLOADS
OFFPEAK
OFFPRINT
OFFPRINTS
OFFPUT
OFFPUTS
OFFS
OFFSADDLE
OFFSADDLED
OFFSADDLES
OFFSADDLING
OFFSCUM
OFFSCUMS
OFFSEASON
OFFSEASONS
OFFSET
OFFSETS
OFFSETTING
OFFSHOOT
OFFSHOOTS
OFFSHORE
OFFSIDE
OFFSIDER
OFFSIDERS
OFFSIDES
OFFSPRING
OFFSPRINGS
OFFTAKE
OFFTAKES
OFLAG
OFLAGS
OFT
OFTEN
OFTENER
OFTENEST
OFTENNESS
OFTENNESSES
OFTTIMES
OGAM
OGAMIC
OGAMS
OGDOAD
OGDOADS
OGEE
OGEES
OGGIN
OGGINS
OGHAM
OGHAMIC
OGHAMS
OGIVAL
OGIVE
OGIVES
OGLE
OGLED
OGLER
OGLERS
OGLES
OGLING
OGLINGS
OGMIC
OGRE
OGREISH
OGRES
OGRESS
OGRESSES
OGRISH
OH
OHM
OHMIC

OHMMETER
OHMMETERS
OHMS
OHO
OHONE
OHOS
OI
OIDIA
OIDIUM
OIK
OIKIST
OIKISTS
OIKS
OIL
OILCAN
OILCANS
OILCLOTH
OILCLOTHS
OILED
OILER
OILERIES
OILERS
OILERY
OILIER
OILIEST
OILILY
OILINESS
OILINESSES
OILING
OILLET
OILLETS
OILNUT
OILNUTS
OILS
OILSKIN
OILSKINS
OILSTONE
OILSTONES
OILY
OINT
OINTED
OINTING
OINTMENT
OINTMENTS
OINTS
OITICICA
OITICICAS
OJIME
OJIMES
OKAPI
OKAPIS
OKAY
OKAYED
OKAYING
OKAYS
OKE
OKES
OKIMONO
OKIMONOS
OKRA
OKRAS
OLD
OLDEN
OLDENED
OLDENING
OLDENS
OLDER
OLDEST
OLDIE
OLDIES

OLDISH
OLDNESS
OLDNESSES
OLDS
OLDSQUAW
OLDSQUAWS
OLDSTER
OLDSTERS
OLDY
OLÉ
OLEACEOUS
OLEANDER
OLEANDERS
OLEARIA
OLEARIAS
OLEASTER
OLEASTERS
OLEATE
OLEATES
OLECRANAL
OLECRANON
OLECRANONS
OLEFIANT
OLEFIN
OLEFINE
OLEFINES
OLEFINS
OLEIC
OLEIN
OLEINS
OLENT
OLEO
OLEOGRAPH
OLEOGRAPHS
OLEOS
OLEUM
OLEUMS
OLFACT
OLFACTED
OLFACTING
OLFACTION
OLFACTIONS
OLFACTIVE
OLFACTORY
OLFACTS
OLIBANUM
OLIBANUMS
OLID
OLIGAEMIA
OLIGAEMIAS
OLIGARCH
OLIGARCHIES
OLIGARCHS
OLIGARCHY
OLIGIST
OLIGISTS
OLIGOPOLIES
OLIGOPOLY
OLIO
OLIOS
OLIPHANT
OLIPHANTS
OLITORIES
OLITORY
OLIVARY
OLIVE
OLIVENITE
OLIVENITES
OLIVER
OLIVERS

OLIVES
OLIVET
OLIVETS
OLIVINE
OLIVINES
OLLA
OLLAMH
OLLAMHS
OLLAS
OLLAV
OLLAVS
OLM
OLMS
OLOGIES
OLOGY
OLOROSO
OLOROSOS
OLPAE
OLPE
OLPES
OLYCOOK
OLYCOOKS
OLYKOEK
OLYKOEKS
OLYMPIAD
OLYMPIADS
OLYMPICS
OM
OMADHAUN
OMADHAUNS
OMASA
OMASAL
OMASUM
OMBRE
OMBRÉ
OMBRELLA
OMBRELLAS
OMBRES
OMBROPHIL
OMBROPHILS
OMBU
OMBÚ
OMBUDSMAN
OMBUDSMEN
OMBÚS
OMBUS
OMEGA
OMEGAS
OMELET
OMELETS
OMELETTE
OMELETTES
OMEN
OMENED
OMENING
OMENS
OMENTA
OMENTAL
OMENTUM
OMER
OMERS
OMERTÀ
OMERTÀS
OMICRON
OMICRONS
OMINOUS
OMINOUSLY
OMISSIBLE
OMISSION
OMISSIONS

OMISSIVE
OMIT
OMITS
OMITTANCE
OMITTANCES
OMITTED
OMITTER
OMITTERS
OMITTING
OMLAH
OMLAHS
OMMATEA
OMMATEUM
OMMATIDIA
OMNEITIES
OMNEITY
OMNIANA
OMNIBUS
OMNIBUSES
OMNIETIES
OMNIETY
OMNIFIC
OMNIFIED
OMNIFIES
OMNIFORM
OMNIFY
OMNIFYING
OMNIUM
OMNIUMS
OMNIVORE
OMNIVORES
OMNIVORIES
OMNIVORY
OMOHYOID
OMOHYOIDS
OMOPHAGIA
OMOPHAGIAS
OMOPHAGIC
OMOPHAGIES
OMOPHAGY
OMOPLATE
OMOPLATES
OMPHACITE
OMPHACITES
OMPHALIC
OMPHALOID
OMPHALOS
OMPHALOSES
OMRAH
OMRAHS
OMS
ON
ONAGER
ONAGERS
ONANISM
ONANISMS
ONANIST
ONANISTIC
ONANISTS
ONBOARD
ONCE
ONCER
ONCERS
ONCES
ONCIDIUM
ONCIDIUMS
ONCOGEN
ONCOGENE
ONCOGENES
ONCOGENIC

ONCOGENS
ONCOLOGIES
ONCOLOGY
ONCOME
ONCOMES
ONCOMETER
ONCOMETERS
ONCOMING
ONCOMINGS
ONCOST
ONCOSTMAN
ONCOSTMEN
ONCOSTS
ONCOTOMIES
ONCOTOMY
ONCUS
ONDATRA
ONDATRAS
ONDINE
ONDINES
ONDING
ONDINGS
ONE
ONEFOLD
ONEIRIC
ONELY
ONENESS
ONENESSES
ONER
ONEROUS
ONEROUSLY
ONERS
ONES
ONESELF
ONEYER
ONEYERS
ONEYRE
ONEYRES
ONFALL
ONFALLS
ONFLOW
ONFLOWS
ONGOING
ONGOINGS
ONION
ONIONED
ONIONING
ONIONS
ONIONY
ONIRIC
ONISCOID
ONKUS
ONLOOKER
ONLOOKERS
ONLOOKING
ONLY
ONNED
ONNING
ONOMASTIC
ONOMASTICS
ONRUSH
ONRUSHES
ONS
ONSET
ONSETS
ONSETTER
ONSETTERS
ONSETTING
ONSETTINGS
ONSHORE

ONSIDE
ONSIDES
ONSLAUGHT
ONSLAUGHTS
ONST
ONSTEAD
ONSTEADS
ONTO
ONTOGENIC
ONTOGENIES
ONTOGENY
ONTOLOGIC
ONTOLOGIES
ONTOLOGY
ONUS
ONUSES
ONWARD
ONWARDLY
ONWARDS
ONYCHA
ONYCHAS
ONYCHIA
ONYCHIAS
ONYCHITE
ONYCHITES
ONYCHITIS
ONYCHITISES
ONYCHIUM
ONYCHIUMS
ONYMOUS
ONYX
ONYXES
OO
OOBIT
OOBITS
OOCYTE
OOCYTES
OODLES
OODLINS
OOF
OOFS
OOFTISH
OOFTISHES
OOGAMIES
OOGAMOUS
OOGAMY
OOGENESES
OOGENESIS
OOGENETIC
OOGENIES
OOGENY
OOGONIA
OOGONIAL
OOGONIUM
OOH
OOHED
OOHING
OOHS
OOIDAL
OOLAKAN
OOLAKANS
OOLITE
OOLITES
OOLITIC
OOLOGIES
OOLOGIST
OOLOGISTS
OOLONG
OOLONGS

OOM
OOMIAC
OOMIACK
OOMIACKS
OOMIACS
OOMIAK
OOMIAKS
OOMPAH
OOMPAHED
OOMPAHING
OOMPAHS
OOMPH
OOMPHS
OOMS
OON
OONS
OONT
OONTS
OOP
OOPED
OOPHORON
OOPHORONS
OOPHYTE
OOPHYTES
OOPING
OOPS
OOR
OORIAL
OORIALS
OORIE
OORIER
OORIEST
OOS
OOSE
OOSES
OOSIER
OOSIEST
OOSPHERE
OOSPHERES
OOSPORE
OOSPORES
OOSY
OOZE
OOZED
OOZES
OOZIER
OOZIEST
OOZILY
OOZINESS
OOZINESSES
OOZING
OOZY
OP
OPACITIES
OPACITY
OPACOUS
OPAH
OPAHS
OPAL
OPALED
OPALINE
OPALINES
OPALISED
OPALIZED
OPALS
OPAQUE
OPAQUED
OPAQUELY
OPAQUER
OPAQUES

OPAQUEST
OPAQUING
OPE
OPED
OPEN
OPENABLE
OPENED
OPENER
OPENERS
OPENEST
OPENING
OPENINGS
OPENLY
OPENNESS
OPENNESSES
OPENS
OPERA
OPERABLE
OPERAND
OPERANDS
OPERANT
OPERANTS
OPERAS
OPERATE
OPERATED
OPERATES
OPERATIC
OPERATING
OPERATION
OPERATIONS
OPERATIVE
OPERATIVES
OPERATOR
OPERATORS
OPERCULA
OPERCULAR
OPERCULUM
OPERETTA
OPERETTAS
OPEROSE
OPEROSELY
OPEROSITIES
OPEROSITY
OPES
OPHIDIAN
OPHIDIANS
OPHIOLITE
OPHIOLITES
OPHIOLOGIES
OPHIOLOGY
OPHITE
OPHITES
OPHITIC
OPHIURAN
OPHIURANS
OPHIURID
OPHIURIDS
OPHIUROID
OPHIUROIDS
OPIATE
OPIATED
OPIATES
OPIATING
OPIFICER
OPIFICERS
OPINABLE
OPINE
OPINED
OPINES
OPING

OPINICUS
OPINICUSES
OPINING
OPINION
OPINIONED
OPINIONS
OPIOID
OPIUM
OPIUMS
OPOBALSAM
OPOBALSAMS
OPODELDOC
OPODELDOCS
OPOPANAX
OPOPANAXES
OPORICE
OPORICES
OPOSSUM
OPOSSUMS
OPPIDAN
OPPIDANS
OPPILATE
OPPILATED
OPPILATES
OPPILATING
OPPONENCIES
OPPONENCY
OPPONENT
OPPONENTS
OPPORTUNE
OPPOSABLE
OPPOSE
OPPOSED
OPPOSER
OPPOSERS
OPPOSES
OPPOSING
OPPOSITE
OPPOSITES
OPPRESS
OPPRESSED
OPPRESSES
OPPRESSING
OPPRESSOR
OPPRESSORS
OPPUGN
OPPUGNANT
OPPUGNANTS
OPPUGNED
OPPUGNER
OPPUGNERS
OPPUGNING
OPPUGNS
OPS
OPSIMATH
OPSIMATHIES
OPSIMATHS
OPSIMATHY
OPSOMANIA
OPSOMANIAS
OPSONIC
OPSONIN
OPSONINS
OPSONIUM
OPSONIUMS
OPT
OPTANT
OPTANTS
OPTATIVE
OPTATIVES

OPTED
OPTIC
OPTICAL
OPTICALLY
OPTICIAN
OPTICIANS
OPTICS
OPTIMA
OPTIMAL
OPTIMATE
OPTIMATES
OPTIME
OPTIMES
OPTIMISE
OPTIMISED
OPTIMISES
OPTIMISING
OPTIMISM
OPTIMISMS
OPTIMIST
OPTIMISTS
OPTIMIZE
OPTIMIZED
OPTIMIZES
OPTIMIZING
OPTIMUM
OPTING
OPTION
OPTIONAL
OPTIONS
OPTOLOGIES
OPTOLOGY
OPTOMETER
OPTOMETERS
OPTOMETRIES
OPTOMETRY
OPTOPHONE
OPTOPHONES
OPTS
OPULENCE
OPULENCES
OPULENT
OPULENTLY
OPULUS
OPULUSES
OPUNTIA
OPUNTIAS
OPUS
OPUSCLE
OPUSCLES
OPUSCULA
OPUSCULE
OPUSCULES
OPUSCULUM
OPUSES
OR
ORACH
ORACHE
ORACHES
ORACIES
ORACLE
ORACLED
ORACLES
ORACLING
ORACULAR
ORACULOUS
ORACY
ORAGIOUS
ORAL
ORALLY

ORALS
ORANG
ORANGE
ORANGEADE
ORANGEADES
ORANGER
ORANGERIES
ORANGERY
ORANGES
ORANGEST
ORANGS
ORANT
ORANTS
ORARIA
ORARIAN
ORARIANS
ORARION
ORARIONS
ORARIUM
ORARIUMS
ORATE
ORATED
ORATES
ORATING
ORATION
ORATIONS
ORATOR
ORATORIAL
ORATORIAN
ORATORIANS
ORATORIES
ORATORIO
ORATORIOS
ORATORS
ORATORY
ORATRESS
ORATRESSES
ORATRIX
ORATRIXES
ORB
ORBED
ORBICULAR
ORBIER
ORBIEST
ORBING
ORBIT
ORBITA
ORBITAL
ORBITALS
ORBITAS
ORBITED
ORBITER
ORBITERS
ORBITIES
ORBITING
ORBITS
ORBITY
ORBS
ORBY
ORC
ORCEIN
ORCEINS
ORCHARD
ORCHARDS
ORCHAT
ORCHATS
ORCHEL
ORCHELLA
ORCHELLAS
ORCHELS

ORCHESES
ORCHESIS
ORCHESTIC
ORCHESTICS
ORCHESTRA
ORCHESTRAS
ORCHID
ORCHIDIST
ORCHIDISTS
ORCHIDS
ORCHIL
ORCHILLA
ORCHILLAS
ORCHILS
ORCHIS
ORCHISES
ORCHITIC
ORCHITIS
ORCHITISES
ORCIN
ORCINE
ORCINES
ORCINOL
ORCINOLS
ORCINS
ORCS
ORD
ORDAIN
ORDAINED
ORDAINER
ORDAINERS
ORDAINING
ORDAINS
ORDALIAN
ORDALIUM
ORDALIUMS
ORDEAL
ORDEALS
ORDER
ORDERED
ORDERER
ORDERERS
ORDERING
ORDERINGS
ORDERLESS
ORDERLIES
ORDERLY
ORDERS
ORDINAIRE
ORDINAIRES
ORDINAL
ORDINALS
ORDINANCE
ORDINANCES
ORDINAND
ORDINANDS
ORDINANT
ORDINANTS
ORDINAR
ORDINARIES
ORDINARS
ORDINARY
ORDINATE
ORDINATED
ORDINATES
ORDINATING
ORDINEE
ORDINEES
ORDNANCE
ORDNANCES

ORDS
ORDURE
ORDURES
ORDUROUS
ORE
OREAD
OREADES
OREADS
ORECROWE
ORECROWED
ORECROWES
ORECROWING
ORECTIC
OREGANO
OREGANOS
OREIDE
OREIDES
OREOLOGIES
OREOLOGY
OREPEARCH
OREPEARCHED
OREPEARCHES
OREPEARCHING
ORES
ORESTUNCK
OREWEED
OREWEEDS
OREXIS
OREXISES
ORF
ORFE
ORFES
ORFS
ORGAN
ORGANA
ORGANDIE
ORGANDIES
ORGANELLE
ORGANELLES
ORGANIC
ORGANICAL
ORGANISE
ORGANISED
ORGANISER
ORGANISERS
ORGANISES
ORGANISING
ORGANISM
ORGANISMS
ORGANIST
ORGANISTS
ORGANITIES
ORGANITY
ORGANIZE
ORGANIZED
ORGANIZER
ORGANIZERS
ORGANIZES
ORGANIZING
ORGANON
ORGANS
ORGANUM
ORGANZA
ORGANZAS
ORGANZINE
ORGANZINES
ORGASM
ORGASMED
ORGASMIC
ORGASMING

ORGASMS	ORIOLES	ORT	OSIERY	OSTEOMAS
ORGASTIC	ORISON	ORTANIQUE	OSMATE	OSTEOPATH
ORGEAT	ORISONS	ORTANIQUES	OSMATES	OSTEOPATHS
ORGEATS	ORLE	ORTHIAN	OSMETERIA	OSTEOTOME
ORGIA	ORLEANS	ORTHICON	OSMIATE	OSTEOTOMES
ORGIAS	ORLEANSES	ORTHICONS	OSMIATES	OSTEOTOMIES
ORGIAST	ORLES	ORTHO	OSMIC	OSTEOTOMY
ORGIASTIC	ORLOP	ORTHOAXES	OSMIOUS	OSTIA
ORGIASTS	ORLOPS	ORTHOAXIS	OSMIUM	OSTIAL
ORGIC	ORMER	ORTHODOX	OSMIUMS	OSTIARIES
ORGIES	ORMERS	ORTHODOXIES	OSMOMETER	OSTIARY
ORGILLOUS	ORMOLU	ORTHODOXY	OSMOMETERS	OSTIATE
ORGONE	ORMOLUS	ORTHOEPIC	OSMOMETRIES	OSTINATO
ORGONES	ORNAMENT	ORTHOEPIES	OSMOMETRY	OSTINATOS
ORGUE	ORNAMENTED	ORTHOEPY	OSMOSE	OSTIOLATE
ORGUES	ORNAMENTING	ORTHOPEDIES	OSMOSED	OSTIOLE
ORGULOUS	ORNAMENTS	ORTHOPEDY	OSMOSES	OSTIOLES
ORGY	ORNATE	ORTHOPOD	OSMOSING	OSTIUM
ORIBI	ORNATELY	ORTHOPODS	OSMOSIS	OSTLER
ORIBIS	ORNATER	ORTHOPTIC	OSMOTIC	OSTLERESS
ORICALCHE	ORNATEST	ORTHOPTICS	OSMOUS	OSTLERESSES
ORICALCHES	ORNERY	ORTHOS	OSMUND	OSTLERS
ORICHALC	ORNIS	ORTHOSES	OSMUNDA	OSTRACA
ORICHALCS	ORNISES	ORTHOSIS	OSMUNDAS	OSTRACEAN
ORIEL	ORNITHIC	ORTHOTIC	OSMUNDS	OSTRACISE
ORIELLED	ORNITHOID	ONTHOTICO	OONADUNG	OGTNACIGED
ORIELS	OROGEN	ORTHOTIST	OSNABURGS	OSTRACISES
ORIENCIES	OROGENIC	ORTHOTISTS	OSPREY	OSTRACISING
ORIENCY	OROGENIES	ORTHOTONE	OSPREYS	OSTRACISM
ORIENT	OROGENY	ORTHROSES	OSSA	OSTRACISMS
ORIENTAL	OROGENY	ORTOLAN	OSSARIUM	OSTRACIZE
ORIENTALS	OROGRAPHIES	ORTOLANS	OSSARIUMS	OSTRACIZED
ORIENTATE	OROGRAPHY	ORTS	OSSEIN	OSTRACIZES
ORIENTATED	OROIDE	ORVAL	OSSEINS	OSTRACIZING
ORIENTATES	OROIDES	ORVALS	OSSELET	OSTRACOD
ORIENTATING	OROLOGIES	ORYX	OSSELETS	OSTRACODS
ORIENTED	OROLOGIST	ORYXES	OSSEOUS	OSTRACON
ORIENTEER	OROLOGISTS	OS	OSSETER	OSTRAKA
ORIENTEERED	OROLOGY	OSCHEAL	OSSETERS	OSTRAKON
ORIENTEERING	OROPESA	OSCILLATE	OSSIA	OSTREGER
ORIENTEERINGS	OROPESAS	OSCILLATED	OSSICLE	OSTREGERS
ORIENTEERS	OROROTUND	OSCILLATES	OSSICLES	OSTRICH
ORIENTING	OROTUND	OSCILLATING	OSSICULAR	OSTRICHES
ORIENTS	ORPHAN	OSCINE	OSSIFIC	OTALGIA
ORIFEX	ORPHANAGE	OSCININE	OSSIFIED	OTALGIAS
ORIFEXES	ORPHANAGES	OSCITANCIES	OSSIFIES	OTALGIES
ORIFICE	ORPHANED	OSCITANCY	OSSIFRAGA	OTALGY
ORIFICES	ORPHANING	OSCITANT	OSSIFRAGAS	OTARIES
ORIFICIAL	ORPHANISM	OSCITATE	OSSIFRAGE	OTARINE
ORIFLAMME	ORPHANISMS	OSCITATED	OSSIFRAGES	OTARY
ORIFLAMMES	ORPHANS	OSCITATES	OSSIFY	OTHER
ORIGAMI	ORPHARION	OSCITATING	OSSIFYING	OTHERNESS
ORIGAMIS	ORPHARIONS	OSCULA	OSSUARIES	OTHERNESSES
ORIGAN	ORPHREY	OSCULAR	OSSUARY	OTHERS
ORIGANE	ORPHREYS	OSCULANT	OSTEAL	OTHERWISE
ORIGANES	ORPIMENT	OSCULAR	OSTEITIS	OTIC
ORIGANS	ORPIMENTS	OSCULATE	OSTEITISES	OTIOSE
ORIGANUM	ORPIN	OSCULATED	OSTENSIVE	OTIOSITIES
ORIGANUMS	ORPINE	OSCULATES	OSTENSORIES	OTIOSITY
ORIGIN	ORPINES	OSCULATING	OSTENSORY	OTITIS
ORIGINAL	ORPINS	OSCULE	OSTENT	OTITISES
ORIGINALS	ORRA	OSCULES	OSTENTS	OTOCYST
ORIGINATE	ORRERIES	OSCULUM	OSTEODERM	OTOCYSTS
ORIGINATED	ORRERY	OSCULUMS	OSTEODERMS	OTOLITH
ORIGINATES	ORRIS	OSHAC	OSTEOGENIES	OTOLITHS
ORIGINATING	ORRISES	OSHACS	OSTEOGENY	OTOLOGIES
ORIGINS	ORS	OSIER	OSTEOID	OTOLOGIST
ORILLION	ORSEILLE	OSIERED	OSTEOLOGIES	OTOLOGISTS
ORILLIONS	ORSEILLES	OSIERIES	OSTEOLOGY	OTOLOGY
ORIOLE	ORSELLIC	OSIERS	OSTEOMA	OTORRHOEA

OTORRHOEAS
OTOSCOPE
OTOSCOPES
OTTAR
OTTARS
OTTAVA
OTTAVAS
OTTAVINO
OTTAVINOS
OTTER
OTTERED
OTTERING
OTTERS
OTTO
OTTOMAN
OTTOMANS
OTTOS
OTTRELITE
OTTRELITES
OU
OUABAIN
OUABAINS
OUAKARI
OUAKARIS
OUBIT
OUBITS
OUBLIETTE
OUBLIETTES
OUCH
OUCHES
OUCHT
OUCHTS
OUGHLIED
OUGHLIES
OUGHLY
OUGHLYING
OUGHT
OUGHTNESS
OUGHTNESSES
OUGHTS
OUGLIE
OUGLIED
OUGLIEING
OUGLIES
OUIJA
OUIJAS
OUISTITI
OUISTITIS
OUK
OUKS
OULACHON
OULACHONS
OULAKAN
OULAKANS
OULK
OULKS
OULONG
OULONGS
OUNCE
OUNCES
OUNDIER
OUNDIEST
OUNDY
OUP
OUPED
OUPH
OUPHE
OUPHES
OUPHS
OUPING

OUPS
OUR
OURALI
OURALIS
OURARI
OURARIS
OUREBI
OUREBIS
OURIE
OURIER
OURIEST
OURN
OUROBOROS
OUROBOROSES
OUROLOGIES
OUROLOGY
OUROSCOPIES
OUROSCOPY
OURS
OURSELF
OURSELVES
OUSEL
OUSELS
OUST
OUSTED
OUSTER
OUSTERS
OUSTING
OUSTITI
OUSTITIS
OUSTS
OUT
OUTACT
OUTACTED
OUTACTING
OUTACTS
OUTAGE
OUTAGES
OUTATE
OUTBACK
OUTBACKER
OUTBACKERS
OUTBACKS
OUTBAR
OUTBARRED
OUTBARRING
OUTBARS
OUTBID
OUTBIDDING
OUTBIDS
OUTBOARD
OUTBOUND
OUTBOUNDS
OUTBOX
OUTBOXED
OUTBOXES
OUTBOXING
OUTBRAG
OUTBRAGGED
OUTBRAGGING
OUTBRAGS
OUTBRAVE
OUTBRAVED
OUTBRAVES
OUTBRAVING
OUTBREAK
OUTBREAKING
OUTBREAKS
OUTBRED
OUTBREED

OUTBREEDING
OUTBREEDINGS
OUTBREEDS
OUTBROKE
OUTBROKEN
OUTBURN
OUTBURNED
OUTBURNING
OUTBURNS
OUTBURNT
OUTBURST
OUTBURSTING
OUTBURSTS
OUTBY
OUTBYE
OUTCAST
OUTCASTE
OUTCASTED
OUTCASTES
OUTCASTING
OUTCASTS
OUTCLASS
OUTCLASSED
OUTCLASSES
OUTCLASSING
OUTCOME
OUTCOMES
OUTCRAFTIED
OUTCRAFTIES
OUTCRAFTY
OUTCRAFTYING
OUTCRIED
OUTCRIES
OUTCROP
OUTCROPPED
OUTCROPPING
OUTCROPS
OUTCROSS
OUTCROSSED
OUTCROSSES
OUTCROSSING
OUTCROSSINGS
OUTCRY
OUTCRYING
OUTDANCE
OUTDANCED
OUTDANCES
OUTDANCING
OUTDARE
OUTDARED
OUTDARES
OUTDARING
OUTDATE
OUTDATED
OUTDATES
OUTDATING
OUTDID
OUTDO
OUTDOES
OUTDOING
OUTDONE
OUTDOOR
OUTDOORS
OUTDOORSY
OUTDRANK
OUTDRINK
OUTDRINKING
OUTDRINKS
OUTDRIVE
OUTDRIVEN

OUTDRIVES
OUTDRIVING
OUTDROVE
OUTDRUNK
OUTDURE
OUTDURED
OUTDURES
OUTDURING
OUTDWELL
OUTDWELLED
OUTDWELLING
OUTDWELLS
OUTDWELT
OUTEAT
OUTEATEN
OUTEATING
OUTEATS
OUTED
OUTEDGE
OUTEDGES
OUTER
OUTERMOST
OUTERS
OUTERWEAR
OUTERWEARS
OUTFACE
OUTFACED
OUTFACES
OUTFACING
OUTFALL
OUTFALLS
OUTFIELD
OUTFIELDS
OUTFIGHT
OUTFIGHTING
OUTFIGHTS
OUTFIT
OUTFITS
OUTFITTED
OUTFITTER
OUTFITTERS
OUTFITTING
OUTFITTINGS
OUTFLANK
OUTFLANKED
OUTFLANKING
OUTFLANKS
OUTFLASH
OUTFLASHED
OUTFLASHES
OUTFLASHING
OUTFLEW
OUTFLIES
OUTFLING
OUTFLINGS
OUTFLOW
OUTFLOWED
OUTFLOWING
OUTFLOWINGS
OUTFLOWN
OUTFLOWS
OUTFLUSH
OUTFLUSHED
OUTFLUSHES
OUTFLUSHING
OUTFLY
OUTFLYING
OUTFOOT
OUTFOOTED
OUTFOOTING

OUTFOOTS
OUTFOUGHT
OUTFOX
OUTFOXED
OUTFOXES
OUTFOXING
OUTFROWN
OUTFROWNED
OUTFROWNING
OUTFROWNS
OUTGAS
OUTGASSED
OUTGASSES
OUTGASSING
OUTGASSINGS
OUTGATE
OUTGATES
OUTGAVE
OUTGIVE
OUTGIVEN
OUTGIVES
OUTGIVING
OUTGIVINGS
OUTGLARE
OUTGLARED
OUTGLARES
OUTGLARING
OUTGO
OUTGOER
OUTGOERS
OUTGOES
OUTGOING
OUTGOINGS
OUTGONE
OUTGREW
OUTGROW
OUTGROWING
OUTGROWN
OUTGROWS
OUTGROWTH
OUTGROWTHS
OUTGUARD
OUTGUARDS
OUTGUN
OUTGUNNED
OUTGUNNING
OUTGUNS
OUTGUSH
OUTGUSHED
OUTGUSHES
OUTGUSHING
OUTHAUL
OUTHAULER
OUTHAULERS
OUTHAULS
OUTHER
OUTHIRE
OUTHIRED
OUTHIRES
OUTHIRING
OUTHIT
OUTHITS
OUTHITTING
OUTHOUSE
OUTHOUSES
OUTHYRE
OUTHYRED
OUTHYRES
OUTHYRING
OUTING

OUTINGS	OUTLOOK	OUTPORT	OUTRELIEF	OUTSHOTS
OUTJEST	OUTLOOKED	OUTPORTS	OUTRELIEFS	OUTSIDE
OUTJESTED	OUTLOOKING	OUTPOST	OUTREMER	OUTSIDER
OUTJESTING	OUTLOOKS	OUTPOSTS	OUTREMERS	OUTSIDERS
OUTJESTS	OUTLUSTRE	OUTPOUR	OUTRIDDEN	OUTSIDES
OUTJET	OUTLUSTRED	OUTPOURED	OUTRIDE	OUTSIGHT
OUTJETS	OUTLUSTRES	OUTPOURER	OUTRIDER	OUTSIGHTS
OUTJUMP	OUTLUSTRING	OUTPOURERS	OUTRIDERS	OUTSIT
OUTJUMPED	OUTLYING	OUTPOURING	OUTRIDES	OUTSITS
OUTJUMPING	OUTMAN	OUTPOURINGS	OUTRIDING	OUTSITTING
OUTJUMPS	OUTMANNED	OUTPOURS	OUTRIGGER	OUTSIZE
OUTJUT	OUTMANNING	OUTPOWER	OUTRIGGERS	OUTSIZED
OUTJUTS	OUTMANS	OUTPOWERED	OUTRIGHT	OUTSIZES
OUTLAID	OUTMANTLE	OUTPOWERING	OUTRIVAL	OUTSKIRT
OUTLAIN	OUTMANTLED	OUTPOWERS	OUTRIVALLED	OUTSKIRTS
OUTLAND	OUTMANTLES	OUTPRAY	OUTRIVALLING	OUTSLEEP
OUTLANDER	OUTMANTLING	OUTPRAYED	OUTRIVALS	OUTSLEEPING
OUTLANDERS	OUTMARCH	OUTPRAYING	OUTROAR	OUTSLEEPS
OUTLANDS	OUTMARCHED	OUTPRAYS	OUTROARED	OUTSLEPT
OUTLASH	OUTMARCHES	OUTPRICE	OUTROARING	OUTSMART
OUTLASHES	OUTMARCHING	OUTPRICED	OUTROARS	OUTSMARTED
OUTLAST	OUTMATCH	OUTPRICES	OUTRODE	OUTSMARTING
OUTLASTED	OUTMATCHED	OUTPRICING	OUTROOP	OUTSMARTS
OUTLASTING	OUTMATCHES	OUTPRIZE	OUTROOPER	OUTSOAR
OUTLASTS	OUTMATCHING	OUTPRIZED	OUTROOPERS	OUTSOARED
OUTLAUNCE	OUTMODE	OUTPRIZED	OUTROOPS	OUTSOARING
OUTLAUNCED	OUTMODED	OUTPRIZING	OUTROOT	OUTSOARS
OUTLAUNCES	OUTMODES	OUTPUT	OUTROOTED	OUTSOLD
OUTLAUNCH	OUTMODING	OUTPUTS	OUTROOTING	OUTSOLE
OUTLAUNCHED	OUTMOST	OUTPUTTING	OUTROOTS	OUTSOLES
OUTLAUNCHES	OUTMOVE	OUTRACE	OUTROPE	OUTSPAN
OUTLAUNCHING	OUTMOVED	OUTRACED	OUTROPER	OUTSPANNED
OUTLAUNCING	OUTMOVES	OUTRACES	OUTROPERS	OUTSPANNING
OUTLAW	OUTMOVING	OUTRACING	OUTROPES	OUTSPANS
OUTLAWED	OUTNAME	OUTRAGE	OUTRUN	OUTSPEAK
OUTLAWING	OUTNAMED	OUTRAGED	OUTRUNNER	OUTSPEAKING
OUTLAWRIES	OUTNAMES	OUTRAGES	OUTRUNNERS	OUTSPEAKS
OUTLAWRY	OUTNAMING	OUTRAGING	OUTRUNNING	OUTSPEND
OUTLAWS	OUTNESS	OUTRAIGNE	OUTRUNS	OUTSPENDING
OUTLAY	OUTNESSES	OUTRAIGNED	OUTRUSH	OUTSPENDS
OUTLAYING	OUTNIGHT	OUTRAIGNES	OUTRUSHED	OUTSPENT
OUTLAYS	OUTNIGHTED	OUTRAIGNING	OUTRUSHES	OUTSPOKE
OUTLEAP	OUTNIGHTING	OUTRAN	OUTRUSHING	OUTSPOKEN
OUTLEAPED	OUTNIGHTS	OUTRANCE	OUTS	OUTSPORT
OUTLEAPING	OUTNUMBER	OUTRANCES	OUTSAIL	OUTSPORTED
OUTLEAPS	OUTNUMBERED	OUTRANK	OUTSAILED	OUTSPORTING
OUTLEAPT	OUTNUMBERING	OUTRANKED	OUTSAILING	OUTSPORTS
OUTLEARN	OUTNUMBERS	OUTRANKING	OUTSAILS	OUTSPRANG
OUTLEARNED	OUTPACE	OUTRANKS	OUTSAT	OUTSPREAD
OUTLEARNING	OUTPACED	OUTRATE	OUTSCOLD	OUTSPREADING
OUTLEARNS	OUTPACES	OUTRATED	OUTSCOLDED	OUTSPREADS
OUTLEARNT	OUTPACING	OUTRATES	OUTSCOLDING	OUTSPRING
OUTLER	OUTPART	OUTRATING	OUTSCOLDS	OUTSPRINGING
OUTLERS	OUTPARTS	OUTRE	OUTSCORN	OUTSPRINGS
OUTLET	OUTPEEP	OUTREACH	OUTSCORNED	OUTSPRUNG
OUTLETS	OUTPEEPED	OUTREACHED	OUTSCORNING	OUTSTAND
OUTLIE	OUTPEEPING	OUTREACHES	OUTSCORNS	OUTSTANDING
OUTLIED	OUTPEEPS	OUTREACHING	OUTSELL	OUTSTANDS
OUTLIER	OUTPEER	OUTRED	OUTSELLING	OUTSTARE
OUTLIERS	OUTPEERED	OUTREDDED	OUTSELLS	OUTSTARED
OUTLIES	OUTPEERING	OUTREDDEN	OUTSET	OUTSTARES
OUTLINE	OUTPEERS	OUTREDDENED	OUTSETS	OUTSTARING
OUTLINEAR	OUTPLAY	OUTREDDENING	OUTSHINE	OUTSTAY
OUTLINED	OUTPLAYED	OUTREDDENS	OUTSHINES	OUTSTAYED
OUTLINES	OUTPLAYING	OUTREDDING	OUTSHINING	OUTSTAYING
OUTLINING	OUTPLAYS	OUTREDS	OUTSHONE	OUTSTAYS
OUTLIVE	OUTPOINT	OUTREIGN	OUTSHOOT	OUTSTEP
OUTLIVED	OUTPOINTED	OUTREIGNED	OUTSHOOTING	OUTSTEPPED
OUTLIVES	OUTPOINTING	OUTREIGNING	OUTSHOOTS	OUTSTEPPING
OUTLIVING	OUTPOINTS	OUTREIGNS	OUTSHOT	OUTSTEPS

OUTSTOOD
OUTSTRAIN
OUTSTRAINED
OUTSTRAINING
OUTSTRAINS
OUTSTRIKE
OUTSTRIKES
OUTSTRIKING
OUTSTRIP
OUTSTRIPPED
OUTSTRIPPING
OUTSTRIPS
OUTSTRUCK
OUTSUM
OUTSUMMED
OUTSUMMING
OUTSUMS
OUTSWEAR
OUTSWEARING
OUTSWEARS
OUTSWELL
OUTSWELLED
OUTSWELLING
OUTSWELLS
OUTSWING
OUTSWINGS
OUTSWOLLEN
OUTSWORE
OUTSWORN
OUTTAKE
OUTTAKEN
OUTTAKES
OUTTAKING
OUTTALK
OUTTALKED
OUTTALKING
OUTTALKS
OUTTELL
OUTTELLING
OUTTELLS
OUTTHINK
OUTTHINKING
OUTTHINKS
OUTTHOUGHT
OUTTOLD
OUTTONGUE
OUTTONGUED
OUTTONGUES
OUTTONGUING
OUTTOOK
OUTTOP
OUTTOPPED
OUTTOPPING
OUTTOPS
OUTTRAVEL
OUTTRAVELLED
OUTTRAVELLING
OUTTRAVELS
OUTTURN
OUTTURNS
OUTVALUE
OUTVALUED
OUTVALUES
OUTVALUING
OUTVENOM
OUTVENOMED
OUTVENOMING
OUTVENOMS
OUTVIE
OUTVIED

OUTVIES
OUTVOICE
OUTVOICED
OUTVOICES
OUTVOICING
OUTVOTE
OUTVOTED
OUTVOTER
OUTVOTERS
OUTVOTES
OUTVOTING
OUTVYING
OUTWALK
OUTWALKED
OUTWALKING
OUTWALKS
OUTWARD
OUTWARDLY
OUTWARDS
OUTWATCH
OUTWATCHED
OUTWATCHES
OUTWATCHING
OUTWEAR
OUTWEARIED
OUTWEARIES
OUTWEARING
OUTWEARS
OUTWEARY
OUTWEARYING
OUTWEED
OUTWEEDED
OUTWEEDING
OUTWEEDS
OUTWEEP
OUTWEEPING
OUTWEEPS
OUTWEIGH
OUTWEIGHED
OUTWEIGHING
OUTWEIGHS
OUTWELL
OUTWELLED
OUTWELLING
OUTWELLS
OUTWENT
OUTWEPT
OUTWICK
OUTWICKED
OUTWICKING
OUTWICKS
OUTWIN
OUTWIND
OUTWINDING
OUTWINDS
OUTWING
OUTWINGED
OUTWINGING
OUTWINGS
OUTWINNING
OUTWINS
OUTWIT
OUTWITH
OUTWITS
OUTWITTED
OUTWITTING
OUTWON
OUTWORE
OUTWORK
OUTWORKER

OUTWORKERS
OUTWORKING .
OUTWORKS
OUTWORN
OUTWORTH
OUTWORTHED
OUTWORTHING
OUTWORTHS
OUTWOUND
OUTWREST
OUTWRESTED
OUTWRESTING
OUTWRESTS
OUTWROUGHT
OUVERT
OUVERTE
OUVRAGE
OUVRAGES
OUVRIER
OUVRIÈRE
OUVRIÈRES
OUVRIERS
OUZEL
OUZELS
OUZO
OUZOS
OVA
OVAL
OVALBUMIN
OVALBUMINS
OVALLY
OVALS
OVARIAN
OVARIES
OVARIOLE
OVARIOLES
OVARIOUS
OVARITIS
OVARITISES
OVARY
OVATE
OVATED
OVATES
OVATING
OVATION
OVATIONS
OVATOR
OVATORS
OVEN
OVENS
OVENWARE
OVENWARES
OVENWOOD
OVENWOODS
OVER
OVERACT
OVERACTED
OVERACTING
OVERACTS
OVERALL
OVERALLED
OVERALLS
OVERARCH
OVERARCHED
OVERARCHES
OVERARCHING
OVERARM
OVERATE
OVERAWE
OVERAWED

OVERAWES
OVERAWING
OVERBEAR
OVERBEARING
OVERBEARS
OVERBEAT
OVERBEATEN
OVERBEATING
OVERBEATS
OVERBID
OVERBIDDING
OVERBIDDINGS
OVERBIDS
OVERBITE
OVERBITES
OVERBLEW
OVERBLOW
OVERBLOWING
OVERBLOWN
OVERBLOWS
OVERBOARD
OVERBOIL
OVERBOILED
OVERBOILING
OVERBOILS
OVERBOLD
OVERBOOK
OVERBOOKED
OVERBOOKING
OVERBOOKS
OVERBORE
OVERBORNE
OVERBOUGHT
OVERBOUND
OVERBOUNDED
OVERBOUNDING
OVERBOUNDS
OVERBROW
OVERBROWED
OVERBROWING
OVERBROWS
OVERBUILD
OVERBUILDING
OVERBUILDS
OVERBUILT
OVERBULK
OVERBULKED
OVERBULKING
OVERBULKS
OVERBURN
OVERBURNED
OVERBURNING
OVERBURNS
OVERBURNT
OVERBUSIED
OVERBUSIES
OVERBUSY
OVERBUSYING
OVERBUY
OVERBUYING
OVERBUYS
OVERBY
OVERCALL
OVERCALLED
OVERCALLING
OVERCALLS
OVERCAME
OVERCARRIED
OVERCARRIES
OVERCARRY

OVERCARRYING
OVERCAST
OVERCASTING
OVERCASTINGS
OVERCASTS
OVERCATCH
OVERCATCHES
OVERCATCHING
OVERCAUGHT
OVERCHECK
OVERCHECKS
OVERCLAD
OVERCLOUD
OVERCLOUDED
OVERCLOUDING
OVERCLOUDS
OVERCLOY
OVERCLOYED
OVERCLOYING
OVERCLOYS
OVERCOAT
OVERCOATS
OVERCOME
OVERCOMES
OVERCOMING
OVERCOUNT
OVERCOUNTED
OVERCOUNTING
OVERCOUNTS
OVERCOVER
OVERCOVERED
OVERCOVERING
OVERCOVERS
OVERCRAW
OVERCRAWED
OVERCRAWING
OVERCRAWS
OVERCROP
OVERCROPPED
OVERCROPPING
OVERCROPS
OVERCROW
OVERCROWD
OVERCROWDED
OVERCROWDING
OVERCROWDS
OVERCROWED
OVERCROWING
OVERCROWS
OVERDATED
OVERDID
OVERDIGHT
OVERDO
OVERDOER
OVERDOERS
OVERDOES
OVERDOING
OVERDONE
OVERDOSE
OVERDOSED
OVERDOSES
OVERDOSING
OVERDRAFT
OVERDRAFTS
OVERDRAW
OVERDRAWING
OVERDRAWN
OVERDRAWS
OVERDRESS
OVERDRESSED

OVERDRESSES
OVERDRESSING
OVERDREW
OVERDRIVE
OVERDRIVEN
OVERDRIVES
OVERDRIVING
OVERDROVE
OVERDUE
OVERDUST
OVERDUSTED
OVERDUSTING
OVERDUSTS
OVERDYE
OVERDYED
OVERDYEING
OVERDYES
OVEREAT
OVEREATEN
OVEREATING
OVEREATS
OVERED
OVEREXERT
OVEREXERTED
OVEREXERTING
OVEREXERTS
OVEREYE
OVEREYED
OVEREYEING
OVEREYES
OVEREYING
OVERFALL
OVERFALLEN
OVERFALLING
OVERFALLS
OVERFAR
OVERFED
OVERFEED
OVERFEEDING
OVERFEEDS
OVERFELL
OVERFILL
OVERFILLED
OVERFILLING
OVERFILLS
OVERFINE
OVERFINER
OVERFIRED
OVERFIRES
OVERFIRING
OVERFISH
OVERFISHED
OVERFISHES
OVERFISHING
OVERFLEW
OVERFLIES
OVERFLOW
OVERFLOWED
OVERFLOWING
OVERFLOWINGS
OVERFLOWN
OVERFLOWS
OVERFLUSH
OVERFLUSHED
OVERFLUSHES
OVERFLUSHING
OVERFLY
OVERFLYING
OVERFOLD
OVERFOLDED

OVERFOLDING
OVERFOLDS
OVERFOND
OVERFREE
OVERFULL
OVERGALL
OVERGALLED
OVERGALLING
OVERGALLS
OVERGANG
OVERGANGED
OVERGANGING
OVERGANGS
OVERGAVE
OVERGET
OVERGETS
OVERGETTING
OVERGIVE
OVERGIVEN
OVERGIVES
OVERGIVING
OVERGLAZE
OVERGLAZED
OVERGLAZES
OVERGLAZING
OVERGLOOM
OVERGLOOMED
OVERGLOOMING
OVERGLOOMS
OVERGOO
OVERGOES
OVERGOING
OVERGOINGS
OVERGONE
OVERGORGE
OVERGORGED
OVERGORGES
OVERGORGING
OVERGOT
OVERGRAIN
OVERGRAINED
OVERGRAINING
OVERGRAINS
OVERGRASS
OVERGRASSED
OVERGRASSES
OVERGRASSING
OVERGRAZE
OVERGRAZED
OVERGRAZES
OVERGRAZING
OVERGRAZINGS
OVERGREAT
OVERGREEN
OVERGREENED
OVERGREENING
OVERGREENS
OVERGREW
OVERGROW
OVERGROWING
OVERGROWN
OVERGROWS
OVERHAILE
OVERHAILED
OVERHAILES
OVERHAILING
OVERHAIR
OVERHAIRS
OVERHALE
OVERHALED

OVERHALES
OVERHALING
OVERHAND
OVERHANDED
OVERHANDING
OVERHANDS
OVERHANG
OVERHANGING
OVERHANGS
OVERHAPPY
OVERHASTE
OVERHASTES
OVERHASTY
OVERHAUL
OVERHAULED
OVERHAULING
OVERHAULS
OVERHEAD
OVERHEADS
OVERHEAR
OVERHEARD
OVERHEARING
OVERHEARS
OVERHEAT
OVERHEATED
OVERHEATING
OVERHEATS
OVERHELD
OVERHENT
OVERHENTING
OVERHENTS
OVERHIT
OVERHITS
OVERHITTING
OVERHOLD
OVERHOLDING
OVERHOLDS
OVERHUNG
OVERING
OVERINKED
OVERISSUE
OVERISSUED
OVERISSUES
OVERISSUING
OVERJOY
OVERJOYED
OVERJOYING
OVERJOYS
OVERJUMP
OVERJUMPED
OVERJUMPING
OVERJUMPS
OVERKEEP
OVERKEEPING
OVERKEEPS
OVERKEPT
OVERKEST
OVERKILL
OVERKILLS
OVERKIND
OVERKING
OVERKINGS
OVERKNEE
OVERLADE
OVERLADED
OVERLADEN
OVERLADES
OVERLADING
OVERLAID
OVERLAIN

OVERLAND
OVERLANDED
OVERLANDING
OVERLANDS
OVERLAP
OVERLAPPED
OVERLAPPING
OVERLAPS
OVERLARD
OVERLARDED
OVERLARDING
OVERLARDS
OVERLAY
OVERLAYING
OVERLAYINGS
OVERLAYS
OVERLEAF
OVERLEAP
OVERLEAPED
OVERLEAPING
OVERLEAPS
OVERLEAPT
OVERLEND
OVERLENDING
OVERLENDS
OVERLENT
OVERLIE
OVERLIER
OVERLIERS
OVERLIES
OVERLIVE
OVERLIVED
OVERLIVES
OVERLIVING
OVERLOAD
OVERLOADED
OVERLOADING
OVERLOADS
OVERLONG
OVERLOOK
OVERLOOKED
OVERLOOKING
OVERLOOKS
OVERLORD
OVERLORDED
OVERLORDING
OVERLORDS
OVERLUSTY
OVERLY
OVERLYING
OVERMAN
OVERMANNED
OVERMANNING
OVERMANS
OVERMAST
OVERMASTED
OVERMASTING
OVERMASTS
OVERMATCH
OVERMATCHED
OVERMATCHES
OVERMATCHING
OVERMEN
OVERMERRY
OVERMOUNT
OVERMOUNTED
OVERMOUNTING
OVERMOUNTS
OVERMUCH
OVERNAME

OVERNAMED
OVERNAMES
OVERNAMING
OVERNEAT
OVERNET
OVERNETS
OVERNETTED
OVERNETTING
OVERNICE
OVERNIGHT
OVERNIGHTS
OVERPAGE
OVERPAID
OVERPAINT
OVERPAINTED
OVERPAINTING
OVERPAINTS
OVERPART
OVERPARTED
OVERPARTING
OVERPARTS
OVERPASS
OVERPASSED
OVERPASSES
OVERPASSING
OVERPAST
OVERPAY
OVERPAYING
OVERPAYS
OVERPEDAL
OVERPEDALLED
OVERPEDALLING
OVERPEDALS
OVERPEER
OVERPEERED
OVERPEERING
OVERPEERS
OVERPERCH
OVERPERCHED
OVERPERCHES
OVERPERCHING
OVERPITCH
OVERPITCHED
OVERPITCHES
OVERPITCHING
OVERPLAST
OVERPLAY
OVERPLAYED
OVERPLAYING
OVERPLAYS
OVERPLIED
OVERPLIES
OVERPLUS
OVERPLUSES
OVERPLY
OVERPLYING
OVERPOISE
OVERPOISED
OVERPOISES
OVERPOISING
OVERPOST
OVERPOSTED
OVERPOSTING
OVERPOSTS
OVERPOWER
OVERPOWERED
OVERPOWERING
OVERPOWERS
OVERPRESS
OVERPRESSED

OVERPRESSES
OVERPRESSING
OVERPRINT
OVERPRINTED
OVERPRINTING
OVERPRINTS
OVERPRIZE
OVERPRIZED
OVERPRIZES
OVERPRIZING
OVERPROOF
OVERPROUD
OVERRACK
OVERRACKED
OVERRACKING
OVERRACKS
OVERRAKE
OVERRAKED
OVERRAKES
OVERRAKING
OVERRAN
OVERRANK
OVERRASH
OVERRATE
OVERRATED
OVERRATES
OVERRATING
OVERRAUGHT
OVERREACH
OVERREACHED
OVERREACHES
OVERREACHING
OVERREACT
OVERREACTED
OVERREACTING
OVERREACTS
OVERREAD
OVERREADING
OVERREADS
OVERRED
OVERREDDED
OVERREDDING
OVERREDS
OVERREN
OVERRENNING
OVERRENS
OVERRIDDEN
OVERRIDE
OVERRIDER
OVERRIDERS
OVERRIDES
OVERRIDING
OVERRIPE
OVERRIPEN
OVERRIPENED
OVERRIPENING
OVERRIPENS
OVERROAST
OVERROASTED
OVERROASTING
OVERROASTS
OVERRODE
OVERRUFF
OVERRUFFED
OVERRUFFING
OVERRUFFS
OVERRULE
OVERRULED
OVERRULER
OVERRULERS

OVERRULES
OVERRULING
OVERRUN
OVERRUNNING
OVERRUNS
OVERS
OVERSAIL
OVERSAILED
OVERSAILING
OVERSAILS
OVERSAW
OVERSCORE
OVERSCORED
OVERSCORES
OVERSCORING
OVERSEA
OVERSEAS
OVERSEE
OVERSEEING
OVERSEEN
OVERSEER
OVERSEERS
OVERSEES
OVERSELL
OVERSELLING
OVERSELLS
OVERSET
OVERSETS
OVERSETTING
OVERSEW
OVERSEWED
OVERSEWING
OVERSEWN
OVERSEWS
OVERSEXED
OVERSHADE
OVERSHADED
OVERSHADES
OVERSHADING
OVERSHINE
OVERSHINES
OVERSHINING
OVERSHIRT
OVERSHIRTS
OVERSHOE
OVERSHOES
OVERSHONE
OVERSHOOT
OVERSHOOTING
OVERSHOOTS
OVERSHOT
OVERSIDE
OVERSIGHT
OVERSIGHTS
OVERSIZE
OVERSIZED
OVERSIZES
OVERSIZING
OVERSKIP
OVERSKIPPED
OVERSKIPPING
OVERSKIPS
OVERSKIRT
OVERSKIRTS
OVERSLEEP
OVERSLEEPING
OVERSLEEPS
OVERSLEPT
OVERSLIP
OVERSLIPPED

OVERSLIPPING
OVERSLIPS
OVERSMAN
OVERSMEN
OVERSOLD
OVERSOUL
OVERSOULS
OVERSOW
OVERSOWED
OVERSOWING
OVERSOWN
OVERSOWS
OVERSPEND
OVERSPENDING
OVERSPENDS
OVERSPENT
OVERSPILL
OVERSPILLS
OVERSPIN
OVERSPINS
OVERSTAFF
OVERSTAFFED
OVERSTAFFING
OVERSTAFFS
OVERSTAIN
OVERSTAINED
OVERSTAINING
OVERSTAINS
OVERSTAND
OVERSTANDING
OVERSTANDS
OVERSTANK
OVERSTARE
OVERSTARED
OVERSTARES
OVERSTARING
OVERSTATE
OVERSTATED
OVERSTATES
OVERSTATING
OVERSTAY
OVERSTAYED
OVERSTAYING
OVERSTAYS
OVERSTEER
OVERSTEERED
OVERSTEERING
OVERSTEERS
OVERSTEP
OVERSTEPPED
OVERSTEPPING
OVERSTEPS
OVERSTINK
OVERSTINKING
OVERSTINKS
OVERSTOCK
OVERSTOCKED
OVERSTOCKING
OVERSTOCKS
OVERSTOOD
OVERSTREW
OVERSTREWED
OVERSTREWING
OVERSTREWN
OVERSTREWS
OVERSTUDIED
OVERSTUDIES
OVERSTUDY
OVERSTUDYING
OVERSTUFF

OVERSTUFFED
OVERSTUFFING
OVERSTUFFS
OVERSTUNK
OVERSWAM
OVERSWAY
OVERSWAYED
OVERSWAYING
OVERSWAYS
OVERSWEAR
OVERSWEARING
OVERSWEARS
OVERSWELL
OVERSWELLED
OVERSWELLING
OVERSWELLS
OVERSWIM
OVERSWIMMING
OVERSWIMS
OVERSWOLLEN
OVERSWORE
OVERSWORN
OVERSWUM
OVERT
OVERTAKE
OVERTAKEN
OVERTAKES
OVERTAKING
OVERTALK
OVERTALKED
OVERTALKING
OVERTALKS
OVERTASK
OVERTASKED
OVERTASKING
OVERTASKS
OVERTAX
OVERTAXED
OVERTAXES
OVERTAXING
OVERTEEM
OVERTEEMED
OVERTEEMING
OVERTEEMS
OVERTHREW
OVERTHROW
OVERTHROWING
OVERTHROWN
OVERTHROWS
OVERTIME
OVERTIMED
OVERTIMER
OVERTIMERS
OVERTIMES
OVERTIMING
OVERTIRE
OVERTIRED
OVERTIRES
OVERTIRING
OVERTLY
OVERTOIL
OVERTOILED
OVERTOILING
OVERTOILS
OVERTONE
OVERTONES
OVERTOOK
OVERTOP
OVERTOPPED
OVERTOPPING

OVERTOPS
OVERTOWER
OVERTOWERED
OVERTOWERING
OVERTOWERS
OVERTRAIN
OVERTRAINED
OVERTRAINING
OVERTRAINS
OVERTRICK
OVERTRICKS
OVERTRIP
OVERTRIPPED
OVERTRIPPING
OVERTRIPS
OVERTRUMP
OVERTRUMPED
OVERTRUMPING
OVERTRUMPS
OVERTRUST
OVERTRUSTED
OVERTRUSTING
OVERTRUSTS
OVERTURE
OVERTURED
OVERTURES
OVERTURING
OVERTURN
OVERTURNED
OVERTURNING
OVERTURNS
OVERUSE
OVERUSED
OVERUSES
OVERUSING
OVERVALUE
OVERVALUED
OVERVALUES
OVERVALUING
OVERVEIL
OVERVEILED
OVERVEILING
OVERVEILS
OVERVIEW
OVERVIEWS
OVERWASH
OVERWASHES
OVERWATCH
OVERWATCHED
OVERWATCHES
OVERWATCHING
OVERWEAR
OVERWEARIED
OVERWEARIES
OVERWEARING
OVERWEARS
OVERWEARY
OVERWEARYING
OVERWEEN
OVERWEENED
OVERWEENING
OVERWEENINGS
OVERWEENS
OVERWEIGH
OVERWEIGHED
OVERWEIGHING
OVERWEIGHS
OVERWENT
OVERWHELM
OVERWHELMED

OVERWHELMING
OVERWHELMINGS
OVERWHELMS
OVERWIND
OVERWINDING
OVERWINDS
OVERWING
OVERWINGED
OVERWINGING
OVERWINGS
OVERWISE
OVERWORD
OVERWORDS
OVERWORE
OVERWORK
OVERWORKED
OVERWORKING
OVERWORKS
OVERWORN
OVERWOUND
OVERWREST
OVERWRESTED
OVERWRESTING
OVERWRESTS
OVERWRITE
OVERWRITES
OVERWRITING
OVERWRITTEN
OVERWROTE
OVERWROUGHT
OVERYEAR
OVERYEARED
OVERYEARING
OVERYEARS
OVIBOS
OVIBOSES
OVIBOVINE
OVICIDE
OVICIDES
OVIDUCAL
OVIDUCT
OVIDUCTAL
OVIDUCTS
OVIFEROUS
OVIFORM
OVIGEROUS
OVINE
OVIPARITIES
OVIPARITY
OVIPAROUS

OVIPOSIT
OVIPOSITED
OVIPOSITING
OVIPOSITS
OVISAC
OVISACS
OVIST
OVISTS
OVOID
OVOIDAL
OVOIDS
OVOLI
OVOLO
OVOTESTES
OVOTESTIS
OVULAR
OVULATE
OVULATED
OVULATES
OVULATING
OVULATION
OVULATIONS
OVULE
OVULES
OVUM
OW
OWCHE
OWCHES
OWE
OWED
OWELTIES
OWELTY
OWER
OWERBY
OWERLOUP
OWERLOUPEN
OWERLOUPING
OWERLOUPIT
OWERLOUPS
OWES
OWING
OWL
OWLED
OWLER
OWLERIES
OWLERS
OWLERY
OWLET
OWLETS
OWLIER

OWLIEST
OWLING
OWLISH
OWLS
OWLY
OWN
OWNED
OWNER
OWNERLESS
OWNERS
OWNERSHIP
OWNERSHIPS
OWNING
OWNS
OWRE
OWRECOME
OWRECOMES
OWRES
OWREWORD
OWREWORDS
OWRIE
OWRIER
OWRIEST
OWSEN
OWT
OWTS
OX
OXALATE
OXALATES
OXALIC
OXALIS
OXALISES
OXAZINE
OXAZINES
OXBLOOD
OXBLOODS
OXEN
OXER
OXERS
OXGANG
OXGANGS
OXGATE
OXGATES
OXHEAD
OXHEADS
OXIDANT
OXIDANTS
OXIDASE
OXIDASES
OXIDATE

OXIDATED
OXIDATES
OXIDATING
OXIDATION
OXIDATIONS
OXIDE
OXIDES
OXIDISE
OXIDISED
OXIDISER
OXIDISERS
OXIDISES
OXIDISING
OXIDIZE
OXIDIZED
OXIDIZER
OXIDIZERS
OXIDIZES
OXIDIZING
OXIME
OXIMES
OXIMETER
OXIMETERS
OXLAND
OXLANDS
OXLIP
OXLIPS
OXONIUM
OXONIUMS
OXSLIP
OXSLIPS
OXTAIL
OXTAILS
OXTER
OXTERED
OXTERING
OXTERS
OXYGEN
OXYGENATE
OXYGENATED
OXYGENATES
OXYGENATING
OXYGENISE
OXYGENISED
OXYGENISES
OXYGENISING
OXYGENIZE
OXYGENIZED
OXYGENIZES
OXYGENIZING

OXYGENOUS
OXYGENS
OXYMEL
OXYMELS
OXYMORON
OXYMORONS
OXYTOCIC
OXYTOCICS
OXYTOCIN
OXYTOCINS
OXYTONE
OXYTONES
OY
OYE
OYER
OYERS
OYES
OYESES
OYEZ
OYEZES
OYS
OYSTER
OYSTERS
OYSTRIGE
OYSTRIGES
OZAENA
OZAENAS
OZEKI
OZEKIS
OZOCERITE
OZOCERITES
OZOKERITE
OZOKERITES
OZONATION
OZONATIONS
OZONE
OZONES
OZONISE
OZONISED
OZONISER
OZONISERS
OZONISES
OZONISING
OZONIZE
OZONIZED
OZONIZER
OZONIZERS
OZONIZES
OZONIZING

P

PA
PABOUCHE
PABOUCHES
PABULAR
PABULOUS
PABULUM
PABULUMS
PACA
PACABLE
PACAS
PACATION
PACATIONS
PACE
PACED
PACEMAKER
PACEMAKERS
PACER
PACERS
PACES
PACEY
PACHA
PACHAK
PACHAKS
PACHALIC
PACHALICS
PACHAS
PACHINKO
PACHINKOS
PACHISI
PACHISIS
PACHYDERM
PACHYDERMS
PACIER
PACIEST
PACIFIC
PACIFICAL
PACIFIED
PACIFIER
PACIFIERS
PACIFIES
PACIFISM
PACIFISMS
PACIFIST
PACIFISTS
PACIFY
PACIFYING
PACING
PACK
PACKAGE
PACKAGED
PACKAGER
PACKAGERS
PACKAGES
PACKAGING
PACKAGINGS
PACKED
PACKER
PACKERS
PACKET
PACKETED
PACKETING
PACKETS
PACKFONG

PACKFONGS
PACKING
PACKINGS
PACKMAN
PACKMEN
PACKS
PACKSHEET
PACKSHEETS
PACKSTAFF
PACKSTAFFS
PACKWAY
PACKWAYS
PACO
PACOS
PACT
PACTA
PACTION
PACTIONAL
PACTIONED
PACTIONING
PACTIONS
PACTS
PACTUM
PACY
PAD
PADANG
PADANGS
PADAUK
PADAUKS
PADDED
PADDER
PADDERS
PADDIES
PADDING
PADDINGS
PADDLE
PADDLED
PADDLER
PADDLERS
PADDLES
PADDLING
PADDLINGS
PADDOCK
PADDOCKS
PADDY
PADELLA
PADELLAS
PADEMELON
PADEMELONS
PADERERO
PADEREROES
PADEREROS
PADISHAH
PADISHAHS
PADLE
PADLES
PADLOCK
PADLOCKED
PADLOCKING
PADLOCKS
PADMA
PADMAS
PADOUK

PADOUKS
PADRE
PADRES
PADRONE
PADRONI
PADS
PADUASOY
PADUASOYS
PADYMELON
PADYMELONS
PAEAN
PAEANS
PAEDERAST
PAEDERASTS
PAEDEUTIC
PAEDEUTICS
PAEDIATRIES
PAEDIATRY
PAEDOLOGIES
PAEDOLOGY
PAELLA
PAELLAS
PAENULA
PAENULAE
PAENULAS
PAEON
PAEONIC
PAEONICS
PAEONIES
PAEONS
PAEONY
PAGAN
PAGANISE
PAGANISED
PAGANISES
PAGANISH
PAGANISING
PAGANISM
PAGANISMS
PAGANIZE
PAGANIZED
PAGANIZES
PAGANIZING
PAGANS
PAGE
PAGEANT
PAGEANTRIES
PAGEANTRY
PAGEANTS
PAGED
PAGEHOOD
PAGEHOODS
PAGER
PAGERS
PAGES
PAGINAL
PAGINATE
PAGINATED
PAGINATES
PAGINATING
PAGING
PAGINGS
PAGLE

PAGLES
PAGOD
PAGODA
PAGODAS
PAGODS
PAGRI
PAGRIS
PAGURIAN
PAGURIANS
PAGURID
PAGURIDS
PAH
PAHOEHOE
PAHOEHOES
PAHS
PAID
PAIDEUTIC
PAIDEUTICS
PAIDLE
PAIDLES
PAIGLE
PAIGLES
PAIK
PAIKED
PAIKING
PAIKS
PAIL
PAILFUL
PAILFULS
PAILLASSE
PAILLASSES
PAILLETTE
PAILLETTES
PAILLON
PAILLONS
PAILS
PAIN
PAINED
PAINFUL
PAINFULLER
PAINFULLEST
PAINFULLY
PAINIM
PAINIMS
PAINING
PAINLESS
PAINS
PAINT
PAINTABLE
PAINTED
PAINTER
PAINTERLY
PAINTERS
PAINTIER
PAINTIEST
PAINTING
PAINTINGS
PAINTRESS
PAINTRESSES
PAINTS
PAINTURE
PAINTURES
PAINTY

PAIOCK
PAIOCKE
PAIOCKES
PAIOCKS
PAIR
PAIRE
PAIRED
PAIRES
PAIRIAL
PAIRIALS
PAIRING
PAIRINGS
PAIRS
PAIRWISE
PAIS
PAISA
PAISANO
PAISANOS
PAISAS
PAISE
PAISLEY
PAISLEYS
PAITRICK
PAITRICKS
PAJAMAS
PAJOCK
PAJOCKE
PAJOCKES
PAJOCKS
PAKAPOO
PAKAPOOS
PAKEHA
PAKEHAS
PAKFONG
PAKFONGS
PAKKA
PAKORA
PAKORAS
PAKTONG
PAKTONGS
PAL
PALABRA
PALABRAS
PALACE
PALACES
PALADIN
PALADINS
PALAESTRA
PALAESTRAE
PALAESTRAS
PALAFITTE
PALAFITTES
PALAMA
PALAMAE
PALAMATE
PALAMINO
PALAMINOS
PALAMPORE
PALAMPORES
PALANKEEN
PALANKEENS
PALANQUIN
PALANQUINS

PALAS	PALISADING	PALMETTES	PALSYING	PANCRATIC
PALASES	PALISADO	PALMETTO	PALTER	PANCREAS
PALATABLE	PALISADOED	PALMETTOES	PALTERED	PANCREASES
PALATABLY	PALISADOES	PALMETTOS	PALTERER	PAND
PALATAL	PALISADOING	PALMFUL	PALTERERS	PANDA
PALATALS	PALISH	PALMFULS	PALTERING	PANDAR
PALATE	PALKEE	PALMHOUSE	PALTERS	PANDARED
PALATED	PALKEES	PALMHOUSES	PALTRIER	PANDARING
PALATES	PALKI	PALMIE	PALTRIEST	PANDARS
PALATIAL	PALKIS	PALMIER	PALTRILY	PANDAS
PALATINE	PALL	PALMIES	PALTRY	PANDATION
PALATINES	PALLA	PALMIEST	PALUDAL	PANDATIONS
PALATING	PALLADIC	PALMIET	PALUDIC	PANDECT
PALAVER	PALLADIUM	PALMIETS	PALUDINAL	PANDECTS
PALAVERED	PALLADIUMS	PALMING	PALUDINE	PANDEMIA
PALAVERER	PALLADOUS	PALMIPED	PALUDISM	PANDEMIAN
PALAVERERS	PALLAE	PALMIPEDE	PALUDISMS	PANDEMIAS
PALAVERING	PALLAH	PALMIPEDES	PALUDOSE	PANDEMIC
PALAVERS	PALLAHS	PALMIPEDS	PALUDOUS	PANDEMICS
PALAY	PALLED	PALMIST	PALUSTRAL	PANDER
PALAYS	PALLET	PALMISTRIES	PALY	PANDERED
PALAZZI	PALLETED	PALMISTRY	PAM	PANDERESS
PALAZZO	PALLETISE	PALMISTS	PAMPA	PANDERESSES
PALE	PALLETISED	PALMITATE	PAMPAS	PANDERING
PALEA	PALLETISES	PALMITATES	PAMPASES	PANDERISM
PALEAE	PALLETISING	PALMITIN	PAMPEAN	PANDERISMS
PALEBUCK	PALLETIZE	PALMITINS	PAMPER	PANDERLY
PALEBUCKS	PALLETIZED	PALMS	PAMPERED	PANDEROUS
PALED	PALLETIZES	PALMY	PAMPERER	PANDERS
PALEFACE	PALLETIZING	PALMYRA	PAMPERERS	PANDIED
PALEFACES	PALLETS	PALMYRAS	PAMPERING	PANDIES
PALELY	PALLIA	PALOLO	PAMPERO	PANDIT
PALEMPORE	PALLIAL	PALOLOS	PAMPEROS	PANDITS
PALEMPORES	PALLIARD	PALOMINO	PAMPERS	PANDOOR
PALENESS	PALLIARDS	PALOMINOS	PAMPHLET	PANDOORS
PALENESSES	PALLIASSE	PALOOKA	PAMPHLETS	PANDORA
PALER	PALLIASSES	PALOOKAS	PAMS	PANDORAS
PALES	PALLIATE	PALP	PAN	PANDORE
PALEST	PALLIATED	PALPABLE	PANACEA	PANDORES
PALESTRA	PALLIATES	PALPABLY	PANACEAN	PANDOUR
PALESTRAE	PALLIATING	PALPAL	PANACEAS	PANDOURS
PALESTRAS	PALLID	PALPATE	PANACHAEA	PANDOWDIES
PALET	PALLIDER	PALPATED	PANACHAEAS	PANDOWDY
PALETOT	PALLIDEST	PALPATES	PANACHE	PANDS
PALETOTS	PALLIDITIES	PALPATING	PANACHES	PANDURA
PALETS	PALLIDITY	PALPATION	PANADA	PANDURAS
PALETTE	PALLIDLY	PALPATIONS	PANADAS	PANDURATE
PALETTES	PALLIER	PALPEBRAL	PANAMA	PANDY
PALEWISE	PALLIEST	PALPED	PANAMAS	PANDYING
PALFREY	PALLING	PALPI	PANARIES	PANE
PALFREYED	PALLIUM	PALPING	PANARY	PANED
PALFREYS	PALLONE	PALPITANT	PANATELLA	PANEGOISM
PALIER	PALLONES	PALPITATE	PANATELLAS	PANEGOISMS
PALIEST	PALLOR	PALPITATED	PANAX	PANEGYRIC
PALIFORM	PALLORS	PALPITATES	PANAXES	PANEGYRICS
PALILALIA	PALLS	PALPITATING	PANCAKE	PANEGYRIES
PALILALIAS	PALLY	PALPS	PANCAKED	PANEGYRY
PALILLOGIES	PALM	PALPUS	PANCAKES	PANEITIES
PALILLOGY	PALMAR	PALS	PANCAKING	PANEITY
PALIMONIES	PALMARIAN	PALSGRAVE	PANCE	PANEL
PALIMONY	PALMARY	PALSGRAVES	PANCES	PANELLED
PALING	PALMATE	PALSIED	PANCHAX	PANELLING
PALINGS	PALMATED	PALSIER	PANCHAXES	PANELLINGS
PALINODE	PALMATELY	PALSIES	PANCHAYAT	PANELLIST
PALINODES	PALMATION	PALSIEST	PANCHAYATS	PANELLISTS
PALINODIES	PALMATIONS	PALSTAFF	PANCHEON	PANELS
PALINODY	PALMED	PALSTAFFS	PANCHEONS	PANES
PALISADE	PALMER	PALSTAVE	PANCHION	PANETTONE
PALISADED	PALMERS	PALSTAVES	PANCHIONS	PANETTONI
PALISADES	PALMETTE	PALSY	PANCOSMIC	PANFUL

PANFULS
PANG
PANGA
PANGAMIC
PANGAMIES
PANGAMY
PANGAS
PANGED
PANGEN
PANGENE
PANGENES
PANGENS
PANGING
PANGLESS
PANGOLIN
PANGOLINS
PANGRAM
PANGRAMS
PANGS
PANHANDLE
PANHANDLED
PANHANDLES
PANHANDLING
PANIC
PANICK
PANICKED
PANICKING
PANICKS
PANICKY
PANICLE
PANICLED
PANICLES
PANICS
PANIM
PANIMS
PANING
PANISC
PANISCS
PANISK
PANISKS
PANISLAM
PANISLAMS
PANLOGISM
PANLOGISMS
PANMICTIC
PANMIXIA
PANMIXIAS
PANMIXIS
PANMIXISES
PANNAGE
PANNAGES
PANNE
PANNED
PANNELLED
PANNES
PANNICK
PANNICKS
PANNICLE
PANNICLES
PANNIER
PANNIERED
PANNIERS
PANNIKEL
PANNIKELL
PANNIKELLS
PANNIKELS
PANNIKIN
PANNIKINS
PANNING
PANNINGS

PANNOSE
PANNUS
PANNUSES
PANOCHA
PANOCHAS
PANOISTIC
PANOPLIED
PANOPLIES
PANOPLY
PANOPTIC
PANORAMA
PANORAMAS
PANORAMIC
PANS
PANSEXUAL
PANSIED
PANSIES
PANSOPHIC
PANSOPHIES
PANSOPHY
PANSPERMIES
PANSPERMY
PANSY
PANT
PANTABLE
PANTABLES
PANTAGAMIES
PANTAGAMY
PANTALEON
PANTALEONS
PANTALETS
PANTALON
PANTALONS
PANTALOON
PANTALOONS
PANTED
PANTER
PANTERS
PANTHEISM
PANTHEISMS
PANTHEIST
PANTHEISTS
PANTHENOL
PANTHENOLS
PANTHER
PANTHERS
PANTIES
PANTIHOSE
PANTILE
PANTILED
PANTILES
PANTILING
PANTILINGS
PANTINE
PANTINES
PANTING
PANTINGLY
PANTINGS
PANTLER
PANTLERS
PANTO
PANTOFFLE
PANTOFFLES
PANTOFLE
PANTOFLES
PANTOMIME
PANTOMIMES
PANTON
PANTONS
PANTOS

PANTOUFLE
PANTOUFLES
PANTOUM
PANTOUMS
PANTRIES
PANTRY
PANTRYMAN
PANTRYMEN
PANTS
PANTUN
PANTUNS
PANZER
PANZERS
PAOLI
PAOLO
PAP
PAPA
PAPABLE
PAPACIES
PAPACY
PAPAIN
PAPAINS
PAPAL
PAPALISE
PAPALISED
PAPALISES
PAPALISING
PAPALISM
PAPALISMS
PAPALIST
PAPALISTS
PAPALIZE
PAPALIZED
PAPALIZES
PAPALIZING
PAPALLY
PAPARAZZI
PAPARAZZO
PAPAS
PAPAW
PAPAWS
PAPAYA
PAPAYAS
PAPE
PAPER
PAPERBACK
PAPERBACKED
PAPERBACKING
PAPERBACKS
PAPERED
PAPERER
PAPERERS
PAPERING
PAPERINGS
PAPERLESS
PAPERS
PAPERWARE
PAPERWARES
PAPERWORK
PAPERWORKS
PAPERY
PAPES
PAPETERIE
PAPETERIES
PAPILIO
PAPILIOS
PAPILLA
PAPILLAE
PAPILLAR
PAPILLARY

PAPILLATE
PAPILLOMA
PAPILLOMAS
PAPILLON
PAPILLONS
PAPILLOSE
PAPILLOTE
PAPILLOTES
PAPILLOUS
PAPILLULE
PAPILLULES
PAPISH
PAPISHER
PAPISHERS
PAPISHES
PAPISM
PAPISMS
PAPIST
PAPISTIC
PAPISTRIES
PAPISTRY
PAPISTS
PAPOOSE
PAPOOSES
PAPPADOM
PAPPADOMS
PAPPED
PAPPIER
PAPPIES
PAPPIEST
PAPPING
PAPPOOSE
PAPPOOSES
PAPPOSE
PAPPOUS
PAPPUS
PAPPUSES
PAPPY
PAPRIKA
PAPRIKAS
PAPS
PAPULA
PAPULAE
PAPULAR
PAPULE
PAPULES
PAPULOSE
PAPULOUS
PAPYRI
PAPYRUS
PAR
PARA
PARABASES
PARABASIS
PARABEMA
PARABEMATA
PARABLE
PARABLED
PARABLES
PARABLING
PARABOLA
PARABOLAS
PARABOLE
PARABOLES
PARABOLIC
PARABRAKE
PARABRAKES
PARACHUTE
PARACHUTED
PARACHUTES

PARACHUTING
PARACLETE
PARACLETES
PARACME
PARACMES
PARACUSES
PARACUSIS
PARADE
PARADED
PARADES
PARADIGM
PARADIGMS
PARADING
PARADISAL
PARADISE
PARADISES
PARADISIC
PARADOS
PARADOSES
PARADOX
PARADOXAL
PARADOXER
PARADOXERS
PARADOXES
PARADOXIES
PARADOXY
PARADROP
PARADROPS
PARAFFIN
PARAFFINE
PARAFFINED
PARAFFINES
PARAFFINING
PARAFFINS
PARAFFINY
PARAFFLE
PARAFFLES
PARAFLE
PARAFLES
PARAFOIL
PARAFOILS
PARAGE
PARAGES
PARAGOGE
PARAGOGES
PARAGOGIC
PARAGOGUE
PARAGOGUES
PARAGON
PARAGONED
PARAGONING
PARAGONS
PARAGRAM
PARAGRAMS
PARAGRAPH
PARAGRAPHED
PARAGRAPHING
PARAGRAPHS
PARAKEET
PARAKEETS
PARALALIA
PARALALIAS
PARALEGAL
PARALEGALS
PARALEXIA
PARALEXIAS
PARALLAX
PARALLAXES
PARALLEL
PARALLELED

PARALLELING
PARALLELS
PARALOGIA
PARALOGIAS
PARALOGIES
PARALOGY
PARALYSE
PARALYSED
PARALYSER
PARALYSERS
PARALYSES
PARALYSING
PARALYSIS
PARALYTIC
PARALYTICS
PARALYZE
PARALYZED
PARALYZER
PARALYZERS
PARALYZES
PARALYZING
PARAMATTA
PARAMATTAS
PARAMECIA
PARAMEDIC
PARAMEDICS
PARAMENT
PARAMENTS
PARAMESE
PARAMESES
PARAMETER
PARAMETERS
PARAMO
PARAMORPH
PARAMORPHS
PARAMOS
PARAMOUNT
PARAMOUNTS
PARAMOUR
PARAMOURS
PARANETE
PARANETES
PARANG
PARANGS
PARANOEA
PARANOEAS
PARANOEIC
PARANOEICS
PARANOIA
PARANOIAC
PARANOIACS
PARANOIAS
PARANOIC
PARANOICS
PARANOID
PARANYM
PARANYMPH
PARANYMPHS
PARANYMS
PARAPET
PARAPETED
PARAPETS
PARAPH
PARAPHED
PARAPHING
PARAPHS
PARAPODIA
PARAQUAT
PARAQUATS
PARAQUITO

PARAQUITOS
PARARHYME
PARARHYMES
PARAS
PARASANG
PARASANGS
PARASCEVE
PARASCEVES
PARASITE
PARASITES
PARASITIC
PARASOL
PARASOLS
PARATAXES
PARATAXIS
PARATHA
PARATHAS
PARATONIC
PARAVAIL
PARAVANE
PARAVANES
PARAVANT
PARAVAUNT
PARAZOA
PARAZOAN
PARAZOANS
PARAZOON
PARBOIL
PARBOILED
PARBOILING
PARBOILS
PARBREAK
PARBREAKED
PARBREAKING
PARBREAKS
PARBUCKLE
PARBUCKLED
PARBUCKLES
PARBUCKLING
PARCEL
PARCELLED
PARCELLING
PARCELS
PARCENARIES
PARCENARY
PARCENER
PARCENERS
PARCH
PARCHED
PARCHEDLY
PARCHES
PARCHESI
PARCHESIS
PARCHING
PARCHMENT
PARCHMENTS
PARCIMONIES
PARCIMONY
PARCLOSE
PARCLOSES
PARD
PARDAL
PARDALE
PARDALES
PARDALIS
PARDALISES
PARDALS
PARDED
PARDI
PARDIE

PARDINE
PARDNER
PARDNERS
PARDON
PARDONED
PARDONER
PARDONERS
PARDONING
PARDONINGS
PARDONS
PARDS
PARDY
PARE
PARECIOUS
PARED
PAREGORIC
PAREGORICS
PAREIRA
PAREIRAS
PARELLA
PARELLAS
PARELLE
PARELLES
PARENESES
PARENESIS
PARENT
PARENTAGE
PARENTAGES
PARENTAL
PARENTED
PARENTING
PARENTINGS
PARENTS
PAREO
PAREOS
PARER
PARERGA
PARERGON
PARERS
PARES
PARESES
PARESIS
PARETIC
PAREU
PAREUS
PARFAIT
PARFAITS
PARFLECHE
PARFLECHES
PARGANA
PARGANAS
PARGASITE
PARGASITES
PARGE
PARGED
PARGES
PARGET
PARGETED
PARGETER
PARGETERS
PARGETING
PARGETINGS
PARGETS
PARGETTED
PARGETTING
PARGETTINGS
PARGING
PARHELIA
PARHELIC
PARHELION

PARHYPATE
PARHYPATES
PARIAH
PARIAHS
PARIAL
PARIALS
PARIETAL
PARIETALS
PARING
PARINGS
PARISCHAN
PARISCHANS
PARISH
PARISHEN
PARISHENS
PARISHES
PARISON
PARISONS
PARITIES
PARITOR
PARITORS
PARITY
PARK
PARKA
PARKAS
PARKEE
PARKEES
PARKER
PARKERS
PARKI
PARKIER
PARKIEST
PARKIN
PARKING
PARKINGS
PARKINS
PARKIS
PARKISH
PARKLAND
PARKLANDS
PARKLIKE
PARKLY
PARKS
PARKWARD
PARKWARDS
PARKWAY
PARKWAYS
PARKY
PARLANCE
PARLANCES
PARLANDO
PARLAY
PARLAYED
PARLAYING
PARLAYS
PARLE
PARLED
PARLES
PARLEY
PARLEYED
PARLEYING
PARLEYS
PARLEYVOO
PARLEYVOOED
PARLEYVOOING
PARLEYVOOS
PARLIES
PARLING
PARLOUR

PARLOURS
PARLOUS
PARLY
PAROCHIAL
PAROCHIN
PAROCHINE
PAROCHINES
PAROCHINS
PARODIC
PARODICAL
PARODIED
PARODIES
PARODIST
PARODISTS
PARODY
PARODYING
PAROEMIA
PAROEMIAC
PAROEMIACS
PAROEMIAL
PAROEMIAS
PAROICOUS
PAROL
PAROLE
PAROLED
PAROLEE
PAROLEES
PAROLES
PAROLING
PARONYM
PARONYMIES
PARONYMS
PARONYMY
PAROQUET
PAROQUETS
PAROTIC
PAROTID
PAROTIDS
PAROTIS
PAROTISES
PAROTITIS
PAROTITISES
PAROUSIA
PAROUSIAS
PAROXYSM
PAROXYSMS
PARPANE
PARPANES
PARPEN
PARPEND
PARPENDS
PARPENS
PARPENT
PARPENTS
PARPOINT
PARPOINTS
PARQUET
PARQUETED
PARQUETING
PARQUETRIES
PARQUETRY
PARQUETS
PARQUETTED
PARQUETTING
PARR
PARRAKEET
PARRAKEETS
PARRAL
PARRALS
PARREL

PARRELS
PARRHESIA
PARRHESIAS
PARRICIDE
PARRICIDES
PARRIED
PARRIES
PARRITCH
PARRITCHES
PARROCK
PARROCKED
PARROCKING
PARROCKS
PARROQUET
PARROQUETS
PARROT
PARROTED
PARROTER
PARROTERS
PARROTING
PARROTRIES
PARROTRY
PARROTS
PARROTY
PARRS
PARRY
PARRYING
PARS
PARSE
PARSEC
PARSECS
PARSED
PARSER
PARSERS
PARSES
PARSIMONIES
PARSIMONY
PARSING
PARSINGS
PARSLEY
PARSLEYS
PARSNEP
PARSNEPS
PARSNIP
PARSNIPS
PARSON
PARSONAGE
PARSONAGES
PARSONIC
PARSONISH
PARSONS
PART
PARTAKE
PARTAKEN
PARTAKER
PARTAKERS
PARTAKES
PARTAKING
PARTAKINGS
PARTAN
PARTANS
PARTED
PARTER
PARTERRE
PARTERRES
PARTERS
PARTI
PARTIAL
PARTIALLY
PARTIALS

PARTIBLE
PARTICLE
PARTICLES
PARTIED
PARTIES
PARTIM
PARTING
PARTINGS
PARTIS
PARTISAN
PARTISANS
PARTITA
PARTITAS
PARTITE
PARTITION
PARTITIONED
PARTITIONING
PARTITIONS
PARTITIVE
PARTITIVES
PARTITURA
PARTITURAS
PARTIZAN
PARTIZANS
PARTLET
PARTLETS
PARTLY
PARTNER
PARTNERED
PARTNERING
PARTNERS
PARTON
PARTONS
PARTOOK
PARTRIDGE
PARTRIDGES
PARTS
PARTURE
PARTURES
PARTWORK
PARTWORKS
PARTY
PARTYING
PARTYISM
PARTYISMS
PARULIS
PARULISES
PARURE
PARURES
PARVENU
PARVENUS
PARVIS
PARVISE
PARVISES
PAS
PASCAL
PASCALS
PASCHAL
PASCUAL
PASEAR
PASEARED
PASEARING
PASEARS
PASEO
PASEOS
PASH
PASHA
PASHALIK
PASHALIKS
PASHAS

PASHED
PASHES
PASHIM
PASHIMS
PASHING
PASHM
PASHMINA
PASHMINAS
PASHMS
PASPALUM
PASPALUMS
PASPIES
PASPY
PASQUILER
PASQUILERS
PASS
PASSABLE
PASSABLY
PASSADE
PASSADES
PASSADO
PASSADOES
PASSADOS
PASSAGE
PASSAGED
PASSAGES
PASSAGING
PASSAMENT
PASSAMENTED
PASSAMENTING
PASSAMENTS
PASSANT
PASSÉ
PASSED
PASSÉE
PASSEMENT
PASSEMENTED
PASSEMENTING
PASSEMENTS
PASSENGER
PASSENGERS
PASSEPIED
PASSEPIEDS
PASSER
PASSERINE
PASSERINES
PASSERS
PASSES
PASSIBLE
PASSIBLY
PASSIM
PASSING
PASSINGS
PASSION
PASSIONAL
PASSIONALS
PASSIONED
PASSIONING
PASSIONS
PASSIVE
PASSIVELY
PASSIVES
PASSIVISM
PASSIVISMS
PASSIVIST
PASSIVISTS
PASSIVITIES
PASSIVITY
PASSKEY
PASSKEYS

PASSLESS
PASSMAN
PASSMEN
PASSMENT
PASSMENTED
PASSMENTING
PASSMENTS
PASSOUT
PASSPORT
PASSPORTS
PASSUS
PASSUSES
PASSWORD
PASSWORDS
PAST
PASTA
PASTANCE
PASTANCES
PASTAS
PASTE
PASTED
PASTEL
PASTELS
PASTER
PASTERN
PASTERNS
PASTERS
PASTES
PASTICCI
PASTICCIO
PASTICHE
PASTICHES
PASTIER
PASTIES
PASTIEST
PASTIL
PASTILLE
PASTILLES
PASTILS
PASTIME
PASTIMES
PASTINESS
PASTINESSES
PASTING
PASTINGS
PASTIS
PASTISES
PASTOR
PASTORAL
PASTORALE
PASTORALES
PASTORALS
PASTORATE
PASTORATES
PASTORLY
PASTORS
PASTRAMI
PASTRAMIS
PASTRIES
PASTRY
PASTS
PASTURAGE
PASTURAGES
PASTURAL
PASTURE
PASTURED
PASTURES
PASTURING
PASTY
PAT

PATACA
PATACAS
PATAGIA
PATAGIAL
PATAGIUM
PATAMAR
PATAMARS
PATBALL
PATBALLS
PATCH
PATCHABLE
PATCHED
PATCHER
PATCHERIES
PATCHERS
PATCHERY
PATCHES
PATCHIER
PATCHIEST
PATCHILY
PATCHING
PATCHINGS
PATCHOCKE
PATCHOCKES
PATCHOULI
PATCHOULIES
PATCHOULIS
PATCHOULY
PATCHWORK
PATCHWORKS
PATCHY
PÂTÉ
PATE
PATED
PATELLA
PATELLAE
PATELLAR
PATELLAS
PATELLATE
PATEN
PATENCIES
PATENCY
PATENS
PATENT
PATENTED
PATENTEE
PATENTEES
PATENTING
PATENTLY
PATENTOR
PATENTORS
PATENTS
PATER
PATERA
PATERAE
PATERCOVE
PATERCOVES
PATERERO
PATEREROES
PATEREROS
PATERNAL
PATERNITIES
PATERNITY
PATERS
PATES
PÂTÉS
PATH
PATHED
PATHETIC
PATHETICS

PATHIC
PATHICS
PATHING
PATHLESS
PATHOGEN
PATHOGENIES
PATHOGENS
PATHOGENY
PATHOLOGIES
PATHOLOGY
PATHOS
PATHOSES
PATHS
PATHWAY
PATHWAYS
PATIBLE
PATIENCE
PATIENCES
PATIENT
PATIENTED
PATIENTING
PATIENTLY
PATIENTS
PATIN
PATINA
PATINAS
PATINATED
PATINE
PATINED
PATINES
PATINS
PATIO
PATIOS
PATLY
PATNESS
PATNESSES
PATOIS
PATONCE
PATRIAL
PATRIALS
PATRIARCH
PATRIARCHS
PATRIATE
PATRIATED
PATRIATES
PATRIATING
PATRICIAN
PATRICIANS
PATRICIDE
PATRICIDES
PATRICK
PATHICKS
PATRICO
PATRICOES
PATRILINIES
PATRILINY
PATRIMONIES
PATRIMONY
PATRIOT
PATRIOTIC
PATRIOTS
PATRISTIC
PATRISTICS
PATROL
PATROLLED
PATROLLER
PATROLLERS
PATROLLING
PATROLMAN
PATROLMEN

PATROLOGIES
PATROLOGY
PATROLS
PATRON
PATRONAGE
PATRONAGED
PATRONAGES
PATRONAGING
PATRONAL
PATRONESS
PATRONESSES
PATRONISE
PATRONISED
PATRONISES
PATRONISING
PATRONIZE
PATRONIZED
PATRONIZES
PATRONIZING
PATRONNE
PATRONNES
PATRONS
PATROON
PATROONS
PATS
PATSIES
PATSY
PATTE
PATTÉ
PATTED
PATTEE
PATTEN
PATTENED
PATTENING
PATTENS
PATTER
PATTERED
PATTERER
PATTERERS
PATTERING
PATTERN
PATTERNED
PATTERNING
PATTERNS
PATTERS
PATTES
PATTIES
PATTING
PATTLE
PATTLES
PATTY
PATULIN
PATULINS
PATULOUS
PATZER
PATZERS
PAUA
PAUAS
PAUCITIES
PAUCITY
PAUGHTIER
PAUGHTIEST
PAUGHTY
PAUL
PAULDRON
PAULDRONS
PAULOWNIA
PAULOWNIAS
PAULS
PAUNCE

PAUNCES
PAUNCH
PAUNCHED
PAUNCHES
PAUNCHIER
PAUNCHIEST
PAUNCHING
PAUNCHY
PAUPER
PAUPERESS
PAUPERESSES
PAUPERISE
PAUPERISED
PAUPERISES
PAUPERISING
PAUPERISM
PAUPERISMS
PAUPERIZE
PAUPERIZED
PAUPERIZES
PAUPERIZING
PAUPERS
PAUSAL
PAUSE
PAUSED
PAUSEFUL
PAUSELESS
PAUSER
PAUSERS
PAUSES
PAUSING
PAUSINGLY
PAUSINGS
PAVAGE
PAVAGES
PAVAN
PAVANE
PAVANES
PAVANS
PAVE
PAVED
PAVEMENT
PAVEMENTED
PAVEMENTING
PAVEMENTS
PAVEN
PAVENS
PAVER
PAVERS
PAVES
PAVID
PAVILION
PAVILIONED
PAVILIONING
PAVILIONS
PAVIN
PAVING
PAVINGS
PAVINS
PAVIOR
PAVIORS
PAVIOUR
PAVIOURS
PAVIS
PAVISE
PAVISES
PAVLOVA
PAVLOVAS
PAVONAZZO
PAVONAZZOS

PAVONE
PAVONES
PAVONIAN
PAVONINE
PAW
PAWA
PAWAS
PAWAW
PAWAWS
PAWED
PAWING
PAWK
PAWKIER
PAWKIEST
PAWKILY
PAWKINESS
PAWKINESSES
PAWKS
PAWKY
PAWL
PAWLS
PAWN
PAWNCE
PAWNCES
PAWNED
PAWNEE
PAWNEES
PAWNER
PAWNERS
PAWNING
PAWNS
PAWNSHOP
PAWNSHOPS
PAWPAW
PAWPAWS
PAWS
PAX
PAXES
PAXIUBA
PAXIUBAS
PAXWAX
PAXWAXES
PAY
PAYABLE
PAYED
PAYEE
PAYEES
PAYER
PAYERS
PAYING
PAYINGS
PAYMASTER
PAYMASTERS
PAYMENT
PAYMENTS
PAYNIM
PAYNIMRIES
PAYNIMRY
PAYNIMS
PAYOLA
PAYOLAS
PAYROLL
PAYROLLS
PAYS
PAYSAGE
PAYSAGES
PAYSAGIST
PAYSAGISTS
PAYSD
PAZAZZ

PAZAZZES
PEA
PEABERRIES
PEABERRY
PEACE
PEACEABLE
PEACEABLY
PEACED
PEACEFUL
PEACELESS
PEACENIK
PEACENIKS
PEACES
PEACETIME
PEACETIMES
PEACH
PEACHED
PEACHER
PEACHERS
PEACHES
PEACHIER
PEACHIEST
PEACHING
PEACHY
PEACING
PEACOCK
PEACOCKED
PEACOCKING
PEACOCKS
PEACOCKY
PEACOD
PEACODS
PEAG
PEAGS
PEAK
PEAKED
PEAKIER
PEAKIEST
PEAKING
PEAKS
PEAKY
PEAL
PEALED
PEALING
PEALS
PEAN
PEANED
PEANING
PEANS
PEANUT
PEANUTS
PEAPOD
PEAPODS
PEAR
PEARCE
PEARCED
PEARCES
PEARCING
PEARE
PEARES
PEARL
PEARLED
PEARLER
PEARLERS
PEARLIER
PEARLIES
PEARLIEST
PEARLIN
PEARLING
PEARLINGS

PEARLINS
PEARLISED
PEARLITE
PEARLITES
PEARLITIC
PEARLIZED
PEARLS
PEARLY
PEARMAIN
PEARMAINS
PEARS
PEARST
PEART
PEARTLY
PEAS
PEASANT
PEASANTRIES
PEASANTRY
PEASANTS
PEASANTY
PEASCOD
PEASCODS
PEASE
PEASECOD
PEASECODS
PEASED
PEASES
PEASEWEEP
PEASEWEEPS
PEASING
PEASON
PEAT
PEATARIES
PEATARY
PEATERIES
PEATERY
PEATIER
PEATIEST
PEATMAN
PEATMEN
PEATS
PEATSHIP
PEATSHIPS
PEATY
PEAVEY
PEAVEYS
PEAVIES
PEAVY
PEAZE
PEAZED
PEAZES
PEAZING
PEBA
PEBAS
PEBBLE
PEBBLED
PEBBLES
PEBBLIER
PEBBLIEST
PEBBLING
PEBBLINGS
PEBBLY
PÉBRINE
PÉBRINES
PEC
PECAN
PECANS
PECCABLE
PECCANCIES
PECCANCY

PECCANT
PECCANTLY
PECCARIES
PECCARY
PECCAVI
PECCAVIS
PECH
PECHED
PECHING
PECHS
PECK
PECKE
PECKED
PECKER
PECKERS
PECKES
PECKING
PECKINGS
PECKISH
PECKS
PECS
PECTEN
PECTIC
PECTIN
PECTINAL
PECTINATE
PECTINEAL
PECTINES
PECTINS
PECTISE
PECTISED
PECTISES
PECTISING
PECTIZE
PECTIZED
PECTIZES
PECTIZING
PECTOLITE
PECTOLITES
PECTORAL
PECTORALS
PECTOSE
PECTOSES
PECULATE
PECULATED
PECULATES
PECULATING
PECULATOR
PECULATORS
PECULIAR
PECULIARS
PECULIUM
PECULIUMS
PECUNIARY
PECUNIOUS
PED
PEDAGOGIC
PEDAGOGICS
PEDAGOGIES
PEDAGOGUE
PEDAGOGUED
PEDAGOGUES
PEDAGOGUING
PEDAGOGY
PEDAL
PEDALIER
PEDALIERS
PEDALLED
PEDALLER
PEDALLERS

PEDALLING
PEDALLINGS
PEDALO
PEDALOES
PEDALOS
PEDALS
PEDANT
PEDANTIC
PEDANTISE
PEDANTISED
PEDANTISES
PEDANTISING
PEDANTISM
PEDANTISMS
PEDANTIZE
PEDANTIZED
PEDANTIZES
PEDANTIZING
PEDANTRIES
PEDANTRY
PEDANTS
PEDATE
PEDATELY
PEDATIFID
PEDDER
PEDDERS
PEDDLE
PEDDLED
PEDDLER
PEDDLERS
PEDDLES
PEDDLING
PEDDLINGS
PEDERASTIES
PEDERASTY
PEDERERO
PEDEREROES
PEDEREROS
PEDESES
PEDESIS
PEDESTAL
PEDESTALLED
PEDESTALLING
PEDESTALS
PEDETIC
PEDICAB
PEDICABS
PEDICEL
PEDICELS
PEDICLE
PEDICLED
PEDICLES
PEDICULAR
PEDICULUS
PEDICULUSES
PEDICURE
PEDICURED
PEDICURES
PEDICURING
PEDIGREE
PEDIGREED
PEDIGREES
PEDIMENT
PEDIMENTS
PEDIPALP
PEDIPALPI
PEDIPALPS
PEDLAR
PEDLARIES
PEDLARS

PEDLARY
PEDOLOGIES
PEDOLOGY
PEDOMETER
PEDOMETERS
PEDRAIL
PEDRAILS
PEDRERO
PEDREROES
PEDREROS
PEDRO
PEDROS
PEDS
PEDUNCLE
PEDUNCLES
PEE
PEECE
PEECES
PEED
PEEING
PEEK
PEEKABO
PEEKABOO
PEEKABOOS
PEEKABOS
PEEKED
PEEKING
PEEKS
PEEL
PEELED
PEELER
PEELERS
PEELING
PEELINGS
PEELS
PEEN
PEENED
PEENGE
PEENGED
PEENGEING
PEENGES
PEENGING
PEENING
PEENS
PEEOY
PEEOYS
PEEP
PEEPE
PEEPED
PEEPER
PEEPERS
PEEPES
PEEPING
PEEPS
PEEPUL
PEEPULS
PEER
PEERAGE
PEERAGES
PEERED
PEERESS
PEERESSES
PEERIE
PEERIER
PEERIES
PEERIEST
PEERING
PEERLESS
PEERS
PEERY

PEES
PEESWEEP
PEESWEEPS
PEETWEET
PEETWEETS
PEEVE
PEEVED
PEEVER
PEEVERS
PEEVES
PEEVING
PEEVISH
PEEVISHLY
PEEWEE
PEEWEES
PEEWIT
PEEWITS
PEG
PEGASUS
PEGASUSES
PEGBOARD
PEGBOARDS
PEGGED
PEGGIES
PEGGING
PEGGINGS
PEGGY
PEGH
PEGHED
PEGHING
PEGHS
PEGMATITE
PEGMATITES
PEGS
PEIGNOIR
PEIGNOIRS
PEIN
PEINCT
PEINCTED
PEINCTING
PEINCTS
PEINED
PEINING
PEINS
PEIRASTIC
PEISE
PEISED
PEISES
PEISHWA
PEISHWAH
PEISHWAHS
PEISHWAS
PEISING
PEIZE
PEIZED
PEIZES
PEIZING
PEJORATE
PEJORATED
PEJORATES
PEJORATING
PEKAN
PEKANS
PEKE
PEKES
PEKOE
PEKOES
PELA
PELAGE
PELAGES

PELAGIAN
PELAGIANS
PELAGIC
PELAS
PELE
PELERINE
PELERINES
PELES
PELF
PELFS
PELHAM
PELHAMS
PELICAN
PELICANS
PELISSE
PELISSES
PELITE
PELITES
PELITIC
PELL
PELLACH
PELLACHS
PELLACK
PELLACKS
PELLAGRA
PELLAGRAS
PELLAGRIN
PELLAGRINS
PELLET
PELLETED
PELLETIFIED
PELLETIFIES
PELLETIFY
PELLETIFYING
PELLETING
PELLETISE
PELLETISED
PELLETISES
PELLETISING
PELLETIZE
PELLETIZED
PELLETIZES
PELLETIZING
PELLETS
PELLICLE
PELLICLES
PELLITORIES
PELLITORY
PELLOCK
PELLOCKS
PELLS
PELLUCID
PELMA
PELMANISM
PELMANISMS
PELMAS
PELMATIC
PELMET
PELMETS
PELOID
PELOIDS
PELOLOGIES
PELOLOGY
PELORIA
PELORIAS
PELORIC
PELORIES
PELORISED
PELORISM
PELORISMS

PELORIZED
PELORUS
PELORUSES
PELORY
PELOTA
PELOTAS
PELT
PELTA
PELTAE
PELTAS
PELTAST
PELTASTS
PELTATE
PELTED
PELTER
PELTERED
PELTERING
PELTERS
PELTING
PELTINGLY
PELTINGS
PELTRIES
PELTRY
PELTS
PELVES
PELVIC
PELVIFORM
PELVIS
PELVISES
PEMBROKE
PEMBROKES
PEMICAN
PEMICANS
PEMMICAN
PEMMICANS
PEMOLINE
PEMOLINES
PEMPHIGUS
PEMPHIGUSES
PEN
PENAL
PENALISE
PENALISED
PENALISES
PENALISING
PENALIZE
PENALIZED
PENALIZES
PENALIZING
PENALLY
PENALTIES
PENALTY
PENANCE
PENANCED
PENANCES
PENANCING
PENATES
PENCE
PENCEL
PENCELS
PENCES
PENCHANT
PENCHANTS
PENCIL
PENCILLED
PENCILLER
PENCILLERS
PENCILLING
PENCILLINGS
PENCILS

PENCRAFT
PENCRAFTS
PEND
PENDANT
PENDANTS
PENDED
PENDENCIES
PENDENCY
PENDENT
PENDENTLY
PENDENTS
PENDICLE
PENDICLER
PENDICLERS
PENDICLES
PENDING
PENDRAGON
PENDRAGONS
PENDS
PENDULAR
PENDULATE
PENDULATED
PENDULATES
PENDULATING
PENDULINE
PENDULOUS
PENDULUM
PENDULUMS
PENE
PENED
PENEPLAIN
PENEPLAINS
PENEPLANE
PENEPLANES
PENES
PENETRANT
PENETRANTS
PENETRATE
PENETRATED
PENETRATES
PENETRATING
PENFOLD
PENFOLDS
PENFUL
PENFULS
PENGUIN
PENGUINRIES
PENGUINRY
PENGUINS
PENHOLDER
PENHOLDERS
PENI
PENIAL
PENIE
PENIES
PENILE
PENILLION
PENING
PENINSULA
PENINSULAS
PENIS
PENISES
PENISTONE
PENISTONES
PENITENCE
PENITENCES
PENITENCIES
PENITENCY
PENITENT
PENITENTS

PENK
PENKNIFE
PENKNIVES
PENKS
PENLIGHT
PENLIGHTS
PENMAN
PENMEN
PENNA
PENNAE
PENNAL
PENNALISM
PENNALISMS
PENNALS
PENNANT
PENNANTS
PENNATE
PENNATULA
PENNATULAE
PENNATULAS
PENNE
PENNED
PENNEECH
PENNEECHS
PENNEECK
PENNEECKS
PENNER
PENNERS
PENNES
PENNIED
PENNIES
PENNIFORM
PENNILESS
PENNILL
PENNILLION
PENNINE
PENNINES
PENNING
PENNINITE
PENNINITES
PENNON
PENNONCEL
PENNONCELS
PENNONED
PENNONS
PENNY
PENNYFEE
PENNYFEES
PENNYLAND
PENNYLANDS
PENOLOGIES
PENOLOGY
PENONCEL
PENONCELS
PENS
PENSÉE
PENSÉES
PENSEL
PENSELS
PENSIL
PENSILE
PENSILITIES
PENSILITY
PENSILS
PENSION
PENSIONED
PENSIONER
PENSIONERS
PENSIONING
PENSIONS

PENSIVE
PENSIVELY
PENSTEMON
PENSTEMONS
PENSTOCK
PENSTOCKS
PENSUM
PENSUMS
PENT
PENTACLE
PENTACLES
PENTACT
PENTACTS
PENTAD
PENTADIC
PENTADS
PENTAGON
PENTAGONS
PENTAGRAM
PENTAGRAMS
PENTALOGIES
PENTALOGY
PENTALPHA
PENTALPHAS
PENTAMERIES
PENTAMERY
PENTANE
PENTANES
PENTANGLE
PENTANGLES
PENTAPODIES
PENTAPODY
PENTARCH
PENTARCHIES
PENTARCHS
PENTARCHY
PENTEL®
PENTELS®
PENTENE
PENTENES
PENTHIA
PENTHIAS
PENTHOUSE
PENTHOUSED
PENTHOUSES
PENTHOUSING
PENTICE
PENTICED
PENTICES
PENTICING
PENTISE
PENTISED
PENTISES
PENTISING
PENTODE
PENTODES
PENTOMIC
PENTOSAN
PENTOSANE
PENTOSANES
PENTOSANS
PENTOSE
PENTOSES
PENTOXIDE
PENTOXIDES
PENTROOF
PENTROOFS
PENTS
PENTYLENE
PENTYLENES

PENUCHE	PEPTIC	PERCOLATED	PERFORATED	PERIDIUM
PENUCHES	PEPTICITIES	PERCOLATES	PERFORATES	PERIDIUMS
PENUCHI	PEPTICITY	PERCOLATING	PERFORATING	PERIDOT
PENUCHIS	PEPTICS	PERCOLIN	PERFORCE	PERIDOTE
PENUCHLE	PEPTIDE	PERCOLINS	PERFORM	PERIDOTES
PENUCHLES	PEPTIDES	PERCUSS	PERFORMED	PERIDOTIC
PENULT	PEPTISE	PERCUSSED	PERFORMER	PERIDOTS
PENULTIMA	PEPTISED	PERCUSSES	PERFORMERS	PERIDROME
PENULTIMAS	PEPTISES	PERCUSSING	PERFORMING	PERIDROMES
PENULTS	PEPTISING	PERCUSSOR	PERFORMINGS	PERIGEAL
PENUMBRA	PEPTIZE	PERCUSSORS	PERFORMS	PERIGEAN
PENUMBRAL	PEPTIZED	PERDENDO	PERFUME	PERIGEE
PENUMBRAS	PEPTIZES	PERDIE	PERFUMED	PERIGEES
PENURIES	PEPTIZING	PERDITION	PERFUMER	PERIGON
PENURIOUS	PEPTONE	PERDITIONS	PERFUMERIES	PERIGONE
PENURY	PEPTONES	PERDU	PERFUMERS	PERIGONES
PENWOMAN	PEPTONISE	PERDUE	PERFUMERY	PERIGONS
PENWOMEN	PEPTONISED	PERDUES	PERFUMES	PERIGYNIES
PEON	PEPTONISES	PERDURE	PERFUMING	PERIGYNY
PEONAGE	PEPTONISING	PERDURED	PERFUMY	PERIKARYA
PEONAGES	PEPTONIZE	PERDURES	PERFUSATE	PERIL
PEONIES	PEPTONIZED	PERDURING	PERFUSATES	PERILLED
PEONISM	PEPTONIZES	PERDUS	PERFUSE	PERILLING
PEONISMS	PEPTONIZING	PERDY	PERFUSED	PERILOUS
PEONS	PER	PÈRE	PERFUSES	PERILS
PEONY	PERACUTE	PEREGAL	PERFUSING	PERILUNE
PEOPLE	PERAEA	PEREGALS	PERFUSION	PERILUNES
PEOPLED	PERAEON	PEREGRINE	PERFUSIONS	PERILYMPH
PEOPLES	PERAEONS	PEREGRINES	PERFUSIVE	PERILYMPHS
PEOPLING	PERAEOPOD	PEREIA	PERGOLA	PERIMETER
PEP	PERAEOPODS	PEREION	PERGOLAS	PERIMETERS
PEPERINO	PERAI	PEREIOPOD	PERGUNNAH	PERIMETRIES
PEPERINOS	PERAIS	PEREIOPODS	PERGUNNAHS	PERIMETRY
PEPEROMIA	PERCALE	PEREIRA	PERHAPS	PERIMORPH
PEPEROMIAS	PERCALES	PEREIRAS	PERI	PERIMORPHS
PEPERONI	PERCALINE	PERENNATE	PERIAGUA	PERINAEAL
PEPERONIS	PERCALINES	PERENNATED	PERIAGUAS	PERINAEUM
PEPFUL	PERCASE	PERENNATES	PERIAKTOI	PERINAEUMS
PEPLOS	PERCE	PERENNATING	PERIAKTOS	PERINATAL
PEPLOSES	PERCEABLE	PERENNIAL	PERIANTH	PERINEAL
PEPLUM	PERCEANT	PERENNIALS	PERIANTHS	PERINEUM
PEPLUMS	PERCED	PERENNITIES	PERIAPT	PERINEUMS
PEPLUS	PERCEIVE	PERENNITY	PERIAPTS	PERIOD
PEPLUSES	PERCEIVED	PÈRES	PERIBLAST	PERIODATE
PEPO	PERCEIVER	PERFAY	PERIBLASTS	PERIODATES
PEPOS	PERCEIVERS	PERFECT	PERIBLEM	PERIODED
PEPPED	PERCEIVES	PERFECTA	PERIBLEMS	PERIODIC
PEPPER	PERCEIVING	PERFECTAS	PERIBOLI	PERIODING
PEPPERED	PERCEIVINGS	PERFECTED	PERIBOLOI	PERIODS
PEPPERER	PERCEN	PERFECTER	PERIBOLOS	PERIOST
PEPPERERS	PERCENTAL	PERFECTERS	PERIBOLUS	PERIOSTS
PEPPERING	PERCEPT	PERFECTEST	PERICARP	PERIOTIC
PEPPERINGS	PERCEPTS	PERFECTI	PERICARPS	PERIOTICS
PEPPERONI	PERCES	PERFECTING	PERICLASE	PERIPATUS
PEPPERONIS	PERCH	PERFECTLY	PERICLASES	PERIPATUSES
PEPPERS	PERCHANCE	PERFECTO	PERICLINE	PERIPETIA
PEPPERY	PERCHED	PERFECTOR	PERICLINES	PERIPETIAS
PEPPIER	PERCHER	PERFECTORS	PERICON	PERIPETIES
PEPPIEST	PERCHERON	PERFECTOS	PERICONES	PERIPETY
PEPPING	PERCHERONS	PERFECTS	PERICOPE	PERIPHERIES
PEPPY	PERCHERS	PERFERVID	PERICOPES	PERIPHERY
PEPS	PERCHES	PERFERVOR	PERICRANIES	PERIPLAST
PEPSIN	PERCHING	PERFERVORS	PERICRANY	PERIPLASTS
PEPSINATE	PERCHINGS	PERFET	PERICYCLE	PERIPLUS
PEPSINATED	PERCIFORM	PERFIDIES	PERICYCLES	PERIPLUSES
PEPSINATES	PERCINE	PERFIDY	PERIDERM	PERIPROCT
PEPSINATING	PERCING	PERFORANS	PERIDERMS	PERIPROCTS
PEPSINE	PERCOCT	PERFORANSES	PERIDIA	PERIPTERIES
PEPSINES	PERCOID	PERFORANT	PERIDIAL	PERIPTERY
PEPSINS	PERCOLATE	PERFORATE	PERIDINIA	PERIQUE

ERIQUES	PERMIT	PERSEVERING	PERTEST	PESAUNT
ERIS	PERMITS	PERSICO	PERTHITE	PESAUNTS
ERISARC	PERMITTED	PERSICOS	PERTHITES	PESETA
ERISARCS	PERMITTER	PERSICOT	PERTHITIC	PESETAS
ERISCIAN	PERMITTERS	PERSICOTS	PERTINENT	PESEWA
ERISCIANS	PERMITTING	PERSIENNE	PERTINENTS	PESEWAS
ERISCOPE	PERMS	PERSIENNES	PERTLY	PESHWA
ERISCOPES	PERMUTATE	PERSIMMON	PERTNESS	PESHWAS
ERISH	PERMUTATED	PERSIMMONS	PERTNESSES	PESKIER
ERISHED	PERMUTATES	PERSING	PERTOOK	PESKIEST
ERISHER	PERMUTATING	PERSIST	PERTS	PESKILY
ERISHERS	PERMUTE	PERSISTED	PERTURB	PESKY
ERISHES	PERMUTED	PERSISTING	PERTURBED	PESO
ERISHING	PERMUTES	PERSISTS	PERTURBER	PESOS
ERISPERM	PERMUTING	PERSON	PERTURBERS	PESSARIES
ERISPERMS	PERN	PERSONA	PERTURBING	PESSARY
ERISTOME	PERNANCIES	PERSONAE	PERTURBS	PESSIMISM
ERISTOMES	PERNANCY	PERSONAGE	PERTUSATE	PESSIMISMS
ERISTYLE	PERNS	PERSONAGES	PERTUSE	PESSIMIST
ERISTYLES	PERONE	PERSONAL	PERTUSED	PESSIMISTS
ERITI	PERONEAL	PERSONAS	PERTUSION	PEST
ERITRICH	PERONES	PERSONATE	PERTUSIONS	PESTER
ERITRICHA	PERONEUS	PERSONATED	PERTUSSAL	PESTERED
ERITUS	PERONEUSES	PERSONATES	PERTUSSIS	PESTERER
ERIWIG	PERORATE	PERSONATING	PERTUSSISES	PESTERERS
ERIWIGGED	PERORATED	PERSONATINGS	PERUKE	PESTERING
ERIWIGGING	PERORATES	PERSONIFIED	PERUKED	PESTEROUS
ERIWIGS	PERORATING	PERSONIFIES	PERUKES	PESTERS
ERJINK	PEROXIDE	PERSONIFY	PERUSAL	PESTFUL
ERJURE	PEROXIDED	PERSONIFYING	PERUSALS	PESTHOUSE
ERJURED	PEROXIDES	PERSONISE	PERUSE	PESTHOUSES
ERJURER	PEROXIDING	PERSONISED	PERUSED	PESTICIDE
ERJURERS	PERPEND	PERSONISES	PERUSER	PESTICIDES
ERJURES	PERPENDED	PERSONISING	PERUSERS	PESTILENT
ERJURIES	PERPENDING	PERSONIZE	PERUSES	PESTLE
ERJURING	PERPENDS	PERSONIZED	PERUSING	PESTLED
ERJUROUS	PERPENT	PERSONIZES	PERV	PESTLES
ERJURY	PERPENTS	PERSONIZING	PERVADE	PESTLING
ERK	PERPETUAL	PERSONNEL	PERVADED	PESTO
ERKED	PERPETUALS	PERSONNELS	PERVADER	PESTOLOGIES
ERKIER	PERPLEX	PERSONS	PERVADERS	PESTOLOGY
ERKIEST	PERPLEXED	PERSPIRE	PERVADES	PESTOS
ERKILY	PERPLEXES	PERSPIRED	PERVADING	PESTS
ERKIN	PERPLEXING	PERSPIRES	PERVASION	PET
ERKINESS	PERRADIAL	PERSPIRING	PERVASIONS	PETAL
ERKINESSES	PERRADII	PERST	PERVASIVE	PETALINE
ERKING	PERRADIUS	PERSUADE	PERVE	PETALISM
ERKINS	PERRIER	PERSUADED	PERVED	PETALISMS
ERKS	PERRIERS	PERSUADER	PERVERSE	PETALLED
ERKY	PERRIES	PERSUADERS	PERVERSER	PETALODIES
ERLITE	PERRON	PERSUADES	PERVERSEST	PETALODY
ERLITES	PERRONS	PERSUADING	PERVERT	PETALOID
ERLITIC	PERRUQUE	PERSUE	PERVERTED	PETALOUS
ERLOUS	PERRUQUES	PERSUED	PERVERTER	PETALS
ERM	PERRY	PERSUES	PERVERTERS	PÉTANQUE
ERMALLOY	PERSANT	PERSUING	PERVERTING	PÉTANQUES
ERMALLOYS	PERSAUNT	PERSWADE	PERVERTS	PETAR
ERMANENT	PERSE	PERSWADED	PERVES	PETARA
ERMEABLE	PERSECUTE	PERSWADES	PERVIATE	PETARAS
ERMEABLY	PERSECUTED	PERSWADING	PERVIATED	PETARD
ERMEANCE	PERSECUTES	PERT	PERVIATES	PETARDS
ERMEANCES	PERSECUTING	PERTAIN	PERVIATING	PETARIES
ERMEASE	PERSEITIES	PERTAINED	PERVICACIES	PETARS
ERMEASES	PERSEITY	PERTAINING	PERVICACY	PETARY
ERMEATE	PERSELINE	PERTAINS	PERVING	PETASUS
ERMEATED	PERSELINES	PERTAKE	PERVIOUS	PETASUSES
ERMEATES	PERSES	PERTAKEN	PERVS	PETAURINE
ERMEATING	PERSEVERE	PERTAKES	PESADE	PETAURIST
ERMED	PERSEVERED	PERTAKING	PESADES	PETAURISTS
ERMING	PERSEVERES	PERTER	PESANT	PETCHARIES
			PESANTE	
			PESANTS	

PETCHARY
PETCOCK
PETCOCKS
PETECHIA
PETECHIAE
PETECHIAL
PETER
PETERED
PETERING
PETERMAN
PETERMEN
PETERS
PETERSHAM
PETERSHAMS
PETHER
PETHERS
PETHIDINE
PETHIDINES
PÉTILLANT
PETIOLAR
PETIOLATE
PETIOLE
PETIOLED
PETIOLES
PETIOLULE
PETIOLULES
PETIT
PETITE
PETITION
PETITIONED
PETITIONING
PETITIONINGS
PETITIONS
PETITORY
PETRARIES
PETRARY
PETRE
PETREL
PETRELS
PETRES
PETRIFIC
PETRIFIED
PETRIFIES
PETRIFY
PETRIFYING
PETROGRAM
PETROGRAMS
PETROL
PETROLAGE
PETROLAGES
PETROLEUM
PETROLEUMS
PETROLEUR
PETROLEURS
PETROLIC
PETROLLED
PETROLLING
PETROLOGIES
PETROLOGY
PETROLS
PETRONEL
PETRONELS
PETROSAL
PETROSALS
PETROUS
PETS
PETTED
PETTEDLY
PETTER
PETTERS

PETTICOAT
PETTICOATS
PETTIER
PETTIES
PETTIEST
PETTIFOG
PETTIFOGGED
PETTIFOGGING
PETTIFOGGINGS
PETTIFOGS
PETTILY
PETTINESS
PETTINESSES
PETTING
PETTINGS
PETTISH
PETTISHLY
PETTITOES
PETTLE
PETTLED
PETTLES
PETTLING
PETTY
PETULANCE
PETULANCES
PETULANCIES
PETULANCY
PETULANT
PETUNIA
PETUNIAS
PETUNTSE
PETUNTSES
PETUNTZE
PETUNTZES
PEW
PEWEE
PEWEES
PEWIT
PEWITS
PEWS
PEWTER
PEWTERER
PEWTERERS
PEWTERS
PEYOTE
PEYOTES
PEYOTISM
PEYOTISMS
PEYOTIST
PEYOTISTS
PEYSE
PEYSED
PEYSES
PEYSING
PEZANT
PEZANTS
PEZIZOID
PFENNIG
PFENNIGE
PFENNIGS
PFENNING
PFENNINGS
PHACOID
PHACOIDAL
PHACOLITE
PHACOLITES
PHACOLITH
PHACOLITHS
PHAEIC
PHAEISM

PHAEISMS
PHAENOGAM
PHAENOGAMS
PHAETON
PHAETONS
PHAGE
PHAGEDENA
PHAGEDENAS
PHAGES
PHAGOCYTE
PHAGOCYTES
PHALANGAL
PHALANGE
PHALANGER
PHALANGERS
PHALANGES
PHALANGID
PHALANGIDS
PHALANX
PHALANXES
PHALAROPE
PHALAROPES
PHALLI
PHALLIC
PHALLIN
PHALLINS
PHALLISM
PHALLISMS
PHALLOID
PHALLUS
PHALLUSES
PHANG
PHANGED
PHANGING
PHANGS
PHANSIGAR
PHANSIGARS
PHANTASIED
PHANTASIES
PHANTASIM
PHANTASIMS
PHANTASM
PHANTASMA
PHANTASMATA
PHANTASMS
PHANTASY
PHANTASYING
PHANTOM
PHANTOMS
PHANTOMY
PHANTOSME
PHANTOSMES
PHARAONIC
PHARE
PHARES
PHARISAIC
PHARMACIES
PHARMACY
PHAROS
PHAROSES
PHARYNGAL
PHARYNGES
PHARYNX
PHARYNXES
PHASE
PHASED
PHASELESS
PHASES
PHASIC
PHASING

PHASIS
PHASMID
PHASMIDS
PHATIC
PHEASANT
PHEASANTS
PHEAZAR
PHEAZARS
PHEER
PHEERE
PHEERES
PHEERS
PHEESE
PHEESED
PHEESES
PHEESING
PHEEZE
PHEEZED
PHEEZES
PHEEZING
PHELLEM
PHELLEMS
PHELLOGEN
PHELLOGENS
PHELLOID
PHELONION
PHELONIONS
PHENACITE
PHENACITES
PHENAKISM
PHENAKISMS
PHENAKITE
PHENAKITES
PHENATE
PHENATES
PHENE
PHENES
PHENETIC
PHENETICS
PHENGITE
PHENGITES
PHENIC
PHENOGAM
PHENOGAMS
PHENOL
PHENOLATE
PHENOLATES
PHENOLIC
PHENOLOGIES
PHENOLOGY
PHENOLS
PHENOMENA
PHENOTYPE
PHENOTYPED
PHENOTYPES
PHENOTYPING
PHENYL
PHENYLIC
PHENYLS
PHEON
PHEONS
PHEROMONE
PHEROMONES
PHESE
PHESED
PHESES
PHESING
PHEW
PHI
PHIAL

PHIALLED
PHIALLING
PHIALS
PHILABEG
PHILABEGS
PHILAMOT
PHILAMOTS
PHILANDER
PHILANDERED
PHILANDERING
PHILANDERS
PHILATELIES
PHILATELY
PHILHORSE
PHILHORSES
PHILIBEG
PHILIBEGS
PHILIPPIC
PHILIPPICS
PHILLABEG
PHILLABEGS
PHILLIBEG
PHILLIBEGS
PHILOGYNIES
PHILOGYNY
PHILOLOGIES
PHILOLOGY
PHILOMATH
PHILOMATHS
PHILOMOT
PHILOMOTS
PHILOPENA
PHILOPENAS
PHILTER
PHILTERS
PHILTRE
PHILTRES
PHIMOSES
PHIMOSIS
PHINNOCK
PHINNOCKS
PHIS
PHISNOMIES
PHISNOMY
PHIZ
PHIZOG
PHIZOGS
PHIZZES
PHLEBITIS
PHLEBITISES
PHLEGM
PHLEGMIER
PHLEGMIEST
PHLEGMON
PHLEGMONS
PHLEGMS
PHLEGMY
PHLOEM
PHLOEMS
PHLOMIS
PHLOMISES
PHLOX
PHLOXES
PHLYCTENA
PHLYCTENAE
PHO
PHOBIA
PHOBIAS
PHOBIC
PHOBISM

PHOBISMS
PHOBIST
PHOBISTS
PHOCA
PHOCAE
PHOCAS
PHOCINE
PHOEBE
PHOEBES
PHOENIXES
PHOH
PHOLADES
PHOLAS
PHON
PHONAL
PHONATE
PHONATED
PHONATES
PHONATING
PHONATION
PHONATIONS
PHONATORY
PHONE
PHONECARD
PHONECARDS
PHONED
PHONEME
PHONEMES
PHONEMIC
PHONEMICS
PHONES
PHONETIC
PHONETICS
PHONETISM
PHONETISMS
PHONETIST
PHONETISTS
PHONEY
PHONEYED
PHONEYING
PHONEYS
PHONIC
PHONICS
PHONIED
PHONIER
PHONIES
PHONIEST
PHONINESS
PHONINESSES
PHONING
PHONMETER
PHONMETERS
PHONOGRAM
PHONOGRAMS
PHONOLITE
PHONOLITES
PHONOLOGIES
PHONOLOGY
PHONON
PHONONS
PHONOPORE
PHONOPORES
PHONOTYPE
PHONOTYPED
PHONOTYPES
PHONOTYPIES
PHONOTYPING
PHONOTYPY
PHONS

PHONY
PHONYING
PHOOEY
PHORMINGES
PHORMINX
PHORMIUM
PHORMIUMS
PHOS
PHOSGENE
PHOSGENES
PHOSPHATE
PHOSPHATED
PHOSPHATES
PHOSPHATING
PHOSPHENE
PHOSPHENES
PHOSPHIDE
PHOSPHIDES
PHOSPHINE
PHOSPHINES
PHOSPHITE
PHOSPHITES
PHOSPHOR
PHOSPHORS
PHOT
PHOTIC
PHOTICS
PHOTISM
PHOTISMS
PHOTO
PHOTOCALL
PHOTOCALLS
PHOTOCELL
PHOTOCELLS
PHOTOCOPIED
PHOTOCOPIES
PHOTOCOPY
PHOTOCOPYING
PHOTOCOPYINGS
PHOTOED
PHOTOFIT
PHOTOFITS
PHOTOGEN
PHOTOGENE
PHOTOGENES
PHOTOGENS
PHOTOGENY
PHOTOGRAM
PHOTOGRAMS
PHOTOING
PHOTOLYSE
PHOTOLYSED
PHOTOLYSES
PHOTOLYSING
PHOTON
PHOTONICS
PHOTONS
PHOTOPHIL
PHOTOPHILS
PHOTOPIA
PHOTOPIAS
PHOTOPIC
PHOTOPSIA
PHOTOPSIAS
PHOTOPSIES
PHOTOPSY
PHOTOS
PHOTOTYPE
PHOTOTYPED

PHOTOTYPES
PHOTOTYPIES
PHOTOTYPING
PHOTOTYPY
PHOTS
PHRASAL
PHRASE
PHRASED
PHRASEMAN
PHRASEMEN
PHRASER
PHRASERS
PHRASES
PHRASIER
PHRASIEST
PHRASING
PHRASINGS
PHRASY
PHRATRIES
PHRATRY
PHREATIC
PHRENESES
PHRENESIS
PHRENETIC
PHRENETICS
PHRENIC
PHRENISM
PHRENISMS
PHRENITIC
PHRENITIS
PHRENITISES
PHRENSIES
PHRENSY
PHRENTICK
PHTHALATE
PHTHALATES
PHTHALEIN
PHTHALEINS
PHTHALIC
PHTHALIN
PHTHALINS
PHTHISES
PHTHISIC
PHTHISICS
PHTHISIS
PHUT
PHUTS
PHYCOCYAN
PHYCOCYANS
PHYCOLOGIES
PHYCOLOGY
PHYLA
PHYLAE
PHYLARCH
PHYLARCHIES
PHYLARCHS
PHYLARCHY
PHYLE
PHYLES
PHYLETIC
PHYLLARIES
PHYLLARY
PHYLLITE
PHYLLITES
PHYLLO
PHYLLODE
PHYLLODES
PHYLLODIES
PHYLLODY
PHYLLOID

PHYLLOME
PHYLLOMES
PHYLLOPOD
PHYLLOPODS
PHYLLOS
PHYLOGENIES
PHYLOGENY
PHYLUM
PHYSALIA
PHYSALIAS
PHYSALIS
PHYSALISES
PHYSIC
PHYSICAL
PHYSICALS
PHYSICIAN
PHYSICIANS
PHYSICISM
PHYSICISMS
PHYSICIST
PHYSICISTS
PHYSICKED
PHYSICKING
PHYSICKY
PHYSICS
PHYSIO
PHYSIOS
PHYSIQUE
PHYSIQUES
PHYTOGENIES
PHYTOGENY
PHYTOLOGIES
PHYTOLOGY
PHYTON
PHYTONS
PHYTOSES
PHYTOSIS
PHYTOTOMIES
PHYTOTOMY
PHYTOTRON
PHYTOTRONS
PI
PIA
PIACEVOLE
PIACULAR
PIAFFE
PIAFFED
PIAFFER
PIAFFERS
PIAFFES
PIAFFING
PIANETTE
PIANETTES
PIANINO
PIANINOS
PIANISM
PIANISMS
PIANIST
PIANISTE
PIANISTES
PIANISTIC
PIANISTS
PIANO
PIANOS
PIARIST
PIARISTS
PIAS
PIASSABA
PIASSABAS
PIASSAVA

PIASSAVAS
PIASTRE
PIASTRES
PIAZZA
PIAZZAS
PIAZZIAN
PIBROCH
PIBROCHS
PIC
PICA
PICADOR
PICADORS
PICAMAR
PICAMARS
PICARIAN
PICARIANS
PICAROON
PICAROONS
PICAS
PICAYUNE
PICAYUNES
PICCADILL
PICCADILLS
PICCANIN
PICCANINS
PICCOLO
PICCOLOS
PICE
PICENE
PICENES
PICEOUS
PICHURIM
PICHURIMS
PICINE
PICK
PICKABACK
PICKABACKS
PICKAPACK
PICKAPACKS
PICKAXE
PICKAXES
PICKBACK
PICKBACKS
PICKED
PICKEER
PICKEERED
PICKEERER
PICKEERERS
PICKEERING
PICKEERS
PICKER
PICKEREL
PICKERELS
PICKERIES
PICKERS
PICKERY
PICKET
PICKETED
PICKETER
PICKETERS
PICKETING
PICKETS
PICKIER
PICKIEST
PICKING
PICKINGS
PICKLE
PICKLED
PICKLER
PICKLERS

PICKLES	PIECEMEAL	PIG	PIGSWILLS	PILFERY
PICKLING	PIECEMEALED	PIGBOAT	PIGTAIL	PILGRIM
PICKLOCK	PIECEMEALING	PIGBOATS	PIGTAILS	PILGRIMER
PICKLOCKS	PIECEMEALS	PIGEON	PIGWASH	PILGRIMERS
PICKMAW	PIECEN	PIGEONED	PIGWASHES	PILGRIMS
PICKMAWS	PIECENED	PIGEONING	PIGWEED	PILHORSE
PICKS	PIECENER	PIGEONRIES	PIGWEEDS	PILHORSES
PICKY	PIECENERS	PIGEONRY	PIKA	PILI
PICNIC	PIECENING	PIGEONS	PIKADELL	PILIFORM
PICNICKED	PIECENS	PIGFEED	PIKADELLS	PILING
PICNICKER	PIECER	PIGFEEDS	PIKAS	PILIS
PICNICKERS	PIECERS	PIGGED	PIKE	PILL
PICNICKING	PIECES	PIGGERIES	PIKED	PILLAGE
PICNICKY	PIECING	PIGGERY	PIKELET	PILLAGED
PICNICS	PIECRUST	PIGGIE	PIKELETS	PILLAGER
PICOCURIE	PIECRUSTS	PIGGIER	PIKEMAN	PILLAGERS
PICOCURIES	PIED	PIGGIES	PIKEMEN	PILLAGES
PICOT	PIEDISH	PIGGIEST	PIKER	PILLAGING
PICOTÉ	PIEDISHES	PIGGIN	PIKERS	PILLAR
PICOTED	PIEDMONT	PIGGING	PIKES	PILLARIST
PICOTEE	PIEDMONTS	PIGGINGS	PIKESTAFF	PILLARISTS
PICOTEES	PIEDNESS	PIGGINS	PIKESTAFFS	PILLARS
PICOTING	PIEDNESSES	PIGGISH	PIKING	PILLAU
PICOTITE	PIEING	PIGGISHLY	PIKUL	PILLAUS
PICOTITES	PIEMAN	PIGGY	PIKULS	PILLED
PICOTS	PIEMEN	PIGGYBACK	PILA	PILLHEAD
PICQUET	PIEND	PIGGYBACKS	PILAFF	PILLHEADS
PICQUETED	PIENDS	PIGHEADED	PILAFFS	PILLICOCK
PICQUETING	PIEPOWDER	PIGHT	PILASTER	PILLICOCKS
PICQUETS	PIEPOWDERS	PIGHTED	PILASTERS	PILLING
PICRA	PIER	PIGHTING	PILAU	PILLION
PICRAS	PIERAGE	PIGHTLE	PILAUS	PILLIONED
PICRATE	PIERAGES	PIGHTLES	PILAW	PILLIONING
PICRATES	PIERCE	PIGHTS	PILAWS	PILLIONS
PICRIC	PIERCED	PIGLET	PILCH	PILLOCK
PICRITE	PIERCER	PIGLETS	PILCHARD	PILLOCKS
PICRITES	PIERCERS	PIGLING	PILCHARDS	PILLORIED
PICS	PIERCES	PIGLINGS	PILCHER	PILLORIES
PICTARNIE	PIERCING	PIGMEAN	PILCHERS	PILLORISE
PICTARNIES	PIERID	PIGMEAT	PILCHES	PILLORISED
PICTOGRAM	PIERIDINE	PIGMEATS	PILCORN	PILLORISES
PICTOGRAMS	PIERIDS	PIGMENT	PILCORNS	PILLORISING
PICTORIAL	PIERROT	PIGMENTAL	PILCROW	PILLORIZE
PICTORIALS	PIERROTS	PIGMENTED	PILCROWS	PILLORIZED
PICTURAL	PIERS	PIGMENTS	PILE	PILLORIZES
PICTURALS	PIERST	PIGMIES	PILEA	PILLORIZING
PICTURE	PIERT	PIGMY	PILEATE	PILLORY
PICTURED	PIES	PIGNERATE	PILEATED	PILLORYING
PICTURES	PIET	PIGNERATED	PILED	PILLOW
PICTURING	PIETÀ	PIGNERATES	PILEI	PILLOWED
PICUL	PIETÀS	PIGNERATING	PILEOUS	PILLOWING
PICULS	PIETIES	PIGNORATE	PILER	PILLOWS
PIDDLE	PIETISM	PIGNORATED	PILERS	PILLOWY
PIDDLED	PIETISMS	PIGNORATES	PILES	PILLS
PIDDLER	PIETIST	PIGNORATING	PILEUM	PILLWORM
PIDDLERS	PIETISTIC	PIGPEN	PILEUS	PILLWORMS
PIDDLES	PIETISTS	PIGPENS	PILEWORK	PILLWORT
PIDDLING	PIETS	PIGS	PILEWORKS	PILLWORTS
PIDDOCK	PIETY	PIGSCONCE	PILEWORT	PILOSE
PIDDOCKS	PIEZO	PIGSCONCES	PILEWORTS	PILOSITIES
PIDGEON	PIFFERARI	PIGSKIN	PILFER	PILOSITY
PIDGEONS	PIFFERARO	PIGSKINS	PILFERAGE	PILOT
PIDGIN	PIFFERO	PIGSNEY	PILFERAGES	PILOTAGE
PIDGINS	PIFFEROS	PIGSNEYS	PILFERED	PILOTAGES
PIE	PIFFLE	PIGSNIE	PILFERER	PILOTED
PIEBALD	PIFFLED	PIGSNIES	PILFERERS	PILOTING
PIEBALDS	PIFFLER	PIGSNY	PILFERIES	PILOTLESS
PIECE	PIFFLERS	PIGSTIES	PILFERING	PILOTS
PIECED	PIFFLES	PIGSTY	PILFERINGS	PILOUS
PIECELESS	PIFFLING	PIGSWILL	PILFERS	PILOW

PILOWS	PINDERS	PINKNESSES	PIOLETS	PIPITS
PILSENER	PINE	PINKO	PION	PIPKIN
PILSENERS	PINEAL	PINKOES	PIONED	PIPKINS
PILSNER	PINEAPPLE	PINKOS	PIONEER	PIPLESS
PILSNERS	PINEAPPLES	PINKROOT	PIONEERED	PIPPED
PILULA	PINED	PINKROOTS	PIONEERING	PIPPIER
PILULAR	PINERIES	PINKS	PIONEERS	PIPPIEST
PILULAS	PINERY	PINKY	PIONER	PIPPIN
PILULE	PINES	PINNA	PIONERS	PIPPING
PILULES	PINETA	PINNACE	PIONEY	PIPPINS
PILUM	PINETUM	PINNACES	PIONEYS	PIPPY
PILUS	PINEY	PINNACLE	PIONIC	PIPS
PIMENT	PINFISH	PINNACLED	PIONIES	PIPSQUEAK
PIMENTO	PINFISHES	PINNACLES	PIONING	PIPSQUEAKS
PIMENTOS	PINFOLD	PINNACLING	PIONINGS	PIPUL
PIMENTS	PINFOLDED	PINNAE	PIONS	PIPULS
PIMIENTO	PINFOLDING	PINNATE	PIONY	PIPY
PIMIENTOS	PINFOLDS	PINNATED	PIOTED	PIQUANCIES
PIMP	PING	PINNATELY	PIOUS	PIQUANCY
PIMPED	PINGED	PINNED	PIOUSLY	PIQUANT
PIMPERNEL	PINGER	PINNER	PIOY	PIQUANTLY
PIMPERNELS	PINGERS	PINNERS	PIOYE	PIQUE
PIMPING	PINGING	PINNET	PIOYES	PIQUED
PIMPLE	PINGLE	PINNETS	PIOYS	PIQUES
PIMPLED	PINGLED	PINNIE	PIP	PIQUET
PIMPLES	PINGLER	PINNIES	PIPA	PIQUETED
PIMPLIER	PINGLERS	PINNING	PIPAGE	PIQUETING
PIMPLIEST	PINGLES	PINNINGS	PIPAGES	PIQUETS
PIMPLY	PINGLING	PINNIPED	PIPAL	PIQUING
PIMPS	PINGO	PINNIPEDE	PIPALS	PIR
PIN	PINGOES	PINNIPEDES	PIPAS	PIRACIES
PIÑA	PINGOS	PINNIPEDS	PIPE	PIRACY
PINACOID	PINGS	PINNOCK	PIPECLAY	PIRAGUA
PINACOIDS	PINGUEFIED	PINNOCKS	PIPECLAYED	PIRAGUAS
PINAFORE	PINGUEFIES	PINNOED	PIPECLAYING	PIRAI
PINAFORED	PINGUEFY	PINNULA	PIPECLAYS	PIRAIS
PINAFORES	PINGUEFYING	PINNULAS	PIPED	PIRANA
PINAKOID	PINGUID	PINNULATE	PIPEFISH	PIRANAS
PINAKOIDS	PINGUIN	PINNULE	PIPEFISHES	PIRANHA
PINAS	PINGUINS	PINNULES	PIPEFUL	PIRANHAS
PINASTER	PINHEAD	PINNY	PIPEFULS	PIRARUCU
PINASTERS	PINHEADS	PINOCHLE	PIPELESS	PIRARUCUS
PINBALL	PINHOLE	PINOCHLES	PIPELIKE	PIRATE
PINBALLS	PINHOLES	PINOCLE	PIPELINE	PIRATED
PINCASE	PINIER	PINOCLES	PIPELINES	PIRATES
PINCASES	PINIES	PINOLE	PIPER	PIRATIC
PINCER	PINIEST	PINOLES	PIPERIC	PIRATICAL
PINCERED	PINING	PIÑON	PIPERINE	PIRATING
PINCERING	PINION	PIÑONS	PIPERINES	PIRAYA
PINCERS	PINIONED	PINOT	PIPERONAL	PIRAYAS
PINCH	PINIONING	PINOTS	PIPERONALS	PIRL
PINCHBECK	PINIONS	PINS	PIPERS	PIRLICUE
PINCHBECKS	PINITE	PINT	PIPES	PIRLICUED
PINCHCOCK	PINITES	PINTA	PIPESTONE	PIRLICUES
PINCHCOCKS	PINK	PINTABLE	PIPESTONES	PIRLICUING
PINCHED	PINKED	PINTABLES	PIPETTE	PIRLS
PINCHER	PINKER	PINTADO	PIPETTED	PIRN
PINCHERS	PINKERTON	PINTADOS	PIPETTES	PIRNIE
PINCHES	PINKERTONS	PINTAIL	PIPETTING	PIRNIES
PINCHFIST	PINKEST	PINTAILED	PIPEWORK	PIRNIT
PINCHFISTS	PINKIE	PINTAILS	PIPEWORKS	PIRNS
PINCHGUT	PINKIER	PINTAS	PIPEWORT	PIROGUE
PINCHGUTS	PINKIES	PINTLE	PIPEWORTS	PIROGUES
PINCHING	PINKIEST	PINTLES	PIPI	PIROSHKI
PINCHINGS	PINKINESS	PINTO	PIPIER	PIROUETTE
PINDAREE	PINKINESSES	PINTOS	PIPIEST	PIROUETTED
PINDAREES	PINKING	PINTS	PIPING	PIROUETTES
PINDARI	PINKINGS	PINXIT	PIPINGS	PIROUETTING
PINDARIS	PINKISH	PINY	PIPIS	PIROZHKI
PINDER	PINKNESS	PIOLET	PIPIT	PIRS

PIS
PISCARIES
PISCARY
PISCATOR
PISCATORS
PISCATORY
PISCATRIX
PISCATRIXES
PISCIFORM
PISCINA
PISCINAE
PISCINAS
PISCINE
PISCINES
PISÉ
PISÉS
PISH
PISHED
PISHES
PISHING
PISHOGUE
PISHOGUES
PISIFORM
PISIFORMS
PISKIES
PISKY
PISMIRE
PISMIRES
PISOLITE
PISOLITES
PISOLITIC
PISS
PISSED
PISSES
PISSING
PISSOIR
PISSOIRS
PISTACHIO
PISTACHIOS
PISTAREEN
PISTAREENS
PISTE
PISTES
PISTIL
PISTILS
PISTOL
PISTOLE
PISTOLEER
PISTOLEERS
PISTOLES
PISTOLET
PISTOLETS
PISTOLLED
PISTOLLING
PISTOLS
PISTON
PISTONS
PIT
PITA
PITAPAT
PITAPATS
PITAPATTED
PITAPATTING
PITARA
PITARAH
PITARAHS
PITARAS
PITAS
PITCH
PITCHED

PITCHER
PITCHERS
PITCHES
PITCHFORK
PITCHFORKED
PITCHFORKING
PITCHFORKS
PITCHIER
PITCHIEST
PITCHING
PITCHINGS
PITCHMAN
PITCHMEN
PITCHPINE
PITCHPINES
PITCHPIPE
PITCHPIPES
PITCHY
PITEOUS
PITEOUSLY
PITFALL
PITFALLS
PITH
PITHBALL
PITHBALLS
PITHEAD
PITHEADS
PITHECOID
PITHED
PITHFUL
PITHIER
PITHIEST
PITHILY
PITHINESS
PITHINESSES
PITHING
PITHLESS
PITHLIKE
PITHOI
PITHOS
PITHS
PITHY
PITIABLE
PITIABLY
PITIED
PITIER
PITIERS
PITIES
PITIFUL
PITIFULLY
PITILESS
PITMAN
PITMEN
PITON
PITONS
PITS
PITTA
PITTANCE
PITTANCES
PITTAS
PITTED
PITTEN
PITTER
PITTERED
PITTERING
PITTERS
PITTING
PITTINGS
PITTITE
PITTITES

PITUITA
PITUITARY
PITUITAS
PITUITE
PITUITES
PITUITRIN
PITUITRINS
PITURI
PITURIS
PITY
PITYING
PITYINGLY
PITYROID
PIÙ
PIUM
PIUMS
PIUPIU
PIUPIUS
PIVOT
PIVOTAL
PIVOTALLY
PIVOTED
PIVOTER
PIVOTERS
PIVOTING
PIVOTINGS
PIVOTS
PIX
PIXEL
PIXELS
PIXES
PIXIE
PIXIES
PIXILATED
PIXY
PIZAZZ
PIZAZZES
PIZE
PIZES
PIZZA
PIZZAIOLA
PIZZAS
PIZZERIA
PIZZERIAS
PIZZICATO
PIZZICATOS
PIZZLE
PIZZLES
PLACABLE
PLACABLY
PLACARD
PLACARDED
PLACARDING
PLACARDS
PLACATE
PLACATED
PLACATES
PLACATING
PLACATION
PLACATIONS
PLACATORY
PLACCAT
PLACCATE
PLACCATES
PLACCATS
PLACE
PLACEBO
PLACEBOS
PLACED
PLACELESS

PLACEMAN
PLACEMEN
PLACEMENT
PLACEMENTS
PLACENTA
PLACENTAE
PLACENTAL
PLACENTALS
PLACENTAS
PLACER
PLACERS
PLACES
PLACET
PLACETS
PLACID
PLACIDER
PLACIDEST
PLACIDITIES
PLACIDITY
PLACIDLY
PLACING
PLACINGS
PLACIT
PLACITA
PLACITORY
PLACITS
PLACITUM
PLACK
PLACKET
PLACKETS
PLACKLESS
PLACKS
PLACODERM
PLACODERMS
PLACOID
PLAFOND
PLAFONDS
PLAGAL
PLAGE
PLAGES
PLAGIARIES
PLAGIARY
PLAGIUM
PLAGIUMS
PLAGUE
PLAGUED
PLAGUES
PLAGUEY
PLAGUIER
PLAGUIEST
PLAGUILY
PLAGUING
PLAGUY
PLAICE
PLAICES
PLAID
PLAIDED
PLAIDING
PLAIDINGS
PLAIDMAN
PLAIDMEN
PLAIDS
PLAIN
PLAINANT
PLAINANTS
PLAINED
PLAINER
PLAINEST
PLAINFUL
PLAINING

PLAININGS
PLAINISH
PLAINLY
PLAINNESS
PLAINNESSES
PLAINS
PLAINSMAN
PLAINSMEN
PLAINSONG
PLAINSONGS
PLAINT
PLAINTFUL
PLAINTIFF
PLAINTIFFS
PLAINTIVE
PLAINTS
PLAINWORK
PLAINWORKS
PLAISTER
PLAISTERS
PLAIT
PLAITED
PLAITER
PLAITERS
PLAITING
PLAITINGS
PLAITS
PLAN
PLANAR
PLANARIAN
PLANARIANS
PLANATION
PLANATIONS
PLANCH
PLANCHED
PLANCHES
PLANCHET
PLANCHETS
PLANCHING
PLANE
PLANED
PLANER
PLANERS
PLANES
PLANET
PLANETARY
PLANETIC
PLANETOID
PLANETOIDS
PLANETS
PLANGENCIES
PLANGENCY
PLANGENT
PLANING
PLANISH
PLANISHED
PLANISHER
PLANISHERS
PLANISHES
PLANISHING
PLANK
PLANKED
PLANKING
PLANKINGS
PLANKS
PLANKTON
PLANKTONS
PLANLESS
PLANNED
PLANNER

PLANNERS
PLANNING
PLANS
PLANT
PLANTA
PLANTABLE
PLANTAGE
PLANTAGES
PLANTAIN
PLANTAINS
PLANTAR
PLANTAS
PLANTED
PLANTER
PLANTERS
PLANTING
PLANTINGS
PLANTLESS
PLANTLET
PLANTLETS
PLANTLING
PLANTLINGS
PLANTS
PLANTSMAN
PLANTSMEN
PLANTULE
PLANTULES
PLANULA
PLANULAE
PLANULAR
PLANULOID
PLANURIA
PLANURIAS
PLANURIES
PLANURY
PLANXTIES
PLANXTY
PLAP
PLAPPED
PLAPPING
PLAPS
PLAQUE
PLAQUES
PLAQUETTE
PLAQUETTES
PLASH
PLASHED
PLASHES
PLASHET
PLASHETS
PLASHIER
PLASHIEST
PLASHING
PLASHINGS
PLASHY
PLASM
PLASMA
PLASMAS
PLASMATIC
PLASMIC
PLASMID
PLASMIDS
PLASMIN
PLASMINS
PLASMODIA
PLASMS
PLAST
PLASTE
PLASTER
PLASTERED

PLASTERER
PLASTERERS
PLASTERING
PLASTERINGS
PLASTERS
PLASTERY
PLASTIC
PLASTICS
PLASTID
PLASTIDS
PLASTIQUE
PLASTIQUES
PLASTISOL
PLASTISOLS
PLASTRAL
PLASTRON
PLASTRONS
PLAT
PLATAN
PLATANE
PLATANES
PLATANNA
PLATANNAS
PLATANS
PLATBAND
PLATE
PLATEASM
PLATEASMS
PLATEAU
PLATEAUED
PLATEAUING
PLATEAUS
PLATEAUX
PLATED
PLATEFUL
PLATEFULS
PLATELET
PLATELETS
PLATEMAN
PLATEMARK
PLATEMARKS
PLATEMEN
PLATEN
PLATER
PLATERS
PLATES
PLATFORM
PLATFORMED
PLATFORMING
PLATFORMINGS
PLATFORMS
PLATIER
PLATIEST
PLATINA
PLATINAS
PLATING
PLATINGS
PLATINIC
PLATINISE
PLATINISED
PLATINISES
PLATINISING
PLATINIZE
PLATINIZED
PLATINIZES
PLATINIZING
PLATINOID
PLATINOIDS

PLATINOUS
PLATINUM
PLATINUMS
PLATITUDE
PLATITUDES
PLATONIC
PLATOON
PLATOONS
PLATS
PLATTED
PLATTER
PLATTERS
PLATTING
PLATTINGS
PLATY
PLATYPUS
PLATYPUSES
PLATYSMA
PLATYSMAS
PLAUDIT
PLAUDITE
PLAUDITS
PLAUSIBLE
PLAUSIBLY
PLAUSIVE
PLAY
PLAYA
PLAYABLE
PLAYAS
PLAYBACK
PLAYBACKS
PLAYBILL
PLAYBILLS
PLAYBOOK
PLAYBOOKS
PLAYBOY
PLAYBOYS
PLAYBUS
PLAYBUSES
PLAYED
PLAYER
PLAYERS
PLAYFUL
PLAYFULLY
PLAYGIRL
PLAYGIRLS
PLAYGROUP
PLAYGROUPS
PLAYHOUSE
PLAYHOUSES
PLAYING
PLAYLET
PLAYLETS
PLAYMATE
PLAYMATES
PLAYROOM
PLAYROOMS
PLAYS
PLAYSOME
PLAYSUIT
PLAYSUITS
PLAYTHING
PLAYTHINGS
PLAYTIME
PLAYTIMES
PLAZA
PLAZAS
PLEA
PLEACH

PLEACHED
PLEACHES
PLEACHING
PLEAD
PLEADABLE
PLEADED
PLEADER
PLEADERS
PLEADING
PLEADINGS
PLEADS
PLEAED
PLEAING
PLEAS
PLEASANCE
PLEASANCES
PLEASANT
PLEASANTER
PLEASANTEST
PLEASE
PLEASED
PLEASEMAN
PLEASEMEN
PLEASER
PLEASERS
PLEASES
PLEASETH
PLEASING
PLEASINGS
PLEASURE
PLEASURED
PLEASURER
PLEASURERS
PLEASURES
PLEASURING
PLEAT
PLEATED
PLEATING
PLEATS
PLEB
PLEBBIER
PLEBBIEST
PLEBBY
PLEBEAN
PLEBEIAN
PLEBEIANS
PLEBIFIED
PLEBIFIES
PLEBIFY
PLEBIFYING
PLEBS
PLECTRA
PLECTRE
PLECTRES
PLECTRON
PLECTRONS
PLECTRUM
PLECTRUMS
PLED
PLEDGE
PLEDGED
PLEDGEE
PLEDGEES
PLEDGEOR
PLEDGEORS
PLEDGER
PLEDGERS
PLEDGES
PLEDGET
PLEDGETS

PLEDGING
PLEDGOR
PLEDGORS
PLEIOMERIES
PLEIOMERY
PLENARILY
PLENARTIES
PLENARTY
PLENARY
PLENILUNE
PLENILUNES
PLENIPO
PLENIPOES
PLENIPOS
PLENISH
PLENISHED
PLENISHES
PLENISHING
PLENISHINGS
PLENIST
PLENISTS
PLENITUDE
PLENITUDES
PLENTEOUS
PLENTIES
PLENTIFUL
PLENTY
PLENUM
PLENUMS
PLEON
PLEONASM
PLEONASMS
PLEONAST
PLEONASTE
PLEONASTES
PLEONASTS
PLEONEXIA
PLEONEXIAS
PLEONS
PLEOPOD
PLEOPODS
PLEROMA
PLEROMAS
PLEROME
PLEROMES
PLESH
PLESHES
PLESSOR
PLESSORS
PLETHORA
PLETHORAS
PLETHORIC
PLEUCH
PLEUCHS
PLEUGH
PLEUGHS
PLEURA
PLEURAE
PLEURAL
PLEURISIES
PLEURISY
PLEURITIC
PLEURITICS
PLEURITIS
PLEURITISES
PLEURON
PLEXIFORM
PLEXOR
PLEXORS
PLEXURE

PLEXURES
PLEXUS
PLEXUSES
PLIABLE
PLIABLY
PLIANCIES
PLIANCY
PLIANT
PLIANTLY
PLICA
PLICAE
PLICAL
PLICATE
PLICATED
PLICATELY
PLICATES
PLICATING
PLICATION
PLICATIONS
PLICATURE
PLICATURES
PLIÉ
PLIED
PLIER
PLIERS
PLIÉS
PLIES
PLIGHT
PLIGHTED
PLIGHTER
PLIGHTERS
PLIGHTFUL
PLIGHTING
PLIGHTS
PLIM
PLIMMED
PLIMMING
PLIMS
PLIMSOLE
PLIMSOLES
PLIMSOLL
PLIMSOLLS
PLINK
PLINKED
PLINKING
PLINKS
PLINTH
PLINTHS
PLISKIE
PLISKIES
PLISSÉ
PLOAT
PLOATED
PLOATING
PLOATS
PLOD
PLODDED
PLODDER
PLODDERS
PLODDING
PLODDINGS
PLODS
PLONG
PLONGD
PLONGE
PLONGED
PLONGES
PLONGING
PLONGS
PLONK

PLONKED
PLONKER
PLONKERS
PLONKING
PLONKS
PLOOK
PLOOKIE
PLOOKIER
PLOOKIEST
PLOOKS
PLOP
PLOPPED
PLOPPING
PLOPS
PLOSION
PLOSIONS
PLOSIVE
PLOSIVES
PLOT
PLOTFUL
PLOTLESS
PLOTS
PLOTTED
PLOTTER
PLOTTERED
PLOTTERING
PLOTTERS
PLOTTIE
PLOTTIES
PLOTTING
PLOTTINGS
PLOTTY
PLOUGH
PLOUGHBOY
PLOUGHBOYS
PLOUGHED
PLOUGHER
PLOUGHERS
PLOUGHING
PLOUGHINGS
PLOUGHMAN
PLOUGHMEN
PLOUGHS
PLOUK
PLOUKIE
PLOUKIER
PLOUKIEST
PLOUKS
PLOUTER
PLOUTERED
PLOUTERING
PLOUTERS
PLOVER
PLOVERS
PLOVERY
PLOW
PLOWED
PLOWING
PLOWS
PLOWTER
PLOWTERED
PLOWTERING
PLOWTERS
PLOY
PLOYS
PLUCK
PLUCKED
PLUCKER
PLUCKERS
PLUCKIER

PLUCKIEST
PLUCKILY
PLUCKING
PLUCKS
PLUCKY
PLUFF
PLUFFED
PLUFFIER
PLUFFIEST
PLUFFING
PLUFFS
PLUFFY
PLUG
PLUGGED
PLUGGER
PLUGGERS
PLUGGING
PLUGGINGS
PLUGS
PLUM
PLUMAGE
PLUMAGED
PLUMAGES
PLUMATE
PLUMB
PLUMBAGO
PLUMBAGOS
PLUMBATE
PLUMBATES
PLUMBED
PLUMBEOUS
PLUMBER
PLUMBERIES
PLUMBERS
PLUMBERY
PLUMBIC
PLUMBING
PLUMBINGS
PLUMBISM
PLUMBISMS
PLUMBITE
PLUMBITES
PLUMBLESS
PLUMBOUS
PLUMBS
PLUMBUM
PLUMBUMS
PLUMCOT
PLUMCOTS
PLUMDAMAS
PLUMDAMASES
PLUME
PLUMED
PLUMELESS
PLUMELET
PLUMELETS
PLUMERIES
PLUMERY
PLUMES
PLUMIER
PLUMIEST
PLUMING
PLUMIPED
PLUMIST
PLUMISTS
PLUMMET
PLUMMETED
PLUMMETING
PLUMMETS
PLUMMIER

PLUMMIEST
PLUMMY
PLUMOSE
PLUMOUS
PLUMP
PLUMPED
PLUMPEN
PLUMPENED
PLUMPENING
PLUMPENS
PLUMPER
PLUMPERS
PLUMPEST
PLUMPIE
PLUMPING
PLUMPISH
PLUMPLY
PLUMPNESS
PLUMPNESSES
PLUMPS
PLUMPY
PLUMS
PLUMULA
PLUMULAE
PLUMULAR
PLUMULATE
PLUMULE
PLUMULES
PLUMULOSE
PLUMY
PLUNDER
PLUNDERED
PLUNDERER
PLUNDERERS
PLUNDERING
PLUNDERS
PLUNGE
PLUNGED
PLUNGER
PLUNGERS
PLUNGES
PLUNGING
PLUNGINGS
PLUNK
PLUNKED
PLUNKER
PLUNKERS
PLUNKING
PLUNKS
PLURAL
PLURALISE
PLURALISED
PLURALISES
PLURALISING
PLURALISM
PLURALISMS
PLURALIST
PLURALISTS
PLURALITIES
PLURALITY
PLURALIZE
PLURALIZED
PLURALIZES
PLURALIZING
PLURALLY
PLURALS
PLURIPARA
PLURIPARAE
PLURIPARAS
PLURISIE

PLURISIES
PLUS
PLUSAGE
PLUSAGES
PLUSED
PLUSES
PLUSH
PLUSHER
PLUSHES
PLUSHEST
PLUSHIER
PLUSHIEST
PLUSHY
PLUSING
PLUSSAGE
PLUSSAGES
PLUSSED
PLUSSES
PLUSSING
PLUTEAL
PLUTEUS
PLUTEUSES
PLUTOCRAT
PLUTOCRATS
PLUTOLOGIES
PLUTOLOGY
PLUTON
PLUTONIUM
PLUTONIUMS
PLUTONOMIES
PLUTONOMY
PLUTONS
PLUVIAL
PLUVIALS
PLUVIOSE
PLUVIOUS
PLY
PLYING
PLYWOOD
PLYWOODS
PNEUMA
PNEUMAS
PNEUMATIC
PNEUMATICS
PNEUMONIA
PNEUMONIAS
PNEUMONIC
PNEUMONICS
PO
POA
POACEOUS
POACH
POACHED
POACHER
POACHERS
POACHES
POACHIER
POACHIEST
POACHING
POACHINGS
POACHY
POAKA
POAKAS
POAKE
POAKES
POAS
POCHARD
POCHARDS
POCHAY
POCHAYED

POCHAYING
POCHAYS
POCHETTE
POCHETTES
POCHOIR
POCHOIRS
POCK
POCKARD
POCKARDS
POCKED
POCKET
POCKETED
POCKETFUL
POCKETFULS
POCKETING
POCKETS
POCKIER
POCKIEST
POCKMANKIES
POCKMANKY
POCKMARK
POCKMARKS
POCKPIT
POCKPITS
POOKO
POCKY
POCO
POD
PODAGRA
PODAGRAL
PODAGRAS
PODAGRIC
PODAGROUS
PODAL
PODALIC
PODDED
PODDIER
PODDIEST
PODDING
PODDY
PODESTA
PODESTAS
PODEX
PODEXES
PODGE
PODGES
PODGIER
PODGIEST
PODGINESS
PODGINESSES
PODGY
PODIA
PODIAL
PODIATRIES
PODIATRY
PODITE
PODITES
PODIUM
PODLEY
PODLEYS
PODOLOGIES
PODOLOGY
PODS
PODSOL
PODSOLIC
PODSOLS
PODZOL
PODZOLS
POEM
POEMATIC

POEMS
POENOLOGIES
POENOLOGY
POESIED
POESIES
POESY
POESYING
POET
POETASTER
POETASTERS
POETASTRIES
POETASTRY
POETESS
POETESSES
POETIC
POETICAL
POETICISE
POETICISED
POETICISES
POETICISING
POETICISM
POETICISMS
POETICIZE
POETICIZED
POETICIZE
POETICIZING
POETICS
POETICULE
POETICULES
POETISE
POETISED
POETISES
POETISING
POETIZE
POETIZED
POETIZES
POETIZING
POETRESSE
POETRESSES
POETRIES
POETRY
POETS
POETSHIP
POETSHIPS
POFFLE
POFFLES
POGGE
POGGES
POGROM
POGROMS
POH
POI
POIGNADO
POIGNADOS
POIGNANCIES
POIGNANCY
POIGNANT
POILU
POILUS
POINADO
POINADOS
POINCIANA
POINCIANAS
POIND
POINDED
POINDER
POINDERS
POINDING
POINDINGS
POINDS

POINT
POINTE
POINTED
POINTEDLY
POINTEL
POINTELS
POINTER
POINTERS
POINTES
POINTIER
POINTIEST
POINTILLÉ
POINTING
POINTINGS
POINTLESS
POINTS
POINTSMAN
POINTSMEN
POINTY
POIS
POISE
POISED
POISER
POISERS
POISING
POISON
POISONED
POISONER
POISONERS
POISONING
POISONOUS
POISONS
POISSON
POISSONS
POITREL
POITRELS
POKAL
POKALS
POKE
POKEBERRIES
POKEBERRY
POKED
POKEFUL
POKEFULS
POKER
POKERISH
POKERS
POKES
POKEWEED
POKEWEEDS
POKIER
POKIEST
POKING
POKY
POLACCA
POLACCAS
POLACRE
POLACRES
POLAR
POLARISE
POLARISED
POLARISER
POLARISERS
POLARISES
POLARISING
POLARITIES
POLARITY
POLARIZE
POLARIZED

POLARIZER
POLARIZERS
POLARIZES
POLARIZING
POLARON
POLARONS
POLARS
POLDER
POLDERED
POLDERING
POLDERS
POLE
POLECAT
POLECATS
POLED
POLEMARCH
POLEMARCHS
POLEMIC
POLEMICAL
POLEMICS
POLEMISE
POLEMISED
POLEMISES
POLEMISING
POLEMIST
POLEMISTS
POLEMIZE
POLEMIZED
POLEMIZES
POLEMIZING
POLENTA
POLENTAS
POLER
POLERS
POLES
POLEY
POLEYN
POLEYNS
POLEYS
POLIANITE
POLIANITES
POLICE
POLICED
POLICEMAN
POLICEMEN
POLICES
POLICIES
POLICING
POLICY
POLING
POLINGS
POLINIA
POLINIC
POLLINIUM
POLLIWIG
POLLIWIGS
POLIO
POLIOS
POLISH
POLISHED
POLISHER
POLISHERS
POLISHES
POLISHING
POLISHINGS
POLITE
POLITELY
POLITER
POLITESSE
POLITESSES
POLITEST
POLITIC
POLITICAL
POLITICK
POLITICKED

POLITICKING
POLITICKINGS
POLITICKS
POLITICLY
POLITICO
POLITICOES
POLITICOS
POLITICS
POLITIES
POLITIQUE
POLITIQUES
POLITY
POLK
POLKA
POLKAS
POLKED
POLKING
POLKS
POLL
POLLACK
POLLACKS
POLLAN
POLLANS
POLLARD
POLLARDED
POLLARDING
POLLARDS
POLLED
POLLEN
POLLENED
POLLENING
POLLENS
POLLENT
POLLER
POLLERS
POLLEX
POLLICAL
POLLICES
POLLICIE
POLLICIES
POLLICY
POLLIES
POLLINATE
POLLINATED
POLLINATES
POLLINATING
POLLING
POLLINGS
POLLINIA
POLLINIC
POLLINIUM
POLLIWIG
POLLIWIGS
POLLIWOG
POLLIWOGS
POLLMAN
POLLMEN
POLLOCK
POLLOCKS
POLLS
POLLSTER
POLLSTERS
POLLUSION
POLLUSIONS
POLLUTANT
POLLUTANTS
POLLUTE
POLLUTED
POLLUTER
POLLUTERS

POLLUTES
POLLUTING
POLLUTION
POLLUTIONS
POLLUTIVE
POLLY
POLLYANNA
POLLYANNAS
POLLYWIG
POLLYWIGS
POLLYWOG
POLLYWOGS
POLO
POLOIST
POLOISTS
POLONAISE
POLONAISES
POLONIE
POLONIES
POLONISE
POLONISED
POLONISES
POLONISING
POLONISM
POLONISMS
POLONIUM
POLONIUMS
POLONIZE
POLONIZED
POLONIZES
POLONIZING
POLONY
POLOS
POLT
POLTED
POLTFEET
POLTFOOT
POLTING
POLTROON
POLTROONS
POLTS
POLVERINE
POLVERINES
POLY
POLYACID
POLYACT
POLYAMIDE
POLYAMIDES
POLYANDRIES
POLYANDRY
POLYARCH
POLYARCHIES
POLYARCHY
POLYAXIAL
POLYAXON
POLYAXONS
POLYBASIC
POLYCONIC
POLYESTER
POLYESTERS
POLYGALA
POLYGALAS
POLYGAM
POLYGAMIC
POLYGAMIES
POLYGAMS
POLYGAMY
POLYGENE
POLYGENES
POLYGENIC

POLYGENIES
POLYGENY
POLYGLOT
POLYGLOTS
POLYGLOTT
POLYGLOTTS
POLYGON
POLYGONAL
POLYGONIES
POLYGONS
POLYGONUM
POLYGONUMS
POLYGONY
POLYGRAPH
POLYGRAPHS
POLYGYNIES
POLYGYNY
POLYHEDRA
POLYLEMMA
POLYLEMMAS
POLYMASTIES
POLYMASTY
POLYMATH
POLYMATHIES
POLYMATHS
POLYMATHY
POLYMER
POLYMERIC
POLYMERIES
POLYMERS
POLYMERY
POLYMORPH
POLYMORPHS
POLYNIA
POLYNIAS
POLYNYA
POLYNYAS
POLYOMINO
POLYOMINOS
POLYONYM
POLYONYMIES
POLYONYMS
POLYONYMY
POLYP
POLYPARIES
POLYPARY
POLYPE
POLYPES
POLYPHAGIES
POLYPHAGY
POLYPHASE
POLYPHON
POLYPHONE
POLYPHONES
POLYPHONIES
POLYPHONS
POLYPHONY
POLYPI
POLYPIDE
POLYPIDES
POLYPIDOM
POLYPIDOMS
POLYPINE
POLYPITE
POLYPITES
POLYPLOID
POLYPOD
POLYPODIES
POLYPODS
POLYPODY

POLYPOID
POLYPOSES
POLYPOSIS
POLYPOUS
POLYPS
POLYPTYCH
POLYPTYCHS
POLYPUS
POLYS
POLYSEME
POLYSEMES
POLYSEMIES
POLYSEMY
POLYSOME
POLYSOMES
POLYSOMIES
POLYSOMY
POLYSTYLE
POLYTENE
POLYTHENE
POLYTHENES
POLYTONAL
POLYTYPIC
POLYURIA
POLYURIAS
POLYVINYL
POLYVINYLS
POLYWATER
POLYWATERS
POLYZOA
POLYZOAN
POLYZOANS
POLYZOARIES
POLYZOARY
POLYZOIC
POLYZONAL
POLYZOOID
POLYZOON
POM
POMACE
POMACEOUS
POMACES
POMADE
POMADED
POMADES
POMADING
POMANDER
POMANDERS
POMATO
POMATOES
POMATUM
POMATUMS
POMBE
POMBES
POME
POMELO
POMELOS
POMEROY
POMEROYS
POMES
POMFRET
POMFRETS
POMMEL
POMMELE
POMMELLED
POMMELLING
POMMELS
POMMETTY
POMMIES
POMMY

POMOERIUM
POMOERIUMS
POMOLOGIES
POMOLOGY
POMP
POMPADOUR
POMPADOURS
POMPANO
POMPANOS
POMPELO
POMPELOS
POMPEY
POMPEYED
POMPEYING
POMPEYS
POMPHOLYX
POMPHOLYXES
POMPIER
POMPION
POMPIONS
POMPOM
POMPOMS
POMPON
POMPONS
POMPOON
POMPOONS
POMPOSITIES
POMPOSITY
POMPOUS
POMPOUSLY
POMPS
POMROY
POMROYS
POMS
POMWATER
POMWATERS
PONCE
PONCEAU
PONCEAUS
PONCEAUX
PONCED
PONCES
PONCHO
PONCHOS
PONCING
POND
PONDAGE
PONDAGES
PONDED
PONDER
PONDERAL
PONDERATE
PONDERATED
PONDERATES
PONDERATING
PONDERED
PONDERER
PONDERERS
PONDERING
PONDEROUS
PONDERS
PONDING
PONDOK
PONDOKKIE
PONDOKKIES
PONDOKS
PONDS
PONDWEED
PONDWEEDS
PONE

PONENT
PONES
PONEY
PONEYS
PONG
PONGED
PONGEE
PONGEES
PONGID
PONGIDS
PONGIER
PONGIEST
PONGING
PONGO
PONGOES
PONGOS
PONGS
PONGY
PONIARD
PONIARDED
PONIARDING
PONIARDS
PONIED
PONIES
PONK
PONKED
PONKING
PONKS
PONS
PONTAGE
PONTAGES
PONTAL
PONTES
PONTIANAC
PONTIANACS
PONTIANAK
PONTIANAKS
PONTIC
PONTIE
PONTIES
PONTIFEX
PONTIFF
PONTIFFS
PONTIFIC
PONTIFICE
PONTIFICES
PONTIFIED
PONTIFIES
PONTIFY
PONTIFYING
PONTIL
PONTILE
PONTILS
PONTLEVIS
PONTLEVISES
PONTON
PONTONEER
PONTONEERS
PONTONIER
PONTONIERS
PONTONS
PONTOON
PONTOONED
PONTOONER
PONTOONERS
PONTOONING
PONTOONS
PONTY
PONY
PONYING

POO
POOCH
POOCHES
POOD
POODLE
POODLES
POODS
POOED
POOF
POOFIER
POOFIEST
POOFS
POOFTAH
POOFTAHS
POOFTER
POOFTERS
POOFY
POOGYE
POOGYEE
POOGYEES
POOGYES
POOH
POOING
POOJA
POOJAH
POOJAHS
POOJAS
POOK
POOKA
POOKAS
POOKING
POOKIT
POOKS
POOL
POOLED
POOLING
POOLS
POOLSIDE
POOLSIDES
POON
POONAC
POONACS
POONS
POONTANG
POONTANGS
POOP
POOPED
POOPING
POOPS
POOR
POORER
POOREST
POORHOUSE
POORHOUSES
POORISH
POORLIER
POORLIEST
POORLY
POORNESS
POORNESSES
POORT
POORTITH
POORTITHS
POORTS
POORWILL
POORWILLS
POOS
POOT
POOTED
POOTER

POOTERS
POOTING
POOTS
POOVE
POOVERIES
POOVERY
POOVES
POOVIER
POOVIEST
POOVY
POP
POPADUM
POPADUMS
POPCORN
POPCORNS
POPE
POPEDOM
POPEDOMS
POPEHOOD
POPEHOODS
POPELING
POPELINGS
POPERIES
POPERIN
POPERINS
POPERY
POPES
POPESHIP
POPESHIPS
POPINJAY
POPINJAYS
POPISH
POPISHLY
POPJOY
POPJOYED
POPJOYING
POPJOYS
POPLAR
POPLARS
POPLIN
POPLINS
POPLITEAL
POPLITIC
POPOVER
POPOVERS
POPPA
POPPADUM
POPPADUMS
POPPAS
POPPED
POPPER
POPPERING
POPPERINGS
POPPERS
POPPET
POPPETS
POPPIED
POPPIES
POPPING
POPPIT
POPPITS
POPPLE
POPPLED
POPPLES
POPPLIER
POPPLIEST
POPPLING
POPPLY
POPPY
POPPYCOCK

POPPYCOCKS
POPRIN
POPRINS
POPS
POPSIES
POPSY
POPULACE
POPULACES
POPULAR
POPULARLY
POPULARS
POPULATE
POPULATED
POPULATES
POPULATING
POPULISM
POPULISMS
POPULIST
POPULISTS
POPULOUS
PORAL
PORBEAGLE
PORBEAGLES
PORCELAIN
PORCELAINS
PORCH
PORCHES
PORCINE
PORCPISCE
PORCPISCES
PORCUPINE
PORCUPINES
PORE
PORED
PORER
PORERS
PORES
PORGE
PORGED
PORGES
PORGIE
PORGIES
PORGING
PORGY
PORIER
PORIEST
PORIFER
PORIFERAL
PORIFERAN
PORIFERS
PORINESS
PORINESSES
PORING
PORISM
PORISMS
PORISTIC
PORK
PORKER
PORKERS
PORKIER
PORKIEST
PORKLING
PORKLINGS
PORKS
PORKY
PORN
PORNO
PORNOMAG
PORNOMAGS
PORNOS

PORNS
POROGAMIC
POROGAMIES
POROGAMY
POROMERIC
POROSCOPE
POROSCOPES
POROSCOPIES
POROSCOPY
POROSE
POROSES
POROSIS
POROSITIES
POROSITY
POROUS
PORPESS
PORPESSE
PORPESSES
PORPHYRIA
PORPHYRIAS
PORPHYRIES
PORPHYRIO
PORPHYRIOS
PORPHYRY
PORPOISE
PORPOISED
PORPOISES
PORPOISING
PORPORATE
PORRECT
PORRECTED
PORRECTING
PORRECTS
PORRENGER
PORRENGERS
PORRIDGE
PORRIDGES
PORRIGO
PORRIGOS
PORRINGER
PORRINGERS
PORT
PORTA
PORTABLE
PORTABLES
PORTAGE
PORTAGES
PORTAGUE
PORTAGUES
PORTAL
PORTALS
PORTANCE
PORTANCES
PORTAS
PORTASES
PORTATE
PORTATILE
PORTATIVE
PORTATIVES
PORTED
PORTEND
PORTENDED
PORTENDING
PORTENDS
PORTENT
PORTENTS
PORTEOUS
PORTEOUSES
PORTER
PORTERAGE

PORTERAGES
PORTERESS
PORTERESSES
PORTERLY
PORTERS
PORTESS
PORTESSE
PORTESSES
PORTFOLIO
PORTFOLIOS
PORTHOLE
PORTHOLES
PORTHORS
PORTHORSES
PORTHOS
PORTHOSES
PORTHOUSE
PORTHOUSES
PORTICO
PORTICOED
PORTICOES
PORTICOS
PORTIER
PORTIÈRE
PORTIÈRES
PORTIEST
PORTIGUE
PORTIGUES
PORTING
PORTION
PORTIONED
PORTIONER
PORTIONERS
PORTIONING
PORTIONS
PORTLAND
PORTLANDS
PORTLAST
PORTLASTS
PORTLIER
PORTLIEST
PORTLY
PORTMAN
PORTMEN
PORTOISE
PORTOISES
PORTOLAN
PORTOLANI
PORTOLANO
PORTOLANOS
PORTOLANS
PORTOUS
PORTOUSES
PORTRAIT
PORTRAITED
PORTRAITING
PORTRAITS
PORTRAY
PORTRAYAL
PORTRAYALS
PORTRAYED
PORTRAYER
PORTRAYERS
PORTRAYING
PORTRAYS
PORTREEVE
PORTREEVES
PORTRESS
PORTRESSES
PORTS

PORTULACA
PORTULACAS
PORTULAN
PORTULANS
PORTY
PORWIGGLE
PORWIGGLES
PORY
POS
POSADA
POSADAS
POSAUNE
POSAUNES
POSE
POSÉ
POSEABLE
POSED
POSER
POSERS
POSES
POSEUR
POSEURS
POSEUSE
POSEUSES
POSH
POSHED
POSHER
POSHES
POSHEST
POSHING
POSHLY
POSHNESS
POSHNESSES
POSHTEEN
POSHTEENS
POSIES
POSIGRADE
POSING
POSINGLY
POSINGS
POSIT
POSITED
POSITING
POSITION
POSITIONED
POSITIONING
POSITIONS
POSITIVE
POSITIVES
POSITON
POSITONS
POSITRON
POSITRONS
POSITS
POSNET
POSNETS
POSOLOGIES
POSOLOGY
POSS
POSSE
POSSED
POSSER
POSSERS
POSSES
POSSESS
POSSESSED
POSSESSES
POSSESSING
POSSESSOR
POSSESSORS

POSSET
POSSETED
POSSETING
POSSETS
POSSIBLE
POSSIBLES
POSSIBLY
POSSIE
POSSIES
POSSING
POSSUM
POSSUMED
POSSUMING
POSSUMS
POST
POSTAGE
POSTAGES
POSTAL
POSTALS
POSTCARD
POSTCARDED
POSTCARDING
POSTCARDS
POSTCODE
POSTCODED
POSTCODES
POSTCODING
POSTDATE
POSTDATED
POSTDATES
POSTDATING
POSTED
POSTEEN
POSTEENS
POSTER
POSTERED
POSTERING
POSTERIOR
POSTERIORS
POSTERITIES
POSTERITY
POSTERN
POSTERNS
POSTERS
POSTFACE
POSTFACES
POSTFIX
POSTFIXED
POSTFIXES
POSTFIXING
POSTHASTE
POSTHASTES
POSTHORSE
POSTHORSES
POSTHOUSE
POSTHOUSES
POSTICHE
POSTICHES
POSTICOUS
POSTIE
POSTIES
POSTIL
POSTILION
POSTILIONS
POSTILLED
POSTILLER
POSTILLERS
POSTILLING
POSTILS
POSTING

POSTINGS
POSTLUDE
POSTLUDES
POSTMAN
POSTMARK
POSTMARKS
POSTMEN
POSTPONE
POSTPONED
POSTPONER
POSTPONERS
POSTPONES
POSTPONING
POSTS
POSTULANT
POSTULANTS
POSTULATA
POSTULATE
POSTULATED
POSTULATES
POSTULATING
POSTURAL
POSTURE
POSTURED
POSTURER
POSTURERS
POSTURES
POSTURING
POSTURIST
POSTURISTS
POSTWOMAN
POSTWOMEN
POSY
POT
POTABLE
POTABLES
POTAGE
POTAGES
POTAMIC
POTASH
POTASHED
POTASHES
POTASHING
POTASS
POTASSA
POTASSAS
POTASSES
POTASSIC
POTASSIUM
POTASSIUMS
POTATION
POTATIONS
POTATO
POTATOES
POTATORY
POTCH
POTCHE
POTCHED
POTCHER
POTCHERS
POTCHES
POTCHING
POTE
POTED
POTEEN
POTEENS
POTENCE
POTENCÉ
POTENCES
POTENCÉS

POTENCIES
POTENCY
POTENT
POTENTATE
POTENTATES
POTENTIAL
POTENTIALS
POTENTISE
POTENTISED
POTENTISES
POTENTISING
POTENTIZE
POTENTIZED
POTENTIZES
POTENTIZING
POTENTLY
POTENTS
POTES
POTFUL
POTFULS
POTGUN
POTGUNS
POTHECARIES
POTHECARY
POTHEEN
POTHEENS
POTHER
POTHERED
POTHERING
POTHERS
POTHERY
POTHOLE
POTHOLER
POTHOLERS
POTHOLES
POTHOLING
POTHOLINGS
POTHOOK
POTHOOKS
POTHOUSE
POTHOUSES
POTICARIES
POTICARY
POTICHE
POTICHES
POTIN
POTING
POTINS
POTION
POTIONS
POTLACH
POTLACHES
POTLATCH
POTLATCHES
POTOMETER
POTOMETERS
POTOROO
POTOROOS
POTS
POTSHERD
POTSHERDS
POTSTONE
POTSTONES
POTT
POTTAGE
POTTAGES
POTTED
POTTER
POTTERED
POTTERER

POTTERERS
POTTERIES
POTTERING
POTTERINGS
POTTERS
POTTERY
POTTIER
POTTIES
POTTIEST
POTTINESS
POTTINESSES
POTTING
POTTINGAR
POTTINGARS
POTTINGER
POTTINGERS
POTTLE
POTTLES
POTTO
POTTOS
POTTS
POTTY
POUCH
POUCHED
POUCHES
POUCHFUL
POUCHFULS
POUCHIER
POUCHIEST
POUCHING
POUCHY
POUDER
POUDERS
POUDRE
POUDRES
POUF
POUFED
POUFFE
POUFFES
POUFS
POUFTAH
POUFTAHS
POUFTER
POUFTERS
POUK
POUKE
POUKES
POUKING
POUKIT
POUKS
POULAINE
POULAINES
POULARD
POULARDS
POULDER
POULDERS
POULDRE
POULDRES
POULDRON
POULDRONS
POULE
POULES
POULP
POULPE
POULPES
POULPS
POULT
POULTER
POULTERER
POULTERERS

POULTERS
POULTICE
POULTICED
POULTICES
POULTICING
POULTRIES
POULTRY
POULTS
POUNCE
POUNCED
POUNCES
POUNCET
POUNCETS
POUNCHING
POUNCING
POUND
POUNDAGE
POUNDAGES
POUNDAL
POUNDALS
POUNDED
POUNDER
POUNDERS
POUNDING
POUNDS
POUPE
POUPED
POUPES
POUPING
POUPT
POUR
POURABLE
POURBOIRE
POURBOIRES
POURED
POURER
POURERS
POURIE
POURIES
POURING
POURINGS
POURPOINT
POURPOINTS
POURS
POURSEW
POURSEWED
POURSEWING
POURSEWS
POURSUE
POURSUED
POURSUES
POURSUING
POURSUIT
POURSUITS
POURSUITT
POURSUITTS
POURTRAHED
POURTRAY
POURTRAYD
POURTRAYED
POURTRAYING
POURTRAYS
POUSOWDIE
POUSOWDIES
POUSSE
POUSSES
POUSSETTE
POUSSETTED
POUSSETTES
POUSSETTING

POUSSIN
POUSSINS
POUT
POUTED
POUTER
POUTERS
POUTHER
POUTHERED
POUTHERING
POUTHERS
POUTIER
POUTIEST
POUTING
POUTINGLY
POUTINGS
POUTS
POUTY
POVERTIES
POVERTY
POW
POWAN
POWANS
POWDER
POWDERED
POWDERIER
POWDERIEST
POWDERING
POWDERS
POWDERY
POWELLISE
POWELLISED
POWELLISES
POWELLISING
POWELLITE
POWELLITES
POWELLIZE
POWELLIZED
POWELLIZES
POWELLIZING
POWER
POWERBOAT
POWERBOATS
POWERED
POWERFUL
POWERING
POWERLESS
POWERPLAY
POWERPLAYS
POWERS
POWIN
POWINS
POWN
POWND
POWNDED
POWNDING
POWNDS
POWNEY
POWNEYS
POWNIE
POWNIES
POWNS
POWNY
POWRE
POWRED
POWRES
POWRING
POWS
POWSOWDIES
POWSOWDY
POWTER

POWTERED
POWTERING
POWTERS
POWWAW
POWWOW
POWWOWED
POWWOWING
POWWOWS
POX
POXED
POXES
POXIER
POXIEST
POXING
POXVIRUS
POXVIRUSES
POXY
POYNANT
POYNT
POYNTED
POYNTING
POYNTS
POYSE
POYSED
POYSES
POYSING
POYSON
POYSONED
POYSONING
POYSONS
POZ
POZZ
POZZIES
POZZOLANA
POZZOLANAS
POZZY
PRAAM
PRAAMS
PRABBLE
PRABBLES
PRACTIC
PRACTICAL
PRACTICALS
PRACTICE
PRACTICED
PRACTICES
PRACTICING
PRACTICK
PRACTICKS
PRACTICS
PRACTICUM
PRACTICUMS
PRACTIQUE
PRACTIQUES
PRACTISE
PRACTISED
PRACTISER
PRACTISERS
PRACTISES
PRACTISING
PRACTIVE
PRACTOLOL
PRACTOLOLS
PRAD
PRADS
PRAEAMBLE
PRAEAMBLES
PRAECOCES
PRAEDIAL
PRAEDIALS

PRAEFECT
PRAEFECTS
PRAELUDIA
PRAENOMEN
PRAENOMENS
PRAENOMINA
PRAESES
PRAESIDIA
PRAETOR
PRAETORS
PRAGMATIC
PRAGMATICS
PRAHU
PRAHUS
PRAIRIE
PRAIRIED
PRAIRIES
PRAISE
PRAISEACH
PRAISEACHS
PRAISED
PRAISEFUL
PRAISER
PRAISERS
PRAISES
PRAISING
PRAISINGS
PRALINE
PRALINES
PRAM
PRAMS
PRANA
PRANAS
PRANAYAMA
PRANAYAMAS
PRANCE
PRANCED
PRANCER
PRANCERS
PRANCES
PRANCING
PRANCINGS
PRANCK
PRANCKE
PRANCKED
PRANCKES
PRANCKING
PRANCKS
PRANDIAL
PRANG
PRANGED
PRANGING
PRANGS
PRANK
PRANKED
PRANKFUL
PRANKIER
PRANKIEST
PRANKING
PRANKINGS
PRANKISH
PRANKLE
PRANKLED
PRANKLES
PRANKLING
PRANKS
PRANKSOME
PRANKSTER
PRANKSTERS
PRANKY

PRASE
PRASES
PRAT
PRATE
PRATED
PRATER
PRATERS
PRATES
PRATFALL
PRATFALLEN
PRATFALLING
PRATFALLS
PRATFELL
PRATIE
PRATIES
PRATING
PRATINGLY
PRATINGS
PRATIQUE
PRATIQUES
PRATS
PRATTED
PRATTING
PRATTLE
PRATTLED
PRATTLER
PRATTLERS
PRATTLES
PRATTLING
PRATY
PRAU
PRAUNCE
PRAUNCED
PRAUNCES
PRAUNCING
PRAUS
PRAVITIES
PRAVITY
PRAWLE
PRAWLES
PRAWLIN
PRAWLINS
PRAWN
PRAWNED
PRAWNING
PRAWNS
PRAXES
PRAXIS
PRAY
PRAYED
PRAYER
PRAYERFUL
PRAYERS
PRAYING
PRAYINGLY
PRAYINGS
PRAYS
PRE
PREACE
PREACED
PREACES
PREACH
PREACHED
PREACHER
PREACHERS
PREACHES
PREACHIER
PREACHIEST
PREACHIFIED
PREACHIFIES

PREACHIFY
PREACHIFYING
PREACHILY
PREACHING
PREACHINGS
PREACHY
PREACING
PREAMBLE
PREAMBLED
PREAMBLES
PREAMBLING
PREASE
PREASED
PREASES
PREASING
PREASSE
PREASSED
PREASSES
PREASSING
PREBEND
PREBENDAL
PREBENDS
PREBIOTIC
PRECAST
PRECATIVE
PRECATORY
PRECEDE
PRECEDED
PRECEDENT
PRECEDENTS
PRECEDES
PRECEDING
PRECEESE
PRECENTOR
PRECENTORS
PRECEPIT
PRECEPITS
PRECEPT
PRECEPTOR
PRECEPTORS
PRECEPTS
PRECESS
PRECESSED
PRECESSES
PRECESSING
PRÉCIEUSE
PRÉCIEUSES
PRECINCT
PRECINCTS
PRECIOUS
PRECIOUSES
PRECIPICE
PRECIPICES
PRÉCIS
PRECISE
PRÉCISED
PRECISELY
PRECISER
PRÉCISES
PRECISEST
PRECISIAN
PRECISIANS
PRÉCISING
PRECISION
PRECISIONS
PRECISIVE
PRECLUDE
PRECLUDED
PRECLUDES
PRECLUDING

PRECOCIAL
PRECOCITIES
PRECOCITY
PRECONISE
PRECONISED
PRECONISING
PRECONIZE
PRECONIZED
PRECONIZES
PRECONIZING
PRECOOK
PRECOOKED
PRECOOKING
PRECOOKS
PRECURRER
PRECURRERS
PRECURSE
PRECURSES
PRECURSOR
PRECURSORS
PREDACITIES
PREDACITY
PREDATE
PREDATED
PREDATES
PREDATING
PREDATION
PREDATIONS
PREDATIVE
PREDATOR
PREDATORS
PREDATORY
PREDEFINE
PREDEFINED
PREDEFINES
PREDEFINING
PREDELLA
PREDELLAS
PREDESIGN
PREDESIGNED
PREDESIGNING
PREDESIGNS
PREDEVOTE
PREDIAL
PREDIALS
PREDICANT
PREDICANTS
PREDICATE
PREDICATED
PREDICATES
PREDICATING
PREDICT
PREDICTED
PREDICTING
PREDICTOR
PREDICTORS
PREDICTS
PREDIED
PREDIES
PREDIGEST
PREDIGESTED
PREDIGESTING
PREDIGESTS
PREDIKANT
PREDIKANTS
PREDILECT
PREDOOM
PREDOOMED
PREDOOMING

PREDOOMS
PREDY
PREDYING
PREE
PREED
PREEING
PREEMIE
PREEMIES
PREEN
PREENED
PREENING
PREENS
PREES
PREEVE
PREEVED
PREEVES
PREEVING
PREFAB
PREFABS
PREFACE
PREFACED
PREFACES
PREFACIAL
PREFACING
PREFADE
PREFADED
PREFADES
PREFADING
PREFARD
PREFATORY
PREFECT
PREFECTS
PREFER
PREFERRED
PREFERRER
PREFERRERS
PREFERRING
PREFERS
PREFIGURE
PREFIGURED
PREFIGURES
PREFIGURING
PREFIX
PREFIXED
PREFIXES
PREFIXING
PREFIXION
PREFIXIONS
PREFLIGHT
PREFORM
PREFORMED
PREFORMING
PREFORMS
PREGGERS
PREGNABLE
PREGNANCE
PREGNANCES
PREGNANCIES
PREGNANCY
PREGNANT
PREHALLUCES
PREHALLUX
PREHEAT
PREHEATED
PREHEATING
PREHEATS
PREHEND
PREHENDED
PREHENDING
PREHENDS

PREHENSOR
PREHENSORS
PREHNITE
PREHNITES
PREHUMAN
PREIF
PREIFE
PREIFES
PREIFS
PREJINK
PREJUDGE
PREJUDGED
PREJUDGES
PREJUDGING
PREJUDICE
PREJUDICED
PREJUDICES
PREJUDICING
PREJUDIZE
PREJUDIZES
PRELACIES
PRELACY
PRELATE
PRELATES
PRELATESS
PRELATESSES
PRELATIAL
PRELATIC
PRELATIES
PRELATION
PRELATIONS
PRELATISE
PRELATISED
PRELATISES
PRELATISH
PRELATISING
PRELATISM
PRELATISMS
PRELATIST
PRELATISTS
PRELATIZE
PRELATIZED
PRELATIZES
PRELATIZING
PRELATURE
PRELATURES
PRELATY
PRELECT
PRELECTED
PRELECTING
PRELECTOR
PRELECTORS
PRELECTS
PRELIM
PRELIMS
PRELUDE
PRELUDED
PRELUDES
PRELUDI
PRELUDIAL
PRELUDING
PRELUDIO
PRELUSION
PRELUSIONS
PRELUSIVE
PRELUSORY
PREMATURE
PREMED
PREMEDIC
PREMEDICS

PREMEDS
PREMIA
PREMIE
PREMIER
PREMIÈRE
PREMIÈRED
PREMIÈRES
PREMIÈRING
PREMIERS
PREMIES
PREMISE
PREMISED
PREMISES
PREMISING
PREMISS
PREMISSES
PREMIUM
PREMIUMS
PREMIX
PREMIXED
PREMIXES
PREMIXING
PREMOLAR
PREMOLARS
PREMONISH
PREMONISHED
PREMONISHES
PREMONISHING
PREMORSE
PREMOSAIC
PREMOTION
PREMOTIONS
PREMOVE
PREMOVED
PREMOVES
PREMOVING
PREMY
PRENASAL
PRENASALS
PRENATAL
PRENOTION
PRENOTIONS
PRENT
PRENTICE
PRENTICES
PRENTS
PRENUBILE
PRENZIE
PREOCCUPIED
PREOCCUPIES
PREOCCUPY
PREOCCUPYING
PREOPTION
PREOPTIONS
PREORAL
PREORALLY
PREORDAIN
PREORDAINED
PREORDAINING
PREORDAINS
PREORDER
PREORDERED
PREORDERING
PREORDERS
PREP
PREPACK
PREPACKED
PREPACKING
PREPACKS
PREPAID

PREPARE
PREPARED
PREPARER
PREPARERS
PREPARES
PREPARING
PREPAY
PREPAYING
PREPAYS
PREPENSE
PREPENSED
PREPENSES
PREPENSING
PREPOLLEX
PREPOLLICES
PREPOTENT
PREPPED
PREPPIER
PREPPIES
PREPPIEST
PREPPING
PREPPY
PREPS
PREPUCE
PREPUCES
PREPUTIAL
PREQUEL
PREQUELS
PRERECORD
PRERECORDED
PRERECORDING
PRERECORDS
PREROSION
PREROSIONS
PRERUPT
PRESA
PRESAGE
PRESAGED
PRESAGER
PRESAGERS
PRESAGES
PRESAGING
PRESBYOPE
PRESBYOPES
PRESBYOPIES
PRESBYOPY
PRESBYTE
PRESBYTER
PRESBYTERS
PRESBYTES
PRESCHOOL
PRESCIENT
PRESCIND
PRESCINDED
PRESCINDING
PRESCINDS
PRESCIOUS
PRESCRIBE
PRESCRIBED
PRESCRIBES
PRESCRIBING
PRESCRIPT
PRESCRIPTS
PRESCUTA
PRESCUTUM
PRESE
PRESELECT
PRESELECTED
PRESELECTING
PRESELECTS

PRESENCE
PRESENCES
PRESENT
PRESENTED
PRESENTEE
PRESENTEES
PRESENTER
PRESENTERS
PRESENTING
PRESENTLY
PRESENTS
PRESERVE
PRESERVED
PRESERVER
PRESERVERS
PRESERVES
PRESERVING
PRESES
PRESET
PRESETS
PRESETTING
PRESIDE
PRESIDED
PRESIDENT
PRESIDENTS
PRESIDES
PRESIDIA
PRESIDIAL
PRESIDING
PRESIDIO
PRESIDIOS
PRESIDIUM
PRESIDIUMS
PRESS
PRESSED
PRESSER
PRESSERS
PRESSES
PRESSFAT
PRESSFATS
PRESSFUL
PRESSFULS
PRESSING
PRESSINGS
PRESSION
PRESSIONS
PRESSMAN
PRESSMEN
PRESSOR
PRESSURE
PRESSURED
PRESSURES
PRESSURING
PREST
PRESTED
PRESTIGE
PRESTIGES
PRESTING
PRESTO
PRESTOS
PRESTS
PRESUME
PRESUMED
PRESUMER
PRESUMERS
PRESUMES
PRESUMING
PRETENCE
PRETENCES
PRETEND

PRETENDED
PRETENDER
PRETENDERS
PRETENDING
PRETENDS
PRETENSE
PRETENSES
PRETERIST
PRETERISTS
PRETERIT
PRETERITE
PRETERITES
PRETERITS
PRETERM
PRETERMIT
PRETERMITS
PRETERMITTED
PRETERMITTING
PRETEXT
PRETEXTS
PRETTIER
PRETTIES
PRETTIEST
PRETTIFIED
PRETTIFIES
PRETTIFY
PRETTIFYING
PRETTILY
PRETTY
PRETTYISH
PRETTYISM
PRETTYISMS
PRETZEL
PRETZELS
PREVAIL
PREVAILED
PREVAILING
PREVAILS
PREVALENT
PREVE
PREVED
PREVENE
PREVENED
PREVENES
PREVENING
PREVENT
PREVENTED
PREVENTER
PREVENTERS
PREVENTING
PREVENTS
PREVERB
PREVERBAL
PREVERBS
PREVES
PREVIEW
PREVIEWED
PREVIEWING
PREVIEWS
PREVING
PREVIOUS
PREVISE
PREVISED
PREVISES
PREVISING
PREVISION
PREVISIONS
PREWYN
PREWYNS
PREX

PREXES
PREXIES
PREXY
PREY
PREYED
PREYFUL
PREYING
PREYS
PREZZIE
PREZZIES
PRIAL
PRIALS
PRIAPIC
PRIAPISM
PRIAPISMS
PRIBBLE
PRIBBLES
PRICE
PRICED
PRICELESS
PRICER
PRICERS
PRICES
PRICEY
PRICIER
PRICIEST
PRICINESS
PRICINESSES
PRICING
PRICK
PRICKED
PRICKER
PRICKERS
PRICKET
PRICKETS
PRICKING
PRICKINGS
PRICKLE
PRICKLED
PRICKLES
PRICKLIER
PRICKLIEST
PRICKLING
PRICKLINGS
PRICKLY
PRICKS
PRICKWOOD
PRICKWOODS
PRICY
PRIDE
PRIDED
PRIDEFUL
PRIDELESS
PRIDES
PRIDIAN
PRIDING
PRIED
PRIEF
PRIEFE
PRIEFES
PRIEFS
PRIER
PRIERS
PRIES
PRIEST
PRIESTED
PRIESTESS
PRIESTESSES
PRIESTING
PRIESTLY

PRIESTS
PRIEVE
PRIEVED
PRIEVES
PRIEVING
PRIG
PRIGGED
PRIGGER
PRIGGERIES
PRIGGERS
PRIGGERY
PRIGGING
PRIGGINGS
PRIGGISH
PRIGGISM
PRIGGISMS
PRIGS
PRILL
PRILLED
PRILLING
PRILLS
PRIM
PRIMA
PRIMACIES
PRIMACY
PRIMAEVAL
PRIMAGE
PRIMAGES
PRIMAL
PRIMALITIES
PRIMALITY
PRIMALLY
PRIMARIES
PRIMARILY
PRIMARY
PRIMATAL
PRIMATE
PRIMATES
PRIMATIAL
PRIMATIC
PRIME
PRIMED
PRIMELY
PRIMENESS
PRIMENESSES
PRIMER
PRIMERO
PRIMEROS
PRIMERS
PRIMES
PRIMEUR
PRIMEURS
PRIMEVAL
PRIMINE
PRIMINES
PRIMING
PRIMINGS
PRIMIPARA
PRIMIPARAE
PRIMIPARAS
PRIMITIAE
PRIMITIAL
PRIMITIAS
PRIMITIVE
PRIMITIVES
PRIMLY
PRIMMED
PRIMMER
PRIMMEST
PRIMMING

PRIMNESS
PRIMNESSES
PRIMO
PRIMORDIA
PRIMOS
PRIMP
PRIMPED
PRIMPING
PRIMPS
PRIMROSE
PRIMROSED
PRIMROSES
PRIMROSING
PRIMROSY
PRIMS
PRIMSIE
PRIMULA
PRIMULAS
PRIMULINE
PRIMULINES
PRIMUS
PRIMUSES
PRIMY
PRINCE
PRINCED
PRINCEDOM
PRINCEDOMS
PRINCEKIN
PRINCEKINS
PRINCELET
PRINCELETS
PRINCELIER
PRINCELIEST
PRINCELY
PRINCES
PRINCESS
PRINCESSE
PRINCESSES
PRINCING
PRINCIPAL
PRINCIPALS
PRINCIPIA
PRINCIPLE
PRINCIPLED
PRINCIPLES
PRINCIPLING
PRINCOCK
PRINCOCKS
PRINCOX
PRINCOXES
PRINK
PRINKED
PRINKING
PRINKS
PRINT
PRINTABLE
PRINTED
PRINTER
PRINTERS
PRINTING
PRINTINGS
PRINTLESS
PRINTS
PRION
PRIONS
PRIOR
PRIORATE
PRIORATES
PRIORESS
PRIORESSES

PRIORIES
PRIORITIES
PRIORITY
PRIORS
PRIORSHIP
PRIORSHIPS
PRIORY
PRISAGE
PRISAGES
PRISE
PRISED
PRISER
PRISERS
PRISES
PRISING
PRISM
PRISMATIC
PRISMOID
PRISMOIDS
PRISMS
PRISMY
PRISON
PRISONED
PRISONER
PRISONERS
PRISONING
PRISONOUS
PRISONS
PRISSIER
PRISSIEST
PRISSY
PRISTINE
PRITHEE
PRIVACIES
PRIVACY
PRIVADO
PRIVADOES
PRIVADOS
PRIVATE
PRIVATEER
PRIVATEERED
PRIVATEERING
PRIVATEERINGS
PRIVATEERS
PRIVATELY
PRIVATES
PRIVATION
PRIVATIONS
PRIVATISE
PRIVATISED
PRIVATISES
PRIVATISING
PRIVATIVE
PRIVATIVES
PRIVATIZE
PRIVATIZED
PRIVATIZES
PRIVATIZING
PRIVET
PRIVETS
PRIVIER
PRIVIES
PRIVIEST
PRIVILEGE
PRIVILEGED
PRIVILEGES
PRIVILEGING
PRIVILY
PRIVITIES
PRIVITY

PRIVY
PRIZABLE
PRIZE
PRIZED
PRIZER
PRIZERS
PRIZES
PRIZING
PRO
PROA
PROAS
PROBABLE
PROBABLES
PROBABLY
PROBALL
PROBAND
PROBANDS
PROBANG
PROBANGS
PROBATE
PROBATED
PROBATES
PROBATING
PROBATION
PROBATIONS
PROBATIVE
PROBATORY
PROBE
PROBED
PROBES
PROBING
PROBIT
PROBITIES
PROBITS
PROBITY
PROBLEM
PROBLEMS
PROBOSCIDES
PROBOSCIS
PROBOSCISES
PROCACITIES
PROCACITY
PROCAINE
PROCAINES
PROCARYON
PROCARYONS
PROCEDURE
PROCEDURES
PROCEED
PROCEEDED
PROCEEDER
PROCEEDERS
PROCEEDING
PROCEEDINGS
PROCEEDS
PROCERITIES
PROCERITY
PROCESS
PROCESSED
PROCESSES
PROCESSING
PROCESSOR
PROCESSORS
PROCIDENT
PROCINCT
PROCINCTS
PROCLAIM
PROCLAIMED
PROCLAIMING
PROCLAIMS

PROCLISES
PROCLISIS
PROCLITIC
PROCLITICS
PROCLIVE
PROCONSUL
PROCONSULS
PROCREANT
PROCREANTS
PROCREATE
PROCREATED
PROCREATES
PROCREATING
PROCTAL
PROCTITIS
PROCTITISES
PROCTOR
PROCTORS
PROCURACIES
PROCURACY
PROCURE
PROCURED
PROCURER
PROCURERS
PROCURES
PROCURESS
PROCURESSES
PROCUREUR
PROCUREURS
PROCURING
PROD
PRODDED
PRODDING
PRODIGAL
PRODIGALS
PRODIGIES
PRODIGY
PRODITOR
PRODITORS
PRODITORY
PRODNOSE
PRODNOSED
PRODNOSES
PRODNOSING
PRODROMAL
PRODROME
PRODROMES
PRODROMI
PRODROMIC
PRODROMUS
PRODS
PRODUCE
PRODUCED
PRODUCER
PRODUCERS
PRODUCES
PRODUCING
PRODUCT
PRODUCTS
PROEM
PROEMBRYO
PROEMBRYOS
PROEMIAL
PROEMS
PROENZYME
PROENZYMES
PROF
PROFACE
PROFANE
PROFANED

PROFANELY
PROFANER
PROFANERS
PROFANES
PROFANING
PROFANITIES
PROFANITY
PROFESS
PROFESSED
PROFESSES
PROFESSING
PROFESSOR
PROFESSORS
PROFFER
PROFFERED
PROFFERER
PROFFERERS
PROFFERING
PROFFERS
PROFILE
PROFILED
PROFILER
PROFILERS
PROFILES
PROFILING
PROFILIST
PROFILISTS
PROFIT
PROFITED
PROFITEER
PROFITEERED
PROFITEERING
PROFITEERINGS
PROFITEERS
PROFITER
PROFITERS
PROFITING
PROFITINGS
PROFITS
PROFLUENT
PROFORMA
PROFORMAS
PROFOUND
PROFOUNDER
PROFOUNDEST
PROFOUNDS
PROFS
PROFUSE
PROFUSELY
PROFUSER
PROFUSERS
PROFUSION
PROFUSIONS
PROG
PROGENIES
PROGENY
PROGERIA
PROGERIAS
PROGESTIN
PROGESTINS
PROGGED
PROGGING
PROGGINS
PROGGINSES
PROGNOSES
PROGNOSIS
PROGRADE
PROGRADED
PROGRADES
PROGRADING

PROGRAM
PROGRAMME
PROGRAMMED
PROGRAMMES
PROGRAMMING
PROGRAMMINGS
PROGRAMS
PROGRESS
PROGRESSED
PROGRESSES
PROGRESSING
PROGS
PROHIBIT
PROHIBITED
PROHIBITING
PROHIBITS
PROIGN
PROIGNED
PROIGNING
PROIGNS
PROIN
PROINE
PROINED
PROINES
PROINING
PROINS
PROJECT
PROJECTED
PROJECTING
PROJECTINGS
PROJECTOR
PROJECTORS
PROJECTS
PROKARYON
PROKARYONS
PROKARYOT
PROKARYOTS
PROKE
PROKED
PROKER
PROKERS
PROKES
PROKING
PROLACTIN
PROLACTINS
PROLAMIN
PROLAMINE
PROLAMINES
PROLAMINS
PROLAPSE
PROLAPSED
PROLAPSES
PROLAPSING
PROLAPSUS
PROLAPSUSES
PROLATE
PROLATED
PROLATELY
PROLATES
PROLATING
PROLATION
PROLATIONS
PROLATIVE
PROLE
PROLED
PROLEG
PROLEGS
PROLEPSES
PROLEPSIS
PROLEPTIC

PROLER
PROLERS
PROLES
PROLETARIES
PROLETARY
PROLICIDE
PROLICIDES
PROLIFIC
PROLINE
PROLINES
PROLING
PROLIX
PROLIXITIES
PROLIXITY
PROLIXLY
PROLL
PROLLED
PROLLER
PROLLERS
PROLLING
PROLLS
PROLOGISE
PROLOGISED
PROLOGISES
PROLOGISING
PROLOGIZE
PROLOGIZED
PROLOGIZES
PROLOGIZING
PROLOGUE
PROLOGUED
PROLOGUES
PROLOGUING
PROLONG
PROLONGE
PROLONGED
PROLONGER
PROLONGERS
PROLONGES
PROLONGING
PROLONGS
PROLUSION
PROLUSIONS
PROLUSORY
PROM
PROMACHOS
PROMACHOSES
PROMENADE
PROMENADED
PROMENADES
PROMENADING
PROMETAL
PROMETALS
PROMINENT
PROMISE
PROMISED
PROMISEE
PROMISEES
PROMISER
PROMISERS
PROMISES
PROMISING
PROMISOR
PROMISORS
PROMISSOR
PROMISSORS
PROMMER
PROMMERS
PROMO
PROMOS

PROMOTE
PROMOTED
PROMOTER
PROMOTERS
PROMOTES
PROMOTING
PROMOTION
PROMOTIONS
PROMOTIVE
PROMOTOR
PROMOTORS
PROMPT
PROMPTED
PROMPTER
PROMPTERS
PROMPTEST
PROMPTING
PROMPTINGS
PROMPTLY
PROMPTS
PROMPTURE
PROMPTURES
PROMS
PROMULGE
PROMULGED
PROMULGING
PROMUSCES
PROMUSCIDES
PROMUSCIS
PROMUSCISES
PRONAOI
PRONAOS
PRONATE
PRONATED
PRONATES
PRONATING
PRONATION
PRONATIONS
PRONATOR
PRONATORS
PRONE
PRONELY
PRONENESS
PRONENESSES
PRONER
PRONES
PRONEST
PRONEUR
PRONEURS
PRONG
PRONGBUCK
PRONGBUCKS
PRONGED
PRONGHORN
PRONGHORNS
PRONGING
PRONGS
PRONOTA
PRONOTAL
PRONOTUM
PRONOUN
PRONOUNCE
PRONOUNCED
PRONOUNCES
PRONOUNCING
PRONOUNCINGS
PRONOUNS
PRONTO
PRONUCLEI

PROO
PROOEMION
PROOEMIONS
PROOEMIUM
PROOEMIUMS
PROOF
PROOFED
PROOFING
PROOFINGS
PROOFLESS
PROOFS
PROOTIC
PROOTICS
PROP
PROPAGATE
PROPAGATED
PROPAGATES
PROPAGATING
PROPAGE
PROPAGED
PROPAGES
PROPAGING
PROPAGULE
PROPAGULES
PROPALE
PROPALED
PROPALES
PROPALING
PROPANE
PROPANES
PROPEL
PROPELLED
PROPELLER
PROPELLERS
PROPELLING
PROPELS
PROPEND
PROPENDED
PROPENDING
PROPENDS
PROPENE
PROPENES
PROPENSE
PROPER
PROPERDIN
PROPERDINS
PROPERLY
PROPERS
PROPERTIED
PROPERTIES
PROPERTY
PROPERTYING
PROPHASE
PROPHASES
PROPHECIES
PROPHECY
PROPHESIED
PROPHESIES
PROPHESY
PROPHESYING
PROPHESYINGS
PROPHET
PROPHETIC
PROPHETS
PROPHYLL
PROPHYLLS
PROPINE
PROPINED
PROPINES
PROPINING

PROPODEON
PROPODEONS
PROPODEUM
PROPODEUMS
PROPOLIS
PROPOLISES
PROPONE
PROPONED
PROPONENT
PROPONENTS
PROPONES
PROPONING
PROPOSAL
PROPOSALS
PROPOSE
PROPOSED
PROPOSER
PROPOSERS
PROPOSES
PROPOSING
PROPOUND
PROPOUNDED
PROPOUNDING
PROPOUNDS
PROPPED
PROPPING
PROPRIETIES
PROPRIETY
PROPS
PROPTOSES
PROPTOSIS
PROPYL
PROPYLA
PROPYLAEA
PROPYLENE
PROPYLENES
PROPYLIC
PROPYLITE
PROPYLITES
PROPYLON
PROPYLS
PRORATE
PRORATED
PRORATES
PRORATING
PRORATION
PRORATIONS
PRORE
PRORECTOR
PRORECTORS
PRORES
PROROGATE
PROROGATED
PROROGATES
PROROGATING
PROROGUE
PROROGUED
PROROGUES
PROROGUING
PROS
PROSAIC
PROSAICAL
PROSAISM
PROSAISMS
PROSAIST
PROSAISTS
PROSATEUR
PROSATEURS
PROSCRIBE
PROSCRIBED

PROSCRIBES
PROSCRIBING
PROSCRIPT
PROSCRIPTS
PROSE
PROSECTOR
PROSECTORS
PROSECUTE
PROSECUTED
PROSECUTES
PROSECUTING
PROSED
PROSELYTE
PROSELYTED
PROSELYTES
PROSELYTING
PROSEMAN
PROSEMEN
PROSER
PROSERS
PROSES
PROSEUCHA
PROSEUCHAE
PROSEUCHE
PROSIER
PROSIEST
PROSILY
PROSIMIAN
PROSIMIANS
PROSINESS
PROSINESSES
PROSING
PROSINGS
PROSIT
PROSODIAL
PROSODIAN
PROSODIANS
PROSODIC
PROSODIES
PROSODIST
PROSODISTS
PROSODY
PROSOPON
PROSOPONS
PROSPECT
PROSPECTED
PROSPECTING
PROSPECTINGS
PROSPECTS
PROSPER
PROSPERED
PROSPERING
PROSPERS
PROSTATE
PROSTATES
PROSTATIC
PROSTRATE
PROSTRATED
PROSTRATES
PROSTRATING
PROSTYLE
PROSTYLES
PROSY
PROTAMINE
PROTAMINES
PROTANDRIES
PROTANDRY
PROTANOPE
PROTANOPES
PROTASES

PROTASIS
PROTATIC
PROTEA
PROTEAN
PROTEAS
PROTEASE
PROTEASES
PROTECT
PROTECTED
PROTECTING
PROTECTOR
PROTECTORS
PROTECTS
PROTÉGÉ
PROTÉGÉE
PROTÉGÉES
PROTÉGÉS
PROTEID
PROTEIDS
PROTEIN
PROTEINIC
PROTEINS
PROTEND
PROTENDED
PROTENDING
PROTENDS
PROTENSE
PROTENSES
PROTEST
PROTESTED
PROTESTER
PROTESTERS
PROTESTING
PROTESTOR
PROTESTORS
PROTESTS
PROTEUS
PROTEUSES
PROTHALLI
PROTHESES
PROTHESIS
PROTHETIC
PROTHORACES
PROTHORAX
PROTHORAXES
PROTHYL
PROTHYLE
PROTHYLES
PROTHYLS
PROTIST
PROTISTIC
PROTISTS
PROTIUM
PROTIUMS
PROTOCOL
PROTOCOLLED
PROTOCOLLING
PROTOCOLS
PROTOGINE
PROTOGINES
PROTOGYNIES
PROTOGYNY
PROTON
PROTONEMA
PROTONEMATA
PROTONIC
PROTONS
PROTOSTAR
PROTOSTARS
PROTOTYPE

PROTOTYPED
PROTOTYPES
PROTOTYPING
PROTOXIDE
PROTOXIDES
PROTOZOA
PROTOZOAN
PROTOZOANS
PROTOZOIC
PROTOZOON
PROTRACT
PROTRACTED
PROTRACTING
PROTRACTS
PROTRUDE
PROTRUDED
PROTRUDES
PROTRUDING
PROTYL
PROTYLE
PROTYLES
PROTYLS
PROUD
PROUDER
PROUDEST
PROUDISH
PROUDLY
PROUDNESS
PROUDNESSES
PROUL
PROULED
PROULER
PROULERS
PROULING
PROULS
PROUSTITE
PROUSTITES
PROVABLE
PROVABLY
PROVAND
PROVANDS
PROVANT
PROVE
PROVEABLE
PROVEABLY
PROVED
PROVEDOR
PROVEDORE
PROVEDORES
PROVEDORS
PROVEN
PROVEND
PROVENDER
PROVENDERED
PROVENDERING
PROVENDERS
PROVENDS
PROVER
PROVERB
PROVERBED
PROVERBING
PROVERBS
PROVERS
PROVES
PROVIANT
PROVIANTS
PROVIDE
PROVIDED
PROVIDENT
PROVIDER

PROVIDERS
PROVIDES
PROVIDING
PROVIDOR
PROVIDORS
PROVINCE
PROVINCES
PROVINE
PROVINED
PROVINES
PROVING
PROVINING
PROVIRAL
PROVIRUS
PROVIRUSES
PROVISION
PROVISIONED
PROVISIONING
PROVISIONS
PROVISO
PROVISOES
PROVISOR
PROVISORS
PROVISORY
PROVISOS
PROVOCANT
PROVOCANTS
PROVOKE
PROVOKED
PROVOKER
PROVOKERS
PROVOKES
PROVOKING
PROVOST
PROVOSTRIES
PROVOSTRY
PROVOSTS
PROW
PROWESS
PROWESSED
PROWESSES
PROWEST
PROWL
PROWLED
PROWLER
PROWLERS
PROWLING
PROWLINGS
PROWLS
PROWS
PROXIES
PROXIMAL
PROXIMATE
PROXIMITIES
PROXIMITY
PROXIMO
PROXY
PROYN
PROYNE
PROYNED
PROYNES
PROYNING
PROYNS
PROZYMITE
PROZYMITES
PRUDE
PRUDENCE
PRUDENCES
PRUDENT
PRUDENTLY

PRUDERIES
PRUDERY
PRUDES
PRUDISH
PRUDISHLY
PRUH
PRUINA
PRUINAS
PRUINE
PRUINES
PRUINOSE
PRUNE
PRUNED
PRUNELLA
PRUNELLAS
PRUNELLE
PRUNELLES
PRUNELLO
PRUNELLOS
PRUNER
PRUNERS
PRUNES
PRUNING
PRUNINGS
PRUNT
PRUNTED
PRUNTS
PRURIENCE
PRURIENCES
PRURIENCIES
PRURIENCY
PRURIENT
PRURIGO
PRURIGOS
PRURITIC
PRURITUS
PRURITUSES
PRUSSIATE
PRUSSIATES
PRUSSIC
PRY
PRYER
PRYERS
PRYING
PRYINGLY
PRYINGS
PRYS
PRYSE
PRYSED
PRYSES
PRYSING
PRYTANEA
PRYTANEUM
PRYTHEE
PSALM
PSALMIST
PSALMISTS
PSALMODIC
PSALMODIES
PSALMODY
PSALMS
PSALTER
PSALTERIA
PSALTERIES
PSALTERS
PSALTERY
PSALTRESS
PSALTRESSES
PSAMMITE
PSAMMITES

PSAMMITIC	PTARMIGANS	PUBLISHES	PUDSIER	PUISSAUNT
PSELLISM	PTERIA	PUBLISHING	PUDSIEST	PUJA
PSELLISMS	PTERIN	PUBS	PUDSY	PUJAS
PSEPHISM	PTERINS	PUCCOON	PUEBLO	PUKE
PSEPHISMS	PTERION	PUCCOONS	PUEBLOS	PUKED
PSEPHITE	PTEROPOD	PUCE	PUER	PUKER
PSEPHITES	PTEROPODS	PUCELAGE	PUERED	PUKERS
PSEPHITIC	PTEROSAUR	PUCELAGES	PUERILE	PUKES
PSEUD	PTEROSAURS	PUCELLE	PUERILISM	PUKING
PSEUDAXES	PTERYGIA	PUCELLES	PUERILISMS	PUKKA
PSEUDAXIS	PTERYGIAL	PUCES	PUERILITIES	PULDRON
PSEUDERIES	PTERYGIUM	PUCK	PUERILITY	PULDRONS
PSEUDERY	PTERYGOID	PUCKA	PUERING	PULE
PSEUDISH	PTERYGOIDS	PUCKER	PUERPERAL	PULED
PSEUDO	PTERYLA	PUCKERED	PUERS	PULER
PSEUDONYM	PTERYLAE	PUCKERING	PUFF	PULERS
PSEUDONYMS	PTILOSES	PUCKERS	PUFFBALL	PULES
PSEUDOPOD	PTILOSIS	PUCKERY	PUFFBALLS	PULICIDE
PSEUDOPODS	PTISAN	PUCKFIST	PUFFED	PULICIDES
PSEUDS	PTISANS	PUCKFISTS	PUFFER	PULIER
PSHAW	PTOMAINE	PUCKISH	PUFFERIES	PULIEST
PSHAWED	PTOMAINES	PUCKS	PUFFERS	PULING
PSHAWING	PTOSES	PUD	PUFFERY	PULINGLY
PSHAWS	PTOSIS	PUDDEN	PUFFIER	PULINGS
PSI	PTYALIN	PUDDENING	PUFFIEST	PULK
PSILOSES	PTYALINS	PUDDENINGS	PUFFILY	PULKA
PSILOSIS	PTYALISE	PUDDENS	PUFFIN	PULKAS
PSILOTIC	PTYALISED	PUDDER	PUFFINESS	PULKHA
PSIONIC	PTYALISES	PUDDERED	PUFFINESSES	PULKHAS
PSIS	PTYALISING	PUDDERING	PUFFING	PULKS
PSOAS	PTYALISM	PUDDERS	PUFFINGLY	PULL
PSOASES	PTYALISMS	PUDDIES	PUFFINGS	PULLED
PSORA	PTYALIZE	PUDDING	PUFFINS	PULLEN
PSORAS	PTYALIZED	PUDDINGS	PUFFS	PULLERS
PSORIASES	PTYALIZES	PUDDINGY	PUFFY	PULLET
PSORIASIS	PTYALIZING	PUDDLE	PUG	PULLETS
PSORIATIC	PTYXES	PUDDLED	PUGGAREE	PULLEY
PSORIC	PTYXIS	PUDDLER	PUGGAREES	PULLEYS
PSST	PTYXISES	PUDDLERS	PUGGED	PULLING
PST	PUB	PUDDLES	PUGGERIES	PULLOVER
PSYCH	PUBERAL	PUDDLIER	PUGGERY	PULLOVERS
PSYCHE	PUBERTAL	PUDDLIEST	PUGGIER	PULLS
PSYCHED	PUBERTIES	PUDDLING	PUGGIES	PULLULATE
PSYCHES	PUBERTY	PUDDLINGS	PUGGIEST	PULLULATED
PSYCHIC	PUBES	PUDDLY	PUGGING	PULLULATES
PSYCHICAL	PUBESCENT	PUDDOCK	PUGGINGS	PULLULATING
PSYCHICS	PUBIC	PUDDOCKS	PUGGISH	PULMO
PSYCHING	PUBIS	PUDDY	PUGGREE	PULMONARY
PSYCHISM	PUBISES	PUDENCIES	PUGGREES	PULMONATE
PSYCHISMS	PUBLIC	PUDENCY	PUGGY	PULMONATES
PSYCHIST	PUBLICAN	PUDENDA	PUGH	PULMONES
PSYCHISTS	PUBLICANS	PUDENDAL	PUGIL	PULMONIC
PSYCHO	PUBLICISE	PUDENDOUS	PUGILISM	PULMONICS
PSYCHOGAS	PUBLICISED	PUDENDUM	PUGILISMS	PULP
PSYCHOGASES	PUBLICISES	PUDENT	PUGILIST	PULPBOARD
PSYCHOID	PUBLICISING	PUDGE	PUGILISTS	PULPBOARDS
PSYCHOIDS	PUBLICIST	PUDGES	PUGILS	PULPED
PSYCHOS	PUBLICISTS	PUDGIER	PUGNACITIES	PULPER
PSYCHOSES	PUBLICITIES	PUDGIEST	PUGNACITY	PULPERS
PSYCHOSIS	PUBLICITY	PUDGINESS	PUGS	PULPIER
PSYCHOTIC	PUBLICIZE	PUDGINESSES	PUH	PULPIEST
PSYCHOTICS	PUBLICIZED	PUDGY	PUIR	PULPIFIED
PSYCHS	PUBLICIZES	PUDIBUND	PUIRER	PULPIFIES
PSYOP	PUBLICIZING	PUDIC	PUIREST	PULPIFY
PSYOPS	PUBLICLY	PUDICITIES	PUISNE	PULPIFYING
PSYWAR	PUBLICS	PUDICITY	PUISNES	PULPILY
PSYWARS	PUBLISH	PUDOR	PUISNY	PULPINESS
PTARMIC	PUBLISHED	PUDORS	PUISSANCE	PULPINESSES
PTARMICS	PUBLISHER	PUDS	PUISSANCES	PULPING
PTARMIGAN	PUBLISHERS	PUDSEY	PUISSANT	PULPIT

PULPITED
PULPITEER
PULPITEERS
PULPITER
PULPITERS
PULPITRIES
PULPITRY
PULPITS
PULPITUM
PULPITUMS
PULPMILL
PULPMILLS
PULPOUS
PULPS
PULPSTONE
PULPSTONES
PULPWOOD
PULPWOODS
PULPY
PULQUE
PULQUES
PULSAR
PULSARS
PULSATE
PULSATED
PULSATES
PULSATILE
PULSATING
PULSATION
PULSATIONS
PULSATIVE
PULSATOR
PULSATORS
PULSATORY
PULSE
PULSED
PULSEJET
PULSEJETS
PULSELESS
PULSES
PULSIDGE
PULSIDGES
PULSIFIC
PULSING
PULSOJET
PULSOJETS
PULTAN
PULTANS
PULTON
PULTONS
PULTOON
PULTOONS
PULTUN
PULTUNS
PULTURE
PULTURES
PULU
PULUS
PULVER
PULVERED
PULVERINE
PULVERINES
PULVERING
PULVERISE
PULVERISED
PULVERISES
PULVERISING
PULVERIZE
PULVERIZED
PULVERIZES

PULVERIZING
PULVEROUS
PULVERS
PULVIL
PULVILIO
PULVILIOS
PULVILLAR
PULVILLE
PULVILLED
PULVILLES
PULVILLI
PULVILLING
PULVILLIO
PULVILLIOS
PULVILLUS
PULVILS
PULVINAR
PULVINARS
PULVINATE
PULVINI
PULVINULE
PULVINULES
PULVINUS
PULWAR
PULWARS
PULY
PUMA
PUMAS
PUMELO
PUMELOS
PUMICATE
PUMICATED
PUMICATES
PUMICATING
PUMICE
PUMICED
PUMICEOUS
PUMICES
PUMICING
PUMIE
PUMIES
PUMMEL
PUMMELLED
PUMMELLING
PUMMELS
PUMP
PUMPED
PUMPER
PUMPERS
PUMPING
PUMPION
PUMPIONS
PUMPKIN
PUMPKINS
PUMPS
PUMY
PUN
PUNA
PUNALUA
PUNALUAN
PUNALUAS
PUNAS
PUNCE
PUNCES
PUNCH
PUNCHED
PUNCHEON
PUNCHEONS
PUNCHER
PUNCHERS

PUNCHES
PUNCHIER
PUNCHIEST
PUNCHING
PUNCHY
PUNCTA
PUNCTATE
PUNCTATED
PUNCTATOR
PUNCTATORS
PUNCTILIO
PUNCTILIOS
PUNCTO
PUNCTOS
PUNCTUAL
PUNCTUATE
PUNCTUATED
PUNCTUATES
PUNCTUATING
PUNCTULE
PUNCTULES
PUNCTUM
PUNCTURE
PUNCTURED
PUNCTURES
PUNCTURING
PUNDIT
PUNDITRIES
PUNDITRY
PUNDITS
PUNDONOR
PUNDONORES
PUNGENCE
PUNGENCES
PUNGENCIES
PUNGENCY
PUNGENT
PUNGENTLY
PUNIER
PUNIEST
PUNILY
PUNINESS
PUNINESSES
PUNISH
PUNISHED
PUNISHER
PUNISHERS
PUNISHES
PUNISHING
PUNITION
PUNITIONS
PUNITIVE
PUNITORY
PUNK
PUNKA
PUNKAH
PUNKAHS
PUNKAS
PUNKINESS
PUNKINESSES
PUNKS
PUNNED
PUNNER
PUNNERS
PUNNET
PUNNETS
PUNNING
PUNNINGS
PUNS
PUNSTER

PUNSTERS
PUNT
PUNTED
PUNTEE
PUNTEES
PUNTER
PUNTERS
PUNTIES
PUNTING
PUNTO
PUNTOS
PUNTS
PUNTSMAN
PUNTSMEN
PUNTY
PUNY
PUP
PUPA
PUPAE
PUPAL
PUPARIA
PUPARIAL
PUPARIUM
PUPAS
PUPATE
PUPATED
PUPATES
PUPATING
PUPATION
PUPATIONS
PUPFISH
PUPFISHES
PUPIL
PUPILAGE
PUPILAGES
PUPILARY
PUPILATE
PUPILLAGE
PUPILLAGES
PUPILLARY
PUPILLATE
PUPILS
PUPPED
PUPPET
PUPPETEER
PUPPETEERS
PUPPETRIES
PUPPETRY
PUPPETS
PUPPIED
PUPPIES
PUPPING
PUPPODUM
PUPPODUMS
PUPPY
PUPPYDOM
PUPPYDOMS
PUPPYHOOD
PUPPYHOODS
PUPPYING
PUPPYISH
PUPPYISM
PUPPYISMS
PUPS
PUPUNHA
PUPUNHAS
PUR
PURBLIND
PURCHASE
PURCHASED

PURCHASER
PURCHASERS
PURCHASES
PURCHASING
PURDAH
PURDAHS
PURDONIUM
PURDONIUMS
PURE
PURED
PURÉE
PURÉED
PURÉEING
PURÉES
PURELY
PURENESS
PURENESSES
PURER
PURES
PUREST
PURFLE
PURFLED
PURFLES
PURFLING
PURFLINGS
PURFLY
PURGATION
PURGATIONS
PURGATIVE
PURGATIVES
PURGATORIES
PURGATORY
PURGE
PURGED
PURGER
PURGERS
PURGES
PURGING
PURGINGS
PURI
PURIFIED
PURIFIER
PURIFIERS
PURIFIES
PURIFY
PURIFYING
PURIM
PURIMS
PURIN
PURINE
PURINES
PURING
PURINS
PURIS
PURISM
PURISMS
PURIST
PURISTIC
PURISTS
PURITAN
PURITANIC
PURITANS
PURITIES
PURITY
PURL
PURLED
PURLER
PURLERS
PURLICUE
PURLICUED

PURLICUES
PURLICUING
PURLIEU
PURLIEUS
PURLIN
PURLINE
PURLINES
PURLING
PURLINGS
PURLINS
PURLOIN
PURLOINED
PURLOINER
PURLOINERS
PURLOINING
PURLOINS
PURLS
PURPIE
PURPIES
PURPLE
PURPLED
PURPLER
PURPLES
PURPLEST
PURPLING
PURPLISH
PURPLY
PURPORT
PURPORTED
PURPORTING
PURPORTS
PURPOSE
PURPOSED
PURPOSELY
PURPOSES
PURPOSING
PURPOSIVE
PURPURA
PURPURAS
PURPURE
PURPUREAL
PURPURES
PURPURIC
PURPURIN
PURPURINS
PURPY
PURR
PURRED
PURRING
PURRINGLY
PURRINGS
PURRS
PURS
PURSE
PURSED
PURSEFUL
PURSEFULS
PURSER
PURSERS
PURSES
PURSEW
PURSEWED
PURSEWING
PURSEWS
PURSIER
PURSIEST
PURSINESS
PURSINESSES
PURSING
PURSLAIN

PURSLAINS
PURSLANE
PURSLANES
PURSUABLE
PURSUAL
PURSUALS
PURSUANCE
PURSUANCES
PURSUANT
PURSUE
PURSUED
PURSUER
PURSUERS
PURSUES
PURSUING
PURSUINGS
PURSUIT
PURSUITS
PURSY
PURTIER
PURTIEST
PURTRAID
PURTRAYD
PURTY
PURULENCE
PURULENCES
PURULENCIES
PURULENCY
PURULENT
PURVEY
PURVEYED
PURVEYING
PURVEYOR
PURVEYORS
PURVEYS
PURVIEW
PURVIEWS
PUS
PUSES
PUSH
PUSHED
PUSHER
PUSHERS
PUSHES
PUSHFUL
PUSHFULLY
PUSHIER
PUSHIEST
PUSHINESS
PUSHINESSES
PUSHING
PUSHINGLY
PUSHROD
PUSHRODS
PUSHY
PUSLE
PUSLED
PUSLES
PUSLING
PUSS
PUSSEL
PUSSELS
PUSSES
PUSSIES
PUSSY
PUSSYFOOT
PUSSYFOOTED
PUSSYFOOTING
PUSSYFOOTS
PUSTULANT

PUSTULANTS
PUSTULAR
PUSTULATE
PUSTULATED
PUSTULATES
PUSTULATING
PUSTULE
PUSTULES
PUSTULOUS
PUT
PUTAMEN
PUTAMINA
PUTATIVE
PUTCHER
PUTCHERS
PUTCHOCK
PUTCHOCKS
PUTCHUK
PUTCHUKS
PUTEAL
PUTEALS
PUTELI
PUTELIS
PUTID
PUTLOCK
PUTLOCKS
PUTLOG
PUTLOGS
PUTOIS
PUTREFIED
PUTREFIES
PUTREFY
PUTREFYING
PUTRID
PUTRIDER
PUTRIDEST
PUTRIDITIES
PUTRIDITY
PUTRIDLY
PUTS
PUTSCH
PUTSCHES
PUTT
PUTTED
PUTTEE
PUTTEES
PUTTEN
PUTTER
PUTTERED
PUTTERING
PUTTERS
PUTTI
PUTTIE
PUTTIED
PUTTIER
PUTTIERS
PUTTIES
PUTTING
PUTTINGS
PUTTO
PUTTOCK
PUTTOCKS
PUTTS
PUTTY
PUTTYING
PUTURE
PUTURES
PUTZ
PUTZES
PUY

PUYS
PUZEL
PUZELS
PUZZEL
PUZZELS
PUZZLE
PUZZLED
PUZZLEDOM
PUZZLEDOMS
PUZZLER
PUZZLERS
PUZZLES
PUZZLING
PUZZOLANA
PUZZOLANAS
PYAEMIA
PYAEMIAS
PYAEMIC
PYAT
PYATS
PYCNIC
PYCNIDIA
PYCNIDIUM
PYCNIDIUMS
PYCNITE
PYCNITES
PYCNON
PYCNONS
PYE
PYEBALD
PYEBALDS
PYEING
PYELITIC
PYELITIS
PYELITISES
PYELOGRAM
PYELOGRAMS
PYEMIA
PYEMIAS
PYENGADU
PYENGADUS
PYES
PYET
PYETS
PYGAL
PYGALS
PYGARG
PYGARGS
PYGIDIA
PYGIDIAL
PYGIDIUM
PYGIDIUMS
PYGMAEAN
PYGMEAN
PYGMIES
PYGMOID
PYGMY
PYGOSTYLE
PYGOSTYLES
PYJAMAED
PYJAMAS
PYKNIC
PYKNOSOME
PYKNOSOMES
PYLON
PYLONS
PYLORIC
PYLORUS
PYLORUSES
PYNE

PYNED
PYNES
PYNING
PYOGENIC
PYOID
PYONER
PYONERS
PYONINGS
PYORRHOEA
PYORRHOEAS
PYOT
PYOTS
PYRACANTH
PYRACANTHS
PYRAL
PYRALID
PYRALIDS
PYRALIS
PYRALISES
PYRAMID
PYRAMIDAL
PYRAMIDED
PYRAMIDES
PYRAMIDIC
PYRAMIDING
PYRAMIDON
PYRAMIDONS
PYRAMIDS
PYRAMIS
PYRAMISES
PYRE
PYRENE
PYRENEITE
PYRENEITES
PYRENES
PYRENOID
PYRENOIDS
PYRES
PYRETHRIN
PYRETHRINS
PYRETHRUM
PYRETHRUMS
PYRETIC
PYREXIA
PYREXIAL
PYREXIAS
PYREXIC
PYRIDINE
PYRIDINES
PYRIDOXIN
PYRIDOXINS
PYRIFORM
PYRITE
PYRITES
PYRITIC
PYRITICAL
PYRITISE
PYRITISED
PYRITISES
PYRITISING
PYRITIZE
PYRITIZED
PYRITIZES
PYRITIZING
PYRITOUS
PYRO
PYROCLAST
PYROCLASTS
PYROGEN
PYROGENIC

PYROGENS
PYROLATER
PYROLATERS
PYROLATRIES
PYROLATRY
PYROLYSE
PYROLYSED
PYROLYSES
PYROLYSING
PYROLYSIS
PYROLYTIC
PYROLYZE
PYROLYZED
PYROLYZES
PYROLYZING

PYROMANCIES
PYROMANCY
PYROMANIA
PYROMANIAS
PYROMETER
PYROMETERS
PYROMETRIES
PYROMETRY
PYROPE
PYROPES
PYROPHONE
PYROPHONES
PYROPUS
PYROPUSES
PYROS

PYROSCOPE
PYROSCOPES
PYROSES
PYROSIS
PYROSOME
PYROSOMES
PYROSTAT
PYROSTATS
PYROXENE
PYROXENES
PYROXENIC
PYROXYLE
PYROXYLES
PYROXYLIC
PYROXYLIN

PYROXYLINS
PYRRHIC
PYRRHICS
PYRRHOUS
PYRROLE
PYRROLES
PYRUVATE
PYRUVATES
PYTHIUM
PYTHIUMS
PYTHON
PYTHONESS
PYTHONESSES
PYTHONIC
PYTHONS

PYURIA
PYURIAS
PYX
PYXED
PYXES
PYXIDES
PYXIDIA
PYXIDIUM
PYXING
PYXIS
PZAZZ
PZAZZES

Q

QADI
QADIS
QALAMDAN
QALAMDANS
QANAT
QANATS
QAT
QATS
QIBLA
QIBLAS
QIGONG
QIGONGS
QINTAR
QINTARS
QUA
QUACK
QUACKED
QUACKERIES
QUACKERY
QUACKING
QUACKLE
QUACKLED
QUACKLES
QUACKLING
QUACKS
QUAD
QUADDED
QUADDING
QUADRANS
QUADRANT
QUADRANTES
QUADRANTS
QUADRAT
QUADRATE
QUADRATED
QUADRATES
QUADRATIC
QUADRATICS
QUADRATING
QUADRATS
QUADRATUS
QUADRATUSES
QUADRELLA
QUADRELLAS
QUADRIC
QUADRIFID
QUADRIGA
QUADRIGAE
QUADRILLE
QUADRILLED
QUADRILLES
QUADRILLING
QUADROON
QUADROONS
QUADRUMAN
QUADRUMANS
QUADRUPED
QUADRUPEDS
QUADRUPLE
QUADRUPLED
QUADRUPLES
QUADRUPLIES
QUADRUPLING

QUADRUPLY
QUADS
QUAERE
QUAERED
QUAEREING
QUAERES
QUAERITUR
QUAESITUM
QUAESITUMS
QUAESTOR
QUAESTORS
QUAFF
QUAFFED
QUAFFER
QUAFFERS
QUAFFING
QUAFFS
QUAG
QUAGGA
QUAGGAS
QUAGGIER
QUAGGIEST
QUAGGY
QUAGMIRE
QUAGMIRED
QUAGMIRES
QUAGMIRIER
QUAGMIRIEST
QUAGMIRING
QUAGMIRY
QUAGS
QUAHAUG
QUAHAUGS
QUAHOG
QUAHOGS
QUAICH
QUAICHS
QUAIGH
QUAIGHS
QUAIL
QUAILED
QUAILING
QUAILINGS
QUAILS
QUAINT
QUAINTER
QUAINTEST
QUAINTLY
QUAIR
QUAIRS
QUAKE
QUAKED
QUAKES
QUAKIER
QUAKIEST
QUAKINESS
QUAKINESSES
QUAKING
QUAKINGLY
QUAKINGS
QUAKY
QUALAMDAN
QUALAMDANS

QUALE
QUALIA
QUALIFIED
QUALIFIER
QUALIFIERS
QUALIFIES
QUALIFY
QUALIFYING
QUALIFYINGS
QUALITIED
QUALITIES
QUALITY
QUALM
QUALMIER
QUALMIEST
QUALMING
QUALMISH
QUALMLESS
QUALMS
QUALMY
QUAMASH
QUAMASHES
QUANDANG
QUANDANGS
QUANDARIES
QUANDARY
QUANDONG
QUANDONGS
QUANGO
QUANGOS
QUANNET
QUANNETS
QUANT
QUANTA
QUANTAL
QUANTED
QUANTIC
QUANTICAL
QUANTICS
QUANTIFIED
QUANTIFIES
QUANTIFY
QUANTIFYING
QUANTING
QUANTISE
QUANTISED
QUANTISES
QUANTISING
QUANTITIES
QUANTITY
QUANTIZE
QUANTIZED
QUANTIZES
QUANTIZING
QUANTONG
QUANTONGS
QUANTS
QUANTUM
QUARENDEN
QUARENDENS
QUARENDER
QUARENDERS
QUARK

QUARKS
QUARREL
QUARRELLED
QUARRELLING
QUARRELLINGS
QUARRELS
QUARRIED
QUARRIER
QUARRIERS
QUARRIES
QUARRY
QUARRYING
QUARRYMAN
QUARRYMEN
QUART
QUARTAN
QUARTANS
QUARTE
QUARTER
QUARTERED
QUARTERING
QUARTERINGS
QUARTERLIES
QUARTERLY
QUARTERN
QUARTERNS
QUARTERS
QUARTES
QUARTET
QUARTETS
QUARTETT
QUARTETTE
QUARTETTES
QUARTETTI
QUARTETTO
QUARTETTS
QUARTIC
QUARTICS
QUARTIER
QUARTIERS
QUARTILE
QUARTILES
QUARTO
QUARTOS
QUARTS
QUARTZ
QUARTZES
QUARTZIER
QUARTZIEST
QUARTZITE
QUARTZITES
QUARTZOSE
QUARTZY
QUASAR
QUASARS
QUASH
QUASHED
QUASHEE
QUASHEES
QUASHES
QUASHIE
QUASHIES
QUASHING

QUASI
QUASSIA
QUASSIAS
QUAT
QUATCH
QUATCHED
QUATCHES
QUATCHING
QUATORZE
QUATORZES
QUATRAIN
QUATRAINS
QUATS
QUAVER
QUAVERED
QUAVERER
QUAVERERS
QUAVERING
QUAVERINGS
QUAVERS
QUAVERY
QUAY
QUAYAGE
QUAYAGES
QUAYD
QUAYS
QUAYSIDE
QUAYSIDES
QUEACH
QUEACHES
QUEACHY
QUEAN
QUEANS
QUEASIER
QUEASIEST
QUEASILY
QUEASY
QUEAZIER
QUEAZIEST
QUEAZY
QUEBRACHO
QUEBRACHOS
QUEECHY
QUEEN
QUEENDOM
QUEENDOMS
QUEENED
QUEENHOOD
QUEENHOODS
QUEENING
QUEENINGS
QUEENITE
QUEENITES
QUEENLESS
QUEENLET
QUEENLETS
QUEENLIER
QUEENLIEST
QUEENLY
QUEENS
QUEENSHIP
QUEENSHIPS
QUEER

QUEERDOM
QUEERDOMS
QUEERED
QUEERER
QUEEREST
QUEERING
QUEERISH
QUEERITIES
QUEERITY
QUEERLY
QUEERNESS
QUEERNESSES
QUEERS
QUEEST
QUEESTS
QUEINT
QUELCH
QUELCHED
QUELCHES
QUELCHING
QUELEA
QUELEAS
QUELL
QUELLED
QUELLER
QUELLERS
QUELLING
QUELLS
QUEME
QUEMED
QUEMES
QUEMING
QUENA
QUENAS
QUENCH
QUENCHED
QUENCHER
QUENCHERS
QUENCHES
QUENCHING
QUENCHINGS
QUENELLE
QUENELLES
QUEP
QUERCETUM
QUERCETUMS
QUERIED
QUERIES
QUERIMONIES
QUERIMONY
QUERIST
QUERISTS
QUERN
QUERNS
QUERULOUS
QUERY
QUERYING
QUERYINGS
QUEST
QUESTANT
QUESTANTS
QUESTED
QUESTER
QUESTERS
QUESTING
QUESTINGS
QUESTION
QUESTIONED
QUESTIONING
QUESTIONINGS

QUESTIONS
QUESTOR
QUESTORS
QUESTRIST
QUESTRISTS
QUESTS
QUETCH
QUETCHED
QUETCHES
QUETCHING
QUETHE
QUETHES
QUETHING
QUETSCH
QUETSCHES
QUETZAL
QUETZALS
QUEUE
QUEUED
QUEUEING
QUEUEINGS
QUEUES
QUEUING
QUEUINGS
QUEY
QUEYN
QUEYNIE
QUEYNIES
QUEYNS
QUEYS
QUIBBLE
QUIBBLED
QUIBBLER
QUIBBLERS
QUIBBLES
QUIBBLING
QUIBBLINGS
QUIBLIN
QUIBLINS
QUICH
QUICHE
QUICHED
QUICHES
QUICHING
QUICK
QUICKBEAM
QUICKBEAMS
QUICKEN
QUICKENED
QUICKENER
QUICKENERS
QUICKENING
QUICKENINGS
QUICKENS
QUICKER
QUICKEST
QUICKIE
QUICKIES
QUICKLIME
QUICKLIMES
QUICKLY
QUICKNESS
QUICKNESSES
QUICKS
QUICKSAND
QUICKSANDS
QUICKSET
QUICKSETS
QUICKSTEP
QUICKSTEPPED

QUICKSTEPPING
QUICKSTEPS
QUID
QUIDAM
QUIDAMS
QUIDDANIES
QUIDDANY
QUIDDIT
QUIDDITIES
QUIDDITS
QUIDDITY
QUIDDLE
QUIDDLED
QUIDDLER
QUIDDLERS
QUIDDLES
QUIDDLING
QUIDNUNC
QUIDNUNCS
QUIDS
QUIESCE
QUIESCED
QUIESCENT
QUIESCES
QUIESCING
QUIET
QUIETED
QUIETEN
QUIETENED
QUIETENING
QUIETENINGS
QUIETENS
QUIETER
QUIETERS
QUIETEST
QUIETING
QUIETINGS
QUIETISM
QUIETISMS
QUIETIST
QUIETISTS
QUIETIVE
QUIETIVES
QUIETLY
QUIETNESS
QUIETNESSES
QUIETS
QUIETSOME
QUIETUDE
QUIETUDES
QUIETUS
QUIETUSES
QUIFF
QUIFFS
QUIGHT
QUIGHTED
QUIGHTING
QUIGHTS
QUILL
QUILLAI
QUILLAIA
QUILLAIAS
QUILLAIS
QUILLAJA
QUILLAJAS
QUILLED
QUILLET
QUILLETS
QUILLING
QUILLINGS

QUILLMAN
QUILLMEN
QUILLON
QUILLONS
QUILLS
QUILLWORT
QUILLWORTS
QUILT
QUILTED
QUILTER
QUILTERS
QUILTING
QUILTINGS
QUILTS
QUIM
QUIMS
QUIN
QUINA
QUINARY
QUINAS
QUINATE
QUINCE
QUINCES
QUINCHE
QUINCHED
QUINCHES
QUINCHING
QUINCUNX
QUINCUNXES
QUINE
QUINELLA
QUINELLAS
QUINES
QUINIC
QUINIDINE
QUINIDINES
QUINIE
QUINIES
QUININE
QUININES
QUINNAT
QUINNATS
QUINOA
QUINOAS
QUINOL
QUINOLINE
QUINOLINES
QUINOLS
QUINONE
QUINONES
QUINQUINA
QUINQUINAS
QUINS
QUINSIED
QUINSIES
QUINSY
QUINT
QUINTA
QUINTAIN
QUINTAINS
QUINTAL
QUINTALS
QUINTAN
QUINTAS
QUINTE
QUINTES
QUINTET
QUINTETS
QUINTETT
QUINTETTE

QUINTETTES
QUINTETTI
QUINTETTO
QUINTETTS
QUINTIC
QUINTILE
QUINTILES
QUINTROON
QUINTROONS
QUINTS
QUINTUPLE
QUINTUPLED
QUINTUPLES
QUINTUPLING
QUINZE
QUINZES
QUIP
QUIPO
QUIPOS
QUIPPED
QUIPPING
QUIPPISH
QUIPS
QUIPSTER
QUIPSTERS
QUIPU
QUIPUS
QUIRE
QUIRED
QUIRES
QUIRING
QUIRISTER
QUIRISTERS
QUIRK
QUIRKED
QUIRKIER
QUIRKIEST
QUIRKING
QUIRKISH
QUIRKS
QUIRKY
QUIRT
QUIRTED
QUIRTING
QUIRTS
QUISLING
QUISLINGS
QUIST
QUISTS
QUIT
QUITCH
QUITCHED
QUITCHES
QUITCHING
QUITE
QUITED
QUITES
QUITING
QUITS
QUITTAL
QUITTALS
QUITTANCE
QUITTANCED
QUITTANCES
QUITTANCING
QUITTED
QUITTER
QUITTERS
QUITTING
QUITTOR

QUITTORS
QUIVER
QUIVERED
QUIVERFUL
QUIVERFULS
QUIVERING
QUIVERINGS
QUIVERISH
QUIVERS
QUIVERY
QUIXOTIC
QUIXOTISM
QUIXOTISMS
QUIXOTRIES
QUIXOTRY
QUIZ
QUIZZED
QUIZZER
QUIZZERIES
QUIZZERS
QUIZZERY

QUIZZES
QUIZZICAL
QUIZZIFIED
QUIZZIFIES
QUIZZIFY
QUIZZIFYING
QUIZZING
QUIZZINGS
QUOAD
QUOD
QUODDED
QUODDING
QUODLIBET
QUODLIBETS
QUODLIN
QUODLINS
QUODS
QUOIF
QUOIFED
QUOIFING
QUOIFS

QUOIN
QUOINED
QUOINING
QUOINS
QUOIST
QUOISTS
QUOIT
QUOITED
QUOITER
QUOITERS
QUOITING
QUOITS
QUOKKA
QUOKKAS
QUOLL
QUOLLS
QUONDAM
QUONK
QUONKED
QUONKING
QUONKS

QUOOKE
QUOP
QUOPPED
QUOPPING
QUOPS
QUORATE
QUORUM
QUORUMS
QUOTA
QUOTABLE
QUOTABLY
QUOTAS
QUOTATION
QUOTATIONS
QUOTATIVE
QUOTATIVES
QUOTE
QUOTED
QUOTER
QUOTERS
QUOTES

QUOTH
QUOTHA
QUOTIDIAN
QUOTIDIANS
QUOTIENT
QUOTIENTS
QUOTING
QUOTITION
QUOTITIONS
QUOTUM
QUOTUMS
QUYTE
QUYTED
QUYTES
QUYTING
QWERTIES
QWERTY
QWERTYS

R

RABANNA	RACAHOUT	RACING	RADIALITIES	RADON
RABANNAS	RACAHOUTS	RACINGS	RADIALITY	RADONS
RABAT	RACCAHOUT	RACISM	RADIALIZE	RADS
RABATINE	RACCAHOUTS	RACISMS	RADIALIZED	RADULA
RABATINES	RACCOON	RACIST	RADIALIZES	RADULAE
RABATMENT	RACCOONS	RACISTS	RADIALIZING	RADULAR
RABATMENTS	RACE	RACK	RADIALLY	RADULATE
RABATO	RACED	RACKED	RADIALS	RAFALE
RABATOES	RACEGOER	RACKER	RADIAN	RAFALES
RABATS	RACEGOERS	RACKERS	RADIANCE	RAFF
RABATTE	RACEGOING	RACKET	RADIANCES	RAFFIA
RABATTED	RACEGOINGS	RACKETED	RADIANCIES	RAFFIAS
RABATTES	RACEHORSE	RACKETEER	RADIANCY	RAFFINATE
RABATTING	RACEHORSES	RACKETEERED	RADIANS	RAFFINATES
RABATTINGS	RACEMATE	RACKETEERING	RADIANT	RAFFINOSE
RABBET	RACEMATES	RACKETEERINGS	RADIANTLY	RAFFINOSES
RABBETED	RACEME	RACKETEERS	RADIANTS	RAFFISH
RABBETING	RACEMED	RACKETER	RADIATE	RAFFISHLY
RABBETS	RACEMES	RACKETERS	RADIATED	RAFFLE
RABBI	RACEMIC	RACKETING	RADIATELY	RAFFLED
RABBIN	RACEMISE	RACKETRIES	RADIATES	RAFFLER
RABBINATE	RACEMISED	RACKETRY	RADIATING	RAFFLERS
RABBINATES	RACEMISES	RACKETS	RADIATION	RAFFLES
RABBINIC	RACEMISING	RACKETT	RADIATIONS	RAFFLING
RABBINISM	RACEMISM	RACKETTS	RADIATIVE	RAFFS
RABBINISMS	RACEMISMS	RACKETY	RADIATOR	RAFT
RABBINIST	RACEMIZE	RACKING	RADIATORS	RAFTED
RABBINISTS	RACEMIZED	RACKINGS	RADIATORY	RAFTER
RABBINITE	RACEMIZES	RACKS	RADICAL	RAFTERED
RABBINITES	RACEMIZING	RACKWORK	RADICALLY	RAFTERING
RABBINS	RACEMOSE	RACKWORKS	RADICALS	RAFTERINGS
RABBIS	RACER	RACLETTE	RADICANT	RAFTERS
RABBIT	RACERS	RACLETTES	RADICATE	RAFTING
RABBITED	RACES	RACLOIR	RADICATED	RAFTMAN
RABBITER	RACEWAY	RACLOIRS	RADICATES	RAFTMEN
RABBITERS	RACEWAYS	RACON	RADICATING	RAFTS
RABBITING	RACH	RACONS	RADICEL	RAFTSMAN
RABBITRIES	RACHE	RACONTEUR	RADICELS	RAFTSMEN
RABBITRY	RACHES	RACONTEURS	RADICES	RAG
RABBITS	RACHIAL	RACOON	RADICLE	RAGA
RABBITY	RACHIDES	RACOONS	RADICLES	RAGAS
RABBLE	RACHIDIAL	RACQUET	RADICULAR	RAGBOLT
RABBLED	RACHIDIAN	RACQUETS	RADICULE	RAGBOLTS
RABBLER	RACHILLA	RACY	RADICULES	RAGDE
RABBLERS	RACHILLAS	RAD	RADII	RAGE
RABBLES	RACHIS	RADAR	RADIO	RAGED
RABBLING	RACHISES	RADARS	RADIOED	RAGEE
RABBLINGS	RACHITIC	RADDLE	RADIOGRAM	RAGEES
RABBONI	RACHITIS	RADDLED	RADIOGRAMS	RAGEFUL
RABBONIS	RACHITISES	RADDLEMAN	RADIOING	RAGER
RABI	RACIAL	RADDLEMEN	RADIOLOGIES	RAGERS
RABIC	RACIALISM	RADDLES	RADIOLOGY	RAGES
RABID	RACIALISMS	RADDLING	RADIONICS	RAGG
RABIDER	RACIALIST	RADDOCKE	RADIOS	RAGGED
RABIDEST	RACIALISTS	RADDOCKES	RADISH	RAGGEDER
RABIDITIES	RACIALLY	RADE	RADISHES	RAGGEDEST
RABIDITY	RACIATION	RADIAL	RADIUM	RAGGEDLY
RABIDLY	RACIATIONS	RADIALE	RADIUMS	RAGGEDY
RABIDNESS	RACIER	RADIALIA	RADIUS	RAGGEE
RABIDNESSES	RACIEST	RADIALISE	RADIUSES	RAGGEES
RABIES	RACILY	RADIALISED	RADIX	RAGGERIES
RABIS	RACINESS	RADIALISES	RADOME	RAGGERY
RACA	RACINESSES	RADIALISING	RADOMES	RAGGIER

RAGGIES
RAGGIEST
RAGGING
RAGGINGS
RAGGLE
RAGGLED
RAGGLES
RAGGLING
RAGGS
RAGGY
RAGI
RAGING
RAGINGLY
RAGINI
RAGINIS
RAGIS
RAGLAN
RAGLANS
RAGMAN
RAGMANS
RAGMEN
RAGMENT
RAGMENTS
RAGOUT
RAGOUTED
RAGOUTING
RAGOUTS
RAGS
RAGSTONE
RAGSTONES
RAGTIME
RAGTIMER
RAGTIMERS
RAGTIMES
RAGULED
RAGULY
RAGWEED
RAGWEEDS
RAGWHEEL
RAGWHEELS
RAGWORK
RAGWORKS
RAGWORM
RAGWORMS
RAGWORT
RAGWORTS
RAH
RAHED
RAHING
RAHS
RAID
RAIDED
RAIDER
RAIDERS
RAIDING
RAIDS
RAIK
RAIKED
RAIKING
RAIKS
RAIL
RAILBUS
RAILBUSES
RAILCARD
RAILCARDS
RAILE
RAILED
RAILER
RAILERS
RAILES

RAILING
RAILINGLY
RAILINGS
RAILLERIES
RAILLERY
RAILLESS
RAILLIES
RAILLY
RAILMAN
RAILMEN
RAILROAD
RAILROADED
RAILROADING
RAILROADS
RAILS
RAILWAY
RAILWAYS
RAIMENT
RAIMENTS
RAIN
RAINBAND
RAINBANDS
RAINBOW
RAINBOWED
RAINBOWS
RAINBOWY
RAINCHECK
RAINCHECKS
RAINCOAT
RAINCOATS
RAINDROP
RAINDROPS
RAINE
RAINED
RAINES
RAINFALL
RAINFALLS
RAINIER
RAINIEST
RAININESS
RAININESSES
RAINING
RAINLESS
RAINPROOF
RAINPROOFED
RAINPROOFING
RAINPROOFS
RAINS
RAINSTORM
RAINSTORMS
RAINTIGHT
RAINY
RAIRD
RAIRDS
RAISABLE
RAISE
RAISEABLE
RAISED
RAISER
RAISERS
RAISES
RAISIN
RAISING
RAISINGS
RAISINS
RAISONNÉ
RAIT
RAITED
RAITING
RAITS

RAIYAT
RAIYATS
RAJ
RAJA
RAJAH
RAJAHS
RAJAHSHIP
RAJAHSHIPS
RAJAS
RAJASHIP
RAJASHIPS
RAJES
RAKE
RAKED
RAKEE
RAKEES
RAKEHELL
RAKEHELLS
RAKEHELLY
RAKER
RAKERIES
RAKERS
RAKERY
RAKES
RAKESHAME
RAKESHAMES
RAKI
RAKING
RAKINGS
RAKIS
RAKISH
RAKISHLY
RAKSHAS
RAKSHASA
RAKSHASAS
RAKSHASES
RALE
RÂLE
RALES
RÂLES
RALLIED
RALLIER
RALLIERS
RALLIES
RALLINE
RALLY
RALLYE
RALLYES
RALLYING
RALLYINGS
RALLYIST
RALLYISTS
RAM
RAMAKIN
RAMAKINS
RAMAL
RAMATE
RAMBLE
RAMBLED
RAMBLER
RAMBLERS
RAMBLES
RAMBLING
RAMBLINGS
RAMBUTAN
RAMBUTANS
RAMCAT
RAMCATS
RAMEAL
RAMEE

RAMEES
RAMEKIN
RAMEKINS
RAMENTA
RAMENTUM
RAMEOUS
RAMEQUIN
RAMEQUINS
RAMFEEZLE
RAMFEEZLED
RAMFEEZLES
RAMFEEZLING
RAMI
RAMIE
RAMIES
RAMIFIED
RAMIFIES
RAMIFORM
RAMIFY
RAMIFYING
RAMIS
RAMMED
RAMMER
RAMMERS
RAMMIES
RAMMING
RAMMISH
RAMMY
RAMOSE
RAMOUS
RAMP
RAMPAGE
RAMPAGED
RAMPAGES
RAMPAGING
RAMPANCIES
RAMPANCY
RAMPANT
RAMPANTLY
RAMPART
RAMPARTED
RAMPARTING
RAMPARTS
RAMPAUGE
RAMPAUGED
RAMPAUGES
RAMPAUGING
RAMPED
RAMPER
RAMPERS
RAMPICK
RAMPICKED
RAMPICKS
RAMPIKE
RAMPIKES
RAMPING
RAMPION
RAMPIONS
RAMPIRE
RAMPIRED
RAMPIRES
RAMPS
RAMPSMAN
RAMPSMEN
RAMROD
RAMRODS
RAMS
RAMSON
RAMSONS
RAMSTAM

RAMULAR
RAMULI
RAMULOSE
RAMULOUS
RAMULUS
RAMUS
RAN
RANA
RANARIAN
RANARIUM
RANARIUMS
RANAS
RANCE
RANCED
RANCEL
RANCELS
RANCES
RANCH
RANCHED
RANCHER
RANCHERIA
RANCHERIAS
RANCHERO
RANCHEROS
RANCHERS
RANCHES
RANCHING
RANCHINGS
RANCHMAN
RANCHMEN
RANCHO
RANCHOS
RANCID
RANCIDER
RANCIDEST
RANCIDITIES
RANCIDITY
RANCING
RANCOR
RANCOROUS
RANCORS
RANCOUR
RANCOURS
RAND
RANDAN
RANDANS
RANDED
RANDEM
RANDEMS
RANDIE
RANDIER
RANDIES
RANDIEST
RANDING
RANDOM
RANDOMISE
RANDOMISED
RANDOMISES
RANDOMISING
RANDOMIZE
RANDOMIZED
RANDOMIZES
RANDOMIZING
RANDOMLY
RANDOMS
RANDON
RANDONS
RANDS
RANDY
RANEE

RANEES
RANG
RANGE
RANGED
RANGELAND
RANGELANDS
RANGER
RANGERS
RANGES
RANGIER
RANGIEST
RANGINESS
RANGINESSES
RANGING
RANGY
RANI
RANIFORM
RANINE
RANIS
RANK
RANKE
RANKED
RANKER
RANKERS
RANKES
RANKEST
RANKING
RANKINGS
RANKLE
RANKLED
RANKLES
RANKLING
RANKLY
RANKNESS
RANKNESSES
RANKS
RANSACK
RANSACKED
RANSACKER
RANSACKERS
RANSACKING
RANSACKS
RANSEL
RANSELS
RANSHAKLE
RANSHAKLED
RANSHAKLES
RANSHAKLING
RANSOM
RANSOMED
RANSOMER
RANSOMERS
RANSOMING
RANSOMS
RANT
RANTED
RANTER
RANTERISM
RANTERISMS
RANTERS
RANTING
RANTINGLY
RANTIPOLE
RANTIPOLED
RANTIPOLES
RANTIPOLING
RANTS
RANULA
RANULAS
RANUNCULI

RANZEL
RANZELMAN
RANZELMEN
RANZELS
RAP
RAPACIOUS
RAPACITIES
RAPACITY
RAPE
RAPED
RAPER
RAPERS
RAPES
RAPHANIA
RAPHANIAS
RAPHE
RAPHES
RAPHIA
RAPHIAS
RAPHIDE
RAPHIDES
RAPHIS
RAPID
RAPIDER
RAPIDEST
RAPIDITIES
RAPIDITY
RAPIDLY
RAPIDNESS
RAPIDNESSES
RAPIDS
RAPIER
RAPIERS
RAPINE
RAPINES
RAPING
RAPIST
RAPISTS
RAPLOCH
RAPLOCHS
RAPPAREE
RAPPAREES
RAPPED
RAPPEE
RAPPEES
RAPPEL
RAPPELLED
RAPPELLING
RAPPELS
RAPPER
RAPPERS
RAPPING
RAPPINGS
RAPPORT
RAPPORTS
RAPS
RAPT
RAPTOR
RAPTORIAL
RAPTORS
RAPTURE
RAPTURED
RAPTURES
RAPTURING
RAPTURISE
RAPTURISED
RAPTURISES
RAPTURISING
RAPTURIST
RAPTURISTS

RAPTURIZE
RAPTURIZED
RAPTURIZES
RAPTURIZING
RAPTUROUS
RARE
RAREBIT
RAREBITS
RAREFIED
RAREFIES
RAREFY
RAREFYING
RARELY
RARENESS
RARENESSES
RARER
RAREST
RARING
RARITIES
RARITY
RAS
RASCAILLE
RASCAILLES
RASCAL
RASCALDOM
RASCALDOMS
RASCALISM
RASCALISMS
RASCALITIES
RASCALITY
RASCALLIEST
RASCALLY
RASCALS
RASCHEL
RASCHELS
RASE
RASED
RASES
RASH
RASHED
RASHER
RASHERS
RASHES
RASHEST
RASHING
RASHLY
RASHNESS
RASHNESSES
RASING
RASORIAL
RASP
RASPATORIES
RASPATORY
RASPBERRIES
RASPBERRY
RASPED
RASPER
RASPERS
RASPIER
RASPIEST
RASPING
RASPINGLY
RASPINGS
RASPS
RASPY
RASSE
RASSES
RAST
RASTA
RASTAFARI

RASTER
RASTERS
RASTRUM
RASTRUMS
RASURE
RASURES
RAT
RATA
RATABLE
RATABLY
RATAFIA
RATAFIAS
RATAN
RATANS
RATAPLAN
RATAPLANS
RATAS
RATBAG
RATBAGS
RATCH
RATCHES
RATCHET
RATCHETS
RATE
RATEABLE
RATEABLY
RATED
RATEL
RATELS
RATEPAYER
RATEPAYERS
RATER
RATERS
RATES
RATFINK
RATFINKS
RATH
RATHE
RATHER
RATHEREST
RATHERIPE
RATHERIPES
RATHERISH
RATHEST
RATHRIPE
RATHRIPES
RATHS
RATIFIED
RATIFIER
RATIFIERS
RATIFIES
RATIFY
RATIFYING
RATINE
RATINES
RATING
RATINGS
RATIO
RATION
RATIONAL
RATIONALE
RATIONALES
RATIONALS
RATIONED
RATIONING
RATIONS
RATIOS
RATITE
RATLIN
RATLINE

RATLINES
RATLING
RATLINGS
RATLINS
RATOON
RATOONED
RATOONER
RATOONERS
RATOONING
RATOONS
RATPACK
RATPACKS
RATPROOF
RATS
RATSBANE
RATSBANES
RATTAN
RATTANS
RATTED
RATTEEN
RATTEENS
RATTEN
RATTENED
RATTENING
RATTENINGS
RATTENS
RATTER
RATTERIES
RATTERS
RATTERY
RATTIER
RATTIEST
RATTING
RATTINGS
RATTISH
RATTLE
RATTLEBAG
RATTLEBAGS
RATTLED
RATTLER
RATTLERS
RATTLES
RATTLIN
RATTLINE
RATTLINES
RATTLING
RATTLINGS
RATTLINS
RATTLY
RATTON
RATTONS
RATTY
RATU
RATUS
RAUCID
RAUCLE
RAUCLER
RAUCLEST
RAUCOUS
RAUCOUSLY
RAUGHT
RAUN
RAUNCH
RAUNCHED
RAUNCHES
RAUNCHIER
RAUNCHIEST
RAUNCHING
RAUNCHY
RAUNGE

RAUNGED	RAY	REACTIVE	REAKING	REANIMATES
RAUNGES	RAYAH	REACTOR	REAKS	REANIMATING
RAUNGING	RAYAHS	REACTORS	REAL	REANNEX
RAUNS	RAYED	REACTS	REALER	REANNEXED
RAVAGE	RAYING	REACTUATE	REALEST	REANNEXES
RAVAGED	RAYLE	REACTUATED	REALGAR	REANNEXING
RAVAGER	RAYLED	REACTUATES	REALGARS	REANS
RAVAGERS	RAYLES	REACTUATING	REALIA	REANSWER
RAVAGES	RAYLESS	READ	REALIGN	REANSWERED
RAVAGING	RAYLET	READABLE	REALIGNED	REANSWERING
RAVE	RAYLETS	READABLY	REALIGNING	REANSWERS
RAVED	RAYLING	READAPT	REALIGNS	REAP
RAVEL	RAYNE	READAPTED	REALISE	REAPED
RAVELIN	RAYNES	READAPTING	REALISED	REAPER
RAVELINS	RAYON	READAPTS	REALISER	REAPERS
RAVELLED	RAYONS	READDRESS	REALISERS	REAPING
RAVELLING	RAYS	READDRESSED	REALISES	REAPPAREL
RAVELLINGS	RAZE	READDRESSES	REALISING	REAPPARELLED
RAVELMENT	RAZED	READDRESSING	REALISM	REAPPARELLING
RAVELMENTS	RAZEE	READER	REALISMS	REAPPARELS
RAVELS	RAZEED	READERS	REALIST	REAPPEAR
RAVEN	RAZEEING	READIED	REALISTIC	REAPPEARED
RAVENED	RAZEES	READIER	REALISTS	REAPPEARING
RAVENER	RAZES	READIES	REALITIES	REAPPEARS
RAVENERS	RAZING	READIEST	REALITY	REAPPLIED
RAVENING	RAZMATAZ	READILY	REALIZE	REAPPLIES
RAVENOUS	RAZMATAZES	READINESS	REALIZED	REAPPLY
RAVENS	RAZMATAZZ	READINESSES	REALIZER	REAPPLYING
RAVER	RAZMATAZZES	READING	REALIZERS	REAPPOINT
RAVERS	RAZOR	READINGS	REALIZES	REAPPOINTED
RAVES	RAZORABLE	READJUST	REALIZING	REAPPOINTING
RAVIN	RAZORS	READJUSTED	REALLIE	REAPPOINTS
RAVINE	RAZURE	READJUSTING	REALLIED	REAPS
RAVINED	RAZURES	READJUSTS	REALLIES	REAR
RAVINES	RAZZ	READMIT	REALLOT	REARED
RAVING	RAZZED	READMITS	REALLOTS	REARER
RAVINGLY	RAZZES	READMITTED	REALLOTTED	REARERS
RAVINGS	RAZZIA	READMITTING	REALLOTTING	REARHORSE
RAVINING	RAZZIAS	READOPT	REALLY	REARHORSES
RAVINS	RAZZING	READOPTED	REALLYING	REARISE
RAVIOLI	RAZZLE	READOPTING	REALM	REARISEN
RAVIOLIS	RAZZLES	READOPTS	REALMLESS	REARISES
RAVISH	RAZZMATAZ	READS	REALMS	REARISING
RAVISHED	RAZZMATAZES	READVANCE	REALNESS	REARLY
RAVISHER	RE	READVANCED	REALNESSES	REARM
RAVISHERS	REABSORB	READVANCES	REALS	REARMED
RAVISHES	REABSORBED	READVANCING	REALTIE	REARMICE
RAVISHING	REABSORBING	READVISE	REALTIES	REARMING
RAW	REABSORBS	READVISED	REALTIME	REARMOST
RAWBONE	REACH	READVISES	REALTOR	REARMOUSE
RAWDONED	REACHABLE	READVISING	REALTORS	REARMS
RAWER	REACHED	READY	REALTY	REAROSE
RAWEST	REACHER	READYING	REAM	REAROUSAL
RAWHEAD	REACHERS	REAEDIFIED	REAME	REAROUSALS
RAWHEADS	REACHES	REAEDIFIES	REAMED	REAROUSE
RAWHIDE	REACHING	REAEDIFY	REAMEND	REAROUSED
RAWHIDES	REACHLESS	REAEDIFYE	REAMENDED	REAROUSES
RAWING	REACQUIRE	REAEDIFYED	REAMENDING	REAROUSING
RAWINGS	REACQUIRED	REAEDIFYES	REAMENDS	REARRANGE
RAWISH	REACQUIRES	REAEDIFYING	REAMER	REARRANGED
RAWLY	REACQUIRING	REAFFIRM	REAMERS	REARRANGES
RAWN	REACT	REAFFIRMED	REAMES	REARRANGING
RAWNESS	REACTANCE	REAFFIRMING	REAMIER	REARREST
RAWNESSES	REACTANCES	REAFFIRMS	REAMIEST	REARRESTED
RAWNS	REACTANT	REAGENCIES	REAMING	REARRESTING
RAWS	REACTANTS	REAGENCY	REAMS	REARRESTS
RAX	REACTED	REAGENT	REAMY	REARS
RAXED	REACTING	REAGENTS	REAN	REARWARD
RAXES	REACTION	REAK	REANIMATE	REARWARDS
RAXING	REACTIONS	REAKED	REANIMATED	

REASCEND
REASCENDED
REASCENDING
REASCENDS
REASCENT
REASCENTS
REASON
REASONED
REASONER
REASONERS
REASONING
REASONINGS
REASONS
REASSERT
REASSERTED
REASSERTING
REASSERTS
REASSESS
REASSESSED
REASSESSES
REASSESSING
REASSIGN
REASSIGNED
REASSIGNING
REASSIGNS
REASSUME
REASSUMED
REASSUMES
REASSUMING
REASSURE
REASSURED
REASSURER
REASSURERS
REASSURES
REASSURING
REAST
REASTED
REASTIER
REASTIEST
REASTING
REASTS
REASTY
REATA
REATAS
REATE
REATES
REATTACH
REATTACHED
REATTACHES
REATTACHING
REATTAIN
REATTAINED
REATTAINING
REATTAINS
REATTEMPT
REATTEMPTED
REATTEMPTING
REATTEMPTS
REAVE
REAVER
REAVERS
REAVES
REAVING
REAWAKE
REAWAKED
REAWAKEN
REAWAKENED
REAWAKENING
REAWAKENINGS
REAWAKENS

REAWAKES
REAWAKING
REAWOKE
REAWOKEN
REBACK
REBACKED
REBACKING
REBACKS
REBAPTISE
REBAPTISED
REBAPTISES
REBAPTISING
REBAPTISM
REBAPTISMS
REBAPTIZE
REBAPTIZED
REBAPTIZES
REBAPTIZING
REBATE
REBATED
REBATER
REBATERS
REBATES
REBATING
REBATO
REBATOES
REBEC
REBECK
REBECKS
REBECS
REBEL
REBELDOM
REBELDOMS
REBELLED
REBELLER
REBELLERS
REBELLING
REBELLION
REBELLIONS
REBELLOW
REBELLOWED
REBELLOWING
REBELS
REBID
REBIDDEN
REBIDDING
REBIDS
REBIND
REBINDING
REBINDS
REBIRTH
REBIRTHS
REBIT
REBITE
REBITES
REBITING
REBITTEN
REBLOOM
REBLOOMED
REBLOOMING
REBLOOMS
REBLOSSOM
REBLOSSOMED
REBLOSSOMING
REBLOSSOMS
REBOANT
REBOATION
REBOATIONS
REBOIL

REBOILED
REBOILING
REBOILS
REBORE
REBORED
REBORES
REBORING
REBORN
REBOUND
REBOUNDED
REBOUNDING
REBOUNDS
REBRACE
REBRACED
REBRACES
REBRACING
REBUFF
REBUFFED
REBUFFING
REBUFFS
REBUILD
REBUILDING
REBUILDS
REBUILT
REBUKABLE
REBUKE
REBUKED
REBUKEFUL
REBUKER
REBUKERS
REBUKES
REBUKING
REBURIAL
REBURIALS
REBURIED
REBURIES
REBURY
REBURYING
REBUS
REBUSES
REBUT
REBUTMENT
REBUTMENTS
REBUTS
REBUTTAL
REBUTTALS
REBUTTED
REBUTTER
REBUTTERS
REBUTTING
REBUTTON
REBUTTONED
REBUTTONING
REBUTTONS
RECAL
RECALESCE
RECALESCED
RECALESCES
RECALESCING
RECALL
RECALLED
RECALLING
RECALLS
RECALMENT
RECALMENTS
RECALS
RECANT
RECANTED
RECANTER
RECANTERS

RECANTING
RECANTS
RECAP
RECAPPED
RECAPPING
RECAPS
RECAPTION
RECAPTIONS
RECAPTOR
RECAPTORS
RECAPTURE
RECAPTURED
RECAPTURES
RECAPTURING
RECAST
RECASTING
RECASTS
RECATCH
RECATCHES
RECATCHING
RECAUGHT
RECCE
RECCED
RECCEED
RECCEING
RECCES
RECCIED
RECCIES
RECCO
RECCOS
RECCY
RECCYING
RECEDE
RECEDED
RECEDES
RECEDING
RECEIPT
RECEIPTED
RECEIPTING
RECEIPTS
RECEIVAL
RECEIVALS
RECEIVE
RECEIVED
RECEIVER
RECEIVERS
RECEIVES
RECEIVING
RECEIVINGS
RECENCIES
RECENCY
RECENSE
RECENSED
RECENSES
RECENSING
RECENSION
RECENSIONS
RECENT
RECENTER
RECENTEST
RECENTLY
RECENTRE
RECENTRED
RECENTRES
RECENTRING
RECEPT
RECEPTION
RECEPTIONS
RECEPTIVE
RECEPTOR

RECEPTORS
RECEPTS
RECESS
RECESSED
RECESSES
RECESSING
RECESSION
RECESSIONS
RECESSIVE
RECESSIVES
RECHARGE
RECHARGED
RECHARGES
RECHARGING
RECHART
RECHARTED
RECHARTER
RECHARTERED
RECHARTERING
RECHARTERS
RECHARTING
RECHARTS
RECHATE
RECHATES
RÉCHAUFFÉ
RÉCHAUFFÉS
RECHEAT
RECHEATED
RECHEATING
RECHEATS
RECHECK
RECHECKED
RECHECKING
RECHECKS
RECHERCHÉ
RECHIE
RECHLESSE
RECIPE
RECIPES
RECIPIENT
RECIPIENTS
RECISION
RECISIONS
RÉCIT
RECITAL
RECITALS
RECITE
RECITED
RECITER
RECITERS
RECITES
RECITING
RÉCITS
RECK
RECKAN
RECKED
RECKING
RECKLESS
RECKLING
RECKLINGS
RECKON
RECKONED
RECKONER
RECKONERS
RECKONING
RECKONINGS
RECKONS
RECKS
RECLAIM
RECLAIMED

RECLAIMER
RECLAIMERS
RECLAIMING
RECLAIMS
RÉCLAME
RÉCLAMES
RECLIMB
RECLIMBED
RECLIMBING
RECLIMBS
RECLINATE
RECLINE
RECLINED
RECLINER
RECLINERS
RECLINES
RECLINING
RECLOSE
RECLOSED
RECLOSES
RECLOSING
RECLOTHE
RECLOTHED
RECLOTHES
RECLOTHING
RECLUSE
RECLUSELY
RECLUSES
RECLUSION
RECLUSIONS
RECLUSIVE
RECLUSORIES
RECLUSORY
RECOGNISE
RECOGNISED
RECOGNISES
RECOGNISING
RECOGNIZE
RECOGNIZED
RECOGNIZES
RECOGNIZING
RECOIL
RECOILED
RECOILER
RECOILERS
RECOILING
RECOILS
RECOINAGE
RECOINAGES
RECOLLECT
RECOLLECTED
RECOLLECTING
RECOLLECTS
RÉCOLLET
RÉCOLLETS
RECOMBINE
RECOMBINED
RECOMBINES
RECOMBINING
RECOMFORT
RECOMFORTED
RECOMFORTING
RECOMFORTS
RECOMMEND
RECOMMENDED
RECOMMENDING
RECOMMENDS
RECOMMIT
RECOMMITS
RECOMMITTED

RECOMMITTING
RECOMPACT
RECOMPACTED
RECOMPACTING
RECOMPACTS
RECOMPOSE
RECOMPOSED
RECOMPOSES
RECOMPOSING
RECONCILE
RECONCILED
RECONCILES
RECONCILING
RECONDITE
RECONFIRM
RECONFIRMED
RECONFIRMING
RECONFIRMS
RECONNECT
RECONNECTED
RECONNECTING
RECONNECTS
RECONQUER
RECONQUERED
RECONQUERING
RECONQUERS
RECONVENE
RECONVENED
RECONVENES
RECONVENING
RECONVERT
RECONVERTED
RECONVERTING
RECONVERTS
RECONVEY
RECONVEYED
RECONVEYING
RECONVEYS
RECORD
RECORDED
RECORDER
RECORDERS
RECORDING
RECORDINGS
RECORDIST
RECORDISTS
RECORDS
RECOUNT
RECOUNTAL
RECOUNTALS
RECOUNTED
RECOUNTING
RECOUNTS
RECOUP
RECOUPED
RECOUPING
RECOUPS
RECOURE
RECOURED
RECOURES
RECOURING
RECOURSE
RECOURSED
RECOURSES
RECOURSING
RECOVER
RECOVERED
RECOVEREE
RECOVEREES
RECOVERER

RECOVERERS
RECOVERIES
RECOVERING
RECOVEROR
RECOVERORS
RECOVERS
RECOVERY
RECOWER
RECOWERED
RECOWERING
RECOWERS
RECOYLE
RECOYLED
RECOYLES
RECOYLING
RECREANCE
RECREANCES
RECREANCIES
RECREANCY
RECREANT
RECREANTS
RECREATE
RECREATED
RECREATES
RECREATING
RECREMENT
RECREMENTS
RECROSS
RECROSSED
RECROSSES
RECROSSING
RECRUIT
RECRUITAL
RECRUITALS
RECRUITED
RECRUITER
RECRUITERS
RECRUITING
RECRUITS
RECTA
RECTAL
RECTALLY
RECTANGLE
RECTANGLES
RECTI
RECTIFIED
RECTIFIER
RECTIFIERS
RECTIFIES
RECTIFY
RECTIFYING
RECTION
RECTIONS
RECTITIC
RECTITIS
RECTITISES
RECTITUDE
RECTITUDES
RECTO
RECTOR
RECTORAL
RECTORATE
RECTORATES
RECTORESS
RECTORESSES
RECTORIAL
RECTORIALS
RECTORIES
RECTORS
RECTORY

RECTOS
RECTRESS
RECTRESSES
RECTRICES
RECTRIX
RECTUM
RECTUMS
RECTUS
RECUILE
RECUILED
RECUILES
RECUILING
RECULE
RECULED
RECULES
RECULING
RECUMBENT
RECUR
RECURE
RECURED
RECURES
RECURING
RECURRED
RECURRENT
RECURRING
RECURS
RECURSION
RECURSIONS
RECURSIVE
RECURVE
RECURVED
RECURVES
RECURVING
RECUSANCE
RECUSANCES
RECUSANCIES
RECUSANCY
RECUSANT
RECUSANTS
RECUSE
RECUSED
RECUSES
RECUSING
RECYCLE
RECYCLED
RECYCLES
RECYCLING
RED
REDACT
REDACTED
REDACTING
REDACTION
REDACTIONS
REDACTOR
REDACTORS
REDACTS
REDAN
REDANS
REDARGUE
REDARGUED
REDARGUES
REDARGUING
REDBACK
REDBACKS
REDBREAST
REDBREASTS
REDBRICK
REDCOAT
REDCOATS
REDD

REDDEN
REDDENDA
REDDENDO
REDDENDOS
REDDENDUM
REDDENED
REDDENING
REDDENS
REDDER
REDDERS
REDDEST
REDDIER
REDDIEST
REDDING
REDDINGS
REDDISH
REDDLE
REDDLED
REDDLEMAN
REDDLEMEN
REDDLES
REDDLING
REDDS
REDDY
REDE
REDEAL
REDEALING
REDEALS
REDEALT
REDECRAFT
REDECRAFTS
REDEEM
REDEEMED
REDEEMER
REDEEMERS
REDEEMING
REDEEMS
REDEFINE
REDEFINED
REDEFINES
REDEFINING
REDELESS
REDELIVER
REDELIVERED
REDELIVERING
REDELIVERS
REDEPLOY
REDEPLOYED
REDEPLOYING
REDEPLOYS
REDES
REDESCEND
REDESCENDED
REDESCENDING
REDESCENDS
REDESIGN
REDESIGNED
REDESIGNING
REDESIGNS
REDEVELOP
REDEVELOPED
REDEVELOPING
REDEVELOPS
REDEYE
REDEYES
REDFISH
REDFISHES
REDHANDED
REDIA
REDIAE

REDID
REDING
REDINGOTE
REDINGOTES
REDIP
REDIPPED
REDIPPING
REDIPS
REDIRECT
REDIRECTED
REDIRECTING
REDIRECTS
REDISTIL
REDISTILLED
REDISTILLING
REDISTILS
REDIVIDE
REDIVIDED
REDIVIDES
REDIVIDING
REDIVIVUS
REDLEG
REDLEGS
REDLY
REDNECK
REDNECKS
REDNESS
REDNESSES
REDO
REDOES
REDOING
REDOLENCE
REDOLENCES
REDOLENCIES
REDOLENCY
REDOLENT
REDONE
REDOUBLE
REDOUBLED
REDOUBLES
REDOUBLING
REDOUBT
REDOUBTED
REDOUBTING
REDOUBTS
REDOUND
REDOUNDED
REDOUNDING
REDOUNDINGS
REDOUNDS
REDOWA
REDOWAS
REDOX
REDPOLL
REDPOLLS
REDRAFT
REDRAFTED
REDRAFTING
REDRAFTS
REDRAW
REDRAWING
REDRAWN
REDRAWS
REDRESS
REDRESSED
REDRESSER
REDRESSERS
REDRESSES
REDRESSING
REDREW

REDRIVE
REDRIVEN
REDRIVES
REDRIVING
REDROVE
REDS
REDSEAR
REDSHANK
REDSHANKS
REDSHARE
REDSHIRE
REDSHORT
REDSKIN
REDSKINS
REDSTART
REDSTARTS
REDSTREAK
REDSTREAKS
REDTOP
REDTOPS
REDUCE
REDUCED
REDUCER
REDUCERS
REDUCES
REDUCIBLE
REDUCING
REDUCTANT
REDUCTANTS
REDUCTASE
REDUCTASES
REDUCTION
REDUCTIONS
REDUCTIVE
REDUIT
REDUITS
REDUNDANT
REDWATER
REDWATERS
REDWING
REDWINGS
REDWOOD
REDWOODS
REE
REEBOK
REEBOKS
REECH
REECHED
REECHES
REECHIE
REECHIER
REECHIEST
REECHING
REECHY
REED
REEDE
REEDED
REEDEN
REEDER
REEDERS
REEDES
REEDIER
REEDIEST
REEDINESS
REEDINESSES
REEDING
REEDINGS
REEDLING
REEDLINGS
REEDS

REEDSTOP
REEDSTOPS
REEDY
REEF
REEFED
REEFER
REEFERS
REEFING
REEFINGS
REEFS
REEK
REEKED
REEKIE
REEKIER
REEKIEST
REEKING
REEKS
REEKY
REEL
REELED
REELER
REELERS
REELING
REELINGLY
REELINGS
REELMAN
REELMEN
REELS
REEN
REENS
REES
REEST
REESTED
REESTIER
REESTIEST
REESTING
REESTS
REESTY
REEVE
REEVED
REEVES
REEVING
REF
REFACE
REFACED
REFACES
REFACING
REFASHION
REFASHIONED
REFASHIONING
REFASHIONS
REFECT
REFECTED
REFECTING
REFECTION
REFECTIONS
REFECTORIES
REFECTORY
REFECTS
REFEL
REFELLED
REFELLING
REFELS
REFER
REFERABLE
REFEREE
REFEREED
REFEREEING
REFEREES
REFERENCE

REFERENCED
REFERENCES
REFERENCING
REFERENDA
REFERENT
REFERENTS
REFERRAL
REFERRALS
REFERRED
REFERRING
REFERS
REFFED
REFFING
REFFO
REFFOS
REFIGURE
REFIGURED
REFIGURES
REFIGURING
REFILL
REFILLED
REFILLING
REFILLS
REFINE
REFINED
REFINEDLY
REFINER
REFINERIES
REFINERS
REFINERY
REFINES
REFINING
REFININGS
REFIT
REFITMENT
REFITMENTS
REFITS
REFITTED
REFITTING
REFITTINGS
REFLAG
REFLAGGED
REFLAGGING
REFLAGS
REFLATE
REFLATED
REFLATES
REFLATING
REFLATION
REFLATIONS
REFLECT
REFLECTED
REFLECTER
REFLECTERS
REFLECTING
REFLECTOR
REFLECTORS
REFLECTS
REFLET
REFLETS
REFLEX
REFLEXED
REFLEXES
REFLEXING
REFLEXION
REFLEXIONS
REFLEXIVE
REFLEXLY
REFLOAT
REFLOATED

REFLOATING
REFLOATS
REFLOW
REFLOWED
REFLOWER
REFLOWERED
REFLOWERING
REFLOWERINGS
REFLOWERS
REFLOWING
REFLOWINGS
REFLOWS
REFLUENCE
REFLUENCES
REFLUENT
REFLUX
REFLUXED
REFLUXES
REFLUXING
REFOOT
REFOOTED
REFOOTING
REFOOTS
REFORM
REFORMADE
REFORMADES
REFORMADO
REFORMADOES
REFORMADOS
REFORMED
REFORMER
REFORMERS
REFORMING
REFORMISM
REFORMISMS
REFORMIST
REFORMISTS
REFORMS
REFORTIFIED
REFORTIFIES
REFORTIFY
REFORTIFYING
REFOUND
REFOUNDED
REFOUNDER
REFOUNDERS
REFOUNDING
REFOUNDS
REFRACT
REFRACTED
REFRACTING
REFRACTOR
REFRACTORS
REFRACTS
REFRAIN
REFRAINED
REFRAINING
REFRAINS
REFRAME
REFRAMED
REFRAMES
REFRAMING
REFREEZE
REFREEZES
REFREEZING
REFRESH
REFRESHED
REFRESHEN
REFRESHENED
REFRESHENING

REFRESHENS
REFRESHER
REFRESHERS
REFRESHES
REFRESHING
REFRINGE
REFRINGED
REFRINGES
REFRINGING
REFROZE
REFROZEN
REFS
REFT
REFUEL
REFUELLED
REFUELLING
REFUELS
REFUGE
REFUGED
REFUGEE
REFUGEES
REFUGES
REFUGIA
REFUGING
REFUGIUM
REFULGENT
REFUND
REFUNDED
REFUNDER
REFUNDERS
REFUNDING
REFUNDS
REFURBISH
REFURBISHED
REFURBISHES
REFURBISHING
REFURNISH
REFURNISHED
REFURNISHES
REFURNISHING
REFUSABLE
REFUSAL
REFUSALS
REFUSE
REFUSED
REFUSENIK
REFUSENIKS
REFUSER
REFUSERS
REFUSES
REFUSING
REFUSION
REFUSIONS
REFUSNIK
REFUSNIKS
REFUTABLE
REFUTABLY
REFUTAL
REFUTALS
REFUTE
REFUTED
REFUTER
REFUTERS
REFUTES
REFUTING
REGAIN
REGAINED
REGAINER
REGAINERS
REGAINING

REGAINS
REGAL
REGALE
REGALED
REGALES
REGALIA
REGALIAN
REGALIAS
REGALING
REGALISM
REGALISMS
REGALIST
REGALISTS
REGALITIES
REGALITY
REGALLY
REGALS
REGAR
REGARD
REGARDANT
REGARDED
REGARDER
REGARDERS
REGARDFUL
REGARDING
REGARDS
REGARS
REGATHER
REGATHERED
REGATHERING
REGATHERS
REGATTA
REGATTAS
REGAVE
REGELATE
REGELATED
REGELATES
REGELATING
REGENCE
REGENCES
REGENCIES
REGENCY
REGENT
REGENTS
REGEST
REGESTS
REGGAE
REGGAES
REGICIDAL
REGICIDE
REGICIDES
RÉGIE
RÉGIES
RÉGIME
REGIMEN
REGIMENS
REGIMENT
REGIMENTED
REGIMENTING
REGIMENTS
RÉGIMES
REGIMINAL
REGINA
REGINAE
REGINAL
REGINAS
REGION
REGIONAL
REGIONARY
REGIONS

REGISSEUR
REGISSEURS
REGISTER
REGISTERED
REGISTERING
REGISTERS
REGISTRAR
REGISTRARS
REGISTRIES
REGISTRY
REGIUS
REGIVE
REGIVEN
REGIVES
REGIVING
REGLET
REGLETS
REGMA
REGMATA
REGNAL
REGNANT
REGOLITH
REGOLITHS
REGORGE
REGORGED
REGORGES
REGORGING
REGRADE
REGRADED
REGRADES
REGRADING
REGRANT
REGRANTED
REGRANTING
REGRANTS
REGRATE
REGRATED
REGRATER
REGRATERS
REGRATES
REGRATING
REGRATINGS
REGRATOR
REGRATORS
REGREDE
REGREDED
REGREDES
REGREDING
REGREET
REGREETED
REGREETING
REGREETS
REGRESS
REGRESSED
REGRESSES
REGRESSING
REGRET
REGRETFUL
REGRETS
REGRETTED
REGRETTING
REGRIND
REGRINDING
REGRINDS
REGROUND
REGROUP
REGROUPED
REGROUPING
REGROUPS
REGROWTH

REGROWTHS
REGUERDON
REGUERDONED
REGUERDONING
REGUERDONS
REGULA
REGULAE
REGULAR
REGULARLY
REGULARS
REGULATE
REGULATED
REGULATES
REGULATING
REGULATOR
REGULATORS
REGULINE
REGULISE
REGULISED
REGULISES
REGULISING
REGULIZE
REGULIZED
REGULIZES
REGULIZING
REGULO
REGULOS
REGULUS
REGULUSES
REGUR
REGURS
REH
REHANDLE
REHANDLED
REHANDLES
REHANDLING
REHANDLINGS
REHASH
REHASHED
REHASHES
REHASHING
REHEAR
REHEARD
REHEARING
REHEARINGS
REHEARS
REHEARSAL
REHEARSALS
REHEARSE
REHEARSED
REHEARSER
REHEARSERS
REHEARSES
REHEARSING
REHEARSINGS
REHEAT
REHEATED
REHEATER
REHEATERS
REHEATING
REHEATS
REHEEL
REHEELED
REHEELING
REHEELS
REHOBOAM
REHOBOAMS
REHOUSE
REHOUSED
REHOUSES

REHOUSING
REHOUSINGS
REHS
REIF
REIFIED
REIFIES
REIFS
REIFY
REIFYING
REIGN
REIGNED
REIGNING
REIGNS
REIK
REIKS
REILLUME
REILLUMED
REILLUMES
REILLUMING
REIMBURSE
REIMBURSED
REIMBURSES
REIMBURSING
REIMPLANT
REIMPLANTED
REIMPLANTING
REIMPLANTS
REIMPORT
REIMPORTED
REIMPORTING
REIMPORTS
REIMPOSE
REIMPOSED
REIMPOSES
REIMPOSING
REIN
REINDEER
REINDEERS
REINED
REINETTE
REINETTES
REINFORCE
REINFORCED
REINFORCES
REINFORCING
REINFORM
REINFORMED
REINFORMING
REINFORMS
REINFUND
REINFUNDED
REINFUNDING
REINFUNDS
REINFUSE
REINFUSED
REINFUSES
REINFUSING
REINHABIT
REINHABITED
REINHABITING
REINHABITS
REINING
REINLESS
REINS
REINSERT
REINSERTED
REINSERTING
REINSERTS
REINSMAN
REINSMEN

REINSPECT
REINSPECTED
REINSPECTING
REINSPECTS
REINSPIRE
REINSPIRED
REINSPIRES
REINSPIRING
REINSTALL
REINSTALLED
REINSTALLING
REINSTALLS
REINSTATE
REINSTATED
REINSTATES
REINSTATING
REINSURE
REINSURED
REINSURER
REINSURERS
REINSURES
REINSURING
REINTER
REINTERRED
REINTERRING
REINTERS
REINVEST
REINVESTED
REINVESTING
REINVESTS
REINVOLVE
REINVOLVED
REINVOLVES
REINVOLVING
REIRD
REIRDS
REIS
REISES
REISSUE
REISSUED
REISSUES
REISSUING
REIST
REISTAFEL
REISTAFELS
REISTED
REISTIER
REISTIEST
REISTING
REISTS
REISTY
REITER
REITERANT
REITERATE
REITERATED
REITERATES
REITERATING
REITERS
REIVE
REIVER
REIVERS
REIVES
REIVING
REJECT
REJECTED
REJECTER
REJECTERS
REJECTING
REJECTION
REJECTIONS

REJECTIVE
REJECTOR
REJECTORS
REJECTS
REJIG
REJIGGED
REJIGGER
REJIGGERED
REJIGGERING
REJIGGERS
REJIGGING
REJIGS
REJOICE
REJOICED
REJOICER
REJOICERS
REJOICES
REJOICING
REJOICINGS
REJOIN
REJOINDER
REJOINDERS
REJOINED
REJOINING
REJOINS
REJÓN
REJONEO
REJONEOS
REJONES
REJOURN
REJOURNED
REJOURNING
REJOURNS
REJUDGE
REJUDGED
REJUDGES
REJUDGING
REKE
REKED
REKES
REKINDLE
REKINDLED
REKINDLES
REKINDLING
REKING
RELÂCHE
RELÂCHES
RELAID
RELAPSE
RELAPSED
RELAPSER
RELAPSERS
RELAPSES
RELAPSING
RELATE
RELATED
RELATER
RELATERS
RELATES
RELATING
RELATION
RELATIONS
RELATIVAL
RELATIVE
RELATIVES
RELATOR
RELATORS
RELAX
RELAXANT
RELAXANTS

RELAXED
RELAXES
RELAXIN
RELAXING
RELAXINS
RELAY
RELAYED
RELAYING
RELAYS
RELEASE
RELEASED
RELEASEE
RELEASEES
RELEASER
RELEASERS
RELEASES
RELEASING
RELEASOR
RELEASORS
RELEGABLE
RELEGATE
RELEGATED
RELEGATES
RELEGATING
RELENT
RELENTED
RELENTING
RELENTINGS
RELENTS
RELET
RELETS
RELETTING
RELEVANCE
RELEVANCES
RELEVANCIES
RELEVANCY
RELEVANT
RELIABLE
RELIABLY
RELIANCE
RELIANCES
RELIANT
RELIC
RELICS
RELICT
RELICTS
RELIDE
RELIE
RELIED
RELIEF
RELIEFS
RELIER
RELIERS
RELIES
RELIEVE
RELIEVED
RELIEVER
RELIEVERS
RELIEVES
RELIEVING
RELIEVO
RELIEVOS
RELIGHT
RELIGHTED
RELIGHTING
RELIGHTS
RELIGIEUX
RELIGION
RELIGIONS
RELIGIOSE

RELIGIOSO
RELIGIOUS
RELIGIOUSES
RELINE
RELINED
RELINES
RELINING
RELIQUARIES
RELIQUARY
RELIQUE
RELIQUES
RELIQUIAE
RELISH
RELISHED
RELISHES
RELISHING
RELIT
RELIVE
RELIVED
RELIVER
RELIVERED
RELIVERING
RELIVERS
RELIVES
RELIVING
RELLISH
RELLISHED
RELLISHES
RELLISHING
RELOAD
RELOADED
RELOADING
RELOADS
RELOCATE
RELOCATED
RELOCATES
RELOCATING
RELUCENT
RELUCT
RELUCTANT
RELUCTATE
RELUCTATED
RELUCTATES
RELUCTATING
RELUCTED
RELUCTING
RELUCTS
RELUME
RELUMED
RELUMES
RELUMINE
RELUMINED
RELUMINES
RELUMING
RELUMINING
RELY
RELYING
REM
REMADE
REMADES
REMAIN
REMAINDER
REMAINDERED
REMAINDERING
REMAINDERS
REMAINED
REMAINING
REMAINS
REMAKE
REMAKES

REMAKING
REMAN
REMAND
REMANDED
REMANDING
REMANDS
REMANENCE
REMANENCES
REMANENCIES
REMANENCY
REMANENT
REMANENTS
REMANET
REMANETS
REMANIÉ
REMANIÉS
REMANNED
REMANNING
REMANS
REMARK
REMARKED
REMARKER
REMARKERS
REMARKING
REMARKS
REMARQUÉ
REMARQUED
REMARQUÉS
REMARRIED
REMARRIES
REMARRY
REMARRYING
REMATCH
REMATCHED
REMATCHES
REMATCHING
REMBLAI
REMBLAIS
REMBLE
REMBLED
REMBLES
REMBLING
REMEAD
REMEADS
REMEASURE
REMEASURED
REMEASURES
REMEASURING
REMEDE
REMEDES
REMEDIAL
REMEDIAT
REMEDIATE
REMEDIED
REMEDIES
REMEDY
REMEDYING
REMEID
REMEIDS
REMEMBER
REMEMBERED
REMEMBERING
REMEMBERS
REMEN
REMENS
REMERCIED
REMERCIES
REMERCY
REMERCYING
REMERGE

EMERGED	REMOTEST	RENEGADES	RENOVATED	REP
EMERGES	REMOTION	RENEGADING	RENOVATES	REPACK
EMERGING	REMOTIONS	RENEGADO	RENOVATING	REPACKED
EMEX	REMOUD	RENEGADOS	RENOVATOR	REPACKING
EMIGATE	REMOULADE	RENEGATE	RENOVATORS	REPACKS
EMIGATED	RÉMOULADE	RENEGATES	RENOWN	REPAID
EMIGATES	REMOULADES	RENEGE	RENOWNED	REPAINT
EMIGATING	RÉMOULADES	RENEGED	RENOWNER	REPAINTED
EMIGES	REMOULD	RENEGER	RENOWNERS	REPAINTING
REMIGIAL	REMOULDED	RENEGERS	RENOWNING	REPAINTINGS
REMIGRATE	REMOULDING	RENEGES	RENOWNS	REPAINTS
REMIGRATED	REMOULDS	RENEGING	RENS	REPAIR
REMIGRATES	REMOUNT	RENEGUE	RENT	REPAIRED
REMIGRATING	REMOUNTED	RENEGUED	RENTABLE	REPAIRER
REMIND	REMOUNTING	RENEGUER	RENTAL	REPAIRERS
REMINDED	REMOUNTS	RENEGUERS	RENTALLER	REPAIRING
REMINDER	REMOVABLE	RENEGUES	RENTALLERS	REPAIRMAN
REMINDERS	REMOVABLY	RENEGUING	RENTALS	REPAIRMEN
REMINDFUL	REMOVAL	RENEW	RENTBOY	REPAIRS
REMINDING	REMOVALS	RENEWABLE	RENTBOYS	REPAND
REMINDS	REMOVE	RENEWAL	RENTE	REPAPER
REMINISCE	REMOVED	RENEWALS	RENTED	REPAPERED
REMINISCED	REMOVER	RENEWED	RENTER	REPAPERING
REMINISCES	REMOVERS	RENEWER	RENTERS	REPAPERS
REMINISCING	REMOVES	RENEWERS	RENTES	REPARABLE
REMISE	REMOVING	RENEWING	RENTIER	REPARABLY
REMISED	REMS	RENEWINGS	RENTIERS	REPARTEE
REMISES	REMUAGE	RENEWS	RENTING	REPARTEED
REMISING	REMUAGES	RENEY	RENTS	REPARTEEING
REMISS	REMUDA	RENEYED	RENUMBER	REPARTEES
REMISSION	REMUDAS	RENEYING	RENUMBERED	REPASS
REMISSIONS	REMUEUR	RENEYS	RENUMBERING	REPASSAGE
REMISSIVE	REMUEURS	RENFIERST	RENUMBERS	REPASSAGES
REMISSLY	REMURMUR	RENFORCE	RENVERSE	REPASSED
REMISSORY	REMURMURED	RENFORCED	RENVERSED	REPASSES
REMIT	REMURMURING	RENFORCES	RENVERSES	REPASSING
REMITMENT	REMURMURS	RENFORCING	RENVERSING	REPAST
REMITMENTS	REN	RENFORST	RENVERST	REPASTED
REMITS	RENAGUE	RENGA	RENVOI	REPASTING
REMITTAL	RENAGUED	RENGAS	RENVOIS	REPASTS
REMITTALS	RENAGUES	RENIED	RENVOY	REPASTURE
REMITTED	RENAGUING	RENIES	RENVOYS	REPASTURES
REMITTEE	RENAL	RENIFORM	RENY	REPAY
REMITTEES	RENAME	RENIG	RENYING	REPAYABLE
REMITTENT	RENAMED	RENIGGED	REOCCUPIED	REPAYING
REMITTER	RENAMES	RENIGGING	REOCCUPIES	REPAYMENT
REMITTERS	RENAMING	RENIGS	REOCCUPY	REPAYMENTS
REMITTING	RENASCENT	RENIN	REOCCUPYING	REPAYS
REMITTOR	RENAY	RENINS	REOFFEND	REPEAL
REMITTORS	RENAYED	RENITENCIES	REOFFENDED	REPEALED
REMNANT	RENAYING	RENITENCY	REOFFENDING	REPEALER
REMNANTS	RENAYS	RENITENT	REOFFENDS	REPEALERS
REMODEL	RENCONTRE	RENMINBI	REOPEN	REPEALING
REMODELLED	RENCONTRES	RENMINBIS	REOPENED	REPEALS
REMODELLING	REND	RENNE	REOPENER	REPEAT
REMODELS	RENDER	RENNED	REOPENERS	REPEATED
REMODIFIED	RENDERED	RENNES	REOPENING	REPEATER
REMODIFIES	RENDERER	RENNET	REOPENS	REPEATERS
REMODIFY	RENDERERS	RENNETS	REORDAIN	REPEATING
REMODIFYING	RENDERING	RENNIN	REORDAINED	REPEATINGS
REMONTANT	RENDERINGS	RENNING	REORDAINING	REPEATS
REMONTANTS	RENDERS	RENNINGS	REORDAINS	REPECHAGE
REMORA	RENDING	RENNINS	REORDER	REPEL
REMORAS	RENDITION	RENOUNCE	REORDERED	REPELLANT
REMORSE	RENDITIONS	RENOUNCED	REORDERING	REPELLANTS
REMORSES	RENDS	RENOUNCER	REORDERS	REPELLED
REMOTE	RENDZINA	RENOUNCERS	REORIENT	REPELLENT
REMOTELY	RENDZINAS	RENOUNCES	REORIENTED	REPELLENTS
REMOTER	RENEGADE	RENOUNCING	REORIENTING	REPELLER
REMOTES	RENEGADED	RENOVATE	REORIENTS	REPELLERS

REPELLING
REPELS
REPENT
REPENTANT
REPENTANTS
REPENTED
REPENTER
REPENTERS
REPENTING
REPENTS
REPEOPLE
REPEOPLED
REPEOPLES
REPEOPLING
REPERCUSS
REPERCUSSED
REPERCUSSES
REPERCUSSING
REPERTORIES
REPERTORY
REPERUSAL
REPERUSALS
REPERUSE
REPERUSED
REPERUSES
REPERUSING
REPETEND
REPETENDS
REPHRASE
REPHRASED
REPHRASES
REPHRASING
REPINE
REPINED
REPINER
REPINERS
REPINES
REPINING
REPININGS
REPIQUE
REPIQUED
REPIQUES
REPIQUING
REPLA
REPLACE
REPLACED
REPLACER
REPLACERS
REPLACES
REPLACING
REPLAN
REPLANNED
REPLANNING
REPLANS
REPLANT
REPLANTED
REPLANTING
REPLANTS
REPLAY
REPLAYED
REPLAYING
REPLAYS
REPLENISH
REPLENISHED
REPLENISHES
REPLENISHING
REPLETE
REPLETED
REPLETES
REPLETING

REPLETION
REPLETIONS
REPLEVIED
REPLEVIES
REPLEVIN
REPLEVINED
REPLEVINING
REPLEVINS
REPLEVY
REPLEVYING
REPLICA
REPLICAS
REPLICATE
REPLICATED
REPLICATES
REPLICATING
REPLIED
REPLIER
REPLIERS
REPLIES
REPLUM
REPLY
REPLYING
REPOINT
REPOINTED
REPOINTING
REPOINTS
REPONE
REPONED
REPONES
REPONING
REPORT
REPORTAGE
REPORTAGES
REPORTED
REPORTER
REPORTERS
REPORTING
REPORTINGS
REPORTS
REPOSAL
REPOSALL
REPOSALLS
REPOSALS
REPOSE
REPOSED
REPOSEDLY
REPOSEFUL
REPOSES
REPOSING
REPOSIT
REPOSITED
REPOSITING
REPOSITOR
REPOSITORS
REPOSITS
REPOSSESS
REPOSSESSED
REPOSSESSES
REPOSSESSING
REPOST
REPOSTED
REPOSTING
REPOSTS
REPOSURE
REPOSURES
REPOT
REPOTS
REPOTTED
REPOTTING

REPOTTINGS
REPOUSSÉ
REPOUSSÉS
REPP
REPPED
REPPING
REPPINGS
REPPS
REPREEVE
REPREEVED
REPREEVES
REPREEVING
REPREHEND
REPREHENDED
REPREHENDING
REPREHENDS
REPRESENT
REPRESENTED
REPRESENTING
REPRESENTS
REPRESS
REPRESSED
REPRESSES
REPRESSING
REPRESSOR
REPRESSORS
REPRIEFE
REPRIEFES
REPRIEVAL
REPRIEVALS
REPRIEVE
REPRIEVED
REPRIEVES
REPRIEVING
REPRIMAND
REPRIMANDED
REPRIMANDING
REPRIMANDS
REPRIME
REPRIMED
REPRIMES
REPRIMING
REPRINT
REPRINTED
REPRINTING
REPRINTS
REPRISAL
REPRISALS
REPRISE
REPRISED
REPRISES
REPRISING
REPRIVE
REPRIVED
REPRIVES
REPRIVING
REPRIZE
REPRIZED
REPRIZES
REPRIZING
REPRO
REPROACH
REPROACHED
REPROACHES
REPROACHING
REPROBACIES
REPROBACY
REPROBATE
REPROBATED
REPROBATES

REPROBATING
REPROCESS
REPROCESSED
REPROCESSES
REPROCESSING
REPRODUCE
REPRODUCED
REPRODUCES
REPRODUCING
REPROOF
REPROOFED
REPROOFING
REPROOFS
REPROS
REPROVAL
REPROVALS
REPROVE
REPROVED
REPROVER
REPROVERS
REPROVES
REPROVING
REPROVINGS
REPRYVE
REPRYVED
REPRYVES
REPRYVING
REPS
REPTANT
REPTATION
REPTATIONS
REPTILE
REPTILES
REPTILIAN
REPTILOID
REPUBLIC
REPUBLICS
REPUBLISH
REPUBLISHED
REPUBLISHES
REPUBLISHING
REPUDIATE
REPUDIATED
REPUDIATES
REPUDIATING
REPUGN
REPUGNANT
REPUGNED
REPUGNING
REPUGNS
REPULP
REPULPED
REPULPING
REPULPS
REPULSE
REPULSED
REPULSES
REPULSING
REPULSION
REPULSIONS
REPULSIVE
REPURE
REPURED
REPURES
REPURIFIED
REPURIFIES
REPURIFY
REPURIFYING
REPURING
REPUTABLE

REPUTABLY
REPUTE
REPUTED
REPUTEDLY
REPUTES
REPUTING
REPUTINGS
REQUERE
REQUERED
REQUERES
REQUERING
REQUEST
REQUESTED
REQUESTER
REQUESTERS
REQUESTING
REQUESTS
REQUICKEN
REQUICKENED
REQUICKENING
REQUICKENS
REQUIEM
REQUIEMS
REQUIGHT
REQUIGHTED
REQUIGHTING
REQUIGHTS
REQUIRE
REQUIRED
REQUIRER
REQUIRERS
REQUIRES
REQUIRING
REQUIRINGS
REQUISITE
REQUISITES
REQUIT
REQUITAL
REQUITALS
REQUITE
REQUITED
REQUITER
REQUITERS
REQUITES
REQUITING
REQUITS
REQUITTED
REQUITTING
REQUOTE
REQUOTED
REQUOTES
REQUOTING
REQUOYLE
REQUOYLED
REQUOYLES
REQUOYLING
RERADIATE
RERADIATED
RERADIATES
RERADIATING
RERAIL
RERAILED
RERAILING
RERAILS
RERAN
REREAD
REREADING
REREADS
REREBRACE
REREBRACES

REREDORSE
REREDORSES
REREDOS
REREDOSES
REREDOSSE
REREDOSSES
REREMICE
REREMOUSE
REREVISE
REREVISED
REREVISES
REREVISING
REREWARD
REREWARDS
REROUTE
REROUTEING
REROUTES
REROUTING
RERUN
RERUNNING
RERUNS
RES
RESAID
RESALE
RESALES
RESALGAR
RESALGARS
RESALUTE
RESALUTED
RESALUTES
RESALUTING
RESAT
RESAY
RESAYING
RESAYS
RESCALE
RESCALED
RESCALES
RESCALING
RESCIND
RESCINDED
RESCINDING
RESCINDS
RESCORE
RESCORED
RESCORES
RESCORING
RESCRIPT
RESCRIPTED
RESCRIPTING
RESCRIPTS
RESCUABLE
RESCUE
RESCUED
RESCUER
RESCUERS
RESCUES
RESCUING
RESEAL
RESEALED
RESEALING
RESEALS
RESEARCH
RESEARCHED
RESEARCHES
RESEARCHING
RESEAT
RESEATED
RESEATING

RESEATS
RÉSEAU
RÉSEAUS
RÉSEAUX
RESECT
RESECTED
RESECTING
RESECTION
RESECTIONS
RESECTS
RESEDA
RESEDAS
RESEIZE
RESEIZED
RESEIZES
RESEIZING
RESELECT
RESELECTED
RESELECTING
RESELECTS
RESELL
RESELLING
RESELLS
RESEMBLE
RESEMBLED
RESEMBLER
RESEMBLERS
RESEMBLES
RESEMBLING
RESENT
RESENTED
RESENTER
RESENTERS
RESENTFUL
RESENTING
RESENTIVE
RESENTS
RESERPINE
RESERPINES
RESERVE
RESERVED
RESERVES
RESERVING
RESERVIST
RESERVISTS
RESERVOIR
RESERVOIRED
RESERVOIRING
RESERVOIRS
RESET
RESETS
RESETTED
RESETTER
RESETTERS
RESETTING
RESETTLE
RESETTLED
RESETTLES
RESETTLING
RESHAPE
RESHAPED
RESHAPES
RESHAPING
RESHIP
RESHIPPED
RESHIPPING
RESHIPS
RESHUFFLE
RESHUFFLED
RESHUFFLES

RESHUFFLING
RESIANCE
RESIANCES
RESIANT
RESIANTS
RESIDE
RESIDED
RESIDENCE
RESIDENCES
RESIDENCIES
RESIDENCY
RESIDENT
RESIDENTS
RESIDER
RESIDERS
RESIDES
RESIDING
RESIDUA
RESIDUAL
RESIDUALS
RESIDUARY
RESIDUE
RESIDUES
RESIDUOUS
RESIDUUM
RESIGN
RESIGNED
RESIGNER
RESIGNERS
RESIGNING
RESIGNS
RESILE
RESILED
RESILES
RESILIENT
RESILING
RESIN
RESINATA
RESINATAS
RESINATE
RESINATES
RESINED
RESINER
RESINERS
RESINIFIED
RESINIFIES
RESINIFY
RESINIFYING
RESINING
RESINISE
RESINISED
RESINISES
RESINISING
RESINIZE
RESINIZED
RESINIZES
RESINIZING
RESINOID
RESINOIDS
RESINOSES
RESINOSIS
RESINOUS
RESINS
RESIST
RESISTANT
RESISTANTS
RESISTED
RESISTENT
RESISTENTS
RESISTING

RESISTIVE
RESISTOR
RESISTORS
RESISTS
RESIT
RESITS
RESITTING
RESKEW
RESKEWED
RESKEWING
RESKEWS
RESKUE
RESKUED
RESKUES
RESKUING
RESNATRON
RESNATRONS
RESOLD
RESOLE
RESOLED
RESOLES
RESOLING
RESOLUBLE
RESOLUTE
RESOLUTES
RESOLVE
RESOLVED
RESOLVENT
RESOLVENTS
RESOLVER
RESOLVERS
RESOLVES
RESOLVING
RESONANCE
RESONANCES
RESONANT
RESONATE
RESONATED
RESONATES
RESONATING
RESONATOR
RESONATORS
RESORB
RESORBED
RESORBENT
RESORBING
RESORBS
RESORCIN
RESORCINS
RESORT
RESORTED
RESORTER
RESORTERS
RESORTING
RESORTS
RESOUND
RESOUNDED
RESOUNDING
RESOUNDS
RESOURCE
RESOURCED
RESOURCES
RESOURCING
RESPEAK
RESPEAKING
RESPEAKS
RESPECT
RESPECTED
RESPECTER
RESPECTERS

RESPECTING
RESPECTS
RESPELL
RESPELLED
RESPELLING
RESPELLS
RESPELT
RESPIRE
RESPIRED
RESPIRES
RESPIRING
RESPITE
RESPITED
RESPITES
RESPITING
RESPLEND
RESPLENDED
RESPLENDING
RESPLENDS
RESPOKE
RESPOKEN
RESPOND
RESPONDED
RESPONDER
RESPONDERS
RESPONDING
RESPONDS
RESPONSA
RESPONSE
RESPONSER
RESPONSERS
RESPONSES
RESPONSOR
RESPONSORS
RESPONSUM
RESPONSUMS
RESPRAY
RESPRAYED
RESPRAYING
RESPRAYS
RESSALDAR
RESSALDARS
REST
RESTAFF
RESTAFFED
RESTAFFING
RESTAFFS
RESTAGE
RESTAGED
RESTAGES
RESTAGING
RESTART
RESTARTED
RESTARTER
RESTARTERS
RESTARTING
RESTARTS
RESTATE
RESTATED
RESTATES
RESTATING
RESTED
RESTEM
RESTEMMED
RESTEMMING
RESTEMS
RESTER
RESTERS
RESTFUL
RESTFULLER

RESTFULLEST	RESURGENT	RETHINK	RETORTED	RETRIEVE
RESTFULLY	RESURGES	RETHINKING	RETORTER	RETRIEVED
RESTIER	RESURGING	RETHINKS	RETORTERS	RETRIEVER
RESTIEST	RESURRECT	RETHOUGHT	RETORTING	RETRIEVERS
RESTIFF	RESURRECTED	RETIAL	RETORTION	RETRIEVES
RESTIFORM	RESURRECTING	RETIARII	RETORTIONS	RETRIEVING
RESTING	RESURRECTS	RETIARIUS	RETORTIVE	RETRIEVINGS
RESTINGS	RESURVEY	RETIARIUSES	RETORTS	RETRIM
RESTITUTE	RESURVEYED	RETIARY	RETOUCH	RETRIMMED
RESTITUTED	RESURVEYING	RETICENCE	RETOUCHED	RETRIMMING
RESTITUTES	RESURVEYS	RETICENCES	RETOUCHER	RETRIMS
RESTITUTING	RET	RETICENCIES	RETOUCHERS	RETRO
RESTIVE	RETABLE	RETICENCY	RETOUCHES	RETROACT
RESTIVELY	RETABLES	RETICENT	RETOUCHING	RETROACTED
RESTLESS	RETAIL	RETICLE	RETOUR	RETROACTING
RESTOCK	RETAILED	RETICLES	RETOURED	RETROACTS
RESTOCKED	RETAILER	RETICULAR	RETOURING	RETROCEDE
RESTOCKING	RETAILERS	RETICULE	RETOURS	RETROCEDED
RESTOCKS	RETAILING	RETICULES	RETRACE	RETROCEDES
RESTORE	RETAILS	RETICULUM	RETRACED	RETROCEDING
RESTORED	RETAIN	RETICULUMS	RETRACES	RETROD
RESTORER	RETAINED	RETIE	RETRACING	RETRODDEN
RESTORERS	RETAINER	RETIED	RETRACT	RETROFIT
RESTORES	RETAINERS	RETIES	RETRACTED	RETROFITS
RESTORING	RETAINING	RETIFORM	RETRACTING	RETROFITTED
RESTRAIN	RETAINS	RETILE	RETRACTOR	RETROFITTING
RESTRAINED	RETAKE	RETILED	RETRACTORS	RETROFITTINGS
RESTRAINING	RETAKEN	RETILES	RETRACTS	RETROFLEX
RESTRAININGS	RETAKER	RETILING	RETRAICT	RETROJECT
RESTRAINS	RETAKERS	RETINA	RETRAICTS	RETROJECTED
RESTRAINT	RETAKES	RETINAE	RETRAIN	RETROJECTING
RESTRAINTS	RETAKING	RETINAL	RETRAINED	RETROJECTS
RESTRICT	RETAKINGS	RETINAS	RETRAINING	RETRORSE
RESTRICTED	RETALIATE	RETINITE	RETRAINS	RETROS
RESTRICTING	RETALIATED	RETINITES	RETRAIT	RETROUSSÉ
RESTRICTS	RETALIATES	RETINITIS	RETRAITE	RETROVERT
RESTRING	RETALIATING	RETINITISES	RETRAITES	RETROVERTED
RESTRINGE	RETAMA	RETINOL	RETRAITS	RETROVERTING
RESTRINGED	RETAMAS	RETINOLS	RETRAITT	RETROVERTS
RESTRINGES	RETARD	RETINUE	RETRAITTS	RETRY
RESTRINGING	RETARDANT	RETINUES	RETRAL	RETRYING
RESTRINGS	RETARDANTS	RETINULA	RETRALLY	RETS
RESTRUNG	RETARDATE	RETINULAE	RETRATE	RETSINA
RESTS	RETARDATES	RETINULAR	RETRATED	RETSINAS
RESTY	RETARDED	RETIRACIES	RETRATES	RETTED
RESTYLE	RETARDER	RETIRACY	RETRATING	RETTERIES
RESTYLED	RETARDERS	RETIRAL	RETREAD	RETTERY
RESTYLES	RETARDING	RETIRALS	RETREADED	RETTING
RESTYLING	RETARDS	RETIRE	RETREADING	RETUND
RESUBMIT	RETCH	RETIRED	RETREADS	RETUNDED
RESUBMITS	RETCHED	RETIREDLY	RETREAT	RETUNDING
RESUBMITTED	RETCHES	RETIREE	RETREATED	RETUNDS
RESUBMITTING	RETCHING	RETIREES	RETREATING	RETUNE
RESULT	RETCHLESS	RETIRER	RETREATS	RETUNED
RESULTANT	RETE	RETIRERS	RETREE	RETUNES
RESULTANTS	RETELL	RETIRES	RETREES	RETUNING
RESULTED	RETELLER	RETIRING	RETRENCH	RETURF
RESULTFUL	RETELLERS	RETITLE	RETRENCHED	RETURFED
RESULTING	RETELLING	RETITLED	RETRENCHES	RETURFING
RESULTS	RETELLS	RETITLES	RETRENCHING	RETURFS
RESUMABLE	RETENE	RETITLING	RETRIAL	RETURN
RESUME	RETENES	RETOLD	RETRIALS	RETURNED
RÉSUMÉ	RETENTION	RETOOK	RETRIBUTE	RETURNEE
RESUMED	RETENTIONS	RETOOL	RETRIBUTED	RETURNEES
RESUMES	RETENTIVE	RETOOLED	RETRIBUTES	RETURNING
RÉSUMÉS	RETES	RETOOLING	RETRIBUTING	RETURNS
RESUMING	RETEXTURE	RETOOLS	RETRIED	RETUSE
RESUPINE	RETEXTURED	RETORSION	RETRIES	RETYING
RESURGE	RETEXTURES	RETORSIONS	RETRIEVAL	REUNIFIED
RESURGED	RETEXTURING	RETORT	RETRIEVALS	REUNIFIES

REUNIFY	REVERBING	REVIEWER	REVULSIONS	RHAPSODES
REUNIFYING	REVERBS	REVIEWERS	REVULSIVE	RHAPSODIC
REUNION	REVERE	REVIEWING	REVVED	RHAPSODIES
REUNIONS	REVERED	REVIEWS	REVVING	RHAPSODY
REUNITE	REVERENCE	REVILE	REVYING	RHATANIES
REUNITED	REVERENCED	REVILED	REW	RHATANY
REUNITES	REVERENCES	REVILER	REWARD	RHEA
REUNITING	REVERENCING	REVILERS	REWARDED	RHEAS
REURGE	REVEREND	REVILES	REWARDER	RHEMATIC
REURGED	REVERENDS	REVILING	REWARDERS	RHENIUM
REURGES	REVERENT	REVILINGS	REWARDFUL	RHENIUMS
REURGING	REVERER	REVISABLE	REWARDING	RHEOCHORD
REUSABLE	REVERERS	REVISAL	REWARDS	RHEOCHORDS
REUSE	REVERES	REVISALS	REWAREWA	RHEOCORD
REUSED	REVERIE	REVISE	REWAREWAS	RHEOCORDS
REUSES	REVERIES	REVISED	REWEIGH	RHEOLOGIC
REUSING	REVERING	REVISER	REWEIGHED	RHEOLOGIES
REUTTER	REVERIST	REVISERS	REWEIGHING	RHEOLOGY
REUTTERED	REVERISTS	REVISES	REWEIGHS	RHEOMETER
REUTTERING	REVERS	REVISING	REWIND	RHEOMETERS
REUTTERS	REVERSAL	REVISION	REWINDING	RHEOSTAT
REV	REVERSALS	REVISIONS	REWINDS	RHEOSTATS
REVALENTA	REVERSE	REVISIT	REWIRE	RHEOTAXES
REVALENTAS	REVERSED	REVISITED	REWIRED	RHEOTAXIS
REVALUE	REVERSELY	REVISITING	REWIRES	RHEOTOME
REVALUED	REVERSER	REVISITS	REWIRING	RHEOTOMES
REVALUES	REVERSERS	REVISOR	REWORD	RHEOTROPE
REVALUING	REVERSES	REVISORS	REWORDED	RHEOTROPES
REVAMP	REVERSI	REVISORY	REWORDING	RHESUS
REVAMPED	REVERSING	REVIVABLE	REWORDS	RHESUSES
REVAMPING	REVERSINGS	REVIVABLY	REWORK	RHETOR
REVAMPS	REVERSION	REVIVAL	REWORKED	RHETORIC
REVANCHE	REVERSIONS	REVIVALS	REWORKING	RHETORICS
REVANCHES	REVERSIS	REVIVE	REWORKS	RHETORISE
REVEAL	REVERSISES	REVIVED	REWOUND	RHETORISED
REVEALED	REVERSO	REVIVER	REWRAP	RHETORISES
REVEALER	REVERSOS	REVIVERS	REWRAPPED	RHETORISING
REVEALERS	REVERT	REVIVES	REWRAPPING	RHETORIZE
REVEALING	REVERTED	REVIVIFIED	REWRAPS	RHETORIZED
REVEALINGS	REVERTING	REVIVIFIES	REWRITE	RHETORIZES
REVEALS	REVERTIVE	REVIVIFY	REWRITES	RHETORIZING
REVEILLE	REVERTS	REVIVIFYING	REWRITING	RHETORS
REVEILLES	REVERY	REVIVING	REWRITTEN	RHEUM
REVEL	REVEST	REVIVINGS	REWROTE	RHEUMATIC
REVELATOR	REVESTED	REVIVOR	REWS	RHEUMATICS
REVELATORS	REVESTING	REVIVORS	REWTH	RHEUMATIZ
REVELLED	REVESTRIES	REVOCABLE	REWTHS	RHEUMATIZES
REVELLER	REVESTRY	REVOCABLY	REX	RHEUMATIZZES
REVELLERS	REVESTS	REVOKE	REYNARD	RHEUMED
REVELLING	REVET	REVOKED	REYNARDS	RHEUMS
REVELLINGS	REVETMENT	REVOKES	RHABDOID	RHEUMY
REVELRIES	REVETMENTS	REVOKING	RHABDOIDS	RHEXES
REVELRY	REVETS	REVOLT	RHABDOM	RHEXIS
REVELS	REVETTED	REVOLTED	RHABDOMS	RHEXISES
REVENANT	REVETTING	REVOLTER	RHABDUS	RHIES
REVENANTS	RÊVEUR	REVOLTERS	RHABDUSES	RHIME
REVENGE	RÊVEURS	REVOLTING	RHACHIDES	RHIMES
REVENGED	RÊVEUSE	REVOLTS	RHACHIS	RHINAL
REVENGER	RÊVEUSES	REVOLUTE	RHACHISES	RHINE
REVENGERS	REVICTUAL	REVOLVE	RHACHITIS	RHINES
REVENGES	REVICTUALLED	REVOLVED	RHACHITISES	RHINITIS
REVENGING	REVICTUALLING	REVOLVER	RHAMPHOID	RHINITISES
REVENGINGS	REVICTUALS	REVOLVERS	RHAPHE	RHINO
REVENGIVE	REVIE	REVOLVES	RHAPHES	RHINOLITH
REVENUE	REVIED	REVOLVING	RHAPHIDE	RHINOLITHS
REVENUED	REVIES	REVOLVINGS	RHAPHIDES	RHINOLOGIES
REVENUES	REVIEW	REVS	RHAPHIS	RHINOLOGY
REVERABLE	REVIEWAL	REVUE	RHAPONTIC	RHINOS
REVERB	REVIEWALS	REVUES	RHAPONTICS	RHIPIDATE
REVERBED	REVIEWED	REVULSION	RHAPSODE	RHIPIDION

RHIPIDIONS	RHOTACISE	RIATAS	RICH	RIDDLE
RHIPIDIUM	RHOTACISED	RIB	RICHED	RIDDLED
RHIPIDIUMS	RHOTACISES	RIBALD	RICHEN	RIDDLER
RHIZIC	RHOTACISING	RIBALDRIES	RICHENED	RIDDLERS
RHIZINE	RHOTACISM	RIBALDRY	RICHENING	RIDDLES
RHIZINES	RHOTACISMS	RIBALDS	RICHENS	RIDDLING
RHIZOBIA	RHOTACIZE	RIBAND	RICHER	RIDDLINGS
RHIZOBIUM	RHOTACIZED	RIBANDED	RICHES	RIDE
RHIZOCARP	RHOTACIZES	RIBANDING	RICHESSE	RIDEABLE
RHIZOCARPS	RHOTACIZING	RIBANDS	RICHESSES	RIDENT
RHIZOCAUL	RHOTIC	RIBATTUTA	RICHEST	RIDER
RHIZOCAULS	RHUBARB	RIBATTUTAS	RICHING	RIDERED
RHIZOID	RHUBARBS	RIBAUD	RICHLY	RIDERLESS
RHIZOIDAL	RHUBARBY	RIBAUDRED	RICHNESS	RIDERS
RHIZOIDS	RHUMB	RIBAUDRIES	RICHNESSES	RIDES
RHIZOME	RHUMBA	RIBAUDRY	RICHT	RIDGE
RHIZOMES	RHUMBAED	RIBAUDS	RICHTED	RIDGEBACK
RHIZOPI	RHUMBAING	RIBBAND	RICHTER	RIDGEBACKS
RHIZOPOD	RHUMBAS	RIBBANDED	RICHTEST	RIDGED
RHIZOPODS	RHUMBS	RIBBANDING	RICHTING	RIDGEL
RHIZOPUS	RHUS	RIBBANDS	RICHTS	RIDGELS
RHIZOPUSES	RHUSES	RIBBED	RICIER	RIDGES
RHO	RHY	RIBBIER	RICIEST	RIDGEWAY
RHODAMINE	RHYME	RIBBIEST	RICIN	RIDGEWAYS
RHODAMINES	RHYMED	RIBBING	RICING	RIDGIER
RHODANATE	RHYMELESS	RIBBINGS	RICINS	RIDGIEST
RHODANATES	RHYMER	RIBBON	RICK	RIDGIL
RHODANIC	RHYMERS	RIBBONED	RICKED	RIDGILS
RHODANISE	RHYMES	RIBBONING	RICKER	RIDGING
RHODANISED	RHYMESTER	RIBBONRIES	RICKERS	RIDGINGS
RHODANISES	RHYMESTERS	RIBBONRY	RICKETILY	RIDGLING
RHODANISING	RHYMING	RIBBONS	RICKETS	RIDGLINGS
RHODANIZE	RHYMIST	RIBBONY	RICKETTY	RIDGY
RHODANIZED	RHYMISTS	RIBBY	RICKETY	RIDICULE
RHODANIZES	RHYNE	RIBCAGE	RICKING	RIDICULED
RHODANIZING	RHYNES	RIBCAGES	RICKLE	RIDICULER
RHODIC	RHYOLITE	RIBIBE	RICKLES	RIDICULERS
RHODIUM	RHYOLITES	RIBIBES	RICKLY	RIDICULES
RHODIUMS	RHYOLITIC	RIBIBLE	RICKS	RIDICULING
RHODOLITE	RHYTA	RIBIBLES	RICKSHA	RIDING
RHODOLITES	RHYTHM	RIBLESS	RICKSHAS	RIDINGS
RHODONITE	RHYTHMAL	RIBLET	RICKSHAW	RIDOTTO
RHODONITES	RHYTHMED	RIBLETS	RICKSHAWS	RIDOTTOS
RHODOPSIN	RHYTHMI	RIBLIKE	RICKSTAND	RIDS
RHODOPSINS	RHYTHMIC	RIBOSE	RICKSTANDS	RIEL
RHODORA	RHYTHMICS	RIBOSES	RICKSTICK	RIELS
RHODORAS	RHYTHMISE	RIBOSOMAL	RICKSTICKS	RIEM
RHODOUS	RHYTHMISED	RIBOSOME	RICKYARD	RIEMPIE
RHOEADINE	RHYTHMISES	RIBOSOMES	RICKYARDS	RIEMPIES
RHOEADINES	RHYTHMISING	RIBS	RICOCHET	RIEMS
RHOMB	RHYTHMIST	RIBSTON	RICOCHETED	RIEVE
RHOMBI	RHYTHMISTS	RIBSTONE	RICOCHETING	RIEVER
RHOMBIC	RHYTHMIZE	RIBSTONES	RICOCHETS	RIEVERS
RHOMBOI	RHYTHMIZED	RIBSTONS	RICOCHETTED	RIEVES
RHOMBOID	RHYTHMIZES	RIBWORK	RICOCHETTING	RIEVING
RHOMBOIDS	RHYTHMIZING	RIBWORKS	RICOTTA	RIFE
RHOMBOS	RHYTHMS	RIBWORT	RICOTTAS	RIFELY
RHOMBS	RHYTHMUS	RIBWORTS	RICTAL	RIFENESS
RHOMBUS	RHYTHMUSES	RICE	RICTUS	RIFENESSES
RHOMBUSES	RHYTINA	RICED	RICTUSES	RIFER
RHONCHAL	RHYTINAS	RICER	RICY	RIFEST
RHONCHI	RHYTON	RICERCAR	RID	RIFF
RHONCHIAL	RIA	RICERCARE	RIDABLE	RIFFLE
RHONCHUS	RIAL	RICERCARES	RIDDANCE	RIFFLED
RHONE	RIALS	RICERCARS	RIDDANCES	RIFFLER
RHONES	RIANCIES	RICERCATA	RIDDED	RIFFLERS
RHOPALIC	RIANCY	RICERCATAS	RIDDEN	RIFFLES
RHOPALISM	RIANT	RICERS	RIDDER	RIFFLING
RHOPALISMS	RIAS	RICES	RIDDERS	RIFFS
RHOS	RIATA	RICEY	RIDDING	RIFLE

RIFLED
RIFLEMAN
RIFLEMEN
RIFLER
RIFLERS
RIFLES
RIFLING
RIFLINGS
RIFT
RIFTE
RIFTED
RIFTIER
RIFTIEST
RIFTING
RIFTLESS
RIFTS
RIFTY
RIG
RIGADOON
RIGADOONS
RIGG
RIGGALD
RIGGALDS
RIGGED
RIGGER
RIGGERS
RIGGING
RIGGINGS
RIGGISH
RIGGS
RIGHT
RIGHTABLE
RIGHTED
RIGHTEN
RIGHTENED
RIGHTENING
RIGHTENS
RIGHTEOUS
RIGHTER
RIGHTERS
RIGHTEST
RIGHTFUL
RIGHTING
RIGHTINGS
RIGHTIST
RIGHTISTS
RIGHTLESS
RIGHTLY
RIGHTNESS
RIGHTNESSES
RIGHTO
RIGHTOS
RIGHTS
RIGHTWARD
RIGHTWARDS
RIGID
RIGIDER
RIGIDEST
RIGIDIFIED
RIGIDIFIES
RIGIDIFY
RIGIDIFYING
RIGIDISE
RIGIDISED
RIGIDISES
RIGIDISING
RIGIDITIES
RIGIDITY
RIGIDIZE
RIGIDIZED

RIGIDIZES
RIGIDIZING
RIGIDLY
RIGIDNESS
RIGIDNESSES
RIGIDS
RIGLIN
RIGLING
RIGLINGS
RIGLINS
RIGMAROLE
RIGMAROLES
RIGOL
RIGOLL
RIGOLLS
RIGOLS
RIGOR
RIGORISM
RIGORISMS
RIGORIST
RIGORISTS
RIGOROUS
RIGORS
RIGOUR
RIGOURS
RIGS
RIGWIDDIE
RIGWIDDIES
RIGWOODIE
RIGWOODIES
RIJSTAFEL
RIJSTAFELS
RILE
RILED
RILES
RILEY
RILIEVI
RILIEVO
RILING
RILL
RILLE
RILLED
RILLES
RILLET
RILLETS
RILLETTES
RILLING
RILLMARK
RILLMARKS
RILLS
RIM
RIMA
RIMAE
RIME
RIMED
RIMER
RIMERS
RIMES
RIMIER
RIMIEST
RIMING
RIMLESS
RIMMED
RIMMING
RIMOSE
RIMOUS
RIMS
RIMU
RIMUS
RIMY

RIN
RIND
RINDED
RINDIER
RINDIEST
RINDING
RINDLESS
RINDS
RINDY
RINE
RINES
RING
RINGBIT
RINGBITS
RINGBONE
RINGBONES
RINGED
RINGENT
RINGER
RINGERS
RINGGIT
RINGGITS
RINGHALS
RINGHALSES
RINGING
RINGINGLY
RINGINGS
RINGLESS
RINGLET
RINGLETED
RINGLETS
RINGMAN
RINGMEN
RINGS
RINGSIDE
RINGSIDER
RINGSIDERS
RINGSIDES
RINGSTAND
RINGSTANDS
RINGSTER
RINGSTERS
RINGTAIL
RINGTAILS
RINGWAY
RINGWAYS
RINGWISE
RINGWORK
RINGWORKS
RINGWORM
RINGWORMS
RINK
RINKED
RINKHALS
RINKHALSES
RINKING
RINKS
RINNING
RINS
RINSABLE
RINSE
RINSED
RINSER
RINSERS
RINSES
RINSIBLE
RINSING
RINSINGS
RIOT
RIOTED

RIOTER
RIOTERS
RIOTING
RIOTINGS
RIOTISE
RIOTISES
RIOTIZE
RIOTIZES
RIOTOUS
RIOTOUSLY
RIOTRIES
RIOTRY
RIOTS
RIP
RIPARIAL
RIPARIAN
RIPARIANS
RIPE
RIPECK
RIPECKS
RIPED
RIPELY
RIPEN
RIPENED
RIPENESS
RIPENESSES
RIPENING
RIPENS
RIPER
RIPERS
RIPES
RIPEST
RIPIENI
RIPIENIST
RIPIENISTS
RIPIENO
RIPIENOS
RIPING
RIPOSTE
RIPOSTED
RIPOSTES
RIPOSTING
RIPP
RIPPED
RIPPER
RIPPERS
RIPPIER
RIPPIERS
RIPPING
RIPPINGLY
RIPPLE
RIPPLED
RIPPLER
RIPPLERS
RIPPLES
RIPPLET
RIPPLETS
RIPPLIER
RIPPLIEST
RIPPLING
RIPPLINGS
RIPPLY
RIPPS
RIPRAP
RIPRAPS
RIPS
RIPT
RIPTIDE
RIPTIDES
RISALDAR

RISALDARS
RISE
RISEN
RISER
RISERS
RISES
RISHI
RISHIS
RISIBLE
RISING
RISINGS
RISK
RISKED
RISKER
RISKERS
RISKFUL
RISKIER
RISKIEST
RISKILY
RISKINESS
RISKINESSES
RISKING
RISKS
RISKY
RISOLUTO
RISOTTO
RISOTTOS
RISP
RISPED
RISPETTI
RISPETTO
RISPING
RISPINGS
RISPS
RISQUE
RISQUÉ
RISQUES
RISSOLE
RISSOLES
RISUS
RISUSES
RIT
RITE
RITELESS
RITENUTO
RITENUTOS
RITES
RITORNEL
RITORNELL
RITORNELLS
RITORNELS
RITS
RITT
RITTED
RITTER
RITTERS
RITTING
RITTS
RITUAL
RITUALISE
RITUALISED
RITUALISES
RITUALISING
RITUALISM
RITUALISMS
RITUALIST
RITUALISTS
RITUALIZE
RITUALIZED
RITUALIZES

RITUALIZING
RITUALLY
RITUALS
RITZIER
RITZIEST
RITZY
RIVA
RIVAGE
RIVAGES
RIVAL
RIVALESS
RIVALESSES
RIVALISE
RIVALISED
RIVALISES
RIVALISING
RIVALITIES
RIVALITY
RIVALIZE
RIVALIZED
RIVALIZES
RIVALIZING
RIVALLED
RIVALLESS
RIVALLING
RIVALRIES
RIVALRY
RIVALS
RIVALSHIP
RIVALSHIPS
RIVAS
RIVE
RIVED
RIVEL
RIVELLED
RIVELLING
RIVELS
RIVEN
RIVER
RIVERAIN
RIVERAINS
RIVERED
RIVERET
RIVERETS
RIVERINE
RIVERLESS
RIVERLIKE
RIVERMAN
RIVERMEN
RIVERS
RIVERSIDE
RIVERSIDES
RIVERWAY
RIVERWAYS
RIVERWEED
RIVERWEEDS
RIVERY
RIVES
RIVET
RIVETED
RIVETER
RIVETERS
RIVETING
RIVETINGS
RIVETS
RIVETTED
RIVETTING
RIVIERA
RIVIERAS
RIVIÈRE

RIVIÈRES
RIVING
RIVLIN
RIVLINS
RIVO
RIVOS
RIVULET
RIVULETS
RIYAL
RIYALS
RIZ
RIZARD
RIZARDS
RIZZAR
RIZZARED
RIZZARING
RIZZARS
RIZZART
RIZZARTS
RIZZER
RIZZERED
RIZZERING
RIZZERS
RIZZOR
RIZZORED
RIZZORING
RIZZORS
ROACH
ROACHED
ROACHES
ROACHING
ROAD
ROADBLOCK
ROADBLOCKS
ROADHOUSE
ROADHOUSES
ROADIE
ROADIES
ROADING
ROADINGS
ROADLESS
ROADMAN
ROADMEN
ROADS
ROADSHOW
ROADSHOWS
ROADSIDE
ROADSIDES
ROADSMAN
ROADSMEN
ROADSTEAD
ROADSTEADS
ROADSTER
ROADSTERS
ROADWAY
ROADWAYS
ROAM
ROAMED
ROAMER
ROAMERS
ROAMING
ROAMS
ROAN
ROANS
ROAR
ROARED
ROARER
ROARERS
ROARIE
ROARIER

ROARIEST
ROARING
ROARINGLY
ROARINGS
ROARS
ROARY
ROAST
ROASTED
ROASTER
ROASTERS
ROASTING
ROASTINGS
ROASTS
ROATE
ROATED
ROATES
ROATING
ROB
ROBALO
ROBALOS
ROBBED
ROBBER
ROBBERIES
ROBBERS
ROBBERY
ROBBING
ROBE
ROBED
ROBES
ROBIN
ROBING
ROBINGS
ROBINIA
ROBINIAS
ROBINS
ROBLE
ROBLES
ROBORANT
ROBORANTS
ROBOT
ROBOTIC
ROBOTICS
ROBOTISE
ROBOTISED
ROBOTISES
ROBOTISING
ROBOTIZE
ROBOTIZED
ROBOTIZES
ROBOTIZING
ROBOTS
ROBS
ROBURITE
ROBURITES
ROBUST
ROBUSTA
ROBUSTAS
ROBUSTER
ROBUSTEST
ROBUSTLY
ROC
ROCAILLE
ROCAILLES
ROCAMBOLE
ROCAMBOLES
ROCH
ROCHES
ROCHET
ROCHETS
ROCK

ROCKAWAY
ROCKAWAYS
ROCKCRESS
ROCKCRESSES
ROCKED
ROCKER
ROCKERIES
ROCKERS
ROCKERY
ROCKET
ROCKETED
ROCKETEER
ROCKETEERS
ROCKETER
ROCKETERS
ROCKETING
ROCKETRIES
ROCKETRY
ROCKETS
ROCKIER
ROCKIERS
ROCKIEST
ROCKILY
ROCKINESS
ROCKINESSES
ROCKING
ROCKINGS
ROCKLAY
ROCKLAYS
ROCKLING
ROCKLINGS
ROCKS
ROCKWATER
ROCKWATERS
ROCKWEED
ROCKWEEDS
ROCKWORK
ROCKWORKS
ROCKY
ROCOCO
ROCOCOS
ROCQUET
ROCQUETS
ROCS
ROD
RODDED
RODDING
RODDINGS
RODE
RODED
RODENT
RODENTS
RODEO
RODEOS
RODES
RODEWAY
RODEWAYS
RODFISHER
RODFISHERS
RODING
RODINGS
RODLESS
RODLIKE
RODMAN
RODMEN
RODS
RODSMAN
RODSMEN
RODSTER
RODSTERS

ROE
ROEBUCK
ROEBUCKS
ROED
ROEMER
ROEMERS
ROENTGEN
ROENTGENS
ROES
ROESTONE
ROESTONES
ROGATION
ROGATIONS
ROGATORY
ROGER
ROGERED
ROGERING
ROGERINGS
ROGERS
ROGUE
ROGUED
ROGUERIES
ROGUERY
ROGUES
ROGUESHIP
ROGUESHIPS
ROGUING
ROGUISH
ROGUISHLY
ROGUY
ROIL
ROILED
ROILIER
ROILIEST
ROILING
ROILS
ROILY
ROIN
ROINED
ROINING
ROINISH
ROINS
ROIST
ROISTED
ROISTER
ROISTERED
ROISTERER
ROISTERERS
ROISTERING
ROISTERS
ROISTING
ROISTS
ROK
ROKE
ROKED
ROKELAY
ROKELAYS
ROKER
ROKES
ROKIER
ROKIEST
ROKING
ROKS
ROKY
ROLAG
ROLAGS
RÔLE
ROLE
RÔLES

ROLES
ROLL
ROLLABLE
ROLLED
ROLLER
ROLLERS
ROLLICK
ROLLICKED
ROLLICKING
ROLLICKINGS
ROLLICKS
ROLLING
ROLLINGS
ROLLMOP
ROLLMOPS
ROLLOCK
ROLLOCKS
ROLLS
ROM
ROMA
ROMAGE
ROMAGES
ROMAIKA
ROMAIKAS
ROMAL
ROMALS
ROMAN
ROMANCE
ROMANCED
ROMANCER
ROMANCERS
ROMANCES
ROMANCING
ROMANCINGS
ROMANS
ROMANTIC
ROMANTICS
ROMAS
ROMAUNT
ROMAUNTS
ROMNEYA
ROMNEYAS
ROMP
ROMPED
ROMPER
ROMPERS
ROMPING
ROMPINGLY
ROMPISH
ROMPISHLY
ROMPS
RONCADOR
RONCADORS
RONDACHE
RONDACHES
RONDAVEL
RONDAVELS
RONDE
RONDEAU
RONDEAUX
RONDEL
RONDELS
RONDES
RONDINO
RONDINOS
RONDO
RONDOS
RONDURE
RONDURES
RONE

RONEO
RONEOED
RONEOING
RONEOS
RONES
RONG
RONGGENG
RONGGENGS
RONNE
RONNING
RONT
RONTE
RONTES
RÖNTGEN
RÖNTGENS
RONTS
RONYON
RONYONS
ROO
ROOD
ROODS
ROOF
ROOFED
ROOFER
ROOFERS
ROOFIER
ROOFIEST
ROOFING
ROOFINGS
ROOFLESS
ROOFS
ROOFY
ROOINEK
ROOINEKS
ROOK
ROOKED
ROOKERIES
ROOKERY
ROOKIE
ROOKIES
ROOKING
ROOKISH
ROOKS
ROOKY
ROOM
ROOMED
ROOMER
ROOMERS
ROOMETTE
ROOMETTES
ROOMFUL
ROOMFULS
ROOMIER
ROOMILY
ROOMIEST
ROOMINESS
ROOMINESSES
ROOMING
ROOMS
ROOMSOME
ROOMY
ROON
ROONS
ROOP
ROOPED
ROOPIER
ROOPIEST
ROOPING
ROOPIT
ROOPS

ROOPY
ROOS
ROOSA
ROOSAS
ROOSE
ROOSED
ROOSES
ROOSING
ROOSTED
ROOSTER
ROOSTERS
ROOSTING
ROOSTS
ROOT
ROOTAGE
ROOTAGES
ROOTED
ROOTEDLY
ROOTER
ROOTERS
ROOTHOLD
ROOTHOLDS
ROOTIER
ROOTIES
ROOTIEST
ROOTING
ROOTINGS
ROOTLE
ROOTLED
ROOTLES
ROOTLESS
ROOTLET
ROOTLETS
ROOTLIKE
ROOTLING
ROOTS
ROOTSTOCK
ROOTSTOCKS
ROOTY
ROPABLE
ROPEABLE
ROPE
ROPEABLE
ROPED
ROPER
ROPERIES
ROPERS
ROPERY
ROPES
ROPEWAY
ROPEWAYS
ROPEWORK
ROPEWORKS
ROPEY
ROPIER
ROPIEST
ROPILY
ROPINESS
ROPINESSES
ROPING
ROPINGS
ROPY
ROQUE
ROQUES
ROQUET
ROQUETED
ROQUETING
ROQUETS
ROQUETTE
ROQUETTES

RORAL
RORE
RORES
RORIC
RORID
RORIE
RORIER
RORIEST
RORQUAL
RORQUALS
RORT
RORTER
RORTERS
RORTIER
RORTIEST
RORTS
RORTY
RORY
ROSACE
ROSACEA
ROSACEAS
ROSACEOUS
ROSACES
ROSAKER
ROSAKERS
ROSALIA
ROSALIAS
ROSARIAN
ROSARIANS
ROSARIUM
ROSARIUMS
ROSARY
ROSCID
ROSE
ROSÉ
ROSEAL
ROSEATE
ROSED
ROSEFISH
ROSEFISHES
ROSELESS
ROSELIKE
ROSELLA
ROSELLAS
ROSELLE
ROSELLES
ROSEMARIES
ROSEMARY
ROSEOLA
ROSEOLAS
ROSERIES
ROSERY
ROSES
ROSÉS
ROSET
ROSETED
ROSETING
ROSETS
ROSETTE
ROSETTED
ROSETTES
ROSETTY
ROSETY
ROSEWOOD
ROSEWOODS
ROSIED
ROSIER
ROSIERE
ROSIERES

ROSIERS
ROSIES
ROSIEST
ROSILY
ROSIN
ROSINATE
ROSINATES
ROSINED
ROSINESS
ROSINESSES
ROSING
ROSINING
ROSINS
ROSINY
ROSIT
ROSITED
ROSITING
ROSITS
ROSMARINE
ROSMARINES
ROSOGLIO
ROSOGLIOS
ROSOLIO
ROSOLIOS
ROSSER
ROSSERS
ROST
ROSTED
ROSTELLAR
ROSTELLUM
ROSTELLUMS
ROSTER
ROSTERED
ROSTERING
ROSTERINGS
ROSTERS
ROSTING
ROSTRA
ROSTRAL
ROSTRATE
ROSTRATED
ROSTRUM
ROSTRUMS
ROSTS
ROSULA
ROSULAS
ROSULATE
ROSY
ROSYING
ROT
ROTA
ROTAL
ROTAPLANE
ROTAPLANES
ROTARIES
ROTARY
ROTAS
ROTATABLE
ROTATE
ROTATED
ROTATES
ROTATING
ROTATION
ROTATIONS
ROTATIVE
ROTATOR
ROTATORS
ROTATORY
ROTAVATE
ROTAVATED

ROTAVATES
ROTAVATING
ROTAVATOR
ROTAVATORS
ROTAVIRUS
ROTAVIRUSES
ROTCH
ROTCHE
ROTCHES
ROTCHIE
ROTCHIES
ROTE
ROTED
ROTENONE
ROTENONES
ROTES
ROTGRASS
ROTGRASSES
ROTGUT
ROTGUTS
ROTHER
ROTHERS
ROTI
ROTIFER
ROTIFERAL
ROTIFERS
ROTING
ROTIS
ROTL
ROTLS
ROTOGRAPH
ROTOGRAPHED
ROTOGRAPHING
ROTOGRAPHS
ROTOLO
ROTOLOS
ROTOR
ROTORS
ROTOVATE
ROTOVATED
ROTOVATES
ROTOVATING
ROTOVATOR
ROTOVATORS
ROTS
ROTTAN
ROTTANS
ROTTED
ROTTEN
ROTTENER
ROTTENEST
ROTTENLY
ROTTENS
ROTTER
ROTTERS
ROTTING
ROTULA
ROTULAS
ROTUND
ROTUNDA
ROTUNDAS
ROTUNDATE
ROTUNDED
ROTUNDER
ROTUNDEST
ROTUNDING
ROTUNDITIES
ROTUNDITY
ROTUNDLY
ROTUNDS

ROTURIER
ROTURIERS
ROUBLE
ROUBLES
ROUCOU
ROUCOUS
ROUÉ
ROUÉS
ROUGE
ROUGED
ROUGES
ROUGH
ROUGHAGE
ROUGHAGES
ROUGHCAST
ROUGHCASTED
ROUGHCASTING
ROUGHCASTS
ROUGHED
ROUGHEN
ROUGHENED
ROUGHENING
ROUGHENS
ROUGHER
ROUGHERS
ROUGHEST
ROUGHIE
ROUGHIES
ROUGHING
ROUGHISH
ROUGHLY
ROUGHNECK
ROUGHNECKS
ROUGHNESS
ROUGHNESSES
ROUGHS
ROUGHT
ROUGHY
ROUGING
ROUL
ROULADE
ROULADES
ROULE
ROULEAU
ROULEAUS
ROULEAUX
ROULES
ROULETTE
ROULETTES
ROULS
ROUM
ROUMING
ROUMINGS
ROUMS
ROUNCE
ROUNCES
ROUNCEVAL
ROUNCEVALS
ROUNCIES
ROUNCY
ROUND
ROUNDARCH
ROUNDED
ROUNDEL
ROUNDELAY
ROUNDELAYS
ROUNDELS
ROUNDER
ROUNDERS
ROUNDEST

ROUNDHAND
ROUNDHANDS
ROUNDING
ROUNDINGS
ROUNDISH
ROUNDLE
ROUNDLES
ROUNDLET
ROUNDLETS
ROUNDLY
ROUNDNESS
ROUNDNESSES
ROUNDS
ROUNDSMAN
ROUNDSMEN
ROUNDURE
ROUNDURES
ROUP
ROUPED
ROUPIER
ROUPIEST
ROUPING
ROUPIT
ROUPS
ROUPY
ROUSANT
ROUSE
ROUSED
ROUSEMENT
ROUSEMENTS
ROUSER
ROUSERS
ROUSES
ROUSING
ROUSINGLY
ROUSSETTE
ROUSSETTES
ROUST
ROUSTED
ROUSTER
ROUSTERS
ROUSTING
ROUSTS
ROUT
ROUTE
ROUTED
ROUTEING
ROUTEMAN
ROUTEMEN
ROUTER
ROUTERS
ROUTES
ROUTH
ROUTHIE
ROUTHIER
ROUTHIEST
ROUTHS
ROUTINE
ROUTINEER
ROUTINEERS
ROUTINELY
ROUTINES
ROUTING
ROUTINGS
ROUTINISE
ROUTINISED
ROUTINISES
ROUTINISING
ROUTINISM
ROUTINISMS

ROUTINIST
ROUTINISTS
ROUTINIZE
ROUTINIZED
ROUTINIZES
ROUTINIZING
ROUTOUS
ROUTOUSLY
ROUTS
ROUX
ROVE
ROVED
ROVER
ROVERS
ROVES
ROVING
ROVINGLY
ROVINGS
ROW
ROWABLE
ROWAN
ROWANS
ROWBOAT
ROWBOATS
ROWDEDOW
ROWDEDOWS
ROWDIER
ROWDIES
ROWDIEST
ROWDILY
ROWDINESS
ROWDINESSES
ROWDY
ROWDYDOW
ROWDYDOWS
ROWDYISH
ROWDYISM
ROWDYISMS
ROWED
ROWEL
ROWELLED
ROWELLING
ROWELS
ROWEN
ROWENS
ROWER
ROWERS
ROWING
ROWINGS
ROWLOCK
ROWLOCKS
ROWME
ROWMES
ROWND
ROWNDED
ROWNDELL
ROWNDELLS
ROWNDING
ROWNDS
ROWS
ROWT
ROWTED
ROWTH
ROWTHS
ROWTING
ROWTS
ROYAL
ROYALET
ROYALETS
ROYALISE

ROYALISED
ROYALISES
ROYALISING
ROYALISM
ROYALISMS
ROYALIST
ROYALISTS
ROYALIZE
ROYALIZED
ROYALIZES
ROYALIZING
ROYALLER
ROYALLEST
ROYALLY
ROYALS
ROYALTIES
ROYALTY
ROYNE
ROYNED
ROYNES
ROYNING
ROYNISH
ROYST
ROYSTED
ROYSTER
ROYSTERED
ROYSTERER
ROYSTERERS
ROYSTERING
ROYSTERS
ROYSTING
ROYSTS
ROZELLE
ROZELLES
ROZET
ROZETED
ROZETING
ROZETS
ROZIT
ROZITED
ROZITING
ROZITS
ROZZER
ROZZERS
RUB
RUBAIYAT
RUBAIYATS
RUBATI
RUBATO
RUBATOS
RUBBED
RUBBER
RUBBERED
RUBBERING
RUBBERISE
RUBBERISED
RUBBERISES
RUBBERISING
RUBBERIZE
RUBBERIZED
RUBBERIZES
RUBBERIZING
RUBBERS
RUBBERY
RUBBET
RUBBING
RUBBINGS
RUBBISH
RUBBISHED
RUBBISHES

RUBBISHING
RUBBISHLY
RUBBISHY
RUBBIT
RUBBLE
RUBBLES
RUBBLIER
RUBBLIEST
RUBBLY
RUBDOWN
RUBDOWNS
RUBE
RUBEFIED
RUBEFIES
RUBEFY
RUBEFYING
RUBELLA
RUBELLAN
RUBELLANS
RUBELLAS
RUBELLITE
RUBELLITES
RUBEOLA
RUBEOLAS
RUBES
RUBESCENT
RUBICELLE
RUBICELLES
RUBICON
RUBICONED
RUBICONING
RUBICONS
RUBICUND
RUBIDIUM
RUBIDIUMS
RUBIED
RUBIER
RUBIES
RUBIEST
RUBIFIED
RUBIFIES
RUBIFY
RUBIFYING
RUBIN
RUBINE
RUBINEOUS
RUBINES
RUBINS
RUBIOUS
RUBLE
RUBLES
RUBRIC
RUBRICAL
RUBRICATE
RUBRICATED
RUBRICATES
RUBRICATING
RUBRICIAN
RUBRICIANS
RUBRICS
RUBS
RUBSTONE
RUBSTONES
RUBY
RUBYING
RUC
RUCHE
RUCHED
RUCHES
RUCHING

RUCHINGS
RUCK
RUCKED
RUCKING
RUCKLE
RUCKLED
RUCKLES
RUCKLING
RUCKS
RUCKSACK
RUCKSACKS
RUCKUS
RUCKUSES
RUCS
RUCTATION
RUCTATIONS
RUCTION
RUCTIONS
RUD
RUDAS
RUDASES
RUDBECKIA
RUDBECKIAS
RUDD
RUDDED
RUDDER
RUDDERS
RUDDIED
RUDDIER
RUDDIES
RUDDIEST
RUDDILY
RUDDINESS
RUDDINESSES
RUDDING
RUDDLE
RUDDLED
RUDDLEMAN
RUDDLEMEN
RUDDLES
RUDDLING
RUDDOCK
RUDDOCKS
RUDDS
RUDDY
RUDDYING
RUDE
RUDELY
RUDENESS
RUDENESSES
RUDER
RUDERAL
RUDERALS
RUDERIES
RUDERY
RUDESBIES
RUDESBY
RUDEST
RUDIMENT
RUDIMENTS
RUDISH
RUDS
RUE
RUED
RUEFUL
RUEFULLY
RUEING
RUEINGS
RUELLE
RUELLES

RUELLIA
RUELLIAS
RUES
RUFESCENT
RUFF
RUFFE
RUFFED
RUFFES
RUFFIAN
RUFFIANED
RUFFIANING
RUFFIANLY
RUFFIANS
RUFFIN
RUFFING
RUFFINS
RUFFLE
RUFFLED
RUFFLER
RUFFLERS
RUFFLES
RUFFLING
RUFFLINGS
RUFFS
RUFOUS
RUGATE
RUGBIES
RUGBY
RUGGED
RUGGEDER
RUGGEDEST
RUGGEDISE
RUGGEDISED
RUGGEDISES
RUGGEDISING
RUGGEDIZE
RUGGEDIZED
RUGGEDIZES
RUGGEDIZING
RUGGEDLY
RUGGER
RUGGERS
RUGGIER
RUGGIEST
RUGGING
RUGGINGS
RUGGY
RUGOSE
RUGOSELY
RUGOSITIES
RUGOSITY
RUGOUS
RUGS
RUGULOSE
RUIN
RUINABLE
RUINATE
RUINATED
RUINATES
RUINATING
RUINATION
RUINATIONS
RUINED
RUINER
RUINERS
RUING
RUINGS
RUINING
RUININGS

RUINOUS
RUINOUSLY
RUINS
RUKH
RUKHS
RULABLE
RULE
RULED
RULELESS
RULER
RULERED
RULERING
RULERS
RULERSHIP
RULERSHIPS
RULES
RULESSE
RULIER
RULIEST
RULING
RULINGS
RULLION
RULLIONS
RULLOCK
RULLOCKS
RULY
RUM
RUMAL
RUMALS
RUMBA
RUMBAED
RUMBAING
RUMBAS
RUMBELOW
RUMBELOWS
RUMBLE
RUMBLED
RUMBLER
RUMBLERS
RUMBLES
RUMBLIER
RUMBLIEST
RUMBLING
RUMBLINGS
RUMBLY
RUMBO
RUMBOS
RUME
RUMEN
RUMES
RUMINA
RUMINANT
RUMINANTS
RUMINATE
RUMINATED
RUMINATES
RUMINATING
RUMINATOR
RUMINATORS
RUMKIN
RUMKINS
RUMLY
RUMMAGE
RUMMAGED
RUMMAGER
RUMMAGERS
RUMMAGES
RUMMAGING
RUMMER
RUMMERS

RUMMEST
RUMMIER
RUMMIES
RUMMIEST
RUMMILY
RUMMINESS
RUMMINESSES
RUMMISH
RUMMY
RUMOR
RUMORED
RUMORING
RUMOROUS
RUMORS
RUMOUR
RUMOURED
RUMOURER
RUMOURERS
RUMOURING
RUMOURS
RUMP
RUMPED
RUMPING
RUMPLE
RUMPLED
RUMPLES
RUMPLESS
RUMPLING
RUMPS
RUMPUS
RUMPUSES
RUMS
RUN
RUNABOUT
RUNABOUTS
RUNAGATE
RUNAGATES
RUNAROUND
RUNAROUNDS
RUNAWAY
RUNAWAYS
RUNCH
RUNCHES
RUNCIBLE
RUNCINATE
RUND
RUNDALE
RUNDALES
RUNDLE
RUNDLED
RUNDLES
RUNDLET
RUNDLETS
RUNDOWN
RUNDOWNS
RUNDS
RUNE
RUNED
RUNES
RUNFLAT
RUNG
RUNGS
RUNIC
RUNKLE
RUNKLED
RUNKLES
RUNKLING
RUNLET
RUNLETS
RUNNABLE

RUNNEL
RUNNELS
RUNNER
RUNNERS
RUNNET
RUNNETS
RUNNIER
RUNNIEST
RUNNING
RUNNINGLY
RUNNINGS
RUNNION
RUNNIONS
RUNNY
RUNRIG
RUNRIGS
RUNS
RUNT
RUNTED
RUNTIER
RUNTIEST
RUNTISH
RUNTS
RUNTY
RUNWAY
RUNWAYS
RUPEE
RUPEES
RUPIA
RUPIAH
RUPIAHS
RUPIAS
RUPTURE
RUPTURED
RUPTURES
RUPTURING
RURAL
RURALISE
RURALISED
RURALISES
RURALISING
RURALISM

RURALISMS
RURALIST
RURALISTS
RURALITIES
RURALITY
RURALIZE
RURALIZED
RURALIZES
RURALIZING
RURALLY
RURALNESS
RURALNESSES
RURALS
RURP
RURPS
RUSA
RUSALKA
RUSALKAS
RUSAS
RUSCUS
RUSCUSES
RUSE
RUSÉ
RUSES
RUSH
RUSHED
RUSHEN
RUSHER
RUSHERS
RUSHES
RUSHIER
RUSHIEST
RUSHINESS
RUSHINESSES
RUSHING
RUSHLIGHT
RUSHLIGHTS
RUSHY
RUSINE
RUSK
RUSKS
RUSMA

RUSMAS
RUSSEL
RUSSELS
RUSSET
RUSSETED
RUSSETING
RUSSETINGS
RUSSETS
RUSSETY
RUSSIA
RUSSIAS
RUST
RUSTED
RUSTIC
RUSTICAL
RUSTICALS
RUSTICATE
RUSTICATED
RUSTICATES
RUSTICATING
RUSTICIAL
RUSTICISE
RUSTICISED
RUSTICISES
RUSTICISING
RUSTICISM
RUSTICISMS
RUSTICITIES
RUSTICITY
RUSTICIZE
RUSTICIZED
RUSTICIZES
RUSTICIZING
RUSTICS
RUSTIER
RUSTIEST
RUSTILY
RUSTINESS
RUSTINESSES
RUSTING
RUSTINGS
RUSTLE

RUSTLED
RUSTLER
RUSTLERS
RUSTLES
RUSTLESS
RUSTLING
RUSTLINGS
RUSTRE
RUSTRED
RUSTRES
RUSTS
RUSTY
RUT
RUTABAGA
RUTABAGAS
RUTACEOUS
RUTH
RUTHENIC
RUTHENIUM
RUTHENIUMS
RUTHFUL
RUTHFULLY
RUTHLESS
RUTHS
RUTILANT
RUTILATED
RUTILE
RUTILES
RUTIN
RUTINS
RUTS
RUTTED
RUTTER
RUTTERS
RUTTIER
RUTTIEST
RUTTING
RUTTINGS
RUTTISH
RUTTY
RYA
RYAL

RYALS
RYAS
RYBAT
RYBATS
RYBAUDRYE
RYBAUDRYES
RYBAULD
RYBAULDS
RYE
RYEPECK
RYEPECKS
RYES
RYFE
RYKE
RYKED
RYKES
RYKING
RYMME
RYMMED
RYMMES
RYMMING
RYND
RYNDS
RYOKAN
RYOKANS
RYOT
RYOTS
RYOTWARI
RYOTWARIS
RYPE
RYPECK
RYPECKS
RYPER
RYTHME
RYTHMED
RYTHMES
RYTHMING
RYVE
RYVED
RYVES
RYVING

S

SAB
SABADILLA
SABADILLAS
SABATON
SABATONS
SABBAT
SABBATIC
SABBATINE
SABBATISE
SABBATISED
SABBATISES
SABBATISING
SABBATISM
SABBATISMS
SABBATIZE
SABBATIZED
SABBATIZES
SABBATIZING
SABBATS
SABELLA
SABELLAS
SABER
SABERED
SABERING
SABERS
SABIN
SABINS
SABLE
SABLED
SABLES
SABLING
SABOT
SABOTAGE
SABOTAGED
SABOTAGES
SABOTAGING
SABOTEUR
SABOTEURS
SABOTIER
SABOTIERS
SABOTS
SABRA
SABRAS
SABRE
SABRED
SABRES
SABRING
SABS
SABULOSE
SABULOUS
SABURRA
SABURRAL
SABURRAS
SAC
SACCADE
SACCADES
SACCADIC
SACCATE
SACCHARIC
SACCHARIN
SACCHARINS
SACCIFORM
SACCOI

SACCOS
SACCOSES
SACCULAR
SACCULE
SACCULES
SACCULI
SACCULUS
SACELLA
SACELLUM
SACHEM
SACHEMDOM
SACHEMDOMS
SACHEMS
SACHET
SACHETS
SACK
SACKAGE
SACKAGES
SACKBUT
SACKBUTS
SACKCLOTH
SACKCLOTHS
SACKED
SACKFUL
SACKFULS
SACKING
SACKINGS
SACKLESS
SACKS
SACLESS
SACQUE
SACQUES
SACRA
SACRAL
SACRALISE
SACRALISED
SACRALISES
SACRALISING
SACRALIZE
SACRALIZED
SACRALIZES
SACRALIZING
SACRAMENT
SACRAMENTED
SACRAMENTING
SACRAMENTS
SACRARIA
SACRARIUM
SACRED
SACREDLY
SACRIFICE
SACRIFICED
SACRIFICES
SACRIFICING
SACRIFIDE
SACRIFIED
SACRIFIES
SACRIFY
SACRIFYING
SACRILEGE
SACRILEGES
SACRING
SACRINGS

SACRIST
SACRISTAN
SACRISTANS
SACRISTIES
SACRISTS
SACRISTY
SACRUM
SACS
SAD
SADDEN
SADDENED
SADDENING
SADDENS
SADDER
SADDEST
SADDHU
SADDHUS
SADDISH
SADDLE
SADDLED
SADDLER
SADDLERIES
SADDLERO
SADDLERY
SADDLES
SADDLING
SADHU
SADHUS
SADISM
SADISMS
SADIST
SADISTIC
SADISTS
SADLY
SADNESS
SADNESSES
SAE
SAECULUM
SAECULUMS
SAETER
SAETERS
SAFARI
SAFARIED
SAFARIING
SAFARIS
SAFE
SAFED
SAFEGUARD
SAFEGUARDED
SAFEGUARDING
SAFEGUARDINGS
SAFEGUARDS
SAFELY
SAFENESS
SAFENESSES
SAFER
SAFES
SAFEST
SAFETIES
SAFETY
SAFFIAN
SAFFIANS
SAFFLOWER

SAFFLOWERS
SAFFRON
SAFFRONED
SAFFRONS
SAFFRONY
SAFING
SAFRANIN
SAFRANINE
SAFRANINES
SAFRANINS
SAFROLE
SAFROLES
SAG
SAGA
SAGACIOUS
SAGACITIES
SAGACITY
SAGAMAN
SAGAMEN
SAGAMORE
SAGAMORES
SAGAPENUM
SAGAPENUMS
SAGAS
SAGATHIES
SAGATHY
SAGE
SAGEBRUSH
SAGEBRUSHES
SAGELY
SAGENE
SAGENES
SAGENESS
SAGENESSES
SAGENITE
SAGENITES
SAGENITIC
SAGER
SAGES
SAGEST
SAGGAR
SAGGARD
SAGGARDS
SAGGARS
SAGGED
SAGGER
SAGGERS
SAGGIER
SAGGIEST
SAGGING
SAGGINGS
SAGGY
SAGIER
SAGIEST
SAGINATE
SAGINATED
SAGINATES
SAGINATING
SAGITTA
SAGITTAL
SAGITTARIES
SAGITTARY
SAGITTAS

SAGITTATE
SAGO
SAGOIN
SAGOINS
SAGOS
SAGOUIN
SAGOUINS
SAGS
SAGUARO
SAGUAROS
SAGUIN
SAGUINS
SAGUM
SAGY
SAHIB
SAHIBA
SAHIBAH
SAHIBAHS
SAHIBAS
SAHIBS
SAI
SAIBLING
SAIBLINGS
SAIC
SAICE
SAICES
SAICK
SAICKS
SAICS
SAID
SAIDEST
SAIDS
SAIDST
SAIGA
SAIGAS
SAIKEI
SAIKEIS
SAIKLESS
SAIL
SAILABLE
SAILBOARD
SAILBOARDS
SAILED
SAILER
SAILERS
SAILIER
SAILIEST
SAILING
SAILINGS
SAILLESS
SAILOR
SAILORING
SAILORINGS
SAILORLY
SAILORS
SAILPLANE
SAILPLANES
SAILS
SAILY
SAIM
SAIMIRI
SAIMIRIS
SAIMS

SAIN
SAINE
SAINED
SAINFOIN
SAINFOINS
SAINING
SAINS
SAINT
SAINTDOM
SAINTDOMS
SAINTED
SAINTESS
SAINTESSES
SAINTFOIN
SAINTFOINS
SAINTHOOD
SAINTHOODS
SAINTING
SAINTISH
SAINTISM
SAINTISMS
SAINTLIER
SAINTLIEST
SAINTLIKE
SAINTLING
SAINTLINGS
SAINTLY
SAINTS
SAINTSHIP
SAINTSHIPS
SAIQUE
SAIQUES
SAIR
SAIRED
SAIRER
SAIREST
SAIRING
SAIRS
SAIS
SAIST
SAITH
SAITHE
SAITHES
SAITHS
SAJOU
SAJOUS
SAKE
SAKER
SAKERET
SAKERETS
SAKERS
SAKES
SAKI
SAKIA
SAKIAS
SAKIEH
SAKIEHS
SAKIS
SAKIYEH
SAKIYEHS
SAKKOI
SAKKOS
SAKKOSES
SAKSAUL
SAKSAULS
SAL
SALAAM
SALAAMED
SALAAMING
SALAAMS

SALABLE
SALABLY
SALACIOUS
SALACITIES
SALACITY
SALAD
SALADE
SALADES
SALADING
SALADINGS
SALADS
SALAL
SALALS
SALAME
SALAMI
SALAMIS
SALAMON
SALAMONS
SALANGANE
SALANGANES
SALARIAT
SALARIATS
SALARIED
SALARIES
SALARY
SALARYING
SALBAND
SALBANDS
SALCHOW
SALCHOWS
SALE
SALEABLE
SALEABLY
SALEP
SALEPS
SALERATUS
SALERATUSES
SALES
SALESGIRL
SALESGIRLS
SALESLADIES
SALESLADY
SALESMAN
SALESMEN
SALET
SALETS
SALEWD
SALEWORK
SALEWORKS
SALFERN
SALFERNS
SALIAUNCE
SALIAUNCES
SALIC
SALICES
SALICET
SALICETA
SALICETS
SALICETUM
SALICETUMS
SALICIN
SALICINE
SALICINES
SALICINS
SALICYLIC
SALIENCE
SALIENCES
SALIENCIES
SALIENCY
SALIENT

SALIENTLY
SALIENTS
SALIFIED
SALIFIES
SALIFY
SALIFYING
SALIGOT
SALIGOTS
SALIMETER
SALIMETERS
SALINA
SALINAS
SALINE
SALINES
SALINITIES
SALINITY
SALIVA
SALIVAL
SALIVARY
SALIVAS
SALIVATE
SALIVATED
SALIVATES
SALIVATING
SALIX
SALLAD
SALLADS
SALLAL
SALLALS
SALLE
SALLEE
SALLEES
SALLES
SALLET
SALLETS
SALLIED
SALLIES
SALLOW
SALLOWED
SALLOWER
SALLOWEST
SALLOWING
SALLOWISH
SALLOWS
SALLOWY
SALLY
SALLYING
SALLYPORT
SALLYPORTS
SALMI
SALMIS
SALMON
SALMONET
SALMONETS
SALMONID
SALMONIDS
SALMONOID
SALMONOIDS
SALMONS
SALON
SALONS
SALOON
SALOONIST
SALOONISTS
SALOONS
SALOOP
SALOOPS
SALOP
SALOPETTE
SALOPETTES

SALOPIAN
SALOPS
SALP
SALPIAN
SALPIANS
SALPICON
SALPICONS
SALPIFORM
SALPINGES
SALPINX
SALPINXES
SALPS
SALS
SALSA
SALSAED
SALSAFIES
SALSAFY
SALSAING
SALSAS
SALSE
SALSES
SALSIFIES
SALSIFY
SALT
SALTANDO
SALTANT
SALTANTS
SALTATE
SALTATED
SALTATES
SALTATING
SALTATION
SALTATIONS
SALTATO
SALTATORY
SALTED
SALTER
SALTERN
SALTERNS
SALTERS
SALTEST
SALTIER
SALTIERS
SALTIEST
SALTILY
SALTINESS
SALTINESSES
SALTING
SALTINGS
SALTIRE
SALTIRES
SALTISH
SALTISHLY
SALTLESS
SALTLY
SALTNESS
SALTNESSES
SALTO
SALTOED
SALTOING
SALTOS
SALTPETER
SALTPETERS
SALTPETRE
SALTPETRES
SALTS
SALTUS
SALTUSES
SALTY
SALUBRITIES

SALUBRITY
SALUE
SALUED
SALUES
SALUING
SALUKI
SALUKIS
SALUTARY
SALUTE
SALUTED
SALUTER
SALUTERS
SALUTES
SALUTING
SALVABLE
SALVAGE
SALVAGED
SALVAGES
SALVAGING
SALVARSAN
SALVARSANS
SALVATION
SALVATIONS
SALVATORIES
SALVATORY
SALVE
SALVED
SALVER
SALVERS
SALVES
SALVETE
SALVETES
SALVIA
SALVIAS
SALVIFIC
SALVING
SALVINGS
SALVO
SALVOES
SALVOR
SALVORS
SALVOS
SAM
SAMAAN
SAMAANS
SAMAN
SAMANS
SAMARA
SAMARAS
SAMARIUM
SAMARIUMS
SAMBA
SAMBAL
SAMBALS
SAMBAR
SAMBARS
SAMBAS
SAMBO
SAMBOS
SAMBUCA
SAMBUCAS
SAMBUR
SAMBURS
SAME
SAMEL
SAMELY
SAMEN
SAMENESS
SAMENESSES
SAMES

SAMEY
SAMFOO
SAMFOOS
SAMFU
SAMFUS
SAMIEL
SAMIELS
SAMIER
SAMIEST
SAMISEN
SAMISENS
SAMITE
SAMITES
SAMIZDAT
SAMIZDATS
SAMLET
SAMLETS
SAMLOR
SAMLORS
SAMNITIS
SAMNITISES
SAMOSA
SAMOSAS
SAMOVAR
SAMOVARS
SAMP
SAMPAN
SAMPANS
SAMPHIRE
SAMPHIRES
SAMPI
SAMPIRE
SAMPIRES
SAMPIS
SAMPLE
SAMPLED
SAMPLER
SAMPLERIES
SAMPLERS
SAMPLERY
SAMPLES
SAMPLING
SAMPLINGS
SAMPS
SAMSHOO
SAMSHOOS
SAMSHU
SAMSHUS
SAMURAI
SAN
SANATIVE
SANATORIA
SANATORY
SANBENITO
SANBENITOS
SANCHO
SANCHOS
SANCTIFIED
SANCTIFIES
SANCTIFY
SANCTIFYING
SANCTIFYINGS
SANCTION
SANCTIONED
SANCTIONING
SANCTIONS
SANCTITIES
SANCTITY
SANCTUARIES
SANCTUARY

SANCTUM
SANCTUMS
SAND
SANDAL
SANDALLED
SANDALS
SANDARAC
SANDARACH
SANDARACHS
SANDARACS
SANDBAG
SANDBAGGED
SANDBAGGING
SANDBAGS
SANDBANK
SANDBANKS
SANDED
SANDER
SANDERS
SANDERSES
SANDHI
SANDHIS
SANDIER
SANDIEST
SANDINESS
SANDINESSES
SANDING
SANDINGS
SANDIVER
SANDIVERS
SANDLING
SANDLINGS
SANDMAN
SANDMEN
SANDPAPER
SANDPAPERED
SANDPAPERING
SANDPAPERS
SANDPIPER
SANDPIPERS
SANDS
SANDSTONE
SANDSTONES
SANDWICH
SANDWICHED
SANDWICHES
SANDWICHING
SANDWORT
SANDWORTS
SANDY
SANDYISH
SANE
SANELY
SANENESS
SANENESSES
SANER
SANEST
SANG
SANGAR
SANGAREE
SANGAREES
SANGARS
SANGFROID
SANGFROIDS
SANGLIER
SANGLIERS
SANGRIA
SANGRIAS
SANGS
SANGUIFIED

SANGUIFIES
SANGUIFY
SANGUIFYING
SANGUINE
SANGUINED
SANGUINES
SANGUINING
SANICLE
SANICLES
SANIDINE
SANIDINES
SANIES
SANIFIED
SANIFIES
SANIFY
SANIFYING
SANIOUS
SANITARIA
SANITARY
SANITATE
SANITATED
SANITATES
SANITATING
SANITIES
SANITISE
SANITISED
SANITISES
SANITISING
SANITIZE
SANITIZED
SANITIZES
SANITIZING
SANITY
SANJAK
SANJAKS
SANK
SANKO
SANKOS
SANNUP
SANNUPS
SANNYASI
SANNYASIN
SANNYASINS
SANNYASIS
SANPAN
SANPANS
SANS
SANSA
SANSAS
SANSEI
SANSEIS
SANSERIF
SANSERIFS
SANTAL
SANTALIN
SANTALINS
SANTALS
SANTIR
SANTIRS
SANTOLINA
SANTOLINAS
SANTON
SANTONICA
SANTONICAS
SANTONIN
SANTONINS
SANTONS
SANTOUR
SANTOURS
SANTUR

SANTURS
SAOUARI
SAOUARIS
SAP
SAPAJOU
SAPAJOUS
SAPAN
SAPANS
SAPEGO
SAPEGOES
SAPELE
SAPELES
SAPFUL
SAPHEAD
SAPHEADED
SAPHEADS
SAPID
SAPIDITIES
SAPIDITY
SAPIDLESS
SAPIENCE
SAPIENCES
SAPIENT
SAPIENTLY
SAPLESS
SAPLING
SAPLINGS
SAPODILLA
SAPODILLAS
SAPOGENIN
SAPOGENINS
SAPONIFIED
SAPONIFIES
SAPONIFY
SAPONIFYING
SAPONIN
SAPONINS
SAPONITE
SAPONITES
SAPOR
SAPOROUS
SAPORS
SAPOTA
SAPOTAS
SAPPAN
SAPPANS
SAPPED
SAPPER
SAPPERS
SAPPHIC
SAPPHICS
SAPPHIRE
SAPPHIRED
SAPPHIRES
SAPPHISM
SAPPHISMS
SAPPHIST
SAPPHISTS
SAPPIER
SAPPIEST
SAPPINESS
SAPPINESSES
SAPPING
SAPPLES
SAPPY
SAPRAEMIA
SAPRAEMIAS
SAPRAEMIC
SAPROBE
SAPROBES

SAPROLITE
SAPROLITES
SAPROPEL
SAPROPELS
SAPROZOIC
SAPS
SAPSAGO
SAPSAGOS
SAPSUCKER
SAPSUCKERS
SAPUCAIA
SAPUCAIAS
SAPWOOD
SAPWOODS
SAR
SARABAND
SARABANDS
SARAFAN
SARAFANS
SARANGI
SARANGIS
SARBACANE
SARBACANES
SARCASM
SARCASMS
SARCASTIC
SARCENET
SARCENETS
SARCOCARP
SARCOCARPS
SARCODE
SARCODES
SARCODIC
SARCOID
SARCOIDS
SARCOLOGIES
SARCOLOGY
SARCOMA
SARCOMAS
SARCOMATA
SARCOMERE
SARCOMERES
SARCONET
SARCONETS
SARCOPTIC
SARCOUS
SARD
SARDANA
SARDANAS
SARDEL
SARDELLE
SARDELLES
SARDELS
SARDINE
SARDINES
SARDIUS
SARDIUSES
SARDONIAN
SARDONIC
SARDONYX
SARDONYXES
SARDS
SARED
SAREE
SAREES
SARGASSO
SARGASSOS
SARGE
SARGES
SARGO

SARGOS
SARGUS
SARGUSES
SARI
SARIN
SARING
SARINS
SARIS
SARK
SARKFUL
SARKFULS
SARKIER
SARKIEST
SARKING
SARKINGS
SARKS
SARKY
SARMENT
SARMENTA
SARMENTS
SARMENTUM
SARNEY
SARNEYS
SARNIE
SARNIES
SAROD
SARODS
SARONG
SARONGS
SARONIC
SAROS
SAROSES
SARPANCH
SARPANCHES
SARRASIN
SARRASINS
SARRAZIN
SARRAZINS
SARS
SARSA
SARSAS
SARSDEN
SARSDENS
SARSEN
SARSENET
SARSENETS
SARSENS
SARSNET
SARSNETS
SARTOR
SARTORIAL
SARTORIAN
SARTORII
SARTORIUS
SARTORIUSES
SARTORS
SARUS
SARUSES
SARZA
SARZAS
SASARARA
SASARARAS
SASH
SASHAY
SASHAYED
SASHAYING
SASHAYS
SASHED
SASHES
SASHIMI

SASHIMIS
SASHING
SASIN
SASINE
SASINES
SASINS
SASKATOON
SASKATOONS
SASQUATCH
SASQUATCHES
SASS
SASSABIES
SASSABY
SASSAFRAS
SASSAFRASES
SASSARARA
SASSARARAS
SASSE
SASSED
SASSES
SASSIER
SASSIEST
SASSING
SASSOLIN
SASSOLINS
SASSOLITE
SASSOLITES
SASSY
SASTRUGA
SASTRUGI
SAT
SATANIC
SATANICAL
SATANISM
SATANISMS
SATANITIES
SATANITY
SATARA
SATARAS
SATCHEL
SATCHELS
SATE
SATED
SATEDNESS
SATEDNESSES
SATEEN
SATEENS
SATELESS
SATELLES
SATELLITE
SATELLITED
SATELLITES
SATELLITING
SATES
SATI
SATIABLE
SATIATE
SATIATED
SATIATES
SATIATING
SATIATION
SATIATIONS
SATIETIES
SATIETY
SATIN
SATINED
SATINET
SATINETS
SATINETTA
SATINETTAS

SATINETTE
SATINETTES
SATING
SATINING
SATINS
SATINWOOD
SATINWOODS
SATINY
SATIRE
SATIRES
SATIRIC
SATIRICAL
SATIRISE
SATIRISED
SATIRISES
SATIRISING
SATIRIST
SATIRISTS
SATIRIZE
SATIRIZED
SATIRIZES
SATIRIZING
SATIS
SATISFIED
SATISFIER
SATISFIERS
SATISFIES
SATISFY
SATISFYING
SATIVE
SATORI
SATORIS
SATRAP
SATRAPAL
SATRAPIC
SATRAPIES
SATRAPS
SATRAPY
SATSUMA
SATSUMAS
SATURABLE
SATURANT
SATURANTS
SATURATE
SATURATED
SATURATES
SATURATING
SATURATOR
SATURATORS
SATURNIC
SATURNINE
SATURNISM
SATURNISMS
SATURNIST
SATURNISTS
SATYR
SATYRA
SATYRAL
SATYRALS
SATYRAS
SATYRESS
SATYRESSES
SATYRIC
SATYRICAL
SATYRID
SATYRIDS
SATYRISK
SATYRISKS
SATYRS
SAUBA

SAUBAS
SAUCE
SAUCED
SAUCEPAN
SAUCEPANS
SAUCER
SAUCERFUL
SAUCERFULS
SAUCERS
SAUCES
SAUCH
SAUCHS
SAUCIER
SAUCIEST
SAUCILY
SAUCINESS
SAUCINESSES
SAUCING
SAUCISSE
SAUCISSES
SAUCISSON
SAUCISSONS
SAUCY
SAUFGARD
SAUFGARDS
SAUGER
SAUGERS
SAUGH
SAUGHS
SAUL
SAULGE
SAULGES
SAULIE
SAULIES
SAULS
SAULT
SAULTS
SAUNA
SAUNAS
SAUNT
SAUNTED
SAUNTER
SAUNTERED
SAUNTERER
SAUNTERERS
SAUNTERING
SAUNTERINGS
SAUNTERS
SAUNTING
SAUNTS
SAUREL
SAURELS
SAURIAN
SAURIANS
SAURIES
SAUROID
SAUROPOD
SAUROPODS
SAURY
SAUSAGE
SAUSAGES
SAUT
SAUTÉ
SAUTÉD
SAUTED
SAUTÉED
SAUTÉING
SAUTÉS
SAUTING
SAUTOIR

SAUTOIRS
SAUTS
SAVABLE
SAVAGE
SAVAGED
SAVAGEDOM
SAVAGEDOMS
SAVAGELY
SAVAGER
SAVAGERIES
SAVAGERY
SAVAGES
SAVAGEST
SAVAGING
SAVAGISM
SAVAGISMS
SAVANNA
SAVANNAH
SAVANNAHS
SAVANNAS
SAVANT
SAVANTS
SAVARIN
SAVARINS
SAVATE
SAVATES
SAVE
SAVED
SAVEGARD
SAVEGARDED
SAVEGARDING
SAVEGARDS
SAVELOY
SAVELOYS
SAVER
SAVERS
SAVES
SAVEY
SAVEYED
SAVEYING
SAVEYS
SAVIN
SAVINE
SAVINES
SAVING
SAVINGLY
SAVINGS
SAVINS
SAVIOUR
SAVIOURS
SAVOR
SAVORED
SAVORIES
SAVORING
SAVOROUS
SAVORS
SAVORY
SAVOUR
SAVOURED
SAVOURIES
SAVOURILY
SAVOURING
SAVOURLY
SAVOURS
SAVOURY
SAVOY
SAVOYS
SAVVEY
SAVVEYED
SAVVEYING

SAVVEYS	SAZES	SCALDINGS	SCANDAL	SCAPUS
SAVVIED	SAZHEN	SCALDINI	SCANDALLED	SCAR
SAVVIES	SAZHENS	SCALDINO	SCANDALLING	SCARAB
SAVVY	SAZZES	SCALDS	SCANDALS	SCARABEE
SAVVYING	SBIRRI	SCALE	SCANDENT	SCARABEES
SAW	SBIRRO	SCALED	SCANDIUM	SCARABOID
SAWAH	SCAB	SCALELESS	SCANDIUMS	SCARABOIDS
SAWAHS	SCABBARD	SCALELIKE	SCANNED	SCARABS
SAWDER	SCABBARDED	SCALENE	SCANNER	SCARCE
SAWDERED	SCABBARDING	SCALER	SCANNERS	SCARCELY
SAWDERING	SCABBARDS	SCALERS	SCANNING	SCARCER
SAWDERS	SCABBED	SCALES	SCANNINGS	SCARCEST
SAWDUST	SCABBIER	SCALIER	SCANS	SCARCITIES
SAWDUSTED	SCABBIEST	SCALIEST	SCANSION	SCARCITY
SAWDUSTING	SCABBING	SCALINESS	SCANSIONS	SCARE
SAWDUSTS	SCABBLE	SCALINESSES	SCANT	SCARECROW
SAWDUSTY	SCABBLED	SCALING	SCANTED	SCARECROWS
SAWED	SCABBLES	SCALINGS	SCANTER	SCARED
SAWER	SCABBLING	SCALL	SCANTEST	SCAREDER
SAWERS	SCABBY	SCALLAWAG	SCANTIER	SCAREDEST
SAWING	SCABIES	SCALLAWAGS	SCANTIES	SCARER
SAWINGS	SCABIOUS	SCALLED	SCANTIEST	SCARERS
SAWN	SCABIOUSES	SCALLION	SCANTILY	SCARES
SAWNEY	SCABRID	SCALLIONS	SCANTING	SCAREY
SAWNEYS	SCABROUS	SCALLOP	SCANTITIES	SCARF
SAWPIT	SCABS	SCALLOPED	SCANTITY	SCARFED
SAWPITS	SCAD	SCALLOPING	SCANTLE	SCARFING
SAWS	SCADS	SCALLOPS	SCANTLED	SCARFINGS
SAWYER	SCAFF	SCALLS	SCANTLES	SCARFISH
SAWYERS	SCAFFIE	SCALLYWAG	SCANTLING	SCARFISHES
SAX	SCAFFIES	SCALLYWAGS	SCANTLINGS	SCARFS
SAXATILE	SCAFFOLD	SCALP	SCANTLY	SCARFSKIN
SAXAUL	SCAFFOLDED	SCALPED	SCANTNESS	SCARFSKINS
SAXAULS	SCAFFOLDING	SCALPEL	SCANTNESSES	SCARIER
SAXES	SCAFFOLDINGS	SCALPELS	SCANTS	SCARIEST
SAXHORN	SCAFFOLDS	SCALPER	SCANTY	SCARIFIED
SAXHORNS	SCAFFS	SCALPERS	SCAPA	SCARIFIER
SAXIFRAGE	SCAG	SCALPING	SCAPAED	SCARIFIERS
SAXIFRAGES	SCAGLIA	SCALPLESS	SCAPAING	SCARIFIES
SAXITOXIN	SCAGLIAS	SCALPRUM	SCAPAS	SCARIFY
SAXITOXINS	SCAGLIOLA	SCALPRUMS	SCAPE	SCARIFYING
SAXONIES	SCAGLIOLAS	SCALPS	SCAPED	SCARING
SAXONITE	SCAGS	SCALY	SCAPEGOAT	SCARIOUS
SAXONITES	SCAIL	SCAM	SCAPEGOATED	SCARLESS
SAXONY	SCAILED	SCAMBLE	SCAPEGOATING	SCARLET
SAXOPHONE	SCAILING	SCAMBLED	SCAPEGOATINGS	SCARLETED
SAXOPHONES	SCAILS	SCAMBLER	SCAPEGOATS	SCARLETING
SAY	SCAITH	SCAMBLERS	SCAPELESS	SCARLETS
SAYABLE	SCAITHED	SCAMBLES	SCAPEMENT	SCARMOGE
SAYED	SCAITHING	SCAMBLING	SCAPEMENTS	SCARMOGES
SAYEDS	SCAITHS	SCAMBLINGS	SCAPES	SCARP
SAYER	SCALA	SCAMEL	SCAPHOID	SCARPED
SAYERS	SCALABLE	SCAMELS	SCAPHOIDS	SCARPER
SAYEST	SCALADE	SCAMMONIES	SCAPHOPOD	SCARPERED
SAYID	SCALADES	SCAMMONY	SCAPHOPODS	SCARPERING
SAYIDS	SCALADO	SCAMP	SCAPI	SCARPERS
SAYING	SCALADOS	SCAMPED	SCAPING	SCARPETTI
SAYINGS	SCALAE	SCAMPER	SCAPOLITE	SCARPETTO
SAYNE	SCALAR	SCAMPERED	SCAPOLITES	SCARPINES
SAYON	SCALARS	SCAMPERING	SCAPPLE	SCARPING
SAYONARA	SCALAWAG	SCAMPERS	SCAPPLED	SCARPINGS
SAYONARAS	SCALAWAGS	SCAMPI	SCAPPLES	SCARPS
SAYONS	SCALD	SCAMPING	SCAPPLING	SCARRE
SAYS	SCALDED	SCAMPINGS	SCAPULA	SCARRED
SAYST	SCALDER	SCAMPIS	SCAPULAE	SCARRES
SAYYID	SCALDERS	SCAMPISH	SCAPULAR	SCARRIER
SAYYIDS	SCALDFISH	SCAMPS	SCAPULARIES	SCARRIEST
SAZ	SCALDFISHES	SCAMS	SCAPULARS	SCARRING
SAZERAC®	SCALDIC	SCAN	SCAPULARY	SCARRINGS
SAZERACS®	SCALDING	SCAND	SCAPULAS	SCARRY

SCARS
SCART
SCARTED
SCARTH
SCARTHS
SCARTING
SCARTS
SCARVES
SCARY
SCAT
SCATCH
SCATCHES
SCATH
SCATHE
SCATHED
SCATHEFUL
SCATHES
SCATHING
SCATHS
SCATOLE
SCATOLES
SCATOLOGIES
SCATOLOGY
SCATS
SCATT
SCATTED
SCATTER
SCATTERED
SCATTERER
SCATTERERS
SCATTERING
SCATTERINGS
SCATTERS
SCATTERY
SCATTIER
SCATTIEST
SCATTING
SCATTS
SCATTY
SCAUD
SCAUDED
SCAUDING
SCAUDS
SCAUP
SCAUPER
SCAUPERS
SCAUPS
SCAUR
SCAURED
SCAURIES
SCAURING
SCAURS
SCAURY
SCAVAGE
SCAVAGER
SCAVAGERS
SCAVAGES
SCAVENGE
SCAVENGED
SCAVENGER
SCAVENGERED
SCAVENGERING
SCAVENGERINGS
SCAVENGERS
SCAVENGES
SCAVENGING
SCAVENGINGS
SCAW
SCAWS
SCAZON

SCAZONS
SCAZONTIC
SCAZONTICS
SCEAT
SCEATT
SCEATTAS
SCEDULE
SCEDULES
SCELERAT
SCELERATE
SCELERATES
SCELERATS
SCENA
SCENARIES
SCENARIO
SCENARIOS
SCENARISE
SCENARISED
SCENARISES
SCENARISING
SCENARIST
SCENARISTS
SCENARIZE
SCENARIZED
SCENARIZES
SCENARIZING
SCENARY
SCEND
SCENDED
SCENDING
SCENDS
SCENE
SCENED
SCENERIES
SCENERY
SCENES
SCENIC
SCENICAL
SCENING
SCENT
SCENTED
SCENTFUL
SCENTING
SCENTINGS
SCENTLESS
SCENTS
SCEPSIS
SCEPSISES
SCEPTIC
SCEPTICAL
SCEPTICS
SCEPTRAL
SCEPTRE
SCEPTRED
SCEPTRES
SCEPTRY
SCERNE
SCERNED
SCERNES
SCERNING
SCHAPPE
SCHAPPED
SCHAPPEING
SCHAPPES
SCHAPSKA
SCHAPSKAS
SCHECHITA
SCHECHITAS
SCHEDULE
SCHEDULED

SCHEDULES
SCHEDULING
SCHEELITE
SCHEELITES
SCHELLUM
SCHELLUMS
SCHELM
SCHELMS
SCHEMA
SCHEMATA
SCHEMATIC
SCHEME
SCHEMED
SCHEMER
SCHEMERS
SCHEMES
SCHEMING
SCHEMINGS
SCHERZI
SCHERZO
SCHERZOS
SCHIAVONE
SCHIAVONES
SCHIEDAM
SCHIEDAMS
SCHILLER
SCHILLERS
SCHILLING
SCHILLINGS
SCHIMMEL
SCHIMMELS
SCHISM
SCHISMA
SCHISMAS
SCHISMS
SCHIST
SCHISTOSE
SCHISTOUS
SCHISTS
SCHIZO
SCHIZOID
SCHIZOIDS
SCHIZONT
SCHIZONTS
SCHIZOPOD
SCHIZOPODS
SCHIZOS
SCHLÄGER
SCHLÄGERS
SCHLEMIEL
SCHLEMIELS
SCHLEMIHL
SCHLEMIHLS
SCHLEP
SCHLEPP
SCHLEPPED
SCHLEPPIER
SCHLEPPIEST
SCHLEPPING
SCHLEPPS
SCHLEPPY
SCHLEPS
SCHLICH
SCHLICHS
SCHLIEREN
SCHLOCK
SCHLOCKS
SCHLOSS
SCHLOSSES
SCHMALTZ

SCHMALTZES
SCHMALTZIER
SCHMALTZIEST
SCHMALTZY
SCHMELZ
SCHMELZES
SCHMO
SCHMOCK
SCHMOCKS
SCHMOE
SCHMOES
SCHMOOZE
SCHMOOZED
SCHMOOZES
SCHMOOZING
SCHMUCK
SCHMUCKS
SCHMUTTER
SCHMUTTERS
SCHNAPPER
SCHNAPPERS
SCHNAPPS
SCHNAPPSES
SCHNAPS
SCHNAPSES
SCHNAUZER
SCHNAUZERS
SCHNELL
SCHNITZEL
SCHNITZELS
SCHNOOK
SCHNOOKS
SCHNORKEL
SCHNORKELS
SCHNORR
SCHNORRED
SCHNORRER
SCHNORRERS
SCHNORRING
SCHNORRS
SCHNOZZLE
SCHNOZZLES
SCHOLAR
SCHOLARCH
SCHOLARCHS
SCHOLARLY
SCHOLARS
SCHOLIA
SCHOLIAST
SCHOLIASTS
SCHOLION
SCHOLIUM
SCHOOL
SCHOOLBAG
SCHOOLBAGS
SCHOOLBOY
SCHOOLBOYS
SCHOOLE
SCHOOLED
SCHOOLERIES
SCHOOLERY
SCHOOLES
SCHOOLING
SCHOOLINGS
SCHOOLMAN
SCHOOLMEN
SCHOOLS
SCHOONER
SCHOONERS
SCHORL

SCHORLS
SCHOUT
SCHOUTS
SCHTICK
SCHTICKS
SCHTIK
SCHTIKS
SCHTOOK
SCHTOOKS
SCHTOOM
SCHTUCK
SCHTUCKS
SCHUIT
SCHUITS
SCHUL
SCHULS
SCHUSS
SCHUSSED
SCHUSSES
SCHUSSING
SCHUYT
SCHUYTS
SCHWA
SCHWAS
SCIAENID
SCIAENOID
SCIAMACHIES
SCIAMACHY
SCIARID
SCIARIDS
SCIATIC
SCIATICA
SCIATICAL
SCIATICAS
SCIENCE
SCIENCED
SCIENCES
SCIENT
SCIENTER
SCIENTIAL
SCIENTISE
SCIENTISED
SCIENTISES
SCIENTISING
SCIENTISM
SCIENTISMS
SCIENTIST
SCIENTISTS
SCIENTIZE
SCIENTIZED
SCIENTIZES
SCIENTIZING
SCILICET
SCILLA
SCILLAS
SCIMITAR
SCIMITARS
SCINCOID
SCINTILLA
SCINTILLAS
SCIOLISM
SCIOLISMS
SCIOLIST
SCIOLISTS
SCIOLOUS
SCIOLTO
SCION
SCIONS
SCIOSOPHIES
SCIOSOPHY

SCIROC
SCIROCCO
SCIROCCOS
SCIROCS
SCIRRHOID
SCIRRHOUS
SCIRRHUS
SCIRRHUSES
SCISSEL
SCISSELS
SCISSIL
SCISSILE
SCISSILS
SCISSION
SCISSIONS
SCISSOR
SCISSORED
SCISSORER
SCISSORERS
SCISSORING
SCISSORS
SCISSURE
SCISSURES
SCIURINE
SCIUROID
SCLAFF
SCLAFFED
SCLAFFING
SCLAFFS
SCLATE
SCLATED
SCLATES
SCLATING
SCLAUNDER
SCLAUNDERS
SCLAVE
SCLAVES
SCLERA
SCLERAL
SCLERAS
SCLERE
SCLEREID
SCLEREIDE
SCLEREIDES
SCLEREIDS
SCLEREMA
SCLEREMAS
SCLERES
SCLERITE
SCLERITES
SCLERITISES
SCLEROID
SCLEROMA
SCLEROMAS
SCLEROSE
SCLEROSED
SCLEROSES
SCLEROSING
SCLEROSIS
SCLEROTAL
SCLEROTALS
SCLEROTIA
SCLEROTIC
SCLEROTICS
SCLEROUS
SCLIFF
SCLIFFS
SCLIM
SCLIMMED

SCLIMMING
SCLIMS
SCOFF
SCOFFED
SCOFFER
SCOFFERS
SCOFFING
SCOFFINGS
SCOFFLAW
SCOFFLAWS
SCOFFS
SCOG
SCOGGED
SCOGGING
SCOGS
SCOINSON
SCOINSONS
SCOLD
SCOLDED
SCOLDER
SCOLDERS
SCOLDING
SCOLDINGS
SCOLDS
SCOLECES
SCOLECID
SCOLECITE
SCOLECITES
SCOLECOID
SCOLEX
SCOLICES
SCOLIOMA
SCOLIOMAS
SCOLIOSES
SCOLIOSIS
SCOLIOTIC
SCOLLOP
SCOLLOPED
SCOLLOPING
SCOLLOPS
SCOLYTOID
SCOMBROID
SCOMFISH
SCOMFISHED
SCOMFISHES
SCOMFISHING
SCONCE
SCONCED
SCONCES
SCONCHEON
SCONCHEONS
SCONCING
SCONE
SCONES
SCONTION
SCONTIONS
SCOOG
SCOOGED
SCOOGING
SCOOGS
SCOOP
SCOOPED
SCOOPER
SCOOPERS
SCOOPFUL
SCOOPFULS
SCOOPING
SCOOPINGS
SCOOPS
SCOOT

SCOOTED
SCOOTER
SCOOTERS
SCOOTING
SCOOTS
SCOPA
SCOPAE
SCOPATE
SCOPE
SCOPES
SCOPULA
SCOPULAS
SCOPULATE
SCORBUTIC
SCORCH
SCORCHED
SCORCHER
SCORCHERS
SCORCHES
SCORCHING
SCORCHINGS
SCORDATO
SCORE
SCORED
SCORELINE
SCORELINES
SCORER
SCORERS
SCORES
SCORIA
SCORIAC
SCORIAE
SCORIFIED
SCORIFIER
SCORIFIERS
SCORIFIES
SCORIFY
SCORIFYING
SCORING
SCORINGS
SCORIOUS
SCORN
SCORNED
SCORNER
SCORNERS
SCORNFUL
SCORNING
SCORNINGS
SCORNS
SCORODITE
SCORODITES
SCORPER
SCORPERS
SCORPIO
SCORPIOID
SCORPION
SCORPIONS
SCORPIOS
SCORSE
SCORSED
SCORSER
SCORSERS
SCORSES
SCORSING
SCOT
SCOTCH
SCOTCHED
SCOTCHES
SCOTCHING
SCOTER

SCOTERS
SCOTIA
SCOTIAS
SCOTOMA
SCOTOMAS
SCOTOMATA
SCOTOMIES
SCOTOMY
SCOTOPIA
SCOTOPIAS
SCOTOPIC
SCOTS
SCOUG
SCOUGED
SCOUGING
SCOUGS
SCOUNDREL
SCOUNDRELS
SCOUP
SCOUPED
SCOUPING
SCOUPS
SCOUR
SCOURED
SCOURER
SCOURERS
SCOURGE
SCOURGED
SCOURGER
SCOURGERS
SCOURGES
SCOURGING
SCOURIE
SCOURIES
SCOURING
SCOURINGS
SCOURS
SCOURSE
SCOURSED
SCOURSES
SCOURSING
SCOUSE
SCOUSES
SCOUT
SCOUTED
SCOUTER
SCOUTERS
SCOUTH
SCOUTHER
SCOUTHERED
SCOUTHERING
SCOUTHERINGS
SCOUTHERS
SCOUTHERY
SCOUTHS
SCOUTING
SCOUTINGS
SCOUTS
SCOW
SCOWDER
SCOWDERED
SCOWDERING
SCOWDERINGS
SCOWDERS
SCOWL
SCOWLED
SCOWLING
SCOWLS
SCOWP
SCOWPED

SCOWPING
SCOWPS
SCOWRER
SCOWRERS
SCOWRIE
SCOWRIES
SCOWS
SCOWTH
SCOWTHER
SCOWTHERED
SCOWTHERING
SCOWTHERS
SCOWTHS
SCRAB
SCRABBED
SCRABBING
SCRABBLE
SCRABBLED
SCRABBLER
SCRABBLERS
SCRABBLES
SCRABBLING
SCRABS
SCRAE
SCRAES
SCRAG
SCRAGGED
SCRAGGIER
SCRAGGIEST
SCRAGGILY
SCRAGGING
SCRAGGLIER
SCRAGGLIEST
SCRAGGLY
SCRAGGY
SCRAGS
SCRAICH
SCRAICHED
SCRAICHING
SCRAICHS
SCRAIGH
SCRAIGHED
SCRAIGHING
SCRAIGHS
SCRAM
SCRAMBLE
SCRAMBLED
SCRAMBLER
SCRAMBLERS
SCRAMBLES
SCRAMBLING
SCRAMBLINGS
SCRAMJET
SCRAMJETS
SCRAMMED
SCRAMMING
SCRAMS
SCRAN
SCRANCH
SCRANCHED
SCRANCHES
SCRANCHING
SCRANNEL
SCRANNY
SCRANS
SCRAP
SCRAPE
SCRAPED
SCRAPER
SCRAPERS

SCRAPES	SCREAM	SCRIBBLINGS	SCRITCHES	SCRUBBINGS
SCRAPIE	SCREAMED	SCRIBBLY	SCRITCHING	SCRUBBY
SCRAPIES	SCREAMER	SCRIBE	SCRIVE	SCRUBLAND
SCRAPING	SCREAMERS	SCRIBED	SCRIVED	SCRUBLANDS
SCRAPINGS	SCREAMING	SCRIBER	SCRIVENER	SCRUBS
SCRAPPED	SCREAMS	SCRIBERS	SCRIVENERS	SCRUFF
SCRAPPIER	SCREE	SCRIBES	SCRIVES	SCRUFFIER
SCRAPPIEST	SCREECH	SCRIBING	SCRIVING	SCRUFFIEST
SCRAPPILY	SCREECHED	SCRIBINGS	SCROBE	SCRUFFS
SCRAPPING	SCREECHER	SCRIBISM	SCROBES	SCRUFFY
SCRAPPLE	SCREECHERS	SCRIBISMS	SCRODDLED	SCRUM
SCRAPPLES	SCREECHES	SCRIECH	SCROFULA	SCRUMMAGE
SCRAPPY	SCREECHIER	SCRIECHED	SCROFULAS	SCRUMMAGED
SCRAPS	SCREECHIEST	SCRIECHING	SCROG	SCRUMMAGES
SCRAT	SCREECHING	SCRIECHS	SCROGGIE	SCRUMMAGING
SCRATCH	SCREECHY	SCRIED	SCROGGIER	SCRUMMED
SCRATCHED	SCREED	SCRIENE	SCROGGIEST	SCRUMMIER
SCRATCHER	SCREEDED	SCRIENES	SCROGGY	SCRUMMIEST
SCRATCHERS	SCREEDER	SCRIES	SCROGS	SCRUMMING
SCRATCHES	SCREEDERS	SCRIEVE	SCROLL	SCRUMMY
SCRATCHIER	SCREEDING	SCRIEVED	SCROLLED	SCRUMP
SCRATCHIEST	SCREEDINGS	SCRIEVES	SCROLLERIES	SCRUMPED
SCRATCHING	SCREEDS	SCRIEVING	SCROLLERY	SCRUMPIES
SCRATCHINGS	SCREEN	SCRIGGLE	SCROLLING	SCRUMPING
SCRATCHY	SCREENED	SCRIGGLED	SCROLLS	SCRUMPS
SCRATS	SCREENER	SCRIGGLES	SCROOGE	SCRUMPY
SCRATTED	SCREENERS	SCRIGGLIER	SCROOGED	SCRUMS
SCRATTING	SCREENING	SCRIGGLIEST	SCROOGES	SCRUNCH
SCRATTLE	SCREENINGS	SCRIGGLING	SCROOGING	SCRUNCHED
SCRATTLED	SCREENS	SCRIGGLY	SCROOP	SCRUNCHES
SCRATTLES	SCREES	SCRIKE	SCROOPED	SCRUNCHIER
SCRATTLING	SCREEVE	SCRIKED	SCROOPING	SCRUNCHIEST
SCRAUCH	SCREEVED	SCRIKES	SCROOPS	SCRUNCHING
SCRAUCHED	SCREEVER	SCRIKING	SCROTAL	SCRUNCHY
SCRAUCHING	SCREEVERS	SCRIM	SCROTUM	SCRUNT
SCRAUCHS	SCREEVES	SCRIMMAGE	SCROTUMS	SCRUNTS
SCRAUGH	SCREEVING	SCRIMMAGED	SCROUGE	SCRUNTY
SCRAUGHED	SCREEVINGS	SCRIMMAGES	SCROUGED	SCRUPLE
SCRAUGHING	SCREICH	SCRIMMAGING	SCROUGER	SCRUPLED
SCRAUGHS	SCREICHED	SCRIMP	SCROUGERS	SCRUPLER
SCRAW	SCREICHING	SCRIMPED	SCROUGES	SCRUPLERS
SCRAWL	SCREICHS	SCRIMPIER	SCROUGING	SCRUPLES
SCRAWLED	SCREIGH	SCRIMPIEST	SCROUNGE	SCRUPLING
SCRAWLER	SCREIGHED	SCRIMPILY	SCROUNGED	SCRUTABLE
SCRAWLERS	SCREIGHING	SCRIMPING	SCROUNGER	SCRUTATOR
SCRAWLIER	SCREIGHS	SCRIMPLY	SCROUNGERS	SCRUTATORS
SCRAWLIEST	SCREW	SCRIMPS	SCROUNGES	SCRUTINIES
SCRAWLING	SCREWBALL	SCRIMPY	SCROUNGING	SCRUTINY
SCRAWLINGS	SCREWBALLS	SCRIMS	SCROUNGINGS	SCRUTO
SCRAWLS	SCREWED	SCRIMSHAW	SCROW	SCRUTOIRE
SCRAWLY	SCREWER	SCRIMSHAWED	SCROWDGE	SCRUTOIRES
SCRAWM	SCREWERS	SCRIMSHAWING	SCROWDGED	SCRUTOS
SCRAWMED	SCREWIER	SCRIMSHAWS	SCROWDGES	SCRUZE
SCRAWMING	SCREWIEST	SCRIMURE	SCROWDGING	SCRUZED
SCRAWMS	SCREWING	SCRIMURES	SCROWL	SCRUZES
SCRAWNIER	SCREWINGS	SCRINE	SCROWLE	SCRUZING
SCRAWNIEST	SCREWS	SCRINES	SCROWLED	SCRY
SCRAWNY	SCREWTOP	SCRIP	SCROWLES	SCRYDE
SCRAWS	SCREWTOPS	SCRIPPAGE	SCROWLING	SCRYER
SCRAY	SCREWY	SCRIPPAGES	SCROWLS	SCRYERS
SCRAYE	SCRIBABLE	SCRIPS	SCROWS	SCRYING
SCRAYES	SCRIBAL	SCRIPT	SCROYLE	SCRYINGS
SCRAYS	SCRIBBLE	SCRIPTED	SCROYLES	SCRYNE
SCREAK	SCRIBBLED	SCRIPTING	SCRUB	SCRYNES
SCREAKED	SCRIBBLER	SCRIPTORY	SCRUBBED	SCUBA
SCREAKIER	SCRIBBLERS	SCRIPTS	SCRUBBER	SCUBAS
SCREAKIEST	SCRIBBLES	SCRIPTURE	SCRUBBERS	SCUCHIN
SCREAKING	SCRIBBLIER	SCRIPTURES	SCRUBBIER	SCUCHINS
SCREAKS	SCRIBBLIEST	SCRITCH	SCRUBBIEST	SCUCHION
SCREAKY	SCRIBBLING	SCRITCHED	SCRUBBING	SCUCHIONS

SCUD
SCUDDALER
SCUDDALERS
SCUDDED
SCUDDER
SCUDDERS
SCUDDING
SCUDDLE
SCUDDLED
SCUDDLES
SCUDDLING
SCUDI
SCUDLER
SCUDLERS
SCUDO
SCUDS
SCUFF
SCUFFED
SCUFFIER
SCUFFIEST
SCUFFING
SCUFFLE
SCUFFLED
SCUFFLER
SCUFFLERS
SCUFFLES
SCUFFLING
SCUFFS
SCUFFY
SCUFT
SCUFTS
SCUG
SCUGGED
SCUGGING
SCUGS
SCUL
SCULK
SCULKED
SCULKING
SCULKS
SCULL
SCULLE
SCULLED
SCULLER
SCULLERIES
SCULLERS
SCULLERY
SCULLES
SCULLING
SCULLINGS
SCULLION
SCULLIONS
SCULLS
SCULP
SCULPED
SCULPIN
SCULPING
SCULPINS
SCULPS
SCULPSIT
SCULPT
SCULPTED
SCULPTING
SCULPTOR
SCULPTORS
SCULPTS
SCULPTURE
SCULPTURED
SCULPTURES
SCULPTURING

SCULPTURINGS
SCULS
SCUM
SCUMBAG
SCUMBAGS
SCUMBER
SCUMBERED
SCUMBERING
SCUMBERS
SCUMBLE
SCUMBLED
SCUMBLES
SCUMBLING
SCUMBLINGS
SCUMFISH
SCUMFISHED
SCUMFISHES
SCUMFISHING
SCUMMED
SCUMMER
SCUMMERS
SCUMMIER
SCUMMIEST
SCUMMING
SCUMMINGS
SCUMMY
SCUMS
SCUNCHEON
SCUNCHEONS
SCUNGE
SCUNGED
SCUNGES
SCUNGIER
SCUNGIEST
SCUNGING
SCUNGY
SCUNNER
SCUNNERED
SCUNNERING
SCUNNERS
SCUP
SCUPPAUG
SCUPPAUGS
SCUPPER
SCUPPERED
SCUPPERING
SCUPPERS
SCUPS
SCUR
SCURF
SCURFIER
SCURFIEST
SCURFS
SCURFY
SCURRED
SCURRIED
SCURRIER
SCURRIERS
SCURRIES
SCURRIL
SCURRILE
SCURRING
SCURRIOUR
SCURRIOURS
SCURRY
SCURRYING
SCURS
SCURVIER
SCURVIES
SCURVIEST

SCURVILY
SCURVY
SCUSE
SCUSED
SCUSES
SCUSING
SCUT
SCUTA
SCUTAGE
SCUTAGES
SCUTAL
SCUTATE
SCUTCH
SCUTCHED
SCUTCHEON
SCUTCHEONS
SCUTCHER
SCUTCHERS
SCUTCHES
SCUTCHING
SCUTCHINGS
SCUTE
SCUTELLA
SCUTELLAR
SCUTELLUM
SCUTES
SCUTIFORM
SCUTIGER
SCUTIGERS
SCUTS
SCUTTER
SCUTTERED
SCUTTERING
SCUTTERS
SCUTTLE
SCUTTLED
SCUTTLER
SCUTTLERS
SCUTTLES
SCUTTLING
SCUTUM
SCYBALA
SCYBALOUS
SCYBALUM
SCYE
SCYES
SCYPHI
SCYPHUS
SCYTALE
SCYTALES
SCYTHE
SCYTHED
SCYTHEMAN
SCYTHEMEN
SCYTHER
SCYTHERS
SCYTHES
SCYTHING
SDAINE
SDAINED
SDAINES
SDAINING
SDAYN
SDAYNED
SDAYNING
SDAYNS
SDEIGNE
SDEIGNED
SDEIGNES
SDEIGNING

SDEIN
SDEINED
SDEINING
SDEINS
SEA
SEABED
SEABEDS
SEABERRIES
SEABERRY
SEABOARD
SEABOARDS
SEABORNE
SEACOAST
SEACOASTS
SEACRAFT
SEACRAFTS
SEACUNNIES
SEACUNNY
SEADROME
SEADROMES
SEAFARER
SEAFARERS
SEAFARING
SEAFARINGS
SEAFOOD
SEAFOODS
SEAGULL
SEAGULLS
SEAHORSE
SEAHORSES
SEAL
SEALANT
SEALANTS
SEALCH
SEALCHS
SEALED
SEALER
SEALERIES
SEALERS
SEALERY
SEALGH
SEALGHS
SEALING
SEALINGS
SEALS
SEALSKIN
SEALSKINS
SEALYHAM
SEALYHAMS
SEAM
SEAMAN
SEAMANLY
SEAMARK
SEAMARKS
SEAME
SEAMED
SEAMEN
SEAMER
SEAMERS
SEAMES
SEAMIER
SEAMIEST
SEAMINESS
SEAMINESSES
SEAMING
SEAMLESS
SEAMOUNT
SEAMOUNTS
SEAMS
SEAMSTER

SEAMSTERS
SEAMY
SEAN
SÉANCE
SÉANCES
SEANED
SEANING
SEANNACHIES
SEANNACHY
SEANS
SEAPLANE
SEAPLANES
SEAPORT
SEAPORTS
SEAQUAKE
SEAQUAKES
SEAR
SEARAT
SEARATS
SEARCE
SEARCED
SEARCES
SEARCH
SEARCHED
SEARCHER
SEARCHERS
SEARCHES
SEARCHING
SEARCING
SEARE
SEARED
SEARER
SEAREST
SEARING
SEARINGS
SEARNESS
SEARNESSES
SEARS
SEAS
SEASATYRE
SEASATYRES
SEASCAPE
SEASCAPES
SEASE
SEASED
SEASES
SEASHELL
SEASHELLS
SEASHORE
SEASHORES
SEASICK
SEASICKER
SEASICKEST
SEASIDE
SEASIDES
SEASING
SEASON
SEASONAL
SEASONED
SEASONER
SEASONERS
SEASONING
SEASONINGS
SEASONS
SEASURE
SEASURES
SEAT
SEATED
SEATER
SEATERS

SEATING	SECONDER	SECURES	SEEDCAKES	SEES
SEATINGS	SECONDERS	SECUREST	SEEDED	SEESAW
SEATLESS	SECONDES	SECURING	SEEDER	SEESAWED
SEATS	SECONDI	SECURITAN	SEEDERS	SEESAWING
SEAWARD	SECONDING	SECURITANS	SEEDIER	SEESAWS
SEAWARDLY	SECONDLY	SECURITIES	SEEDIEST	SEETHE
SEAWARDS	SECONDO	SECURITY	SEEDILY	SEETHED
SEAWAY	SECONDS	SED	SEEDINESS	SEETHER
SEAWAYS	SECRECIES	SEDAN	SEEDINESSES	SEETHERS
SEAWEED	SECRECY	SEDANS	SEEDING	SEETHES
SEAWEEDS	SECRET	SEDATE	SEEDINGS	SEETHING
SEAWORTHY	SECRETA	SEDATED	SEEDLESS	SEETHINGS
SEAZE	SECRETAGE	SEDATELY	SEEDLING	SEEWING
SEAZED	SECRETAGES	SEDATER	SEEDLINGS	SEG
SEAZES	SECRETARIES	SEDATES	SEEDLIP	SEGAR
SEAZING	SECRETARY	SEDATEST	SEEDLIPS	SEGARS
SEBACEOUS	SECRETE	SEDATING	SEEDNESS	SEGGAR
SEBACIC	SECRETED	SEDATION	SEEDNESSES	SEGGARS
SEBATE	SECRETES	SEDATIONS	SEEDS	SEGHOL
SEBATES	SECRETIN	SEDATIVE	SEEDSMAN	SEGHOLATE
SEBESTEN	SECRETING	SEDATIVES	SEEDSMEN	SEGHOLATES
SEBESTENS	SECRETINS	SEDENT	SEEDY	SEGHOLS
SEBIFIC	SECRETION	SEDENTARY	SEEING	SEGMENT
SEBUM	SECRETIONS	SEDERUNT	SEEINGS	SEGMENTAL
SEBUMS	SECRETIVE	SEDERUNTS	SEEK	SEGMENTED
SEBUNDIES	SECRETLY	SEDES	SEEKER	SEGMENTING
SEBUNDY	SECRETORY	SEDGE	SEEKERS	SEGMENTS
SEC	SECRETS	SEDGED	SEEKING	SEGNO
SECANT	SECS	SEDGELAND	SEEKS	SEGNOS
SECANTS	SECT	SEDGELANDS	SEEL	SEGO
SECATEUR	SECTARIAL	SEDGES	SEELD	SEGOL
SECATEURS	SECTARIAN	SEDGIER	SEELED	SEGOLATE
SECCO	SECTARIANS	SEDGIEST	SEELIER	SEGOLATES
SECCOS	SECTARIES	SEDGY	SEELIEST	SEGOLS
SECEDE	SECTARY	SEDILE	SEELING	SEGOS
SECEDED	SECTATOR	SEDILIA	SEELINGS	SEGREANT
SECEDER	SECTATORS	SEDIMENT	SEELS	SEGREGATE
SECEDERS	SECTILE	SEDIMENTED	SEELY	SEGREGATED
SECEDES	SECTILITIES	SEDIMENTING	SEEM	SEGREGATES
SECEDING	SECTILITY	SEDIMENTS	SEEMED	SEGREGATING
SECERN	SECTION	SEDITION	SEEMELESS	SEGS
SECERNED	SECTIONAL	SEDITIONS	SEEMER	SEGUE
SECERNENT	SECTIONED	SEDITIOUS	SEEMERS	SEGUED
SECERNENTS	SECTIONING	SEDUCE	SEEMING	SEGUEING
SECERNING	SECTIONS	SEDUCED	SEEMINGLY	SEGUES
SECERNS	SECTOR	SEDUCER	SEEMINGS	SEI
SECESH	SECTORAL	SEDUCERS	SEEMLESS	SEICENTO
SECESHER	SECTORED	SEDUCES	SEEMLESSE	SEICENTOS
SECESHERS	SECTORIAL	SEDUCING	SEEMLIER	SEICHE
SECESHES	SECTORIALS	SEDUCINGS	SEEMLIEST	SEICHES
SECESSION	SECTORING	SEDUCTION	SEEMLIHED	SEIF
SECESSIONS	SECTORS	SEDUCTIONS	SEEMLIHEDS	SEIFS
SECKEL	SECTS	SEDUCTIVE	SEEMLY	SEIGNEUR
SECKELS	SECULAR	SEDUCTOR	SEEMLYHED	SEIGNEURS
SECLUDE	SECULARLY	SEDUCTORS	SEEMLYHEDS	SEIGNIOR
SECLUDED	SECULARS	SEDULITIES	SEEMS	SEIGNIORIES
SECLUDES	SECULUM	SEDULITY	SEEN	SEIGNIORS
SECLUDING	SECULUMS	SEDULOUS	SEEP	SEIGNIORY
SECLUSION	SECUND	SEDUM	SEEPAGE	SEIGNORAL
SECLUSIONS	SECUNDINE	SEDUMS	SEEPAGES	SEIGNORIES
SECLUSIVE	SECUNDINES	SEE	SEEPED	SEIGNORY
SECODONT	SECUNDUM	SEEABLE	SEEPIER	SEIL
SECODONTS	SECURABLE	SEECATCH	SEEPIEST	SEILED
SECOND	SECURANCE	SEECATCHIE	SEEPING	SEILING
SECONDARIES	SECURANCES	SEED	SEEPS	SEILS
SECONDARY	SECURE	SEEDBED	SEEPY	SEINE
SECONDE	SECURED	SEEDBEDS	SEER	SEINED
SECONDED	SECURELY	SEEDBOX	SEERESS	SEINER
SECONDEE	SECURER	SEEDBOXES	SEERESSES	SEINERS
SECONDEES	SECURERS	SEEDCAKE	SEERS	SEINES

SEINING
SEININGS
SEIS
SEISE
SEISED
SEISES
SEISIN
SEISING
SEISINS
SEISM
SEISMAL
SEISMIC
SEISMICAL
SEISMISM
SEISMISMS
SEISMS
SEITIES
SEITY
SEIZABLE
SEIZE
SEIZED
SEIZER
SEIZERS
SEIZES
SEIZIN
SEIZING
SEIZINGS
SEIZINS
SEIZURE
SEIZURES
SEJANT
SEJEANT
SEKOS
SEKOSES
SEKT
SEKTS
SEL
SELACHIAN
SELACHIANS
SELADANG
SELADANGS
SELAH
SELAHS
SELCOUTH
SELD
SELDOM
SELDSEEN
SELDSHOWN
SELE
SELECT
SELECTED
SELECTING
SELECTION
SELECTIONS
SELECTIVE
SELECTOR
SELECTORS
SELECTS
SELENATE
SELENATES
SELENIC
SELENIDE
SELENIDES
SELENIOUS
SELENITE
SELENITES
SELENITIC
SELENIUM
SELENIUMS
SELENOUS

SELES
SELF
SELFED
SELFHOOD
SELFHOODS
SELFING
SELFISH
SELFISHLY
SELFISM
SELFISMS
SELFIST
SELFISTS
SELFLESS
SELFNESS
SELFNESSES
SELFS
SELICTAR
SELICTARS
SELKIE
SELKIES
SELL
SELLABLE
SELLE
SELLER
SELLERS
SELLES
SELLING
SELLOTAPE
SELLOTAPED
SELLOTAPES
SELLOTAPING
SELLS
SELS
SELTZER
SELTZERS
SELVA
SELVAGE
SELVAGED
SELVAGEE
SELVAGEES
SELVAGES
SELVAGING
SELVAS
SELVEDGE
SELVEDGED
SELVEDGES
SELVEDGING
SELVES
SEMANTEME
SEMANTEMES
SEMANTIC
SEMANTICS
SEMANTRA
SEMANTRON
SEMAPHORE
SEMAPHORED
SEMAPHORES
SEMAPHORING
SEMATIC
SEMBLABLE
SEMBLABLES
SEMBLABLY
SEMBLANCE
SEMBLANCES
SEMBLANT
SEMBLANTS
SEMBLE
SEMBLED
SEMBLES
SEMBLING

SEMÉ
SEMÉE
SEMEIA
SEMEION
SEMEIOTIC
SEMEIOTICS
SEMEME
SEMEMES
SEMEN
SEMENS
SEMESTER
SEMESTERS
SEMESTRAL
SEMI
SEMIANGLE
SEMIANGLES
SEMIBREVE
SEMIBREVES
SEMIBULL
SEMIBULLS
SEMICOLON
SEMICOLONS
SEMICOMA
SEMICOMAS
SEMIE
SEMIES
SEMIFINAL
SEMIFINALS
SEMIFLUID
SEMIFLUIDS
SEMILOG
SEMILUNE
SEMILUNES
SEMINAL
SEMINALLY
SEMINAR
SEMINARIES
SEMINARS
SEMINARY
SEMINATE
SEMINATED
SEMINATES
SEMINATING
SEMIOLOGIES
SEMIOLOGY
SEMIOTIC
SEMIOTICS
SEMIPED
SEMIPEDS
SEMIPLUME
SEMIPLUMES
SEMIS
SEMISES
SEMITAR
SEMITARS
SEMITAUR
SEMITAURS
SEMITONE
SEMITONES
SEMITONIC
SEMIVOWEL
SEMIVOWELS
SEMMIT
SEMMITS
SEMOLINA
SEMOLINAS
SEMPER
SEMPITERN
SEMPLE
SEMPLER

SEMPLEST
SEMPLICE
SEMPRE
SEMPSTER
SEMPSTERS
SEMSEM
SEMSEMS
SEMUNCIA
SEMUNCIAE
SEMUNCIAL
SEMUNCIAS
SEN
SENARIES
SENARII
SENARIUS
SENARY
SENATE
SENATES
SENATOR
SENATORS
SEND
SENDAL
SENDALS
SENDED
SENDER
SENDERS
SENDING
SENDINGS
SENDS
SENECIO
SENECIOS
SENEGA
SENEGAS
SENESCENT
SENESCHAL
SENESCHALS
SENGREEN
SENGREENS
SENILE
SENILELY
SENILITIES
SENILITY
SENIOR
SENIORITIES
SENIORITY
SENIORS
SENNA
SENNACHIE
SENNACHIES
SENNAS
SENNET
SENNETS
SENNIGHT
SENNIGHTS
SENNIT
SENNITS
SENS
SENSA
SENSATION
SENSATIONS
SENSE
SENSED
SENSEFUL
SENSELESS
SENSES
SENSIBLE
SENSIBLER
SENSIBLES
SENSIBLEST
SENSIBLY

SENSILE
SENSILLA
SENSILLUM
SENSING
SENSINGS
SENSISM
SENSISMS
SENSIST
SENSISTS
SENSITISE
SENSITISED
SENSITISES
SENSITISING
SENSITIVE
SENSITIVES
SENSITIZE
SENSITIZED
SENSITIZES
SENSITIZING
SENSOR
SENSORIAL
SENSORIES
SENSORIUM
SENSORIUMS
SENSORS
SENSORY
SENSUAL
SENSUALLY
SENSUALTIES
SENSUALTY
SENSUISM
SENSUISMS
SENSUIST
SENSUISTS
SENSUM
SENSUOUS
SENT
SENTED
SENTENCE
SENTENCED
SENTENCER
SENTENCERS
SENTENCES
SENTENCING
SENTIENCE
SENTIENCES
SENTIENCIES
SENTIENCY
SENTIENT
SENTIENTS
SENTIMENT
SENTIMENTS
SENTINEL
SENTINELLED
SENTINELLING
SENTINELS
SENTING
SENTRIES
SENTRY
SENTS
SENVIES
SENVY
SENZA
SEPAD
SEPADDED
SEPADDING
SEPADS
SEPAL
SEPALINE
SEPALODIES

SEPALODY
SEPALOID
SEPALOUS
SEPALS
SEPARABLE
SEPARABLY
SEPARATE
SEPARATED
SEPARATES
SEPARATING
SEPARATOR
SEPARATORS
SEPARATUM
SEPARATUMS
SEPHEN
SEPHENS
SEPIA
SEPIAS
SEPIMENT
SEPIMENTS
SEPIOLITE
SEPIOLITES
SEPIOST
SEPIOSTS
SEPIUM
SEPIUMS
SEPOY
SEPOYS
SEPPUKU
SEPPUKUS
SEPS
SEPSES
SEPSIS
SEPT
SEPTA
SEPTAL
SEPTARIA
SEPTARIAN
SEPTARIUM
SEPTATE
SEPTATION
SEPTATIONS
SEPTEMFID
SEPTEMVIR
SEPTEMVIRI
SEPTEMVIRS
SEPTENARIES
SEPTENARY
SEPTENNIA
SEPTET
SEPTETS
SEPTETT
SEPTETTE
SEPTETTES
SEPTETTS
SEPTIC
SEPTICITIES
SEPTICITY
SEPTIFORM
SEPTIMAL
SEPTIME
SEPTIMES
SEPTIMOLE
SEPTIMOLES
SEPTLEVA
SEPTLEVAS
SEPTS
SEPTUM
SEPTUOR
SEPTUORS

SEPTUPLE
SEPTUPLED
SEPTUPLES
SEPTUPLET
SEPTUPLETS
SEPTUPLING
SEPULCHRE
SEPULCHRED
SEPULCHRES
SEPULCHRING
SEPULTURE
SEPULTURED
SEPULTURES
SEPULTURING
SEQUACITIES
SEQUACITY
SEQUEL
SEQUELA
SEQUELAE
SEQUELS
SEQUENCE
SEQUENCED
SEQUENCES
SEQUENCING
SEQUENT
SEQUENTS
SEQUESTER
SEQUESTERED
SEQUESTERING
SEQUESTERS
SEQUIN
SEQUINS
SEQUOIA
SEQUOIAS
SERA
SÉRAC
SÉRACS
SERAFILE
SERAFILES
SERAGLIO
SERAGLIOS
SERAI
SERAIL
SERAILS
SERAIS
SERAL
SERANG
SERANGS
SERAPE
SERAPES
SERAPH
SERAPHIC
SERAPHIM
SERAPHIMS
SERAPHIN
SERAPHINE
SERAPHINES
SERAPHINS
SERAPHS
SERASKIER
SERASKIERS
SERDAB
SERDABS
SERE
SERED
SEREIN
SEREINS
SERENADE
SERENADED
SERENADER

SERENADERS
SERENADES
SERENADING
SERENATA
SERENATAS
SERENATE
SERENATES
SERENE
SERENED
SERENELY
SERENER
SERENES
SERENESS
SERENESSES
SERENEST
SERENING
SERENITIES
SERENITY
SERER
SERES
SEREST
SERF
SERFAGE
SERFAGES
SERFDOM
SERFDOMS
SERFHOOD
SERFHOODS
SERFISH
SERFS
SERFSHIP
SERFSHIPS
SERGE
SERGEANCIES
SERGEANCY
SERGEANT
SERGEANTS
SERGES
SERIAL
SERIALISE
SERIALISED
SERIALISES
SERIALISING
SERIALISM
SERIALISMS
SERIALIST
SERIALISTS
SERIALITIES
SERIALITY
SERIALIZE
SERIALIZED
SERIALIZES
SERIALIZING
SERIALLY
SERIALS
SERIATE
SERIATED
SERIATELY
SERIATES
SERIATIM
SERIATING
SERIATION
SERIATIONS
SERIC
SERICEOUS
SERICIN
SERICINS
SERICITE
SERICITES
SERICITIC

SERICON
SERICONS
SERIEMA
SERIEMAS
SERIES
SERIF
SERIFS
SERIGRAPH
SERIGRAPHS
SERIN
SERINETTE
SERINETTES
SERING
SERINGA
SERINGAS
SERINS
SERIOUS
SERIOUSLY
SERIPH
SERIPHS
SERJEANCIES
SERJEANCY
SERJEANT
SERJEANTIES
SERJEANTS
SERJEANTY
SERK
SERKALI
SERKALIS
SERKS
SERMON
SERMONED
SERMONEER
SERMONEERS
SERMONER
SERMONERS
SERMONET
SERMONETS
SERMONIC
SERMONING
SERMONINGS
SERMONISE
SERMONISED
SERMONISES
SERMONISH
SERMONISING
SERMONIZE
SERMONIZED
SERMONIZES
SERMONIZING
SERMONS
SEROLOGIES
SEROLOGY
SERON
SERONS
SEROON
SEROONS
SEROSA
SEROSAE
SEROSAS
SEROSITIES
SEROSITY
SEROTINE
SEROTINES
SEROTONIN
SEROTONINS
SEROTYPE
SEROTYPED
SEROTYPES
SEROTYPING

SEROTYPINGS
SEROUS
SEROW
SEROWS
SERPENT
SERPENTED
SERPENTING
SERPENTRIES
SERPENTRY
SERPENTS
SERPIGINES
SERPIGO
SERPIGOES
SERPULA
SERPULAE
SERPULITE
SERPULITES
SERR
SERRA
SERRAE
SERRAN
SERRANID
SERRANIDS
SERRANOID
SERRANOIDS
SERRANS
SERRAS
SERRATE
SERRATED
SERRATES
SERRATING
SERRATION
SERRATIONS
SERRATURE
SERRATURES
SERRATUS
SERRATUSES
SERRE
SERRED
SERREFILE
SERREFILES
SERRES
SERRICORN
SERRIED
SERRIES
SERRING
SERRS
SERRULATE
SERRY
SERRYING
SERUEWE
SERUEWED
SERUEWES
SERUEWING
SERUM
SERUMS
SERVAL
SERVALS
SERVANT
SERVANTED
SERVANTING
SERVANTRIES
SERVANTRY
SERVANTS
SERVE
SERVED
SERVER
SERVERIES
SERVERS
SERVERY

ERVES
ERVEWE
ERVEWED
ERVEWES
ERVEWING
ERVICE
ERVICED
ERVICES
ERVICING
ERVIENT
ERVIETTE
ERVIETTES
ERVILE
ERVILELY
ERVILES
ERVILISM
ERVILISMS
ERVILITIES
ERVILITY
ERVING
ERVINGS
ERVITOR
ERVITORS
ERVITUDE
ERVITUDES
ERVO
ESAME
ESAMES
ESAMOID
ESAMOIDS
ESE
ESELI
ESELIS
ESEY
ESS
ESSA
ESSES
ESSILE
ESSION
ESSIONAL
ESSIONS
ESSPOOL
ESSPOOLS
ESTERCE
ESTERCES
ESTERTIA
ESTET
ESTETS
ESTETT
ESTETTE
ESTETTES
ESTETTO
ESTETTOS
ESTETTS
ESTINA
ESTINAS
ESTINE
ESTINES
ESTON
ESTONS
ET
ETA
ETACEOUS
ETAE
ETBACK
ETBACKS
ETNESS
ETNESSES
ETON
ETONS

SETOSE
SETS
SETT
SETTEE
SETTEES
SETTER
SETTERED
SETTERING
SETTERS
SETTING
SETTINGS
SETTLE
SETTLED
SETTLER
SETTLERS
SETTLES
SETTLING
SETTLINGS
SETTLOR
SETTLORS
SETTS
SETUALE
SETUALES
SETWALL
SETWALLS
SEVEN
SEVENFOLD
SEVENS
SEVENTEEN
SEVENTEENS
SEVENTH
SEVENTHLY
SEVENTHS
SEVENTIES
SEVENTY
SEVER
SEVERABLE
SEVERAL
SEVERALLY
SEVERALS
SEVERALTIES
SEVERALTY
SEVERANCE
SEVERANCES
SEVERED
SEVERELY
SEVERER
SEVEREST
SEVERIES
SEVERING
SEVERITIES
SEVERITY
SEVERS
SEVERY
SEW
SEWAGE
SEWAGES
SEWED
SEWEL
SEWELLEL
SEWELLELS
SEWELS
SEWEN
SEWENS
SEWER
SEWERAGE
SEWERAGES
SEWERED
SEWERING

SEWERINGS
SEWERS
SEWIN
SEWING
SEWINGS
SEWINS
SEWN
SEWS
SEX
SEXED
SEXENNIAL
SEXER
SEXERS
SEXES
SEXFID
SEXFOIL
SEXFOILS
SEXIER
SEXIEST
SEXINESS
SEXINESSES
SEXING
SEXISM
SEXISMS
SEXIST
SEXISTS
SEXLESS
SEXOLOGIES
SEXOLOGY
SEXPOT
SEXPOTS
SEXT
SEXTAN
SEXTANS
SEXTANSES
SEXTANT
SEXTANTAL
SEXTANTS
SEXTET
SEXTETS
SEXTETT
SEXTETTE
SEXTETTES
SEXTETTS
SEXTILE
SEXTILES
SEXTOLET
SEXTOLETS
SEXTON
SEXTONESS
SEXTONESSES
SEXTONS
SEXTS
SEXTUOR
SEXTUORS
SEXTUPLE
SEXTUPLED
SEXTUPLES
SEXTUPLET
SEXTUPLETS
SEXTUPLING
SEXUAL
SEXUALISE
SEXUALISED
SEXUALISES
SEXUALISING
SEXUALISM
SEXUALISMS
SEXUALIST
SEXUALISTS

SEXUALITIES
SEXUALITY
SEXUALIZE
SEXUALIZED
SEXUALIZES
SEXUALIZING
SEXUALLY
SEXVALENT
SEXY
SEY
SEYEN
SEYENS
SEYS
SEYSURE
SEYSURES
SEZ
SFERICS
SFORZANDI
SFORZANDO
SFORZANDOS
SFORZATI
SFORZATO
SFORZATOS
SFUMATO
SFUMATOS
SGRAFFITI
SGRAFFITO
SH
SHABBIER
SHABBIEST
SHABBILY
SHABBLE
SHABBLES
SHABBY
SHABRACK
SHABRACKS
SHACK
SHACKLE
SHACKLED
SHACKLES
SHACKLING
SHACKS
SHAD
SHADBERRIES
SHADBERRY
SHADBUSH
SHADBUSHES
SHADDOCK
SHADDOCKS
SHADE
SHADED
SHADELESS
SHADES
SHADIER
SHADIEST
SHADILY
SHADINESS
SHADINESSES
SHADING
SHADINGS
SHADOOF
SHADOOFS
SHADOW
SHADOWED
SHADOWER
SHADOWERS
SHADOWIER
SHADOWIEST
SHADOWING
SHADOWINGS

SHADOWS
SHADOWY
SHADS
SHADUF
SHADUFS
SHADY
SHAFT
SHAFTED
SHAFTER
SHAFTERS
SHAFTING
SHAFTINGS
SHAFTLESS
SHAFTS
SHAG
SHAGEARED
SHAGGED
SHAGGIER
SHAGGIEST
SHAGGILY
SHAGGING
SHAGGY
SHAGREEN
SHAGREENS
SHAGROON
SHAGROONS
SHAGS
SHAH
SHAHS
SHAIKH
SHAIKHS
SHAIRN
SHAIRNS
SHAITAN
SHAITANS
SHAKABLE
SHAKE
SHAKEABLE
SHAKED
SHAKEN
SHAKER
SHAKERISM
SHAKERISMS
SHAKERS
SHAKES
SHAKIER
SHAKIEST
SHAKILY
SHAKINESS
SHAKINESSES
SHAKING
SHAKINGS
SHAKO
SHAKOES
SHAKOS
SHAKT
SHAKUDO
SHAKUDOS
SHAKY
SHALE
SHALED
SHALES
SHALIER
SHALIEST
SHALING
SHALL
SHALLI
SHALLIS
SHALLON
SHALLONS

SHALLOON	SHAMPOOING	SHARK	SHAWL	SHED
SHALLOONS	SHAMPOOS	SHARKED	SHAWLED	SHEDDER
SHALLOP	SHAMROCK	SHARKER	SHAWLING	SHEDDERS
SHALLOPS	SHAMROCKS	SHARKERS	SHAWLINGS	SHEDDING
SHALLOT	SHAMS	SHARKING	SHAWLLESS	SHEDDINGS
SHALLOTS	SHAMUS	SHARKINGS	SHAWLS	SHEDS
SHALLOW	SHAMUSES	SHARKS	SHAWM	SHEEL
SHALLOWED	SHAN	SHARKSKIN	SHAWMS	SHEELED
SHALLOWER	SHANACHIE	SHARKSKINS	SHAWS	SHEELING
SHALLOWEST	SHANACHIES	SHARN	SHAY	SHEELS
SHALLOWING	SHAND	SHARNIER	SHAYA	SHEEN
SHALLOWINGS	SHANDIES	SHARNIEST	SHAYAS	SHEENED
SHALLOWLY	SHANDRIES	SHARNS	SHAYS	SHEENIER
SHALLOWS	SHANDRY	SHARNY	SHCHI	SHEENIES
SHALM	SHANDS	SHARP	SHCHIS	SHEENIEST
SHALMS	SHANDY	SHARPED	SHE	SHEENING
SHALOM	SHANGHAI	SHARPEN	SHEA	SHEENS
SHALOT	SHANGHAIED	SHARPENED	SHEADING	SHEENY
SHALOTS	SHANGHAIING	SHARPENER	SHEADINGS	SHEEP
SHALT	SHANGHAIS	SHARPENERS	SHEAF	SHEEPDOG
SHALWAR	SHANK	SHARPENING	SHEAFED	SHEEPDOGS
SHALWARS	SHANKED	SHARPENS	SHEAFIER	SHEEPFOLD
SHALY	SHANKING	SHARPER	SHEAFIEST	SHEEPFOLDS
SHAM	SHANKS	SHARPERS	SHEAFING	SHEEPIER
SHAMA	SHANNIES	SHARPEST	SHEAFS	SHEEPIEST
SHAMAN	SHANNY	SHARPIE	SHEAFY	SHEEPISH
SHAMANIC	SHANS	SHARPIES	SHEAL	SHEEPMEAT
SHAMANISM	SHANTIES	SHARPING	SHEALED	SHEEPMEATS
SHAMANISMS	SHANTUNG	SHARPINGS	SHEALING	SHEEPSKIN
SHAMANIST	SHANTUNGS	SHARPISH	SHEALINGS	SHEEPSKINS
SHAMANISTS	SHANTY	SHARPLY	SHEALS	SHEEPWALK
SHAMANS	SHANTYMAN	SHARPNESS	SHEAR	SHEEPWALKS
SHAMAS	SHANTYMEN	SHARPNESSES	SHEARED	SHEEPY
SHAMATEUR	SHAPABLE	SHARPS	SHEARER	SHEER
SHAMATEURS	SHAPE	SHASH	SHEARERS	SHEERED
SHAMBLE	SHAPEABLE	SHASHES	SHEARING	SHEERER
SHAMBLED	SHAPED	SHASHLIK	SHEARINGS	SHEEREST
SHAMBLES	SHAPELESS	SHASHLIKS	SHEARLING	SHEERING
SHAMBLING	SHAPELIER	SHASTER	SHEARLINGS	SHEERLY
SHAMBLINGS	SHAPELIEST	SHASTERS	SHEARMAN	SHEERS
SHAMBOLIC	SHAPELY	SHASTRA	SHEARMEN	SHEET
SHAME	SHAPEN	SHASTRAS	SHEARS	SHEETED
SHAMED	SHAPER	SHAT	SHEAS	SHEETIER
SHAMEFAST	SHAPERS	SHATTER	SHEATH	SHEETIEST
SHAMEFUL	SHAPES	SHATTERED	SHEATHE	SHEETING
SHAMELESS	SHAPING	SHATTERING	SHEATHED	SHEETINGS
SHAMER	SHAPINGS	SHATTERS	SHEATHES	SHEETS
SHAMERS	SHAPS	SHATTERY	SHEATHIER	SHEETY
SHAMES	SHARD	SHAUCHLE	SHEATHIEST	SHEHITA
SHAMIANA	SHARDED	SHAUCHLED	SHEATHING	SHEHITAH
SHAMIANAH	SHARDS	SHAUCHLES	SHEATHINGS	SHEHITAHS
SHAMIANAHS	SHARE	SHAUCHLIER	SHEATHS	SHEHITAS
SHAMIANAS	SHARECROP	SHAUCHLIEST	SHEATHY	SHEIK
SHAMING	SHARECROPPED	SHAUCHLING	SHEAVE	SHEIKDOM
SHAMISEN	SHARECROPPING	SHAUCHLY	SHEAVED	SHEIKDOMS
SHAMISENS	SHARECROPS	SHAVE	SHEAVES	SHEIKH
SHAMMED	SHARED	SHAVED	SHEAVING	SHEIKHDOM
SHAMMER	SHAREMAN	SHAVELING	SHEBANG	SHEIKHDOMS
SHAMMERS	SHAREMEN	SHAVELINGS	SHEBANGS	SHEIKHS
SHAMMIES	SHARER	SHAVEN	SHEBEEN	SHEIKS
SHAMMING	SHARERS	SHAVER	SHEBEENED	SHEILA
SHAMMY	SHARES	SHAVERS	SHEBEENER	SHEILAS
SHAMOY	SHARESMAN	SHAVES	SHEBEENERS	SHEILING
SHAMOYED	SHARESMEN	SHAVIE	SHEBEENING	SHEILINGS
SHAMOYING	SHARIA	SHAVIES	SHEBEENINGS	SHEKEL
SHAMOYS	SHARIAS	SHAVING	SHEBEENS	SHEKELS
SHAMPOO	SHARIAT	SHAVINGS	SHECHITA	SHELDDUCK
SHAMPOOED	SHARIATS	SHAW	SHECHITAH	SHELDDUCKS
SHAMPOOER	SHARING	SHAWED	SHECHITAHS	SHELDRAKE
SHAMPOOERS	SHARINGS	SHAWING	SHECHITAS	SHELDRAKES

SHELDUCK
SHELDUCKS
SHELF
SHELFED
SHELFIER
SHELFIEST
SHELFING
SHELFROOM
SHELFROOMS
SHELFS
SHELFY
SHELL
SHELLAC
SHELLACKED
SHELLACKING
SHELLACKINGS
SHELLACS
SHELLBACK
SHELLBACKS
SHELLBARK
SHELLBARKS
SHELLDUCK
SHELLDUCKS
SHELLED
SHELLER
SHELLERS
SHELLFIRE
SHELLFIRES
SHELLFISH
SHELLFISHES
SHELLFUL
SHELLFULS
SHELLIER
SHELLIEST
SHELLING
SHELLINGS
SHELLS
SHELLWORK
SHELLWORKS
SHELLY
SHELTER
SHELTERED
SHELTERER
SHELTERERS
SHELTERING
SHELTERINGS
SHELTERS
SHELTERY
SHELTIE
SHELTIES
SHELTY
SHELVE
SHELVED
SHELVES
SHELVIER
SHELVIEST
SHELVING
SHELVINGS
SHELVY
SHEMOZZLE
SHEMOZZLED
SHEMOZZLES
SHEMOZZLING
SHEND
SHENDING
SHENDS
SHENT
SHEPHERD
SHEPHERDED
SHEPHERDING

SHEPHERDS
SHERBET
SHERBETS
SHERD
SHERDS
SHERE
SHEREEF
SHEREEFS
SHERIA
SHERIAS
SHERIAT
SHERIATS
SHERIF
SHERIFF
SHERIFFS
SHERIFIAN
SHERIFS
SHERRIES
SHERRIS
SHERRISES
SHERRY
SHES
SHET
SHETLAND
SHETS
SHETTING
SHEUCH
SHEUCHED
SHEUCHING
SHEUCHS
SHEUGH
SHEUGHED
SHEUGHING
SHEUGHS
SHEVA
SHEVAS
SHEW
SHEWBREAD
SHEWBREADS
SHEWED
SHEWEL
SHEWELS
SHEWING
SHEWN
SHEWS
SHIATSU
SHIATSUS
SHIBUICHI
SHIBUICHIS
SHICKER
SHICKERED
SHICKERS
SHICKSA
SHICKSAS
SHIDDER
SHIDDERS
SHIED
SHIEL
SHIELD
SHIELDED
SHIELDER
SHIELDERS
SHIELDING
SHIELDS
SHIELDUCK
SHIELDUCKS
SHIELED
SHIELING
SHIELINGS
SHIELS

SHIER
SHIERS
SHIES
SHIEST
SHIFT
SHIFTED
SHIFTER
SHIFTERS
SHIFTIER
SHIFTIEST
SHIFTILY
SHIFTING
SHIFTINGS
SHIFTLESS
SHIFTS
SHIFTY
SHIGELLA
SHIGELLAS
SHIITAKE
SHIKAR
SHIKAREE
SHIKAREES
SHIKARI
SHIKARIS
SHIKARS
SHIKSA
SHIKSAS
SHIKSE
SHIKSES
SHILL
SHILLABER
SHILLABERS
SHILLED
SHILLELAH
SHILLELAHS
SHILLING
SHILLINGS
SHILLS
SHILPIT
SHILY
SHIM
SHIMMER
SHIMMERED
SHIMMERING
SHIMMERINGS
SHIMMERS
SHIMMERY
SHIMMIED
SHIMMIES
SHIMMY
SHIMMYING
SHIMOZZLE
SHIMOZZLES
SHIMS
SHIN
SHINDIES
SHINDIG
SHINDIGS
SHINDY
SHINE
SHINED
SHINELESS
SHINER
SHINERS
SHINES
SHINESS
SHINESSES
SHINGLE
SHINGLED
SHINGLER

SHINGLERS
SHINGLES
SHINGLIER
SHINGLIEST
SHINGLING
SHINGLINGS
SHINGLY
SHINIER
SHINIEST
SHININESS
SHININESSES
SHINING
SHININGLY
SHINNE
SHINNED
SHINNES
SHINNIED
SHINNIES
SHINNING
SHINNY
SHINNYING
SHINS
SHINTIES
SHINTY
SHINY
SHIP
SHIPBOARD
SHIPBOARDS
SHIPFUL
SHIPFULS
SHIPLAP
SHIPLAPPED
SHIPLAPPING
SHIPLAPS
SHIPLESS
SHIPMAN
SHIPMATE
SHIPMATES
SHIPMEN
SHIPMENT
SHIPMENTS
SHIPPED
SHIPPEN
SHIPPENS
SHIPPER
SHIPPERS
SHIPPING
SHIPPINGS
SHIPPO
SHIPPON
SHIPPONS
SHIPPOS
SHIPPOUND
SHIPPOUNDS
SHIPS
SHIPSHAPE
SHIPWRECK
SHIPWRECKED
SHIPWRECKING
SHIPWRECKS
SHIPYARD
SHIPYARDS
SHIR
SHIRALEE
SHIRALEES
SHIRE
SHIREMAN
SHIREMEN
SHIRES
SHIRK

SHIRKED
SHIRKER
SHIRKERS
SHIRKING
SHIRKS
SHIRR
SHIRRA
SHIRRAS
SHIRRED
SHIRRING
SHIRRINGS
SHIRRS
SHIRS
SHIRT
SHIRTED
SHIRTIER
SHIRTIEST
SHIRTING
SHIRTINGS
SHIRTLESS
SHIRTS
SHIRTY
SHIT
SHITE
SHITES
SHITING
SHITS
SHITTAH
SHITTAHS
SHITTIER
SHITTIEST
SHITTIM
SHITTIMS
SHITTING
SHITTY
SHIV
SHIVAREE
SHIVAREED
SHIVAREEING
SHIVAREES
SHIVE
SHIVER
SHIVERED
SHIVERING
SHIVERINGS
SHIVERS
SHIVERY
SHIVES
SHIVOO
SHIVOOS
SHIVS
SHIVVED
SHIVVING
SHLEMIEL
SHLEMIELS
SHLEP
SHLEPPED
SHLEPPING
SHLEPS
SHLIMAZEL
SHLIMAZELS
SHLOCK
SHLOCKS
SHMOOSE
SHMOOSED
SHMOOSES
SHMOOSING
SHMOOZE
SHMOOZED
SHMOOZES

SHMOOZING	SHOGUNS	SHORESMAN	SHOUTERS	SHRADDHAS
SHOAL	SHOJI	SHORESMEN	SHOUTHER	SHRANK
SHOALED	SHOJIS	SHOREWARD	SHOUTHERED	SHRAPNEL
SHOALER	SHOLA	SHOREWARDS	SHOUTHERING	SHRAPNELS
SHOALEST	SHOLAS	SHORING	SHOUTHERS	SHRED
SHOALIER	SHONE	SHORINGS	SHOUTING	SHREDDED
SHOALIEST	SHOO	SHORN	SHOUTINGS	SHREDDER
SHOALING	SHOOED	SHORT	SHOUTS	SHREDDERS
SHOALINGS	SHOOGIE	SHORTAGE	SHOVE	SHREDDIER
SHOALNESS	SHOOGIED	SHORTAGES	SHOVED	SHREDDIEST
SHOALNESSES	SHOOGIEING	SHORTCAKE	SHOVEL	SHREDDING
SHOALS	SHOOGIES	SHORTCAKES	SHOVELER	SHREDDINGS
SHOALWISE	SHOOGLE	SHORTCUT	SHOVELERS	SHREDDY
SHOALY	SHOOGLED	SHORTCUTS	SHOVELFUL	SHREDLESS
SHOAT	SHOOGLES	SHORTED	SHOVELFULS	SHREDS
SHOATS	SHOOGLIER	SHORTEN	SHOVELLED	SHREEK
SHOCHET	SHOOGLIEST	SHORTENED	SHOVELLER	SHREEKED
SHOCHETIM	SHOOGLING	SHORTENER	SHOVELLERS	SHREEKING
SHOCK	SHOOGLY	SHORTENERS	SHOVELLING	SHREEKS
SHOCKED	SHOOING	SHORTENING	SHOVELS	SHREIK
SHOCKER	SHOOK	SHORTENINGS	SHOVER	SHREIKED
SHOCKERS	SHOOKS	SHORTENS	SHOVERS	SHREIKING
SHOCKING	SHOOL	SHORTER	SHOVES	SHREIKS
SHOCKS	SHOOLED	SHORTEST	SHOVING	SHREW
SHOD	SHOOLING	SHORTFALL	SHOW	SHREWD
SHODDIER	SHOOLS	SHORTFALLS	SHOWBIZ	SHREWDER
SHODDIES	SHOON	SHORTGOWN	SHOWBIZZES	SHREWDEST
SHODDIEST	SHOOS	SHORTGOWNS	SHOWBIZZY	SHREWDLY
SHODDILY	SHOOT	SHORTHAND	SHOWBREAD	SHREWED
SHODDY	SHOOTABLE	SHORTHANDS	SHOWBREADS	SHREWING
SHODER	SHOOTER	SHORTIE	SHOWCARD	SHREWISH
SHODERS	SHOOTERS	SHORTIES	SHOWCARDS	SHREWMICE
SHOE	SHOOTING	SHORTING	SHOWCASE	SHREWS
SHOEBILL	SHOOTINGS	SHORTISH	SHOWCASED	SHRIECH
SHOEBILLS	SHOOTIST	SHORTLY	SHOWCASES	SHRIECHED
SHOEBLACK	SHOOTISTS	SHORTNESS	SHOWCASING	SHRIECHES
SHOEBLACKS	SHOOTS	SHORTNESSES	SHOWED	SHRIECHING
SHOED	SHOP	SHORTS	SHOWER	SHRIEK
SHOEHORN	SHOPBOARD	SHORTY	SHOWERED	SHRIEKED
SHOEHORNED	SHOPBOARDS	SHOT	SHOWERFUL	SHRIEKER
SHOEHORNING	SHOPE	SHOTE	SHOWERIER	SHRIEKERS
SHOEHORNS	SHOPFUL	SHOTES	SHOWERIEST	SHRIEKING
SHOEING	SHOPFULS	SHOTFIRER	SHOWERING	SHRIEKINGS
SHOEINGS	SHOPHAR	SHOTFIRERS	SHOWERINGS	SHRIEKS
SHOELESS	SHOPHARS	SHOTGUN	SHOWERS	SHRIEVAL
SHOEMAKER	SHOPHROTH	SHOTGUNS	SHOWERY	SHRIEVE
SHOEMAKERS	SHOPMAN	SHOTMAKER	SHOWGHE	SHRIEVED
SHOER	SHOPMEN	SHOTMAKERS	SHOWGHES	SHRIEVES
SHOERS	SHOPPED	SHOTPROOF	SHOWGIRL	SHRIEVING
SHOES	SHOPPER	SHOTS	SHOWGIRLS	SHRIFT
SHOESHINE	SHOPPERS	SHOTT	SHOWIER	SHRIFTS
SHOESHINES	SHOPPIER	SHOTTED	SHOWIEST	SHRIGHT
SHOFAR	SHOPPIEST	SHOTTEN	SHOWILY	SHRIGHTS
SHOFARS	SHOPPING	SHOTTING	SHOWINESS	SHRIKE
SHOFROTH	SHOPPINGS	SHOTTLE	SHOWINESSES	SHRIKED
SHOG	SHOPPY	SHOTTLES	SHOWING	SHRIKES
SHOGGED	SHOPS	SHOTTS	SHOWINGS	SHRIKING
SHOGGING	SHOPWORN	SHOUGH	SHOWMAN	SHRILL
SHOGGLE	SHORAN	SHOUGHS	SHOWMANLY	SHRILLED
SHOGGLED	SHORANS	SHOULD	SHOWMEN	SHRILLER
SHOGGLES	SHORE	SHOULDER	SHOWN	SHRILLEST
SHOGGLIER	SHORED	SHOULDERED	SHOWPIECE	SHRILLING
SHOGGLIEST	SHORELESS	SHOULDERING	SHOWPIECES	SHRILLINGS
SHOGGLING	SHORELINE	SHOULDERINGS	SHOWPLACE	SHRILLS
SHOGGLY	SHORELINES	SHOULDERS	SHOWPLACES	SHRILLY
SHOGS	SHOREMAN	SHOULDEST	SHOWROOM	SHRIMP
SHOGUN	SHOREMEN	SHOULDST	SHOWROOMS	SHRIMPED
SHOGUNAL	SHORER	SHOUT	SHOWS	SHRIMPER
SHOGUNATE	SHORERS	SHOUTED	SHOWY	SHRIMPERS
SHOGUNATES	SHORES	SHOUTER	SHRADDHA	SHRIMPING

SHRIMPINGS	SHTCHIS	SHY	SICKED	SIDEROSES
SHRIMPS	SHTETL	SHYER	SICKEN	SIDEROSIS
SHRINAL	SHTETLS	SHYERS	SICKENED	SIDERS
SHRINE	SHTICK	SHYEST	SICKENER	SIDES
SHRINED	SHTICKS	SHYING	SICKENERS	SIDESMAN
SHRINES	SHTOOK	SHYISH	SICKENING	SIDESMEN
SHRINING	SHTOOKS	SHYLY	SICKENINGS	SIDESWIPE
SHRINK	SHTOOM	SHYNESS	SICKENS	SIDESWIPES
SHRINKAGE	SHTUCK	SHYNESSES	SICKER	SIDEWALK
SHRINKAGES	SHTUCKS	SHYSTER	SICKERLY	SIDEWALKS
SHRINKER	SHTUM	SHYSTERS	SICKEST	SIDEWARD
SHRINKERS	SHTUMM	SI	SICKIE	SIDEWARDS
SHRINKING	SHUBUNKIN	SIAL	SICKIES	SIDEWAY
SHRINKS	SHUBUNKINS	SIALIC	SICKING	SIDEWAYS
SHRITCH	SHUCK	SIALOGRAM	SICKISH	SIDEWISE
SHRITCHED	SHUCKED	SIALOGRAMS	SICKISHLY	SIDHA
SHRITCHES	SHUCKER	SIALOID	SICKLE	SIDHAS
SHRITCHING	SHUCKERS	SIALOLITH	SICKLED	SIDING
SHRIVE	SHUCKING	SIALOLITHS	SICKLEMAN	SIDINGS
SHRIVED	SHUCKINGS	SIALON	SICKLEMEN	SIDLE
SHRIVEL	SHUCKS	SIALONS	SICKLES	SIDLED
SHRIVELLED	SHUDDER	SIALS	SICKLIED	SIDLES
SHRIVELLING	SHUDDERED	SIAMANG	SICKLIER	SIDLING
SHRIVELS	SHUDDERING	SIAMANGS	SICKLIES	SIEGE
SHRIVEN	SHUDDERINGS	SIAMESE	SICKLIEST	SIEGED
SHRIVER	SHUDDERS	SIAMESED	SICKLILY	SIEGER
SHRIVERS	SHUDDERY	SIAMESES	SICKLY	SIEGERS
SHRIVES	SHUFFLE	SIAMESING	SICKLYING	SIEGES
SHRIVING	SHUFFLED	SIAMEZE	SICKMAN	SIEGING
SHRIVINGS	SHUFFLER	SIAMEZED	SICKMEN	SIELD
SHROFF	SHUFFLERS	SIAMEZES	SICKNESS	SIEMENS
SHROFFAGE	SHUFFLES	SIAMEZING	SICKNESSES	SIEN
SHROFFAGES	SHUFFLING	SIB	SICKNURSE	SIENNA
SHROFFED	SHUFFLINGS	SIBB	SICKNURSES	SIENNAS
SHROFFING	SHUFTI	SIBBS	SICKROOM	SIENS
SHROFFS	SHUFTIES	SIBILANCE	SICKROOMS	SIENT
SHROUD	SHUFTIS	SIBILANCES	SICKS	SIENTS
SHROUDED	SHUFTY	SIBILANCIES	SICLIKE	SIERRA
SHROUDIER	SHUL	SIBILANCY	SICS	SIERRAN
SHROUDIEST	SHULS	SIBILANT	SIDA	SIERRAS
SHROUDING	SHUN	SIBILANTS	SIDALCEA	SIESTA
SHROUDINGS	SHUNLESS	SIBILATE	SIDALCEAS	SIESTAS
SHROUDS	SHUNNED	SIBILATED	SIDAS	SIETH
SHROUDY	SHUNNING	SIBILATES	SIDDHA	SIETHS
SHROVE	SHUNS	SIBILATING	SIDDHAS	SIEVE
SHROVED	SHUNT	SIBILOUS	SIDDHI	SIEVED
SHROVES	SHUNTED	SIBLING	SIDDHIS	SIEVERT
SHROVING	SHUNTER	SIBLINGS	SIDDUR	SIEVERTS
SHROW	SHUNTERS	SIBS	SIDDURIM	SIEVES
SHROWD	SHUNTING	SIBSHIP	SIDE	SIEVING
SHROWED	SHUNTINGS	SIBSHIPS	SIDEARM	SIFAKA
SHROWING	SHUNTS	SIBYL	SIDEARMS	SIFAKAS
SHROWS	SHUSH	SIBYLS	SIDEBOARD	SIFFLE
SHRUB	SHUSHED	SIC	SIDEBOARDS	SIFFLED
SHRUBBED	SHUSHES	SICCAN	SIDEBURNS	SIFFLES
SHRUBBERIES	SHUSHING	SICCAR	SIDECAR	SIFFLING
SHRUBBERY	SHUT	SICCATIVE	SIDECARS	SIFT
SHRUBBIER	SHUTS	SICCATIVES	SIDED	SIFTED
SHRUBBIEST	SHUTTER	SICCED	SIDELIGHT	SIFTER
SHRUBBING	SHUTTERED	SICCING	SIDELIGHTS	SIFTERS
SHRUBBY	SHUTTERING	SICCITIES	SIDELING	SIFTING
SHRUBLESS	SHUTTERINGS	SICCITY	SIDELOCK	SIFTINGLY
SHRUBS	SHUTTERS	SICE	SIDELOCKS	SIFTINGS
SHRUG	SHUTTING	SICES	SIDELONG	SIFTS
SHRUGGED	SHUTTLE	SICH	SIDER	SIGH
SHRUGGING	SHUTTLED	SICILIANA	SIDERAL	SIGHED
SHRUGS	SHUTTLES	SICILIANE	SIDEREAL	SIGHER
SHRUNK	SHUTTLING	SICILIANO	SIDERITE	SIGHERS
SHRUNKEN	SHWA	SICILIANOS	SIDERITES	SIGHFUL
SHTCHI	SHWAS	SICK	SIDERITIC	SIGHING

SIGHINGLY
SIGHS
SIGHT
SIGHTED
SIGHTER
SIGHTERS
SIGHTING
SIGHTLESS
SIGHTLIER
SIGHTLIEST
SIGHTLY
SIGHTS
SIGHTSAW
SIGHTSEE
SIGHTSEEING
SIGHTSEEINGS
SIGHTSEEN
SIGHTSEER
SIGHTSEERS
SIGHTSEES
SIGIL
SIGILLARY
SIGILLATE
SIGILS
SIGISBEI
SIGISBEO
SIGLA
SIGMA
SIGMAS
SIGMATE
SIGMATED
SIGMATES
SIGMATIC
SIGMATING
SIGMATION
SIGMATIONS
SIGMATISM
SIGMATISMS
SIGMATRON
SIGMATRONS
SIGMOID
SIGMOIDAL
SIGN
SIGNAL
SIGNALISE
SIGNALISED
SIGNALISES
SIGNALISING
SIGNALIZE
SIGNALIZED
SIGNALIZES
SIGNALIZING
SIGNALLED
SIGNALLER
SIGNALLERS
SIGNALLING
SIGNALLINGS
SIGNALLY
SIGNALMAN
SIGNALMEN
SIGNALS
SIGNARIES
SIGNARY
SIGNATORIES
SIGNATORY
SIGNATURE
SIGNATURES
SIGNBOARD
SIGNBOARDS
SIGNED

SIGNER
SIGNERS
SIGNET
SIGNETED
SIGNETS
SIGNEUR
SIGNEURIE
SIGNEURIES
SIGNIEUR
SIGNIEURS
SIGNIFICS
SIGNIFIED
SIGNIFIER
SIGNIFIERS
SIGNIFIES
SIGNIFY
SIGNIFYING
SIGNING
SIGNIOR
SIGNIORS
SIGNLESS
SIGNOR
SIGNORA
SIGNORAS
SIGNORE
SIGNORES
SIGNORI
SIGNORIA
SIGNORIAL
SIGNORIAS
SIGNORIES
SIGNORINA
SIGNORINAS
SIGNORS
SIGNORY
SIGNPOST
SIGNPOSTED
SIGNPOSTING
SIGNPOSTS
SIGNS
SIKA
SIKAS
SIKE
SIKES
SILAGE
SILAGED
SILAGES
SILAGING
SILANE
SILANES
SILASTIC
SILASTICS
SILD
SILDS
SILE
SILED
SILEN
SILENCE
SILENCED
SILENCER
SILENCERS
SILENCES
SILENCING
SILENE
SILENES
SILENS
SILENT
SILENTER
SILENTEST
SILENTLY

SILENTS
SILENUS
SILENUSES
SILER
SILERS
SILES
SILESIA
SILESIAS
SILEX
SILEXES
SILICA
SILICANE
SILICANES
SILICAS
SILICATE
SILICATED
SILICATES
SILICATING
SILICEOUS
SILICIC
SILICIDE
SILICIDES
SILICIFIED
SILICIFIES
SILICIFY
SILICIFYING
SILICIOUS
SILICIUM
SILICIUMS
SILICLE
SILICLES
SILICON
SILICONE
SILICONES
SILICONS
SILICOSES
SILICOSIS
SILICOTIC
SILICOTICS
SILICULA
SILICULAS
SILICULE
SILICULES
SILING
SILIQUA
SILIQUAS
SILIQUE
SILIQUES
SILIQUOSE
SILK
SILKED
SILKEN
SILKENED
SILKENING
SILKENS
SILKIE
SILKIER
SILKIES
SILKIEST
SILKILY
SILKINESS
SILKINESSES
SILKING
SILKS
SILKTAIL
SILKTAILS
SILKWEED
SILKWEEDS
SILKWORM
SILKWORMS

SILKY
SILL
SILLABUB
SILLABUBS
SILLADAR
SILLADARS
SILLER
SILLERS
SILLIER
SILLIES
SILLIEST
SILLILY
SILLINESS
SILLINESSES
SILLOCK
SILLOCKS
SILLS
SILLY
SILO
SILOED
SILOING
SILOS
SILPHIA
SILPHIUM
SILPHIUMS
SILT
SILTATION
SILTATIONS
SILTED
SILTIER
SILTIEST
SILTING
SILTS
SILTSTONE
SILTSTONES
SILTY
SILURID
SILURIDS
SILURIST
SILURISTS
SILUROID
SILUROIDS
SILVA
SILVAE
SILVAN
SILVANS
SILVAS
SILVATIC
SILVER
SILVERED
SILVERIER
SILVERIEST
SILVERING
SILVERINGS
SILVERISE
SILVERISED
SILVERISES
SILVERISING
SILVERIZE
SILVERIZED
SILVERIZES
SILVERIZING
SILVERLY
SILVERN
SILVERS
SILVERY
SIM
SIMA
SIMAR
SIMARRE

SIMARRES
SIMARS
SIMAS
SIMI
SIMIAL
SIMIAN
SIMIANS
SIMILAR
SIMILARLY
SIMILE
SIMILES
SIMILISE
SIMILISED
SIMILISES
SIMILISING
SIMILIZE
SIMILIZED
SIMILIZES
SIMILIZING
SIMILOR
SIMILORS
SIMIOUS
SIMIS
SIMITAR
SIMITARS
SIMKIN
SIMKINS
SIMMER
SIMMERED
SIMMERING
SIMMERS
SIMNEL
SIMNELS
SIMONIAC
SIMONIACS
SIMONIES
SIMONIOUS
SIMONIST
SIMONISTS
SIMONY
SIMOOM
SIMOOMS
SIMOON
SIMOONS
SIMORG
SIMORGS
SIMP
SIMPAI
SIMPAIS
SIMPATICO
SIMPER
SIMPERED
SIMPERER
SIMPERERS
SIMPERING
SIMPERS
SIMPKIN
SIMPKINS
SIMPLE
SIMPLED
SIMPLER
SIMPLERS
SIMPLES
SIMPLESSE
SIMPLESSES
SIMPLEST
SIMPLETON
SIMPLETONS
SIMPLEX
SIMPLICES

SIMPLIFIED	SING	SINOEKETE	SIRENE	SIT
SIMPLIFIES	SINGABLE	SINOEKETES	SIRENES	SITAR
SIMPLIFY	SINGALONG	SINOPIA	SIRENIAN	SITARS
SIMPLIFYING	SINGALONGS	SINOPIAS	SIRENIANS	SITATUNGA
SIMPLING	SINGE	SINOPIS	SIRENIC	SITATUNGAS
SIMPLINGS	SINGED	SINOPISES	SIRENS	SITCOM
SIMPLISM	SINGEING	SINOPITE	SIRES	SITCOMS
SIMPLISMS	SINGER	SINOPITES	SIRGANG	SITDOWN
SIMPLIST	SINGERS	SINS	SIRGANGS	SITDOWNS
SIMPLISTE	SINGES	SINSYNE	SIRI	SITE
SIMPLISTS	SINGING	SINTER	SIRIASES	SITED
SIMPLY	SINGINGLY	SINTERED	SIRIASIS	SITES
SIMPS	SINGINGS	SINTERING	SIRIH	SITFAST
SIMS	SINGLE	SINTERS	SIRIHS	SITFASTS
SIMULACRA	SINGLED	SINTERY	SIRING	SITH
SIMULACRE	SINGLES	SINUATE	SIRIS	SITHE
SIMULACRES	SINGLET	SINUATED	SIRKAR	SITHED
SIMULANT	SINGLETON	SINUATELY	SIRKARS	SITHEN
SIMULANTS	SINGLETONS	SINUATION	SIRLOIN	SITHENCE
SIMULAR	SINGLETS	SINUATIONS	SIRLOINS	SITHENS
SIMULARS	SINGLING	SINUITIS	SIRNAME	SITHES
SIMULATE	SINGLINGS	SINUITISES	SIRNAMED	SITHING
SIMULATED	SINGLY	SINUOSE	SIRNAMES	SITING
SIMULATES	SINGS	SINUOSITIES	SIRNAMING	SITIOLOGIES
SIMULATING	SINGSONG	SINUOSITY	SIROC	SITIOLOGY
SIMULATOR	SINGSONGED	SINUOUS	SIROCCO	SITOLOGIES
SIMULATORS	SINGSONGING	SINUOUSLY	SIROCCOS	SITOLOGY
SIMULCAST	SINGSONGS	SINUS	SIROCS	SITREP
SIMULCASTED	SINGSPIEL	SINUSES	SIRRAH	SITREPS
SIMULCASTING	SINGSPIELS	SINUSITIS	SIRRAHS	SITS
SIMULCASTS	SINGULAR	SINUSITISES	SIRRED	SITTAR
SIMULIUM	SINGULARS	SINUSOID	SIRREE	SITTARS
SIMULIUMS	SINGULT	SINUSOIDS	SIRREES	SITTER
SIMURG	SINGULTS	SIP	SIRRING	SITTERS
SIMURGH	SINGULTUS	SIPE	SIRS	SITTINE
SIMURGHS	SINGULTUSES	SIPED	SIRUP	SITTING
SIMURGS	SINICAL	SIPES	SIRUPED	SITTINGS
SIN	SINICISE	SIPHON	SIRUPING	SITUATE
SINAPISM	SINICISED	SIPHONAGE	SIRUPS	SITUATED
SINAPISMS	SINICISES	SIPHONAGES	SIRVENTE	SITUATES
SINCE	SINICISING	SIPHONAL	SIRVENTES	SITUATING
SINCERE	SINICIZE	SIPHONATE	SIS	SITUATION
SINCERELY	SINICIZED	SIPHONED	SISAL	SITUATIONS
SINCERER	SINICIZES	SIPHONET	SISALS	SITULA
SINCEREST	SINICIZING	SIPHONETS	SISERARIES	SITULAE
SINCERITIES	SINING	SIPHONIC	SISERARY	SITUS
SINCERITY	SINISTER	SIPHONING	SISES	SITUTUNGA
SINCIPUT	SINISTRAL	SIPHONS	SISKIN	SITUTUNGAS
SINCIPUTS	SINISTRALS	SIPHUNCLE	SISKINS	SITZKRIEG
SIND	SINK	SIPHUNCLES	SISS	SITZKRIEGS
SINDED	SINKAGE	SIPING	SISSERARIES	SIVER
SINDING	SINKAGES	SIPPED	SISSERARY	SIVERS
SINDINGS	SINKER	SIPPER	SISSES	SIWASH
SINDON	SINKERS	SIPPERS	SISSIER	SIWASHES
SINDONS	SINKIER	SIPPET	SISSIES	SIX
SINDS	SINKIEST	SIPPETS	SISSIEST	SIXAINE
SINE	SINKING	SIPPING	SISSOO	SIXAINES
SINECURE	SINKINGS	SIPPLE	SISSOOS	SIXER
SINECURES	SINKS	SIPPLED	SISSY	SIXERS
SINED	SINKY	SIPPLES	SIST	SIXES
SINES	SINLESS	SIPPLING	SISTED	SIXFOLD
SINEW	SINLESSLY	SIPS	SISTER	SIXPENCE
SINEWED	SINNED	SIR	SISTERED	SIXPENCES
SINEWING	SINNER	SIRCAR	SISTERING	SIXPENNIES
SINEWLESS	SINNERED	SIRCARS	SISTERLY	SIXPENNY
SINEWS	SINNERING	SIRDAR	SISTERS	SIXSCORE
SINEWY	SINNERS	SIRDARS	SISTING	SIXSCORES
SINFONIA	SINNET	SIRE	SISTRA	SIXTE
SINFONIAS	SINNETS	SIRED	SISTRUM	SIXTEEN
SINFUL	SINNING	SIREN	SISTS	SIXTEENER

SIXTEENERS
SIXTEENMO
SIXTEENMOS
SIXTEENS
SIXTEENTH
SIXTEENTHS
SIXTES
SIXTH
SIXTHLY
SIXTHS
SIXTIES
SIXTIETH
SIXTIETHS
SIXTY
SIZABLE
SIZAR
SIZARS
SIZARSHIP
SIZARSHIPS
SIZE
SIZEABLE
SIZED
SIZEL
SIZELS
SIZER
SIZERS
SIZES
SIZIER
SIZIEST
SIZINESS
SIZINESSES
SIZING
SIZINGS
SIZY
SIZZLE
SIZZLED
SIZZLER
SIZZLERS
SIZZLES
SIZZLING
SIZZLINGS
SJAMBOK
SJAMBOKKED
SJAMBOKKING
SJAMBOKS
SKA
SKAIL
SKAILED
SKAILING
SKAILS
SKAITH
SKAITHED
SKAITHING
SKAITHS
SKALD
SKALDIC
SKALDS
SKART
SKARTH
SKARTHS
SKARTS
SKAS
SKAT
SKATE
SKATED
SKATER
SKATERS
SKATES
SKATING
SKATINGS

SKATOLE
SKATOLES
SKATOLOGIES
SKATOLOGY
SKATS
SKATT
SKATTS
SKAW
SKAWS
SKEAN
SKEANS
SKEAR
SKEARED
SKEARIER
SKEARIEST
SKEARING
SKEARS
SKEARY
SKEDADDLE
SKEDADDLED
SKEDADDLES
SKEDADDLING
SKEELIER
SKEELIEST
SKEELY
SKEER
SKEERED
SKEERIER
SKEERIEST
SKEERING
SKEERS
SKEERY
SKEESICKS
SKEET
SKEETER
SKEETERS
SKEETS
SKEG
SKEGGER
SKEGGERS
SKEGS
SKEIGH
SKEIGHER
SKEIGHEST
SKEIN
SKEINS
SKELDER
SKELDERED
SKELDERING
SKELDERS
SKELETAL
SKELETON
SKELETONS
SKELF
SKELFS
SKELLIE
SKELLIED
SKELLIER
SKELLIES
SKELLIEST
SKELLOCH
SKELLOCHED
SKELLOCHING
SKELLOCHS
SKELLUM
SKELLUMS
SKELLY
SKELLYING
SKELM
SKELMS

SKELP
SKELPED
SKELPING
SKELPINGS
SKELPS
SKELTER
SKELTERED
SKELTERING
SKELTERS
SKENE
SKENES
SKEO
SKEOS
SKEP
SKEPFUL
SKEPFULS
SKEPPED
SKEPPING
SKEPS
SKEPSIS
SKEPSISES
SKEPTIC
SKEPTICS
SKER
SKERRED
SKERRICK
SKERRICKS
SKERRIES
SKERRING
SKERRY
SKERS
SKETCH
SKETCHED
SKETCHER
SKETCHERS
SKETCHES
SKETCHIER
SKETCHIEST
SKETCHILY
SKETCHING
SKETCHY
SKEW
SKEWBALD
SKEWBALDS
SKEWED
SKEWER
SKEWERED
SKEWERING
SKEWERS
SKEWEST
SKEWING
SKEWS
SKI
SKIABLE
SKIAGRAM
SKIAGRAMS
SKIAGRAPH
SKIAGRAPHS
SKIAMACHIES
SKIAMACHY
SKIASCOPIES
SKIASCOPY
SKIATRON
SKIATRONS
SKID
SKIDDED
SKIDDING
SKIDOO
SKIDOOS
SKIDPAN

SKIDPANS
SKIDS
SKIED
SKIER
SKIERS
SKIES
SKIEY
SKIEYER
SKIEYEST
SKIFF
SKIFFED
SKIFFING
SKIFFLE
SKIFFLES
SKIFFS
SKIING
SKIINGS
SKIJORING
SKIJORINGS
SKILFUL
SKILFULLY
SKILL
SKILLED
SKILLESS
SKILLET
SKILLETS
SKILLIER
SKILLIES
SKILLIEST
SKILLING
SKILLINGS
SKILLION
SKILLIONS
SKILLS
SKILLY
SKIM
SKIMMED
SKIMMER
SKIMMERS
SKIMMIA
SKIMMIAS
SKIMMING
SKIMMINGS
SKIMP
SKIMPED
SKIMPIER
SKIMPIEST
SKIMPILY
SKIMPING
SKIMPS
SKIMPY
SKIMS
SKIN
SKINFLICK
SKINFLICKS
SKINFLINT
SKINFLINTS
SKINFOOD
SKINFOODS
SKINFUL
SKINFULS
SKINHEAD
SKINHEADS
SKINK
SKINKED
SKINKER
SKINKERS
SKINKING
SKINKS
SKINLESS

SKINNED
SKINNER
SKINNERS
SKINNIER
SKINNIEST
SKINNING
SKINNY
SKINS
SKINT
SKINTER
SKINTEST
SKIO
SKIOS
SKIP
SKIPJACK
SKIPJACKS
SKIPPED
SKIPPER
SKIPPERED
SKIPPERING
SKIPPERINGS
SKIPPERS
SKIPPET
SKIPPETS
SKIPPING
SKIPPINGS
SKIPS
SKIRL
SKIRLED
SKIRLING
SKIRLINGS
SKIRLS
SKIRMISH
SKIRMISHED
SKIRMISHES
SKIRMISHING
SKIRMISHINGS
SKIRR
SKIRRED
SKIRRET
SKIRRETS
SKIRRING
SKIRRS
SKIRT
SKIRTED
SKIRTER
SKIRTERS
SKIRTING
SKIRTINGS
SKIRTLESS
SKIRTS
SKIS
SKIT
SKITE
SKITED
SKITES
SKITING
SKITS
SKITTER
SKITTERED
SKITTERING
SKITTERS
SKITTISH
SKITTLE
SKITTLED
SKITTLES
SKITTLING
SKIVE
SKIVED
SKIVER

KIVERED	SKRIMPING	SKYLARKS	SLAGGING	SLASHED
KIVERING	SKRIMPS	SKYLIGHT	SLAGGY	SLASHER
KIVERS	SKRUMP	SKYLIGHTS	SLAGS	SLASHERS
KIVES	SKRUMPED	SKYLINE	SLAID	SLASHES
KIVIE	SKRUMPING	SKYLINES	SLAIN	SLASHING
KIVIER	SKRUMPS	SKYMAN	SLAINTE	SLASHINGS
KIVIEST	SKRY	SKYMEN	SLAIRG	SLAT
KIVING	SKRYER	SKYR	SLAIRGED	SLATE
KIVINGS	SKRYERS	SKYRE	SLAIRGING	SLATED
KIVVIES	SKRYING	SKYRED	SLAIRGS	SLATER
KIVVY	SKUA	SKYRES	SLAISTER	SLATERS
KIVY	SKUAS	SKYRING	SLAISTERED	SLATES
KLATE	SKUDLER	SKYROCKET	SLAISTERIES	SLATHER
KLATED	SKUDLERS	SKYROCKETED	SLAISTERING	SLATHERED
KLATES	SKUG	SKYROCKETING	SLAISTERS	SLATHERING
KLATING	SKUGGED	SKYROCKETS	SLAISTERY	SLATHERS
KLENT	SKUGGING	SKYRS	SLAKE	SLATIER
KLENTED	SKUGS	SKYSAIL	SLAKED	SLATIEST
KLENTING	SKULK	SKYSAILS	SLAKELESS	SLATINESS
KLENTS	SKULKED	SKYSCAPE	SLAKES	SLATINESSES
KLIFF	SKULKER	SKYSCAPES	SLAKING	SLATING
KLIFFS	SKULKERS	SKYTE	SLALOM	SLATINGS
KLIM	SKULKING	SKYTED	SLALOMED	SLATS
KLIMMED	SKULKINGS	SKYTES	SLALOMING	SLATTED
KLIMMING	SKULKS	SKYTING	SLALOMS	SLATTER
KLIMO	SKULL	SKYWARD	SLAM	SLATTERED
KOAL	SKULLCAP	SKYWARDS	SLAMMAKIN	SLATTERING
KOFF	SKULLCAPS	SKYWAY	SLAMMAKINS	SLATTERN
KOFFED	SKULLS	SKYWAYS	SLAMMED	SLATTERNS
KOFFING	SKULPIN	SLAB	SLAMMER	SLATTERS
KOFFS	SKULPINS	SLABBED	SLAMMERS	SLATTERY
KOKIAAN	SKUMMER	SLABBER	SLAMMING	SLATTING
KOKIAANS	SKUMMERED	SLABBERED	SLAMS	SLATY
KOL	SKUMMERING	SLABBERER	SLANDER	SLAUGHTER
KOLIA	SKUMMERS	SLABBERERS	SLANDERED	SLAUGHTERED
KOLION	SKUNK	SLABBERING	SLANDERER	SLAUGHTERING
KOLLIE	SKUNKED	SLABBERS	SLANDERERS	SLAUGHTERS
KOLLIES	SKUNKING	SLABBERY	SLANDERING	SLAVE
KOLLY	SKUNKS	SLABBIER	SLANDERS	SLAVED
KRAN	SKURRIED	SLABBIEST	SLANE	SLAVER
KRANS	SKURRIES	SLABBING	SLANES	SLAVERED
KREAKIER	SKURRY	SLABBY	SLANG	SLAVERER
KREAKIEST	SKURRYING	SLABS	SLANGED	SLAVERERS
KREAKY	SKUTTLE	SLABSTONE	SLANGIER	SLAVERIES
KREEN	SKUTTLED	SLABSTONES	SLANGIEST	SLAVERING
KREENE	SKUTTLES	SLACK	SLANGILY	SLAVERS
KREENES	SKUTTLING	SLACKED	SLANGING	SLAVERY
KREENS	SKY	SLACKEN	SLANGINGS	SLAVES
KREIGH	SKYBORN	SLACKENED	SLANGISH	SLAVEY
KREIGHED	SKYCLAD	SLACKENING	SLANGS	SLAVEYS
KREIGHING	SKYER	SLACKENINGS	SLANGULAR	SLAVING
KREIGHS	SKYERS	SLACKENS	SLANGY	SLAVISH
KRIECH	SKYEY	SLACKER	SLANT	SLAVISHLY
KRIECHED	SKYIER	SLACKERS	SLANTED	SLAVOCRAT
KRIECHING	SKYIEST	SLACKEST	SLANTING	SLAVOCRATS
KRIECHS	SKYING	SLACKING	SLANTLY	SLAW
KRIED	SKYISH	SLACKLY	SLANTS	SLAWS
KRIEGH	SKYJACK	SLACKNESS	SLANTWAYS	SLAY
KRIEGHED	SKYJACKED	SLACKNESSES	SLANTWISE	SLAYED
KRIEGHING	SKYJACKER	SLACKS	SLAP	SLAYER
KRIEGHS	SKYJACKERS	SLADANG	SLAPJACK	SLAYERS
KRIES	SKYJACKING	SLADANGS	SLAPJACKS	SLAYING
KRIK	SKYJACKINGS	SLADE	SLAPPED	SLAYS
KRIKS	SKYJACKS	SLADES	SLAPPER	SLEAVE
KRIMMAGE	SKYLAB	SLAE	SLAPPERS	SLEAVED
KRIMMAGED	SKYLABS	SLAES	SLAPPING	SLEAVES
KRIMMAGES	SKYLARK	SLAG	SLAPS	SLEAVING
KRIMMAGING	SKYLARKED	SLAGGED	SLAPSTICK	SLEAZE
KRIMP	SKYLARKING	SLAGGIER	SLAPSTICKS	SLEAZES
KRIMPED	SKYLARKINGS	SLAGGIEST	SLASH	SLEAZIER

SLEAZIEST
SLEAZILY
SLEAZY
SLED
SLEDDED
SLEDDING
SLEDDINGS
SLEDED
SLEDGE
SLEDGED
SLEDGER
SLEDGERS
SLEDGES
SLEDGING
SLEDGINGS
SLEDS
SLEE
SLEECH
SLEECHES
SLEECHIER
SLEECHIEST
SLEECHY
SLEEK
SLEEKED
SLEEKEN
SLEEKENED
SLEEKENING
SLEEKENS
SLEEKER
SLEEKERS
SLEEKEST
SLEEKIER
SLEEKIEST
SLEEKING
SLEEKINGS
SLEEKIT
SLEEKLY
SLEEKNESS
SLEEKNESSES
SLEEKS
SLEEKY
SLEEP
SLEEPER
SLEEPERS
SLEEPERY
SLEEPIER
SLEEPIEST
SLEEPILY
SLEEPING
SLEEPINGS
SLEEPLESS
SLEEPRY
SLEEPS
SLEEPY
SLEER
SLEEST
SLEET
SLEETED
SLEETIER
SLEETIEST
SLEETING
SLEETS
SLEETY
SLEEVE
SLEEVED
SLEEVER
SLEEVERS
SLEEVES
SLEEVING
SLEEVINGS

SLEEZIER
SLEEZIEST
SLEEZY
SLEIDED
SLEIGH
SLEIGHED
SLEIGHING
SLEIGHINGS
SLEIGHS
SLEIGHT
SLEIGHTS
SLENDER
SLENDERER
SLENDEREST
SLENDERLY
SLEPT
SLEUTH
SLEUTHED
SLEUTHING
SLEUTHS
SLEW
SLEWED
SLEWING
SLEWS
SLEY
SLEYS
SLICE
SLICED
SLICER
SLICERS
SLICES
SLICING
SLICINGS
SLICK
SLICKED
SLICKEN
SLICKENED
SLICKENING
SLICKENS
SLICKER
SLICKERS
SLICKEST
SLICKING
SLICKINGS
SLICKLY
SLICKNESS
SLICKNESSES
SLICKS
SLID
SLIDDEN
SLIDDER
SLIDDERED
SLIDDERING
SLIDDERS
SLIDDERY
SLIDE
SLIDED
SLIDER
SLIDERS
SLIDES
SLIDING
SLIDINGLY
SLIDINGS
SLIER
SLIEST
SLIGHT
SLIGHTED
SLIGHTER
SLIGHTEST
SLIGHTING

SLIGHTISH
SLIGHTLY
SLIGHTS
SLILY
SLIM
SLIME
SLIMED
SLIMES
SLIMIER
SLIMIEST
SLIMILY
SLIMINESS
SLIMINESSES
SLIMING
SLIMLINE
SLIMLY
SLIMMED
SLIMMER
SLIMMERS
SLIMMEST
SLIMMING
SLIMMINGS
SLIMMISH
SLIMNESS
SLIMNESSES
SLIMS
SLIMSIER
SLIMSIEST
SLIMSY
SLIMY
SLING
SLINGER
SLINGERS
SLINGING
SLINGS
SLINGSHOT
SLINGSHOTS
SLINK
SLINKER
SLINKERS
SLINKIER
SLINKIEST
SLINKING
SLINKS
SLINKSKIN
SLINKSKINS
SLINKWEED
SLINKWEEDS
SLINKY
SLIP
SLIPE
SLIPES
SLIPFORM
SLIPPAGE
SLIPPAGES
SLIPPED
SLIPPER
SLIPPERED
SLIPPERIER
SLIPPERIEST
SLIPPERING
SLIPPERS
SLIPPERY
SLIPPIER
SLIPPIEST
SLIPPING
SLIPPY
SLIPRAIL
SLIPRAILS
SLIPS

SLIPSHOD
SLIPSLOP
SLIPSLOPS
SLIPT
SLIPWARE
SLIPWARES
SLIPWAY
SLIPWAYS
SLISH
SLISHES
SLIT
SLITHER
SLITHERED
SLITHERIER
SLITHERIEST
SLITHERING
SLITHERS
SLITHERY
SLITS
SLITTER
SLITTERS
SLITTING
SLIVE
SLIVED
SLIVEN
SLIVER
SLIVERED
SLIVERING
SLIVERS
SLIVES
SLIVING
SLIVOVIC
SLIVOVICA
SLIVOVICAS
SLIVOVICS
SLIVOVITZ
SLIVOVITZES
SLIVOWITZ
SLIVOWITZES
SLOAN
SLOANS
SLOB
SLOBBER
SLOBBERED
SLOBBERING
SLOBBERS
SLOBBERY
SLOBBIER
SLOBBIEST
SLOBBY
SLOBLAND
SLOBLANDS
SLOBS
SLOCKEN
SLOCKENED
SLOCKENING
SLOCKENS
SLOE
SLOEBUSH
SLOEBUSHES
SLOES
SLOETHORN
SLOETHORNS
SLOETREE
SLOETREES
SLOG
SLOGAN
SLOGANEER
SLOGANEERED
SLOGANEERING

SLOGANEERINGS
SLOGANEERS
SLOGANISE
SLOGANISED
SLOGANISES
SLOGANISING
SLOGANISINGS
SLOGANIZE
SLOGANIZED
SLOGANIZES
SLOGANIZING
SLOGANIZINGS
SLOGANS
SLOGGED
SLOGGER
SLOGGERS
SLOGGING
SLOGS
SLOID
SLOIDS
SLOKEN
SLOKENED
SLOKENING
SLOKENS
SLOOM
SLOOMED
SLOOMIER
SLOOMIEST
SLOOMING
SLOOMS
SLOOMY
SLOOP
SLOOPS
SLOOT
SLOOTS
SLOP
SLOPE
SLOPED
SLOPES
SLOPEWISE
SLOPIER
SLOPIEST
SLOPING
SLOPINGLY
SLOPPED
SLOPPIER
SLOPPIEST
SLOPPILY
SLOPPING
SLOPPY
SLOPS
SLOPWORK
SLOPWORKS
SLOPY
SLOSH
SLOSHED
SLOSHES
SLOSHIER
SLOSHIEST
SLOSHING
SLOSHY
SLOT
SLOTH
SLOTHED
SLOTHFUL
SLOTHING
SLOTHS
SLOTS
SLOTTED
SLOTTER

SLOTTERS
SLOTTING
SLOUCH
SLOUCHED
SLOUCHER
SLOUCHERS
SLOUCHES
SLOUCHIER
SLOUCHIEST
SLOUCHING
SLOUCHY
SLOUGH
SLOUGHED
SLOUGHIER
SLOUGHIEST
SLOUGHING
SLOUGHS
SLOUGHY
SLOVE
SLOVEN
SLOVENLIER
SLOVENLIEST
SLOVENLY
SLOVENRIES
SLOVENRY
SLOVENS
SLOW
SLOWBACK
SLOWBACKS
SLOWCOACH
SLOWCOACHES
SLOWED
SLOWER
SLOWEST
SLOWING
SLOWINGS
SLOWISH
SLOWLY
SLOWNESS
SLOWNESSES
SLOWPOKE
SLOWPOKES
SLOWS
SLOYD
SLOYDS
SLUB
SLUBB
SLUBBED
SLUBBER
SLUBBERED
SLUBBERING
SLUBBERINGS
SLUBBERS
SLUBBIER
SLUBBIEST
SLUBBING
SLUBBINGS
SLUBBS
SLUBBY
SLUBS
SLUDGE
SLUDGES
SLUDGIER
SLUDGIEST
SLUDGY
SLUE
SLUED
SLUEING
SLUES
SLUG

SLUGFEST
SLUGFESTS
SLUGGABED
SLUGGABEDS
SLUGGARD
SLUGGARDS
SLUGGED
SLUGGER
SLUGGERS
SLUGGING
SLUGGISH
SLUGHORN
SLUGHORNE
SLUGHORNES
SLUGHORNS
SLUGS
SLUICE
SLUICED
SLUICES
SLUICIER
SLUICIEST
SLUICING
SLUICY
SLUING
SLUIT
SLUITS
SLUM
SLUMBER
SLUMBERED
SLUMBERER
SLUMBERERS
SLUMBERING
SLUMBERINGS
SLUMBERS
SLUMBERY
SLUMBROUS
SLUMBRY
SLUMMED
SLUMMER
SLUMMIER
SLUMMIEST
SLUMMING
SLUMMINGS
SLUMMOCK
SLUMMOCKED
SLUMMOCKING
SLUMMOCKS
SLUMMY
SLUMP
SLUMPED
SLUMPIER
SLUMPICOT
SLUMPING
SLUMPS
SLUMPY
SLUMS
SLUNG
SLUNK
SLUR
SLURB
SLURBS
SLURP
SLURPED
SLURPING
SLURPS
SLURRED
SLURRIES
SLURRING
SLURRY

SLURS
SLUSE
SLUSES
SLUSH
SLUSHED
SLUSHES
SLUSHIER
SLUSHIEST
SLUSHING
SLUSHY
SLUT
SLUTS
SLUTTERIES
SLUTTERY
SLUTTISH
SLY
SLYBOOTS
SLYER
SLYEST
SLYISH
SLYLY
SLYNESS
SLYNESSES
SLYPE
SLYPES
SMA
SMACK
SMACKED
SMACKER
SMACKERS
SMACKING
SMACKINGS
SMACKS
SMAIK
SMAIKS
SMALL
SMALLAGE
SMALLAGES
SMALLED
SMALLER
SMALLEST
SMALLING
SMALLISH
SMALLNESS
SMALLNESSES
SMALLPOX
SMALLPOXES
SMALLS
SMALM
SMALMED
SMALMIER
SMALMIEST
SMALMILY
SMALMING
SMALMS
SMALMY
SMALT
SMALTI
SMALTITE
SMALTITES
SMALTO
SMALTOS
SMALTS
SMARAGD
SMARAGDS
SMARM
SMARMED
SMARMIER
SMARMIEST
SMARMILY

SMARMING
SMARMS
SMARMY
SMART
SMARTARSE
SMARTARSES
SMARTASS
SMARTASSES
SMARTED
SMARTEN
SMARTENED
SMARTENING
SMARTENS
SMARTER
SMARTEST
SMARTIE
SMARTIES
SMARTING
SMARTLY
SMARTNESS
SMARTNESSES
SMARTS
SMARTY
SMASH
SMASHED
SMASHER
SMASHEROO
SMASHEROOS
SMASHERS
SMASHES
SMASHING
SMASHINGS
SMATCH
SMATCHED
SMATCHES
SMATCHING
SMATTER
SMATTERED
SMATTERER
SMATTERERS
SMATTERING
SMATTERINGS
SMATTERS
SMEAR
SMEARED
SMEARIER
SMEARIEST
SMEARILY
SMEARING
SMEARS
SMEARY
SMEATH
SMEATHS
SMECTIC
SMEDDUM
SMEDDUMS
SMEE
SMEECH
SMEECHED
SMEECHES
SMEECHING
SMEEK
SMEEKED
SMEEKING
SMEEKS
SMEES
SMEETH
SMEETHS
SMEGMA
SMEGMAS

SMELL
SMELLED
SMELLER
SMELLERS
SMELLIER
SMELLIEST
SMELLING
SMELLINGS
SMELLS
SMELLY
SMELT
SMELTED
SMELTER
SMELTERIES
SMELTERS
SMELTERY
SMELTING
SMELTINGS
SMELTS
SMEUSE
SMEUSES
SMEW
SMEWS
SMICKER
SMICKERED
SMICKERING
SMICKERINGS
SMICKERS
SMICKET
SMICKETS
SMICKLY
SMIDDIES
SMIDDY
SMIDGEN
SMIDGENS
SMIDGEON
SMIDGEONS
SMIDGIN
SMIDGINS
SMIGHT
SMIGHTING
SMIGHTS
SMILAX
SMILAXES
SMILE
SMILED
SMILEFUL
SMILELESS
SMILER
SMILERS
SMILES
SMILET
SMILETS
SMILING
SMILINGLY
SMILINGS
SMILODON
SMILODONS
SMIR
SMIRCH
SMIRCHED
SMIRCHES
SMIRCHING
SMIRK
SMIRKED
SMIRKIER
SMIRKIEST
SMIRKING
SMIRKS
SMIRKY

SMIRR
SMIRRED
SMIRRIER
SMIRRIEST
SMIRRING
SMIRRS
SMIRRY
SMIRS
SMIT
SMITE
SMITER
SMITERS
SMITES
SMITH
SMITHED
SMITHERIES
SMITHERS
SMITHERY
SMITHIED
SMITHIES
SMITHING
SMITHS
SMITHY
SMITHYING
SMITING
SMITS
SMITTED
SMITTEN
SMITTING
SMITTLE
SMOCK
SMOCKED
SMOCKING
SMOCKINGS
SMOCKS
SMOG
SMOGGIER
SMOGGIEST
SMOGGY
SMOGS
SMOILE
SMOILED
SMOILES
SMOILING
SMOKABLE
SMOKE
SMOKED
SMOKELESS
SMOKER
SMOKERS
SMOKES
SMOKIER
SMOKIES
SMOKIEST
SMOKILY
SMOKINESS
SMOKINESSES
SMOKING
SMOKINGS
SMOKO
SMOKOS
SMOKY
SMOLDER
SMOLDERED
SMOLDERING
SMOLDERS
SMOLT
SMOLTS
SMOOCH
SMOOCHED

SMOOCHES
SMOOCHING
SMOOR
SMOORED
SMOORING
SMOORS
SMOOT
SMOOTED
SMOOTH
SMOOTHE
SMOOTHED
SMOOTHEN
SMOOTHENED
SMOOTHENING
SMOOTHENS
SMOOTHER
SMOOTHERS
SMOOTHES
SMOOTHEST
SMOOTHIE
SMOOTHIES
SMOOTHING
SMOOTHINGS
SMOOTHISH
SMOOTHLY
SMOOTHS
SMOOTING
SMOOTS
SMØRBRØD
SMØRBRØDS
SMORE
SMORED
SMORES
SMORING
SMORZANDO
SMORZATO
SMOTE
SMOTHER
SMOTHERED
SMOTHERER
SMOTHERERS
SMOTHERING
SMOTHERINGS
SMOTHERS
SMOTHERY
SMOUCH
SMOUCHED
SMOUCHES
SMOUCHING
SMOULDER
SMOULDERED
SMOULDERING
SMOULDERINGS
SMOULDERS
SMOULDRY
SMOUS
SMOUSE
SMOUSED
SMOUSER
SMOUSERS
SMOUSES
SMOUSING
SMOUT
SMOUTED
SMOUTING
SMOUTS
SMOWT
SMOWTS
SMOYLE
SMOYLED

SMOYLES
SMOYLING
SMUDGE
SMUDGED
SMUDGER
SMUDGERS
SMUDGES
SMUDGIER
SMUDGIEST
SMUDGILY
SMUDGING
SMUDGY
SMUG
SMUGGED
SMUGGER
SMUGGEST
SMUGGING
SMUGGLE
SMUGGLED
SMUGGLER
SMUGGLERS
SMUGGLES
SMUGGLING
SMUGGLINGS
SMUGLY
SMUGNESS
SMUGNESSES
SMUGS
SMUR
SMURRED
SMURRIER
SMURRIEST
SMURRING
SMURRY
SMURS
SMUT
SMUTCH
SMUTCHED
SMUTCHES
SMUTCHING
SMUTS
SMUTTED
SMUTTIER
SMUTTIEST
SMUTTILY
SMUTTING
SMUTTY
SMYTRIE
SMYTRIES
SNAB
SNABBLE
SNABBLED
SNABBLES
SNABBLING
SNABS
SNACK
SNACKED
SNACKING
SNACKS
SNAFFLE
SNAFFLED
SNAFFLES
SNAFFLING
SNAFU
SNAFUS
SNAG
SNAGGED
SNAGGIER
SNAGGIEST
SNAGGING

SNAGGY
SNAGS
SNAIL
SNAILED
SNAILERIES
SNAILERY
SNAILIER
SNAILIEST
SNAILING
SNAILS
SNAILY
SNAKE
SNAKEBIRD
SNAKEBIRDS
SNAKEBITE
SNAKEBITES
SNAKED
SNAKELIKE
SNAKEROOT
SNAKEROOTS
SNAKES
SNAKESKIN
SNAKESKINS
SNAKEWEED
SNAKEWEEDS
SNAKEWISE
SNAKEWOOD
SNAKEWOODS
SNAKIER
SNAKIEST
SNAKILY
SNAKINESS
SNAKINESSES
SNAKING
SNAKISH
SNAKY
SNAP
SNAPHANCE
SNAPHANCES
SNAPPED
SNAPPER
SNAPPERED
SNAPPERING
SNAPPERS
SNAPPIER
SNAPPIEST
SNAPPILY
SNAPPING
SNAPPINGS
SNAPPISH
SNAPPY
SNAPS
SNAPSHOT
SNAPSHOTS
SNAR
SNARE
SNARED
SNARER
SNARERS
SNARES
SNARIER
SNARIEST
SNARING
SNARINGS
SNARK
SNARKS
SNARL
SNARLED
SNARLER
SNARLERS

SNARLIER
SNARLIEST
SNARLING
SNARLINGS
SNARLS
SNARLY
SNARRED
SNARRING
SNARS
SNARY
SNASH
SNASHED
SNASHES
SNASHING
SNASTE
SNASTES
SNATCH
SNATCHED
SNATCHER
SNATCHERS
SNATCHES
SNATCHIER
SNATCHIEST
SNATCHILY
SNATCHING
SNATCHY
SNATH
SNATHE
SNATHES
SNATHS
SNAZZIER
SNAZZIEST
SNAZZY
SNEAD
SNEADS
SNEAK
SNEAKED
SNEAKER
SNEAKERS
SNEAKEUP
SNEAKEUPS
SNEAKIER
SNEAKIEST
SNEAKILY
SNEAKING
SNEAKISH
SNEAKS
SNEAKSBIES
SNEAKSBY
SNEAKY
SNEAP
SNEAPED
SNEAPING
SNEAPS
SNEATH
SNEATHS
SNEB
SNEBBE
SNEBBED
SNEBBES
SNEBBING
SNEBS
SNECK
SNECKED
SNECKING
SNECKS
SNED
SNEDDED
SNEDDING
SNEDS

SNEE
SNEED
SNEEING
SNEER
SNEERED
SNEERER
SNEERERS
SNEERIER
SNEERIEST
SNEERING
SNEERINGS
SNEERS
SNEERY
SNEES
SNEESH
SNEESHAN
SNEESHANS
SNEESHES
SNEESHIN
SNEESHING
SNEESHINGS
SNEESHINS
SNEEZE
SNEEZED
SNEEZER
SNEEZERS
SNEEZES
SNEEZIER
SNEEZIEST
SNEEZING
SNEEZINGS
SNEEZY
SNELL
SNELLED
SNELLER
SNELLEST
SNELLING
SNELLS
SNELLY
SNIB
SNIBBED
SNIBBING
SNIBS
SNICK
SNICKED
SNICKER
SNICKERED
SNICKERING
SNICKERS
SNICKET
SNICKETS
SNICKING
SNICKS
SNIDE
SNIDELY
SNIDENESS
SNIDENESSES
SNIDER
SNIDES
SNIDEST
SNIFF
SNIFFED
SNIFFER
SNIFFERS
SNIFFIER
SNIFFIEST
SNIFFILY
SNIFFING
SNIFFINGS
SNIFFLE

SNIFFLED
SNIFFLER
SNIFFLERS
SNIFFLES
SNIFFLING
SNIFFS
SNIFFY
SNIFT
SNIFTED
SNIFTER
SNIFTERED
SNIFTERING
SNIFTERS
SNIFTIER
SNIFTIEST
SNIFTING
SNIFTS
SNIFTY
SNIG
SNIGGED
SNIGGER
SNIGGERED
SNIGGERER
SNIGGERERS
SNIGGERING
SNIGGERINGS
SNIGGERS
SNIGGING
SNIGGLE
SNIGGLED
SNIGGLER
SNIGGLERS
SNIGGLES
SNIGGLING
SNIGGLINGS
SNIGS
SNIP
SNIPE
SNIPED
SNIPER
SNIPERS
SNIPES
SNIPIER
SNIPIEST
SNIPING
SNIPINGS
SNIPPED
SNIPPER
SNIPPERS
SNIPPET
SNIPPETS
SNIPPETY
SNIPPIER
SNIPPIEST
SNIPPING
SNIPPINGS
SNIPPY
SNIPS
SNIPY
SNIRT
SNIRTLE
SNIRTLED
SNIRTLES
SNIRTLING
SNIRTS
SNITCH
SNITCHED
SNITCHER
SNITCHERS
SNITCHES

SNITCHING
SNIVEL
SNIVELLED
SNIVELLER
SNIVELLERS
SNIVELLING
SNIVELLY
SNIVELS
SNOB
SNOBBERIES
SNOBBERY
SNOBBIER
SNOBBIEST
SNOBBISH
SNOBBISM
SNOBBISMS
SNOBBY
SNOBLING
SNOBLINGS
SNOBS
SNOD
SNODDED
SNODDING
SNODDIT
SNODS
SNOEK
SNOEKS
SNOG
SNOGGED
SNOGGING
SNOGS
SNOKE
SNOKED
SNOKES
SNOKING
SNOOD
SNOODED
SNOODING
SNOODS
SNOOK
SNOOKED
SNOOKER
SNOOKERED
SNOOKERING
SNOOKERS
SNOOKING
SNOOKS
SNOOL
SNOOLED
SNOOLING
SNOOLS
SNOOP
SNOOPED
SNOOPER
SNOOPERS
SNOOPING
SNOOPS
SNOOT
SNOOTED
SNOOTFUL
SNOOTFULS
SNOOTIER
SNOOTIEST
SNOOTING
SNOOTS
SNOOTY
SNOOZE
SNOOZED
SNOOZER
SNOOZERS

SNOOZES
SNOOZING
SNOOZLE
SNOOZLED
SNOOZLES
SNOOZLING
SNORE
SNORED
SNORER
SNORERS
SNORES
SNORING
SNORINGS
SNORKEL
SNORKELS
SNORT
SNORTED
SNORTER
SNORTERS
SNORTIER
SNORTIEST
SNORTING
SNORTINGS
SNORTS
SNORTY
SNOT
SNOTS
SNOTTED
SNOTTER
SNOTTERED
SNOTTERIES
SNOTTERING
SNOTTERS
SNOTTERY
SNOTTIER
SNOTTIES
SNOTTIEST
SNOTTILY
SNOTTING
SNOTTY
SNOUT
SNOUTED
SNOUTIER
SNOUTIEST
SNOUTING
SNOUTS
SNOUTY
SNOW
SNOWBALL
SNOWBALLED
SNOWBALLING
SNOWBALLS
SNOWCAP
SNOWCAPS
SNOWDRIFT
SNOWDRIFTS
SNOWDROP
SNOWDROPS
SNOWED
SNOWFALL
SNOWFALLS
SNOWFLAKE
SNOWFLAKES
SNOWFLECK
SNOWFLECKS
SNOWFLICK
SNOWFLICKS
SNOWIER
SNOWIEST
SNOWILY

SNOWINESS
SNOWINESSES
SNOWING
SNOWISH
SNOWK
SNOWKED
SNOWKING
SNOWKS
SNOWLESS
SNOWLIKE
SNOWLINE
SNOWLINES
SNOWMAN
SNOWMEN
SNOWS
SNOWSCAPE
SNOWSCAPES
SNOWSLIP
SNOWSLIPS
SNOWSTORM
SNOWSTORMS
SNOWY
SNUB
SNUBBE
SNUBBED
SNUBBER
SNUBBERS
SNUBBES
SNUBBIER
SNUBBIEST
SNUBBING
SNUBBINGS
SNUBBISH
SNUBBY
SNUBS
SNUCK
SNUDGE
SNUDGED
SNUDGES
SNUDGING
SNUFF
SNUFFBOX
SNUFFBOXES
SNUFFED
SNUFFER
SNUFFERS
SNUFFIER
SNUFFIEST
SNUFFING
SNUFFINGS
SNUFFLE
SNUFFLED
SNUFFLER
SNUFFLERS
SNUFFLES
SNUFFLING
SNUFFLINGS
SNUFFS
SNUFFY
SNUG
SNUGGED
SNUGGER
SNUGGERIES
SNUGGERY
SNUGGEST
SNUGGING
SNUGGLE
SNUGGLED
SNUGGLES
SNUGGLING

SNUGLY
SNUGNESS
SNUGNESSES
SNUGS
SNUSH
SNUSHED
SNUSHES
SNUSHING
SNUZZLE
SNUZZLED
SNUZZLES
SNUZZLING
SO
SOAK
SOAKAGE
SOAKAGES
SOAKAWAY
SOAKAWAYS
SOAKED
SOAKEN
SOAKER
SOAKERS
SOAKING
SOAKINGLY
SOAKINGS
SOAKS
SOAP
SOAPBERRIES
SOAPBERRY
SOAPBOX
SOAPBOXES
SOAPED
SOAPIE
SOAPIER
SOAPIES
SOAPIEST
SOAPILY
SOAPINESS
SOAPINESSES
SOAPING
SOAPLESS
SOAPS
SOAPSTONE
SOAPSTONES
SOAPWORT
SOAPWORTS
SOAPY
SOAR
SOARAWAY
SOARE
SOARED
SOARES
SOARING
SOARINGLY
SOARINGS
SOARS
SOB
SOBBED
SOBBING
SOBBINGLY
SOBBINGS
SOBEIT
SOBER
SOBERED
SOBERER
SOBEREST
SOBERING
SOBERISE
SOBERISED
SOBERISES

SOBERISING
SOBERIZE
SOBERIZED
SOBERIZES
SOBERIZING
SOBERLY
SOBERNESS
SOBERNESSES
SOBERS
SOBOLE
SOBOLES
SOBRIETIES
SOBRIETY
SOBRIQUET
SOBRIQUETS
SOBS
SOC
SOCAGE
SOCAGER
SOCAGERS
SOCAGES
SOCCAGE
SOCCAGES
SOCCER
SOCCERS
SOCIABLE
SOCIABLES
SOCIABLY
SOCIAL
SOCIALISE
SOCIALISED
SOCIALISES
SOCIALISING
SOCIALISM
SOCIALISMS
SOCIALIST
SOCIALISTS
SOCIALITE
SOCIALITES
SOCIALITIES
SOCIALITY
SOCIALIZE
SOCIALIZED
SOCIALIZES
SOCIALIZING
SOCIALLY
SOCIALS
SOCIATE
SOCIATES
SOCIATIVE
SOCIETAL
SOCIETARY
SOCIETIES
SOCIETY
SOCIOGRAM
SOCIOGRAMS
SOCIOLOGIES
SOCIOLOGY
SOCIOPATH
SOCIOPATHS
SOCK
SOCKED
SOCKER
SOCKERS
SOCKET
SOCKETED
SOCKETING
SOCKETS
SOCKEYE
SOCKEYES

SOCKING
SOCKO
SOCKS
SOCLE
SOCLES
SOCMAN
SOCMEN
SOCS
SOD
SODA
SODAIC
SODAIN
SODAINE
SODALITE
SODALITES
SODALITIES
SODALITY
SODAMIDE
SODAMIDES
SODAS
SODDED
SODDEN
SODDENED
SODDENING
SODDENS
SODDIER
SODDIEST
SODDING
SODDY
SODGER
SODGERS
SODIC
SODIUM
SODIUMS
SODOMIES
SODOMISE
SODOMISED
SODOMISES
SODOMISING
SODOMITE
SODOMITES
SODOMITIC
SODOMIZE
SODOMIZED
SODOMIZES
SODOMIZING
SODOMY
SODS
SOEVER
SOFA
SOFAR
SOFARS
SOFAS
SOFFIONI
SOFFIT
SOFFITS
SOFT
SOFTA
SOFTAS
SOFTBACK
SOFTBACKS
SOFTBALL
SOFTBALLS
SOFTED
SOFTEN
SOFTENED
SOFTENER
SOFTENERS
SOFTENING
SOFTENINGS

SOFTENS
SOFTER
SOFTEST
SOFTHEAD
SOFTHEADS
SOFTIE
SOFTIES
SOFTING
SOFTISH
SOFTLING
SOFTLINGS
SOFTLY
SOFTNESS
SOFTNESSES
SOFTS
SOFTWARE
SOFTWARES
SOFTWOOD
SOFTWOODS
SOFTY
SOG
SOGER
SOGERS
SOGGED
SOGGIER
SOGGIEST
SOGGILY
SOGGINESS
SOGGINESSES
SOGGING
SOGGINGS
SOGGY
SOGS
SOH
SOHS
SOIGNÉ
SOIGNÉE
SOIL
SOILED
SOILIER
SOILIEST
SOILINESS
SOILINESSES
SOILING
SOILINGS
SOILLESS
SOILS
SOILURE
SOILURES
SOILY
SOIRÉE
SOIRÉES
SOJA
SOJAS
SOJOURN
SOJOURNED
SOJOURNER
SOJOURNERS
SOJOURNING
SOJOURNINGS
SOJOURNS
SOKE
SOKEMAN
SOKEMANRIES
SOKEMANRY
SOKEMEN
SOKEN
SOKENS
SOKES
SOL

SOLA
SOLACE
SOLACED
SOLACES
SOLACING
SOLACIOUS
SOLAH
SOLAHS
SOLAN
SOLAND
SOLANDER
SOLANDERS
SOLANDS
SOLANINE
SOLANINES
SOLANO
SOLANOS
SOLANS
SOLANUM
SOLANUMS
SOLAR
SOLARISE
SOLARISED
SOLARISES
SOLARISING
SOLARISM
SOLARISMS
SOLARIST
SOLARISTS
SOLARIUM
SOLARIUMS
SOLARIZE
SOLARIZED
SOLARIZES
SOLARIZING
SOLARS
SOLAS
SOLATION
SOLATIONS
SOLATIUM
SOLATIUMS
SOLD
SOLDADO
SOLDADOS
SOLDAN
SOLDANS
SOLDE
SOLDER
SOLDERED
SOLDERER
SOLDERERS
SOLDERING
SOLDERINGS
SOLDERS
SOLDES
SOLDI
SOLDIER
SOLDIERED
SOLDIERIES
SOLDIERING
SOLDIERINGS
SOLDIERLY
SOLDIERS
SOLDIERY
SOLDO
SOLDS
SOLE
SOLECISE
SOLECISED
SOLECISES

SOLECISING
SOLECISM
SOLECISMS
SOLECIST
SOLECISTS
SOLECIZE
SOLECIZED
SOLECIZES
SOLECIZING
SOLED
SOLEIN
SOLELY
SOLEMN
SOLEMNER
SOLEMNESS
SOLEMNESSES
SOLEMNEST
SOLEMNIFIED
SOLEMNIFIES
SOLEMNIFY
SOLEMNIFYING
SOLEMNISE
SOLEMNISED
SOLEMNISES
SOLEMNISING
SOLEMNITIES
SOLEMNITY
SOLEMNIZE
SOLEMNIZED
SOLEMNIZES
SOLEMNIZING
SOLEMNLY
SOLEN
SOLENESS
SOLENESSES
SOLENETTE
SOLENETTES
SOLENODON
SOLENODONS
SOLENOID
SOLENOIDS
SOLENS
SOLER
SOLERA
SOLERAS
SOLERS
SOLES
SOLEUS
SOLEUSES
SOLFATARA
SOLFATARAS
SOLFEGGI
SOLFEGGIO
SOLFERINO
SOLFERINOS
SOLI
SOLICIT
SOLICITED
SOLICITIES
SOLICITING
SOLICITINGS
SOLICITOR
SOLICITORS
SOLICITS
SOLICITY
SOLID
SOLIDARE
SOLIDARES
SOLIDARY
SOLIDATE

SOLIDATED
SOLIDATES
SOLIDATING
SOLIDER
SOLIDEST
SOLIDI
SOLIDIFIED
SOLIDIFIES
SOLIDIFY
SOLIDIFYING
SOLIDISH
SOLIDISM
SOLIDISMS
SOLIDIST
SOLIDISTS
SOLIDITIES
SOLIDITY
SOLIDLY
SOLIDNESS
SOLIDNESSES
SOLIDS
SOLIDUM
SOLIDUMS
SOLIDUS
SOLILOQUIES
SOLILOQUY
SOLING
SOLIPED
SOLIPEDS
SOLIPSISM
SOLIPSISMS
SOLIPSIST
SOLIPSISTS
SOLITAIRE
SOLITAIRES
SOLITARIES
SOLITARY
SOLITO
SOLITON
SOLITONS
SOLITUDE
SOLITUDES
SOLIVE
SOLIVES
SOLLAR
SOLLARS
SOLLER
SOLLERET
SOLLERETS
SOLLERS
SOLO
SOLOED
SOLOING
SOLOIST
SOLOISTS
SOLONCHAK
SOLONCHAKS
SOLONETS
SOLONETSES
SOLONETZ
SOLONETZES
SOLOS
SOLS
SOLSTICE
SOLSTICES
SOLUBLE
SOLUM
SOLUMS
SOLUS
SOLUTE

SOLUTES
SOLUTION
SOLUTIONED
SOLUTIONING
SOLUTIONS
SOLUTIVE
SOLVABLE
SOLVATE
SOLVATED
SOLVATES
SOLVATING
SOLVATION
SOLVATIONS
SOLVE
SOLVED
SOLVENCIES
SOLVENCY
SOLVENT
SOLVENTS
SOLVER
SOLVERS
SOLVES
SOLVING
SOMA
SOMAS
SOMASCOPE
SOMASCOPES
SOMATIC
SOMATISM
SOMATISMS
SOMATIST
SOMATISTS
SOMBRE
SOMBRED
SOMBRELY
SOMBRER
SOMBRERO
SOMBREROS
SOMBRES
SOMBREST
SOMBRING
SOMBROUS
SOME
SOMEBODIES
SOMEBODY
SOMEDAY
SOMEDEAL
SOMEDELE
SOMEGATE
SOMEHOW
SOMEONE
SOMEONES
SOMEPLACE
SOMERSET
SOMERSETS
SOMERSETTED
SOMERSETTING
SOMETHING
SOMETHINGS
SOMETIME
SOMETIMES
SOMEWAY
SOMEWAYS
SOMEWHAT
SOMEWHATS
SOMEWHEN
SOMEWHERE
SOMEWHILE
SOMEWHY
SOMEWISE

SOMITAL
SOMITE
SOMITES
SOMITIC
SOMMELIER
SOMMELIERS
SOMNIAL
SOMNIFIC
SOMNOLENT
SON
SONANCE
SONANCES
SONANCIES
SONANCY
SONANT
SONANTS
SONAR
SONARS
SONATA
SONATAS
SONATINA
SONATINAS
SONCE
SONCES
SONDAGE
SONDAGES
SONDE
SONDELI
SONDELIS
SONDES
SONE
SONERI
SONERIS
SONES
SONG
SONGBIRD
SONGBIRDS
SONGBOOK
SONGBOOKS
SONGCRAFT
SONGCRAFTS
SONGFEST
SONGFESTS
SONGFUL
SONGFULLY
SONGLESS
SONGMAN
SONGMEN
SONGS
SONGSMITH
SONGSMITHS
SONGSTER
SONGSTERS
SONIC
SONICS
SONLESS
SONNE
SONNES
SONNET
SONNETARY
SONNETED
SONNETEER
SONNETEERED
SONNETEERING
SONNETEERINGS
SONNETEERS
SONNETING
SONNETINGS
SONNETISE
SONNETISED

SONNETISES
SONNETISING
SONNETIST
SONNETISTS
SONNETIZE
SONNETIZED
SONNETIZES
SONNETIZING
SONNETRIES
SONNETRY
SONNETS
SONNIES
SONNY
SONOBUOY
SONOBUOYS
SONOGRAPH
SONOGRAPHS
SONORANT
SONORANTS
SONORITIES
SONORITY
SONOROUS
SONS
SONSE
SONSES
SONSHIP
SONSHIPS
SONSIE
SONSIER
SONSIEST
SONSY
SONTAG
SONTAGS
SONTIES
SONUANCE
SONUANCES
SOOGEE
SOOGEED
SOOGEEING
SOOGEES
SOOGIE
SOOGIED
SOOGIEING
SOOGIES
SOOJEY
SOOJEYS
SOOK
SOOKS
SOOLE
SOOLED
SOOLES
SOOLING
SOOM
SOOMED
SOOMING
SOOMS
SOON
SOONER
SOONEST
SOOP
SOOPED
SOOPING
SOOPINGS
SOOPS
SOOPSTAKE
SOOT
SOOTE
SOOTED
SOOTERKIN
SOOTERKINS

SOOTES	SOPPINESS	SOREHON	SORROWFUL	SOUGHS
SOOTFLAKE	SOPPINESSES	SOREHONS	SORROWING	SOUGHT
SOOTFLAKES	SOPPING	SOREL	SORROWINGS	SOUK
SOOTH	SOPPINGS	SORELL	SORROWS	SOUKS
SOOTHE	SOPPY	SORELLS	SORRY	SOUL
SOOTHED	SOPRA	SORELS	SORRYISH	SOULDAN
SOOTHER	SOPRANI	SORELY	SORT	SOULDANS
SOOTHERED	SOPRANINI	SORENESS	SORTABLE	SOULDIER
SOOTHERING	SOPRANINO	SORENESSES	SORTANCE	SOULDIERED
SOOTHERS	SOPRANINOS	SORER	SORTANCES	SOULDIERING
SOOTHES	SOPRANIST	SORES	SORTATION	SOULDIERS
SOOTHEST	SOPRANISTS	SOREST	SORTATIONS	SOULED
SOOTHFAST	SOPRANO	SOREX	SORTED	SOULFUL
SOOTHFUL	SOPRANOS	SOREXES	SORTER	SOULFULLY
SOOTHING	SOPS	SORGHO	SORTERS	SOULLESS
SOOTHINGS	SORA	SORGHOS	SORTES	SOULS
SOOTHLICH	SORAGE	SORGHUM	SORTIE	SOUM
SOOTHLY	SORAGES	SORGHUMS	SORTIED	SOUMED
SOOTHS	SORAL	SORGO	SORTIEING	SOUMING
SOOTHSAID	SORAS	SORGOS	SORTIES	SOUMINGS
SOOTHSAY	SORB	SORI	SORTILEGE	SOUMS
SOOTHSAYING	SORBARIA	SORICINE	SORTILEGES	SOUND
SOOTHSAYINGS	SORBARIAS	SORICOID	SORTILEGIES	SOUNDED
SOOTHSAYS	SORBATE	SORING	SORTILEGY	SOUNDER
SOOTIER	SORBATES	SORITES	SORTING	SOUNDERS
SOOTIEST	SORBED	SORITIC	SORTINGS	SOUNDEST
SOOTILY	SORBENT	SORITICAL	SORTITION	SOUNDING
SOOTINESS	SORBENTS	SORN	SORTITIONS	SOUNDINGS
SOOTINESSES	SORBET	SORNED	SORTMENT	SOUNDLESS
SOOTING	SORBETS	SORNER	SORTMENTS	SOUNDLY
SOOTLESS	SORBING	SORNERS	SORTS	SOUNDNESS
SOOTS	SORBITOL	SORNING	SORUS	SOUNDNESSES
SOOTY	SORBITOLS	SORNINGS	SOS	SOUNDS
SOP	SORBO	SORNS	SOSS	SOUP
SOPH	SORBOS	SOROBAN	SOSSED	SOUPÇON
SOPHA	SORBS	SOROBANS	SOSSES	SOUPÇONS
SOPHAS	SORBUS	SOROCHE	SOSSING	SOUPER
SOPHERIC	SORBUSES	SOROCHES	SOSSINGS	SOUPERS
SOPHERIM	SORCERER	SORORAL	SOSTENUTO	SOUPIER
SOPHIA	SORCERERS	SORORATE	SOT	SOUPIEST
SOPHIAS	SORCERESS	SORORATES	SOTERIAL	SOUPLE
SOPHIC	SORCERESSES	SORORIAL	SOTS	SOUPLED
SOPHICAL	SORCERIES	SORORISE	SOTTED	SOUPLES
SOPHISM	SORCEROUS	SORORISED	SOTTING	SOUPLING
SOPHISMS	SORCERY	SORORISES	SOTTINGS	SOUPS
SOPHIST	SORD	SORORISING	SOTTISH	SOUPSPOON
SOPHISTER	SORDA	SORORITIES	SOTTISHLY	SOUPSPOONS
SOPHISTERS	SORDES	SORORITY	SOTTISIER	SOUPY
SOPHISTIC	SORDID	SORORIZE	SOTTISIERS	SOUR
SOPHISTICS	SORDIDER	SORORIZED	SOU	SOURCE
SOPHISTRIES	SORDIDEST	SORORIZES	SOUARI	SOURCED
SOPHISTRY	SORDIDLY	SORORIZING	SOUARIS	SOURCES
SOPHISTS	SORDINE	SOROSES	SOUBISE	SOURCING
SOPHOMORE	SORDINES	SOROSIS	SOUBISES	SOURCINGS
SOPHOMORES	SORDINI	SOROSISES	SOUBRETTE	SOURDINE
SOPHS	SORDINO	SORPTION	SOUBRETTES	SOURDINES
SOPITE	SORDO	SORPTIONS	SOUCE	SOURDOUGH
SOPITED	SORDOR	SORRA	SOUCED	SOURDOUGHS
SOPITES	SORDORS	SORRAS	SOUCES	SOURED
SOPITING	SORDS	SORREL	SOUCHONG	SOURER
SOPOR	SORE	SORRELS	SOUCHONGS	SOUREST
SOPORIFIC	SORED	SORRIER	SOUCING	SOURING
SOPORIFICS	SOREDIA	SORRIEST	SOUCT	SOURINGS
SOPOROSE	SOREDIAL	SORRILY	SOUFFLE	SOURISH
SOPOROUS	SOREDIATE	SORRINESS	SOUFFLÉ	SOURISHLY
SOPORS	SOREDIUM	SORRINESSES	SOUFFLES	SOURLY
SOPPED	SOREE	SORROW	SOUFFLÉS	SOURNESS
SOPPIER	SOREES	SORROWED	SOUGH	SOURNESSES
SOPPIEST	SOREHEAD	SORROWER	SOUGHED	SOUROCK
SOPPILY	SOREHEADS	SORROWERS	SOUGHING	SOUROCKS

OURPUSS	SOVIETIZE	SOX	SPAEMEN	SPANGED
OURPUSSES	SOVIETIZED	SOY	SPAER	SPANGHEW
OURS	SOVIETIZES	SOYA	SPAERS	SPANGHEWED
OURSE	SOVIETIZING	SOYAS	SPAES	SPANGHEWING
OURSES	SOVIETS	SOYLE	SPAEWIFE	SPANGHEWS
OUS	SOVRAN	SOYLED	SPAEWIVES	SPANGING
OUSE	SOVRANS	SOYLES	SPAGERIC	SPANGLE
OUSED	SOVRANTIES	SOYS	SPAGERICS	SPANGLED
OUSES	SOVRANTY	SOZZLE	SPAGERIST	SPANGLER
OUSEWIFE	SOVS	SOZZLED	SPAGERISTS	SPANGLERS
OUSEWIVES	SOW	SOZZLES	SPAGHETTI	SPANGLES
OUSING	SOWANS	SOZZLIER	SPAGHETTIS	SPANGLET
OUSINGS	SOWAR	SOZZLIEST	SPAGIRIC	SPANGLETS
OUSLIK	SOWARREE	SOZZLING	SPAGIRICS	SPANGLIER
OUSLIKS	SOWARREES	SOZZLY	SPAGIRIST	SPANGLIEST
OUT	SOWARRIES	SPA	SPAGIRISTS	SPANGLING
OUTACHE	SOWARRY	SPACE	SPAGYRIC	SPANGLINGS
OUTACHES	SOWARS	SPACED	SPAGYRICS	SPANGLY
OUTANE	SOWCE	SPACELESS	SPAGYRIST	SPANGS
OUTANES	SOWCED	SPACEMAN	SPAGYRISTS	SPANIEL
OUTAR	SOWCES	SPACEMEN	SPAHEE	SPANIELLED
OUTARS	SOWCING	SPACER	SPAHEES	SPANIELLING
OUTENEUR	SOWED	SPACERS	SPAHI	SPANIELS
OUTENEURS	SOWENS	SPACES	SPAHIS	SPANING
OUTER	SOWER	SPACESHIP	SPAIN	SPANK
OUTERLY	SOWERS	SPACESHIPS	SPAINED	SPANKED
OUTERS	SOWF	SPACEY	SPAING	SPANKER
OUTH	SOWFED	SPACIAL	SPAINGS	SPANKERS
OUTHED	SOWFF	SPACIER	SPAINING	SPANKING
OUTHER	SOWFFED	SPACIEST	SPAINS	SPANKINGS
OUTHERED	SOWFFING	SPACING	SPAIRGE	SPANKS
OUTHERING	SOWFFS	SPACINGS	SPAIRGED	SPANLESS
OUTHERLY	SOWFING	SPACIOUS	SPAIRGES	SPANNED
OUTHERN	SOWFS	SPACY	SPAIRGING	SPANNER
OUTHERNS	SOWING	SPADASSIN	SPAKE	SPANNERS
OUTHERS	SOWINGS	SPADASSINS	SPALD	SPANNING
OUTHING	SOWL	SPADE	SPALDS	SPANS
OUTHINGS	SOWLE	SPADED	SPALE	SPANSULE
OUTHLAND	SOWLED	SPADEFUL	SPALES	SPANSULES
OUTHLANDS	SOWLES	SPADEFULS	SPALL	SPAR
OUTHMOST	SOWLING	SPADEMAN	SPALLE	SPARABLE
OUTHPAW	SOWLS	SPADEMEN	SPALLED	SPARABLES
OUTHPAWS	SOWM	SPADER	SPALLES	SPARAXIS
OUTHRON	SOWMED	SPADERS	SPALLING	SPARAXISES
OUTHRONS	SOWMING	SPADES	SPALLS	SPARD
OUTHS	SOWMS	SPADESMAN	SPALPEEN	SPARE
OUTHSAID	SOWN	SPADESMEN	SPALPEENS	SPARED
OUTHSAY	SOWND	SPADEWORK	SPALT	SPARELESS
OUTHSAYING	SOWNDED	SPADEWORKS	SPALTED	SPARELY
OUTHSAYS	SOWNDING	SPADGER	SPALTING	SPARENESS
OUTHWARD	SOWNDS	SPADGERS	SPALTS	SPARENESSES
OUTHWARDS	SOWNE	SPADICES	SPAMMIER	SPARER
OUTS	SOWNES	SPADILLE	SPAMMIEST	SPARERS
OUVENIR	SOWP	SPADILLES	SPAMMY	SPARES
OUVENIRED	SOWPS	SPADILLIO	SPAN	SPAREST
OUVENIRING	SOWS	SPADILLIOS	SPANAEMIA	SPARGE
OUVENIRS	SOWSE	SPADILLO	SPANAEMIAS	SPARGED
OV	SOWSED	SPADILLOS	SPANAEMIC	SPARGER
OVENANCE	SOWSES	SPADING	SPANCEL	SPARGERS
OVENANCES	SOWSING	SPADIX	SPANCELLED	SPARGES
OVEREIGN	SOWSSE	SPADO	SPANCELLING	SPARGING
OVEREIGNS	SOWSSED	SPADOES	SPANCELS	SPARID
OVIET	SOWSSES	SPADONES	SPANDREL	SPARIDS
OVIETIC	SOWSSING	SPADOS	SPANDRELS	SPARING
OVIETISE	SOWTER	SPADROON	SPANDRIL	SPARINGLY
OVIETISED	SOWTERS	SPADROONS	SPANDRILS	SPARK
OVIETISES	SOWTH	SPAE	SPANE	SPARKE
OVIETISING	SOWTHED	SPAED	SPANED	SPARKED
OVIETISM	SOWTHING	SPAEING	SPANES	SPARKES
OVIETISMS	SOWTHS	SPAEMAN	SPANG	SPARKING

SPARKISH
SPARKLE
SPARKLED
SPARKLER
SPARKLERS
SPARKLES
SPARKLESS
SPARKLET
SPARKLETS
SPARKLIES
SPARKLING
SPARKLINGS
SPARKLY
SPARKS
SPARLING
SPARLINGS
SPAROID
SPAROIDS
SPARRE
SPARRED
SPARRER
SPARRERS
SPARRES
SPARRING
SPARRINGS
SPARROW
SPARROWS
SPARRY
SPARS
SPARSE
SPARSEDLY
SPARSELY
SPARSER
SPARSEST
SPARSITIES
SPARSITY
SPART
SPARTAN
SPARTEINE
SPARTEINES
SPARTERIE
SPARTERIES
SPARTH
SPARTHE
SPARTHES
SPARTHS
SPARTS
SPAS
SPASM
SPASMATIC
SPASMED
SPASMIC
SPASMING
SPASMODIC
SPASMS
SPASTIC
SPASTICS
SPAT
SPATE
SPATES
SPATFALL
SPATFALLS
SPATHE
SPATHED
SPATHES
SPATHIC
SPATHOSE
SPATIAL
SPATIALLY
SPÄTLESE

SPÄTLESEN
SPÄTLESES
SPATS
SPATTED
SPATTEE
SPATTEES
SPATTER
SPATTERED
SPATTERING
SPATTERS
SPATTING
SPATULA
SPATULAR
SPATULAS
SPATULATE
SPATULE
SPATULES
SPAUL
SPAULD
SPAULDS
SPAULS
SPAVIE
SPAVIES
SPAVIN
SPAVINED
SPAVINS
SPAW
SPAWL
SPAWLED
SPAWLING
SPAWLS
SPAWN
SPAWNED
SPAWNER
SPAWNERS
SPAWNING
SPAWNINGS
SPAWNS
SPAWS
SPAY
SPAYAD
SPAYADS
SPAYD
SPAYDS
SPAYED
SPAYING
SPAYS
SPEAK
SPEAKABLE
SPEAKER
SPEAKERS
SPEAKING
SPEAKINGS
SPEAKS
SPEAL
SPEALS
SPEAN
SPEANED
SPEANING
SPEANS
SPEAR
SPEARED
SPEARFISH
SPEARFISHES
SPEARHEAD
SPEARHEADED
SPEARHEADING
SPEARHEADS
SPEARIER
SPEARIEST

SPEARING
SPEARMAN
SPEARMEN
SPEARMINT
SPEARMINTS
SPEARS
SPEARWORT
SPEARWORTS
SPEARY
SPEAT
SPEATS
SPEC
SPECCIES
SPECCY
SPECIAL
SPECIALLY
SPECIALS
SPECIALTIES
SPECIALTY
SPECIATE
SPECIATED
SPECIATES
SPECIATING
SPECIE
SPECIES
SPECIFIC
SPECIFICS
SPECIFIED
SPECIFIES
SPECIFY
SPECIFYING
SPECIMEN
SPECIMENS
SPECIOUS
SPECK
SPECKED
SPECKIER
SPECKIEST
SPECKING
SPECKLE
SPECKLED
SPECKLES
SPECKLESS
SPECKLING
SPECKS
SPECKY
SPECS
SPECTACLE
SPECTACLES
SPECTATE
SPECTATED
SPECTATES
SPECTATING
SPECTATOR
SPECTATORS
SPECTER
SPECTERS
SPECTRA
SPECTRAL
SPECTRE
SPECTRES
SPECTRUM
SPECULA
SPECULAR
SPECULATE
SPECULATED
SPECULATES
SPECULATING
SPECULUM
SPED

SPEECH
SPEECHED
SPEECHES
SPEECHFUL
SPEECHIFIED
SPEECHIFIES
SPEECHIFY
SPEECHIFYING
SPEECHING
SPEED
SPEEDBALL
SPEEDBALLS
SPEEDED
SPEEDER
SPEEDERS
SPEEDFUL
SPEEDIER
SPEEDIEST
SPEEDILY
SPEEDING
SPEEDINGS
SPEEDLESS
SPEEDO
SPEEDOS
SPEEDS
SPEEDSTER
SPEEDSTERS
SPEEDWAY
SPEEDWAYS
SPEEDWELL
SPEEDWELLS
SPEEDY
SPEEL
SPEELED
SPEELER
SPEELERS
SPEELING
SPEELS
SPEER
SPEERED
SPEERING
SPEERINGS
SPEERS
SPEIR
SPEIRED
SPEIRING
SPEIRINGS
SPEIRS
SPEISS
SPEISSES
SPEKBOOM
SPEKBOOMS
SPELAEAN
SPELD
SPELDED
SPELDER
SPELDERED
SPELDERING
SPELDERS
SPELDIN
SPELDING
SPELDINGS
SPELDINS
SPELDRIN
SPELDRING
SPELDRINGS
SPELDRINS
SPELDS
SPELEAN
SPELIKIN

SPELIKINS
SPELK
SPELKS
SPELL
SPELLABLE
SPELLBIND
SPELLBINDING
SPELLBINDS
SPELLBOUND
SPELLDOWN
SPELLDOWNS
SPELLED
SPELLER
SPELLERS
SPELLFUL
SPELLICAN
SPELLICANS
SPELLIKIN
SPELLIKINS
SPELLING
SPELLINGS
SPELLS
SPELT
SPELTER
SPELTERS
SPELTS
SPENCE
SPENCER
SPENCERS
SPENCES
SPEND
SPENDABLE
SPENDALL
SPENDALLS
SPENDER
SPENDERS
SPENDING
SPENDINGS
SPENDS
SPENT
SPEOS
SPEOSES
SPERLING
SPERLINGS
SPERM
SPERMARIA
SPERMARIES
SPERMARY
SPERMATIA
SPERMATIC
SPERMATICS
SPERMATID
SPERMATIDS
SPERMIC
SPERMOUS
SPERMS
SPERRE
SPERRED
SPERRES
SPERRING
SPERSE
SPERSED
SPERSES
SPERSING
SPERST
SPERTHE
SPERTHES
SPET
SPETCH
SPETCHES

SPETS
SPETSNAZ
SPETSNAZES
SPETTING
SPETZNAZ
SPETZNAZES
SPEW
SPEWED
SPEWER
SPEWERS
SPEWIER
SPEWIEST
SPEWINESS
SPEWINESSES
SPEWING
SPEWS
SPEWY
SPHACELUS
SPHACELUSES
SPHAER
SPHAERE
SPHAERES
SPHAERITE
SPHAERITES
SPHAERS
SPHAGNOUS
SPHEAR
SPHEARE
SPHEARES
SPHEARS
SPHENDONE
SPHENDONES
SPHENE
SPHENES
SPHENIC
SPHENODON
SPHENODONS
SPHENOID
SPHENOIDS
SPHERAL
SPHERE
SPHERED
SPHERES
SPHERIC
SPHERICAL
SPHERICS
SPHERIER
SPHERIEST
SPHERING
SPHEROID
SPHEROIDS
SPHERULAR
SPHERULE
SPHERULES
SPHERY
SPHINCTER
SPHINCTERS
SPHINGES
SPHINGID
SPHINGIDS
SPHINX
SPHINXES
SPHYGMIC
SPHYGMOID
SPHYGMUS
SPHYGMUSES
SPIAL
SPIALS
SPIC
SPICA

SPICAS
SPICATE
SPICATED
SPICCATO
SPICCATOS
SPICE
SPICED
SPICER
SPICERIES
SPICERS
SPICERY
SPICES
SPICIER
SPICIEST
SPICILEGE
SPICILEGES
SPICILY
SPICINESS
SPICINESSES
SPICING
SPICK
SPICKER
SPICKEST
SPICKNEL
SPICKNELS
SPICKS
SPICS
SPICULA
SPICULAR
SPICULAS
SPICULATE
SPICULE
SPICULES
SPICULUM
SPICY
SPIDE
SPIDER
SPIDERIER
SPIDERIEST
SPIDERS
SPIDERY
SPIE
SPIED
SPIEL
SPIELED
SPIELER
SPIELERS
SPIELING
SPIELS
SPIES
SPIFF
SPIFFIER
SPIFFIEST
SPIFFING
SPIFFY
SPIGHT
SPIGHTED
SPIGHTING
SPIGHTS
SPIGNEL
SPIGNELS
SPIGOT
SPIGOTS
SPIK
SPIKE
SPIKED
SPIKELET
SPIKELETS
SPIKENARD
SPIKENARDS

SPIKES
SPIKIER
SPIKIEST
SPIKILY
SPIKINESS
SPIKINESSES
SPIKING
SPIKS
SPIKY
SPILE
SPILED
SPILES
SPILIKIN
SPILIKINS
SPILING
SPILINGS
SPILITE
SPILITES
SPILITIC
SPILL
SPILLAGE
SPILLAGES
SPILLED
SPILLER
SPILLERS
SPILLIKIN
SPILLIKINS
SPILLING
SPILLINGS
SPILLOVER
SPILLOVERS
SPILLS
SPILLWAY
SPILLWAYS
SPILOSITE
SPILOSITES
SPILT
SPILTH
SPILTHS
SPIN
SPINA
SPINACH
SPINACHES
SPINAE
SPINAGE
SPINAGES
SPINAL
SPINAR
SPINARS
SPINAS
SPINATE
SPINDLE
SPINDLED
SPINDLES
SPINDLIER
SPINDLIEST
SPINDLING
SPINDLINGS
SPINDLY
SPINDRIFT
SPINDRIFTS
SPINE
SPINED
SPINEL
SPINELESS
SPINELS
SPINES
SPINET
SPINETS
SPINETTE

SPINETTES
SPINIER
SPINIEST
SPINIFEX
SPINIFEXES
SPINIFORM
SPININESS
SPININESSES
SPINK
SPINKS
SPINNAKER
SPINNAKERS
SPINNER
SPINNERET
SPINNERETS
SPINNERIES
SPINNERS
SPINNERY
SPINNET
SPINNETS
SPINNEY
SPINNEYS
SPINNIES
SPINNING
SPINNINGS
SPINNY
SPINODE
SPINODES
SPINOSE
SPINOSITIES
SPINOSITY
SPINOUS
SPINOUT
SPINOUTS
SPINS
SPINSTER
SPINSTERS
SPINTEXT
SPINTEXTS
SPINULATE
SPINULE
SPINULES
SPINULOSE
SPINULOUS
SPINY
SPIRACLE
SPIRACLES
SPIRACULA
SPIRAEA
SPIRAEAS
SPIRAL
SPIRALISM
SPIRALISMS
SPIRALIST
SPIRALISTS
SPIRALITIES
SPIRALITY
SPIRALLED
SPIRALLING
SPIRALLY
SPIRALS
SPIRANT
SPIRANTS
SPIRASTER
SPIRASTERS
SPIRATED
SPIRATION
SPIRATIONS
SPIRE
SPIREA

SPIREAS
SPIRED
SPIRELESS
SPIREME
SPIREMES
SPIRES
SPINEWISE
SPIRIC
SPIRICS
SPIRIER
SPIRIEST
SPIRILLA
SPIRILLAR
SPIRILLUM
SPIRING
SPIRIT
SPIRITED
SPIRITFUL
SPIRITING
SPIRITINGS
SPIRITISM
SPIRITISMS
SPIRITIST
SPIRITISTS
SPIRITOSO
SPIRITOUS
SPIRITS
SPIRITUAL
SPIRITUALS
SPIRITUEL
SPIRITUS
SPIRITUSES
SPIRITY
SPIRLING
SPIRLINGS
SPIROID
SPIRT
SPIRTED
SPIRTING
SPIRTLE
SPIRTLES
SPIRTS
SPIRY
SPIT
SPITAL
SPITALS
SPITCHER
SPITE
SPITED
SPITEFUL
SPITEFULLER
SPITEFULLEST
SPITES
SPITFIRE
SPITFIRES
SPITING
SPITS
SPITTED
SPITTEN
SPITTER
SPITTERS
SPITTING
SPITTINGS
SPITTLE
SPITTLES
SPITTOON
SPITTOONS
SPITZ
SPITZES
SPIV

SPIVS
SPIVVERIES
SPIVVERY
SPIVVIER
SPIVVIEST
SPIVVY
SPLASH
SPLASHED
SPLASHER
SPLASHERS
SPLASHES
SPLASHIER
SPLASHIEST
SPLASHILY
SPLASHING
SPLASHINGS
SPLASHY
SPLAT
SPLATCH
SPLATCHED
SPLATCHES
SPLATCHING
SPLATS
SPLATTED
SPLATTER
SPLATTERED
SPLATTERING
SPLATTERS
SPLATTING
SPLATTINGS
SPLAY
SPLAYED
SPLAYING
SPLAYS
SPLEEN
SPLEENFUL
SPLEENISH
SPLEENS
SPLEENY
SPLENDENT
SPLENDID
SPLENDOR
SPLENDORS
SPLENDOUR
SPLENDOURS
SPLENETIC
SPLENETICS
SPLENIA
SPLENIAL
SPLENIC
SPLENII
SPLENITIS
SPLENITISES
SPLENIUM
SPLENIUMS
SPLENIUS
SPLENIUSES
SPLENT
SPLENTED
SPLENTING
SPLENTS
SPLEUCHAN
SPLEUCHANS
SPLICE
SPLICED
SPLICES
SPLICING
SPLIFF
SPLIFFS
SPLINE

SPLINED
SPLINES
SPLINING
SPLINT
SPLINTED
SPLINTER
SPLINTERED
SPLINTERING
SPLINTERS
SPLINTERY
SPLINTING
SPLINTS
SPLIT
SPLITS
SPLITTED
SPLITTER
SPLITTERS
SPLITTING
SPLODGE
SPLODGED
SPLODGES
SPLODGIER
SPLODGIEST
SPLODGILY
SPLODGING
SPLODGY
SPLORE
SPLORES
SPLOSH
SPLOSHED
SPLOSHES
SPLOSHING
SPLOTCH
SPLOTCHED
SPLOTCHES
SPLOTCHIER
SPLOTCHIEST
SPLOTCHING
SPLOTCHY
SPLURGE
SPLURGED
SPLURGES
SPLURGIER
SPLURGIEST
SPLURGING
SPLURGY
SPLUTTER
SPLUTTERED
SPLUTTERING
SPLUTTERINGS
SPLUTTERS
SPLUTTERY
SPODE
SPODES
SPODIUM
SPODIUMS
SPODUMENE
SPODUMENES
SPOFFISH
SPOFFY
SPOIL
SPOILAGE
SPOILAGES
SPOILED
SPOILER
SPOILERS
SPOILFUL
SPOILING
SPOILS
SPOILSMAN

SPOILSMEN
SPOILT
SPOKE
SPOKEN
SPOKES
SPOKESMAN
SPOKESMEN
SPOKEWISE
SPOLIATE
SPOLIATED
SPOLIATES
SPOLIATING
SPOLIATION
SPOLIATOR
SPOLIATORS
SPONDAIC
SPONDEE
SPONDEES
SPONDULIX
SPONDYL
SPONDYLS
SPONGE
SPONGED
SPONGEOUS
SPONGER
SPONGERS
SPONGES
SPONGIER
SPONGIEST
SPONGILY
SPONGIN
SPONGING
SPONGINS
SPONGIOSE
SPONGIOUS
SPONGOID
SPONGY
SPONSAL
SPONSALIA
SPONSIBLE
SPONSING
SPONSINGS
SPONSION
SPONSIONS
SPONSON
SPONSONS
SPONSOR
SPONSORED
SPONSORING
SPONSORS
SPONTOON
SPONTOONS
SPOOF
SPOOFED
SPOOFER
SPOOFERIES
SPOOFERS
SPOOFERY
SPOOFING
SPOOFS
SPOOK
SPOOKED
SPOOKERIES
SPOOKERY
SPOOKIER
SPOOKIEST
SPOOKILY
SPOOKING
SPOOKISH
SPOOKS
SPOOKY

SPOOL
SPOOLED
SPOOLER
SPOOLERS
SPOOLING
SPOOLS
SPOOM
SPOOMED
SPOOMING
SPOOMS
SPOON
SPOONBILL
SPOONBILLS
SPOONED
SPOONEY
SPOONEYS
SPOONFUL
SPOONFULS
SPOONIER
SPOONIES
SPOONIEST
SPOONILY
SPOONING
SPOONMEAT
SPOONMEATS
SPOONS
SPOONWAYS
SPOONWISE
SPOONY
SPOOR
SPOORED
SPOORER
SPOORERS
SPOORING
SPOORS
SPORADIC
SPORANGIA
SPORE
SPORES
SPORIDESM
SPORIDESMS
SPORIDIA
SPORIDIAL
SPORIDIUM
SPOROCARP
SPOROCARPS
SPOROCYST
SPOROCYSTS
SPOROGENIES
SPOROGENY
SPOROPHYL
SPOROPHYLS
SPORRAN
SPORRANS
SPORT
SPORTABLE
SPORTANCE
SPORTANCES
SPORTED
SPORTER
SPORTERS
SPORTFUL
SPORTIER
SPORTIEST
SPORTILY
SPORTING
SPORTIVE
SPORTLESS
SPORTS
SPORTSMAN

SPORTSMEN
SPORTY
SPORULAR
SPORULATE
SPORULATED
SPORULATES
SPORULATING
SPORULE
SPORULES
SPOSH
SPOSHES
SPOSHY
SPOT
SPOTLESS
SPOTLIGHT
SPOTLIGHTED
SPOTLIGHTING
SPOTLIGHTS
SPOTLIT
SPOTS
SPOTTE
SPOTTED
SPOTTER
SPOTTERS
SPOTTES
SPOTTIER
SPOTTIEST
SPOTTILY
SPOTTING
SPOTTINGS
SPOTTY
SPOUSAGE
SPOUSAGES
SPOUSAL
SPOUSALS
SPOUSE
SPOUSED
SPOUSES
SPOUSING
SPOUT
SPOUTED
SPOUTER
SPOUTERS
SPOUTIER
SPOUTIEST
SPOUTING
SPOUTLESS
SPOUTS
SPOUTY
SPRACK
SPRACKLE
SPRACKLED
SPRACKLES
SPRACKLING
SPRAD
SPRAG
SPRAGGED
SPRAGGING
SPRAGS
SPRAICKLE
SPRAICKLED
SPRAICKLES
SPRAICKLING
SPRAID
SPRAIN
SPRAINED
SPRAINING
SPRAINS
SPRAINT
SPRAINTS

SPRANG
SPRANGLE
SPRANGLED
SPRANGLES
SPRANGLING
SPRAT
SPRATS
SPRATTLE
SPRATTLED
SPRATTLES
SPRATTLING
SPRAUCHLE
SPRAUCHLED
SPRAUCHLES
SPRAUCHLING
SPRAUNCIER
SPRAUNCIEST
SPRAUNCY
SPRAWL
SPRAWLED
SPRAWLER
SPRAWLERS
SPRAWLIER
SPRAWLIEST
SPRAWLING
SPRAWLS
SPRAWLY
SPRAY
SPRAYED
SPRAYER
SPRAYERS
SPRAYEY
SPRAYIER
SPRAYIEST
SPRAYING
SPRAYS
SPREAD
SPREADER
SPREADERS
SPREADING
SPREADINGS
SPREADS
SPREAGH
SPREAGHS
SPREATHE
SPREATHED
SPREATHES
SPREATHING
SPREAZE
SPREAZED
SPREAZES
SPREAZING
SPRECHERIES
SPRECHERY
SPRECKLED
SPRED
SPREDD
SPREDDE
SPREDDEN
SPREDDES
SPREDDING
SPREDDS
SPREDS
SPREE
SPREED
SPREEING
SPREES
SPREETHE
SPREETHED
SPREETHES

SPREETHING
SPREEZE
SPREEZED
SPREEZES
SPREEZING
SPRENT
SPRIG
SPRIGGED
SPRIGGIER
SPRIGGIEST
SPRIGGING
SPRIGGY
SPRIGHT
SPRIGHTED
SPRIGHTING
SPRIGHTLIER
SPRIGHTLIEST
SPRIGHTLY
SPRIGHTS
SPRIGS
SPRING
SPRINGAL
SPRINGALD
SPRINGALDS
SPRINGALS
SPRINGBOK
SPRINGBOKS
SPRINGE
SPRINGED
SPRINGER
SPRINGERS
SPRINGES
SPRINGIER
SPRINGIEST
SPRINGILY
SPRINGING
SPRINGINGS
SPRINGLE
SPRINGLES
SPRINGLET
SPRINGLETS
SPRINGS
SPRINGY
SPRINKLE
SPRINKLED
SPRINKLER
SPRINKLERS
SPRINKLES
SPRINKLING
SPRINKLINGS
SPRINT
SPRINTED
SPRINTER
SPRINTERS
SPRINTING
SPRINTINGS
SPRINTS
SPRIT
SPRITE
SPRITEFUL
SPRITELY
SPRITES
SPRITS
SPRITSAIL
SPRITSAILS
SPRITZER
SPRITZERS
SPRITZIG
SPRITZIGS
SPROCKET

SPROCKETS
SPROD
SPRODS
SPROG
SPROGS
SPRONG
SPROUT
SPROUTED
SPROUTING
SPROUTINGS
SPROUTS
SPRUCE
SPRUCED
SPRUCELY
SPRUCER
SPRUCES
SPRUCEST
SPRUCING
SPRUE
SPRUES
SPRUG
SPRUGS
SPRUIK
SPRUIKED
SPRUIKER
SPRUIKERS
SPRUIKING
SPRUIKS
SPRUIT
SPRUITS
SPRUNG
SPRUSH
SPRUSHED
SPRUSHES
SPRUSHING
SPRY
SPRYER
SPRYEST
SPRYLY
SPRYNESS
SPRYNESSES
SPUD
SPUDDED
SPUDDIER
SPUDDIEST
SPUDDING
SPUDDINGS
SPUDDY
SPUDS
SPUE
SPUED
SPUEING
SPUES
SPUILZIE
SPUILZIED
SPUILZIEING
SPUILZIES
SPUING
SPULE
SPULEBANE
SPULEBANES
SPULEBONE
SPULEBONES
SPULES
SPULYE
SPULYED
SPULYEING
SPULYES
SPULYIE
SPULYIED

SPULYIEING
SPULYIES
SPULZIE
SPULZIED
SPULZIEING
SPULZIES
SPUME
SPUMED
SPUMES
SPUMIER
SPUMIEST
SPUMING
SPUMOUS
SPUMY
SPUN
SPUNGE
SPUNGES
SPUNK
SPUNKED
SPUNKIE
SPUNKIER
SPUNKIES
SPUNKIEST
SPUNKING
SPUNKS
SPUNKY
SPUR
SPURGE
SPURGES
SPURIAE
SPURIOUS
SPURLESS
SPURLING
SPURLINGS
SPURN
SPURNE
SPURNED
SPURNER
SPURNERS
SPURNES
SPURNING
SPURNINGS
SPURNS
SPURRED
SPURRER
SPURRERS
SPURREY
SPURREYS
SPURRIER
SPURRIERS
SPURRIES
SPURRIEST
SPURRING
SPURRINGS
SPURRY
SPURS
SPURT
SPURTED
SPURTING
SPURTLE
SPURTLES
SPURTS
SPUTA
SPUTNIK
SPUTNIKS
SPUTTER
SPUTTERED
SPUTTERER
SPUTTERERS
SPUTTERING

SPUTTERINGS
SPUTTERS
SPUTTERY
SPUTUM
SPY
SPYAL
SPYALS
SPYGLASS
SPYGLASSES
SPYING
SPYINGS
SPYMASTER
SPYMASTERS
SPYRE
SPYRES
SQUAB
SQUABASH
SQUABASHED
SQUABASHES
SQUABASHING
SQUABBED
SQUABBER
SQUABBEST
SQUABBIER
SQUABBIEST
SQUABBING
SQUABBISH
SQUABBLE
SQUABBLED
SQUABBLER
SQUABBLERS
SQUABBLES
SQUABBLING
SQUABBY
SQUABS
SQUACCO
SQUACCOS
SQUAD
SQUADDIES
SQUADDY
SQUADRON
SQUADRONE
SQUADRONED
SQUADRONES
SQUADRONING
SQUADRONS
SQUADS
SQUAIL
SQUAILED
SQUAILER
SQUAILERS
SQUAILING
SQUAILINGS
SQUAILS
SQUALID
SQUALIDER
SQUALIDEST
SQUALIDLY
SQUALL
SQUALLED
SQUALLER
SQUALLERS
SQUALLIER
SQUALLIEST
SQUALLING
SQUALLINGS
SQUALLS
SQUALLY
SQUALOID
SQUALOR

SQUALORS	SQUAWKINGS	SQUIDGE	SQUIRMIER	STACKED
SQUAMA	SQUAWKS	SQUIDGED	SQUIRMIEST	STACKER
SQUAMAE	SQUAWKY	SQUIDGES	SQUIRMING	STACKERS
SQUAMATE	SQUAWMAN	SQUIDGIER	SQUIRMS	STACKET
SQUAME	SQUAWMEN	SQUIDGIEST	SQUIRMY	STACKETS
SQUAMELLA	SQUAWS	SQUIDGING	SQUIRR	STACKING
SQUAMELLAS	SQUEAK	SQUIDGY	SQUIRRED	STACKINGS
SQUAMES	SQUEAKED	SQUIDS	SQUIRREL	STACKS
SQUAMOSAL	SQUEAKER	SQUIER	SQUIRRELLED	STACKYARD
SQUAMOSALS	SQUEAKERIES	SQUIERS	SQUIRRELLING	STACKYARDS
SQUAMOSE	SQUEAKERS	SQUIFF	SQUIRRELS	STACTE
SQUAMOUS	SQUEAKERY	SQUIFFER	SQUIRRELY	STACTES
SQUAMULA	SQUEAKIER	SQUIFFERS	SQUIRRING	STADDA
SQUAMULAS	SQUEAKIEST	SQUIFFIER	SQUIRRS	STADDAS
SQUAMULE	SQUEAKILY	SQUIFFIEST	SQUIRT	STADDLE
SQUAMULES	SQUEAKING	SQUIFFY	SQUIRTED	STADDLES
SQUANDER	SQUEAKINGS	SQUIGGLE	SQUIRTER	STADE
SQUANDERED	SQUEAKS	SQUIGGLED	SQUIRTERS	STADES
SQUANDERING	SQUEAKY	SQUIGGLES	SQUIRTING	STADIA
SQUANDERINGS	SQUEAL	SQUIGGLIER	SQUIRTINGS	STADIAL
SQUANDERS	SQUEALED	SQUIGGLIEST	SQUIRTS	STADIALS
SQUARE	SQUEALER	SQUIGGLING	SQUISH	STADIAS
SQUARED	SQUEALERS	SQUIGGLY	SQUISHED	STADIUM
SQUARELY	SQUEALING	SQUILGEE	SQUISHES	STADIUMS
SQUARER	SQUEALINGS	SQUILGEED	SQUISHIER	STAFF
SQUARERS	SQUEALS	SQUILGEEING	SQUISHIEST	STAFFAGE
SQUARES	SQUEAMISH	SQUILGEES	SQUISHING	STAFFAGES
SQUAREST	SQUEEDGE	SQUILL	SQUISHY	STAFFED
SQUARING	SQUEEDGED	SQUILLS	SQUIT	STAFFER
SQUARINGS	SQUEEDGES	SQUINANCIES	SQUITCH	STAFFERS
SQUARISH	SQUEEDGING	SQUINANCY	SQUITCHES	STAFFING
SQUARROSE	SQUEEGEE	SQUINCH	SQUITS	STAFFROOM
SQUARSON	SQUEEGEED	SQUINCHES	SRADDHA	STAFFROOMS
SQUARSONS	SQUEEGEEING	SQUINIED	SRADDHAS	STAFFS
SQUASH	SQUEEGEES	SQUINIES	ST	STAG
SQUASHED	SQUEEZE	SQUINNIED	STAB	STAGE
SQUASHER	SQUEEZED	SQUINNIES	STABBED	STAGED
SQUASHERS	SQUEEZER	SQUINNY	STABBER	STAGER
SQUASHES	SQUEEZERS	SQUINNYING	STABBERS	STAGERIES
SQUASHIER	SQUEEZES	SQUINT	STABBING	STAGERS
SQUASHIEST	SQUEEZIER	SQUINTED	STABBINGS	STAGERY
SQUASHILY	SQUEEZIEST	SQUINTER	STABILE	STAGES
SQUASHING	SQUEEZING	SQUINTERS	STABILES	STAGEY
SQUASHY	SQUEEZINGS	SQUINTEST	STABILISE	STAGGARD
SQUAT	SQUEEZY	SQUINTING	STABILISED	STAGGARDS
SQUATNESS	SQUEG	SQUINTINGS	STABILISES	STAGGED
SQUATNESSES	SQUEGGED	SQUINTS	STABILISING	STAGGER
SQUATS	SQUEGGER	SQUINY	STABILITIES	STAGGERED
SQUATTED	SQUEGGERS	SQUINYING	STABILITY	STAGGERER
SQUATTER	SQUEGGING	SQUIRAGE	STABILIZE	STAGGERERS
SQUATTERED	SQUEGGINGS	SQUIRAGES	STABILIZED	STAGGERING
SQUATTERING	SQUEGS	SQUIRALTIES	STABILIZES	STAGGERINGS
SQUATTERS	SQUELCH	SQUIRALTY	STABILIZING	STAGGERS
SQUATTEST	SQUELCHED	SQUIRARCH	STABLE	STAGGING
SQUATTIER	SQUELCHER	SQUIRARCHS	STABLED	STAGHORN
SQUATTIEST	SQUELCHERS	SQUIRE	STABLER	STAGHORNS
SQUATTING	SQUELCHES	SQUIREAGE	STABLERS	STAGHOUND
SQUATTLE	SQUELCHIER	SQUIREAGES	STABLES	STAGHOUNDS
SQUATTLED	SQUELCHIEST	SQUIRED	STABLEST	STAGIER
SQUATTLES	SQUELCHING	SQUIREDOM	STABLING	STAGIEST
SQUATTLING	SQUELCHINGS	SQUIREDOMS	STABLINGS	STAGILY
SQUATTY	SQUELCHY	SQUIREEN	STABLISH	STAGINESS
SQUAW	SQUIB	SQUIREENS	STABLISHED	STAGINESSES
SQUAWK	SQUIBBED	SQUIRELY	STABLISHES	STAGING
SQUAWKED	SQUIBBING	SQUIRES	STABLISHING	STAGINGS
SQUAWKER	SQUIBBINGS	SQUIRESS	STABLY	STAGNANCIES
SQUAWKERS	SQUIBS	SQUIRESSES	STABS	STAGNANCY
SQUAWKIER	SQUID	SQUIRING	STACCATO	STAGNANT
SQUAWKIEST	SQUIDDED	SQUIRM	STACCATOS	STAGNATE
SQUAWKING	SQUIDDING	SQUIRMED	STACK	STAGNATED

STAGNATES
STAGNATING
STAGS
STAGY
STAID
STAIDER
STAIDEST
STAIDLY
STAIDNESS
STAIDNESSES
STAIG
STAIGS
STAIN
STAINED
STAINER
STAINERS
STAINING
STAININGS
STAINLESS
STAINS
STAIR
STAIRCASE
STAIRCASES
STAIRED
STAIRFOOT
STAIRFOOTS
STAIRHEAD
STAIRHEADS
STAIRS
STAIRWAY
STAIRWAYS
STAIRWISE
STAITH
STAITHE
STAITHES
STAITHS
STAKE
STAKED
STAKES
STAKING
STALACTIC
STALAG
STALAGMA
STALAGMAS
STALAGS
STALE
STALED
STALELY
STALEMATE
STALEMATED
STALEMATES
STALEMATING
STALENESS
STALENESSES
STALER
STALES
STALEST
STALING
STALK
STALKED
STALKER
STALKERS
STALKIER
STALKIEST
STALKING
STALKINGS
STALKLESS
STALKO
STALKOES
STALKS

STALKY
STALL
STALLAGE
STALLAGES
STALLED
STALLING
STALLINGS
STALLION
STALLIONS
STALLMAN
STALLMEN
STALLS
STALWART
STALWARTS
STALWORTH
STALWORTHS
STAMEN
STAMENED
STAMENS
STAMINA
STAMINAL
STAMINAS
STAMINATE
STAMINEAL
STAMINODE
STAMINODES
STAMINODIES
STAMINODY
STAMINOID
STAMMEL
STAMMELS
STAMMER
STAMMERED
STAMMERER
STAMMERERS
STAMMERING
STAMMERINGS
STAMMERS
STAMNOI
STAMNOS
STAMP
STAMPED
STAMPEDE
STAMPEDED
STAMPEDES
STAMPEDING
STAMPEDO
STAMPEDOED
STAMPEDOING
STAMPEDOS
STAMPER
STAMPERS
STAMPING
STAMPINGS
STAMPS
STANCE
STANCES
STANCH
STANCHED
STANCHEL
STANCHELLED
STANCHELLING
STANCHELS
STANCHER
STANCHERED
STANCHERING
STANCHERS
STANCHES
STANCHEST
STANCHING

STANCHINGS
STANCHION
STANCHIONED
STANCHIONING
STANCHIONS
STANCHLY
STANCK
STAND
STANDARD
STANDARDS
STANDEN
STANDER
STANDERS
STANDGALE
STANDGALES
STANDING
STANDINGS
STANDISH
STANDISHES
STANDS
STANE
STANED
STANES
STANG
STANGED
STANGING
STANGS
STANHOPE
STANHOPES
STANIEL
STANIELS
STANING
STANK
STANKS
STANNARIES
STANNARY
STANNATE
STANNATES
STANNATOR
STANNATORS
STANNEL
STANNELS
STANNIC
STANNITE
STANNITES
STANNOUS
STANYEL
STANYELS
STANZA
STANZAIC
STANZAS
STANZE
STANZES
STANZO
STANZOES
STANZOS
STAP
STAPEDES
STAPEDIAL
STAPEDII
STAPEDIUS
STAPEDIUSES
STAPELIA
STAPELIAS
STAPES
STAPH
STAPHS
STAPHYLE
STAPHYLES
STAPLE

STAPLED
STAPLER
STAPLERS
STAPLES
STAPLING
STAPPED
STAPPING
STAPPLE
STAPPLES
STAPS
STAR
STARAGEN
STARAGENS
STARBOARD
STARBOARDED
STARBOARDING
STARBOARDS
STARCH
STARCHED
STARCHER
STARCHERS
STARCHES
STARCHIER
STARCHIEST
STARCHILY
STARCHING
STARCHY
STARDOM
STARDOMS
STARE
STARED
STARER
STARERS
STARES
STARETS
STARETSES
STARETZ
STARETZES
STARFISH
STARFISHES
STARING
STARINGLY
STARINGS
STARK
STARKED
STARKEN
STARKENED
STARKENING
STARKENS
STARKER
STARKERS
STARKEST
STARKING
STARKLY
STARKNESS
STARKNESSES
STARKS
STARLESS
STARLET
STARLETS
STARLIGHT
STARLIGHTS
STARLIKE
STARLING
STARLINGS
STARLIT
STARN
STARNED
STARNIE
STARNIES

STARNING
STARNS
STAROSTA
STAROSTAS
STAROSTIES
STAROSTY
STARR
STARRED
STARRIER
STARRIEST
STARRILY
STARRING
STARRINGS
STARRS
STARRY
STARS
STARSHINE
STARSHINES
STARSPOT
STARSPOTS
START
STARTED
STARTER
STARTERS
STARTFUL
STARTING
STARTINGS
STARTISH
STARTLE
STARTLED
STARTLER
STARTLERS
STARTLES
STARTLING
STARTLINGS
STARTLISH
STARTLY
STARTS
STARVE
STARVED
STARVES
STARVING
STARVINGS
STARWORT
STARWORTS
STASES
STASH
STASHED
STASHES
STASHIE
STASHIES
STASHING
STASIDION
STASIDIONS
STASIMA
STASIMON
STASIS
STATABLE
STATAL
STATANT
STATE
STATED
STATEDLY
STATEHOOD
STATEHOODS
STATELESS
STATELIER
STATELIEST
STATELILY
STATELY

STATEMENT	STAYING	STEARATES	STEENBOK	STEINBOCKS
STATEMENTS	STAYINGS	STEARD	STEENBOKS	STEINED
STATER	STAYLESS	STEARE	STEENBRAS	STEINING
STATEROOM	STAYNE	STEARED	STEENBRASES	STEININGS
STATEROOMS	STAYNED	STEARES	STEENED	STEINS
STATERS	STAYNES	STEARIC	STEENING	STELA
STATES	STAYNING	STEARIN	STEENINGS	STELAE
STATESIDE	STAYRE	STEARINE	STEENKIRK	STELAR
STATESMAN	STAYRES	STEARINES	STEENKIRKS	STELE
STATESMEN	STAYS	STEARING	STEENS	STELENE
STATEWIDE	STAYSAIL	STEARINS	STEEP	STELES
STATIC	STAYSAILS	STEARS	STEEPED	STELL
STATICAL	STEAD	STEARSMAN	STEEPEN	STELLAR
STATICS	STEADED	STEARSMEN	STEEPENED	STELLATE
STATING	STEADFAST	STEATITE	STEEPENING	STELLATED
STATION	STEADIED	STEATITES	STEEPENS	STELLED
STATIONAL	STEADIER	STEATITIC	STEEPER	STELLIFIED
STATIONED	STEADIES	STEATOMA	STEEPERS	STELLIFIES
STATIONER	STEADIEST	STEATOMAS	STEEPEST	STELLIFY
STATIONERS	STEADILY	STEATOSES	STEEPIER	STELLIFYING
STATIONING	STEADING	STEATOSIS	STEEPIEST	STELLIFYINGS
STATIONS	STEADINGS	STED	STEEPING	STELLING
STATISM	STEADS	STEDD	STEEPISH	STELLION
STATISMS	STEADY	STEDDE	STEEPLE	STELLIONS
STATIST	STEADYING	STEDDED	STEEPLED	STELLS
STATISTIC	STEAK	STEDDES	STEEPLES	STELLULAR
STATISTICS	STEAKS	STEDDIED	STEEPLY	STEM
STATISTS	STEAL	STEDDIES	STEEPNESS	STEMBOK
STATIVE	STEALE	STEDDING	STEEPNESSES	STEMBOKS
STATOCYST	STEALED	STEDDS	STEEPS	STEMBUCK
STATOCYSTS	STEALER	STEDDY	STEEPY	STEMBUCKS
STATOLITH	STEALERS	STEDDYING	STEER	STEME
STATOLITHS	STEALES	STEDE	STEERABLE	STEMED
STATOR	STEALING	STEDED	STEERAGE	STEMES
STATORS	STEALINGS	STEDES	STEERAGES	STEMING
STATUA	STEALS	STEDFAST	STEERED	STEMLESS
STATUARIES	STEALT	STEDING	STEERER	STEMLET
STATUARY	STEALTH	STEDS	STEERERS	STEMLETS
STATUAS	STEALTHIER	STEED	STEERIES	STEMMA
STATUE	STEALTHIEST	STEEDED	STEERING	STEMMATA
STATUED	STEALTHS	STEEDIED	STEERINGS	STEMME
STATUES	STEALTHY	STEEDIES	STEERLING	STEMMED
STATUETTE	STEAM	STEEDING	STEERLINGS	STEMMES
STATUETTES	STEAMBOAT	STEEDS	STEERS	STEMMING
STATURE	STEAMBOATS	STEEDY	STEERSMAN	STEMPEL
STATURED	STEAMED	STEEDYING	STEERSMEN	STEMPELS
STATURES	STEAMER	STEEK	STEERY	STEMPLE
STATUS	STEAMERS	STEEKING	STEEVE	STEMPLES
STATUTE	STEAMIE	STEEKIT	STEEVED	STEMS
STATUTES	STEAMIER	STEEKS	STEEVELY	STEMSON
STATUTORY	STEAMIES	STEEL	STEEVER	STEMSONS
STAUNCH	STEAMIEST	STEELBOW	STEEVES	STEN
STAUNCHED	STEAMILY	STEELBOWS	STEEVEST	STENCH
STAUNCHER	STEAMING	STEELD	STEEVING	STENCHED
STAUNCHES	STEAMINGS	STEELED	STEEVINGS	STENCHES
STAUNCHEST	STEAMS	STEELIER	STEGNOSES	STENCHIER
STAUNCHING	STEAMSHIP	STEELIEST	STEGNOSIS	STENCHIEST
STAUNCHLY	STEAMSHIPS	STEELING	STEGNOTIC	STENCHING
STAVE	STEAMY	STEELINGS	STEGODON	STENCHY
STAVED	STEAN	STEELS	STEGODONS	STENCIL
STAVES	STEANE	STEELWORK	STEGODONT	STENCILLED
STAVING	STEANED	STEELWORKS	STEGODONTS	STENCILLING
STAW	STEANES	STEELY	STEGOMYIA	STENCILLINGS
STAWED	STEANING	STEELYARD	STEGOMYIAS	STENCILS
STAWING	STEANINGS	STEELYARDS	STEGOSAUR	STEND
STAWS	STEANS	STEEM	STEGOSAURS	STENDED
STAY	STEAR	STEEMED	STEIL	STENDING
STAYED	STEARAGE	STEEMING	STEILS	STENDS
STAYER	STEARAGES	STEEMS	STEIN	STENGAH
STAYERS	STEARATE	STEEN	STEINBOCK	STENGAHS

STENLOCK
STENLOCKS
STENNED
STENNING
STENOPAIC
STENOSED
STENOSES
STENOSIS
STENOTIC
STENOTYPE
STENOTYPES
STENOTYPIES
STENOTYPY
STENS
STENT
STENTED
STENTING
STENTOR
STENTORS
STENTOUR
STENTOURS
STENTS
STEP
STEPBAIRN
STEPBAIRNS
STEPCHILD
STEPCHILDREN
STEPDAME
STEPDAMES
STEPHANE
STEPHANES
STEPNEY
STEPNEYS
STEPPE
STEPPED
STEPPER
STEPPERS
STEPPES
STEPPING
STEPS
STEPSON
STEPSONS
STEPT
STEPWISE
STERADIAN
STERADIANS
STERCORAL
STERCULIA
STERCULIAS
STERE
STEREO
STEREOED
STEREOING
STEREOME
STEREOMES
STEREOS
STERES
STERIC
STERIGMA
STERIGMATA
STERILE
STERILISE
STERILISED
STERILISES
STERILISING
STERILITIES
STERILITY
STERILIZE
STERILIZED
STERILIZES

STERILIZING
STERLET
STERLETS
STERLING
STERLINGS
STERN
STERNAGE
STERNAGES
STERNAL
STERNEBRA
STERNEBRAE
STERNED
STERNER
STERNEST
STERNING
STERNITE
STERNITES
STERNITIC
STERNLY
STERNMOST
STERNNESS
STERNNESSES
STERNPORT
STERNPORTS
STERNS
STERNSON
STERNSONS
STERNUM
STERNUMS
STERNWARD
STERNWARDS
STERNWAY
STERNWAYS
STEROID
STEROIDS
STEROL
STEROLS
STERVE
STERVED
STERVES
STERVING
STET
STETS
STETTED
STETTING
STEVEDORE
STEVEDORED
STEVEDORES
STEVEDORING
STEVEN
STEVENS
STEW
STEWARD
STEWARDRIES
STEWARDRY
STEWARDS
STEWARTRIES
STEWARTRY
STEWED
STEWER
STEWERS
STEWIER
STEWIEST
STEWING
STEWINGS
STEWPAN
STEWPANS
STEWPOND
STEWPONDS
STEWPOT

STEWPOTS
STEWS
STEWY
STEY
STEYER
STEYEST
STHENIC
STIBBLE
STIBBLER
STIBBLERS
STIBBLES
STIBIAL
STIBINE
STIBINES
STIBIUM
STIBIUMS
STIBNITE
STIBNITES
STICCADO
STICCADOES
STICCADOS
STICCATO
STICCATOES
STICCATOS
STICH
STICHERA
STICHERON
STICHERONS
STICHIC
STICHIDIA
STICHOI
STICHOS
STICHS
STICK
STICKED
STICKER
STICKERS
STICKFUL
STICKFULS
STICKIED
STICKIER
STICKIES
STICKIEST
STICKILY
STICKING
STICKINGS
STICKIT
STICKJAW
STICKJAWS
STICKLE
STICKLED
STICKLER
STICKLERS
STICKLES
STICKLING
STICKS
STICKUP
STICKUPS
STICKWORK
STICKWORKS
STICKY
STICKYING
STIDDIE
STIDDIED
STIDDIEING
STIDDIES
STIDDYING
STIE
STIED
STIES
STIEVE

STIEVELY
STIEVER
STIEVEST
STIFF
STIFFED
STIFFEN
STIFFENED
STIFFENER
STIFFENERS
STIFFENING
STIFFENINGS
STIFFENS
STIFFER
STIFFEST
STIFFING
STIFFISH
STIFFLY
STIFFNESS
STIFFNESSES
STIFFS
STIFLE
STIFLED
STIFLER
STIFLERS
STIFLES
STIFLING
STIFLINGS
STIGMA
STIGMAS
STIGMATA
STIGMATIC
STIGMATICS
STIGME
STIGMES
STILB
STILBENE
STILBENES
STILBITE
STILBITES
STILBS
STILE
STILED
STILES
STILET
STILETS
STILETTO
STILETTOED
STILETTOING
STILETTOS
STILING
STILL
STILLAGE
STILLAGES
STILLED
STILLER
STILLERS
STILLEST
STILLIER
STILLIEST
STILLING
STILLINGS
STILLION
STILLIONS
STILLNESS
STILLNESSES
STILLS
STILLY
STILT
STILTED
STILTEDLY

STILTER
STILTERS
STILTIER
STILTIEST
STILTING
STILTINGS
STILTISH
STILTS
STILTY
STIME
STIMED
STIMES
STIMIE
STIMIED
STIMIES
STIMING
STIMULANT
STIMULANTS
STIMULATE
STIMULATED
STIMULATES
STIMULATING
STIMULI
STIMULUS
STIMY
STIMYING
STING
STINGAREE
STINGAREES
STINGED
STINGER
STINGERS
STINGIER
STINGIEST
STINGILY
STINGING
STINGINGS
STINGLESS
STINGO
STINGOS
STINGS
STINGY
STINK
STINKARD
STINKARDS
STINKER
STINKERS
STINKHORN
STINKHORNS
STINKING
STINKINGS
STINKS
STINT
STINTED
STINTEDLY
STINTER
STINTERS
STINTIER
STINTIEST
STINTING
STINTINGS
STINTLESS
STINTS
STINTY
STIPA
STIPAS
STIPE
STIPEL
STIPELS
STIPEND

STIPENDS
STIPES
STIPITATE
STIPITES
STIPPLE
STIPPLED
STIPPLER
STIPPLERS
STIPPLES
STIPPLING
STIPPLINGS
STIPULAR
STIPULARY
STIPULATE
STIPULATED
STIPULATES
STIPULATING
STIPULE
STIPULED
STIPULES
STIR
STIRABOUT
STIRABOUTS
STIRE
STIRED
STIRES
STIRING
STIRK
STIRKS
STIRLESS
STIRP
STIRPES
STIRPS
STIRRA
STIRRAH
STIRRAHS
STIRRAS
STIRRE
STIRRED
STIRRER
STIRRERS
STIRRES
STIRRING
STIRRINGS
STIRRUP
STIRRUPS
STIRS
STISHIE
STISHIES
STITCH
STITCHED
STITCHER
STITCHERIES
STITCHERS
STITCHERY
STITCHES
STITCHING
STITCHINGS
STITHIED
STITHIES
STITHY
STITHYING
STIVE
STIVED
STIVER
STIVERS
STIVES
STIVIER
STIVIEST
STIVING

STIVY
STOA
STOAE
STOAI
STOAS
STOAT
STOATS
STOB
STOBS
STOCCADO
STOCCADOS
STOCCATA
STOCCATAS
STOCK
STOCKADE
STOCKADED
STOCKADES
STOCKADING
STOCKED
STOCKFISH
STOCKFISHES
STOCKIER
STOCKIEST
STOCKILY
STOCKINET
STOCKINETS
STOCKING
STOCKINGS
STOCKISH
STOCKIST
STOCKISTS
STOCKLESS
STOCKMAN
STOCKMEN
STOCKPILE
STOCKPILED
STOCKPILES
STOCKPILING
STOCKPILINGS
STOCKS
STOCKTAKE
STOCKTAKES
STOCKWORK
STOCKWORKS
STOCKY
STOCKYARD
STOCKYARDS
STODGE
STODGED
STODGER
STODGERS
STODGES
STODGIER
STODGIEST
STODGILY
STODGING
STODGY
STOEP
STOEPS
STOGEY
STOGEYS
STOGIE
STOGIES
STOGY
STOIC
STOICAL
STOICALLY
STOICISM
STOICISMS
STOIT

STOITED
STOITER
STOITERED
STOITERING
STOITERS
STOITING
STOITS
STOKE
STOKED
STOKEHOLD
STOKEHOLDS
STOKER
STOKERS
STOKES
STOKING
STOLA
STOLAS
STOLE
STOLED
STOLEN
STOLES
STOLID
STOLIDER
STOLIDEST
STOLIDITIES
STOLIDITY
STOLIDLY
STOLN
STOLON
STOLONS
STOMA
STOMACH
STOMACHAL
STOMACHED
STOMACHER
STOMACHERS
STOMACHIC
STOMACHICS
STOMACHING
STOMACHS
STOMACHY
STOMATA
STOMATAL
STOMATIC
STOMODAEA
STOMODEA
STOMODEUM
STOMODEUMS
STOMP
STOMPED
STOMPING
STOMPS
STOND
STONDS
STONE
STONECHAT
STONECHATS
STONECROP
STONECROPS
STONED
STONEFISH
STONEFISHES
STONEHAND
STONEHANDS
STONELESS
STONEN
STONER
STONERN
STONERS
STONES

STONESHOT
STONESHOTS
STONEWALL
STONEWALLED
STONEWALLING
STONEWALLINGS
STONEWALLS
STONEWARE
STONEWARES
STONEWORK
STONEWORKS
STONEWORT
STONEWORTS
STONG
STONIED
STONIER
STONIES
STONIEST
STONILY
STONINESS
STONINESSES
STONING
STONINGS
STONK
STONKER
STONKERED
STONKERING
STONKERS
STONKS
STONN
STONNE
STONNED
STONNES
STONNING
STONNS
STONY
STONYING
STOOD
STOODEN
STOOGE
STOOGED
STOOGES
STOOGING
STOOK
STOOKED
STOOKER
STOOKERS
STOOKING
STOOKS
STOOL
STOOLBALL
STOOLBALLS
STOOLED
STOOLIE
STOOLIES
STOOLING
STOOLS
STOOP
STOOPE
STOOPED
STOOPER
STOOPERS
STOOPES
STOOPING
STOOPS
STOOR
STOORS
STOOSHIE
STOOSHIES
STOP

STOPE
STOPED
STOPES
STOPING
STOPINGS
STOPLESS
STOPPAGE
STOPPAGES
STOPPED
STOPPER
STOPPERED
STOPPERING
STOPPERS
STOPPING
STOPPINGS
STOPPLE
STOPPLED
STOPPLES
STOPPLING
STOPS
STORABLE
STORAGE
STORAGES
STORAX
STORAXES
STORE
STORED
STOREMAN
STOREMEN
STORER
STOREROOM
STOREROOMS
STORERS
STORES
STOREY
STOREYED
STOREYS
STORGE
STORGES
STORIATED
STORIED
STORIES
STORIETTE
STORIETTES
STORING
STORK
STORKS
STORM
STORMED
STORMFUL
STORMIER
STORMIEST
STORMILY
STORMING
STORMINGS
STORMLESS
STORMS
STORMY
STORNELLI
STORNELLO
STORY
STORYETTE
STORYETTES
STORYING
STORYINGS
STOT
STOTINKA
STOTINKI
STOTIOUS
STOTS

STOTTED
STOTTER
STOTTERED
STOTTERING
STOTTERS
STOTTING
STOUN
STOUND
STOUNDED
STOUNDING
STOUNDS
STOUNING
STOUNS
STOUP
STOUPS
STOUR
STOURIER
STOURIEST
STOURS
STOURY
STOUSH
STOUSHED
STOUSHES
STOUSHING
STOUT
STOUTEN
STOUTENED
STOUTENING
STOUTENS
STOUTER
STOUTEST
STOUTH
STOUTHRIE
STOUTHRIES
STOUTHS
STOUTISH
STOUTLY
STOUTNESS
STOUTNESSES
STOUTS
STOVAINE
STOVAINES
STOVE
STOVED
STOVEPIPE
STOVEPIPES
STOVER
STOVERS
STOVES
STOVIES
STOVING
STOVINGS
STOW
STOWAGE
STOWAGES
STOWAWAY
STOWAWAYS
STOWDOWN
STOWDOWNS
STOWED
STOWER
STOWERS
STOWING
STOWINGS
STOWLINS
STOWN
STOWND
STOWNDED
STOWNDING
STOWNDS

STOWNLINS
STOWRE
STOWRES
STOWS
STRABISM
STRABISMS
STRACK
STRAD
STRADDLE
STRADDLED
STRADDLES
STRADDLING
STRADIOT
STRADIOTS
STRADS
STRAE
STRAES
STRAFE
STRAFED
STRAFES
STRAFF
STRAFFED
STRAFFING
STRAFFS
STRAFING
STRAG
STRAGGLE
STRAGGLED
STRAGGLER
STRAGGLERS
STRAGGLES
STRAGGLIER
STRAGGLIEST
STRAGGLING
STRAGGLINGS
STRAGGLY
STRAGS
STRAICHT
STRAICHTER
STRAICHTEST
STRAIGHT
STRAIGHTED
STRAIGHTER
STRAIGHTEST
STRAIGHTING
STRAIGHTS
STRAIK
STRAIKED
STRAIKING
STRAIKS
STRAIN
STRAINED
STRAINER
STRAINERS
STRAINING
STRAININGS
STRAINS
STRAINT
STRAINTS
STRAIT
STRAITED
STRAITEN
STRAITENED
STRAITENING
STRAITENS
STRAITER
STRAITEST
STRAITING
STRAITLY
STRAITS

STRAK
STRAKE
STRAKES
STRAMAÇON
STRAMAÇONS
STRAMASH
STRAMASHED
STRAMASHES
STRAMASHING
STRAMAZON
STRAMAZONS
STRAMMEL
STRAMMELS
STRAMP
STRAMPED
STRAMPING
STRAMPS
STRAND
STRANDED
STRANDING
STRANDS
STRANGE
STRANGELY
STRANGER
STRANGERED
STRANGERING
STRANGERS
STRANGEST
STRANGLE
STRANGLED
STRANGLER
STRANGLERS
STRANGLES
STRANGLING
STRANGURIES
STRANGURY
STRAP
STRAPLESS
STRAPPADO
STRAPPADOED
STRAPPADOING
STRAPPADOS
STRAPPED
STRAPPER
STRAPPERS
STRAPPIER
STRAPPIEST
STRAPPING
STRAPPINGS
STRAPPY
STRAPS
STRAPWORT
STRAPWORTS
STRASS
STRASSES
STRATA
STRATAGEM
STRATAGEMS
STRATEGIC
STRATEGICS
STRATEGIES
STRATEGY
STRATH
STRATHS
STRATI
STRATIFIED
STRATIFIES
STRATIFY
STRATIFYING
STRATONIC

STRATOSE
STRATOUS
STRATUM
STRATUS
STRATUSES
STRAUCHT
STRAUCHTED
STRAUCHTER
STRAUCHTEST
STRAUCHTING
STRAUCHTS
STRAUGHT
STRAUGHTED
STRAUGHTER
STRAUGHTEST
STRAUGHTING
STRAUGHTS
STRAUNGE
STRAVAIG
STRAVAIGED
STRAVAIGING
STRAVAIGS
STRAW
STRAWED
STRAWEN
STRAWIEST
STRAWING
STRAWLESS
STRAWN
STRAWS
STRAWY
STRAY
STRAYED
STRAYER
STRAYERS
STRAYING
STRAYINGS
STRAYLING
STRAYLINGS
STRAYS
STREAK
STREAKED
STREAKER
STREAKERS
STREAKIER
STREAKIEST
STREAKILY
STREAKING
STREAKINGS
STREAKS
STREAKY
STREAM
STREAMED
STREAMER
STREAMERS
STREAMIER
STREAMIEST
STREAMING
STREAMINGS
STREAMLET
STREAMLETS
STREAMS
STREAMY
STREEK
STREEKED
STREEKING
STREEKS
STREEL
STREELED

STREELING
STREELS
STREET
STREETAGE
STREETAGES
STREETED
STREETFUL
STREETFULS
STREETIER
STREETIEST
STREETS
STREETWAY
STREETWAYS
STREETY
STREIGHT
STREIGNE
STREIGNED
STREIGNES
STREIGNING
STRELITZ
STRELITZES
STRELITZI
STRENE
STRENES
STRENGTH
STRENGTHS
STRENUITIES
STRENUITY
STRENUOUS
STREP
STREPENT
STREPS
STRESS
STRESSED
STRESSES
STRESSFUL
STRESSING
STRESSOR
STRESSORS
STRETCH
STRETCHED
STRETCHER
STRETCHERED
STRETCHERING
STRETCHERS
STRETCHES
STRETCHIER
STRETCHIEST
STRETCHING
STRETCHY
STRETTA
STRETTE
STRETTI
STRETTO
STREW
STREWAGE
STREWAGES
STREWED
STREWER
STREWERS
STREWING
STREWINGS
STREWMENT
STREWMENTS
STREWN
STREWS
STREWTH
STRIA
STRIAE
STRIATA

STRIATE
STRIATED
STRIATES
STRIATING
STRIATION
STRIATIONS
STRIATUM
STRIATUMS
STRIATURE
STRIATURES
STRICH
STRICHES
STRICKEN
STRICKLE
STRICKLED
STRICKLES
STRICKLING
STRICT
STRICTER
STRICTEST
STRICTISH
STRICTLY
STRICTURE
STRICTURES
STRID
STRIDDEN
STRIDDLE
STRIDDLED
STRIDDLES
STRIDDLING
STRIDE
STRIDENCE
STRIDENCES
STRIDENCIES
STRIDENCY
STRIDENT
STRIDES
STRIDING
STRIDLING
STRIDOR
STRIDORS
STRIDS
STRIFE
STRIFEFUL
STRIFES
STRIFT
STRIFTS
STRIG
STRIGA
STRIGAE
STRIGATE
STRIGGED
STRIGGING
STRIGIL
STRIGILS
STRIGINE
STRIGOSE
STRIGS
STRIKE
STRIKEOUT
STRIKEOUTS
STRIKER
STRIKERS
STRIKES
STRIKING
STRIKINGS
STRING
STRINGED
STRINGENT
STRINGER

STRINGERS
STRINGIER
STRINGIEST
STRINGILY
STRINGING
STRINGINGS
STRINGS
STRINGY
STRINKLE
STRINKLED
STRINKLES
STRINKLING
STRINKLINGS
STRIP
STRIPE
STRIPED
STRIPES
STRIPEY
STRIPIER
STRIPIEST
STRIPING
STRIPINGS
STRIPLING
STRIPLINGS
STRIPPED
STRIPPER
STRIPPERS
STRIPPING
STRIPPINGS
STRIPS
STRIPY
STRIVE
STRIVED
STRIVEN
STRIVER
STRIVERS
STRIVES
STRIVING
STRIVINGS
STROAM
STROAMED
STROAMING
STROAMS
STROBE
STROBES
STROBIC
STROBILA
STROBILAE
STROBILE
STROBILES
STROBILI
STROBILUS
STRODDLE
STRODDLED
STRODDLES
STRODDLING
STRODE
STRODLE
STRODLED
STRODLES
STRODLING
STROKE
STROKED
STROKEN
STROKER
STROKERS
STROKES
STROKING
STROKINGS
STROLL

STROLLED
STROLLER
STROLLERS
STROLLING
STROLLINGS
STROLLS
STROMA
STROMATA
STROMATIC
STROMB
STROMBS
STROMBUS
STROMBUSES
STROND
STRONDS
STRONG
STRONGARM
STRONGARMED
STRONGARMING
STRONGARMS
STRONGER
STRONGEST
STRONGISH
STRONGLY
STRONGMAN
STRONGMEN
STRONGYLE
STRONGYLES
STRONTIA
STRONTIAN
STRONTIANS
STRONTIAS
STRONTIUM
STRONTIUMS
STROOK
STROOKE
STROOKEN
STROOKES
STROP
STROPHE
STROPHES
STROPHIC
STROPPED
STROPPIER
STROPPIEST
STROPPING
STROPPY
STROPS
STROSSERS
STROUD
STROUDING
STROUDINGS
STROUDS
STROUP
STROUPS
STROUT
STROUTED
STROUTING
STROUTS
STROVE
STROW
STROWED
STROWER
STROWERS
STROWING
STROWINGS
STROWN
STROWS
STROY
STROYED

STROYING
STROYS
STRUCK
STRUCKEN
STRUCTURE
STRUCTURED
STRUCTURES
STRUCTURING
STRUDEL
STRUDELS
STRUGGLE
STRUGGLED
STRUGGLER
STRUGGLERS
STRUGGLES
STRUGGLING
STRUGGLINGS
STRUM
STRUMA
STRUMAE
STRUMATIC
STRUMITIS
STRUMITISES
STRUMMED
STRUMMEL
STRUMMELS
STRUMMING
STRUMOSE
STRUMOUS
STRUMPET
STRUMPETED
STRUMPETING
STRUMPETS
STRUMS
STRUNG
STRUNT
STRUNTED
STRUNTING
STRUNTS
STRUT
STRUTS
STRUTTED
STRUTTER
STRUTTERS
STRUTTING
STRUTTINGS
STRYCHNIA
STRYCHNIAS
STRYCHNIC
STRYFULL
STUB
STUBBED
STUBBIER
STUBBIES
STUBBIEST
STUBBING
STUBBLE
STUBBLED
STUBBLES
STUBBLIER
STUBBLIEST
STUBBLY
STUBBORN
STUBBORNED
STUBBORNING
STUBBORNS
STUBBY
STUBS
STUCCO
STUCCOED

STUCCOER
STUCCOERS
STUCCOING
STUCCOS
STUCK
STUCKS
STUD
STUDDED
STUDDEN
STUDDING
STUDDINGS
STUDDLE
STUDDLES
STUDENT
STUDENTRIES
STUDENTRY
STUDENTS
STUDIED
STUDIEDLY
STUDIER
STUDIERS
STUDIES
STUDIO
STUDIOS
STUDIOUS
STUDS
STUDWORK
STUDWORKS
STUDY
STUDYING
STUFF
STUFFED
STUFFER
STUFFERS
STUFFIER
STUFFIEST
STUFFILY
STUFFING
STUFFINGS
STUFFS
STUFFY
STUGGIER
STUGGIEST
STUGGY
STULL
STULLS
STULM
STULMS
STULTIFIED
STULTIFIES
STULTIFY
STULTIFYING
STUM
STUMBLE
STUMBLED
STUMBLER
STUMBLERS
STUMBLES
STUMBLIER
STUMBLIEST
STUMBLING
STUMBLY
STUMER
STUMERS
STUMM
STUMMED
STUMMEL
STUMMELS
STUMMING
STUMP

STUMPAGE
STUMPAGES
STUMPED
STUMPER
STUMPERS
STUMPIER
STUMPIES
STUMPIEST
STUMPILY
STUMPING
STUMPS
STUMPY
STUMS
STUN
STUNG
STUNK
STUNKARD
STUNNED
STUNNER
STUNNERS
STUNNING
STUNNINGS
STUNS
STUNSAIL
STUNSAILS
STUNT
STUNTED
STUNTING
STUNTMAN
STUNTMEN
STUNTS
STUPA
STUPAS
STUPE
STUPED
STUPEFIED
STUPEFIER
STUPEFIERS
STUPEFIES
STUPEFY
STUPEFYING
STUPENT
STUPES
STUPID
STUPIDER
STUPIDEST
STUPIDITIES
STUPIDITY
STUPIDLY
STUPIDS
STUPING
STUPOR
STUPOROUS
STUPORS
STUPRATE
STUPRATED
STUPRATES
STUPRATING
STURDIED
STURDIER
STURDIES
STURDIEST
STURDILY
STURDY
STURE
STURGEON
STURGEONS
STURMER
STURMERS
STURNINE

STURNOID
STURT
STURTED
STURTING
STURTS
STUSHIE
STUSHIES
STUTTER
STUTTERED
STUTTERER
STUTTERERS
STUTTERING
STUTTERINGS
STUTTERS
STY
STYE
STYED
STYES
STYING
STYLAR
STYLATE
STYLE
STYLED
STYLELESS
STYLES
STYLET
STYLETS
STYLI
STYLIFORM
STYLING
STYLISE
STYLISED
STYLISES
STYLISH
STYLISHLY
STYLISING
STYLIST
STYLISTIC
STYLISTICS
STYLISTS
STYLITE
STYLITES
STYLIZE
STYLIZED
STYLIZES
STYLIZING
STYLO
STYLOBATE
STYLOBATES
STYLOID
STYLOIDS
STYLOS
STYLUS
STYLUSES
STYME
STYMED
STYMES
STYMIE
STYMIED
STYMIEING
STYMIES
STYMING
STYMYING
STYPSIS
STYPSISES
STYPTIC
STYPTICAL
STYPTICS
STYRAX
STYRAXES

STYRE
STYRED
STYRENE
STYRENES
STYRES
STYRING
SUABILITIES
SUABILITY
SUABLE
SUASIBLE
SUASION
SUASIONS
SUASIVE
SUASIVELY
SUASORY
SUAVE
SUAVELY
SUAVER
SUAVEST
SUAVITIES
SUAVITY
SUB
SUBACID
SUBACRID
SUBACT
SUBACTION
SUBACTIONS
SUBACUTE
SUBADAR
SUBADARS
SUBADULT
SUBADULTS
SUBAERIAL
SUBAGENCIES
SUBAGENCY
SUBAGENT
SUBAGENTS
SUBAH
SUBAHDAR
SUBAHDARIES
SUBAHDARS
SUBAHDARY
SUBAHS
SUBAHSHIP
SUBAHSHIPS
SUBALPINE
SUBALTERN
SUBALTERNS
SUBAQUA
SUBARCTIC
SUBARID
SUBASTRAL
SUBATOM
SUBATOMIC
SUBATOMICS
SUBATOMS
SUBBASAL
SUBBASALS
SUBBED
SUBBING
SUBBINGS
SUBBRANCH
SUBBRANCHES
SUBBREED
SUBBREEDS
SUBCANTOR
SUBCANTORS

SUBCAUDAL
SUBCLASS
SUBCLASSES
SUBCLAUSE
SUBCLAUSES
SUBCOSTA
SUBCOSTAE
SUBCOSTAL
SUBCOSTALS
SUBDEACON
SUBDEACONS
SUBDEAN
SUBDEANS
SUBDEW
SUBDEWED
SUBDEWING
SUBDFWS
SUBDIVIDE
SUBDIVIDED
SUBDIVIDES
SUBDIVIDING
SUBDOLOUS
SUBDUABLE
SUBDUAL
SUBDUALS
SUBDUCE
SUBDUCED
SUBDUCES
SUBDUCING
SUBDUCT
SUBDUCTED
SUBDUCTING
SUBDUCTS
SUBDUE
SUBDUED
SUBDUEDLY
SUBDUER
SUBDUERS
SUBDUES
SUBDUING
SUBDUPLE
SUBEDAR
SUBEDARS
SUBEDIT
SUBEDITED
SUBEDITING
SUBEDITOR
SUBEDITORS
SUBEDITS
SUBENTIRE
SUBEQUAL
SUBER
SUBERATE
SUBERATES
SUBERECT
SUBEREOUS
SUBERIC
SUBERIN
SUBERINS
SUBERISE
SUBERISED
SUBERISES
SUBERISING
SUBERIZE
SUBERIZED
SUBERIZES
SUBERIZING
SUBEROSE
SUBEROUS
SUBERS

SUBFAMILIES
SUBFAMILY
SUBFEU
SUBFEUED
SUBFEUING
SUBFEUS
SUBFLOOR
SUBFLOORS
SUBFUSC
SUBFUSCS
SUBFUSK
SUBFUSKS
SUBGENERA
SUBGENUS
SUBGENUSES
SUBGRADE
SUBGRADES
SUBGROUP
SUBGROUPS
SUBHUMAN
SUBIMAGINES
SUBIMAGO
SUBIMAGOS
SUBINCISE
SUBINCISED
SUBINCISES
SUBINCISING
SUBITO
SUBJACENT
SUBJECT
SUBJECTED
SUBJECTING
SUBJECTS
SUBJOIN
SUBJOINED
SUBJOINING
SUBJOINS
SUBJUGATE
SUBJUGATED
SUBJUGATES
SUBJUGATING
SUBLATE
SUBLATED
SUBLATES
SUBLATING
SUBLATION
SUBLATIONS
SUBLEASE
SUBLEASED
SUBLEASES
SUBLEASING
SUBLESSEE
SUBLESSEES
SUBLESSOR
SUBLESSORS
SUBLET
SUBLETHAL
SUBLETS
SUBLETTER
SUBLETTERS
SUBLETTING
SUBLETTINGS
SUBLIMATE
SUBLIMATED
SUBLIMATES
SUBLIMATING
SUBLIME
SUBLIMED
SUBLIMELY
SUBLIMER

SUBLIMES
SUBLIMEST
SUBLIMING
SUBLIMINGS
SUBLIMISE
SUBLIMISED
SUBLIMISES
SUBLIMISING
SUBLIMITIES
SUBLIMITY
SUBLIMIZE
SUBLIMIZED
SUBLIMIZES
SUBLIMIZING
SUBLINEAR
SUBLUNAR
SUBLUNARIES
SUBLUNARS
SUBLUNARY
SUBLUNATE
SUBMAN
SUBMARINE
SUBMARINED
SUBMARINES
SUBMARINING
SUBMEN
SUBMENTAL
SUBMENTUM
SUBMENTUMS
SUBMERGE
SUBMERGED
SUBMERGES
SUBMERGING
SUBMERSE
SUBMERSED
SUBMERSES
SUBMERSING
SUBMICRON
SUBMICRONS
SUBMISS
SUBMISSLY
SUBMIT
SUBMITS
SUBMITTED
SUBMITTER
SUBMITTERS
SUBMITTING
SUBMITTINGS
SUBMUCOSA
SUBMUCOSAE
SUBMUCOUS
SUBNEURAL
SUBNIVEAL
SUBNIVEAN
SUBNORMAL
SUBNORMALS
SUBOCTAVE
SUBOCTAVES
SUBOCULAR
SUBOFFICE
SUBOFFICES
SUBORDER
SUBORDERS
SUBORN
SUBORNED
SUBORNER
SUBORNERS
SUBORNING
SUBORNS
SUBOVATE

SUBOXIDE
SUBOXIDES
SUBPHYLA
SUBPHYLUM
SUBPLOT
SUBPLOTS
SUBPOENA
SUBPOENAED
SUBPOENAING
SUBPOENAS
SUBPRIOR
SUBPRIORS
SUBREGION
SUBREGIONS
SUBROGATE
SUBROGATED
SUBROGATES
SUBROGATING
SUBS
SUBSACRAL
SUBSCRIBE
SUBSCRIBED
SUBSCRIBES
SUBSCRIBING
SUBSCRIBINGS
SUBSCRIPT
SUBSCRIPTS
SUBSEA
SUBSECIVE
SUBSELLIA
SUBSERE
SUBSERES
SUBSERIES
SUBSERVE
SUBSERVED
SUBSERVES
SUBSERVING
SUBSET
SUBSETS
SUBSHRUB
SUBSHRUBS
SUBSIDE
SUBSIDED
SUBSIDES
SUBSIDIES
SUBSIDING
SUBSIDISE
SUBSIDISED
SUBSIDISES
SUBSIDISING
SUBSIDIZE
SUBSIDIZED
SUBSIDIZES
SUBSIDIZING
SUBSIDY
SUBSIST
SUBSISTED
SUBSISTING
SUBSISTS
SUBSIZAR
SUBSIZARS
SUBSOIL
SUBSOILED
SUBSOILER
SUBSOILERS
SUBSOILING
SUBSOILINGS
SUBSOILS
SUBSOLAR
SUBSONIC

SUBSTAGE
SUBSTAGES
SUBSTANCE
SUBSTANCES
SUBSTRACT
SUBSTRACTED
SUBSTRACTING
SUBSTRACTS
SUBSTRATA
SUBSTRATE
SUBSTRATES
SUBSTRUCT
SUBSTRUCTED
SUBSTRUCTING
SUBSTRUCTS
SUBSTYLAR
SUBSTYLE
SUBSTYLES
SUBSULTUS
SUBSULTUSES
SUBSUME
SUBSUMED
SUBSUMES
SUBSUMING
SUBSYSTEM
SUBSYSTEMS
SUBTACK
SUBTACKS
SUBTEEN
SUBTEENS
SUBTENANT
SUBTENANTS
SUBTEND
SUBTENDED
SUBTENDING
SUBTENDS
SUBTENSE
SUBTENSES
SUBTEXT
SUBTEXTS
SUBTIL
SUBTILE
SUBTILELY
SUBTILER
SUBTILEST
SUBTILETIES
SUBTILETY
SUBTILISE
SUBTILISED
SUBTILISES
SUBTILISING
SUBTILIST
SUBTILISTS
SUBTILITIES
SUBTILITY
SUBTILIZE
SUBTILIZED
SUBTILIZES
SUBTILIZING
SUBTILLY
SUBTILTIES
SUBTILTY
SUBTITLE
SUBTITLED
SUBTITLES
SUBTITLING
SUBTLE
SUBTLER
SUBTLEST
SUBTLETIES

SUBTLETY
SUBTLIST
SUBTLISTS
SUBTLY
SUBTONIC
SUBTONICS
SUBTOPIA
SUBTOPIAN
SUBTOPIAS
SUBTOTAL
SUBTOTALLED
SUBTOTALLING
SUBTOTALS
SUBTRACT
SUBTRACTED
SUBTRACTING
SUBTRACTS
SUBTRIBE
SUBTRIBES
SUBTRIST
SUBTROPIC
SUBTROPICS
SUBTRUDE
SUBTRUDED
SUBTRUDES
SUBTRUDING
SUBTYPE
SUBTYPES
SUBUCULA
SUBUCULAS
SUBULATE
SUBUNGUAL
SUBUNIT
SUBUNITS
SUBURB
SUBURBAN
SUBURBANS
SUBURBIA
SUBURBIAS
SUBURBS
SUBURSINE
SUBVASSAL
SUBVASSALS
SUBVERSAL
SUBVERSALS
SUBVERSE
SUBVERSED
SUBVERSES
SUBVERSING
SUBVERST
SUBVERT
SUBVERTED
SUBVERTER
SUBVERTERS
SUBVERTING
SUBVERTS
SUBVIRAL
SUBWARDEN
SUBWARDENS
SUBWAY
SUBWAYS
SUBZERO
SUBZONAL
SUBZONE
SUBZONES
SUCCADE
SUCCADES
SUCCEED
SUCCEEDED
SUCCEEDER

SUCCEEDERS
SUCCEEDING
SUCCEEDS
SUCCENTOR
SUCCENTORS
SUCCÈS
SUCCESS
SUCCESSES
SUCCESSOR
SUCCESSORS
SUCCI
SUCCINATE
SUCCINATES
SUCCINCT
SUCCINCTER
SUCCINCTEST
SUCCINIC
SUCCINITE
SUCCINITES
SUCCINUM
SUCCINUMS
SUCCOR
SUCCORED
SUCCORIES
SUCCORING
SUCCORS
SUCCORY
SUCCOSE
SUCCOTASH
SUCCOTASHES
SUCCOUR
SUCCOURED
SUCCOURER
SUCCOURERS
SUCCOURING
SUCCOURS
SUCCOUS
SUCCUBA
SUCCUBAE
SUCCUBAS
SUCCUBI
SUCCUBINE
SUCCUBOUS
SUCCUBUS
SUCCUBUSES
SUCCULENT
SUCCULENTS
SUCCUMB
SUCCUMBED
SUCCUMBING
SUCCUMBS
SUCCURSAL
SUCCURSALS
SUCCUS
SUCCUSS
SUCCUSSED
SUCCUSSES
SUCCUSSING
SUCH
SUCHLIKE
SUCHNESS
SUCHNESSES
SUCHWISE
SUCK
SUCKED
SUCKEN
SUCKENER
SUCKENERS
SUCKENS
SUCKER

SUCKERED
SUCKERING
SUCKERS
SUCKET
SUCKETS
SUCKING
SUCKINGS
SUCKLE
SUCKLED
SUCKLER
SUCKLERS
SUCKLES
SUCKLING
SUCKLINGS
SUCKS
SUCRASE
SUCRASES
SUCRE
SUCRES
SUCRIER
SUCRIERS
SUCROSE
SUCROSES
SUCTION
SUCTIONS
SUCTORIAL
SUCTORIAN
SUCTORIANS
SUCURUJÚ
SUCURUJÚS
SUD
SUDAMEN
SUDAMINA
SUDAMINAL
SUDANIC
SUDARIES
SUDARIUM
SUDARIUMS
SUDARY
SUDATE
SUDATED
SUDATES
SUDATING
SUDATION
SUDATIONS
SUDATORIES
SUDATORY
SUDD
SUDDEN
SUDDENLY
SUDDENTIES
SUDDENTY
SUDDER
SUDDERS
SUDDS
SUDOR
SUDORAL
SUDORIFIC
SUDORIFICS
SUDOROUS
SUDORS
SUDS
SUDSER
SUDSERS
SUDSIER
SUDSIEST
SUDSY
SUE
SUEABLE
SUED

SUEDE
SUÈDE
SUEDED
SUÈDED
SUEDES
SUÈDES
SUEDETTE
SUEDETTES
SUEDING
SUÈDING
SUER
SUERS
SUES
SUET
SUETIER
SUETIEST
SUETS
SUETTY
SUETY
SUFFER
SUFFERED
SUFFERER
SUFFERERS
SUFFERING
SUFFERINGS
SUFFERS
SUFFETE
SUFFETES
SUFFICE
SUFFICED
SUFFICER
SUFFICERS
SUFFICES
SUFFICING
SUFFIX
SUFFIXAL
SUFFIXED
SUFFIXES
SUFFIXING
SUFFLATE
SUFFLATED
SUFFLATES
SUFFLATING
SUFFOCATE
SUFFOCATED
SUFFOCATES
SUFFOCATING
SUFFOCATINGS
SUFFRAGAN
SUFFRAGANS
SUFFRAGE
SUFFRAGES
SUFFUSE
SUFFUSED
SUFFUSES
SUFFUSING
SUFFUSION
SUFFUSIONS
SUGAR
SUGARED
SUGARIER
SUGARIEST
SUGARING
SUGARINGS
SUGARLESS
SUGARS
SUGARY
SUGGEST
SUGGESTED
SUGGESTER

SUGGESTERS
SUGGESTING
SUGGESTS
SUI
SUICIDAL
SUICIDE
SUICIDES
SUIDIAN
SUILLINE
SUING
SUINGS
SUINT
SUINTS
SUIT
SUITABLE
SUITABLY
SUITE
SUITED
SUITES
SUITING
SUITINGS
SUITOR
SUITORED
SUITORING
SUITORS
SUITRESS
SUITRESSES
SUITS
SUIVEZ
SUJEE
SUJEES
SUK
SUKH
SUKHS
SUKIYAKI
SUKIYAKIS
SUKS
SULCAL
SULCALISE
SULCALISED
SULCALISES
SULCALISING
SULCALIZE
SULCALIZED
SULCALIZES
SULCALIZING
SULCATE
SULCATED
SULCATION
SULCATIONS
SULCI
SULCUS
SULFA
SULFATE
SULFATED
SULFATES
SULFATING
SULFUR
SULFURED
SULFURING
SULFURS
SULK
SULKED
SULKIER
SULKIES
SULKIEST
SULKILY
SULKINESS
SULKINESSES
SULKING

SULKS
SULKY
SULLAGE
SULLAGES
SULLEN
SULLENER
SULLENEST
SULLENLY
SULLENS
SULLIED
SULLIES
SULLY
SULLYING
SULPHA
SULPHATE
SULPHATED
SULPHATES
SULPHATIC
SULPHATING
SULPHIDE
SULPHIDES
SULPHITE
SULPHITES
SULPHONE
SULPHONES
SULPHONIC
SULPHUR
SULPHURED
SULPHURET
SULPHURETS
SULPHURIC
SULPHURING
SULPHURS
SULPHURY
SULTAN
SULTANA
SULTANAS
SULTANATE
SULTANATES
SULTANESS
SULTANESSES
SULTANIC
SULTANS
SULTRIER
SULTRIEST
SULTRILY
SULTRY
SUM
SUMAC
SUMACH
SUMACHS
SUMACS
SUMATRA
SUMATRAS
SUMLESS
SUMMA
SUMMAE
SUMMAND
SUMMANDS
SUMMAR
SUMMARIES
SUMMARILY
SUMMARISE
SUMMARISED
SUMMARISES
SUMMARISING
SUMMARIST
SUMMARISTS
SUMMARIZE
SUMMARIZED

SUMMARIZES
SUMMARIZING
SUMMARY
SUMMAT
SUMMATE
SUMMATED
SUMMATES
SUMMATING
SUMMATION
SUMMATIONS
SUMMATIVE
SUMMATS
SUMMED
SUMMER
SUMMERED
SUMMERIER
SUMMERIEST
SUMMERING
SUMMERINGS
SUMMERLY
SUMMERS
SUMMERSET
SUMMERSETS
SUMMERSETTED
SUMMERSETTING
SUMMERY
SUMMING
SUMMINGS
SUMMIST
SUMMISTS
SUMMIT
SUMMITEER
SUMMITEERS
SUMMITRIES
SUMMITRY
SUMMITS
SUMMON
SUMMONED
SUMMONER
SUMMONERS
SUMMONING
SUMMONS
SUMMONSED
SUMMONSES
SUMMONSING
SUMO
SUMOS
SUMOTORI
SUMOTORIS
SUMP
SUMPH
SUMPHISH
SUMPHS
SUMPIT
SUMPITAN
SUMPITANS
SUMPITS
SUMPS
SUMPSIMUS
SUMPSIMUSES
SUMPTER
SUMPTERS
SUMPTUARY
SUMPTUOUS
SUMS
SUN
SUNBATH
SUNBATHE
SUNBATHED
SUNBATHER

SUNBATHERS	SUNN	SUPERFINE	SUPPING	SURAS
SUNBATHES	SUNNED	SUPERFLUX	SUPPLANT	SURAT
SUNBATHING	SUNNIER	SUPERFLUXES	SUPPLANTED	SURATS
SUNBATHINGS	SUNNIEST	SUPERFUSE	SUPPLANTING	SURBAHAR
SUNBATHS	SUNNILY	SUPERFUSED	SUPPLANTS	SURBAHARS
SUNBEAM	SUNNINESS	SUPERFUSES	SUPPLE	SURBASE
SUNBEAMED	SUNNINESSES	SUPERFUSING	SUPPLED	SURBASED
SUNBEAMS	SUNNING	SUPERGLUE	SUPPLER	SURBASES
SUNBEAMY	SUNNS	SUPERGLUES	SUPPLES	SURBATE
SUNBED	SUNNY	SUPERHEAT	SUPPLEST	SURBATED
SUNBEDS	SUNPROOF	SUPERHEATED	SUPPLIAL	SURBATES
SUNBELT	SUNRAY	SUPERHEATING	SUPPLIALS	SURBATING
SUNBELTS	SUNRAYS	SUPERHEATS	SUPPLIANT	SURBED
SUNBLOCK	SUNRISE	SUPERHET	SUPPLIANTS	SURBEDDED
SUNBLOCKS	SUNRISES	SUPERHIVE	SUPPLICAT	SURBEDDING
SUNBOW	SUNRISING	SUPERHIVES	SUPPLICATS	SURBEDS
SUNBOWS	SUNRISINGS	SUPERING	SUPPLIED	SURBET
SUNBRIGHT	SUNS	SUPERIOR	SUPPLIER	SURCEASE
SUNBURN	SUNSCREEN	SUPERIORS	SUPPLIERS	SURCEASED
SUNBURNED	SUNSCREENS	SUPERMAN	SUPPLIES	SURCEASES
SUNBURNING	SUNSET	SUPERMART	SUPPLING	SURCEASING
SUNBURNS	SUNSETS	SUPERMARTS	SUPPLY	SURCHARGE
SUNBURNT	SUNSHINE	SUPERMEN	SUPPLYING	SURCHARGED
SUNBURST	SUNSHINES	SUPERNAL	SUPPORT	SURCHARGES
SUNBURSTS	SUNSHINY	SUPERNOVA	SUPPORTED	SURCHARGING
SUNDAE	SUNSPOT	SUPERNOVAE	SUPPORTER	SURCINGLE
SUNDAES	SUNSPOTS	SUPERNOVAS	SUPPORTERS	SURCINGLED
SUNDARI	SUNSTONE	SUPERPLUS	SUPPORTING	SURCINGLES
SUNDARIS	SUNSTONES	SUPERPLUSES	SUPPORTINGS	SURCINGLING
SUNDER	SUNSTROKE	SUPERPOSE	SUPPORTS	SURCOAT
SUNDERED	SUNSTROKES	SUPERPOSED	SUPPOSAL	SURCOATS
SUNDERER	SUNSTRUCK	SUPERPOSES	SUPPOSALS	SURCULI
SUNDERERS	SUNSUIT	SUPERPOSING	SUPPOSE	SURCULOSE
SUNDERING	SUNSUITS	SUPERS	SUPPOSED	SURCULUS
SUNDERINGS	SUNTAN	SUPERSALT	SUPPOSER	SURCULUSES
SUNDERS	SUNTANNED	SUPERSALTS	SUPPOSERS	SURD
SUNDIAL	SUNTANS	SUPERSEDE	SUPPOSES	SURDITIES
SUNDIALS	SUNTRAP	SUPERSEDED	SUPPOSING	SURDITY
SUNDOWN	SUNTRAPS	SUPERSEDES	SUPPOSINGS	SURDS
SUNDOWNS	SUNWARD	SUPERSEDING	SUPPRESS	SURE
SUNDRA	SUNWARDS	SUPERSTAR	SUPPRESSED	SURED
SUNDRAS	SUNWISE	SUPERSTARS	SUPPRESSES	SURELY
SUNDRI	SUP	SUPERTAX	SUPPRESSING	SURENESS
SUNDRIES	SUPAWN	SUPERTAXES	SUPPURATE	SURENESSES
SUNDRIS	SUPAWNS	SUPERVENE	SUPPURATED	SURER
SUNDRY	SUPER	SUPERVENED	SUPPURATES	SURES
SUNFAST	SUPERABLE	SUPERVENES	SUPPURATING	SUREST
SUNFLOWER	SUPERABLY	SUPERVENING	SUPREMACIES	SURETIED
SUNFLOWERS	SUPERADD	SUPERVISE	SUPREMACY	SURETIES
SUNG	SUPERADDED	SUPERVISED	SUPRÊME	SURETY
SUNGAR	SUPERADDING	SUPERVISES	SUPREME	SURETYING
SUNGARS	SUPERADDS	SUPERVISING	SUPREMELY	SURF
SUNGLASS	SUPERATE	SUPINATE	SUPREMER	SURFACE
SUNGLASSES	SUPERATED	SUPINATED	SUPREMES	SURFACED
SUNGLOW	SUPERATES	SUPINATES	SUPRÊMES	SURFACER
SUNGLOWS	SUPERATING	SUPINATING	SUPREMEST	SURFACERS
SUNHAT	SUPERB	SUPINATOR	SUPREMITIES	SURFACES
SUNHATS	SUPERBER	SUPINATORS	SUPREMITY	SURFACING
SUNK	SUPERBEST	SUPINE	SUPREMO	SURFACINGS
SUNKEN	SUPERBITIES	SUPINELY	SUPREMOS	SURFBOARD
SUNKET	SUPERBITY	SUPINES	SUPS	SURFBOARDS
SUNKETS	SUPERBLY	SUPPAWN	SUQ	SURFED
SUNKIE	SUPERCOLD	SUPPAWNS	SUQS	SURFEIT
SUNKIES	SUPERCOOL	SUPPEAGO	SUR	SURFEITED
SUNKS	SUPERCOOLED	SUPPEAGOES	SURA	SURFEITER
SUNLESS	SUPERCOOLING	SUPPED	SURAH	SURFEITERS
SUNLIGHT	SUPERCOOLS	SUPPER	SURAHS	SURFEITING
SUNLIGHTS	SUPERED	SUPPERED	SURAL	SURFEITINGS
SUNLIKE	SUPERETTE	SUPPERING	SURANCE	SURFEITS
SUNLIT	SUPERETTES	SUPPERS	SURANCES	SURFER

SURFERS
SURFICIAL
SURFIER
SURFIEST
SURFING
SURFINGS
SURFMAN
SURFMEN
SURFS
SURFY
SURGE
SURGED
SURGEFUL
SURGELESS
SURGENT
SURGEON
SURGEONCIES
SURGEONCY
SURGEONS
SURGERIES
SURGERY
SURGES
SURGICAL
SURGIER
SURGIEST
SURGING
SURGINGS
SURGY
SURICATE
SURICATES
SURING
SURLIER
SURLIEST
SURLILY
SURLINESS
SURLINESSES
SURLOIN
SURLOINS
SURLY
SURMASTER
SURMASTERS
SURMISAL
SURMISALS
SURMISE
SURMISED
SURMISER
SURMISERS
SURMISES
SURMISING
SURMISINGS
SURMOUNT
SURMOUNTED
SURMOUNTING
SURMOUNTINGS
SURMOUNTS
SURMULLET
SURMULLETS
SURNAME
SURNAMED
SURNAMES
SURNAMING
SURPASS
SURPASSED
SURPASSES
SURPASSING
SURPLICE
SURPLICED
SURPLICES
SURPLUS
SURPLUSES

SURPRISAL
SURPRISALS
SURPRISE
SURPRISED
SURPRISER
SURPRISERS
SURPRISES
SURPRISING
SURPRISINGS
SURQUEDIES
SURQUEDRIES
SURQUEDRY
SURQUEDY
SURRA
SURRAS
SURREAL
SURREBUT
SURREBUTS
SURREBUTTED
SURREBUTTING
SURREINED
SURREJOIN
SURREJOINED
SURREJOINING
SURREJOINS
SURRENDER
SURRENDERED
SURRENDERER
SURRENDERING
SURRENDERS
SURRENDRIES
SURRENDRY
SURREY
SURREYS
SURROGACIES
SURROGACY
SURROGATE
SURROGATES
SURROUND
SURROUNDED
SURROUNDING
SURROUNDINGS
SURROUNDS
SURROYAL
SURROYALS
SURTAX
SURTAXED
SURTAXES
SURTAXING
SURTITLE
SURTITLES
SURTOUT
SURTOUTS
SURUCUCU
SURUCUCUS
SURVEILLE
SURVEILLED
SURVEILLES
SURVEILLING
SURVEW
SURVEWE
SURVEWED
SURVEWES
SURVEWING
SURVEWS
SURVEY
SURVEYAL
SURVEYALS
SURVEYED
SURVEYING
SURVEYINGS

SURVEYOR
SURVEYORS
SURVEYS
SURVIEW
SURVIEWED
SURVIEWING
SURVIEWS
SURVIVAL
SURVIVALS
SURVIVE
SURVIVED
SURVIVES
SURVIVING
SURVIVOR
SURVIVORS
SUS
SUSCEPTOR
SUSCEPTORS
SUSCITATE
SUSCITATED
SUSCITATES
SUSCITATING
SUSES
SUSHI
SUSHIS
SUSLIK
SUSLIKS
SUSPECT
SUSPECTED
SUSPECTING
SUSPECTS
SUSPENCE
SUSPEND
SUSPENDED
SUSPENDER
SUSPENDERS
SUSPENDING
SUSPENDS
SUSPENS
SUSPENSE
SUSPENSES
SUSPENSOR
SUSPENSORS
SUSPICION
SUSPICIONED
SUSPICIONING
SUSPICIONS
SUSPIRE
SUSPIRED
SUSPIRES
SUSPIRING
SUSS
SUSSARARA
SUSSARARAS
SUSSED
SUSSES
SUSSING
SUSTAIN
SUSTAINED
SUSTAINER
SUSTAINERS
SUSTAINING
SUSTAININGS
SUSTAINS
SUSTINENT
SUSURRANT
SUSURRATE
SUSURRATED
SUSURRATES
SUSURRATING

SUSURRUS
SUSURRUSES
SUTILE
SUTLER
SUTLERIES
SUTLERS
SUTLERY
SUTOR
SUTORIAL
SUTORIAN
SUTORS
SUTRA
SUTRAS
SUTTEE
SUTTEEISM
SUTTEEISMS
SUTTEES
SUTTLE
SUTTLED
SUTTLES
SUTTLETIE
SUTTLETIES
SUTTLING
SUTTLY
SUTURAL
SUTURALLY
SUTURE
SUTURED
SUTURES
SUTURING
SUVERSED
SUZERAIN
SUZERAINS
SVASTIKA
SVASTIKAS
SVELTE
SVELTER
SVELTEST
SWAB
SWABBED
SWABBER
SWABBERS
SWABBING
SWABS
SWACK
SWAD
SWADDIES
SWADDLE
SWADDLED
SWADDLER
SWADDLERS
SWADDLES
SWADDLING
SWADDY
SWADS
SWAG
SWAGE
SWAGED
SWAGES
SWAGGED
SWAGGER
SWAGGERED
SWAGGERER
SWAGGERERS
SWAGGERING
SWAGGERINGS
SWAGGERS
SWAGGIE
SWAGGIES
SWAGGING

SWAGING
SWAGMAN
SWAGMEN
SWAGS
SWAGSHOP
SWAGSHOPS
SWAGSMAN
SWAGSMEN
SWAIN
SWAINING
SWAININGS
SWAINISH
SWAINS
SWALE
SWALED
SWALES
SWALIER
SWALIEST
SWALING
SWALINGS
SWALLET
SWALLETS
SWALLOW
SWALLOWED
SWALLOWER
SWALLOWERS
SWALLOWING
SWALLOWS
SWALY
SWAM
SWAMI
SWAMIS
SWAMP
SWAMPED
SWAMPER
SWAMPERS
SWAMPIER
SWAMPIEST
SWAMPING
SWAMPLAND
SWAMPLANDS
SWAMPS
SWAMPY
SWAN
SWANG
SWANHERD
SWANHERDS
SWANK
SWANKED
SWANKER
SWANKERS
SWANKEST
SWANKEY
SWANKEYS
SWANKIER
SWANKIES
SWANKIEST
SWANKING
SWANKPOT
SWANKPOTS
SWANKS
SWANKY
SWANLIKE
SWANNERIES
SWANNERY
SWANNIER
SWANNIEST
SWANNY
SWANS
SWANSDOWN

SWANSDOWNS
SWAP
SWAPPED
SWAPPER
SWAPPERS
SWAPPING
SWAPPINGS
SWAPS
SWAPT
SWARAJ
SWARAJES
SWARAJISM
SWARAJISMS
SWARAJIST
SWARAJISTS
SWARD
SWARDED
SWARDIER
SWARDIEST
SWARDING
SWARDS
SWARDY
SWARE
SWARF
SWARFED
SWARFING
SWARFS
SWARM
SWARMED
SWARMER
SWARMERS
SWARMING
SWARMINGS
SWARMS
SWART
SWARTH
SWARTHIER
SWARTHIEST
SWARTHS
SWARTHY
SWARTIER
SWARTIEST
SWARTNESS
SWARTNESSES
SWARTY
SWARVE
SWARVED
SWARVES
SWARVING
SWASH
SWASHED
SWASHER
SWASHERS
SWASHES
SWASHIER
SWASHIEST
SWASHING
SWASHINGS
SWASHWORK
SWASHWORKS
SWASHY
SWASTIKA
SWASTIKAS
SWAT
SWATCH
SWATCHES
SWATH
SWATHE
SWATHED
SWATHES

SWATHIER
SWATHIEST
SWATHING
SWATHS
SWATHY
SWATS
SWATTED
SWATTER
SWATTERED
SWATTERING
SWATTERS
SWATTING
SWATTINGS
SWAY
SWAYBACK
SWAYBACKS
SWAYED
SWAYER
SWAYERS
SWAYING
SWAYINGS
SWAYL
SWAYLED
SWAYLING
SWAYLINGS
SWAYLS
SWAYS
SWAZZLE
SWAZZLES
SWEAL
SWEALED
SWEALING
SWEALINGS
SWEALS
SWEAR
SWEARD
SWEARDS
SWEARER
SWEARERS
SWEARING
SWEARINGS
SWEARS
SWEAT
SWEATED
SWEATER
SWEATERS
SWEATIER
SWEATIEST
SWEATING
SWEATINGS
SWEATS
SWEATY
SWEDE
SWEDES
SWEE
SWEED
SWEEING
SWEEL
SWEELED
SWEELING
SWEELS
SWEENEY
SWEENEYS
SWEENIES
SWEENY
SWEEP
SWEEPBACK
SWEEPBACKS
SWEEPER
SWEEPERS

SWEEPIER
SWEEPIEST
SWEEPING
SWEEPINGS
SWEEPS
SWEEPY
SWEER
SWEERED
SWEERT
SWEES
SWEET
SWEETED
SWEETEN
SWEETENED
SWEETENER
SWEETENERS
SWEETENING
SWEETENINGS
SWEETENS
SWEETER
SWEETEST
SWEETFISH
SWEETFISHES
SWEETIE
SWEETIES
SWEETING
SWEETINGS
SWEETISH
SWEETLY
SWEETMEAL
SWEETMEAT
SWEETMEATS
SWEETNESS
SWEETNESSES
SWEETPEA
SWEETPEAS
SWEETS
SWEETWOOD
SWEETWOODS
SWEETY
SWEIR
SWEIRNESS
SWEIRNESSES
SWEIRT
SWELCHIE
SWELCHIES
SWELL
SWELLDOM
SWELLDOMS
SWELLED
SWELLER
SWELLERS
SWELLEST
SWELLING
SWELLINGS
SWELLISH
SWELLS
SWELT
SWELTED
SWELTER
SWELTERED
SWELTERING
SWELTERINGS
SWELTERS
SWELTING
SWELTRIER
SWELTRIEST
SWELTRY
SWELTS
SWEPT

SWEPTBACK
SWEPTWING
SWERF
SWERFED
SWERFING
SWERFS
SWERVE
SWERVED
SWERVER
SWERVERS
SWERVES
SWERVING
SWERVINGS
SWEVEN
SWEVENS
SWIDDEN
SWIDDENS
SWIES
SWIFT
SWIFTED
SWIFTER
SWIFTERS
SWIFTEST
SWIFTING
SWIFTLET
SWIFTLETS
SWIFTLY
SWIFTNESS
SWIFTNESSES
SWIFTS
SWIG
SWIGGED
SWIGGER
SWIGGERS
SWIGGING
SWIGS
SWILL
SWILLED
SWILLER
SWILLERS
SWILLING
SWILLINGS
SWILLS
SWIM
SWIMMABLE
SWIMMER
SWIMMERET
SWIMMERETS
SWIMMERS
SWIMMIER
SWIMMIEST
SWIMMING
SWIMMINGS
SWIMMY
SWIMS
SWIMSUIT
SWIMSUITS
SWIMWEAR
SWIMWEARS
SWINDGE
SWINDGED
SWINDGES
SWINDGING
SWINDLE
SWINDLED
SWINDLER
SWINDLERS
SWINDLES
SWINDLING
SWINDLINGS

SWINE
SWINEHERD
SWINEHERDS
SWINEHOOD
SWINEHOODS
SWINERIES
SWINERY
SWING
SWINGBOAT
SWINGBOATS
SWINGE
SWINGED
SWINGEING
SWINGER
SWINGERS
SWINGES
SWINGING
SWINGINGS
SWINGISM
SWINGISMS
SWINGLE
SWINGLED
SWINGLES
SWINGLING
SWINGLINGS
SWINGS
SWINGTREE
SWINGTREES
SWINISH
SWINISHLY
SWINK
SWINKED
SWINKING
SWINKS
SWIPE
SWIPED
SWIPER
SWIPERS
SWIPES
SWIPEY
SWIPIER
SWIPIEST
SWIPING
SWIPPLE
SWIPPLES
SWIRE
SWIRES
SWIRL
SWIRLED
SWIRLIER
SWIRLIEST
SWIRLING
SWIRLS
SWIRLY
SWISH
SWISHED
SWISHER
SWISHERS
SWISHES
SWISHEST
SWISHIER
SWISHIEST
SWISHING
SWISHINGS
SWISHY
SWISSING
SWISSINGS
SWITCH
SWITCHED
SWITCHEL

SWITCHELS
SWITCHES
SWITCHING
SWITCHINGS
SWITCHMAN
SWITCHMEN
SWITCHY
SWITH
SWITHER
SWITHERED
SWITHERING
SWITHERS
SWITS
SWITSES
SWIVEL
SWIVELLED
SWIVELLING
SWIVELS
SWIVET
SWIVETS
SWIZ
SWIZZES
SWIZZLE
SWIZZLED
SWIZZLES
SWIZZLING
SWOB
SWOBBED
SWOBBER
SWOBBERS
SWOBBING
SWODS
SWOLLEN
SWOLN
SWONE
SWONES
SWOON
SWOONED
SWOONING
SWOONINGS
SWOONS
SWOOP
SWOOPED
SWOOPING
SWOOPS
SWOOSH
SWOOSHED
SWOOSHES
SWOOSHING
SWOP
SWOPPED
SWOPPER
SWOPPERS
SWOPPING
SWOPPINGS
SWOPS
SWOPT
SWORD
SWORDED
SWORDER
SWORDERS
SWORDFISH
SWORDFISHES
SWORDING
SWORDLESS
SWORDMAN
SWORDMEN
SWORDPLAY
SWORDPLAYS
SWORDS

SWORDSMAN
SWORDSMEN
SWORE
SWORN
SWOT
SWOTS
SWOTTED
SWOTTER
SWOTTERS
SWOTTING
SWOTTINGS
SWOUN
SWOUND
SWOUNDED
SWOUNDING
SWOUNDS
SWOUNE
SWOUNED
SWOUNES
SWOUNING
SWOUNS
SWOWND
SWOWNDS
SWOWNE
SWOWNES
SWOZZLE
SWOZZLES
SWUM
SWUNG
SWY
SYBARITE
SYBARITES
SYBARITIC
SYBBE
SYBBES
SYBIL
SYBILS
SYBO
SYBOE
SYBOES
SYBOTIC
SYBOTISM
SYBOTISMS
SYBOW
SYBOWS
SYCAMINE
SYCAMINES
SYCAMORE
SYCAMORES
SYCE
SYCEE
SYCEES
SYCES
SYCOMORE
SYCOMORES
SYCONIUM
SYCONIUMS
SYCOPHANT
SYCOPHANTS
SYCOSES
SYCOSIS
SYE
SYED
SYEING
SYEN
SYENITE
SYENITES
SYENITIC
SYENS
SYES

SYKE
SYKER
SYKES
SYLLABARIES
SYLLABARY
SYLLABI
SYLLABIC
SYLLABICS
SYLLABIFIED
SYLLABIFIES
SYLLABIFY
SYLLABIFYING
SYLLABISE
SYLLABISED
SYLLABISES
SYLLABISING
SYLLABISM
SYLLABISMS
SYLLABIZE
SYLLABIZED
SYLLABIZES
SYLLABIZING
SYLLABLE
SYLLABLED
SYLLABLES
SYLLABLING
SYLLABUB
SYLLABUBS
SYLLABUS
SYLLABUSES
SYLLEPSES
SYLLEPSIS
SYLLEPTIC
SYLLOGISE
SYLLOGISED
SYLLOGISES
SYLLOGISING
SYLLOGISM
SYLLOGISMS
SYLLOGIZE
SYLLOGIZED
SYLLOGIZES
SYLLOGIZING
SYLPH
SYLPHID
SYLPHIDE
SYLPHIDES
SYLPHIDS
SYLPHINE
SYLPHISH
SYLPHS
SYLVA
SYLVAE
SYLVAN
SYLVANER
SYLVANERS
SYLVANITE
SYLVANITES
SYLVANS
SYLVAS
SYLVATIC
SYLVIA
SYLVIAS
SYLVIINE
SYLVINE
SYLVINES
SYLVINITE
SYLVINITES
SYLVITE
SYLVITES

SYMAR
SYMARS
SYMBION
SYMBIONS
SYMBIONT
SYMBIONTS
SYMBIOSES
SYMBIOSIS
SYMBIOTIC
SYMBOL
SYMBOLE
SYMBOLES
SYMBOLIC
SYMBOLICS
SYMBOLISE
SYMBOLISED
SYMBOLISES
SYMBOLISING
SYMBOLISM
SYMBOLISMS
SYMBOLIST
SYMBOLISTS
SYMBOLIZE
SYMBOLIZED
SYMBOLIZES
SYMBOLIZING
SYMBOLLED
SYMBOLLING
SYMBOLOGIES
SYMBOLOGY
SYMBOLS
SYMITAR
SYMITARE
SYMITARES
SYMITARS
SYMMETRAL
SYMMETRIC
SYMMETRIES
SYMMETRY
SYMPATHIES
SYMPATHIN
SYMPATHINS
SYMPATHY
SYMPHILE
SYMPHILES
SYMPHILIES
SYMPHILY
SYMPHONIC
SYMPHONIES
SYMPHONY
SYMPHYSES
SYMPHYSIS
SYMPHYTIC
SYMPLOCE
SYMPLOCES
SYMPODIA
SYMPODIAL
SYMPODIUM
SYMPOSIA
SYMPOSIAC
SYMPOSIAL
SYMPOSIUM
SYMPTOM
SYMPTOMS
SYMPTOSES
SYMPTOSIS
SYMPTOTIC
SYNAGOGAL
SYNAGOGUE
SYNAGOGUES

SYNANDRIA
SYNANGIA
SYNANGIUM
SYNANGIUMS
SYNANTHIC
SYNANTHIES
SYNANTHY
SYNAPHEA
SYNAPHEAS
SYNAPHEIA
SYNAPHEIAS
SYNAPSE
SYNAPSES
SYNAPSIS
SYNAPTASE
SYNAPTASES
SYNAPTE
SYNAPTES
SYNAPTIC
SYNARCHIES
SYNARCHY
SYNASTRIES
SYNASTRY
SYNAXES
SYNAXIS
SYNC
SYNCARP
SYNCARPIES
SYNCARPS
SYNCARPY
SYNCED
SYNCH
SYNCHED
SYNCHING
SYNCHRONIES
SYNCHRONY
SYNCHS
SYNCHYSES
SYNCHYSIS
SYNCING
SYNCLINAL
SYNCLINALS
SYNCLINE
SYNCLINES
SYNCOPAL
SYNCOPATE
SYNCOPATED
SYNCOPATES
SYNCOPATING
SYNCOPE
SYNCOPES
SYNCOPIC
SYNCOPTIC
SYNCRETIC
SYNCS
SYNCYTIA
SYNCYTIAL
SYNCYTIUM
SYNCYTIUMS
SYND
SYNDACTYL
SYNDED
SYNDESES
SYNDESIS
SYNDET
SYNDETIC
SYNDETS
SYNDIC
SYNDICAL
SYNDICATE

SYNDICATED
SYNDICATES
SYNDICATING
SYNDICS
SYNDING
SYNDINGS
SYNDROME
SYNDROMES
SYNDROMIC
SYNDS
SYNE
SYNECHIA
SYNECHIAS
SYNECTIC
SYNECTICS
SYNED
SYNEDRIA
SYNEDRIAL
SYNEDRION
SYNEDRIUM
SYNERESES
SYNERESIS
SYNERGIC
SYNERGID
SYNERGIDS
SYNERGIES
SYNERGISE
SYNERGISED
SYNERGISES
SYNERGISING
SYNERGISM
SYNERGISMS
SYNERGIST
SYNERGISTS
SYNERGIZE
SYNERGIZED
SYNERGIZES
SYNERGIZING
SYNERGY
SYNES

SYNESES
SYNESIS
SYNFUEL
SYNFUELS
SYNGAMIC
SYNGAMIES
SYNGAMOUS
SYNGAMY
SYNGENEIC
SYNGRAPH
SYNGRAPHS
SYNING
SYNIZESES
SYNIZESIS
SYNOD
SYNODAL
SYNODALS
SYNODIC
SYNODICAL
SYNODS
SYNODSMAN
SYNODSMEN
SYNOECETE
SYNOECETES
SYNOECISE
SYNOECISED
SYNOECISES
SYNOECISING
SYNOECISM
SYNOECISMS
SYNOECIZE
SYNOECIZED
SYNOECIZES
SYNOECIZING
SYNOEKETE
SYNOEKETES
SYNOICOUS
SYNONYM
SYNONYMIC
SYNONYMIES

SYNONYMS
SYNONYMY
SYNOPSES
SYNOPSIS
SYNOPSISE
SYNOPSISED
SYNOPSISES
SYNOPSISING
SYNOPSIZE
SYNOPSIZED
SYNOPSIZES
SYNOPSIZING
SYNOPTIC
SYNOPTIST
SYNOPTISTS
SYNOVIA
SYNOVIAL
SYNOVIAS
SYNOVITIC
SYNOVITIS
SYNOVITISES
SYNROC
SYNROCS
SYNTACTIC
SYNTAGMA
SYNTAGMATA
SYNTAN
SYNTANS
SYNTAX
SYNTAXES
SYNTECTIC
SYNTEXIS
SYNTEXISES
SYNTHESES
SYNTHESIS
SYNTHETIC
SYNTHETICS
SYNTONIC
SYNTONIES
SYNTONIN

SYNTONINS
SYNTONISE
SYNTONISED
SYNTONISES
SYNTONISING
SYNTONIZE
SYNTONIZED
SYNTONIZES
SYNTONIZING
SYNTONOUS
SYNTONY
SYPE
SYPED
SYPES
SYPHILIS
SYPHILISE
SYPHILISED
SYPHILISES
SYPHILISING
SYPHILIZE
SYPHILIZED
SYPHILIZES
SYPHILIZING
SYPHILOID
SYPHILOMA
SYPHILOMAS
SYPHON
SYPHONED
SYPHONING
SYPHONS
SYPING
SYREN
SYRENS
SYRINGA
SYRINGAS
SYRINGE
SYRINGEAL
SYRINGED
SYRINGES
SYRINGING

SYRINX
SYRINXES
SYRLYE
SYRPHID
SYRPHIDS
SYRTES
SYRTIS
SYRUP
SYRUPED
SYRUPING
SYRUPS
SYRUPY
SYSSITIA
SYSSITIAS
SYSTALTIC
SYSTEM
SYSTEMED
SYSTEMIC
SYSTEMISE
SYSTEMISED
SYSTEMISES
SYSTEMISING
SYSTEMIZE
SYSTEMIZED
SYSTEMIZES
SYSTEMIZING
SYSTEMS
SYSTOLE
SYSTOLES
SYSTOLIC
SYSTYLE
SYSTYLES
SYTHE
SYTHES
SYVER
SYVERS
SYZYGIAL
SYZYGIES
SYZYGY

T

TA
TAAL
TAALS
TAB
TABANID
TABANIDS
TABARD
TABARDS
TABARET
TABARETS
TABASHEER
TABASHEERS
TABASHIR
TABASHIRS
TABBED
TABBIED
TABBIES
TABBINET
TABBINETS
TABBING
TABBOULEH
TABBOULEHS
TABBY
TABBYHOOD
TABBYHOODS
TABBYING
TABEFIED
TABEFIES
TABEFY
TABEFYING
TABELLION
TABELLIONS
TABERDAR
TABERDARS
TABES
TABESCENT
TABETIC
TABID
TABINET
TABINETS
TABLA
TABLAS
TABLATURE
TABLATURES
TABLE
TABLEAU
TABLEAUX
TABLED
TABLEFUL
TABLEFULS
TABLELAND
TABLELANDS
TABLES
TABLET
TABLETED
TABLETING
TABLETS
TABLEWISE
TABLING
TABLINGS
TABLOID
TABLOIDS
TABOGGAN

TABOGGANED
TABOGGANING
TABOGGANS
TABOO
TABOOED
TABOOING
TABOOS
TABOR
TABORED
TABORER
TABORERS
TABORET
TABORETS
TABORIN
TABORING
TABORINS
TABORS
TABOUR
TABOURED
TABOURET
TABOURETS
TABOURIN
TABOURING
TABOURINS
TABOURS
TABRERE
TABRERES
TABRET
TABRETS
TABS
TABU
TABUED
TABUING
TABULA
TABULAE
TABULAR
TABULARLY
TABULATE
TABULATED
TABULATES
TABULATING
TABULATOR
TABULATORS
TABUN
TABUNS
TABUS
TACAHOUT
TACAHOUTS
TACAMAHAC
TACAMAHACS
TACE
TACES
TACET
TACH
TACHE
TACHES
TACHISM
TACHISME
TACHISMES
TACHISMS
TACHIST
TACHISTE
TACHISTES

TACHISTS
TACHOGRAM
TACHOGRAMS
TACHYLITE
TACHYLITES
TACHYLYTE
TACHYLYTES
TACHYON
TACHYONS
TACIT
TACITLY
TACITNESS
TACITNESSES
TACITURN
TACK
TACKED
TACKER
TACKERS
TACKET
TACKETS
TACKETY
TACKIER
TACKIES
TACKIEST
TACKINESS
TACKINESSES
TACKING
TACKINGS
TACKLE
TACKLED
TACKLER
TACKLERS
TACKLES
TACKLING
TACKLINGS
TACKS
TACKSMAN
TACKSMEN
TACKY
TACO
TACONITE
TACONITES
TACOS
TACT
TACTFUL
TACTFULLY
TACTIC
TACTICAL
TACTICIAN
TACTICIANS
TACTICITIES
TACTICITY
TACTICS
TACTILE
TACTILIST
TACTILISTS
TACTILITIES
TACTILITY
TACTION
TACTIONS
TACTISM
TACTISMS
TACTLESS

TACTS
TACTUAL
TACTUALLY
TAD
TADPOLE
TADPOLES
TADS
TADVANCE
TAE
TAED
TAEDIUM
TAEDIUMS
TAEING
TAEL
TAELS
TAENIA
TAENIAE
TAENIAS
TAENIASES
TAENIASIS
TAENIATE
TAENIOID
TAES
TAFFEREL
TAFFERELS
TAFFETA
TAFFETAS
TAFFETASES
TAFFETIES
TAFFETY
TAFFIES
TAFFRAIL
TAFFRAILS
TAFFY
TAFIA
TAFIAS
TAG
TAGETES
TAGGED
TAGGER
TAGGERS
TAGGING
TAGHAIRM
TAGHAIRMS
TAGLIONI
TAGLIONIS
TAGMEME
TAGMEMES
TAGMEMIC
TAGMEMICS
TAGRAG
TAGRAGS
TAGS
TAGUAN
TAGUANS
TAHA
TAHAS
TAHINA
TAHINAS
TAHINI
TAHINIS
TAHR
TAHRS

TAHSIL
TAHSILDAR
TAHSILDARS
TAHSILS
TAI
TAIGA
TAIGAS
TAIGLE
TAIGLED
TAIGLES
TAIGLING
TAIL
TAILARD
TAILARDS
TAILBACK
TAILBACKS
TAILED
TAILING
TAILINGS
TAILLESS
TAILLEUR
TAILLEURS
TAILLIE
TAILLIES
TAILOR
TAILORED
TAILORESS
TAILORESSES
TAILORING
TAILORINGS
TAILORS
TAILPIECE
TAILPIECES
TAILPLANE
TAILPLANES
TAILRACE
TAILRACES
TAILS
TAILSKID
TAILSKIDS
TAILYE
TAILYES
TAILZIE
TAILZIES
TAINT
TAINTED
TAINTING
TAINTLESS
TAINTS
TAINTURE
TAINTURES
TAIPAN
TAIPANS
TAIRA
TAIRAS
TAIS
TAISCH
TAISCHES
TAISH
TAISHES
TAIT
TAITS
TAIVER

TAIVERED
TAIVERING
TAIVERS
TAIVERT
TAJ
TAJES
TAK
TAKA
TAKABLE
TAKAHE
TAKAHEA
TAKAHEAS
TAKAHES
TAKAMAKA
TAKAMAKAS
TAKAS
TAKE
TAKEABLE
TAKEN
TAKEOVER
TAKEOVERS
TAKER
TAKERS
TAKES
TAKIER
TAKIEST
TAKIN
TAKING
TAKINGLY
TAKINGS
TAKINS
TAKS
TAKY
TALA
TALAK
TALAKS
TALANT
TALANTS
TALAPOIN
TALAPOINS
TALAQ
TALAQS
TALAR
TALARIA
TALARS
TALAS
TALAUNT
TALAUNTS
TALAYOT
TALAYOTS
TALBOT
TALBOTS
TALBOTYPE
TALBOTYPES
TALC
TALCKIER
TALCKIEST
TALCKY
TALCOSE
TALCOUS
TALCS
TALCUM
TALCUMS
TALE
TALEFUL
TALEGALLA
TALEGALLAS
TALENT
TALENTED
TALENTS

TALES
TALESMAN
TALESMEN
TALI
TALION
TALIONIC
TALIONS
TALIPAT
TALIPATS
TALIPED
TALIPEDS
TALIPES
TALIPOT
TALIPOTS
TALISMAN
TALISMANS
TALK
TALKABLE
TALKATHON
TALKATHONS
TALKATIVE
TALKED
TALKER
TALKERS
TALKFEST
TALKFESTS
TALKIE
TALKIES
TALKING
TALKINGS
TALKS
TALL
TALLAGE
TALLAGED
TALLAGES
TALLAGING
TALLAT
TALLATS
TALLBOY
TALLBOYS
TALLENT
TALLENTS
TALLER
TALLEST
TALLET
TALLETS
TALLIABLE
TALLIATE
TALLIATED
TALLIATES
TALLIATING
TALLIED
TALLIER
TALLIERS
TALLIES
TALLITH
TALLITHS
TALLNESS
TALLNESSES
TALLOT
TALLOTS
TALLOW
TALLOWED
TALLOWING
TALLOWISH
TALLOWS
TALLOWY
TALLY
TALLYING
TALLYMAN

TALLYMEN
TALLYSHOP
TALLYSHOPS
TALMA
TALMAS
TALON
TALONED
TALONS
TALPA
TALPAE
TALPAS
TALUK
TALUKDAR
TALUKDARS
TALUKS
TALUS
TALUSES
TALWEG
TALWEGS
TAM
TAMABLE
TAMAL
TAMALE
TAMALES
TAMALS
TAMANDUA
TAMANDUAS
TAMANOIR
TAMANOIRS
TAMANU
TAMANUS
TAMARA
TAMARACK
TAMARACKS
TAMARAS
TAMARI
TAMARILLO
TAMARILLOS
TAMARIN
TAMARIND
TAMARINDS
TAMARINS
TAMARIS
TAMARISK
TAMARISKS
TAMASHA
TAMASHAS
TAMBER
TAMBERS
TAMBOUR
TAMBOURA
TAMBOURAS
TAMBOURED
TAMBOURIN
TAMBOURING
TAMBOURINS
TAMBOURS
TAMBURA
TAMBURAS
TAMBURIN
TAMBURINS
TAME
TAMEABLE
TAMED
TAMELESS
TAMELY
TAMENESS
TAMENESSES
TAMER
TAMERS

TAMES
TAMEST
TAMIN
TAMINE
TAMINES
TAMING
TAMINGS
TAMINS
TAMIS
TAMISE
TAMISES
TAMMIES
TAMMY
TAMP
TAMPED
TAMPER
TAMPERED
TAMPERER
TAMPERERS
TAMPERING
TAMPERINGS
TAMPERS
TAMPING
TAMPINGS
TAMPION
TAMPIONS
TAMPON
TAMPONADE
TAMPONADES
TAMPONAGE
TAMPONAGES
TAMPONED
TAMPONING
TAMPONS
TAMPS
TAMS
TAN
TANA
TANADAR
TANADARS
TANAGER
TANAGERS
TANAGRA
TANAGRAS
TANAGRINE
TANAISTE
TANAISTES
TANAS
TANDEM
TANDEMS
TANDOORI
TANDOORIS
TANE
TANG
TANGA
TANGAS
TANGED
TANGELO
TANGELOS
TANGENCIES
TANGENCY
TANGENT
TANGENTS
TANGERINE
TANGERINES
TANGHIN
TANGHININ
TANGHININS
TANGHINS
TANGIBLE

TANGIBLES
TANGIBLY
TANGIE
TANGIER
TANGIES
TANGIEST
TANGING
TANGLE
TANGLED
TANGLER
TANGLERS
TANGLES
TANGLIER
TANGLIEST
TANGLING
TANGLINGS
TANGLY
TANGO
TANGOED
TANGOING
TANGOIST
TANGOISTS
TANGOS
TANGRAM
TANGRAMS
TANGS
TANGUN
TANGUNS
TANGY
TANIST
TANISTRIES
TANISTRY
TANISTS
TANK
TANKA
TANKAGE
TANKAGES
TANKARD
TANKARDS
TANKAS
TANKED
TANKER
TANKERS
TANKFUL
TANKFULS
TANKIA
TANKIAS
TANKING
TANKINGS
TANKS
TANLING
TANLINGS
TANNA
TANNABLE
TANNAGE
TANNAGES
TANNAH
TANNAHS
TANNAS
TANNATE
TANNATES
TANNED
TANNER
TANNERIES
TANNERS
TANNERY
TANNEST
TANNIC
TANNIN
TANNING

TANNINGS	TAPERNESS	TARANTISM	TAROTS	TARTARS
TANNINS	TAPERNESSES	TARANTISMS	TARP	TARTER
TANREC	TAPERS	TARANTULA	TARPAN	TARTEST
TANRECS	TAPERWISE	TARANTULAS	TARPANS	TARTIER
TANS	TAPES	TARAS	TARPAULIN	TARTIEST
TANSIES	TAPESTRIED	TARAXACUM	TARPAULINS	TARTINE
TANSY	TAPESTRIES	TARAXACUMS	TARPON	TARTINES
TANTALATE	TAPESTRY	TARBOGGIN	TARPONS	TARTINESS
TANTALATES	TAPESTRYING	TARBOGGINED	TARPS	TARTINESSES
TANTALIC	TAPET	TARBOGGINING	TARRAGON	TARTISH
TANTALISE	TAPETA	TARBOGGINS	TARRAGONS	TARTLET
TANTALISED	TAPETAL	TARBOOSH	TARRAS	TARTLETS
TANTALISES	TAPETI	TARBOOSHES	TARRASES	TARTLY
TANTALISING	TAPETIS	TARBOUSH	TARRE	TARTNESS
TANTALISINGS	TAPETS	TARBOUSHES	TARRED	TARTNESSES
TANTALISM	TAPETUM	TARBUSH	TARRES	TARTRATE
TANTALISMS	TAPEWORM	TARBUSHES	TARRIANCE	TARTRATES
TANTALITE	TAPEWORMS	TARCEL	TARRIANCES	TARTS
TANTALITES	TAPING	TARCELS	TARRIED	TARTY
TANTALIZE	TAPIOCA	TARDIED	TARRIER	TARWEED
TANTALIZED	TAPIOCAS	TARDIER	TARRIERS	TARWEEDS
TANTALIZES	TAPIR	TARDIES	TARRIES	TARWHINE
TANTALIZING	TAPIROID	TARDIEST	TARRIEST	TARWHINES
TANTALIZINGS	TAPIRS	TARDILY	TARRINESS	TASAR
TANTALUM	TAPIS	TARDINESS	TARRINESSES	TASARS
TANTALUMS	TAPISES	TARDINESSES	TARRING	TASH
TANTALUS	TAPIST	TARDIVE	TARRINGS	TASHED
TANTALUSES	TAPISTS	TARDY	TARROCK	TASHES
TANTARA	TAPLASH	TARDYING	TARROCKS	TASHING
TANTARARA	TAPLASHES	TARE	TARROW	TASIMETER
TANTARARAS	TAPPA	TARED	TARROWED	TASIMETERS
TANTARAS	TAPPAS	TARES	TARROWING	TASK
TANTI	TAPPED	TARGE	TARROWS	TASKED
TANTIVIES	TAPPER	TARGED	TARRY	TASKER
TANTIVY	TAPPERS	TARGES	TARRYING	TASKERS
TANTO	TAPPET	TARGET	TARS	TASKING
TANTONIES	TAPPETS	TARGETED	TARSAL	TASKINGS
TANTONY	TAPPICE	TARGETEER	TARSALGIA	TASKS
TANTRA	TAPPICED	TARGETEERS	TARSALGIAS	TASLET
TANTRAS	TAPPICES	TARGETING	TARSALS	TASLETS
TANTRIC	TAPPICING	TARGETS	TARSEL	TASS
TANTRUM	TAPPING	TARGING	TARSELS	TASSE
TANTRUMS	TAPPINGS	TARIFF	TARSI	TASSEL
TANYARD	TAPPIT	TARIFFED	TARSIA	TASSELL
TANYARDS	TAPROOM	TARIFFING	TARSIAS	TASSELLED
TAOISEACH	TAPROOMS	TARIFFS	TARSIER	TASSELLING
TAOISEACHS	TAPROOT	TARING	TARSIERS	TASSELLINGS
TAP	TAPROOTS	TARLATAN	TARSIOID	TASSELLS
TAPA	TAPS	TARLATANS	TARSUS	TASSELLY
TAPACOLO	TAPSMAN	TARMAC	TART	TASSELS
TAPACOLOS	TAPSMEN	TARMACKED	TARTAN	TASSES
TAPACULO	TAPSTER	TARMACKING	TARTANA	TASSET
TAPACULOS	TAPSTERS	TARMACS	TARTANAS	TASSETS
TAPADERA	TAPSTRY	TARN	TARTANE	TASSIE
TAPADERAS	TAPU	TARNAL	TARTANED	TASSIES
TAPADERO	TAPUS	TARNATION	TARTANES	TASSWAGE
TAPADEROS	TAR	TARNISH	TARTANS	TASTABLE
TAPAS	TARA	TARNISHED	TARTAR	TASTE
TAPE	TARAKIHI	TARNISHER	TARTARE	TASTED
TAPED	TARAKIHIS	TARNISHERS	TARTARES	TASTEFUL
TAPELESS	TARAND	TARNISHES	TARTARIC	TASTELESS
TAPELINE	TARANDS	TARNISHING	TARTARISE	TASTER
TAPELINES	TARANTARA	TARNS	TARTARISED	TASTERS
TAPEN	TARANTARAED	TARO	TARTARISES	TASTES
TAPER	TARANTARAING	TAROC	TARTARISING	TASTEVIN
TAPERED	TARANTARAS	TAROCS	TARTARIZE	TASTEVINS
TAPERER	TARANTAS	TAROK	TARTARIZED	TASTIER
TAPERERS	TARANTASES	TAROKS	TARTARIZES	TASTIEST
TAPERING	TARANTASS	TAROS	TARTARIZING	TASTILY
TAPERINGS	TARANTASSES	TAROT	TARTARLY	TASTING

TASTINGS	TAUNTING	TAWSE	TEACHERS	TEASES
TASTY	TAUNTINGS	TAWSES	TEACHES	TEASING
TAT	TAUNTS	TAWT	TEACHIE	TEASINGLY
TATAMI	TAUPE	TAWTED	TEACHING	TEASINGS
TATAMIS	TAUPES	TAWTIE	TEACHINGS	TEASPOON
TATE	TAUPIE	TAWTIER	TEACHLESS	TEASPOONS
TATER	TAUPIES	TAWTIEST	TEACUP	TEAT
TATERS	TAUREAN	TAWTING	TEACUPFUL	TEATED
TATES	TAURIC	TAWTS	TEACUPFULS	TEATIME
TATH	TAURIFORM	TAX	TEACUPS	TEATIMES
TATHED	TAURINE	TAXA	TEAD	TEATS
TATHING	TAUS	TAXABLE	TEADE	TEAZE
TATHS	TAUT	TAXABLY	TEADES	TEAZED
TATIE	TAUTED	TAXAMETER	TEADS	TEAZEL
TATIES	TAUTEN	TAXAMETERS	TEAED	TEAZELED
TATLER	TAUTENED	TAXATION	TEAGLE	TEAZELING
TATLERS	TAUTENING	TAXATIONS	TEAGLED	TEAZELLED
TATOU	TAUTENS	TAXATIVE	TEAGLES	TEAZELLING
TATOUS	TAUTER	TAXED	TEAGLING	TEAZELS
TATS	TAUTEST	TAXER	TEAING	TEAZES
TATT	TAUTING	TAXERS	TEAK	TEAZING
TATTED	TAUTIT	TAXES	TEAKS	TEAZLE
TATTER	TAUTLY	TAXI	TEAL	TEAZLED
TATTERED	TAUTNESS	TAXIARCH	TEALS	TEAZLES
TATTERING	TAUTNESSES	TAXIARCHS	TEAM	TEAZLING
TATTERS	TAUTOG	TAXICAB	TEAMED	TEBBAD
TATTERY	TAUTOGS	TAXICABS	TEAMER	TEBBADS
TATTIE	TAUTOLOGIES	TAXIDERMIES	TEAMERS	TECH
TATTIER	TAUTOLOGY	TAXIDERMY	TEAMING	TECHIER
TATTIES	TAUTOMER	TAXIED	TEAMINGS	TECHIEST
TATTIEST	TAUTOMERS	TAXIES	TEAMS	TECHNIC
TATTILY	TAUTONYM	TAXIING	TEAMSTER	TECHNICAL
TATTINESS	TAUTONYMS	TAXIMAN	TEAMSTERS	TECHNICS
TATTINESSES	TAUTS	TAXIMEN	TEAMWISE	TECHNIQUE
TATTING	TAVER	TAXIMETER	TEAMWORK	TECHNIQUES
TATTINGS	TAVERED	TAXIMETERS	TEAMWORKS	TECHS
TATTLE	TAVERING	TAXING	TEAPOT	TECHY
TATTLED	TAVERN	TAXINGS	TEAPOTS	TECKEL
TATTLER	TAVERNA	TAXIS	TEAPOY	TECKELS
TATTLERS	TAVERNAS	TAXIWAY	TEAPOYS	TECTIFORM
TATTLES	TAVERNER	TAXIWAYS	TEAR	TECTONIC
TATTLING	TAVERNERS	TAXMAN	TEARAWAY	TECTONICS
TATTLINGS	TAVERNS	TAXMEN	TEARAWAYS	TECTORIAL
TATTOO	TAVERS	TAXON	TEARER	TECTRICES
TATTOOED	TAVERT	TAXONOMER	TEARERS	TECTRIX
TATTOOER	TAW	TAXONOMERS	TEARFUL	TED
TATTOOERS	TAWDRIER	TAXONOMIC	TEARFULLY	TEDDED
TATTOOING	TAWDRIES	TAXONOMIES	TEARIER	TEDDER
TATTOOIST	TAWDRIEST	TAXONOMY	TEARIEST	TEDDERS
TATTOOISTS	TAWDRILY	TAXOR	TEARING	TEDDIES
TATTOOS	TAWDRY	TAXORS	TEARLESS	TEDDING
TATTOW	TAWED	TAXYING	TEARS	TEDDY
TATTOWED	TAWER	TAYBERRIES	TEARY	TEDESCA
TATTOWING	TAWERIES	TAYBERRY	TEAS	TEDESCHE
TATTOWS	TAWERS	TAYRA	TEASE	TEDESCHI
TATTS	TAWERY	TAYRAS	TEASED	TEDESCO
TATTY	TAWIE	TAZZA	TEASEL	TEDIER
TATU	TAWING	TAZZAS	TEASELED	TEDIEST
TATUED	TAWINGS	TAZZE	TEASELER	TEDIOSITIES
TATUING	TAWNEY	TCHICK	TEASELERS	TEDIOSITY
TATUS	TAWNEYS	TCHICKED	TEASELING	TEDIOUS
TAU	TAWNIER	TCHICKING	TEASELINGS	TEDIOUSLY
TAUBE	TAWNIES	TCHICKS	TEASELLED	TEDISOME
TAUBES	TAWNIEST	TE	TEASELLER	TEDIUM
TAUGHT	TAWNINESS	TEA	TEASELLERS	TEDIUMS
TAULD	TAWNINESSES	TEABERRIES	TEASELLING	TEDS
TAUNT	TAWNY	TEABERRY	TEASELLINGS	TEDY
TAUNTED	TAWPIE	TEACH	TEASELS	TEE
TAUNTER	TAWPIES	TEACHABLE	TEASER	TEED
TAUNTERS	TAWS	TEACHER	TEASERS	TEEHEE

TEEHEED
TEEHEEING
TEEHEES
TEEING
TEEL
TEELS
TEEM
TEEMED
TEEMER
TEEMERS
TEEMFUL
TEEMING
TEEMLESS
TEEMS
TEEN
TEENAGE
TEENAGED
TEENAGER
TEENAGERS
TEEND
TEENDED
TEENDING
TEENDS
TEENE
TEENED
TEENES
TEENIER
TEENIEST
TEENING
TEENS
TEENSIER
TEENSIEST
TEENSY
TEENTIER
TEENTIEST
TEENTSIER
TEENTSIEST
TEENTSY
TEENTY
TEENY
TEEPEE
TEEPEES
TEER
TEERED
TEERING
TEERS
TEES
TEETER
TEETERED
TEETERING
TEETERS
TEETH
TEETHE
TEETHED
TEETHES
TEETHING
TEETHINGS
TEETOTAL
TEETOTALS
TEETOTUM
TEETOTUMS
TEF
TEFF
TEFFS
TEFS
TEG
TEGG
TEGGS
TEGMEN
TEGMENTAL

TEGMENTUM
TEGMENTUMS
TEGMINA
TEGS
TEGUEXIN
TEGUEXINS
TEGULA
TEGULAE
TEGULAR
TEGULARLY
TEGULATED
TEGUMENT
TEGUMENTS
TEHEE
TEHEED
TEHEEING
TEHEES
TEHR
TEHRS
TEIL
TEILS
TEIND
TEINDED
TEINDING
TEINDS
TEKNONYMIES
TEKNONYMY
TEKTITE
TEKTITES
TEL
TELA
TELAE
TELAMON
TELAMONES
TELARY
TELD
TELECAST
TELECASTED
TELECASTING
TELECASTS
TELECHIR
TELECHIRS
TELECINE
TELECINES
TELECOM
TELECOMS
TELEDU
TELEDUS
TELEFILM
TELEFILMS
TELEGA
TELEGAS
TELEGENIC
TELEGONIES
TELEGONY
TELEGRAM
TELEGRAMS
TELEGRAPH
TELEGRAPHED
TELEGRAPHING
TELEGRAPHS
TELEMARK
TELEMARKED
TELEMARKING
TELEMARKS
TELEMETER
TELEMETERED
TELEMETERING
TELEMETERS
TELEMETRIES

TELEMETRY
TELEOLOGIES
TELEOLOGY
TELEONOMIES
TELEONOMY
TELEOSAUR
TELEOSAURS
TELEOST
TELEOSTS
TELEPATH
TELEPATHED
TELEPATHIES
TELEPATHING
TELEPATHS
TELEPATHY
TELEPHEME
TELEPHEMES
TELEPHONE
TELEPHONED
TELEPHONES
TELEPHONIES
TELEPHONING
TELEPHONY
TELEPHOTO
TELERGIC
TELERGIES
TELERGY
TELESALE
TELESALES
TELESCOPE
TELESCOPED
TELESCOPES
TELESCOPIES
TELESCOPING
TELESCOPY
TELESEME
TELESEMES
TELESES
TELESIS
TELESM
TELESMS
TELESTIC
TELESTICH
TELESTICHS
TELETEX
TELETEXES
TELETEXT
TELETEXTS
TELETHON
TELETHONS
TELETRON
TELETRONS
TELEVIEW
TELEVIEWED
TELEVIEWING
TELEVIEWS
TELEVISE
TELEVISED
TELEVISES
TELEVISING
TELEVISOR
TELEVISORS
TELEX
TELEXED
TELEXES
TELEXING
TELIC
TELL
TELLABLE
TELLAR

TELLARED
TELLARING
TELLARS
TELLER
TELLERED
TELLERING
TELLERS
TELLIES
TELLING
TELLINGLY
TELLINGS
TELLS
TELLTALE
TELLTALES
TELLURAL
TELLURATE
TELLURATES
TELLURIAN
TELLURIANS
TELLURIC
TELLURIDE
TELLURIDES
TELLURION
TELLURIONS
TELLURISE
TELLURISED
TELLURISES
TELLURISING
TELLURITE
TELLURITES
TELLURIUM
TELLURIUMS
TELLURIZE
TELLURIZED
TELLURIZES
TELLURIZING
TELLUROUS
TELLY
TELOPHASE
TELOPHASES
TELOS
TELOSES
TELPHER
TELPHERS
TELS
TELSON
TELSONS
TELT
TEMBLOR
TEMBLORES
TEME
TEMED
TEMENOS
TEMENOSES
TEMERITIES
TEMERITY
TEMEROUS
TEMES
TEMP
TEMPED
TEMPER
TEMPERA
TEMPERAS
TEMPERATE
TEMPERATED
TEMPERATES
TEMPERATING
TEMPERED
TEMPERER
TEMPERERS

TEMPERING
TEMPERINGS
TEMPERS
TEMPEST
TEMPESTED
TEMPESTING
TEMPESTS
TEMPI
TEMPING
TEMPLAR
TEMPLATE
TEMPLATES
TEMPLE
TEMPLED
TEMPLES
TEMPLET
TEMPLETS
TEMPO
TEMPORAL
TEMPORALS
TEMPORARIES
TEMPORARY
TEMPORE
TEMPORISE
TEMPORISED
TEMPORISES
TEMPORISING
TEMPORISINGS
TEMPORIZE
TEMPORIZED
TEMPORIZES
TEMPORIZING
TEMPORIZINGS
TEMPOS
TEMPS
TEMPT
TEMPTABLE
TEMPTED
TEMPTER
TEMPTERS
TEMPTING
TEMPTINGS
TEMPTRESS
TEMPTRESSES
TEMPTS
TEMPURA
TEMPURAS
TEMS
TEMSE
TEMSED
TEMSES
TEMSING
TEMULENCE
TEMULENCES
TEMULENCIES
TEMULENCY
TEMULENT
TEN
TENABLE
TENACE
TENACES
TENACIOUS
TENACITIES
TENACITY
TENACULUM
TENACULUMS
TENAIL
TENAILLE
TENAILLES
TENAILLON

TENAILLONS	TENETS	TENTED	TEQUILAS	TERMINAL
TENAILS	TENFOLD	TENTER	TEQUILLA	TERMINALS
TENANCIES	TENIA	TENTERED	TEQUILLAS	TERMINATE
TENANCY	TENIAE	TENTERING	TERAI	TERMINATED
TENANT	TENIAS	TENTERS	TERAIS	TERMINATES
TENANTED	TENIOID	TENTFUL	TERAKIHI	TERMINATING
TENANTING	TENNÉ	TENTFULS	TERAKIHIS	TERMINER
TENANTRIES	TENNER	TENTH	TERAPH	TERMINERS
TENANTRY	TENNERS	TENTHLY	TERAPHIM	TERMING
TENANTS	TENNÉS	TENTHS	TERAPHIMS	TERMINI
TENCH	TENNIS	TENTIE	TERAS	TERMINISM
TENCHES	TENNISES	TENTIER	TERATA	TERMINISMS
TEND	TENON	TENTIEST	TERATISM	TERMINIST
TENDANCE	TENONED	TENTIGO	TERATISMS	TERMINISTS
TENDANCES	TENONER	TENTIGOS	TERATOGEN	TERMINUS
TENDED	TENONERS	TENTING	TERATOGENS	TERMINUSES
TENDENCE	TENONING	TENTINGS	TERATOID	TERMITARIES
TENDENCES	TENONS	TENTORIA	TERATOMA	TERMITARY
TENDENCIES	TENOR	TENTORIAL	TERATOMATA	TERMITE
TENDENCY	TENORIST	TENTORIUM	TERBIC	TERMITES
TENDENZ	TENORISTS	TENTORIUMS	TERBIUM	TERMLESS
TENDENZEN	TENORITE	TENTS	TERBIUMS	TERMLIES
TENDER	TENORITES	TENTWISE	TERCE	TERMLY
TENDERED	TENOROON	TENTY	TERCEL	TERMOR
TENDERER	TENOROONS	TENUE	TERCELET	TERMORS
TENDERERS	TENORS	TENUES	TERCELETS	TERMS
TENDEREST	TENOTOMIES	TENUIOUS	TERCELS	TERN
TENDERING	TENOTOMY	TENUIS	TERCES	TERNAL
TENDERINGS	TENOUR	TENUITIES	TERCET	TERNARIES
TENDERISE	TENOURS	TENUITY	TERCETS	TERNARY
TENDERISED	TENPENCE	TENUOUS	TERCIO	TERNATE
TENDERISES	TENPENCES	TENUOUSLY	TERCIOS	TERNATELY
TENDERISING	TENPENNY	TENURABLE	TEREBENE	TERNE
TENDERIZE	TENPINS	TENURE	TEREBENES	TERNED
TENDERIZED	TENREC	TENURES	TEREBINTH	TERNES
TENDERIZES	TENRECS	TENURIAL	TEREBINTHS	TERNING
TENDERIZING	TENS	TENUTO	TEREBRA	TERNION
TENDERLY	TENSE	TENZON	TEREBRAE	TERNIONS
TENDERS	TENSED	TENZONS	TEREBRANT	TERNS
TENDING	TENSELY	TEOCALLI	TEREBRANTS	TERPENE
TENDINOUS	TENSENESS	TEOCALLIS	TEREBRAS	TERPENES
TENDON	TENSENESSES	TEOSINTE	TEREBRATE	TERPENOID
TENDONS	TENSER	TEOSINTES	TEREBRATED	TERPENOIDS
TENDRE	TENSES	TEPAL	TEREBRATES	TERPINEOL
TENDRES	TENSEST	TEPALS	TEREBRATING	TERPINEOLS
TENDRIL	TENSIBLE	TEPEE	TEREDINES	TERRA
TENDRILS	TENSILE	TEPEES	TEREDO	TERRACE
TENDRON	TENSILITIES	TEPEFIED	TEREDOS	TERRACED
TENDRONS	TENSILITY	TEPEFIES	TEREFA	TERRACES
TENDS	TENSING	TEPEFY	TEREFAH	TERRACING
TENE	TENSION	TEPEFYING	TEREK	TERRACINGS
TENEBRAE	TENSIONS	TEPHIGRAM	TEREKS	TERRAE
TENEBRIO	TENSITIES	TEPHIGRAMS	TERETE	TERRAIN
TENEBRIOS	TENSITY	TEPHRA	TERF	TERRAINS
TENEBRISM	TENSIVE	TEPHRAS	TERFE	TERRAMARA
TENEBRISMS	TENSON	TEPHRITE	TERFES	TERRAMARE
TENEBRIST	TENSONS	TEPHRITES	TERFS	TERRANE
TENEBRISTS	TENSOR	TEPHRITIC	TERGAL	TERRANES
TENEBRITIES	TENSORS	TEPHROITE	TERGITE	TERRAPIN
TENEBRITY	TENT	TEPHROITES	TERGITES	TERRAPINS
TENEBROSE	TENTACLE	TEPID	TERGUM	TERRARIA
TENEBROUS	TENTACLED	TEPIDARIA	TERGUMS	TERRARIUM
TENEMENT	TENTACLES	TEPIDER	TERIYAKI	TERRARIUMS
TENEMENTS	TENTACULA	TEPIDEST	TERIYAKIS	TERRAS
TENENDUM	TENTAGE	TEPIDITIES	TERM	TERRASES
TENENDUMS	TENTAGES	TEPIDITY	TERMAGANT	TERRAZZO
TENES	TENTATION	TEPIDLY	TERMAGANTS	TERRAZZOS
TENESMUS	TENTATIONS	TEPIDNESS	TERMED	TERREEN
TENESMUSES	TENTATIVE	TEPIDNESSES	TERMER	TERREENS
TENET	TENTATIVES	TEQUILA	TERMERS	TERRELLA

TERRELLAS	TESSELLAR	TESTUDOS	TEUCH	THALLUS
TERRENE	TESSERA	TESTY	TEUCHAT	THALLUSES
TERRENELY	TESSERACT	TETANAL	TEUCHATS	THALWEG
TERRENES	TESSERACTS	TETANIC	TEUCHER	THALWEGS
TERRET	TESSERAE	TETANIES	TEUCHEST	THAN
TERRETS	TESSERAL	TETANISE	TEUCHTER	THANA
TERRIBLE	TESSITURA	TETANISED	TEUCHTERS	THANADAR
TERRIBLES	TESSITURAS	TETANISES	TEUGH	THANADARS
TERRIBLY	TEST	TETANISING	TEUGHER	THANAGE
TERRICOLE	TESTA	TETANIZE	TEUGHEST	THANAGES
TERRICOLES	TESTABLE	TETANIZED	TEW	THANAH
TERRIER	TESTACIES	TETANIZES	TEWART	THANAHS
TERRIERS	TESTACY	TETANIZING	TEWARTS	THANAS
TERRIES	TESTAMENT	TETANOID	TEWED	THANATISM
TERRIFIC	TESTAMENTS	TETANUS	TEWEL	THANATISMS
TERRIFIED	TESTAMUR	TETANUSES	TEWELS	THANATIST
TERRIFIES	TESTAMURS	TETANY	TEWHIT	THANATISTS
TERRIFY	TESTAS	TETCHIER	TEWHITS	THANATOID
TERRIFYING	TESTATE	TETCHIEST	TEWING	THANE
TERRINE	TESTATION	TETCHILY	TEWIT	THANEDOM
TERRINES	TESTATIONS	TETCHY	TEWITS	THANEDOMS
TERRIT	TESTATOR	TÊTE	TEWS	THANEHOOD
TERRITORIES	TESTATORS	TÊTES	TEXAS	THANEHOODS
TERRITORY	TESTATRICES	TETHER	TEXASES	THANES
TERRITS	TESTATRIX	TETHERED	TEXT	THANESHIP
TERNON	TESTATRIXES	TETHERING	TEXTBOOK	THANESHIPS
TERRORISE	TESTATUM	TETHERS	TEXTBOOKS	THANK
TERRORISED	TESTATUMS	TETRA	TEXTILE	THANKED
TERRORISES	TESTE	TETRACID	TEXTILES	THANKEE
TERRORISING	TESTED	TETRACT	TEXTORIAL	THANKER
TERRORISM	TESTEE	TETRACTS	TEXTS	THANKERS
TERRORISMS	TESTEES	TETRAD	TEXTUAL	THANKFUL
TERRORIST	TESTER	TETRADIC	TEXTUALLY	THANKING
TERRORISTS	TESTERN	TETRADITE	TEXTUARIES	THANKINGS
TERRORIZE	TESTERNED	TETRADITES	TEXTUARY	THANKLESS
TERRORIZED	TESTERNING	TETRADS	TEXTURAL	THANKS
TERRORIZES	TESTERNS	TETRAGON	TEXTURE	THANNA
TERRORIZING	TESTERS	TETRAGONS	TEXTURED	THANNAH
TERRORS	TESTES	TETRAGRAM	TEXTURES	THANNAHS
TERRY	TESTICLE	TETRAGRAMS	TEXTURING	THANNAS
TERSE	TESTICLES	TETRALOGIES	TEXTURISE	THAR
TERSELY	TESTIER	TETRALOGY	TEXTURISED	THARS
TERSENESS	TESTIEST	TETRAPLA	TEXTURISES	THAT
TERSENESSES	TESTIFIED	TETRAPLAS	TEXTURISING	THATAWAY
TERSER	TESTIFIER	TETRAPOD	TEXTURIZE	THATCH
TERSEST	TESTIFIERS	TETRAPODIES	TEXTURIZED	THATCHED
TERSION	TESTIFIES	TETRAPODS	TEXTURIZES	THATCHER
TERSIONS	TESTIFY	TETRAPODY	TEXTURIZING	THATCHERS
TERTIA	TESTIFYING	TETRARCH	THACK	THATCHES
TERTIAL	TESTILY	TETRARCHIES	THACKS	THATCHING
TERTIALS	TESTIMONIED	TETRARCHS	THAE	THATCHINGS
TERTIAN	TESTIMONIES	TETRARCHY	THAGI	THATCHT
TERTIANS	TESTIMONY	TETRAS	THAGIS	THATNESS
TERTIARIES	TESTIMONYING	TETRAXON	THAIM	THATNESSES
TERTIARY	TESTINESS	TETRAXONS	THAIRM	THAUMATIN
TERTIAS	TESTINESSES	TETRODE	THAIRMS	THAUMATINS
TERTIUS	TESTING	TETRODES	THALAMI	THAW
TERTIUSES	TESTINGS	TETRONAL	THALAMIC	THAWED
TERTS	TESTIS	TETRONALS	THALAMUS	THAWER
TERVALENT	TESTON	TETROXIDE	THALASSIC	THAWERS
TERZETTA	TESTONS	TETROXIDES	THALER	THAWIER
TERZETTAS	TESTOON	TETRYL	THALERS	THAWIEST
TERZETTI	TESTOONS	TETRYLS	THALIAN	THAWING
TERZETTO	TESTRIL	TETTER	THALLI	THAWINGS
TERZETTOS	TESTRILL	TETTERED	THALLIC	THAWLESS
TES	TESTRILLS	TETTERING	THALLINE	THAWS
TESLA	TESTRILS	TETTEROUS	THALLIUM	THAWY
TESLAS	TESTS	TETTERS	THALLIUMS	THE
TESSELLA	TESTUDINES	TETTIX	THALLOID	THEACEOUS
TESSELLAE	TESTUDO	TETTIXES	THALLOUS	THEANDRIC

THEARCHIC
THEARCHIES
THEARCHY
THEATER
THEATERS
THEATRAL
THEATRE
THEATRES
THEATRIC
THEATRICS
THEAVE
THEAVES
THEBAINE
THEBAINES
THECA
THECAE
THECAL
THECATE
THECODONT
THECODONTS
THEE
THEED
THEEING
THEEK
THEEKED
THEEKING
THEEKS
THEES
THEFT
THEFTBOOT
THEFTBOOTS
THEFTBOTE
THEFTBOTES
THEFTS
THEFTUOUS
THEGITHER
THEGN
THEGNS
THEIC
THEICS
THEINE
THEINES
THEIR
THEIRS
THEISM
THEISMS
THEIST
THEISTIC
THEISTS
THELEMENT
THELEMENTS
THELF
THELVES
THELYTOKIES
THELYTOKY
THEM
THEMA
THEMATA
THEMATIC
THEME
THEMED
THEMES
THEMING
THEMSELVES
THEN
THENABOUT
THENABOUTS
THENAR
THENARS
THENCE

THENS
THEOCRACIES
THEOCRACY
THEOCRASIES
THEOCRASY
THEOCRAT
THEOCRATS
THEODICIES
THEODICY
THEOGONIC
THEOGONIES
THEOGONY
THEOLOGER
THEOLOGERS
THEOLOGIC
THEOLOGIES
THEOLOGUE
THEOLOGUES
THEOLOGY
THEOMACHIES
THEOMACHY
THEOMANCIES
THEOMANCY
THEOMANIA
THEOMANIAS
THEONOMIES
THEONOMY
THEOPATHIES
THEOPATHY
THEOPHAGIES
THEOPHAGY
THEOPHANIES
THEOPHANY
THEORBIST
THEORBISTS
THEORBO
THEORBOS
THEOREM
THEOREMS
THEORETIC
THEORETICS
THEORIC
THEORICS
THEORIES
THEORIQUE
THEORIQUES
THEORISE
THEORISED
THEORISER
THEORISERS
THEORISES
THEORISING
THEORIST
THEORISTS
THEORIZE
THEORIZED
THEORIZER
THEORIZERS
THEORIZES
THEORIZING
THEORY
THEOSOPH
THEOSOPHIES
THEOSOPHS
THEOSOPHY
THEOTOKOI
THEOTOKOS
THEOW
THEOWS
THERALITE

THERALITES
THERAPIES
THERAPIST
THERAPISTS
THERAPSID
THERAPSIDS
THERAPY
THERBLIG
THERBLIGS
THERE
THEREAT
THEREAWAY
THEREBY
THEREFOR
THEREFORE
THEREFROM
THEREIN
THEREINTO
THERENESS
THERENESSES
THEREOF
THEREON
THEREOUT
THERES
THERETO
THEREUNTO
THEREUPON
THEREWITH
THERIAC
THERIACA
THERIACAL
THERIACAS
THERIACS
THERM
THERMAE
THERMAL
THERMALLY
THERMALS
THERMIC
THERMICAL
THERMION
THERMIONS
THERMITE
THERMITES
THERMOS
THERMOSES
THERMOTIC
THERMOTICS
THERMS
THEROID
THEROLOGIES
THEROLOGY
THEROPOD
THEROPODS
THESAURUS
THESAURUSES
THESE
THESES
THESIS
THESPIAN
THESPIANS
THETA
THETAS
THETCH
THETCHED
THETCHES
THETCHING
THETE
THETES
THETHER

THETIC
THETICAL
THEURGIC
THEURGIES
THEURGIST
THEURGISTS
THEURGY
THEW
THEWED
THEWES
THEWIER
THEWIEST
THEWLESS
THEWS
THEWY
THEY
THIAMIN
THIAMINE
THIAMINES
THIAMINS
THIASUS
THIASUSES
THIAZIDE
THIAZIDES
THIBET
THIBETS
THIBLE
THIBLES
THICK
THICKED
THICKEN
THICKENED
THICKENER
THICKENERS
THICKENING
THICKENINGS
THICKENS
THICKER
THICKEST
THICKET
THICKETED
THICKETS
THICKETY
THICKHEAD
THICKHEADS
THICKING
THICKISH
THICKLY
THICKNESS
THICKNESSES
THICKO
THICKOES
THICKOS
THICKS
THICKSET
THICKSETS
THICKSKIN
THICKSKINS
THICKY
THIEF
THIEVE
THIEVED
THIEVERIES
THIEVERY
THIEVES
THIEVING
THIEVINGS
THIEVISH
THIG
THIGGER

THIGGERS
THIGGING
THIGGINGS
THIGGIT
THIGH
THIGHS
THIGS
THILK
THILL
THILLER
THILLERS
THILLS
THIMBLE
THIMBLED
THIMBLES
THIMBLING
THIN
THINE
THING
THINGAMIES
THINGAMY
THINGHOOD
THINGHOODS
THINGIER
THINGIES
THINGIEST
THINGNESS
THINGNESSES
THINGS
THINGUMMIES
THINGUMMY
THINGY
THINK
THINKABLE
THINKER
THINKERS
THINKING
THINKINGS
THINKS
THINLY
THINNED
THINNER
THINNERS
THINNESS
THINNESSES
THINNEST
THINNING
THINNINGS
THINNISH
THINS
THIOL
THIOLS
THIOUREA
THIOUREAS
THIR
THIRAM
THIRAMS
THIRD
THIRDED
THIRDING
THIRDINGS
THIRDLY
THIRDS
THIRDSMAN
THIRDSMEN
THIRL
THIRLAGE
THIRLAGES
THIRLED
THIRLING

THIRLS
THIRST
THIRSTED
THIRSTER
THIRSTERS
THIRSTFUL
THIRSTIER
THIRSTIEST
THIRSTILY
THIRSTING
THIRSTS
THIRSTY
THIRTEEN
THIRTEENS
THIRTIES
THIRTIETH
THIRTIETHS
THIRTY
THIRTYISH
THIS
THISNESS
THISNESSES
THISTLE
THISTLES
THISTLIER
THISTLIEST
THISTLY
THITHER
THIVEL
THIVELS
THLIPSES
THLIPSIS
THO
THOFT
THOFTS
THOLE
THOLED
THOLES
THOLI
THOLING
THOLOBATE
THOLOBATES
THOLOI
THOLOS
THOLUS
THON
THONDER
THONG
THONGED
THONGS
THORACES
THORACIC
THORAX
THORAXES
THORITE
THORITES
THORIUM
THORIUMS
THORN
THORNBACK
THORNBACKS
THORNED
THORNIER
THORNIEST
THORNING
THORNLESS
THORNS
THORNSET
THORNTREE
THORNTREES

THORNY
THORON
THORONS
THOROUGH
THOROUGHER
THOROUGHEST
THOROUGHS
THORP
THORPE
THORPES
THORPS
THOSE
THOTHER
THOU
THOUGH
THOUGHT
THOUGHTED
THOUGHTEN
THOUGHTS
THOUING
THOUS
THOUSAND
THOUSANDS
THOWEL
THOWELS
THOWL
THOWLESS
THOWLS
THRAE
THRALLIUM
THRALDOMS
THRALL
THRALLDOM
THRALLDOMS
THRALLED
THRALLING
THRALLS
THRANG
THRANGED
THRANGING
THRANGS
THRAPPLE
THRAPPLED
THRAPPLES
THRAPPLING
THRASH
THRASHED
THRASHER
THRASHERS
THRASHES
THRASHING
THRASHINGS
THRASONIC
THRAVE
THRAVES
THRAW
THRAWARD
THRAWART
THRAWING
THRAWN
THRAWS
THREAD
THREADED
THREADEN
THREADER
THREADERS
THREADIER
THREADIEST
THREADING
THREADS

THREADY
THREAP
THREAPING
THREAPIT
THREAPS
THREAT
THREATED
THREATEN
THREATENED
THREATENING
THREATENINGS
THREATENS
THREATFUL
THREATING
THREATS
THREAVE
THREAVES
THREE
THREEFOLD
THREENESS
THREENESSES
THREEP
THREEPING
THREEPIT
THREEPS
THREES
THREESOME
THREESOMES
THRENE
THRENED
THRENETIC
THRENODE
THRENODES
THRENODIC
THRENODIES
THRENODY
THRENOS
THRENOSES
THREONINE
THREONINES
THRESH
THRESHED
THRESHEL
THRESHELS
THRESHER
THRESHERS
THRESHES
THRESHING
THRESHINGS
THRESHOLD
THRESHOLDS
THRETTIES
THRETTY
THREW
THRICE
THRID
THRIDACE
THRIDACES
THRIDDED
THRIDDING
THRIDS
THRIFT
THRIFTIER
THRIFTIEST
THRIFTILY
THRIFTS
THRIFTY
THRILL
THRILLANT
THRILLED

THRILLER
THRILLERS
THRILLIER
THRILLIEST
THRILLING
THRILLS
THRILLY
THRIMSA
THRIMSAS
THRIP
THRIPS
THRIPSES
THRISSEL
THRISSELS
THRIST
THRISTED
THRISTING
THRISTLE
THRISTLES
THRISTS
THRISTY
THRIVE
THRIVED
THRIVEN
THRIVER
THRIVERS
THRIVES
THRIVING
THRIVINGS
THRO
THROAT
THROATED
THROATIER
THROATIEST
THROATILY
THROATS
THROATY
THROB
THROBBED
THROBBING
THROBBINGS
THROBLESS
THROBS
THROE
THROED
THROEING
THROES
THROMBI
THROMBIN
THROMBINS
THROMBOSE
THROMBOSED
THROMBOSES
THROMBOSING
THROMBUS
THRONE
THRONED
THRONES
THRONG
THRONGED
THRONGFUL
THRONGING
THRONGINGS
THRONGS
THRONING
THROPPLE
THROPPLED
THROPPLES
THROPPLING
THROSTLE

THROSTLES
THROTTLE
THROTTLED
THROTTLER
THROTTLERS
THROTTLES
THROTTLING
THROTTLINGS
THROUGH
THROUGHLY
THROVE
THROW
THROWE
THROWER
THROWERS
THROWES
THROWING
THROWINGS
THROWN
THROWS
THROWSTER
THROWSTERS
THRU
THRUM
THRUMMED
THRUMMER
THRUMMERS
THRUMMIER
THRUMMIEST
THRUMMING
THRUMMINGS
THRUMMY
THRUMS
THRUSH
THRUSHES
THRUST
THRUSTED
THRUSTER
THRUSTERS
THRUSTING
THRUSTINGS
THRUSTS
THRUTCH
THRUTCHED
THRUTCHES
THRUTCHING
THRUWAY
THRUWAYS
THRYMSA
THRYMSAS
THUD
THUDDED
THUDDING
THUDS
THUG
THUGGEE
THUGGEES
THUGGERIES
THUGGERY
THUGGISM
THUGGISMS
THUGS
THUJA
THUJAS
THULIA
THULIAS
THULITE
THULITES
THULIUM
THULIUMS

THUMB	THYMIDINES	TICKLERS	TIERS	TILE
THUMBED	THYMIER	TICKLES	TIES	TILED
THUMBIER	THYMIEST	TICKLIER	TIETAC	TILEFISH
THUMBIEST	THYMINE	TICKLIEST	TIETACK	TILEFISHES
THUMBING	THYMINES	TICKLING	TIETACKS	TILER
THUMBKINS	THYMOCYTE	TICKLINGS	TIETACS	TILERIES
THUMBLESS	THYMOCYTES	TICKLISH	TIFF	TILERS
THUMBLING	THYMOL	TICKLY	TIFFANIES	TILERY
THUMBLINGS	THYMOLS	TICKS	TIFFANY	TILES
THUMBNAIL	THYMUS	TICKY	TIFFED	TILING
THUMBNAILS	THYMUSES	TICS	TIFFIN	TILINGS
THUMBPOT	THYMY	TID	TIFFING	TILL
THUMBPOTS	THYRATRON	TIDAL	TIFFINGS	TILLABLE
THUMBS	THYRATRONS	TIDBIT	TIFFINS	TILLAGE
THUMBY	THYREOID	TIDBITS	TIFFS	TILLAGES
THUMP	THYRISTOR	TIDDIER	TIFT	TILLED
THUMPED	THYRISTORS	TIDDIES	TIFTED	TILLER
THUMPER	THYROID	TIDDIEST	TIFTING	TILLERED
THUMPERS	THYROIDS	TIDDLE	TIFTS	TILLERING
THUMPING	THYROXIN	TIDDLED	TIG	TILLERS
THUMPS	THYROXINE	TIDDLER	TIGE	TILLIER
THUNDER	THYROXINES	TIDDLERS	TIGER	TILLIEST
THUNDERED	THYROXINS	TIDDLES	TIGERISH	TILLING
THUNDERER	THYRSE	TIDDLEY	TIGERISM	TILLINGS
THUNDERERS	THYRSES	TIDDLEYS	TIGERISMS	TILLITE
THUNDERING	THYRSI	TIDDLIER	TIGERLY	TILLITES
THUNDERINGS	THYRSOID	TIDDLIES	TIGERS	TILLS
THUNDERS	THYRSUS	TIDDLIEST	TIGERY	TILLY
THUNDERY	THYSELF	TIDDLING	TIGES	TILS
THUNDROUS	TI	TIDDLY	TIGGED	TILT
THURIBLE	TIAR	TIDDY	TIGGING	TILTABLE
THURIBLES	TIARA	TIDE	TIGHT	TILTED
THURIFER	TIARAED	TIDED	TIGHTEN	TILTER
THURIFERS	TIARAS	TIDELESS	TIGHTENED	TILTERS
THURIFIED	TIARS	TIDEMARK	TIGHTENER	TILTH
THURIFIES	TIBIA	TIDEMARKS	TIGHTENERS	TILTHS
THURIFY	TIBIAE	TIDEMILL	TIGHTENING	TILTING
THURIFYING	TIBIAL	TIDEMILLS	TIGHTENS	TILTINGS
THUS	TIBIAS	TIDES	TIGHTER	TILTS
THUSES	TIC	TIDIED	TIGHTEST	TIMARIOT
THUSNESS	TICAL	TIDIER	TIGHTISH	TIMARIOTS
THUSNESSES	TICALS	TIDIES	TIGHTLY	TIMBAL
THUSWISE	TICCA	TIDIEST	TIGHTNESS	TIMBALE
THWACK	TICE	TIDILY	TIGHTNESSES	TIMBALES
THWACKED	TICED	TIDINESS	TIGHTS	TIMBALS
THWACKER	TICES	TIDINESSES	TIGHTWAD	TIMBER
THWACKERS	TICH	TIDING	TIGHTWADS	TIMBERED
THWACKING	TICHES	TIDINGS	TIGLON	TIMBERING
THWACKINGS	TICHIER	TIDIVATE	TIGLONS	TIMBERINGS
THWACKS	TICHIEST	TIDIVATED	TIGON	TIMBERS
THWAITE	TICHY	TIDIVATES	TIGONS	TIMBÓ
THWAITES	TICING	TIDIVATING	TIGRESS	TIMBÓS
THWART	TICK	TIDS	TIGRESSES	TIMBRE
THWARTED	TICKED	TIDY	TIGRINE	TIMBREL
THWARTER	TICKEN	TIDYING	TIGRISH	TIMBRELS
THWARTERS	TICKENS	TIE	TIGROID	TIMBRES
THWARTING	TICKER	TIED	TIGS	TIME
THWARTINGS	TICKERS	TIELESS	TIKA	TIMED
THWARTLY	TICKET	TIER	TIKAS	TIMELESS
THWARTS	TICKETED	TIERCE	TIKE	TIMELIER
THY	TICKETING	TIERCÉ	TIKES	TIMELIEST
THYINE	TICKETS	TIERCEL	TIKI	TIMELY
THYLACINE	TICKEY	TIERCELET	TIKIS	TIMENOGUY
THYLACINES	TICKEYS	TIERCELETS	TIL	TIMENOGUYS
THYLOSE	TICKIES	TIERCELS	TILAPIA	TIMEOUS
THYLOSES	TICKING	TIERCERON	TILAPIAS	TIMEOUSLY
THYLOSIS	TICKINGS	TIERCERONS	TILBURIES	TIMEPIECE
THYME	TICKLE	TIERCES	TILBURY	TIMEPIECES
THYMES	TICKLED	TIERED	TILDE	TIMER
THYMIDINE	TICKLER	TIERING	TILDES	TIMERS

TIMES
TIMESCALE
TIMESCALES
TIMETABLE
TIMETABLED
TIMETABLES
TIMETABLING
TIMID
TIMIDER
TIMIDEST
TIMIDITIES
TIMIDITY
TIMIDLY
TIMIDNESS
TIMIDNESSES
TIMING
TIMINGS
TIMIST
TIMISTS
TIMOCRACIES
TIMOCRACY
TIMON
TIMONEER
TIMONEERS
TIMONS
TIMOROUS
TIMORSOME
TIMOTHIES
TIMOTHY
TIMOUS
TIMOUSLY
TIMPANI
TIMPANIST
TIMPANISTS
TIMPANO
TIMPS
TIN
TINAJA
TINAJAS
TINAMOU
TINAMOUS
TINCAL
TINCALS
TINCHEL
TINCHELS
TINCT
TINCTED
TINCTING
TINCTS
TINCTURE
TINCTURED
TINCTURES
TINCTURING
TIND
TINDAL
TINDALS
TINDED
TINDER
TINDERS
TINDERY
TINDING
TINDS
TINE
TINEA
TINEAS
TINED
TINEID
TINEIDS
TINES
TINFOIL

TINFOILS
TINFUL
TINFULS
TING
TINGE
TINGED
TINGES
TINGING
TINGLE
TINGLED
TINGLER
TINGLERS
TINGLES
TINGLIER
TINGLIEST
TINGLING
TINGLINGS
TINGLISH
TINGLY
TINGS
TINGUAITE
TINGUAITES
TINHORN
TINHORNS
TINIER
TINIEST
TININESS
TININESSES
TINING
TINK
TINKED
TINKER
TINKERED
TINKERING
TINKERINGS
TINKERS
TINKING
TINKLE
TINKLED
TINKLER
TINKLERS
TINKLES
TINKLIER
TINKLIEST
TINKLING
TINKLINGS
TINKLY
TINKS
TINMAN
TINMEN
TINNED
TINNER
TINNERS
TINNIE
TINNIER
TINNIES
TINNIEST
TINNING
TINNINGS
TINNITUS
TINNITUSES
TINNY
TINPOT
TINPOTS
TINS
TINSEL
TINSELLED
TINSELLING
TINSELLY
TINSELRIES

TINSELRY
TINSELS
TINSEY
TINSEYS
TINSMITH
TINSMITHS
TINSNIPS
TINSTONE
TINSTONES
TINT
TINTED
TINTER
TINTERS
TINTIER
TINTIEST
TINTINESS
TINTINESSES
TINTING
TINTINGS
TINTLESS
TINTS
TINTY
TINTYPE
TINTYPES
TINWARE
TINWARED
TINY
TIP
TIPI
TIPIS
TIPPED
TIPPER
TIPPERS
TIPPET
TIPPETS
TIPPIER
TIPPIEST
TIPPING
TIPPINGS
TIPPLE
TIPPLED
TIPPLER
TIPPLERS
TIPPLES
TIPPLING
TIPPY
TIPS
TIPSIER
TIPSIEST
TIPSIFIED
TIPSIFIES
TIPSIFY
TIPSIFYING
TIPSILY
TIPSINESS
TIPSINESSES
TIPSTAFF
TIPSTAFFS
TIPSTAVES
TIPSTER
TIPSTERS
TIPSY
TIPT
TIPTOE
TIPTOED
TIPTOEING
TIPTOES
TIPTOP
TIPTOPS
TIPULA

TIPULAS
TIRADE
TIRADES
TIRASSE
TIRASSES
TIRE
TIRED
TIREDER
TIREDEST
TIREDNESS
TIREDNESSES
TIRELESS
TIRELING
TIRELINGS
TIRES
TIRESOME
TIRING
TIRINGS
TIRL
TIRLED
TIRLING
TIRLS
TIRO
TIROES
TIROS
TIRR
TIRRED
TIRRING
TIRRIT
TIRRITS
TIRRIVEE
TIRRIVEES
TIRRIVIE
TIRRIVIES
TIRRS
TIS
TISANE
TISANES
TISICK
TISICKS
TISSUE
TISSUED
TISSUES
TISSUING
TISWAS
TISWASES
TIT
TITAN
TITANATE
TITANATES
TITANIC
TITANITE
TITANITES
TITANIUM
TITANIUMS
TITANOUS
TITANS
TITBIT
TITBITS
TITCH
TITCHES
TITE
TITELY
TITER
TITERS
TITFER
TITFERS
TITHABLE
TITHE
TITHED

TITHER
TITHERS
TITHES
TITHING
TITHINGS
TITI
TITIAN
TITIANS
TITILLATE
TITILLATED
TITILLATES
TITILLATING
TITIS
TITIVATE
TITIVATED
TITIVATES
TITIVATING
TITLARK
TITLARKS
TITLE
TITLED
TITLELESS
TITLER
TITLERS
TITLES
TITLING
TITLINGS
TITMICE
TITMOSE
TITMOUSE
TITOKI
TITOKIS
TITRATE
TITRATED
TITRATES
TITRATING
TITRATION
TITRATIONS
TITRE
TITRES
TITS
TITTED
TITTER
TITTERED
TITTERER
TITTERERS
TITTERING
TITTERINGS
TITTERS
TITTIES
TITTING
TITTIVATE
TITTIVATED
TITTIVATES
TITTIVATING
TITTLE
TITTLEBAT
TITTLEBATS
TITTLED
TITTLES
TITTLING
TITTUP
TITTUPED
TITTUPING
TITTUPS
TITTUPY
TITTY
TITUBANCIES
TITUBANCY
TITUBANT

TITUBATE
TITUBATED
TITUBATES
TITUBATING
TITULAR
TITULARIES
TITULARLY
TITULARS
TITULARY
TITULE
TITULED
TITULES
TITULING
TITUP
TITUPED
TITUPING
TITUPS
TITUPY
TIZWAS
TIZWASES
TIZZ
TIZZES
TIZZIES
TIZZY
TMESES
TMESIS
TO
TOAD
TOADFISH
TOADFISHES
TOADFLAX
TOADFLAXES
TOADGRASS
TOADGRASSES
TOADIED
TOADIES
TOADRUSH
TOADRUSHES
TOADS
TOADSTOOL
TOADSTOOLS
TOADY
TOADYING
TOADYISH
TOADYISM
TOADYISMS
TOAST
TOASTED
TOASTER
TOASTERS
TOASTIE
TOASTIES
TOASTING
TOASTINGS
TOASTS
TOASTY
TOAZE
TOAZED
TOAZES
TOAZING
TOBACCO
TOBACCOES
TOBACCOS
TOBIES
TOBOGGAN
TOBOGGANED
TOBOGGANING
TOBOGGANINGS
TOBOGGANS
TOBOGGIN

TOBOGGINED
TOBOGGINING
TOBOGGINS
TOBY
TOCCATA
TOCCATAS
TOCCATINA
TOCCATINAS
TOCHER
TOCHERED
TOCHERING
TOCHERS
TOCO
TOCOLOGIES
TOCOLOGY
TOCOS
TOCSIN
TOCSINS
TOD
TODAY
TODAYS
TODDE
TODDED
TODDES
TODDIES
TODDING
TODDLE
TODDLED
TODDLER
TODDLERS
TODDLES
TODDLING
TODDY
TODIES
TODS
TODY
TOE
TOECAP
TOECAPS
TOECLIP
TOECLIPS
TOED
TOEING
TOENAIL
TOENAILS
TOES
TOFF
TOFFEE
TOFFEES
TOFFIER
TOFFIES
TOFFIEST
TOFFISH
TOFFS
TOFFY
TOFORE
TOFT
TOFTS
TOFU
TOFUS
TOG
TOGA
TOGAED
TOGAS
TOGATE
TOGATED
TOGE
TOGED
TOGES
TOGETHER

TOGGED
TOGGERIES
TOGGERY
TOGGING
TOGGLE
TOGGLED
TOGGLES
TOGGLING
TOGS
TOGUE
TOGUES
TOHEROA
TOHEROAS
TOHO
TOHOS
TOIL
TOILE
TOILED
TOILER
TOILERS
TOILES
TOILET
TOILETED
TOILETING
TOILETRIES
TOILETRY
TOILETS
TOILETTE
TOILETTES
TOILFUL
TOILINET
TOILINETS
TOILING
TOILINGS
TOILLESS
TOILS
TOILSOME
TOISE
TOISEACH
TOISEACHS
TOISECH
TOISECHS
TOISES
TOISON
TOISONS
TOKAMAK
TOKAMAKS
TOKE
TOKED
TOKEN
TOKENED
TOKENING
TOKENISM
TOKENISMS
TOKENS
TOKES
TOKING
TOKO
TOKOLOGIES
TOKOLOGY
TOKOLOSHE
TOKOLOSHES
TOKOS
TOLA
TOLAS
TOLBOOTH
TOLDOOTHS
TOLD
TOLE
TOLED

TOLERABLE
TOLERABLY
TOLERANCE
TOLERANCES
TOLERANT
TOLERATE
TOLERATED
TOLERATES
TOLERATING
TOLERATOR
TOLERATORS
TOLES
TOLING
TOLINGS
TOLL
TOLLABLE
TOLLAGE
TOLLAGES
TOLLBOOTH
TOLLBOOTHS
TOLLDISH
TOLLDISHES
TOLLED
TOLLER
TOLLERS
TOLLGATE
TOLLGATES
TOLLING
TOLLINGS
TOLLMAN
TOLLMEN
TOLLS
TOLSEL
TOLSELS
TOLSEY
TOLSEYS
TOLT
TOLTER
TOLTERED
TOLTERING
TOLTERS
TOLTS
TOLU
TOLUATE
TOLUATES
TOLUENE
TOLUENES
TOLUIC
TOLUIDINE
TOLUIDINES
TOLUOL
TOLUOLS
TOLUS
TOLZEY
TOLZEYS
TOM
TOMAHAWK
TOMAHAWKED
TOMAHAWKING
TOMAHAWKS
TOMALLEY
TOMALLEYS
TOMAN
TOMANS
TOMATO
TOMATOES
TOMB
TOMBAC
TOMBACS
TOMBAK

TOMBAKS
TOMBED
TOMBIC
TOMBING
TOMBLESS
TOMBOC
TOMBOCS
TOMBOLA
TOMBOLAS
TOMBOLO
TOMBOLOS
TOMBOY
TOMBOYISH
TOMBOYS
TOMBS
TOMBSTONE
TOMBSTONES
TOME
TOMENTOSE
TOMENTOUS
TOMENTUM
TOMENTUMS
TOMES
TOMFOOL
TOMFOOLED
TOMFOOLING
TOMFOOLS
TOMIAL
TOMIUM
TOMIUMS
TOMMIED
TOMMIES
TOMMY
TOMMYING
TOMOGRAM
TOMOGRAMS
TOMOGRAPH
TOMOGRAPHS
TOMORROW
TOMORROWS
TOMPION
TOMPIONS
TOMPON
TOMPONS
TOMS
TOMTIT
TOMTITS
TON
TONAL
TONALITE
TONALITES
TONALITIES
TONALITY
TONANT
TONDI
TONDINI
TONDINO
TONDINOS
TONDO
TONDOS
TONE
TONED
TONELESS
TONEME
TONEMES
TONEMIC
TONES
TONETIC
TONEY
TONG

TONGA
TONGAS
TONGS
TONGUE
TONGUED
TONGUELET
TONGUELETS
TONGUES
TONGUING
TONGUINGS
TONIC
TONICITIES
TONICITY
TONICS
TONIER
TONIES
TONIEST
TONIGHT
TONIGHTS
TONING
TONISH
TONISHLY
TONITE
TONITES
TONK
TONKED
TONKER
TONKERS
TONKING
TONKS
TONLET
TONLETS
TONNAG
TONNAGE
TONNAGES
TONNAGS
TONNE
TONNEAU
TONNEAUS
TONNELL
TONNELLS
TONNES
TONNISH
TONNISHLY
TONOMETER
TONOMETERS
TONOMETRIES
TONOMETRY
TONS
TONSIL
TONSILLAR
TONSILS
TONSOR
TONSORIAL
TONSORS
TONSURE
TONSURED
TONSURES
TONTINE
TONTINER
TONTINERS
TONTINES
TONUS
TONUSES
TONY
TOO
TOOART
TOOARTS
TOOK
TOOL

TOOLBAG
TOOLBAGS
TOOLBOX
TOOLBOXES
TOOLED
TOOLER
TOOLERS
TOOLHOUSE
TOOLHOUSES
TOOLING
TOOLINGS
TOOLKIT
TOOLKITS
TOOLMAKER
TOOLMAKERS
TOOLMAN
TOOLMEN
TOOLROOM
TOOLROOMS
TOOLS
TOOM
TOOMED
TOOMER
TOOMEST
TOOMING
TOOMO
TOON
TOONS
TOORIE
TOORIES
TOOT
TOOTED
TOOTER
TOOTERS
TOOTH
TOOTHACHE
TOOTHACHES
TOOTHCOMB
TOOTHCOMBS
TOOTHED
TOOTHFUL
TOOTHFULS
TOOTHIER
TOOTHIEST
TOOTHING
TOOTHLESS
TOOTHPICK
TOOTHPICKS
TOOTHS
TOOTHSOME
TOOTHWASH
TOOTHWASHES
TOOTHWORT
TOOTHWORTS
TOOTHY
TOOTING
TOOTLE
TOOTLED
TOOTLES
TOOTLING
TOOTS
TOOTSIE
TOOTSIES
TOOTSY
TOP
TOPARCH
TOPARCHIES
TOPARCHS
TOPARCHY
TOPAZ

TOPAZES
TOPAZINE
TOPCOAT
TOPCOATS
TOPE
TOPECTOMIES
TOPECTOMY
TOPED
TOPEE
TOPEES
TOPEK
TOPEKS
TOPER
TOPERS
TOPES
TOPFULL
TOPHI
TOPHUS
TOPI
TOPIARIAN
TOPIARIES
TOPIARIST
TOPIARISTS
TOPIARY
TOPIC
TOPICAL
TOPICALLY
TOPICS
TOPING
TOPIS
TOPKNOT
TOPKNOTS
TOPLESS
TOPLOFTY
TOPMAKER
TOPMAKERS
TOPMAKING
TOPMAKINGS
TOPMAN
TOPMAST
TOPMASTS
TOPMEN
TOPMINNOW
TOPMINNOWS
TOPMOST
TOPOI
TOPOLOGIC
TOPOLOGIES
TOPOLOGY
TOPONYM
TOPONYMAL
TOPONYMIC
TOPONYMICS
TOPONYMIES
TOPONYMS
TOPONYMY
TOPOS
TOPPED
TOPPER
TOPPERS
TOPPING
TOPPINGLY
TOPPINGS
TOPPLE
TOPPLED
TOPPLES
TOPPLING
TOPS
TOPSAIL
TOPSAILS

TOPSIDE
TOPSIDES
TOPSMAN
TOPSMEN
TOPSPIN
TOPSPINS
TOQUE
TOQUES
TOR
TORAN
TORANA
TORANAS
TORANS
TORBANITE
TORBANITES
TORC
TORCH
TORCHED
TORCHER
TORCHÈRE
TORCHÈRES
TORCHERS
TORCHES
TORCHING
TORCHON
TORCHONS
TORCS
TORCULAR
TORCULARS
TORDION
TORDIONS
TORE
TOREADOR
TOREADORS
TORERO
TOREROS
TORES
TOREUTIC
TOREUTICS
TORGOCH
TORGOCHS
TORI
TORIC
TORII
TORIIS
TORMENT
TORMENTED
TORMENTIL
TORMENTILS
TORMENTING
TORMENTINGS
TORMENTOR
TORMENTORS
TORMENTS
TORMENTUM
TORMENTUMS
TORMINA
TORMINAL
TORMINOUS
TORN
TORNADE
TORNADES
TORNADIC
TORNADO
TORNADOES
TOROID
TOROIDAL
TOROIDS
TORPEDO
TORPEDOED

TORPEDOER
TORPEDOERS
TORPEDOES
TORPEDOING
TORPEDOS
TORPEFIED
TORPEFIES
TORPEFY
TORPEFYING
TORPID
TORPIDITIES
TORPIDITY
TORPIDLY
TORPIDS
TORPITUDE
TORPITUDES
TORPOR
TORPORS
TORQUATE
TORQUATED
TORQUE
TORQUED
TORQUES
TORR
TORREFIED
TORREFIES
TORREFY
TORREFYING
TORRENT
TORRENTS
TORRET
TORRETS
TORRID
TORRIDER
TORRIDEST
TORRIDITIES
TORRIDITY
TORRS
TORS
TORSADE
TORSADES
TORSE
TORSEL
TORSELS
TORSES
TORSION
TORSIONAL
TORSIONS
TORSIVE
TORSK
TORSKS
TORSO
TORSOS
TORT
TORTE
TORTEN
TORTES
TORTILE
TORTILITIES
TORTILITY
TORTILLA
TORTILLAS
TORTIOUS
TORTIVE
TORTOISE
TORTOISES
TORTRICES
TORTRICID
TORTRICIDS
TORTRIX

TORTS
TORTUOUS
TORTURE
TORTURED
TORTURER
TORTURERS
TORTURES
TORTURING
TORTURINGS
TORTUROUS
TORUFFLED
TORULA
TORULAS
TORULIN
TORULINS
TORULOSE
TORULOSES
TORULOSIS
TORULUS
TORULUSES
TORUS
TOSE
TOSED
TOSES
TOSH
TOSHACH
TOSHACHS
TOSHED
TOSHER
TOSHERS
TOSHES
TOSHIER
TOSHIEST
TOSHING
TOSHY
TOSING
TOSS
TOSSED
TOSSEN
TOSSER
TOSSERS
TOSSES
TOSSIER
TOSSIEST
TOSSILY
TOSSING
TOSSINGS
TOSSPOT
TOSSPOTS
TOSSY
TOST
TOT
TOTAL
TOTALISE
TOTALISED
TOTALISER
TOTALISERS
TOTALISES
TOTALISING
TOTALITIES
TOTALITY
TOTALIZE
TOTALIZED
TOTALIZER
TOTALIZERS
TOTALIZES
TOTALIZING
TOTALLED
TOTALLING
TOTALLY

TOTALS
TOTARA
TOTARAS
TOTE
TOTED
TOTEM
TOTEMIC
TOTEMISM
TOTEMISMS
TOTEMIST
TOTEMISTS
TOTEMS
TOTES
TOTHER
TOTIENT
TOTIENTS
TOTING
TOTITIVE
TOTITIVES
TOTS
TOTTED
TOTTER
TOTTERED
TOTTERER
TOTTERERS
TOTTERING
TOTTERINGS
TOTTERS
TOTTERY
TOTTIE
TOTTIER
TOTTIES
TOTTIEST
TOTTING
TOTTINGS
TOTTY
TOUCAN
TOUCANET
TOUCANETS
TOUCANS
TOUCH
TOUCHABLE
TOUCHÉ
TOUCHED
TOUCHER
TOUCHERS
TOUCHES
TOUCHIER
TOUCHIEST
TOUCHILY
TOUCHING
TOUCHINGS
TOUCHLESS
TOUCHWOOD
TOUCHWOODS
TOUCHY
TOUGH
TOUGHEN
TOUGHENED
TOUGHENER
TOUGHENERS
TOUGHENING
TOUGHENINGS
TOUGHENS
TOUGHER
TOUGHEST
TOUGHIE
TOUGHIES
TOUGHISH
TOUGHLY

TOUGHNESS
TOUGHNESSES
TOUGHS
TOUK
TOUKS
TOUN
TOUNS
TOUPEE
TOUPEES
TOUPET
TOUPETS
TOUR
TOURACO
TOURACOS
TOURED
TOURER
TOURERS
TOURING
TOURINGS
TOURISM
TOURISMS
TOURIST
TOURISTIC
TOURISTS
TOURISTY
TOURNEDOS
TOURNEY
TOURNEYED
TOURNEYER
TOURNEYERS
TOURNEYING
TOURNEYS
TOURNURE
TOURNURES
TOURS
TOUSE
TOUSED
TOUSER
TOUSERS
TOUSES
TOUSIER
TOUSIEST
TOUSING
TOUSINGS
TOUSLE
TOUSLED
TOUSLES
TOUSLING
TOUSTIE
TOUSY
TOUT
TOUTED
TOUTER
TOUTERS
TOUTIE
TOUTIER
TOUTIEST
TOUTING
TOUTS
TOUZE
TOUZED
TOUZES
TOUZING
TOUZLE
TOUZLED
TOUZLES
TOUZLING
TOVARISH
TOVARISHES
TOW

TOWAGE
TOWAGES
TOWARD
TOWARDLY
TOWARDS
TOWBAR
TOWBARS
TOWED
TOWEL
TOWELLED
TOWELLING
TOWELLINGS
TOWELS
TOWER
TOWERED
TOWERIER
TOWERIEST
TOWERING
TOWERLESS
TOWERS
TOWERY
TOWHEE
TOWHEES
TOWIER
TOWIEST
TOWING
TOWINGS
TOWLINE
TOWLINES
TOWMON
TOWMOND
TOWMONDS
TOWMONS
TOWMONT
TOWMONTS
TOWN
TOWNEE
TOWNEES
TOWNHOUSE
TOWNHOUSES
TOWNIE
TOWNIER
TOWNIES
TOWNIEST
TOWNISH
TOWNLAND
TOWNLANDS
TOWNLING
TOWNLINGS
TOWNLY
TOWNS
TOWNSCAPE
TOWNSCAPED
TOWNSCAPES
TOWNSCAPING
TOWNSCAPINGS
TOWNSFOLK
TOWNSFOLKS
TOWNSHIP
TOWNSHIPS
TOWNSKIP
TOWNSKIPS
TOWNSMAN
TOWNSMEN
TOWNY
TOWPATH
TOWPATHS
TOWROPE
TOWROPES
TOWS

TOWSE
TOWSED
TOWSER
TOWSERS
TOWSES
TOWSIER
TOWSIEST
TOWSING
TOWSY
TOWT
TOWTED
TOWTING
TOWTS
TOWY
TOWZE
TOWZED
TOWZES
TOWZING
TOXAEMIA
TOXAEMIAS
TOXAEMIC
TOXAPHENE
TOXAPHENES
TOXIC
TOXICAL
TOXICALLY
TOXICANT
TOXICANTS
TOXICITIES
TOXICITY
TOXIN
TOXINS
TOXOCARA
TOXOCARAS
TOXOID
TOXOIDS
TOXOPHILIES
TOXOPHILY
TOY
TOYED
TOYER
TOYERS
TOYING
TOYINGS
TOYISH
TOYISHLY
TOYLESOME
TOYLSOM
TOYMAN
TOYMEN
TOYS
TOYSHOP
TOYSHOPS
TOYSOME
TOYWOMAN
TOYWOMEN
TOZE
TOZED
TOZES
TOZIE
TOZIES
TOZING
TRABEATE
TRABEATED
TRABECULA
TRABECULAE
TRACE
TRACEABLE
TRACEABLY
TRACED

TRACELESS	TRADENAME	TRAIPSING	TRANSCENDED	TRANSMUTES
TRACER	TRADENAMES	TRAIPSINGS	TRANSCENDING	TRANSMUTING
TRACERIED	TRADER	TRAIT	TRANSCENDS	TRANSOM
TRACERIES	TRADERS	TRAITOR	TRANSE	TRANSOMS
TRACERS	TRADES	TRAITORLY	TRANSECT	TRANSONIC
TRACERY	TRADESMAN	TRAITORS	TRANSECTED	TRANSONICS
TRACES	TRADESMEN	TRAITRESS	TRANSECTING	TRANSPIRE
TRACHEA	TRADING	TRAITRESSES	TRANSECTS	TRANSPIRED
TRACHEAE	TRADINGS	TRAITS	TRANSENNA	TRANSPIRES
TRACHEAL	TRADITION	TRAJECT	TRANSENNAS	TRANSPIRING
TRACHEARIES	TRADITIONS	TRAJECTED	TRANSEPT	TRANSPORT
TRACHEARY	TRADITIVE	TRAJECTING	TRANSEPTS	TRANSPORTED
TRACHEATE	TRADITOR	TRAJECTS	TRANSES	TRANSPORTING
TRACHEID	TRADITORS	TRAM	TRANSFARD	TRANSPORTINGS
TRACHEIDE	TRADS	TRAMMEL	TRANSFECT	TRANSPORTS
TRACHEIDES	TRADUCE	TRAMMELLED	TRANSFECTED	TRANSPOSE
TRACHEIDS	TRADUCED	TRAMMELLING	TRANSFECTING	TRANSPOSED
TRACHITIS	TRADUCER	TRAMMELS	TRANSFECTS	TRANSPOSES
TRACHITISES	TRADUCERS	TRAMP	TRANSFER	TRANSPOSING
TRACHOMA	TRADUCES	TRAMPED	TRANSFERRED	TRANSPOSINGS
TRACHOMAS	TRADUCING	TRAMPER	TRANSFERRING	TRANSSHIP
TRACHYTE	TRADUCINGS	TRAMPERS	TRANSFERS	TRANSSHIPPED
TRACHYTES	TRAFFIC	TRAMPET	TRANSFIX	TRANSSHIPPING
TRACHYTIC	TRAFFICKED	TRAMPETS	TRANSFIXED	TRANSSHIPPINGS
TRACING	TRAFFICKING	TRAMPETTE	TRANSFIXES	TRANSSHIPS
TRACINGS	TRAFFICKINGS	TRAMPETTES	TRANSFIXING	TRANSUDE
TRACK	TRAFFICS	TRAMPING	TRANSFORM	TRANSUDED
TRACKAGE	TRAGEDIAN	TRAMPLE	TRANSFORMED	TRANSUDES
TRACKAGES	TRAGEDIANS	TRAMPLED	TRANSFORMING	TRANSUDING
TRACKED	TRAGEDIED	TRAMPLER	TRANSFORMINGS	TRANSUME
TRACKER	TRAGEDY	TRAMPLERS	TRANSFORMS	TRANSUMED
TRACKERS	TRAGELAPH	TRAMPLES	TRANSFUSE	TRANSUMES
TRACKING	TRAGELAPHS	TRAMPLING	TRANSFUSED	TRANSUMING
TRACKINGS	TRAGI	TRAMPLINGS	TRANSFUSES	TRANSUMPT
TRACKLESS	TRAGIC	TRAMPOLIN	TRANSFUSING	TRANSUMPTS
TRACKMAN	TRAGICAL	TRAMPOLINS	TRANSHIP	TRANSVEST
TRACKMEN	TRAGOPAN	TRAMPS	TRANSHIPPED	TRANSVESTED
TRACKROAD	TRAGOPANS	TRAMS	TRANSHIPPING	TRANSVESTING
TRACKROADS	TRAGULE	TRAMWAY	TRANSHIPPINGS	TRANSVESTS
TRACKS	TRAGULES	TRAMWAYS	TRANSHIPS	TRANT
TRACKWAY	TRAGULINE	TRANCE	TRANSHUME	TRANTED
TRACKWAYS	TRAGUS	TRANCED	TRANSHUMED	TRANTER
TRACT	TRAHISON	TRANCEDLY	TRANSHUMES	TRANTERS
TRACTABLE	TRAHISONS	TRANCES	TRANSHUMING	TRANTING
TRACTATE	TRAIK	TRANCHE	TRANSIENT	TRANTS
TRACTATES	TRAIKED	TRANCHES	TRANSIENTS	TRAP
TRACTATOR	TRAIKING	TRANCHET	TRANSIRE	TRAPAN
TRACTATORS	TRAIKIT	TRANCHETS	TRANSIRES	TRAPANNED
TRACTED	TRAIKS	TRANCING	TRANSIT	TRAPANNING
TRACTILE	TRAIL	TRANECT	TRANSITED	TRAPANS
TRACTING	TRAILED	TRANECTS	TRANSITING	TRAPE
TRACTION	TRAILER	TRANGAM	TRANSITS	TRAPED
TRACTIONS	TRAILERED	TRANGAMS	TRANSLATE	TRAPES
TRACTIVE	TRAILERING	TRANGLE	TRANSLATED	TRAPESED
TRACTOR	TRAILERS	TRANGLES	TRANSLATES	TRAPESES
TRACTORS	TRAILING	TRANKUM	TRANSLATING	TRAPESING
TRACTRIX	TRAILS	TRANKUMS	TRANSMEW	TRAPESINGS
TRACTRIXES	TRAIN	TRANNIE	TRANSMEWED	TRAPEZE
TRACTS	TRAINABLE	TRANNIES	TRANSMEWING	TRAPEZED
TRACTUS	TRAINED	TRANNY	TRANSMEWS	TRAPEZES
TRACTUSES	TRAINEE	TRANQUIL	TRANSMIT	TRAPEZIA
TRAD	TRAINEES	TRANQUILLER	TRANSMITS	TRAPEZIAL
TRADABLE	TRAINER	TRANQUILLEST	TRANSMITTED	TRAPEZING
TRADE	TRAINERS	TRANSACT	TRANSMITTING	TRAPEZIUM
TRADEABLE	TRAINING	TRANSACTED	TRANSMOVE	TRAPEZIUMS
TRADED	TRAININGS	TRANSACTING	TRANSMOVED	TRAPEZIUS
TRADEFUL	TRAINS	TRANSACTS	TRANSMOVES	TRAPEZIUSES
TRADELESS	TRAIPSE	TRANSAXLE	TRANSMOVING	TRAPEZOID
TRADEMARK	TRAIPSED	TRANSAXLES	TRANSMUTE	TRAPEZOIDS
TRADEMARKS	TRAIPSES	TRANSCEND	TRANSMUTED	TRAPING

TRAPPEAN
TRAPPED
TRAPPER
TRAPPERS
TRAPPIER
TRAPPIEST
TRAPPING
TRAPPINGS
TRAPPY
TRAPS
TRAPUNTO
TRAPUNTOS
TRASH
TRASHED
TRASHERIES
TRASHERY
TRASHES
TRASHIER
TRASHIEST
TRASHILY
TRASHING
TRASHTRIE
TRASHTRIES
TRASHY
TRASS
TRASSES
TRATTORIA
TRATTORIAS
TRATTORIE
TRAUCHLE
TRAUCHLED
TRAUCHLES
TRAUCHLING
TRAUMA
TRAUMAS
TRAUMATA
TRAUMATIC
TRAVAIL
TRAVAILED
TRAVAILING
TRAVAILS
TRAVE
TRAVEL
TRAVELLED
TRAVELLER
TRAVELLERS
TRAVELLING
TRAVELLINGS
TRAVELS
TRAVERSAL
TRAVERSALS
TRAVERSE
TRAVERSED
TRAVERSER
TRAVERSERS
TRAVERSES
TRAVERSING
TRAVERSINGS
TRAVERTIN
TRAVERTINS
TRAVES
TRAVESTIED
TRAVESTIES
TRAVESTY
TRAVESTYING
TRAVIS
TRAVISES
TRAVOIS
TRAWL
TRAWLED

TRAWLER
TRAWLERS
TRAWLING
TRAWLINGS
TRAWLS
TRAY
TRAYBIT
TRAYBITS
TRAYFUL
TRAYFULS
TRAYNE
TRAYNED
TRAYNES
TRAYNING
TRAYS
TREACHER
TREACHERIES
TREACHERS
TREACHERY
TREACHOUR
TREACHOURS
TREACLE
TREACLED
TREACLES
TREACLIER
TREACLIEST
TREACLING
TREACLY
TREAD
TREADER
TREADERS
TREADING
TREADINGS
TREADLE
TREADLED
TREADLER
TREADLERS
TREADLES
TREADLING
TREADLINGS
TREADMILL
TREADMILLS
TREADS
TREAGUE
TREAGUES
TREASON
TREASONS
TREASURE
TREASURED
TREASURER
TREASURERS
TREASURES
TREASURIES
TREASURING
TREASURY
TREAT
TREATABLE
TREATED
TREATER
TREATERS
TREATIES
TREATING
TREATINGS
TREATISE
TREATISES
TREATMENT
TREATMENTS
TREATS
TREATY
TREBLE

TREBLED
TREBLES
TREBLING
TREBLY
TREBUCHET
TREBUCHETS
TRECENTO
TRECENTOS
TRECK
TRECKED
TRECKING
TRECKS
TREDDLE
TREDDLED
TREDDLES
TREDDLING
TREDILLE
TREDILLES
TREDRILLE
TREDRILLES
TREE
TREED
TREEING
TREELESS
TREEN
TREENAIL
TREENAILS
TREENS
TREES
TREESHIP
TREESHIPS
TREETOP
TREETOPS
TREF
TREFA
TREFOIL
TREFOILED
TREFOILS
TREGETOUR
TREGETOURS
TREHALA
TREHALAS
TREILLAGE
TREILLAGES
TREILLE
TREILLES
TREK
TREKKED
TREKKER
TREKKERS
TREKKING
TREKS
TRELLIS
TRELLISED
TRELLISES
TRELLISING
TREMA
TREMAS
TREMATIC
TREMATODE
TREMATODES
TREMATOID
TREMATOIDS
TREMBLANT
TREMBLE
TREMBLED
TREMBLER
TREMBLERS
TREMBLES
TREMBLIER

TREMBLIEST
TREMBLING
TREMBLINGS
TREMBLY
TRÉMIE
TREMIE
TREMIES
TRÉMIES
TREMOLANT
TREMOLANTS
TREMOLITE
TREMOLITES
TREMOLO
TREMOLOS
TREMOR
TREMORS
TREMULANT
TREMULANTS
TREMULATE
TREMULATED
TREMULATES
TREMULATING
TREMULOUS
TRENAIL
TRENAILS
TRENCH
TRENCHAND
TRENCHANT
TRENCHARD
TRENCHARDS
TRENCHED
TRENCHER
TRENCHERS
TRENCHES
TRENCHING
TREND
TRENDED
TRENDIER
TRENDIES
TRENDIEST
TRENDING
TRENDS
TRENDY
TRENISE
TRENISES
TRENTAL
TRENTALS
TREPAN
TREPANG
TREPANGS
TREPANNED
TREPANNER
TREPANNERS
TREPANNING
TREPANNINGS
TREPANS
TREPHINE
TREPHINED
TREPHINES
TREPHINING
TREPID
TREPIDANT
TREPIDER
TREPIDEST
TREPONEMA
TREPONEMAS
TREPONEMATA
TRESPASS
TRESPASSED
TRESPASSES

TRESPASSING
TRESS
TRESSED
TRESSEL
TRESSELS
TRESSES
TRESSIER
TRESSIEST
TRESSING
TRESSURE
TRESSURED
TRESSURES
TRESSY
TRESTLE
TRESTLES
TRET
TRETS
TREVALLIES
TREVALLY
TREVIS
TREVISES
TREVISS
TREVISSES
TREW
TREWS
TREWSMAN
TREWSMEN
TREY
TREYBIT
TREYBITS
TREYS
TREZ
TREZES
TRIABLE
TRIACID
TRIACT
TRIACTINE
TRIAD
TRIADIC
TRIADIST
TRIADISTS
TRIADS
TRIAGE
TRIAGES
TRIAL
TRIALISM
TRIALISMS
TRIALIST
TRIALISTS
TRIALITIES
TRIALITY
TRIALLIST
TRIALLISTS
TRIALOGUE
TRIALOGUES
TRIALS
TRIANGLE
TRIANGLED
TRIANGLES
TRIAPSAL
TRIARCH
TRIARCHIES
TRIARCHS
TRIARCHY
TRIATHLON
TRIATHLONS
TRIATIC
TRIATICS
TRIATOMIC
TRIAXIAL

TRIAXIALS	TRICKERIES	TRIERARCH	TRIKES	TRINING
TRIAXON	TRICKERS	TRIERARCHS	TRIKING	TRINITIES
TRIAXONS	TRICKERY	TRIERS	TRILBIES	TRINITRIN
TRIBADE	TRICKIER	TRIES	TRILBY	TRINITRINS
TRIBADES	TRICKIEST	TRIETERIC	TRILBYS	TRINITY
TRIBADIC	TRICKILY	TRIETHYL	TRILD	TRINKET
TRIBADIES	TRICKING	TRIFACIAL	TRILEMMA	TRINKETED
TRIBADISM	TRICKINGS	TRIFECTA	TRILEMMAS	TRINKETER
TRIBADISMS	TRICKISH	TRIFECTAS	TRILINEAR	TRINKETERS
TRIBADY	TRICKLE	TRIFFID	TRILITH	TRINKETING
TRIBAL	TRICKLED	TRIFFIDS	TRILITHIC	TRINKETINGS
TRIBALISM	TRICKLES	TRIFFIDY	TRILITHON	TRINKETRIES
TRIBALISMS	TRICKLESS	TRIFID	TRILITHONS	TRINKETRY
TRIBALIST	TRICKLET	TRIFLE	TRILITHS	TRINKETS
TRIBALISTS	TRICKLETS	TRIFLED	TRILL	TRINKUM
TRIBALLY	TRICKLIER	TRIFLER	TRILLED	TRINKUMS
TRIBASIC	TRICKLIEST	TRIFLERS	TRILLING	TRINOMIAL
TRIBBLE	TRICKLING	TRIFLES	TRILLINGS	TRINOMIALS
TRIBBLES	TRICKLINGS	TRIFLING	TRILLION	TRINS
TRIBE	TRICKLY	TRIFOCAL	TRILLIONS	TRIO
TRIBELESS	TRICKS	TRIFOCALS	TRILLIUM	TRIODE
TRIBES	TRICKSIER	TRIFOLIES	TRILLIUMS	TRIODES
TRIBESMAN	TRICKSIEST	TRIFOLIUM	TRILLO	TRIOLET
TRIBESMEN	TRICKSOME	TRIFOLIUMS	TRILLOES	TRIOLETS
TRIBLET	TRICKSTER	TRIFOLY	TRILLS	TRIONES
TRIBLETS	TRICKSTERS	TRIFORIA	TRILOBATE	TRIONYM
TRIBOLOGIES	TRICKSY	TRIFORIUM	TRILOBE	TRIONYMAL
TRIBOLOGY	TRICKY	TRIFORM	TRILOBED	TRIONYMS
TRIBRACH	TRICLINIA	TRIFORMED	TRILOBES	TRION
TRIBRACHS	TRICLINIC	TRIG	TRILOBITE	TRIORS
TRIBUNAL	TRICOLOR	TRIGAMIES	TRILOBITES	TRIOS
TRIBUNALS	TRICOLORS	TRIGAMIST	TRILOGIES	TRIOXIDE
TRIBUNATE	TRICOLOUR	TRIGAMISTS	TRILOGY	TRIOXIDES
TRIBUNATES	TRICOLOURS	TRIGAMOUS	TRIM	TRIP
TRIBUNE	TRICORN	TRIGAMY	TRIMARAN	TRIPE
TRIBUNES	TRICORNE	TRIGGED	TRIMARANS	TRIPEDAL
TRIBUTARIES	TRICORNES	TRIGGER	TRIMER	TRIPEMAN
TRIBUTARY	TRICORNS	TRIGGERED	TRIMERIC	TRIPEMEN
TRIBUTE	TRICOT	TRIGGERING	TRIMEROUS	TRIPERIES
TRIBUTER	TRICOTS	TRIGGERS	TRIMERS	TRIPERY
TRIBUTERS	TRICROTIC	TRIGGEST	TRIMESTER	TRIPES
TRIBUTES	TRICUSPID	TRIGGING	TRIMESTERS	TRIPEWIFE
TRICAR	TRICYCLE	TRIGLOT	TRIMETER	TRIPEWIVES
TRICARS	TRICYCLED	TRIGLOTS	TRIMETERS	TRIPHONE
TRICE	TRICYCLER	TRIGLY	TRIMETHYL	TRIPHONES
TRICED	TRICYCLERS	TRIGLYPH	TRIMETRIC	TRIPITAKA
TRICEPS	TRICYCLES	TRIGLYPHS	TRIMLY	TRIPITAKAS
TRICEPSES	TRICYCLIC	TRIGNESS	TRIMMED	TRIPLANE
TRICERION	TRICYCLING	TRIGNESSES	TRIMMER	TRIPLANES
TRICERIONS	TRICYCLINGS	TRIGON	TRIMMERS	TRIPLE
TRICES	TRIDACNA	TRIGONAL	TRIMMEST	TRIPLED
TRICHINA	TRIDACNAS	TRIGONIC	TRIMMING	TRIPLES
TRICHINAE	TRIDACTYL	TRIGONOUS	TRIMMINGS	TRIPLET
TRICHINAS	TRIDARN	TRIGONS	TRIMNESS	TRIPLETS
TRICHITE	TRIDARNS	TRIGRAM	TRIMNESSES	TRIPLEX
TRICHITES	TRIDE	TRIGRAMS	TRIMS	TRIPLEXES
TRICHITIC	TRIDENT	TRIGRAPH	TRIMTAB	TRIPLIED
TRICHOID	TRIDENTAL	TRIGRAPHS	TRIMTABS	TRIPLIES
TRICHOME	TRIDENTED	TRIGS	TRIN	TRIPLING
TRICHOMES	TRIDENTS	TRIGYNIAN	TRINAL	TRIPLINGS
TRICHORD	TRIDUAN	TRIGYNOUS	TRINARY	TRIPLOID
TRICHORDS	TRIDUUM	TRIHEDRAL	TRINDLE	TRIPLOIDIES
TRICHOSES	TRIDUUMS	TRIHEDRALS	TRINDLED	TRIPLOIDY
TRICHOSIS	TRIDYMITE	TRIHEDRON	TRINDLES	TRIPLY
TRICHROIC	TRIDYMITES	TRIHEDRONS	TRINDLING	TRIPLYING
TRICHROME	TRIE	TRIHYBRID	TRINE	TRIPOD
TRICING	TRIECIOUS	TRIHYBRIDS	TRINED	TRIPODAL
TRICK	TRIED	TRIHYDRIC	TRINES	TRIPODIES
TRICKED	TRIENNIAL	TRIKE	TRINGLE	TRIPODS
TRICKER	TRIER	TRIKED	TRINGLES	TRIPODY

TRIPOLI
TRIPOLIS
TRIPOS
TRIPOSES
TRIPPANT
TRIPPED
TRIPPER
TRIPPERS
TRIPPERY
TRIPPET
TRIPPETS
TRIPPING
TRIPPINGS
TRIPPLE
TRIPPLED
TRIPPLER
TRIPPLERS
TRIPPLES
TRIPPLING
TRIPS
TRIPSES
TRIPSIS
TRIPTANE
TRIPTANES
TRIPTOTE
TRIPTOTES
TRIPTYCH
TRIPTYCHS
TRIPTYQUE
TRIPTYQUES
TRIPUDIA
TRIPUDIUM
TRIPUDIUMS
TRIQUETRA
TRIQUETRAS
TRIRADIAL
TRIREME
TRIREMES
TRISAGION
TRISAGIONS
TRISECT
TRISECTED
TRISECTING
TRISECTOR
TRISECTORS
TRISECTS
TRISEME
TRISEMES
TRISEMIC
TRISHAW
TRISHAWS
TRISKELE
TRISKELES
TRISKELIA
TRISMUS
TRISMUSES
TRISOME
TRISOMES
TRISOMIC
TRISOMIES
TRISOMY
TRIST
TRISTE
TRISTFUL
TRISTICH
TRISTICHS
TRISUL
TRISULA
TRISULAS
TRISULS

TRITE
TRITELY
TRITENESS
TRITENESSES
TRITER
TRITES
TRITEST
TRITHEISM
TRITHEISMS
TRITHEIST
TRITHEISTS
TRITIATE
TRITIATED
TRITIATES
TRITIATING
TRITICAL
TRITICALE
TRITICALES
TRITICISM
TRITICISMS
TRITIDE
TRITIDES
TRITIUM
TRITIUMS
TRITON
TRITONE
TRITONES
TRITONIA
TRITONIAS
TRITONS
TRITURATE
TRITURATED
TRITURATES
TRITURATING
TRIUMPH
TRIUMPHAL
TRIUMPHALS
TRIUMPHED
TRIUMPHER
TRIUMPHERS
TRIUMPHING
TRIUMPHINGS
TRIUMPHS
TRIUMVIR
TRIUMVIRI
TRIUMVIRIES
TRIUMVIRS
TRIUMVIRY
TRIUNE
TRIUNES
TRIUNITIES
TRIUNITY
TRIVALENT
TRIVALVE
TRIVALVED
TRIVALVES
TRIVET
TRIVETS
TRIVIA
TRIVIAL
TRIVIALLY
TRIVIUM
TRIVIUMS
TRIZONAL
TRIZONE
TRIZONES
TROAD
TROADE
TROADES
TROADS

TROAT
TROATED
TROATING
TROATS
TROCAR
TROCARS
TROCHAIC
TROCHAICS
TROCHAL
TROCHE
TROCHEE
TROCHEES
TROCHES
TROCHI
TROCHILIC
TROCHILUS
TROCHILUSES
TROCHISK
TROCHISKS
TROCHITE
TROCHITES
TROCHLEA
TROCHLEAR
TROCHLEAS
TROCHOID
TROCHOIDS
TROCHUS
TROCHUSES
TROCK
TROCKED
TROCKING
TROCKS
TROD
TRODDEN
TRODE
TRODES
TRODS
TROELIE
TROELIES
TROELY
TROG
TROGGED
TROGGING
TROGGS
TROGON
TROGONS
TROGS
TROIKA
TROIKAS
TROILISM
TROILISMS
TROILIST
TROILISTS
TROILITE
TROILITES
TROKE
TROKED
TROKES
TROKING
TROLL
TROLLED
TROLLER
TROLLERS
TROLLEY
TROLLEYS
TROLLIES
TROLLING
TROLLINGS
TROLLOP
TROLLOPED

TROLLOPEE
TROLLOPEES
TROLLOPING
TROLLOPS
TROLLOPY
TROLLS
TROLLY
TROMBONE
TROMBONES
TROMINO
TROMINOES
TROMINOS
TROMMEL
TROMMELS
TROMP
TROMPE
TROMPES
TROMPS
TRON
TRONA
TRONAS
TRONC
TRONCS
TRONE
TRONES
TRONS
TROOLIE
TROOLIES
TROOP
TROOPED
TROOPER
TROOPERS
TROOPIAL
TROOPIALS
TROOPING
TROOPS
TROPARIA
TROPARION
TROPE
TROPED
TROPES
TROPHESIES
TROPHESY
TROPHI
TROPHIC
TROPHIED
TROPHIES
TROPHY
TROPHYING
TROPIC
TROPICAL
TROPICS
TROPING
TROPISM
TROPISMS
TROPIST
TROPISTIC
TROPISTS
TROPOLOGIES
TROPOLOGY
TROPPO
TROSSERS
TROT
TROTH
TROTHED
TROTHFUL
TROTHING
TROTHLESS
TROTHS
TROTLINE

TROTLINES
TROTS
TROTTED
TROTTER
TROTTERS
TROTTING
TROTTINGS
TROTTOIR
TROTTOIRS
TROTYL
TROTYLS
TROUBLE
TROUBLED
TROUBLER
TROUBLERS
TROUBLES
TROUBLING
TROUBLINGS
TROUBLOUS
TROUGH
TROUGHS
TROULE
TROULED
TROULES
TROULING
TROUNCE
TROUNCED
TROUNCER
TROUNCERS
TROUNCES
TROUNCING
TROUNCINGS
TROUPE
TROUPED
TROUPER
TROUPERS
TROUPES
TROUPIAL
TROUPIALS
TROUPING
TROUSE
TROUSERED
TROUSERS
TROUSES
TROUSSEAU
TROUSSEAUS
TROUSSEAUX
TROUT
TROUTER
TROUTERS
TROUTFUL
TROUTIER
TROUTIEST
TROUTING
TROUTINGS
TROUTLESS
TROUTLET
TROUTLETS
TROUTLING
TROUTLINGS
TROUTS
TROUTY
TROUVÈRE
TROUVÈRES
TROUVEUR
TROUVEURS
TNOVER
TROVERS
TROW
TROWED

TROWEL	TRUFFLE	TRUSTIER	TSUNAMI	TUCHUN
TROWELLED	TRUFFLED	TRUSTIES	TSUNAMIS	TUCHUNS
TROWELLER	TRUFFLES	TRUSTIEST	TUAN	TUCK
TROWELLERS	TRUG	TRUSTILY	TUANS	TUCKAHOE
TROWELLING	TRUGS	TRUSTING	TUART	TUCKAHOES
TROWELS	TRUING	TRUSTLESS	TUARTS	TUCKED
TROWING	TRUISM	TRUSTS	TUATARA	TUCKER
TROWS	TRUISMS	TRUSTY	TUATARAS	TUCKERBAG
TROWSERS	TRUISTIC	TRUTH	TUATH	TUCKERBAGS
TROY	TRULL	TRUTHFUL	TUATHS	TUCKERBOX
TROYS	TRULLS	TRUTHIER	TUB	TUCKERBOXES
TRUANCIES	TRULY	TRUTHIEST	TUBA	TUCKERED
TRUANCY	TRUMEAU	TRUTHLESS	TUBAE	TUCKERING
TRUANT	TRUMEAUX	TRUTHLIKE	TUBAGE	TUCKERS
TRUANTED	TRUMP	TRUTHS	TUBAGES	TUCKET
TRUANTING	TRUMPED	TRUTHY	TUBAL	TUCKETS
TRUANTRIES	TRUMPERIES	TRY	TUBAR	TUCKING
TRUANTRY	TRUMPERY	TRYE	TUBAS	TUCKS
TRUANTS	TRUMPET	TRYER	TUBATE	TUCOTUCO
TRUCAGE	TRUMPETED	TRYERS	TUBBED	TUCOTUCOS
TRUCAGES	TRUMPETER	TRYING	TUBBER	TUCUTUCO
TRUCE	TRUMPETERS	TRYINGLY	TUBBERS	TUCUTUCOS
TRUCELESS	TRUMPETING	TRYINGS	TUBBIER	TUFA
TRUCES	TRUMPETINGS	TRYP	TUBBIEST	TUFACEOUS
TRUCHMAN	TRUMPETS	TRYPS	TUBBINESS	TUFAS
TRUCHMANS	TRUMPING	TRYPSIN	TUBBINESSES	TUFF
TRUCHMEN	TRUMPINGS	TRYPSINS	TUBBING	TUFFE
TRUCIAL	TRUMPS	TRYPTIC	TUBBINGS	TUFFES
TRUCK	TRUNCAL	TRYSAIL	TUBBISH	TUFFET
TRUCKAGE	TRUNCATE	TRYSAILS	TUBBY	TUFFETS
TRUCKAGES	TRUNCATED	TRYST	TUBE	TUFFS
TRUCKED	TRUNCATES	TRYSTED	TUBECTOMIES	TUFT
TRUCKER	TRUNCATING	TRYSTER	TUBECTOMY	TUFTED
TRUCKERS	TRUNCHEON	TRYSTERS	TUBED	TUFTER
TRUCKING	TRUNCHEONED	TRYSTING	TUBEFUL	TUFTERS
TRUCKINGS	TRUNCHEONING	TRYSTS	TUBEFULS	TUFTIER
TRUCKLE	TRUNCHEONS	TSADDIK	TUBELESS	TUFTIEST
TRUCKLED	TRUNDLE	TSADDIKIM	TUBER	TUFTING
TRUCKLER	TRUNDLED	TSADDIKS	TUBERCLE	TUFTINGS
TRUCKLERS	TRUNDLES	TSADDIQ	TUBERCLED	TUFTS
TRUCKLES	TRUNDLING	TSADDIQIM	TUBERCLES	TUFTY
TRUCKLING	TRUNK	TSADDIQS	TUBERCULA	TUG
TRUCKLINGS	TRUNKED	TSAMBA	TUBERCULE	TUGGED
TRUCKMAN	TRUNKFISH	TSAMBAS	TUBERCULES	TUGGER
TRUCKMEN	TRUNKFISHES	TSAR	TUBEROSE	TUGGERS
TRUCKS	TRUNKFUL	TSARDOM	TUBEROSES	TUGGING
TRUCULENT	TRUNKFULS	TSARDOMS	TUBEROUS	TUGGINGLY
TRUDGE	TRUNKING	TSAREVICH	TUBERS	TUGGINGS
TRUDGED	TRUNKINGS	TSAREVICHES	TUBES	TUGRIK
TRUDGEN	TRUNKS	TSAREVNA	TUBFAST	TUGRIKS
TRUDGENS	TRUNNION	TSAREVNAS	TUBFASTS	TUGS
TRUDGEON	TRUNNIONS	TSARINA	TUBFISH	TUI
TRUDGEONS	TRUQUAGE	TSARINAS	TUBFISHES	TUILLE
TRUDGER	TRUQUAGES	TSARISM	TUBFUL	TUILLES
TRUDGERS	TRUQUEUR	TSARISMS	TUBFULS	TUILLETTE
TRUDGES	TRUQUEURS	TSARIST	TUBICOLAR	TUILLETTES
TRUDGING	TRUSS	TSARISTS	TUBICOLE	TUILYIE
TRUDGINGS	TRUSSED	TSARITSA	TUBICOLES	TUILYIED
TRUE	TRUSSER	TSARITSAS	TUBIFORM	TUILYIEING
TRUED	TRUSSERS	TSARS	TUBING	TUILYIES
TRUEING	TRUSSES	TSESSEBE	TUBINGS	TUILZIE
TRUEMAN	TRUSSING	TSESSEBES	TUBS	TUILZIED
TRUEMEN	TRUSSINGS	TSETSE	TUBULAR	TUILZIEING
TRUENESS	TRUST	TSETSES	TUBULATE	TUILZIES
TRUENESSES	TRUSTED	TSIGANE	TUBULATED	TUIS
TRUEPENNIES	TRUSTEE	TSIGANES	TUBULATES	TUISM
TRUEPENNY	TRUSTEES	TSOTSI	TUBULATING	TUISMS
TRUER	TRUSTER	TSOTSIS	TUBULE	TUITION
TRUES	TRUSTERS	TSUBA	TUBULES	TUITIONAL
TRUEST	TRUSTFUL	TSUBAS	TUBULOUS	TUITIONS

TULAREMIA
TULAREMIAS
TULAREMIC
TULBAN
TULBANS
TULCHAN
TULCHANS
TULE
TULES
TULIP
TULIPANT
TULIPANTS
TULIPS
TULLE
TULLES
TULWAR
TULWARS
TUM
TUMBLE
TUMBLED
TUMBLER
TUMBLERS
TUMBLES
TUMBLING
TUMBLINGS
TUMBREL
TUMBRELS
TUMBRIL
TUMBRILS
TUMEFIED
TUMEFIES
TUMEFY
TUMEFYING
TUMESCE
TUMESCED
TUMESCENT
TUMESCES
TUMESCING
TUMID
TUMIDITIES
TUMIDITY
TUMIDLY
TUMIDNESS
TUMIDNESSES
TUMMIES
TUMMY
TUMOR
TUMOROUS
TUMORS
TUMOUR
TUMOURS
TUMP
TUMPED
TUMPHIES
TUMPHY
TUMPING
TUMPS
TUMPY
TUMS
TUMULAR
TUMULARY
TUMULI
TUMULT
TUMULTED
TUMULTING
TUMULTS
TUMULUS
TUN
TUNA
TUNABLE

TUNABLY
TUNAS
TUNBELLIES
TUNBELLY
TUND
TUNDED
TUNDING
TUNDRA
TUNDRAS
TUNDS
TUNDUN
TUNDUNS
TUNE
TUNEABLE
TUNED
TUNEFUL
TUNEFULLY
TUNELESS
TUNER
TUNERS
TUNES
TUNESMITH
TUNESMITHS
TUNGSTATE
TUNGSTATES
TUNGSTEN
TUNGSTENS
TUNIC
TUNICATE
TUNICATED
TUNICATES
TUNICIN
TUNICINS
TUNICKED
TUNICLE
TUNICLES
TUNICS
TUNIER
TUNIEST
TUNING
TUNINGS
TUNNAGE
TUNNAGES
TUNNED
TUNNEL
TUNNELLED
TUNNELLER
TUNNELLERS
TUNNELLING
TUNNELLINGS
TUNNELS
TUNNIES
TUNNING
TUNNINGS
TUNNY
TUNS
TUNY
TUP
TUPEK
TUPEKS
TUPELO
TUPELOS
TUPIK
TUPIKS
TUPPED
TUPPENCE
TUPPENCES
TUPPENNIES
TUPPENNY
TUPPING

TUPS
TUPTOWING
TUQUE
TUQUES
TURACIN
TURACINS
TURACO
TURACOS
TURBAN
TURBAND
TURBANDS
TURBANED
TURBANS
TURBANT
TURBANTS
TURBARIES
TURBARY
TURBID
TURBIDITE
TURBIDITES
TURBIDITIES
TURBIDITY
TURBIDLY
TURBINAL
TURBINALS
TURBINATE
TURBINATES
TURBINE
TURBINED
TURBINES
TURBIT
TURBITH
TURBITHS
TURBITS
TURBO
TURBOCAR
TURBOCARS
TURBOFAN
TURBOFANS
TURBOND
TURBONDS
TURBOPROP
TURBOPROPS
TURBOS
TURBOT
TURBOTS
TURBULENT
TURCOPOLE
TURCOPOLES
TURD
TURDINE
TURDION
TURDIONS
TURDOID
TURDS
TUREEN
TUREENS
TURF
TURFED
TURFEN
TURFIER
TURFIEST
TURFINESS
TURFINESSES
TURFING
TURFINGS
TURFITE
TURFITES
TURFMAN
TURFMEN

TURFS
TURFY
TURGENT
TURGENTLY
TURGID
TURGIDITIES
TURGIDITY
TURGIDLY
TURGOR
TURGORS
TURION
TURIONS
TURKEY
TURKEYS
TURKIES
TURKIESES
TURKIS
TURKISES
TURLOUGH
TURLOUGHS
TURM
TURME
TURMERIC
TURMERICS
TURMES
TURMOIL
TURMOILED
TURMOILING
TURMOILS
TURMS
TURN
TURNABOUT
TURNABOUTS
TURNAGAIN
TURNAGAINS
TURNBACK
TURNBACKS
TURNCOAT
TURNCOATS
TURNCOCK
TURNCOCKS
TURNDUN
TURNDUNS
TURNED
TURNER
TURNERIES
TURNERS
TURNERY
TURNING
TURNINGS
TURNIP
TURNIPED
TURNIPING
TURNIPS
TURNKEY
TURNKEYS
TURNOFF
TURNOFFS
TURNOVER
TURNOVERS
TURNPIKE
TURNPIKES
TURNROUND
TURNROUNDS
TURNS
TURNSKIN
TURNSKINS
TURNSOLE
TURNSOLES
TURNSPIT

TURNSPITS
TURNSTILE
TURNSTILES
TURNSTONE
TURNSTONES
TURNTABLE
TURNTABLES
TURPETH
TURPETHS
TURPITUDE
TURPITUDES
TURPS
TURQUOISE
TURQUOISES
TURRET
TURRETED
TURRETS
TURRIBANT
TURRIBANTS
TURTLE
TURTLED
TURTLER
TURTLERS
TURTLES
TURTLING
TURTLINGS
TURVES
TUSCHE
TUSCHES
TUSH
TUSHED
TUSHERIES
TUSHERY
TUSHES
TUSHING
TUSK
TUSKAR
TUSKARS
TUSKED
TUSKER
TUSKERS
TUSKIER
TUSKIEST
TUSKING
TUSKLESS
TUSKS
TUSKY
TUSSAH
TUSSAHS
TUSSAL
TUSSEH
TUSSEHS
TUSSER
TUSSERS
TUSSIS
TUSSISES
TUSSIVE
TUSSLE
TUSSLED
TUSSLES
TUSSLING
TUSSOCK
TUSSOCKS
TUSSOCKY
TUSSORE
TUSSORES
TUT
TUTANIA
TUTANIAS
TUTEE

TUTEES	TWADDLES	TWEENIES	TWILIGHTED	TWISTED
TUTELAGE	TWADDLIER	TWEENY	TWILIGHTING	TWISTER
TUTELAGES	TWADDLIEST	TWEER	TWILIGHTS	TWISTERS
TUTELAR	TWADDLING	TWEERED	TWILIT	TWISTIER
TUTELARIES	TWADDLINGS	TWEERING	TWILL	TWISTIEST
TUTELARS	TWADDLY	TWEERS	TWILLED	TWISTING
TUTELARY	TWAE	TWEEST	TWILLIES	TWISTINGS
TUTENAG	TWAES	TWEET	TWILLING	TWISTS
TUTENAGS	TWAFALD	TWEETED	TWILLS	TWISTY
TUTIORISM	TWAIN	TWEETER	TWILLY	TWIT
TUTIORISMS	TWAINS	TWEETERS	TWILT	TWITCH
TUTIORIST	TWAITE	TWEETING	TWILTED	TWITCHED
TUTIORISTS	TWAITES	TWEETS	TWILTING	TWITCHER
TUTMAN	TWAL	TWEEZE	TWILTS	TWITCHERS
TUTMEN	TWALHOURS	TWEEZED	TWIN	TWITCHES
TUTOR	TWALPENNIES	TWEEZERS	TWINE	TWITCHIER
TUTORAGE	TWALPENNY	TWEEZES	TWINED	TWITCHIEST
TUTORAGES	TWALS	TWEEZING	TWINER	TWITCHING
TUTORED	TWANG	TWELFTH	TWINERS	TWITCHINGS
TUTORESS	TWANGED	TWELFTHLY	TWINES	TWITCHY
TUTORESSES	TWANGIER	TWELFTHS	TWINGE	TWITE
TUTORIAL	TWANGIEST	TWELVE	TWINGED	TWITES
TUTORIALS	TWANGING	TWELVEMO	TWINGES	TWITS
TUTORING	TWANGINGS	TWELVEMOS	TWINGING	TWITTED
TUTORINGS	TWANGLE	TWELVES	TWINIER	TWITTEN
TUTORISE	TWANGLED	TWENTIES	TWINIEST	TWITTENS
TUTORISED	TWANGLES	TWENTIETH	TWINING	TWITTER
TUTORISES	TWANGLING	TWENTIETHS	TWININGLY	TWITTERED
TUTORISING	TWANGLINGS	TWENTY	TWININGS	TWITTERER
TUTORISM	TWANGS	TWENTYISH	TWINK	TWITTERERS
TUTORISMS	TWANGY	TWERP	TWINKED	TWITTERING
TUTORIZE	TWANK	TWERPS	TWINKING	TWITTERINGS
TUTORIZED	TWANKAY	TWIBILL	TWINKLE	TWITTERS
TUTORIZES	TWANKAYS	TWIBILLS	TWINKLED	TWITTERY
TUTORIZING	TWANKS	TWICE	TWINKLER	TWITTING
TUTORS	TWAS	TWICER	TWINKLERS	TWITTINGS
TUTORSHIP	TWASOME	TWICERS	TWINKLES	TWIZZLE
TUTORSHIPS	TWASOMES	TWICHILD	TWINKLING	TWIZZLED
TUTRESS	TWAT	TWICHILDREN	TWINKLINGS	TWIZZLES
TUTRESSES	TWATS	TWIDDLE	TWINKS	TWIZZLING
TUTRICES	TWATTLE	TWIDDLED	TWINLING	TWO
TUTRIX	TWATTLED	TWIDDLER	TWINLINGS	TWOER
TUTRIXES	TWATTLER	TWIDDLERS	TWINNED	TWOERS
TUTS	TWATTLERS	TWIDDLES	TWINNING	TWOFOLD
TUTSAN	TWATTLES	TWIDDLIER	TWINNINGS	TWONESS
TUTSANS	TWATTLING	TWIDDLIEST	TWINS	TWONESSES
TUTTED	TWATTLINGS	TWIDDLING	TWINSHIP	TWOPENCE
TUTTI	TWAY	TWIDDLINGS	TWINSHIPS	TWOPENCES
TUTTIES	TWAYS	TWIDDLY	TWINTER	TWOPENNIES
TUTTING	TWEAK	TWIER	TWINTERS	TWOPENNY
TUTTIS	TWEAKED	TWIERS	TWINY	TWOS
TUTTY	TWEAKING	TWIFOLD	TWIRE	TWOSEATER
TUTU	TWEAKS	TWIFORKED	TWIRED	TWOSEATERS
TUTUS	TWEE	TWIFORMED	TWIRES	TWOSOME
TUTWORK	TWEED	TWIG	TWIRING	TWOSOMES
TUTWORKER	TWEEDIER	TWIGGED	TWIRL	TWOSTROKE
TUTWORKERS	TWEEDIEST	TWIGGEN	TWIRLED	TWYER
TUTWORKS	TWEEDLE	TWIGGER	TWIRLER	TWYERE
TUXEDO	TWEEDLED	TWIGGERS	TWIRLERS	TWYERES
TUXEDOES	TWEEDLES	TWIGGIER	TWIRLIER	TWYERS
TUXEDOS	TWEEDLING	TWIGGIEST	TWIRLIEST	TWYFOLD
TUYERE	TWEEDS	TWIGGING	TWIRLING	TWYFORKED
TUYERES	TWEEDY	TWIGGY	TWIRLS	TWYFORMED
TUZZ	TWEEL	TWIGHT	TWIRLY	TYCHISM
TUZZES	TWEELED	TWIGHTED	TWIRP	TYCHISMS
TWA	TWEELING	TWIGHTING	TWIRPS	TYCOON
TWADDLE	TWEELS	TWIGHTS	TWISCAR	TYCOONATE
TWADDLED	TWEELY	TWIGS	TWISCARS	TYCOONATES
TWADDLER	TWEENESS	TWIGSOME	TWIST	TYCOONERIES
TWADDLERS	TWEENESSES	TWILIGHT	TWISTABLE	TYCOONERY

TYCOONS
TYDE
TYE
TYED
TYEING
TYES
TYG
TYGS
TYING
TYKE
TYKES
TYKISH
TYLECTOMIES
TYLECTOMY
TYLER
TYLERS
TYLOPOD
TYLOPODS
TYLOSES
TYLOSIS
TYLOTE
TYLOTES
TYMBAL
TYMBALS
TYMP
TYMPAN
TYMPANA
TYMPANAL
TYMPANI
TYMPANIC
TYMPANICS

TYMPANIES
TYMPANIST
TYMPANISTS
TYMPANO
TYMPANS
TYMPANUM
TYMPANY
TYMPS
TYND
TYNDE
TYNE
TYNED
TYNES
TYNING
TYPAL
TYPE
TYPECAST
TYPECASTING
TYPECASTS
TYPED
TYPES
TYPEWRITE
TYPEWRITES
TYPEWRITING
TYPEWRITINGS
TYPEWRITTEN
TYPEWROTE
TYPHLITIC
TYPHLITIS
TYPHLITISES
TYPHOID

TYPHOIDAL
TYPHOIDS
TYPHON
TYPHONIAN
TYPHONIC
TYPHONS
TYPHOON
TYPHOONS
TYPHOUS
TYPHUS
TYPHUSES
TYPIC
TYPICAL
TYPICALLY
TYPIFIED
TYPIFIER
TYPIFIERS
TYPIFIES
TYPIFY
TYPIFYING
TYPING
TYPINGS
TYPIST
TYPISTS
TYPO
TYPOLOGIES
TYPOLOGY
TYPOMANIA
TYPOMANIAS
TYPOS
TYPTO

TYPTOED
TYPTOING
TYPTOS
TYRAMINE
TYRAMINES
TYRAN
TYRANED
TYRANING
TYRANNE
TYRANNED
TYRANNES
TYRANNESS
TYRANNESSES
TYRANNIC
TYRANNIES
TYRANNING
TYRANNIS
TYRANNISE
TYRANNISED
TYRANNISES
TYRANNISING
TYRANNIZE
TYRANNIZED
TYRANNIZES
TYRANNIZING
TYRANNOUS
TYRANNY
TYRANS
TYRANT
TYRANTED
TYRANTING

TYRANTS
TYRE
TYRED
TYRELESS
TYRES
TYRO
TYROES
TYRONES
TYROSINE
TYROSINES
TYSTIE
TYSTIES
TYTE
TYTHE
TYTHED
TYTHES
TYTHING
TZADDIK
TZADDIKIM
TZADDIKS
TZADDIQ
TZADDIQIM
TZADDIQS
TZAR
TZARS
TZIGANIES
TZIGANY
TZIMMES

U

UAKARI
UAKARIS
UBEROUS
UBERTIES
UBERTY
UBIETIES
UBIETY
UBIQUE
UBIQUITIES
UBIQUITY
UDAL
UDALLER
UDALLERS
UDALS
UDDER
UDDERED
UDDERFUL
UDDERLESS
UDDERS
UDO
UDOMETER
UDOMETERS
UDOMETRIC
UDOS
UDS
UEY
UEYS
UFO
UFOLOGIES
UFOLOGIST
UFOLOGISTS
UFOLOGY
UFOS
UG
UGGED
UGGING
UGH
UGHS
UGLI
UGLIED
UGLIER
UGLIES
UGLIEST
UGLIFIED
UGLIFIES
UGLIFY
UGLIFYING
UGLILY
UGLINESS
UGLINESSES
UGLIS
UGLY
UGLYING
UGS
UGSOME
UHLAN
UHLANS
UHURU
UHURUS
UINTAHITE
UINTAHITES
UINTAITE
UINTAITES

UITLANDER
UITLANDERS
UKASE
UKASES
UKELELE
UKELELES
UKULELE
UKULELES
ULCER
ULCERATE
ULCERATED
ULCERATES
ULCERATING
ULCERED
ULCERING
ULCEROUS
ULCERS
ULE
ULEMA
ULEMAS
ULES
ULEX
ULEXES
ULICHON
ULICHONS
ULICON
ULICONS
ULIGINOUS
ULIKON
ULIKONS
ULITIS
ULITISES
ULLAGE
ULLAGED
ULLAGES
ULLAGING
ULLING
ULLINGS
ULMACEOUS
ULMIN
ULMINS
ULNA
ULNAE
ULNAR
ULNARE
ULNARIA
ULOSES
ULOSIS
ULOTRICHIES
ULOTRICHY
ULSTER
ULSTERED
ULSTERS
ULTERIOR
ULTIMA
ULTIMACIES
ULTIMACY
ULTIMAS
ULTIMATA
ULTIMATE
ULTIMATES
ULTIMATUM
ULTIMO

ULTION
ULTIONS
ULTRA
ULTRAISM
ULTRAISMS
ULTRAIST
ULTRAISTS
ULTRARED
ULTRAS
ULULANT
ULULATE
ULULATED
ULULATES
ULULATING
ULULATION
ULULATIONS
ULYIE
ULYIES
ULZIE
ULZIES
UM
UMBEL
UMBELLAR
UMBELLATE
UMBELLULE
UMBELLULES
UMBELS
UMBER
UMBERED
UMBERING
UMBERS
UMBERY
UMBILICAL
UMBILICI
UMBILICUS
UMBILICUSES
UMBLES
UMBO
UMBONAL
UMBONATE
UMBONES
UMBOS
UMBRA
UMBRAE
UMBRAGE
UMBRAGED
UMBRAGES
UMBRAGING
UMBRAL
UMBRAS
UMBRATED
UMBRATIC
UMBRATILE
UMBRE
UMBREL
UMBRELLA
UMBRELLAS
UMBRELLO
UMBRELLOES
UMBRELLOS
UMBRELS
UMBRERE
UMBRERES

UMBRES
UMBRETTE
UMBRETTES
UMBRIERE
UMBRIERES
UMBRIL
UMBRILS
UMBROSE
UMBROUS
UMIAK
UMIAKS
UMLAUT
UMLAUTED
UMLAUTING
UMLAUTS
UMPH
UMPIRAGE
UMPIRAGES
UMPIRE
UMPIRED
UMPIRES
UMPIRING
UMPTEEN
UMPTEENTH
UMPTIETH
UMPTY
UMQUHILE
UMWHILE
UN
UNABASHED
UNABATED
UNABLE
UNACCUSED
UNACHING
UNACTABLE
UNACTED
UNACTIVE
UNADAPTED
UNADMIRED
UNADOPTED
UNADORED
UNADORNED
UNADVISED
UNAFRAID
UNAIDABLE
UNAIDED
UNAIMED
UNAIRED
UNAKING
UNALIGNED
UNALIKE
UNALIST
UNALISTS
UNALIVE
UNALLAYED
UNALLIED
UNALLOYED
UNALTERED
UNAMAZED
UNAMENDED
UNAMERCED
UNAMIABLE
UNAMUSED

UNAMUSING
UNANCHOR
UNANCHORED
UNANCHORING
UNANCHORS
UNANELED
UNANIMITIES
UNANIMITY
UNANIMOUS
UNANXIOUS
UNAPPAREL
UNAPPARELLED
UNAPPARELLING
UNAPPARELS
UNAPPLIED
UNAPT
UNAPTLY
UNAPTNESS
UNAPTNESSES
UNARGUED
UNARISEN
UNARM
UNARMED
UNARMING
UNARMS
UNARTFUL
UNASHAMED
UNASKED
UNASSAYED
UNASSUMED
UNASSURED
UNATONED
UNATTIRED
UNAU
UNAUS
UNAVENGED
UNAVOIDED
UNAVOWED
UNAWARE
UNAWARES
UNAWED
UNBACKED
UNBAFFLED
UNBAG
UNBAGGED
UNBAGGING
UNBAGS
UNBAITED
UNBAKED
UNBALANCE
UNBALANCED
UNBALANCES
UNBALANCING
UNBANDED
UNBANKED
UNBAPTISE
UNBAPTISED
UNBAPTISES
UNBAPTISING
UNBAPTIZE
UNBAPTIZED
UNBAPTIZES
UNBAPTIZING

UNBAR	UNBIAS	UNBOSOMING	UNCAGED	UNCHEWED
UNBARBED	UNBIASED	UNBOSOMS	UNCAGES	UNCHILD
UNBARE	UNBIASES	UNBOUGHT	UNCAGING	UNCHILDED
UNBARED	UNBIASING	UNBOUND	UNCALLED	UNCHILDING
UNBARES	UNBIASSED	UNBOUNDED	UNCANDID	UNCHILDS
UNBARING	UNBIASSES	UNBOWED	UNCANDOUR	UNCHOSEN
UNBARK	UNBIASSING	UNBOX	UNCANDOURS	UNCHRISOM
UNBARKED	UNBID	UNBOXED	UNCANNIER	UNCHURCH
UNBARKING	UNBIDDEN	UNBOXES	UNCANNIEST	UNCHURCHED
UNBARKS	UNBIND	UNBOXING	UNCANNILY	UNCHURCHES
UNBARRED	UNBINDING	UNBRACE	UNCANNY	UNCHURCHING
UNBARRING	UNBINDINGS	UNBRACED	UNCANONIC	UNCI
UNBARS	UNBINDS	UNBRACES	UNCAP	UNCIAL
UNBASHFUL	UNBISHOP	UNBRACING	UNCAPABLE	UNCIALS
UNBATED	UNBISHOPED	UNBRAIDED	UNCAPE	UNCIFORM
UNBATHED	UNBISHOPING	UNBRASTE	UNCAPED	UNCINATE
UNBE	UNBISHOPS	UNBRED	UNCAPES	UNCINATED
UNBEAR	UNBITT	UNBREECH	UNCAPING	UNCINI
UNBEARDED	UNBITTED	UNBREECHED	UNCAPPED	UNCINUS
UNBEARING	UNBITTING	UNBREECHES	UNCAPPING	UNCIPHER
UNBEARS	UNBITTS	UNBREECHING	UNCAPS	UNCIPHERED
UNBEATEN	UNBLAMED	UNBRIDGED	UNCAREFUL	UNCIPHERING
UNBED	UNBLENDED	UNBRIDLE	UNCARING	UNCIPHERS
UNBEDDED	UNBLENT	UNBRIDLED	UNCART	UNCIVIL
UNBEDDING	UNBLESS	UNBRIDLES	UNCARTED	UNCIVILLY
UNBEDS	UNBLESSED	UNBRIDLING	UNCARTING	UNCLAD
UNBEEN	UNBLESSES	UNBRIZZED	UNCARTS	UNCLAIMED
UNBEGET	UNBLESSING	UNBROKE	UNCASE	UNCLASP
UNBEGETS	UNBLEST	UNBROKEN	UNCASED	UNCLASPED
UNBEGETTING	UNBLIND	UNBRUISED	UNCASES	UNCLASPING
UNBEGGED	UNBLINDED	UNBRUSED	UNCASHED	UNCLASPS
UNBEGOT	UNBLINDING	UNBRUSHED	UNCASING	UNCLASSED
UNBEGOTTEN	UNBLINDS	UNBUCKLE	UNCATE	UNCLASSY
UNBEGUILE	UNBLOCK	UNBUCKLED	UNCAUGHT	UNCLE
UNBEGUILED	UNBLOCKED	UNBUCKLES	UNCAUSED	UNCLEAN
UNBEGUILES	UNBLOCKING	UNBUCKLING	UNCE	UNCLEANED
UNBEGUILING	UNBLOCKS	UNBUDDED	UNCEASING	UNCLEANER
UNBEGUN	UNBLOODED	UNBUILD	UNCERTAIN	UNCLEANEST
UNBEING	UNBLOODY	UNBUILDING	UNCES	UNCLEANLY
UNBEINGS	UNBLOTTED	UNBUILDS	UNCESSANT	UNCLEAR
UNBEKNOWN	UNBLOWED	UNBUILT	UNCHAIN	UNCLEARED
UNBELIEF	UNBLOWN	UNBUNDLE	UNCHAINED	UNCLEARER
UNBELIEFS	UNBLUNTED	UNBUNDLED	UNCHAINING	UNCLEAREST
UNBELIEVE	UNBODIED	UNBUNDLES	UNCHAINS	UNCLEARLY
UNBELIEVED	UNBODING	UNBUNDLING	UNCHANCIER	UNCLED
UNBELIEVES	UNBOLT	UNBUNDLINGS	UNCHANCIEST	UNCLENCH
UNBELIEVING	UNBOLTED	UNBURDEN	UNCHANCY	UNCLENCHED
UNBELOVED	UNBOLTING	UNBURDENED	UNCHANGED	UNCLENCHES
UNBELT	UNBOLTS	UNBURDENING	UNCHARGE	UNCLENCHING
UNBELTED	UNBONE	UNBURDENS	UNCHARGED	UNCLES
UNBELTING	UNBONED	UNBURIED	UNCHARGES	UNCLESHIP
UNBELTS	UNBONES	UNBURIES	UNCHARGING	UNCLESHIPS
UNBEND	UNBONING	UNBURNED	UNCHARITIES	UNCLEW
UNBENDED	UNBONNET	UNBURNT	UNCHARITY	UNCLEWED
UNBENDING	UNBONNETED	UNBURROW	UNCHARM	UNCLEWING
UNBENDINGS	UNBONNETING	UNBURROWED	UNCHARMED	UNCLEWS
UNBENDS	UNBONNETS	UNBURROWING	UNCHARMING	UNCLING
UNBENIGN	UNBOOKED	UNBURROWS	UNCHARMS	UNCLIPPED
UNBENT	UNBOOKISH	UNBURTHEN	UNCHARNEL	UNCLIPT
UNBEREFT	UNBOOT	UNBURTHENED	UNCHARNELLED	UNCLOAK
UNBERUFEN	UNBOOTED	UNBURTHENING	UNCHARNELLING	UNCLOAKED
UNBESEEM	UNBOOTING	UNBURTHENS	UNCHARNELS	UNCLOAKING
UNBESEEMED	UNBOOTS	UNBURY	UNCHARTED	UNCLOAKS
UNBESEEMING	UNBORE	UNBURYING	UNCHARY	UNCLOG
UNBESEEMS	UNBORN	UNBUSY	UNCHASTE	UNCLOGGED
UNBESPEAK	UNBORNE	UNBUTTON	UNCHECK	UNCLOGGING
UNBESPEAKING	UNBOSOM	UNBUTTONED	UNCHECKED	UNCLOGS
UNBESPEAKS	UNBOSOMED	UNBUTTONING	UNCHECKING	UNCLOSE
UNBESPOKE	UNBOSOMER	UNBUTTONS	UNCHECKS	UNCLOSED
UNBESPOKEN	UNBOSOMERS	UNCAGE	UNCHEERED	UNCLOSES

UNCLOSING
UNCLOTHE
UNCLOTHED
UNCLOTHES
UNCLOTHING
UNCLOUD
UNCLOUDED
UNCLOUDING
UNCLOUDS
UNCLOUDY
UNCLOVEN
UNCLUTCH
UNCLUTCHED
UNCLUTCHES
UNCLUTCHING
UNCO
UNCOCK
UNCOCKED
UNCOCKING
UNCOCKS
UNCOIL
UNCOILED
UNCOILING
UNCOILS
UNCOINED
UNOOLT
UNCOLTED
UNCOLTING
UNCOLTS
UNCOMBED
UNCOMBINE
UNCOMBINED
UNCOMBINES
UNCOMBINING
UNCOMELY
UNCOMMON
UNCOMMONER
UNCOMMONEST
UNCONCERN
UNCONCERNS
UNCONFINE
UNCONFINED
UNCONFINES
UNCONFINING
UNCONFORM
UNCONGEAL
UNCONGEALED
UNCONGEALING
UNCONGEALS
UNCOOKED
UNCOOL
UNCOPE
UNCOPED
UNCOPES
UNCOPING
UNCORD
UNCORDED
UNCORDIAL
UNCORDING
UNCORDS
UNCORK
UNCORKED
UNCORKING
UNCORKS
UNCORRUPT
UNCOS
UNCOSTLY
UNCOUNTED
UNCOUPLE
UNCOUPLED

UNCOUPLES
UNCOUPLING
UNCOURTLY
UNCOUTH
UNCOUTHER
UNCOUTHEST
UNCOUTHLY
UNCOVER
UNCOVERED
UNCOVERING
UNCOVERS
UNCOWL
UNCOWLED
UNCOWLING
UNCOWLS
UNCOYNED
UNCRATE
UNCRATED
UNCRATES
UNCRATING
UNCREATE
UNCREATED
UNCREATES
UNCREATING
UNCROPPED
UNCROSS
UNCROSSED
UNCROSSES
UNCROSSING
UNCROWDED
UNCROWN
UNCROWNED
UNCROWNING
UNCROWNS
UNCRUDDED
UNCRUMPLE
UNCRUMPLED
UNCRUMPLES
UNCRUMPLING
UNCTION
UNCTIONS
UNCTUOUS
UNCULLED
UNCURABLE
UNCURBED
UNCURDLED
UNCURED
UNCURIOUS
UNCURL
UNCURLED
UNCURLING
UNCURLS
UNCURRENT
UNCURSE
UNCURSED
UNCURSES
UNCURSING
UNCURTAIN
UNCURTAINED
UNCURTAINING
UNCURTAINS
UNCUS
UNCUT
UNDAM
UNDAMAGED
UNDAMMED
UNDAMMING
UNDAMNED
UNDAMPED
UNDAMS

UNDASHED
UNDATE
UNDATED
UNDAUNTED
UNDAWNING
UNDAZZLE
UNDAZZLED
UNDAZZLES
UNDAZZLING
UNDE
UNDÉ
UNDEAD
UNDEAF
UNDEAFED
UNDEAFING
UNDEAFS
UNDEALT
UNDEAR
UNDEBASED
UNDECAYED
UNDECEIVE
UNDECEIVED
UNDECEIVES
UNDECEIVING
UNDECENT
UNDECIDED
UNDECIMAL
UNDECK
UNDECKED
UNDECKING
UNDECKS
UNDEE
UNDÉE
UNDEEDED
UNDEFACED
UNDEFIDE
UNDEFIED
UNDEFILED
UNDEFINED
UNDEIFIED
UNDEIFIES
UNDEIFY
UNDEIFYING
UNDELAYED
UNDELIGHT
UNDELIGHTS
UNDELUDED
UNDER
UNDERACT
UNDERACTED
UNDERACTING
UNDERACTS
UNDERARM
UNDERBEAR
UNDERBEARING
UNDERBEARINGS
UNDERBEARS
UNDERBID
UNDERBIDDING
UNDERBIDS
UNDERBIT
UNDERBITE
UNDERBITES
UNDERBITING
UNDERBITTEN
UNDERBORE
UNDERBORNE
UNDERBOUGHT
UNDERBRED
UNDERBUSH

UNDERBUSHED
UNDERBUSHES
UNDERBUSHING
UNDERBUY
UNDERBUYING
UNDERBUYS
UNDERCARD
UNDERCARDS
UNDERCART
UNDERCARTS
UNDERCAST
UNDERCASTS
UNDERCLAD
UNDERCLAY
UNDERCLAYS
UNDERCLUB
UNDERCLUBBED
UNDERCLUBBING
UNDERCLUBS
UNDERCOAT
UNDERCOATS
UNDERCOOK
UNDERCOOKS
UNDERCOOL
UNDERCOOLED
UNDERCOOLING
UNDERCOOLS
UNDERCUT
UNDERCUTS
UNDERCUTTING
UNDERDECK
UNDERDECKS
UNDERDID
UNDERDO
UNDERDOER
UNDERDOERS
UNDERDOES
UNDERDOG
UNDERDOGS
UNDERDOING
UNDERDONE
UNDERDRAW
UNDERDRAWING
UNDERDRAWINGS
UNDERDRAWN
UNDERDRAWS
UNDERDREW
UNDERFED
UNDERFEEDING
UNDERFEEDS
UNDERFELT
UNDERFELTS
UNDERFIRE
UNDERFIRED
UNDERFIRES
UNDERFIRING
UNDERFLOW
UNDERFLOWS
UNDERFONG
UNDERFONGED
UNDERFONGING
UNDERFONGS
UNDERFOOT
UNDERFOOTED
UNDERFOOTING
UNDERFOOTS
UNDERFUR
UNDERFURS
UNDERGIRD

UNDERGIRDED
UNDERGIRDING
UNDERGIRDS
UNDERGIRT
UNDERGO
UNDERGOES
UNDERGOING
UNDERGONE
UNDERGOWN
UNDERGOWNS
UNDERGRAD
UNDERGRADS
UNDERHAND
UNDERHANDS
UNDERHUNG
UNDERKEEP
UNDERKEEPING
UNDERKEEPS
UNDERKEPT
UNDERKING
UNDERKINGS
UNDERLAID
UNDERLAIN
UNDERLAP
UNDERLAPPED
UNDERLAPPING
UNDERLAPS
UNDERLAY
UNDERLAYING
UNDERLAYS
UNDERLET
UNDERLETTING
UNDERLETTINGS
UNDERLIE
UNDERLIES
UNDERLINE
UNDERLINED
UNDERLINES
UNDERLING
UNDERLINGS
UNDERLINING
UNDERLIP
UNDERLIPS
UNDERLYING
UNDERMAN
UNDERMANNED
UNDERMANNING
UNDERMEN
UNDERMINE
UNDERMINED
UNDERMINES
UNDERMINING
UNDERMININGS
UNDERMOST
UNDERN
UNDERNOTE
UNDERNOTED
UNDERNOTES
UNDERNOTING
UNDERNS
UNDERPAID
UNDERPASS
UNDERPASSES
UNDERPAY
UNDERPAYING
UNDERPAYS
UNDERPEEP
UNDERPEEPED

UNDERPEEPING
UNDERPEEPS
UNDERPIN
UNDERPINNED
UNDERPINNING
UNDERPINNINGS
UNDERPINS
UNDERPLAY
UNDERPLAYED
UNDERPLAYING
UNDERPLAYS
UNDERPLOT
UNDERPLOTS
UNDERPROP
UNDERPROPPED
UNDERPROPPING
UNDERPROPS
UNDERRAN
UNDERRATE
UNDERRATED
UNDERRATES
UNDERRATING
UNDERRUN
UNDERRUNNING
UNDERRUNNINGS
UNDERRUNS
UNDERSAID
UNDERSAY
UNDERSAYE
UNDERSAYES
UNDERSAYING
UNDERSAYS
UNDERSEA
UNDERSEAL
UNDERSEALED
UNDERSEALING
UNDERSEALINGS
UNDERSEALS
UNDERSELF
UNDERSELL
UNDERSELLING
UNDERSELLS
UNDERSELVES
UNDERSET
UNDERSETS
UNDERSETTING
UNDERSHOT
UNDERSIDE
UNDERSIDES
UNDERSIGN
UNDERSIGNED
UNDERSIGNING
UNDERSIGNS
UNDERSKIES
UNDERSKY
UNDERSOIL
UNDERSOILS
UNDERSOLD
UNDERSONG
UNDERSONGS
UNDERTAKE
UNDERTAKEN
UNDERTAKES
UNDERTAKING
UNDERTAKINGS
UNDERTANE
UNDERTIME
UNDERTIMES
UNDERTINT
UNDERTINTS

UNDERTONE
UNDERTONES
UNDERTOOK
UNDERTOW
UNDERTOWS
UNDERUSE
UNDERUSED
UNDERUSES
UNDERUSING
UNDERVEST
UNDERVESTS
UNDERWAY
UNDERWEAR
UNDERWEARS
UNDERWENT
UNDERWING
UNDERWINGS
UNDERWIT
UNDERWITS
UNDERWOOD
UNDERWOODS
UNDERWORK
UNDERWORKED
UNDERWORKING
UNDERWORKS
UNDERWROUGHT
UNDESERT
UNDESERTS
UNDESERVE
UNDESERVED
UNDESERVES
UNDESERVING
UNDESIRED
UNDEVOUT
UNDID
UNDIES
UNDIGHT
UNDIGHTING
UNDIGHTS
UNDIGNIFIED
UNDIGNIFIES
UNDIGNIFY
UNDIGNIFYING
UNDILUTED
UNDIMMED
UNDINE
UNDINES
UNDINISM
UNDINISMS
UNDINTED
UNDIPPED
UNDIVIDED
UNDIVINE
UNDO
UNDOCK
UNDOCKED
UNDOCKING
UNDOCKS
UNDOER
UNDOERS
UNDOES
UNDOING
UNDOINGS
UNDONE
UNDOOMED
UNDOUBLE
UNDOUBLED
UNDOUBLES
UNDOUBLING
UNDOUBTED

UNDRAINED
UNDRAPED
UNDRAW
UNDRAWING
UNDRAWN
UNDRAWS
UNDREADED
UNDREAMED
UNDREAMT
UNDRESS
UNDRESSED
UNDRESSES
UNDRESSING
UNDRESSINGS
UNDREST
UNDREW
UNDRIED
UNDRILLED
UNDRIVEN
UNDROSSY
UNDROWNED
UNDRUNK
UNDUBBED
UNDUG
UNDULANCIES
UNDULANCY
UNDULANT
UNDULATE
UNDULATED
UNDULATES
UNDULATING
UNDULLED
UNDULOSE
UNDULOUS
UNDULY
UNDUTEOUS
UNDUTIFUL
UNDYED
UNDYING
UNDYINGLY
UNEARED
UNEARNED
UNEARTH
UNEARTHED
UNEARTHING
UNEARTHLIER
UNEARTHLIEST
UNEARTHLY
UNEARTHS
UNEASE
UNEASES
UNEASIER
UNEASIEST
UNEASILY
UNEASY
UNEATABLE
UNEATEN
UNEATH
UNEATHES
UNEDGE
UNEDGED
UNEDGES
UNEDGING
UNEDITED
UNEFFACED
UNELATED
UNELECTED
UNEMPTIED
UNENDING

UNENDOWED
UNENGAGED
UNENTERED
UNENVIED
UNENVIOUS
UNENVYING
UNEQUABLE
UNEQUAL
UNEQUALLY
UNEQUALS
UNERRING
UNESPIED
UNESSAYED
UNESSENCE
UNESSENCED
UNESSENCES
UNESSENCING
UNETH
UNETHICAL
UNEVEN
UNEVENER
UNEVENEST
UNEVENLY
UNEXALTED
UNEXCITED
UNEXPIRED
UNEXPOSED
UNEXTINCT
UNEXTREME
UNEYED
UNFABLED
UNFACT
UNFACTS
UNFADABLE
UNFADED
UNFADING
UNFAILING
UNFAIR
UNFAIRED
UNFAIRER
UNFAIREST
UNFAIRING
UNFAIRLY
UNFAIRS
UNFAITH
UNFAITHS
UNFALLEN
UNFAMED
UNFANNED
UNFASTEN
UNFASTENED
UNFASTENING
UNFASTENS
UNFAULTY
UNFAZED
UNFEARED
UNFEARFUL
UNFEARING
UNFED
UNFEED
UNFEELING
UNFEIGNED
UNFELLED
UNFELT
UNFENCED
UNFETTER
UNFETTERED
UNFETTERING
UNFETTERS
UNFEUDAL

UNFEUED
UNFIGURED
UNFILDE
UNFILED
UNFILIAL
UNFILLED
UNFILMED
UNFINE
UNFIRED
UNFIRM
UNFISHED
UNFIT
UNFITLY
UNFITNESS
UNFITNESSES
UNFITS
UNFITTED
UNFITTER
UNFITTEST
UNFITTING
UNFIX
UNFIXED
UNFIXES
UNFIXING
UNFIXITIES
UNFIXITY
UNFLAWED
UNFLEDGED
UNFLESH
UNFLESHED
UNFLESHES
UNFLESHING
UNFLESHLY
UNFLOORED
UNFLUSH
UNFLUSHED
UNFLUSHES
UNFLUSHING
UNFOCUSED
UNFOLD
UNFOLDED
UNFOLDER
UNFOLDERS
UNFOLDING
UNFOLDINGS
UNFOLDS
UNFOOL
UNFOOLED
UNFOOLING
UNFOOLS
UNFOOTED
UNFORBID
UNFORCED
UNFORGED
UNFORGOT
UNFORM
UNFORMAL
UNFORMED
UNFORMING
UNFORMS
UNFORTUNE
UNFORTUNES
UNFOUGHT
UNFOUND
UNFOUNDED
UNFRAMED
UNFRANKED
UNFRAUGHT
UNFRAUGHTED
UNFRAUGHTING

UNFRAUGHTS	UNGLAZED	UNHALLOW	UNHEATED	UNHUMBLED
UNFREE	UNGLOSSED	UNHALLOWED	UNHEDGED	UNHUNG
UNFREEMAN	UNGLOVE	UNHALLOWING	UNHEEDED	UNHUNTED
UNFREEMEN	UNGLOVED	UNHALLOWS	UNHEEDFUL	UNHURRIED
UNFREEZE	UNGLOVES	UNHALSED	UNHEEDILY	UNHURT
UNFREEZES	UNGLOVING	UNHAND	UNHEEDING	UNHURTFUL
UNFREEZING	UNGLUE	UNHANDED	UNHEEDY	UNHUSK
UNFRETTED	UNGLUED	UNHANDILY	UNHELE	UNHUSKED
UNFRIEND	UNGLUES	UNHANDING	UNHELED	UNHUSKING
UNFRIENDS	UNGLUING	UNHANDLED	UNHELES	UNHUSKS
UNFROCK	UNGOD	UNHANDS	UNHELING	UNI
UNFROCKED	UNGODDED	UNHANDY	UNHELM	UNIAXIAL
UNFROCKING	UNGODDING	UNHANG	UNHELMED	UNICITIES
UNFROCKS	UNGODLIER	UNHANGED	UNHELMING	UNICITY
UNFROZE	UNGODLIEST	UNHANGING	UNHELMS	UNICOLOR
UNFROZEN	UNGODLIKE	UNHANGS	UNHELPED	UNICOLOUR
UNFUELLED	UNGODLILY	UNHAPPIED	UNHELPFUL	UNICORN
UNFUMED	UNGODLY	UNHAPPIER	UNHEPPEN	UNICORNS
UNFUNDED	UNGODS	UNHAPPIES	UNHEROIC	UNICYCLE
UNFUNNY	UNGORD	UNHAPPIEST	UNHERST	UNICYCLES
UNFURL	UNGORED	UNHAPPILY	UNHEWN	UNIDEAL
UNFURLED	UNGORGED	UNHAPPY	UNHIDDEN	UNIFIABLE
UNFURLING	UNGOT	UNHAPPYING	UNHINGE	UNIFIC
UNFURLS	UNGOTTEN	UNHARBOUR	UNHINGED	UNIFIED
UNFURNISH	UNGOWN	UNHARBOURED	UNHINGES	UNIFIER
UNFURNISHED	UNGOWNED	UNHARBOURING	UNHINGING	UNIFIERS
UNFURNISHES	UNGOWNING	UNHARBOURS	UNHIP	UNIFIES
UNFURNISHING	UNGOWNS	UNHARDY	UNHIRED	UNIFILAR
UNFURRED	UNGRACED	UNHARMED	UNHITCH	UNIFORM
UNGAIN	UNGRADED	UNHARMFUL	UNHITCHED	UNIFORMED
UNGAINFUL	UNGRASSED	UNHARMING	UNHITCHES	UNIFORMING
UNGAINLIER	UNGRAVELY	UNHARNESS	UNHITCHING	UNIFORMLY
UNGAINLIEST	UNGRAZED	UNHARNESSED	UNHIVE	UNIFORMS
UNGAINLY	UNGROOMED	UNHARNESSES	UNHIVED	UNIFY
UNGALLANT	UNGROUND	UNHARNESSING	UNHIVES	UNIFYING
UNGALLED	UNGROWN	UNHASP	UNHIVING	UNIFYINGS
UNGARBLED	UNGRUDGED	UNHASPED	UNHOARD	UNILLUMED
UNGAUGED	UNGUAL	UNHASPING	UNHOARDED	UNILOBAR
UNGAZED	UNGUARD	UNHASPS	UNHOARDING	UNILOBED
UNGEAR	UNGUARDED	UNHASTING	UNHOARDS	UNIMBUED
UNGEARED	UNGUARDING	UNHASTY	UNHOLIER	UNIMPEDED
UNGEARING	UNGUARDS	UNHAT	UNHOLIEST	UNIMPOSED
UNGEARS	UNGUENT	UNHATCHED	UNHOLILY	UNINCITED
UNGENIAL	UNGUENTS	UNHATS	UNHOLPEN	UNINDEXED
UNGENTEEL	UNGUES	UNHATTED	UNHOLY	UNINJURED
UNGENTLE	UNGUESSED	UNHATTING	UNHOMELY	UNINSURED
UNGENTLY	UNGUIDED	UNHATTINGS	UNHONEST	UNINURED
UNGENUINE	UNGUIFORM	UNHAUNTED	UNHOOD	UNINVITED
UNGERMANE	UNGUILTY	UNHEAD	UNHOODED	UNION
UNGET	UNGUIS	UNHEADED	UNHOODING	UNIONISE
UNGETS	UNGULA	UNHEADING	UNHOODS	UNIONISED
UNGETTING	UNGULAE	UNHEADS	UNHOOK	UNIONISES
UNGHOSTLY	UNGULATE	UNHEAL	UNHOOKED	UNIONISING
UNGIFTED	UNGULATES	UNHEALED	UNHOOKING	UNIONISM
UNGILD	UNGULED	UNHEALING	UNHOOKS	UNIONISMS
UNGILDED	UNGUM	UNHEALS	UNHOOP	UNIONIST
UNGILDING	UNGUMMED	UNHEALTH	UNHOOPED	UNIONISTS
UNGILDS	UNGUMMING	UNHEALTHIER	UNHOOPING	UNIONIZE
UNGILT	UNGUMS	UNHEALTHIEST	UNHOOPS	UNIONIZED
UNGIRD	UNGYVE	UNHEALTHS	UNHOPED	UNIONIZES
UNGIRDED	UNGYVED	UNHEALTHY	UNHOPEFUL	UNIONIZING
UNGIRDING	UNGYVES	UNHEARD	UNHORSE	UNIONS
UNGIRDS	UNGYVING	UNHEARSE	UNHORSED	UNIPAROUS
UNGIRT	UNHABLE	UNHEARSED	UNHORSES	UNIPED
UNGIRTH	UNHACKED	UNHEARSES	UNHORSING	UNIPEDS
UNGIRTHED	UNHAILED	UNHEARSING	UNHOUSE	UNIPLANAR
UNGIRTHING	UNHAIR	UNHEART	UNHOUSED	UNIPOD
UNGIRTHS	UNHAIRED	UNHEARTED	UNHOUSES	UNIPODS
UNGIVING	UNHAIRING	UNHEARTING	UNHOUSING	UNIPOLAR
UNGLAD	UNHAIRS	UNHEARTS	UNHUMAN	UNIQUE

UNIQUELY	UNKENNELS	UNLEADING	UNLOOSED	UNMEEK
UNIQUER	UNKENT	UNLEADS	UNLOOSEN	UNMEET
UNIQUES	UNKEPT	UNLEAL	UNLOOSENED	UNMEETLY
UNIQUEST	UNKET	UNLEARN	UNLOOSENING	UNMELTED
UNIRONED	UNKID	UNLEARNED	UNLOOSENS	UNMERITED
UNIS	UNKIND	UNLEARNING	UNLOOSES	UNMET
UNISERIAL	UNKINDER	UNLEARNS	UNLOOSING	UNMETED
UNISEX	UNKINDEST	UNLEARNT	UNLOPPED	UNMEW
UNISEXUAL	UNKINDLED	UNLEASED	UNLORD	UNMEWED
UNISON	UNKINDLIER	UNLEASH	UNLORDED	UNMEWING
UNISONAL	UNKINDLIEST	UNLEASHED	UNLORDING	UNMEWS
UNISONANT	UNKINDLY	UNLEASHES	UNLORDLY	UNMILKED
UNISONOUS	UNKING	UNLEASHING	UNLORDS	UNMILLED
UNISONS	UNKINGED	UNLED	UNLOSABLE	UNMINDED
UNIT	UNKINGING	UNLESS	UNLOST	UNMINDFUL
UNITAL	UNKINGLIER	UNLET	UNLOVABLE	UNMINGLED
UNITARIAN	UNKINGLIEST	UNLICH	UNLOVE	UNMIRY
UNITARIANS	UNKINGLY	UNLICKED	UNLOVED	UNMISSED
UNITARY	UNKINGS	UNLID	UNLOVELY	UNMIXED
UNITE	UNKISS	UNLIDDED	UNLOVES	UNMIXEDLY
UNITED	UNKISSED	UNLIDDING	UNLOVING	UNMOANED
UNITEDLY	UNKISSES	UNLIDS	UNLUCKIER	UNMODISH
UNITER	UNKISSING	UNLIGHTED	UNLUCKIEST	UNMONEYED
UNITERS	UNKNELLED	UNLIKABLE	UNLUCKILY	UNMONIED
UNITES	UNKNIGHT	UNLIKE	UNLUCKY	UNMOOR
UNITIES	UNKNIGHTED	UNLIKELIER	UNMADE	UNMOORED
UNITING	UNKNIGHTING	UNLIKELIEST	UNMAILED	UNMOORING
UNITINGS	UNKNIGHTS	UNLIKELY	UNMAIMED	UNMOORS
UNITION	UNKNIT	UNLIKES	UNMAKABLE	UNMORAL
UNITIONS	UNKNITS	UNLIMBER	UNMAKE	UNMOTIVED
UNITISE	UNKNITTED	UNLIMBERED	UNMAKES	UNMOULD
UNITISED	UNKNITTING	UNLIMBERING	UNMAKING	UNMOULDED
UNITISES	UNKNOT	UNLIMBERS	UNMAKINGS	UNMOULDING
UNITISING	UNKNOTS	UNLIME	UNMAN	UNMOULDS
UNITIVE	UNKNOTTED	UNLIMES	UNMANACLE	UNMOUNT
UNITIVELY	UNKNOTTING	UNLIMING	UNMANACLED	UNMOUNTED
UNITIZE	UNKNOWING	UNLIMITED	UNMANACLES	UNMOUNTING
UNITIZED	UNKNOWN	UNLINE	UNMANACLING	UNMOUNTS
UNITIZES	UNKNOWNS	UNLINEAL	UNMANAGED	UNMOURNED
UNITIZING	UNLACE	UNLINED	UNMANLIER	UNMOVABLE
UNITS	UNLACED	UNLINES	UNMANLIEST	UNMOVABLY
UNITY	UNLACES	UNLINING	UNMANLIKE	UNMOVED
UNIVALENT	UNLACING	UNLINK	UNMANLY	UNMOVEDLY
UNIVALENTS	UNLADE	UNLINKED	UNMANNED	UNMOVING
UNIVALVE	UNLADED	UNLINKING	UNMANNING	UNMOWN
UNIVALVES	UNLADEN	UNLINKS	UNMANS	UNMUFFLE
UNIVERSAL	UNLADES	UNLISTED	UNMANTLE	UNMUFFLED
UNIVERSALS	UNLADING	UNLIT	UNMANTLED	UNMUFFLES
UNIVERSE	UNLADINGS	UNLIVABLE	UNMANTLES	UNMUFFLING
UNIVERSES	UNLAID	UNLIVE	UNMANTLING	UNMUSICAL
UNIVOCAL	UNLASH	UNLIVED	UNMANURED	UNMUZZLE
UNIVOCALS	UNLASHED	UNLIVELY	UNMARD	UNMUZZLED
UNJADED	UNLASHES	UNLIVES	UNMARKED	UNMUZZLES
UNJEALOUS	UNLASHING	UNLIVING	UNMARRED	UNMUZZLING
UNJOINT	UNLAST	UNLOAD	UNMARRIED	UNMUZZLINGS
UNJOINTED	UNLASTE	UNLOADED	UNMARRIES	UNNAIL
UNJOINTING	UNLATCH	UNLOADER	UNMARRY	UNNAILED
UNJOINTS	UNLATCHED	UNLOADERS	UNMARRYING	UNNAILING
UNJOYFUL	UNLATCHES	UNLOADING	UNMASK	UNNAILS
UNJOYOUS	UNLATCHING	UNLOADINGS	UNMASKED	UNNAMABLE
UNJUST	UNLAW	UNLOADS	UNMASKER	UNNAMED
UNJUSTER	UNLAWED	UNLOCATED	UNMASKERS	UNNANELD
UNJUSTEST	UNLAWFUL	UNLOCK	UNMASKING	UNNATIVE
UNJUSTLY	UNLAWING	UNLOCKED	UNMASKINGS	UNNATURAL
UNKED	UNLAWS	UNLOCKING	UNMASKS	UNNEATH
UNKEMPT	UNLAY	UNLOCKS	UNMATCHED	UNNEEDED
UNKENNED	UNLAYING	UNLOGICAL	UNMATED	UNNEEDFUL
UNKENNEL	UNLAYS	UNLOOKED	UNMATURED	UNNERVE
UNKENNELLED	UNLEAD	UNLOOSE	UNMEANING	UNNERVED
UNKENNELLING	UNLEADED		UNMEANT	UNNERVES

UNNERVING	UNPEGS	UNPLUMBS	UNPROVIDE	UNREALLY
UNNEST	UNPEN	UNPLUME	UNPROVIDED	UNREAPED
UNNESTED	UNPENNED	UNPLUMED	UNPROVIDES	UNREASON
UNNESTING	UNPENNIED	UNPLUMES	UNPROVIDING	UNREASONS
UNNESTS	UNPENNING	UNPLUMING	UNPROVOKE	UNREAVE
UNNETHES	UNPENS	UNPOETIC	UNPROVOKED	UNREAVED
UNNETTED	UNPENT	UNPOINTED	UNPROVOKES	UNREAVES
UNNOBLE	UNPEOPLE	UNPOISED	UNPROVOKING	UNREAVING
UNNOBLED	UNPEOPLED	UNPOISON	UNPRUNED	UNREBATED
UNNOBLES	UNPEOPLES	UNPOISONED	UNPULLED	UNREBUKED
UNNOBLING	UNPEOPLING	UNPOISONING	UNPURGED	UNRECKED
UNNOTED	UNPERCH	UNPOISONS	UNPURSE	UNRED
UNNOTICED	UNPERCHED	UNPOLICED	UNPURSED	UNREDREST
UNOBEYED	UNPERCHES	UNPOLISH	UNPURSES	UNREDUCED
UNOBVIOUS	UNPERCHING	UNPOLISHED	UNPURSING	UNREEL
UNOFFERED	UNPERFECT	UNPOLISHES	UNPURSUED	UNREELED
UNOFTEN	UNPERPLEX	UNPOLISHING	UNQUALIFIED	UNREELING
UNOILED	UNPERPLEXED	UNPOLITE	UNQUALIFIES	UNREELS
UNOPENED	UNPERPLEXES	UNPOLITIC	UNQUALIFY	UNREEVE
UNOPPOSED	UNPERPLEXING	UNPOLLED	UNQUALIFYING	UNREEVED
UNORDER	UNPERSON	UNPOPE	UNQUEEN	UNREEVES
UNORDERED	UNPERSONED	UNPOPED	UNQUEENED	UNREEVING
UNORDERING	UNPERSONING	UNPOPES	UNQUEENING	UNREFINED
UNORDERLY	UNPERSONS	UNPOPING	UNQUEENLIER	UNREFUTED
UNORDERS	UNPERVERT	UNPOPULAR	UNQUEENLIEST	UNREIN
UNOWNED	UNPERVERTED	UNPOSED	UNQUEENLY	UNREINED
UNOWNED	UNPERVERTING	UNPOSTED	UNQUEENS	UNREINING
UNPACK	UNPERVERTS	UNPOTABLE	UNQUELLED	UNREINS
UNPACKED	UNPICK	UNPRAISE	UNQUIET	UNRELATED
UNPACKER	UNPICKED	UNPRAISED	UNQUIETED	UNRELAXED
UNPACKERS	UNPICKING	UNPRAISES	UNQUIETING	UNREMOVED
UNPACKING	UNPICKS	UNPRAISING	UNQUIETLY	UNRENEWED
UNPACKINGS	UNPIERCED	UNPRAY	UNQUIETS	UNRENT
UNPACKS	UNPILOTED	UNPRAYED	UNQUOTE	UNREPAID
UNPAGED	UNPIN	UNPRAYING	UNQUOTED	UNREPAIR
UNPAID	UNPINKED	UNPRAYS	UNQUOTES	UNREPAIRS
UNPAINED	UNPINKT	UNPREACH	UNQUOTING	UNRESERVE
UNPAINFUL	UNPINNED	UNPREACHED	UNRACED	UNRESERVES
UNPAINT	UNPINNING	UNPREACHES	UNRACKED	UNREST
UNPAINTED	UNPINS	UNPREACHING	UNRAISED	UNRESTFUL
UNPAINTING	UNPITIED	UNPRECISE	UNRAKE	UNRESTING
UNPAINTS	UNPITIFUL	UNPREDICT	UNRAKED	UNRESTS
UNPAIRED	UNPITYING	UNPREDICTED	UNRAKES	UNREVISED
UNPALSIED	UNPLACE	UNPREDICTING	UNRAKING	UNREVOKED
UNPANEL	UNPLACED	UNPREDICTS	UNRATED	UNRHYMED
UNPANELLED	UNPLACES	UNPREPARE	UNRAVEL	UNRIBBED
UNPANELLING	UNPLACING	UNPREPARED	UNRAVELLED	UNRID
UNPANELS	UNPLAGUED	UNPREPARES	UNRAVELLING	UNRIDABLE
UNPANGED	UNPLAINED	UNPREPARING	UNRAVELLINGS	UNRIDDEN
UNPANNEL	UNPLAIT	UNPRESSED	UNRAVELS	UNRIDDLE
UNPANNELLED	UNPLAITED	UNPRETTY	UNRAZORED	UNRIDDLED
UNPANNELLING	UNPLAITING	UNPRICED	UNREACHED	UNRIDDLER
UNPANNELS	UNPLAITS	UNPRIEST	UNREAD	UNRIDDLERS
UNPAPER	UNPLANKED	UNPRIESTED	UNREADIER	UNRIDDLES
UNPAPERED	UNPLANNED	UNPRIESTING	UNREADIEST	UNRIDDLING
UNPAPERING	UNPLANTED	UNPRIESTS	UNREADILY	UNRIFLED
UNPAPERS	UNPLEASED	UNPRIMED	UNREADY	UNRIG
UNPARED	UNPLEATED	UNPRINTED	UNREAL	UNRIGGED
UNPARTIAL	UNPLEDGED	UNPRISON	UNREALISE	UNRIGGING
UNPATHED	UNPLIABLE	UNPRISONED	UNREALISED	UNRIGHT
UNPAVED	UNPLIABLY	UNPRISONING	UNREALISES	UNRIGHTS
UNPAY	UNPLIANT	UNPRISONS	UNREALISING	UNRIGS
UNPAYABLE	UNPLUCKED	UNPRIZED	UNREALISM	UNRIMED
UNPAYING	UNPLUG	UNPROP	UNREALISMS	UNRINGED
UNPAYS	UNPLUGGED	UNPROPER	UNREALITIES	UNRIP
UNPEELED	UNPLUGGING	UNPROPPED	UNREALITY	UNRIPE
UNPEERED	UNPLUGS	UNPROPPING	UNREALIZE	UNRIPENED
UNPEG	UNPLUMB	UNPROPS	UNREALIZED	UNRIPER
UNPEGGED	UNPLUMBED	UNPROVED	UNREALIZES	UNRIPEST
UNPEGGING	UNPLUMBING	UNPROVEN	UNREALIZING	UNRIPPED

UNRIPPING
UNRIPPINGS
UNRIPS
UNRISEN
UNRIVEN
UNRIVET
UNRIVETED
UNRIVETING
UNRIVETS
UNROBE
UNROBED
UNROBES
UNROBING
UNROLL
UNROLLED
UNROLLING
UNROLLS
UNROOF
UNROOFED
UNROOFING
UNROOFS
UNROOST
UNROOSTED
UNROOSTING
UNROOSTS
UNROOT
UNROOTED
UNROOTING
UNROOTS
UNROPE
UNROPED
UNROPES
UNROPING
UNROSINED
UNROTTED
UNROTTEN
UNROUGED
UNROUGH
UNROUND
UNROUNDED
UNROUNDING
UNROUNDS
UNROUSED
UNROVE
UNROYAL
UNROYALLY
UNRUBBED
UNRUDE
UNRUFFE
UNRUFFLE
UNRUFFLED
UNRUFFLES
UNRUFFLING
UNRULE
UNRULED
UNRULES
UNRULIER
UNRULIEST
UNRULY
UNRUMPLED
UNS
UNSADDLE
UNSADDLED
UNSADDLES
UNSADDLING
UNSAFF
UNSAFELY
UNSAFER
UNSAFEST
UNSAFETIES

UNSAFETY
UNSAID
UNSAILED
UNSAINED
UNSAINT
UNSAINTED
UNSAINTING
UNSAINTLIER
UNSAINTLIEST
UNSAINTLY
UNSAINTS
UNSALABLE
UNSALTED
UNSALUTED
UNSAPPED
UNSASHED
UNSATABLE
UNSATED
UNSATIATE
UNSATING
UNSAVED
UNSAVOURY
UNSAY
UNSAYABLE
UNSAYING
UNSAYS
UNSCALE
UNSCALED
UNSCALES
UNSCALING
UNSCANNED
UNSCARRED
UNSCARY
UNSCATHED
UNSCENTED
UNSCOURED
UNSCREW
UNSCREWED
UNSCREWING
UNSCREWS
UNSCYTHED
UNSEAL
UNSEALED
UNSEALING
UNSEALS
UNSEAM
UNSEAMED
UNSEAMING
UNSEAMS
UNSEASON
UNSEASONED
UNSEASONING
UNSEASONS
UNSEAT
UNSEATED
UNSEATING
UNSEATS
UNSECRET
UNSECULAR
UNSECURED
UNSEDUCED
UNSEEABLE
UNSEEDED
UNSEEING
UNSEEL
UNSEELED
UNSEELING
UNSEELS
UNSEEMING
UNSEEMINGS

UNSEEMLIER
UNSEEMLIEST
UNSEEMLY
UNSEEN
UNSEENS
UNSEIZED
UNSELDOM
UNSELF
UNSELFED
UNSELFING
UNSELFISH
UNSELFS
UNSELVES
UNSENSE
UNSENSED
UNSENSES
UNSENSING
UNSENT
UNSERIOUS
UNSET
UNSETS
UNSETTING
UNSETTLE
UNSETTLED
UNSETTLES
UNSETTLING
UNSETTLINGS
UNSEVERED
UNSEW
UNSEWED
UNSEWING
UNSEWN
UNSEWS
UNSEX
UNSEXED
UNSEXES
UNSEXING
UNSEXUAL
UNSEXIST
UNSHACKLE
UNSHACKLED
UNSHACKLES
UNSHACKLING
UNSHADED
UNSHADOW
UNSHADOWED
UNSHADOWING
UNSHADOWS
UNSHAKED
UNSHAKEN
UNSHALE
UNSHALED
UNSHALING
UNSHAMED
UNSHAPE
UNSHAPED
UNSHAPELIER
UNSHAPELIEST
UNSHAPELY
UNSHAPEN
UNSHAPES
UNSHAPING
UNSHARED
UNSHAVED
UNSHAVEN
UNSHEATHE
UNSHEATHED
UNSHEATHES
UNSHEATHING

UNSHED
UNSHELL
UNSHELLED
UNSHELLING
UNSHELLS
UNSHENT
UNSHEWN
UNSHIP
UNSHIPPED
UNSHIPPING
UNSHIPS
UNSHOCKED
UNSHOD
UNSHOE
UNSHOED
UNSHOEING
UNSHOES
UNSHOOT
UNSHOOTED
UNSHOOTING
UNSHOOTS
UNSHORN
UNSHOT
UNSHOUT
UNSHOUTED
UNSHOUTING
UNSHOUTS
UNSHOWN
UNSHRIVED
UNSHRIVEN
UNSHROUD
UNSHROUDED
UNSHROUDING
UNSHROUDS
UNSHRUBD
UNSHUNNED
UNSHUT
UNSHUTS
UNSHUTTER
UNSHUTTERED
UNSHUTTERING
UNSHUTTERS
UNSHUTTING
UNSICKER
UNSICKLED
UNSIFTED
UNSIGHING
UNSIGHT
UNSIGHTED
UNSIGHTLIER
UNSIGHTLIEST
UNSIGHTLY
UNSIGNED
UNSINEW
UNSINEWED
UNSINEWING
UNSINEWS
UNSISTING
UNSIZABLE
UNSIZED
UNSKILFUL
UNSKILLED
UNSKIMMED
UNSKINNED
UNSLAIN
UNSLAKED
UNSLING
UNSLINGING
UNSLINGS
UNSLUICE

UNSLUICED
UNSLUICES
UNSLUICING
UNSLUNG
UNSMART
UNSMILING
UNSMITTEN
UNSMOOTH
UNSMOOTHED
UNSMOOTHING
UNSMOOTHS
UNSMOTE
UNSNAP
UNSNAPPED
UNSNAPPING
UNSNAPS
UNSNARL
UNSNARLED
UNSNARLING
UNSNARLS
UNSNECK
UNSNECKED
UNSNECKING
UNSNECKS
UNSNUFFED
UNSOAPED
UNSOCIAL
UNSOCKET
UNSOCKETED
UNSOCKETING
UNSOCKETS
UNSOD
UNSODDEN
UNSOFT
UNSOILED
UNSOLACED
UNSOLD
UNSOLDER
UNSOLDERED
UNSOLDERING
UNSOLDERS
UNSOLEMN
UNSOLID
UNSOLIDLY
UNSOLVED
UNSONSY
UNSOOTE
UNSORTED
UNSOUGHT
UNSOUL
UNSOULED
UNSOULING
UNSOULS
UNSOUND
UNSOUNDED
UNSOUNDER
UNSOUNDEST
UNSOUNDLY
UNSOURCED
UNSOURED
UNSOWN
UNSPAR
UNSPARED
UNSPARING
UNSPARRED
UNSPARRING
UNSPARD
UNSPEAK
UNSPEAKING
UNSPEAKS

UNSPED
UNSPELL
UNSPELLED
UNSPELLING
UNSPELLS
UNSPENT
UNSPHERE
UNSPHERED
UNSPHERES
UNSPHERING
UNSPIDE
UNSPIED
UNSPILLED
UNSPILT
UNSPOILED
UNSPOILT
UNSPOKE
UNSPOKEN
UNSPOTTED
UNSPRUNG
UNSPUN
UNSQUARED
UNSTABLE
UNSTABLER
UNSTABLEST
UNSTACK
UNSTACKED
UNSTACKING
UNSTACKS
UNSTUCK
UNUTAID
UNSTAINED
UNSTAMPED
UNSTARCH
UNSTARCHED
UNSTARCHES
UNSTARCHING
UNSTATE
UNSTATED
UNSTATES
UNSTATING
UNSTAYED
UNSTAYING
UNSTEADIED
UNSTEADIER
UNSTEADIES
UNSTEADIEST
UNSTEADY
UNSTEADYING
UNSTEEL
UNSTEELED
UNSTEELING
UNSTEELS
UNSTEP
UNSTEPPED
UNSTEPPING
UNSTEPS
UNSTERILE
UNSTICK
UNSTICKING
UNSTICKS
UNSTIFLED
UNSTILLED
UNSTINTED
UNSTITCH
UNSTITCHED
UNSTITCHES
UNSTITCHING
UNSTOCK
UNSTOCKED
UNSTOCKING

UNSTOCKS
UNSTOP
UNSTOPPED
UNSTOPPER
UNSTOPPERED
UNSTOPPERING
UNSTOPPERS
UNSTOPPING
UNSTOPS
UNSTOW
UNSTOWED
UNSTOWING
UNSTOWS
UNSTRAP
UNSTRAPPED
UNSTRAPPING
UNSTRAPS
UNSTRING
UNSTRINGED
UNSTRINGING
UNSTRINGS
UNSTRIP
UNSTRIPED
UNSTRIPPED
UNSTRIPPING
UNSTRIPS
UNSTRUCK
UNSTRUNG
UNSTUCK
UNSTUDIED
UNSTUFFED
UNSTUFFY
UNSTUFT
UNSUBDUED
UNSUBJECT
UNSUBTLE
UNSUCCESS
UNSUCCESSES
UNSUCKED
UNSUIT
UNSUITED
UNSUITING
UNSUITS
UNSULLIED
UNSUMMED
UNSUNG
UNSUNNED
UNSUNNY
UNSUPPLE
UNSURE
UNSURED
UNSURER
UNSUREST
UNSUSPECT
UNSWADDLE
UNSWADDLED
UNSWADDLES
UNSWADDLING
UNSWATHE
UNSWATHED
UNSWATHES
UNSWATHING
UNSWAYED
UNSWEAR
UNSWEARING
UNSWEARINGS
UNSWEARS
UNSWEET
UNSWEPT
UNSWORE

UNSWORN
UNTACK
UNTACKED
UNTACKING
UNTACKLE
UNTACKLED
UNTACKLES
UNTACKLING
UNTACKS
UNTAILED
UNTAINTED
UNTAKEN
UNTAMABLE
UNTAMABLY
UNTAME
UNTAMED
UNTAMES
UNTAMING
UNTANGLE
UNTANGLED
UNTANGLES
UNTANGLING
UNTANNED
UNTAPPED
UNTARRED
UNTASTED
UNTAUGHT
UNTAX
UNTAXED
UNTAXES
UNTAXING
UNTEACH
UNTEACHES
UNTEACHING
UNTEAM
UNTEAMED
UNTEAMING
UNTEAMS
UNTEMPER
UNTEMPERED
UNTEMPERING
UNTEMPERS
UNTEMPTED
UNTENABLE
UNTENANT
UNTENANTED
UNTENANTING
UNTENANTS
UNTENDED
UNTENDER
UNTENT
UNTENTED
UNTENTING
UNTENTS
UNTENTY
UNTESTED
UNTETHER
UNTETHERED
UNTETHERING
UNTETHERS
UNTHANKED
UNTHATCH
UNTHATCHED
UNTHATCHES
UNTHATCHING
UNTHAW
UNTHAWED
UNTHAWING
UNTHAWS
UNTHINK

UNTHINKING
UNTHINKS
UNTHOUGHT
UNTHREAD
UNTHREADED
UNTHREADING
UNTHREADS
UNTHRIFT
UNTHRIFTS
UNTHRIFTY
UNTHRONE
UNTHRONED
UNTHRONES
UNTHRONING
UNTIDIED
UNTIDIER
UNTIDIES
UNTIDIEST
UNTIDILY
UNTIDY
UNTIDYING
UNTIE
UNTIED
UNTIES
UNTIL
UNTILE
UNTILED
UNTILES
UNTILLING
UNTILLED
UNTIMELIER
UNTIMELIEST
UNTIMELY
UNTIMEOUS
UNTIN
UNTINGED
UNTINNED
UNTINNING
UNTINS
UNTIRABLE
UNTIRED
UNTIRING
UNTITLED
UNTO
UNTOILING
UNTOLD
UNTOMB
UNTOMBED
UNTOMBING
UNTOMBS
UNTONED
UNTORN
UNTOUCHED
UNTOWARD
UNTRACE
UNTRACED
UNTRACES
UNTRACING
UNTRACKED
UNTRADED
UNTRAINED
UNTREAD
UNTREADING
UNTREADS
UNTREATED
UNTRESSED
UNTRIDE
UNTRIED
UNTRIM
UNTRIMMED

UNTRIMMING
UNTRIMS
UNTROD
UNTRODDEN
UNTRUE
UNTRUER
UNTRUEST
UNTRUISM
UNTRUISMS
UNTRULY
UNTRUSS
UNTRUSSED
UNTRUSSER
UNTRUSSERS
UNTRUSSES
UNTRUSSING
UNTRUSSINGS
UNTRUST
UNTRUSTS
UNTRUSTY
UNTRUTH
UNTRUTHS
UNTUCK
UNTUCKED
UNTUCKING
UNTUCKS
UNTUMBLED
UNTUNABLE
UNTUNABLY
UNTUNE
UNTUNED
UNTUNEFUL
UNTUNES
UNTUNING
UNTURBID
UNTURF
UNTURFED
UNTURFING
UNTURFS
UNTURN
UNTURNED
UNTURNING
UNTURNS
UNTUTORED
UNTWINE
UNTWINED
UNTWINES
UNTWINING
UNTWIST
UNTWISTED
UNTWISTING
UNTWISTINGS
UNTWISTS
UNTYING
UNTYINGS
UNTYPABLE
UNTYPICAL
UNURGED
UNUSABLE
UNUSABLY
UNUSED
UNUSEFUL
UNUSHERED
UNUSUAL
UNUSUALLY
UNUTTERED
UNVAIL
UNVAILE
UNVAILED
UNVAILES

UNVAILING
UNVAILS
UNVALUED
UNVARIED
UNVARYING
UNVEIL
UNVEILED
UNVEILER
UNVEILERS
UNVEILING
UNVEILINGS
UNVEILS
UNVENTED
UNVERSED
UNVEXED
UNVIABLE
UNVIEWED
UNVIRTUE
UNVIRTUES
UNVISITED
UNVISOR
UNVISORED
UNVISORING
UNVISORS
UNVITAL
UNVIZARD
UNVIZARDED
UNVIZARDING
UNVIZARDS
UNVOCAL
UNVOICE
UNVOICED
UNVOICES
UNVOICING
UNVOICINGS
UNVULGAR
UNWAGED
UNWAKED
UNWAKENED
UNWALLED
UNWANTED
UNWARDED
UNWARE
UNWARELY
UNWARES
UNWARIE
UNWARIER
UNWARIEST
UNWARILY
UNWARLIKE
UNWARMED
UNWARNED
UNWARPED
UNWARY
UNWASHED
UNWASHEN
UNWASTED
UNWASTING
UNWATCHED
UNWATER
UNWATERED
UNWATERING
UNWATERS
UNWATERY
UNWAYED
UNWEAL
UNWEALS
UNWEANED
UNWEAPON
UNWEAPONED

UNWEAPONING
UNWEAPONS
UNWEARIED
UNWEARY
UNWEAVE
UNWEAVES
UNWEAVING
UNWEBBED
UNWED
UNWEDDED
UNWEEDED
UNWEENED
UNWEETING
UNWEIGHED
UNWELCOME
UNWELDY
UNWELL
UNWEPT
UNWET
UNWETTED
UNWHIPPED
UNWHIPT
UNWIELDIER
UNWIELDIEST
UNWIELDY
UNWIFELIER
UNWIFELIEST
UNWIFELY
UNWIGGED
UNWILFUL
UNWILL
UNWILLED
UNWILLING
UNWILLS
UNWIND
UNWINDING
UNWINDINGS
UNWINDS
UNWINGED
UNWINKING
UNWIPED
UNWIRE
UNWIRED
UNWIRES
UNWIRING
UNWISDOM
UNWISDOMS
UNWISE
UNWISELY
UNWISER
UNWISEST
UNWISH
UNWISHED
UNWISHES
UNWISHFUL
UNWISHING
UNWIST
UNWIT
UNWITCH
UNWITCHED
UNWITCHES
UNWITCHING
UNWITS
UNWITTED
UNWITTILY
UNWITTING
UNWITTY
UNWIVE
UNWIVED
UNWIVES

UNWIVING
UNWOMAN
UNWOMANED
UNWOMANING
UNWOMANLIER
UNWOMANLIEST
UNWOMANLY
UNWOMANS
UNWON
UNWONT
UNWONTED
UNWOODED
UNWOOED
UNWORDED
UNWORK
UNWORKED
UNWORKING
UNWORKS
UNWORLDLIER
UNWORLDLIEST
UNWORLDLY
UNWORMED
UNWORN
UNWORRIED
UNWORTH
UNWORTHIER
UNWORTHIEST
UNWORTHS
UNWORTHY
UNWOUND
UNWOUNDED
UNWOVE
UNWOVEN
UNWRAP
UNWRAPPED
UNWRAPPING
UNWRAPS
UNWREAKED
UNWREATHE
UNWREATHED
UNWREATHES
UNWREATHING
UNWRINKLE
UNWRINKLED
UNWRINKLES
UNWRINKLING
UNWRITE
UNWRITES
UNWRITING
UNWRITTEN
UNWROTE
UNWROUGHT
UNWRUNG
UNYEANED
UNYOKE
UNYOKED
UNYOKES
UNYOKING
UNZEALOUS
UNZIP
UNZIPPED
UNZIPPING
UNZIPS
UNZONED
UP
UPADAISY
UPAITHRIC
UPAS
UPASES
UPBEAR

UPBEARING
UPBEARS
UPBEAT
UPBIND
UPBINDING
UPBINDS
UPBLEW
UPBLOW
UPBLOWING
UPBLOWN
UPBLOWS
UPBOIL
UPBOILED
UPBOILING
UPBOILS
UPBORE
UPBORNE
UPBOUND
UPBOUNDEN
UPBRAID
UPBRAIDED
UPBRAIDER
UPBRAIDERS
UPBRAIDING
UPBRAIDINGS
UPBRAIDS
UPBRAST
UPBRAY
UPBRAYED
UPBRAYING
UPBRAYS
UPBREAK
UPBREAKING
UPBREAKS
UPBRING
UPBRINGING
UPBRINGINGS
UPBRINGS
UPBROKE
UPBROKEN
UPBROUGHT
UPBUILD
UPBUILDING
UPBUILDINGS
UPBUILDS
UPBUILT
UPBURNING
UPBURST
UPBURSTING
UPBURSTS
UPBY
UPBYE
UPCAST
UPCASTING
UPCASTS
UPCATCH
UPCATCHES
UPCATCHING
UPCAUGHT
UPCHEARD
UPCHEER
UPCHEERED
UPCHEERING
UPCHEERS
UPCLIMB
UPCLIMBED
UPCLIMBING
UPCLIMBS
UPCLOSE
UPCLOSED

UPCLOSES
UPCLOSING
UPCOAST
UPCOIL
UPCOILED
UPCOILING
UPCOILS
UPCOME
UPCOMES
UPCURL
UPCURLED
UPCURLING
UPCURLS
UPCURVED
UPDATE
UPDATED
UPDATES
UPDATING
UPDRAG
UPDRAGGED
UPDRAGGING
UPDRAGS
UPDRAW
UPDRAWING
UPDRAWN
UPDRAWS
UPDREW
UPFILL
UPFILLED
UPFILLING
UPFILLINGS
UPFILLS
UPFLOW
UPFLOWED
UPFLOWING
UPFLOWS
UPFLUNG
UPFOLLOW
UPFOLLOWED
UPFOLLOWING
UPFOLLOWS
UPFRONT
UPFURL
UPFURLED
UPFURLING
UPFURLS
UPGANG
UPGANGS
UPGATHER
UPGATHERED
UPGATHERING
UPGATHERS
UPGAZE
UPGAZED
UPGAZES
UPGAZING
UPGO
UPGOES
UPGOING
UPGOINGS
UPGONE
UPGRADE
UPGRADED
UPGRADES
UPGRADING
UPGREW
UPGROW
UPGROWING
UPGROWINGS
UPGROWN

UPGROWS
UPGROWTH
UPGROWTHS
UPGUSH
UPGUSHED
UPGUSHES
UPGUSHING
UPHAND
UPHANG
UPHANGING
UPHANGS
UPHAUD
UPHAUDING
UPHAUDS
UPHEAP
UPHEAPED
UPHEAPING
UPHEAPINGS
UPHEAPS
UPHEAVAL
UPHEAVALS
UPHEAVE
UPHEAVED
UPHEAVES
UPHEAVING
UPHELD
UPHILD
UPHILL
UPHILLS
UPHOARD
UPHOARDED
UPHOARDING
UPHOARDS
UPHOIST
UPHOISTED
UPHOISTING
UPHOISTS
UPHOLD
UPHOLDER
UPHOLDERS
UPHOLDING
UPHOLDINGS
UPHOLDS
UPHOLSTER
UPHOLSTERED
UPHOLSTERING
UPHOLSTERS
UPHOORD
UPHOORDED
UPHOORDING
UPHOORDS
UPHROE
UPHROES
UPHUDDEN
UPHUNG
UPHURL
UPHURLED
UPHURLING
UPHURLS
UPJET
UPJETS
UPJETTED
UPJETTING
UPKEEP
UPKEEPS
UPKNIT
UPKNITS
UPKNITTED
UPKNITTING
UPLAID

UPLAND
UPLANDER
UPLANDERS
UPLANDISH
UPLANDS
UPLAY
UPLAYING
UPLAYS
UPLEAD
UPLEADING
UPLEADS
UPLEAN
UPLEANED
UPLEANING
UPLEANS
UPLEANT
UPLEAP
UPLEAPED
UPLEAPING
UPLEAPS
UPLEAPT
UPLED
UPLIFT
UPLIFTED
UPLIFTER
UPLIFTERS
UPLIFTING
UPLIFTINGS
UPLIFTS
UPLIGHTED
UPLIGHTER
UPLIGHTERS
UPLOCK
UPLOCKED
UPLOCKING
UPLOCKS
UPLOOK
UPLOOKED
UPLOOKING
UPLOOKS
UPLYING
UPMAKE
UPMAKER
UPMAKERS
UPMAKES
UPMAKING
UPMAKINGS
UPMOST
UPON
UPPED
UPPER
UPPERCUT
UPPERCUTS
UPPERMOST
UPPERS
UPPILED
UPPING
UPPINGS
UPPISH
UPPISHLY
UPPITY
UPRAISE
UPRAISED
UPRAISES
UPRAISING
UPRAN
UPRATE
UPRATED
UPRATES
UPRATING

UPREAR
UPREARED
UPREARING
UPREARS
UPREST
UPRESTS
UPRIGHT
UPRIGHTED
UPRIGHTING
UPRIGHTLY
UPRIGHTS
UPRISAL
UPRISALS
UPRISE
UPRISEN
UPRISES
UPRISING
UPRISINGS
UPRIST
UPRISTS
UPRIVER
UPROAR
UPROARED
UPROARING
UPROARS
UPROLL
UPROLLED
UPROLLING
UPROLLS
UPROOT
UPROOTAL
UPROOTALS
UPROOTED
UPROOTER
UPROOTERS
UPROOTING
UPROOTINGS
UPROOTS
UPROSE
UPROUSE
UPROUSED
UPROUSES
UPROUSING
UPRUN
UPRUNNING
UPRUNS
UPRUSH
UPRUSHED
UPRUSHES
UPRUSHING
UPRYST
UPS
UPSEE
UPSEES
UPSEND
UPSENDING
UPSENDS
UPSENT
UPSET
UPSETS
UPSETTER
UPSETTERS
UPSETTING
UPSETTINGS
UPSEY
UPSEYS
UPSHOOT
UPSHOOTING
UPSHOOTS
UPSHOT

UPSHOTS
UPSIDE
UPSIDES
UPSIES
UPSILON
UPSILONS
UPSITTING
UPSITTINGS
UPSPAKE
UPSPEAK
UPSPEAKING
UPSPEAKS
UPSPEAR
UPSPEARED
UPSPEARING
UPSPEARS
UPSPOKE
UPSPOKEN
UPSPRANG
UPSPRING
UPSPRINGING
UPSPRINGS
UPSPRUNG
UPSTAGE
UPSTAGED
UPSTAGES
UPSTAGING
UPSTAIR
UPSTAIRS
UPSTAND
UPSTANDING
UPSTANDS
UPSTARE
UPSTARED
UPSTARES
UPSTARING
UPSTART
UPSTARTED
UPSTARTING
UPSTARTS
UPSTATE
UPSTAY
UPSTAYED
UPSTAYING
UPSTAYS
UPSTOOD
UPSTREAM
UPSTREAMED
UPSTREAMING
UPSTREAMS
UPSTROKE
UPSTROKES
UPSURGE
UPSURGED
UPSURGES
UPSURGING
UPSWARM
UPSWARMED
UPSWARMING
UPSWARMS
UPSWAY
UPSWAYED
UPSWAYING
UPSWAYS
UPSWEEP
UPSWEEPS
UPSWELL
UPSWELLED
UPSWELLING
UPSWELLS

UPSWEPT
UPSWING
UPSWINGS
UPSWOLLEN
UPSY
UPTAK
UPTAKE
UPTAKEN
UPTAKES
UPTAKING
UPTAKS
UPTEAR
UPTEARING
UPTEARS
UPTHREW
UPTHROW
UPTHROWING
UPTHROWN
UPTHROWS
UPTHRUST
UPTHRUSTING
UPTHRUSTS
UPTHUNDER
UPTHUNDERED
UPTHUNDERING
UPTHUNDERS
UPTIE
UPTIED
UPTIES
UPTIGHT
UPTIGHTER
UPTIGHTEST
UPTILT
UPTILTED
UPTILTING
UPTILTS
UPTOOK
UPTORE
UPTORN
UPTOWN
UPTOWNS
UPTRAIN
UPTRAINED
UPTRAINING
UPTRAINS
UPTREND
UPTRENDS
UPTRILLED
UPTURN
UPTURNED
UPTURNING
UPTURNINGS
UPTURNS
UPTYING
UPVALUE
UPVALUED
UPVALUES
UPVALUING
UPWAFT
UPWAFTED
UPWAFTING
UPWAFTS
UPWARD
UPWARDLY
UPWARDS
UPWELL
UPWELLED
UPWELLING
UPWELLINGS
UPWELLS

UPWENT
UPWHIRL
UPWHIRLED
UPWHIRLING
UPWHIRLS
UPWIND
UPWINDING
UPWINDS
UPWOUND
UPWROUGHT
UR
URACHUS
URACHUSES
URACIL
URACILS
URAEMIA
URAEMIAS
URAEMIC
URAEUS
URAEUSES
URALI
URALIS
URALITE
URALITES
URALITIC
URALITISE
URALITISED
URALITISES
URALITISING
URALITIZE
URALITIZED
URALITIZES
URALITIZING
URANIAN
URANIC
URANIDE
URANIDES
URANIN
URANINITE
URANINITES
URANINS
URANISCUS
URANISCUSES
URANISM
URANISMS
URANITE
URANITES
URANITIC
URANIUM
URANIUMS
URANOLOGIES
URANOLOGY
URANOUS
URANYL
URANYLS
URAO
URAOS
URARI
URARIS
URATE
URATES
URBAN
URBANE
URBANELY
URBANER
URBANEST
URBANISE
URBANISED
URBANISES
URBANISING

URBANITE
URBANITES
URBANITIES
URBANITY
URBANIZE
URBANIZED
URBANIZES
URBANIZING
URCEOLATE
URCEOLI
URCEOLUS
URCEOLUSES
URCHIN
URCHINS
URD
URDÉ
URDEE
URDÉE
URDS
URDY
URE
UREA
UREAL
UREAS
UREDIA
UREDINE
UREDINES
UREDINIA
UREDINIAL
UREDINIUM
UREDINOUS
UREDIUM
UREDO
UREDOSORI
UREIDE
UREIDES
UREMIA
UREMIAS
UREMIC
URENA
URENAS
URENT
URES
URESES
URESIS
URETER
URETERAL
URETERIC
URETERS
URETHAN
URETHANE
URETHANES
URETHANS
URETHRA
URETHRAE
URETHRAL
URETHRAS
URETIC
URGE
URGED
URGENCE
URGENCES
URGENCIES
URGENCY
URGENT
URGENTLY
URGER
URGERS
URGES
URGING

URGINGS
URIAL
URIALS
URIC
URICASE
URICASES
URIDINE
URIDINES
URINAL
URINALS
URINANT
URINARIES
URINARY
URINATE
URINATED
URINATES
URINATING
URINATION
URINATIONS
URINATIVE
URINATOR
URINATORS
URINE
URINED
URINES
URINING
URINOLOGIES
URINOLOGY
URINOUS
URITE
URITES
URMAN
URMANS
URN
URNAL
URNED
URNFIELD
URNFIELDS
URNFUL
URNFULS
URNING
URNINGS
URNS
UROCHORD
UROCHORDS
UROCHROME
UROCHROMES
URODELAN
URODELANS
URODELE
URODELES
URODELOUS
UROGRAPHIES
UROGRAPHY
UROKINASE
UROKINASES
UROLAGNIA
UROLAGNIAS
UROLITH
UROLITHS
UROLOGIC
UROLOGIES
UROLOGIST
UROLOGISTS
UROLOGY
UROMERE
UROMERES
UROPOD
UROPODS
UROPYGIAL

UROPYGIUM
UROPYGIUMS
UROSCOPIES
UROSCOPY
UROSES
UROSIS
UROSOME
UROSOMES
UROSTEGE
UROSTEGES
UROSTYLE
UROSTYLES
URSINE
URSON
URSONS
URTICA
URTICANT
URTICARIA
URTICARIAS
URTICAS
URTICATE
URTICATED
URTICATES
URTICATING
URUBU
URUBUS
URUS
URUSES
URVA
URVAS
US
USABLE
USAGE
USAGER
USAGERS
USAGES
USANCE
USANCES
USE
USED
USEFUL
USEFULLY
USELESS
USELESSLY
USER
USERS
USES
USHER
USHERED
USHERESS
USHERESSES
USHERETTE
USHERETTES
USHERING
USHERINGS
USHERS
USHERSHIP
USHERSHIPS
USING
USNEA
USNEAS
USTION
USTIONS
USUAL
USUALLY
USUALNESS
USUALNESSES
USUALS
USUCAPION
USUCAPIONS

USUCAPT
USUCAPTED
USUCAPTING
USUCAPTS
USUFRUCT
USUFRUCTED
USUFRUCTING
USUFRUCTS
USURE
USURED
USURER
USURERS
USURES
USURESS
USURESSES
USURIES
USURING
USURIOUS
USUROUS
USURP
USURPED
USURPEDLY
USURPER
USURPERS
USURPING
USURPINGS
USURPS
USURY
USWARD
USWARDS
UT
UTAS
UTASES
UTE
UTENSIL
UTENSILS
UTERI
UTERINE
UTERITIS
UTERITISES
UTEROTOMIES
UTEROTOMY
UTERUS
UTES
UTILE
UTILISE
UTILISED
UTILISER
UTILISERS
UTILISES
UTILISING
UTILITIES
UTILITY
UTILIZE
UTILIZED
UTILIZER
UTILIZERS
UTILIZES
UTILIZING
UTIS
UTISES
UTMOST
UTMOSTS
UTOPIA
UTOPIAN
UTOPIANS
UTOPIAS
UTOPIAST
UTOPIASTS
UTOPISM

UTOPISMS
UTOPIST
UTOPISTS
UTRICLE
UTRICLES
UTRICULAR
UTRICULI
UTRICULUS
UTS
UTTER

UTTERABLE
UTTERANCE
UTTERANCES
UTTERED
UTTERER
UTTERERS
UTTEREST
UTTERING
UTTERINGS
UTTERLESS

UTTERLY
UTTERMOST
UTTERMOSTS
UTTERNESS
UTTERNESSES
UTTERS
UTU
UTUS
UVA
UVAROVITE

UVAROVITES
UVAS
UVEA
UVEAL
UVEAS
UVEITIS
UVEITISES
UVULA
UVULAE
UVULAR

UVULARLY
UVULAS
UVULITIS
UVULITISES
UXORIAL
UXORICIDE
UXORICIDES
UXORIOUS

V

VAC
VACANCE
VACANCES
VACANCIES
VACANCY
VACANT
VACANTLY
VACATE
VACATED
VACATES
VACATING
VACATION
VACATIONED
VACATIONING
VACATIONS
VACATUR
VACATURS
VACCINAL
VACCINATE
VACCINATED
VACCINATES
VACCINATING
VACCINE
VACCINES
VACCINIA
VACCINIAL
VACCINIAS
VACCINIUM
VACCINIUMS
VACHERIN
VACHERINS
VACILLANT
VACILLATE
VACILLATED
VACILLATES
VACILLATING
VACKED
VACKING
VACS
VACUA
VACUATE
VACUATED
VACUATES
VACUATING
VACUATION
VACUATIONS
VACUIST
VACUISTS
VACUITIES
VACUITY
VACUOLAR
VACUOLATE
VACUOLE
VACUOLES
VACUOUS
VACUOUSLY
VACUUM
VACUUMED
VACUUMING
VACUUMS
VADE
VADED
VADES

VADING
VAE
VAES
VAGABOND
VAGABONDED
VAGABONDING
VAGABONDS
VAGAL
VAGARIES
VAGARIOUS
VAGARISH
VAGARY
VAGI
VAGILE
VAGILITIES
VAGILITY
VAGINA
VAGINAE
VAGINAL
VAGINALLY
VAGINANT
VAGINAS
VAGINATE
VAGINATED
VAGINITIS
VAGINITISES
VAGINULA
VAGINULAE
VAGINULE
VAGINULES
VAGITUS
VAGITUSES
VAGRANCIES
VAGRANCY
VAGRANT
VAGRANTS
VAGROM
VAGUE
VAGUED
VAGUELY
VAGUENESS
VAGUENESSES
VAGUER
VAGUES
VAGUEST
VAGUING
VAGUS
VAHINE
VAHINES
VAIL
VAILED
VAILING
VAILS
VAIN
VAINER
VAINESSE
VAINESSES
VAINEST
VAINGLORIED
VAINGLORIES
VAINGLORY
VAINGLORYING
VAINLY

VAINNESS
VAINNESSES
VAIR
VAIRÉ
VAIRIER
VAIRIEST
VAIRS
VAIRY
VAIVODE
VAIVODES
VAKASS
VAKASSES
VAKEEL
VAKEELS
VAKIL
VAKILS
VALANCE
VALANCED
VALANCES
VALE
VALENCE
VALENCES
VALENCIES
VALENCY
VALENTINE
VALENTINES
VALERIAN
VALERIANS
VALES
VALET
VALETA
VALETAS
VALETE
VALETED
VALETES
VALETING
VALETINGS
VALETS
VALGOUS
VALGUS
VALGUSES
VALI
VALIANCE
VALIANCES
VALIANCIES
VALIANCY
VALIANT
VALIANTLY
VALIANTS
VALID
VALIDATE
VALIDATED
VALIDATES
VALIDATING
VALIDER
VALIDEST
VALIDITIES
VALIDITY
VALIDLY
VALIDNESS
VALIDNESSES
VALINE
VALINES

VALIS
VALISE
VALISES
VALLAR
VALLARY
VALLECULA
VALLECULAE
VALLEY
VALLEYS
VALLONIA
VALLONIAS
VALLUM
VALLUMS
VALONEA
VALONEAS
VALONIA
VALONIAS
VALOR
VALORISE
VALORISED
VALORISES
VALORISING
VALORIZE
VALORIZED
VALORIZES
VALORIZING
VALOROUS
VALORS
VALOUR
VALOURS
VALSE
VALSED
VALSES
VALSING
VALUABLE
VALUABLES
VALUABLY
VALUATE
VALUATED
VALUATES
VALUATING
VALUATION
VALUATIONS
VALUATOR
VALUATORS
VALUE
VALUED
VALUELESS
VALUER
VALUERS
VALUES
VALUING
VALUTA
VALUTAS
VALVAL
VALVAR
VALVASSOR
VALVASSORS
VALVATE
VALVE
VALVED
VALVELESS
VALVELET

VALVELETS
VALVES
VALVING
VALVULA
VALVULAE
VALVULAR
VALVULE
VALVULES
VAMBRACE
VAMBRACED
VAMBRACES
VAMOOSE
VAMOOSED
VAMOOSES
VAMOOSING
VAMOSE
VAMOSED
VAMOSES
VAMOSING
VAMP
VAMPED
VAMPER
VAMPERS
VAMPING
VAMPINGS
VAMPIRE
VAMPIRED
VAMPIRES
VAMPIRIC
VAMPIRING
VAMPIRISE
VAMPIRISED
VAMPIRISES
VAMPIRISING
VAMPIRISM
VAMPIRISMS
VAMPIRIZE
VAMPIRIZED
VAMPIRIZES
VAMPIRIZING
VAMPISH
VAMPLATE
VAMPLATES
VAMPS
VAN
VANADATE
VANADATES
VANADIC
VANADIUM
VANADIUMS
VANADOUS
VANDAL
VANDALISE
VANDALISED
VANDALISES
VANDALISING
VANDALISM
VANDALISMS
VANDALIZE
VANDALIZED
VANDALIZES
VANDALIZING
VANDALS

VANDYKE
VANDYKED
VANDYKES
VANDYKING
VANE
VANED
VANELESS
VANES
VANESSA
VANESSAS
VANG
VANGS
VANGUARD
VANGUARDS
VANILLA
VANILLAS
VANILLIN
VANILLINS
VANISH
VANISHED
VANISHER
VANISHERS
VANISHES
VANISHING
VANISHINGS
VANITAS
VANITASES
VANITIES
VANITORIES
VANITORY
VANITY
VANNED
VANNER
VANNERS
VANNING
VANNINGS
VANQUISH
VANQUISHED
VANQUISHES
VANQUISHING
VANS
VANT
VANTAGE
VANTAGED
VANTAGES
VANTAGING
VANTBRACE
VANTBRACES
VANTS
VANWARD
VAPID
VAPIDER
VAPIDEST
VAPIDITIES
VAPIDITY
VAPIDLY
VAPIDNESS
VAPIDNESSES
VAPOR
VAPORABLE
VAPORED
VAPORETTI
VAPORETTO
VAPORETTOS
VAPORIFIC
VAPORING
VAPORISE
VAPORISED
VAPORISER
VAPORISERS

VAPORISES
VAPORISING
VAPORIZE
VAPORIZED
VAPORIZER
VAPORIZERS
VAPORIZES
VAPORIZING
VAPOROUS
VAPORS
VAPOUR
VAPOURED
VAPOURER
VAPOURERS
VAPOURING
VAPOURINGS
VAPOURISH
VAPOURS
VAPOURY
VAPULATE
VAPULATED
VAPULATES
VAPULATING
VAQUERO
VAQUEROS
VARA
VARACTOR
VARACTORS
VARAN
VARANS
VARAS
VARDIES
VARDY
VARE
VAREC
VARECH
VARECHS
VARECS
VARES
VAREUSE
VAREUSES
VARGUEÑO
VARGUEÑOS
VARIABLE
VARIABLES
VARIABLY
VARIANCE
VARIANCES
VARIANT
VARIANTS
VARIATE
VARIATED
VARIATES
VARIATING
VARIATION
VARIATIONS
VARIATIVE
VARICELLA
VARICELLAS
VARICES
VARICOSE
VARIED
VARIEDLY
VARIEGATE
VARIEGATED
VARIEGATES
VARIEGATING
VARIER
VARIERS
VARIES

VARIETAL
VARIETIES
VARIETY
VARIFORM
VARIOLA
VARIOLAR
VARIOLAS
VARIOLATE
VARIOLATED
VARIOLATES
VARIOLATING
VARIOLE
VARIOLES
VARIOLITE
VARIOLITES
VARIOLOID
VARIOLOUS
VARIORUM
VARIORUMS
VARIOUS
VARIOUSLY
VARISCITE
VARISCITES
VARISTOR
VARISTORS
VARIX
VARLET
VARLETESS
VARLETESSES
VARLETRIES
VARLETRY
VARLETS
VARLETTO
VARLETTOS
VARMENT
VARMENTS
VARMINT
VARMINTS
VARNA
VARNAS
VARNISH
VARNISHED
VARNISHER
VARNISHERS
VARNISHES
VARNISHING
VARNISHINGS
VARROA
VARROAS
VARSAL
VARSITIES
VARSITY
VARTABED
VARTABEDS
VARUS
VARUSES
VARVE
VARVED
VARVEL
VARVELLED
VARVELS
VARVES
VARY
VARYING
VARYINGS
VAS
VASA
VASAL
VASCULA
VASCULAR

VASCULUM
VASCULUMS
VASE
VASECTOMIES
VASECTOMY
VASES
VASIFORM
VASOMOTOR
VASSAIL
VASSAILS
VASSAL
VASSALAGE
VASSALAGES
VASSALESS
VASSALESSES
VASSALLED
VASSALLING
VASSALRIES
VASSALRY
VASSALS
VAST
VASTER
VASTEST
VASTIDITIES
VASTIDITY
VASTIER
VASTIEST
VASTITIES
VASTITUDE
VASTITUDES
VASTITY
VASTLY
VASTNESS
VASTNESSES
VASTS
VASTY
VAT
VATFUL
VATFULS
VATIC
VATICIDE
VATICIDES
VATICINAL
VATMAN
VATMEN
VATS
VATTED
VATTING
VAU
VAUDOO
VAUDOOS
VAUDOUX
VAULT
VAULTAGE
VAULTAGES
VAULTED
VAULTER
VAULTERS
VAULTING
VAULTINGS
VAULTS
VAULTY
VAUNCE
VAUNCED
VAUNCES
VAUNCING
VAUNT
VAUNTAGE
VAUNTAGES
VAUNTED

VAUNTER
VAUNTERIES
VAUNTERS
VAUNTERY
VAUNTFUL
VAUNTING
VAUNTINGS
VAUNTS
VAURIEN
VAURIENS
VAUS
VAUT
VAUTE
VAUTED
VAUTES
VAUTING
VAUTS
VAVASORIES
VAVASORY
VAVASOUR
VAVASOURS
VAWARD
VAWARDS
VAWTE
VAWTED
VAWTES
VAWTING
VEAL
VEALE
VEALES
VEALIER
VEALIEST
VEALS
VEALY
VECTOR
VECTORED
VECTORIAL
VECTORING
VECTORINGS
VECTORS
VEDALIA
VEDALIAS
VEDETTE
VEDETTES
VEDUTA
VEDUTE
VEDUTISTA
VEDUTISTI
VEE
VEENA
VEENAS
VEER
VEERED
VEERIES
VEERING
VEERINGLY
VEERINGS
VEERS
VEERY
VEES
VEG
VEGA
VEGAN
VEGANIC
VEGANISM
VEGANISMS
VEGANS
VEGAS
VEGETABLE
VEGETABLES

VEGETABLY
VEGETAL
VEGETALS
VEGETANT
VEGETATE
VEGETATED
VEGETATES
VEGETATING
VEGETATINGS
VEGETE
VEGETIVE
VEGETIVES
VEGGIE
VEGGIES
VEGIE
VEGIES
VEHEMENCE
VEHEMENCES
VEHEMENCIES
VEHEMENCY
VEHEMENT
VEHICLE
VEHICLES
VEHICULAR
VEHM
VEHME
VEHMIC
VEHMIQUE
VEIL
VEILED
VEILIER
VEILIEST
VEILING
VEILINGS
VEILLESS
VEILLEUSE
VEILLEUSES
VEILS
VEILY
VEIN
VEINED
VEINIER
VEINIEST
VEINING
VEININGS
VEINLET
VEINLETS
VEINOUS
VEINS
VEINSTONE
VEINSTONES
VEINSTUFF
VEINSTUFFS
VEINY
VELA
VELAMEN
VELAMINA
VELAR
VELARIA
VELARIC
VELARISE
VELARISED
VELARISES
VELARISING
VELARIUM
VELARIZE
VELARIZED
VELARIZES
VELARIZING
VELARS

VELATE
VELATED
VELATURA
VELATURAS
VELD
VELDS
VELDSKOEN
VELDSKOENS
VELDT
VELDTS
VELE
VELES
VELETA
VELETAS
VELIGER
VELIGERS
VELL
VELLEITIES
VELLEITY
VELLENAGE
VELLENAGES
VELLET
VELLETS
VELLICATE
VELLICATED
VELLICATES
VELLICATING
VELLON
VELLONS
VELLS
VELLUM
VELLUMS
VELOCE
VELOCITIES
VELOCITY
VELODROME
VELODROMES
VELOUR
VELOURS
VELOUTÉ
VELOUTÉS
VELOUTINE
VELOUTINES
VELSKOEN
VELSKOENS
VELUM
VELURE
VELURED
VELURES
VELURING
VELVERET
VELVERETS
VELVET
VELVETED
VELVETEEN
VELVETEENS
VELVETING
VELVETINGS
VELVETS
VELVETY
VENA
VENAE
VENAL
VENALITIES
VENALITY
VENALLY
VENATIC
VENATICAL
VENATION
VENATIONS

VENATOR
VENATORS
VEND
VENDACE
VENDACES
VENDAGE
VENDAGES
VENDANGE
VENDANGES
VENDED
VENDEE
VENDEES
VENDER
VENDERS
VENDETTA
VENDETTAS
VENDEUSE
VENDEUSES
VENDIBLE
VENDIBLES
VENDIBLY
VENDING
VENDIS
VENDISES
VENDISS
VENDISSES
VENDITION
VENDITIONS
VENDOR
VENDORS
VENDS
VENDUE
VENDUES
VENEER
VENEERED
VENEERER
VENEERERS
VENEERING
VENEERINGS
VENEERS
VENEFIC
VENEFICAL
VENERABLE
VENERABLY
VENERATE
VENERATED
VENERATES
VENERATING
VENERATOR
VENERATORS
VENEREAL
VENEREAN
VENEREANS
VENEREOUS
VENERER
VENERERS
VENERIES
VENERY
VENEWE
VENEWES
VENEY
VENEYS
VENGE
VENGEABLE
VENGEABLY
VENGEANCE
VENGEANCES
VENGED
VENGEFUL
VENGEMENT

VENGEMENTS
VENGER
VENGERS
VENGES
VENGING
VENIAL
VENIALITIES
VENIALITY
VENIALLY
VENIN
VENINS
VENIRE
VENIREMAN
VENIREMEN
VENIRES
VENISON
VENISONS
VENITE
VENITES
VENNEL
VENNELS
VENOM
VENOMED
VENOMING
VENOMOUS
VENOMS
VENOSE
VENOSITIES
VENOSITY
VENOUS
VENT
VENTAGE
VENTAGES
VENTAIL
VENTAILE
VENTAILES
VENTAILS
VENTANA
VENTANAS
VENTAYLE
VENTAYLES
VENTED
VENTER
VENTERS
VENTIDUCT
VENTIDUCTS
VENTIFACT
VENTIFACTS
VENTIGE
VENTIGES
VENTIL
VENTILATE
VENTILATED
VENTILATES
VENTILATING
VENTILS
VENTING
VENTINGS
VENTOSE
VENTOSITIES
VENTOSITY
VENTRAL
VENTRALLY
VENTRALS
VENTRE
VENTRED
VENTRES
VENTRICLE
VENTRICLES
VENTRING

VENTRINGS
VENTROUS
VENTS
VENTURE
VENTURED
VENTURER
VENTURERS
VENTURES
VENTURI
VENTURING
VENTURINGS
VENTURIS
VENTUROUS
VENUE
VENUES
VENULE
VENULES
VENUS
VENUSES
VENVILLE
VENVILLES
VERACIOUS
VERACITIES
VERACITY
VERANDA
VERANDAH
VERANDAHS
VERANDAS
VERATRIN
VERATRINE
VERATRINES
VERATRINS
VERATRUM
VERATRUMS
VERB
VERBAL
VERBALISE
VERBALISED
VERBALISES
VERBALISING
VERBALISM
VERBALISMS
VERBALIST
VERBALISTS
VERBALITIES
VERBALITY
VERBALIZE
VERBALIZED
VERBALIZES
VERBALIZING
VERBALLED
VERBALLING
VERBALLY
VERBALS
VERBARIAN
VERBARIANS
VERBATIM
VERBENA
VERBENAS
VERBERATE
VERBERATED
VERBERATES
VERBERATING
VERBIAGE
VERBIAGES
VERBICIDE
VERBICIDES
VERBLESS
VERBOSE
VERBOSELY

VERBOSER
VERBOSEST
VERBOSITIES
VERBOSITY
VERBS
VERDANCIES
VERDANCY
VERDANT
VERDANTLY
VERDELHO
VERDELHOS
VERDERER
VERDERERS
VERDEROR
VERDERORS
VERDET
VERDETS
VERDICT
VERDICTS
VERDIGRIS
VERDIGRISED
VERDIGRISES
VERDIGRISING
VERDIT
VERDITER
VERDITERS
VERDITS
VERDOY
VERDURE
VERDURED
VERDURES
VERDUROUS
VERECUND
VERGE
VERGED
VERGENCIES
VERGENCY
VERGER
VERGERS
VERGES
VERGING
VERGLAS
VERGLASES
VERIDICAL
VERIER
VERIEST
VERIFIED
VERIFIER
VERIFIERS
VERIFIES
VERIFY
VERIFYING
VERILY
VERISM
VERISMO
VERISMOS
VERISMS
VERIST
VERISTIC
VERISTS
VERITABLE
VERITABLY
VERITIES
VERITY
VERJUICE
VERJUICED
VERJUICES
VERKRAMP
VERLIG
VERLIGTE

VERLIGTES
VERMEIL
VERMEILED
VERMEILING
VERMEILLE
VERMEILLED
VERMEILLES
VERMEILLING
VERMEILS
VERMELL
VERMELLS
VERMES
VERMIAN
VERMICIDE
VERMICIDES
VERMICULE
VERMICULES
VERMIFORM
VERMIFUGE
VERMIFUGES
VERMIL
VERMILIES
VERMILION
VERMILIONED
VERMILIONING
VERMILIONS
VERMILLED
VERMILLING
VERMILS
VERMILY
VERMIN
VERMINATE
VERMINATED
VERMINATES
VERMINATING
VERMINED
VERMINOUS
VERMINS
VERMINY
VERMIS
VERMISES
VERMOUTH
VERMOUTHS
VERNAL
VERNALISE
VERNALISED
VERNALISES
VERNALISING
VERNALITIES
VERNALITY
VERNALIZE
VERNALIZED
VERNALIZES
VERNALIZING
VERNALLY
VERNANT
VERNATION
VERNATIONS
VERNICLE
VERNICLES
VERNIER
VERNIERS
VERONAL
VERONALS
VERONICA
VERONICAS
VÉRONIQUE
VERQUERE
VERQUERES
VERQUIRE

VERQUIRES
VERREL
VERRELS
VERREY
VERRUCA
VERRUCAE
VERRUCAS
VERRUCOSE
VERRUCOUS
VERRUGA
VERRUGAS
VERRY
VERS
VERSAL
VERSALS
VERSANT
VERSANTS
VERSATILE
VERSE
VERSED
VERSELET
VERSELETS
VERSER
VERSERS
VERSES
VERSET
VERSETS
VERSICLE
VERSICLES
VERSIFIED
VERSIFIER
VERSIFIERS
VERSIFIES
VERSIFORM
VERSIFY
VERSIFYING
VERSIN
VERSINE
VERSINES
VERSING
VERSINGS
VERSINS
VERSION
VERSIONAL
VERSIONER
VERSIONERS
VERSIONS
VERSO
VERSOS
VERST
VERSTS
VERSUS
VERSUTE
VERT
VERTEBRA
VERTEBRAE
VERTEBRAL
VERTED
VERTEX
VERTICAL
VERTICALS
VERTICES
VERTICIL
VERTICILS
VERTICITIES
VERTICITY
VERTIGINES
VERTIGO
VERTIGOES
VERTIGOS

VERTING
VERTIPORT
VERTIPORTS
VERTS
VERTU
VERTUE
VERTUES
VERTUOUS
VERTUS
VERVAIN
VERVAINS
VERVE
VERVEL
VERVELLED
VERVELS
VERVEN
VERVENS
VERVES
VERVET
VERVETS
VERY
VESICA
VESICAE
VESICAL
VESICANT
VESICANTS
VESICATE
VESICATED
VESICATES
VESICATING
VESICLE
VESICLES
VESICULA
VESICULAE
VESICULAR
VESPA
VESPAS
VESPER
VESPERAL
VESPERS
VESPIARIES
VESPIARY
VESPINE
VESPOID
VESSAIL
VESSAILS
VESSEL
VESSELS
VEST
VESTA
VESTAL
VESTALS
VESTAS
VESTED
VESTIARIES
VESTIARY
VESTIBULE
VESTIBULED
VESTIBULES
VESTIBULING
VESTIGE
VESTIGES
VESTIGIA
VESTIGIAL
VESTIGIUM
VESTIMENT
VESTIMENTS
VESTING
VESTINGS
VESTITURE

VESTITURES
VESTMENT
VESTMENTS
VESTRAL
VESTRIES
VESTRY
VESTRYMAN
VESTRYMEN
VESTS
VESTURAL
VESTURE
VESTURED
VESTURER
VESTURERS
VESTURES
VESTURING
VESUVIAN
VESUVIANS
VET
VETCH
VETCHES
VETCHIER
VETCHIEST
VETCHLING
VETCHLINGS
VETCHY
VETERAN
VETERANS
VETIVER
VETIVERS
VETKOEK
VETKOEKS
VETO
VETOED
VETOES
VETOING
VETS
VETTED
VETTING
VETTURA
VETTURAS
VETTURINI
VETTURINO
VEX
VEXATION
VEXATIONS
VEXATIOUS
VEXATORY
VEXED
VEXEDLY
VEXEDNESS
VEXEDNESSES
VEXER
VEXERS
VEXES
VEXILLA
VEXILLARIES
VEXILLARY
VEXILLUM
VEXING
VEXINGLY
VEXINGS
VEZIR
VEZIRS
VIA
VIABILITIES
VIABILITY
VIABLE
VIADUCT
VIADUCTS

VIAE	VICED	VIDEOS	VIGOROUS	VILLEIN
VIAL	VICENARY	VIDEOTAPE	VIGORS	VILLEINS
VIALFUL	VICENNIAL	VIDEOTAPES	VIGOUR	VILLENAGE
VIALFULS	VICEREINE	VIDEOTEX	VIGOURS	VILLENAGES
VIALLED	VICEREINES	VIDEOTEXES	VIHARA	VILLI
VIALS	VICEROY	VIDEOTEXT	VIHARAS	VILLIAGO
VIAMETER	VICEROYS	VIDEOTEXTS	VIHUELA	VILLIAGOES
VIAMETERS	VICES	VIDETTE	VIHUELAS	VILLIAGOS
VIAND	VICESIMAL	VIDETTES	VIKING	VILLIFORM
VIANDS	VICIATE	VIDIMUS	VIKINGISM	VILLOSE
VIAS	VICIATED	VIDIMUSES	VIKINGISMS	VILLOSITIES
VIATICA	VICIATES	VIDUAGE	VIKINGS	VILLOSITY
VIATICALS	VICIATING	VIDUAGES	VILAYET	VILLOUS
VIATICUM	VICINAGE	VIDUAL	VILAYETS	VILLS
VIATICUMS	VICINAGES	VIDUITIES	VILD	VILLUS
VIATOR	VICINAL	VIDUITY	VILDE	VIM
VIATORIAL	VICING	VIDUOUS	VILDLY	VIMANA
VIATORS	VICINITIES	VIE	VILDNESS	VIMANAS
VIBE	VICINITY	VIED	VILDNESSES	VIMINEOUS
VIBES	VICIOSITIES	VIELLE	VILE	VIMS
VIBEX	VICIOSITY	VIELLES	VILELY	VIN
VIBICES	VICIOUS	VIER	VILENESS	VINA
VIBIST	VICIOUSLY	VIERS	VILENESSES	VINACEOUS
VIBISTS	VICOMTE	VIES	VILER	VINAL
VIBRACULA	VICOMTES	VIEW	VILEST	VINAS
VIBRAHARP	VICTIM	VIEWABLE	VILIACO	VINASSE
VIBRAHARPS	VICTIMISE	VIEWDATA	VILIACOES	VINASSES
VIBRANCIES	VICTIMISED	VIEWDATAS	VILIACOS	VINCA
VIBRANCY	VICTIMISES	VIEWED	VILIAGO	VINCAS
VIBRANT	VICTIMISING	VIEWER	VILIAGOES	VINCIBLE
VIBRATE	VICTIMIZE	VIEWERS	VILIAGOS	VINCULA
VIBRATED	VICTIMIZED	VIEWIER	VILIFIED	VINCULUM
VIBRATES	VICTIMIZES	VIEWIEST	VILIFIER	VINDALOO
VIBRATILE	VICTIMIZING	VIEWINESS	VILIFIERS	VINDALOOS
VIBRATING	VICTIMS	VIEWINESSES	VILIFIES	VINDEMIAL
VIBRATION	VICTOR	VIEWING	VILIFY	VINDICATE
VIBRATIONS	VICTORESS	VIEWINGS	VILIFYING	VINDICATED
VIBRATIVE	VICTORESSES	VIEWLESS	VILIPEND	VINDICATES
VIBRATO	VICTORIA	VIEWLY	VILIPENDED	VINDICATING
VIBRATOR	VICTORIAS	VIEWPHONE	VILIPENDING	VINE
VIBRATORS	VICTORIES	VIEWPHONES	VILIPENDS	VINED
VIBRATORY	VICTORINE	VIEWPOINT	VILL	VINEGAR
VIBRATOS	VICTORINES	VIEWPOINTS	VILLA	VINEGARED
VIBRIO	VICTORS	VIEWS	VILLADOM	VINEGARING
VIBRIOS	VICTORY	VIEWY	VILLADOMS	VINEGARS
VIBRIOSES	VICTRESS	VIFDA	VILLAGE	VINEGARY
VIBRIOSIS	VICTRESSES	VIFDAS	VILLAGER	VINER
VIBRISSA	VICTRIX	VIGESIMAL	VILLAGERIES	VINERIES
VIBRISSAE	VICTRIXES	VIGIA	VILLAGERS	VINERS
VIBRONIC	VICTUAL	VIGIAS	VILLAGERY	VINERY
VIBS	VICTUALLED	VIGIL	VILLAGES	VINES
VIBURNUM	VICTUALLING	VIGILANCE	VILLAGIO	VINEW
VIBURNUMS	VICTUALS	VIGILANCES	VILLAGIOES	VINEWED
VICAR	VICUÑA	VIGILANT	VILLAGIOS	VINEWING
VICARAGE	VICUÑAS	VIGILANTE	VILLAGREE	VINEWS
VICARAGES	VIDAME	VIGILANTES	VILLAGREES	VINEYARD
VICARATE	VIDAMES	VIGILS	VILLAIN	VINEYARDS
VICARATES	VIDE	VIGNERON	VILLAINIES	VINIER
VICARESS	VIDELICET	VIGNERONS	VILLAINS	VINIEST
VICARESSES	VIDENDA	VIGNETTE	VILLAINY	VINING
VICARIAL	VIDENDUM	VIGNETTED	VILLAN	VINO
VICARIATE	VIDEO	VIGNETTER	VILLANAGE	VINOLENT
VICARIATES	VIDEODISC	VIGNETTERS	VILLANAGES	VINOLOGIES
VICARIES	VIDEODISCS	VIGNETTES	VILLANIES	VINOLOGY
VICARIOUS	VIDEOED	VIGNETTING	VILLANOUS	VINOS
VICARS	VIDEOFIT	VIGOR	VILLANS	VINOSITIES
VICARSHIP	VIDEOFITS	VIGORISH	VILLANY	VINOSITY
VICARSHIPS	VIDEOGRAM	VIGORISHES	VILLAR	VINOUS
VICARY	VIDEOGRAMS	VIGORO	VILLAS	VINS
VICE	VIDEOING	VIGOROS	VILLATIC	VINT

VINTAGE	VIRELAYS	VIRTUOSA	VISIES	VISUALS
VINTAGED	VIREMENT	VIRTUOSE	VISILE	VITA
VINTAGER	VIREMENTS	VIRTUOSI	VISILES	VITAE
VINTAGERS	VIRENT	VIRTUOSIC	VISING	VITAL
VINTAGES	VIREO	VIRTUOSO	VISION	VITALISE
VINTAGING	VIREOS	VIRTUOSOS	VISIONAL	VITALISED
VINTAGINGS	VIRES	VIRTUOUS	VISIONARIES	VITALISER
VINTED	VIRESCENT	VIRTUS	VISIONARY	VITALISERS
VINTING	VIRETOT	VIRUCIDAL	VISIONED	VITALISES
VINTNER	VIRETOTS	VIRUCIDE	VISIONER	VITALISING
VINTNERS	VIRGA	VIRUCIDES	VISIONERS	VITALISM
VINTRIES	VIRGAS	VIRULENCE	VISIONING	VITALISMS
VINTRY	VIRGATE	VIRULENCES	VISIONINGS	VITALIST
VINTS	VIRGATES	VIRULENCIES	VISIONIST	VITALISTS
VINY	VIRGE	VIRULENCY	VISIONISTS	VITALITIES
VINYL	VIRGER	VIRULENT	VISIONS	VITALITY
VINYLS	VIRGERS	VIRUS	VISIT	VITALIZE
VIOL	VIRGES	VIRUSES	VISITABLE	VITALIZED
VIOLA	VIRGIN	VIS	VISITANT	VITALIZER
VIOLABLE	VIRGINAL	VISA	VISITANTS	VITALIZERS
VIOLABLY	VIRGINALLED	VISAED	VISITATOR	VITALIZES
VIOLAS	VIRGINALLING	VISAGE	VISITATORS	VITALIZING
VIOLATE	VIRGINALS	VISAGED	VISITE	VITALLY
VIOLATED	VIRGINED	VISAGES	VISITED	VITALS
VIOLATES	VIRGINING	VISAGIST	VISITEE	VITAMIN
VIOLATING	VIRGINITIES	VISAGISTE	VISITEES	VITAMINE
VIOLATION	VIRGINITY	VISAGISTES	VISITER	VITAMINES
VIOLATIONS	VIRGINIUM	VISAGISTS	VISITERS	VITAMINS
VIOLATIVE	VIRGINIUMS	VISAING	VISITES	VITASCOPE
VIOLATOR	VIRGINLY	VISAS	VISITING	VITASCOPES
VIOLATORS	VIRGINS	VISCACHA	VISITINGS	VITATIVE
VIOLD	VIRGULATE	VISCACHAS	VISITOR	VITE
VIOLENCE	VIRGULE	VISCERA	VISITORS	VITELLARY
VIOLENCES	VIRGULES	VISCERAL	VISITRESS	VITELLI
VIOLENT	VIRICIDAL	VISCERATE	VISITRESSES	VITELLIN
VIOLENTED	VIRICIDE	VISCERATED	VISITS	VITELLINE
VIOLENTING	VIRICIDES	VISCERATES	VISIVE	VITELLINES
VIOLENTLY	VIRID	VISCERATING	VISNE	VITELLINS
VIOLENTS	VIRIDIAN	VISCID	VISNES	VITELLUS
VIOLER	VIRIDIANS	VISCIDITIES	VISNOMIE	VITEX
VIOLERS	VIRIDITE	VISCIDITY	VISNOMIES	VITEXES
VIOLET	VIRIDITES	VISCIN	VISNOMY	VITIABLE
VIOLETS	VIRIDITIES	VISCINS	VISON	VITIATE
VIOLIN	VIRIDITY	VISCOSE	VISONS	VITIATED
VIOLINIST	VIRILE	VISCOSES	VISOR	VITIATES
VIOLINISTS	VIRILISED	VISCOSITIES	VISORED	VITIATING
VIOLINS	VIRILISM	VISCOSITY	VISORING	VITIATION
VIOLIST	VIRILISMS	VISCOUNT	VISORS	VITIATIONS
VIOLISTS	VIRILITIES	VISCOUNTIES	VISTA	VITIATOR
VIOLONE	VIRILITY	VISCOUNTS	VISTAED	VITIATORS
VIOLONES	VIRILIZED	VISCOUNTY	VISTAING	VITICETA
VIOLS	VIRION	VISCOUS	VISTAL	VITICETUM
VIPER	VIRIONS	VISCUM	VISTALESS	VITICETUMS
VIPERINE	VIRL	VISCUMS	VISTAS	VITICIDE
VIPERISH	VIRLS	VISCUS	VISTO	VITICIDES
VIPEROUS	VIROGENE	VISE	VISTOS	VITILIGO
VIPERS	VIROGENES	VISÉ	VISUAL	VITILIGOS
VIRAEMIA	VIROID	VISED	VISUALISE	VITIOSITIES
VIRAEMIAS	VIROIDS	VISÉED	VISUALISED	VITIOSITY
VIRAEMIC	VIROLOGIES	VISÉING	VISUALISES	VITRAGE
VIRAGO	VIROLOGY	VISES	VISUALISING	VITRAGES
VIRAGOES	VIROSE	VISÉS	VISUALIST	VITRAIL
VIRAGOISH	VIROSES	VISIBLE	VISUALISTS	VITRAIN
VIRAGOS	VIROSIS	VISIBLES	VISUALITIES	VITRAINS
VIRAL	VIROUS	VISIBLY	VISUALITY	VITRAUX
VIRANDA	VIRTU	VISIE	VISUALIZE	VITREOUS
VIRANDAS	VIRTUAL	VISIED	VISUALIZED	VITREUM
VIRANDO	VIRTUALLY	VISIEING	VISUALIZES	VITREUMS
VIRANDOS	VIRTUE	VISIER	VISUALIZING	VITRIC
VIRELAY	VIRTUES	VISIERS	VISUALLY	VITRICS

VITRIFIED	VIXENISH	VOCATION	VOLARY	VOLUBIL
VITRIFIES	VIXENLY	VOCATIONS	VOLATIC	VOLUBLE
VITRIFORM	VIXENS	VOCATIVE	VOLATILE	VOLUBLY
VITRIFY	VIZAMENT	VOCATIVES	VOLATILES	VOLUCRINE
VITRIFYING	VIZAMENTS	VOCES	VOLCANIAN	VOLUME
VITRINE	VIZARD	VOCODER	VOLCANIC	VOLUMED
VITRINES	VIZARDED	VOCODERS	VOLCANISE	VOLUMES
VITRIOL	VIZARDING	VOCULAR	VOLCANISED	VOLUMETER
VITRIOLIC	VIZARDS	VOCULE	VOLCANISES	VOLUMETERS
VITRIOLS	VIZCACHA	VOCULES	VOLCANISING	VOLUMINAL
VITTA	VIZCACHAS	VODKA	VOLCANISM	VOLUMING
VITTAE	VIZIER	VODKAS	VOLCANISMS	VOLUMIST
VITTATE	VIZIERATE	VOE	VOLCANIST	VOLUMISTS
VITTLE	VIZIERATES	VOES	VOLCANISTS	VOLUNTARIES
VITTLES	VIZIERIAL	VOGIE	VOLCANIZE	VOLUNTARY
VITULAR	VIZIERS	VOGIER	VOLCANIZED	VOLUNTEER
VITULINE	VIZIES	VOGIEST	VOLCANIZES	VOLUNTEERED
VIVA	VIZIR	VOGUE	VOLCANIZING	VOLUNTEERING
VIVACE	VIZIRATE	VOGUED	VOLCANO	VOLUNTEERS
VIVACIOUS	VIZIRATES	VOGUES	VOLCANOES	VOLUSPA
VIVACITIES	VIZIRIAL	VOGUEY	VOLE	VOLUSPAS
VIVACITY	VIZIRS	VOGUIER	VOLED	VOLUTE
VIVAED	VIZIRSHIP	VOGUIEST	VOLENS	VOLUTED
VIVAING	VIZIRSHIPS	VOGUING	VOLERIES	VOLUTES
VIVAMENTE	VIZOR	VOGUISH	VOLERY	VOLUTIN
VIVANDIER	VIZORED	VOICE	VOLES	VOLUTINS
VIVANDIERS	VIZORING	VOICED	VOLET	VOLUTION
VIVARIA	VIZORS	VOICEFUL	VOLETS	VOLUTIONS
VIVARIES	VIZSLA	VOICELESS	VOLING	VOLUTOID
VIVARIUM	VIZSLAS	VOICER	VOLITANT	VOLVA
VIVARIUMS	VIZY	VOICERS	VOLITATE	VOLVAS
VIVARY	VIZZIE	VOICES	VOLITATED	VOLVATE
VIVAS	VIZZIED	VOICING	VOLITATES	VOLVE
VIVAT	VIZZIEING	VOICINGS	VOLITATING	VOLVED
VIVDA	VIZZIES	VOID	VOLITIENT	VOLVES
VIVDAS	VLEI	VOIDABLE	VOLITION	VOLVING
VIVE	VLEIS	VOIDANCE	VOLITIONS	VOLVULUS
VIVELY	VLIES	VOIDANCES	VOLITIVE	VOLVULUSES
VIVENCIES	VLY	VOIDED	VOLITIVES	VOMER
VIVENCY	VOAR	VOIDEE	VOLKSRAAD	VOMERINE
VIVER	VOARS	VOIDEES	VOLKSRAADS	VOMERS
VIVERRINE	VOCABLE	VOIDER	VOLLEY	VOMICA
VIVERS	VOCABLES	VOIDERS	VOLLEYED	VOMICAS
VIVES	VOCABULAR	VOIDING	VOLLEYING	VOMIT
VIVIANITE	VOCAL	VOIDINGS	VOLLEYS	VOMITED
VIVIANITES	VOCALIC	VOIDNESS	VOLOST	VOMITING
VIVID	VOCALION	VOIDNESSES	VOLOSTS	VOMITINGS
VIVIDER	VOCALIONS	VOIDS	VOLPINO	VOMITIVE
VIVIDEST	VOCALISE	VOILÀ	VOLPINOS	VOMITIVES
VIVIDITIES	VOCALISED	VOILE	VOLPLANE	VOMITO
VIVIDITY	VOCALISER	VOILES	VOLPLANED	VOMITORIA
VIVIDLY	VOCALISERS	VOISINAGE	VOLPLANES	VOMITORIES
VIVIDNESS	VOCALISES	VOISINAGES	VOLPLANING	VOMITORY
VIVIDNESSES	VOCALISING	VOITURE	VOLS	VOMITOS
VIVIFIC	VOCALISM	VOITURES	VOLT	VOMITS
VIVIFIED	VOCALISMS	VOITURIER	VOLTA	VOODOO
VIVIFIER	VOCALIST	VOITURIERS	VOLTAGE	VOODOOED
VIVIFIERS	VOCALISTS	VOIVODE	VOLTAGES	VOODOOING
VIVIFIES	VOCALITIES	VOIVODES	VOLTAIC	VOODOOISM
VIVIFY	VOCALITY	VOL	VOLTAISM	VOODOOISMS
VIVIFYING	VOCALIZE	VOLA	VOLTAISMS	VOODOOIST
VIVIPARIES	VOCALIZED	VOLABLE	VOLTE	VOODOOISTS
VIVIPARY	VOCALIZER	VOLAE	VOLTES	VOODOOS
VIVISECT	VOCALIZERS	VOLAGE	VOLTIGEUR	VOR
VIVISECTED	VOCALIZES	VOLAGEOUS	VOLTIGEURS	VORACIOUS
VIVISECTING	VOCALIZING	VOLANT	VOLTINISM	VORACITIES
VIVISECTS	VOCALLY	VOLANTE	VOLTINISMS	VORACITY
VIVO	VOCALNESS	VOLANTES	VOLTMETER	VORAGO
VIVRES	VOCALNESSES	VOLAR	VOLTMETERS	VORAGOES
VIXEN	VOCALS	VOLARIES	VOLTS	VORANT

VORPAL	VOUCHSAFED	VOX	VULCANISMS	VULNERATES
VORRED	VOUCHSAFES	VOYAGE	VULCANIST	VULNERATING
VORRING	VOUCHSAFING	VOYAGED	VULCANISTS	VULNING
VORS	VOUDOU	VOYAGER	VULCANITE	VULNS
VORTEX	VOUDOUED	VOYAGERS	VULCANITES	VULPICIDE
VORTEXES	VOUDOUING	VOYAGES	VULCANIZE	VULPICIDES
VORTICAL	VOUDOUS	VOYAGEUR	VULCANIZED	VULPINE
VORTICES	VOUGE	VOYAGEURS	VULCANIZES	VULPINISM
VORTICISM	VOUGES	VOYAGING	VULCANIZING	VULPINISMS
VORTICISMS	VOULGE	VOYEUR	VULCANS	VULPINITE
VORTICIST	VOULGES	VOYEURISM	VULGAR	VULPINITES
VORTICISTS	VOULU	VOYEURISMS	VULGARER	VULSELLA
VORTICITIES	VOUSSOIR	VOYEURS	VULGAREST	VULSELLAE
VORTICITY	VOUSSOIRED	VRAIC	VULGARIAN	VULSELLUM
VORTICOSE	VOUSSOIRING	VRAICKER	VULGARIANS	VULTURE
VOTARESS	VOUSSOIRS	VRAICKERS	VULGARISE	VULTURES
VOTARESSES	VOUTSAFE	VRAICKING	VULGARISED	VULTURINE
VOTARIES	VOUTSAFED	VRAICKINGS	VULGARISES	VULTURISH
VOTARIST	VOUTSAFES	VRAICS	VULGARISING	VULTURISM
VOTARISTS	VOUTSAFING	VRIL	VULGARISM	VULTURISMS
VOTARY	VOW	VRILS	VULGARISMS	VULTURN
VOTE	VOWED	VROOM	VULGARITIES	VULTURNS
VOTED	VOWEL	VROOMED	VULGARITY	VULTUROUS
VOTEEN	VOWELISE	VROOMING	VULGARIZE	VULVA
VOTEENS	VOWELISED	VROOMS	VULGARIZED	VULVAL
VOTELESS	VOWELISES	VROUW	VULGARIZES	VULVAR
VOTER	VOWELISING	VROUWS	VULGARIZING	VULVAS
VOTERS	VOWELIZE	VUG	VULGARLY	VULVATE
VOTES	VOWELIZED	VUGGIER	VULGARS	VULVIFORM
VOTING	VOWELIZES	VUGGIEST	VULGATE	VULVITIS
VOTIVE	VOWELIZING	VUGGY	VULGATES	VULVITISES
VOUCH	VOWELLED	VUGS	VULGO	VUM
VOUCHED	VOWELLESS	VULCAN	VULGUS	VUMMED
VOUCHEE	VOWELLING	VULCANIAN	VULGUSES	VUMMING
VOUCHEES	VOWELLY	VULCANIC	VULN	VUMS
VOUCHER	VOWELS	VULCANISE	VULNED	VYING
VOUCHERS	VOWESS	VULCANISED	VULNERARIES	VYINGLY
VOUCHES	VOWESSES	VULCANISES	VULNERARY	
VOUCHING	VOWING	VULCANISING	VULNERATE	
VOUCHSAFE	VOWS	VULCANISM	VULNERATED	

W

WABAIN	WADSETTS	WAGGONING	WAISTBOATS	WALDHORNS
WABAINS	WADY	WAGGONS	WAISTCOAT	WALDS
WABBLE	WAE	WAGHALTER	WAISTCOATS	WALE
WABBLED	WAEFUL	WAGHALTERS	WAISTED	WALED
WABBLER	WAENESS	WAGING	WAISTER	WALER
WABBLERS	WAENESSES	WAGMOIRE	WAISTERS	WALERS
WABBLES	WAES	WAGMOIRES	WAISTLINE	WALES
WABBLIER	WAESOME	WAGON	WAISTLINES	WALI
WABBLIEST	WAESUCKS	WAGONAGE	WAISTS	WALIER
WABBLING	WAFER	WAGONAGES	WAIT	WALIES
WABBLY	WAFERED	WAGONED	WAITE	WALIEST
WABOOM	WAFERING	WAGONER	WAITED	WALING
WABOOMS	WAFERS	WAGONERS	WAITER	WALIS
WABSTER	WAFERY	WAGONETTE	WAITERAGE	WALISE
WABSTERS	WAFF	WAGONETTES	WAITERAGES	WALISES
WACKE	WAFFED	WAGONFUL	WAITERING	WALK
WACKES	WAFFING	WAGONFULS	WAITERINGS	WALKABLE
WACKIER	WAFFLE	WAGONING	WAITERS	WALKABOUT
WACKIEST	WAFFLED	WAGONS	WAITES	WALKABOUTS
WACKINESS	WAFFLES	WAGS	WAITING	WALKED
WACKINESSES	WAFFLING	WAGTAIL	WAITINGLY	WALKER
WACKY	WAFFS	WAGTAILS	WAITINGS	WALKERS
WAD	WAFT	WAHINE	WAITRESS	WALKING
WADD	WAFTAGE	WAHINES	WAITRESSES	WALKINGS
WADDED	WAFTAGES	WAHOO	WAITS	WALKS
WADDIE	WAFTED	WAHOOS	WAIVE	WALKWAY
WADDIED	WAFTER	WAID	WAIVED	WALKWAYS
WADDIES	WAFTERS	WAIDE	WAIVER	WALL
WADDING	WAFTING	WAIF	WAIVERS	WALLA
WADDINGS	WAFTINGS	WAIFED	WAIVES	WALLABA
WADDLE	WAFTS	WAIFING	WAIVING	WALLABAS
WADDLED	WAFTURE	WAIFS	WAIVODE	WALLABIES
WADDLES	WAFTURES	WAIFT	WAIVODES	WALLABY
WADDLING	WAG	WAIFTS	WAIWODE	WALLAH
WADDS	WAGE	WAIL	WAIWODES	WALLAHS
WADDY	WAGED	WAILED	WAKE	WALLAROO
WADDYING	WAGELESS	WAILER	WAKED	WALLAROOS
WADE	WAGENBOOM	WAILERS	WAKEFUL	WALLAS
WADED	WAGENBOOMS	WAILFUL	WAKEFULLY	WALLED
WADER	WAGER	WAILING	WAKELESS	WALLER
WADERS	WAGERED	WAILINGLY	WAKEMAN	WALLERS
WADES	WAGERER	WAILINGS	WAKEMEN	WALLET
WADI	WAGERERS	WAILS	WAKEN	WALLETS
WADIES	WAGERING	WAIN	WAKENED	WALLFISH
WADING	WAGERS	WAINAGE	WAKENER	WALLFISHES
WADINGS	WAGES	WAINAGES	WAKENERS	WALLIER
WADIS	WAGGED	WAINED	WAKENING	WALLIES
WADMAAL	WAGGERIES	WAINING	WAKENINGS	WALLIEST
WADMAALS	WAGGERY	WAINS	WAKENS	WALLING
WADMAL	WAGGING	WAINSCOT	WAKER	WALLINGS
WADMALS	WAGGISH	WAINSCOTED	WAKERIFE	WALLOP
WADMOL	WAGGISHLY	WAINSCOTING	WAKERS	WALLOPED
WADMOLL	WAGGLE	WAINSCOTINGS	WAKES	WALLOPER
WADMOLLS	WAGGLED	WAINSCOTS	WAKIKI	WALLOPERS
WADMOLS	WAGGLES	WAINSCOTTED	WAKIKIS	WALLOPING
WADS	WAGGLIER	WAINSCOTTING	WAKING	WALLOPINGS
WADSET	WAGGLIEST	WAINSCOTTINGS	WAKINGS	WALLOPS
WADSETS	WAGGLING	WAIST	WALD	WALLOW
WADSETT	WAGGLY	WAISTBAND	WALDFLUTE	WALLOWED
WADSETTED	WAGGON	WAISTBANDS	WALDFLUTES	WALLOWER
WADSETTER	WAGGONED	WAISTBELT	WALDGRAVE	WALLOWERS
WADSETTERS	WAGGONER	WAISTBELTS	WALDGRAVES	WALLOWING
WADSETTING	WAGGONERS	WAISTBOAT	WALDHORN	WALLOWINGS

WALLOWS
WALLPAPER
WALLPAPERS
WALLS
WALLSEND
WALLSENDS
WALLWORT
WALLWORTS
WALLY
WALLYDRAG
WALLYDRAGS
WALNUT
WALNUTS
WALRUS
WALRUSES
WALTIER
WALTIEST
WALTY
WALTZ
WALTZED
WALTZER
WALTZERS
WALTZES
WALTZING
WALTZINGS
WALY
WAMBLE
WAMBLED
WAMBLES
WAMBLIER
WAMBLIEST
WAMBLING
WAMBLINGS
WAMBLY
WAME
WAMED
WAMEFUL
WAMEFULS
WAMES
WAMMUS
WAMMUSES
WAMPEE
WAMPEES
WAMPISH
WAMPISHED
WAMPISHES
WAMPISHING
WAMPUM
WAMPUMS
WAMPUS
WAMPUSES
WAMUS
WAMUSES
WAN
WANCHANCY
WAND
WANDER
WANDERED
WANDERER
WANDERERS
WANDERING
WANDERINGS
WANDEROO
WANDEROOS
WANDERS
WANDLE
WANDOO
WANDOOS
WANDS
WANE

WANED
WANES
WANEY
WANG
WANGAN
WANGANS
WANGLE
WANGLED
WANGLER
WANGLERS
WANGLES
WANGLING
WANGLINGS
WANGS
WANGUN
WANGUNS
WANHOPE
WANHOPES
WANIER
WANIEST
WANIGAN
WANIGANS
WANING
WANINGS
WANK
WANKED
WANKER
WANKERS
WANKING
WANKLE
WANKS
WANLE
WANLY
WANNED
WANNEL
WANNER
WANNESS
WANNESSES
WANNEST
WANNING
WANNISH
WANS
WANT
WANTAGE
WANTAGES
WANTED
WANTER
WANTERS
WANTHILL
WANTHILLS
WANTIES
WANTING
WANTINGS
WANTON
WANTONED
WANTONER
WANTONEST
WANTONING
WANTONISE
WANTONISED
WANTONISES
WANTONISING
WANTONIZE
WANTONIZED
WANTONIZES
WANTONIZING
WANTONLY
WANTONS
WANTS
WANTY

WANWORDY
WANWORTH
WANWORTHS
WANY
WANZE
WANZED
WANZES
WANZING
WAP
WAPENSHAW
WAPENSHAWS
WAPENTAKE
WAPENTAKES
WAPINSHAW
WAPINSHAWS
WAPITI
WAPITIS
WAPPED
WAPPEND
WAPPER
WAPPERED
WAPPERING
WAPPERS
WAPPING
WAPS
WAR
WARATAH
WARATAHS
WARBIER
WARBIEST
WARBLE
WARBLED
WARBLER
WARBLERS
WARBLES
WARBLING
WARBLINGS
WARBY
WARD
WARDED
WARDEN
WARDENED
WARDENING
WARDENRIES
WARDENRY
WARDENS
WARDER
WARDERED
WARDERING
WARDERS
WARDING
WARDINGS
WARDOG
WARDOGS
WARDRESS
WARDRESSES
WARDROBE
WARDROBER
WARDROBERS
WARDROBES
WARDROP
WARDROPS
WARDS
WARDSHIP
WARDSHIPS
WARE
WARED
WAREHOUSE
WAREHOUSED
WAREHOUSES

WAREHOUSING
WAREHOUSINGS
WARELESS
WARES
WARFARE
WARFARED
WARFARER
WARFARERS
WARFARES
WARFARIN
WARFARING
WARFARINGS
WARFARINS
WARHABLE
WARHEAD
WARHEADS
WARIER
WARIEST
WARILY
WARIMENT
WARIMENTS
WARINESS
WARINESSES
WARING
WARISON
WARISONS
WARK
WARKS
WARLIKE
WARLING
WARLINGS
WARLOCK
WARLOCKRIES
WARLOCKRY
WARLOCKS
WARLORD
WARLORDS
WARM
WARMAN
WARMBLOOD
WARMBLOODS
WARMED
WARMEN
WARMER
WARMERS
WARMEST
WARMING
WARMINGS
WARMLY
WARMNESS
WARMNESSES
WARMONGER
WARMONGERS
WARMS
WARMTH
WARMTHS
WARN
WARNED
WARNER
WARNERS
WARNING
WARNINGLY
WARNINGS
WARNS
WARP
WARPATH
WARPATHS
WARPED
WARPER
WARPERS

WARPING
WARPINGS
WARPLANE
WARPLANES
WARPS
WARRAGAL
WARRAGALS
WARRAGLE
WARRAGLES
WARRAGUL
WARRAGULS
WARRAN
WARRAND
WARRANDED
WARRANDING
WARRANDS
WARRANED
WARRANING
WARRANS
WARRANT
WARRANTED
WARRANTEE
WARRANTEES
WARRANTER
WARRANTERS
WARRANTIES
WARRANTING
WARRANTINGS
WARRANTOR
WARRANTORS
WARRANTS
WARRANTY
WARRAY
WARRAYED
WARRAYING
WARRAYS
WARRE
WARRED
WARREN
WARRENER
WARRENERS
WARRENS
WARREY
WARREYED
WARREYING
WARREYS
WARRIGAL
WARRIGALS
WARRING
WARRIOR
WARRIORS
WARRISON
WARRISONS
WARS
WARSHIP
WARSHIPS
WARSLE
WARSLED
WARSLES
WARSLING
WARST
WART
WARTED
WARTIER
WARTIEST
WARTIME
WARTIMES
WARTLESS
WARTS
WARTWEED

WARTWEEDS
WARTWORT
WARTWORTS
WARTY
WARWOLF
WARWOLVES
WARY
WAS
WASE
WASES
WASH
WASHABLE
WASHED
WASHEN
WASHER
WASHERED
WASHERIES
WASHERING
WASHERMAN
WASHERMEN
WASHERS
WASHERY
WASHES
WASHIER
WASHIEST
WASHINESS
WASHINESSES
WASHING
WASHINGS
WASHLAND
WASHLANDS
WASHROOM
WASHROOMS
WASHY
WASP
WASPIE
WASPIER
WASPIES
WASPIEST
WASPISH
WASPISHLY
WASPS
WASPY
WASSAIL
WASSAILED
WASSAILER
WASSAILERS
WASSAILING
WASSAILINGS
WASSAILRIES
WASSAILRY
WASSAILS
WASSERMAN
WASSERMEN
WAST
WASTAGE
WASTAGES
WASTE
WASTED
WASTEFUL
WASTEL
WASTELAND
WASTELANDS
WASTELS
WASTENESS
WASTENESSES
WASTER
WASTERED
WASTERFUL
WASTERIES

WASTERIFE
WASTERIFES
WASTERING
WASTERS
WASTERY
WASTES
WASTFULL
WASTING
WASTINGS
WASTNESS
WASTNESSES
WASTREL
WASTRELS
WASTRIES
WASTRY
WASTS
WAT
WATCH
WATCHABLE
WATCHCASE
WATCHCASES
WATCHED
WATCHER
WATCHERS
WATCHES
WATCHET
WATCHETS
WATCHFUL
WATCHING
WATCHMAN
WATCHMEN
WATCHWORD
WATCHWORDS
WATE
WATER
WATERAGE
WATERAGES
WATERED
WATERER
WATERERS
WATERFALL
WATERFALLS
WATERIER
WATERIEST
WATERING
WATERINGS
WATERISH
WATERLESS
WATERLILIES
WATERLILY
WATERLOG
WATERLOGGED
WATERLOGGING
WATERLOGS
WATERMAN
WATERMARK
WATERMARKED
WATERMARKING
WATERMARKS
WATERMEN
WATERS
WATERSHED
WATERSHEDS
WATERSIDE
WATERSIDES
WATERWAY
WATERWAYS
WATERWORK
WATERWORKS
WATERY

WATS
WATT
WATTAGE
WATTAGES
WATTER
WATTEST
WATTLE
WATTLED
WATTLES
WATTLING
WATTLINGS
WATTMETER
WATTMETERS
WATTS
WAUCHT
WAUCHTED
WAUCHTING
WAUCHTS
WAUFF
WAUFFED
WAUFFING
WAUFFS
WAUGH
WAUGHED
WAUGHING
WAUGHS
WAUGHT
WAUGHTED
WAUGHTING
WAUGHTS
WAUK
WAUKED
WAUKING
WAUKRIFE
WAUKS
WAUL
WAULED
WAULING
WAULINGS
WAULK
WAULKED
WAULKING
WAULKS
WAULS
WAUR
WAURED
WAURING
WAURS
WAURST
WAVE
WAVEBAND
WAVEBANDS
WAVED
WAVEFORM
WAVEFORMS
WAVEFRONT
WAVEFRONTS
WAVEGUIDE
WAVEGUIDES
WAVELESS
WAVELET
WAVELETS
WAVELIKE
WAVELLITE
WAVELLITES
WAVEMETER
WAVEMETERS
WAVER
WAVERED
WAVERER

WAVERERS
WAVERING
WAVERINGS
WAVEROUS
WAVERS
WAVERY
WAVES
WAVESHAPE
WAVESHAPES
WAVESON
WAVESONS
WAVEY
WAVEYS
WAVIER
WAVIES
WAVIEST
WAVINESS
WAVINESSES
WAVING
WAVINGS
WAVY
WAW
WAWE
WAWES
WAWL
WAWLED
WAWLING
WAWLINGS
WAWLS
WAWS
WAX
WAXBERRIES
WAXBERRY
WAXBILL
WAXBILLS
WAXED
WAXEN
WAXER
WAXERS
WAXES
WAXIER
WAXIEST
WAXINESS
WAXINESSES
WAXING
WAXINGS
WAXWING
WAXWINGS
WAXWORK
WAXWORKER
WAXWORKERS
WAXWORKS
WAXY
WAY
WAYBREAD
WAYBREADS
WAYED
WAYFARE
WAYFARED
WAYFARER
WAYFARERS
WAYFARES
WAYFARING
WAYFARINGS
WAYGONE
WAYGOOSE
WAYGOOSES
WAYING
WAYLAID
WAYLAY

WAYLAYER
WAYLAYERS
WAYLAYING
WAYLAYS
WAYLESS
WAYMARK
WAYMARKED
WAYMARKING
WAYMARKS
WAYMENT
WAYMENTED
WAYMENTING
WAYMENTS
WAYS
WAYSIDE
WAYSIDES
WAYWARD
WAYWARDLY
WAYWISER
WAYWISERS
WAYWORN
WAYZGOOSE
WAYZGOOSES
WAZIR
WAZIRS
WE
WEAK
WEAKEN
WEAKENED
WEAKENER
WEAKENERS
WEAKENING
WEAKENS
WEAKER
WEAKEST
WEAKFISH
WEAKFISHES
WEAKLIER
WEAKLIEST
WEAKLING
WEAKLINGS
WEAKLY
WEAKNESS
WEAKNESSES
WEAL
WEALD
WEALDS
WEALS
WEALSMAN
WEALSMEN
WEALTH
WEALTHIER
WEALTHIEST
WEALTHILY
WEALTHS
WEALTHY
WEAMB
WEAMBS
WEAN
WEANED
WEANEL
WEANELS
WEANER
WEANERS
WEANING
WEANLING
WEANLINGS
WEANS
WEAPON
WEAPONED

WEAPONRIES
WEAPONRY
WEAPONS
WEAR
WEARABLE
WEARED
WEARER
WEARERS
WEARIED
WEARIER
WEARIES
WEARIEST
WEARIFUL
WEARILESS
WEARILY
WEARINESS
WEARINESSES
WEARING
WEARINGS
WEARISH
WEARISOME
WEARS
WEARY
WEARYING
WEASAND
WEASANDS
WEASEL
WEASELED
WEASELER
WEASELERS
WEASELING
WEASELLED
WEASELLER
WEASELLERS
WEASELLING
WEASELLY
WEASELS
WEATHER
WEATHERED
WEATHERING
WEATHERINGS
WEATHERLY
WEATHERS
WEAVE
WEAVED
WEAVER
WEAVERS
WEAVES
WEAVING
WEAVINGS
WEAZAND
WEAZANDS
WEAZEN
WEAZENED
WEAZENING
WEAZENS
WEB
WEBBED
WEBBIER
WEBBIEST
WEBBING
WEBBINGS
WEBBY
WEBER
WEBERS
WEBS
WEBSTER
WEBSTERS
WEBWHEEL
WEBWHEELS

WEBWORM
WEBWORMS
WECHT
WECHTS
WED
WEDDED
WEDDING
WEDDINGS
WEDELN
WEDELNED
WEDELNING
WEDELNS
WEDGE
WEDGED
WEDGES
WEDGEWISE
WEDGIE
WEDGIES
WEDGING
WEDGINGS
WEDLOCK
WEDLOCKS
WEDS
WEE
WEED
WEEDED
WEEDER
WEEDERIES
WEEDERS
WEEDERY
WEEDICIDE
WEEDICIDES
WEEDIER
WEEDIEST
WEEDINESS
WEEDINESSES
WEEDING
WEEDINGS
WEEDLESS
WEEDS
WEEDY
WEEING
WEEK
WEEKDAY
WEEKDAYS
WEEKE
WEEKEND
WEEKENDED
WEEKENDING
WEEKENDS
WEEKES
WEEKLIES
WEEKLY
WEEKNIGHT
WEEKNIGHTS
WEEKS
WEEL
WEELS
WEEM
WEEMS
WEEN
WEENED
WEENIER
WEENIEST
WEENING
WEENS
WEENY
WEEP
WEEPER
WEEPERS

WEEPHOLE
WEEPHOLES
WEEPIE
WEEPIER
WEEPIES
WEEPIEST
WEEPING
WEEPINGLY
WEEPINGS
WEEPS
WEEPY
WEER
WEES
WEEST
WEET
WEETE
WEETEN
WEETING
WEETINGLY
WEETLESS
WEEVER
WEEVERS
WEEVIL
WEEVILED
WEEVILLED
WEEVILLY
WEEVILS
WEEVILY
WEFT
WEFTAGE
WEFTAGES
WEFTE
WEFTED
WEFTES
WEFTING
WEFTS
WEID
WEIDS
WEIGELA
WEIGELAS
WEIGH
WEIGHABLE
WEIGHAGE
WEIGHAGES
WEIGHED
WEIGHER
WEIGHERS
WEIGHING
WEIGHINGS
WEIGHS
WEIGHT
WEIGHTED
WEIGHTIER
WEIGHTIEST
WEIGHTILY
WEIGHTING
WEIGHTINGS
WEIGHTS
WEIGHTY
WEIL
WEILS
WEIR
WEIRD
WEIRDED
WEIRDER
WEIRDEST
WEIRDIE
WEIRDIES
WEIRDING
WEIRDLY

WEIRDNESS
WEIRDNESSES
WEIRDO
WEIRDOS
WEIRDS
WEIRED
WEIRING
WEIRS
WEISE
WEISED
WEISES
WEISING
WEIZE
WEIZED
WEIZES
WEIZING
WEKA
WEKAS
WELAWAY
WELCH
WELCHED
WELCHER
WELCHERS
WELCHES
WELCHING
WELCOME
WELCOMED
WELCOMER
WELCOMERS
WELCOMES
WELCOMING
WELD
WELDABLE
WELDED
WELDER
WELDERS
WELDING
WELDINGS
WELDLESS
WELDMENT
WELDMENTS
WELDMESH
WELDMESH®
WELDMESHES
WELDMESHES®
WELDOR
WELDORS
WELDS
WELFARE
WELFARES
WELFARISM
WELFARISMS
WELFARIST
WELFARISTS
WELK
WELKE
WELKED
WELKES
WELKIN
WELKING
WELKINS
WELKS
WELKT
WELL
WELLADAY
WELLANEAR
WELLAWAY
WELLED
WELLIE
WELLIES

WELLING
WELLINGS
WELLS
WELLY
WELSH
WELSHED
WELSHER
WELSHERS
WELSHES
WELSHING
WELT
WELTED
WELTER
WELTERED
WELTERING
WELTERS
WELTING
WELTS
WEM
WEMB
WEMBS
WEMS
WEN
WENCH
WENCHED
WENCHER
WENCHERS
WENCHES
WENCHING
WEND
WENDED
WENDIGO
WENDIGOS
WENDING
WENDS
WENNIER
WENNIEST
WENNISH
WENNY
WENS
WENT
WENTS
WEPT
WERE
WEREGILD
WEREGILDS
WEREWOLF
WEREWOLVES
WERGILD
WERGILDS
WERNERITE
WERNERITES
WERSH
WERSHER
WERSHEST
WERT
WERWOLF
WERWOLVES
WESAND
WESANDS
WEST
WESTBOUND
WESTED
WESTER
WESTERED
WESTERING
WESTERINGS
WESTERLIES
WESTERLY
WESTERN

WESTERNER	WHALLY	WHEEL	WHENEVER	WHIDDING
WESTERNERS	WHAM	WHEELBASE	WHENS	WHIDS
WESTERNS	WHAMMED	WHEELBASES	WHERE	WHIFF
WESTERS	WHAMMING	WHEELED	WHEREAS	WHIFFED
WESTING	WHAMPLE	WHEELER	WHEREAT	WHIFFER
WESTINGS	WHAMPLES	WHEELERS	WHEREBY	WHIFFERS
WESTLIN	WHAMS	WHEELIE	WHEREFOR	WHIFFET
WESTMOST	WHANG	WHEELIER	WHEREFORE	WHIFFIER
WESTS	WHANGAM	WHEELIES	WHEREFORES	WHIFFIEST
WESTWARD	WHANGAMS	WHEELIEST	WHEREFROM	WHIFFING
WESTWARDS	WHANGED	WHEELING	WHEREIN	WHIFFINGS
WET	WHANGEE	WHEELINGS	WHEREINTO	WHIFFLE
WETBACK	WHANGEES	WHEELMAN	WHERENESS	WHIFFLED
WETBACKS	WHANGING	WHEELMEN	WHERENESSES	WHIFFLER
WETHER	WHANGS	WHEELS	WHEREOF	WHIFFLERIES
WETHERS	WHAP	WHEELWORK	WHEREON	WHIFFLERS
WETLAND	WHAPPED	WHEELWORKS	WHEREOUT	WHIFFLERY
WETLANDS	WHAPPING	WHEELY	WHERES	WHIFFLES
WETLY	WHAPS	WHEEN	WHERESO	WHIFFLING
WETNESS	WHARE	WHEENGE	WHERETO	WHIFFLINGS
WETNESSES	WHARES	WHEENGED	WHEREUNTO	WHIFFS
WETS	WHARF	WHEENGES	WHEREUPON	WHIFFY
WETTED	WHARFAGE	WHEENGING	WHEREVER	WHIFT
WETTER	WHARFAGES	WHEENS	WHEREWITH	WHIFTS
WETTEST	WHARFED	WHEEPLE	WHEREWITHS	WHIG
WETTING	WHARFING	WHEEPLED	WHERRET	WHIGGED
WETTISH	WHARFINGS	WHEEPLES	WHERRETED	WHIGGING
WEX	WHARFS	WHEEPLING	WHERRETING	WHIGS
WEXE	WHARVE	WHEESHT	WHERRETS	WHILE
WEXED	WHARVES	WHEESHTED	WHERRIES	WHILED
WEXES	WHAT	WHEESHTING	WHERRY	WHILES
WEXING	WHATEN	WHEESHTS	WHERRYMAN	WHILING
WEY	WHATEVER	WHEEZE	WHERRYMEN	WHILK
WEYARD	WHATNA	WHEEZED	WHET	WHILLIED
WEYS	WHATNESS	WHEEZES	WHETHER	WHILLIES
WEYWARD	WHATNESSES	WHEEZIER	WHETS	WHILLY
WEZAND	WHATNOT	WHEEZIEST	WHETSTONE	WHILLYING
WEZANDS	WHATNOTS	WHEEZILY	WHETSTONES	WHILLYWHA
WHACK	WHATS	WHEEZING	WHETTED	WHILLYWHAED
WHACKED	WHATSIS	WHEEZINGS	WHETTER	WHILLYWHAING
WHACKER	WHATSISES	WHEEZLE	WHETTERS	WHILLYWHAS
WHACKERS	WHATSIT	WHEEZLED	WHETTING	WHILOM
WHACKIER	WHATSITS	WHEEZLES	WHEUGH	WHILST
WHACKIEST	WHATSO	WHEEZLING	WHEUGHED	WHIM
WHACKING	WHATTEN	WHEEZY	WHEUGHING	WHIMBREL
WHACKINGS	WHAUP	WHEFT	WHEUGHS	WHIMBRELS
WHACKO	WHAUPS	WHEFTS	WHEW	WHIMMED
WHACKOES	WHAUR	WHELK	WHEWED	WHIMMIER
WHACKOS	WHAURS	WHELKED	WHEWING	WHIMMIEST
WHACKS	WHEAL	WHELKIER	WHEWS	WHIMMING
WHACKY	WHEALS	WHELKIEST	WHEY	WHIMMY
WHAISLE	WHEAR	WHELKS	WHEYEY	WHIMPER
WHAISLED	WHEARE	WHELKY	WHEYIER	WHIMPERED
WHAISLES	WHEAT	WHELM	WHEYIEST	WHIMPERER
WHAISLING	WHEATEAR	WHELMED	WHEYISH	WHIMPERERS
WHAIZLE	WHEATEARS	WHELMING	WHEYS	WHIMPERING
WHAIZLED	WHEATEN	WHELMS	WHICH	WHIMPERINGS
WHAIZLES	WHEATS	WHELP	WHICHEVER	WHIMPERS
WHAIZLING	WHEE	WHELPED	WHICKER	WHIMPLE
WHALE	WHEECH	WHELPING	WHICKERED	WHIMPLED
WHALEBONE	WHEECHED	WHELPS	WHICKERING	WHIMPLES
WHALEBONES	WHEECHING	WHEMMLE	WHICKERS	WHIMPLING
WHALED	WHEECHS	WHEMMLED	WHID	WHIMS
WHALER	WHEEDLE	WHEMMLES	WHIDAH	WHIMSEY
WHALERIES	WHEEDLED	WHEMMLING	WHIDAHS	WHIMSEYS
WHALERS	WHEEDLER	WHEN	WHIDDED	WHIMSICAL
WHALERY	WHEEDLERS	WHENAS	WHIDDER	WHIMSIER
WHALES	WHEEDLES	WHENCE	WHIDDERED	WHIMSIES
WHALING	WHEEDLING	WHENCES	WHIDDERING	WHIMSIEST
WHALINGS	WHEEDLINGS	WHENCEVER	WHIDDERS	

WHIMSILY
WHIMSY
WHIN
WHINCHAT
WHINCHATS
WHINE
WHINED
WHINER
WHINERS
WHINES
WHINGE
WHINGED
WHINGEING
WHINGEINGS
WHINGER
WHINGERS
WHINGES
WHINIARD
WHINIARDS
WHINIER
WHINIEST
WHININESS
WHININESSES
WHINING
WHININGLY
WHININGS
WHINNIED
WHINNIER
WHINNIES
WHINNIEST
WHINNY
WHINNYING
WHINS
WHINSTONE
WHINSTONES
WHINY
WHINYARD
WHINYARDS
WHIP
WHIPBIRD
WHIPBIRDS
WHIPCAT
WHIPCATS
WHIPCORD
WHIPCORDS
WHIPCORDY
WHIPJACK
WHIPJACKS
WHIPLASH
WHIPLASHED
WHIPLASHES
WHIPLASHING
WHIPLIKE
WHIPPED
WHIPPER
WHIPPERS
WHIPPET
WHIPPETS
WHIPPIER
WHIPPIEST
WHIPPING
WHIPPINGS
WHIPPY
WHIPS
WHIPSTAFF
WHIPSTAFFS
WHIPSTALL
WHIPSTALLED
WHIPSTALLING
WHIPSTALLS

WHIPSTER
WHIPSTERS
WHIPT
WHIPWORM
WHIPWORMS
WHIR
WHIRL
WHIRLED
WHIRLER
WHIRLERS
WHIRLIGIG
WHIRLIGIGS
WHIRLING
WHIRLINGS
WHIRLPOOL
WHIRLPOOLS
WHIRLS
WHIRLWIND
WHIRLWINDS
WHIRR
WHIRRED
WHIRRET
WHIRRETED
WHIRRETING
WHIRRETS
WHIRRIED
WHIRRIES
WHIRRING
WHIRRINGS
WHIRRS
WHIRRY
WHIRRYING
WHIRS
WHIRTLE
WHIRTLES
WHISH
WHISHED
WHISHES
WHISHING
WHISHT
WHISHTED
WHISHTING
WHISHTS
WHISK
WHISKED
WHISKER
WHISKERED
WHISKERS
WHISKERY
WHISKET
WHISKETS
WHISKEY
WHISKEYS
WHISKIES
WHISKING
WHISKS
WHISKY
WHISPER
WHISPERED
WHISPERER
WHISPERERS
WHISPERING
WHISPERINGS
WHISPERS
WHISPERY
WHISS
WHISSED
WHISSES
WHISSING
WHIST

WHISTED
WHISTING
WHISTLE
WHISTLED
WHISTLER
WHISTLERS
WHISTLES
WHISTLING
WHISTLINGS
WHISTS
WHIT
WHITE
WHITEBAIT
WHITEBAITS
WHITEBASS
WHITEBASSES
WHITEBEAM
WHITEBEAMS
WHITECAP
WHITECAPS
WHITED
WHITEFISH
WHITEFISHES
WHITEHEAD
WHITEHEADS
WHITELY
WHITEN
WHITENED
WHITENER
WHITENERS
WHITENESS
WHITENESSES
WHITENING
WHITENINGS
WHITENS
WHITER
WHITES
WHITEST
WHITEWALL
WHITEWALLS
WHITEWARE
WHITEWARES
WHITEWASH
WHITEWASHED
WHITEWASHES
WHITEWASHING
WHITEWING
WHITEWINGS
WHITEWOOD
WHITEWOODS
WHITEY
WHITEYS
WHITHER
WHITHERED
WHITHERING
WHITHERS
WHITIER
WHITIES
WHITIEST
WHITING
WHITINGS
WHITISH
WHITLING
WHITLINGS
WHITLOW
WHITLOWS
WHITRET
WHITRETS
WHITS
WHITSTER

WHITSTERS
WHITTAW
WHITTAWER
WHITTAWERS
WHITTAWS
WHITTER
WHITTERED
WHITTERING
WHITTERS
WHITTLE
WHITTLED
WHITTLER
WHITTLERS
WHITTLES
WHITTLING
WHITTLINGS
WHITTRET
WHITTRETS
WHITY
WHIZ
WHIZZ
WHIZZED
WHIZZER
WHIZZERS
WHIZZES
WHIZZING
WHIZZINGS
WHO
WHOA
WHODUNNIT
WHODUNNITS
WHOEVER
WHOLE
WHOLEFOOD
WHOLEFOODS
WHOLEMEAL
WHOLEMEALS
WHOLENESS
WHOLENESSES
WHOLES
WHOLESALE
WHOLESALES
WHOLESOME
WHOLESOMER
WHOLESOMEST
WHOLISM
WHOLISMS
WHOLISTIC
WHOLLY
WHOM
WHOMBLE
WHOMBLED
WHOMBLES
WHOMBLING
WHOMEVER
WHOMMLE
WHOMMLED
WHOMMLES
WHOMMLING
WHOOBUB
WHOOBUBS
WHOOP
WHOOPED
WHOOPEE
WHOOPEES
WHOOPER
WHOOPERS
WHOOPING
WHOOPINGS
WHOOPS

WHOOSH
WHOOSHED
WHOOSHES
WHOOSHING
WHOOT
WHOOTED
WHOOTING
WHOOTS
WHOP
WHOPPED
WHOPPER
WHOPPERS
WHOPPING
WHOPPINGS
WHOPS
WHORE
WHORED
WHOREDOM
WHOREDOMS
WHORES
WHORESON
WHORESONS
WHORING
WHORISH
WHORISHLY
WHORL
WHORLED
WHORLS
WHORT
WHORTS
WHOSE
WHOSEVER
WHOSO
WHOSOEVER
WHOT
WHOW
WHUMMLE
WHUMMLED
WHUMMLES
WHUMMLING
WHUNSTANE
WHUNSTANES
WHY
WHYDAH
WHYDAHS
WHYEVER
WICK
WICKED
WICKEDER
WICKEDEST
WICKEDLY
WICKEN
WICKENS
WICKER
WICKERED
WICKERS
WICKET
WICKETS
WICKIES
WICKING
WICKS
WICKY
WIDDIES
WIDDLE
WIDDLED
WIDDLES
WIDDLING
WIDDY
WIDE
WIDELY

WIDEN
WIDENED
WIDENER
WIDENERS
WIDENESS
WIDENESSES
WIDENING
WIDENS
WIDER
WIDES
WIDEST
WIDGEON
WIDGEONS
WIDGET
WIDGETS
WIDISH
WIDOW
WIDOWED
WIDOWER
WIDOWERS
WIDOWHOOD
WIDOWHOODS
WIDOWING
WIDOWS
WIDTH
WIDTHS
WIDTHWAYS
WIDTHWISE
WIEL
WIELD
WIELDABLE
WIELDED
WIELDER
WIELDERS
WIELDIER
WIELDIEST
WIELDING
WIELDLESS
WIELDS
WIELDY
WIELS
WIFE
WIFEHOOD
WIFEHOODS
WIFELESS
WIFELIER
WIFELIEST
WIFELY
WIG
WIGAN
WIGANS
WIGEON
WIGEONS
WIGGED
WIGGERIES
WIGGERY
WIGGING
WIGGINGS
WIGGLE
WIGGLED
WIGGLER
WIGGLERS
WIGGLES
WIGGLIER
WIGGLIEST
WIGGLING
WIGGLY
WIGHT
WIGHTED
WIGHTING

WIGHTLY
WIGHTS
WIGLESS
WIGS
WIGWAG
WIGWAGGED
WIGWAGGING
WIGWAGS
WIGWAM
WIGWAMS
WILD
WILDCAT
WILDCATS
WILDCATTED
WILDCATTING
WILDED
WILDER
WILDERED
WILDERING
WILDERS
WILDEST
WILDFIRE
WILDFIRES
WILDGRAVE
WILDGRAVES
WILDING
WILDINGS
WILDISH
WILDLIFE
WILDLIFES
WILDLY
WILDNESS
WILDNESSES
WILDOAT
WILDOATS
WILDS
WILE
WILED
WILEFUL
WILES
WILFUL
WILFULLY
WILI
WILIER
WILIEST
WILILY
WILINESS
WILINESSES
WILING
WILIS
WILL
WILLABLE
WILLED
WILLEMITE
WILLEMITES
WILLER
WILLERS
WILLEST
WILLET
WILLETS
WILLEY
WILLEYED
WILLEYING
WILLEYS
WILLIE
WILLIED
WILLIES
WILLING
WILLINGLY
WILLIWAW

WILLIWAWS
WILLOW
WILLOWED
WILLOWING
WILLOWISH
WILLOWS
WILLOWY
WILLS
WILLY
WILLYARD
WILLYART
WILLYING
WILT
WILTED
WILTING
WILTS
WILY
WIMBLE
WIMBLED
WIMBLES
WIMBLING
WIMBREL
WIMBRELS
WIMP
WIMPIER
WIMPIEST
WIMPISH
WIMPLE
WIMPLED
WIMPLES
WIMPLING
WIMPS
WIMPY
WIN
WINCE
WINCED
WINCER
WINCERS
WINCES
WINCEY
WINCEYS
WINCH
WINCHED
WINCHES
WINCHING
WINCHMAN
WINCHMEN
WINCING
WINCINGS
WINCOPIPE
WINCOPIPES
WIND
WINDAC
WINDACS
WINDAGE
WINDAGES
WINDAS
WINDASES
WINDBLOW
WINDBLOWS
WINDBURN
WINDBURNS
WINDED
WINDER
WINDERS
WINDFALL
WINDFALLS
WINDIER
WINDIEST
WINDIGO

WINDIGOS
WINDILY
WINDINESS
WINDINESSES
WINDING
WINDINGLY
WINDINGS
WINDLASS
WINDLASSED
WINDLASSES
WINDLASSING
WINDLE
WINDLES
WINDLESS
WINDMILL
WINDMILLED
WINDMILLING
WINDMILLS
WINDOCK
WINDOCKS
WINDORE
WINDORES
WINDOW
WINDOWED
WINDOWING
WINDOWINGS
WINDOWS
WINDPIPE
WINDPIPES
WINDRING
WINDROSE
WINDROSES
WINDROW
WINDROWED
WINDROWING
WINDROWS
WINDS
WINDSES
WINDSHIP
WINDSHIPS
WINDSTORM
WINDSTORMS
WINDSURF
WINDSURFED
WINDSURFING
WINDSURFINGS
WINDSURFS
WINDSWEPT
WINDTHROW
WINDTHROWS
WINDWARD
WINDWARDS
WINDY
WINE
WINED
WINERIES
WINERY
WINES
WINEY
WING
WINGBEAT
WINGBEATS
WINGDING
WINGDINGS
WINGE
WINGED
WINGEDLY
WINGEING
WINGER
WINGERS

WINGES
WINGIER
WINGIEST
WINGING
WINGLESS
WINGLET
WINGLETS
WINGS
WINGSPAN
WINGSPANS
WINGY
WINIER
WINIEST
WINING
WINK
WINKED
WINKER
WINKERS
WINKING
WINKINGLY
WINKINGS
WINKLE
WINKLER
WINKLERS
WINKLES
WINKS
WINN
WINNA
WINNABLE
WINNER
WINNERS
WINNING
WINNINGLY
WINNINGS
WINNLE
WINNLES
WINNOCK
WINNOCKS
WINNOW
WINNOWED
WINNOWER
WINNOWERS
WINNOWING
WINNOWINGS
WINNOWS
WINNS
WINO
WINOS
WINS
WINSEY
WINSEYS
WINSOME
WINSOMELY
WINSOMER
WINSOMEST
WINTER
WINTERED
WINTERIER
WINTERIEST
WINTERING
WINTERISE
WINTERISED
WINTERISES
WINTERISING
WINTERIZE
WINTERIZED
WINTERIZES
WINTERIZING
WINTERLY
WINTERS

WINTERY	WISENESS	WITHDRAWS	WITWANTON	WOLDS
WINTLE	WISENESSES	WITHDREW	WITWANTONED	WOLF
WINTLED	WISENT	WITHE	WITWANTONING	WOLFED
WINTLES	WISENTS	WITHED	WITWANTONS	WOLFER
WINTLING	WISER	WITHER	WIVE	WOLFERS
WINTRIER	WISES	WITHERED	WIVED	WOLFING
WINTRIEST	WISEST	WITHERING	WIVEHOOD	WOLFINGS
WINTRY	WISH	WITHERINGS	WIVEHOODS	WOLFISH
WINY	WISHBONE	WITHERITE	WIVERN	WOLFISHLY
WINZE	WISHBONES	WITHERITES	WIVERNS	WOLFKIN
WINZES	WISHED	WITHERS	WIVES	WOLFKINS
WIPE	WISHER	WITHES	WIVING	WOLFLING
WIPED	WISHERS	WITHHAULT	WIZARD	WOLFLINGS
WIPEOUT	WISHES	WITHHELD	WIZARDLY	WOLFRAM
WIPEOUTS	WISHFUL	WITHHOLD	WIZARDRIES	WOLFRAMS
WIPER	WISHFULLY	WITHHOLDEN	WIZARDRY	WOLFS
WIPERS	WISHING	WITHHOLDING	WIZARDS	WOLFSBANE
WIPES	WISHINGS	WITHHOLDS	WIZEN	WOLFSBANES
WIPING	WISING	WITHIER	WIZENED	WOLLIES
WIPINGS	WISKET	WITHIES	WIZENING	WOLLY
WIRE	WISKETS	WITHIEST	WIZENS	WOLVE
WIRED	WISP	WITHIN	WIZIER	WOLVED
WIREDRAW	WISPED	WITHING	WIZIERS	WOLVER
WIREDRAWING	WISPIER	WITHOUT	WO	WOLVERENE
WIREDRAWINGS	WISPIEST	WITHOUTEN	WOAD	WOLVERENES
WIREDRAWN	WISPING	WITHS	WOADED	WOLVERINE
WIREDRAWS	WISPS	WITHSTAND	WOADS	WOLVERINES
WIREDREW	WISPY	WITHSTANDING	WOBBEGONG	WOLVERS
WIRELESS	WISSED	WITHSTANDS	WOBBEGONGS	WOLVES
WIRELESSED	WISSES	WITHSTOOD	WOBBLE	WOLVING
WIRELESSES	WISSING	WITHWIND	WOBBLED	WOLVINGS
WIRELESSING	WIST	WITHWINDS	WOBBLER	WOLVISH
WIREPHOTO	WISTARIA	WITHY	WOBBLERS	WOLVISHLY
WIREPHOTOS	WISTARIAS	WITHYWIND	WOBBLES	WOMAN
WIREN	WISTED	WITHYWINDS	WOBBLIER	WOMANED
WIRERS	WISTERIA	WITING	WOBBLIES	WOMANHOOD
WIRES	WISTERIAS	WITLESS	WOBBLIEST	WOMANHOODS
WIRETAP	WISTFUL	WITLESSLY	WOBBLING	WOMANING
WIRETAPPED	WISTFULLY	WITLING	WOBBLINGS	WOMANISE
WIRETAPPING	WISTING	WITLINGS	WOBBLY	WOMANISED
WIRETAPS	WISTITI	WITLOOF	WOBEGONE	WOMANISER
WIREWORK	WISTITIS	WITLOOFS	WOCK	WOMANISERS
WIREWORKS	WISTLY	WITNESS	WOCKS	WOMANISES
WIREWOVE	WISTS	WITNESSED	WODGE	WOMANISH
WIRIER	WIT	WITNESSER	WODGES	WOMANISING
WIRIEST	WITAN	WITNESSERS	WOE	WOMANIZE
WIRILY	WITCH	WITNESSES	WOEBEGONE	WOMANIZED
WIRINESS	WITCHED	WITNESSING	WOEFUL	WOMANIZER
WIRINESSES	WITCHEN	WITS	WOEFULLER	WOMANIZERS
WIRING	WITCHENS	WITTED	WOEFULLEST	WOMANIZES
WIRINGS	WITCHERIES	WITTER	WOEFULLY	WOMANIZING
WIRRICOW	WITCHERY	WITTERED	WOEFULNESS	WOMANKIND
WIRRICOWS	WITCHES	WITTERING	WOEFULNESSES	WOMANKINDS
WIRY	WITCHETTIES	WITTERS	WOES	WOMANLIER
WIS	WITCHETTY	WITTICISM	WOESOME	WOMANLIEST
WISARD	WITCHING	WITTICISMS	WOFUL	WOMANLY
WISARDS	WITCHINGS	WITTIER	WOFULLY	WOMANS
WISDOM	WITCHKNOT	WITTIEST	WOFULNESS	WOMB
WISDOMS	WITCHKNOTS	WITTILY	WOFULNESSES	WOMBAT
WISE	WITE	WITTINESS	WOG	WOMBATS
WISEACRE	WITED	WITTINESSES	WOGGLE	WOMBED
WISEACRES	WITELESS	WITTING	WOGGLES	WOMBING
WISECRACK	WITES	WITTINGLY	WOGS	WOMBS
WISECRACKED	WITGAT	WITTINGS	WOIWODE	WOMBY
WISECRACKING	WITGATS	WITTOL	WOIWODES	WOMEN
WISECRACKS	WITH	WITTOLLY	WOK	WOMENFOLK
WISED	WITHAL	WITTOLS	WOKE	WOMENFOLKS
WISELING	WITHDRAW	WITTY	WOKEN	WOMENKIND
WISELINGS	WITHDRAWING	WITWALL	WOKS	WOMENKINDS
WISELY	WITHDRAWN	WITWALLS	WOLD	WOMERA

WOMERAS	WOODMICE	WOOLSEYS	WORKER	WORRISOME
WON	WOODMOUSE	WOOLWARD	WORKERIST	WORRIT
WONDER	WOODNESS	WOOLWORK	WORKERISTS	WORRITED
WONDERED	WOODNESSES	WOOLWORKS	WORKERS	WORRITING
WONDERER	WOODRUFF	WOOMERA	WORKFOLK	WORRITS
WONDERERS	WOODRUFFS	WOOMERANG	WORKFOLKS	WORRY
WONDERFUL	WOODS	WOOMERANGS	WORKFORCE	WORRYCOW
WONDERING	WOODSHED	WOOMERAS	WORKFORCES	WORRYCOWS
WONDERINGS	WOODSHEDDED	WOON	WORKFUL	WORRYGUTS
WONDEROUS	WOODSHEDDING	WOONED	WORKHORSE	WORRYING
WONDERS	WOODSHEDS	WOONING	WORKHORSES	WORRYINGS
WONDRED	WOODSIER	WOONS	WORKHOUSE	WORRYWART
WONDROUS	WOODSIEST	WOORALI	WORKHOUSES	WORRYWARTS
WONED	WOODSMAN	WOORALIS	WORKING	WORSE
WONGA	WOODSMEN	WOORARA	WORKINGS	WORSED
WONGAS	WOODSY	WOORARAS	WORKLESS	WORSEN
WONING	WOODWALE	WOOS	WORKLOAD	WORSENED
WONINGS	WOODWALES	WOOSEL	WORKLOADS	WORSENESS
WONKIER	WOODWARD	WOOSELL	WORKMAN	WORSENESSES
WONKIEST	WOODWARDS	WOOSELLS	WORKMANLY	WORSENING
WONKY	WOODWIND	WOOSELS	WORKMEN	WORSENS
WONNED	WOODWINDS	WOOSH	WORKPIECE	WORSER
WONNING	WOODWORK	WOOSHED	WORKPIECES	WORSES
WONS	WOODWORKS	WOOSHES	WORKPLACE	WORSHIP
WONT	WOODWORM	WOOSHING	WORKPLACES	WORSHIPPED
WONTED	WOODWORMS	WOOT	WORKROOM	WORSHIPPING
WONTING	WOODWOSE	WOOTZ	WORKROOMS	WORSHIPS
WONTLESS	WOODWOSES	WOOTZES	WORKS	WORSING
WONTS	WOODY	WOOZIER	WORKSHOP	WORST
WOO	WOODYARD	WOOZIEST	WORKSHOPS	WORSTED
WOOBUT	WOODYARDS	WOOZILY	WORKSOME	WORSTEDS
WOOBUTS	WOOED	WOOZINESS	WORKTOP	WORSTING
WOOD	WOOER	WOOZINESSES	WORKTOPS	WORSTS
WOODBIND	WOOERS	WOOZY	WORKWEAR	WORT
WOODBINDS	WOOF	WOP	WORKWEARS	WORTH
WOODBINE	WOOFED	WOPPED	WORLD	WORTHED
WOODBINES	WOOFER	WOPPING	WORLDED	WORTHFUL
WOODBLOCK	WOOFERS	WOPS	WORLDLIER	WORTHIED
WOODBLOCKS	WOOFIER	WORCESTER	WORLDLIEST	WORTHIER
WOODCHIP	WOOFIEST	WORCESTERS	WORLDLING	WORTHIES
WOODCHIPS	WOOFS	WORD	WORLDLINGS	WORTHIEST
WOODCHUCK	WOOFY	WORDAGE	WORLDLY	WORTHILY
WOODCHUCKS	WOOING	WORDAGES	WORLDS	WORTHING
WOODCOCK	WOOINGLY	WORDBOOK	WORLDWIDE	WORTHLESS
WOODCOCKS	WOOINGS	WORDBOOKS	WORM	WORTHS
WOODCRAFT	WOOL	WORDBOUND	WORMED	WORTHY
WOODCRAFTS	WOOLD	WORDED	WORMER	WORTHYING
WOODCUT	WOOLDED	WORDIER	WORMERIES	WORTLE
WOODCUTS	WOOLDER	WORDIEST	WORMERS	WORTLES
WOODED	WOOLDERS	WORDILY	WORMERY	WORTS
WOODEN	WOOLDING	WORDINESS	WORMIER	WOS
WOODENER	WOOLDINGS	WORDINESSES	WORMIEST	WOSBIRD
WOODENEST	WOOLDS	WORDING	WORMING	WOSBIRDS
WOODENLY	WOOLFAT	WORDINGS	WORMS	WOST
WOODHOUSE	WOOLFATS	WORDISH	WORMWOOD	WOT
WOODHOUSES	WOOLFELL	WORDLESS	WORMWOODS	WOTCHER
WOODIE	WOOLFELLS	WORDS	WORMY	WOTS
WOODIER	WOOLLED	WORDSMITH	WORN	WOTTED
WOODIES	WOOLLEN	WORDSMITHS	WORRAL	WOTTEST
WOODIEST	WOOLLENS	WORDY	WORRALS	WOTTETH
WOODINESS	WOOLLIER	WORE	WORREL	WOTTING
WOODINESSES	WOOLLIES	WORK	WORRELS	WOUBIT
WOODING	WOOLLIEST	WORKABLE	WORRICOW	WOUBITS
WOODLAND	WOOLLY	WORKADAY	WORRICOWS	WOULD
WOODLANDS	WOOLMAN	WORKADAYS	WORRIED	WOULDS
WOODLESS	WOOLMEN	WORKBOAT	WORRIER	WOULDST
WOODLICE	WOOLS	WORKBOATS	WORRIERS	WOUND
WOODLOUSE	WOOLSACK	WORKBOOK	WORRIES	WOUNDABLE
WOODMAN	WOOLSACKS	WORKBOOKS	WORRIMENT	WOUNDED
WOODMEN	WOOLSEY	WORKED	WORRIMENTS	WOUNDER

WOUNDERS	WRASTED	WRENCH	WRINKLIEST	WRY
WOUNDILY	WRASTING	WRENCHED	WRINKLING	WRYBILL
WOUNDING	WRASTS	WRENCHES	WRINKLY	WRYBILLS
WOUNDINGS	WRATE	WRENCHING	WRIST	WRYER
WOUNDLESS	WRATH	WRENCHINGS	WRISTBAND	WRYEST
WOUNDS	WRATHED	WRENS	WRISTBANDS	WRYING
WOUNDWORT	WRATHFUL	WREST	WRISTIER	WRYLY
WOUNDWORTS	WRATHIER	WRESTED	WRISTIEST	WRYNECK
WOUNDY	WRATHIEST	WRESTER	WRISTLET	WRYNECKS
WOURALI	WRATHILY	WRESTERS	WRISTLETS	WRYNESS
WOURALIS	WRATHING	WRESTING	WRISTS	WRYNESSES
WOVE	WRATHLESS	WRESTLE	WRISTY	WRYTHEN
WOVEN	WRATHS	WRESTLED	WRIT	WUD
WOW	WRATHY	WRESTLER	WRITABLE	WUDDED
WOWED	WRAWL	WRESTLERS	WRITATIVE	WUDDING
WOWEE	WRAWLED	WRESTLES	WRITE	WUDS
WOWF	WRAWLING	WRESTLING	WRITER	WULFENITE
WOWFER	WRAWLS	WRESTLINGS	WRITERESS	WULFENITES
WOWFEST	WRAXLE	WRESTS	WRITERESSES	WULL
WOWING	WRAXLED	WRETCH	WRITERLY	WULLED
WOWS	WRAXLES	WRETCHED	WRITERS	WULLING
WOWSER	WRAXLING	WRETCHES	WRITES	WULLS
WOWSERS	WRAXLINGS	WRETHE	WRITHE	WUNNER
WOX	WREAK	WRETHED	WRITHED	WUNNERS
WOXEN	WREAKED	WRETHES	WRITHEN	WURLEY
WRACK	WREAKED	WHETHING	WRITHES	WURLEYS
WRACKED	WREAKER	WRICK	WRITHING	WURLIES
WRACKFUL	WREAKERS	WRICKED	WRITHINGS	WURST
WRACKING	WREAKES	WRICKING	WRITHLED	WURSTS
WRACKS	WREAKFUL	WRICKS	WRITING	WURTZITE
WRAITH	WREAKING	WRIED	WRITINGS	WURTZITES
WRAITHS	WREAKLESS	WRIER	WRITS	WUSHU
WRANGLE	WREAKS	WRIES	WRITTEN	WUSHUS
WRANGLED	WREATH	WRIEST	WRIZLED	WUTHER
WRANGLER	WREATHE	WRIGGLE	WROATH	WUTHERED
WRANGLERS	WREATHED	WRIGGLED	WROATHS	WUTHERING
WRANGLES	WREATHEN	WRIGGLER	WROKE	WUTHERS
WRANGLING	WREATHER	WRIGGLERS	WROKEN	WUZZLE
WRANGLINGS	WREATHERS	WRIGGLES	WRONG	WUZZLED
WRAP	WREATHES	WRIGGLIER	WRONGED	WUZZLES
WRAPOVER	WREATHIER	WRIGGLIEST	WRONGER	WUZZLING
WRAPOVERS	WREATHIEST	WRIGGLING	WRONGERS	WYANDOTTE
WRAPPAGE	WREATHING	WRIGGLINGS	WRONGEST	WYANDOTTES
WRAPPAGES	WREATHS	WRIGGLY	WRONGFUL	WYE
WRAPPED	WREATHY	WRIGHT	WRONGING	WYES
WRAPPER	WRECK	WRIGHTS	WRONGLY	WYN
WRAPPERED	WRECKAGE	WRING	WRONGNESS	WYND
WRAPPERING	WRECKAGES	WRINGED	WRONGNESSES	WYNDS
WRAPPERS	WRECKED	WRINGER	WRONGOUS	WYNN
WRAPPING	WRECKER	WRINGERS	WRONGS	WYNNS
WRAPPINGS	WRECKERS	WHINGING	WROOT	WYNS
WRAPROUND	WRECKFISH	WRINGINGS	WROOTED	WYSIWYG
WRAPROUNDS	WRECKFISHES	WRINGS	WROOTING	WYTE
WRAPS	WRECKFUL	WRINKLE	WROOTS	WYTED
WRAPT	WRECKING	WRINKLED	WROTE	WYTES
WRASSE	WRECKINGS	WRINKLES	WROTH	WYTING
WRASSES	WRECKS	WRINKLIER	WROUGHT	WYVERN
WRAST	WREN	WRINKLIES	WRUNG	WYVERNS

X

XANTHATE	XENOLITHS	XERASIAS	XOANONS	XYLOMETER
XANTHATES	XENOMANIA	XERIC	XYLEM	XYLOMETERS
XANTHEIN	XENOMANIAS	XEROCHASIES	XYLEMS	XYLONIC
XANTHEINS	XENOMENIA	XEROCHASY	XYLENE	XYLONITE
XANTHENE	XENOMENIAS	XERODERMA	XYLENES	XYLONITES
XANTHENES	XENON	XERODERMAS	XYLENOL	XYLOPHAGE
XANTHIC	XENONS	XEROMA	XYLENOLS	XYLOPHAGES
XANTHIN	XENOPHILE	XEROMAS	XYLIC	XYLOPHONE
XANTHINE	XENOPHILES	XEROMORPH	XYLITOL	XYLOPHONES
XANTHINES	XENOPHOBE	XEROMORPHS	XYLITOLS	XYLORIMBA
XANTHINS	XENOPHOBES	XEROPHAGIES	XYLOCARP	XYLORIMBAS
XANTHOMA	XENOPHOBIES	XEROPHAGY	XYLOCARPS	XYLOSE
XANTHOMAS	XENOPHOBY	XEROPHILIES	XYLOGEN	XYLOSES
XANTHOUS	XENOPHYA	XEROPHILY	XYLOGENS	XYLYL
XEBEC	XENOPHYAS	XEROPHYTE	XYLOGRAPH	XYLYLS
XEBECS	XENOTIME	XEROPHYTES	XYLOGRAPHS	XYST
XENIA	XENOTIMES	XEROSES	XYLOID	XYSTER
XENIAL	XENURINE	XEROSIS	XYLOIDIN	XYSTERS
XENIAS	XERAFIN	XEROSTOMA	XYLOIDINE	XYSTI
XENIUM	XERAFINS	XEROSTOMAS	XYLOIDINES	XYSTOI
XENOCRYST	XERANSES	XEROTES	XYLOIDINS	XYSTOS
XENOCRYSTS	XERANSIS	XEROTIC	XYLOL	XYSTOSES
XENOGAMIES	XERANTIC	XI	XYLOLOGIES	XYSTS
XENOGAMY	XERAPHIM	XIPHOID	XYLOLOGY	XYSTUS
XENOGRAFT	XERAPHIMS	XIPHOIDAL	XYLOLS	XYSTUSES
XENOGRAFTS	XERARCH	XIS	XYLOMA	
XENOLITH	XERASIA	XOANON	XYLOMAS	

Y

YABBER
YABBERED
YABBERING
YABBERS
YABBIE
YABBIES
YABBY
YACCA
YACCAS
YACHT
YACHTED
YACHTER
YACHTERS
YACHTING
YACHTINGS
YACHTS
YACHTSMAN
YACHTSMEN
YACK
YACKED
YACKER
YACKERS
YACKING
YACKS
YAFF
YAFFED
YAFFING
YAFFLE
YAFFLES
YAFFS
YAGER
YAGERS
YAGGER
YAGGERS
YAH
YAHOO
YAHOOS
YAK
YAKHDAN
YAKHDANS
YAKKA
YAKKAS
YAKKED
YAKKER
YAKKERS
YAKKING
YAKS
YAKUZA
YALD
YALE
YALES
YAM
YAMEN
YAMENS
YAMMER
YAMMERED
YAMMERING
YAMMERINGS
YAMMERS
YAMS
YAMULKA
YAMULKAS
YANG

YANGS
YANK
YANKED
YANKER
YANKERS
YANKIE
YANKIES
YANKING
YANKS
YAOURT
YAOURTS
YAP
YAPOCK
YAPOCKS
YAPOK
YAPOKS
YAPON
YAPONS
YAPP
YAPPED
YAPPER
YAPPERS
YAPPING
YAPPS
YAPS
YAPSTER
YAPSTERS
YARD
YARDAGE
YARDAGES
YARDANG
YARDANGS
YARDED
YARDING
YARDLAND
YARDLANDS
YARDMAN
YARDMEN
YARDS
YARDSTICK
YARDSTICKS
YARDWAND
YARDWANDS
YARE
YARELY
YARER
YAREST
YARFA
YARFAS
YARMULKA
YARMULKAS
YARMULKE
YARMULKES
YARN
YARNED
YARNING
YARNS
YARPHA
YARPHAS
YARR
YARROW
YARROWS
YARRS

YARTA
YARTAS
YARTO
YARTOS
YASHMAK
YASHMAKS
YATAGAN
YATAGANS
YATAGHAN
YATAGHANS
YATE
YATES
YATTER
YATTERED
YATTERING
YATTERINGS
YATTERS
YAUD
YAUDS
YAULD
YAUP
YAUPON
YAUPONS
YAW
YAWED
YAWEY
YAWING
YAWL
YAWLED
YAWLING
YAWLS
YAWN
YAWNED
YAWNIER
YAWNIEST
YAWNING
YAWNINGLY
YAWNINGS
YAWNS
YAWNY
YAWP
YAWPED
YAWPER
YAWPERS
YAWPING
YAWPS
YAWS
YAWY
YBET
YBLENT
YBORE
YBOUND
YBOUNDEN
YBRENT
YCLAD
YCLED
YCLEEPE
YCLEPED
YCLEPT
YCOND
YDRAD
YDRED
YE

YEA
YEAD
YEADING
YEADS
YEAH
YEALDON
YEALDONS
YEALM
YEALMED
YEALMING
YEALMS
YEAN
YEANED
YEANING
YEANLING
YEANLINGS
YEANS
YEAR
YEARD
YEARDED
YEARDING
YEARDS
YEARLIES
YEARLING
YEARLINGS
YEARLONG
YEARLY
YEARN
YEARNED
YEARNING
YEARNINGS
YEARNS
YEARS
YEAS
YEAST
YEASTED
YEASTIER
YEASTIEST
YEASTING
YEASTS
YEASTY
YEDE
YEDES
YEDING
YEED
YEEDING
YEEDS
YEGG
YEGGMAN
YEGGMEN
YEGGS
YELD
YELDRING
YELDRINGS
YELDROCK
YELDROCKS
YELK
YELKS
YELL
YELLED
YELLING
YELLINGS
YELLOCH

YELLOCHED
YELLOCHING
YELLOCHS
YELLOW
YELLOWED
YELLOWER
YELLOWEST
YELLOWING
YELLOWISH
YELLOWS
YELLOWY
YELLS
YELM
YELMED
YELMING
YELMS
YELP
YELPED
YELPER
YELPERS
YELPING
YELPINGS
YELPS
YELT
YELTS
YEN
YENNED
YENNING
YENS
YENTA
YENTAS
YEOMAN
YEOMANLY
YEOMANRIES
YEOMANRY
YEOMEN
YEP
YEPS
YERBA
YERBAS
YERD
YERDED
YERDING
YERDS
YERK
YERKED
YERKING
YERKS
YERSINIA
YERSINIAE
YERSINIAS
YES
YESES
YESHIVA
YESHIVAH
YESHIVAHS
YESHIVAS
YESHIVOTH
YESK
YESKED
YESKING
YESKS
YESSES

YEST
YESTER
YESTERDAY
YESTERDAYS
YESTEREVE
YESTEREVES
YESTERN
YESTREEN
YESTS
YESTY
YET
YETI
YETIS
YETT
YETTS
YEUK
YEUKED
YEUKING
YEUKS
YEVE
YEVEN
YEVES
YEVING
YEW
YEWEN
YEWS
YEX
YEXED
YEXES
YEXING
YFERE
YGLAUNST
YGO
YGOE
YIBBLES
YICKER
YICKERED
YICKERING
YICKERS
YIELD
YIELDABLE
YIELDED
YIELDER
YIELDERS
YIELDING
YIELDINGS
YIELDS
YIKKER
YIKKERED
YIKKERING
YIKKERS
YILL
YILLS
YIN
YINCE
YINS
YIP
YIPPED
YIPPEE
YIPPIES
YIPPING
YIPPY
YIPS
YIRD
YIRDED
YIRDING
YIRDS
YIRK

YIRKED
YIRKING
YIRKS
YITE
YITES
YLEM
YLEMS
YLIKE
YLKE
YMOLT
YMOLTEN
YMPE
YMPES
YMPING
YMPT
YNAMBU
YNAMBUS
YO
YOB
YOBBISH
YOBBISHLY
YOBBO
YOBBOES
YOBBOS
YOBS
YOCK
YOCKED
YOCKING
YOCKS
YOD
YODE
YODEL
YODELLED
YODELLER
YODELLERS
YODELLING
YODELS
YODLE
YODLED
YODLER
YODLERS
YODLES
YODLING
YOGA
YOGAS
YOGH
YOGHOURT
YOGHOURTS
YOGHS
YOGHURT
YOGHURTS
YOGI
YOGIC
YOGIN
YOGINI
YOGINIS
YOGINS
YOGIS
YOGISM
YOGISMS
YOGURT
YOGURTS
YOHIMBINE
YOHIMBINES
YOICK
YOICKED
YOICKING
YOICKS

YOICKSED
YOICKSES
YOICKSING
YOJAN
YOJANA
YOJANAS
YOJANS
YOK
YOKE
YOKED
YOKEL
YOKELISH
YOKELS
YOKES
YOKING
YOKINGS
YOKKED
YOKKING
YOKS
YOKUL
YOLD
YOLDRING
YOLDRINGS
YOLK
YOLKED
YOLKIER
YOLKIEST
YOLKS
YOLKY
YOMP
YOMPED
YOMPING
YOMPS
YON
YOND
YONDER
YONDERLY
YONGTHLY
YONI
YONIS
YONKER
YONKERS
YONKS
YONT
YOOP
YOOPS
YOPPER
YOPPERS
YORE
YORES
YORK
YORKED
YORKER
YORKERS
YORKIE
YORKIES
YORKING
YORKS
YOS
YOU
YOUK
YOUKED
YOUKING
YOUKS
YOUNG
YOUNGER
YOUNGEST
YOUNGISH

YOUNGLING
YOUNGLINGS
YOUNGLY
YOUNGNESS
YOUNGNESSES
YOUNGS
YOUNGSTER
YOUNGSTERS
YOUNGTH
YOUNGTHLY
YOUNGTHS
YOUNKER
YOUNKERS
YOUR
YOURN
YOURS
YOURSELF
YOURSELVES
YOURT
YOURTS
YOUTH
YOUTHFUL
YOUTHHEAD
YOUTHHEADS
YOUTHHOOD
YOUTHHOODS
YOUTHIER
YOUTHIEST
YOUTHLY
YOUTHS
YOUTHSOME
YOUTHY
YOW
YOWE
YOWES
YOWIE
YOWIES
YOWL
YOWLED
YOWLEY
YOWLEYS
YOWLING
YOWLINGS
YOWLS
YOWS
YPIGHT
YPLAST
YPLIGHT
YPSILOID
YPSILON
YPSILONS
YRAPT
YRAVISHED
YRENT
YRIVD
YSAME
YSHEND
YSHENDING
YSHENDS
YSHENT
YSLAKED
YTOST
YTTERBIA
YTTERBIAS
YTTERBIUM
YTTERBIUMS
YTTRIA
YTTRIAS

YTTRIC
YTTRIOUS
YTTRIUM
YTTRIUMS
YU
YUAN
YUCA
YUCAS
YUCCA
YUCCAS
YUCK
YUCKED
YUCKER
YUCKERS
YUCKIER
YUCKIEST
YUCKING
YUCKS
YUCKY
YUFT
YUFTS
YUG
YUGA
YUGAS
YUGS
YUK
YUKE
YUKED
YUKES
YUKIER
YUKIEST
YUKING
YUKKIER
YUKKIEST
YUKKY
YUKS
YUKY
YULAN
YULANS
YULE
YULES
YULETIDE
YULETIDES
YUMMIER
YUMMIEST
YUMMY
YUMP
YUMPIE
YUMPIES
YUMPS
YUNX
YUNXES
YUP
YUPON
YUPONS
YUPPIE
YUPPIES
YUPPY
YUPS
YURT
YURTS
YUS
YWIS
YWRAKE
YWROKE
YWROKEN

Z

ZABAIONE
ZABAIONES
ZABETA
ZABETAS
ZABRA
ZABRAS
ZABTIEH
ZABTIEHS
ZACK
ZACKS
ZADDIK
ZADDIKIM
ZADDIKS
ZAFFER
ZAFFERS
ZAFFRE
ZAFFRES
ZAG
ZAGGED
ZAGGING
ZAGS
ZAIRE
ZAKUSKA
ZAKUSKI
ZAMAN
ZAMANG
ZAMANGS
ZAMANS
ZAMARRA
ZAMARRAS
ZAMARRO
ZAMARROS
ZAMBO
ZAMBOMBA
ZAMBOMBAS
ZAMBOORAK
ZAMBOORAKS
ZAMBOS
ZAMIA
ZAMIAS
ZAMINDAR
ZAMINDARI
ZAMINDARIS
ZAMINDARS
ZAMOUSE
ZAMOUSES
ZAMPOGNA
ZAMPOGNAS
ZANDER
ZANDERS
ZANELLA
ZANELLAS
ZANIED
ZANIER
ZANIES
ZANIEST
ZANJA
ZANJAS
ZANJERO
ZANJEROS
ZANTE
ZANTES
ZANY
ZANYING
ZANYISM

ZANYISMS
ZANZE
ZANZES
ZAP
ZAPATA
ZAPATEADO
ZAPATEADOS
ZAPOTILLA
ZAPOTILLAS
ZAPPED
ZAPPIER
ZAPPIEST
ZAPPING
ZAPPY
ZAPS
ZAPTIAH
ZAPTIAHS
ZAPTIEH
ZAPTIEHS
ZARAPE
ZARAPES
ZARATITE
ZARATITES
ZAREBA
ZAREBAS
ZAREEBA
ZAREEBAS
ZARF
ZARFS
ZARIBA
ZARIBAS
ZARNEC
ZARNECS
ZARNICH
ZARNICHS
ZARZUELA
ZARZUELAS
ZASTRUGA
ZASTRUGI
ZATI
ZATIS
ZAX
ZAXES
ZEA
ZEAL
ZEALANT
ZEALANTS
ZEALFUL
ZEALLESS
ZEALOT
ZEALOTISM
ZEALOTISMS
ZEALOTRIES
ZEALOTRY
ZEALOTS
ZEALOUS
ZEALOUSLY
ZEALS
ZEAS
ZEBEC
ZEBECK
ZEBECKS
ZEBECS
ZEBRA
ZEBRAS

ZEBRASS
ZEBRASSES
ZEBRINE
ZEBRINNIES
ZEBRINNY
ZEBROID
ZEBRULA
ZEBRULAS
ZEBRULE
ZEBRULES
ZEBU
ZEBUB
ZEBUBS
ZEBUS
ZECCHINE
ZECCHINES
ZECCHINI
ZECCHINO
ZECCHINOS
ZED
ZEDOARIES
ZEDOARY
ZEDS
ZEE
ZEES
ZEIN
ZEINS
ZEITGEIST
ZEITGEISTS
ZEK
ZEKS
ZEL
ZELANT
ZELANTS
ZELOSO
ZELOTYPIA
ZELOTYPIAS
ZELS
ZEMINDAR
ZEMINDARI
ZEMINDARIES
ZEMINDARIS
ZEMINDARS
ZEMINDARY
ZEMSTVO
ZEMSTVOS
ZENANA
ZENANAS
ZENDIK
ZENDIKS
ZENITH
ZENITHAL
ZENITHS
ZEOLITE
ZEOLITES
ZEOLITIC
ZEPHYR
ZEPHYRS
ZEPPELIN
ZEPPELINS
ZERDA
ZERDAS
ZEREBA
ZEREBAS
ZERIBA

ZERIBAS
ZERO
ZEROED
ZEROING
ZEROS
ZEROTH
ZERUMBET
ZERUMBETS
ZEST
ZESTFUL
ZESTFULLY
ZESTIER
ZESTIEST
ZESTS
ZESTY
ZETA
ZETAS
ZETETIC
ZETETICS
ZEUGMA
ZEUGMAS
ZEUGMATIC
ZEUXITE
ZEUXITES
ZEZE
ZEZES
ZHO
ZHOMO
ZHOMOS
ZHOS
ZIBELINE
ZIBELINES
ZIBELLINE
ZIBELLINES
ZIBET
ZIBETS
ZIFF
ZIFFIUS
ZIFFIUSES
ZIFFS
ZIG
ZIGAN
ZIGANKA
ZIGANKAS
ZIGANS
ZIGGED
ZIGGING
ZIGGURAT
ZIGGURATS
ZIGS
ZIGZAG
ZIGZAGGED
ZIGZAGGING
ZIGZAGGY
ZIGZAGS
ZIKKURAT
ZIKKURATS
ZILA
ZILAS
ZILCH
ZILCHES
ZILLAH
ZILLAHS
ZILLION
ZILLIONS

ZILLIONTH
ZILLIONTHS
ZIMB
ZIMBI
ZIMBIS
ZIMBS
ZIMMER
ZIMMERS
ZIMOCCA
ZIMOCCAS
ZINC
ZINCED
ZINCIER
ZINCIEST
ZINCIFIED
ZINCIFIES
ZINCIFY
ZINCIFYING
ZINCING
ZINCITE
ZINCITES
ZINCKED
ZINCKIER
ZINCKIEST
ZINCKIFIED
ZINCKIFIES
ZINCKIFY
ZINCKIFYING
ZINCKING
ZINCKY
ZINCO
ZINCODE
ZINCODES
ZINCOID
ZINCOS
ZINCOUS
ZINCS
ZINCY
ZINEB
ZINEBS
ZINFANDEL
ZINFANDELS
ZING
ZINGED
ZINGEL
ZINGELS
ZINGIBER
ZINGIBERS
ZINGIER
ZINGIEST
ZINGING
ZINGS
ZINGY
ZINKE
ZINKED
ZINKENITE
ZINKENITES
ZINKES
ZINKIER
ZINKIEST
ZINKIFIED
ZINKIFIES
ZINKIFY
ZINKIFYING
ZINKING

ZINKY
ZINNIA
ZINNIAS
ZIP
ZIPPED
ZIPPER
ZIPPERED
ZIPPERS
ZIPPIER
ZIPPIEST
ZIPPING
ZIPPY
ZIPS
ZIPTOP
ZIRCALLOY
ZIRCALLOYS
ZIRCON
ZIRCONIA
ZIRCONIAS
ZIRCONIC
ZIRCONIUM
ZIRCONIUMS
ZIRCONS
ZIT
ZITHER
ZITHERN
ZITHERNS
ZITHERS
ZITS
ZIZ
ZIZEL
ZIZELS
ZIZZ
ZIZZED
ZIZZES
ZIZZING
ZLOTY
ZLOTYS
ZO
ZOA
ZOARIUM
ZOARIUMS
ZOBO
ZOBOS
ZOBU
ZOBUS
ZOCCO
ZOCCOLO
ZOCCOLOS
ZOCCOS
ZODIAC
ZODIACAL
ZODIACS
ZOEA
ZOEAE
ZOEAL
ZOEAS
ZOECHROME
ZOECHROMES
ZOEFORM
ZOETIC
ZOETROPE
ZOETROPES
ZOETROPIC
ZOIATRIA
ZOIATRIAS
ZOIATRICS
ZOIC
ZOISITE
ZOISITES
ZOISM

ZOISMS
ZOIST
ZOISTS
ZOMBI
ZOMBIE
ZOMBIES
ZOMBIISM
ZOMBIISMS
ZOMBIS
ZOMBORUK
ZOMBORUKS
ZONA
ZONAE
ZONAL
ZONARY
ZONATE
ZONATED
ZONATION
ZONATIONS
ZONDA
ZONDAS
ZONE
ZONED
ZONELESS
ZONES
ZONING
ZONINGS
ZONKED
ZONOID
ZONULA
ZONULAR
ZONULAS
ZONULE
ZONULES
ZONULET
ZONULETS
ZOO
ZOOBIOTIC
ZOOBLAST
ZOOBLASTS
ZOOCHORE
ZOOCHORES
ZOOCHORIES
ZOOCHORY
ZOOCYTIA
ZOOCYTIUM
ZOOEA
ZOOEAE
ZOOEAL
ZOOEAS
ZOOECIA
ZOOECIUM
ZOOGAMETE
ZOOGAMETES
ZOOGAMIES
ZOOGAMOUS
ZOOGAMY
ZOOGENIC
ZOOGENIES
ZOOGENOUS
ZOOGENY
ZOOGLOEA
ZOOGLOEAS
ZOOGLOEIC
ZOOGONIES
ZOOGONOUS
ZOOGONY
ZOOGRAFT
ZOOGRAFTS
ZOOGRAPHIES
ZOOGRAPHY

ZOOID
ZOOIDAL
ZOOIDS
ZOOKS
ZOOLATER
ZOOLATERS
ZOOLATRIA
ZOOLATRIAS
ZOOLATRIES
ZOOLATRY
ZOOLITE
ZOOLITES
ZOOLITH
ZOOLITHIC
ZOOLITHS
ZOOLITIC
ZOOLOGIES
ZOOLOGIST
ZOOLOGISTS
ZOOLOGY
ZOOM
ZOOMANCIES
ZOOMANCY
ZOOMANTIC
ZOOMED
ZOOMETRIC
ZOOMETRIES
ZOOMETRY
ZOOMING
ZOOMORPH
ZOOMORPHIES
ZOOMORPHS
ZOOMORPHY
ZOOMS
ZOON
ZOONAL
ZOONIC
ZOONITE
ZOONITES
ZOONITIC
ZOONOMIA
ZOONOMIAS
ZOONOMIC
ZOONOMIES
ZOONOMIST
ZOONOMISTS
ZOONOMY
ZOONOSES
ZOONOSIS
ZOONOTIC
ZOONS
ZOOPATHIES
ZOOPATHY
ZOOPERAL
ZOOPERIES
ZOOPERIST
ZOOPERISTS
ZOOPERY
ZOOPHAGAN
ZOOPHAGANS
ZOOPHILE
ZOOPHILES
ZOOPHILIA
ZOOPHILIAS
ZOOPHILIES
ZOOPHILY
ZOOPHOBIA
ZOOPHOBIAS
ZOOPHORIC
ZOOPHORUS
ZOOPHORUSES

ZOOPHYTE
ZOOPHYTES
ZOOPHYTIC
ZOOPLASTIES
ZOOPLASTY
ZOOS
ZOOSCOPIC
ZOOSCOPIES
ZOOSCOPY
ZOOSPERM
ZOOSPERMS
ZOOSPORE
ZOOSPORES
ZOOSPORIC
ZOOTAXIES
ZOOTAXY
ZOOTECHNIES
ZOOTECHNY
ZOOTHECIA
ZOOTHEISM
ZOOTHEISMS
ZOOTHOME
ZOOTHOMES
ZOOTOMIC
ZOOTOMIES
ZOOTOMIST
ZOOTOMISTS
ZOOTOMY
ZOOTOXIN
ZOOTOXINS
ZOOTROPE
ZOOTROPES
ZOOTROPHIES
ZOOTROPHY
ZOOTYPE
ZOOTYPES
ZOOTYPIC
ZOOZOO
ZOOZOOS
ZOPILOTE
ZOPILOTES
ZOPPO
ZORGITE
ZORGITES
ZORIL
ZORILLE
ZORILLES
ZORILLO
ZORILLOS
ZORILS
ZORINO
ZORINOS
ZORRO
ZORROS
ZOS
ZOSTER
ZOSTERS
ZOUNDS
ZOWIE
ZUCCHETTO
ZUCCHETTOS
ZUCCHINI
ZUCCHINIS
ZUCHETTA
ZUCHETTAS
ZUCHETTO
ZUCHETTOS
ZUFFOLI
ZUFFOLO
ZUFOLI
ZUFOLO

ZUGZWANG
ZUGZWANGS
ZULU
ZULUS
ZUMBOORUK
ZUMBOORUKS
ZUPA
ZUPAN
ZUPANS
ZUPAS
ZURF
ZURFS
ZUZ
ZUZES
ZYGAENID
ZYGAENINE
ZYGAENOID
ZYGAL
ZYGANTRA
ZYGANTRUM
ZYGANTRUMS
ZYGODONT
ZYGOMA
ZYGOMAS
ZYGOMATIC
ZYGON
ZYGONS
ZYGOPHYTE
ZYGOPHYTES
ZYGOSE
ZYGOSES
ZYGOSIS
ZYGOSPERM
ZYGOSPERMS
ZYGOSPORE
ZYGOSPORES
ZYGOTE
ZYGOTES
ZYGOTIC
ZYLONITE
ZYLONITES
ZYMASE
ZYMASES
ZYME
ZYMES
ZYMIC
ZYMITE
ZYMITES
ZYMOGEN
ZYMOGENIC
ZYMOGENS
ZYMOID
ZYMOLOGIC
ZYMOLOGIES
ZYMOLOGY
ZYMOLYSES
ZYMOLYSIS
ZYMOLYTIC
ZYMOME
ZYMOMES
ZYMOMETER
ZYMOMETERS
ZYMOSES
ZYMOSIS
ZYMOTIC
ZYMOTICS
ZYMURGIES
ZYMURGY
ZYTHUM
ZYTHUMS